Civil War Almanac

John C. Fredriksen

Checkmark Books®
An imprint of Infobase Publishing

Civil War Almanac

Copyright © 2008, 2007 by John C. Fredriksen

Checkmark Books
An imprint of Infobase Publishing
132 West 31st Street
New York NY 10001

ISBN-13: 978-0-8160-6459-5 (hardcover)
ISBN-13: 978-0-8160-7554-6 (paperback)

Library of Congress Cataloging-in-Publication Data

Fredriksen, John C.
Civil War almanac / John C. Fredriksen.
    p. cm.
Includes bibliographical references and index.
Audience: Grades 9–12.
ISBN 0-8160-6459-8 (hardcover : alk. paper)—ISBN 0-8160-7554-9 (pbk : alk. paper)
 1. United States—History—Civil War, 1861–1865—Miscellanea.
2. Almanacs, American. I. Title.
E468.F85 2007
973.702′02—dc22   2006029985

Checkmark Books are available at special discounts when purchased in bulk quantities for businesses, associations, institutions or sales promotions. Please call our Special Sales Department in New York at (212) 967-8800 or (800) 322-8755.

You can find Facts On File on the World Wide Web at http://www.factsonfile.com

Text design by Erika K. Arroyo
Cover design by Salvatore Luongo
Illustrations by Dale Williams

Printed in the United States of America

VB Hermitage 10 9 8 7 6 5 4 3 2 1

This book is printed on acid-free paper and contains 30% post-consumer recycled content.

CONTENTS

Introduction   v

Chronology   1

Biographies   603

Appendix   799

Maps   801

Bibliography   816

Index   829

INTRODUCTION

By 1860, America's uneasy coexistence with slavery was headed for a violent and dramatic denouement. The election of Abraham Lincoln to the presidency in November proved a catalyst that unleashed long-suppressed urgings for secession among the Southern polity. Commencing with South Carolina in December, the national union quickly unraveled as a majority of slave-holding states voted to end their association with the United States voluntarily, much as the thirteen colonies had departed the British Empire in 1776. Lincoln, who had never campaigned to abolish the "peculiar institution" and, instead, had sought merely to contain it, suddenly confronted a crisis that neither he nor the nation had ever envisioned and for which they were certainly unprepared. The new Confederate States of America underscored its determination to achieve national sovereignty by firing on the Union garrison at Fort Sumter, Charleston, in April 1861. This singular act in and of itself became an immediate catalyst for Northern opinion. Heretofore hesitant as to civil conflict, Northern sentiment suddenly fell in lockstep behind the president in a war to preserve America. The ensuing conflagration proved bigger, more costly, and ultimately more cleansing than any of the contestants could have imagined in the balmy days prior to Bull Run, when myriads of raw recruits merrily tramped off in gaudy uniforms to martial music, beneath flowing banners. By the time the guns fell silent four years later, more than 620,000 of them lay dead, a bigger toll than that exacted in World War II. Large swaths of the South lay in ruins with cities gutted, thousands displaced, and grinding poverty a common lot for years to come. Yet the incubus of slavery had finally been expunged from the political landscape and exchanged for citizenship under a constitution that trumpeted equality for all. But the magnitude of the slaughter and the inspiring heroics and willing sacrifice on both sides forever seared America's consciousness. Appreciably, the Civil War remains a topic of continuing fascination and seemingly endless discourse, as exemplified by the sheer volume of books, essays, and movies produced annually on the subject.

The book you hold is designed to highlight military facets and occurrences as they transpired in the United States throughout the period 1861–65. Due to the sheer scope of events covered and constraints on word length, only passing references can be made to events in other spheres such as politics and diplomacy. In essaying this task, I chose a relatively conventional format made up of two distinct but integral parts. The first is a near-daily almanac of happenings arrayed along a topical/geographical axis. Because the thrust of this almanac is preponderantly military in tenor, great emphasis is paid to recording battles and skirmishes on land, significant troop movements, promotions or demotions of leading personnel, and the capture of individual vessels at sea. Daily subject content varies as to actual events recorded, but in cases in which more than one event transpires the invariable order is diplomacy, politics, North, South, West, Southwest, and naval. Given the expanse of the conflict, some explanation of geographical boundaries is also in order. North refers to Union states from Maryland to Vermont; South covers the Confederacy from Virginia to Florida and then Southern states as far as Louisiana; the West begins at the Shenandoah Valley and extends across the northern tier of the Middle South to regions astride the Mississippi River. Southwest refers to Texas, California, and the Indian Territory. Naval includes both actions at sea and on and along numerous inland waterways. The second part of this book consists of a biographical dictionary containing 107 detailed sketches of military and naval figures associated (Lincoln and Davis are included because of their roles as commander in chief) with this war. All entries are uniform in style and consist of a name, title, dates, text, and bibliography. Special care has also been given to the selection of photos chosen to insure good visuals and subjects in military, not civilian, attire. Textual cross-references, where relevant, then are indicated by small capital letters. In sum, this book is especially designed to afford prospective users immediate access to chronological data, with varying degrees of useful detail contingent upon relative significance, while the biographies proffer a useful cross-section of notable personalities relevant to the military equation, 1861–65.

The Civil War remains a perennially popular topic for reference books, and library shelves abound with almanaclike publications. However, most share an Achilles' heel in that they either contain outdated bibliographic citations or lack them completely. By contrast, I feel it incumbent as an author of reference books to list only the very latest scholarship available, seeing how older items usually are cited in their bibliographies and footnotes anyway. I achieve this by repeatedly combing the Library of Congress and WorldCat Web sites, along with frequent forays into periodical databases found at any college library. Inquiring minds are thereby exposed to rich and varied sources such as master's theses and doctoral dissertations in addition to more traditional materials such as books and articles. Readers can thus enjoy the fullest and most recent intellectual discourse on events and personages covered in this book. Moreover, I also append a detailed bibliography of the very latest Civil War publications, 2000–05, listing materials that would not fit logically in the essays. These two compilations, mutually exclusive, render this almanac very much a reference source for 21st-century scholars, students, or general readers.

I hope that the *Civil War Almanac* will promote a chronological sense for the complex interplay of strategic events and tactical variables on land and sea, 1861–65, that took place in the course of so large and protracted a struggle. It will go far to update or replace existing volumes on the topic and bring to the attention of students and scholars the latest trends in scholarship. I wish to thank my editor, Owen Lancer, for calling this project to my attention. I found it challenging to research and daunting to compile; in sum, it has been a valuable learning experience for myself and one for which I am very grateful.

—John C. Fredriksen, Ph.D.

# CHRONOLOGY

1860

February 1
POLITICS: After 44 ballots, Democrat William F. Pennington emerges as Speaker of the U.S. House of Representatives. He does so only after the withdrawal of fellow Democrat John Sherman, whose own candidacy was hobbled by his endorsement of an antislavery tract. The contest highlights growing factionalism within the Democratic Party over that "peculiar institution."

February 2
POLITICS: Senator Jefferson Davis of Mississippi introduces extreme resolutions defending the legality of slavery in both slaves states and the territories, which also guarantee the return of fugitive slaves to rightful owners.

February 23
POLITICS: The Kansas Territorial Legislature adopts the antislavery Wynadotte Constitution over the veto of Governor Samuel Medary.

February 27
POLITICS: Abraham Lincoln, speaking at New York's Cooper Union in his first memorable eastern address, strongly denounces the extremism of "popular sovereignty" and remains conciliatory and reassuring toward the South. However, he reiterates his adamant opposition toward the extension of slavery in the territories.

April 23–May 3
POLITICS: In the face of a mounting sectional schism, the Democratic Party holds its nominating convention at Charleston, South Carolina. However, when the majority fails to approve a territorial slave code, representatives from Alabama, Arkansas, Florida, Georgia, Louisiana, and South Carolina withdraw in protest on April 30. The remaining participants, unable to muster a two-thirds majority behind any one candidate, vote instead to adjourn and reassemble on June 18.

May 9–10
POLITICS: Baltimore, Maryland, is the site of the Constitutional Union Party nominating convention; this entity is formed from remnants of the American and Whig parties. They choose John Bell of Tennessee as their candidate for president with Edward Everett of Massachusetts as his vice president. They also strongly denounce sectionalism and secessionism.

May 16

POLITICS: The Republican Party convenes its nominating convention in Chicago, Illinois. The leading candidate, William H. Seward, is regarded as too radical on the issue of abolition, so he succumbs on the third ballot to Abraham Lincoln of Illinois. Hannibal Hamlin of Maine is then selected as vice president. Lincoln triumphs by positing himself as a moderate on the subject of slavery; he opposes its expansion into the territories but pledges not to interfere where it already exists.

May 24–25

POLITICS: The U.S. Senate, controlled 36 to 26 by the Democrats, adopts Senator Jefferson Davis's proslavery resolutions. However, the acrimony this engenders only widens the rift between northern and southern delegates, particularly within the Democratic Party.

June 11

POLITICS: Southern Democrats who abandoned the party convention in Charleston, South Carolina, assemble in Richmond, Virginia, to plan a strategy session. They vote to reconvene again in Baltimore on the 28th.

June 18–23

POLITICS: The Democratic Party reconvenes its nominating convention in Baltimore, Maryland, in the absence of many Southern delegates. They nonetheless nominate Stephen A. Douglas for president with Herschel V. Johnson of Georgia as his vice presidential running mate. Their platform also endorses the notion of "popular sovereignty" in the territories.

June 28

POLITICS: Southern delegates, who previously had absented themselves from the Democratic Party convention, likewise convene in Baltimore, Maryland, as National Democrats. They nominate former vice president John C. Breckinridge of Kentucky as their standard-bearer with Joseph Lane of Oregon as vice president; the party's platform unequivocally supports the expansion of slavery into the territories.

August 31

DIPLOMACY: Secretary of State Lewis Cass, alarmed by a major French incursion into Mexico, warns the government of Napoleon III that military occupation of that country is unacceptable to the United States.

November 6

POLITICS: Abraham Lincoln and Hannibal Hamlin win the presidential contest by carrying 18 free states with 1,866,452 popular votes and 180 electoral votes—although none are from Southern states. The Northern Democratic ticket of Stephen A. Douglas and Herschel V. Johnson registers second with 1,376,957 votes and 12 electoral votes while the competing Southern Democratic ticket of John C. Breckinridge and Joseph Lane are third with 11 slave states, 849,781 votes, and 72 electoral votes. Finishing fourth is the Constitutional Unionist ticket of John Bell and Edward Everett with 588,879 popular votes and 39 electoral votes. Lincoln's triumph proves short-lived and precipitates secessionist tremors throughout the South.

November 7
POLITICS: Defiant authorities in Charleston, South Carolina, take umbrage over Abraham Lincoln's recent victory; they raise the traditional Palmetto flag over the city and detain a U.S. officer caught in the act of transferring military supplies from the Charleston arsenal to Fort Moultrie.

November 9
POLITICS: President James Buchanan summons his very divided cabinet to discuss the possible secession crisis. Northerners Lewis Cass, Jeremiah S. Black, and Joseph Holt clearly favor preserving the Union by armed force if necessary, whereas Southerners Howell Cobb, Jacob Thompson, and John B. Floyd oppose military intervention of any kind.
SOUTH: Partisans in Charleston, South Carolina, attempt to seize U.S. arms stored at Fort Moultrie.

A campaign banner for Republican candidates Abraham Lincoln and Hannibal Hamlin, printed in *Harper's Weekly* *(Library of Congress)*

November 10
POLITICS: The South Carolina legislature reacts to Abraham Lincoln's victory by authorizing a convention to contemplate secession from the Union. Senators James Chestnut and James H. Hammond from that state also resign from the government.

November 13
POLITICS: The South Carolina legislature authorizes raising 10,000 volunteers to defend the state from a possible invasion by U.S. forces.

November 14
POLITICS: Georgia congressman Alexander H. Stephens addresses the state legislature at Milledgeville and implores them to oppose secession and uphold constitutional law.

November 15
SOUTH: Major Robert Anderson, U.S. Army, himself a Southerner and sympathetic toward the issue of slavery, is ordered to take command of the garrison at Fort Moultrie in Charleston Harbor.

NAVAL: Lieutenant Thomas A. Craven, commanding naval installations at Key West, Florida, orders landing parties to secure nearby Forts Taylor and Jefferson against possible seizure by "bands of lawless men."

November 18
POLITICS: The Georgia legislature, following South Carolina's lead, procures $1 million to purchase arms and begin to train troops.

November 20
POLITICS: President Buchanan is advised by Attorney General Jeremiah S. Black of his obligation to protect public property from illegal seizure and of the necessity of refraining from military force unless violence is initiated by the secessionists. He is further counseled not to wage offensive warfare against rebellious states but rather to rely on the courts to uphold the law.

November 23
SOUTH: Major Robert Anderson reports on the defensive weaknesses of Fort Moultrie, Charleston Harbor, and suggests transferring the garrison to nearby Fort Sumter, offshore.

November 30
POLITICS: The Mississippi state legislature begins to draw up articles of secession.

December 1
POLITICS: The Florida legislature convenes in order to ponder and debate the growing sectional crisis.

December 3
POLITICS: The 36th Congress convenes its second session in Washington, D.C.

December 4
POLITICS: President James Buchanan makes his final State of the Union message to Congress, noting with trepidation that different sections of the Union were "now arrayed against each other." He attributes the mounting crisis to the machinations of free states, and he questions the constitutionality of using military force to interfere with secession. Buchanan nonetheless opposes secession, despite his strong sympathies for the South.

December 5
POLITICS: President-elect Abraham Lincoln strongly rebukes President James Buchanan's recent State of the Union address.

December 6
POLITICS: The House of Representatives appoints the Committee of Thirty-Three, with one member representing each state, to discuss the present crisis and to suggest possible solutions.

December 8
POLITICS: Secretary of the Treasury Howell Cobb, a Georgian, feels that secession is inevitable at this juncture and tenders his resignation. He is succeeded briefly by Philip F. Thomas of Maryland.

President-elect Abraham Lincoln approaches political rival William H. Seward and asks him to serve as secretary of state under his new administration. Seward readily agrees, although less out of altruism than from a sense that the "incompetent" Lincoln needed an experienced politician to serve as his de facto "prime minister."

December 10
POLITICS: A delegation of South Carolinians meets with President James Buchanan in Washington, D.C., assuring him that U.S. troops and installations will not be disturbed in the event of secession. The president remains unconvinced and begins to mobilize military resources for action. Buchanan continues wrestling with the issue of dispatching reinforcements to the South, however.

The South Carolina legislature endorses a secession convention that is set to convene in Columbia on December 17.

December 11
SOUTH: Major Don C. Buell arrives at Fort Moultrie, Charleston Harbor, with instructions from the War Department for Major Robert Anderson. Apparently, Secretary of War John B. Floyd, a Virginian, refuses to dispatch reinforcements there to avoid provoking a confrontation.

December 12
POLITICS: Secretary of State Lewis Cass, furious over President James Buchanan's unwillingness to send military reinforcements and protect military installations in Charleston, South Carolina, resigns in protest.

The Committee of Thirty-Three, meeting in the U.S. House of Representatives, concocts more than 30 well-intentioned suggestions for avoiding war and secession—none of which prove viable.

December 13
POLITICS: President James Buchanan declines to send reinforcements to Fort Sumter, South Carolina, despite the urging of several cabinet members.

In Washington, D.C., seven senators and 23 representatives from across the South sign a manifesto encouraging secession and independence.

December 14
POLITICS: The Georgia state legislature entreats Alabama, Florida, Mississippi, and South Carolina to appoint delegates for a possible secession convention. All willingly comply.

December 17
POLITICS: The secession convention convenes in Columbia, South Carolina.

Attorney General Jeremiah S. Black, a close confidant of President James Buchanan, is appointed as temporary secretary of state to succeed Lewis Cass. However, Black cannot prevail on Buchanan to reinforce the threatened posts; the president is convinced that the Southern polity will be more pliable if new troops are withheld.

December 18
POLITICS: In an attempt to stave off violence and conciliate Southerners, Senator John J. Crittenden of Kentucky promulgates the Crittenden Compromise, restrict-

ing slavery to the boundaries of the old Missouri Compromise (1819) and extending that line across the continent. Slavery is thus kept out of northern territories, but otherwise the "peculiar institution" is left intact. Significantly, President-elect Abraham Lincoln opposes the measure.

December 19

POLITICS: Delegates to the South Carolina Convention declare that no Federal soldiers can be sent to the forts in Charleston Harbor.

December 20

POLITICS: In light of the mounting sectional crisis, the U.S. Senate appoints the Committee of Thirteen to investigate state affairs and seek possible solutions.

Democrat Edward M. Stanton is appointed attorney general to replace Jeremiah S. Black.

The South Carolina State Convention meeting at Charleston votes 169 to 0—unanimously—to secede from the United States, declaring all prior associations with that entity null and void. This single act sets in motion a chain of events culminating in a mammoth military confrontation between North and South. Charleston's inhabitants nonetheless slip into near-delirious celebrations.

December 22

POLITICS: The South Carolina State Convention demands that the federal government yield control of Fort Moultrie, Fort Sumter, and the U.S. arsenal in Charleston to state authorities. Three commissioners are then dispatched to Washington, D.C., to reiterate those demands.

December 24

POLITICS: Governor Francis W. Pickens of South Carolina declares his state free and independent from the United States, consistent with the "Declaration of Immediate Causes" issued by the convention.

In Washington, D.C., Senator William J. Seward proffers a last-minute constitutional amendment mandating that Congress must not interfere with slavery as it exists in the states. He also seeks jury trials for any fugitive slaves apprehended in free states.

December 26

SOUTH: Major Robert Anderson, commanding the Union garrison at Fort Moultrie, South Carolina, remains cognizant of the dangers to his command. Henceforth, under the cover of darkness, he surreptitiously transfers soldiers from the mainland to the more defensible position at nearby Fort Sumter in Charleston Harbor. This is a large, pentagonal-shaped, casemate (brick) structure that was first constructed on an artificial island in 1829 but never was completed fully. Anderson also undertakes his move without prior authorization from Secretary of War John B. Floyd. Once situated, his soldiers begin to mount cannons and to strengthen their defensive works.

December 27

POLITICS: President James Buchanan expresses his surprise and regrets to Southern congressmen that the garrison of Charleston shifted itself to Fort Sumter, but he declines ordering them back to the mainland.

South: South Carolina state forces occupy Fort Moultrie and Castle Pinckney in Charleston Harbor. This constitutes the first overt act of military aggression against the U.S. government.

Naval: South Carolina forces seize the U.S. revenue cutter *William Aiken* in Charleston Harbor.

December 28

Politics: A South Carolina delegation arrives in Washington, D.C., demanding that President James Buchanan transfer all Federal troops from Charleston. He receives them only as private citizens and again declines all demands for removing U.S. troops. Meanwhile, General in Chief Winfield Scott opposes abandoning the fort and urges Secretary of War John B. Floyd to dispatch immediate supplies and reinforcements.

December 29

Politics: President James Buchanan requests and receives the resignation of Secretary of War John B. Floyd after Floyd insists on removing Federal forces from Charleston, South Carolina, and the president declines.

December 30

Politics: Continuing seizure of Federal property by South Carolina authorities prompts threats of additional resignations among President James Buchanan's cabinet if he fails to take more forceful action.

South: The U.S. arsenal at Charleston, South Carolina, is seized by state forces. They also occupy all remaining Federal property in the city save one—Fort Sumter in the harbor.

December 31

Politics: Postmaster General Joseph Holt is appointed acting secretary of war following the resignation of John B. Floyd. President James Buchanan also refuses another demand by South Carolina commissioners to withdraw Federal troops from Charleston. Upon repeated insistence by Secretary of State Jeremiah S. Black, he finally and reluctantly orders the army and navy departments to mobilize troops and ships for the relief of Fort Sumter. Lines are being drawn inexorably in the sand and will have to be crossed soon.

The Senate Committee of Thirteen fails to reach agreement on any possible political solutions, including the so-called "Crittenden Compromise."

1861

January 2

Politics: President James Buchanan refuses to accept a letter from the South Carolina commissioners. The nominally sympathetic executive then instructs that preparations be made to reinforce the garrison at Fort Sumter, Charleston. General Winfield Scott then prevails upon the president to dispatch reinforcements by means of a civilian steamer, which would arrive more quickly than a warship—and attract less attention.

NORTH: The defense of Washington, D.C., is entrusted to Colonel Charles P. Stone, who begins to organize the District of Columbia militia.

SOUTH: South Carolina forces seize the inactive post of Fort Johnson in Charleston Harbor.

NAVAL: The USS *Brooklyn* at Norfolk, Virginia, receives orders to ready itself for a possible relief effort at Fort Sumter, Charleston Harbor.

January 3

POLITICS: The War Department summarily cancels former secretary of war John B. Floyd's instructions to transfer heavy cannon from Pittsburgh, Pennsylvania, to various points throughout the South.

The South Carolina commission departs Washington, D.C., deeming its mission a failure.

The Delaware legislature, although permitting slavery, votes unanimously to remain in the Union.

The Florida State Convention assembles in Tallahassee to weigh secession.

SOUTH: Fort Pulaski, near the mouth of the Savannah River, is peacefully occupied by Georgia state troops on the orders of Governor Joseph E. Brown.

January 4

SOUTH: The U.S. arsenal at Mount Vernon, Mobile, is occupied by Alabama state forces under orders from Governor Andrew B. Moore.

January 5

POLITICS: Senators from seven Southern states—Alabama, Arkansas, Florida, Georgia, Louisiana, Mississippi, and Texas—confer in Washington, D.C., over the possibility of secession. They ultimately urge slaves states to leave the union and establish a confederacy of their own.

SOUTH: The Federal installations of Fort Morgan and Fort Gaines, which guard the entrance to Mobile Bay, Alabama, are taken over by state forces.

NAVAL: A detachment of 40 U.S. Marines is detailed from the Washington Navy Yard and shuttled to Fort Washington on the Maryland side of the Potomac River, as a precaution against seizure.

The supply vessel *Star of the West* departs New York for Fort Sumter, South Carolina, carrying food, supplies, and 250 soldiers as reinforcements. The warship USS *Brooklyn,* originally intended for the mission, is detained by General Winfield Scott, who feels that use of a civilian vessel is less provocative.

January 6

POLITICS: Governor Thomas H. Hicks of Maryland, which is a slave state, wades in heavily against secession.

SOUTH: The U.S. arsenal at Apalachicola, Florida, is seized by state forces.

January 7

POLITICS: The U.S. House of Representatives approves Major Robert Anderson's recent and unauthorized transfer of Federal forces to Fort Sumter, South Carolina.

State conventions in Mississippi and Alabama begin to debate secession.

SOUTH: The U.S. Army post of Fort Marion, St. Augustine, is seized by Florida forces.

January 8
POLITICS: President James Buchanan urges Congress to consider adopting the Crittenden Compromise.

Secretary of the Interior Jacob Thompson, the last remaining Southerner in President James Buchanan's cabinet, tenders his resignation over the *Star of the West*'s departure. Before leaving Washington, D.C., he cables authorities in Charleston, South Carolina, that the transport has been dispatched.

SOUTH: Federal troops garrisoning Fort Barrancas, Pensacola, fire warning shots at a group of individuals approaching them.

January 9
POLITICS: The Mississippi State Convention meeting at Jackson votes to secede on a vote of 84 to 15—becoming the second state to depart.

SOUTH: Fort Johnson, North Carolina, is expropriated by state forces.

Artillery manned by South Carolina state forces at Fort Moultrie and Morris Island fire on the transport *Star of the West* as it approaches Charleston Harbor. No damage is inflicted and it returns to New York unscathed. Technically speaking, these are the first shots of the Civil War, and Major Robert Anderson, commanding the Fort Sumter garrison, protests the action to Governor Francis W. Pickens. However, Anderson orders the garrison to stand down and makes no attempt to interfere.

NAVAL: A detachment of 30 U.S. Marines marches from the Washington Navy Yard to occupy Fort McHenry, Baltimore harbor, until they can be relieved by regular army troops.

January 10
POLITICS: Senator Jefferson Davis addresses the Senate, requesting immediate action on and approval of Southern demands. However, he decries any use of force and seeks to resolve the crisis through constitutional means.

William H. Seward gains appointment as secretary of state.

The Florida State Convention adopts secession on a 62 to 7 vote, becoming the third state to secede.

SOUTH: Fort Caswell, North Carolina, is seized by state forces.

Federal troops under Lieutenant Adam J. Slemmer, garrisoning Fort Barrancas at Pensacola, Florida, spike their cannon and relocate offshore to Fort Pickens on nearby Santa Rosa Island. Local troops soon confiscate the navy yard, but Fort Pickens remains in Union hands for the duration of hostilities.

The U.S. arsenal and barracks at Baton Rouge, Louisiana, are confiscated by state forces under Braxton Bragg on the orders of Governor Thomas O. Moore.

January 11
POLITICS: The Mississippi delegation to the U.S. House of Representatives walks out of Congress.

The New York legislature underscores its determination to uphold the Union by passing several pro-government resolutions.

The Alabama State Convention at Montgomery approves secession on a 61 to 39 vote, becoming the fourth state to secede.

SOUTH: South Carolina governor Francis W. Pickens demands the surrender of Fort Sumter, Charleston Harbor. Major Robert Anderson politely yet curtly declines.

Louisiana state forces occupy the U.S. Marine Hospital in New Orleans, along with Fort Jackson and Fort St. Philip on the Mississippi River.

January 12

POLITICS: The Ohio legislature votes overwhelmingly to support continuation of the Union.

SOUTH: The Federal outposts of Fort Barrancas, Fort McCree, and the Pensacola Navy Yard are occupied by Florida state forces. However, continuing demands for the surrender of Fort Pickens offshore are ignored.

January 13

POLITICS: President James Buchanan entertains an envoy dispatched from South Carolina governor Francis W. Pickens, declaring that Fort Sumter will not be surrendered to state authorities. The president also receives a messenger from Major Robert Anderson, who alerts him of the worsening situation there.

SOUTH: An unofficial truce emerges between South Carolina authorities and the garrison at Fort Sumter, Charleston Harbor.

January 14

POLITICS: The U.S. House Committee of Thirty-Three fails to agree on any compromise solution. Chairman Thomas Corwin next proposes a constitutional amendment to protect slavery where it exists; it passes but is never ratified by any state.

The South Carolina legislature summarily declares that any Union attempt to reinforce Fort Sumter is tantamount to war.

SOUTH: Federal forces under Captain John M. Brannan hurriedly garrison Fort Taylor on Key West, Florida, transforming it into a coaling station of strategic significance.

The Federal installation at Fort Pike, New Orleans, is occupied by Louisiana state forces.

January 15

SOUTH: Major Robert Anderson receives a second summons to surrender Fort Sumter, Charleston Harbor; he declines again.

WEST: Colonel Albert S. Johnston assumes command of the newly formed Department of the Pacific (California and Oregon).

The commander of Fort Pickens, Florida, again refuses a summons to surrender his post.

January 16

POLITICS: The U.S. Senate effectively defeats the Crittenden Compromise; insisting that the U.S. Constitution must be obeyed, not amended.

January 18
POLITICS: Former postmaster general Joseph Holt becomes secretary of war.

The legislature of Massachusetts votes to offer the federal government both men and money to preserve the Union.

SOUTH: South Carolina officials make a third demand for the surrender of Major Robert Anderson and Fort Sumter, Charleston Harbor, which is declined.

Fort Pickens, Florida, turns down a third demand to surrender.

Fort Jefferson, Key West, Florida, is occupied by Federal forces under Major Lewis G. Arnold, and subsequently serves as a detention center for political prisoners.

NAVAL: Alabama state forces seize the lighthouse tender USS *Alert* at Mobile.

January 19
POLITICS: The Georgia State Convention in Milledgeville approves secession on a 208 to 89 vote, becoming the fifth state to secede.

The Virginia General Assembly entreats all states to send delegates to a National Peace Convention in Washington, D.C.

January 20
SOUTH: Mississippi forces occupy Fort Massachusetts on Ship Island, at the mouth of the Mississippi River.

January 21
POLITICS: Jefferson Davis of Mississippi together with Clement C. Clay and Benjamin Fitzpatrick of Alabama and Stephen R. Mallory and David L. Yulee of Florida make a dramatic departure from the U.S. Senate chamber in Washington, D.C., and head for home. Nonetheless, Davis remains deeply troubled by the course of events and allegedly prays for peace that evening.

The New York legislature agrees to uphold the Union by force, if necessary.

NORTH: Rabid abolitionist Wendell Phillips hails the decision of slave states to secede, feeling that their continued presence is detrimental to the United States.

January 22
POLITICS: New York governor Edwin Morgan orders all weapons and gunpowder previously sold to Georgia impounded. This prompts a sharp rebuke from Governor Joseph E. Brown, who seizes several Northern vessels in retaliation.

The Wisconsin legislature votes to agree with New York's stand on the Union.

January 23
POLITICS: The Massachusetts legislature votes in agreement with New York's pledge to support the Union.

NAVAL: Commander John A. B. Dahlgren removes cannon and ammunition from the Washington Navy Yard in the event of a possible attack, storing the latter in the attic of a building.

January 24
SOUTH: The U.S. arsenal at Augusta, Georgia, is seized by state forces.

Naval: Federal forces from Fortress Monroe, Virginia, are loaded onboard ships and dispatched to reinforce Fort Pickens, Florida. The squadron consists of the USS *Brooklyn, Sabine, Macedonia,* and *St. Louis.*

January 26
Politics: At Baton Rouge, the Louisiana State Convention approves secession on a vote of 113 to 17, becoming the sixth state to secede.
South: Georgia forces occupy the Oglethorpe barracks and Fort Jackson, Savannah, as per orders from Governor Joseph E. Brown.

January 28
South: The Federal installation at Fort Macomb, New Orleans, is occupied by Louisiana forces.

January 29
Politics: Following a congressional vote, Kansas joins the Union as the 34th state; significantly, its constitution explicitly outlaws slavery.
Naval: Louisiana forces seize the U.S. revenue cutter *Robert McClelland* at New Orleans.

To avoid provoking a fight, the Navy Department orders a Marine Corps detachment onboard the USS *Brooklyn,* steaming for Fort Pickens, Florida, not to disembark unless that post is attacked.

January 30
Naval: The U.S. revenue cutter *Lewis Cass* surrenders to state forces at Mobile Bay, Alabama.

January 31
South: Louisiana officials orchestrate the seizure of the U.S. Mint and Customs House at New Orleans, along with the U.S. revenue schooner *Washington.*

February 1
Politics: The Texas State Convention, convening in Austin, votes 166 to 7 in favor of secession, becoming the seventh state to secede. A public referendum is also scheduled to solicit public opinion on the measure.

February 3
Politics: Senators Judah P. Benjamin and John Slidell of Louisiana withdraw from the U.S. Senate and return home.

February 4
Politics: The Peace Convention, summoned by Virginia, assembles in Washington, D.C., under former president John Tyler. It consists of 131 members from 21 states, but none of the seceded states are represented.

Representatives from Alabama, Florida, Georgia, Louisiana, Mississippi, and South Carolina assemble in Montgomery, Alabama, and a Provisional Congress of the Confederate States of America forms with Howell Cobb of Georgia serving as president.

February 5
POLITICS: President James Buchanan reiterates to South Carolina officials his determination that Fort Sumter, Charleston Harbor, will not be surrendered to state authorities.

The Peace Conference convening in Washington, D.C., earnestly votes to resolve the outbreak of sectional violence both diplomatically and constitutionally.

February 7
POLITICS: The Secession Convention at Montgomery, Alabama, begins to draft plans for a provisional form of government, a confederacy of states.

The Choctaw Nation declares its allegiance to the South.

February 8
POLITICS: President James Buchanan authorizes a $25 million loan for current expenses and redemption of treasury notes.

Southern delegates at Montgomery, Alabama, proffer and unanimously approve the Provisional Constitution of the Confederate States—thereby founding the Confederacy. This document, while similar to its Northern equivalent, explicitly declares and protects the right to own slaves. While the importation of slaves remains banned, the existing fugitive slave law is strengthened.

WEST: The U.S. Arsenal at Little Rock, Arkansas, is seized by state troops under orders of Governor Henry M. Rector.

February 9
POLITICS: Jefferson Davis of Mississippi, who is absent from the constitutional convention in Montgomery, Alabama, is unanimously elected provisional president of the Confederate States of America. Alexander H. Stephens of Georgia likewise becomes provisional vice president. Moreover, the Provisional Congress of the Confederacy pledges that all laws extant under the U.S. Constitution, which do not conflict with the Confederate constitution, will be maintained.

Voters in Tennessee roundly defeat a move to convene a secession convention, 68,282 to 59,449.

WEST: General David E. Twiggs appoints a military commission to confer with civilian authorities in Texas.

NAVAL: The steamer USS *Brooklyn* arrives at Pensacola, Florida, to reinforce the garrison at Fort Pickens, but a Marine Corps detachment remains onboard so as not to upset the status quo.

February 10
POLITICS: In Mississippi, a rather surprised Jefferson Davis is alerted by telegram of his election to the Confederate presidency. He has been anticipating a military commission, but nonetheless he agrees to the appointment.

February 11
POLITICS: President-elect Abraham Lincoln departs Springfield, Illinois, and wends his way toward Washington, D.C. He will never return alive.

Jefferson Davis travels from his plantation in Brierfield, Mississippi, to attend inauguration ceremonies at Montgomery, Alabama.

February 12
POLITICS: The Provisional Congress of the Confederacy at Montgomery, Alabama, votes to establish a Peace Commission to the United States.
WEST: State forces seize U.S. Army munitions stored at Napoleon, Arkansas.

February 13
POLITICS: The electoral college completes counting all votes and declares Abraham Lincoln the new chief executive.
WEST: A detachment of U.S. Army troops under Colonel Bernard J. Dowling defeats a band of Chiricahua Apaches at Apache Pass, Arizona; in January 1894 he receives the Congressional Medal of Honor for this action.

February 15
NAVAL: Lieutenant Raphael Semmes resigns his U.S. Navy commission and leaves for the South.

February 16
POLITICS: President-elect Jefferson Davis arrives at Montgomery, Alabama, amid thunderous applause.
WEST: The U.S. arsenal at San Antonio, Texas, is seized by state forces under Ben McCulloch.

Texas civilian commissioners demand the surrender of all Federal posts and property within their state.

February 18
POLITICS: Jefferson Davis of Mississippi is inaugurated as provisional president of the Confederate States of America, declaring, "Obstacles may retard, but they cannot long prevent the progress of a movement sanctified by its justice and sustained by a virtuous people." Alexander H. Stephens of Georgia, who initially opposed secession, then becomes vice president. Military bands then serenade the proceedings with a catchy air popularly known as "Dixie," which gradually gains wide acceptance as an unofficial national anthem of the Confederacy.
WEST: In an act widely condemned as treasonable, General David E. Twiggs surrenders all U.S. Army installations in Texas to state authorities.

February 19
POLITICS: The Confederate Convention in Montgomery, Alabama, elects Judah P. Benjamin of Louisiana attorney general, Christopher G. Memminger of South Carolina secretary of the treasury, John H. Reagan of Texas postmaster general, Robert Toombs of Georgia secretary of state, and Leroy P. Walker of Alabama secretary of war.
SOUTH: Louisiana forces appropriate the U.S. Paymaster's Office in New Orleans.

Colonel Carlos A. Waite replaces General David E. Twiggs as commander of the Department of Texas.

February 20

POLITICS: The Provisional Confederate Congress, acting in the absence of an established body, declares the Mississippi River open to commerce. It also passes legislation creating a Department of the Navy.

February 21

POLITICS: President Jefferson Davis receives a missive from South Carolina governor Francis W. Pickens requesting immediate action on Fort Sumter. Pickens regards the continuing presence of the Federal garrison an affront to "honor and safety."

The former U.S. senator from Florida, Stephen R. Mallory, is chosen as Confederate secretary of the navy.

SOUTHWEST: Federal troops abandon Camp Cooper, Texas.

February 22

POLITICS: While in Baltimore, Maryland, President-elect Abraham Lincoln is warned of a possible attempt on his life and completes his journey to Washington, D.C., on board a secret train.

WEST: A mass gathering at San Francisco, California, declares itself for the Union.

February 23

POLITICS: President-elect Abraham Lincoln arrives in Washington, D.C., amidst a mounting sense of national foreboding.

Texas voters affirm secession by a margin of three to one.

February 25

POLITICS: Judah P. Benjamin is sworn in as Confederate attorney general; this multitalented individual will hold several positions within the new government.

February 26

SOUTHWEST: Federal forces under Captain Edmund Kirby-Smith abandon Camp Colorado, Texas.

February 27

POLITICS: As a continuing gesture to avoid hostilities, President Jefferson Davis appoints three commissioners for possible peace negotiations in Washington, D.C.

The Peace Commission suggests adoption of no less than six constitutional amendments to forestall any possibility of violence.

NAVAL: Congress authorizes the Navy Department's request for seven heavily armed steam sloops to augment the existing fleet strength.

February 28

POLITICS: The House of Representatives adopts an amendment proposed by Thomas Corwin that reaffirms slavery's status where it already exists. President-elect Abraham Lincoln fully concurs with the legislation.

Calls for a state convention to weigh the possibility of secession are narrowly defeated by a popular vote held in North Carolina.

The Confederate Congress agrees to a $15 million domestic loan.

WEST: The Colorado Territory is formed from the western part of the Kansas Territory and William Gilpin gains appointment as governor.

March 1
POLITICS: President-elect Abraham Lincoln appoints Pennsylvania politician Simon Cameron his new secretary of war.

The Provisional Confederate States of America assumes formal control of events at Charleston, South Carolina.

SOUTH: Pierre G. T. Beauregard is commissioned brigadier general, C.S.A.

Major Robert Anderson alerts the government that the garrison at Fort Sumter, Charleston Harbor, must be either supplied, reinforced, or evacuated without further delay. He is running out of provisions rapidly and must capitulate soon by default.

March 2
POLITICS: The U.S. Senate refuses compromise resolutions advanced by the Peace Convention, over the objections of Kentucky senator John J. Crittenden. This act concludes all attempts at political compromise.

WEST: President James Buchanan approves establishment of the new territories of Nevada and Dakota.

NAVAL: The U.S. revenue schooner *Henry Dodge* is captured by state forces at Galveston, Texas.

March 3
POLITICS: President-elect Abraham Lincoln dines with his cabinet for the first time and tours the Senate. Meanwhile, General Winfield Scott, commander in chief of the U.S. Army, dourly informs Secretary of State William H. Seward that mounting a major relief effort to rescue Fort Sumter, Charleston Harbor, appears impractical.

SOUTH: President Jefferson Davis appoints General Pierre G. T. Beauregard commander of Confederate forces in the vicinity of Charleston, South Carolina. He is instructed to prepare for military action against the Federal garrison sequestered inside Fort Sumter in the harbor.

March 4
POLITICS: Abraham Lincoln is formally inaugurated as the 16th president of a less-than-united United States, and he is sworn in by Chief Justice Roger B. Taney. His first address declares that the Union is "perpetual" and cannot be undone by secession. The chief executive also reiterates his stance to preserve all Federal property within the states now seceded. Moreover, he affirms his belief that slavery cannot be allowed in the territories, but he is willing to leave it intact where it already exists. He remains conciliatory, assures the South it will not be attacked, and appeals to "the better angels of our nature." Hannibal Hamlin of Maine becomes vice president, along with William H. Seward as secretary of state, Salmon P. Chase as secretary of the treasury, and Edward Bates as attorney general.

The Confederate Convention assembled at Montgomery, Alabama, officially adopts the "Stars and Bars" flag of seven stars and three stripes as its official symbol.

NAVAL: The Navy Department, which currently operates 42 warships, recalls all but three from foreign stations to assist in the impending crisis.

March 5
POLITICS: President Abraham Lincoln discusses the plight of Major Robert Anderson at Fort Sumter, South Carolina. The major telegraphs him that his supplies are due to run out within four to six weeks, after which he will have little recourse but to surrender. Furthermore, both Anderson and General Winfield Scott concur that the post cannot be held successfully with less than 20,000 troops. Time is running out for a peaceful solution, but Lincoln continues nuancing the delicate situation.

March 6
POLITICS: The Confederate Congress authorizes recruitment of 100,000 volunteers for 12 months. President Jefferson Davis appoints Martin J. Crawford, John Forsyth, and A. B. Roman special commissioners to deal with Republican officeholders in Washington, D.C., once it becomes apparent that President Abraham Lincoln refuses to receive them.

March 7
POLITICS: Gideon Welles, a former Connecticut newspaper editor, is sworn in as the 24th secretary of the navy.

The Missouri State Convention displays a strong pro-Union streak and votes against secession, yet also considers the Crittenden Compromise a possible avenue for avoiding war.
SOUTH: Braxton Bragg and Samuel Cooper are appointed brigadier generals in the Confederate army.
SOUTHWEST: Federal forces abandon Ringgold Barracks and Camp Verde, Texas.

March 9
POLITICS: At Montgomery, Alabama, the Confederate Convention authorizes the raising of military forces. Delegates also pass a coinage bill and issue treasury notes in denominations from $50 to $1 million.

March 11
POLITICS: The constitution of the Confederacy is unanimously adopted by the Confederate Convention at Montgomery, Alabama, and passed along to constituent states for ratification. It is based primarily on the U.S. Constitution but differs in explicitly condoning the practice of slavery.
SOUTH: General Braxton Bragg assumes command of Confederate forces in Florida and proves himself to be a competent disciplinarian and organizer.

March 12
SOUTHWEST: Federal forces abandon Fort McIntosh, Texas.

March 13
POLITICS: Despite pressure from within his own cabinet, President Abraham Lincoln directly orders Secretary of State William H. Seward not to receive Confederate

emissaries. Through this expedient, he avoids any appearance of recognition of the Confederate government in Montgomery. He also dispatches former navy officer Gustavus V. Fox on a mission to Fort Sumter, South Carolina, to evaluate all possibilities of succoring the garrison.

WEST: Captain Nathaniel Lyon, a pugnacious, aggressive officer by nature, becomes commander of the U.S. arsenal at St. Louis, Missouri.

March 15

POLITICS: President Abraham Lincoln inquires of his cabinet whether or not a relief attempt ought to be mounted to resupply the garrison of Fort Sumter, Charleston Harbor. The majority, especially Secretary of State William H. Seward, view such a move as provocative and advise against it.

The Confederate Congress thanks the state of Louisiana for enriching its coffers with $536,000 appropriated from the U.S. Mint at New Orleans.

SOUTHWEST: Camp Wood, Texas, is abandoned by Federal forces.

March 16

DIPLOMACY: President Jefferson Davis appoints three special ministers, William L. Yancey, Pierre A. Rost, and Dudley Mann, to visit Europe in a quest for diplomatic recognition. They are instructed to use cotton as economic leverage, whenever possible, for securing support.

POLITICS: The Confederate Convention at Montgomery, Alabama, adjourns.

SOUTHWEST: The Arizona Territory Convention at Mesilla votes in favor of secession.

March 17

SOUTHWEST: Federal troops abandon Camp Hudson, Texas.

NAVAL: Agents of the Confederate navy department arrive in New Orleans to arrange for the purchase and construction of gunboats.

March 18

DIPLOMACY: President Abraham Lincoln appoints Charles Francis Adams as minister to Great Britain.

POLITICS: The Arkansas State Convention defeats the move to secede on a 39 to 35 vote and then schedules a public referendum on the issue that summer.

SOUTH: Lieutenant Adam J. Slemmer, commanding Fort Pickens, Florida, returns four fugitive slaves to their owners.

General Braxton Bragg forbids the passing of supplies or communications to either Fort Pickens, Florida, or the navy squadron offshore.

SOUTHWEST: Governor Sam Houston of Texas, having refused to take an oath of allegiance to the Confederacy, is forced to retire from office.

March 19

SOUTHWEST: Federal forces abandon Forts Clark, Inge, and Lancaster, Texas.

March 20

SOUTHWEST: Federal troops yield Fort Brown and Fort Duncan, Texas.

NAVAL: The sloop USS *Isabella,* stocked with supplies for the garrison at Pensacola, is seized by state forces at Mobile, Alabama.

March 21

NAVAL: Former navy officer Gustavus V. Fox, pursuant to orders from President Abraham Lincoln, reconnoiters Fort Sumter and Charleston Harbor, South Carolina, with a view toward relieving the garrison.

March 22

WEST: Governor Claiborne F. Jackson fails to convince his fellow Missourians to join the Confederacy, after which the polity sharply divides into pro- and anti-Federal camps.

Colonel William W. Loring becomes commander of the Department of New Mexico.

March 26

SOUTHWEST: Colonel Earl Van Dorn arrives in Texas to support the Confederate cause.

March 28

POLITICS: To break the impasse, President Abraham Lincoln resolves to mount a seaborne expedition to succor the Federal garrison at Fort Sumter, Charleston Harbor, and he orders it to sail no later than April 6, 1861. His cabinet also divides on the matter, 3 to 2 in favor with Secretary of War Simon Cameron abstaining. In effect, the wily president is maneuvering his Southern counterpart into firing the first shot.

SOUTHWEST: Federal forces abandon Fort Mason, Texas.

March 31

POLITICS: President Abraham Lincoln orders a relief expedition to assist the Federal garrison at Fort Pickens, Florida, guarding the entrance to Pensacola harbor.

SOUTHWEST: Federal forces abandon Fort Bliss, Texas.

NAVAL: Secretary of the Navy Gideon Welles orders 250 personnel transferred from the New York Navy Yard to Norfolk, Virginia, to bolster the garrison.

April 1

POLITICS: Secretary of State William H. Seward strongly recommends that President Abraham Lincoln abandon Fort Sumter, Charleston Harbor, while more tenable posts along the Gulf of Mexico be fortified. He also suggests that a war with Europe would serve as a "panacea" to unify the country. Lincoln courteously thanks the secretary for such sage advice—then declares that he intends to run his own administration.

April 3

NAVAL: Confederate artillery on Morris Island, Charleston Harbor, fires upon the Union vessel *Rhoda H. Shannon.*

April 4

POLITICS: President Abraham Lincoln approves the strategy suggested by Gustavus V. Fox and informs Major Robert Anderson at Fort Sumter, Charleston, of an impending relief expedition. However, he still grants that officer complete latitude on any response necessary should the Confederates attack.

The Virginia State Convention in Richmond rejects an ordinance of secession, 89 to 45.

April 5

SOUTHWEST: Federal forces abandon Fort Quitman, Texas.

NAVAL: A squadron consisting of USS *Pawnee, Pocahontas,* and U.S. revenue cutter *Harriet Lane* are assembled under the command of Captain Samuel Mercer. Meanwhile, the *Powhatan* continues steaming toward Fort Pickens, Florida.

April 6

POLITICS: South Carolina governor Francis W. Pickens is advised by President Abraham Lincoln that an expedition is being mounted to supply—not reinforce—the garrison at Fort Sumter, Charleston Harbor. Moreover, if no resistance is encountered, he pledges that no additional troops will be dispatched.

NAVAL: Lieutenant John L. Worden is ordered overland to Fort Pickens; he carries secret orders for the squadron offshore to land reinforcements.

April 7

SOUTH: To increase pressure on Major Robert Anderson, General Pierre G. T. Beauregard forbids any further communications between Fort Sumter, Charleston Harbor, and the shore.

General Braxton Bragg, commanding Confederate forces in Pensacola, requests and receives permission to fire on any reinforcements being landed at Fort Pickens from the squadron offshore.

April 8

SOUTH: In response to the approaching relief expedition to Fort Sumter, Charleston Harbor, Confederate authorities begin to undertake military preparations around the harbor.

NAVAL: Federal troops onboard the U.S. revenue cutter *Harriet Lane* land to bolster the garrison of Fort Pickens, Florida.

April 10

NAVAL: The steamer *Baltic* departs New York in a second attempt to relieve the garrison at Fort Sumter, Charleston Harbor, with naval agent Gustavus V. Fox onboard. En route, it is joined by the USS *Pawnee* off Hampton Roads, Virginia.

Lieutenant John L. Worden arrives at Pensacola, Florida, on official business and receives permission from General Braxton Bragg to visit Fort Pickens.

April 11

POLITICS: Three Confederate peace emissaries depart Washington, D.C., having failed to reach an agreeable solution with Secretary of State William H. Steward. Meanwhile, Federal troops are ordered into the nation's capital, which is completely surrounded by potentially hostile territory.

SOUTH: As a sovereign entity, the Confederate government cannot allow the presence of foreign troops—or their flag—in a major port. The impending arrival of a Union supply ship to further sustain the Fort Sumter garrison constitutes an egregious affront to Southern independence and cannot be permitted. Therefore, General Pierre G. T. Beauregard is ordered by Confederate authorities to demand the immediate capitulation of Fort Sumter, Charleston Harbor. He receives careful instructions not to take offensive action if Major Robert Anderson agrees to evacuate by a strict time table. However, when these new terms are delivered to the Union commander, he flatly refuses. As a sop to Southern sensitivities, Anderson also informs Beauregard that he is nearly out of supplies and must yield by April 15, regardless. The Federals receive a deadline of 24 hours.

SOUTHWEST: Colonel Earl Van Dorn becomes Confederate commander in Texas and is ordered to arrest any U.S. soldiers refusing to join the Southern cause.

April 12

SOUTH: At 3:20 A.M., the tempo of events dramatically escalates once General Pierre G. T. Beauregard dispatches Colonel James Chesnut and Captain Stephen D. Lee to Fort Sumter, Charleston Harbor. They demand a precise time for the evacuation of that post. Major Robert Anderson, acknowledging the inevitable, declares noontime on April 15, provided he does not receive additional supplies or instructions from the government. Anderson then is informed summarily that the Confederates will commence bombarding within one hour. The Civil War, a monumental struggle in military history and a defining moment for the United States, is about to unfold.

At 4:30 A.M., the shoreline around Charleston Harbor erupts into flame as 18 mortars and 30 heavy cannon, backed by 7,000 troops, bombard Fort Sumter. Major Robert Anderson, commanding only 85 men, 43 civilian engineers, and 48 cannon, weathers the storm and waits until daybreak before responding with six cannon of his own. Captain Abner Doubleday receives the honor of firing the first Union shot of the war.

NAVAL: The USS *Pawnee,* the U.S. revenue cutter *Harriet Lane,* and the steamship *Baltic,* commanded by Gustavus V. Fox, arrive in Charleston Harbor, South Carolina, with supplies for Fort Sumter. Having appeared too late to reinforce the garrison they remain helpless spectators as the fort is bombarded.

The naval squadron consisting of USS *Sabine, Brooklyn, St. Louis,* and *Wynandotte* begins to land reinforcements at Fort Pickens, Florida.

April 13

SOUTH: After 34 hours of continuous shelling, a lucky Confederate shot slices through Fort Sumter's flagstaff at 12:48 P.M., while hotshot ignites several fires. This act induces former Texas senator Louis T. Wigfall to commandeer a boat, row out to the fort, and again demand its surrender. At this juncture, Major Robert Anderson concludes this is the wiser course, and he raises a white flag at 2:30 P.M. Firing upon Fort Sumter then ceases and surrender ceremonies are planned for the following day. Curiously, the Federals have sustained no casualties despite 4,000 shells hitting their post. The garrison, for its part, managed to fire off 1,000 rounds, again with little damage to the city or its military facilities. But this perceived Southern aggression galvanizes heretofore tepid sentiments throughout the

North, granting President Abraham Lincoln the political wherewithal necessary for waging war.

SOUTHWEST: Federal forces abandon Fort Davis, Texas.

NAVAL: Relief ships under Gustavus V. Fox continue loitering outside Charleston Harbor, South Carolina, unwilling to approach closer in the face of hostile fire.

His mission completed, Navy lieutenant John L. Worden returns to Washington, D.C., from Fort Pickens, Florida. En route, he is arrested by Confederate authorities near Montgomery, Alabama, and is imprisoned.

The USS *Sabine* assumes blockading stations off Pensacola, Florida.

April 14

SOUTH: Major Robert Anderson formally capitulates Fort Sumter, Charleston Harbor, to Confederate authorities. Ironically, despite the intensity of the bombardment, the only fatalities, two killed and four wounded, occur when a pile of ordnance accidently ignites during a 100-gun salute to the U.S. flag. Anderson's surrender also signals the eruption of euphoric celebrations on the shore and in the city. The captives are subsequently entertained by the cream of Charleston society and depart onboard the provisional squadron commanded by Gustavus V. Fox. "We have met them and we have conquered," Governor Francis Pickens subsequently crows as the first act in a long and bloody drama concludes.

Interior view of Fort Sumter on April 14, 1861, after its evacuation *(National Archives)*

April 15

POLITICS: In a move designed to deny the Confederacy diplomatic recognition, President Abraham Lincoln declares not war but, rather, a state of insurrection and calls for raising 75,000 three-month volunteers to suppress it. However, service by African Americans is declined. He also requests a special meeting of Congress to convene on July 4, Independence Day. Not surprisingly, Lincoln's call to arms is ignored entirely by the governments of North Carolina, Kentucky, and Virginia. However, New York's legislature militantly embraces the Union cause and votes $3 million to support war efforts.

Federal installations at Fort Macon, North Carolina, are seized by state forces.

NAVAL: Naval authorities apprehend 17 Southern vessels at New York harbor.

April 16

POLITICS: Virginia governor John Lechter informs President Abraham Lincoln that his state will not furnish troops for what he considers the "subjugation" of the South.

SOUTH: North Carolina state forces seize Forts Caswell and Johnson.

SOUTHWEST: Federal forces abandon Fort Washita, Chickasaw Nation.

April 17

POLITICS: Secessionists gather in Baltimore in large numbers.

The Virginia State Convention, reacting strongly against President Abraham Lincoln's call for troops, votes 88 to 55 for secession. The proposal is then forwarded to the public for ratification.

President Jefferson Davis begins to solicit applications for Confederate letters of marque and reprisal, in effect, establishing a force of privateers.

WEST: The governments of Missouri and Tennessee refuse to raise the requisite numbers of militia forces.

NAVAL: Southern sympathizers attempt to block Gosport Navy Yard, Norfolk, Virginia, by placing obstacles in the channel, but the attempt proves ineffectual.

The USS *Powhatan* under Lieutenant David D. Porter arrives at Fort Pickens, Florida, and disembarks an additional 600 troops to bolster the sailors and marines already deployed. Thus the best harbor on the Gulf of Mexico is secured for use by Union forces for the remainder of the war.

April 18

NORTH: The 6th Massachusetts rides the rails from New York to Baltimore, Maryland, en route to Washington, D.C.

Colonel Robert E. Lee declines an offer from Abraham Lincoln to command all Union forces. Lee does not support secession, but he feels compelled to follow his native state of Virginia.

Five companies of Pennsylvania Volunteers arrive to protect Washington, D.C.

SOUTH: Virginia forces seize the U.S. Customs Office at Richmond.

Colonel Harvey Brown takes command of Fort Pickens, Pensacola, and establishes the new Department of Florida.

WEST: Lieutenant Roger Jones orders his command of 50 men to burn the U.S. armory at Harper's Ferry, western Virginia, thereby preventing its tooling facilities from falling into enemy hands. Fire destroys the buildings and with it some 15,000 rifled muskets, but the local population extinguishes the flames before valuable factory equipment is destroyed.

Arkansas state forces seize U.S. Army stores at Pine Bluff.

NAVAL: Captain Hiram Paulding is ordered to assemble 1,000 U.S. Marines for the purpose of burning Federal supplies and equipment in the Norfolk Navy Yard, Virginia.

April 19

POLITICS: To interrupt any flow of food or war materiel from abroad, President Abraham Lincoln declares a naval blockade of the Confederate coastline. This effort encompasses all the ports of South Carolina, Georgia, Alabama, Florida, Mississippi, Louisiana, and Texas and so overwhelms the relatively small U.S. Navy that its implementation is gradual, by stages. This is the only part of General Winfield Scott's so-called Anaconda Plan that is enacted from the onset of the war, and Lincoln does so after the urging of Secretary of State William H. Seward. In time the blockade intensifies to reach stranglehold proportions and emerges as a major factor in the downfall of the Confederacy.

NORTH: The 6th Massachusetts, transferring between railroad stations in Baltimore, Maryland, is violently attacked by rioters. Shots are exchanged; four soldiers are killed and 36 are wounded. These are the first Union casualties incurred by hostile action; 11 civilians were also slain. Seething Southerners also begin to cut rail and telegraph lines leading to the capital. For several anxious days, Washington, D.C., remains temporarily cut off from the rest of the country.

Dorothea Dix volunteers to recruit and direct women nurses for the Federal army.

NAVAL: Captain Samuel F. Du Pont embarks from Philadelphia, Pennsylvania, with reinforcements for the beleaguered Union capital. The 8th Massachusetts under General Benjamin F. Butler also sails for Annapolis, Maryland, aboard the ferryboat *Maryland*.

The steam transport *Star of the West* is seized by state forces under General Earl Van Dorn at Indianola, Texas.

Southern-born captain David G. Farragut remains loyal to the Union and relocates his family from Norfolk, Virginia, to New York.

April 20

NORTH: Colonel Robert E. Lee tenders his resignation from the U.S. Army.

To obstruct the passage of Federal troops to Washington, D.C., secessionist mobs burn several railways out of Baltimore, Maryland. This forces Federal troops to arrive by water and then rebuild the tracks as they proceed on foot.

The 8th Massachusetts under General Benjamin F. Butler parades through Annapolis en route to Washington, D.C.

SOUTH: The 4th Massachusetts arrives at Fortress Monroe, on the tip of the Yorktown Peninsula, Virginia.

WEST: Confederate sympathizers seize the U.S. arsenal at Liberty, Missouri.

NAVAL: Captain Charles S. McCauley hurriedly and prematurely orders the Gosport Navy Yard in Norfolk, Virginia, burned and evacuated. He does so despite the arrival of 1,000 U.S. Marines under Commodore Hiram Paulding as reinforcements. The resulting destruction is less than complete, and the dry docks become operative again in a few weeks. The Confederates also retrieve no less than 1,200 heavy naval cannon, which they implant at fortifications as far west as Vicksburg, Mississippi. Among the aged vessels hurriedly destroyed or scuttled are ships of the line USS *Pennsylvania, Columbus, Delaware*; frigates *Raritan, Columbia, Merrimac*; and sloops *Dolphin, Germantown,* and *Plymouth*—mostly obsolete but potentially useful for enforcing the initial Union blockade. McCauley's badly botched withdrawal from Norfolk proves an embarrassing windfall for the Confederate war effort.

The venerable USS *Constitution*, "Old Ironsides" of War of 1812 fame, is towed safely offshore from Annapolis by the steamer USS *Maryland*.

The U.S. Naval Academy at Annapolis is abandoned and transferred north to Newport, Rhode Island. The buildings remain occupied by Federal troops for the remainder of the war.

Texas authorities confiscate the U.S. Coast survey schooner *Twilight* at Aransas Pass.

April 21

NORTH: Rioting and civil disorder continue in Baltimore, Maryland, including sabotage of nearby railroad lines.

WEST: Pro-Union delegates meeting in Monongahela County in western Virginia discuss a secession movement of their own from the Confederacy.

NAVAL: Confederate forces rapidly reoccupy Gosport Navy Yard, Norfolk, Virginia, and commence reconstruction efforts. Due to the hasty Union withdrawal, many tons of valuable weapons and equipment are recovered. Among the vessels salvaged is the old steam frigate USS *Merrimack,* which in a few months is reincarnated as the ironclad ram CSS *Virginia.*

The USS *Saratoga* captures the cargo vessel *Nightingale,* which is found laden with 961 African slaves. The U.S. government officially banned trafficking in human cargo in 1808.

April 22

NORTH: The 7th New York arrives at Annapolis, Maryland, onboard the steamer *Boston.*

SOUTH: The U.S. arsenal at Fayetteville, North Carolina, is captured by state forces.

WEST: Militia begins to arrive at Cairo, Illinois, at the confluence of the Ohio and Mississippi rivers.

Governor Henry M. Rector of Arkansas refuses to provide his quota of militia for government use.

NAVAL: Captain Franklin Buchanan, commanding the Washington Navy Yard, tenders his resignation in anticipation of Maryland's seemingly impending secession—he is not reinstated once his state remains loyal, and he ultimately joins the Confederacy. Buchanan is succeeded by Captain John A. B. Dahlgren.

April 23
POLITICS: President Jefferson Davis offers aid to Confederate sympathizers in Missouri if they attack and seize the U.S. arsenal in St. Louis.
NORTH: An assembly of free African Americans in Boston, Massachusetts, demands that Federal laws preventing their enrollment in state militia be repealed.

General George B. McClellan gains appointment as major general, U.S. Army.
SOUTH: General Robert E. Lee becomes commander of Virginia state forces.
WEST: The Federal installation at Fort Smith, Arkansas, is seized by state forces.
SOUTHWEST: U.S. Army officers taken at San Antonio, Texas, are treated as prisoners of war.
NAVAL: The defenses of Washington, D.C., are enhanced by the arrival of USS *Pawnee* under Captain Hiram Paulding.

April 24
NAVAL: The Navy Department formally begins to evacuate the U.S. Naval Academy at Annapolis, Maryland, whereupon Captain S. Blake loads faculty and midshipmen onto the iconic frigate USS *Constitution*.

The USS *Cumberland* captures the Confederate vessels *Young America* and *George M. Smith* off Hampton Roads, Virginia, both heavily laden with military supplies and ammunition.

April 25
NORTH: The 8th Massachusetts under General Benjamin F. Butler defiantly parades through Washington, D.C., following a lengthy march around Baltimore, Maryland.
WEST: In a daring preemptive raid, Union Captain James H. Stokes arrives at St. Louis, Missouri, by steamer, removes 12,000 muskets from the U.S. arsenal there, and returns the weapons to Alton, Illinois, for militia use. This proves a critical blow to pro-Confederate militias forming in the region.

General Edwin V. Sumner replaces Colonel Albert S. Johnston as commander of the Department of the Pacific.
SOUTHWEST: Fort Stockton, Texas, is abandoned by Federal forces.

Major Caleb C. Sibley capitulates 420 Federal troops to Colonel Earl Van Dorn at Indianola, Texas.

April 26
POLITICS: Georgia governor Joseph E. Brown orders all debts owed to Northerners repudiated.
SOUTH: General Joseph E. Johnston arrives and receives command of Virginia state forces defending the capital of Richmond.
NAVAL: The USS *Commerce* captures Confederate blockade-runner *Lancaster* off Havre de Grace, Maryland.

Confederate secretary of the navy Stephen R. Mallory proposes constructing new classes of steam-powered armored warships to offset the stark Union advantage in numbers.

April 27

POLITICS: President Abraham Lincoln authorizes suspension of writs of habeas corpus between Philadelphia, Pennsylvania, and Washington, D.C. General Winfield Scott is entrusted with adjudicating all incidents arising from the move.

NORTH: General Robert Patterson, Pennsylvania militia, takes command of the Department of Pennsylvania.

The 8th New York makes a belated appearance in the streets of Washington, D.C.

General Benjamin F. Butler assumes command of the Department of Annapolis, Maryland.

SOUTH: The Virginia Convention proffers its capital of Richmond as an alternative to Montgomery, Alabama.

WEST: Confederate colonel Thomas J. Jackson receives command of Virginia troops in the vicinity of Harper's Ferry.

The steamer *Helmick* is seized with military stores intended for the Confederacy at Cairo, Illinois.

NAVAL: President Abraham Lincoln extends the Union blockade to encompass the coasts of Virginia and North Carolina. Secretary of the Navy Gideon Welles also authorizes the interdiction of Confederate privateers at sea.

April 29

POLITICS: The Maryland House of Delegates decisively votes down secession by a margin of 53 to 13.

The provisional Confederate Congress convenes its second session at Montgomery, Alabama, granting President Jefferson Davis war powers and authority to raise volunteers, make loans, issue letters of marque, and command land and naval forces. They do so in direct reaction to President Abraham Lincoln's insurrection declaration and his call for volunteers.

NORTH: Elizabeth Blackwell, the nation's first female doctor, establishes the Women's Central Association for Relief to better coordinate the myriads of smaller war-relief groups. Her organization serves as a precursor for the much larger U.S. Sanitation Commission.

April 30

SOUTHWEST: Colonel William H. Emory evacuates Fort Washita in Indian Territory near the Texas border and heads north toward Fort Leavenworth, Texas. His withdrawal renders the neighboring Five Civilized Tribes—Cherokee, Chickasaw, Creek, Choctaw, and Seminole—vulnerable to Confederate influence.

May 1

NORTH: Soldiers killed in the Baltimore riots are interred with full military honors in Boston, Massachusetts.

SOUTH: General Robert E. Lee orders that additional Confederate forces be concentrated in the vicinity of Harper's Ferry, Virginia, presently commanded by Colonel Thomas J. Jackson.

Joseph E. Johnston is appointed brigadier general, C.S.A.

WEST: Governor Samuel W. Black of the Nebraska Territory calls out volunteer forces to assist the Union.

NAVAL: The USS *Commerce* captures the Confederate steam tug *Lioness* at the mouth of the Patapsco River, Maryland.

The first U.S. Navy vessels establish a blockade of the James River and Hampton Roads, Virginia.

The USS *Hatteras* seizes the Confederate vessel *Magnolia* in the Gulf of Mexico.

May 3

NORTH: President Abraham Lincoln issues a new call for 42,000 three-year volunteers, with 10 new regiments for the U.S. Army and an additional 18,000 seamen for the navy. This brings available manpower ceilings to 156,000 for the army and 25,000 for the navy.

General Winfield Scott, the senior American commander, unveils his so-called Anaconda Plan for defeating the rising tide of secessionism to President Abraham Lincoln. Basically, this entails a gunboat-supported drive down the Mississippi River by 60,000 troops, commencing at Cairo, Illinois, and ending in the Gulf of Mexico. Concurrently, the U.S. Navy would establish a tight blockade of the Southern coast to strangle Confederate trade with Europe. Derided at first by younger general officers who preferred a swift and decisive military campaign, the Scott plan is not adopted formally until 1864, and then in slightly modified form. Nonetheless, the aged "Old Fuss and Feathers" Scott provided a viable, war-winning strategy that ultimately preserved the Union. Lincoln spends nearly three years finding a general to execute it forcefully.

WEST: The Department of the Ohio is formed (Illinois, Indiana, Ohio).

U.S. ordnance stores are seized at Kansas City, Missouri.

May 4

WEST: Confederate sympathizers appropriate U.S. ordnance stores in Kansas City, Missouri.

SOUTHWEST: Fort Arbuckle, Indian Territory, is abandoned by Federal forces.

NAVAL: The USS *Cumberland* captures the *Mary and Virginia* and the *Theresa C.* attempting to run the blockade off Fortress Monroe, Virginia.

The CSS *Star of the West* is recommissioned in the Confederate navy at New Orleans, Louisiana, as a receiving ship.

May 5

NORTH: To deter attempted sabotage, troops under General Benjamin F. Butler occupy buildings along the Baltimore and Ohio Railroad.

SOUTH: Confederate forces temporarily evacuate the town of Alexandria, Virginia, situated on the Potomac River directly across from Washington, D.C.

NAVAL: The USS *Valley City* captures the Confederate vessel *J. O'Neil* off Pamlico River, North Carolina.

May 6

POLITICS: President Jefferson Davis signs a bill passed by the Confederate Congress, declaring a state of war with the United States.

The state legislature in Arkansas approves secession by 69 to 1, becoming the ninth state to depart, while the government of Tennessee likewise votes 66 to 25 to authorize a public referendum on the issue.

WEST: The Confederate-leaning Missouri State Militia under General Daniel M. Frost establishes a training camp near St. Louis at the behest of Governor Claiborne Jackson. Meanwhile, Captain Nathaniel Lyon, commanding the garrison at St. Louis, refuses all public demands to remove his troops from the city.

NAVAL: The Confederate Congress mandates the issuance of letters of marque and reprisal to privateers.

May 7

POLITICS: The Tennessee state legislature formally votes to join the Confederacy while riots erupt between pro- and antisecessionist sympathizers in Knoxville. The eastern half of the state remains a strong Unionist enclave throughout the war.

NORTH: President Abraham Lincoln appoints newly repatriated Major Robert Anderson to recruiting duties in his native state of Kentucky.

NAVAL: The U.S. Naval Academy staff, students, and supplies finally board the steamer USS *Baltic* and the venerable frigate USS *Constitution* at Annapolis, prior to relocating to Newport, Rhode Island.

The USS *Yankee* receives the fire of Confederate batteries stationed at Gloucester Point, Virginia.

May 9

POLITICS: President Jefferson Davis authorizes enlisting more than 400,000 volunteers for three years or the duration of the war. The quotas are met enthusiastically at first.

NORTH: Maryland's pro-Union stance forces all secessionist military units to evacuate the state.

SOUTHWEST: Colonel William H. Emory abandons Fort Cobb in the Chickasaw Indian Nation.

A detachment of Federal troops under Colonel Isaac V. D. Reeve surrenders to Colonel Earl Van Dorn at San Lucas Spring, Texas.

NAVAL: The frigate USS *Constitution* and the steamer *Baltic* arrive at Newport, Rhode Island, with faculty and midshipmen, to reestablish the U.S. Naval Academy.

Confederate secretary of the navy Stephen R. Mallory orders Commander James D. Bulloch to England as Confederate naval agent. There, Bulloch engages in a battle of wits with U.S. Minister Charles Francis Adams while clandestinely acquiring ships, guns, and munitions.

May 10

POLITICS: President Jefferson Davis urges the Confederate Congress to purchase six warships, arms, and supplies from abroad.

SOUTH: General Robert E. Lee is made commander of Confederate troops in Virginia.

WEST: Violence erupts in St. Louis, Missouri, between secessionist sympathizers and U.S. Army troops, backed by a large German-speaking population. About two dozen civilians and two soldiers die in the fighting as Captain Nathaniel Lyon energetically takes General Daniel M. Frost and 625 Confederates prisoner at Camp Jackson. However, his rashness induces many undecided citizens to join secessionist ranks, and 30 citizens die in subsequent rioting.

Naval: Confederate secretary of the navy Stephen R. Mallory alerts the Committee of Naval Affairs, Confederate Congress, that the acquisition of a heavily armed iron ship is "a matter of the first necessity."

The steamer USS *Niagara* under Captain William W. McKean assumes a blockading position off Charleston, South Carolina.

May 11

South: Ben McCulloch is appointed brigadier general, C.S.A.

West: Continuing secessionist unrest in St. Louis, Missouri, results in seven civilian deaths at the hands of the 5th Reserve Regiment. Colonel William S. Harney also arrives back in town to succeed Captain Nathaniel Lyon as garrison commander.

Naval: The USS *Pawnee* arrives off Alexandria, Virginia, to protect anchored Union vessels from attack.

May 12

Naval: The USS *Niagara* captures the Confederate blockade-runner *General Parkhill* at sea while approaching Charleston, South Carolina.

May 13

Diplomacy: In a move that antagonizes the Lincoln administration, the government of Great Britain recognizes both the North and the South as belligerents. This amounts to a discreet nod in terms of recognizing the Confederacy as an equal partner in the upcoming struggle, but Queen Victoria's adherence to strict neutrality dashes Southern hopes for military intervention on their behalf.

Politics: Virginia delegates from the western portion of the state, who disagree with secession, convene a convention of their own at Wheeling. There, they discuss joining the Union as a new state.

North: Baltimore is reoccupied and secured by Federal forces under General Benjamin F. Butler, who both occupies Federal Hill and imposes martial law without prior authorization.

West: General George B. McClellan is appointed commander of the Department of the Ohio.

Southwest: General Ben McCulloch becomes Confederate commander of the Indian Territory.

Naval: The blockade of Pensacola, Florida, resumes under the USS *Sabine*.

May 14

Diplomacy: U.S. minister Charles Francis Adams arrives in London, England, where it is expected his pristine abolitionist credentials will resonate favorably at the Court of St. James.

NORTH: John C. Frémont, a popular explorer and one-time presidential candidate, becomes a major general, U.S. Army. Irvin McDowell and Montgomery C. Meigs also are appointed brigadier generals.

General Benjamin F. Butler consolidates his grip on Baltimore, Maryland, and arrests noted secessionists, including Ross Winans, who had invented a steam cannon. Governor Thomas H. Hicks also issues a call for four regiments to defend Maryland and the national capital.

SOUTH: Robert E. Lee is appointed brigadier general, C.S.A.

WEST: Major Robert Anderson is instructed by President Abraham Lincoln to assist Kentucky Unionists wherever possible, despite the state's avowed neutrality.

The South needs rolling stock, so Colonel Thomas J. Jackson orders the seizure of trains and railroad cars at Harper's Ferry, Virginia.

NAVAL: The USS *Minnesota* captures Confederate schooners *Mary Willis, Delaware Farmer,* and *Emily Ann* off Hampton Roads, Virginia.

May 15

NORTH: Major Robert Anderson, defender of Fort Sumter and regarded as a Northern hero, is promoted several steps to brigadier general, U.S. Army.

SOUTH: General Benjamin Butler relinquishes command of the Department of Annapolis and arrives at Fortress Monroe, Virginia, where he advances to major general of volunteers. He is succeeded by General George Cadwalader.

WEST: General Joseph E. Johnston assumes command of Confederate forces near Harper's Ferry, Virginia.

Colonel William S. Harney, commanding at St. Louis, Missouri, implores citizens to ignore secessionist attempts to raise militia. However, he takes no active steps to interfere, which raises eyebrows among union supporters.

NAVAL: The USS *Bainbridge* is ordered to New Grenada (Panama) to protect American shipping from possible Confederate privateers.

May 16

POLITICS: Tennessee is encouraged to enter the Confederacy at the urging of Governor Isham Harris.

SOUTH: Samuel Cooper gains appointment as a full general and senior leader in the Confederate army.

WEST: William S. Rosecrans is promoted to brigadier general, U.S. Army.

Union troops enter Potosi, Missouri, and begin to round up suspected Confederate sympathizers.

NAVAL: The Navy Department orders Commander John Rodgers to establish naval forces on western rivers and to cooperate with troops under General John C. Frémont.

May 17

POLITICS: President Jefferson Davis agrees to a $50 million loan to the Confederate government along with the distribution of treasury notes. He also signs legislation admitting North Carolina into the Confederacy.

NAVAL: The USS *Minnesota* seizes the Confederate bark *Star* at sea en route to Bremen, Germany.

WEST: The California legislature votes its support for the Union.

SOUTHWEST: Chief John Ross declares neutrality for Cherokee throughout the Indian Territory, although the tribe continues splintering into pro- and antisecessionist factions.

May 18

POLITICS: Arkansas formally joins the Confederate States of America.

WEST: Missouri politician Francis Blair contacts President Abraham Lincoln concerning his suspicions about Colonel William S. Harney, commanding officer at St. Louis.

NAVAL: U.S. Navy ships blockade the mouth of the Rappahannock River, Virginia.

The Confederate schooner *Savannah* is commissioned as a privateer.

May 19

WEST: The Confederate garrison at Harper's Ferry in western Virginia is strengthened by additional troops.

NAVAL: Warships USS *Monticello* and *Thomas Freeborn* trade fire with a Confederate battery at Sewell's Point, Virginia.

The CSS *Lady Davis* seizes the Union ship *A. B. Thompson* near Charleston, South Carolina.

May 20

POLITICS: The Provisional Confederate Congress elects to relocate itself from Montgomery, Alabama, to Richmond, Virginia, where it will remain until 1865. This is calculated to strengthen the Old Dominion's ties to the Confederacy but also shifts the locus of the war northward.

At the behest of Governor Beriah Magoffin, the legislature of the strategic state of Kentucky declares neutrality in the upcoming struggle.

The North Carolina State Convention at Raleigh votes to become the 10th state to secede and also ratifies the Confederate Constitution.

SOUTH: William W. Loring is appointed brigadier general, C.S.A.

NAVAL: The USS *Crusader* captures Confederate blockade-runner *Neptune* off Fort Taylor, Florida.

May 21

DIPLOMACY: A bellicose secretary of state William H. Seward issues Dispatch No. 10 for Minister Charles F. Adams in London, which threatens war with England. In light of prevailing military and political realities, Adams simply ignores it.

POLITICS: The Provisional Confederate Congress adjourns its second Session.

SOUTH: General John B. Magruder arrives to take command of Confederate forces at Yorktown, Virginia. Among his best units there is the 1st North Carolina under Colonel Daniel H. Hill.

WEST: General William S. Harney, commanding Federal forces in Missouri, enters into a convention with Missouri State Guard commander General Sterling Price. He then agrees not to introduce Federal troops into the state if the Southerners can maintain order. Both Congressman Francis P. Blair and Captain Nathaniel Lyon condemn the agreement, regarding it as treasonous.

NAVAL: USS *Pocahontas* captures the Confederate steamer *James Guy* off Machdoc Creek, Virginia.

The venerable frigate USS *Constellation,* the navy's oldest operating warship, captures the slaver *Triton* off the west coast of Africa.

May 23

POLITICS: A popular vote for secession in Virginia is 97,750 in favor and 32,134 against. However, efforts continue in the 50 western counties to remain within the Union.

SOUTH: General Benjamin F. Butler, commanding Fortress Monroe, Virginia, refuses to return three runaways slaves to their owner by declaring them "contraband of war." This sets an important precedent for allowing thousands of slaves to escape to Union lines and freedom.

John B. Floyd, the former secretary of war, becomes a brigadier general, C.S.A.

Virginia general Benjamin Huger assumes command at Norfolk, Virginia.

WEST: Federal troops commence extended operations against Indians on the Eel and Mad rivers of California for the next three weeks.

NAVAL: The USS *Mississippi* suffers sabotage to its steam condensers and is forced back to Boston, Massachusetts, for repairs.

May 24

SOUTH: About 13,000 Union soldiers under General Samuel P. Heintzelman occupy Alexandria and Arlington Heights, Virginia, bolstering the defenses of Washington, D.C. The North now enjoys another solid lodgment on Old Dominion soil. However, when 24-year-old Colonel Elmer E. Ellsworth of the 11th New York Regiment (Fire Zouaves) removes a Confederate flag from a hotel in Alexandria, he is shot by innkeeper James T. Jackson, who is then himself killed. Ellsworth enjoys the melancholy distinction of becoming the North's first officer fatality. Both men are enshrined as martyrs by their respective side.

NAVAL: The USS *Pawnee* under Commander Stephen C. Rowan receives the surrender of Alexandria, Virginia, which is occupied promptly by Federal forces under Commodore John A. B. Dahlgren.

May 25

POLITICS: President Abraham Lincoln attends the funeral of Colonel Elmer E. Ellsworth after his remains lay in state at the White House. "So much of promised usefulness to one's country, and of bright hopes for one's self and friends," a somber Lincoln writes, "have rarely been so suddenly dashed, as in his fall."

NORTH: Secessionist John Merryman is imprisoned by Union authorities in Baltimore, Maryland, for recruiting Confederate troops and sabotaging railroad lines and bridges. Chief Justice Roger B. Taney, acting in the capacity of a Federal circuit court judge, issues a writ of habeas corpus on his behalf to release him, but the commanding officer recognizes no authority other than the commander in chief's. Taney subsequently countered that only Congress possesses the power to suspend habeas corpus.

SOUTH: To forestall Confederate moves against Washington, D.C., Union forces destroy seven miles of bridges and rail line between Alexandria and Leesburg, Virginia.

NAVAL: The USS *Pawnee* captures the Confederate steamer *Thomas Collyer* at Alexandria, Virginia.

The USS *Minnesota* captures the Confederate bark *Winfred* off Hampton Roads, Virginia.

May 26

POLITICAL: U.S. postmaster general Francis P. Blair announces the suspension of all service with Confederate states.

WEST: General George B. McClellan orders three columns of Union forces to advance on Grafton in western Virginia to secure the Baltimore and Ohio Railroad. This forms the most important link between the capital and the western states.

NAVAL: The sloop USS *Powhatan* under Lieutenant David D. Porter takes up blockading positions off Mobile, Alabama.

Commander Charles H. Poor of the USS *Brooklyn* assumes blockading stations off New Orleans, Louisiana.

May 27

POLITICS: Chief Justice Roger B. Taney again declares the suspension of the writ of habeas corpus unconstitutional, which President Abraham Lincoln promptly ignores in light of circumstances.

SOUTH: To enlarge the Northern staging area around Fortress Monroe, Virginia, General Benjamin F. Butler advances eight miles and occupies Newport News.

May 28

SOUTH: General Irvin McDowell is appointed commander of the Department of Northeastern Virginia, including newly acquired Alexandria.

NAVAL: The USS *Union* assumes blockading positions off Savannah, Georgia.

May 29

NORTH: Dorothea L. Dix approaches Secretary of War Simon Cameron and offers to assist organizing hospital services for Federal forces.

SOUTH: Albert S. Johnston is appointed a full general in the Confederate army.

The first Confederate Congress convenes its first session in Richmond, Virginia.

NAVAL: The Potomac Flotilla, consisting of steamers USS *Thomas Freeborn, Anacostia, Resolute,* and *Pawnee,* bombard Southern batteries at Aquia Creek, Virginia, for the next three days.

Commander John R. Goldsborough and the steamer USS *Union* establish a blockade off Savannah, Georgia.

The USS *Powhatan* under Lieutenant David D. Porter captures the Confederate schooner *Mary Clinton* near the Southwest Pass, Mississippi River.

The Confederate privateer *J. C. Calhoun* captures the Union brig *Panama* and takes it to New Orleans.

May 30

POLITICS: Secretary of War Simon Cameron instructs General Benjamin F. Butler at Fortress Monroe, Virginia, that fugitive slaves who cross Union lines are not to be returned but, rather, fed and given work around military installations.

WEST: Federal forces under Colonel Benjamin F. Kelley occupy Grafton, western Virginia, to secure passage of the Baltimore and Ohio Railroad as well as encourage the activities of pro-Union inhabitants. General George B. McClellan next dispatches a brigade under General Thomas A. Morris to seize the town at Philippi, west of strategic Harper's Ferry.

NAVAL: Confederate forces raise the scuttled USS *Merrimac* at Norfolk, Virginia, and commence reconstruction work.

The USS *Quaker City* captures the Confederate schooner *Lynchburg* at sea.

May 31

WEST: General John C. Frémont supersedes General William S. Harney as Union commander in Missouri. His prior agreement with General Sterling Price not to introduce Federal troops in the region also is abrogated.

Federal troops, newly removed from Indian Territory, reestablish themselves at Fort Leavenworth, Kansas.

NAVAL: The USS *Perry* seizes the Confederate blockade runner *Hannah M. Johnson* at sea.

June 1

DIPLOMACY In a major defeat for Confederate privateering, the government of Great Britain forbids armed vessels of either side from bringing prizes into English ports. However, this stance does not prevent British shipyards from clandestinely constructing warships for use by the Confederate navy.

SOUTH: Skirmishing commences between Union and Confederate forces at Arlington Mills and Fairfax County Courthouse, Virginia. Captain John Q. Marr becomes the South's earliest officer fatality.

NAVAL: The USS *Union* captures the Confederate vessel *F. W. Johnson* off the North Carolina coast.

June 2

SOUTH: General Pierre G. T. Beauregard, formerly commanding at Charleston, South Carolina, succeeds General Milledge L. Bonham as head of Confederate forces at Manassas Junction, Virginia.

June 3

POLITICS: Democrat Stephen A. Douglas, the "Little Giant" who defeated Abraham Lincoln in his bid for the Senate, dies in Chicago, Illinois, at the age of 48. The North loses one of its most eloquent and forceful spokespeople.

WEST: A brigade of Indiana troops under General Thomas A. Morris surprises and easily defeats a Confederate detachment under Colonel George A. Porterfield at Philippi, in western Virginia. The Northerners successfully attack his camp and send the defenders scurrying with the loss of 15 men, their baggage, and several flags out of roughly 1,000 men who were engaged. Thomas loses two men wounded. This victory, greatly exaggerated in the press as the "Philippi Races," clears the Kanawha Valley of enemy forces and provides greater impetus for the region to break with the Confederacy. General George B. McClellan, commanding but not directly involved in the action, receives both credit and increasing political attention.

June 4

NAVAL: The brig USS *Perry* captures the Confederate privateer *Savannah* at sea, releasing its prize, the American brig *Joseph*.

June 5

NORTH: Federal authorities and U.S. marshals seize powder works in Connecticut and Delaware to prevent possible shipments to the Confederacy.

SOUTH: Earl Van Dorn is appointed brigadier general, C.S.A.

NAVAL: The USS *Quaker City* captures the Confederate ship *General Greene* off the Chesapeake Capes.

The U.S. revenue cutter *Harriet Lane* engages Confederate forces at Pig Point, Hampton Roads, Virginia.

The USS *Niagara* captures the Confederate vessel *Aid* off Mobile, Alabama.

June 6

SOUTH: Colonel John B. Magruder, commanding Confederate forces outside of Yorktown, Virginia, dispatches Colonel Daniel H. Hill and his 1st North Carolina to nearby Big Bethel to observe Union movements. This places them only eight miles from the main Union force gathered at Hampton.

WEST: Responsibility for Missouri is transferred to the Department of the Ohio under General George B. McClellan.

General Henry A. Wise, former Virginia governor, is appointed Confederate commander of the Kanawha Valley, western Virginia.

June 8

POLITICS: Tennessee voters approve secession by a margin of 104,913 to 47,238, and it joins the Confederacy as the 11th and final state to do so. However, the eastern sections of the state remain active in the Union cause.

SOUTH: General Robert S. Garnett is appointed commander of Confederate forces in northwestern Virginia. Governor John Lechter, to enhance the defenses of his state further, transfers all Virginia troops to Confederate control.

NAVAL: The USS *Resolute* captures the Confederate vessel *Somerset* at Breton's Bay, Georgia.

The USS *Mississippi* establishes a blockade off Key West, Florida.

June 9

NORTH: The U.S. Sanitary Commission is founded and organized to provide nursing, sanitation, and other support activities to Federal forces.

SOUTH: General Benjamin F. Butler decides to dislodge Confederate forces entrenched at Big Bethel, Virginia, only eight miles from his main position in Hampton. To do so, he orders the brigade of General Ebenezer Pierce—composed of five

New York regiments, one from Massachusetts and Vermont, and a section of the 2nd U.S. Artillery out from Newport News—on a night march. The transit goes badly, with many units becoming lost. Worse, the 5th New York (Zouaves), resplendent in their gray uniforms, are mistaken for Confederates and are fired upon, sustaining 21 casualties. Butler's plan, which calls for an attack by four converging columns, also proves overly complicated for his inexperienced recruits to execute properly.

NAVAL: The USS *Massachusetts* captures the British blockade-runner *Perthshire* off Pensacola, Florida.

June 10

NORTH: Dorothea L. Dix becomes superintendent of woman nurses to help supervise medical activities within the U.S. Army.

Colonel Charles Stone leads the 14th U.S. Infantry from Washington, D.C., and embarks at Edward's Ferry across the Potomac River en route to Rockville, Maryland.

SOUTH: Federal forces under General Ebenezer Pierce, numbering 4,400, attack 1,500 Confederates led by Colonel John B. Magruder at Big Bethel, Virginia. The green Union troops are committed piecemeal against enemy entrenchments by their commander and are beaten back, principally by the well-trained 1st North Carolina of Colonel Daniel H. Hill. After badly bungling the effort, Pierce withdraws with eight killed, 53 wounded, and five missing. Among the slain is Major Theodore Winthrop, a noted journalist and member of General Benjamin F. Butler's staff. Southern losses are one killed and seven wounded; news of this successful encounter causes joyous celebrations at Richmond. Consequently, both Magruder and Hill gain promotion to brigadier general. Major George W. Randolph, who handled Magruder's artillery, ultimately rises to Confederate secretary of war.

WEST: Federal captain Nathaniel Lyon, commanding the St. Louis garrison, storms out of negotiations with pro-Southern Missouri governor Claiborne F. Jackson and Home Guard commander General Sterling Price. He then "declares war" on the state of Missouri and prepares to dispense his opponents by force. Meanwhile, Claiborne issues an urgent appeal for 50,000 volunteers to fend off Federal troops.

NAVAL: Confederate lieutenant John M. Brooke, a gifted naval engineer, receives orders to convert the former stream frigate USS *Merrimack* into the ironclad CSS *Virginia.*

The USS *Union* captures the Confederate vessel *Hallie Jackson* off Savannah, Georgia.

June 11

POLITICS: Pro-Union delegates meeting at Wheeling, Virginia, form an alternate government in the westernmost reaches of that state and elect Francis H. Pierpont as governor, along with two U.S. senators.

WEST: Colonel Lew Wallace and his 11th Indiana depart Cumberland, Maryland, and advance against Romney in western Virginia, which he intends to occupy.

SOUTHWEST: Colonel William W. Loring resigns his commission as commander of the New Mexico Territory to join the Confederacy and is succeeded by Colonel Edward R. S. Canby.

June 13

WEST: Colonel Lew Wallace and his 11th Indiana brush aside Confederate pickets and occupy Romney in western Virginia.

Pro-Southern militia under Governor Claiborne F. Jackson evacuate St. Louis, Missouri, and set out for the capital at Jefferson City.

NAVAL: The USS *Mississippi* seizes the schooner *Frost King* at Key West, Florida.

June 14

NORTH: Federal troops under Colonel Charles P. Stone skirmish with Confederates at Seneca Falls, Maryland. At Point of Rocks, Maryland, engineers also remove a 100-ton boulder obstructing the Baltimore and Ohio Railroad, rolled there from overhanging cliffs by retreating Confederates.

SOUTH: Robert E. Lee is promoted to full general, C.S.A.

WEST: General Joseph E. Johnston evacuates Harper's Ferry, Virginia, in the face of converging columns under Generals Robert Patterson and George B. McClellan.

Confederate sympathizers under Governor Claiborne F. Jackson hastily depart Jefferson City, Missouri, as Federal forces draw nearer.

NAVAL: The USS *Sumter* captures the slaver *Falmouth* off the West African coast.

June 15

WEST: Federal troops under Captain Nathaniel Lyon forcibly occupy the capital of Jefferson City, Missouri, while 1,500 poorly armed and trained Confederate sympathizers under Governor Claiborne F. Jackson encamp at nearby Booneville.

June 16

WEST: Confederate forces under General Robert S. Garnett seize Laurel Hill in western Virginia and subsequently occupy a similar strong position at Rich Mountain. Badly outnumbered by troops of the nearby Department of the Ohio under General George B. McClellan, he initiates a series of raids on his line of communications to keep Union forces off balance.

June 17

DIPLOMACY: The government of Spain declares its neutrality but, following Britain's lead, recognizes the Confederacy as a belligerent power.

POLITICS: Unionist delegates meeting in Wheeling, Virginia, unanimously declare their independence from the Confederacy.

NORTH: President Abraham Lincoln is treated to a demonstration of balloon technology by Professor Thaddeus S. C. Lowe. Military observers who are present appreciate the potential use of such technology as battlefield reconnaissance platforms.

Union forces under Colonel Charles P. Stones skirmish with Confederates at Conrad's Ferry, Maryland.

SOUTH: In a clever little action, Colonel Maxcy Gregg of the 1st South Carolina Infantry ambushes and captures a locomotive at Vienna, Virginia. Ohio troops are subsequently dispatched there to repair the tracks.

WEST: Pro-Union inhabitants of Greeneville, Tennessee, rally to keep their region of the state out of the Confederacy.

Union General Nathaniel Lyon and 1,700 men aggressively pursue retreating Missouri State Guard under Governor Claiborne F. Jackson up the Missouri River. He then disembarks and attacks 1,500 poorly armed secessionists at Camp Bacon near Boonville. Jackson forms a line to resist an onslaught by the 1st Missouri Infantry and 2nd Missouri Rifles, but his stand is shattered by artillery fire from Lyon's two cannon. In 20 minutes, the governor and his consorts flee to the southwest corner of the state. Both sides lose three dead and 10 wounded apiece, with an additional 60 guardsmen captured. More important, Union forces now control the lower Missouri River—and Lyon sternly warns all inhabitants against possible acts of treason. He then dispatches a column of pro-Union Missouri Volunteers to prevent General Sterling Price from linking up with Confederate forces under General Ben McCulloch in Arkansas.

NAVAL: The USS *Massachusetts* takes the Confederate schooner *Achilles* off Ship Island, Mississippi.

June 18

NAVAL: The USS *Union* captures the blockade-runner *Amelia* at Charleston, South Carolina.

June 19

POLITICAL: Pro-Union delegates meeting at Wheeling, Virginia, elect Francis H. Pierpont provisional governor of the western portion of that state.

WEST: An attack on Cole Camp, Missouri, by German-speaking pro-Unionists is repulsed by secessionist militia. This small victory stiffens the resolve of the fleeing Southerners.

SOUTHWEST: Cherokee chief John Ross repeats his stance of neutrality and reminds fellow tribesmen of previous obligations to the United States.

NAVAL: The USS *Massachusetts* captures the Confederate brig *Nahum Stetson* off Pass al'Outre, Louisiana.

June 20

WEST: The governor of Kansas calls on citizens to organize and repel any pro-secessionist attacks emanating from Missouri.

June 22

SOUTH: Colonel Harvey Brown, commanding Fort Pickens, Florida, informs the War Department that he will not return fugitive slaves to their owners unless ordered to do so.

WEST: Pro-Union sympathizers gather in Greeneville, Tennessee, and formally declare their allegiance to the Federal government.

June 23

SOUTH: Professor Thaddeus S. C. Lowe rises in his balloon to observe Confederate deployments at Falls Church, Virginia.

NAVAL: Armored conversion of the ex-USS *Merrimac* into the new ironclad CSS *Virginia* continues in earnest at Norfolk, Virginia.

The USS *Massachusetts* seizes Confederate schooners *Trois Frese, Olive Branch, Fanny,* and *Basile* in the Gulf of Mexico. It also catches a Mexican schooner, *Brilliant,* as it attempts to slip through the blockade.

June 24
NORTH: In Washington, D.C., President Abraham Lincoln observes demonstrations of rifled cannon and the "Coffee Mill," an experimental, rapid-firing weapon.
NAVAL: The USS *Pawnee* and *Thomas Freeborn* again engage Confederate batteries at Mathias Point, Virginia.

June 25
SOUTH: Leonidas Polk is appointed major general, C.S.A.

June 26
NORTH: General Nathaniel P. Banks is directed to arrest George P. Jane, marshal of Baltimore, Maryland, police, for secessionist activity. He is ordered to apprehend him as discreetly as possible.
WEST: Colonel Lew Wallace skirmishes with Confederates at Patterson Creek, in western Virginia.
NAVAL: The USS *Minnesota* captures the Confederate bark *Sally Magee* off Hampton Roads, Virginia.

June 27
NORTH: A major strategy session is called in Washington, D.C., with representatives of the army, navy, and coast survey in attendance. The newly created Blockade Strategy Board includes Captain Samuel F. Du Pont, Commander Charles H. Davis, and other military notables and becomes a key planning body. The policies they promulgate remain in effect to the end of the war.
NAVAL: A landing party from the USS *Resolute* burns a Confederate supply depot on the southern shore of the Potomac River.

Confederate forces repel an attempt to land forces at Mathias Point, Virginia, by gunboats USS *Pawnee* and *Thomas Freeborn.* Commander James H. Ward, a former superintendent of the U.S. Naval Academy, is killed in action, becoming the first U.S. Navy officer fatality.

June 28
NAVAL: The Blockade Strategy Board resolves to seize a port in South Carolina and Georgia to serve as coaling stations for the blockading fleet offshore.

Confederates posing as passengers under George N. Hollins, C.S.N., board and capture the passenger steamer *St. Nicholas* at Baltimore and then sail into Chesapeake Bay. Hollins hopes to encounter and surprise the USS *Pawnee,* but it fails to appear.

Confederate privateer *Jefferson Davis* slips past the blockade at Charleston, South Carolina, and commences a successful career raiding Union commerce.

June 29
POLITICAL: Amid mounting war fever, President Abraham Lincoln is briefed on military strategy by Generals Winfield Scott and Irvin McDowell. However, Scott

is against committing untrained levies to combat at this stage and argues—unsuccessfully—against seeking victory in a single, decisive campaign.

NORTH: The Washington, D.C., garrison is bolstered by the arrival of the 11th Massachusetts and 12th New York, which encamp about the White House.

SOUTH: A surprise Confederate raid against Harper's Ferry destroys several boats and bridges before withdrawing.

June 30

NAVAL: The USS *Reliance* destroys the Confederate sloop *Passenger* in the Potomac River.

Captain Raphael Semmes, commanding CSS *Sumter,* evades the USS *Brooklyn* off New Orleans, Louisiana, and commences his celebrated career as a commerce raider.

July 1

POLITICS: The War Department decrees that military volunteers will be recruited from both Kentucky and Tennessee, despite the former's neutrality and the latter's secession.

NORTH: At Baltimore, Maryland, Federal troops arrest four members of the local police force for secessionist activities.

NAVAL: The USS *Minnesota* captures the Confederate schooner *Sally Mears* off Hampton Roads, Virginia.

July 2

POLITICS: The new pro-Union legislature of western Virginia convenes at Wheeling.

NORTH: President Abraham Lincoln confers with General John C. Frémont over strategy in the vital and sensitive region of Missouri, which remains wracked by secessionist unrest.

WEST: General Robert Patterson continues advancing into the Shenandoah Valley and crosses the Potomac River at Williamsport, Maryland, to pin down Confederate forces there. Patterson also wins a minor clash at Hoke's Run, Virginia. General Joseph E. Johnston, meanwhile, prepares to hold off Patterson while shifting the bulk of his troops to Confederate troops near Washington, D.C.

NAVAL: The USS *South Carolina* under Commander James Alden assumes blockading positions off Galveston, Texas.

July 3

WEST: General Robert Patterson continues advancing down the Shenandoah Valley and occupies Martinsburg, Virginia. Outnumbered, General Joseph E. Johnston falls back on Winchester, Virginia.

SOUTHWEST: Union forces abandon Fort McLane in the New Mexico Territory. Meanwhile, the new Western Department arises, consisting of Missouri, Arkansas, Kansas, New Mexico, and the Indian Territory.

NAVAL: CSS *Sumter* under Captain Raphael Semmes captures the American vessel *Golden Rocket* off Cuba.

July 4

POLITICS: President Abraham Lincoln addresses a special session of the 37th Congress and pleads for $4 million—and an additional 400,000 men. Having exhausted all avenues for peaceful settlement, he makes clear his intention of waging war solely against the Confederate government—not the South itself. He also explains and justifies his recent suspension of habeas corpus strictly as a wartime expedient.

SOUTH: Joseph E. Johnston is appointed a full general, C.S.A.

WEST: Union and Confederate forces briefly skirmish at Harper's Ferry, Virginia.

NAVAL: The USS *South Carolina* captures the Confederate blockade-runners *Shark, Venus, Ann Ryan, McCanfield, Louisa,* and *Dart* of Galveston, Texas.

July 5

SOUTH: Contending forces under Generals Benjamin Butler and John B. Magruder skirmish near Curtis's Farm, Newport News, Virginia.

WEST: Colonel Franz Sigel, leading a German-speaking detachment of 1,100 volunteers, advances on a larger force of 4,000 Missouri militia under Governor Claiborne F. Jackson near Carthage. The Confederates decide to attack Sigel's line, which is posted on a hill. The Northerners, who lack cavalry to guard their flanks, pelt Jackson's line with some small artillery, which so unnerves their commander that he orders his 2,000 unharmed state cavalry to take shelter in adjoining woods. Sigel, however, interprets this move as a threat to his flank, so he sounds a retreat. Union losses are 13 dead and 31 wounded to a Confederate tally of 40 killed and 64 injured. Sigel subsequently falls back on the army of General Nathaniel Lyon while Jackson moves to unite with forces under General Sterling Price. Elsewhere, General Ben McCulloch captures a detachment of 80 Union soldiers at Neosho.

NAVAL: The USS *South Carolina* captures the Confederate blockade-runners *Falcon* and *Coralia* off Galveston, Texas.

The USS *Dana* captures the Confederate sloop *Teaser* in Nanjemoy Creek, Maryland.

July 6

WEST: George B. McClellan, commanding the Department of the Ohio, orders an Indiana brigade under General Thomas A. Morris to depart Philippi in western Virginia and march toward Confederate troop concentrations at Laurel Hill. He will take the main force of three brigades simultaneously in a movement against enemy forces at nearby Rich Mountain.

NAVAL: Confederate privateer *Jefferson Davis* seizes Union vessels *Enchantress* and *John Welsh* off Cape Hatteras, North Carolina.

The USS *South Carolina* captures the Confederate schooner *George Baker* off Galveston, Texas.

Confederate raider CSS *Sumter* under Captain Raphael Semmes docks at Havana, Cuba, with six Northern prizes in tow.

July 7

NORTH: Union and Confederate troops skirmish at Great Falls, Maryland.

SOUTH: Contending forces skirmish heavily at Bellington and Laurel Hill in western Virginia.

WEST: Union troops arrive at the foot of Laurel Hill in western Virginia. A force of two regiments under Colonel Robert L. McCook probes defenses erected there by Confederate general Robert S. Gannett, and heavy skirmishing erupts.

General Nathaniel Lyon, commanding Union forces at Springfield, Missouri, is reinforced by troops under Major Samuel D. Sturgis. He now possesses 7,000 men but remains outnumbered two to one by invigorated Confederate forces.

NAVAL: The USS *Pocahontas* engages and damages the CSS *George Page* in Aquia Creek, Virginia.

The Confederate privateer *Jefferson Davis* seizes the Northern ship *S. J. Waring* off New Jersey.

The USS *South Carolina* captures the Confederate schooner *Sam Houston* off Galveston, Texas.

July 8

WEST: Union forces attack and disperse a camp of secessionist militia at Florida, Missouri.

Confederate general Henry H. Sibley receives orders to march from Texas and drive Union forces out of the neighboring New Mexico Territory.

While cruising the Potomac River, the screw tug *Resolute* espies and retrieves two mysterious looking objects, which turn out to be the First Confederate "torpedoes" (mines) encountered during the war.

July 9

POLITICS: The U.S. House of Representatives resolves not to oblige Union soldiers to return fugitive slaves.

WEST: General George B. McClellan, angered by guerrilla attacks on his supply lines in the Allegheny Mountains of western Virginia, resolves to attack Confederate forces under General Robert S. Garnett near Beverly. He gathers up four brigades totaling 15,000 troops and marches to Rich Mountain.

Colonel Robert F. Smith, 16th Illinois, skirmishes with Confederates around Monroe Station, Missouri.

NAVAL: The USS *South Carolina* destroys the Confederate schooner *Tom Hicks* off Galveston, Texas.

Confederate privateer *Jefferson Davis* captures the Union brig *Mary E. Thompson* and the schooner *Mary Goodell.*

July 10

POLITICS: President Abraham Lincoln assures General Simon B. Buckner, head of the Kentucky militia, that Union forces will not violate his state's neutrality.

The Creek Nation concludes a peace treaty with Colonel Albert Pike of the Confederacy.

SOUTH: Daniel H. Hill is appointed brigadier general, C.S.A.

WEST: Having reconnoitered enemy positions, General George B. McClellan commences his offensive in western Virginia by dispatching General William S. Rosecrans to dislodge enemy troops from Rich Mountain while another force under

Colonel Thomas A. Morris advances upon Confederates concentrated at Laurel Hill.

SOUTHWEST: Federal forces abandon Fort Breckinridge, New Mexico Territory.

NAVAL: The USS *Minnesota* captures the Confederate brig *Amy Warwick* in Hampton Roads, Virginia.

July 11

POLITICS: The U.S. Senate formally expels absent members from Arkansas, North Carolina, Texas, and Virginia. One senator from Tennessee is also ejected, but Andrew Johnson, a loyalist from the eastern region of that state, retains his seat.

NORTH: General Nathaniel P. Banks becomes commander of the Department of Annapolis.

WEST: General William S. Rosecrans and 2,000 Union troops attack Colonel John Pegram's 1,300 Confederates at Rich Mountain, western Virginia, after marching all night through a heavy downpour. Assisted by local Unionist guide David Hart, the Northerners snake down a secret path turning the Confederate left flank. A stout fight ensues, and Rosecrans drives back a 300-man advance guard before moving on Pegram's main body. The Confederates hastily abandon their position and flee to nearby Beverly. Victory here places Union forces astride General Robert S. Garnett's lines of communication, and he likewise withdraws from Laurel Hill, closely pursued by the main force under General George B. McClellan. Union losses are 12 killed and 62 wounded; Confederate casualties are given as 72.

NAVAL: The USS *South Carolina* seizes the Confederate ship *T. J. Chambers* off Galveston, Texas.

July 12

POLITICS: Colonel Albert Pike arranges treaties between the Confederacy and the Choctaw and Chickasaw tribes of the Indian Territory.

SOUTH: Continued skirmishing erupts between Union and Confederate forces near Newport News, Virginia.

WEST: Colonel John Pegram surrenders 555 men to General William S. Rosecrans at Beverly, western Virginia, which is then occupied by the main Union army under General George B. McClellan. In the same theater, General Jacob D. Cox's Federal troops advance to engage General Henry A. Wise's Confederates in the Great Kanawha Valley. Southern forces under General Robert S. Garnett, anxious to escape the closing pincer movement, hurriedly move from Kaler's Ford on the Cheat River to nearby Corrick's Ford.

July 13

POLITICS: The House of Representatives expels Missouri member John Clark on a vote of 94 to 45.

WEST: General Robert S. Garnett and his Confederates are defeated again at Corrick's Ford (Carricksford) in western Virginia by General Thomas A. Morris's Indiana brigade. After hard slogging through heavy rainfall and steep terrain, the Federals catch Garnett while fording the Cheat River and maul the 23rd Virginia, which constitutes his rear guard. Garnett himself was in the act of rallying his skirmishers when he is struck down and killed. Confederate resistance collapses as Morris captures one cannon and 40 wagons. Union casualties are reported variously from 10 to 53 while the Confederates admit to 20. Garnett is also the first general officer on either side killed in action. McClellan, elevated by success to the status of national hero, next orders the bulk of his forces to advance on nearby Romney.

NAVAL: The USS *Massachusetts* captures the Confederate schooner *Hiland* off Ship Island, Mississippi.

July 14

WEST: Command of Confederate forces in western Virginia reverts to General Henry R. Jackson. Meanwhile, the Union push under General Robert Patterson stalls south of Harper's Ferry after encountering General Joseph E. Johnston's troops. Patterson's overall timidity and reluctance to give battle earns him the unflattering nickname "Granny" from his troops.

NAVAL: The USS *Daylight* under Commander Samuel Lockwood establishes a formal blockade of Wilmington, North Carolina.

July 15

WEST: Confederate forces effect a full retreat from Harper's Ferry in western Virginia.

July 16

SOUTH: Anxious to maintain the strategic initiative on the heel of victories in western Virginia, General Irvin McDowell orders his 32,000 men onto Manassas Junction. Here, the Manassas Gap and Orange and Alexandria railroads intersect only 30 miles southeast of Washington, D.C. "On to Richmond!" becomes a national mantra—although McDowell manages to traverse only six miles to Fairfax Court House. Another two days are required to reach Centreville, 22 miles from the capital, and the delay grants Confederate forces under General Pierre G. T. Beauregard a badly needed respite. The latter musters only 22,000 men, thinly spread along an eight-mile defensive position behind Bull Run Creek, while awaiting reinforcements from the Shenandoah. Previously, both McDowell and General in Chief Winfield Scott expressed reservations to President Lincoln about committing such raw soldiery to combat, but they were overruled by political considerations.

WEST: Skirmishing continues between General Jacob D. Cox's Federals and Confederates under General Henry A. Wise at Barboursville, western Virginia.

NAVAL: The Blockade Strategy Board informs navy secretary Gideon Welles of the importance of interdicting Confederate shipping. They then suggest using "stone fleets" (scuttled vessels) to obstruct Southern waterways.

The USS *St. Lawrence* captures the British blockade-runner *Herald* while running the blockade out of Beaufort, North Carolina.

In a reversal of fortune, the Confederate prize crew onboard the captured *S. J. Waring* is overcome by its crew—led on by William Tilghman, an African-American sailor. The ship arrives at New York six days later.

July 17

SOUTH: President Jefferson Davis orders General Joseph E. Johnston to reinforce General Pierre G. T. Beauregard in Virginia. In the face of General Robert Patterson's lethargic pursuit, Johnston expertly disengages from the Shenandoah Valley and races 11,000 men east by train to Manassas, Virginia. For the first time in military history, large numbers of troops are shuttled strategically from one front to the other by rail, bringing Confederate numbers up nearly to match Union strength.

WEST: Scarey Town, western Virginia, occasions minor actions between General Jacob D. Cox and General Henry A. Wise, C.S.A.

July 18

DIPLOMACY: Secretary of State William H. Seward instructs American ministers in Britain and France to endorse the previously rejected 1856 Declaration of Paris, which outlawed privateering. However, this move is scuttled subsequently when neither government proves willing to apply it to the Confederacy.

SOUTH: General Irvin McDowell dispatches a reconnaissance in force under General Daniel Tyler toward Confederate forces collected at Centreville, Virginia. He is instructed specifically not to bring on a general engagement. After ascertaining intelligence from the local populace, Tyler accompanies Colonel Israel B. Richardson's command as it probes Confederate positions along Blackburn's Ford on Bull Run Creek. This is on the extreme right of General Pierre G. T. Beauregard's line, then arrayed eight miles along and behind Bull Run Creek. Richardson then deploys two cannon and the 1st Massachusetts, who enthusiastically engage enemy skirmishers until they are staggered by volleys fired from three Virginia brigades under Colonel James Longstreet. After heavy fighting, Richardson orders his force withdrawn, but Tyler, against orders, brings additional cannon and regiments into the fray. These skirmish with Confederates across the creek for an hour before the 12th New York makes an ill-advised charge and is blasted back by Southerners lurking in the dense forestry. Then Longstreet, assisted by the brigade of General Jubal A. Early, counterattacks across the line, but his raw troops give way to confusion. Both sides then draw off to sort themselves out, but the Federal attempts to cross the creek are thwarted. Losses are 19 Union killed and 38 wounded to a Confederate tally of 15 dead and 53 wounded. This minor affair, nonetheless, bolsters Southern morale for the impending fight at Bull Run. McDowell further compounds Northern problems by wasting two more days gathering supplies and conducting additional reconnaissance.

Richard H. Anderson is appointed brigadier general, C.S.A.

NAVAL: The USS *Yankee* captures the Confederate schooner *Favorite* on the Yeocomico River, Virginia.

July 19

WEST: General John Pope, newly arrived in northern Missouri, warns the inhabitants that treasonable activity will be punished promptly, "without awaiting civil process."

NAVAL: The captain-general of Cuba releases all prizes brought into Cuban waters by Captain Raphael Semmes of CSS *Sumter*.

July 20

POLITICS: The *New York Tribune* adopts the pejorative term *Copperhead* (a poisonous snake) for any Northern politician opposing the war effort.

The third session of the first provisional Confederate Congress convenes in Richmond, Virginia. President Jefferson Davis declares that Arkansas, North Carolina, Tennessee, and Virginia have allied themselves with the Confederacy and that the new capital now is established firmly at Richmond.

SOUTH: General Joseph E. Johnston arrives at Manassas Junction with reinforcements and technically succeeds General Pierre P. T. Beauregard as senior commander. Both leaders make preparations to receive an attack delivered by General Irvin McDowell to their front. McDowell, meanwhile, decides that the Confederate right is too strong to assail frontally—as demonstrated by the affair at Blackburn's Ford—and he seeks an unguarded crossing point nearer to Beauregard's left flank. When intelligence is received on the relatively weak defenses around Sudley Ford, McDowell devises a concerted plan to crush the Confederates.

The Union attack is slated to begin with feints launched by General Daniel Tyler's First Division, marching west from Centreville along Warrenton Pike, until it makes demonstrations at the stone bridge where the pike crosses Bull Run. Meanwhile, the Second and Third Divisions under Generals David Hunter and Samuel P. Heintzelman would move west behind Tyler before passing him to suddenly descend on Sudley's Ford at about 7:00 A.M. Once across, these two divisions—totaling 13,000 men—would sweep around the Confederate left and rear, destroying them. An additional feint was intended for Blackburn's Ford by one brigade of Colonel S. D. Miles Fourth Division on the far right, while his remaining brigade remained in reserve. All told, McDowell conceived a viable enough strategy, but he entrusted it to men and officers who simply were too inexperienced to execute it properly.

Curiously, General Beauregard also intended to assail the enemy's left, but his operational orders proved contradictory. Many Southern commanders mistakenly assumed they were to remain in place and the attack never developed. Had they moved, spectators would have witnessed both armies, numbering in the thousands, simultaneously turn each other's flank and ultimately reverse their positions.

WEST: General William W. Loring assumes control of the Confederate's Northwestern Army in western Virginia.

NAVAL: The USS *Mount Vernon* seizes the Confederate sloop *Wild Pigeon* on the Rappahannock River.

The USS *Albatross* captures the former prize vessel *Enchantress* off Hatteras Inlet, North Carolina.

July 21

SOUTH: A momentous day begins with early morning movements by General Daniel Tyler's division, which is roused from its camps and begins to grope through the darkness at 2:00 A.M. Four hours later, his cannon begins to lob shells at Confederate forces behind the stone bridge crossing Bull Run. However, Colonel Nathan G. Evans deduces that Tyler's movement is merely a demonstration, and he rushes troops to the vicinity of Sudley's Ford. General David Hunter, meanwhile, is equally tardy in

The Fourth Alabama, depicted firing the opening shots of the first major battle of the Civil War *(The National Guard Heritage)*

his movements, and it is not until 9:30 A.M. that Union flanking forces are able to ford Bull Run and work their way south. Evans, however, cobbles together 900 men to oppose their advance on Matthews Hill, and he withstands repeated piecemeal attacks. Gradually, Confederate reinforcements arrive under Colonel Francis S. Bartow and General Barnard Bee while additional Union forces likewise are fed into the fray. After two hours of heavy fighting, the Southerners give way in confusion, and the Federals resume advancing in the direction of Henry House Hill.

General Beauregard nearly compromises his own defensive position with a stream of conflicting orders that keep most of his units stationary instead of moving toward his threatened left flank. One unit that did arrive is a brigade of five Virginia regiments under General Thomas J. Jackson. These quickly deploy on Henry House Hill, assisted by several cannon, and they resist ferociously a Union onslaught by 18,000 men. Jackson's stand enables the survivors of Evans's, Bartow's, and Bee's commands to rally behind him. McDowell also arrives to direct matters personally, but he compromises his numerical superiority by launching piecemeal attacks that are easily repelled. Worse, two Union batteries brought up in support are outgunned and eventually are captured by blue-clad Confederate forces who were mistaken for Federals. Jackson's aggressive defense greatly inspires the Southerners, and General Bee allegedly exclaims: "There is Jackson standing like a stonewall. Rally behind the Virginians!" McDowell continues committing additional forces to battle, but at 4:00 P.M., a Confederate brigade under Colonel Philip St. George Cocke arrives and sweeps the Federals from Henry House Hill. The Union army's offensive, spent by its exertions, begins to sputter out in the intense summer heat.

Meanwhile, a separate struggle unfolds west of Henry House Hill along Chinn Ridge. Union troops under Colonel Oliver O. Howard successfully storm the heights, which places them astride Jackson's flank, poised to drive him off. But as Howard maneuvers to perform exactly that, he is himself outflanked by Confederate brigades under Generals Arnold Elzay and Jubal A. Early and is thrown back. Sensing victory and the exhausted state of his antagonists, Beauregard orders a sudden advance by the entire line of Confederates. Flushed with success, they surge forward, shrieking their trademark battlecry, the "Rebel Yell." McDowell's units, finally bested, give ground in orderly fashion initially and recross Bull Run without undue hazard. However, a lucky Confederate shell suddenly turns over a wagon on the Cub Run Bridge, and utter panic ensues. The exhausted, demoralized soldiers run—headlong into the well-dressed and merry throng of civilians gathered by the roadside to witness what they anticipated would be a clear Union triumph. President Jefferson Davis, arriving on the battlefield during the final stages, urges an all-out pursuit to the gates of Washington, D.C. General Joseph E. Johnston, however, perceiving the disorganized and fatigued nature of his men, declines. Fighting gradually peters out after 10 hours of combat.

The first major engagement of the Civil War ends in a tactical triumph for the Confederacy. Southern losses are 387 killed and 1,582 wounded (1,982) to a Union tally of 460 killed, 1,124 wounded, and 1,132 missing (2,896). The spoils of battle also prove impressive, and they include 28 cannon, 37 caissons, 500,000 rounds of ammunition, and nine regimental colors. In retrospect, Bull Run did little to alter the strategic balance of the war. While minuscule in comparison to later encounters, it demonstrated to both sides that the ensuing struggle would be prolonged and costly.

General Pierre G. T. Beauregard is appointed full general, C.S.A. Jubal A. Early also becomes a brigadier general.

WEST: General Nathaniel P. Banks succeeds General Robert Patterson as commander of the Department of the Shenandoah, western Virginia. The latter's failure to pin down Confederate forces in the region proves a major factor in the Union defeat at Bull Run.

General Jacob D. Dox and Henry A. Wise continue skirmishing at Charlestown, western Virginia.

Skirmishing ensues with Native Americans along the Eel River, California.

NAVAL: The U.S. Marine Corps receives its baptism of fire at Bull Run when a battalion commanded by Major John Reynolds loses with 9 killed, 19 wounded, and 16 missing.

The USS *Albatross* engages the CSS *Beaufort* in Oregon Inlet, North Carolina, forcing it to retreat.

The Confederate privateer *Jefferson Davis* seizes the Union bark *Alvarado* at sea.

July 22

POLITICS: Consistent with the Crittenden Resolution, the U.S. House of Representatives votes for war to preserve governance under the Constitution, save the Union, and maintain the status quo with regard to slavery. The measure is likewise approved by the Senate.

NORTH: The three-month enlistment term of many Union volunteers begins to expire, allowing many of them to be discharged. President Abraham Lincoln counters by signing two bills authorizing 1 million three-year volunteers.

SOUTH: General Barnard Bee, C.S.A., succumbs of wounds received at Bull Run.

WEST: General George B. McClellan is ordered to succeed General Irvin McDowell, who is now disgraced.

The Missouri State Convention, convening at Jefferson City, votes overwhelmingly in favor of the Union and also relocates the capital to St. Louis. Secessionist governor Claiborne F. Jackson, meanwhile, declares himself the only legitimate political authority in Missouri.

Federal troops under General Thomas Sweeney occupy Forsyth, Missouri.

General William J. Hardee, C.S.A., assumes command of Confederate forces in northern Arkansas.

July 23

NORTH: General John A. Dix assumes control of the Department of Maryland.

WEST: General William S. Rosecrans succeeds General George B. McClellan as commander of the Department of the Ohio once the latter transfers to Virginia.

SOUTHWEST: Federal forces abandon Fort Buchanan, New Mexico Territory.

July 24

POLITICS: Congress authorizes the position of assistant secretary of the navy, along with legislation "for the temporary increase in the navy."

WEST: General Jacob D. Cox engages and disperses Confederate forces under General Henry A. Wise at Tyler Mountain in western Virginia. The town of Charleston subsequently is evacuated in the face of mounting Union pressure, and the Kanawha Valley is now free of Southern forces. Wise, meanwhile, retreats in the direction of Gauley Bridge.

July 25

POLITICS: Congress authorizes the recruitment of volunteers, offering those who serve two years a $100 bonus.

Tennessee senator Andrew Johnson moves to adopt the Crittenden Resolution in the U.S. Senate, and it passes 30 to 5. This mandates and reaffirms that the war is being fought for the preservation of the Union and not to abolish slavery.

Confederate secretary of state Robert Toombs, having resigned to join the army, is replaced by Robert M. T. Hunter.

South: John La Mountain conducts the first balloon reconnaissance flights at Fortress Monroe, Virginia.

West: General Nathaniel P. Banks formally succeeds General Robert Patterson as commander of Union forces in the Shenandoah Valley.

General John C. Frémont, a celebrated explorer, becomes commander of the Western Department with headquarters at St. Louis, Missouri.

Skirmishes continue between pro-Union and pro-Confederate forces at Harrisville and Dug Springs, Missouri.

Southwest: A small Federal detachment of 500 men under Major Isaac Lynde repulses a Confederate attack upon their position at Mesilla, New Mexico Territory.

Naval: Congress passes legislation intending to overhaul and improve U.S. Marine Corps organization.

The USS *Resolute* docks at Washington, D.C., with two schooners and one sloop as prizes.

The Confederate privateer *Mariner* captures the Union schooner *Nathaniel Chase* off Ocracoke, North Carolina.

The Confederate privateer *Gordon* seizes the Union brig *William McGilvery* off Cape Hatteras, North Carolina.

The Confederate privateer *Dixie* takes the Union schooner *Mary Alice* off the Florida east coast.

The Confederate raider CSS *Sumter* under Captain Raphael Semmes captures the schooner *Abby Bradford* in the Caribbean.

July 26

West: General Felix K. Zollicoffer assumes command of Confederate forces in eastern Tennessee.

Southwest: Major Isaac Lynde surrenders 500 men to a smaller Confederate force under Captain John Baylor at Fort Fillmore, New Mexico Territory. Lynde is disgraced and subsequently is drummed out of the service, but he eventually makes his way back onto the retirement list.

July 27

Politics: President Abraham Lincoln confers with General George B. McClellan, newly arrived in Washington, D.C. The chief executive urges a strategic offensive with advances into Tennessee by way of Virginia and Kentucky. McClellan, who is not as easily stampeded into action as his predecessor, respectfully demurs.

Naval: The Confederate raider CSS *Sumter* under Captain Raphael Semmes takes the Union bark *Joseph Maxwell* near Venezuela.

July 28

South: In light of the deteriorating situation in western Virginia and the death of General Robert Garnett at Carricksford, General Robert E. Lee is ordered to take command of Confederate forces there.

West: Confederate forces occupy New Madrid, Missouri, on the Mississippi River.

NAVAL: The USS *Union* destroys the Confederate brig *B. T. Martin* north of Cape Hatteras, North Carolina, once it is run aground by its crew.

The Confederate privateer *Gordon* seizes the Union schooner *Protector* off Cape Hatteras, North Carolina.

The USS *St. Lawrence* sinks the Confederate privateer *Petrel* off Charleston, South Carolina.

July 29

POLITICS: Horace Greeley, the previously hawkish editor of the *New York Tribune,* writes to President Abraham Lincoln and suggests peaceful negotiations to end the fighting.

WEST: General John Pope assumes command of Union forces in North Missouri. He takes active measures to protect railroads from sabotage and suppresses local unrest.

NAVAL: The USS *Yankee* and *Reliance* engage Confederate batteries erected at Marlborough Point, Virginia.

Four U.S. Navy steamers trade shots with a Confederate battery at Aquia Creek, Virginia, for several hours.

July 30

POLITICS: The Missouri State Convention votes 56–25 to declare the gubernatorial seat open, thereby deposing Confederate-leaning Claiborne F. Jackson as chief executive.

SOUTH: General Benjamin F. Butler seeks clarification of orders from the War Department as to policies respecting the great number of escaped African Americans in his camp.

WEST: Union forces under General Jacob D. Cox advance from Charleston and into the Great Kanawha River valley of western Virginia.

July 31

POLITICS: Pro-Union forces in Missouri are bolstered by the election of Hamilton R. Gamble as governor.

WEST: President Abraham Lincoln elevates Ulysses S. Grant, an obscure former army officer, to general of volunteers in Illinois.

General John Pope sternly issues Order No. 3 for the purpose of restoring order to northern Missouri and restricting activities by Confederate sympathizers.

General Sterling Price and his Missouri State Guard unite with Texas troops under General Ben McCulloch and Arkansas forces under General Nicholas B. Pearce at Cassville, Missouri. Their combined forces number in excess of 12,000 men—twice the number of Union general Nathaniel Lyon.

NAVAL: The Confederate privateer *Dixie* captures the Union bark *Glenn* at sea and removes it to Beaufort, North Carolina.

August 1

SOUTH: President Jefferson Davis urges General Joseph E. Johnston to maintain the strategic initiative with further offensive actions against Union forces still in Virginia.

WEST: General Robert E. Lee succeeds General William W. Loring as head of Confederate forces in western Virginia.

A Confederate force of 12,000 men under Generals Ben McCulloch and Sterling Price march up Telegraph Road from Cassville, Missouri, to Springfield, 50 miles distant.

SOUTHWEST: Skirmishing erupts between Confederate and Union sympathizers in Arizona and New Mexico Territories after Captain John Baylor declares the entire region for the South.

NAVAL: Gustavus V. Fox, a former naval officer, gains appointment as assistant secretary of the navy.

August 2
POLITICS: Congress approves virtually all of President Abraham Lincoln's acts and appropriations deemed necessary to pursue the war effort, along with issuances of bonds and tariff increases. To better secure funding for the war effort, Congress also passes its first-ever national income tax of 3 percent on incomes of more than $800, along with higher tariffs. Seamen are also enlisted for the duration of the war.

WEST: Union forces under General Nathaniel Lyon and Confederates under General Ben McCulloch clash at Dug Springs, Missouri. Lyon, badly outnumbered, prepares to retrograde back on Springfield and regroup. Consequently, commanding General John C. Frémont dispatches reinforcements down the Mississippi River to assist him.

SOUTHWEST: Union forces evacuate Fort Stanton, New Mexico Territory, in light of recent Confederate successes elsewhere.

August 3
POLITICS: Governor Isham G. Harris of Tennessee seeks to visit with authorities in Richmond, Virginia, and discuss weakening Confederate control of his state.

WEST: Federal forces skirmish with Indians in the Upper Pitt River valley, California.

NAVAL: Congress directs the Department of the Navy to design and construct three ironclad prototypes. They also institute a three-officer "Ironclad Board" to study and recommend construction and deployment of ironclad warships. This body ultimately includes Commodore Joseph Smith, Captain Hiram Paulding, and Commander Charles H. Davis.

In an early application of aerial reconnaissance, John La Mountain lifts off from the deck of USS *Fanny* off Hampton Roads, Virginia, to observe Confederate gun positions along Sewell's Point.

The USS *Wabash* recaptures the Union vessel *Mary Alice* from the Confederate privateer *Dixie* and also seizes the blockade-runner *Sarah Starr* off Charleston, South Carolina.

The USS *South Carolina* engages Confederate shore batteries off Galveston, Texas.

August 4
NAVAL: A cutter dispatched from the USS *Thomas Freeborn* cuts out and captures the Confederate schooner *Pocahontas* and the sloop *Mary Grey* in Pohick Creek, Virginia.

August 5

Politics: The first session of the 37th Congress concludes its monumental, 34-day special session and adjourns.

West: General Nathaniel Lyon evacuates Dug Springs, Missouri, in the face of superior Confederate numbers and continues falling back upon Springfield.

Naval: The USS *Jamestown* burns the Confederate prize bark *Alvarado* off Fernandina, Florida.

The Confederate privateer *Jefferson Davis* captures the Union brig *Santa Clara* near Puerto Rico.

August 6

Politics: President Abraham Lincoln signs the First Confiscation Act, which emancipates all African-American slaves found in the employ of Confederate armed forces, either as laborers or as soldiers.

North: General Ambrose E. Burnside is appointed brigadier general, U.S. Army.

West: Union forces ignore Kentucky neutrality by establishing "Dick Robinson," a military camp near Lexington.

Advanced elements of Confederate forces under Generals Ben McCulloch and Sterling Price reach Wilson's Creek, 10 miles from Springfield, Missouri.

August 7

South: Confederate forces under General John B. Magruder abandon and burn Hampton, Virginia, denying its use to Union forces.

West: The steamer *Luella* ferries Federal troops under Major John McDonald, 8th Missouri, on an expedition against Price's Landing, Missouri.

Naval: The U.S. government authorizes construction of seven ironclad gunboats under engineer James B. Eads of St. Louis, Missouri, for riverine service: USS *Cairo, Carondelet, Cincinnati, Louisville, Mound City, Pittsburgh,* and *St. Louis.* These are subsequently designed by contractor Samuel M. Pooks, and his ships, incorporating a "humpbacked" design, are popularly referred to as "Pooks's Turtles." The vessels gradually emerge as the nucleus of Union naval power along strategic western water routes.

The USS *Massachusetts* captures the Confederate blockade-runner *Charles Henry* off Ship Island, Mississippi.

August 8

Politics: Secretary of War Simon Cameron declares that citizens are not obliged to obey the Fugitive Slave Law as it pertains to secessionists. He further orders General Benjamin F. Butler not to return any escaped slaves to their Confederate owners.

West: General Ulysses S. Grant takes command of Union forces at Ironton, Missouri.

Naval: The USS *Santee* captures the Confederate schooner *C. P. Knapp* in the Gulf of Mexico.

August 9

West: A force of 12,000 Confederates under Generals Ben McCulloch and Sterling Price converge on Springfield, Missouri, in the vicinity of Wilson's Creek, 10 miles to the southwest. Once rested, they intend to attack and overpower Union-held positions in the city on the following day. But rather than abandon Springfield without a fight, General Nathaniel Lyon boldly decides on a preemptive strike of his own. Commanding 4,200 men, he is assisted by a German-speaking detachment of 1,200 soldiers under Colonel Franz Sigel, who marches circuitously to take the Confederates from behind.

NAVAL: The Confederate privateer *York* captures the Union schooner *George C. Baker* and then promptly relinquishes it to the USS *Union. York* is run ashore soon after at Cape Hatteras and burned by its crew.

August 10

WEST: General Ulysses S. Grant skirmishes with Confederate forces at Potosi, Missouri.

Union general Nathaniel Lyon initiates the Battle of Wilson's Creek by storming Confederate campsites at 5:30 A.M. They drive General Sterling Price back and occupy a prominent ridge crest that is soon to be christened "Bloody Hill." The Southerners, overcoming their initial surprise, redress their lines and rebuff a Union column under Captain Joseph Plummer, who tries to storm artillery posted on their right. Sigel, meanwhile, stealthily advances on the Confederate camp from the south and routs Southern cavalry deployed there. General Ben McCulloch, however, reacts quickly to this new threat and dispatches troops that drive Sigel back, securing the Confederate rear. Their success here is due largely to Colonel Louis Hebert's 3rd Louisiana, clad in gray uniforms like many Union troops, who advance to close range and unleash a volley, staggering the defenders. Attention then swings back to Battle Hill, where the struggle continues raging.

Lyon, unaware of Sigel's debacle, holds his ground as Price launches two frontal attacks in superior strength. The Northerners staunchly repel the Missouri State Guard and drive them back with considerable loss. But as Lyon brings up the 1st Iowa and 2nd Kansas to bolster his own line, a bullet strikes and kills him. Command then devolves upon Major Samuel D. Sturgis. The Union lines, somewhat more constricted, easily fight off a charge by Confederate cavalry and brace themselves for a third charge by Price, now reinforced by McCulloch's Texans. The Confederates come on in great strength and grimly fight their way up the slopes, charging at one point to within 20 paces of Sturgis's position. Federal forces are hard pressed but their line still holds and the Southerners fall back a third time.

At this juncture, Sturgis is apprised of Sigel's failure. He also observes Southerners massing for a fourth assault upon his line, already exhausted and low on ammunition after five hours of continuous combat. Sturgis consequently gives orders to retreat, which the men perform in orderly fashion. The equally battered Confederates under McCulloch occupy the Union position, but they decline to pursue. Despite Southern advantages in numbers, losses at Wilson's Creek proved nearly equal, with the Federals suffering 258 killed, 873 wounded, and 186 missing (1,317) to a Southern tally of 277 killed and 945 injured (1,230), rates of 25.5 percent and 12 percent, respectively. The South has won the Civil War's second pitched engagement, while Lyon is the first Northern general slain in combat. The victory also revives Confederate fortunes in Missouri, and Price continues his march to St. Louis. McCulloch and Nicholas Pearce (Brigadier General of Arkansas forces), meanwhile, hasten back to Arkansas.

August 11

WEST: General John B. Floyd is appointed head of Confederate forces in the Kanawha Valley, western Virginia.

General Jeff Thompson assumes command of the Confederate-leaning Missouri State Guard.

NAVAL: The Confederate blockade-runner *Louisa,* closely pursed by the USS *Penguin,* strikes a shoal off Cape Fear, North Carolina, and sinks.

August 12

WEST: Mescalero Apache raiders under Chief Nicholas attack and kill 15 Confederates at Big Bend, Texas.

NAVAL: The wooden gunboats USS *Tyler, Lexington,* and *Conestoga* drop anchor off Cairo, Illinois, and guard the confluence of the Ohio and Mississippi rivers. These are stopgap designs intending to serve until the new ironclads are in commission, but they prove entirely successful.

August 13

NAVAL: The USS *Powhatan* under Lieutenant David D. Porter recaptures the Union schooner *Abby Bradford* near the mouth of the Mississippi River.

August 14

NORTH: A mutiny by discontented volunteers in the 79th New York Regiment near Washington, D.C., is suppressed.

WEST: General John C. Frémont declares martial law in St. Louis, Missouri, and begins to confiscate Confederate property.

SOUTHWEST: General Paul O. Hebert succeeds General Earl Van Dorn as commander of Confederate forces in Texas.

August 15

POLITICS: President Jefferson Davis orders all remaining Northerners out of Confederate territory within 40 days.

NORTH: Disruptions in the 2nd Maine result in 60 transfers from the Army of the Potomac to the distant Dry Tortugas, Florida.

SOUTH: George B. Crittenden is appointed brigadier general, C.S.A.

WEST: General Robert Anderson, formerly commander at Fort Sumter, takes charge of the Department of the Cumberland (Tennessee and Kentucky). However, he continually suffers from nervous exhaustion brought on by his recent ordeal and retires shortly afterward.

In view of Confederate successes in Missouri, General John C. Frémont pleads with the War Department for immediate reinforcements. President Abraham Lincoln, cognizant of the threat to this important border state, authorizes the transfer of troops.

Major John McDonald and men of the 8th Missouri are ferried by the steamer *Hannibal City* on an expedition against Saint Genevieve, Missouri.

Federal troops skirmish with Indians near Kellogg's Lake, California.

Naval: Gunboats USS *Tyler* and *Conestoga* conduct a reconnaissance down the Mississippi River and scout for Confederate fortifications, while the USS *Lexington* performs similar tasks upstream as far as Cape Girardeau, Missouri.

The USS *Resolute* bombards Confederate troops assembled at Mathias Point, Virginia.

August 16
Politics: President Abraham Lincoln reiterates that the South remains in a state of insurrection and declares that all commercial intercourse between loyal and rebellious states is prohibited.
West: Union and Confederate sympathizers clash at Fredericktown and Kirksville, Missouri.

August 17
North: The new Department of the Potomac is constituted by merging the Departments of Northeastern Virginia, Washington, and the Shenandoah.

Henry W. Halleck is promoted to major general, U.S. Army.
South: The venerable General John E. Wool replaces General Benjamin F. Butler as head of the Department of Virginia, with headquarters at Fortress Monroe at the tip of Yorktown Peninsula.

August 18
Politics: New York newspapers *Journal of Commerce, Daily News, Day Book,* and *Freeman's Journal* are banned summarily from publishing for alleged disloyalty.
South: Troopers of the 1st New York Cavalry skirmish with Confederates 12 miles south of Alexandria, Virginia.
Naval: The successful Confederate privateer *Jefferson Davis* runs aground on a sandbar and is destroyed off St. Augustine, Florida.

August 19
Politics: The Southern-leaning editor of the Massachusetts *Essex County Democrat* is accosted by a mob, tarred, and feathered. Newspaper offices in Easton and West Chester, Pennsylvania, are also accosted by pro-Union mobs because of suspected pro-Southern sympathies.

Proslavery expatriates from Missouri petition for their state to join the Confederacy even after they have been driven from office.
North: George H. Thomas is appointed brigadier general, U.S. Army.

General Henry W. Halleck is summoned from California to Washington, D.C.
West: Union forces defeat the Missouri Home Guard at Charleston, Missouri, directly across the river from Cairo, Illinois.
Navy: Secretary of the Navy Gideon Welles orders 200 U.S. Marines to join the Potomac Flotilla for the purpose of scouring the countryside for Confederate depots and supplies.

August 20
North: General George B. McClellan formally takes command of the newly constituted Department and Army of the Potomac. This vaunted force becomes a permanent fixture in the struggle for Virginia during the next four years.

John F. Reynolds is appointed brigadier general, U.S. Army.

South: General Richard C. Gatlin becomes commander of the Confederate forces in North Carolina.

August 21
South: General John B. Grayson assumes control of Confederate forces in the Department of Middle and East Florida.

General Roswell S. Ripley takes charge of Confederate forces in the Department of South Carolina.

West: Union and Confederate sympathizers clash at Jonesboro, Missouri.

Naval: The USS *Vandalia* captures the Confederate blockade-runner *Henry Middleton* off Charleston, South Carolina.

August 22
Naval: Commander John Rodgers drives an estimated 600 Confederates from Commerce, Missouri, preventing them from erecting batteries there.

The Federal gunboat USS *Lexington* impounds the steamer *W. B. Terry* at Paducah, Kentucky, for trading with the enemy. Nearby Confederate forces abscond with the steamer *Samuel Orr* and sail it up the Tennessee River.

August 23
Southwest: Union and Confederate forces skirmish near Fort Craig, New Mexico Territory.

Naval: The steamers USS *Release* and *Yankee* trade salvos with Confederate batteries at the mouth of Potomac Creek, Virginia.

August 24
Diplomacy: President Jefferson Davis appoints James M. Mason of Virginia special commissioner to Great Britain, John Slidell of Louisiana special commissioner to France, and Pierre A. Rost of Louisiana special commissioner to Spain. Each is specifically instructed to seek diplomatic recognition for the Confederacy and, with it, the ability to acquire arms and ammunition.

Politics: President Abraham Lincoln informs Governor Beriah Magoffin that he refuses to order the withdrawal of Union troops, despite Kentucky's professed neutrality.

North: The Department of the Potomac is enlarged through absorption of the Department of Pennsylvania.

August 25
West: The encampment of General Henry A. Wise in western Virginia is beset by an outbreak of measles. His force also skirmishes with Federal troops at Piggot's Mill.

Southwest: Federal troops under Lieutenant John R. Pulliam fight with hostile Indians near Fort Stanton, New Mexico Territory.

Confederate troops under Colonel John R. Baylor skirmish with hostile Apaches near Fort Bliss, Texas.

August 26

WEST: Confederates under General John B. Floyd surprise Colonel Erastus B. Tyler's 27th Ohio Regiment in their camp at Cross Lanes (Summersville), western Virginia, routing them.

Union and Confederate forces skirmish heavily at Wayne Court House and Blue's House in the westernmost reaches of Virginia.

NAVAL: A combined expedition assembles at Hampton Roads, Virginia, under Commodore Silas H. Stringham, consisting of the USS *Cumberland, Fanny, Harriet Lane, Minnesota, Monticello, Pawnee, Susquehanna,* and *Wabash.* This powerful force mounts 143 heavy, rifled cannon. Stringham, a capable veteran of many years with the Mediterranean squadron, is well versed in the newest fort-reduction tactics perfected during the Crimean War; he takes onboard 900 soldiers of the 9th Massachusetts and 20th New York under General Benjamin F. Butler. The expedition weighs anchor and makes for Hatteras Inlet, North Carolina, to eliminate privateering operations there. This is also the first large-scale amphibious operation of the war and is intended as a demonstration of Union naval prowess.

The USS *Daylight* attacks and recaptures the Union schooner *Monticello* in the Rappahannock River, Virginia.

The tug USS *Fanny* captures the Confederate sloop *Emma* off the mouth of the Manokin River, Maryland.

Captain Andrew H. Foote is appointed to replace Captain John Rodgers as commander of the gunboat flotilla of the western rivers.

August 27

NAVAL: The naval expedition under Commodore Silas H. Stringham anchors off Hatteras Inlet and makes preparations to land troops and attack nearby Forts Clark and Hatteras. These are garrisoned by 350 men of the 7th North Carolina under Colonel William F. Mountain. They are situated poorly to contend with such a powerful force. Mountain possesses only 12 small, smoothbore cannon in two open positions, and he is thus outgunned and outnumbered.

August 28

NORTH: The Federal garrison at Fort Ellsworth, Washington, D.C., under General William B. Franklin is augmented by the arrival of 400 sailors deployed from the Washington Navy Yard.

SOUTH: The 2nd and 3rd Michigan skirmish with Confederate forces near Bailey's Cross Roads, Virginia.

WEST: General Nathaniel Lyon, recently slain at Wilson's Creek, is interred with full military honors at St. Louis, Missouri.

NAVAL: The USS *Yankee* captures the Confederate schooner *Remittance* off Piney Point, Virginia.

To seal off Pamlico Sound, an important blockade-running route, a combined expedition of eight warships and two transports under Commodore Silas H. Stringham drops anchor off Hatteras Inlet, North Carolina. A preliminary landing of some 300 men nearly goes awry when high surfs swamps many of the landing boats. Nonetheless, at 10 A.M., Stringham forms his vessels into a fast-moving circle, which continuously bombards the Confederate positions with accurate, plunging fire. The Southern artillery in the forts lack sufficient range to hit back, and the defenders gradually drift away before reinforcements arrive under Commodore Samuel Barron.

The U.S. revenue cutter *R. R. Cuyler* attacks and burns the Confederate ship *Finland* as it attempts to run the blockade off Apalachicola, Florida.

August 29

SOUTH: General Benjamin F. Butler lands 900 soldiers and occupies Forts Hatteras and Clark at Hatteras Inlet, North Carolina. The Confederate garrison under Commodore Samuel Barron offers scant resistance before surrendering their posts, which are secured without any Federal fatalities. Butler is ordered to abandon the position after its defenses are dismantled, but noting how control of the inlet strangles Confederate shipping out of Pamlico Sound, he decides to retain them—a wise decision subsequently upheld by the War Department. The Union has secured its first foothold on Southern territory, and Hatteras Inlet performs useful service as a coaling station and supply depot for the blockading squadron offshore. Coming on the heels of Bull Run, the victory also raises Northern morale.

August 30

WEST: Without prior authorization, General Charles Frémont proclaims a conditional emancipation declaration in Missouri and frees slaves belonging to Confederate sympathizers. He also orders the death penalty for any Southern guerrillas apprehended behind Union lines. President Abraham Lincoln, after hearing of Frémont's actions, declares them "dictatorial" and potentially alienating for Union sympathizers in Kentucky.

NAVAL: In a brisk action, the Confederate steam tug *Harmony* attacks and damages the USS *Savannah* at Newport News, Virginia.

August 31

POLITICS: The third session of the Provisional Confederate Congress adjourns.

NORTH: George G. Meade is promoted to brigadier general, U.S. Army.

SOUTH: The 3rd New Jersey Regiment skirmishes with Confederate forces at Munson's Hill, Virginia.

WEST: General William S. Rosecrans takes three brigades of Ohio troops, 6,000 strong and marches south from Clarksburg, western Virginia, intending to attack the Confederate camp of General John B. Floyd at Carnifex Ferry.

NAVAL: The Union Navy Department abolishes the daily rum ration for sailors.

The CSS *Teaser* approaches and bombards Union forces at Newport News, Virginia.

The USS *George Peabody* captures the Confederate brig *Henry C. Brooks* in Hatteras Inlet, North Carolina.

The USS *Jamestown* apprehends the British blockade-runner *Aigburth* off the Florida coast.

September 1

POLITICS: President Abraham Lincoln is greatly relieved by word of Federal success at Hatteras Inlet, North Carolina, a welcome victory that raises Northern morale.

WEST: Skirmishing continues at Blue Creek, Boone Court House, and Burlington, in the western reaches of Virginia.

Arriving at Cape Girardeau, General Ulysses S. Grant takes nominal command of Union forces in southeastern Missouri.

SOUTH: Mary Chase, an African-American freedwoman, starts the first school for contrabands (escaped slaves) in Alexandria, Virginia.

NAVAL: The USS *Dana* captures the Confederate schooner *T. J. Evans* as it runs the blockade off Clay Island, Maryland.

September 2

POLITICS: President Abraham Lincoln, eager to appease slaveholding border states, instructs General Charles C. Frémont to "modify" his emancipation declaration—in effect, he countermands it.

SOUTH: Colonel Harvey Brown, commanding Fort Pickens, Florida, orders a sortie across Pensacola Bay to destroy a Confederate floating dry dock, which he believes is intended to be sunk in the channel as an obstacle.

WEST: General Leonidas Polk assumes command of all Confederate forces in Department No. 2, encompassing Tennessee, Arkansas, and Missouri.

General Jeff Thompson threatens retaliatory measures for any Confederate sympathizers executed under General Charles C. Frémont's directive.

September 3

NORTH: Oliver O. Howard, Daniel E. Sickles, and Lew Wallace are promoted to brigadier generals, U.S. Army.

WEST: In a major development, General Leonidas Polk orders Confederate forces to violate Kentucky neutrality and preempt any possible Union advances there. General Gideon Pillow responds by occupying Hickman, Chalk Cliffs, and Columbus, establishing a continuous war front that now stretches from Kansas to the Atlantic.

General Gideon J. Pillow and Colonel William H. L. Wallace arrange prisoner exchanges to take place in Missouri.

September 4

NORTH: Union forces under General George A. McCall skirmish with Confederates at Great Falls, Maryland.

WEST: General Ulysses S. Grant arrives at Cairo, Illinois, to evaluate the new and potentially advantageous situation in Kentucky.

In the face of Confederate pressure, General Stephen A. Hurlbut evacuates Shelbina, Missouri.

NAVAL: The USS *Jamestown* seizes and scuttles the Confederate schooner *Colonel Long* off the Georgia coast.

The gunboat CSS *Yankee*, assisted by Confederate batteries at Hickman, Kentucky, trades shots with gunboats USS *Tyler* and *Lexington* near Cairo, Illinois.

September 5
WEST: General Ulysses S. Grant prepares his forces at Cairo, Illinois, for an immediate occupation of Paducah, Kentucky, at the confluence of the Tennessee and Ohio rivers. Significantly, the mouth of the Cumberland River is also nearby.
NAVAL: Captain Andrew H. Foote reports for duty at St. Louis, Missouri, replacing Commander John Rodgers.

September 6
DIPLOMACY: The U.S. consul in London, England, is alerted to the purchase of steamers *Bermuda, Adelaide,* and *Victoria* by Confederate agents.
WEST: Union forces under General Ulysses S. Grant advance south from Cairo, Illinois, to Paducah, Kentucky, at the mouth of the Tennessee River, to forestall a Confederate takeover. He also appoints General Charles F. Smith to command troops in western Kentucky once he returns to Cairo. This minor action wields big strategic consequences as it precludes Southern attempts to establish a main line of defense behind the Ohio River.
NAVAL: The gunboats USS *Tyler* and *Lexington* under Commander John Rodgers provide useful support for General Ulysses S. Grant's occupation of Paducah and Smithland, Kentucky, at the mouths of the Tennessee and Cumberland rivers. The operation proceeds smoothly and demonstrates both Grant's understanding of naval power and his uncanny knack for juggling combined operations.

September 7
WEST: Colonel Alvin P. Hovey leads the 24th Indiana on an expedition to Big Springs, Missouri.

September 8
WEST: General Ulysses S. Grant girds for an engagement at Lucas Bend, Missouri, supported by gunfire from USS *Conestoga* and *Lexington.*

General John Pope initiates military operations against Confederate guerrilla bands in northern Missouri.

September 9
POLITICAL: President Abraham Lincoln is advised by his cabinet to relieve the erratic but popular General Charles C. Frémont of command in Missouri. The president nonetheless relents for the time being and instructs General David Hunter to convey troops there as reinforcements.
WEST: Action looms as Federal troops under General William S. Rosecrans advance to Carnifex Ferry in western Virginia, skirmishing with Confederate outposts en route.
NAVAL: The USS *Cambridge* captures the Confederate schooner *Louisa Agnes* off Nova Scotia, Canada.

September 10
SOUTH: General Albert S. Johnston is appointed commander of Confederate forces in the West.

WEST: General William S. Rosecrans and 6,000 Federal troops strike 2,000 Confederates under General John B. Floyd at Carnifex Ferry on a bend in the Gauley River in western Virginia. Previously, Floyd was warned by General Henry B. Wise not to encamp with his back to the river, but he ignored this sound dictum. The Union troops press forward and clear a heavily wooded area, capturing many Confederate supplies. Rosecrans then views Floyd's fortified camp on the bluffs and pauses to regroup before resuming the fight on the morrow. Floyd, however, quickly evacuates his command across the river under the cover of darkness and destroys the ferry to avoid pursuit. Union forces sustain 17 killed and 141 wounded to Confederate claims of only 20, but Rosecrans's offensive tightens the Federal grip on western Virginia. Curiously, General Wise is blamed for not reinforcing Floyd in a timely manner, and ultimately he is relieved.

General Robert E. Lee prepares his command to pass over to the offensive. He formulates a complicated plan to isolate and storm the Union outpost atop Cheat Mountain, as possession of this strategic point would severe Union communications along several mountain passes and the Staunton-Parkersburg Turnpike. However, his efforts are hampered by General William W. Loring, who outranked Lee in the prewar regular army and strongly resents subordination to him. Despite Lee's best efforts to cultivate cordiality, Loring remains sullen and uncooperative.

General George H. Thomas assumes command of the Union training camp Dick Robinson in eastern Kentucky.

General John McClernand leads Federal troops on a reconnaissance of Norfolk, Missouri.

NAVAL: In a sharp action, gunboats USS *Conestoga* and *Lexington* attack and silence a Confederate battery at Lucas Bend, Missouri, and also damage the Confederate gunboat CSS *Yankee*.

The USS *Pawnee* apprehends the Confederate schooner *Susan Jane* in Hatteras Inlet, North Carolina.

The USS *Cambridge* intercepts the British blockade-runner *Revere* off Beaufort, North Carolina.

September 11

POLITICS: President Abraham Lincoln orders the emancipation declaration of General John C. Frémont modified to conform with acts of Congress.

The Kentucky legislature, angered by Confederate violation of its neutrality, demands the immediate removal of all Southern troops. A similar bill applying to Northern forces is defeated by pro-Unionists.

SOUTH: Confederate cavalry under Colonel J. E. B. Stuart clash with Union troops under General William F. Smith outside Lewinsville, Virginia. In light of their good conduct, General George B. McClellan restores the colors of the 79th New York.

WEST: General Robert E. Lee and 15,000 Confederates launch an overly intricate and unsuccessful attack on 2,000 Union soldiers under General J. J. Reynolds at Cheat Mountain Summit and Elkwater, western Virginia. The Confederates are hampered at the onset by rough terrain and heavy rainfall, but after prodigious efforts, they position themselves without arousing Northern concern. The main strike force under Colonel Albert Rust, 3rd Arkansas, numbering 2,000 men, then prepares to storm the summit of Cheat Mountain, guarded by only 300 men of the 14th Indiana under Colonel Nathan Kimball. Rust, unfortunately, is misled by prisoners into thinking he is actually outnumbered. Then, alarmed by the supposed approach of Union reinforcements, he unceremoniously withdraws without attacking—the signal for which Lee and his army in the Tygart Valley are waiting.

After several hours, Lee, realizing that the element of surprise is compromised, calls off General William W. Loring's attack on Reynolds's main force at Elkwater and retreats. Union casualties are 21 killed and 60 captured to Southern losses of about 100. It is an inauspicious debut for a general soon hailed as the Confederacy's premier soldier.

NAVAL: The USS *South Carolina* captures the *Soledad Cos* off Galveston, Texas.

September 12

POLITICS: President Abraham Lincoln dispatches a personal emissary to St. Louis who is to instruct General John C. Frémont to modify his emancipation declaration, which the president considers a dire threat to Kentucky's allegiance. He also orders Federal troops to arrest 31 members of the Maryland legislature who are suspected of collusion with the enemy.

SOUTH: Braxton Bragg is promoted to major general, C.S.A.

WEST: Simon B. Buckner, the Confederate-leaning head of Kentucky militia forces, calls on inhabitants to resist a Union invasion of the state.

A Confederate force of 7,000 men under General Sterling Price approaches a smaller Union garrison of 3,600 under Colonel James Mulligan at Lexington, Missouri.

Union forces under Colonel Jefferson C. Davis skirmish with Confederates at Booneville, Missouri.

September 13

SOUTH: President Jefferson Davis and General Joseph E. Johnston heatedly argue about the seniority of Confederate generals, the beginning of a permanent estrangement between the two men.

WEST: General Robert E. Lee, learning that Union general Joseph J. Reynolds has reinforced Colonel Nathan Kimball atop Cheat Mountain, launches a reconnaissance in force to ascertain Northern intentions. Colonel John A. Washington, his aide-de-camp, is killed in the process.

General Sterling Price, seeking to maintain the strategic initiative, marches from Wilson's Creek toward Lexington, Missouri—midway between Kansas City and St. Louis— with 7,000 Missouri State Guardsmen. There his advance troops skirmish with the picket's of Colonel James A. Mulligan, 23rd Illinois, and he elects to surround and besiege the town. Mulligan, who commands only 3,600 men and seven cannon within a strongly fortified post, has no choice but to await reinforcements promised by General John C. Frémont.

Naval: The CSS *Patrick Henry* under Commander John R. Tucker trades fire with the USS *Savannah* and *Louisiana* off Newport News, Virginia; neither side scores any hits.

The USS *Susquehanna* captures the British blockade-runner *Argonaut* at sea as it makes its way to Key West, Florida.

September 14

South: Simon B. Buckner is appointed brigadier general, C.S.A.

Southwest: Colonel George Wright, 9th U.S. Infantry, is appointed commander of Federal forces in Southern California.

Naval: The USS *Albatross* captures the Confederate schooner *Alabama* off the mouth of the Potomac River.

Lieutenant John H. Russell fights the first pitched naval engagement of the war at Pensacola, Florida, by sailing the frigate USS *Colorado* past Confederate batteries at night and then leading 100 sailors and marines on a cutting-out expedition. Russell's men storm and capture the privateer *Judah* after hand-to-hand fighting, burn it to the waterline, and withdraw unimpeded. Several enemy artillery pieces are also taken and spiked while ashore. Russell subsequently receives personal thanks from President Abraham Lincoln and is feted by the Navy Department. General Braxton Bragg, however, begins to plan a Confederate retaliatory response.

September 15

Politics: President Abraham Lincoln confers with his cabinet about the necessity of removing General John C. Frémont as commander of Missouri.

South: The 28th Pennsylvania Volunteers under Colonel John W. Geary skirmish with Confederates at Pritchards Mill, Virginia.

West: General Robert E. Lee, bested at Cheat Mountain, directs the evacuation of Confederates from the westernmost counties of Virginia. Consequently, he earns the unflattering nickname of "Granny." More important, recent operations reflect badly on Lee as a leader, and soon after he is transferred to South Carolina—a quiet sector.

General Albert S. Johnston arrives to replace General Leonidas Polk as commander of Confederate Department No. 2.

General John C. Frémont has politician Frank P. Blair, his most vocal critic, arrested in St. Louis, Missouri.

September 16

West: Confederate General Sterling Price is reinforced and tightens his grip around Lexington, Missouri, while Union defenders under Colonel James A. Mulligan, 23rd Illinois, await promised assistance from St. Louis. Unknown to Mulligan, General John C. Frémont fails to help the beleaguered garrison.

Naval: The Ironclad Board recommends to Secretary of the Navy Gideon Welles the construction of three new ironclad warships—*Monitor, Galena,* and *New Ironsides.* The former is a revolutionary new turreted design promulgated by Swedish engineer John Ericsson.

The USS *Pawnee* dispatches a landing party against Confederate fortifications on Beacon Island, North Carolina, and subsequently closes the Oracoke Inlet to enemy shipping.

Armed boats from the USS *Massachusetts* seize and occupy Ship Island, Mississippi, on the Gulf of Mexico. This lodges a Union naval base for the still-forming Gulf Blockade Squadron, midway between New Orleans, Louisiana, and Mobile, Alabama.

The gunboat USS *Conestoga* captures the Confederate steamers *V. R. Stephenson* and *Gazelle* on the Cumberland River, Kentucky.

September 17

WEST: General Benjamin M. Prentiss takes charge of Federal forces north of the Hannibal and St. Joseph Railroad, Missouri.

NAVAL: Confederate forces hastily evacuate Ship Island, Mississippi, after fighting landing parties from the USS *Massachusetts*.

September 18

POLITICS: The Kentucky legislature authorizes the use of force to expel Confederate forces from the state.

WEST: Bowling Green, Kentucky, falls to advancing Confederate forces under General Simon B. Buckner, who is newly appointed, and his Central Division of Kentucky.

General Sterling Price's Confederates fiercely assail the Union perimeter at Lexington, Missouri, and cut the garrison off from their water supply. Progress accelerates once the Confederates seize the brick, two-story Anderson house 100 yards outside the Union perimeter, previously used as a hospital and which now serves as a sniper platform for firing into their camp. At day's end—with few losses to either side—Price calls off the attack and allows the intense heat to do its work. Artillery wagons and pieces of ordnance arrive in his camp during the night in preparation for a final assault.

SOUTHWEST: General Paul O. Hebert assumes command of Confederate forces in the Department of Texas.

NAVAL: Commodore Samuel F. Du Pont wins appointment as commander of the South Atlantic Blockading Squadron.

The USS *Rescue* captures the Confederate schooner *Harford* on the Potomac River.

September 19

SOUTH: Earl Van Dorn is promoted to major general, C.S.A.

WEST: Advancing Confederate forces under General Felix K. Zollicoffer drive Union troops from Barboursville, Kentucky. The Southerners then commence the erection of strong defensive positions across Cumberland Gap, Bowling Green, and Columbus.

General Sterling Price's Confederates continue besieging Lexington, Missouri, which now is being reinforced by artillery units. Union forces under Colonel James A. Mulligan resist stoutly, unaware that a nearby relief column of 3,000 men under General Samuel D. Sturgis has been turned back.

NAVAL: The North Atlantic Blockading Squadron under Commodore Louis M. Goldman is ordered to commence operations from the southernmost boundary of North Carolina up through Virginia.

The USS *Gemsbok* seizes the Confederate schooner *Harmony* off Oracoke, North Carolina.

September 20
WEST: Confederate forces abandon Mayfield, Kentucky, in the face of a Union advance, while General Robert Anderson is ordered to establish his headquarters at Louisville.

Colonel J. Mulligan, 23rd Illinois Regiment, surrenders 3,600 Union troops to General Sterling Price at Lexington, Missouri, after a nine-day siege. Price's men ingeniously employed dampened bales of hemp as moveable breastworks, which they pushed ahead of their advance. Outnumbered, surrounded, and lacking water, Mulligan's officers vote to capitulate. Confederate losses are only 25 killed and 72 wounded while Mulligan suffers 39 killed and 120 wounded. Price also seizes seven cannon and 3,000 rifles, which are distributed among his poorly equipped forces. The inability of Union troops to raise the siege causes many in St. Louis and Washington, D.C., to question the competence of General John C. Frémont.

September 21
WEST: General Robert E. Lee arrives and takes personal command of Confederate forces in the Valley of the Kanawha, western Virginia, to oppose advancing Federals under General William S. Rosecrans.

General Ormsby M. Mitchel assumes command of Federal forces in the Department of the Ohio.

General Albert S. Johnston issues a call for 30,000 volunteers from Tennessee for service in the West.

General Leonidas Polk assumes command of the Western Division in Confederate Department No. 2.

NAVAL: A boat launched from the USS *Seminole* attacks and seizes the Confederate sloop *Maryland* on the Potomac River.

September 22
SOUTH: General Joseph E. Johnston issues a call for 10,000 volunteers from Arkansas and Missouri for service in Department No. 2 (Tennessee).

WEST: General Ulysses S. Grant conducts a reconnaissance in the direction of Columbus, Kentucky, and fights a skirmish at Mayfield Creek.

Federal jayhawkers under James H. Lane attack and burn the town of Osceola, Missouri.

NAVAL: The USS *Gemsbok* captures the Confederate schooner *Mary E. Pindar* off Federal Point, North Carolina.

September 23
NORTH: Winfield S. Hancock becomes a brigadier general, U.S. Army.

WEST: Sharp engagements erupt at Romney, Mechanicsburg Gap, and Hanging Rock in western Virginia as Federal forces advance.

General Felix K. Zollicoffer wages a sharp skirmish with Federal troops at Albany, Kentucky.

General Charles C. Frémont closes a St. Louis paper that blamed him for the surrender of Lexington, Missouri.

NAVAL: Commodore Louis M Goldsborough formally takes charge of the North Atlantic Blockading Squadron.

The USS *Cambridge* intercepts the British schooner *Julia* as it approached Beaufort, North Carolina.

The gunboat USS *Lexington* sails down the Ohio River to Owensboro, Kentucky, in a show of force to thwart Confederate sympathizers.

September 24

NORTH: Colonel John Geary and his 28th Pennsylvania Volunteers skirmish with Confederate forces at Point of Rocks, Maryland.

SOUTH: James Ewell Brown (J. E. B.) Stuart is appointed brigadier general of Confederate cavalry.

NAVAL: The USS *Dart* captures the Confederate schooner *Cecelia* off the Louisiana coast.

September 25

SOUTH: In Richmond, Virginia, President Jefferson Davis and General Joseph E. Johnston engage in another heated contretemps, this time over strategy and the allocation of reinforcements.

General William F. Smith leads Federal troops on a reconnaissance near Lewinsville, Virginia.

General Gustavus W. Smith assumes command of the II Corps, Army of Northern Virginia.

WEST: Federal troops under General William S. Rosecrans continue advancing into the Kanawha Valley, western Virginia, intent on eliminating Confederate forces under General Robert E. Lee. A skirmish is fought near Chapmansville.

Confederate general Henry A. Wise is relieved of command in western Virginia following continuous disagreements with his superior, General John P. Floyd.

Union forces occupy Smithland, Kentucky.

SOUTHWEST: The Department of Southern California is organized.

NAVAL: The Navy Department authorizes the employment of African-American "contrabands" on board naval vessels. They will begin to draw pay at the rank of "boy": 10 dollars per month and one ration per day.

The USS *Jacob Bell* and *Seminole* engage Confederate artillery at Freestone Point, Virginia.

Confederate raider CSS *Sumter* under Captain Raphael Semmes captures the Union ship *Joseph Park* off South America.

September 26

WEST: Confederate troops under General Felix K. Zollicoffer capture Salt Works (Clay County), Kentucky, after skirmishing at Laurel Bridge.

General Simon B. Buckner's Confederates destroy the locks at the mouth of Muddy River, Kentucky.

September 27

NORTH: President Abraham Lincoln and General George B. McClellan engage in heated discussions over resuming the offensive in Virginia. The general feels that the Army of the Potomac is not yet ready for prolonged operations, whereas Lincoln is being criticized for the general's alleged inactivity.

September 28

SOUTH: Thomas C. Hindman is appointed brigadier general, C.S.A.

Colonel Edward D. Baker and his 71st Pennsylvania wage a successful skirmish near Vanderburgh's House, Virginia.

NAVAL: The USS *Susquehanna* captures Confederate schooner *San Juan* as it approaches Elizabeth City, North Carolina.

September 29

SOUTH: Fatalities result when the 69th Pennsylvania accidentally fires into the 71st Pennsylvania at Munson's Hill, Virginia.

General Daniel H. Hill is ordered from Virginia to North Carolina in anticipation of Union activity there.

WEST: The 12th Kentucky under Colonel William A. Hoskins skirmishes with Confederates at Albany, Kentucky, and Travisville, Tennessee.

NAVAL: The USS *Susquehanna* seizes the Confederate schooner *Baltimore* off Hatteras Inlet, North Carolina.

September 30

NAVAL: The USS *Dart* captures the Confederate schooner *Zavalla* off Vermillion Bay, Louisiana.

The USS *Niagara* captures the Confederate pilot boat *Frolic* on the South West Pass of the Mississippi River.

SOUTHWEST: Confederate scout Captain R. Hardeman leads an action against hostile Native Americans near Camp Robledo, New Mexico Territory.

October 1

POLITICS: President Abraham Lincoln appoints General Benjamin F. Butler to command the Department of New England, created largely for the purpose of raising and training new troops for future operations. He also requests action on a large naval expedition to the southeastern coast to establish a coaling station.

At Centreville, Virginia, President Jefferson Davis and Generals Joseph E. Johnston, Pierre G. T. Beauregard, and Gustavus W. Smith continue debating strategy. At length, they finally agree to consolidate their positions and restrain from launching offensive operations into Northern territory until at least the following spring.

NAVAL: Secretary of the Navy Gideon Welles opposes issuing letters of marque and reprisal against the South as it inadvertently would imply recognition of the South's national sovereignty.

A Confederate squadron consisting of CSS *Curlew, Raleigh,* and *Junaluska* captures the supply steamer USS *Fanny* while conveying troops off Pamlico Sound, North Carolina.

October 2

POLITICS: The Confederacy reaches an accord with the Osage in the Indian Territory.

Governor Andrew B. Moore of Alabama warns tradespeople against charging exorbitant prices for their services.

SOUTH: Union forces prevail in a large skirmish at Chapmansville, Virginia, while other fighting rages at Springfield Station.

WEST: Pro-Union forces from Cairo, Illinois, attack a Southern camp at Charleston, Missouri, where statewide intermittent strife continues.

October 3

DIPLOMACY: Louisiana governor Thomas O. Moore summarily bans cotton exports in an attempt to force Britain and France to recognize the Confederacy's independence.

SOUTH: General Henry W. Slocum dispatches the 26th New York to capture Pohick Church, Virginia, from Confederate forces.

The 31st New York, dispatched by General William B. Franklin, skirmishes with Confederate cavalry at Springfield Station, Virginia.

WEST: General Joseph J. Reynolds advances from Cheat Mountain with 5,000 men to dislodge a Confederate force stationed at Camp Bartow, along the southern fork of the Greenbrier River in western Virginia. The 1,800 Southerners under General Henry R. Jackson give ground slowly before making a stand behind the river. Reynolds then deploys his men and makes two determined attacks covered by artillery fire but is easily repulsed. Unable to turn Jackson's flanks, Reynold simply withdraws back to Cheat Mountain, and an impasse settles over the region. Union losses are reported as eight killed and 36 wounded to a Confederate tally of six killed, 33 wounded, and 13 missing.

NAVAL: The USS *Sam Houston* arrives off Galveston, Texas, where it sinks the Confederate schooner *Reindeer.*

October 4

NORTH: Colonel Charles P. Stone skirmishes with Confederate forces at Edwards Ferry, Maryland.

SOUTH: Confederate forces fail to dislodge Union defenders, commanded by General John E. Wool, near Chicamacomico, North Carolina.

WEST: The Confederacy concludes a treaty with the Shawnee, Seneca, and Cherokee in the Indian Territory.

SOUTHWEST: Colonel George Wright, 9th U.S. Infantry, assumes command of the new District of Southern California.

NAVAL: President Abraham Lincoln approves a contract for constructing the U.S. Navy's first ironclad warships; among the intended vessels is John Ericsson's revolutionary USS *Monitor.*

The USS *South Carolina* takes Confederate schooners *Ezilda* and *Joseph H. Toone* at the Southwest Pass of the Mississippi River.

October 5
SOUTH: General Joseph K. F. Mansfield takes charge of Union forces garrisoning Hatteras Inlet, North Carolina.

SOUTHWEST: Pro-Union forces sweep through Oak Grove and Temecula Ranch, California, in an attempt to flush out Confederate sympathizers.

NAVAL: At Chincoteague, Virginia, the USS *Louisiana* dispatches two boats, which attack and destroy a Confederate schooner being outfitted as a privateer.

Heavy fire from the USS *Monticello* proves instrumental in repulsing Confederate troops and steamers as they attacked Hatteras Inlet, North Carolina.

October 6
NAVAL: The USS *Flag* captures the blockade-running schooner *Alert* off Charleston, South Carolina.

October 7
POLITICS: President Abraham Lincoln dispatches Secretary of War Simon Cameron with a letter to General Samuel R. Curtis to inquire if General John C. Frémont should be replaced as commander in Missouri.

SOUTH: William J. Hardee, Thomas J. Jackson, James Longstreet, and John B. Magruder gain promotion to major generals, C.S.A.

General Braxton Bragg extends his military authority over all of Alabama.

WEST: Eager to restore his flagging reputation, General Charles Frémont advances 40,000 men from St. Louis, Missouri, toward Lexington. The move prompts General Sterling Price to withdraw south.

NAVAL: The steam-powered ironclad CSS *Virginia* (nee *Merrimack*), completely armored and redesigned by Confederate engineer John M. Brooke, makes its brief but ominous debut off Hampton Roads, Virginia.

The USS *Louisiana* captures the Confederate schooner *S. T. Carrison* off Wallops Island, Virginia.

The gunboat USS *Tyler* exchanges shots with Confederate artillery posted at Iron Bluffs near Columbus, Kentucky.

General Ulysses S. Grant, accompanied by gunboats USS *Lexington* and *Tyler,* conducts a reconnaissance of Lucas Bend, Missouri.

October 8
WEST: General Robert Anderson, who is ailing and commands the Department of the Cumberland, is superseded by General William T. Sherman at Louisville, Kentucky.

October 9
SOUTH: General Braxton Bragg orders 1,000 Confederates under General Richard H. Anderson across Pensacola Bay to attack Union-held Fort Pickens on Santa Rosa Island, Florida. The Southerners, under cover of darkness, safely land and drive the 6th New York from its camp. Union commander Colonel Harvey Brown then brings

out several companies of regulars from the fort, assisted by artillery. These troops skirmish heavily with the Confederates, which dissuades Anderson from attacking further. A quick sweep by Union troops nets several stragglers as the Confederates withdraw, but the bulk of Anderson's troops reach the mainland intact. Brown reports losses of 13 killed, 27 wounded, and 21 missing, whereas Anderson loses 18 dead, 39 wounded, and 30 captured.

NAVAL: American naval vessels guarding the Head of Passes, Mississippi River, are attacked by the Confederate steamer CSS *Ivy*. No damage is incurred by either side, but the impressive range of Southern naval ordnance is noted by the Federals.

October 10

POLITICS: President Jefferson Davis, writing to General Gustavus W. Smith, briefly ponders the use of African-American slaves by Confederate forces as laborers.

WEST: General Ormsby M. Mitchel is ordered on an expedition into the heart of pro-Union East Tennessee.

NAVAL: Accurate shooting by the USS *Daylight* silences a Confederate battery at Lynnhaven Bay, Virginia, after it begins to shell the Union vessel *John Clark*.

Confederate forces attack and capture the American sloop *William Batty* in Tampa Bay, Florida.

October 11

SOUTH: Edmund Kirby-Smith is appointed major general, C.S.A.

WEST: General William S. Rosecrans assumes command of Union forces in the Department of Western Virginia.

NAVAL: The USS *Union* dispatches three boat crews under Lieutenant Abram D. Harrell, which cut out and burn a Confederate privateer in Dumfries Creek, Virginia.

October 12

WEST: General John C. Frémont's advance results in heavy skirmishes at Clintonville and Pomme de Terre (Cameron), Missouri. Confederate partisans under Missouri militiaman Jeff Thompson also raid Ironton from their home base in Stoddard County.

NAVAL: Covered by rain and darkness, the Confederate steamer *Theodora* runs the Union blockade off Charleston, South Carolina, and makes for Cuba. On board are special commissioners James M. Mason and John Slidell.

The USS *Dale* captures the Confederate schooner *Specie* east of Jacksonville, Florida.

Newly launched Confederate rammer CSS *Manassas* under Commodore George N. Hollins departs New Orleans, Louisiana, and ventures down the Mississippi River with the armed steamers *Ivy* and *James L. Day*. While clearing the Head of Passes, they encounter a Union squadron consisting of the USS *Richmond, Vincennes, Water Witch, Nightingale,* and *Preble*. A stiff engagement develops in which *Manassas* successfully rams *Richmond* and *Vincennes*, running them aground. The action concludes soon after, and Hollins steams back upstream. The Union vessels subsequently are refloated, and the blockade resumes.

The confederate privateer *Sallie* captures the Union brig *Granada* at sea.

The first Union ironclad, USS *St. Louis,* is launched at Carondelet, Missouri.

October 13
SOUTH: General Thomas Williams succeeds General James K. F. Mansfield as commander of Union forces at Hatteras Inlet, North Carolina.

NAVAL: The USS *Keystone State* seizes the Confederate steamer *Salvor* near Tortugas Island, Florida.

October 14
POLITICS: To discourage treasonable activity, President Abraham Lincoln orders General Winfield Scott to suspend writs of habeas corpus anywhere in the region from Maine to Washington, D.C.

Secretary of War Simon Cameron orders General Thomas W. Sherman to organize and arm fugitive slaves into military squads at Port Royal, South Carolina.

SOUTH: General Braxton Bragg formally takes charge of the newly constituted Department of Alabama and West Florida.

WEST: Former Virginia attorney turned Confederate raider Jeff Thompson establishes his home base in southeastern Missouri.

SOUTHWEST: Colonel James H. Carleton, 1st California Infantry, replaces Colonel George Wright as commander of the District of Southern California.

NAVAL: Lieutenant A. Murray of the USS *Louisiana* administers loyalty oaths to the inhabitants of Chincoteague Island, Virginia.

October 15
SOUTH: Colonel Isaac M. Tucker and the 2nd New Jersey Regiment skirmish with Confederates at Little River Turnpike, Virginia.

WEST: Confederate raiders under Jeff Thompson attack a Union outpost at Potosi, Missouri, taking 33 prisoners of the 38th Illinois and burning the Big River Bridge.

NAVAL: The USS *Roanoke, Flag, Monticello,* and *Vandalia* capture and sink the Confederate blockade-runner *Thomas Watson* off Stono Reef, Charleston, South Carolina.

October 16
POLITICS: President Jefferson Davis denies requests by Confederate soldiers to return home to serve in their state militia.

WEST: Confederate cavalry under Colonel Ashby Turner clashes with Union forces near Harper's Ferry in western Virginia.

Union forces reoccupy Lexington, Missouri.

NAVAL: The USS *South Carolina* captures the Confederate schooner *Edward Barnard* near South West Pass, Mississippi River.

October 17
NAVAL: After some deliberation, Commodore Samuel F. Du Pont informs U.S. Navy secretary Gideon Welles that Port Royal, South Carolina, is an inviting target and would constitute an important asset to the continuing blockade effort.

The Confederate privateer *Sallie* captures the Federal brig *Betsey Ames* on the Bahama Banks.

October 18

POLITICAL: President Abraham Lincoln meets with his cabinet about continuing dissatisfaction with General in Chief Winfield Scott and his probable retirement. He also experiences problems prying troops from the armies of Generals William T. Sherman and George B. McClellan for the upcoming coastal expedition.

SOUTH: General Israel B. Richardson takes Union forces on a reconnaissance of the Occoquan River, Virginia.

WEST: Confederate raiders under Jeff Thompson skirmish with Colonel Joseph B. Plummer's 11th Missouri Regiment around Wardensburg, Missouri.

SOUTHWEST: General Mansfield Lovell replaces General David E. Twiggs as commander of Confederate Department No. 1 (Louisiana and Texas).

NAVAL: The USS *Gemsbok* captures the Confederate brig *Ariel* off Wilmington, Delaware.

October 19

NAVAL: USS *Massachusetts* and CSS *Florida* wage an inconclusive battle in the Mississippi Sound, but Union forces are alarmed by the apparent longer range of Confederate ordnance.

October 20

SOUTH: General George B. McClellan, eager to test Confederate responses and pressured by Radical Republicans to assume the offensive, orders politician-turned-soldier Colonel Charles P. Stone to dispatch troops from his base at Poolesville, Maryland, and demonstrate before enemy lines near Leesburg, Virginia. Stone elects to send a single brigade of 1,700 men under the inexperienced colonel Edward D. Baker, a political appointee and close friend of President Abraham Lincoln. He is ordered to make a "slight demonstration" to test Confederate reactions. When word of Baker's advance reaches Confederate colonel Nathan G. Evans, he energetically makes preparations to receive the intruders.

Union forces under General George A. McCall occupy Dranesville, Virginia, below the Potomac River. He is supposed to be acting in concert with forces dispatched to Leesburg by Colonel Edward P. Stone, but he withdraws his troops without informing the latter.

WEST: Colonel William P. Carlin advances his 38th Illinois to Pilot Knob, Missouri.

Colonel George Wright replaces General Edwin V. Sumner as commander of the Department of the Pacific.

October 21

SOUTH: Acting upon faulty intelligence, Colonel Isaac D. Baker ferries 1,700 men of his brigade across the Potomac River at Ball's Bluff, Virginia, a 100-foot ledge overlooking the waterway. He does so without first reconnoitering the area for enemy troops and remains unaware that Colonel Nathan G. Evans's Confederates are posted in the woods above him. Federal troops clamber up the slope, but senior officer express concern about having their backs against a river. At this juncture the milling soldiers are fired on by Southerners from higher up, enjoying the advantage of position. An unequal battle ensues for three and a half hours until Baker is killed and his command succumbs to panic. Evans then charges down hill and routs the remaining defenders, many of whom tumble over the bluffs and drown while fording the Potomac. Losses in this affair are 49 Union troops killed, 158 wounded, and 714 captured to a Confederate tally of 33 killed, 115 wounded, and one missing. President Abraham Lincoln is notably shaken upon hearing of the death of Baker, a good friend and close confidant.

Nathan G. Evans is promoted to brigadier general, C.S.A., for his performance at Ball's Bluff.

General John B. Magruder skirmishes with Union forces at Young's Mills (Newport News), Virginia.

General John B. Grayson, C.S.A., dies of illness in Tallahassee, Florida.

WEST: Confederates under General Felix K. Zollicoffer skirmish heavily with the Union troops of General Albin F. Schoepf at Rockcastle Hills, Kentucky.

Colonel J. B. Plummer engages in a three-hour battle with Confederate forces near Fredericktown, Missouri, and occupies the town.

October 22
SOUTH: The Confederate Department of Virginia organizes under General Joseph E. Johnston while General Pierre G. T. Beauregard retains command of the District of the Potomac.

General Theophilus Holmes takes command of the Aquia District of Virginia.

General James H. Trapier assumes control of the Confederate Department of Middle and East Florida.

WEST: General Benjamin F. Kelley takes charge of Union forces in the Department of Harper's Ferry.

General Thomas J. Jackson is ordered to lead Confederate forces in the Shenandoah Valley of western Virginia.

NAVAL: Captain Thomas T. Craven, commanding the Potomac River Flotilla, informs superiors that Confederate batteries control access to the Potomac at all points below Alexandria, Virginia.

October 23
WEST: Skirmishing erupts between Union and Confederate forces at West Liberty and Hodgeville, Kentucky. The strength of enemy defenses alarms General William T. Sherman, who is anxious to forestall further Confederate advances into that state.

NAVAL: Crew members of the captured Confederate privateer *Savannah* are tried in New York on charges of piracy and threatened with execution. Though convicted, the sentences are never carried out.

October 24
POLITICS: President Abraham Lincoln relieves General John C. Frémont of command in Missouri and replaces him with General David Hunter. He also attends the funeral of Colonel Edward D. Baker, his close friend, lately killed at Ball's Bluff.

WEST: The inhabitants of western Virginia overwhelmingly endorse plans for forming their own state.

Colonel R. D. Anderson and his 14th Tennessee attack the Union position of Camp Joe Underwood, Kentucky.

Western Union finalizes its transcontinental telegraph; viable communication with the entire country now becomes possible.

October 25

WEST: Union cavalry under Major Charles Zagonyi defeat opposing Confederate forces and occupy Springfield, Missouri.

NAVAL: Swedish inventor and engineer John Ericsson begins to construct his revolutionary, one-turret warship USS *Monitor* at Greenpoint, New York, by laying its keel.

The USS *Rhode Island* captures the Confederate schooner *Aristides* off Charlotte Harbor, Florida.

October 26

SOUTH: General Alexander R. Lawton takes command of the Confederate Department of Georgia.

WEST: Continued skirmishing under General Benjamin F. Kelley at Romney and South Branch Bridge in western Virginia removes the last remaining Confederate forces from the theater.

General John C. Frémont and General Sterling Price of the Missouri Home Guard agree on a prisoner exchange.

NAVAL: CSS *Nashville* successfully clears the blockade out of Charleston, South Carolina.

The gunboat USS *Conestoga* ferries Federal troops to Eddyville, Kentucky, for an impending advance on Saratoga by General Charles F. Smith.

October 27

WEST: General John C. Frémont shepherds his army toward Springfield, Missouri, in the mistaken belief that the main Confederate force under General Sterling Price encamps there. In fact, Price has retreated long since to safety thanks to Frémont's lethargic movements.

NAVAL: The USS *Santee* captures the Confederate brig *Delta* off Galveston, Texas.

October 28

NORTH: Union troops under General Joseph Hooker engage Confederate batteries near Budd's Ferry, Maryland.

WEST: General Albert S. Johnston relieves General Simon B. Buckner as commander of the Confederate Army Corps of Kentucky at Bowling Green.

Federal forces under General Chester Harding advance toward Fulton, Missouri.

NAVAL: Lieutenant Alfred Hopkins of the USS *Louisiana* leads a three-boat expedition that attacks and burns three Confederate vessels anchored in the Chincoteague Inlet, Virginia.

October 29

NAVAL: A huge combined expedition of 17 warships, 25 supply ships, and 25 transports under Commodore Samuel F. Du Pont, conveying 13,000 Union troops under General Thomas W. Sherman, departs Hampton Roads, Virginia. The largest American armada assembled to date, the flotilla is intended to capture Port Royal, South Carolina, midway between Charleston and Savannah, Georgia. En route, the armada is buffeted by heavy seas off the coast and is scattered widely.

October 30

SOUTH: President Jefferson Davis complains to General Pierre G. T. Beauregard about publishing excerpts from Beauregard's report on the Battle of First Manassas "to exalt yourself at my expense." Thereafter, the two leaders are never reconciled.
WEST: Confederate forces near Fort Donelson, Tennessee, begin to sink stone-filled barges on the Cumberland River as an obstacle to Federal gunboats.
NAVAL: The Confederate privateer *Sallie* seizes the American brig *B. K. Eaton* at sea.

October 31

POLITICS: Secessionist-leaning Missouri legislators meet at Neosho, Missouri, and vote to join the Confederacy. The state continues to be claimed simultaneously by both belligerents.
NORTH: Ailing, 75-year-old General in Chief Winfield Scott, once the military doyen of his age, voluntarily resigns as general in chief of Union forces. He then retires in virtual isolation to the U.S. Military Academy at West Point, New York, for the remainder of the war.
WEST: Union soldiers repulse Confederate attackers at Morgantown, Kentucky, with few casualties to either side.

November 1

NORTH: The 34-year-old general George B. McClellan gains appointment as general in chief to succeed the ailing Winfield Scott. In light of his youth, dash, and reputation, much is expected of him.
WEST: Confederate forces under General John B. Floyd botch an attack on General William S. Rosecrans's troops at Gauley Bridge and Cotton Hill in western Virginia. After being repulsed, the Southerners withdraw completely from the area.

General Ulysses S. Grant arrives at Cairo, Illinois, to take charge of the District of Southeast Missouri. Rumpled and nondescript in appearance, he proves to be aggressively disposed and begins to formulate plans to evict Confederate forces from their strong point along the bluffs at Columbus, Kentucky.

General John C. Frémont finally concludes a prisoner-exchange agreement with General Sterling Price, and he also pledges to release civilians held in military detention. The agreement subsequently is negated by President Abraham Lincoln for exceeding local military authority.
NAVAL: The Union armada under Commodore Samuel F. Du Pont continues being buffeted by high seas off Cape Hatteras, North Carolina, and remains widely scattered.

Portrait of a Confederate soldier *(Library of Congress)*

November 2

SOUTH: Former vice president John C. Breckinridge is appointed brigadier general, C.S.A.

WEST: General John C. Frémont, who has proven incorrigible, is relieved of command of the Department of the West at Springfield, Missouri, and is temporarily replaced by General David Hunter.

Southern partisans under General Jeff Thompson are the object of a Federal offensive at Bird's Point, Cape Girardeau, and Ironton, Missouri.

NAVAL: The USS *Sabine* rescues a battalion of U.S. Marines from the sinking transport *Governor* near Georgetown, South Carolina, before it founders.

British steamer *Bermuda* successfully runs the blockade at Charleston, South Carolina.

November 3

NORTH: Union troops under General Oliver O. Howard advance into southern Maryland to clear out remaining pockets of Confederate troops.

November 4

POLITICS: President Jefferson Davis, frustrated in his inability to reach an agreement with General Pierre G. T. Beauregard concerning strategy, solicits support and advice from General Samuel Cooper and General Robert E. Lee. He also is increasingly aware of rumors concerning his alleged military ineptitude.

SOUTH: General John A. Dix forbids all African Americans from entering beyond closely prescribed military lines.

WEST: General Thomas J. "Stonewall" Jackson arrives as commander of Confederate forces in the Shenandoah Valley, headquartered at Winchester, Virginia.

NAVAL: A large naval expedition under Commodore Samuel F. Du Pont gathers off Port Royal Sound, South Carolina. Meanwhile, Confederate vessels under Commodore Josiah Tattnall fire on the coast survey ship *Vixen* and USS *Ottawa* as they reconnoiter the two-mile-wide entrance into the channel. No damage results as the Union ships complete their mission and withdraw.

November 5

SOUTH: General Robert E. Lee assumes responsibilities as head of the newly constituted Department of South Carolina, Georgia, and East Florida.

WEST: Union troops under General William Nelson occupy Prestonburg, Kentucky.

General John C. Frémont, still commanding the Department of the West, orders General Ulysses S. Grant on a diversionary attack against Columbus, Kentucky, to cover Union thrusts in southeastern Missouri. He anticipates that this maneuver will keep Confederate forces preoccupied and unable to cross the Mississippi River and interfere.

NAVAL: The USS *Ottawa, Pembina, Seneca,* and *Pawnee* attack and disperse a Confederate squadron under Commodore Josiah Tattnall in Port Royal Sound, and begin to shell neighboring Forts Walker and Beauregard on the north and south sides of the sound.

November 6

POLITICS: President Jefferson Davis is elected permanent chief executive of the Confederate States of America and is slated to serve a six-year term. Vice President Alexander Stephens likewise is reelected, as are members of the first permanent Confederate Congress.

Portrait of a Union officer *(Library of Congress)*

WEST: General Ulysses S. Grant embarks from Cairo, Illinois, with two brigades of infantry, some cavalry, and an artillery battery for an amphibious descent on nearby Belmont, Missouri. To cover his actions, he orders General Charles F. Smith, commanding Union forces at Paducah, Kentucky, to demonstrate against the main Confederate force under General Leonidas Polk at Columbus, directly opposite Belmont.

NAVAL: The USS *Rescue* attacks and burns the Confederate schooner *Ada* in Curratoman Creek, Virginia.

The USS *Lawrence* captures the British blockade-runner *Fanny Lee* off Darien, Georgia.

November 7

WEST: General Don C. Buell is chosen to command Union forces in Kentucky, and he receives instructions from General George B. McClellan on the legal status of fugitive African-American slaves.

Approximately 3,000 Union troops under General Ulysses S. Grant disembark at Hunter's Farm, three miles above his objective at Belmont, Missouri. His opponent, General Gideon Pillow, commands 2,500 men, and once the firing commences, General Leonidas Polk rushes an additional 2,500 men across the Mississippi River. Meanwhile, Grant's men launch into the Confederates, who are saddled by Pillow's inept leadership and are routed in a four-hour fight. Enthusiastic Union troops storm into the Confederate camp, and, despite the entreaties of Grant and other officers, they embark on headlong plundering. This allows Pillow to regroup and receive reinforcements under Polk, who arrives in person to take charge. With Confederate forces now interposed between his men and his water transport, Grant has little choice but to cut his way through enemy lines to the riverbank—and safety. Union forces again prevail in stiff fighting and successfully embark while vengeful Confederates fire on them from the shoreline. Grant himself nearly stumbles into advancing Confederates in the woods and almost is captured. His first battle proves somewhat of a botched draw, with Federal troops sustaining 607 casualties to a Confederate tally of 641. But, most important, the affair demonstrates Grant's willingness to undertake the offensive, along with his aptitude for combined operations employing both troops and gunboats.

NAVAL: The South Atlantic Blockading Squadron of 77 vessels under Commodore Samuel F. Du Pont disembarks 16,000 troops under General Thomas W. Sherman off Port Royal Sound, South Carolina, halfway between Charleston and Savannah, Georgia. The Union vessels steam directly into the sound, assume a circling oval formation, and subject the Confederates to a steady stream of accurate gunfire from 154 heavy cannon. Forts Beauregard and Walker, whose crews are largely untrained, respond with a sputtering fire from 41 guns that mainly falls short. Ironically, the Southerners are commanded by General Thomas F. Drayton, whose brother, Percival Drayton, is a Union naval commander. By 3:30 P.M., both fortifications are abandoned and overrun by the combined assault. Confederate defenders under Commodore Josiah Tattnall can only harass their antagonists, but they do manage to rescue the garrison at Hilton Head and ferry them ashore. Despite spectacular pyrotechnics, losses are extremely light, with Du Pont losing eight killed and six wounded while Drayton reports 11 killed and 48 wounded. The Union has acquired a second firm lodging on the Confederate coastline; Port Royal Sound/Hilton Head emerges as a major coaling base for the blockading squadrons.

The wooden gunboats USS *Tyler* and *Lexington* afford useful fire support for Union forces at Belmont, Missouri, allowing them to escape a Confederate pursuit to the water's edge. Their success underscores the growing utility and flexibility of naval craft for riverine operations throughout the West.

The British mail steamer *Trent* departs Havana, Cuba, bound for the Danish island of St. Thomas in the Caribbean. Confederate agents James M. Mason and John Slidell are onboard.

November 8

SOUTH: Federal forces under General Thomas W. Sherman advance inland from Hilton Head, South Carolina, toward the city of Beaufort.

General Robert E. Lee arrives at his new headquarters in Savannah, Georgia. Hearing of the success of Union forces at Port Royal Sound, he orders the coastline evacuated save for the garrison of Fort Pulaski, Georgia.

WEST: Pro-Union agitators rise up and attack Southern forces in the mountainous region of eastern Tennessee, destroying railroad lines and forcing General Felix K. Zollicoffer to request immediate reinforcements.

Union troops under General William Nelson engage Confederate forces at Ivy Mountain, Kentucky. While at Prestonburg, Nelson had become aware of Southern recruiting activities under Colonel John S. Williams at Piketon, 28 miles distant, and resolved to entrap them. He then dispatches Colonel Joshua W. Sill, two regiments, and some cannon on a circuitous route to cut Williams off near the Virginia state line. Nelson himself marches three regiments and two batteries directly toward Piketown. The Confederates, badly outnumbered and armed mostly with muskets and shotguns, rapidly fall back to Ivy Mountain and position themselves along a bend in the road. Nelson's troops are then fought to a standstill. The second column under Sill never arrives. Williams manages to disengage and return to Virginia intact. Nelson reports six killed and 24 wounded; Southern losses are unknown.

NAVAL: The USS *Rescue* shells a Confederate battery at Urbana Creek, Virginia, and subsequently nets a large enemy schooner.

In a potentially disastrous move, the screw sloop USS *San Jacinto* under irascible Captain Charles Wilkes, boards the British mail packet *Trent* in Old Bahama Channel and forcibly removes Southern envoys James M. Mason and John Slidell. This proves an egregious violation of international law involving the rights of neutrals on the high seas and threatens to precipitate a war with Great Britain.

A cutting-out expedition under Lieutenant James E. Jouett, launched from USS *Santee,* surprises and burns the Confederate schooner *Royal Yacht* at Galveston, Texas.

November 9

SOUTH: Union forces under Generals Joseph Hooker and Daniel E. Sickles advance on Mathias Point, York River, Virginia.

Federal troops under General Thomas W. Sherman, assisted by gunboats, advance from Port Royal, South Carolina, and capture the city of Beaufort on the Broad River. This severs a vital communications link between Charleston and Savannah, Georgia. Department commander General Robert E. Lee expresses concern to the government in Richmond about the Union's apparent ability to land troops anywhere at will.

George B. Crittenden is promoted to major general, C.S.A.

WEST: In a major shake-up of command, General Henry W. Halleck becomes commander of Federal troops in the newly created Department of Missouri (Missouri, Arkansas, Illinois, and western Kentucky) while General Don C. Buell replaces General William T. Sherman as head of the Department of the Cumberland, subsequently enlarged and renamed the Department of the Ohio (Indiana, Michigan, Tennessee, and western Kentucky).

The Department of Kansas is organized under General David Hunter.

SOUTHWEST: The Department of New Mexico is reorganized under Colonel Edward R. S. Canby, U.S. Army.

November 11

NORTH: Thaddeus Lowe, Union chief of army aeronautics, rides an observation balloon launched from the *G. W. Parke Custis* anchored in the Potomac River. In nearby Washington, D.C., a torchlight parade is held honoring General George B. McClellan, now publicly heralded as savior of the Union.

WEST: General Jacob D. Cox's Federal troops skirmish with Confederate forces at Gauley Bridge in western Virginia.

General Leonidas Polk is wounded when a large Confederate cannon at Columbus, Kentucky, explodes while being test-fired.

General George B. Crittenden assumes command of Confederate troops in the District of Cumberland Gap, Tennessee. His chief subordinate, Felix K. Zollicoffer, is assigned to southeastern Kentucky but is to remain south of the Cumberland River.

Pitched battles erupt between Union Jayhawkers and Southern Bushwhackers at Little Blue, Missouri.

November 12

SOUTH: Renewed Federal reconnaissance of Occoquan Creek by Federal troops under General Samuel P. Heintzelman.

NAVAL: The British-built steamer *Fingal* arrives with a cargo of military stores at Savannah, Georgia. The vessel subsequently is armed and rechristened CSS *Atlanta*.

November 13

POLITICS: George B. Lincoln contemptuously snubs President Abraham Lincoln when the latter calls on his headquarters by retiring to bed. Henceforth, the general will be summoned to the White House when consultations become necessary.

NAVAL: The USS *Water Witch* captures the British blockade-runner *Cornucopia* off Mobile, Alabama.

November 14

NORTH: General Joseph Hooker fights a minor engagement at Mattawoman Creek, Maryland.

NAVAL: The U.S. revenue cutter *Mary* attacks and captures the Confederate privateer *Neva* at San Francisco, California.

November 15

POLITICS: President Abraham Lincoln and his cabinet begin to focus attention on strategic New Orleans, Louisiana, the Confederacy's second-largest city and a port of great significance. In selecting a naval leader to spearhead an amphibious expedition against it, Secretary Gideon Welles chooses Captain David G. Farragut, a 60-year-old Tennessean and War of 1812 veteran known for his aggressive disposition. Welles has been persuaded to do so by Captain David D. Porter, Farragut's stepbrother.

The U.S. Christian Commission is organized as a wartime extension of the Young Men's Christian Association (YMCA). The commission is designated to provide supplies and extend other assistance to Union troops.

WEST: General Don C. Buell arrives at Louisville, Kentucky, as commander of the Department of the Ohio, replacing General William T. Sherman. The president is counting on him for an early advance into pro-Union eastern Tennessee.

A camp occupied by Union sympathizers near Chattanooga, Tennessee, is overrun by Confederate forces. Their leader, William B. Carter, is captured but subsequently escapes.

SOUTHWEST: A mixed Confederate force of 1,400 Texans under Colonel Douglas H. Cooper with allied Cherokee, Choctaw, and Chickasaw warriors arrives at Canadian Creek, Indian Territory, intending to fight a reputed 1,000 pro-Union Creek Indians stationed there under Opothleyahola. However, once arrived, they discovered that the enemy has withdrawn, so Cooper sets off in pursuit toward nearby Round Mountain.

NAVAL: The USS *San Jacinto* under Captain John Wilkes arrives at Fortress Monroe, Virginia, with captured Confederate emissaries James M. Mason and John Slidell onboard. This is the government's first inkling of what had transpired at sea, and Wilkes is hailed as a hero in the press.

The USS *Dale* captures the British schooner *Mabel* east of Jacksonville, Florida.

November 16
POLITICS: To preclude a potentially ruinous war with Great Britain, Postmaster General Montgomery Blair and Senator Charles Sumner of Massachusetts urge the immediate release of Confederate envoys James M. Mason and John Slidell.

NAVAL: Confederate navy secretary Stephen R. Mallory accepts bids for four, heavily armed seagoing ironclads.

November 17
NAVAL: The USS *Connecticut* captures the British schooner *Adeline* off Cape Canaveral, Florida, uncovering a large cache of military stores and supplies onboard.

November 18
POLITICS: The fifth session of the Provisional Confederate Congress convenes.

Confederate Kentuckians meet at Russellville and adopt a secession ordinance. Like Missouri, Kentucky has separate legislatures in both Union and Confederate camps.

A convention of loyal North Carolinians convenes at Hatteras to denounce secession and reaffirm their loyalty to the Union. Marble Taylor Nash is then elected provisional governor of the state.

SOUTH: The 1st Virginia Cavalry under Colonel Fitzhugh Lee skirmishes with Union forces at Fairfax Courthouse, Virginia.

WEST: General Albert S. Johnston repeats his call for a complete mobilization by all militia and volunteers from Tennessee.

Guerrillas under General Jeff Thompson seize a Federal steamer at Price's Landing, Missouri.

General George Wright formally accepts command of the Department of the Pacific.

SOUTHWEST: A detachment of the 9th Texas under Colonel Douglas H. Cooper, assisted by allied Cherokees, fights a skirmish with Creek warriors under Opothleyahola at Round Mountain, Indian Territory. The pro-Union Native Americans are defeated yet skillfully extricate themselves.

NAVAL: Commodore David D. Porter is tasked with acquiring and supplying gunboats for the long-anticipated campaign against New Orleans, Louisiana.

The USS *Monticello* exchanges fire with Confederate artillery near New Inlet, North Carolina.

Heavy and accurate fire from the gunboat USS *Conestoga* silences a Confederate battery at Canton, Kentucky, and disperses accompanying troops.

November 19
NAVAL: The CSS *Nashville* captures and burns the Union clipper *Harvey Birch* at sea.

November 20
NORTH: General George B. McClellan, a superb organizer and disciplinarian, reviews 70,000 men of the Army of the Potomac near Washington, D.C. In contrast with amateurish forces hastily assembled the previous summer, visitors comment favorably on the martial ardor and discipline of all ranks. However, it remains to be seen if McClellan will aggressively engage enemy forces who are defending the Confederate capital, Richmond, Virginia.

WEST: General John B. Floyd hastily withdraws from the Gauley River region of western Virginia, abandoning or destroying valuable tents and other equipment.

General Thomas C. Hindman leads Confederate forces in a skirmish at Brownsville, Kentucky.

General Henry W. Halleck, newly arrived at the Department of the Missouri in St. Louis, declares General Orders No. 3, excluding African-American slaves from military camps in the Department of the Missouri.

SOUTHWEST: Pursuing Union forces corner and capture Confederate sympathizers under Daniel Showalter at Warner's Ranch, southeast of Los Angeles, California.

November 21
POLITICS: The Confederate cabinet is reorganized with Judah P. Benjamin succeeding LeRoy P. Walker as secretary of war.

NORTH: John M. Schofield is appointed brigadier general, U.S. Army.

WEST: Confederate general Lloyd Tilghman becomes commander of strategic Forts Henry and Donelson on the Tennessee and Cumberland rivers, respectively. These are the lynchpins of Confederate defense in the central region of the war and critical to the Southern war effort.

General Albert S. Johnston again summons 10,000 volunteers from Mississippi to assist in the defense of Columbus, Kentucky.

NAVAL: The USS *New London,* assisted by the *R. R. Cuyler* and *Massachusetts,* seizes the Confederate schooner *Olive* in Mississippi Sound. Hours later, they also seize the steamer *Anna.*

November 22
SOUTHWEST: General Albert Pike is appointed commander of the newly instituted Confederate Department of the Indian Territory.
NAVAL: The Navy Department is authorized to recruit an additional 500 marines and officers.

The USS *Niagara* and *Richmond* engage in a two-day duel with Confederate artillery based in Fort McRee, Pensacola, Florida. The vessels are assisted by fire from neighboring Fort Pickens; Confederate positions sustain heavy damage, as does the *Richmond.*

November 23
WEST: Union troops under General George H. Thomas stage a demonstration from Danville, Kentucky, toward eastern Tennessee.
NAVAL: The Confederate raider CSS *Sumter* under Captain Raphael Semmes evades the USS *Iroquois* at Martinique and heads for Europe.

November 24
WEST: Colonel Nathan B. Forrest mounts a prolonged cavalry raid against union garrisons Caseyville and Eddyville, Kentucky, initiating what becomes a spectacular partisan career.
NAVAL: The USS *San Jacinto* under Captain John Wilkes docks in Boston, Massachusetts, whereupon captured Confederate commissioners James M. Mason and John Slidell are imprisoned at Fort Warren.

A U.S. Navy squadron consisting of the USS *Flag, August, Pocahontas, Seneca,* and *Savannah,* the whole under Commander John Rodgers, disembark forces on Tybee Island and seal off the mouth of the Savannah River, Georgia. This acquisition places nearby Fort Pulaski, Savannah's principal fortification, within Union grasp.

November 25
SOUTH: Confederate secretary of war Judah P. Benjamin orders pro-Union guerrillas captured in Tennessee to be tried by court-martial and hanged if found guilty of burning bridges.
NAVAL: The USS *Penguin* captures the Confederate blockade-runner *Albion* near Edisto, North Carolina.

The Confederate raider CSS *Sumter* under Captain Raphael Semmes takes the Union brig *Montmorenci* off the Leeward Islands.

November 26
POLITICS: A constituent convention gathers at Wheeling, Virginia, and adopts a resolution to secede from Virginia and establish a separate state.
NORTH: A banquet honoring Captain Charles Wilkes is held in Boston as diplomats begin to weigh the diplomatic implications of his actions.

South: General George A. McCall leads Union forces on an expedition to Dranesville, Virginia, engaging in several skirmishes en route.

Naval: Commodore Josiah Tattnall sorties with three armed steamers against Union vessels off Cockspur Roads, Georgia. The Confederates withdraw after failing to lure their opponents to within range of Fort Pulaski's guns.

The Confederate raider CSS *Sumter* under Captain Raphael Semmes seizes and burns the American schooner *Arcade* north of the Leeward Islands.

November 27

Diplomacy: Indignation runs high in Great Britain as word of the *Trent* affair circulates. Signs and editorials declaring an "outrage on the British flag" begin to manifest publicly while war seems in the offing.

West: General Don C. Buell, commanding the Department of the Ohio, is encouraged by General George B. McClellan to advance into the Tennessee heartland.

Naval: A large Union naval expedition, destined for Ship Island, Mississippi, departs Hampton Roads, Virginia. This is the preliminary step for launching an expedition against New Orleans, Louisiana.

The USS *Vincennes* boards and seizes the British blockade-runner *Empress* after it runs aground at the mouth of the Mississippi River.

November 28

Politics: The Confederate Congress inducts Missouri into the Confederacy as the 12th state.

West: General Benjamin M. Prentiss assumes control of Union forces in the Department of North Missouri.

Naval: The USS *New London* captures the blockade-runner *Lewis* and the schooner *A. J. View* off Ship Island, Mississippi.

November 29

South: In an act of defiance, farmers in the vicinity of Charleston, South Carolina, and Savannah, Georgia, burn cotton crops rather than see them confiscated by Northern forces.

West: General John M. Schofield takes command of the Union militia in Missouri.

Naval: Lieutenant John L. Worden is exchanged and arrives back in Washington, D.C., after seven months of close confinement in Alabama.

November 30

Diplomacy: The British cabinet, headed by Foreign Secretary Lord John Russell, greatly incensed by the *Trent* affair, demands a formal apology and the immediate release of detained Confederate agents James M. Mason and John Slidell. The British minister to the United States, Lord Lyons, is also instructed to depart Washington, D.C., if a proper response is not forthcoming within one week.

West: A raid by Confederate bushwhackers captures horses belonging to Federal troops under Benjamin F. Kelley.

Naval: The USS *Savannah* attacks and captures the Confederate schooner *E. J. Waterman* after it grounds on Tybee Island, Georgia.

The USS *Wanderer* captures the British blockade-runner *Telegraph* near Indian Keys, Florida.

December 1

DIPLOMACY: The British cabinet prepares for war with the United States by dispatching 6,000 troops to Canada and sending Admiral Sir Alexander Milne to Halifax, Nova Scotia, with 40 vessels mounting 1,273 guns.

POLITICS: U.S. secretary of war Simon Cameron reports to President Abraham Lincoln as to what should be done with the thousands of African-American slaves flocking into Union lines. The president, desperate to maintain the loyalty of border states Delaware, Maryland, Kentucky, and Missouri, orders all mention of emancipation or military service struck from the report, preferring instead to allow Congress to address the issue after the war. The president also inquires of General George B. McClellan exactly when he intends to resume offensive operations in Virginia.

WEST: A brigade of Federal troops under General Albin Schoeph advances to engage General Felix K. Zollicoffer's Confederates at Mill Springs and Somerset, Kentucky.

Confederate authorities in Tennessee hang several pro-Union guerrillas charged with burning bridges.

NAVAL: The gunboat USS *Penguin* captures the blockade-runner *Albion* off Charleston, South Carolina, along with a cargo of commodities worth $100,000.

The USS *Seminole* captures the Confederate sloop *Lida* off St. Simon's Sound, Georgia.

The USS *New London* captures the Confederate sloop *Advocate* in Mississippi Sound.

December 2

POLITICS: The second session of the 37th Congress convenes in Washington, D.C.

Secretary of War Simon Cameron reveals that U.S. military forces comprise 20,334 army soldiers and 640,637 volunteers.

WEST: General Henry Halleck is authorized to suspend writs of habeas corpus within the Department of Missouri.

NAVAL: Secretary of the Navy Gideon Welles informs President Abraham Lincoln that 153 enemy vessels have been captured in the previous year. Moreover, he declares naval manpower at 22,000 men and, once all new vessels on the stocks are afloat, that the navy possesses 264 warships of various description.

The CSS *Patrick Henry* under Commander John R. Tucker attacks four Union steamers off Newport News, Virginia, and withdraws two hours later after sustaining damage.

December 3

POLITICS: President Abraham Lincoln, in his message to Congress, suggests that slaves appropriated from Southern owners be allowed to emigrate. He also reiterates his belief that the Union must be preserved by all means at the government's disposal.

South: Confederate forces at Vienna, Virginia, capture a detachment of the 3rd Pennsylvania Cavalry.

West: The 13th Illinois under Colonel John B. Wyman skirmishes with Confederates at Salem, Missouri, while Major George C. Marshall leads the 2nd Missouri Cavalry on a reconnaissance through Saline County.

General John Pope is installed as commander of all Federal forces between the Missouri and Osage rivers.

Naval: Two regiments, the first troops of General Benjamin F. Butler's expedition, arrive by sea at Ship Island, Mississippi. The locale is converted rapidly into a major staging area for future operations against New Orleans, Louisiana.

The USS *Santiago de Cuba* captures the British blockade-runner *Victoria* at sea.

The Confederate raider CSS *Sumter* under Captain Raphael Semmes captures and burns the Union ship *Vigilant* at sea near the West Indies.

December 4

Diplomacy: The British government forbids all exports to the United States, especially materials capable of being used for armaments.

Politics: The U.S. Senate formerly expels former vice president John C. Breckinridge of Kentucky on a vote of 36 to 0. Since the previous November, Breckinridge has been serving as a Confederate major general.

Southern Presbyterians gather in Augusta, Georgia, to separate themselves from their Northern counterparts. They then found the Assembly of the Presbyterian Church in the Confederate States of America.

West: Newly arrived at his headquarters at St. Louis, Missouri, General Henry W. Halleck authorizes continuing punitive measures against Confederate sympathizers in his region. These include the death penalty for any citizen caught assisting rebel guerrillas.

Colonel John H. Morgan leads a successful Confederate mounted raid, which burns the Bacon Creek Bridge near Munfordville, Kentucky.

Armed citizens of Dunksburg, Missouri, unite to repel a Confederate raiding party.

Naval: The USS *Montgomery* is attacked by the Confederate steamers *Florida* and *Pamlico* at Horn Island Pass, Mississippi Sound. No damage to either side ensues.

December 5

Politics: Congress introduces petitions and bills mandating the abolition of slavery.

West: General William J. Hardee assumes command of the Confederate Central Army of Kentucky.

Colonel John B. Wyman of the 13th Illinois commences an expedition to Current Hills, Missouri.

Naval: A naval squadron consisting of the USS *Ottawa*, *Seneca*, and *Pembina* conducts a reconnaissance in force along Wassaw Sound, Georgia.

December 6

Political: Pro-Union newspaper editor William G. Brownlow is arrested by Confederate authorities on charges of treason in Knoxville, Tennessee.

SOUTH: General George G. Meade conducts a successful Union foraging expedition through Gunnell's Farm in Dranesville, Virginia.

NAVAL: The USS *Augusta* seizes the British blockade-runner *Cheshire* off South Carolina.

December 7

WEST: Confederate forces occupy Glasgow, Missouri, without a fight.

NAVAL: The USS *Santiago de Cuba* under Commander Daniel B. Ridgley stops the British ship *Eugenia Smith* at sea and removes Confederate purchasing agent J. W. Zacharie of New Orleans, Louisiana. Coming on the heels of the *Trent* affair, this act exacerbates tensions between the two nations.

December 8

NORTH: The American Bible Society begins to distribute as many as 7,000 Bibles a day to Union soldiers and sailors.

SOUTHWEST: Pro-Union Chief Opothleyahola and Creek 1,000 warriors arrive at Bird Creek (Chusto-Talasah), Indian Territory, and assume defensive positions while pursued by Confederate and allied Indian forces. The chief then dispatches a messenger to the hostile tribes indicating that he does not wish to spill Indian blood, but word of Creek determination to fight unsettles many of Colonel Douglas H. Cooper's warriors. Native Americans begin to desert him.

NAVAL: The USS *Rhode Island* captures the British blockade-runner *Phantom* off Cape Lookout, North Carolina.

The Confederate raider CSS *Sumter* under Captain Raphael Semmes captures and burns the Union bark *Eben Dodge* at sea.

December 9

POLITICS: In light of recent military disasters at Bull Run and Ball's Bluff, Congress votes 33-3 to establish an oversight committee to monitor the conduct of the war. This becomes known infamously as the Joint Committee on the Conduct of the War and is the bane of many senior Union officers.

SOUTHWEST: Pro-Confederate Cherokee, Chickasaw, and Choctaw, assisted by the 9th Texas under Colonel Douglas H. Cooper, attack pro-Union Creek under Opotheyahola at Bird Creek (Chusto-Talasah), Indian Territory. With his Texans in the center, Cherokees on the left, and Choctaws and Chickasaws on the right, Cooper advances on the Creeks in unison. Resistance proves fierce initially, but finally both of Opothleyahola's flanks retreat, and he falls back with the center. Cooper's losses amount to 15 killed and 37 wounded, while Creek casualties, never tallied, are probably heavier. However, supply shortages dog the Confederate column, and they fail to pursue the fleeing Creek, who eventually make it to Kansas.

NAVAL: The USS *Harriet Lane,* supported by the Potomac Flotilla, engages Confederate artillery at Freestone Point, Virginia.

The USS *New London* seizes the Confederate schooner *Delight* and sloops *Express* and *Osceola* off Cat Island Passage, Mississippi.

December 10

POLITICS: The Confederate Congress admits the expatriate Kentucky "government" into the Confederacy as its 13th state. It thus joins Missouri as having representatives in both belligerent camps.

NAVAL: A landing party under Lieutenant James W. A. Nicholson of the USS *Isaac Smith* captures an abandoned Confederate fort on Otter Island in the Ashepoo River, South Carolina. It subsequently is turned over to Federal forces.

December 11

SOUTH: The city of Charleston, South Carolina, is ravaged by a destructive fire that consumes half of the city.

NAVAL: The USS *South Carolina* captures the Confederate sloop *Florida* as it attempts to run the blockade off Savannah, Georgia.

The USS *Bienville* captures the Confederate schooner *Sarah and Caroline* off St. John's River, Florida.

December 12

NAVAL: Gunfire from the USS *Isaac Smith* covers a landing by U.S. Marines as they destroy a Confederate base in the Ashepoo River, South Carolina. In this manner, Union forces are slowly expanding their base of operations out from Port Royal Sound.

The USS *Alabama* captures the British ship *Admiral* as it attempts to run the blockade off Savannah, Georgia.

December 13

WEST: Newly appointed Union general Robert H. Milroy decides to attack Confederate positions atop nearby Allegheny Mountain in western Virginia. He marches 830 men from Cheat Mountain directly to his objective, then garrisoned by 1,200 Confederates under General Edward Johnson, while another column under Colonel Gideon C. Moody with 930 men takes a circuitous route 12 miles around the enemy's left flank. However, when Moody is delayed several hours by poor terrain, Milroy attacks alone. Charging up the heavily wooded slopes, he is handily repulsed, at which point Johnson charges downhill and completely disperses his antagonists. By the time Moody's column arrives on the scene, the Southerners are ready for him, and both sides engage in a five-hour firefight across the mountain slope. At length, Moody withdraws back toward Cheat Mountain. Union losses are 20 dead, 107 wounded, and 10 missing while the Confederates record 20 killed, 98 wounded, and 28 missing.

December 14

SOUTHWEST: General Henry H. Sibley assumes control of Confederate forces along the Upper Rio Grande River and the New Mexico and Arizona Territories.

December 15

NAVAL: The USS *Stars and Stripes* captures the Confederate blockade-runner *Charity* off Cape Hatteras, North Carolina, while the USS *Jamestown* seizes the sloop *Havelock* at nearby Cape Fear.

December 16
POLITICS: Congressman Clement Vallandigham of Ohio, soon vilified as a "Copperhead," introduces a resolution commending Captain Charles Wilkes for his role in the *Trent* affair.

December 17
DIPLOMACY: Armed forces of Britain, Spain, and France attack and occupy Veracruz, Mexico, ostensibly seeking reparations for foreign debts. However, once Napoleon III begins to maneuver to seize political control of that nation, the other two belligerents withdraw their troops. The French regime seeks to take advantage of America's preoccupation with domestic strife for its own gain.

SOUTH: Confederate troops skirmish and then evacuate Rockville, South Carolina, in the face of advancing Union forces from nearby Hilton Head.

WEST: General Thomas J. Jackson commences operations against Dam No. 5 on the Potomac River, western Virginia.

Union and Confederate forces under Generals Alexander M. McCook and Thomas C. Hindman, respectively, fight a heavy skirmish at Rowlett's Station, Green River, Kentucky, which results in 17 Northern casualties to 33 killed and 55 wounded Southerners.

NAVAL: The U.S. Navy scuttles a "stone fleet" of seven old vessels at the entrance of Savannah Harbor, Georgia. This is comprised of wooden sailing vessels, heavily laden with stones to impede navigation.

Commodore Henry H. Foote institutes regular Sunday services onboard his fleet of gunboats on the Cumberland River.

December 18
WEST: General John Pope reconnoiters Confederate positions along Blackwater Creek, Missouri, prompting General Sterling Price to withdraw.

December 19
DIPLOMACY: Lord Lyons, British minister to the United States, informally alerts Secretary of State William H. Seward of his instructions, namely, his government's insistence that the Americans must unconditionally release the Southern commissioners James M. Mason and John Slidell, who had been illegally removed from the British vessel *Trent*. Seward asks Lyons to make a formal presentation of his government's demands on December 23.

SOUTH: General George A. McCall orders General Edward O. C. Ord to take his 3rd Brigade of Pennsylvania Reserves, march up the Leesburg Pike from Camp Pierpont, and forage in the vicinity of Dranesville, Virginia. Ord takes with him the 6th, 9th, 10th, and 12th Pennsylvania Reserves, and a squadron of the 1st Pennsylvania Cavalry, and he is further buttressed by the attached 13th Pennsylvania "Bucktails."

NAVAL: Confederates destroy the lighthouse on Morris Island, Charleston Harbor, to deny its use to the enemy.

December 20
POLITICS: The influential Joint Committee on the Conduct of the War is instituted formally in the U.S. Congress following a disastrous defeat at Ball's Bluff during the

previous October. It is staffed largely by such Radical Republicans as Benjamin F. Wade of Ohio and Zachariah Chandler of Michigan and is tasked with closely scrutinizing the conduct of president and senior commanders throughout the war.

SOUTH: To obviate mounting shortages of animal fodder and food supplies, Generals Joseph E. Johnston and George B. McClellan dispatch competing foraging expeditions in the vicinity of Dranesville, Virginia. The Union effort, led by General Edward O. C. Ord, consists of five infantry regiments, an artillery battery, and a cavalry squadron. The 1,800 Confederates are led by General J. E. B. Stuart with an almost identical force, though hobbled by a very large wagon train. The Northern troops occupy Dranesville first where Colonel Thomas Kane observes Stuart's approach and warns Ord, who rushes up the balance of his force. Stuart remains oblivious to danger until his 1st Kentucky and 6th South Carolina, who had previously fired on each other by mistake, suddenly encounter the 9th Pennsylvania in an adjoining woods. Stuart nonetheless marches up and deploys his remaining troops with alacrity, pushing the Federals back under the cover of their artillery. But Kane's troops subsequently rally around a two-story brick house, which the Confederates attack and are repulsed. The 11th Virginia then swings forward to outflank the Northerners when it is suddenly assailed in the flank by concealed companies of the 10th Pennsylvania and also is driven back. Stuart then calls off the battle and withdraws back to Centreville, having sustained 43 killed, 143 wounded, and eight missing (194) to a Union tally of seven killed and 61 wounded. All told, it is an inauspicious debut for the South's most celebrated cavalryman.

NAVAL: To further deter Confederate blockade-runners, Captain Charles H. Davis scuttles 16 old whaling vessels, heavily laden with heavy rocks, in the main channel of Charleston Harbor, South Carolina.

December 21

POLITICS: The U.S. Congress institutes the Navy Medal of Honor as the nation's highest military award granted to that service. Curiously, it is intended for enlisted ranks, and commissioned officers are not eligible until 1915.

December 22

WEST: General Henry W. Halleck reiterates, in no uncertain terms, that any individuals found sabotaging Union railroads or telegraph lines are to be shot immediately.

December 23

DIPLOMACY: British minister to the United States Lord Lyons formally submits a note to Secretary of State William H. Seward in which his government demands the release of Confederate agents James M. Mason and John Slidell. The American government has one week to respond satisfactorily, after which time Britain will withdraw its ambassador.

WEST: To break up a concentration of Confederate troops and recruits in southeastern Kentucky, Colonel James A. Garfield is dispatched toward Prestonburg with 1,100 infantry and 450 cavalry with orders to drive the enemy back to Virginia.

Union cavalry under General John Pope reach Lexington, Missouri.

December 24

SOUTH: In light of his poor performance, General Henry A. Wise is dismissed from the Virginia theater and reassigned to a quiet sector in North Carolina.

NAVAL: The USS *Gem of the Sea* captures and sinks the British blockade-runner *Prince of Wales* off Georgetown, South Carolina.

December 25

POLITICS: President Abraham Lincoln celebrates Christmas with his family and later that day confers with legal authorities about the disposition of imprisoned Confederate envoys.

WEST: General Ulysses S. Grant orders the expulsion of all fugitive African Americans from Fort Holt, Kentucky.

General Samuel R. Curtis assumes command of Federal forces in the Southwest District of Missouri.

Colonel George G. Todd and his 10th Missouri Infantry advance upon Danville, Missouri.

NAVAL: The USS *Fernandina* captures the Confederate schooner *William H. Northrup* off Cape Fear, North Carolina.

Confederate navy secretary Stephen R. Mallory implores General Leonidas Polk at Columbus, Kentucky, to furlough troops so that they can assist in the construction of ironclads at Memphis, Tennessee.

December 26

DIPLOMACY: An international crisis is averted when President Abraham Lincoln's cabinet concurs that the seizure of James M. Mason and John Slidell is illegal and that the two captives should be released and allowed to continue to Europe. Secretary of State William H. Seward authorizes their release from confinement at Fort Warren, Boston, blaming the entire matter on a "misunderstanding" by Captain John Wilkes.

SOUTH: Confederate Brigadier General Philip St. George Cocke commits suicide after a lengthy illness in Powhatan, Virginia.

WEST: Martial law is again declared in St. Louis, Missouri, and around its attendant railroads by General Henry W. Halleck.

NAVAL: Commodore Josiah Tattnall sorties from the Savannah River, Georgia, with the CSS *Savannah, Resolute, Sampson, Ida,* and *Barton* and temporarily forces a Union blockading squadron into deeper waters.

The USS *Rhode Island* captures the Confederate schooner *Venus* at Sabine Pass off the Louisiana coast.

December 27

POLITICS: Secretary of State William H. Seward alerts the House and Senate Foreign Relations Committees as to President Abraham Lincoln's decision to release Confederate agents James M. Mason and John Slidell from captivity at Fort Warren in Boston, Massachusetts. He also provides British ambassador Lord Lyons with a lengthy diplomatic note—not an apology—explaining the American response.

WEST: Union and Confederate forces clash at Hallsville, Missouri, and General Benjamin M. Prentiss scatters the Southern garrison lodged there.

December 28

WEST: General Lew Wallace leads Union forces on an expedition against Camp Beauregard and Viola, Kentucky.

Confederate cavalry under Colonel Nathan B. Forrest engage the Union forces of General Thomas L. Crittenden. Forrest leads a detachment of 300 Confederate cavalry toward Sacramento, Kentucky. En route, he encounters a smaller force of 168 Union men under Major Eli Murray. After skirmishing breaks out, Forrest recalls his line to reorganize, which Murray misinterprets as a retreat. The Union troopers charge headlong against twice their number and are hit on both flanks before scattering. Forrest, consistent with his nature, is in the thick of fighting and kills two Union officers. His Confederates sustain two dead, having killed 11 and taken 40 prisoner. Triumphant in this first of many scrapes, the future "Wizard of the Saddle" takes his command back to Greenville, hotly pursued by 500 Union troopers under Colonel James Jackson.

General Benjamin M. Prentiss skirmishes with Confederate forces at Mount Zion Church, Missouri.

NAVAL: The USS *New London* seizes the schooner *Gipsy* in Mississippi Sound.

December 29

WEST: Occupation of Beckley and Suttonville by Union forces in western Virginia further consolidates their grip on the region.

Confederate partisans under General Jeff Thompson unsuccessfully attack the Union steamer *City of Alton* near Commerce, Missouri.

NAVAL: The CSS *Sea Bird* dodges Union gunfire and captures an unnamed Union schooner near Hampton Roads, Virginia.

December 30

NAVAL: The USS *Santee* captures the Confederate schooner *Garonne* off Galveston, Texas.

December 31

POLITICS: Noting the inactivity of Union forces in the East, President Abraham Lincoln anxiously cables General Henry W. Halleck in St. Louis, Missouri, in hopes of hearing of offensive operations in that theater soon. "Are you and General Buell in concert?" he inquires.

NAVAL: A landing party dispatched from USS *Mount Vernon* captures and destroys a light ship off Wilmington, North Carolina, which has been outfitted as a gunboat.

An attack by army troops and sailors from gunboats USS *Ottawa, Pembina,* and *Seneca* disperses Confederate forces at Port Royal Ferry and along the Coosaw River. This preemptive strike removes the threat of Southern artillery emplacements that would isolate Union forces on Port Royal Island.

The USS *Augusta* captures the Confederate schooner *Island Belle* as it ran the blockade near Bull's Bay, South Carolina.

A large landing party from USS *Water Witch, New London,* and *Henry Lewis* attacks and captures Biloxi, Mississippi. The Confederate schooner *Captain Spedden* is also seized, and an artillery battery is demolished.

1862

January 1

DIPLOMACY: Confederate agents James M. Mason and John Slidell board the HMS *Rinaldo* off Provincetown, Massachusetts, and sail for Halifax en route to Great Britain.

NORTH: General in Chief George B. McClellan remains sidelined by illness as President Abraham Lincoln frets over his continuing military inactivity.

SOUTH: Federal troops skirmish heavily as they advance toward Port Royal Ferry on the Coosaw River, South Carolina, attempting to enlarge their bridgehead.

Union and Confederate batteries exchange fire in the vicinity of Fort Pickens and Fort Barancas, Pensacola, Florida.

WEST: General Thomas J. Jackson, eager to secure the lightly defended town of Romney in western Virginia, orders his Stonewall brigade and 8,500 troops under General William W. Loring out of their winter abodes at Winchester. However, no sooner do they leave than the temperature plunges to freezing, and soldiers, marching without heavy overcoats, suffer severely.

General George H. Thomas takes 5,000 Union soldiers on a march from Lebanon, Kentucky, toward the Tennessee state line.

Generals Henry W. Halleck at St. Louis, Missouri, and Don C. Buell at Louisville, Kentucky, are encouraged by the War Department to undertake offensive operations against Confederate forces at Columbus and Nashville.

A detachment of the 1st Kansas Cavalry burns the settlement of Dayton, Missouri.

NAVAL: The USS *Yankee* and *Anacostia* exchange fire with Confederate batteries along Cockpit Point on the Potomac River. The latter receives slight damage.

Commodore Andrew H. Foote dispatches the Federal gunboat USS *Lexington* down the Ohio River to assist the *Conestoga* in protecting Union citizens along the river banks.

January 2

NAVAL: Taking advantage of a heavy fog, the Confederate steamer *Ella Warley* evades the USS *Mohican* and slips into Charleston, South Carolina, with a valuable cargo.

January 3

POLITICS: President Jefferson Davis expresses anxiety over the recent Union seizure of Ship Island, Mississippi, and its probable future use as a base of operations against New Orleans, Louisiana.

SOUTH: Union and Confederate outposts skirmish in the vicinity of Big Bethel, Virginia.

WEST: Confederates under General Thomas J. Jackson continue slogging through freezing, damp weather from Winchester, Virginia, and up the Shenandoah Valley to destroy the Baltimore and Ohio Railroad and dams on the Chesapeake and Ohio Canal.

General George B. Crittenden arrives at Mills Springs, Kentucky, to take command of Confederate forces mistakenly deployed north of the Cumberland River by General Felix K. Zollicoffer.

January 4
WEST: The town of Bath, western Virginia, falls to Confederate forces under General Thomas J. Jackson.

January 5
NORTH: Confederate artillery under General Thomas J. Jackson briefly bombard Union positions in and around Hancock, Maryland. Jackson then retires to Unger's Store to rest his shivering troops.

January 6
POLITICAL: President Abraham Lincoln ignores cries by Radical Republican senators to replace General George B. McClellan, then ill from typhoid fever, over allegations of military inactivity. He also continues urging General Don C. Buell, commanding the Army of the Ohio in Kentucky, to assume an offensive posture.
SOUTH: Henry Heth is appointed brigadier general, C.S.A.
NAVAL: In response to critical shortages of trained manpower, Commodore Andrew H. Foote suggests drafting soldiers to serve on the gunboat fleet. The army proves reluctant to do so, and General Ulysses S. Grant recommends that the guardhouses be emptied to assist the navy.

January 7
NORTH: General Ambrose E. Burnside is appointed commander of the future Department of North Carolina.
WEST: Confederate troops begin to shift from Hancock, Maryland, toward Romney, western Virginia. En route, a Union detachment at Blue's Gap scatters its Confederate opposites and captures two cannon. General Thomas J. Jackson nonetheless determines to capture Romney, possession of which grants him control of the South Branch Valley, Potomac River.
NAVAL: The Federal gunboat USS *Conestoga,* recently returned from a reconnaissance of Confederate positions at Fort Donelson, Tennessee, alerts Commodore Andrew H. Foote as to the intrinsic strength of that position and the danger it poses to a naval assault.

January 8
POLITICS: President Jefferson Davis contacts fugitive Missouri governor Claiborne F. Jackson and assures him that his state is not being neglected by the Confederate government. He also presses the governor to raise additional manpower to offset Union advantages.

January 9
POLITICS: President Abraham Lincoln expresses dismay that Generals Henry W. Halleck and Don C. Buell still fail to initiate offensive measures anywhere in the West.

NAVAL: Commodore David G. Farragut of the USS *Hartford* is appointed commander of the Western Gulf Blockading Squadron. In this capacity, he is responsible for orchestrating the capture of New Orleans, Louisiana, an essential facet of Union strategy. Farragut, cognizant of the need to maintain utmost secrecy, instructs his wife to burn any correspondence he exchanges with her.

January 10

POLITICS: President Abraham Lincoln displays concern to Secretary of War Simon Cameron over the apparent lack of military activity in the West.

Confederate-leaning Missourians Waldo P. Johnson and Trusten Polk are expelled from the U.S. Senate.

WEST: Believing themselves heavily outnumbered, Union forces abandon strategic Romney, western Virginia, to advancing Confederates under General Thomas J. Jackson. That esteemed leader also engages in a bitter contretemps with General William W. Loring about charges that he abused his soldiers by marching them during bitterly cold weather.

General James A. Garfield wages an indecisive pitched battle against Confederates under General Humphrey Marshall at Middle Fork near Prestonburg, Kentucky. Marshall gathers 2,200 men slightly west of the town, largely underequipped and in varied states of training and health. Garfield advances against them with 1,100 infantry and 450 cavalry, although his march from Louisa encounters rough, swampy terrain. The battle begins as Union troops attempt to force the Southerners from two hills while Marshall simultaneously tries to turn the Northern left flank. A confused stalemate ensues until Garfield receives 700 reinforcements in the late afternoon. Humphrey, unable to counter Union numbers, withdraws, conceding the field of battle to Garfield. Losses in this minor affair are 10 Confederates killed, 15 wounded, and 25 captured to a Union tally of one killed and 20 injured. Garfield nonetheless is congratulated by General Don C. Buell and is promoted to brigadier general.

Generals Ulysses S. Grant and John A. McClernand ready their forces at Cairo, Illinois, for a concerted campaign to evict Confederates from their stronghold at Columbus, Kentucky.

The Trans-Mississippi District of Confederate Department No. 2 is organized with General Earl Van Dorn as commander.

NAVAL: In light of the advanced state of the Confederate ironclad CSS *Virginia,* officers at the Navy Department ponder probable defensive measures against it. Commodore Louis M. Goldsborough orders the steam tugs USS *Dragon* and *Zouave* off Hampton Roads, Virginia, to tow the sail frigates *Congress* and *Cumberland* to any position deemed advantageous.

Commodore Andrew H. Foote's gunboats begin to ferry Union troops up and down the Tennessee and Mississippi rivers to mask General Ulysses S. Grant's forthcoming advance on Fort Henry, Tennessee.

January 11

POLITICS: Secretary of War Simon Cameron resigns from office amidst charges of corruption and mismanagement. President Lincoln subsequently nominates former attorney general Edwin M. Stanton, a confidant of General George B. McClellan, as his successor. The appointment proves fortuitous, for Stanton infuses military administration with new energy and efficiency.

SOUTH: The Department of Key West, Florida, is organized with General John M. Brannan as commander.

NAVAL: Commodore Louis M. Goldsborough assembles a squadron consisting of the USS *Henry Brinker, Delaware, Philadelphia, Hunchback, Morse, Southfield, Commodore Barney,* and *Commodore Perry* and the schooner *Howard* off Hampton Roads, Virginia. His immediate objective is the capture of Roanoke Island, North Carolina.

Commander David D. Porter of the gunboat USS *Essex,* along with the *St. Louis,* engage Confederate vessels and positions along the Mississippi River near Lucas Bend, Missouri. The Southerners subsequently withdraw under the cover of their batteries at Columbus, Kentucky.

January 12

WEST: The 37th Ohio conducts antiguerrilla sweeps around Logan County Court House and in the Guyandotte Valley, western Virginia.

NAVAL: A naval expedition of 100 vessels under Commodore Louis M. Goldsborough departs Hampton Roads, Virginia, in preparation for an attack on strategic Roanoke Island, North Carolina. He is accompanied by 15,000 Federal troops under General Ambrose E. Burnside.

The USS *Pensacola* successfully runs past Confederate batteries on the Potomac River at Cockpit and Shipping Points, Virginia.

January 13

POLITICS: President Abraham Lincoln again urges generals Henry W. Halleck and Don C. Buell of the necessity to commence offensive operations in the West. He finds their passivity disconcerting.

NORTH: General George B. McClellan refuses to consult with either the president or other officials as to his impending plan of operations. Moreover, he disagrees with Lincoln's overall strategy of attacking along a broad front.

NAVAL: Lieutenant John L. Worden, still convalescing from months of captivity, is appointed to take command of the revolutionary USS *Monitor,* then under construction on Long Island, New York.

Commodore Louis M. Goldsborough and his 100-ship expedition arrive off Hatteras Inlet, North Carolina. Once on station, he reiterates orders that gunners must be trained completely and familiar with the new Bormann fuzes fitted to 9-inch shrapnel shells.

January 14

WEST: Confederates under General Thomas J. Jackson occupy the strategic hamlet of Romney, western Virginia, amid mounting friction with his unruly subordinate, General William W. Loring.

NAVAL: Three Federal gunboats on the Mississippi River begin to probe the Confederate defenses of Columbus, Kentucky, with a brief bombardment.

January 15
POLITICS: Ohioan Edwin M. Stanton is confirmed by the U.S. Senate as the new secretary of war to replace outgoing Simon Cameron of Pennsylvania.
SOUTH: Confederate general Lovell Mansfield confiscates 14 civilian steamers at New Orleans, Louisiana, and impresses them to bolster that city's defenses.
NAVAL: Commodore Andrew H. Foote advises subordinates against wasting scarce ammunition for his scarcely trained gunboat squadron, urging all hands to make every shot count.

January 16
WEST: General Felix K. Zollicoffer disregards orders from General George B. Crittenden by maintaining Confederate troops north of the Cumberland River, Kentucky, where they must fight with the river to their backs. Shortly after, Crittenden arrives with reinforcements, and he decides that the water is running too high to recross safely. He then makes the most of his subordinate's rashness by planning to engage an oncoming Union column at Logan's Cross Roads, nine miles distant.
NAVAL: Accurate gunfire from the USS *Hatteras,* followed up by boat crews and marines, destroys seven vessels, a railroad depot, and a telegraph office at Cedar Keys, Florida.

The USS *Albatross* captures and sinks the British blockade-runner *York* off Bogue Inlet, North Carolina.

The Union enhances it grip on western waters after the Ead gunboats *Carondelet, St. Louis,* and *Cincinnati* are commissioned. This brings the total of armored river gunboats to seven, and they prove indispensable in asserting Union control of strategic waterways.

January 17
WEST: General George H. Thomas arrives from Somerset, Kentucky, and takes charge of 4,000 Union troops in the vicinity of Logan's Crossroads. The nearest Confederate forces are only 10 miles distant at Mills Springs on the Cumberland River, so he anticipates an attack.

General Charles F. Smith boards a gunboat and begins to probe in the direction of Confederate-held Fort Henry on the Tennessee River.
NAVAL: The USS *Connecticut* seizes the British blockade-runner *Emma* off the Florida coast.

Federal gunboats USS *Conestoga* and *Lexington* conduct a preliminary reconnaissance of the Tennessee River past Confederate-held Fort Henry. The detailed knowledge they acquire helps formulate plans for its swift capture.

January 18
POLITICS: Former president John Tyler dies in Richmond, Virginia, at the age of 62.
WEST: 4,000 Union troops under General George H. Thomas, having enticed Confederate troops north of the Cumberland River to attack, encamp at Mill Springs, Kentucky. Strong reconnaissance parties sent toward the river return with positive information that General George B. Crittenden's Confederates are advancing and

that they intend to strike the Union camp at dawn. With trademark thoroughness, Thomas methodically and unhurriedly prepares to receive the enemy while ordering two nearby brigades in support.

NAVAL: The USS *Kearsarge* sails to Cádiz, Spain, in order to halt the depredations of the CSS *Sumter*.

The CSS *Sumter* under Captain Raphael Semmes seizes and burns the Union barks *Neapolitan* and *Investigator* in the Strait of Gibraltar.

Union vessels USS *Midnight* and *Rachel Seaman* bombard Confederate positions at Velasco, Texas.

January 19

WEST: At daybreak, a force of 4,000 Confederates under Generals Felix K. Zollicoffer and William H. Carroll marches 10 miles to attack the Union encampment at Logan's Cross Roads, Kentucky. Despite heavy rain and mud, the Southerners slam into Northern pickets at daybreak, driving them back to the main defense line, commanded by General Mahlon D. Manson. General George H. Thomas then rallies his men and withstands several assaults until the 10th Indiana, tired and out of ammunition, bolts for the rear. Thomas counters by feeding the 4th Kentucky under Colonel Speed S. Fry into line, which drives the Confederates back into a ravine. The two forces then trade shots for several tense minutes as they sort themselves out. The Confederates emerge and charge one more time while Thomas, expecting this move, stations the newly arrived brigade of General Samuel P. Carter obliquely, whose troops rake the Southerners with a deadly enfilade fire. At this confused juncture, Zollicoffer mistakenly gallops into Fry's position in the fog and is shot dead in the saddle. The Confederates waver until Crittenden arrives in person to lead another brigade forward. This charge is also fought to a standstill and, judging the moment right, Thomas orders the 12th Kentucky and 9th Ohio to turn both Confederate flanks. Crittenden's men break under this latest onslaught and flee back to their Beech Grove encampment.

The ensuing Union pursuit proves somewhat slow owing to the poor state of the roads, so Thomas only arrives outside Crittenden's camp at Mills Springs that evening. He determines to attack in force on the morrow, but Crittenden evacuates his Confederates by boat across the swollen Cumberland River and withdraws rapidly back to Nashville. Thomas subsequently captures their supply train, 12 cannon, and 1,000 horses. Confederate losses are 125 killed, 309 wounded, and 99 missing to 40 Union dead, 207 wounded, and 15 missing. Mills Springs is the first in a series of disasters, which negates the Southern defensive line in Kentucky. More significantly, the victory revives Union sentiments throughout the region and delivers to Union forces control of the Cumberland Gap—an important invasion route into eastern Tennessee.

NAVAL: The USS *Itasca* captures the Confederate schooner *Lizzie Weston* off the Florida coast.

January 20

NAVAL: At the behest of Secretary of the Navy Gideon Welles, the Union Gulf Blockading Squadron is reorganized into two distinct formations: The Eastern Gulf

Blockading Squadron and the Western Blockading Squadron, with the latter commanded by Commodore David G. Farragut. His fleet consists of 17 steam warships and 19 mortar boats under his foster brother, Commander David D. Porter. At this time Farragut announces word of his impending campaign against New Orleans, Louisiana, to the crews.

Union boarding parties from the USS *R. R. Cuyler,* in concert with the *Huntsville* and *Potomac,* capture the Confederate schooner *J. W. Wilder* off Mobile, Alabama.

January 21
West: Union forces under General John A. McClernand advance on the Confederate stronghold at Columbus, Kentucky, but they do not engage.
Naval: The USS *Ethan Allen* captures the Confederate schooner *Olive Branch* off Cedar Keys along the Florida coast.

January 22
South: General Henry A. Wise becomes commander of Confederate forces in the vicinity of Hatteras Inlet, North Carolina, then under an impending Union assault from the sea.
Naval: The Federal gunboat USS *Lexington* trades fire with Confederate batteries at Fort Henry on the Tennessee River. General Charles F. Smith is onboard as an observer.

January 23
West: General Thomas J. Jackson leads his Stonewall Brigade out from Romney, western Virginia, and back down to Winchester. The town, however, remains garrisoned by troops under the uncooperative general William W. Loring. Worse, Loring feels that Jackson deliberately has left his troops in an exposed position only 20 miles from Union lines, so he and other officers violate the chain of command by petitioning friends in the Confederate Congress for redress and a change in orders.

At St. Louis, Missouri, General Henry W. Halleck strengthens existing martial law provisions, making it illegal for individuals to conduct subversive activities. This includes the failure of pro-Southern inhabitants to pay assessments to support pro-Union fugitives; their property is now subject to seizure.
Naval: Commodore Louis M. Goldsborough reports slow but steady progress working his warships and heavily laden transports over the bar at Pamlico Sound, North Carolina.

The Federal schooner USS *Samuel Rotan* seizes the Confederate steamer *Calhoun* in East Bay, Mississippi River.

Commodore Andrew H. Foote, citing chronic manpower shortages, pleads with Secretary of the Navy Gideon Welles to broach the subject with the War Department and arrange a draft of army troops to fill out his gunboat squadron.

January 24
West: The small Confederate command of General Humphrey Marshall is ordered withdrawn from Martindale, Kentucky, and back into Virginia via Pound Gap.

NAVAL: The USS *Mercedita* forces the Confederate schooner *Julia* aground at the mouth of the Mississippi River.

January 25
NAVAL: The USS *Arthur* captures the Confederate schooner *J. J. McNeil* off Pass Cavallo, Texas.

January 26
SOUTH: General Pierre G. T. Beauregard transfers from the Eastern Theater to the West and becomes subordinate to General Albert S. Johnston. Command in Virginia remains with General Joseph E. Johnston, still smarting from his contretemps with President Jefferson Davis.

NAVAL: A second stone fleet is sunk to obstruct Maffitt's Channel, Charleston Harbor.

Captain Charles H. Davis leads USS *Ottawa* and *Seneca* on a reconnaissance of Wassaw Sound, Georgia, in the vicinity of strategic Fort Pulaski. He is accompanied by 2,400 men under General Horatio G. Wright.

January 27
DIPLOMACY: Emperor Napoleon III declares that the American conflict infringes on trade relations with France, but he will observe a policy of strict neutrality.

POLITICS: President Abraham Lincoln, exasperated by a lack of initiative by Union commanders, composes General War Order No. 1. This mandates a general offensive against the Confederacy from various points along the line. February 22—George Washington's birthday—is selected as the deadline to commence combined operations by both army and navy forces.

January 28
WEST: Colonel John H. Morgan leads Confederate cavalry in an action against Union forces near Greensburg and Lebanon, Kentucky.

NAVAL: Off Hatteras Inlet, North Carolina, Commodore Louis M. Goldsborough informs the secretary of the navy that getting army transports over the bar has delayed operations, but he puts the time to good use by aggressively reconnoitering Confederate positions on Roanoke Island.

The USS *De Soto* captures the Confederate blockade-runner *Major Barbour* off Isle Derniere, Louisiana.

Commodore Andrew H. Foote advises senior general Henry W. Halleck to commence operations against Forts Henry and Donelson before the water levels on the Tennessee and Cumberland rivers begin to recede.

January 29
WEST: Union forces began an intensive manhunt around Blue Springs, Missouri, looking for noted guerrilla William C. Quantrill.

NAVAL: The USS storeship *Supply* seizes the Confederate schooner *Stephen Hart* off Sarasota, Florida.

January 30
DIPLOMACY: Recently released Confederate envoys James M. Mason and John Slidell arrive at Southampton, England, and are cordially received.

WEST: General Henry W. Halleck, at St. Louis, Missouri, finally authorizes combined operations against Confederate positions at Forts Henry and Donelson, Tennessee. Because recent rains have reduced existing roads to quagmires, he orders all troop movements conducted by gunboat. General Ulysses S. Grant wastes no time putting his command in motion.

NAVAL: John Ericsson's revolutionary ironclad USS *Monitor,* derided by onlookers as "a cheesebox on a raft," is launched at Greenpoint, Long Island, amid thunderous applause. Trial and acceptance runs begin immediately.

The USS *Kingfisher* captures the Confederate blockade-runner *Teresita* in the Gulf of Mexico.

The Federal gunboat USS *Conestoga* conducts a final reconnaissance of the Tennessee River in preparation for movement against Confederate-held Fort Henry.

January 31

DIPLOMACY: Queen Victoria of Great Britain further dashes Southern hopes by reiterating her government's stance of observing strict neutrality in matters of war. Nonetheless, the British advise Confederate agents of European displeasure over having Southern ports blocked by obstacles.

POLITICS: President Abraham Lincoln issues Special War Order No. 1, which mandates an advance on Manassas Junction, Virginia, by the Army of the Potomac no later than February 22, 1862. General George B. McClellan, however, simply ignores the directive and continues honing his recruits to a fine edge.

Congress passes the Railways and Telegraph Act, empowering the president to commandeer any rail facility deemed essential for the conduct of the war effort.

Radical Republicans demand that General George B. McClellan attack Southern positions immediately, along with actively freeing slaves and enlisting them in the military. The general, however, steadfastly declines to turn a war to save the Union into a social crusade to free African Americans held in bondage.

WEST: Confederate secretary of war Judah P. Benjamin, at the behest of friends in the Confederate Congress, orders General Thomas J. Jackson to relocate Confederate troops from the town of Romney, western Virginia, and back to Winchester. An angry Jackson, aware that General William W. Loring has violated the chain of command behind his back, complies with the order—then resigns from the army. Fortunately for the Confederacy, President Jefferson Davis refuses to accept, and, assisted by Virginia governor John Lechter, he persuades Jackson to remain with the army.

February 1

SOUTHWEST: Confederate forces under General Henry H. Sibley advance from El Paso, Texas, into the New Mexico Territory, intent on conquering the entire region for the South.

NAVAL: The USS *Portsmouth* captures the Confederate steamer *Labuan* near the mouth of the Rio Grande.

The USS *Montgomery* seizes the Confederate schooner *Isabel* in the Gulf of Mexico.

February 2

WEST: General Ulysses S. Grant departs Cairo, Illinois, on his campaign against the Confederate-held Fort Henry on the Tennessee River. He embarks 17,000 troops, transporting them on Commodore Andrew H. Foote's gunboats. Grant intends to land on Panther Creek west of the fort, march inland, and quickly seal off the garrison's avenue of escape.

NAVAL: The USS *Hartford,* flagship of Commodore David G. Farragut, departs Hampton Roads, Virginia, en route to Ship Island, Mississippi, there to take charge of the Western Gulf Blockading Squadron prior to an amphibious descent on New Orleans, Louisiana.

Commodore Andrew H. Foote orders Lieutenant Seth L. Phelps to take the timberclad gunboats USS *Conestoga, Lexington,* and *Tyler* on an independent foray down the Tennessee River and destroy the railroad bridge at Danville, Tennessee. Phelps is then at liberty to venture downstream as far as the water depth allows him.

February 3

POLITICS: President Abraham Lincoln and General George B. McClellan continue at loggerheads over an exact timetable for resuming offensive operations in Virginia. They also differ on strategy, the president leaning toward a direct, overland campaign and the general wishing to sidestep Confederate defenses by landing on the enemy coast.

WEST: General Ulysses S. Grant continues his Fort Henry offensive by dispatching Federal gunboats up the Tennessee River while army transports continue departing from Cairo, Illinois.

NAVAL: The Federal government resolves to treat Confederate privateersmen as prisoners of war rather than to prosecute them as pirates. This eliminates any chance that Union naval personnel might be hanged in retaliation.

The CSS *Nashville* weighs anchor at Southampton, England, and sails off while the USS *Tuscarora* is detained in port for 24 hours, pursuant to international law. As a precaution, the British government assigns HMS *Shannon* to observe the Union gunboat closely until the deadline passes.

Commodore Andrew H. Foote diverts Federal gunboats USS *Essex* and *St. Louis* from Paducah, Kentucky, to assist troop landings 65 miles downstream at Pine Bluff. He then leads a riverine spearhead of four gunboats and several rams on an action that precipitates the Confederacy's ultimate downfall.

February 4

POLITICS: Members of the Confederate Congress at Richmond, Virginia, debate virtues and vices of utilizing free African Americans for service in the Confederate army. Such a commonsense remedy to address endemic manpower shortages is never seriously entertained, however.

WEST: General Lloyd Tilghman, commanding at Fort Henry, Tennessee, learns of the large Union expedition that is bearing down on him and telegraphs General Leonidas Polk for immediate reinforcements.

NAVAL: The gunboat squadron of Commodore Andrew H. Foote, consisting of the USS *Essex, Carondelet, St. Louis, Cincinnati, Conestoga, Tyler,* and *Lexington,* assume bombardment positions on the Tennessee River and begin to sound out the defenses of Confederate-held Fort Henry. One Southerner is killed and three wounded during this preliminary exchange. Several moored mines, or torpedoes, have also been worked free by the fast currents and are examined closely by naval personnel.

February 5

DIPLOMACY: The British government lifts all restrictions against transporting guns, ammunition, and other military stores to Confederate ports.

NORTH: The poem "Battle Hymn of the Republic" by Julia Ward Howe appears in an issue of *Atlantic Monthly.* It is musically arranged to the popular tune "John Brown's Body."

WEST: General Charles F. Smith lands Union troops and seizes the unfinished works of Fort Heiman on the Tennessee River, directly opposite Fort Henry, Tennessee. General Lloyd Tilghman considers his position hopeless and prepares to evacuate the bulk of his garrison to Fort Donelson.

NAVAL: The USS *Keystone State* apprehends the British blockade-runner *Mars* off Fernandina, Florida.

February 6

WEST: General Ulysses S. Grant commences his strategic flanking movement with a concerted drive against Confederate-held Fort Henry on the Tennessee River. This is a wretchedly situated, low-lying earthwork near the riverbank, susceptible to flooding when the Tennessee runs high. Grant disembarks 17,000 troops under Generals John A. McClernand and Charles F. Smith two miles below the fort, but they bog down in swampy terrain and advance slowly. Meanwhile, Confederate general Lloyd Tilghman hurriedly evacuates his 3,400-man garrison to Fort Donelson, 10 miles distant on the Cumberland River before all escape is cut off. Little combat ensues, but a Union cavalry detachment pursues the fleeing Confederates, seizing six cannon and 38 stragglers.

NAVAL: The USS *Sciota* captures the Confederate sloop *Margaret* off Isle au Breton, Louisiana.

The powerful ironclad CSS *Louisiana* is launched at Jefferson City, Louisiana.

Commodore Andrew H. Foote leads a flotilla of four ironclads and three wooden gunboats against Confederate Fort Henry on the Tennessee River, and they open fire at a range of 1,700 yards. General Lloyd Tilghman remains behind with 100 artillerists and 17 cannon to mount an "honorable" defense while his garrison escapes overland. Foote, closing to 600 yards, maintains a tremendous cannonade that disables Tilghman's artillery pieces in a two-hour action. Southerner gunners nonetheless fight well against great odds, striking their antagonists 59 times and scoring a direct hit on the USS *Essex,* which bursts its boilers and scalds several sailors. Several naval officers then row through the sallyport and onto the flooded parade ground to accept Tilgham's surrender at 2:00 P.M. Thus the first Union riverine offensive succeeds almost effortlessly. Union losses are 11 killed, 31 injured, and five missing to

Flag Officer Andrew H. Foote's gunboats attacking Fort Henry, February 6, 1862 *(Library of Congress)*

five Confederates dead, six wounded, five missing, and 70 captured. To underscore his strategic mobility, Foote hurriedly deploys several gunboats downstream, which destroy railroad bridges over the Tennessee River as far south as Muscle Shoals, Alabama. More important, a major invasion route into the center of the South has been pried open. Grant now begins to formulate an attack on Fort Donelson, 10 miles away along the Cumberland River.

NAVAL: The fall of Fort Donelson signals Lieutenant Seth L. Phelps to begin his sojourn down the Tennessee River with the gunboats USS *Conestoga, Lexington,* and *Tyler.* It is a clear demonstration of the Union's ability to project military strength down the western waterways.

February 7

WEST: Federal troops reoccupy Romney, western Virginia, as Confederates under General William W. Loring are withdrawn back to Winchester.

General Ulysses S. Grant, having secured Fort Henry, maps out his strategy for attacking Fort Donelson, Tennessee, on the Cumberland River. Unlike Fort Henry, this is a spacious, well-sited position encompassing 100 acres within its outworks, being both amply garrisoned and well armed with heavy cannon. On a lesser note, General John A. McClernand informs Commodore Andrew H. Foote of his decision to rename Fort Henry Fort Foote in his honor.

At Bowling Green, Kentucky, Confederate general Albert S. Johnston confers with William J. Hardee and Pierre G. T. Beauregard as to his rapidly deteriorating position. Reacting to Fort Henry's fall, he orders troops under General Gideon Pillow at Clarksville, Tennessee, and those of General John B. Floyd at Bowling Green, Kentucky, to march rapidly to the defense of Fort Donelson. Their mission is to stave off Union forces long enough to allow the main portion of the army to withdraw safely to Nashville. Entrusting the inexperienced Floyd and Pillow to undertake such a vital mission bears serious consequences for the Confederacy.

NAVAL: A large naval expedition under Commodore Louis M. Goldsborough leaves its anchorage at Hatteras Inlet, North Carolina, steams into Croatan Sound, and attacks Roanoke Island. The flotilla encounters little resistance and brushes aside Captain William F. Lynch's seven-gunboat flotilla with accurate naval gunfire. The defenders gradually flee upstream, burning the CSS *Curlew* to prevent its capture. Then 10,000 troops under General Ambrose E. Burnside splash ashore at Ashby Point and encamp for the evening. General Henry M. Wise, the regional commander, is absent due to illness, so Confederate leadership devolves upon Colonel Henry M. Shaw. Shaw possesses only 2,500 men and a few ill-served cannon. Inexplicably, strategic Roanoke remains undermanned and poorly situated to receive an attack long anticipated.

The USS *Bohio* captures the Confederate schooner *Eugenie* in the Gulf of Mexico.

The Federal gunboat USS *Conestoga* under Lieutenant S. L. Phelps surprises Confederate shipping on the Tennessee River, forcing the Confederates to burn the steamers *Samuel Orr, Appleton Belle,* and *Lynn Boyd.* While stopping at Perry's Landing the crewmen are surprised but pleased to be lauded and assisted by local pro-Unionists.

February 8

POLITICS: The administration of President Jefferson Davis in Richmond, Virginia, reels from the news of the loss of Fort Henry and Roanoke Island, and a sense of mounting gloom pervades the Confederacy.

SOUTH: The three brigades of Generals Jesse Reno, John G. Parke, and John G. Foster, totaling 10,000 men, advance on Confederate defensive works on the northern end of Roanoke Island, North Carolina. This consists of three small forts and three cannon, manned by 2,500 troops under Colonel Henry M. Shaw. As one Union brigade engages the Southerners frontally, General Ambrose E. Burnside directs the other two into adjoining swamps on a three-hour flanking march. The 9th New York Zouaves then charges the main Confederate work as the rest of the force simultaneously turns both flanks. Southern defenses crumble under the onslaught and surrender. Union casualties total 37 killed, 214 wounded, and 13 missing to a Confederate tally of 23 killed, and 2,500 captured. This constitutes the first major Union land victory, and it greatly boosts Northern morale. Moreover, possession of Roanoke Island grants Burnside a platform on Albemarle Sound from which he can suppress blockade-runners and launch expeditions toward the interior. Its fall also compromises communications with Norfolk, Virginia, and proves a major factor in its abandonment.

In light of the Roanoke disaster, the Confederate Congress tasks an investigative committee to explore General Henry A. Wise's behavior and allegations of incompetence against General Benjamin Huger, overall theater commander, and Secretary of War Judah P. Benjamin.

WEST: The recent fall of Fort Henry, Tennessee, prompts General Albert S. Johnston to order Confederate forces under General William J. Hardee to abandon the south bank of the Cumberland River for Nashville.

NAVAL: Federal gunboats depart Roanoke Island, North Carolina, and begin to sail up the Pasquotank River toward Elizabeth City.

The Federal gunboat USS *Conestoga* attacks and captures the Confederate steamers *Sallie Wood* and CSS *Muscle* on the Mississippi River near Chickasaw, Alabama. Three other vessels are likewise destroyed to prevent capture, bringing recent naval losses for the Confederacy to nine. Dropping anchor at Florence, Alabama, Lieutenant Seth L. Phelps respects the wishes of local citizens not to destroy their railroad bridge, and instead his bluejackets simply tap into the local telegraph office and eavesdrop on Confederate communications.

February 9

WEST: General Gideon J. Pillow supplants Generals Bushrod J. Johnson and Simon B. Buckner as commander of Confederate-held Fort Donelson, Tennessee.

NAVAL: The Federal gunboats USS *Tyler, Conestoga,* and *Lexington* seize the Confederate steamer *Eastport* on the Tennessee River and also attack a deserted Confederate army camp, which they burn.

February 10

WEST: Union general Samuel R. Curtis, commanding the 12,000-man Army of the Southwest, departs Rolla, Missouri, and marches against the 8,000 Missouri Home Guard under General Sterling Price. He intends to drive them deep into Arkansas to preclude any possible interference with the main Union thrust then unfolding down the Mississippi River.

NAVAL: A Federal naval flotilla headed by Commander Stephen C. Rowan of the USS *Delaware* sails up the Pasquotank River and attacks Confederate gunboats and batteries off Elizabeth City, North Carolina. The Southerners are drubbed in a very sharp action and hurriedly scuttle the CSS *Seabird, Black Warrior, Fanny,* and *Forrest.* Artillery positions at Cobb's Point also are destroyed by Union naval gunfire.

Captain Franklin Buchanan complains that he still lacks the necessary trained crew members to man his nearly completed steam ram CSS *Virginia* at Norfolk, Virginia.

Commodore Andrew H. Foote feverishly repairs his gunboats at Cairo, Illinois, after requests by General Henry W. Halleck for their immediate deployment on the Cumberland River against Fort Donelson.

The three-gunboat expedition of Lieutenant Seth L. Phelps concludes its foray down the Tennessee River by arriving back at Fort Donelson, Tennessee. They arrive with three captured Confederate steamers of which one, the *Eastport,* is armed and impressed into Union service. Phelps's raid constitutes one of the most successful endeavors of riverine warfare in the western theater.

February 11

POLITICS: The U.S. Military Rail Roads are established by Secretary of War Edwin M. Stanton. These are adopted to insure the safe and efficient coordination of military transport along thousands of miles of rail line nationwide. Consequently, railborne Union logistics achieve a degree of effectiveness unmatched by its Southern counterpart.

WEST: Union forces under Generals John A. McClernand and Charles F. Smith begin to march 15,000 men from Fort Henry to Fort Donelson on the Cumberland River, Tennessee, although impeded by heavy rains. The latter fort's garrison, meanwhile, has been strengthened by the arrival of Confederates under General Gideon Pillow.

February 12

SOUTH: General Ambrose E. Burnside pushes Federal forces inland and seizes Edenton, North Carolina, as he expands his occupation perimeter beyond Roanoke Island and vicinity.

WEST: General Ulysses S. Grant directs 15,000 Union troops 10 miles overland to invest Fort Donelson on the Cumberland River, Tennessee, now defended by 21,000 Confederates under General John B. Floyd, who is newly arrived. The Federal troops of Generals John A. McClernand and Charles F. Smith conduct the actual siege operations in concert with naval support from the gunboat USS *Carondelet.*

February 13

WEST: Southern forces under General William J. Hardee evacuate Bowling Green, Kentucky, just ahead of advancing Union forces.

Outside Fort Donelson, Tennessee, General John A. McClernand disobeys instructions not to precipitate a general action by deeply probing the Confederate defenses. He then attempts storming a battery at the enemy's center, being heavily repulsed.

The Union Army of the Southwest under General Samuel L. Curtis advances and occupies Springfield, Missouri.

NAVAL: The USS *Pembina,* while sounding the Savannah River, Georgia, observes numerous Confederate torpedoes at low tide. The majority subsequently are sunk or exploded by rifle fire.

February 14

POLITICS: President Abraham Lincoln invokes a general amnesty and pardons all political prisoners who consent to a loyalty oath.

WEST: Bowling Green, Kentucky, is occupied by Union troops under General Ormsby M. Mitchel.

Generals John B. Floyd and Gideon Pillow, despite rebuffing a Union gunboat squadron, conclude that their position at Fort Donelson on the Cumberland River is hopeless. They begin to plan a sortie for the next day, intending to break through Union lines and march to safety.

NAVAL: The experimental ironclad USS *Galena* is launched at Mystic, Connecticut.

Armed boats from the USS *Restless* capture and burn the Confederate sloop *Edisto* and the schooners *Wandoo, Elizabeth,* and *Theodore Stoney* near Bull's Bay, North Carolina.

At 3:00 P.M., Union commodore Andrew H. Foote's gunboat squadron begins a concerted bombardment against Fort Donelson on the Cumberland River, at one point closing to within 400 yards. However, heavy Confederate guns are situated on a 150-foot high bluff, and they subject Foote's vessels to severe plunging fire. The one-sided exchange continues for 90 minutes, and three of four ironclads present are badly damaged and drift helplessly downstream. Foote himself is severely wounded by a splinter and orders his battered armada withdrawn. Losses to naval personnel are 11 killed and 43 wounded. The USS *St. Louis* receives no less than 59 hits and loses its steering, as does the *Louisville.* Little damage has been inflicted upon the Confederates, but the attack unnerves generals John B. Floyd and Gideon Pillow.

February 15

SOUTH: William W. Loring gains appointment as major general, C.S.A.

WEST: Confederate defenders under Generals John B. Floyd and Gideon Pillow suddenly sortie from Fort Donelson, Tennessee, at 6:00 A.M. The attack succeeds completely and penetrates the division of General John A. McClernand. General Ulysses S. Grant, meanwhile, who is on the river flotilla conferring with Commodore Andrew H. Foote, hastily repairs back to the lines to direct a counterattack. He is assisted inadvertently by the Confederates, who, despite having opened an escape route, begin to bicker among themselves about what to do next. As they dither, Grant directs General Charles F. Smith's troops to assail the Confederate right, which he suspects has been weakened, and they gain the outer ramparts of Fort Donelson. Additional forces under General Lew Wallace also charge and contain the Confederate thrust, driving them back inside their post.

That night, Grant obtains additional reinforcements, which bring his total manpower up to 27,000. After heated consultations, the Confederate leaders prepare to surrender; however, neither Floyd nor Pillow wish to be taken prisoner, and that night they ferry themselves across the Cumberland along with 5,000 troops. Some cavalry under Colonel Nathan B. Forrest also determine to escape and wade into the flooded landscape at night to safety.

General Albert S. Johnston arrives in Nashville, Tennessee, to coordinate rapidly crumbling Confederate defenses. As a precaution, Governor Isham Harris removes all state papers and flees south.

General John M. Schofield assumes command of the District of St. Louis, Missouri.

SOUTHWEST: A Confederate column of 3,000 men under General Henry H. Sibley, marching from Mesilla, advances on Union-held Fort Craig, New Mexico Territory. This post is presently garrisoned by 1,000 regulars under Colonel Edward R. S. Canby.

NAVAL: Commodore Josiah Tattnall leads Confederate gunboats on an attack against Union batteries stationed at Venus Point on the Savannah River, but they are gradually beaten back.

February 16

WEST: The Confederate bastion of Fort Donelson, Tennessee, surrenders to General Ulysses S. Grant. Previously, Confederate generals John B. Floyd and Gideon Pillow abandoned their command and ignominiously fled, leaving Generals Simon B. Buckner and Bushrod R. Johnson to their fate. When Buckner, an old acquaintance of Grant's, requests terms, the latter brusquely responds: "No terms except unconditional and immediate surrender can be accepted. I propose to move immediately upon your works." He then takes 15,000 Confederates prisoner, along with 20,000 stands of arms, 48 field pieces, 57 heavy cannon, and considerable supplies. The Southerners also sustain 1,500 combat-related casualties. Union losses are 500 killed, 2,108 wounded, and 221 captive or missing (2,832). For winning the first significant western land action, the victorious Grant is lionized in the Northern press and hailed as "Unconditional Surrender Grant." He also gains promotion to major general.

The loss of Fort Donelson renders the Confederate defensive cordon across Kentucky and Tennessee untenable, prompting General Albert S. Johnston to withdraw his Army of Central Kentucky back toward Murfreesboro. An invasion route to the Deep South is now flung wide open.

SOUTHWEST: The Confederate column of General Henry H. Sibley arrives outside Fort Craig, New Mexico Territory. Sibley, however, deems the post too strong to attack and decides to bypass it, possibly luring the garrison out to do battle on the nearby floodplains.

NAVAL: Accurate shelling by the Union gunboat USS *St. Louis* destroys the Tennessee Ironworks near Dover on the Cumberland River.

February 17

POLITICS: The fifth session of the Confederate Provisional Congress adjourns at Richmond, Virginia.

NORTH: Ulysses S. Grant gains promotion to major general of volunteers, U.S. Army.

WEST: Two Confederate regiments advancing to reinforce Fort Donelson fall captive to Union forces.

NAVAL: The formidable Confederate ironclad CSS *Virginia* is commissioned—with Captain Franklin Buchanan, equally redoubtable, at the helm.

Commodore Andrew H. Foote proceeds with several gunboats and mortar boats down the Cumberland River toward Confederate-held Clarksville, Tennessee.

February 18

POLITICS: The first-ever elected Confederate Congress convenes at Richmond, Virginia.

NAVAL: The USS *Ethan Allen* captures the Confederate schooner *Spitfire* and the sloops *Atlanta* and *Caroline* in Clearwater harbor, Florida.

February 19

POLITICS: The Confederate Congress in Richmond, Virginia, orders the release of 2,000 Federal prisoners.

WEST: Union troops commanded by General Charles F. Smith seize and occupy Clarksville, Tennessee, and Fort Defiance.

SOUTHWEST: General Henry H. Sibley orders his Confederate column of 2,600 men across the Rio Grande toward Valverde Ford, five miles north of Union-held Fort Craig, New Mexico Territory, to threaten its line of communications. As anticipated, Colonel Edward R. S. Canby, rather than remain in his works, sorties the 2,800 man garrison—mostly untrained New Mexico Volunteers—and marches to prevent the Southerners from crossing the river.

NAVAL: The USS *Monitor* begins sea trials in New York harbor, where some propulsion deficiencies are noted.

The USS *Delaware* and *Commodore Perry* conduct an armed reconnaissance down the Chowan River, North Carolina. At length they encounter Confederate forces near the town of Winton, and they withdraw.

The USS *Brooklyn* and *South Carolina* capture the Confederate steamer *Magnolia* in the Gulf of Mexico.

Commodore Andrew H. Foote helps capture Fort Defiance and Clarksville, Tennessee, which Confederate forces hastily evacuate on his approach. The commodore then urges General William F. Smith to advance quickly on Nashville while the Cumberland River still runs high.

February 20

POLITICS: President Abraham Lincoln's 12-year-old son William Wallace ("Willie") Lincoln dies at the White House from typhoid fever.

In light of the twin disasters at Forts Henry and Donelson, the Confederate government authorizes an evacuation of troops from Columbus, Kentucky.

Tennessee governor Isham Harris relocates the Confederate state capital to Memphis as Nashville is threatened by advancing Union forces.

SOUTH: General John E. Wool, commanding Union forces at Fortress Monroe, Virginia, receives disturbing intelligence that the ironclad CSS *Virginia* is deploying against them soon.

WEST: General Albert S. Johnston reassembles his scattered Confederate forces at Murfreesboro, Tennessee.

NAVAL: The new Federal ironclad USS *Monitor* is ordered south to Hampton Roads, Virginia, to reinforce the blockade effort there.

Commodore Louis M. Goldsborough comments on the strength of Confederate river obstacles at New Bern, North Carolina, to Assistant Navy Secretary Gustavus Fox.

Union troops, supported by the USS *Delaware* and *Commodore Perry,* disembark and capture the town of Winton, North Carolina, on the Chowan River.

Commodore David G. Farragut arrives at Ship Island, Mississippi, and prepares to launch what Secretary of the Navy Gideon Welles has deemed "the most important operation of the war"—the expedition against New Orleans, Louisiana.

Landing parties from the USS *New London* seize 12 sloops on Cat Island, Mississippi, suspected of serving as pilot vessels for blockade-runners.

The USS *Portsmouth* captures the Confederate sloop *Pioneer* off Boca Chica, Texas.

February 21

POLITICS: Colonel Charles P. Stone is removed from command and arrested by the Committee on the Conduct of the War. He is blamed with betraying troops defeated at Ball's Bluff the previous October and remains imprisoned for 189 days without trial. Stone is eventually pardoned and released, but his fate is held as an example to others who could be scrutinized by the committee.

NORTH: Nathaniel Gordon, a convicted slave trader, is hanged in New York City, which is the first such punishment rendered for this outlawed practice.

SOUTH: Command of the Department of Florida passes to General Lewis G. Arnold.

SOUTHWEST: Union troops under Colonel Edwin R. S. Canby engage General Henry H. Sibley's marauding Confederates at Valverde, New Mexico Territory, roughly five miles north of strategic Fort Craig. Because Sibley is sidelined with illness, actual combat operations devolve on Colonel Thomas Green. The initial Union assault pushes the Texan vanguard back from the fords and into a ravine, pinning them there. The hard-pressed Green, seeing that the key to Canby's position is a battery of six cannon under Captain Alexander McRae, temporarily abandons his left wing, masses the bulk of his forces on the right, and then charges the guns. These fall after a difficult struggle, and the captured ordnance is then turned on its previous owners. Canby consequently orders his troops to disengage and march back to Fort Craig. Federal losses are given as 68 killed, 160 wounded, and 35 missing, compared to 36 slain Southerners, 150 wounded, and one missing. Sibley's troops prevail in combat, but lacking heavy artillery and possessing but three days' supplies, they elect to bypass Fort Craig altogether and continue marching toward Albuquerque. The fort and its garrison remain a menace to Confederate lines of communication.

February 22

POLITICS: President Jefferson Davis is inaugurated as the first elected chief executive of the Confederate States of America. His ensuing address places the blame for the present hostilities squarely on the North, and he states that he considers the North's stance against states rights to violate principles of the American Revolution. Alexander H. Stevens continues as vice president. From this point on, Southerners view their constitution and administration as permanent, not provisional.

SOUTH: The 5th Pennsylvania Cavalry under Colonel Max Friedman executes an expedition to Vienna and Flint Hill, Virginia.

WEST: The Army of Ohio under General Don C. Buell marches south from Bowling Green, Kentucky, toward Nashville, Tennessee.

NAVAL: Union naval vessels begin to penetrate the Savannah River to isolate Fort Pulaski, Georgia.

Commodore David G. Farragut orders the coast survey to study all Mississippi River passes to establish the safest passage.

February 23

POLITICS: U.S. senator Andrew Johnson of Tennessee is nominated to serve as military governor of the pro-Union, eastern portion of his state by President Abraham Lincoln.

SOUTH: General Benjamin F. Butler is tapped to serve as commander of the newly constituted Department of the Gulf.

West: General Albert S. Johnston takes charge of the Confederate Central Army in Tennessee, gathering its strength at Murfreesboro.

Confederate forces under General Nathan B. Forrest evacuate Nashville, Tennessee, now threatened by advancing Union troops under General Don C. Buell.

General John Pope gains appointment as commander of the Army of Mississippi at Commerce, Missouri.

Fayetteville, Arkansas, is occupied by Federal troops under General Samuel R. Curtis.

Naval: The USS *Harriet Lane* captures the Confederate schooner *Joanna Ward* off the Florida coast.

Commodore Andrew H. Foote, accompanied by General George W. Cullum, army chief of staff, takes his entire flotilla of four ironclads, three "woodenclads," and three transport vessels down the Mississippi River to observe formidable Confederate positions at Columbus, Kentucky. Concurrently, the USS *Tyler* is dispatched to scout the Tennessee River as far south as Eastport, Mississippi.

February 24

West: The much-ravaged town of Harper's Ferry, strategically located at the confluence of the Potomac and Shenandoah rivers, is reoccupied by Union troops of General Nathaniel P. Bank's division.

The Army of the Ohio under General Don C. Buell arrives on the north bank of the Cumberland River, opposite Nashville.

Naval: Captain Franklin Buchanan, CSS *Virginia*, is ordered by Confederate secretary of the navy Stephen R. Mallory to sortie his James River squadron against Union naval forces off nearby Hampton Roads as soon as practicable.

February 25

Politics: The Legal Tender Act is approved by President Abraham Lincoln. This is the nation's first government-sponsored paper money system. The new currency, known popularly as greenbacks, is intended only as a wartime expedient to allow the Treasury Department to pay bills. Ultimately, $400 million are in circulation by war's end.

The War Department is authorized to commandeer all telegraph lines and services to facilitate military communications.

West: Union general William Nelson, assisted by the gunboat USS *Cairo*, bloodlessly occupies Nashville, Tennessee. This is the first Southern state capital and significant industrial center captured by the North. It thereupon serves as a base of operations for the Army of the Ohio. Nashville's fate also signals that Kentucky and western Tennessee are irretrievably lost to the South. Meanwhile, Confederate forces continue their precipitous withdrawal from the line of the Cumberland River.

General Edmund Kirby-Smith is ordered to take command of Southern forces in East Tennessee.

Naval: The new Union ironclad USS *Monitor* is commissioned at Long Island, New York, with Lieutenant John L. Worden commanding. It features a revolutionary design that incorporates a single, rotating turret housing two 11-inch Dalhgren smoothbore cannon. Largely submerged underwater, the ship incorporates a forced-draft ventilation system for its crew.

The USS *R. B. Forbes* grounds in a gale off Nag's Head, North Carolina, and is burned to prevent capture.

The USS *Mohican* and *Bienville* capture the British blockade-runner *Arrow* near Fernandina, Florida.

The USS *Kingfisher* seizes the Confederate blockade-runner *Lion* after a three-day chase in the Gulf of Mexico.

The USS *Cairo*, escorting seven steam transports, assists in the capture of Nashville, Tennessee.

February 26
SOUTH: Ambrose P. Hill is appointed brigadier general, C.S.A.

NAVAL: The CSS *Nashville* captures and burns the Union schooner *Robert Gilfillan* at sea.

The USS *Bienville* captures the Confederate schooner *Alert* off St. Johns, Florida.

February 27
POLITICS: Like his northern counterpart, President Jefferson Davis finds it necessary to suspend writs of habeas corpus as a wartime expedient. He then declares martial law in Norfolk and Portsmouth, Virginia, then threatened by Union forces.

NAVAL: The much-anticipated departure of USS *Monitor* is delayed by ammunition shortages and intractable steering failures.

Lack of gunpowder delays the sailing of the Confederate ironclad CSS *Virginia* at Norfolk, Virginia.

February 28
POLITICS: An anxious president Jefferson Davis advises General Joseph E. Johnston, commanding Confederate forces in Virginia, to formulate contingency plans for evacuating men and materiel to safety if necessary.

SOUTH: Union forces are unable to initiate action at Harper's Ferry, western Virginia, because boats provided them for a pontoon bridge prove too large for the canal locks.

General Samuel Jones becomes commander of the Department of Alabama and West Florida following General Braxton Bragg's departure.

WEST: Federal troops occupy Charleston in western Virginia.

General John Pope's Army of the Mississippi advances from Commerce, Missouri, down the western shore of the Mississippi River toward the Confederate enclave of New Madrid. This strongly fortified post houses 7,500 men under General John P. McCown, with 19 heavy guns and a flotilla of gunboats under Captain George N. Hollins.

SOUTHWEST: Advancing Confederate forces capture the town of Tucson in the western New Mexico Territory. The region then elects a delegation to attend Congress in Richmond.

NAVAL: CSS *Nashville* skirts Union blockaders and runs safely into Beaufort, North Carolina.

March 1

NORTH: David Hunter and Irvin McDowell are promoted to major general, U.S. Army.

SOUTH: Martial law is declared in Richmond, Virginia, by Confederate authorities under General John H. Winder.

WEST: General Henry W. Halleck, commanding the Department of the West, orders General Ulysses S. Grant to cross the Tennessee River and move against Eastport, Mississippi.

Confederate general Pierre G. T. Beauregard begins to distribute troops on a line stretching from Columbus, Kentucky, past Island No. 10 on the Mississippi River and Fort Pillow, Tennessee, as far south as Corinth, Mississippi. General Albert S. Johnston also starts to move his command from Murfreesboro, Tennessee, toward an eventual union with Beauregard at Corinth, Mississippi.

SOUTHWEST: Federal forces abandon Albuquerque, New Mexico, to advancing Confederates under General Henry H. Sibley.

NAVAL: The USS *Mount Vernon* captures the British blockade-runner *British Queen* off Wilmington, North Carolina.

Federal gunboats USS *Tyler* and *Lexington* engage a Confederate battery guarding Pittsburgh Landing, Tennessee. However, when sailors and army sharpshooters land to scout the position, several casualties are incurred. Henceforth, Commodore Andrew H. Foote forbids naval personnel from disembarking to fight ashore.

Commodore Andrew H. Foote requests the Navy Department for $20,000 to repair and arm the captured Confederate steamer *Eastport,* which he describes as a fine vessel more than 100 feet long.

March 2

WEST: Confederate forces under General Leonidas Polk finally abandon their strong point at Columbus, Kentucky, and retreat south. Its garrison and armament of 140 cannon are subsequently relocated across the Mississippi River to New Madrid, Missouri, and Island No. 10 under General John P. McCown. The Confederate Kentucky line, previously stretching as far east as Cumberland Gap, has now completely vanished.

General Earl Van Dorn arrives at the Boston Mountains, Arkansas, to take command of the Confederate Trans-Mississippi District. There, he unites his forces with those of General Sterling Price and Ben McCulloch into the new Army of the West and countermands their withdrawal from Missouri. Disregarding poor logistical arrangements and freezing weather, Van Dorn orders his men north to confront pursuing Union forces.

March 3

SOUTH: John Bell Hood is appointed brigadier general, C.S.A.

General Robert E. Lee is recalled from Charleston, South Carolina to Richmond, Virginia, to act as a military adviser for President Jefferson Davis.

WEST: Martinsburg, western Virginia, is occupied by Federal troops.

General Henry W. Halleck accuses General Ulysses S. Grant of sloppy administration, and he orders him detained at Fort Henry, Tennessee, until further notice.

General John Pope directs 18,000 men of the Union Army of the Mississippi into siege operations against New Madrid, Missouri, on the Mississippi River.

SOUTHWEST: Advancing Confederates under General Henry H. Sibley capture Cubero, New Mexico Territory.

NAVAL: A naval expedition under Commodore Samuel F. Du Pont attacks and captures Cumberland Island and Sound, Georgia, along with Fernandina and Amelia Island, Florida. Fort Clinch, seized by a crew from the USS *Ottawa*, is the first Federal fortification retaken in the war. The North thus gains another valuable lodgment on the southern Atlantic seaboard while the entire coast of Georgia falls under Union control.

March 4

POLITICS: The U.S. Senate confirms Tennessee senator Andrew Johnson as military governor of Tennessee with a rank of brigadier general.

SOUTH: Patrick R. Cleburne is appointed brigadier general, C.S.A.

General John C. Pemberton succeeds Robert E. Lee as commander of the Department of South Carolina, Georgia, and East Florida.

WEST: General Charles F. Smith is appointed to lead Union advances down the Tennessee River in light of General Ulysses S. Grant's disciplinary difficulties.

General Earl Van Dorn marches 16,000 men from the Boston Mountains toward Missouri. He remains intent on engaging the Union Army of the Southwest under General Samuel R. Curtis somewhere in the extreme northeastern corner of Arkansas.

SOUTHWEST: Santa Fe, New Mexico Territory, is occupied by Confederates under General Henry H. Sibley.

NAVAL: The USS *Santiago de Cuba* seizes the Confederate sloop *O. K.* off Cedar Keys, Florida.

Federal gunboats USS *Cincinnati* and *Louisville* reconnoiter recently abandoned Confederate works at Columbus, Kentucky, previously hailed as "the Gibraltar of the West." Union troops arrive shortly after by river transport.

March 5

WEST: As Federal troops under General Nathaniel P. Banks advance from Harper's Ferry, western Virginia, and into the Shenandoah Valley, skirmishing erupts at Bunker Hill and Pohick Church.

Union forces under General Charles F. Smith position themselves at Savannah, Tennessee, several miles northeast of Corinth, Mississippi.

General Pierre G. T. Beauregard arrives at Jackson, Tennessee, taking charge of the newly established Confederate Army of the Mississippi. General Albert S. Johnston likewise continues massing troops at Corinth, Mississippi, determined to contest any probable Union thrusts down the Tennessee River.

March 6

POLITICS: President Abraham Lincoln urges Congress to offer monetary compensation to any state that willingly abolishes slavery. The measure is rejected soundly by state legislatures.

The Confederate Congress authorizes military authorities to destroy any cotton, tobacco, or other stores deemed of use to the enemy if they cannot be safely relocated.

SOUTH: Sterling Price is appointed major general, C.S.A.

After interminable delays, General George B. McClellan orders the Army of the Potomac southward against Manassas, Virginia. Concurrently, Confederate forces under General Joseph E. Johnston make preparations to fall back on Fredericksburg.

Union forces reoccupy Leesburg, Virginia.

WEST: A force of 10,500 Union troops under General Samuel R. Curtis entrenches itself along Sugar Creek near Pea Ridge and Elkhorn Tavern, Arkansas, in anticipation of a major Confederate assault. After General Earl Van Dorn tests the Union position and finds it too strong to be attacked frontally, he prepares for a prolonged night march around Curtis to cut him off from Missouri—then attack from behind. The Confederate Army of the West has also been recently reinforced by three Cherokee regiments under General Albert Pike and Colonel Stand Watie.

NAVAL: USS *Water Witch* captures the Confederate schooner *William Mallory* near St. Andrew's Bay, Florida.

The USS *Monitor* under Lieutenant John L. Worden departs New York while under tow by tug *Seth Law* and heads for Hampton Roads, Virginia.

The USS *Pursuit* seizes the Confederate schooner *Anna Belle* off Apalachicola, Florida.

March 7

SOUTH: Pressured by the ponderous Army of the Potomac, General Joseph E. Johnston withdraws Confederate forces from Evansport, Dumfries, Manassas, and Occoquan and heads south toward Fredericksburg, Virginia.

A Union landing party commanded by General Thomas W. Sherman captures Fort Clinch on Fernandina Island, Florida.

WEST: Confederate cavalry under Colonel Ashby Turner skirmish with Union forces near Winchester, western Virginia.

Confederate forces under General Earl Van Dorn conduct a complicated night march around the Army of the Southwest near Pea Ridge, northwestern Arkansas. The main strike force under General Sterling Price positions itself behind and opposite the Union left wing, but fatigued Texans of General Ben McCulloch's division deploying against Curtis's right cannot close the gap. Thus two wings of the Confederate army remain widely separated and unable to act in concert. Van Dorn himself is ill and directs operations from an ambulance in the rear of his line. General Samuel R. Curtis, quickly perceiving the danger posed to his command, simply orders his entire line to "about face." The new threat is immediately countered and negates whatever advantage Van Dorn's wearying march sought to achieve. The action commences across the line when Price's Missourians launch two desperate charges that are beaten back. McCulloch's column, however, stumbles badly when both he and his second in command, General James M. McIntosh, are killed. A third charge by Price manages to drive back Curtis's right, but prompt Union counterattacks regain lost ground. A similar effort is made against Pike's Cherokee on the left with good results. A fourth attack at sunset pushes the Union line back 800 yards but still fails to break it. Fighting then subsides with nightfall.

March 8

POLITICS: President Abraham Lincoln issues General War Order No. 2, which reorganizes the Army of the Potomac into four corps. It also stipulates that at least one corps be left behind for the defense of Washington, D.C. General Irvin McDowell's command draws the assignment.

Unionist William G. Brownlow is released from confinement and allowed to cross over to Union lines in eastern Tennessee.

SOUTH: Union forces advance and occupy Leesburg, Virginia.

WEST: Resurgent Confederate forces under General John B. Floyd reoccupy Chattanooga and Knoxville, Tennessee, forcing Unionists in the region to flee.

Confederate cavalryman Colonel John H. Morgan raids the suburbs of Nashville, Tennessee.

Fighting resumes at Pea Ridge, Arkansas, when Confederate artillery bombard the position of General Samuel R. Curtis, who constricts and consolidates his line. However, when Van Dorn's guns are silenced for want of ammunition, Curtis deduces that Van Dorn's entire force must likewise be low, and he orders General Franz Sigel to attack across the front. A surging blue tide sweeps across the battlefield of Confederates as Van Dorn, his army shattered, orders a complete withdrawal. Union losses amount to 20 killed, 980 wounded, and 201 missing, while the Southerners sustain roughly 2,000 casualties, including 300 captured. Pea Ridge is the first major Union victory in the Far West and thwarts Confederate hopes of invading Missouri for the next two years.

NAVAL: The ironclad ram CSS *Virginia* under Captain Franklin Buchanan sorties from Norfolk, Virginia, and engages wooden ships of the Union blockading squadron off Newport News. Buchanan first maneuvers and slams into the sloop USS *Cumberland,* breaking off its metallic ram and sinking that hapless vessel. The *Virginia* then receives heavy fire from the frigate *Congress,* whose cannon balls simply rebound off heavy iron plate. Buchanan next riddles his opponent at close range, driving it ashore and reducing *Congress* to a burning hulk. A third vessel, *Minnesota,* grounds itself in anticipation of being attacked. Buchanan, who is wounded by gunfire from the shoreline, relinquishes command to Lieutenant Catesby ap Roger Jones, who breaks off the action. Union casualties are two vessels sunk and roughly 300 sailors killed and wounded. Moreover, the death knell of wooden warships has sounded.

The USS *Monitor* under Lieutenant John L. Worden, having survived a perilous transit from New York, arrives off Hampton Roads, Virginia, in the evening.

The USS *Bohio* captures the Confederate schooner *Henry Travers* off Southwest Pass, Mississippi River.

March 9

SOUTH: The Army of the Potomac under General George B. McClellan fails to establish contact with enemy forces and returns to Alexandria, Virginia. Meanwhile, the

Turret of the USS *Monitor*. Photo taken after the battle with the CSS *Virginia*. Note dents in the turret next to the gun ports. *(Naval Historical Foundation)*

Confederate army under General Joseph E. Johnston retreats farther south and positions itself behind the Rappahannock River.

WEST: General Edmund Kirby-Smith arrives at Knoxville to command Confederate forces in East Tennessee.

NAVAL: At about 9:00 A.M., Lieutenant Catesby ap Roger Jones takes the undamaged ironclad CSS *Virginia* out of Norfolk, intending to finish off the grounded USS *Minnesota*. As he approaches his quarry, he is startled to see the low-lying and strange-looking *Monitor* sail directly into his path. During the next four hours, the two iron giants duel to the death before thousands of spectators onshore. Both vessels, heavily armed and armored, fire repeatedly at close range yet fail to inflict serious damage. Jones next tries ramming the *Monitor*, but Lieutenant John L. Worden simply dodges his lumbering adversary while firing away. At length, a lucky Confederate shot strikes Worden's pilothouse, wounding his eye with a splinter. His successor, Lieutenant S. Dana Greene, draws off to assess matters and reload, while

Virginia inadvertently grounds in shallow water. Once Jones frees himself, he makes a final lunge at the *Minnesota* and then, mindful of lowering tides, steams back to Norfolk. This dramatic but inconclusive confrontation heralds the dawn of iron warships in naval warfare.

Landing parties from USS *Anacostia* and *Yankee* occupy and raze abandoned Confederate batteries at Cockpit Point and Evansport, Virginia.

The USS *Mohican* and *Pocahontas* seize St. Simon's and Jekyl islands at New Brunswick, Georgia.

The USS *Pinola* captures the Confederate schooner *Cora* in the Gulf of Mexico and deposits it at Ship Island, Mississippi.

March 10

POLITICS: President Abraham Lincoln pays a bedside visit to Lieutenant John L. Worden, seriously wounded in the fight between the USS *Monitor* and the CSS *Virginia.*

SOUTH: John P. McCown is promoted to major general, C.S.A.

NAVAL: The Union tug USS *Whitehall* is accidentally lost to fire off Fortress Monroe, Virginia.

Commodore David G. Farragut methodically begins to work his deep-draft warships over the bar and into the Mississippi River below New Orleans, Louisiana.

March 11

POLITICS: President Abraham Lincoln, disillusioned by General George B. McClellan's lack of aggressiveness, issues War Order No. 3. This removes the slow-to-act leader as general in chief, although he is retained as command of the Army of the Potomac. Henceforth, all generals are to report directly to Secretary of War Edwin M. Stanton.

President Jefferson Davis refuses to accept the reports of General John B. Floyd and Gideon Pillow on the fall of Fort Donelson, and he unceremoniously relieves both of command.

NORTH: The Department of Western Virginia is absorbed by the Mountain Department and is granted to General John C. Frémont.

General Henry W. Halleck is appointed commander of all Union forces in the West through an amalgamation of the Departments of Kansas, the Missouri, and the Ohio into the new Department of the Mississippi.

WEST: General Thomas J. Jackson departs Winchester, western Virginia, at the head of 4,600 men, and he marches up the valley toward Mount Jackson. He is shadowed cautiously by 18,000 Federals under General Nathaniel P. Banks.

NAVAL: A landing party from the USS *Wabash* captures and occupies St. Augustine, Florida.

Confederate authorities at Pensacola, Florida, fearing a Union naval thrust against them, burn two gunboats to prevent their capture.

March 12

SOUTH: Federal troops under General Ambrose E. Burnside board army transports at Roanoke Island, North Carolina, for an expedition against New Bern on the Neuse River.

WEST: Union forces advance and reoccupy Winchester in western Virginia as Confederates under General Thomas J. Jackson withdraw farther up the Shenandoah Valley.

General John Pope receives and deploys heavy siege artillery to facilitate his siege of New Madrid, Missouri, on the Mississippi River.

NAVAL: The USS *Gem of the Sea* captures the British blockade-runner *Fair Play* off Georgetown, South Carolina.

A landing party from the USS *Ottawa* seizes and occupies Jacksonville, Florida.

Federal gunboats USS *Tyler* and *Lexington* cruise down the Tennessee River and trade shots with a Confederate battery at Chickasaw, Alabama.

March 13

POLITICS: President Abraham Lincoln approves of plans for operations along the Virginia coast by forces under General George B. McClellan. He urges the general "at all events, move such remainder of the army at once in pursuit of the enemy."

New army regulations forbid army officers from returning fugitive African-American slaves back to their owners. Failure to comply is punishable by court-martial.

SOUTH: General George B. McClellan convenes a war conference at Fairfax Court House, Virginia, and finalizes his strategy against Richmond. Rather than campaign overland from Urbana on the Rappahannock River, he elects to ship the entire Army of the Potomac up the York and James rivers to outflank strong Confederate defenses. To that end, his force is reorganized into five corps under generals Irvin McDowell (I Corps), Edwin V. Sumner (II Corps), Samuel P. Heintzelman (III Corps), Erasmus D. Keyes (IV Corps), and Nathaniel P. Banks (V Corps).

General Ambrose E. Burnside lands three brigades of 12,000 Union soldiers at Slocum's Creek on the Neuse River, North Carolina, supported by 13 gunboats. His objective is New Bern, that state's second-largest city and an important railhead. After learning of his approach, Confederate general Lawrence O. Branch constricts his 4,000-man garrison within defensive works six miles south of New Bern and awaits their approach.

WEST: A heavy bombardment from General John Pope's siege guns at Point Pleasant, Missouri, induces Confederate forces under General John P. McCown to evacuate their base at New Madrid for Island No. 10, abandoning mounds of valuable supplies in the process.

General William T. Sherman begins to probe from the Union lodgment at Pittsburg Landing on the Tennessee River and into the surrounding Mississippi countryside.

NAVAL: A naval expedition lands 12,000 Federal troops under General Ambrose E. Burnside on the Neuse River, North Carolina.

Commander David D. Porter assembles his mortar-ship flotilla at Ship Island, Mississippi, to assist in the upcoming New Orleans campaign.

Captain George N. Hollins reassembles his Confederate gunboat squadron at Island No. 10 in the Mississippi River following the fall of New Madrid, Missouri. His squadron then consists of CSS *Livingston, Polk,* and *Pontchartrain.*

March 14

SOUTH: 12,000 Federal troops under General Ambrose E. Burnside land and advance through rain and mud toward New Bern, North Carolina, the former colonial capital. Confederate defenders under General Lawrence O. Branch resist doughtily for several hours until a militia unit in his center suddenly cracks. The gap is exploited by the brigades of generals Jesse Reno and John G. Foster, and Branch retreats toward Kinston. The 26th and 33rd North Carolina under Colonels Zebulon B. Vance and Robert F. Hoke, respectively, are trapped behind enemy lines, yet both energetically grope for a ford across the Trent River and escape certain capture. New Bern is subsequently occupied by Burnside's victorious forces that afternoon. Union losses are 92 killed, 391 wounded, and one missing for a Confederate total of 64 dead, 101 injured, and 413 captured. The loss in materiel to the Confederates is significant, and the Union gains another base for projecting its strength inland. Burnside gains promotion to major general for the effort, while Confederate general Richard C. Gatlin is sacked for failing to prepare New Bern's defenses in advance.

General George Stoneman conducts a Federal reconnaissance toward Cedar Run, Virginia.

General James H. Trapier assumes command of the Confederate Department of Middle and East Florida.

WEST: General William S. Rosecrans takes charge of the Union Mountain Department.

Commanding General William W. Halleck orders the Army of the Ohio under General Don C. Buell to proceed south from Nashville toward Savannah, Georgia.

Confederates under General Edmund Kirby-Smith skirmish with Union forces at Big Creek Gap and Jacksonboro, Tennessee.

General John Pope overruns the Confederate enclave at New Madrid, Missouri, as defenders under General John P. McCown flee to Island No. 10 in the nearby Mississippi River.

NAVAL: Naval landing parties at New Bern, North Carolina, under Commander Stephen C. Rowan capture two Confederate steamers, sizable cotton supplies, and a howitzer battery.

The division of General Stephen Hurlbut joins General William T. Sherman's force that is already deploying at Pittsburg Landing, Tennessee.

Commodore Andrew H. Foote departs Cairo, Illinois, with seven gunboats for an attack on Island No. 10 in the Mississippi River.

March 15

SOUTH: The Department of the South under General David Hunter absorbs the Department of Florida.

WEST: General Ulysses S. Grant is exonerated of misconduct by General Henry W. Halleck and resumes command of Union forces in Tennessee.

NAVAL: Commodore Andrew H. Foote's flotilla of six gunboats and 121 mortar boats unleashes a preliminary bombardment of Confederate defenses on Island No. 10 in the Mississippi River.

March 16

WEST: General James Garfield and 600 Union volunteers attack and destroy a Confederate encampment under General Humphrey Marshall at Pound Gap, Tennessee.

Colonel John H. Morgan leads Confederate raiders in and around Gallatin, Tennessee.

Federal troops under General John Pope, in concert with Commodore Andrew H. Foote's gunboat flotilla, initiate combined operations against Confederate positions on Island No. 10 in the Mississippi River. This post, well manned and heavily armed, presents a formidable obstacle to all river navigation.

NAVAL: Federal gunboats USS *Yankee* and *Anacostia* duel with Confederate batteries at Aquia Creek, Virginia.

The USS *Owasco* captures Confederate schooners *Eugenia* and *President* in the Gulf of Mexico.

March 17

SOUTH: The Army of the Potomac—105,000 strong—begins to embark at Alexandria, Virginia, for an amphibious transit to Fortress Monroe on the York and James rivers. Through this maneuver, General George B. McClellan aspires to outflank Confederate defenses guarding Richmond.

NAVAL: The CSS *Nashville* slips past blockading vessels USS *Cambridge* and *Gemsbok* off Beaufort, North Carolina. The Navy Department was quite embarrassed by its failure to stop the raider, and Assistant Secretary Gustavus V. Fox described the affair as "a Bull Run for the Navy."

Commodore Andrew H. Foote engages Confederate batteries on Island No. 10 with his gunboat flotilla. Some damage is inflicted ashore, but both USS *Benton* and *Cincinnati* receive damage when a gun burst on *St. Louis* kills and wounds several sailors.

March 18

POLITICS: President Jefferson Davis appoints Confederate secretary of war Judah P. Benjamin his new secretary of state to replace Robert M. T. Hunter, who was elected to the Confederate Senate.

NORTH: Ambrose E. Burnside is promoted to major general, U.S. Army.

WEST: The advance guard of Confederate forces under General Albert S. Johnston trudge into Corinth, Mississippi, from Murfreesboro, Tennessee.

NAVAL: The British blockade-runner *Emily St. Pierre* falls captive to the Union blockading squadron off Charleston, South Carolina. However, once at sea, the prize crew is overpowered, and the vessel sails on to Liverpool, England.

March 19

SOUTH: General Joseph R. Anderson assumes command of the Confederate Department of North Carolina.

WEST: Confederates under General Thomas J. Jackson successfully skirmish with the Union troops of General James Shield at Strasburg, western Virginia.

Colonel Powell Clayton leads the 5th Kansas Cavalry on a mounted expedition to Carthage, Missouri.

SOUTHWEST: Union forces skirmish with Indians at Bishop's Creek, Owen's River valley, California.

NAVAL: The gunboat squadron under Commodore Andrew H. Foote continues flailing away at Confederate defenses on Island No. 10 in the Mississippi River, meeting heavy resistance.

March 20

NORTH: General Nathaniel P. Banks and his V Corps are ordered out of the Shenandoah Valley to the defense of Washington, D.C.

SOUTH: Federal forces under General Oliver O. Howard conduct a reconnaissance of Manassas Junction, Virginia.

General Ambrose E. Burnside leads a strong Union force overland against Washington, North Carolina, from New Bern.

General Benjamin F. Butler accedes to command of the Department of the Gulf at Ship Island, Mississippi, prior to operations against New Orleans, Louisiana.

WEST: Confederates under General Thomas J. Jackson depart Strasburg, Virginia, and advance toward Mount Jackson.

March 21

NORTH: Samuel R. Curtis, William S. Rosecrans, and Lew Wallace gain appointment as major generals, U.S. Army.

SOUTH: Union troops under General Ambrose E. Burnside advance and seize Washington, North Carolina.

WEST: Confederate cavalry under Colonel Turner Ashby alert General Thomas J. Jackson that General Nathaniel P. Banks is withdrawing two divisions from Winchester in the Shenandoah Valley. Jackson, fearing that these reinforcements are destined to assist the Army of the Potomac's drive on Richmond, determines to lure them back. He immediately puts two brigades in motion toward Kernstown.

Confederates under General Edmund Kirby-Smith skirmish with Union forces at Cumberland Gap, Tennessee.

March 22

NORTH: Don C. Buell, John Pope, and Franz Sigel are appointed major generals, U.S. Army.

The Middle Department, headquartered at Baltimore, is constituted under General John A. Dix.

SOUTH: General Mansfield Lovell, commanding the Confederate garrison at New Orleans, reports that he has six steamers for the defense of the city but that the inhabitants are dismayed once the bulk of Confederate naval assets deploy upriver.

WEST: Preliminary skirmishing erupts at Kernstown, western Virginia, between Confederate cavalry under Colonel Turner Ashby and Union forces under General James Shield. Ashby then mistakenly reports to General Thomas J. Jackson that Union strength is about 4,000 men, the same as his own. In fact, Shield possesses twice as many men, with most of them hidden in nearby copses.

The 2nd Kansas Cavalry under Colonel Robert B. Mitchell skirmishes with the Confederate guerrillas of William C. Quantrill outside Independence, Missouri.

NAVAL: The future CSS *Florida,* presently disguised as the British steamer *Oreto,* departs Liverpool for Nassau. There, the vessel is to be renamed and outfitted with four seven-inch guns. This was the first English vessel built expressly for the Confederate navy and clandestinely secured through the efforts of agent James D. Bulloch.

A naval landing party from USS *Penguin* and *Henry Andrew* engages Confederate forces while reconnoitering ashore at Mosquito Inlet, Florida, suffering three killed.

March 23

POLITICS: George W. Randolph is appointed Confederate secretary of war.

SOUTH: General Ambrose E. Burnside orders Union forces under General John G. Parke against Confederate-held Fort Macon (Beaufort), North Carolina. Defenders in the old stone fort, garrisoned by 400 men under Colonel Moses J. White, are summoned to surrender, but White refuses.

WEST: General Thomas J. Jackson concludes an impressive two-day march by covering 41 miles in two days. He then initiates his diversionary Shenandoah Valley strategy by attacking 9,000 Union troops under General James Shields at Kernstown, Virginia, south of Winchester. His force of 4,500 in three brigades advances confidently and flanks the Union left, driving them back. However, Union commander General Nathan Kimball continuously feeds more men into the fray and fights the Southerners to a draw. A crisis erupts when the Stonewall brigade of General Richard B. Garnett runs out of ammunition and departs without orders, creating a gap in Jackson's line. As increasing numbers of Federal troops surge forward, Jackson's entire line falls back in semiconfusion, losing 80 killed, 355 wounded, and 263 captured (718) men, along with a number of cannon and wagons. Union losses totaled 118 dead, 450 injured, and 22 captives (590).

Kernstown, while a Confederate tactical defeat, harbors immense strategic implications for both contenders. Union authorities are convinced that Jackson would not have attacked down the Shenandoah until he had been massively reinforced, and now Washington, D.C., is perceived as in danger. Accordingly, President Abraham Lincoln orders the I Corps of General Irvin McDowell to be detained indefinitely at the capital, thereby depriving the Army of the Potomac of its services during the upcoming Peninsula Campaign. The two divisions of General Nathaniel P. Banks are likewise frozen at Harper's Ferry and are rendered unavailable as reinforcements. The defeat at Kernstown also heralds the start of Jackson's dazzling Shenandoah Valley campaign, one of the Civil War's legendary endeavors.

Union soldiers commence digging a 12-mile-long, 50-foot wide canal on the Mississippi River to allow Union gunboats to bypass Confederate defensive works at Island No. 10.

March 24

SOUTH: General John B. Magruder, commanding Confederate forces in Virginia's Yorktown Peninsula region, advises superiors in Richmond that Union soldiers are arriving at nearby Fortress Monroe.

General Theophilus H. Holmes becomes commander of the Department of North Carolina.

WEST: The continuing unpopularity of emancipation is underscored when radical abolitionist Wendell Phillips is pelted with eggs and stones in Cincinnati, Ohio.

General Albert S. Johnston completes his concentration of Confederate forces at Corinth, Mississippi, while Union troops under General Ulysses S. Grant consolidate their position at Pittsburg Landing, 20 miles distant.

March 25

WEST: General Henry W. Halleck, commanding at St. Louis, expresses alarm to Commodore Andrew H. Foote on the receipt of intelligence that the Confederates are constructing a huge ironclad (CSS *Arkansas*) downstream capable of destroying his smaller Union gunboats.

SOUTHWEST: Major John M. Chivington of the 1st Colorado Volunteers is ordered to attack a Confederate force lodged near Santa Fe, New Mexico Territory. He arrives at the far end of La Glorietta Pass that evening, captures several sentinels, and prepares to storm the enemy camp at dawn.

NAVAL: Confederate secretary of the navy Stephen R. Mallory orders Commodore Josiah Tattnall to replace the wounded Captain Franklin Buchanan at Norfolk, Virginia.

CSS *Oregon* and *Pamlico* engage the USS *New London* off Pass Christian, Mississippi, but subsequently withdraw when their rifled ordnance jams and no damage is inflicted. Meanwhile, an armada of transport vessels arrives off Ship Island, Mississippi, bearing the army of General Benjamin F. Butler.

The USS *Cayuga* captures the Confederate schooner *Jessie L. Cox* at sea.

Landing parties from the Federal gunboat USS *Cairo* occupy recently abandoned Fort Zollicoffer below Nashville, seizing guns and other equipment.

March 26

SOUTH: Daniel H. Hill is promoted to major general, C.S.A.

General John H. Winder is tapped to serve as commander of the Confederate Department of Henrico, which includes Petersburg, Virginia.

SOUTHWEST: A skirmish between Union and Confederate cavalry near Denver City, Colorado Territory, results in 50 Southern prisoners.

In an early morning raid, Colonel John M. Chivington, 1st Colorado Infantry, advances through Glorieta Pass, New Mexico Territory, and attacks Confederate forces under Major Charles L. Pryon that are encamped at Johnson's Ranch. Federal troops capture the 30-man advance guard and then storm the enemy camp. The surprised Confederates respond with artillery fire that stabilizes their line, but Chivington redeploys to catch the Texans in a crossfire, and the Texans retire in confusion. A last-minute charge by Union cavalry against the Confederate rear guard nets several prisoners; Chivington then orders his men back to Kozlowski's Ranch to regroup. Union losses are 19 dead, 5 wounded, and 3 missing while the Southerners report 16 killed, 30 injured, and 79 missing. The shaken Pyron immediately sends for reinforcements.

NAVAL: Armed boats dispatched by the USS *Delaware* capture Confederate schooners *Albemarle* and *Lion* in Pantego Creek, North Carolina.

March 27

SOUTH: Colonel Jonathan W. Geary and the 28th Pennsylvania conduct a reconnaissance of the region between Middleburg and White Plains, Virginia.

General Joseph E. Johnston is ordered to reinforce the Confederate Army of the Peninsula at Yorktown, Virginia, under General John B. Magruder.

WEST: Secretary of War Edwin M. Stanton tells engineer Charles Ellet to commence construction of numerous steam rams at Pittsburgh, Pennsylvania, and Cincinnati, Ohio, capable of thwarting the new Confederate ironclad being assembled at Memphis, Tennessee.

SOUTHWEST: Colonel William R. Scurry's 4th Texas arrives at Johnson's Ranch, New Mexico Territory, to reinforce a detachment under Major Charles L. Pyron. The Confederates then brace themselves for an anticipated Union attack, and when it fails to materialize, Pyron resumes the offensive by marching through Glorieta Pass.

NAVAL: An armed boat from the USS *Restless* captures the Confederate schooner *Julia Warden* and burns the sloop *Mary Louisa* and the schooner *George Washington* off the South Carolina coast.

Commodore Samuel F. Du Pont informs the Navy Department that Confederate batteries have withdrawn from Skiddaway and Greene Island off the Georgia coast, granting his fleet control of Wassaw and Ossabaw sounds, along with the mouths of the Vernon and Wilmington rivers. The approaches to Savannah, Georgia, are now open.

March 28

SOUTH: General Oliver O. Howard's Union troops occupy Shipping Point, Virginia, to sever the Orange and Alexandria Railroad.

WEST: Union general Washington Morgan and his 7th Division are ordered to secure the Cumberland Gap in Tennessee, a strategic mountain pass connecting Tennessee, Kentucky, and western Virginia.

SOUTHWEST: A Union detachment at Johnson's Ranch near Glorietta Ranch, New Mexico Territory, is reinforced by a detachment under Colonel John P. Slough. Slough decides to attack the Confederates at nearby Apache Canyon and orders Major John Chivington, 1st Colorado Volunteers, and 450 men to march circuitously west around and to their right and rear. As this movement unfolds, a Confederate column under Colonel William R. Scurry simultaneously advances through Glorieta Pass and attacks Slough at Pigeon's Ranch. They drive the defenders hard but are gradually stopped by superior artillery and nightfall.

Meanwhile, Chivington marches around Apache Canyon and happens upon the lightly guarded Confederate baggage train at Johnson's Ranch. He immediately attacks, burning 90 supply wagons and killing 800 draft animals. Chivington then retraces his steps and rejoins Slough's main force at Koslowski's Ranch. The engagements at Glorieta Pass prove disastrous to Confederate fortunes in the Southwest. The loss of their entire commissary marked the end of General Henry H. Sibley's offensive, and he has little recourse but to withdraw back to Texas. Scurry reports his losses as 36 dead, 60 injured, and 25 missing out of 1,100, while Slough sustains 31 killed, 50 wounded, and 30 missing out of 1,345 engaged.

NAVAL: Armed boats under Lieutenant Thomas F. Stevens venture up St. John's River, Florida, and capture and raise the racing yacht *America*, which had been scuttled by Confederate sympathizers. The vessel subsequently is taken into U.S. naval service.

Commander Henry H. Bell takes the USS *Kennebec* on a close reconnaissance of Confederate river defenses below Forts Jackson and St. Philip, below New Orleans, Louisiana. This information allows Commodore David G. Farragut to formulate a precise plan of operations to bypass the forts.

March 29
SOUTH: Advanced elements of General John G. Parke's brigade land on Bogue Banks, Beaufort, North Carolina, and begin to surround nearby Fort Morgan.
WEST: Command of the Mountain Department switches from General William S. Rosecrans to General John C. Frémont.

General Albert S. Johnston assembles his Army of the Mississippi at Corinth, Mississippi, by amalgamating the Armies of Kentucky and Mississippi into a single structure with General Pierre G. T. Beauregard as second in command together with commanders Leonidas Polk (I Corps), Braxton Bragg (II Corps), William J. Hardee (III Corps), and George B. Crittenden (Reserve).
NAVAL: An armed boat from USS *Restless* captures the Confederate schooner *Lydia and Mary* in the Santee River, South Carolina.

The USS *R. R. Cuyler* captures the Confederate schooner *Grace E. Baker* off the Cuban coast.

March 30
WEST: Federal troops occupy Union City, Tennessee.

March 31
NORTH: The division of Union general Louis Blenker is ordered up from General George B. McClellan's Army of the Potomac by President Abraham Lincoln for the defense of Washington, D.C.
SOUTH: General David Hunter assumes command of the newly enlarged Department of the South (South Carolina, Georgia, Florida), with headquarters at Hilton Head, South Carolina.
WEST: Federal forces under General Lew Wallace skirmish with Confederates along the Purdy Road, Adamsville, Tennessee.

Federal troops occupy Union City, Tennessee.

Confederate general William W. Mackall arrives to replace General John P. McCown as commander of New Madrid Bend and Island No. 10 in the Mississippi River. McCown is relieved over his premature abandonment of New Madrid, Missouri, on March 13.

April 1
SOUTH: Headquarters, Army of the Potomac, is transferred from Alexandria to Fortress Monroe, Virginia.
WEST: Confederates under General Thomas J. Jackson withdraw up the Shenandoah Valley, screened by cavalry under Colonel Ashby Turner.

General Nathaniel P. Banks directs an advance of Federal troops from Strasburg, Virginia, to Woodstock and Edenburg.

General Benjamin Cheatham leads a Confederate reconnaissance of Federal positions at Pittsburg Landing, Tennessee, and reports that General Ulysses S. Grant apparently has divided his force.

NAVAL: CSS *Gaines* recaptures the former Confederate schooner *Isabelle* off Mobile, Alabama.

A combined expedition escorted by Federal gunboat USS St. *Louis* captures Fort No. 1 on the Tennessee shore, above Island No. 10 in the Mississippi River. The guns are spiked, and the expedition withdraws unmolested.

April 2

NORTH: Confederate spy Rose Greenhow is expelled from Washington, D.C., by Federal authorities.

SOUTH: General George B. McClellan and his staff arrive at Fortress Monroe, Virginia, preparatory to advancing on Confederate defenses at nearby Yorktown.

WEST: Skirmishing continues between opposing vedettes outside Pittsburg Landing, Tennessee, as General Pierre G. T. Beauregard conceives an overly complex order of battle. He places all three Confederate corps in three successive waves of attack, a tactic exacerbating mass confusion in the swirl of battle. The necessity of attacking gains additional currency once it is learned that the Army of the Ohio under General Don C. Buell departed Nashville and is only a few days away from joining General Ulysses S. Grant. General Albert S. Johnston determines to embark on a violent preemptive strike that, if successful, will prevent Federal forces from combining in overwhelming strength.

NAVAL: The USS *Mount Vernon, Fernandina,* and *Cambridge* capture and burn the Confederate schooner *Kate* off Wilmington, North Carolina.

April 3

POLITICS: The U.S. Senate abolishes slavery in the District of Columbia on a 29 to 14 vote.

Secretary of War Edwin M. Stanton, encouraged by the course of events thus far, mistakenly orders all U.S. recruiting offices closed.

NORTH: President Abraham Lincoln is angered that General George B. McClellan disobeys orders and assigns less than 20,000 men to the defense of Washington, D.C. He therefore insists that one full army corps be retained at the capital. Lincoln also orders offensive operations against Richmond, Virginia, to commence as soon as possible.

SOUTH: General George B. McClellan makes final preparations to direct his massive Army of the Potomac into combat. A talented disciplinarian and organizer, he commands a well-appointed force of 112,000 men.

WEST: Massed Confederate forces under General Albert S. Johnston decamp from Corinth, Mississippi, and grope toward Union positions at Pittsburg Landing, Tennessee. Their advance is dogged by driving rain and poor marching discipline, which many senior commanders fear will alert the defenders to their approach.

NAVAL: The USS *Susquehanna* captures the British blockade-runner *Coquette* off Charleston, South Carolina.

Commodore Samuel F. Du Pont orders the USS *Mohican* to reconnoiter up the Wilmington River and establish the best avenues of approach to Fort Pulaski, Georgia.

Armed boats dispatched from the USS *Isaac Smith* seize the British blockade-runner *British Empire* in Matanzas Inlet, Florida.

Armed boats from the USS *Mercedita* and *Sagamore* capture Apalachicola, Florida, seizing schooners *New Island, Floyd,* and *Rose,* along with the sloop *Octavia.*

April 4

NORTH: The new Departments of the Rappahannock and Shenandoah are constituted under Generals Irvin McDowell (I Corps) and Nathaniel P. Banks (V Corps), respectively.

SOUTH: With his army of 112,000 men assembled on the Yorktown Peninsula, General George B. McClellan begins his long-awaited drive on Richmond, Virginia. His first objective is to capture Yorktown and establish a base between the James and York rivers. In contrast to the slap-dash Union forces of the previous year, the Army of the Potomac is well trained and led, well equipped, and eager to prove its mettle in combat.

WEST: Confederate forces under General Albert S. Johnston continue advancing on Pittsburg Landing, Tennessee, impeded by heavy rains, yet Union forces remain blissfully ignorant of their approach.

NAVAL: The USS *Pursuit* captures the Confederate sloop *Lafayette* in St. Joseph's Bay, Florida.

A Union squadron consisting of USS *J. P. Jackson, New London,* and *Hatteras* lands 1,200 sailors and marines at Pass Christian, Mississippi. Confederate vessels CSS *Carondelet, Pamlico,* and *Oregon* briefly oppose their passage and then withdraw.

The USS *J. P. Jackson* captures the Confederate steamer *P. C. Wallis* off New Orleans, Louisiana.

Under the cover of darkness and rain, the USS *Carondelet* under Commander Henry Walke dashes past Confederate batteries on Island No. 10 in the Mississippi River. As a precaution, the vessel is outfitted with cordwood piled around its boilers, thickened deck planking, and an anchor chain placed as additional armor. The Southerners are now cut off from reinforcements downstream, and Union troops under General John Pope can safely cross the Mississippi River to the Tennessee shore.

April 5

POLITICS: General Andrew Johnson, military governor of his home state of Tennessee, suspends several city officials in Nashville for refusing to take an oath of allegiance.

SOUTH: The Army of the Potomac begins its Peninsula campaign with an advance on Yorktown, Virginia, then energetically defended by 15,000 Confederates under General John B. Magruder. Magruder cannot possibly match his adversary in strength, so he conducts elaborate ruses such as erecting false "Quaker guns" along his line and continually marches troops to give an impression of greater numbers. General George B. McClellan is completely duped by the deception, and rather than aggressively probe Confederate defenses along the Yorktown–Warwick River line, he commences siege operations. His overly cautious demeanor keeps the Army of the Potomac fixed in place for a month.

Union forces take and occupy Edisto Island, South Carolina.

WEST: Massed Confederates under General Albert S. Johnston prepare to strike at Union positions along Pittsburg Landing, Tennessee. Despite entreaties by General Pierre G. T. Beauregard and others to relent, Johnston determines to hit the invaders hard on the morrow. "I would fight them if they were a million," he reputedly declares. Curiously, the army of General Ulysses S. Grant bivouacs quiescently in camp, unaware of the swift fate rapidly descending on it.

NAVAL: Commodore David G. Farragut takes the USS *Iroquois* on a close reconnaissance of Forts Jackson and St. Philip on the Mississippi River. Farragut personally views the fortifications from a mast despite heavy enemy fire.

An armed boat launched from USS *Montgomery* captures and sinks the Confederate schooner *Columbia* near San Luis Pass, Texas.

April 6

SOUTH: Braxton Bragg is promoted to full general, C.S.A.

As General George B. McClellan dithers before Yorktown, Virginia, General Joseph E. Johnston accelerates a transfer of troops there from the Rappahannock River.

WEST: A Federal expedition advances from Greeneville, Tennessee, into the Laurel Valley, North Carolina.

On this momentous day, the Battle of Shiloh erupts at dawn as 44,000 Confederates under General Albert S. Johnston surprise 39,000 Federal troops under General Ulysses S. Grant in camp. Grant is then at his headquarters in Savannah, seven miles distant, and actual leadership devolves on General William T. Sherman. Despite continuing signs of an enemy presence to his front, Sherman takes no precautions. Consequently, the massed Southerners spill out of the adjoining woods at 5:30 A.M., and Union forces suffer complete tactical surprise. The three divisions of Generals Sherman, John A. McClernand, and Benjamin Prentiss attempt to form defensive lines but are repeatedly swept back by a surging gray tide. But Prentiss is luckier; he rallies 3,000 troops along a sunken road surrounded by densely wooded thickets situated directly in the enemy's path. Johnston's men sweep across various parts of the field and ultimately lap around both of Grant's flanks, but his drive in the center falters in the face of stout resistance from Prentiss's small band. They fight so fiercely that the Southerners dub this portion of the battlefield the "Hornets' Nest." General Braxton Bragg, wishing to maintain pressure on Prentiss to keep his forces pinned in position, forsakes maneuvering and launches no less than 12 frontal assaults—all of which are blasted back with heavy losses. General Johnston himself is hit while directing combat from his saddle, and he bleeds to death at about 2:30 P.M. General Pierre G. T. Beauregard then assumes tactical control

The 9th Illinois Infantry at the battle in Shiloh, Tennessee, where their 90-minute stand helped prepare the way for a great Union counterattack the next day *(National Guard Heritage)*

of the battle and orders up 62 cannon to bombard the Federals into submission. A tremendous pounding ensues, and Prentiss finally surrenders 2,000 battered survivors at 5:30 P.M. Beauregard is finally free to lead victorious Confederates against the final Union line.

Meanwhile, Grant returns to camp shortly after the fighting commences and begins to reorganize a coherent defense. The gallant stand of the Hornets' Nest grants him precious little time to sort out his shaken units, bring up new troops, and reestablish a defensive perimeter. He also orders the division of General Lew Wallace, stationed at Crump's Landing seven miles away, to march immediately toward Pittsburg Landing. As it turns out, that general botches his line of march and fails to arrive in a timely manner. Meanwhile, as the exhausted Confederates, low on ammunition and disorganized by intense combat push forward, they begin to lose impetus. Grant then strings his survivors out along a ridge crest fronting Pittsburg Landing, deploys his reserve artillery, and receives timely assistance from two navy gunboats on the Tennessee River. Beauregard briefly tests Grant's new line and judges it too compact and well defended to hit frontally with his exhausted soldiers.

He suspends the attack and determines to renew it in the morning. Unknown to the Confederates, Union positions are strengthened materially by the tardy arrival of Wallace's division that evening, along with elements of General Don C. Buell's Army of the Ohio. Grant, manifestly strengthened by this infusion of fresh troops and now enjoying numerical superiority, determines to strike first the following day.

NAVAL: The USS *Pursuit* captures the Confederate steamer *Florida* at North Bay, Florida.

The USS *Carondelet* drops farther down the Mississippi River on a reconnaissance foray from New Madrid, Missouri, to Tiptonville, where armed parties disembark and spike a Confederate shore battery.

Throughout the engagement at Shiloh, heavy and accurate fire from Federal gunboats USS *Tyler* and *Lexington* assists last-ditch Union defenses.

April 7

POLITICS: The U.S. government concludes a new agreement with Great Britain for more aggressive suppression of the slave trade.

SOUTH: Colonel Thomas J. Lucas leads the 16th Indiana on a reconnaissance over the Rappahannock River into Virginia.

Unions forces embark for an amphibious descent on Elizabeth City, North Carolina.

WEST: General John Pope lands four regiments across the Mississippi River to Tiptonville, Tennessee, severing the supply lines of Confederate-held Island No. 10. The garrison is now completely isolated.

General Ormsby M. Mitchel recruits noted Union spy James J. Andrews for a clandestine raid behind Confederate lines to sabotage railroad links between Atlanta, Georgia, and Chattanooga, Tennessee. Andrews then solicits 22 volunteers from General Joshua W. Sill's Ohio brigade and gradually slips them in by small teams to Marietta, Georgia.

The struggle at Shiloh resumes at 7:30 A.M. as Union forces under General Ulysses S. Grant, newly reinforced, mount a spirited counterattack to regain ground lost in the previous day's fighting. The Confederates under General Pierre G. T. Beauregard resist gamely but slowly yield to superior numbers. The blue tide advances inexorably across the field, and by 2:30, the Southerners are in full retreat back to Corinth, 23 miles away. Both sides then begin the grim business of tallying the results of their work.

Casualties at Shiloh shock both North and South alike due to their sheer enormity. Grant, with 65,000 men engaged, loses 1,754 killed, 8,408 wounded, and 2,885 missing (13,047) while the 44,400 Confederates present sustain 1,728 dead, 8,012 injured, and 959 missing (10,694). The grim reality of the Civil War and the carnage it ultimately entails finally emerge in bold relief. Worse, the Confederates staked everything on an all-out assault that failed. Once defeated, their position in the West erodes even further, and only the solitary bastion at Vicksburg, Mississippi, stands between the South and gradual dismemberment. Nor did the victorious Grant escape recriminations for such slaughter; even though Sherman technically commanded at the onset and is culpable of being surprised in camp, Grant's reputation as "the Butcher" begins to be heard in some quarters.

NAVAL: The Confederate raider CSS *Sumter* is laid up at Gibraltar and abandoned by Captain Raphael Semmes after experiencing boiler difficulties. In the course of its brief career, it seized no less than 18 Northern vessels.

The Federal ironclads USS *Pensacola* and *Mississippi* traverse the bar at the Passes and enter the Mississippi River, prior to moving against New Orleans, Louisiana.

The Federal gunboat USS *Pittsburgh* sails past Island No. 10 on the Mississippi River and joins the *Carondelet* in covering General John Pope's army, then ferrying to the Tennessee side. The gunboat squadron under Commodore Andrew H. Foote also captures heavy ordnance and several Confederate steamers moored there. He consequently receives a vote of thanks from Congress.

April 8

POLITICS: President Jefferson Davis proclaims martial law in East Tennessee to suppress activities of pro-Union inhabitants.

SOUTH: General Joseph Finegan assumes control of the Confederate Department of Middle and Eastern Florida.

WEST: General William W. Mackall surrenders the Confederate garrison of 4,500 men on Island No. 10 to General John Pope. Union forces sustain seven killed, 14 wounded, and seven missing, principally among naval personnel. They also capture 109 heavy cannon, four steamers, and vast quantities of military supplies while extending Union control of the Mississippi River as far south as Fort Pillow, Tennessee. Considering the difficult terrain and currents encountered, Pope performed well. Moreover, his victory constitutes another serious breech of Confederate defenses. President Abraham Lincoln consequently assigns him to command the newly organized Army of Virginia back east.

Federal troops under General Ulysses S. Grant advance from Pittsburg Landing, Tennessee, in pursuit of General Pierre G. T. Beauregard's withdrawing Confederates. General William T. Sherman pursues them briefly but is capably contained by General Nathan B. Forrest's rear guard.

SOUTHWEST: Pursuing Union forces under Colonel Edward R. S. Canby harry General Henry H. Sibley's Confederates as they retreat from Albuquerque, New Mexico Territory.

NAVAL: Commodore David G. Farragut runs the last of his West Gulf Blockading Squadron vessels over the Southwest Pass bar and into the Mississippi River. He then assembles 24 warships, mounting 200 large-caliber guns and 19 mortar schooners under Commander David D. Porter, at Head of Passes. But before steaming toward New Orleans, Louisiana, Farragut must first encounter and bypass Forts Jackson and St. Philip, 80 miles from the city.

April 9

POLITICS: President Abraham Lincoln, flummoxed by General George B. McClellan's lack of aggressiveness, confers with his cabinet over what to do. The chief executive then suggests several lines of attack for the Army of the Potomac to consider and entreats McClellan to attack immediately, insisting, "But you must act."

The Confederate Congress approves a conscription measure over the protest of many politicians who consider the practice a violation of their liberties.

WEST: Command of the Confederate Missouri State Guard passes to General Mosby M. Parsons.

NAVAL: Confederate secretary of the navy Stephen R. Mallory, convinced that the biggest threat to New Orleans, Louisiana, is the Mississippi River squadron of Commodore Andrew H. Foote, refuses to allow the Confederate squadron at Fort Pillow, Tennessee, to shift theaters.

Union forces evacuate Jacksonville, Florida, under the cover of USS *Ottawa, Pembina,* and *Ellen.*

April 10

POLITICS: President Abraham Lincoln signs a joint congressional resolution stipulating gradual emancipation of African-American slaves. It is aimed primarily at the border states and offers "pecuniary aid" in exchange for voluntary compliance.

SOUTH: General Joseph E. Johnston takes command of Confederate forces in the Peninsula District of Virginia, and reinforcements gradually bring Southern manpower up to 34,000. Johnston nonetheless remains pessimistic about resisting the Army of the Potomac, thrice his size, for long.

After weeks of methodical preparation, Union artillery commanded by Captain Quincy A. Gilmore commence shelling Fort Pulaski on Cockspur Island in Savannah harbor. This strategic post, boasting masonry walls seven and a half feet thick, is occupied by Colonel Charles H. Olmstead, 48 cannon, and a garrison of 385 Confederates. Gilmore, meanwhile, directs the placement of 11 batteries on Tybee Island, containing 36 heavy guns and mortars that ring the fort at a distance between 1,650 and 3,400 yards. Union general Thomas W. Sherman implores Olmstead to surrender, but he haughtily replies: "I am here to defend this fort, not to surrender it." Gilmore then gives the order to fire at 8:15 A.M., and his highly accurate, rifled Parrott cannons loose penetrating shells that systematically decimate Fort Pulaski's defenses. By nightfall several large breeches are observed in Olmstead's walls, through which Union shells begin to strike his reinforced gunpowder magazine.

WEST: General John M. Schofield assumes command of Union forces in Missouri while General Samuel R. Curtis heads the new District of Kansas.

NAVAL: The USS *Whitehead* captures the Confederate schooners *Comet* and *J. J. Crittenden* and the sloop *America* in Newbegun Creek, North Carolina.

A detachment from USS *Wabash* manned Battery Sigel during the capture of Fort Pulaski, Georgia. They are cordially invited to come ashore and participate by General David Hunter, overall army commander.

The USS *Keystone State* runs the British blockade-runner *Liverpool* aground at North Inlet, South Carolina, where it was burned by its crew.

Gunboat USS *Kanawha* seizes blockade-runners *Southern Independence, Victoria, Charlotte,* and *Cuba* off Mobile, Alabama.

April 11

POLITICS: Following the Senate's cue, the U.S. House of Representatives votes 93–39 to abolish slavery gradually in the District of Columbia.

SOUTH: Fort Pulaski, Georgia, surrenders to Union captain Quincy A. Gilmore following a heavy bombardment by 5,275 shells from nearby Tybee Island. Union losses are one killed while the Confederates sustain one dead, 13 wounded, and 360 captured. This battle marks the first tactical employment of long-range, rifled cannon with impressive results against masonry defenses. Moreover, the Union victory here jeopardizes the city of Savannah, Georgia, eliminating it as a blockade-running port.

WEST: General Henry W. Halleck supersedes General Ulysses S. Grant at Pittsburg Landing, Tennessee, although he still commands the District of West Tennessee. Leadership of the Army of the Tennessee temporarily reverts to General George H. Thomas.

Union forces under General Ormsby M. Mitchel sever the Memphis and Charleston Railroad by occupying Huntsville, Alabama. They defeat the Confederates of General Edmund Kirby-Smith en route, taking several hundred prisoners in the process.

NAVAL: The Confederate ironclad CSS *Virginia* under Commodore Josiah Tattnall suddenly reappears off Hampton Roads, Virginia. Escorting vessels CSS *Jamestown* and Raleigh under Captain John R. Tucker capture three Union transports but fail to bring on a second duel with the USS *Monitor* offshore.

April 12

SOUTH: General Joseph E. Johnston's command authority is enlarged to include the Departments of Norfolk and the Peninsula, Virginia.

General John B. Magruder's Confederate army at Yorktown, Virginia, is augmented by additional divisions under General James Longstreet, Daniel H. Hill, and Gustavus W. Smith. These are arrayed against the full might of the Army of the Potomac, then consisting of the II Corps of General Edwin V. Sumner, the III Corps of General Samuel Heintzelman, and the IV Corps under General Erasmus Keyes. General William B. Franklin's division, detached from I Corps, also hovers in reserve.

WEST: Cavalry dispatched by General Benjamin F. Kelley snares numerous Confederate operatives in Valley River and Boothville in western Virginia.

Major James J. Andrews and 22 Union volunteers steal the Confederate locomotive *General* and three freight cars at Big Shanty, Georgia, and then head north toward Chattanooga, Tennessee. Their mission is to destroy railroad bridges leading into the city, but the plan is thwarted by rainy weather. Worse, Confederate soldiers hotly pursue in another engine, and the chase continues for 90 miles. When the *General* finally runs out of steam and is abandoned, Andrews and his men flee to the woods where the majority are captured. Andrews and seven volunteers, seized out of uniform, are executed as spies on June 7, 1862, but eight men eventually escape captivity while the rest are exchanged. The raiders become the U.S. Army's first recipients of the Congressional Medal of Honor in March 1863. This affair enters popular folklore as the "Great Locomotive Chase."

NAVAL: Secretary of the Navy Gideon Welles implores President Abraham Lincoln to forbid the export of anthracite coal abroad and thus keep it out of Confederate hands. Since this fuel burns cleanly, it allows blockade-runners to approach ports without detection, whereas steam engines powered by regular coal belch forth black clouds more easily perceived at sea.

April 13

SOUTH: General David Hunter, commanding the vicinity of Fort Pulaski, Georgia, declares his region free of slavery and unilaterally begins to free all African Americans within his jurisdiction.

WEST: Federal troops under General Ormsby M. Mitchel occupy Decatur, Alabama, on the Tennessee River.

SOUTHWEST: Union troops under Colonel Edward R. S. Canby skirmish with retreating Confederates at Peralta, New Mexico Territory.

General James H. Carleton leads a column of troops from California into western Arizona and ultimately drives remaining Confederate forces out of New Mexico Territory.

NAVAL: USS *Beauregard* shells the Confederate garrison at Fort Brooke, Tampa Bay, Florida, after it refuses his surrender summons.

A coastal survey party under Ferdinand H. Gerdes begins to map the Mississippi River approaches below Forts Jackson and St. Philip.

Federal gunboats USS *Tyler* and *Lexington* convey Union troops from Shiloh, Tennessee, to Chickasaw, Alabama, and destroy a bridge operated by the Memphis and Charleston Railroad.

April 14

SOUTH: John C. Breckinridge and Thomas C. Hindman are appointed major generals, C.S.A.

A high-level war meeting convenes in Richmond, Virginia, whereby General Joseph E. Johnston, badly outnumbered by the 112,000 strong Army of the Potomac, pleads with superiors to abandon the Yorktown–Warwick River line before General George B. McClellan attacks in overwhelming strength. However, President Jefferson Davis and his chief military adviser, General Robert E. Lee, demur, observing that withdrawing necessitates the abandonment of Norfolk and its valuable naval facilities.

WEST: In Missouri, Union forces tangle with Confederate irregulars under William C. Quantrill.

NAVAL: The Potomac Flotilla sails down the Rappahannock River, Virginia, shelling Confederate positions and capturing three vessels.

Federal mortar boats under Commodore Andrew H. Foote commence bombarding Fort Pillow, Tennessee, on the Mississippi River. This fortification is located 60 miles south of Island No. 10 and guards the northern approaches to Memphis. Intermittent bombardment continues for the next seven weeks.

April 15

SOUTH: At a special war council held in Richmond, Virginia, President Jefferson Davis breaks the strategic impasse by ordering General Joseph E. Johnston to move his army to Yorktown on the Virginia Peninsula and reinforce General John B. Magruder. A somewhat disgruntled Johnston returns to his command and prepares to march.

A detachment of the 1st Maine Cavalry under Captain Robert F. Dyer is repulsed at Bealeton, Virginia.

WEST: Confederate troops commanded by General Earl Van Dorn are ordered to Memphis, Tennessee.

SOUTHWEST: Pursuing Union forces under Colonel Edward R. S. Canby continue skirmishing with General Henry H. Sibley's Confederates at Peralta, 20 miles south of Albuquerque, New Mexico Territory. The Southerners are bested in a series of running battles as they retire toward Fort Bliss.

NAVAL: The USS *Chenango,* anchored at New York, experiences a boiler explosion that kills 25 sailors.

The USS *Keystone State* captures the Confederate blockade-runner *Success* off Georgetown, South Carolina.

April 16

POLITICS: President Abraham Lincoln signs a bill outlawing slavery in the District of Columbia on a compensated basis—$300 per slave. However, slaves escaping from masters loyal to the Union still remain subject to return under the existing Fugitive Slave Law.

With Union forces only 10 miles from his capital and a stream of bad news from the West, President Jefferson Davis authorizes conscription to maintain Confederate military manpower levels. Consequently, all white males aged 18 to 35 become eligible for three years of service. This is the first conscription legislation in U.S. history.

SOUTH: Union General William F. Smith tests Confederate defenses on the Virginia Peninsula by probing Dam No. 1 along the Warwick River line. He then attacks at Burnt Chimneys with the 3rd, 4th, and 6th Vermont regiments and is repelled with 165 casualties. This small reverse convinces General George B. McClellan of the necessity to erect siege works to flush the defenders from their lines.

An advance to Whitemarsh Island, Georgia, by Union general Quincy A. Gilmore results in heavy skirmishing.

WEST: Union forces attack and occupy Tuscumbia, Alabama.

NAVAL: Commodore David G. Farragut begins to mass 17 warships of his West Gulf Blockading Squadron, including the gunboat squadron of Commodore David D. Porter, below Forts Jackson and St. Philip, Louisiana. These aged structures, one on each side of the Mississippi River, are situated 12 miles above Head of Passes, mount 90 cannon, and are further abetted by a "Mosquito Squadron" of small warships under Captain George N. Hollis. Unfortunately for the defenders, the waterway runs extremely high, which floods Confederate defensive positions and lifts Unions vessel above numerous obstacles placed in their path to block them.

April 17

SOUTH: General Irvin McDowell and his Federal troops skirmish near Falmouth, Virginia, and occupy neighboring Fredericksburg.

New Confederate reinforcements bring the strength of General Joseph E. Johnston's force along the Yorktown-Warwick River line up to 53,000. He nonetheless remains badly outnumbered by the nearby Army of the Potomac, which fields roughly twice as many troops.

WEST: Union forces under General Nathaniel P. Banks occupy Mount Jackson in western Virginia, following a skirmish at Rude's Hill. Confederate forces under General Thomas J. Jackson continue withdrawing before them.

The 36th Ohio under Major Ebenezer B. Andrews tangles with Confederate irregulars between Summerville and Addison, western Virginia.

Quick action by General Edmund Kirby-Smith's Confederates snares 475 Union stragglers at Woodson's Gap, Tennessee.

NAVAL: Commodore David G. Farragut's fleet of 17 warships begins to wend its way up the Mississippi River toward New Orleans, Louisiana. He is also accompanied by a flotilla of 20 mortar boats under Commander David D. Porter.

April 18

NORTH: In an attempt to promote younger, more vigorous leadership, Congress suspends seniority within the ranks of the Army Medical Bureau.

SOUTH: General Joseph Finegan takes charge of the Confederate Department of Middle and East Florida.

General Irvin McDowell marches south and occupies the towns of Falmouth and Yorktown, Virginia.

WEST: General Robert E. Lee orders General Edward Johnson and his Army of the Northwest to coordinate his movements in the Shenandoah Valley.

NAVAL: Landing parties from the USS *Crusader* attack Edisto Island, South Carolina.

Commodore David G. Farragut dispatches Commander David D. Porter with 20 mortar boats to bombard Forts Jackson and St. Philip on the Mississippi River. Porter, convinced he can neutralize these positions with firepower alone, pelts them with 200-pound mortar shells for the next five days. Farragut's movement positions him only 70 miles below the strategic port of New Orleans, Louisiana, and Confederates pin their hopes on the two old forts and an array of sunken hulks and river chains to prevent further Union progress upstream.

April 19

SOUTH: The forces of Generals Ambrose E. Burnside and Benjamin Huger tangle at South Mills, Camden County, South Carolina.

WEST: Sparta in western Virginia is occupied by Federal troops under General Nathaniel P. Banks. Confederates under General Thomas J. Jackson, meanwhile, strike their encampment at Rude Hill and head farther south.

NAVAL: The USS *Huron* captures the Confederate schooner *Glide* off Charleston, South Carolina.

Artillery fire from Fort Jackson, Louisiana, sinks the Federal mortar boat USS *Maria J. Carlton.*

Under the cover of darkness, the USS *Itasca* and *Pinola* advance below Forts Jackson and St. Philip to cut the chain and remove obstructions placed on the Mississippi River. They are assisted greatly by the absence of fire rafts that would have illuminated them as targets—a major Confederate oversight. The river gradually is rendered navigable for Commodore David G. Farragut's fleet.

April 20

SOUTH: General Irvin McDowell confers with President Abraham Lincoln at Aquia Creek, Virginia, and subsequently accompanies him to Washington, D.C.

WEST: General Edward Johnson's Confederate army of the Northwest retreats eastward from Shenandoah Mountain, western Virginia, pressured by a larger Union forces under General John C. Frémont.

NAVAL: The Potomac Flotilla captures nine Confederate vessels at the mouth of the Rappahannock River, Virginia.

April 21

POLITICS: To offset the manpower advantages of the North, the Confederate government authorizes creation of guerrilla formations by passing the Partisan Ranger Act and then adjourns its first session.

Members of the Brownlow family and several other Union sympathizers are evicted from Confederate-held East Tennessee.

WEST: Union forces under General John Pope, having secured Island No. 10, cross back over the Mississippi to assist ongoing efforts in Tennessee.

NAVAL: The Federal gunboat USS *Tyler* seizes the Confederate steamer *Alfred Robb* on the Tennessee River.

April 22

POLITICS: Secretary of War Edwin M. Stanton appoints engineer and inventor Herman Haupt to serve as chief of construction and transportation for U.S. military railroads. The appointment proves fortuitous, and Haupt discharges his duties with efficiency and dispatch.

SOUTH: Advancing Union forces occupy Harrisonburg, Virginia.

General William B. Franklin's division arrives at Fortress Monroe, Virginia, to reinforce the Army of the Potomac.

WEST: General Nathaniel P. Banks occupies Luray in western Virginia.

NAVAL: Armed boats from the USS *Arthur* capture three Confederate vessels at Aransas Pass, Texas, and then just as quickly yield them to attacking enemy troops.

April 23

NAVAL: The USS *Lockwood, Whitehead,* and *Putnam* sink a schooner at the mouth of the Albemarle and Chesapeake Canal near Elizabeth City, North Carolina, closing another useful waterway to the South.

Commodore David G. Farragut, impatient for success and concluding that the bombardment of Forts Jackson and St. Philip is having no effect, decides to run his entire fleet past the fortifications at night.

April 24

NAVAL: The CSS *Nashville,* crammed with 60,000 stands of arms and 40 tons of gunpowder, successfully runs the Union blockade and slips into Wilmington, North Carolina.

At 2:00 A.M. in the predawn darkness, Commodore David G. Farragut runs his fleet of 17 vessels past Forts Jackson and St. Philip on the Mississippi River, in

Flag Officer Farragut's squadron passes the forts on the Mississippi, April 24, 1862, and the U.S. frigate *Mississippi* destroys the rebel ram *Manassas*. Lithograph by Currier & Ives *(Library of Congress)*

three divisions. Confederate defenders under General Johnson K. Duncan unleash a heavy cannonade, but they inflict very little loss. Farragut's flagship, USS *Hartford*, is briefly endangered by a fire raft while the USS *Varuna* is rammed and sinks. But in the ensuing scrape, Commander John K. Mitchell's Southern squadron, including CSS *Warrior, Stonewall Jackson, General Lovell*, and *Breckinridge*, along with steamers *Star, Belle Algerine*, and gunboat *General Quitman*, all succumb to concentrated Union fire. The armored ram CSS *Manassas* is also run ashore and destroyed. With this single, decisive stroke, the fate of New Orleans, Louisiana, is decided. Farragut then sails directly down to the helpless city, intent on bombarding it into submission. Union losses tally 39 killed and 146 wounded while the Confederates sustain nine dead and 33 injured.

April 25
NORTH: George H. Thomas is promoted to major general, U.S. Army.
SOUTH: Federal forces under General John G. Parke commence the bombardment of Fort Macon on Bogue Banks Island off Beaufort, North Carolina. The Confederate garrison only could sputter in reply with a few old cannon while sustaining 25 casualties. At length, Colonel Moses J. White surrenders, and 300 Southerners pass into captivity. The main Union force under General Ambrose E. Burnside is now at liberty to conduct deep forays into the surrounding countryside.

General David Hunter proclaims martial law in his Department of the South (South Carolina, Georgia, Florida).

Confederate general Mansfield Lovell and his 4,000 soldiers quickly slip out of New Orleans, Louisiana, and escape inland before Union occupation forces arrive.

WEST: Charles F. Smith, a talented Union general, dies of a septic leg infection at Savannah, Tennessee.

NAVAL: The USS *Maratanza* bombards Gloucester and Yorktown, Virginia, to assist the Army of the Potomac.

The squadron of Commander Samuel Lockwood, consisting of USS *Daylight, State of Georgia, Chippewa,* and *Gemsbok,* bombards Fort Macon, North Carolina, into submission. Confederate blockade-runners *Alliance* and *Gondar* are also captured.

The USS *Santiago de Cuba* captures the Confederate blockade-runner *Ella Warley* off Port Royal, South Carolina.

The Union flotilla under Commodore David G. Farragut captures the city of New Orleans, Louisiana, following a brief duel with Confederate gunners at English Turn. The Mississippi River is running high and enables the fleet to point its guns over the levee. Union landing parties are met nonetheless by angry, hostile demonstrations at the water's edge while hundreds of valuable cotton bales are burned to prevent capture. But the Confederacy loses its largest and wealthiest seaport while the North acquires a splendid base for operations directly into the Southern heartland.

NAVAL: The uncompleted CSS *Mississippi,* one of the largest and most powerful ironclads afloat, is destroyed by Confederate authorities at New Orleans, Louisiana, to prevent its capture.

The USS *Katahdin* captures the Confederate schooner *John Gilpin* below New Orleans, Louisiana.

April 26

POLITICS: President Abraham Lincoln pays a courtesy call on the French warship *Gassendi,* anchored at the Washington Navy Yard.

NORTH: Alfred H. Terry is appointed a brigadier general, U.S. Army.

SOUTH: Fort Macon, North Carolina, is occupied by Union forces under General John G. Parke.

WEST: Union forces under General Nathaniel P. Banks advance into New Market, western Virginia.

NAVAL: The USS *Onward* destroys the Confederate schooner *Chase* off Raccoon Key, South Carolina.

The USS *Flambeau* captures the Confederate blockade-runner *Active* off Stono Inlet, South Carolina.

The USS *Santiago de Cuba* captures the Confederate schooner *Mersey* off Charleston, South Carolina.

The USS *Uncas* captures the Confederate schooner *Belle* off Charleston, South Carolina.

April 27

SOUTH: General Joseph E. Johnston orders General Benjamin Huger to evacuate Norfolk, Virginia, and salvage as much equipment as possible from the Gosport Navy Yard.

NAVAL: The USS *Mercedita* captures the Confederate steamer *Bermuda* northeast of Abaco.

The USS *Wamsutta* and *Potomska* trade fire with dismounted Confederate cavalry at Wookville Island, Riceboro River, Georgia.

U.S. naval forces accept the surrender of Fort Livingston on Bastian Bay, Louisiana, and crew members from the USS *Kittatinny* hoist the Stars and Stripes flag over its ramparts. Nearby Forts Quitman, Pike, and Wood also capitulate that afternoon.

April 28

NORTH: James H. Carleton is appointed brigadier general, U.S. Army.

SOUTH: General John H. Forney assumes command of the Confederate Department of Alabama and West Florida.

WEST: General John Pope directs a skirmish against Confederates at Monterey, Tennessee.

NAVAL: Confederate Forts Jackson and St. Philip on the Mississippi River mutiny against the commanding general, John K. Duncan and surrender 900 prisoners to Union forces under Commander David D. Porter. The unfinished ironclad CSS *Louisiana,* the *Defiance,* and the *McRae* are also burned to prevent capture.

The British steamer *Oreto* arrives at Nassau, Bahamas, where Confederate sailors wait to man it. It eventually emerges as the CSS *Florida.*

April 29

SOUTH: A skittish general Joseph E. Johnston, cognizant of the vast array of Union siege artillery being mounted against his army along the Yorktown–Warwick River line, informs superiors that he is withdrawing inland as soon as it becomes practical. Johnston reasons that it is better to sacrifice Norfolk than his entire army and suggests a new concentration closer to Richmond.

Timothy Webster, a talented spy working for Allan Pinkerton's Federal Secret Service, is hanged by Confederate authorities at Richmond, Virginia.

The 29th Massachusetts skirmishes at Batchelder's Creek, North Carolina.

City officials formally surrender New Orleans, Louisiana, to Federal authorities. Raising of the U.S. flag over the Customs House arouses much indignation from the inhabitants.

WEST: General Thomas J. Jackson departs Staunton, western Virginia, by dispatching cavalry under Colonel Turner Ashby toward Harrisonburg while he leads the main force toward Port Republic.

Union forces occupy Purdy, Tennessee.

General Henry W. Halleck prepares to move from Pittsburg Landing, Tennessee, against Confederate forces under General Pierre G. T. Beauregard at Corinth, Mississippi. Halleck commands in excess of 100,000 troops.

NAVAL: Landing parties from the gunboat USS *E. B. Hale* destroy a Confederate battery on the Dawho River, South Carolina. On the return route, their vessel is ambushed downstream by troops under General Nathan G. Evans, but Lieutenant Alexander C. Rhind, who previously orders his crew and passengers to lay on the deck, sustains no losses and returns to Edisto Island unharmed.

The USS *Kanawha* captures the British blockade-runner *Annie* in the Gulf of Mexico.

April 30

WEST: Confederate forces under General Thomas J. Jackson march from Elk Run, western Virginia, toward Staunton in a driving rain. There, he intends to confront the 20,000-man army under General John C. Frémont, then advancing from the west. For the next four days, Jackson hounds his command as they cover 92 miles on foot and then ride another 25 miles by rail. This proves one of the most impressive forced marches of the entire war and garners to troops involved the sobriquet of Jackson's "Foot Cavalry."

General Henry W. Halleck finalizes a reorganization of his Armies of the Mississippi to include General Ulysses S. Grant as second in command, George H. Thomas and the Army of the Tennessee (right wing), John Pope and the Army of the Mississippi (left wing), John A. McClernand (reserve wing), and Don C. Buell and the Army of the Ohio. This aggregate of 120,000 troops is the largest military force ever assembled in North America to date. Halleck then orders a concerted, cautious advance on the strategic railroad junction at Corinth, Mississippi, presently defended by 53,000 Confederates under General Pierre G. T. Beauregard.

NAVAL: The USS *Santiago de Cuba* captures the Confederate schooner *Maria* off Port Royal, South Carolina.

May 1

NORTH: William T. Sherman is appointed major general, U.S. Army.

WEST: General Richard S. Ewell takes his 8,500-man division to Swift Run Gap, western Virginia, where he relieves forces under General Thomas J. Jackson.

SOUTH: General George B. McClellan begins to deploy heavy siege ordnance to facilitate the fall of Yorktown, Virginia.

New Orleans, Louisiana, is occupied formally by 15,000 Federal troops under General Benjamin F. Butler, who ushers in a period of controversial and acrimonious administration.

WEST: Union troops under General Jacob D. Cox skirmish with Confederates in the Stone River valley in western Virginia.

NAVAL: The USS *Marblehead* bombards Confederate positions at Yorktown, Virginia.

The USS *Jamestown* captures the British blockade-runner *Intended* off the North Carolina coast.

The USS *Huron* captures the Confederate schooner *Albert* off Charleston, South Carolina.

The USS *Onward* forces the crew of the Confederate schooner *Sarah* to scuttle their own vessel.

The USS *Hatteras* captures the Confederate schooner *Magnolia* near Berwick Bay, Louisiana.

May 2

NORTH: John Gibbon is appointed brigadier general, U.S. Army.

SOUTH: Edward Stanly becomes Federal military governor of North Carolina.

The Army of the Potomac, stalled before illusionary defenses along the Yorktown–Warwick River line in Virginia's Yorktown Peninsula, readies a huge battery of more than 100 heavy guns and mortars. General George B. McClellan prepares to blast the Confederates out of their entrenchments rather than risk heavy casualties from a frontal assault.

WEST: General James G. Blunt takes charge of the newly reconstituted Department of Kansas.

NAVAL: The USS *Restless* captures the British blockade-runner *Flash* off the South Carolina coast.

May 3

SOUTH: General Joseph E. Johnston begins to withdraw 55,000 Confederate troops from Yorktown, Virginia, before heavy Union siege ordnance starts to shoot. At midnight, Southern artillery erupts along the line to distract Union attention from the operation. General George B. McClellan, observing Confederate works the following day, is surprised but relieved that Johnston's army has vanished. The Army of the Potomac now begins to move up the Yorktown Peninsula as the retreating Southerners funnel through Williamsburg toward Richmond.

WEST: Skirmishing occurs between General Henry W. Halleck and General Pierre G. T. Beauregard at Farmington, Mississippi, as Union forces begin their belated advance on Corinth.

NAVAL: The USS *R. R. Cuyler* captured the Confederate schooner *Jane* off Tampa Bay, Florida.

May 4

SOUTH: After a month-long siege, Union forces finally occupy the Confederate Yorktown-Warwick River line of Virginia's Yorktown Peninsula. General George B. McClellan methodically begins to pursue the enemy by advancing upon the old colonial capital of Williamsburg in overwhelming strength. The movement of both sides is hampered by continual downpours, which turn the roads to mud.

Skirmishing erupts between cavalry forces of Generals George B. Stoneman and J. E. B. Stuart near Williamsburg, Virginia. Fighting there induces a rear guard to form under General James Longstreet, who occupies a prepositioned line of redoubts centering on a bastion dubbed Fort Magruder. The Confederates enjoy the better of the day's fighting once General Lafayette McLaws charges and overturns Union cavalry and artillery commanded by General Philip St. George Cooke.

WEST: Skirmishing continues between General Henry W. Halleck and Pierre G. T. Beauregard at Farmington Heights, Mississippi.

SOUTHWEST: Confederate forces evacuate Tucson, New Mexico Territory, ahead of the "California column" of General James H. Carleton. Meanwhile, the main

Southern force under General Henry H. Sibley straggles into El Paso, Texas, after an arduous, failed endeavor.

NAVAL: The USS *Corwin* captures the Confederate schooner *Director* in the York River, Virginia.

Crew members of the USS *Wachusetts* hoist the U.S. flag over Gloucester Point, Virginia, while two Confederate schooners are captured.

The USS *Calhoun* captures the Confederate schooner *Charles Henry* of St. Joseph, Louisiana, and also raises the American flag over nearby Fort Pike.

The USS *Somerset* captures the Confederate steamer *Circassian* at sea.

May 5

POLITICS: President Abraham Lincoln and Secretary of War Edwin M. Stanton board the steamer *Miami* and sail to Hampton Roads, Virginia, to prod General George B. McClellan into greater action.

Congress authorizes creation of the Department of Agriculture.

SOUTH: A Union force of 41,000 men commanded by General Edwin V. Sumner confronts a determined Confederate rear guard numbering 32,000 at Williamsburg, Virginia. Sumner initially brings up two divisions under Generals Joseph Hooker and William F. Smith, who deploy to attack the defenders head on. However, Confederate forces under General James Longstreet are positioned ably at Fort Magruder in the center of the line and repulse Hooker's onslaught with heavy casualties. At this juncture, the commanding general, Joseph E. Johnston, gallops up with reinforcements, although he allows Longstreet to continue fighting. Longstreet, sensing confusion in Union ranks, suddenly launches a sharp counterattack against their left, pushing Hooker's men back in confusion and capturing several cannon. For several desperate minutes, it appears that his division might be destroyed piecemeal, save for the appearance of reinforcements under General Philip Kearny, who promptly drives the disorganized Southerners back inside their works.

On the Confederate left, events shape up more favorably for the North. General Smith detaches General William S. Hancock's brigade on a two-hour, circuitous march around Longstreet's flank, and by dint of adroit maneuvering, he suddenly appears behind the Confederate line at about 3:00 P.M. Hancock then pours in a heavy artillery fire on the defenders until two Confederate brigades under General Jubal A. Early and Daniel H. Hill are ordered up to outflank him. Unfortunately, both commanders are disoriented by the intervening march and deploy directly in front of Hancock's well-positioned troops. The aggressive Early and Hill nonetheless launch disjointed frontal assaults against the Union line, which are blasted back with heavy losses. But despite this tactical success, Sumner fails to follow it up with a decisive attack of his own, and an impasse settles across the battlefield. Fighting stops by nightfall, the Confederates withdraw unmolested, Johnston resumes his retrograde movement back toward Richmond.

Williamsburg, the first encounter of the Peninsula campaign, is both indecisive and characterized by heavy casualties: the Union suffers 456 killed, 1,410 wounded, and 373 missing (2,239) while the Confederacy lose 133 dead and 1,570 injured (1,703). Thanks to Sumner's mishandling of events, Union forces waged a contest that they should have won easily, whereas the Confederates again manage to avoid decisive defeat.

WEST: General Thomas J. Jackson's Confederates occupy Staunton in western Virginia, where he unites with General Edward Johnson's Army of the Northwest. Both men then advance with 10,000 men against nearby Union forces under General Robert H. Milroy.

NAVAL: An armed boat from the USS *Corwin* captures the Confederate sloop *Water Witch* near Gloucester, Virginia.

The USS *Calhoun* captures the Confederate schooner *Rover* on Lake Pontchartrain, Louisiana.

May 6

SOUTH: Williamsburg, Virginia, is occupied by the Army of the Potomac under General George B. McClellan.

WEST: General Thomas J. Jackson bests Union troops under General Nathaniel P. Banks in a heavy skirmish at Harrisonburg, western Virginia, and then marches his Confederates on a 35-mile trek through the mountains toward McDowell. Banks, meanwhile, withdraws in confusion to New Market.

NAVAL: The USS *Ottawa* seizes the Confederate schooner *General C. C. Pinckney* off Charleston, South Carolina.

The USS *Calhoun* captures the Confederate steamer *Whiteman* on Lake Pontchartrain, Louisiana.

May 7

SOUTH: Union and Confederate forces under Generals William B. Franklin and Gustavus W. Smith clash at Eltham's Landing, Virginia, to contest the road from Yorktown to Richmond. Franklin lands part of his division on the south bank of the York River to harass the Confederate left flank as it withdraws from Williamsburg. Smith, tasked with guarding the passage of the entire Confederate baggage train, is cognizant of the danger posed by Franklin's presence and orders General William C. Whiting's division to dislodge him. The Confederates, particularly General John B. Hood's Texas brigade, press the Union pickets hard, pushing them through the woods and under the cover of gunboats in the river. At that point Whiting relents and withdraws, and Franklin's men do not follow. The Confederate wagon train thereby retires intact. Southern losses amount to 48, whereas the Union sustains 186, including 46 captured.

The 6th Pennsylvania Cavalry under Major Robert Morris conducts a reconnaissance toward Mulberry Point on the James River, Virginia.

WEST: General Thomas J. Jackson nudges his footsore host from Staunton to the outskirts of McDowell, western Virginia, tangling with the pickets of General Robert H. Milroy's brigade en route. As the 10,000 Confederates deploy to engage the next morning, Milroy receives timely reinforcements in the form of General Robert C. Schenk's brigade, which brings Union numbers up to 6,000.

General Braxton Bragg gains command of the Confederate Army of Mississippi.

NAVAL: President Abraham Lincoln visits and examines the USS *Monitor* off Fortress Monroe, Virginia.

USS *Wachusetts, Chocura,* and *Sebago* ascend the York River and assist the landing of army troops at West Point, Virginia.

The USS *Currituck* captures the Confederate vessels *American Coaster* and *Planter* in the Pamunkey River, Virginia.

May 8

SOUTH: Union forces begin to occupy Baton Rouge, Louisiana.

WEST: 10,000 Confederates under General Thomas J. Jackson move forward to engage 6,000 Federal troops under Generals Robert H. Milroy and Robert C. Schenk at McDowell, western Virginia. Union troops initially are posted near the town, dominated by nearby Setlinger's Hill. When Milroy perceives Jackson's troop advancing toward that strategic point, he considers retreating until Schenk convinces him to attack and cover their withdrawal. Commencing at 4:30 P.M., Union troops charge up the heavily wooded hill, firing into an open copse into which Southerners deployed and inflicting heavy casualties. But Confederates under General Edward Johnson's Army of the Northwest grimly repulse every attack and hold their ground as Jackson labors to bring up additional troops. After a surprisingly stiff fight of four hours, Milroy finally issues orders to retreat. This is successfully accomplished without Southern interference.

Confederate cavalry under Colonel Turner Ashby mount a pursuit, but the bulk of Union forces escape intact. McDowell is an inauspicious debut for Jackson's celebrated Valley Campaign, for his losses are twice that of his opponents— 116 killed and 300 wounded, and 4 missing to 34 Union dead, 220 injured, and 5 missing. Southerners were further deprived of the services of General Johnson, an excellent commander, who is seriously injured and requires a lengthy convalescence. Consequently, his Army of the Northwest is absorbed into Jackson's Army of the Valley.

General William W. Loring is assigned to command the Army of Southwest Virginia.

Union forces under General Henry W. Halleck pause within a few miles of their objective at Corinth, Mississippi, as his "offensive" assumes more the nature of a siege.

NAVAL: The USS *Monitor, Dacotah, Naugatuck, Seminole,* and *Susquehanna* bombard Confederate batteries at Sewell's Point, Virginia, under the direction of President Abraham Lincoln, who also orders the monitor *Galena* up the James River to support General George B. McClellan.

A landing party from the USS *Iroquois* captures the city of Baton Rouge, Louisiana, and also seizes the local arsenal.

Three rams of the Confederate River Defense Fleet briefly sortie on the Mississippi River from Fort Pillow, Tennessee, but they quickly withdraw after confronting larger Union gunboats.

May 9

SOUTH: President Abraham Lincoln diplomatically admonishes General George B. McClellan for not moving more vigorously on the Confederate capital at Richmond, Virginia.

Confederate forces begin to evacuate the port of Norfolk, Virginia, where great quantities of valuable supplies are abandoned.

General David Hunter declares all African-American slaves in the Department of the South (Florida, Georgia, South Carolina) emancipated. Furthermore, all willing slaves are to be armed and incorporated into the military.

Retreating Confederate forces burn and evacuate the navy yard at Pensacola, Florida, destroying the unfinished ironclad CSS *Fulton* in the process.

WEST: General Thomas J. Jackson pursues Federal forces fleeing toward Franklin, western Virginia.

Skirmishing continues between the forces of General Henry W. Halleck and Pierre G. T. Beauregard near Corinth, Mississippi, as Union forces continue inching toward their objective.

NAVAL: Commodore Andrew H. Foote, wounded at the capture of Fort Donelson, is relieved by Captain Charles H. Davis above Fort Pillow, Tennessee.

May 10

SOUTH: The Gosport Navy Yard at Norfolk, Virginia, is occupied by Union forces under General John E. Wool, whose movements are partially directed from offshore by President Abraham Lincoln. The mighty ram CSS *Virginia* now is deprived of a berth as it draws too much water to be sequestered up the James River.

Confederate forces, informed of the fall of New Orleans, promptly evacuate Pensacola, Florida. Union forces under General Lewis G. Arnold then reclaim the base and the navy yard, which functions as a supply depot for various blockading squadrons.

WEST: Union force prevail in a skirmish with Confederates at Bloomfield, Missouri, and capture their supplies.

The impasse continues outside Corinth, Mississippi, as Union forces slowly advance.

NAVAL: The ironclad USS *New Ironsides* is launched at Philadelphia, Pennsylvania.

The USS *Unadilla* captures the Confederate schooner *Mary Theresa* off Charleston, South Carolina.

The scratch-built Confederate River Defense Fleet of eight converted steam rams under Captain James E. Montgomery bravely sorties at Plum Run Bend on the Mississippi River, just north of Fort Pillow, Tennessee. He is seriously outgunned, and his vessels are lightly armed and protected by cotton bales, but their relatively high speed gives them tactical advantages in cramped waters. He then engages seven U.S. ironclads under Commodore Charles H. Davis in one of few squadron actions of the Civil War. Montgomery appears suddenly off Craigshead Point, and he directly attacks the gunboat USS *Cincinnati* and *Gunboat No. 16*. The *Cincinnati* is rammed several times by CSS *General Bragg, General Sterling Price,* and *General Sumter,* yet fights valiantly and inflicts considerable damage before sinking in shallow water. Montgomery's ships then move up to meet Davis's ironclads as they move downstream to engage. The *Mound City* is rammed by the *General Van Dorn,* losing its bow, and grounds itself to avoid sinking. But once the heavy ironclad *Carondelet* moves into firing range, it punishes the Confederates with rifled cannon fire. *General Sumter, Colonel Levell,* and *General Van Dorn* all sustain serious damage before Montgomery signals them to withdraw back to Fort Pillow. The *Cincinnati* and *Mound City* are raised subsequently and repaired but, in view of this rough experience, Davis appeals to the Navy Department for several of the speedy, new Ellet rams.

May 11
WEST: Colonel John H. Morgan's Confederate cavalry seize a train of the Louisville and Nashville Railroad at Cave City, Kentucky.

NAVAL: Because the CSS *Virginia* draws too much water to operate up the James River, Commodore Josiah Tattnall scuttles it off Craney Island, Virginia, to prevent capture. The Northern Blockading Fleet under Commodore Louis M. Goldsborough now enjoys unfettered passage upriver as far as Drewry's Bluff. He makes immediate preparations to dispatch an expedition in the direction of Richmond, Virginia.

The USS *Bainbridge* captures the Confederate schooner *Newcastle* in the Atlantic.

The USS *Kittatinny* captures the British blockade-runner *Julia* off the Southwest Pass, Mississippi River.

The USS *Hatteras* captures the Confederate steamer *Governor A. Mouton* at Berwick Bay, Louisiana.

May 12
POLITICS: President Abraham Lincoln declares the captured ports of Beaufort, North Carolina, Port Royal, South Carolina, and New Orleans, Louisiana, open to trade. He hopes that the resumption of commercial activities will encourage and strengthen political bonds to the North.

Pro-Union sympathizers hold a convention in Nashville, Tennessee, under the watchful eye of Union forces.

SOUTH: The Army of the Potomac under General George B. McClellan advances to White House, Virginia, coming within 22 miles of the Confederate capital at Richmond.

WEST: General Thomas J. Jackson's pursuit of Union forces fleeing from McDowell, western Virginia, falters due to rain and mud. He thereupon stops at Franklin and turns east to confront advancing columns under General Nathaniel P. Banks.

Troops under General Henry W. Halleck seize Natchez, Mississippi, but their advance on Corinth sputters into a continuing series of skirmishes at Farmington.

NAVAL: The USS *Maratanza* and other gunboats sail up the Pamunkey River in support of the Army of the Potomac.

Crew members of the former CSS *Virginia* are collected under Lieutenant Catesby Ap Roger Jones at Drewry's Bluff on the James River, where they man an artillery battery. This is a formidable position, rising 100 feet above the river and only seven miles downriver from Richmond, Virginia. At length, they are joined by General George W. C. Lee, engineering officer and eldest son of General Robert E. Lee, who supervises the construction of redoubts and also directs the placement of numerous hulks in the river to block any Union passage.

May 13

SOUTH: The seemingly inexorable approach of the Army of the Potomac toward Richmond places the Confederate capital in a panic. President Jefferson Davis sends his wife Varina out of the city for safety.

Martial law is declared in Charleston, South Carolina.

WEST: Union troops under General John C. Frémont occupy Franklin, western Virginia, as Confederates under General Thomas J. Jackson withdraw through the Shenandoah Valley.

Rogersville, Alabama, is captured by Federal troops under General Ormsby M. Mitchel.

NAVAL: Harbor pilot Robert Smalls and eight fellow African-American consorts abscond with the Confederate steamer *Planter* and sail it from Charleston Harbor, South Carolina, before surrendering to the USS *Onward* offshore.

The USS *Bohio* captures the Confederate schooner *Deer Island* in the Mississippi Sound.

The USS *Calhoun* captures the Confederate gunboat *Corypheus* at Bayou Bonfouca, Louisiana.

The USS *Iroquois* and *Oneida* under Commander David G. Farragut capture and occupy Natchez, Mississippi, as Union forces gradually move toward the citadel of Vicksburg.

May 14

SOUTH: After skirmishing at Gaines's Cross Roads, Union forces halt at the White House on the Pamunkey River, only 20 miles from Richmond, Virginia. General George B. McClellan, though enjoying numerical superiority over his adversaries, awaits additional reinforcements from General Irwin McDowell.

NAVAL: The USS *Calhoun* captures the Confederate schooner *Venice* on Lake Pontchartrain, Louisiana.

May 15

SOUTH: As General George B. McClellan closes in on Richmond, Virginia, Confederate forces under General Joseph E. Johnston retire along the Chickahominy River to within three miles of the capital.

The 15th Massachusetts under Colonel Thomas J. C. Armory scouts and skirmishes at Trenton Bridge and Pollocksville, North Carolina.

Rude behavior by New Orleans ladies toward Union occupiers angers General Benjamin F. Butler and prompts him to issue his infamous General Order No. 28, the so-called Woman Order. This stipulates that any woman disposed to act disrespectfully toward Union soldiers will be arrested and treated as a prostitute. The act triggers waves of outrage and indignation across the South—and Butler is ultimately threatened with hanging if apprehended. For this reason, he gains the infamous moniker of "Beast Butler."

WEST: General Thomas J. Jackson's Confederates depart McDowell, western Virginia, and return to the Shenandoah Valley.

General Henry Heth, following the defeat of a Confederate detachment under General Humphrey Marshall, falls back on Jackson's River Depot in western Virginia.

General John C. Frémont conducts small actions at Princeton and Ravenswood, western Virginia.

NAVAL: The armed vessel designated "290"—destined to become the infamous CSS *Alabama*—is launched at Liverpool, England.

Commodore John Rodgers leads the ironclads USS *Monitor, Galena,* and *Naugatuck* up the James River, accompanied by three wooden warships. En route, they encounter formidable Confederate defensives along Drewry's Bluff, seven miles from Richmond, Virginia, and give battle. Southern artillery, manned mostly by naval personnel under Commander Ebenezer Ferrand and enjoying a clear advantage of position, unleash a devastating plunging fire. The Union vessels scarcely can elevate their guns high enough to fire back in return. During a four-hour engagement, *Galena* is struck 40 times and is seriously damaged, losing 13 killed and 11 wounded. The *Naugatuck* also suffers when its 100-pound Parrott gun explodes while firing. Wooden gunboats *Aroostoock* and *Port Royal* wisely shy away from the proceedings and hover out of range. Seriously outgunned and unable to circumvent obstacles in his path, Rodgers disengages and limps back to Norfolk—Richmond is saved. For heroism under fire, Corporal John B. Mackie also becomes the first member of the U.S. Marine Corps eligible for the Congressional Medal of Honor.

The USS *Sea Foam* under Matthew Vassar captures the Confederate sloops *Sarah* and *New Eagle* off Ship Island, Mississippi.

May 16

NORTH: The venerable John E. Wool is promoted to major general.

SOUTH: General George B. McClellan establishes his headquarters at the stately mansion at the White House, Virginia, on the Pamunkey River. The property was formerly owned by General Robert E. Lee.

Union and Confederate forces clash briefly near Princeton, Virginia.

General Benjamin F. Butler continues tightening the screws at New Orleans, Louisiana, by closing down the newspapers *Bee* and *Delta.*

WEST: Federal troops capture the Confederate steamer *Daniel E. Miller* at Hornersville, Missouri.

NAVAL: Union naval forces under Commander Samuel P. Lee ascend the Mississippi River, pausing only to bombard Grand Gulf, Mississippi, en route.

May 17

SOUTH: General Irvin McDowell's I Corps, stationed at Fredericksburg, Virginia, finally is ordered south against the Confederate capital at Richmond, in concert with the Army of the Potomac.

WEST: Union troops under General Jacob D. Cox commence to move across the Flat Top Mountains of western Virginia, with a view toward severing the Virginia and Tennessee Railroad. To prevent this, General Humphrey Marshall assembles two brigades under himself and General Henry Heth, with which he prepares to assault Cox's headquarters at Princeton. Marshall plans to attack from the east on the following day while Heth is ordered to strike from the south. But Marshall arrives at Princeton that night and, detecting weak Union defenses, attacks and easily captures the town with support. He then learns from captured papers that additional Union forces were en route and falls back. Heth never rendezvoused as ordered, but Cox, fearing himself outnumbered, withdraws from Princeton completely. Thus the Virginia and Tennessee Railroad is spared while Humphrey's aggressive move captures 29 Union prisoners.

General Henry W. Halleck continues his snail-like approach to Corinth, Mississippi, stopping today to skirmish with Confederates at Russell's House.

NAVAL: The USS *Sebago* and *Currituck* escort the troop transport *Seth Low* several miles down the Pamunkey River, Virginia, forcing Confederates to burn or scuttle 17 vessels to prevent capture. However, the river at this point becomes so narrow that the gunboats are obliged to run backward for several miles before turning their bows around.

The USS *Hatteras* captures the Confederate sloop *Poody* off Vermillion Bay, Louisiana.

May 18

SOUTH: General William B. Franklin takes charge of the VI Corps, Army of the Potomac, while General Fitz John Porter assumes command of the V Corps.

WEST: Advancing Confederates under General Thomas J. Jackson skirmish with General Nathaniel P. Banks at Woodstock, western Virginia.

NAVAL: The USS *Hunchback* and *Shawsheen* capture the Confederate schooner *Smoot* at Potecasi Creek, North Carolina.

Commander Stephen P. Lee demands the surrender of Vicksburg, Mississippi, but Confederate general Martin L. Smith defiantly refuses. More than a year will lapse before the "Gibraltar of the West" succumbs to Union forces.

May 19

POLITICS: President Abraham Lincoln countermands General David Hunter's unauthorized emancipation order as it affects the Department of the South (South Carolina, Georgia, Florida).

SOUTH: The 4th Georgia attacks a Union landing party along the banks of the James River at City Point, Virginia.

WEST: Confederates under General Thomas J. Jackson begin to march up the Shenandoah Valley toward New Market.

Union forces under General Isaac F. Quinby sail down the Mississippi River to attack Fort Pillow near Memphis, Tennessee.

NAVAL: Federal gunboats USS *Unadilla*, *Pembina*, and *Ottawa* ascend the Stono River, South Carolina, and commence bombarding Confederate positions on Cole Island.

The USS *Whitehead* captures the Confederate schooner *Eugenia* in Bennet's Creek, North Carolina.

May 20

POLITICS: Congress passes the Homestead Act, which insures settlers 160 acres of land if they remain sedentary for five years and work their plots. Southerners heretofore opposed the measure fearing it would attract overwhelming numbers of antislavery homesteaders to the territories. Three million acres are ultimately distributed among 25,000 citizens by war's end, which in turn facilitates the oncoming tide of western settlement.

SOUTH: Having advanced briefly, General George B. McClellan halts only eight miles from the Confederate capital at Richmond, Virginia. He then divides the Army of the Potomac along both banks of the Chickahominy River while awaiting General Irvin McDowell's I Corps to arrive from Washington, D.C.

General Erasmus D. Keyes leads the IV Corps in operations at Bottom's Bridge on the Chickahominy River, Virginia.

WEST: General Thomas J. Jackson's rapidly moving command swells to 17,000 men with the addition of General Richard S. Ewell's contingent in the Luray Valley, western Virginia. He determines to apply maximum pressure in the Shenandoah Valley to prevent General Nathaniel P. Banks from reinforcing General George B. McClellan's Army of the Potomac.

SOUTHWEST: Union forces reoccupy Tucson in the New Mexico Territory.

NAVAL: Armed boats from USS *Hunchback* and *Whitehead* capture the Confederate schooner *Winter Shrub* in Keel's Creek, North Carolina.

The Federal gunboat USS *Oneida* arrives off Vicksburg, Mississippi, and shells the town.

May 21

SOUTH: Stalled eight miles from the Confederate capital of Richmond, Virginia, and ignoring his clear numerical superiority over the Confederates, General George B. McClellan calls for reinforcements. Meanwhile, the I Corps of General Irvin McDowell continues marching overland toward Richmond, Virginia.

WEST: Confederates under General Thomas J. Jackson move northward in the Luray Valley via passes in the Massanutten Mountains and approach the isolated Union outpost at Fort Royal. His movements are masked effectively by cavalry under Colonel Turner Ashby, which completely confounds Union general Nathaniel P. Banks.

NAVAL: Armed boats from the USS *Hunchback* capture the Confederate schooner *Winter Shrub* at Keel's Creek, North Carolina.

May 22

SOUTH: The 6th Pennsylvania Cavalry (Rush's Lancers) conduct reconnaissance operations around the New Castle and Hanovertown ferries, Virginia.

WEST: Confederate forces under General Thomas J. Jackson depart Luray Gap and advance on Front Royal, western Virginia. He intends to surprise and overwhelm the small Union garrison there.

General Henry W. Halleck continues his leisurely advance toward Corinth, Mississippi, with reconnaissance probes of nearby Iuka and Burnsville.

NAVAL: The USS *Mount Vernon* captures the Confederate steamer *Constitution* at Wilmington, North Carolina.

The USS *Whitehead* captures the Confederate sloop *Ella D* off Keel's Creek, North Carolina.

May 23

SOUTH: Ashby Turner is promoted to brigadier general, C.S.A.

President Abraham Lincoln arrives at Fredericksburg, Virginia, and confers with General Irvin McDowell, whose 20,000 troops suddenly are diverted away from Richmond and into the Shenandoah Valley.

WEST: A force of 17,000 Confederates under General Thomas J. Jackson suddenly appears before a rather surprised Union outpost at Front Royal, Virginia. It is garrisoned by 1,000 men of the 1st Maryland under Colonel John R. Kenly, who remains ignorant of enemy strength and intentions. As the Confederates race down the road to engage the defenders, General Richard Taylor is hailed by notorious spy Belle Boyd, who relays useful intelligence as to Union dispositions about the town. Thus informed, Jackson pushes forward men of his own 1st Maryland, C.S.A., to clear Front Royal and prevent Federal troops from burning two valuable bridges. As Southerners pour into town and vengeful Marylanders from both sides clash, Kenly tries to effect an orderly withdrawal, but his command disintegrates around him. A quick pursuit by the 6th Virginia Cavalry nets Kenly and most of his command outside Cedarville, three miles distant. Union losses in this unequal struggle amount to 904, mostly captured, while Confederate losses are about 50. Both Jackson and the main Union army under General Nathaniel P. Banks continue racing north to Winchester.

Federal troops under General Jacob D. Cox defeat Confederate forces of General Henry Heth at Lewisburg, western Virginia.

May 24

POLITICS: The defeat at Front Royal stings Union authorities into action, and President Abraham Lincoln directs General John C. Frémont to advance into the Shenandoah Valley and confront Confederate forces there. General George B. McClellan is also advised that promised reinforcements are not forthcoming at this time.

SOUTH: Colonel Richard Rush takes his 6th Pennsylvania Cavalry on a scouting mission toward Hanover Court House, Virginia.

WEST: Pursuing Confederates under General Thomas J. Jackson maneuver to intercept Federal forces under General Nathaniel P. Banks at Newtown, western Virginia, but they are slowed by the delaying actions of General John P. Hatch's Union cavalry. Finally brushing aside his opponents, Jackson roughly handles Bank's rearguard and wagon train, taking prisoners and several vehicles. He then trundles up his limping legions and marches them on this latest rapid excursion toward Winchester. Jackson's alarming success prompts President Abraham Lincoln to order General Irwin McDowell to halt at Fredericksburg, Virginia, whereupon he is redirected into the Shenandoah Valley. Lincoln hopes that rapid action will cut off all Confederate escape routes.

NAVAL: The USS *Bienville* seizes the British blockade-runner *Stettin* off Charleston, South Carolina.

The USS *Amanda* and *Bainbridge* capture the Confederate steamer *Swan* off the Tortugas, Florida.

May 25

NORTH: President Abraham Lincoln, chafing over the stalled Union offensive, again urges General George B. McClellan to resume advancing. "I think the time is near when you must either attack Richmond or give up the job and come to the defense of Washington," he blithely declares.

SOUTH: The 3rd Pennsylvania Cavalry under Lieutenant Frank C. Davis advances toward the James River from Bottom's Bridge, Virginia.

The Army of the Potomac, slowly advancing on Richmond, Virginia, is divided by the Chickahominy River, with three Union Corps on its north bank and two below. Confederate commander Joseph E. Johnston, desperate to prevent General George B. McClellan from uniting with the 30,000 men of I Corps under General Irvin McDowell near Fredericksburg, starts to plan to attack Union forces along the river's north bank. By throwing his whole weight against the separated corps of Generals Edwin V. Sumner, William B. Franklin, and Fitz John Porter, he hopes to defeat the Federals in detail before marching north to deal with McDowell.

WEST: Having prevailed over Union forces below Winchester, General Thomas J. Jackson hurriedly marches his weary forces toward another engagement. He even disregards his own religious predilection for observing the Sabbath to hurry the men forward. Jackson then perceives the 7,000 men of General Nathaniel P. Banks deployed along a low range of hills just south of the city, with Colonel Dudley Donnelly's 1st Brigade covering the left flank and Colonel George H. Gordon's 3rd brigade arrayed on the right. Jackson seeks to overpower his adversary quickly and sends three brigades of Generals Charles S. Winder, William B. Taliaferro, and John A. Campbell against Banks's center on Bower's Hill. When these veterans recoil from concentrated infantry and artillery fire, General Richard S. Ewell's division likewise is advanced against the Union right while General Richard Taylor's Louisiana brigade simultaneously hits their left. Taylor leads his men on a wild charge that scatters his opponents, and the entire Union line buckles and breaks. Union troops then stampede through the town and do not rally until they cross the Potomac River into Maryland, 35 miles distant—completely out of the Shenandoah Valley. Jackson, lacking sufficient cavalry to pursue, turns south.

Banks's tactical ineptitude costs him 62 killed, 329 wounded, and 1,714 missing (2,019) while the Confederates barely sustain 400 casualties. During the past three days, Jackson captures 3,030 prisoners, 9,000 firearms, and such a trove of quartermaster stores that Confederates refer to their vanquished adversary as "Commissary Banks." Moreover, Jackson is now poised threateningly only 50 miles from Washington, D.C., a fact mandating General James Shield's recall back to Shenandoah. Ultimately, 40,000 Union troops are withheld from service in the Peninsula campaign because of Jackson's success in the Shenandoah Valley.

General Pierre G. T. Beauregard decides to abandon Corinth, Mississippi, to superior Union numbers and to preserve his army of 50,000 men. He then concocts a number of clever stratagems to convince General Henry W. Halleck that the Confederates actually are being reinforced and that they intend to fight.

NAVAL: Federal and Confederate gunboats exchange fire near the James and Dixon Island, Charleston Harbor.

Colonel Charles Ellet assembles seven steam-powered rams of the Army Mississippi Ram Fleet outside Fort Pillow, Tennessee. There they join the flotilla of Union gunboats under Commodore Charles H. Davis, already deployed.

May 26

SOUTH: Ambrose P. Hill is promoted to major general, C.S.A.

WEST: Defeated Union forces under General Nathaniel P. Banks filter across the Potomac River into Williamsport, Maryland. General Thomas J. Jackson's Confederates, meanwhile, occupy Winchester, Virginia, as additional Federal columns under General John C. Frémont and Irvin McDowell maneuver to cut his retreat.

SOUTHWEST: The Confederate Trans-Mississippi Department is expanded to include Arkansas, the Indian Territory, Missouri, West Louisiana, and Texas.

NAVAL: The USS *Huron* captures the British blockade-runner *Cambria* off Charleston, South Carolina.

The USS *Brooklyn*, assisted by gunboats *Kineo* and *Katahdin*, bombards Grand Gulf, Mississippi.

The USS *Pursuit* captures the Confederate schooner *Andromeda* off the Cuban coast.

Lieutenant Isaac N. Brown is ordered to command the armored ram CSS *Arkansas* at Yazoo City, Mississippi, and oversee its completion.

May 27

SOUTH: With the Army of the Potomac poised only eight miles from Richmond, General George B. McClellan evinces concern for his right flank, situated north of the Chickahominy River. His attention specifically is drawn to Hanover Court House, a village on the Virginia Central Railroad just south of the Pamunkey River, where Confederates allegedly are concentrating in strength. To clear them out, he assigns the V Corps under General Fitz John Porter, who braves a heavy downpour and muddy roads to reach his objective at noon. The 25th New York, his most advanced unit, makes contact with 4,000 men of a North Carolina brigade commanded by Lawrence O. Branch, whose 28th North Carolina resists stoutly. Porter feeds additional men into the line and then mistakenly directs them north in search of the main Confederate body. Sensing an advantage, Branch orders an all-out assault on the Federals to his immediate front, never cognizant of how badly outnumbered he is. The Confederates consequently butt up against General John H. Martindale's brigade of Maine and New York troops, assisted by Massachusetts artillery. Branch's men press the Yankees hard and are on the verge of breaking them when Porter, hearing the fighting in his rear, hurriedly returns to the scene. The North Carolinians yield ground slowly after Branch orders a retreat and fighting sputters out once darkness falls. Union forces then tear up the railroad tracks, burn some bridges, and retrace their steps. Although the fight at Hanover Court House is technically an inconclusive skirmish, it occasions heavy casualties. Porter sustains 62 killed, 223 wounded, and 70 missing to a Confederate tally of 73 dead, 192 injured, and 730 captured.

WEST: As Union forces under General Nathaniel P. Banks continue crossing the Potomac River to safety, General Thomas J. Jackson's Confederates engage their rear guard at Loudoun Heights, western Virginia, threatening Harper's Ferry.

NAVAL: The USS *Bienville* captures the British blockade-runner *Patras* off Bull's Island, South Carolina.

The USS *Santiago de Cuba* seizes the Confederate schooner *Lucy C. Holmes* off Charleston, South Carolina.

May 28

POLITICS: President Jefferson Davis expresses disappointment that General Joseph E. Johnston has not commenced an offensive against the much-larger Army of the Potomac. Nonetheless, he insists: "We are steadily developing for a great battle, and under God's favor I trust for a decisive victory."

WEST: Skirmishing continues between General Henry W. Halleck and Pierre G. T. Beauregard outside Corinth, Mississippi.

The Confederate Department of West Louisiana is designated under General Paul O. Hebert.

NAVAL: Assistant Secretary of the Navy Gustavus V. Fox begins to push legislators to abolish the Navy's rum ration.

The USS *State of Georgia* and *Victoria* capture the Confederate steamer *Nassau* off Fort Caswell, North Carolina.

May 29

SOUTH: Confederate cavalry under General J. E. B. Stuart arrive at Richmond, Virginia, with news that the much-feared approach of General Irvin McDowell's I Corps from the vicinity of Fredericksburg will not materialize. Apparently, the success of General Thomas J. Jackson in the Shenandoah Valley has panicked the Northerners, who then order McDowell to redeploy there. This development prompts General Joseph E. Johnston, commanding Confederate forces in Virginia, to cancel his impending lunge at three Union corps on the north bank of the Chickahominy River in favor of attacking the remaining two Union corps on the south bank of the river.

Union forces skirmish outside South Anna River, Virginia, and also capture the town of Ashland.

WEST: Roughly 50,000 Federal troops under Generals Irvin McDowell, John C. Frémont, and Nathaniel P. Banks begin to concentrate in the vicinity of Harper's Ferry, western Virginia, to cut off and possibly capture the Confederates of General Thomas J. Jackson. All are encouraged by an anxious president Abraham Lincoln, who urges, "Put in all the speed you can." But the wily Jackson begins another one of his rapid disengagements from Front Royal and rapidly transits south to Winchester.

Superior Union numbers prompt General Pierre G. T. Beauregard finally to abandon Corinth, Mississippi, and he withdraws 50,000 men toward Tupelo. To cover the move, Beauregard orders troops and trains to make as much noise as possible to give the impression that reinforcements actually are arriving.

NAVAL: The USS *Keystone* captures the British blockade-runner *Elizabeth* off Charleston, South Carolina.

The USS *Bienville* seizes blockade-runners *Providence*, *Rebecca*, and *La Criolla* off Charleston, South Carolina.

May 30

POLITICS: President Abraham Lincoln, anxious for good news from either Richmond or the Shenandoah Valley, urges all his field commanders to fight.

SOUTH: General Joseph E. Johnston makes a close reconnaissance of Union forces looming within 10 miles of Richmond, Virginia, and he observes that they are physically divided by the rain-swollen Chickahominy River. He decides to concentrate 51,000 men against the combined 34,000 men of III and IV Corps of General Samuel P. Heintzelman and Erasmus D. Keyes, now unsupported on the south bank. Johnston then promulgates a tactically sound if somewhat overcomplicated plan with attacks delivered down three main roads, which is designed to catch the Federals from three different directions. The main strike forces are commanded by Generals James Longstreet, Daniel H. Hill, and Benjamin Huger. However, Johnston's plan is compromised by an overreliance on oral commands, instead of written orders, that further complicates matters for his inexperienced troops.

WEST: Confederates under General Thomas J. Jackson withdraw from Winchester, western Virginia, to avoid being engulfed by three converging Union columns. General Ashby Turner and some Confederate cavalry remain behind as a rear guard. However, when a division under Colonel Nathan Kimball approach the town, Turner panics and abandons his command. A quick charge by the 1st Rhode Island Cavalry recaptures Front Royal, along with 156 Confederate prisoners. The town subsequently is secured by Federal troops under General James Shield.

Union forces under General Henry W. Halleck secure 2,000 Confederate prisoners at Corinth, Mississippi, following the withdrawal of General Pierre G. T. Beauregard. Previously, Beauregard ordered his troops to cook three days of rations to give the impression that he was preparing to fight. He also had troops cheer arriving trains during evacuation measures to give the appearance that he was receiving reinforcements. Halleck thus secured a vital transportation link and severed the vital Memphis and Charleston and Mobile and Ohio railroads, but he nonetheless is criticized for a dilatory pace while campaigning. It has taken him 30 days to cover the 22-mile distance from Pittsburg Landing.

May 31

NORTH: Edward R. S. Canby is promoted to brigadier general, U.S. Army.

SOUTH: As Federal forces under General George B. McClellan continue their glacial advance on Richmond, Virginia, topography requires him to split his forces on both banks of the rain-swollen Chickahominy River. The raging water then washes away all available bridges, and Confederate general Joseph E. Johnston seeks to avail himself of an opportunity to destroy the isolated II and IV Corps, under Generals Samuel P. Heintzelman and Erasmus D. Keyes, respectively, on the south bank. But the impending Confederate assault, through well planned, remains hobbled from the onset by poor staff work and overreliance on verbal orders. Consequently, wholesale confusion ensues as the troops of General James Longstreet inadvertently assume a line of advance previously assigned to Generals Benjamin Huger and D. H. Hill. Hours are lost as the intermingling commands extricate themselves from a tangle of regiments, brigades, and divisions. It is not until 1:00 P.M. that Hill's division finally positions itself to strike Union forces in the vicinity of Seven Pines.

The Confederate attack kicks off amid stiff resistance and heavy casualties. By dint of hard fighting, Hill manages to evict General Silas Casey's Federals from their position and storms several batteries, but Union forces promptly re-form and establish new lines to the rear. Excited Confederate units continue arriving on the battlefield in slovenly order and deliver their assaults piecemeal, so General Keyes stems their advance with reinforcements of his own and counterattacks. These are repulsed after more severe fighting and Longstreet orders an advance across the line to clinch the victory. The hard-charging Southerners drive their opponents from the field, but Union resistance proves insurmountable, and their line re-forms anew and holds. Fighting finally peters out along the line at about 6:00 P.M., and both sides withdraw to lick their wounds and assess damage.

Johnston's secondary attack at Fair Oaks fared little better. Here, Union troops under the redoubtable general Phil Kearny fiercely resist General W. H. C. Whiting's advance and expertly repulse him. Meanwhile, troops from General Edwin V. Sumner's II Corps manage to throw a bridge across the Chickahominy and begin to funnel into the fracas. These forces have been personally ordered here by General George B. McClellan, who is sick and takes no further part in the fighting. As Whiting's attack falters again, General Johnston rides up to supervise matters personally, when a musket ball suddenly thuds into his shoulder. Confederate command devolves to a dithering General Gustavus W. Smith, who withdraws his remaining troops from the field. That evening, Smith reconsiders and issues orders to resume fighting on the following day.

WEST: Adroit maneuvering by General Thomas J. Jackson extricates his army from closing pincers formed by Generals Irwin McDowell and John C. Frémont, and he retires in driving rain from Winchester, western Virginia, to Strasburg.

General Thomas C. Hindman assumes control of the Confederate Trans-Mississippi Department.

NAVAL: The USS *Philadelphia* captures the Confederate schooner *W. F. Harris* in Core Sound, North Carolina.

The USS *Keystone State* captures the British blockade-runner *Cora* off Charleston, South Carolina.

June 1

POLITICS: President Abraham Lincoln telegrams and implores General George B. McClellan to "Hold all your ground, or yield any inch by inch and in good order."

NORTH: Joseph Hooker is appointed major general, U.S. Army.

The Department of Virginia is enlarged with General John E. Wool assigned to the Middle Department and General John A. Dix to head Fortress Monroe, Virginia; all are now under the overall command of General George B. McClellan.

SOUTH: Confederate forces at Seven Pines, Virginia, resume their offensive against the Army of the Potomac. General Gustavus W. Smith orders General D. H. Hill to attack, assisted by additional soldiers under General James Longstreet, but once again Southern plans miscarry. The Confederates deliver their charges fiercely but in piecemeal fashion, which enables Union troops to repulse them. At length, General Robert E. Lee arrives from Richmond to succeed Smith, and he orders the battle stopped at 1 P.M. Both sides sustain severe casualties: The Southerners, who did most of the attacking, lose 980 killed, 4,749 wounded, and 405 missing (6,134) to a

Union tally of 790 dead, 3,594 injured, and 647 missing (5,031). The erstwhile cautious McClellan, who retains the battlefield, could claim a tactical victory, but there follows one portentous, unforeseen consequence: When the skittish General Smith asks to be relieved, President Jefferson Davis assigns Robert E. Lee to succeed him. A corner has been turned in the course of military events of the Civil War—and a dazzling new chapter is about to unfold.

WEST: Confederates under General Thomas J. Jackson and Federals under General Irvin McDowell skirmish at Mount Carmel, western Virginia.

June 2

WEST: Union cavalry under General George Bayard brush aside Confederates under General Turner Ashby near Woodstock, western Virginia, as the Federal pursuit of General Thomas J. Jackson intensifies.

Union forces under General John Pope cautiously begin to follow General Pierre G. T. Beauregard's retreating Confederates at Rienzi, Mississippi.

NAVAL: The USS *Unadilla, Pembina, E. B. Hale, Ellen,* and *Henry Andrew* provide supporting gunfire as troops land on James Island, South Carolina.

Armed boats from the USS *Kingfisher* are attacked in the Aucilla River, Florida, suffering two killed and nine wounded.

An armed boat from the USS *New London* captures the Confederate yachts *Comet* and *Algerine* off Near Basin, Louisiana.

June 3

SOUTH: Colonel George F. Shepley, 12th Maine, becomes military governor of Louisiana.

WEST: Fort Pillow, Tennessee, below Island No. 10 on the Mississippi River, is abandoned by Confederate forces following the fall of Corinth, Mississippi.

NAVAL: USS *Gem of the Sea* captures the blockade-runner *Mary Stewart* off the mouth of the South Santee River, South Carolina.

The USS *Montgomery* captures the British schooner *Will-o'-the-Wisp* off the mouth of the Rio Grande, Texas.

Prolonged bombardment by Federal gunboats on the Mississippi River convinces Confederate defenders to abandon Fort Pillow, Tennessee. The nearby city of Memphis likewise is all but undefended, save for a weak Confederate naval squadron.

June 4

WEST: General Thomas J. Jackson's Confederates pause briefly to skirmish at Big Bend, western Virginia, as he withdraws southward down the Shenandoah Valley.

General Ormsby M. Mitchel skirmishes outside Huntsville, Alabama, where he begins to threaten Chattanooga, Tennessee.

Southern farmers along the Yazoo River begin to burn vast crops of cotton to prevent their capture by advancing Union forces.

NAVAL: Fort Pillow on the Mississippi River is abandoned by Confederate forces and the gunboat flotilla under Commodore Charles H. Davis completely bypasses it.

June 5

POLITICS: In another deft blow against slavery, the United States formally recognizes the largely black nations of Liberia and Haiti, and President Abraham Lincoln appoints diplomatic representatives.

SOUTH: The Union drive on Richmond, Virginia, is stalled by inclement weather while Confederates under the heretofore little-known General Robert E. Lee begin to gird for a decisive counterstrike.

The 24th Massachusetts under Colonel Francis A. Osborn fights a pitched battle at Tranter's Creek, North Carolina.

NAVAL: Confederates destroy the steamer *Havana* at Deadman's Bay, Florida, to prevent its capture by USS *Ezilda*.

Having ignored Fort Pillow, Tennessee, four Union gunboats and five rams under Commodore Charles H. Davis and Colonel Charles Ellet steam down the Mississippi River to capture Memphis, Tennessee.

A tug escorting the USS *Benton* captures the Confederate steamer *Sovereign* off Island No. 37 in the Mississippi River.

June 6

WEST: Confederate cavalry leader General Ashby Turner is mortally wounded in a rearguard action near Harrisonburg, western Virginia. Meanwhile, the main column under General Thomas J. Jackson rapidly retrogrades toward Port Republic, covering over 100 miles in five days.

NAVAL: At 4:20 A.M., Union gunboats under Commodore Charles H. Davis weigh anchor off Island No. 45, two miles north of Memphis, Tennessee, and head for the city. He commands the ironclads USS *Benton, Louisville, Carondelet, Cairo,* and *St. Louis,* along with the small but very potent fleet of army rams under Colonel Charles Ellet. Suddenly, Confederates under Captain James E. Montgomery sortie a small squadron of steam rams, *General Beauregard, General Bragg, General Price, General Van Dorn, General Thompson, Colonel Lovell, Sumter,* and *Little Rebel.* At 5:40 A.M., contact is established between the opposing armadas, and cannonading commences below the city as thousands throng the riverbanks to observe. Davis feigns a retreat while Montgomery pursues until he is surprised amidships by Ellet's rams sailing downstream, four abreast. A confused and violent melee erupts as the majority of Confederate vessels systematically are rammed, disabled by superior Union gunfire, and sunk. Only *Van Dorn* escapes the wreckage and slips downstream to safety. On the Union side, *Queen of the West* is rammed and grounds itself to prevent sinking. Confederate losses in this lopsided encounter are nearly 100 killed and wounded with another 100 captured. The only Union casualty, Colonel Ellet, is wounded superficially by a gunshot through the kneecap and dies two weeks later from infection.

Davis, having dispensed with his adversary, wastes no time claiming Memphis as his prize. Two officers row ashore to the city fathers and demand an immediate surrender, which is received at 10:00 A.M. Handfuls of Confederate troops under General Jeff Thompson slip out of the city beforehand and escape. But all of western Tennessee is now firmly in Union hands and Memphis—the Confederacy's fifth

Lithograph by Middleton, Strobridge & Co. In the foreground are various Confederate ships shown sinking, burning, and being rammed, with Federal warships in the background. The city of Memphis is in the right distance, with a wharf boat by the shore. *(Naval Historical Foundation)*

largest city—functions as a vital staging area for subsequent operations against Vicksburg, Mississippi.

The USS *Pembina* captures the Confederate schooner *Rowena* in the Stono River, South Carolina.

June 7
SOUTH: Federal cavalry patrols reach the outskirts of Richmond, Virginia.

General Benjamin F. Butler orders Louisianan William B. Mumford hanged for removing and destroying the U.S. flag atop the New Orleans Mint.

WEST: Federal troops under General Ormsby M. Mitchel attack Confederate positions at Chattanooga, Tennessee, and are repulsed by General Edmund Kirby Smith.

The important rail center at Jackson, Tennessee, falls to Union forces.

NAVAL: The USS *Anacostia* captures the Confederate sloop *Monitor* in the Piankatank River, Virginia.

The USS *Wissahickon* and *Itasca* begin prolonged exchanges of fire with Confederate artillery stationed at Grand Gulf, Mississippi.

June 8
SOUTH: Unionists are defeated in a heavy skirmish on St. John's Island, South Carolina, and subsequently withdraw back to Legareville.

WEST: The main portion of the Army of the Valley under General Thomas J. Jackson reposes at Port Republic, western Virginia, prior to advancing against the Union forces of General James Shields. Early this morning, a surprise raid by Union cavalry nearly overruns Jackson's headquarters in town, capturing three staff officers. But quick action by nearby Confederates repulses the Federals, costing them four cannon.

Seven miles away, General Richard S. Ewell's force of 5,000 men assumes defensive positions at Cross Keys, western Virginia, anticipating a major thrust by Federal troops under General John C. Frémont. He deploys his three brigades along the crest on the south bank of Mill Creek with artillery concentrated toward his center. At length, Frémont approaches Ewell's position from Port Republic with 12,000 men and begins a desultory series of artillery exchanges and half-hearted reconnaissance probes at about 10:00 A.M. Fighting commences in earnest when Union troops under General Julius Stahel haphazardly deploy against Ewell's right and run headlong into General Issac R. Trimble's eager Confederates. The 15th Alabama, in particular, allows the Federals to approach their position in a cornfield when they suddenly rise up and unleash several crushing volleys at point-blank range. Trimble then chases the chastised Yankees down the Keezletown Road even as Union reinforcements under General Henry Bohlen's brigade arrive to assist.

In the center of Ewell's line, General Robert H. Milroy advances to contact before deciding his position is too strong to carry frontally. However, the Confederate right experiences increasing pressure from General Robert C. Schenck's brigade, and Ewell dispatches General Richard Taylor's troops to buttress that flank. But before more serious fighting develops, Frémont suddenly orders his units disengaged, and he falls back down the Keezletown Road. The Confederates follow cautiously and by nightfall occupy the former Union position. Trimble subsequently begs Ewell to pursue vigorously, but that general, acting under Jackson's strict instructions, maintains his defensive posture. The affair at Cross Keyes is but a skirmish, yet it constitutes another timid performance by Frémont. Confederate losses are recorded as 288 while the Union suffers 684 casualties, nearly half among the serried ranks of the 8th New York. Later that evening, Ewell prepares to march and join Jackson at Port Republic on the following day.

General Irvin McDowell's I Corps again is ordered to depart the Shenandoah Valley and march south to assist the attack on Richmond, Virginia.

NAVAL: The USS Penobscot burns the Confederate schooner Sereta off Shallotte Inlet, North Carolina.

June 9

SOUTH: General John E. Wool assumes command of the Middle Military Department, Virginia.

WEST: Confederates under General Thomas J. Jackson cross a narrow wagon bridge over the North River to attack General Erastus B. Tyler's brigade at Port Republic. Tyler arrays his 3,000 men in a line anchored by a seven-gun battery occupying a charcoal plant, which stands on a hilltop. As the Stonewall brigade under General Charles S. Winder files onto the field at about 7:00 A.M., it receives heavy fire from Tyler's entire force and sustains heavy losses. Nonetheless, he advances to within 200 yards of the Union line and bravely maintains an unequal contest for an hour.

Meanwhile, Jackson orders the Louisiana brigade of General Richard Taylor against the Union left to storm their commanding battery on the hill. Braving heavy fire, Taylor accomplishes just that, although he loses the captured guns twice before prevailing on an excruciating third try. As this drama unfolds, the Stonewall brigade recoils in disorder until bolstered by General Richard S. Ewell's division. By 11:00 A.M., Tyler, now badly outnumbered, orders a withdrawal, which degenerates into a rout. The Union army of General Charles C. Frémont also makes a late appearance across the river but is unable to intervene because Ewell burned all the bridges behind him. Frémont's troops could only shell the field from afar, which does little to assist Tyler's shattered command. Union losses amount to 1,108, including 558 prisoners, while the Southerners incur roughly 800 casualties.

Port Republic, although it reflects somewhat badly on Jackson's combat leadership, is the sixth and final encounter of his remarkable Valley campaign. Since the previous March, Jackson's infamous "Foot Cavalry," whose strength peaked at 17,000 men, have slogged 676 miles, won four pitched battles and several skirmishes, and defied all attempts by 60,000 Federals to snare him. Campaign losses also favor the South, amounting to 3,100 Confederates and more than 5,000 Union troops. But most important, Jackson's endeavors repeatedly siphon off manpower assets that are badly needed before Richmond. With Frémont and Shields safely disposed of, Jackson is now at liberty to depart the Shenandoah Valley and reinforce General Robert E. Lee on the Peninsula. "God has been our shield," he modestly concludes, "and to His name be all the glory."

The division of Union general James Shields is ordered from the Shenandoah Valley to rejoin the I Corps of General Irvin McDowell near Fredericksburg, Virginia.

NAVAL: The USS *Commodore Perry, Shawsheen,* and *Ceres* land and disembark troops at Hamilton, North Carolina, capturing the Confederate steamer *Wilson* in the process.

June 10

WEST: The glacial-acting General Henry W. Halleck authorizes General Ulysses S. Grant, John Pope, and Don C. Buell to resume heading their respective corps. Grant, as the senior leader, rebounds as theater commander and the tempo of events rapidly escalates.

NAVAL: The Federal gunboats USS *Iroquois* and *Katahdin* join *Wissahickon* and *Itasca* in a concerted bombardment of Grand Gulf, Mississippi.

The Federal gunboat USS *Mound City* is damaged by Confederate artillery fire eight miles below Saint Charles on the White River, Arkansas.

June 11

DIPLOMATIC: British prime minister Lord Palmerston protests the behavior of General William F. Butler toward civilians at New Orleans to U.S. minister Charles F. Adams.

SOUTH: General David Hunter, commanding the Department of the South, temporarily leaves and orders his successor, General Henry W. Benham, to refrain from initiating major engagements.

WEST: General John C. Frémont is ordered to withdraw his army from Port Republic and back to Mount Jackson in western Virginia.

SOUTHWEST: Confederate guerrillas under William C. Quantrill unsuccessfully attack a Federal mail escort at Pink Hill, Missouri.

NAVAL: The USS *Susquehanna* captures the Confederate blockade-runner *Princeton* in the Gulf of Mexico.

The USS *Bainbridge* captures the Confederate schooner *Biagorry* in the Gulf of Mexico.

June 12

SOUTH: The Army of the Potomac is strengthened by the arrival of a division commanded by General George A. McCall.

At 2:00 A.M., General J. E. B. Stuart bursts into his headquarters and declares: "Gentlemen, in ten minutes every man must be in the saddle." His 1,200 Virginian troopers then commence a dramatic and celebrated ride from Richmond, Virginia, and around the Army of the Potomac. Stuart is tasked with verifying rumors that parts of General George B. McClellan's right flank are "up in the air" to facilitate a new Confederate offensive envisioned by General Robert E. Lee.

To further confuse Northern military intelligence, General Robert E. Lee dispatches sizable reinforcements to the Shenandoah region to give the impression of a major offensive developing there.

June 13

SOUTH: General J. E. B. Stuart's cavalry reach a threshold after passing through Old Church, Virginia, on the right flank of General George B. McClellan's army. En route, he tangles briefly with a detachment of the 5th U.S. Cavalry, which results in the death of Captain William Latane, 9th Virginia Cavalry—his sole fatality, who is subsequently enshrined as a Southern martyr. No Confederate unit had ever penetrated Union lines this far, but rather than retrace his steps, Stuart boldly plunges ahead and begins his circuitous ride to fame.

June 14

SOUTH: General J. E. B. Stuart's cavalry destroy the bridge over the Chickahominy River at Forge Site to prevent a Union pursuit, and they gallop around the Army of the Potomac's left flank. Ironically, Stuart is chased by Federal cavalry under his father-in-law and fellow Virginian, Colonel Philip St. George Cooke.

NAVAL: The USS *William G. Anderson* captures the Confederate schooner *Montebello* in the Jordan River, Mississippi.

The tug USS *Spitfire* captures the Confederate steamer *Clara Dolsen* in the White River, Arkansas.

June 15

POLITICS: With amazing perspicacity, President Abraham Lincoln informs a worried general John C. Frémont that Confederate reinforcements headed for the Shenandoah Valley are probably a ruse to mask General Thomas J. Jackson's movement toward Richmond, Virginia.

SOUTH: General Robert E. Lee formally orders General Thomas J. Jackson, then in the Shenandoah Valley, to join the Army of Northern Virginia on the Peninsula. Lee seeks to annihilate General George B. McClellan's army before it can be reinforced by General Irvin McDowell's I Corps.

General J. E. B. Stuart gallops into Richmond, Virginia, ahead of his troopers with important military intelligence about the Army of the Potomac, which he recently circumnavigated. His 100-mile jaunt captures 165 prisoners, 260 mules and horses, and renders him the darling of the Southern press. More significant, he brings General Robert E. Lee accurate information about the disposition of Union General Fitz John Porter's V Corps, presently unsupported on the north bank of the Chickahominy River. Stuart discerns that Porter's right flank lies unprotected by natural obstacles and is, hence, "in the air." Lee, eager to break the military impasse near Richmond, begins to concoct a plan for Porter's demise.

Federals under General Daniel Sickles advance on Seven Pines, Virginia, skirmishing en route.

WEST: Union troops under General William T. Sherman skirmish heavily at Tallahatchie Bridge, Mississippi.

NAVAL: The USS *Corwin* captures the Confederate schooner *Starlight* on the Potopotank River, Virginia.

The USS *Tahoma* and *Somerset* shell a Confederate lighthouse at St. Mary's River, Florida, and subsequently land parties ashore, which capture and burn a battery and a barracks.

June 16

SOUTH: The remainder of General J. E. B. Stuart's Confederate cavalry completes its spectacular jaunt around the Union army and canters back to Richmond, Virginia.

At 2:00 A.M., General Henry W. Benham rouses the divisions of General Horatio G. Wright and Isaac I. Stevens from their encampment on James Island, a swampy neck southwest of Charleston, South Carolina. He then orders them to attack Confederate fortifications at nearby Secessionville. This is despite standing orders from his commanding officer, General David Hunter, not to initiate major engagements during his absence. The local Confederate commander, Colonel Thomas G. Lamar of the 1st South Carolina Artillery, is alert to Benham's intentions and prepares a two-mile long position, heavily defended by cannon, to receive the enemy. Possessing but 500 men, Lamar also requests reinforcements from his district commander, General Nathan G. Evans. Federal forces advance stealthily through the darkness, manage to capture an entire Confederate picket, and then confront swampy terrain that funnels their attack directly toward the Confederate works. At 4:00 A.M., Benham orders the first wave of his 6,000 men forward, and they are bloodily repulsed by Lamar's six-inch Columbiad cannon. Two more waves also advance and bravely struggle up the parapet, but the defenders, reinforced now to a strength of 1,500 men, easily shoot down their opponents. At length, Benham ceases the slaughter at 9:30 A.M. and marches back to camp.

The Battle of Secessionville was a minor disaster for the Union and a setback in its campaign to seize Charleston, South Carolina. Benham's recklessness cost his army 107 killed, 487 wounded, and 80 captured to a Confederate tally of 52 dead, 144 injured, and 8 missing. Evans is so pleased with Lamar's performance that his fortifications are officially renamed Fort Lamar in his honor. Benham, however, is subsequently relieved from command and discharged from uniform the following August.

NAVAL: The USS *Somerset* captures the Confederate schooner *Curlew* off Cedar Keys, Florida.

Confederates sink the steamers *Eliza G.* and *Mary Patterson* in the White River, Arkansas, to impede the passage of Union vessels.

June 17

NORTH: General John C. Frémont resigns his commission rather than be subordinated to General John Pope in the new Army of Virginia. He is replaced by General Franz Sigel.

WEST: Confederate forces under General Thomas J. Jackson hurriedly march toward Richmond, Virginia, to join the Army of Northern Virginia under General Robert E. Lee.

General Braxton Bragg, a close friend and confidant of President Jefferson Davis, succeeds the General Pierre G. T. Beauregard, who is ailing, as commander of the Confederate Western Department. The aggressive Bragg is a capable strategist and an accomplished logistician, but his garrulous disposition and indecisive nature alienate all but the most faithful subordinates. Many ranking Confederates openly loath serving under him.

NAVAL: Union forces, assisted by the Federal gunboat USS *New London*, attack Confederate troops at Pass Manchac, Louisiana.

Captain Charles H. Davis is promoted to commodore and commander of U.S. Navy forces along the Mississippi River.

At the behest of General Henry W. Halleck, a naval squadron consisting of the USS *Mound City, St. Louis, Lexington,* and *Conestoga,* engages Confederate batteries at St. Charles, Arkansas. *Mound City* sustains heavy damage when exploding boilers kill or wound 10 sailors, but troops land ashore and successfully carry the position. Victory here closes off the White River to Confederate traffic.

June 18

SOUTH: Union general Samuel D. Sturgis receives command of the Reserve Army Corps in Virginia.

WEST: Federal forces under General George W. Morgan advance and occupy the Cumberland Gap, where mountain trails connecting Tennessee, Kentucky, and Virginia strategically converge. This movement also stirs up long-suppressed Union sentiments throughout the region.

Recent adverse developments prompt the garrison of Vicksburg, Mississippi, to commence building an extensive network of defensive works.

SOUTHWEST: General Paul O. Hebert takes charge of the Confederate District of Texas.

NAVAL: Admiral David G. Farragut begins to assemble his squadron and mortar boat fleet prior to sailing past the guns of Vicksburg on the Mississippi River.

June 19

POLITICS: President Abraham Lincoln signs legislation outlawing slavery in the territories.

SOUTH: The 20th Indiana under Colonel William L. Brown skirmishes along Charles City Road outside Richmond, Virginia, before withdrawing.

At James Island, South Carolina, General Henry W. Benham is arrested for his role in the aborted attack upon Secessionville, and the Judge Advocate General's Office, after weighing the evidence against him, strongly recommends that his brigadier's commission be revoked.

NAVAL: Commander Matthew F. Maury reports to Confederate secretary of the navy Stephen R. Mallory of mining operations on the James River. He also mentions the use of galvanic batteries and the existence of the CSS *Teaser,* the first naval vessel outfitted as a minelayer. It also carries the first Confederate reconnaissance balloon.

The USS *Florida* captures the sloop *Ventura* off Grant's Pass, Mobile Bay, Alabama.

June 20

WEST: General Braxton Bragg arrives at Tupelo, Mississippi, and assumes command of the Confederate Western Department from General Pierre G. T. Beauregard.

A detachment of 3,000 Union troops under General William Thomas boards Admiral David G. Farragut's fleet and heads up the Mississippi River from Baton Rouge. He is ordered to establish a base camp opposite Vicksburg, Mississippi, where a canal can be cut to permit river traffic to bypass the city's formidable armament. Thomas's movement induces General Earl Van Dorn, commanding the Department of Southern Mississippi, to accelerate fortifying the city.

NAVAL: The USS *Keystone State* captures the British blockade-runner *Sarah* off Charleston, South Carolina.

The USS *Madgie* captures the Confederate schooner *Southern Belle* near Darien, South Carolina.

Armed boats from the USS *Albatross* capture the Confederate steam tug *Treaty* and schooner *Louisa* off Georgetown, South Carolina.

The USS *Beauregard* seizes the British blockade-runner *Lucy* at Deadman's Point, Florida.

June 21

SOUTH: Union and Confederate forces skirmish heavily along the Chickahominy River near Richmond, Virginia. Expectations for decisive military action mount, but the nerve-wracking impasse continues.

WEST: General Jeff Thompson's Confederate guerrilla evade a Union attack at Coldwater Station, Mississippi.

NAVAL: Landing parties from the USS *Crusader* and *Planter* drive up the Wadmelaw River, South Carolina, capture Simmons Bluff, and destroy a Confederate encampment there.

The USS *Bohio* captures the Confederate sloop *L. Rebecca* in the Gulf of Mexico.

June 22
SOUTH: The Sisters of Charity dispatch 30 members to serve as nurses in the Army of the Potomac at Fortress Monroe, Virginia.

Union general Erasmus D. Keyes leads a large reconnaissance party in the vicinity of White Oak Swamp, 16 miles south of Richmond, Virginia.

June 23
POLITICS: President Abraham Lincoln, disillusioned by General George B. McClellan's fabled cautiousness, ventures to West Point, New York, and confers with former general in chief Winfield Scott over strategy.

SOUTH: General Robert E. Lee assembles his commanders at the Dabb's House near Richmond, Virginia, and outlines his offensive against the Army of the Potomac's right wing under General Fitz John Porter. He plans to concentrate no less than 55,000 men against Porter's 30,000-strong V Corps by throwing the combined weight of Generals Thomas J. Jackson, James Longstreet, Daniel H. Hill, and Ambrose P. Hill at it in a single, coordinated strike. The lynchpin of Confederate hopes falls on Jackson's Army of the Valley, which is expected to force march to the battlefield and take Porter from behind once he is pinned down frontally by the others. Concurrently, Generals Benjamin Huger and John B. Magruder will fix McClellan's army before Richmond with 25,000 men until Lee's return. Jackson, who had arrived only recently at Richmond alone from the Shenandoah Valley, immediately rejoins his command to accelerate its passage.

WEST: Union general Benjamin Alvord takes charge of the District of Oregon.

June 24
SOUTH: Skirmishing erupts as the Army of the Potomac resumes its belated advance by pressing down on Mechanicsville, Virginia. Confederate forces evacuate White House Landing on their approach.

WEST: General Earl Van Dorn continues fortifying Vicksburg, Mississippi, as 3,000 Federal troops begin encamping nearby across the river.

June 25
SOUTH: The Army of the Potomac edges to within six miles of the Confederate capital at Richmond, Virginia, the closest Union forces will approach in three years. General George B. McClellan, desiring to place heavy cannon on the outskirts of the city and bombard it, orders Oak Grove, a section of swampy, wooded terrain to his front, wrested from the enemy. General Samuel P. Heintzelman's III Corps then advances to dislodge the defenders under General Benjamin Huger and heavy fighting erupts along the front. General Joseph Hooker's division also plunges into the woods at 8:30 A.M., soon supported by the forces led by General Phil Kearny. But the Confederates of General Ambrose R. Wright resist stoutly, slowing Hooker's advance and enabling the brigade of General Robert Ransom to arrive and assist. The exposed Union brigade under General Daniel E. Sickles suddenly breaks and runs for cover, and McClellan next orders all his troops back to their original starting positions. After sorting themselves out and bringing up additional artillery, the Federals advance back upon Oak Grove, methodically raking the Southerners with

heavy canister fire. Wright and Ransom both yield ground before darkness envelopes the battlefield and fighting stops. The Union acquires Oak Grove at a cost of 68 killed, 503 wounded, and 55 missing (626), while the Confederates lose 66 dead, 362 injured, and 12 missing (441)—a trifling toll in light of what follows. McClellan congratulates himself on advancing his front another 600 yards toward Richmond, then waxes worried over intelligence that General Thomas J. Jackson's Army of the Valley is approaching. The Army of the Potomac thus concludes its only offensive action of the Peninsula campaign; no one could anticipate that the strategic initiative is passing suddenly into Southern hands.

WEST: The new Army of Virginia is constituted under General John Pope in western Virginia, an amalgam of forces commanded by Generals Irvin McDowell, John C. Frémont, and Nathaniel P. Banks.

To counter the growth of pro-Southern civic organizations, the Union League is organized at Pekin, Illinois, to bolster Northern morale and assist the war effort.

General Thomas Williams division arrives opposite Vicksburg, Mississippi, and establishes a base camp near Swampy Toe.

June 26

SOUTH: Throughout the morning, three Confederate divisions under General James Longstreet, Daniel H. Hill, and Ambrose P. Hill concentrate 47,000 men in the vicinity of Mechanicsville, Virginia. Opposing them are the 30,000-man V Corps of General Fitz John Porter, strongly entrenched behind Beaver Dam Creek. However, Confederate success hinges completely on the arrival of General Thomas J. Jackson's corps in the rear of Union defenses. The Southerners wait patiently for Jackson, whose very arrival constitutes the signal to attack, but he fails to materialize or even establish contact with other commands. His uncharacteristic dilatoriness proves too much for the aggressive A. P. Hill, who orders a frontal assault against Porter at 3:00 P.M. Well-positioned Union forces experience little difficulty blasting back the enthusiastic Confederates, who launch several brave but piecemeal assaults. Three brigades are then committed against the Union right, which likewise are slaughtered by the concentrated artillery and musketry fire of General John F. Reynolds's command.

Meanwhile, Jackson's exhausted men finally trudge into Pole Green—three miles from the scene of fighting—where he expects to confer with other commanders. But finding the place deserted with no orders awaiting him, the exhausted general orders his fatigued troops into bivouacs. Back at Mechanicsville, President Jefferson Davis also makes an unexpected appearance at Lee's headquarters, just as brigade-sized attacks by Generals Dorsey Pender and Roswell Ripley are launched. Both men are rebuffed with heavy losses and, with the onset of twilight, the fighting tapers off and stops. Lee's battle plan misfires spectacularly with a loss of 1,484 Confederates to 361 Federals. Union forces waged a set piece defense against steep odds and prevailed in this, the first of the Seven Day's Battles—but victory held unintended consequences. Lee's sudden pugnaciousness completely unnerves General George B. McClellan, who suddenly orders the victorious Porter to abandon his otherwise strong position. The V Corps is now to concentrate four miles east at Gaines' Mill.

In a major move, General George B. McClellan also decides to shift his base of operations from the Pamunkey River to Harrison's Landing on the James River, and he implores Commodore Louis M. Goldsborough to send the bulk of his provision transports there. This is the first move in what many participants on either side begin to ridicule as "the Great Skedaddle."

WEST: The new Federal Army of Virginia under General John Pope assumes responsibility for the former Mountain Department, along with those of the Rappahannock and Shenandoah. General Nathaniel P. Banks commands the II Corps while Irvin McDowell is reassigned the III Corps. General Franz Sigel ultimately is tapped to succeed John C. Frémont as chief of I Corps.

NAVAL: An armed boat from the USS *Mount Vernon* attacks and burns the Confederate blockade-runner Emily off Wilmington, North Carolina, despite heavy fire from nearby Fort Caswell.

The USS *Kensington,* accompanied by mortar boats *Horace Beals* and *Sarah Bruen,* attack and level a Confederate battery at Cole's Creek on the Mississippi River, prior to moving on Vicksburg, Mississippi.

June 27

POLITICS: President Abraham Lincoln formally accepts the resignation of the controversial explorer, soldier, and politician John C. Frémont.

SOUTH: The Union V Corps under General Fitz John Porter retires four miles southeast from Mechanicsville, Virginia, and establishes a new defensive perimeter along a swampy plateau near Gaines' Mill. His 30,000 men deploy in a semicircular line, with General George Sykes's division of U.S. Army regulars holding the right and General George W. Morrell's division on the left and with ample artillery covering his center. The position is buttressed further by the presence of Boatswain Swamp to the front, itself a nearly impassable obstacle.

The Army of Northern Virginia under General Robert E. Lee sharply pursues the Federals and determines to deliver a crushing blow with 56,000 men. To that end, Lee commits the entire division of General Ambrose P. Hill against Porter's center at 2:30 P.M., which is staggered by a maelstrom of artillery and musketry fire. A New York brigade under Colonel Gouverneur K. Warren also distinguishes itself by slamming into the flank of General Maxcy Gregg's South Carolina brigade and driving them off. As this transpires, General James Longstreet's division arrives on the battlefield, but he delays attacking pending the arrival of General Thomas J. Jackson's corps. Jackson, who missed the previous day's fighting at Mechanicsville, performs equally poorly this day and fails to position his men before 3:00 P.M. Meanwhile, Lee resumes attacking Porter's line by forwarding divisions under Generals Daniel H. Hill and Richard S. Ewell up against Porter's left while General George E. Pickett's brigade performs a diversionary thrust on the right. Both attacks, bravely delivered, again are repulsed bloodily by the withering fire of Sykes's regulars and supporting cannon.

Lee's own sloppy staff work means that he cannot assemble the bulk of his army on the field prior to 7:00 P.M. Undeterred by losses, he determines to make a final charge on the tiring Federals, spearheaded by 4,000 fresh troops. Foremost among these is the Texas brigade under General John B. Hood, which takes frightful losses yet crashes through Porter's defenses, netting 14 cannon. This signals the retreat of Union forces, which are covered by a suicidal charge of the U.S. 5th and 2nd Cavalry. As the victorious but weary Confederates surmount the plateau, Porter withdraws in good order toward Chickahominy Creek and closer to General George B. McClellan's main force. Gaines' Mill proves to be the most sanguine of the Seven Days' battles, with Confederate losses of 1,483 dead, 6,401 wounded, and 108 missing (7,993) versus a Union tally of 894 killed, 3,114 wounded, and 2,829 captured (6,837). The combined might of the Army of Virginia had failed again to destroy an isolated Union corps, but Lee's aggressiveness convinces McClellan to abandon Richmond altogether and retreat toward the James River. The much-vaunted Union offensive unravels.

WEST: Federal troops across from Vicksburg, Mississippi, begin digging a canal to alter a bend in the Mississippi River.

General Braxton Bragg directs 3,000 men of General John P. McCown's division to transit by rail from Tupelo, Mississippi, to Chattanooga, Tennessee, and there they join the army of General Edmund Kirby-Smith. The movement takes six days and proceeds smoothly, which convinces Bragg that larger transfers of men and supplies could be shuttled to that theater before Union forces can respond.

NAVAL: The USS *Bienville* captures the Confederate schooner *Morning Star* off Wilmington, North Carolina.

The USS *Cambridge* destroys the blockade-runner *Modern Greece* off Wilmington, North Carolina.

The USS *Bohio* captures the Confederate sloop *Wave* near Mobile, Alabama.

Admiral David G. Farragut formulates plans to run his squadron past the guns of Vicksburg, Mississippi. That accomplished, he will unite with the gunboat flotilla under Admiral Charles H. Davis on the Mississippi River.

June 28

SOUTH: General George B. McClellan withdraws from Richmond and bitterly concludes that he is losing the campaign due to a lack of promised reinforcements. Meanwhile, the Confederates hastily regroup and reorganize to maintain their strategic initiative. General Robert E. Lee, having analyzed McClellan's temperament, now orders his army on an intricate march down four different roads in an attempt to surround and possibly cripple his opponent. He also directs the 11,000-man force under General John B. Magruder to harass the withdrawal of Union forces until the main Confederate body is brought up.

Confederate forces under Colonel George T. Anderson attack a small Union detachment at Garnett's and Golding's farms, Virginia, but they are repulsed in heavy fighting. That night, another force under General (and former Confederate secretary of state) Robert Toombs also probes the Union line only to suffer another defeat. Casualties are recorded as 461 Confederates and 361 Federals.

Federal forces evacuate James Island, South Carolina, temporarily suspending their campaign to capture the city of Charleston.

WEST: Colonel Philip Sheridan takes a brigade of Union cavalry to Boonesboro, 20 miles south of Corinth, Mississippi, and establishes a fortified outpost. He is scouting for possible offensive activity by Confederates under General Braxton Bragg.

General Earl Van Dorn arrives back at Vicksburg, Mississippi, and resumes control of the city's defenses.

NAVAL: Navy vessels sortie from their anchorage at Fortress Monroe, Virginia, and sail to Harrison's Landing to secure communications for the Army of the Potomac as it retires from Richmond.

The USS *Braziliera* captures the Confederate schooner *Chance* off Wassaw Sound, Georgia.

At 2:00 A.M., Admiral David G. Farragut and Commander David D. Porter slip their respective commands past Confederate batteries at Vicksburg, Mississippi, suffering 15 killed and 30 wounded—a trivial toll considering the heavy ordnance poured on them. The mightiest Confederate bastion in the West is about to be challenged.

June 29

SOUTH: The Confederate Department of Alabama and West Florida is disbanded.

General John B. Magruder, advancing east from Williamsburg, Virginia, with 11,000 men, cautiously probes the region for Union forces. He is ordered by General Robert E. Lee to pursue retreating Federal forces aggressively and possibly to destroy their rear guard. Previously, Magruder made arrangements with Generals Thomas J. Jackson and Benjamin Huger to provide cover and support for both of his flanks, but neither force materializes—Jackson is delayed constructing a bridge over Chickahominy Creek while Huger's troops take the wrong road and become lost. Contact with Union troops finally is established at Allen's Farm at about 9:00 A.M., although Magruder suddenly finds himself confronting the entire II Corps of 26,000 men under General Edwin V. Sumner, backed by 40 cannon. He nonetheless attacks and enjoys reasonable success until Federal defenses stiffen. Magruder then suspends the battle at 11:00 A.M. and assumes defensive positions. The equally timorous Sumner then withdraws to new positions at Savage's Station and assumes defensive lines of his own.

Magruder, still unsupported by either Jackson or Huger, cautiously resumes his advance at about 4:00 P.M. and, within the hour, tangles with Sumner's pickets. But Sumner, despite the preponderance of his force, declines to attack and simply lobs shells at Confederate positions for several hours. Confederate General Richard Griffith, reconnoitering Union lines closely, is killed in consequence. Stiff fighting then ensues between the divisions of General Lafayette McLaws and John Sedgwick until an unexpected thunderstorm erupts at about 9:00 P.M., and combat ceases. Thus far, Magruder's "pursuit" availed him little beyond 626 casualties. Sumner's mishandling of affairs cost him 919 men, and he abandons 2,500 sick and injured soldiers before leaving. A major Confederate advance has been stalled. Overnight, the II Corps withdraws to new positions at White Oak Swamp and Glendale.

WEST: General Franz Sigel formally assumes command of the Army of Virginia's I Corps.

NAVAL: The USS *Marblehead* and *Chocura*, anchored in the Pamunkey River, Virginia, provide cover fire for the Army of the Potomac as it withdraws from the vicinity of White House. Transports and armed escorts also sortie up the James and Chickahominy rivers in support of General George B. McClellan.

The USS *Susquehanna* and *Kanawha* capture the British blockade-runner *Ann* off Mobile, Alabama.

The Federal gunboat USS *Lexington* takes fire from Confederate forces on the White River, Arkansas, near St. Charles.

June 30

SOUTH: General Robert E. Lee, intent on destroying at least a portion of General George B. McClellan's Army of the Potomac, issues another set of complicated attack plans to catch the fleeing Federals in a pincer at Glendale, near the junctions of the Charles City Road, Long Bridge Road, and Quaker Road. Orders then are sent out to the divisions of John B. Magruder, Benjamin Huger, Thomas J. Jackson, James Longstreet, and Ambrose P. Hill to converge on Union forces from front, flank, and rear, crushing them. But, once again, Lee is stymied by inept staff work, and his strategy quickly goes awry. Magruder, for his part, becomes lost and spends the entire day marching to and fro behind Confederate lines without seeing action. Huger likewise is unable to surmount obstacles placed in his path along the Charles City Road, and he fails to advance in time. The usually astute Jackson then turns in one of the most lethargic performances of his career by simply remaining north of White Oak Swamp and swapping cannonballs with General William B. Franklin's VI Corps. By 4:00 P.M. that afternoon, an exasperated Lee could count only 19,000 men of Longstreet's and Hill's divisions on the field, and these are seriously depleted by previous fighting.

At length, Longstreet and Hill charge the center of the Union line, posted behind White Oak Swamp Creek, and crash into the division of General George A. McCall, capturing him. But before they can exploit their advantage and seize a vital crossroads, fresh forces under Generals Joseph Hooker, Phil Kearney, and John Sedgewick rush up to engage them. Savage hand-to-hand fighting finally evicts the Confederates and fighting concludes with nightfall. The Union line of retreat is saved. Lee's losses at White Oak are 638 dead, 2,814 wounded, and 221 missing (3,673) while McClellan sustains 297 killed, 1,696 wounded, and 1,804 missing (3,797). Despite a fine performance by his troops, the Union leader continues shifting his base of operations toward Harrison's Landing on the James River and assumes new defensive positions along Malvern Hill, two miles distant.

NAVAL: The USS *South Carolina* is detached from the South Atlantic Blockading Squadron to join the *Wyandotte* off Mosquito Inlet, New Smyrna, Florida, recently used by blockade-runners from Nassau.

The USS *Quaker City* captures the Confederate brig *Model* in the Gulf of Mexico.

The Federal gunboat USS *Lexington* trades fire with Confederate batteries on the White River, Arkansas.

July 1

POLITICS: To meet mounting wartime expenditures, President Lincoln raises the federal income tax to 3 percent on incomes of more than $600 per annum. (The first income tax passed in 1861 was never enacted). The Bureau of Internal Revenue is also founded to collect the levies. Congress then passes the Pacific Railway Act, authorizing construction of the first transcontinental railroad.

SOUTH: Unable to destroy the Army of the Potomac at White Oak Swamp the previous day, General Robert E. Lee is convinced that, nevertheless, General George B. McClellan's force is demoralized by the sledgehammer blows he has dealt them. Now, with Union forces poised to reach Harrison's Landing on the James River safely, he hopes to deliver one last and possibly crushing blow against them at Malvern Hill, a 150-foot high-rise flanked by swamps and other obstacles. That position is defended ably by the V Corps of General Fitz John Porter, who arrays his troops in a defensive semicircle along its crest. Porter's secure flanks also promise to funnel any Confederate assault directly up the center of his waiting line, crowned by 100 pieces of field artillery. The approach is covered further by a thick belt of skirmishers from Colonel Hiram Berdan's elite regiment of green-clad sharpshooters. Finally, even if endangered, Porter could call on any one of four Union additional corps deployed to his rear for assistance.

Confederate general Daniel H. Hill, on surveying the obvious strength of Porter's position, advises Lee to relent, but the general remains determined to attack. Orders then go out for the divisions of General Thomas J. Jackson to deploy against the Union left, that of John B. Magruder to hit their center and of Benjamin Huger's to assail their right. General James Longstreet, meanwhile, strongly suggests that Confederate artillery be massed along either flank and pointed at the center to catch Union gunners in a crossfire. However, as happened repeatedly all week, Lee's sound plan is vexed and undone due to staff errors and misunderstandings. Magruder becomes lost again, countermarching fruitlessly for several hours, and he arrives to find that his position has been taken up by Huger. The Confederate attack, when it developed at 1:00 P.M., is also delivered piecemeal and subject to defeat in detail. The heavy Southern columns present excellent targets to Porter's well-drilled gunners, who rip their formation apart with a deluge of shot, canister, and grape. For several hours, the valiant gray coats fling themselves at the Union position, only to be blasted downhill in tangled heaps. The one-sided slaughter continues until darkness finally closes the contest. Lee's final lunge at McClellan proves catastrophic: His troops sustain losses totaling 869 killed, 4,241 wounded, and 540 missing (5,650) while Union casualties amount to 314 dead, 1,875 wounded, and 818 missing (3,007). A stunned general Daniel H. Hill characterizes Malvern Hill not as war; rather, he says, "it was murder." Porter and other Union generals implore McClellan to counterattack immediately and to resume the drive on Richmond, but he characteristically refuses. The Army of the Potomac then withdraws a final five miles overnight and reestablishes itself at Harrison's Landing, safely under the guns of the Union navy.

The Seven Days' campaign reaches its bloody conclusion with Union forces pushed far from the Southern capital. The Confederacy is preserved for another three and a half years at a cost of 3,286 killed, 15,909 wounded, and 946 missing (20,141). The Army of the Potomac, which handles itself well under excruciating circumstances—not the least of which is McClellan's timorous leadership—loses 1,734 dead, 8,062 injured, and 6,063 missing (15,849). Most important of all, the campaign defines General Robert E. Lee as an assertive, imaginative, and offensive-minded battle captain, much given to bold and calculated risks. Warfare in the eastern theater now largely revolves around his actions.

WEST: Union forces under General Philip H. Sheridan engage a larger force of 4,700 Confederates under General James R. Chalmers at Booneville, Mississippi, 20 miles south of Corinth. Chalmers presses hard against Sheridan's pickets, carrying the latest Colt revolving rifles, and they make little headway. But Sheridan, while badly outnumbered, orders his 2nd Michigan and 2nd Iowa Cavalry to slip around Chalmer's line and attack his rear. When this move finally transpires at about 3:30 P.M., the Confederates are unnerved completely and withdraw in good order, hotly pursued by Federal troopers. Only 728 Union troops are engaged in this fine defensive action, and they lose one killed, 24 wounded, and 16 missing. Sheridan reportedly counts 65 Confederate dead on the field. Moreover, his aggressive handling of troops catches the attention of General Henry W. Halleck, who arranges for a promotion to brigadier general 10 weeks hence.

NAVAL: Commodore John Rodgers directs naval cannon fire from the gunboats *Galena, Aroostook,* and *Jacob Bell* against General Robert E. Lee's right flank at Malvern Hill, Virginia, facilitating the final Union withdrawal.

The USS *DeSoto* captures the British schooner *William* off Sabine Pass, Texas.

The Western Flotilla under Commodore Charles H. Davis unites with the naval expedition of Admiral David G. Farragut above Vicksburg, Mississippi. Freshwater and saltwater squadrons thereby are joined for the first time after remarkable efforts by both.

July 2

POLITICS: President Abraham Lincoln authorizes the "Ironclad test oath" to extract loyalty from all federal employees, and the oath eventually is extended to include federal contractors, attorneys, jurors, and passport applicants. Furthermore, citizens in Federal-occupied regions of the South likewise are required to pledge their allegiance. Lincoln also signs the Land Grant College Act (or Morrill Act), which transfers public lands to educational institutions throughout the North.

SOUTH: General George B. McClellan concludes his overall withdrawal to Harrison's Landing, Virginia, derided by many as the "Great Skedaddle."

WEST: The Confederate districts of the Mississippi and of the Gulf are constituted under Generals Earl Van Dorn and John H. Forney, respectively.

NAVAL: The USS *Western World* captures the British blockade-runner *Volante* in Winyah Bay, South Carolina.

July 3

POLITICS: President Abraham Lincoln and General George B. McClellan both endure a firestorm of criticism and recrimination over the recent Peninsula campaign's failure.

WEST: General Sterling Price becomes commander of the Confederate Army of the West.

NAVAL: The USS *Quaker City* captures the British blockade-runner *Lilla* off Hole-in-the-Wall, Virginia.

The USS *Hatteras* captures the Confederate schooner *Sarah* off Sabine Pass, Texas.

July 4

POLITICS: General George B. McClellan again advises President Abraham Lincoln that the objective of military operations should be the preservation of the Union, not the elimination of slavery.

NORTH: Philip Kearny, Fitz John Porter, and John Sedgwick are each appointed major general, U.S. Army.

WEST: Confederate cavalry under Colonel John H. Morgan depart Knoxville, Tennessee, with 867 troopers, starting the first of three celebrated raids. Morgan's objective is the town of Gallatin, Tennessee, where he intends to cut the Louisville and Nashville Railroad, then supplying the army of General Don C. Buell.

SOUTHWEST: Pro-union German settlers under Fritz Teneger rally at Bear Creek, Texas, and organize three armed companies for their own protection.

NAVAL: The USS *Maratanza* attacks and captures CSS *Teaser* at Haxall's on the James River, Virginia, as it lays torpedoes. The vessel was also preparing to conduct balloon reconnaissance operations with a device stitched together from old silk frocks.

The USS *Rhode Island* captures the British blockade-runner *R. O. Bryan* off the Texas coast.

July 5

WEST: General William J. Hardee temporarily takes charge of the Army of the Mississippi.

NAVAL: The U.S. Navy Department is reorganized by Act of Congress into eight divisions: Yards and Docks, Equipment and Recruiting, Navigation, Ordnance, Construction and Repair, Steam Engineering, Provisions and Clothing, and Medicine and Surgery.

The USS *Hatteras* captures the Confederate sloop *Elizabeth* off the Louisiana coast.

July 6

SOUTH: General Ambrose E. Burnside sails from the Department of North Carolina with reinforcements slated for the Army of the Potomac, Virginia. His successor is General John G. Foster.

WEST: General Nathan B. Forrest begins to assemble cavalry in Mississippi for an extended raid through Tennessee.

NAVAL: Commodore John Wilkes assumes command of the James River Flotilla, presently a division within the North Atlantic Blockading Squadron under Commodore Louis M. Goldsborough.

July 7

SOUTH: President Abraham Lincoln visits General George B. McClellan at Harrison's Landing, Virginia, to discuss recent events. The general blames his recent setback on a lack of promised reinforcements, and he also urges the president to adopt more conservative approaches to both strategy—and politics.

WEST: Union forces under Generals Samuel R. Curtis and Frederick Steele defeat a body of Confederates at Cache, Arkansas.

NAVAL: The James River Flotilla under Commodore John Rodgers actively escorts and convoys army transports supporting the Army of the Potomac, Virginia.

The USS *Tahoma* captures the Confederate schooner *Uncle Mose* off Yucatán Bank, Mexico.

The USS *Quaker City* and *Huntsville* seize the British schooner *Adela* off the Bahama Islands.

July 8

WEST: Federal troops attack a camp occupied by Confederate guerrilla William C. Quantrill at Pleasant Hill, Missouri.

NAVAL: President Abraham Lincoln arrives onboard the USS *Areil* at Harrison's Landing, Virginia.

Armed boats from the USS *Flag* and *Restless* capture the blockade-runner *Emilie* in Bulls Bay, South Carolina.

July 9

WEST: Tompkinsville, Kentucky, is captured by Confederate cavalry under Colonel John H. Morgan, along with 400 Union prisoners.

NAVAL: An expedition consisting of Federal gunboats USS *Commodore Perry, Shawsheen,* and *Ceres* steams up the Roanoke River, North Carolina, and captures the town of Hamilton, along with the Confederate steamer *Wilson.*

The USS *Arthur* captures the Confederate schooner *Reindeer* off Aransas Pass, Texas.

July 10

WEST: The newly designated Army of Virginia under General John Pope positions itself in the Shenandoah Valley and reminds inhabitants of their obligation to assist Union efforts. He also promises harsh justice for any treasonable or harmful activities against military personnel.

Confederate raider Colonel John H. Morgan captures a Union depot at Glasgow, Kentucky, and issues a dispatch urging inhabitants to "rise and arm, and drive the Hessian invaders from their soil."

Union forces apprehend 90 Confederate guerrillas as they drill between Gallatin and Hartsville, Tennessee.

NAVAL: The USS *Arthur* apprehends the Confederate sloop *Belle Italia* at Aransas Pass, Texas, while the sloop *Monte Christo* is burned to prevent capture.

July 11

POLITICAL: Congress authorizes compensation for the families of Union sailors killed in the action against the CSS *Virginia* at Hampton Roads, Virginia.

NORTH: General Henry W. Halleck gains appointment as general in chief of Union forces.

WEST: Colonel John H. Morgan's occupation of Lebanon, Kentucky, alarms the countryside as far as Cincinnati, Ohio, Evansville, Indiana, and neighboring Lexington and Louisville.

July 12

NORTH: The Congressional Medal of Honor, established in 1861 to honor naval personnel, is expanded to include soldiers.

WEST: Union forces under General Samuel R. Curtis arrive at Helena, Arkansas, from Missouri.

NAVAL: The USS *Mercedita* captures Confederate blockade-runners *Victoria* and *Ida* off Hole-in-the-Wall, Abaco, Bahamas.

Faced with falling water levels on the Yazoo River, the large Confederate ironclad CSS *Arkansas,* under Lieutenant Isaac N. Brown, sorties into the Mississippi River and steams south toward Vicksburg, Mississippi.

July 13

POLITICS: President Abraham Lincoln seeks congressional action to compensate states that are willing to abolish slavery voluntarily. He also informs Secretary of State William H. Seward and Secretary of the Navy Gideon Welles of his intention to read an initial "emancipation proclamation" to the full cabinet on July 22.

SOUTH: Having skirmished with Confederates forces, Union troops burn a bridge along the Rapidan River, Virginia.

WEST: Colonel Nathan B. Forrest and 1,000 Confederate cavalry capture Murfreesboro, Tennessee, by defeating a Union garrison of 1,200 men. He does so by overrunning the camps of the 9th Michigan and 7th Pennsylvania Cavalry before bluffing the still intact 3rd Minnesota to surrender. "I did not come here to make a half job of it," he declares to subordinates after being warned about approaching reinforcements, "I intend to have them all." Union casualties are 29 killed and 120 wounded while Forrest suffers 25 killed and about 50 wounded.

Confederate cavalry under Colonel John H. Morgan raid the vicinity of Harrodsburg, Kentucky.

All remaining Missouri State Guard troops east of the Mississippi River are ordered home to become part of the army under General Thomas C. Hindman.

July 14

POLITICS: President Abraham Lincoln approves legislation for a Federal pension system to assist all widows and children of Union soldiers killed in the war. Meanwhile, 20 representatives from border states announce their opposition to the president's compensated emancipation plan.

SOUTH: Richard H. Anderson is appointed major general, C.S.A.

WEST: General John Pope rallies soldiers of his Army of Virginia in declaring that "The strongest position a soldier should desire to occupy is one from which he can most easily advance against the enemy." He then positions his men between Washington, D.C., and Confederate forces to draw their attention from General George B. McClellan.

Confederate cavalry under Colonel John H. Morgan skirmish with Union forces at Mackville, Kentucky.

July 15

SOUTHWEST: Apaches under Mangas Coloradas and Cochise engage California troops at the Battle of Apache Pass, New Mexico Territory.

NAVAL: Union vessels USS *Carondelet, Tyler,* and *Queen of the West* under Captain Charles H. Davis attack the newly built Confederate ironclad CSS *Arkansas* under Lieutenant Isaac N. Brown once it emerges from the Yazoo River onto the Mississippi. After a heavy exchange of fire, which badly damages *Carondelet* and *Tyler, Arkansas* dashes through 16 Union vessels comprising Commodore David G. Farragut's blockading fleet and steams unscathed on to Vicksburg, Mississippi. Brown then anchors safely under the city's big guns, but Farragut, angered over being surprised, directs his fleet past Vicksburg in broad daylight and attacks the Confederate intruder. Both sides sustain damage, but the *Arkansas* remains afloat and a menace to Union shipping throughout the region. In light of falling water levels on the Mississippi, Farragut continues to New Orleans to recoup his losses. Moreover, Davis's mishandling of the *Arkansas* sortie leads to his eventual replacement by David D. Porter.

July 16

DIPLOMACY: Confederate agent John Slidell requests the French government under Emperor Napoleon III to grant diplomatic recognition.

POLITICS: The western gunboat fleet, constructed and managed by the War Department, is formally transferred by Congress to the Navy Department.

NORTH: Alfred Pleasonton is appointed brigadier general of cavalry.

WEST: General Ulysses S. Grant has his District of West Tennessee enlarged to include the District of the Mississippi and the two armies they contain.

SOUTHWEST: General Theophilus H. Holmes becomes commander of the Confederate Trans-Mississippi Department.

NAVAL: David G. Farragut is formally promoted to rear admiral by Congress, the first officer in United States naval history to hold that rank. President Abraham Lincoln also signs legislation conferring similar promotions on all sitting flag officers.

The USS *Huntsville* captures the British schooner *Agnes* off Abaco, Bahamas.

July 17

POLITICS: President Abraham Lincoln approves the Second Confiscation Act, which mandates freedom for any African-American slaves reaching Union lines. Those wishing to emigrate from the United States will also receive assistance. Various kinds of property useful to the Confederate war effort also are subject to seizure. However, escaped slaves in loyal, border states remain subject to return under the Fugitive Slave Law.

The second session of the 37th Congress adjourns.

SOUTH: General John Pope's Federal troops capture Gordonsville, Virginia, then functioning as a Confederate supply base.

General Daniel H. Hill transfers to the Department of North Carolina.

WEST: Following General Henry S. Halleck's departure for Washington, D.C., General Ulysses S. Grant formally resumes his role as commander of troops in the western theater.

NAVAL: An armed party of sailors and marines from USS *Potomac, New London,* and *Grey Cloud* ascends the Pascagoula River, Mississippi, on an expedition, but it is turned back by Confederate cavalry.

July 18

WEST: A small party of Confederate raiders under Captain Adam R. Johnson cross the Ohio River and briefly seize the town of Newburg, Indiana. He then employs two fake cannon constructed from stove pipes across the river to bluff local Indiana Home Guards into compliance lest he "shell" the town. After absconding with guns stored in the Federal arsenal there, the raiders slip quickly back across the river, chased and shelled by a Union gunboat. Hereafter, Johnson is convivially nicknamed "Stovepipe." Two Union soldiers are wounded in the raid, which prompts Governor Oliver P. Morton to wire the War Department for reinforcements.

Confederate cavalry under Colonel John H. Morgan attack and capture the town of Cynthiana, Kentucky, leaving 17 Union and 24 Confederate soldiers dead. He also seizes 400 prisoners.

The Confederate Department No. 2 is enlarged to include Mississippi, East Louisiana, and West Florida.

NAVAL: Secretary of the Navy Gideon Welles directs naval flag officers to select three enlisted boys annually to become candidates at the U.S. Naval Academy.

July 19

POLITICS: Horace Greeley, editor of the *New York Tribune,* composes a letter to President Abraham Lincoln and calls on him to free the slaves as a means of weakening the Confederacy.

John S. Phelps of Missouri is named military governor of Arkansas.

NAVAL: The U.S. Congress approves a pension bill guaranteeing a lifetime subsidy to all naval personnel injured in the line of duty.

A Confederate court of inquiry acquits Commodore Josiah Tattnall for his destruction of the CSS *Virginia* on May 11, 1862.

July 20

WEST: Colonel John H. Morgan's raiders are surprised by Union cavalry at Owensville, Kentucky, and are dispersed.

July 21

POLITICS: President Abraham Lincoln discusses with the cabinet the possible employment of African-American soldiers. No action is taken.

SOUTH: Nathan B. Forrest is appointed brigadier general, C.S.A.

WEST: Union forces occupy Luray in western Virginia.

The Confederate Army of Mississippi under General Braxton Bragg advances toward Chattanooga, Tennessee, while command of the District of Tennessee reverts to General Sterling Price.

NAVAL: The USS *Huntsville* captures the Confederate steamer *Reliance* in the Bahama Channel.

Federal steamers *Clara Dolsen* and *Rob Roy,* along with the tug *Restless,* embark troops at Cairo, Illinois, and transport them to nearby Evansville prior to recapturing Henderson, Kentucky, from Confederate irregulars.

The transport USS *Sallie Woods* is destroyed by Confederate artillery at Argyle Landing on the Mississippi River.

July 22

POLITICS: President Abraham Lincoln unveils a draft of his Emancipation Proclamation to his cabinet, stipulating a grant of freedom to all African Americans held in bondage throughout the Confederacy. However, he heeds Secretary of State William H. Seward's advice to postpone the document's unveiling until after a significant military victory by the North. Secretary of War Edwin M. Stanton also announces that the army can appropriate personal property for military purposes and also employ any freed African Americans as paid laborers.

Federal and Confederate officials reach agreement on a cartel for exchanging prisoners of war. It functions effectively until the fall of 1863 when Union complaints over the treatment of black soldiers force its cancellation.

WEST: Generals John A. Dix and Ambrose E. Burnside assume command of the VII and IX Corps, respectively, in the Department of Virginia.

Confederate raiders under Colonel John H. Morgan return to Livingston, Tennessee, after a spectacular raid through Kentucky. The Federals also learn that a Confederate operative working for Morgan had tapped into their telegraph lines and intercepted army dispatches for the past 12 days.

NAVAL: The USS *Essex* under Captain William B. Porter, accompanied by the ram *Queen of the West,* resumes attacking the Confederate ironclad CSS *Arkansas* off Vicksburg, Mississippi. Both Union vessels are driven off without seriously damaging their opponent, which defiantly steams past Vicksburg's batteries, challenging its opponents to fight. *Queen of the West* nonetheless strikes the ironclad with a heavy broadside and damages its engines before the action concludes.

July 23

NORTH: General Henry W. Halleck, newly arrived as general in chief in Washington, D.C., discusses the possibility of joint operations between Generals George B. McClellan and John Pope.

SOUTH: Union cavalry under Colonel Hugh J. Kirkpatrick, advancing from Fredericksburg, Virginia, raid Confederate supplies gathered at Carmel Church until driven back by General J. E. B. Stuart.

WEST: General John Pope tightens restriction on the inhabitants of the Shenandoah region by insisting that all military-age males take an oath of allegiance or face deportation to the South. Violators, if caught, would be summarily executed and their property would be confiscated.

General Braxton Bragg skillfully transfers by rail 31,000 Confederate troops from Tupelo, Mississippi, to Chattanooga, Tennessee—a distance of 776 miles—in the largest Confederate railroad movement of the war. By invading Kentucky, both Bragg and General Edmund Kirby-Smith intend to take the Union Army of the Ohio from behind. However, in his place Bragg leaves behind two independent commands: Generals Sterling Price at Tupelo and Earl Van Dorn at Vicksburg, each with 16,000 men apiece. A clear line of authority between the two headstrong leaders is never clearly established, again with detrimental effects for the South.

July 24
POLITICS: Martin Van Buren, the eighth president of the United States, dies in Kinderhook, New York, aged 80 years.

SOUTH: Fitzhugh Lee is appointed brigadier general, C.S.A.

Union forces attack and rout a Confederate detachment at Benton's Ferry, Louisiana.

Federal troops under General John Gibbon commence the reconnoitering of Orange Court House, Virginia, from Fredericksburg.

General John G. Foster initiates a Union overland campaign against Trenton, North Carolina, from New Bern.

NAVAL: Falling water levels on the Mississippi River and rising sickness induce Admiral David G. Farragut to remove his squadron from below Vicksburg, Mississippi, to New Orleans, Louisiana, following a two-month hiatus. His experience outside Vicksburg has convinced him that naval forces alone can never take the city. That will require the services of a large, well-equipped army.

The gunboat flotilla of Admiral Charles H. Davis on the Mississippi River steams off toward Helena, Arkansas, from which a steady flow of men and supplies from Texas and Arkansas originates. Both Davis and General Samuel R. Curtis plan sweeping raids along the Arkansas shore and interdict enemy lines of communication.

The USS *Octorara* captures the British blockade-runner *Tubal* Cain off Savannah, Georgia.

The USS *Quaker City* captures the blockade-runner *Orion* off Key West, Florida.

July 25
SOUTH: J. E. B. Stuart is appointed major general, C.S.A.

WEST: Confederate cavalry under General Joseph Wheeler penetrate 70 miles behind Union lines from Holly Springs, Mississippi, and attacks bridges and communications.

NAVAL: The Confederate steamer *Cuba* skirts the Union blockade and enters Mobile, Alabama.

July 26
WEST: General Braxton Bragg's men compel a Federal retreat from Spangler's Mill at Jonesboro, Alabama.

NAVAL: Confederates burn the Union schooner *Louisia Reed* in the James River.

The Southern steamer *Romain* successfully runs the Union blockade off Charleston, South Carolina.

July 27
NORTH: John Buford is appointed brigadier general of cavalry, U.S. Army.

NAVAL: The USS *Yankee* and *Satellite* capture the Confederate schooner *J. W. Sturges* in Chippoak Creek, Virginia.

July 28

POLITICS: Confederate governors of Texas, Missouri, Arkansas, and Louisiana appeal to President Jefferson Davis for men, supplies, money, and a senior commanding general to bolster their military defenses.

SOUTH: Richard Taylor is appointed major general, C.S.A.

Captain Charles D. Sanford conducts the 12th Massachusetts Cavalry on a reconnaissance expedition from Bachelder's Creek, North Carolina, down the Neuse River Road.

WEST: Colonel John H. Morgan's raiders arrive at Livingston, Tennessee.

Confederate forces are ejected from Bollinger's Mills, Missouri, by Federal troops.

NAVAL: The USS *Hatteras* captures the Confederate brig *Josephine* off Ship Shoal, Louisiana.

July 29

SOUTH: General John Pope departs Washington, D.C., to join the Army of Virginia in the field.

WEST: Federal authorities arrest Confederate spy Bell Boyd at Warrenton, Virginia, and she is sent to the Old Capital Prison in Washington, D.C.

Advance elements of the Confederate Army of Mississippi arrive at Chattanooga, Tennessee, constituting a strategic transfer of resources from the Deep South back to its center. General Braxton Bragg skillfully cobbles together a force of 30,000 men there for an offensive into Kentucky.

Confederate cavalry rout General John Logan's troopers at Hatchie Bottom, Tennessee.

Union forces rout Confederate defenders at Moore's Mills, Missouri, inflicting 62 killed and 100 wounded for a Northern loss of 16 dead and 30 injured.

NAVAL: Ship "290," christened *Enrica*, departs Liverpool, England, ostensibly for sea trials. It actually is headed for Nassau for service with the Confederate navy as the infamous commerce raider CSS *Alabama*.

The USS *Mount Vernon* and *Mystic* capture the British blockade-runner *Napier* near Wilmington, North Carolina.

July 30

SOUTH: General George B. McClellan, commanding the Army of the Potomac, Virginia, receives orders to transfer all sick and wounded soldiers from Harrison's Landing. This is a preliminary step for relocating his entire command back to Washington, D.C.

At New Orleans, Louisiana, General Benjamin Butler further roils public sentiments by confiscating a load of church bells cast in Boston; he orders them auctioned.

SOUTHWEST: Major Alfred Hobby arrives at Corpus Christi, Texas, with 300 men of the 8th Texas. His purpose is to guard the town against attacks mounted by the offshore Union squadron under Captain John W. Kittredge.

July 31

DIPLOMACY: U.S. minister Charles F. Adams badgers Foreign Secretary Lord Russell not to allow the newly launched *Enrica* (the future CSS *Alabama*) to leave port. The British government dithers for five days before Lord Russell issues the requested orders, but Confederate agents slip aboard and it sails away under the pretense of conducting sea trials. Ultimately, this vessel accounts for the destruction of 60 Union merchant ships and becomes a major source of friction between the two governments.

POLITICS: President Jefferson Davis directs that any Union officer captured from General John Pope's Army of Virginia is to be treated as a felon. This is in retaliation for the order that hostile Southern citizens should be shot for treason under Pope's draconian administration of the Shenandoah Valley.

WEST: General Braxton Bragg and Genevoe Edmund Kirby-Smith confer at Chattanooga, Tennessee, and hammer out a strategy for the upcoming campaign in Kentucky. The former, while senior, fails to exert his authority over Kirby-Smith, who insists on a virtually independent command. The Confederate offensive thus is compromised from the onset and promises to be poorly coordinated.

NAVAL: The USS *Cimarron* engages a Confederate battery at Coggin's Point, Virginia, after it sinks two army transports.

The USS *Magnolia* captures the Confederate steamer *Memphis* off Cape Romain, South Carolina.

August 1

NORTH: George Crook is appointed brigadier general, U.S. Army.

SOUTH: Federal and Confederate artillery duels at Harrison's Landing, Virginia.

WEST: A heavy skirmish erupts at Newark, Missouri, with Confederates losing 100 killed and wounded while capturing 70 Union troops.

SOUTHWEST: Fritz Teneger convinces 65 pro-Union German settlers at Turtle Creek, Texas, to cross the Rio Grande into Mexico, sail to New Orleans, and join the Union army there. When Confederate authorities learn of the plan they dispatch 94 men to intercept them.

NAVAL: The USS *Thomas Freeborn* captures the Confederate schooner *Mail* in the Coan River, Virginia.

The USS *Penobscot* captures the Confederate sloop *Lizzie* off New Inlet, North Carolina.

August 2

DIPLOMACY: Secretary of State William H. Seward orders American minister to Britain Charles F. Adams to officially ignore any British overtures for mediation.

SOUTH: Malvern Hill, Virginia, is reoccupied by Union troops under General George B. McClellan.

Union forces under General John Pope storm into Orange Court House, Virginia, killing 11 Confederates and taking 52 prisoners for a loss of five wounded.

NAVAL: English authorities prepare to release CSS *Florida* for sea duty after it had been seized at Nassau. August 3

SOUTH: General Henry W. Halleck orders the Army of the Potomac to begin shifting from Harrison's Landing on the Yorktown Peninsula to Aquia Landing near Fredericksburg, Virginia, to protect the national capital better. The transfer occasions much umbrage from General George B. McClellan, who seeks a renewed offensive against Richmond.

WEST: General Jeff Thompson's Confederates are defeated near Memphis, Tennessee.

NAVAL: The USS *Santiago de Cuba* seizes the blockade-runner *Columbia* north of Abaco, Bahamas, along with its cargo of several thousand British-made Enfield rifles, 12 cannon, and tons of munitions.

The Confederate ironclad CSS *Arkansas,* despite persistent engine problems, is ordered out of its berth at Vicksburg, Mississippi, and steams downstream to assist an attack on Baton Rouge, Louisiana. Lieutenant Henry K. Stevens, fearing the worse for his temperamental warship, complies only reluctantly.

August 4
POLITICS: President Abraham Lincoln issues a call for 300,000 drafted militia to serve nine months; this levy was never enacted. But despite persistent manpower shortages, he declines the services of two African-Americans regiments from Indiana, suggesting instead that they be employed as laborers.

SOUTH: Confederate cavalry under General J. E. B. Stuart commence an expedition from Hanover Court House to Fredericksburg, Virginia.

General Ambrose E. Burnside's IX Corps arrives at Aquia Creek, near Fredericksburg, Virginia, to assist the Army of Virginia under General John Pope.

At New Orleans, Louisiana, General Benjamin F. Butler assesses "secessionists" $341,000 to assist the city's poor.

NAVAL: The USS *Huron* captures the Confederate schooner *Aquilla* near Charleston, South Carolina.

The USS *Unadilla* captures the British steamer *Lodona* as it ran the blockade at Hell Gate, Georgia.

August 5
SOUTH: General John Gibbon leads a Federal expedition from Fredericksburg, Virginia, to Frederick's Hall Station, skirmishing en route.

General John C. Breckinridge is ordered by General Earl Van Dorn to attack the Union enclave at Baton Rouge, Louisiana, with a force of 2,600 Confederates, accompanied by the ironclad CSS *Arkansas*. An important part of his mission is to secure Port Hudson on the Mississippi River halfway between Vicksburg and Baton Rouge and to fortify it as a choke point. The Union garrison of 2,500 men under General Thomas Williams deploys to receive him, and a sharp action erupts in very dense fog at about 4:30 A.M. Confusion reigns on both sides but a party of Southerners under General Charles Clark gradually flanks the Union left and pushes the defenders back into the city. Williams is killed while rallying his disorganized troops, but the Confederate advance is thwarted by accurate gunfire from Union gunboats anchored offshore. Fighting finally subsides at about 10:00 A.M. when Breckinridge, realizing that the *Arkansas* is not coming, orders his men back. The Confederates then return to Vicksburg, Mississippi, pausing only to fortify Port Hudson en route. Union losses are 84 dead and 299 wounded to a Southern tally of 84 dead and 372 injured. General Clark, severely wounded, is abandoned on the battlefield and captured.

NAVAL: Union forces commence an expedition up the White River, Arkansas, accompanied by the gunboats *Benton, Iatan, Louisville,* and *Mound City.*

The large Confederate ironclad CSS *Arkansas* under Lieutenant Henry K. Stevens continues down the Mississippi River to assist the expedition against Baton Rouge, Louisiana. Stevens's mission is to neutralize Union gunboats offshore; however, his ship experiences a broken propellor shaft en route to the city, and he is unable to support military efforts ashore. Confederate troops driving against Union positions thus are deprived of badly needed naval support and largely are repulsed by Federal gunboats enfilading their right flank.

August 6
NORTH: William S. Rosecrans is promoted to major general, U.S. Army.

SOUTH: Heavy skirmishing is reported at Malvern Hill and Thornburg, Virginia, and Federal forces withdraw.

WEST: A large skirmish takes place between Federals under General John D. Cox and Confederates under General William W. Loring at Packs Ferry, western Virginia.

Union general Robert L. McCook is murdered by Confederate guerrillas while riding in an ambulance near Decherd, Tennessee.

A starving band of Mdewkanton Santee (Sioux) tribe members arrive at the Lower Agency, where chief Little Crow (Taoyateduta) pleads with Agent Andrew J. Myrick for promised foodstuffs. However, war activities delay the arrival of treaty payments from Washington, D.C., and local authorities refuse to lend Little Crow the credit necessary to feed his people. Despite desperate entreaties for help, Myrick rebuffs the Native Americans, declaring: "So far as I am concerned, if they are hungry, let them eat grass." The chiefs angrily depart the agency, incensed at official indifference.

NAVAL: A Federal naval flotilla under Commander David D. Porter of the USS *Essex* attacks and damages the ironclad CSS *Arkansas,* mechanically unsound and suffering from engine trouble, near Baton Rouge, Louisiana. Once the *Arkansas* is grounded, Stevens orders it set afire and scuttled. The Confederacy never again deploys such a large warship on the Mississippi.

August 7
SOUTH: A force of 24,000 Confederates under General Thomas J. Jackson decamps Gordonsville, Virginia, and marches north to Orange Court House. However, because General Ambrose P. Hill completely misinterprets Jackson's orders and fails to leave camp, the usually hard-marching Southerners cover only eight miles. The incident remains a sore point between the two leaders for the rest of their lives.

SOUTHWEST: Union troops under General Edward R. S. Canby defeat Confederate stragglers near Fort Fillmore, New Mexico Territory.

NAVAL: President Abraham Lincoln, Secretary of War Edwin M. Stanton, and Secretary of State William H. Seward are guests of Admiral John A. B. Dahlgren at the Washington Navy Yard, were they witness the test firing of an experimental repeating cannon christened "Rafael."

The CSS *Florida* sails from Nassau to commence a celebrated raiding career under Lieutenant John N. Maffitt.

August 8

POLITICS: Secretary of War Edwin Stanton suspends writs of habeas corpus throughout the country to facilitate cases against treason and draft evasion.

NORTH: Federal authorities release and parole Confederate spy Belle Boyd from Old Capitol Prison, Washington, D.C., citing lack of evidence to detain her further.

SOUTH: General John Pope orders General Nathaniel P. Banks's division of 9,000 men to proceed south on the Culpeper Road.

General Thomas J. Jackson departs from Orange Court House, Virginia, crosses the Rapidan River with 24,000 men, and advances to evict 9,000 Union troops under General Nathaniel P. Banks from Culpeper County.

WEST: The Army of Mississippi of 30,000 men under General Braxton Bragg departs Chattanooga, Tennessee, and invades Kentucky.

Union and Confederate forces clash heavily at Cumberland Gap, Tennessee, with losses of three Union dead and 15 wounded to 125 Southern casualties.

A spate of attacks on trains by Confederate guerrillas near Huntsville, Alabama, forces Union authorities to arrest secessionist clergy members and place them as passengers on the trains.

August 9

WEST: Aware that Confederates under General Thomas J. Jackson are converging on his position near Cedar Mountain, nine miles south of Culpeper, Virginia, General Nathaniel P. Banks deploys his 9,000 men at its base with cavalry covering open farmland along Cedar Run while his artillery unlimbers atop nearby hills. The overconfident Jackson then approaches from the south with General Richard S. Ewell's division on his right and General Henry S. Winder to his left. His third division under General Ambrose P. Hill is strung out several miles to the rear, en route. After preliminary artillery duels and a hasty, improper reconnaissance, Jackson orders his two divisions forward around 4:30 P.M. The men march sloppily across the field with a considerable gap between them. Jackson, however, is unaware that Banks has stationed two brigades under Generals Samuel W. Crawford and George Gordon in the woods to the left of Winder. These suddenly emerge and hit the Confederates hard, routing Winder's command, including the famous Stonewall Brigade. As General Jubal A. Early advances on the Union center, he also sustains serious losses from Federal artillery and halts to dress ranks. Banks then commits all his reserves to the onslaught, which outflank Jackson and threaten to roll up his line. Confusion increases once the capable Winder is killed by artillery fire, and his command scatters. Jackson grows so perturbed by these unexpected reverses that he draws his sword—allegedly for the only time in the war—grasps a flag, and commences rallying his men. For a few moments it appears that Banks had achieved a startling upset over the previously unstoppable Confederates.

Events began to turn in Jackson's favor at about 5:30 P.M., once the first elements of Hill's division came trudging up the road. These forces plug gaps in the sagging

Confederate line and begin to drive the tiring and outnumbered Federals back. After a failed charge by the 1st Pennsylvania Cavalry, which loses 95 men out of 164, Banks withdraws his men, and the Confederates retain possession of the field. Jackson's losses are 223 killed, 1,060 wounded, and 31 missing (1,334) to a Union tally of 314 killed, 1,445 wounded, and 622 captured (2,353)—a toll that leads participants to dub the encounter "Slaughter Mountain." His victory is tempered by the loss of the capable and talented Winder. Nonetheless, Cedar Mountain forces General Pope to postpone a general advance south, thereby granting General Robert E. Lee additional time to dispatch General James Longstreet north to reinforce Jackson.

August 10

SOUTH: Having elected not to renew the struggle at Cedar Mountain, Virginia, Generals Nathaniel P. Banks and Thomas J. Jackson arrange a truce to collect and bury their dead.

SOUTHWEST: Texas troops under Lieutenant C. D. Macrae attack a sleeping camp of 65 pro-Union German settlers along the Nueces River, Texas, killing 19, wounding nine, and capturing the rest. The nine injured are subsequently removed from camp and executed. Confederate losses are two killed and 18 wounded. The affair permanently dampens outward German disaffection in Texas.

NAVAL: The USS *Resolute* seizes the Confederate schooner *S. S. Jones* off the Virginia coast.

Union forces capture the Confederate steamer *General Lee* outside of Fort Pulaski, Georgia.

Admiral David G. Farragut, in response to guerrilla attacks from the shore on his vessels, partially destroys the town of Donaldsonville, Louisiana, warning inhabitants that the rest will be destroyed if the sniping persists.

August 11

SOUTH: Confederate forces under General Thomas J. Jackson withdraw south of the Rapidan River and back to Gordonsville, Virginia.

WEST: Confederate raiders under William C. Quantrill capture and briefly hold Independence, Missouri.

General Ulysses S. Grant, headquartered at Corinth, Mississippi, declares that all fugitive African American slaves will be employed in his department as laborers.

August 12

WEST: Colonel John H. Morgan stealthily seizes Gallatin, Tennessee, along with 124 Union soldiers under Colonel William P. Boone, without firing a shot. His troopers then destroy tunnels belonging to the Louisville and Nashville Railroad, cutting the supply lines of General Don C. Buell and halting his advance on Chattanooga, Tennessee, for three months.

A Union expedition leaves Fort Leavenworth, Kansas, to secure Independence, Missouri, from Confederate irregulars.

NAVAL: The USS *Arthur* captures the Confederate armed schooner *Breaker* off Aransas Pass, Texas, while the schooners *Elma* and *Hannah* are burned to prevent being captured.

August 13

SOUTH: General Robert E. Lee begins to advance his Army of Northern Virginia from the Peninsula to Gordonsville, Virginia. He begins by dispatching 30,000 troops under General James Longstreet by rail, where they are scheduled to link up with the corps of General Thomas J. Jackson.

SOUTHWEST: Captain John W. Kittredge, commanding U.S. Navy vessels off Corpus Christi, Texas, lands under a flag of truce and urges Confederate authorities to evacuate civilians in light of his impending attack.

WEST: Confederates wage an unsuccessful fight at Yellow Creek, Missouri, losing 60 captives to Union forces.

NAVAL: A collision between Union steamers *George Peabody* and *West Point* on the Potomac River, Virginia, results in 83 deaths, mostly convalescents.

The USS *Kensington* captures the Confederate schooner *Troy* off Sabine Pass, Texas.

August 14

POLITICS: President Abraham Lincoln confers with a delegation of free African Americans at the White House and suggests Central America as a possible venue for colonization. The suggestion is badly received by many black leaders, particularly Frederick Douglass, who accuses the president of "contempt for Negroes."

SOUTH: The III and V Corps are taken by transports from Harrison's Landing, Virginia, and deposited at Aquia Creek near Fredericksburg.

Colonel Charles A. Heckman leads the 9th New Jersey on a reconnaissance from Newport, North Carolina, toward Swansborough.

NAVAL: The USS *Pocahontas* and steam tug *Treaty* exchange fire with Confederate forces on the Black River near Georgetown, South Carolina. This interference allows the steamer *Nina* to escape capture.

August 15

SOUTH: General Robert E. Lee's Army of Northern Virginia reposes at Gordonsville, Virginia, 54,000 strong. From there, he deduces that a lightning strike by Confederate cavalry on bridges over the Rappahannock would isolate Union general John Pope's Army of Virginia on the south bank and was liable to be defeated in detail. He plans to order the march immediately but is dissuaded by General Fitzhugh Lee, who feels that his cavalry horses are worn and require rest.

NAVAL: Commander John Rodgers of the USS *Galena,* in concert with *Port Royal* and *Satellite,* covers the Army of the Potomac as it embarks at Harrison's Landing, Virginia, and is transported over the Chickahominy River.

The USS *Arthur* captures the Confederate steamer *A. B.* after it grounds at the entrance of the Nueces River, Corpus Christi, Texas.

August 16

SOUTH: The Army of the Potomac is relocated completely from Harrison's Landing to Aquia Creek (Alexandria), Virginia, to protect Washington, D.C., better. This withdrawal concludes the so-called Peninsula campaign.

The Army of Northern Virginia under General Robert E. Lee continues advancing toward Gordonsville, Virginia, in anticipation of engaging General John Pope's Army of Virginia.

WEST: General Edmund Kirby-Smith departs Knoxville, Tennessee, with 10,000 men and plunges through the Cumberland Gap and into Kentucky. This act initiates a major Southern offensive to reclaim that state for the Confederacy.

NAVAL: A naval expedition consisting of the USS *Mound City, Benton,* and *General Bragg,* assisted by rams *Monarch, Samson, Lioness,* and *Switzerland,* convey army troops under Colonel Charles R. Woods up the Mississippi River as far as the Yazoo River. They repeatedly land parties along the shore to capture batteries and disperse troop encampments.

August 17

SOUTH: General J. E. B. Stuart assumes command of all Confederate cavalry in the Army of Northern Virginia.

WEST: Half-starved Sioux tribe members stage an uprising in southwest Minnesota by killing five settlers on their farm in Acton Township. Chief Little Crow, when informed of the action, realizes that war with the whites is inevitable and takes to the warpath. The result is a savage, six-week uprising claiming approximately 600 lives.

NAVAL: An armed party from the USS *Ellis* destroys a Confederate battery and a nearby saltworks at Swansboro, North Carolina.

The USS *Sachem, Reindeer, Bella Italia,* and *Corypheus* shell Confederate positions at Corpus Christi, Texas. However, steady fire from Confederate shore emplacements commanded by Major Alfred Hobby keep the Union vessels at a distance. After an ineffectual four-hour exchange, Captain John W. Kittredge calls off his attack and prepares to renew the struggle on the morrow.

Off Nassau, Bahamas, Lieutenant John N. Maffitt assumes formal command of the newly armed and commissioned Confederate raider CSS *Florida.* However, his initial cruise is beset by an outbreak of yellow fever among the crew.

August 18

POLITICS: President Jefferson Davis, addressing the newly convened second session of the Confederate Congress, excoriates the behavior of Union general Benjamin F. Butler at New Orleans.

SOUTH: The Union Army of Virginia under General John Pope withdraws behind the Rappahannock River in the face of advancing Confederate forces. He there awaits reinforcements from General George B. McClellan's 100,000-strong Army of the Potomac.

WEST: General Kirby-Smith and 10,000 Confederates occupy the town of Barboursville, Kentucky. From there, impending supply shortages induce him to commence moving against Lexington.

Confederate forces recapture the town of Clarksville, Tennessee, without a shot being fired. The garrison commander, Col. R. Mason of the 71st Ohio, subsequently is dismissed from the service for cowardice.

Rampaging Sioux warriors attack the Upper and Lower Indian agencies, Minnesota, killing 20 people, including Agent Andrew J. Myrick, whose mouth is symbolically stuffed with the very grass he told the tribes to eat. A detachment of 46 soldiers under Captain John Marsh, 5th Minnesota, advances to rescue the workers and is ambushed at Redwood Ferry and nearly annihilated with the loss of 24 soldiers.

NAVAL: A landing party of 30 sailors and a howitzer disembark from USS *Bella Italia* near Corpus Christi, Texas. A party of 25 men from the 8th Texas engages them on the beach for several tense minutes, at which point Captain John W. Kittredge suspends his attack and returns to the ships offshore. Confederate losses are one dead and a handful wounded.

August 19

NORTH: James B. McPherson is appointed brigadier general, U.S. Army.

SOUTH: General John Pope continues relocating 51,000 Union troops from the Rapidan River to behind the Rappahannock River, Virginia, while awaiting additional forces under General George B. McClellan.

WEST: The Union Department of the Ohio is reconstituted (Illinois, Indiana, Michigan, Ohio, Wisconsin, and eastern Kentucky) under General Horatio G. Wright.

Confederate cavalry under Colonel John H. Morgan begin to probe and raid along the Louisiana and Nashville Railroad.

Federal troops commence a four-month expedition against the Snake Indians of Idaho.

NAVAL: The USS *St. Louis* runs the Confederate steamer *Swallow* aground below Memphis, Tennessee, and then burns it.

August 20

SOUTH: Skirmishes erupt between Federal troops under General John Pope and advancing Confederates under General Thomas J. Jackson at Raccoon Ford, Stevensburg, Brandy Station, and Kelly's Ford, Virginia. Meanwhile, after continuing delays, General Robert E. Lee abandons his plan to strike at bridges over the Rappahannock River to isolate the Army of Virginia under General John Pope.

The Confederate Trans-Mississippi Department absorbs the Districts of Arkansas, Louisiana, and Texas, with General Richard Taylor commanding the District of West Louisiana.

WEST: A mob of Mdewkanton Santee (Sioux) warriors hastily attacks the outskirts of New Ulm, Minnesota, and are repulsed by armed settlers and militia.

SOUTHWEST: General Hamilton P. Bee arrives at Corpus Christi, Texas, to help organize Confederate defenses there.

August 21

POLITICS: The Federal government begins to issue postage stamps to raise money.

Confederate military authorities issue orders to execute any Northern officers found commanding African-American troops. Generals David Hunter and John W. Phelps, in particular, are to be treated as felons if captured for their role in freeing and arming slaves for service in the Union army. Ironically, Phelps resigns his commission this same day because the government has disavowed his efforts.

South: Confederate forces attempting to cross the Rappahannock River are rebuffed strongly by Union troops, suffering 700 casualties and 2,000 prisoners.

West: General Braxton Bragg positions his Confederates above Chattanooga, Tennessee, while the city of Gallatin surrenders.

A large gathering of Mdewkanton band Santee (Sioux) warriors under Chief Little Crow attacks Fort Ridgely, Minnesota, and is repulsed by 180 soldiers and three cannon commanded by Lieutenant Timothy Sheehan. The garrison loses six killed and 20 wounded while Santee losses are considerably heavier. The Indians draw off but continue the siege while awaiting reinforcements.

Naval: The USS *Bienville* captures the British blockade-runner Eliza in the Atlantic.

Union forces evacuate Baton Rouge, Louisiana, covered by the USS *Essex* and *Gunboat No. 7.*

August 22

South: General J. E. B. Stuart crosses the Rappahannock River with 1,500 troopers and two cannon, intending to sever the Orange and Alexandria Railroad, a major Union supply artery. They soon occupy the town of Warrenton, Virginia, without any sign of the enemy and subsequently advance on Catlett's Station under a driving rainstorm.

General Benjamin F. Butler issues orders to recruit African-American slaves into the Union army at New Orleans, Louisiana.

West: Confederate cavalry under General Albert G. Jenkins begin an extended raid into western Virginia and Ohio.

Chief Little Crow of the Mdewkanton band of Santee (Sioux) is joined by 400 warriors from the Sisseton and Wahpeton bands, for a total of nearly 800. These forces then make another aborted attack on the 180-man garrison at Fort Ridgley, Minnesota, and are repulsed with 100 casualties. Federal troops sustain three killed and 13 wounded.

Naval: Secretary of the Navy Gideon Welles instructs Admiral Louis M. Goldsborough to cooperate closely with the army during its evacuation from Fortress Monroe, Virginia.

The USS *Keystone State* captures the British schooner *Fanny* off St. Simon's Sound, Georgia.

August 23

South: Northern and Southern artillery duel along the Rappahannock River for five hours.

General J. E. B. Stuart is informed by a captured African American that Catlett's Station, Virginia, is the headquarters of General John Pope. Stuart then attacks with 1,500 troopers under the cover of a rainstorm. They seize 300 prisoners and Pope's personal baggage and uniform, along with his military correspondence. Once in receipt of the latter, General Robert E. Lee is apprised of Union intentions to unite Pope's 51,000-man Army of Virginia with the 100,000-strong Army of the Potomac under General George B. McClellan. Lee, realizing he never could counter such a force successfully, begins to formulate plans to disperse Pope before the two forces can merge.

WEST: General Horatio G. Wright formally accepts command of the Department of the Ohio.

As a Confederate column under General Edmund Kirby-Smith marches on Lexington, Kentucky, the cavalry of his van under Colonel John S. Scott drive off a Union detachment from Big Hill, south of Richmond, where other Federal forces have begun to mass.

The town of New Ulm, Minnesota, is attacked again by 400 rampaging Mdewkanton Santee (Sioux) warriors under Chief Little Crow. The town, stoutly defended by civilians under Judge Charles Flandreu, nearly is consumed by fire, but the Sioux are repulsed and withdraw. The whites lose 36 dead and 23 wounded; Native American losses are unknown but presumed equally heavy.

NAVAL: The USS *Bienville* captures the British blockade-runner *Louisa* near Cape Romain, South Carolina.

The USS *Adirondack* grounds on a reef off Man of War Cay, Little Bahamas, and is abandoned.

The USS *James S. Chambers* captures the Confederate schooner *Corelia* off the Cuban coast.

The USS *Essex* shells Bayou Sara, Louisiana, after guerrillas fire on a landing party.

August 24

SOUTH: In a stunningly bold maneuver, General Robert E. Lee divides the Army of Northern Virginia by detaching 25,000 men of General Thomas J. Jackson's corps on a rapid march to destroy the Orange and Alexandria Railroad, thereby cutting Union general John Pope's supply line. Through this expedient, Lee hopes to draw Union forces up from central Virginia where he can deal with them in the open. Meanwhile, the 30,000 Confederates under General James Longstreet are to remain stationary until Jackson's men are in place.

WEST: General John P. McCown temporarily assumes command of the Department of East Tennessee.

NAVAL: The USS *Henry Andrew* is wrecked in a gale near Cape Henry, Virginia.

The USS *Isaac N. Seymour* sinks in the Neuse River, North Carolina.

The USS *Stars and Stripes* captures British blockade-runner *Mary Elizabeth* off Wilmington, North Carolina.

The USS yacht *Corypheus* captures the Confederate schooner *Water Witch* off Aransas Bay, Texas.

Having received its armament, CSS *Alabama* is commissioned into the Confederate navy off Terceira, Azores, with celebrated raider Raphael Semmes as captain.

August 25

POLITICS: To placate Radical Republicans and alleviate manpower shortages, Secretary of War Edwin M. Stanton authorizes the recruitment of as many as 5,000 African-American soldiers. Orders are then dispatched to General Rufus Saxton, military governor of the South Carolina Sea Islands, to raise five regiments of black troops for military service.

SOUTH: General Thomas J. Jackson's corps detaches from the Army of Northern Virginia and advances to the Rappahannock River. He then commences a wide flanking movement around General John Pope's right flank to cut his line of communications. Jackson's command consists of three crack divisions under Generals Richard S. Ewell, Ambrose P. Hill, and William Taliaferro. By dint of hard slogging, the Southerners cover 56 miles in only two days—one of the most impressive performances of the entire war—and arrive behind the Union Army of Virginia. Through this expedient, Jackson also interposes himself between Pope and the Union capital at Washington, D.C.

WEST: The settlement of New Ulm, Minnesota, is evacuated in the face of possible renewed Sioux attacks. Nearly 1,000 survivors pack up their belongings and flee 30 miles east to Mankato.

August 26
SOUTH: In a surprise move, Confederate forces led by General Isaac Trimble storm into Manassas Junction, Virginia, capturing General John Pope's main supply base. The nominally malnourished Confederates of General Thomas J. Jackson, famously looking more like scarecrows than soldiers, gleefully gorge themselves on the cornucopia within their grasp. At the cost of 12 casualties, the Southerners also net 300 prisoners, eight cannon, and 175 horses.

WEST: General James H. Carleton, takes command of the Department of New Mexico.

NAVAL: Captain Franklin Buchanan is promoted to rear admiral for his conduct in the engagement involving the CSS *Virginia* on March 8, 1862. He remains the only Southerner so honored.

A joint expedition under General Samuel R. Curtis and Commodore Charles H. Davis captures the Confederate steamer *Fair Play* on the Yazoo River in Arkansas. More than 1,200 imported English Enfield rifles are seized.

August 27
SOUTH: Union and Confederate forces begin to grope around the old battlefield of Manassas, Virginia, in anticipation of a major clash. General John Pope, stung by the capture of his supply base at Manassas Junction, rapidly marches from behind the Rappahannock River in search of Confederates under General Thomas J. Jackson. Jackson, meanwhile, ambushes a New Jersey brigade under General George W. Taylor, killing the general, inflicting 135 casualties, and taking 300 prisoners. He then digs in along the Warrenton Turnpike and awaits the balance of the army under General James Longstreet.

The Union division of General Joseph Hooker wins a skirmish at Kettle Run, Virginia, against General Richard S. Ewell, driving him from the field. Hooker's success induces General Thomas J. Jackson to abandon Manassas, and he falls back on Groveton on the Warrenton Turnpike.

WEST: General Nathan B. Forrest is repulsed by the Union garrison at Round Mountain, Tennessee.

Confederate cavalry under General Joseph Wheeler fords the Tennessee River at Chattanooga, ahead of General Braxton Bragg's Army of Mississippi.

A relief column commanded of 1,400 soldiers under Colonel Henry H. Sibley arrives at Fort Sibley, Minnesota, from distant Fort Snelling. Meanwhile, a detachment of troops under Major Joseph R. Brown is ambushed by the Santee (Sioux) at Birch Coulee, losing 16 killed and 44 wounded.

NAVAL: The USS *South Carolina* destroys the Confederate schooner *Patriot* off Mosquito Inlet, Florida.

The USS *Santiago de Cuba* captures the Confederate blockade-runner *Lavinia* off Abaco, Bahamas.

August 28

NORTH: Confederate spy Belle Boyd is released from Old Capital Prison in Washington, D.C., for lack of evidence and sent South with a warning not to return.

SOUTH: Generals Robert E. Lee and James Longstreet force a passage through Thoroughfare Gap, Virginia, to engage the main Union army. In the process, they engage and brush aside a Union division under General James B. Ricketts and cavalry forces under General John Buford.

Two Confederate divisions of General Thomas J. Jackson surprise and engage a force of 2,800 Union troops under General Rufus King at Groveton, Virginia. However, as the heady Southerners advance anticipating an easy victory, they run headlong into the western brigade of General John Gibbon near Brawner's Farm. An intense firefight ensues at 100 yards between Gibbon's black-hatted troops and the famous Stonewall Brigade under General William B. Taliaferro—with both sides oblivious to the carnage marking their respective lines. At length, Jackson tries clinching the victory by outflanking Gibbon, but he is thwarted by a valiant stand by the 19th Indiana under Colonel Solomon Meredith behind a stone wall. After two hours of fierce fighting, both sides withdraw exhausted. Jackson loses not only 1,200 men out of 4,500 present but also the service of Generals Taliaferro and Richard S. Ewell, both seriously injured. General King, who was sidelined for most of the battle by an epileptic seizure, sustains 1,100 casualties out of 2,800 engaged. And for their splendid performance in this, their first engagement, Gibbon's troops gained the famous moniker of "Iron Brigade."

By deliberately precipitating a fight at Groveton, Jackson sought to lure the Army of Virginia under General John Pope to his vicinity, where it could be attacked and destroyed in detail by the combined Confederate force. Pope, as anticipated, took the bait, marched north, and began to concentrate his forces near Jackson's position.

WEST: General Braxton Bragg's Confederate Army of Mississippi, soon to be redesignated the Army of Tennessee, proceeds north from Chattanooga into Kentucky, several days behind a second column under General Edmund Kirby-Smith.

NAVAL: The Federal gunboat USS *Pittsburgh,* accompanied by the steamers *Iatan* and *White Cloud,* leads an expedition from Helena, Arkansas, to Eunice.

August 29

SOUTH: General Thomas J. Jackson begins to assume strong defensive positions behind an unfinished railroad near Groveton, Virginia, as Union forces under General John Pope mass 65,000 men for an attack. The Second Battle of Manassas begins as blue-coated columns under General Franz Sigel and General Joseph Hooker assail Jackson's line, safely ensconced behind an unfinished railroad, from which he easily repels their advance. The problem is that Pope, while enjoying local superiority in numbers, squanders his advantage through piecemeal attacks. Next came the brigades of General Philip Kearny and John F. Reynolds. These forces charge Jackson's left flank and drive General Ambrose P. Hill's defenders hard along Stony Ridge, but they are finally repulsed by timely reinforcements under General Jubal A. Early. On Pope's left flank, the V Corps of General Fitz John Porter deploys and prepares to engage when it detects the approach of General James Longstreet and 30,000 Confederates. This brings available Southern strength up to 55,000 men. Porter immediately notifies Pope of the danger to his army, but he ignores it and remains fixated on Jackson's unbroken line to his front. He also orders Porter to attack Jackson immediately, but Porter demurs and prepares to receive Longstreet. This insubordination ultimately costs Porter his military career, but it probably spared the Army of Virginia from annihilation.

After a hard day of fighting and heavy losses, Pope compounds his difficulties this evening as he perceives Jackson withdrawing slightly to readjust and shorten his line. He mistakenly misinterprets this as a Confederate retreat and, instead of making arrangements to counter Longstreet's corps on his left, begins to deploy

The Second Battle of Bull Run/Manassas August 29, 1862 *(Library of Congress)*

his men for a pursuit. Longstreet, meanwhile, has been ordered by General Robert E. Lee to attack Union forces directly to his front, but he dallies, not knowing the enemy's strength. Thus, the first day of strife at Second Manassas ends with sizable portions of both contesting armies unwilling or unable to engage.

General Pierre G. T. Beauregard relieves General John C. Pemberton as commander of the Department of South Carolina and Georgia.

WEST: The advance guard of General Edmund Kirby-Smith's Confederate column skirmishes with Union forces under General Mahlon D. Manson at Rogersville, outside Richmond, Kentucky. Both sides then summon reinforcements in expectation of a full-scale battle.

WEST: General Frederick Steele assumes command of the Union Army of the Southwest in Arkansas.

NAVAL: The USS *Pittsburgh*, escorting the steamers *White Cloud* and *Iatan*, bombards Confederate emplacements at Carson's Landing on the Mississippi River.

Commodore John Wilkes is transferred from the James River Flotilla to the command of the Potomac Flotilla.

August 30

SOUTH: General Gustavus W. Smith assumes command of Richmond, Virginia, defenses.

The Second Battle of Manassas rages on as Union troops who were ordered by General John Pope to pursue supposedly defeated Confederate forces instead find them deployed in strong defensive positions. Nonetheless, Pope directs General Fitz John Porter to attack the Confederate right, and waves of blue-coated infantry surge forward. Porter makes three concerted charges on General Thomas J. Jackson's men; the first two are repulsed with heavy losses, while the third, delivered directly into Confederate lines, bends yet fails to break them. But Jackson endures several heart-stopping moments as his ammunition begins to give out, and several units have no recourse but to pick up rocks and hurl them at the enemy. Federal troops under Generals Franz Sigel and Joseph Hooker likewise press back Jackson's left wing severely before grinding to a halt. Suddenly, a roll of cannon fire rakes Porter's left flank as General James Longstreet's massed artillery opens fire. This is followed up by a massed charge, spearheaded by General John B. Hood's Texas brigade, which simply rolls up the Union left. Jackson, seeing his blue-clad opponents suddenly waver, orders his own men to charge the enemy in front, and Pope's entire army dissolves. Desperate fighting ensues as a handful of intact Union brigades labor to stem the Confederate tide, first along Chinn Ridge and then Henry House Hill, and their sacrifice enables the Army of Virginia to escape to Centreville. A tough division of U.S. Army regulars under General George Sykes distinguishes itself by trading lives and space for time. A heavy downpour also dampens the ensuing Confederate pursuit. Pope's army, roughly handled, thus escapes to fight another day. General Robert E. Lee, by dint of an exceptionally bold tactical gambit, flawlessly executed, scores another impressive victory for the Southern cause.

Losses at Second Manassas are severe with Pope reporting 1,724 killed, 8,372 wounded, and 5,958 missing (16,054) while Lee counts 1,481 dead, 7,627 injured, and 89 missing (9,197). Moreover, with Pope in headlong retreat and the strategic initiative firmly in his grasp, Lee remains positioned to take the war northward into Maryland. That night, he orders Jackson's perpetually exhausted corps on another forced march to Chantilly in a final attempt to cut Pope's withdrawal toward Washington, D.C.

WEST: General Mahlon D. Manson, bolstered by the arrival of troops under General Charles Cruft, pours 6,500 Union troops—mostly new recruits—into defensive positions six miles below Richmond, Kentucky. His pickets then detect the approach of a Confederate division under General Patrick R. Cleburne, and fighting erupts along the line. When Cleburne sustains a severe mouth injury, he is succeeded by Colonel Preston Smith. The veteran Confederates easily dislodge Manson from his post, and he falls back forming a new line two miles below Richmond at Rogersville. Fighting resumes, and Smith, now reinforced by General James Churchill's division to a strength of 6,850 men, rebuffs a Union counterattack. The discouraged Federals fall back in confusion through the streets of Richmond. There, they are rallied forcefully by newly arrived General William "Bull" Nelson, who stands six-foot, six-inches and weighs 300 pounds. But the Confederates easily disperse this third line, and the Northerners quit the field completely. Kirby-Smith losses are 98 killed, 492 wounded, and 10 missing while Union losses tally 206 killed, 844 wounded, and 4,303 captured. General Nelson is among the wounded, while Manson is captured along with his artillery and wagon train. Worse, as surviving Union troops stampede for Louisville, Kirby-Smith's invasion route is clear as far as the Ohio River.

SOUTHWEST: The Union Department of Arizona is created from the New Mexico Territory.

NAVAL: The large new ironclad monitor USS *Passaic* is launched at Greenpoint, New York.

The USS *R. R. Cuyler* captures the Confederate schooner *Anne Sophie* east of Jacksonville, Florida.

August 31

SOUTH: The Union Army of Virginia under General John Pope consolidates and regroups at Centreville, Virginia, while General Robert E. Lee dispatches Confederates under General Thomas J. Jackson on a forced march around Pope's left flank to possibly cut his retreat to Washington, D.C. This move presages what Lee anticipates will be a decisive blow to destroy the Federal force altogether. After a difficult slog through mud and rain, Jackson arrives at Chantilly and awaits promised reinforcements under General James Longstreet.

Federal troops evacuate Fredericksburg, Virginia, abandoning great quantities of military stores.

A stiff action ensues at Weldon, Virginia, where 100 Confederates are left dead on the ground in exchange for five Union soldiers killed.

WEST: Confederates capture Weston in western Virginia.

NAVAL: The USS *William G. Anderson* captures the Confederate schooner *Lily* off the Louisiana coast.

Confederate forces capture the Union transport *W. B. Terry* after it grounds at Duck River Shoals on the Tennessee River.

September 1

SOUTH: Confederates forces under General Thomas J. Jackson, deployed around Ox Hill and Chantilly, Virginia, are accosted suddenly by Union forces from General Joseph Hooker's division. Jackson initially intended to engage the marauders beforehand but is dissuaded from doing so by General J. E. B. Stuart, who finds their position too strong to assail. Fighting commences at about 4:00 P.M. when Union troops under General Isaac I. Stevens, IX Corps, advance down Warrenton Pike and charge. This clash coincides with a tremendous downpour that does little to temper the ferocity of the combatants. Stevens's attack forces a Louisiana brigade to recoil when he is killed suddenly and his line falters. A determined advance by the Stonewall brigade under General William E. Starke likewise is repelled. Union troops are then bolstered by the appearance of General Philip Kearny's brigade, which plunges into the Confederates and plugs a gap in the Union line. Unfortunately, Kearny, while conducting a personal reconnaissance ahead of his troops, stumbles into Confederate lines and is shot dead. By 6:30 P.M., fighting dies down, and both sides withdraw. Losses in this brief but deadly conflict are estimated at 500 Confederates and 700 Federals; the Union army is weakened further by the loss of two effective leaders. After Chantilly, the curtain lowers on the spectacular Second Manassas campaign.

General Ormsby M. Mitchel assumes control of the Department of South Carolina.

WEST: The approach of Confederate forces under General Edmund Kirby-Smith into Kentucky causes consternation in the capital at Lexington, and the legislature votes to adjourn and relocate to Louisville.

General John P. McCown is appointed commander of the Confederate Department of East Tennessee.

NAVAL: Commodore Louis M. Goldsborough is relieved as commander of the North Atlantic Blockading squadron and replaced by Samuel P. Lee.

The Confederate raider CSS *Florida* under Lieutenant John N. Maffitt puts into Havana, Cuba, beset by an outbreak of yellow fever.

September 2

NORTH: President Abraham Lincoln, ignoring the advice of his cabinet, restores General George B. McClellan as head of the Army of the Potomac, a decision immediately hailed by soldiers in the ranks. The bumbling and recently disgraced general John Pope, meanwhile, continues on without an official command.

WEST: Union forces abandon Winchester, in the Shenandoah Valley, Virginia.

Confederate cavalry under General Albert G. Jenkins captures the Union garrison at Spencer Court House, western Virginia.

Lexington, Kentucky, is occupied by Confederates under General Edmund Kirby-Smith.

Martial law is declared in Cincinnati, Ohio, for fear of a Confederate attack from neighboring Richmond, Kentucky.

A detachment of soldiers is attacked in camp at Birch Coulee, Minnesota, by a band of Santee (Sioux) warriors under Big Eagle (Wambdi Tanka). They manage to keep the attackers at bay for the next 31 hours.

NAVAL: The USS *Restless* captures the Confederate sloop *John Thompson* off the South Carolina coast.

September 3

POLITICS: Kentuckian Joseph Holt is appointed judge advocate general of the United States.

NORTH: General John Pope remonstrates to General in Chief Henry W. Halleck that his recent debacle is due to General Fitz John Porter's refusal to obey orders and George B. McClellan's failure to provide timely support.

SOUTH: General Robert E. Lee, unable to find appreciable openings in Washington, D.C.'s defenses, declines to attack and instead advances toward Leesburg, Virginia, and the Potomac River.

WEST: Generals Alpheus S. Williams and Jesse L. Reno take command of the II Corps and III Corps, respectively, in the Army of Virginia.

Confederate forces reoccupy Winchester, Virginia, while skirmishing erupts at Harper's Ferry, Falls Church, and Bunker Hill.

General Edmund Kirby-Smith's Confederates occupy the provisional Confederate state capital at Frankfort, Kentucky, amid cheering supporters.

NAVAL: The USS *Essex* under Commander William D. Porter bombards the city of Natchez, Mississippi, and it surrenders.

September 4

POLITICS: The Naval Investigating Committee of the Confederate Congress reports favorably on the activities of Secretary of the Navy Stephen R. Mallory, despite the loss of New Orleans and other naval setbacks.

NORTH: The 40,000 men of the Army of Northern Virginia cross the Potomac River at White's Ford, Virginia, and into Maryland.

Union troops begin to evacuate Frederick, Maryland.

SOUTH: Federal forces, ambushed by Texas Rangers at Boutte Station, Louisiana, vigorously pursue their assailants into nearby swamps, capturing several.

WEST: General Albert G. Jenkins takes Confederate cavalry briefly across the Ohio River for a raid in the Point Pleasant region of western Virginia and then returns.

Confederate cavalry under Colonel John H. Morgan unite with the army of General Edmund Kirby-Smith at Lexington, Kentucky.

NAVAL: The USS *Shepherd Knapp* captures the Confederate bark *Fannie Laurie* near the South Edisto River, South Carolina.

The CSS *Florida* under Lieutenant John N. Maffitt plunges past the USS *Oneida*, *Winona*, and *Rachel Seaman* and enters into Mobile Bay, Alabama. His success results in an official rebuke for local commanders and calls for better management of the blockade effort.

The USS *William G. Anderson* captures the Confederate schooner *Theresa* in the Gulf of Mexico.

September 5
NORTH: General John Pope is formally relieved of command and is recalled back to Washington, D.C., for reassignment. General in Chief Henry W. Halleck orders that his Army of Virginia is to be consolidated within the Army of the Potomac under General George B. McClellan.

SOUTH: General John M. Brannan temporarily takes command of the Department of South Carolina.

WEST: Confederates under General William W. Loring commence campaigning in the Kanawha Valley, western Virginia.

Union troops advance from Fort Donelson, Tennessee, toward Confederate-held Clarksville.

General Don C. Buell withdraws the Army of the Ohio from northern Alabama and back toward Murfreesboro, Tennessee.

General Benjamin H. Grierson leads a mounted reconnaissance to Holly Springs, Mississippi, skirmishing en route.

The Union Department of the Northwest is created out of Wisconsin, Iowa, Minnesota, and the Nebraska and Dakota territories.

NAVAL: The Confederate raider CSS *Alabama* under Captain Raphael Semmes seizes and burns the Union whaler *Ocmulgee* near the Azores.

September 6
NORTH: General John Pope receives the military equivalent of political exile by assuming command of the Department of the Northwest (Wisconsin, Iowa, Minnesota, and the Nebraska and Dakota territories). There he is concerned primarily with curbing a deadly Sioux uprising under Little Crow.

Confederate troops under General Thomas J. Jackson occupy Frederick, Maryland, expecting to be greeted as liberators, yet they are coolly received by the inhabitants.

SOUTH: Federal forces abandon the depot at Aquila Creek, Virginia, leaving tons of valuable supplies.

NAVAL: The USS *Louisiana* assists repelling a Confederate attack on Washington, North Carolina, while an accidental explosion destroys the U.S. Army gunboat *Picket*.

September 7
NORTH: The Union capital at Washington, D.C., panics as Confederate forces under General Robert E. Lee occupy Frederick, Maryland—within striking distance. General George B. McClellan, hastily reappointed commander of the Army of the Potomac, advances north from the capital to engage them.

General Joseph Hooker relieves Irvin McDowell as commander of III Corps, Army of Virginia.

WEST: Clarksville, Tennessee, is occupied by Union forces, as is Bowling Green, Kentucky. Meanwhile, as Confederate general Braxton Bragg marches the Army of Mississippi into Kentucky, he bypasses Union troops under General Don C. Buell at Murfreesboro and Nashville, Tennessee.

NAVAL: The CSS *Alabama* under Captain Raphael Semmes captures and burns the Union schooner *Starlight* off the Azores.

The USS *Essex* under Commodore David D. Porter receives 14 hits as it cruises past Confederate batteries at Port Hudson, Louisiana, on the lower Mississippi River.

September 8
NORTH: The defenses of Washington, D.C., are entrusted to General Nathaniel P. Banks. Meanwhile, General Robert E. Lee issues a proclamation to the inhabitants of Maryland, reassuring them that "We know no enemies among you, and will protect all, of every opinion." Attitudes toward the Confederates remain nonetheless tepid.
WEST: A mounted expedition rides from Fort Leavenworth, Kansas, in pursuit of William C. Quantrill's Confederate guerrillas.
NAVAL: Armed boats from USS *Kingfisher* destroy saltworks along St. Joseph's Bay, Florida.

Commodore John Wilkes assembles the West India Squadron (a mobile or "flying squadron") consisting of USS *Wachusett, Dacotah, Cimarron, Sonoma, Tioga, Octorara,* and *Santiago de Cuba.* He is tasked with halting the depredations by the Confederate raiders CSS *Alabama* and *Florida.*

The CSS *Alabama* under Captain Raphael Semmes captures and burns the Union whaling vessel *Ocean Rover* off the Azores.

September 9
NORTH: As the Army of Northern Virginia filters through Frederick, Maryland, General Robert E. Lee grows concerned that a sizable Union garrison at Harper's Ferry, below him, could threaten his rear. Therefore, he composes Special Order No. 191, which audaciously dispatches the corps of General Thomas J. Jackson back into the Shenandoah Valley to capture that strategic position, while the divisions of Generals Lafayette McLaws and John G. Walker take different routes to the same objective. Lee then instructs General James Longstreet's corps to advance toward Hagerstown, Maryland, daringly—and dangerously—splitting his army in two.
SOUTH: General Samuel P. Heintzelman takes charge of the Washington, D.C., defenses south of the Potomac.

Fighting erupts at Williamsburg, Virginia, where Union forces prevail after a heavy skirmish.
NAVAL: The CSS *Alabama* under Captain Raphael Semmes captures and burns the Union whaling vessels *Alert* and *Weather Gauge* off the Azores.

September 10
NORTH: The Confederate corps of General Thomas J. Jackson and the divisions of General Lafayette McLaws and John G. Walker march from their cantonments near Frederick, Maryland, and commence a converging movement on Harper's Ferry in western Virginia. Meanwhile, General James Longstreet is also sent in the direction of Hagerstown, leaving the Army of Northern Virginia badly scattered and subject to defeat in detail. Timing is thus essential as the larger Army of the Potomac under General George B. McClellan is feared to be bearing down on General Robert E.

Lee. Lee, while advancing with Longstreet, deploys the division of General Daniel H. Hill to guard the passages around South Mountain as a precaution. Meanwhile McClellan, on learning that Lee has abandoned Frederick, moves up cautiously to occupy that position.

WEST: The inhabitants of Cincinnati, Ohio, brace themselves for a possible Confederate raid across the Ohio River from approaching Confederates under General Edmund Kirby-Smith.

September 11

NORTH: Governor Andrew G. Curtin of Pennsylvania, alarmed by the Confederate incursion into neighboring Maryland, calls for 50,000 militia to defend the state.

Hagerstown, Maryland, is occupied by General Robert E. Lee's Confederate forces while the Army of the Potomac under General George B. McClellan inches up to former Southern positions at Frederick.

WEST: Confederates under General Edmund Kirby-Smith capture Maysville, Kentucky, within range of Cincinnati, Ohio. His approach results in thousands of marksmen and squirrel hunters from the Ohio Valley volunteering their services as home guards.

NAVAL: The USS *Patroon* and *Uncas* trade shots with Confederate artillery at St. John's Bluff, Florida, and withdraw after receiving damage.

Armed parties from USS *Sagamore* land at St. Andrew's Bay, Florida, to destroy Confederate saltworks.

September 12

NORTH: As a precaution, the Pennsylvania state archives and treasury relocate from Harrisburg and Philadelphia to New York.

The former Union Army of Virginia is disbanded and absorbed into the Army of the Potomac with its I, II, and III Corps redesignated as I, XI, and XII Corps.

Confederate troops abandon Frederick, Maryland, in the face of pursuing Union forces. This afternoon, General George B. McClellan arrives with 75,000 men from the Army of the Potomac, who begin to scour the countryside for elusive Southerners.

WEST: General Thomas J. Jackson shepherds his corps into the Shenandoah Valley toward Harper's Ferry, western Virginia. A detachment of 2,000 Union troops under General Julius White abandons Martinsdale on their approach and flees to join the main garrison at the ferry.

The town of Glasgow, Kentucky, falls to Confederates under General Edmund Kirby-Smith.

September 13

NORTH: Private Barton W. Mitchell of the 27th Indiana accidentally finds a copy of General Robert E. Lee's Special Order No. 191 wrapped around a cigar. When Mitchell brings his trophy to the attention of Colonel Robert H. Chilton, Chilton immediately dispatches, through channels, the information to commanding General George B. McClellan. McClellan, in turn, suddenly realizes that the Confederates are badly dispersed and subject to defeat by division. Inexplicably, he waits almost 16 hours before putting troops in motion while his golden opportunity ebbs.

General John Sedgwick assumes command of XII Corps, Army of the Potomac.

WEST: Harper's Ferry in western Virginia is enveloped by a three-pronged Confederate movement. General Lafayette McLaws's division occupies neighboring Maryland Heights across the river after a six-hour battle with Union defenders, while General John G. Walker's division positions itself on nearby Loudoun Heights. Subsequently, three more divisions under General Thomas J. Jackson align themselves along School House Ridge to cut off the town. The 12,000-man Union garrison under Colonel Dixon S. Miles thus is trapped speedily by 23,000 Confederates enjoying superiority in both numbers and position. However, Jackson labors under a strict timetable to seize the town within two days—or abandon it and rejoin the badly dispersed main army.

Union forces evacuate Charleston in western Virginia under pressure from Confederates under General William W. Loring.

General Kirby-Smith's Confederates occupy Frankfort, Kentucky, a two-day march from Cincinnati, Ohio.

The Union garrison at Munfordville, Kentucky, is surrounded by a brigade of Mississippi troops under General James R. Chalmers. He summons Union commander Colonel John T. Wilder to surrender. Wilder refuses.

NAVAL: The CSS *Alabama* under Captain Raphael Semmes seizes and burns the Union whaler *Altamaha* off the Azores.

September 14

NORTH: General George B. McClellan sorties the entire Army of the Potomac, intending to catch dispersed Confederates under General Robert E. Lee before they can regroup. He orders the IX Corps under General Jesse L. Reno and the I Corps of General Joseph Hooker to march their respective ways through Fox and Turner's Gap at South Mountain by 9:00 A.M. The pass is held by 3,000 men under General Daniel H. Hill, who, though completely surprised by the attack, resists tenaciously in rough terrain. Hill nonetheless takes a terrific pounding with General Samuel Garland killed and his brigade of North Carolinians largely captured. But at 4:00 P.M., General James Longstreet arrives with reinforcements and feeds brigades under Robert Rodes and John B. Hood back into the fray. The Union attack, now abetted by Hooker's corps and additional troops under General Ambrose E. Burnside, finally clears South Mountain by 10. P.M., with 28,500 Federals pressing on 17,850 Confederates. But because of their slow movements, Northerners lose a golden opportunity to catch the Southerners who besiege Harper's Ferry from behind and destroy them. Nonetheless, Lee is fortunate to draw off the bulk of his army intact. Losses in this severe action amount to 443 Union dead—including General Reno—1,807 wounded, and 75 missing (2,325) to a Confederate tally of 325 killed, 1,560 wounded, and 800 missing (2,685).

Cognizant of General Robert E. Lee's dispersed Army of Northern Virginia, General George B. McClellan dispatches the VI Corps under General William B. Franklin to advance with all haste through Crampton's Gap, Maryland. Once through, he is at liberty to trap the vastly outnumbered division of General Layfayette McLaws near Harper's Ferry and destroy it. Franklin proceeds as ordered and, on approaching Crampton's Gap, encounters advanced elements of a small Confederate holding force under Colonel William A. Parham—an understrength infantry and cavalry brigade totaling 1,000 men. For most of the day, Franklin's two divisions of 12,800 men under General Henry Slocum and William F. Smith methodically batter their way up the slopes of Crampton's Gap, systematically flushing Parham from the densely wooded terrain. The Confederates receive reinforcements in the form of a brigade under General Howell Cobb, but these too are dispersed. By 6:00 P.M., the exhausted, outnumbered Southerners begin to stream down the mountainside in confusion and are rallied in Pleasant Valley only by General McLaws himself. Union casualties tally 533, the Confederates about 800.

Franklin is well positioned to pitch full-force into McLaws division at Harper's Ferry, trapping it against the Potomac River. However, he vastly overestimates the size of Confederate forces opposing him and, as darkness approaches, encamps for the evening instead. Franklin's dilatoriness holds fatal consequences for the Union garrison at Harper's Ferry.

General Jacob D. Cox assumes control of IX Corps, Army of the Potomac.

WEST: Confederate artillery ranges across Union positions at Harper's Ferry, western Virginia, to bombard the garrison of Colonel Dixon S. Miles into submission. The shelling is intense and intimidating, but it injures very few soldiers. Worse, in light of Union advances after the Battle of South Mountain, Jackson must seize the town no later than the morrow, lest General Robert E. Lee be forced to cancel his invasion of Maryland. That night, he slips around General Ambrose P. Hill's division of 3,000 men on the Union left on Bolivar's Heights, prior to launching a general assault. Meanwhile, 1,400 Union cavalry under Colonel Benjamin F. "Grimes" Davis, an enterprising Mississippian in Federal employ, find an unguarded road, and he gallops the 8th New York and 12th Illinois cavalries to safety. Adding insult to injury, Davis also seizes a Confederate supply train of 97 wagons en route to Maryland.

The Army of the Ohio under General Don C. Buell approaches Bowling Green, Kentucky, to stave off a Confederate advance against his rear.

As the main Confederate force under General Braxton Bragg approaches Munfordville, Kentucky, Mississippi troops under General James R. Chalmers launch an attack. The Union commander, Colonel John T. Wilder, reinforced overnight to a strength of 4,000 men, rebuffs the assault on his two blockhouses. Southern losses are 35 killed and 253 wounded to a Federal tally of 15 dead and 57 injured. Chalmers then again demands Wilder's surrender. He again refuses.

General Sterling Price occupies Iuka, Mississippi, with 15,000 soldiers prior to joining General Braxton Bragg in Tennessee. This places him only 20 miles southeast of the main Union staging area at Corinth, and General Ulysses S. Grant sees an opportunity to trap and destroy the exposed Confederates. He therefore orders columns under General Williams S. Rosecrans and Edward O. C. Ord to approach Iuka from two directions to catch the Confederates in a pincer movement.

NAVAL: The CSS *Alabama* under Captain Raphael Semmes captures and burns the Union whaler *Benjamin Tucker* off the Azores.

September 15

NORTH: General Robert E. Lee instructs his Army of Northern Virginia, presently strung out along the hills of Sharpsburg, Maryland, to begin to consolidate and to thwart an attack by superior Union forces. He also orders General Thomas J. Jackson to depart the Shenandoah Valley and rejoin him with all possible haste.

General Joseph Mansfield is appointed commander of the XII Corps, Army of the Potomac.

WEST: After a prolonged bombardment in which Colonel Dixon A. Miles is mortally wounded, General Julius White surrenders the Union garrison at Harper's Ferry, western Virginia, to General Thomas J. Jackson. This proves another stunning setback for the Union. For a loss of 39 dead and 247 injured, the Southerners kill 44, wound 173, and take 12,520 prisoners, a like number of small arms, 73 cannon, tons of valuable equipment, and innumerable livestock. This is the largest Union capitulation of the Civil War, and it represents the largest number of Americans captured in a single action until Bataan in 1942. Jackson quickly rounds up his prisoners and proceeds with celerity to Antietam Creek, Maryland, where a major engagement seems in the offing. Lethargic Union leadership proves General Robert E. Lee's greatest ally in the race to concentrate his army.

General Braxton Bragg envelopes the town of Mundfordville, Kentucky, and besieges the Union garrison there under Colonel John T. Wilder. Intent on settling the matter by a coup de main, Bragg sends one corps under General Leonidas Polk to the north side while another under General William J. Hardee deploys on the south side. Curiously, Bragg is dissuaded from attacking by General Simon B. Buckner, who owns a house in Munfordville and fears for the lives of former neighbors.

Confederates under General Edmund Kirby-Smith advance briefly on Covington, Kentucky—directly opposite Cincinnati, Ohio—and then falls back to Lexington.

General Sterling Price's Southerners occupy the town of Iuka, Mississippi, apparently unaware of Union forces bearing down on them.

NAVAL: The USS *Thomas Freeborn* burns the Confederate schooner *Arctic* in the Great Wicomico River, Maryland.

September 16

POLITICS: The Confederate Congress issues a vote of thanks to Commander Ebenezer Farrand, senior naval officer commanding at Drewry's Bluff on May 15, 1862.

NORTH: General Robert E. Lee, buoyed by the recent seizure of Harper's Ferry, determines not to leave Maryland without a fight and positions his army along a series of low hills at Sharpsburg (Antietam). He initially musters only 18,000 troops, but glacial movements by the Army of the Potomac allows two divisions of General Thomas J. Jackson's corps to arrive and deploy on the Confederate left flank. Jackson's final division under General Ambrose P. Hill is still at Harper's Ferry, 17 miles distant, processing paroles and gathering captured supplies. Hill is ordered to march immediately once he completes his work there. Toward evening, General

George B. McClellan and the main Union army arrive and make a leisurely deployment with 75,000 men—nearly twice the Confederates's strength.

West: General John Pope, newly appointed commander of the Department of the Northwest, arrives at St. Paul, Minnesota, to direct military operations against the Santee (Sioux).

Naval: The Confederate raider CSS *Alabama* under Captain Raphael Semmes captures and burns the Union whaler *Courser* off the Azores.

September 17

North: The Battle of Antietam commences at 5:30 A.M. when 12,000 soldiers of General Joseph Hooker's I Corps advance against the Confederate left under General Thomas J. Jackson. In stiff fighting Hooker sweeps away the first rows of defenders past the North Wood and onto a nearby Cornfield. Suddenly, General John B. Hood's Texas Brigade bursts on the scene, crashes into Hooker's Federals, and hurls them back. Action recommences when the XII Corps under General Joseph Mansfield approaches to the left of Hooker, seizes the East Woods, and begins to press Jackson back from Dunker Church. Severe fighting ensues and, once Mansfield is killed in action, the Confederates again drive the Northerners back. Fighting then flares anew when General John Sedgwick's division of General Edwin V. Sumner's Corps charges back into the West Woods and is riddled from three sides by Jackson's remaining troops. Sedgwick hastily falls back as two fresh Confederate divisions are shunted over from the right flank by General Robert E. Lee. Jackson is then ordered to counterattack across the line and he does so, being heavily repulsed in turn. The frightful carnage attests to little gain by either army, but Jackson still stands his ground. Momentum consequently shifts to the Confederate center where an equally brutal contest is shaping up.

General Daniel H. Hill, without additional support, commands 5,000 men deployed along the length of a sunken road. At midday, he is hit by two remaining divisions of Sumner's V Corps, and a tremendous firefight erupts along the line. Both sides endure grievous casualties but Hill clings tenaciously to his embattlements. The Southern position then is suddenly compromised when an officer mistakenly takes his regiment out of line and Union reinforcements pour through. Hill then withdraws through a deadly enfilade fire that drops men in clumps and bequeaths to his position the unsavory nickname of "Bloody Lane." The Confederate center is now laid bare after tremendous sacrifice, and all General George B. McClellan needs to do is to order the 25,000 man V Corps under General Fitz John Porter out of reserves and forward. This he fails to do, again squandering an excellent chance to destroy the Army of Northern Virginia.

As fighting dies down across Lee's center, the locus of combat shifts again to the Confederate right. Here the IX Corps under General Ambrose E. Burnside makes several ineffectual attempts to cross a stone bridge over Antietam Creek, which finally succeeds at 3:00 P.M. Burnside then brings up four fresh divisions against the Confederates, whose right flank has been picked clean by earlier fighting, and he is opposed by only 500 Georgia infantry under Colonel Robert Toombs. Another moment of decision has arrived, and swift marching would have destroyed

Battle of Antietam/Sharpsburg September 17, 1862 *(Library of Congress)*

the Confederates, but Burnside advances slowly. Just as he begins to position units to attack, his own left is assailed suddenly by General Ambrose P. Hill's "Light Division," which has been marched rapidly from Harper's Ferry since noon. Furious fighting drives the Federals back to their starting point at about 4:00 P.M., which saves the Confederate army. When McClellan declines to resume the contest, the fighting ends at about 5:00 P.M.

Antietam is technically a drawn battle, but it exacts a horrific toll for both contestants. McClellan, with 75,000 present (although 25,000 were not engaged) suffers 2,108 killed, 9,549 wounded, and 753 missing (12,410). Lee, who can ill-afford such attrition, loses almost as many: 1,512 killed, 7,816 wounded, and 1,844 missing (11,172). The combined total of 3,500 dead and 17,000 wounded renders this the single bloodiest day in American military history, a toll unexceeded by any battle in any conflict, including World War II. The battle also underscores McClellan's inadequacy as a combat commander for he continually frittered away his numerical superiority in uncoordinated, piecemeal attacks. Lee, meanwhile, is fortunate enough to survive intact and has little recourse but to conclude his Maryland campaign on a very bloody note and retreat back into Virginia. His failure also grants President

Abraham Lincoln the military pretext he is seeking to announce his Emancipation Proclamation.

Generals George G. Meade and Alpheus S. Williams become commanders of the I Corps and XII Corps, Army of the Potomac, respectively.

SOUTH: General Ormsby M. Mitchel becomes commander of the Department of the South (South Carolina, Georgia, Florida),

WEST: General Braxton Bragg's 30,000 Confederates capture 4,000 Federal troops under Colonel John T. Wilder at Munfordsville, Kentucky, but only after a unique play of chivalry unfolds. Wilder, an amateur soldier, is perplexed at what to do next and arrives unannounced at General Simon B. Buckner's headquarters under a flag of truce. He is seeking Buckner's personal advice as a gentleman. Buckner willingly obliges his adversary by leading him around Confederate lines to highlight their stark superiority in numbers. Only then does Wilder agree to lay down his arms, and his entire command is paroled and released. Bragg's success subsequently forces Union general George W. Morgan back through the Cumberland Gap, exposing newly emergent Unionists in eastern Tennessee to retaliation.

NAVAL: The CSS *Alabama* under Captain Raphael Semmes captures and burns the Union whaler *Virginia* off the Azores.

The USS *William G. Anderson* seizes the Confederate schooner *Reindeer* in the Gulf of Mexico.

September 18

NORTH: General Robert E. Lee disengages and begins to ferry the Army of Northern Virginia across the Potomac at Blackford's Ford, Maryland, and back into Virginia. He departs, leaving thousands of casualties in his wake. Superior Union forces under General George B. McClellan, however, fail to interfere or even actively to pursue.

SOUTH: General Earl Van Dorn, commanding the Confederate garrison at Vicksburg, Mississippi, orders General Sterling Price and his 15,000 men to rendezvous with him at Pocahontas, Tennessee, and to assist the campaign of General Braxton Bragg. He remains unaware that two Union columns are closing on Price's base at Iuka, to prevent him from doing exactly that.

SOUTHWEST: General James H. Carleton succeeds General Edward R. S. Canby to command the Department of New Mexico.

NAVAL: The Confederate raider CSS *Alabama* under Captain Raphael Semmes captures and burns the Union whaler *Elisha Dunbar* off the Azores.

September 19

NORTH: Pursuing Union forces skirmish with withdrawing Confederates at Boteler's Ford on the Potomac River near Shepherdstown Ford, Maryland. General Robert E. Lee previously had posted chief of artillery General William N. Pendleton at the ford with 45 cannon, a small detachment of infantry, and orders to hold off pursuers until the next day. Around noon, General Fitz John Porter's V Corps appears on the other bank and begins to slip infantry brigades of General Charles Griffin and Colonel James Barnes across the river. As heavy fighting breaks across the line, Pendleton loses his nerve, gallops back to Lee's headquarters, and announces that all his artillery has been captured. Counteracting this loss, General Thomas J. Jackson is instructed to push General Ambrose P. Hill's division toward the ford and block any possible Union pursuit.

The Confederate Department of North Carolina and Southern Virginia is established with General Gustavus W. Smith as commander.

WEST: The 30,000-man Army of Tennessee of General Braxton Bragg occupies Glasgow, Kentucky, 30 miles east of Bowling Green.

Union columns of 9,000 men each under Generals William S. Rosecrans and Edward O. C. Ord march west and south of Iuka, Mississippi, attempting to crush 15,000 Confederates under General Sterling Price between them. However, Price's cavalry alert him of their approach, and he prepares to attack Rosecrans before both columns unite. General Henry Little's division then spearheads the assault, crumpling the Union left and seizing nine cannon of the 11th Ohio Battery. Fortunately for Rosecrans, he is able to rush up reinforcements and form a new line 600 yards to the rear, which the Confederates assail but, after the death of General Little, fail to break. As night falls, Price abandons his attack and withdraws. Casualties include 86 Southerners killed, 408 wounded, and 200 captured to Union losses of 141 men dead, 613 injured, and 36 missing.

In a curious turn of events, Ord's force, which could have tipped the balance decisively, never budges. He is ordered to move as soon as he hears the sound of gunfire, but owing to a phenomenon called acoustic shadow, he never hears a shot. Moreover, Ord assumes that smoke rising on the skyline is that of Iuka being burned to prevent capture. Rosecrans thus is forced to bear the brunt of battle unsupported, which allows Price to escape. This embarrassment also generates considerable friction among Rosecrans, Ord, and Ulysses S. Grant. Nevertheless, the discouraged Price withdraws southward, now unable to support the army of General Braxton Bragg in Tennessee. He thereupon elects to link up with Confederate forces under General Earl Van Dorn in Mississippi, who is himself planning an eventual attack on Corinth.

The Department of the Missouri is reconstituted while that of Kansas is disbanded.

NAVAL: The Federal ram USS *Queen of the West* trades shots with Confederate batteries and infantry near Bolivar, Mississippi.

September 20

SOUTH: A Confederate division under General Ambrose. P. Hill advances against two Union brigades crossing Boteler's Ford into Virginia. As he deploys to attack, several of his brigades come under severe fire from 70 Union cannon posted across the river. The Confederates nonetheless charge and drive the Federals back across the stream in a stiff fight. The 118th Pennsylvania is particularly hard hit, being forced over a high bluff and into the Potomac River while Confederates man the high bank, shooting at them as they swim. As events turn out, General William N. Pendleton's alarm is completely unfounded: the Southerners lose only four cannon. Thereafter Pendleton is restricted to administrative functions. Casualties in this sharp action total 261 Confederates and 363 Federals. With his rear now secure, General Robert E. Lee next orders the main army back upon Opequon Creek.

WEST: General Braxton Bragg takes his army of 30,000 men out of Munfordville, Kentucky, and proceeds northeast to Bardsville. There, he hopes to engage the looming Army of the Ohio under General Don C. Buell.

NAVAL: Admiral Samuel F. Du Pont warns Assistant Secretary of the Navy Gustavus V. Fox of the perils of attacking so heavily a fortified port as Charleston, South Carolina. "It is a cul de sac," he declares, "and resembles a porcupine's hide turned outside in than anything else, with no outlet—you go into the bag—no running forts as at New Orleans." His admonitions go unheeded by the Navy Department.

The USS *Albatross* captures the Confederate schooner *Two Sisters* near the Rio Grande, Texas.

September 21

SOUTH: Union forces crossing the Potomac River into Virginia skirmish heavily with Confederates at Shepherdstown before disengaging.

WEST: General Braxton Bragg advances Confederate forces toward Bardstown, Kentucky, for the purpose of uniting with General Edmund Kirby-Smith. Meanwhile, Union forces under General Don C. Buell occupy Louisville ahead of the Southerners. Other Federal troops recapture Mumsfordville.

NAVAL: The USS *Albatross* captures the Confederate schooner *Two Sisters* off the Rio Grande River, Texas.

September 22

POLITICS: The Emancipation Proclamation is unveiled by President Abraham Lincoln, which promises freedom for all African Americans currently held in secessionist states. However, he carefully skirts the issue as it pertains to slaveholding border states. Public reaction in the North decidedly is mixed and ranges from wild enthusiasm in New England to angry protests elsewhere. But his stance lessens chances that France or Britain will intervene on the Confederacy's behalf to preserve the institution of slavery, long banned in Europe.

WEST: Union forces reoccupy Harper's Ferry in western Virginia.

NAVAL: The USS *Wyandank* captures the Confederate schooner *Southerner* on the Coan River, Virginia.

September 23

POLITICS: President Abraham Lincoln's Emancipation Proclamation first appears in the Northern press; reaction is mixed and ranges from antipathy to admiration.

WEST: The Department of the Tennessee arises with General George H. Thomas as commander.

After Confederate guerrillas attack the steamer *Eugene* on the Mississippi River near Randolph, Tennessee, Union troops land and raze the town in retaliation.

Little Crow's band of 800 Mdewkanton Santee (Sioux) warriors flee up the Minnesota Valley, pursed by 1,600 volunteer and troops under Colonel Henry H. Sibley. Sibley then encamps for the evening at Lone Tree Lake (reported as Wood Lake), and Little Wolf suddenly turns on his pursuers and prepares to attack at dawn. Fortunately for Sibley, when several of his men attempt to desert, they run headlong into the Indian ambush, and the entire camp is alerted. The ensuing Santee assault is heavily repelled by artillery, and Chief Mankato, along with 30 of his warriors, is killed. The Americans sustain seven dead and 30 wounded. Sibley then presses ahead, and the bulk of the Santee nation surrenders en masse. The Union troops rescue 269 white hostages while taking 2,000 Native Americans prisoners. Several captives will hang for their role in the uprising, but the bulk of the tribe's members are slated for eventual settlement along the Niobrara River, Nebraska Territory.

NAVAL: The USS *Alabama* captures the British blockade-runner *Nelly* near Ossabaw Sound, Georgia.

September 24

POLITICS: President Abraham Lincoln authorizes suspension of all writs of habeas corpus as enunciated by Secretary of War Edwin M. Stanton. Furthermore, military trials are now required for all persons suspected of dodging the draft or encouraging disloyal practices.

A three-day conference of Union governors convenes in Altoona, Pennsylvania, at the behest of Governor Andrew G. Curtin. They gather to pledge continuing support for the president and to discuss new ideas on how to best prosecute the war.

The Confederate Congress adopts the seal of the Confederacy.

SOUTH: General Pierre G. T. Beauregard replaces General John C. Pemberton as commander of the Confederate Department of South Carolina and Georgia.

WEST: General Samuel R. Curtis takes charge of the Department of Missouri.

September 25

WEST: The Army of the Ohio under General Don C. Buell reaches Louisville, Kentucky, and prepares for a possible confrontation with Confederate forces under General Braxton Bragg.

NAVAL: The USS *Florida* captures the British schooner *Agnes* as it tries running the blockade at St. Andrew's Sound, Georgia.

The USS *Kensington* and *Rachel Seaman,* assisted by mortar schooner *Henry James,* shell Confederate batteries along Sabine Pass, Texas. The city then surrenders to landing parties who go ashore, march inland, and burn a bridge.

September 26

NAVAL: Admiral Samuel F. Du Pont proposes employing floating, coal-carrying hulks, attended by coaling schooners, that can directly transfer fuel to ships still on station. This visionary suggestion anticipates the 20th-century practice of employing fleet oilers to fuel warships at sea.

The USS *State of Georgia* and *Mystic* sink an unnamed blockade-runner off New Inlet, North Carolina.

September 27

POLITICS: The Second Confederate Conscription Act is enacted, mandating that all men between 35 and 45 years of age are subject to conscription. It does make allowances for religious conscientious objectors, provided that they pay a $500 exemption tax.

South: The first regiment of former African-American slaves, the *Chasseurs d'Afrique,* musters into Union service at New Orleans, Louisiana, at the behest of General Benjamin F. Butler.

Naval: The USS *Kittatinny* captures the Confederate schooner *Emma* off the Texas coast.

September 28

West: The armies of General Sterling Price and Earl Van Dorn unite at Ripley, Tennessee, prior to offensive operations against the vital railroad junction at Corinth, Mississippi. Van Dorn, who enjoys seniority over Price, enjoys grudging overall command.

Naval: The USS *State of Georgia* and *Mystic* capture the British blockade-runner *Sunbeam* off New Inlet, North Carolina.

September 29

South: General John F. Reynolds becomes commander of the I Corps, Army of the Potomac.

West: Union general Jefferson C. Davis has a heated contretemps with his superior, General William "Bull" Nelson, and fatally shoots him at a hotel in Louisville, Kentucky.

The combined armies of Generals Earl Van Dorn and Sterling Price, numbering 22,000 men, depart Ripley, Mississippi, and begin to maneuver toward the important railroad junction at Corinth.

September 30

West: The Army of Mississippi under General Braxton Bragg begins to concentrate at Bardstown, Kentucky, 30 miles southeast of General Don C. Buell's main Union force at Louisville.

A strong detachment of 4,500 Union and territorial troops under General Colonel Edward Salomon skirmishes with a small Confederate detachment at Newtonia, Missouri; the skirmish rapidly escalates into a battle as reinforcements arrive from both sides. Newly arrived Southerners under Colonel Douglas H. Cooper are handled roughly by Salomon's men, firing from enfilade, and they are rescued only by the timely appearance of Colonel Joseph O. Shelby's 5th Missouri Cavalry and several battalions of mounted Cherokee, Chickasaw, and Choctaw. This new infusion of numbers gives Cooper 6,000 men, and he presses the Federals hard on both flanks. Salomon consequently orders his men to retreat toward Sarcoxie, which is accomplished under close pursuit. Cooper reports his losses at 12 killed, 63 wounded, and three missing; Union casualties number about 400.

October 1

West: President Abraham Lincoln confers with General George B. McClellan at Harper's Ferry, western Virginia, over impending strategy.

The 50,000-man Army of the Ohio under General Don C. Buell departs Louisville, Kentucky, in four columns; three of these will concentrate at Perryville while a fourth is assigned to demonstrate toward Confederate-held Frankfort. Their movements are complicated by incessant heat and growing lack of water.

General John C. Pemberton arrives at Vicksburg, Mississippi, supplanting Earl Van Dorn as commander of the Department of Mississippi and East Louisiana.

NAVAL: All army vessels of the Western Gunboat Fleet are formally transferred from the War Department to the Navy Department. Command of the newly designated Mississippi Squadron now devolves on Captain David D. Porter, who replaces the less aggressive, scientifically oriented Charles H. Davis.

October 2

POLITICS: President Abraham Lincoln sets up his tent right next to General George B. McClellan's headquarters in an attempt to spur the reluctant dragon into action.

WEST: The Army of the Ohio under General Don C. Buell slowly begins to press on Bardstown, Kentucky, prior to a further advance toward Frankfort, the provisional Confederate capital. His movement is detected by scouts commanded by General Patrick R. Cleburne, who then alert Confederate headquarters.

A force of 22,000 Confederates under Generals Earl Van Dorn and Sterling Price enter Chewalla, Tennessee, 10 miles northwest of their intended target, Corinth, Mississippi. By this subterfuge, Van Dorn hopes to dupe the Union commander, General William S. Rosecrans, into thinking that his forces actually are marching north into Tennessee to assist General Braxton Bragg.

October 3

SOUTH: A combined expedition under General John M. Brannon captures a Confederate battery at St. John's Bluff and then occupies Jacksonville, Florida.

WEST: Confederate forces numbering 22,000 troops under General Earl van Dorn and Sterling Price attack 23,000 Union troops commanded by General William S. Rosecrans at Corinth, Mississippi. Van Dorn arrays his three divisions under Generals Mansfield Lovell, Dabney Maury, and Louis Hebert in an arc along the northern fringes of the town. Rosecrans, meanwhile, deploys his men in several, mutually supporting lines of defense with all intervals between covered by carefully sited cannon. These fortifications lie 400 yards distant from the main defensive lines constructed in town. The impetuous Van Dorn encounters the first line of Union earthworks at about 9:30 A.M., after which the Confederates, with great gallantry and heavy losses, grind the defenders back toward their second line. This action, however, has the effect of further concentrating and compacting the Union line, and resistance stiffens while heat, fatigue, and a lack of water weaken the Southerners. By nightfall, Van Dorn redeploys his command in a semicircle around Rosecrans's fieldworks and five lunettes (fixed batteries). Ignoring heavy casualties, he intends to attack on the morrow and clinch the victory before Union reinforcements arrive from outlying areas.

NAVAL: The USS *Commodore Perry, Hunchback,* and *Whitehead* trade shots with Confederate forces along the Blackwater River, Virginia, for six hours. However, they are thwarted in their attempt to reach Franklin by obstacles thrown into the river.

The USS *Westfield, Harriet Lane, Owasco,* and *Clifton,* accompanied by the mortar schooner *Henry James,* pound Confederate positions at Galveston, Texas. Landing parties subsequently arrive ashore and capture the city.

The Confederate raider CSS *Alabama* under Captain Raphael Semmes seizes and burns the Union ship *Brilliant* on the high seas.

October 4

POLITICS: In the Confederate-held capital of Frankfort, Kentucky, Governor Richard Hawes is sworn into office with General Braxton Bragg in attendance. However, the attendant festivities are cancelled when word of 20,000 approaching Union troops arrives.

NORTH: President Abraham Lincoln returns from the headquarters of General George B. McClellan after a day of visiting the campsite and hospitals.

WEST: At 4:00 A.M., Confederate forces under General Earl Van Dorn resume attacking General William S. Rosecrans's defensive works at Corinth, Mississippi. General Louis Hebert previously reported himself ill and is replaced by General Martin E. Green, a switch entailing some command confusion. Worse still for the Confederates, General Mansfield Lovell, fearful of wasting his men in headlong attacks against an entrenched foe, remains deliberately unengaged. By dint of hard fighting and heavy sacrifice, part of Green's force storms and seizes the Robinson lunette, Rosecrans's main battery, while his remaining brigades force their way into the town. In both instances, they encounter intractable resistance and soon are evicted in vicious hand-to-hand fighting. Van Dorn finally concedes defeat at about 1:00 P.M. and orders a withdrawal back to Ripley. Rosecrans, astutely planning and conducting an able defense in depth, finally prevails in one of the war's most hard-fought encounters. Federal losses are put at 355 killed, 1,841 wounded, and 324 missing (2,520) while Van Dorn sustains 473 dead, 1,997 injured, and 1,763 captured or missing (4,233)—losses the Confederacy could ill afford in this theater. Generals Lovell and Hebert are also relieved of command, pending a military tribunal. Control of western Tennessee and northern Mississippi begins to pass irrevocably into Union hands, and the locus of war in the West gradually shifts to Vicksburg.

Confederate Indians under Colonel Douglas H. Cooper retreat from Newtonia, Missouri, and back onto the Indian Territory in the face of Union advances directed by General John M. Schofield. Cooper's cavalry, under Colonel Joseph O. Shelby, withdraws separately to the Boston Mountains in southwestern Arkansas and regroups.

NAVAL: Landing parties from the USS *Thomas Freeborn* occupy Dumfries, Virginia, to destroy the telegraph office and its numerous wires.

Armed boats from USS *Somerset* and *Tahoma* destroy Confederate saltworks at Depot Key, Florida.

October 5

DIPLOMACY: British prime minister Lord Palmerston and Foreign Secretary Lord Russell had been leaning in favor of recognizing the Confederacy, a fact made easier by the embarrassing Union defeats of the spring and summer. Their plans are derailed on receiving word of Antietam and the Emancipation Proclamation as much of British public opinion finds the preservation of slavery unpalatable.

WEST: Confederate forces under General Braxton Bragg withdraw from Bardstown, Kentucky, cautiously pursued by the Army of the Ohio under General Don C. Buell.

General Earl Van Dorn's Confederates retreat from Corinth, Mississippi, to Holly Springs. They are intercepted by Union troops under General Edward O. C. Ord along the Hatchie River, Tennessee. An intense but indecisive clash erupts, and the Southerners continue retrograding, covered by cavalry under General Joseph Wheeler. This movement signifies the end of the hard-fought, but badly waged Corinth campaign.

October 6

NORTH: President Abraham Lincoln, frustrated at the dithering of General George C. McClellan, orders General Henry W. Halleck to prod the general to advance into Virginia to engage the enemy. "The President directs that you cross the Potomac and give battle to the enemy or drive him south," Halleck's telegram reads, "Your army must move now while the roads are good." McClellan, as usual, largely ignores the directive.

General Jacob D. Cox is promoted to major general, U.S. Army.

SOUTH: General Joseph Finegan becomes commander of Confederate forces in East Florida; those in West Florida are assigned to General John H. Forney.

WEST: The Army of the Ohio under General Don C. Buell occupies Bardstown, Kentucky, as Confederates under General Braxton Bragg continue withdrawing toward Harrodsburg. Skirmishing intensifies as the two forces close.

NAVAL: The USS *Rachel Seaman* captures the British blockade-runner *Dart* off Sabine Pass, Texas.

October 7

NORTH: General George B. McClellan, who is himself opposed to the Emancipation Proclamation, issues a general order reminding many disgruntled officers of their legal subordination to civilian authority.

General Darius N. Couch replaces General Edwin V. Sumter aa commander of II Corps, Army of the Potomac.

WEST: The III Corps of General Charles C. Gilbert, Army of the Ohio, trudges down the Springfield Road near the vicinity of Perryville, Kentucky, suffering greatly from intense heat. He then dispatches General Philip Sheridan's brigade to seize nearby watering holes from enemy skirmishers commanded by General William J. Hardee lurking to his front. Gilbert's arrival induces General Braxton Bragg to begin to mass the 16,000 men of his Army of Mississippi for an attack. However, due to poor cavalry reconnaissance, Bragg remains unaware that two more Union corps under General Don C. Buell also arrive later in the day, granting him a total of 25,000 men. An additional 32,000 Federal troops are also within marching distance.

General Gordon Granger assumes command of the Union Army of Kentucky.

Union general Eugene A. Carr becomes commander of the Army of the Southwest.

NAVAL: The army transport *Darlington* attacks and captures the Confederate steamer *Governor Milton* in St. John's River, Florida.

Confederate raider CSS *Alabama* under Captain Raphael Semmes captures and burns the Union bark *Wave Crest* and the brig *Dunkirk* off Nova Scotia.

October 8

NORTH: James N. McPherson is promoted to major general, U.S. Army.

General Orlando B. Wilcox succeeds General Jacob D. Cox as head of IX Corps, Army of the Potomac.

WEST: General Franz Sigel leads a reconnaissance from Fairfax Court House to Aldie, Virginia, skirmishing en route.

General Don C. Buell arranges his 25,000 men for battle near Perryville, Kentucky. Today, he deploys the I Corps of General Alexander McCook on his left, the III Corps of General Charles Gilbert in his center, and the II Corps under General Thomas Crittenden on his right. Previously, Confederates under General Leonidas Polk had advanced to attack the Union force, then reported as a single corps, but Polk assumes defensive positions after perceiving their superior numbers. At 10:00 A.M., General Braxton Bragg arrives at the front and orders the Confederates forward against the Union left, regardless. General William J. Hardee is also directed to position his troops along the center to keep Union forces at bay. Bragg's attack kicks off at about 2:00 P.M. when Polk's command, infiltrating through a ravine that remained propitiously undefended, suddenly turns McCook's left flank and violently drives him back. The Federals stumble away in confusion for nearly a mile before new lines can be stabilized. Buell, meanwhile, remains in his tent at some distance to the rear, unaware of the fighting owing to "acoustic shadow." This phenomenon prevents the noise of battle from being heard at headquarters, although the general is eventually alerted by messengers. Buell then spurs his horse onward, arriving on the field at about 4:00 P.M.

In the re-formed center, Gilbert's III Corps handily repulses a Confederate attack by Colonel Samuel Powell's brigade as troops under General Phil Sheridan begin to press through their lines. Sheridan, however, lends no assistance to the hard-pressed McCook on his left, having been ordered by Buell to ignore that sector. Fighting rages on until darkness when Bragg, though he wins a tactical victory of sorts, finally perceives that he is badly outnumbered. That evening he issues orders to fall back on Harrodsburg, capably screened by horsemen under Colonel Joseph Wheeler. The Battle of Perryville proves a costly encounter for both sides: Buell records his losses as 845 killed, 2,851 wounded, and 515 missing (4,211) while Bragg sustains 510 killed, 2,635 wounded, and 251 missing (3,405). Buell's casualties, although slightly heavier, also constitute a smaller percentage of his overall force, whereas the Confederates suffer a staggering loss rate of 20 percent. Moreover, Perryville signals the end of Bragg's promising Kentucky campaign; hereafter, the state is secured and brought more firmly into the Union fold.

NAVAL: Confederates burn the steamer *Blanche* off Havana, Cuba, to prevent its capture by the USS *Montgomery*.

The Confederate raider CSS *Alabama* under Captain Raphael Semmes captures and then releases the Union packet *Tonawanda* on bond off Nova Scotia.

October 9
SOUTH: James Longstreet and Edmund Kirby-Smith are promoted to lieutenant general, C.S.A.

October 10
POLITICS: President Jefferson Davis encourages the Confederate Congress to draft 4,500 African Americans for the purpose of constructing fortifications in and around Richmond, Virginia.
NORTH: 1,800 Confederate cavalry under General J. E. B. Stuart clatter out of Darkesville, Virginia, and ford the Potomac River near Black Creek, Maryland. Their orders are to destroy the Cumberland Valley Railroad bridge near Chambersburg, Pennsylvania, a major supply artery for the Army of the Potomac. This is the genesis of Stuart's second celebrated foray around General George B. McClellan's army.
SOUTH: William J. Hardee, Thomas J. Jackson, John C. Pemberton, and Leonidas Polk gain appointment as lieutenant generals, C.S.A.

John B. Hood and George E. Pickett are appointed major generals, C.S.A.
SOUTHWEST: General John B. Magruder is assigned command of the Department of Texas.

October 11
POLITICS: President Jefferson Davis modifies the draft law to exempt all persons owning 20 or more slaves. This rule serves to heighten a pervasive sense of class conflict, and many politicians accuse Davis of waging "a rich man's war and a poor man's fight."
NORTH: Chambersburg, Pennsylvania, is captured briefly and held by Confederate general J. E. B. Stuart, who destroys several locomotives, paroles 300 Union prisoners, and makes off with 500 horses. However, his main objective, the iron railroad bridge in town, could not be wrecked in time. Stuart then cuts east to Cashtown, south to Emmitsburg, Maryland, and finally fords the Potomac at White's Ferry. His latest venture covers 180 miles in two days without serious Union opposition, and he also seizes 1,200 horses.
WEST: Union forces reoccupy Harrodsburg, Kentucky, in the wake of retreating Confederates under General Braxton Bragg.
NAVAL: The USS *Monticello* captures the British schooner *Revere* off Frying Pan Shoals, North Carolina.

The USS *Maratanza* is damaged by Confederate artillery fire off Cape Fear, North Carolina.

The Confederate raider CSS *Alabama* under Captain Raphael Semmes captures and burns the Union vessel *Manchester*. Reading captured New York newspapers, he also learns of the dispositions of several U.S. Navy warships looking for him.

October 12
SOUTH: Confederate cavalry under General J. E. B. Stuart recross the Potomac near Poolesville, Virginia, completing another famous sojourn from the saddle.

The military results of the raid prove insignificant, but they completely discourage General George B. McClellan, rendering him even more cautious than usual.

WEST: General Earl Van Dorn is appointed formally commander of all Confederate forces in Mississippi.

Federal troops gather at Ozark, Missouri, to begin a campaign headed for Yellville, Arkansas.

NAVAL: The USS *Restless* captures the Confederate schooner *Elmira Cornelius* off the South Carolina coast.

Confederate commander and noted oceanographer Matthew F. Maury skillfully pilots the *Herald* past the Union blockade off Charleston, South Carolina, and then sails for Britain to purchase warships for the South.

October 13

POLITICS: The second session, first Confederate Congress, adjourns in Richmond, Virginia.

NORTH: President Abraham Lincoln again urges General George B. McClellan to resume offensive operations. "Are you not being overcautious when you assume that you cannot do what the enemy is constantly doing?" the president inquires pointedly. McClellan nonetheless refuses to budge and spends several days reorganizing the Army of the Potomac.

WEST: General Jacob D. Cox accepts command of the Federal District of Western Virginia.

Defeated Confederates under General Braxton Bragg and Edmund Kirby-Smith filter through the Cumberland Gap and back into Tennessee. The much-heralded Kentucky offensive fails, representing the high point of Confederate fortunes in the center region.

NAVAL: The USS *America* seizes the Confederate schooner *David Crockett* as it runs the blockade off Charleston, South Carolina.

October 14

POLITICS: Elections held in Pennsylvania, Iowa, Ohio, and Indiana result in Democratic Party gains. The new members largely oppose emancipation and favor peaceful accommodation with the Confederacy.

WEST: General John C. Pemberton assumes command of the Department of Mississippi and East Louisiana at Vicksburg from General Earl Van Dorn.

NAVAL: The USS *Memphis* captures the British blockade-runner *Ouachita* off Cape Romain, South Carolina.

October 15

NORTH: Troops from the Army of the Potomac advance from Sharpsburg, Maryland, to Smithfield in western Virginia, while also conducting reconnaissance operations in and around Harper's Ferry.

WEST: General John H. Morgan proposes to General Edmund Kirby-Smith another protracted raid on Union lines of communication throughout central Kentucky. Permission is granted.

NAVAL: Landing parties from the USS *Fort Henry,* while scouting up the Apalachicola River, Florida, encounter and capture the Confederate sloop *G. L. Brockenborough.*

Armed boats from the USS *Rachel Seaman* and *Kensington* bombard and destroy a railroad bridge at Taylor's Bayou, Texas, to prevent the transit of heavy cannon through Sabine Pass. They then burn schooners *Stonewall* and *Lone Star,* along with a Confederate barracks.

The Confederate raider CSS *Alabama* under Captain Raphael Semmes captures and burns the Union bark *Lamplighter* off Nova Scotia.

October 16

NORTH: Several Pennsylvania counties experience violent resistance to a Federal militia draft.

General George B. McClellan finally is prodded into launching two probing actions from Sharpsburg, Maryland, and Harper's Ferry, Virginia.

WEST: General John Echols supplants General William W. Loring as commander of the Confederate Department of Western Virginia.

Confederate forces under General Braxton Bragg continue their leisurely withdrawal through the Cumberland Gap bottleneck without interference from Union forces under General Don C. Buell.

The Department of the Tennessee is resurrected with General Ulysses S. Grant as commander. He begins to marshal men and resources for an immediate campaign against Vicksburg, Mississippi.

October 17

WEST: Colonel John H. Morgan takes 1,800 cavalry and departs from the Confederate camp, 25 miles southeast of Richmond, Kentucky, on his second major raid of the war. He rides toward the lightly guarded town of Lexington, intending to storm it.

October 18

WEST: Colonel John H. Morgan and 1,800 raiders suddenly attack and evict the Union garrison from Lexington, Kentucky, seizing both the town and 125 prisoners. During the next 12 days, Morgan cuts a circuitous swath across Kentucky, damaging railroad tracks and bridges.

October 19

WEST: General Braxton Bragg continues leading elements of his defeated Army of Tennessee south through the Cumberland Gap, Kentucky. General Don C. Buell is subject to increasing criticism for allowing Confederate forces to withdraw unmolested.

October 20

NORTH: General Henry W. Slocum is appointed commander of XII Corps, Army of the Potomac.

WEST: Union forces collecting on the Gallatin Pike near Nashville, Tennessee, repulse a cavalry attack by General Nathan B. Forrest.

Confederate marauders operating near Bardstown, Kentucky, capture a train of 81 Union wagons.

President Abraham Lincoln instructs former-politician-turned general John A. McClernand to command the newly formed Army of the Mississippi and with it to mount an expedition with troops from Indiana, Illinois, and Iowa against Vicksburg, Mississippi. This action complicates, and infringes on, efforts already underway by General Ulysses S. Grant.

October 21

POLITICS: President Abraham Lincoln urges elections in Tennessee for new state and congressional officials.

President Jefferson Davis advises General Theophilus H. Holmes of Confederate plans for an offensive to clear Tennessee and Arkansas of Federal forces.

NAVAL: The USS *Louisville* and the troop transport *Meteor* capture Bledsoe's Landing and Hamblin's Landing, Arkansas, burning both towns in retaliation for guerrilla attacks on vessels.

October 22

WEST: General Braxton Bragg leisurely evacuates the last of his Confederate forces through the Cumberland Gap, two weeks after his defeat at Perryville and unimpeded by Union troops under General Don C. Buell.

Confederate cavalry under General Joseph Wheeler capture London, Kentucky.

Union forces prevail in a heavy engagement at Maysville, Arkansas, capturing Confederate artillery and horses.

NAVAL: The USS *Penobscot* seizes the British brig *Robert Bruce* off Cape Fear, North Carolina.

The USS *Ellis* destroys the blockade-runner *Adelaide* off New Topsail Inlet, North Carolina.

Battery crews from the USS *Wabash* man three 12-pounder boat howitzers and assist Union troops in a battle at Pocotaglico (Yemassee), South Carolina. The Northerners nonetheless are repulsed and withdraw.

October 23

NAVAL: The CSS *Alabama* under Captain Raphael Semmes captures and burns the Union bark *Lafayette* near Halifax, Nova Scotia.

October 24

WEST: General Don C. Buell is sacked as commander of the Army of the Ohio for failing to aggressively pursue and destroy General Braxton Bragg's defeated army, now safely reposing at Knoxville and Chattanooga, Tennessee.

Command of the Department of the Cumberland passes to General William S. Rosecrans.

A Federal expedition out of Independence, Missouri, skirmishes heavily with Confederate irregulars near Greenton, Chapel Hill, and Hopewell.

NAVAL: The Confederate raider SS *Alabama* under Captain Raphael Semmes captures and burns the Federal whaler *Lafayette* off Halifax, Nova Scotia.

An armed party of mounted sailors from the USS *Baron de Kalb* skirmishes with Confederates scouts at Hopefield, Arkansas, and captures them after a running fight of nine miles.

October 25

POLITICS: President Abraham Lincoln again urges General George B. McClellan to commit the Army of the Potomac to offensive operations in Virginia. When the general informs the president of his fatigued horses, an angry chief executive cables back, "Will you pardon me for asking what the horses of your army have done since the battle of Antietam that fatigue anything?"

SOUTH: Union forces under General Benjamin F. Butler attack and seize Donaldsonville, Louisiana, from Confederates under General Godfrey Weitzel.

WEST: General Ulysses S. Grant receives control of the newly constituted XIII Corps within the Department of the Tennessee.

October 26

NORTH: General Samuel P. Heintzelman succeeds Nathaniel P. Banks as commander of the Washington, D.C., defenses.

SOUTH: After continual prodding, General George B. McClellan finally crosses the Potomac River back into Virginia, but he moves so slowly that General Robert E. Lee's Confederates easily interpose themselves between the invaders and Richmond. Nevertheless, President Abraham Lincoln "rejoiced" at the news.

WEST: The Union Army of the Mississippi under General John A. McClernand is disbanded and reassigned, largely through the machinations of General Ulysses S. Grant.

NAVAL: The Confederate raider CSS *Alabama* under Captain Raphael Semmes captures and burns the Union schooner *Crenshaw* off Halifax, Nova Scotia.

October 27

WEST: General William S. Rosecrans receives command of the XIV Corps in Tennessee.

Union forces prevail in a heavy skirmish at Labadieville, Louisiana, losing 18 killed and 74 wounded to a Southern tally of six killed, 15 wounded, and 208 captured.

NAVAL: Boats from the USS *Flag* capture the British steamer *Anglia* in Bulls Bay, South Carolina.

October 28

SOUTH: General George B. McClellan continues advancing—albeit it at a snail's pace—against Confederate forces at Warrenton, Virginia. General Robert E. Lee counters by falling back to prevent being encircled.

WEST: Confederate general John C. Breckinridge becomes commander of the Army of Middle Tennessee.

Roughly 1,000 Federals under General Samuel R. Curtis of the Army of the Frontier prepare to engage three times their number at Fayetteville, Arkansas, as the latter continues retreating through the Boston Mountains.

NAVAL: A quick raid by Confederates under Lieutenant John T. Wood, C.S.N., captures and burns the Union ship *Alleghanian* off the mouth of the Rappahannock River, Chesapeake Bay.

The USS *Montgomery* captures the Confederate steamer *Caroline* off Pensacola, Florida.

The USS *Sagamore* captures the British blockade-runner *Trier* at Indian River Inlet, Florida.

The Confederate raider CSS *Alabama* under Captain Raphael Semmes captures and burns the Union bark *Lauraetta* off Halifax, Nova Scotia.

October 29

POLITICS: President Abraham Lincoln, ignoring the dilatory pace of General George B. McClelland's movement in Virginia, nonetheless is relieved to see the army in motion. "When you get entirely across the river let me know," he pens, "What do you know of the enemy."

The steady stream of bad news from the West convinces President Jefferson Davis that the Confederacy lacks the resources to defend everything. "Our only alternatives are to abandon important points," he cautions, "or to use our limited resources as effectively as circumstances will permit."

WEST: Pursuing Federal troops recapture 200 head of cattle from Confederate cavalry under General J. E. B. Stuart at Petersburg, western Virginia.

NAVAL: Landing parties from the USS *Ellis* destroy Confederate saltworks at New Topsail Inlet, North Carolina.

The USS *Dan* bombards Sabine Pass, Texas. Landing parties subsequently capture and burn a mill and several buildings.

The CSS *Alabama* under Captain Raphael Semmes seizes the old vessel *Baron de Castine*, which he converts into a cartel vessel, deposits 45 prisoners, and releases on a ransom bond.

October 30

DIPLOMACY: Emperor Napoleon III suggests that France, Russia, and Great Britain conduct a joint mediation effort to end the American war. Failing that, he recommends recognition of the Confederacy.

NORTH: Command of III Corps, Army of the Potomac, passes from General Samuel P. Heintzelman to General George Stoneman.

SOUTH: Joseph Wheeler is appointed brigadier general, C.S.A.

General John M. Brannan resumes command of the Union Department of the South following the death of Ormsby M. Mitchel from illness at Beaufort, South Carolina.

WEST: General William S. Rosecrans formally supplants General Don C. Buell as head of the Department of the Cumberland.

NAVAL: The U.S. Navy Department announces a $500,000 reward for the capture of the Confederate raider "290" (CSS *Alabama*). A dozen warships, better employed elsewhere, are necessarily sent off in pursuit.

The USS *Daylight* captures the Confederate schooner *Racer* near New Topsail Inlet, North Carolina.

The USS *Connecticut* captures the British schooner *Hermosa* at the mouth of the Sabine River, Texas.

October 31

WEST: Union forces under General Ulysses S. Grant begin to mass 30,000 troops at Grand Junction, Tennessee, in preparation for an advance on Vicksburg, Mississippi.

NAVAL: To compensate for its lack of warships, the Confederate Congress authorizes a Torpedo Bureau under General Gabriel J. Rains and an embryonic Naval Submarine Battery Service headed by Lieutenant Hunter Davidson. The numerous devices they test and deploy prove a menace to Union vessels at sea, in harbors, and especially on rivers—ultimately sinking 40 ships.

The USS *Reliance* captures the Confederate sloop *Pointer* off Alexandria, Virginia.

Landing parties from the USS *Mahaska* destroy a Confederate artillery emplacement on Wormley's Creek and West Point, Virginia.

The USS *Commodore Perry, Hetzel, Hunchback, Valley City,* and the gunboat *Vidette* shell a Confederate camp at Plymouth, North Carolina.

The USS *Restless* captures the Confederate sloop *Susan McPherson* off the South Carolina coast.

November 1
SOUTH: General Benjamin F. Butler, commanding the garrison of New Orleans, Louisiana, imposes new restrictions on movements in and out of the city. He also emancipates all the African-American slaves from nonloyal owners.
WEST: General Braxton Bragg assumes control over all Confederate forces in the Department of East Tennessee. To that end, the Army of Mississippi and the Army of Kentucky are merged into a new entity, the Army of Tennessee.

Colonel John H. Morgan concludes his second successful raid through Kentucky by arriving at Springfield, Tennessee.

General Ulysses S. Grant prepares his 30,000 troops at Grand Junction, Tennessee, and orders three columns to advance down the Mississippi Central Railroad toward the important rail junction at Holly Springs.

Federal forces commence sweeps against Confederate guerrillas under William C. Quantrill in Boone and Jackson counties, Missouri.
NAVAL: The USS *Thomas Freeborn* captures three Confederate vessels on the Potomac River near Maryland Point.

The USS *Louisville* captures the Confederate steamer *Evansville* near Island No. 36 on the Mississippi River.

The Confederate raider CSS *Alabama* under Captain Raphael Semmes captures and burns the Union whaler *Levi Starbuck* off Bermuda.

November 3
SOUTH: General James Longstreet's corps deploys along Culpeper Court House, Virginia, and assumes blocking positions in front of the Army of the Potomac under General George B. McClellan.

Union landings on the coasts of Georgia and Florida involve the 1st South Carolina Volunteers under Colonel Thomas W. Higginson, the first African-American unit committed to combat operations.
WEST: Confederate guerrillas under William C. Quantrill attack and capture a Union wagon train at Harrisonville, Missouri.
NAVAL: Commander Henry K. Thatcher contacts Assistant Naval Secretary Gustavus V. Fox and implores that more warships be deployed to the Mediterranean station to prelude any chance of Confederate commerce raiding there.

The USS *Penobscot* runs the British blockade-runner *Pathfinder* aground at Shallotte Inlet, North Carolina.

Federal gunboats USS *Kinsman, Estella, St. Mary, Calhoun,* and *Diana* attack the CSS *Cotton* and Confederate shore batteries at Berwick Bay, Louisiana, and are repulsed.

November 4

POLITICS: Northern Democrats win significant elections in New York, New Jersey, Illinois, and Wisconsin, but Republican victories in California and Michigan offset these losses, and the party maintains control of the U.S. House of Representatives.

NORTH: Richard J. Gatling receives a government patient for his revolutionary, rapid-fire Gatling gun, a precursor to modern machine guns. Functional models are developed by the end of the war but rarely are committed to combat operations.

WEST: Union troops under General Ulysses S. Grant occupy La Grange, Tennessee, prior to a coordinated descent on Vicksburg with forces already collected at Grand Junction.

NAVAL: The USS *Jacob Bell* captures and burns the Confederate schooner *Robert Wilbur* on Nomini Creek, a tributary of the Potomac River.

The USS *Coeur de Lion, Teaser,* and *S. H. Poole* evacuate Union sympathizers off Gwynn's Island, Virginia.

The USS *Daylight* and *Mount Vernon* run the British blockade-runner *Sophia* aground at Masonboro Inlet, North Carolina.

A large naval expedition consisting of the USS *Hetzel, Commodore Perry, Hunchback, Valley City,* and *Seymour,* accompanied by the army gunboat *Vidette,* advance on Hamilton, North Carolina, but they withdraw once troops under General John G. Foster fail to rendezvous as planned.

The USS *Hale* captures the Confederate pilot boat *Wave* off Nassau Sound, Florida.

November 5

NORTH: President Abraham Lincoln, exasperated by General George B. McClellan's dilatoriness, finally orders him replaced by General Ambrose E. Burnside as commander of the Army of the Potomac.

WEST: Confederate cavalry under General Nathan B. Forrest skirmishes with General James S. Negley's Union troops at Nashville, Tennessee.

NAVAL: The USS *Louisiana* captures the Confederate schooner *Alice L. Webb* off Rose Bay, North Carolina.

November 6

SOUTH: Generals James Longstreet and Thomas J. Jackson receive command of the 1st and 2nd Army Corps in the Army of Northern Virginia, respectively.

WEST: General Ulysses S. Grant orders an extended reconnaissance of the region from La Grange, Tennessee, into neighboring Mississippi.

Federal forces out of Fort Scott, Kansas, skirmish with Confederate guerrillas under William C. Quantrill.

NAVAL: The USS *Teaser* captures the Confederate sloop *Grapeshot* in Chesapeake Bay.

November 7

North: General George B. McClellan formally steps down as commander of the Army of the Potomac. While never popular with politicians, "Little Mac" remains adored by his men.

West: Generals Leonidas Polk and William J. Hardee receive command of the 1st and 2nd Corps, Army of the Mississippi, respectively.

The Union Army of the Cumberland under General William S. Rosecrans begins to march from Kentucky to Nashville, Tennessee.

Naval: Armed parties from the USS *Potomska* and the army transport *Darlington* disembark on the Sapelo River, Georgia, and destroy Confederate saltworks at Fairhope.

The USS *Kinsman* and the steamer *Seger* burn the Confederate steamers *Osprey* and *J. P. Smith* at Bayou Cheval, Louisiana.

On the urging of Admiral David D. Porter, President Abraham Lincoln authorizes the army's Ellet Rams on the Mississippi River to be transferred to the Mississippi Squadron over War Department objections.

November 8

South: General William C. Whiting assumes command of Confederate defenses on Cape Fear River, North Carolina.

After a stormy and controversial tenure commanding the Department of the Gulf at New Orleans, General Benjamin F. Butler is replaced by General Nathaniel P. Banks. To preempt any celebrations by the populace, Butler peremptorily closes all breweries and distilleries within his jurisdiction.

West: Confederate colonel John D. Imboden's partisan rangers capture St. George in western Virginia.

General Ulysses S. Grant continues massing several thousand Union troops near La Grange, Tennessee, prior to leading them across the state line into Mississippi and, ultimately, to the Confederate citadel of Vicksburg. He plans his axis of attack down the Mississippi Central Railroad leading directly into the city.

Naval: The USS *Resolute* captures the Confederate sloop *Capitola* off Glymount, Maryland.

The Confederate raider CSS *Alabama* under Captain Raphael Semmes captures and burns the Union vessel *T. B. Wales* near Bermuda.

November 9

South: General Ambrose E. Burnside assumes command of the Army of the Potomac, a position he never really sought and initially tried to refuse. Acting on his instructions, Union cavalry under Colonel Ulric Dahlgren dash spectacularly through Confederate positions at Fredericksburg, Virginia, taking 54 prisoners for a loss of one killed. This affair proves that the town's defenses are weak, and Burnside begins to draw up plans for an offensive there.

West: Partisan rangers under Colonel John D. Imboden skirmish with Federal troops under General Benjamin F. Kelley on the South Fork of the Potomac.

Naval: A combined Army-Navy landing party from the USS *Louisiana* captures Greenville, North Carolina.

November 10

NORTH: General Joseph Hooker replaces Fitz John Porter as V Corps commander in the Army of the Potomac. Porter is slated to undergo court-martial proceedings for his role at Second Manassas.

SOUTH: General George B. McClellan, highly respected and beloved by the men he commanded, bids a final farewell to his Army of the Potomac at Warrenton, Virginia.

WEST: The Confederate Department of Western Virginia passes to General John S. Williams.

November 11

NAVAL: The USS *Kensington* captures the Confederate schooner *Course* off the coast of Florida.

November 12

NAVAL: The USS *Kensington* captures the British blockade-runner *Maria* off the coast of Florida.

November 13

WEST: The important rail junction at Holly Springs, Mississippi, is occupied by Union forces as part of a larger campaign directed at Vicksburg by General Ulysses S. Grant.

General Braxton Bragg leads the Confederate Army of Tennessee from Chattanooga, Tennessee, toward Murfreesboro. There, he intends to unite with forces under General John C. Breckinridge.

November 14

NORTH: Newly installed General Ambrose E. Burnside, commanding the Army of the Potomac, effects a major reorganization of his charge by placing Generals Joseph Hooker, Edwin V. Sumner, and William B. Franklin as commanders of the Right, Center, and Left Grand Divisions, respectively. Their respective commands then are organized as "grand divisions" of two corps each. He also prepares for an immediate advance toward Fredericksburg, Virginia, prior to an eventual move on Richmond.

WEST: The Confederate Army of Tennessee under General Braxton Bragg begins to concentrate around Tullahoma, Tennessee.

November 15

POLITICS: George W. Randolph resigns suddenly as Confederate secretary of war.

NORTH: General Ambrose E. Burnside initiates an advance on Falmouth, Virginia, by first launching a feint toward Warrenton. An excellent organizer, Burnside's troops cover 40 miles in two days of hard slogging and arrive opposite the town of Fredericksburg on the Rappahannock River. His alacrity also leaves the Confederates perplexed as to his locale and intentions.

NAVAL: President Abraham Lincoln and several cabinet members narrowly escape injury when an experimental Hyde rocket accidentally explodes during a demonstration at the Washington Navy Yard.

The Confederate raider CSS *Alabama* under Captain Raphael Semmes steams into Martinique harbor, followed closely by the USS *San Jacinto,* which establishes a loose blockade.

November 16

NORTH: Generals Daniel Butterfield and William F. Smith assume command of the V Corps and VI Corps, respectively.

NAVAL: The USS *T. A. Ward* captures the Confederate sloop *G. W. Greene* along St. Jerome's Creek, Maryland.

November 17

POLITICS: General Gustavus W. Smith is appointed acting Confederate secretary of war at the behest of President Jefferson Davis.

SOUTH: The Union Right Grand Division under General Edwin V. Sumner deploys at Falmouth, Virginia, just across from Fredericksburg on the Rappahannock River. This move concludes an impressive 40-mile march by the usually plodding Army of the Potomac, one orchestrated by the new commander, General Ambrose E. Burnside. This maneuver proves so stealthy that Confederate general Robert E. Lee temporarily loses contact with his adversary's whereabouts. Moreover, Fredericksburg at this time is only lightly defended, but despite Sumner's urging, Burnside declines to send troops across the Rappahannock and occupy it. Worse, pontoon bridges and other equipment that Burnside requested have failed to materialize due to bureaucratic snares, and, by waiting for them to arrive, he gradually loses his advantage of surprise.

NAVAL: The USS *Cambridge* runs the British blockade-runner *J. W. Pindar* aground at Masonboro Inlet, North Carolina, burning it.

The USS *Kanawha* and *Kennebec* chase an unnamed Confederate blockade-runner ashore near Mobile, Alabama.

November 18

SOUTH: The Army of the Potomac under General Ambrose E. Burnside continues occupying Falmouth, Virginia, behind the Rappahannock River and directly opposite the heights of Fredericksburg. However, Burnside takes no offensive actions during the next three weeks, allowing Confederates under General James Longstreet to arrive and greatly strengthen their defensive arrangements.

NAVAL: The USS *Monticello* runs the British blockade-runners *Ariel* and *Ann Maria* aground near Shallotte Inlet, North Carolina, burning them.

November 19

SOUTH: General Ambrose E. Burnside arrives to take charge of the Army of the Potomac at Falmouth, Virginia. The Army of Northern Virginia, meanwhile, begins to adjust defensive arrangements near Fredericksburg by posting General James Longstreet's corps at Culpeper while Confederate cavalry under General J. E. B. Stuart occupy Warrenton Junction.

WEST: General Ulysses S. Grant continues probing Confederate lines from Grand Junction, Tennessee, toward Ripley, Mississippi, prior to advancing on Vicksburg.

NAVAL: USS *Wissahickon* and *Dawn*, while blockading the CSS *Nashville* in Ossabaw Sound, Georgia, trade fire with Fort McAllister on the Ogeechee River. *Wissahickon* sustains serious damage and draws off.

The Confederate raider CSS *Alabama* under Captain Raphael Semmes departs Martinique under the cover of a storm, eluding the blockading USS *San Jacinto*.

November 20

SOUTH: General Robert E. Lee arrives at Fredericksburg to direct the Army of Northern Virginia personally as a buildup of troops continues on both sides.

WEST: General Braxton Bragg's Confederate Army of Tennessee is reconstituted with three corps commanded by Generals Edmund Kirby-Smith, Leonidas Polk, and William J. Hardee.

NAVAL: The USS *Seneca* captures the Confederate schooner *Annie Dees* off Charleston, South Carolina.

The USS *Montgomery* captures the Confederate sloop *William E. Chester* in Pensacola Bay, Florida.

November 21

POLITICS: James A. Seddon succeeds George W. Randolph as Confederate secretary of war.

SOUTH: General Ambrose E. Burnside demands that the mayor of Fredericksburg, Virginia, surrender. When he refuses, Burnside strongly advises him to evacuate women and children from the town.

WEST: General Braxton Bragg dispatches Confederate cavalry under General Nathan B. Forrest to disrupt Union lines of communication in western Tennessee.

November 22

POLITICS: Secretary of War Edwin M. Stanton releases the majority of political prisoners in army custody.

SOUTH: General Ambrose E. Burnside reverses himself and assures the mayor of Fredericksburg, Virginia, that he will not fire into the town. In exchange, he expects no hostile action on behalf of its inhabitants.

NAVAL: Joint army-navy landing parties from the USS *Mahaska* capture Matthews Court House, Virginia, destroying numerous saltworks in the area. They also seize three schooners, several small boats, and ample provisions.

November 23

NAVAL: An armed party from the USS *Ellis* under Lieutenant William B. Cushing seizes two schooners off Jacksonville, North Carolina, before they ground and are burned by crews. Cushing later escapes in one of the captured vessels.

November 24

WEST: Confederates under General Thomas J. Jackson march from Winchester, western Virginia, toward the main army at Fredericksburg, Virginia.

President Jefferson Davis elevates General Joseph E. Johnston to commander of Confederate troops in the west, succeeding Generals John C. Pemberton and Braxton Bragg. His military authority embraces the regions of western North

Carolina, Tennessee, northern Georgia, Alabama, Mississippi, and eastern Louisiana. Johnston is tasked specifically with guiding Pemberton in the defense of Vicksburg, Mississippi.

Union troops scour Jasper and Barton counties, Missouri, in search of Confederate bushwhackers under William C. Quantrill.

NAVAL: The USS *Reliance* captures the Confederate longboat *New Moon* on the Potomac River near Alexandria, Virginia.

Landing parties from the USS *Monticello* capture and destroy Confederate saltworks at Little River Inlet, North Carolina.

November 25

WEST: General Samuel Jones succeeds General John S. Williams as commander of the Confederate Western Department of Virginia.

NAVAL: The USS *Kittatinny* captures the British blockade-runner *Matilda* at sea.

November 26

NORTH: President Abraham Lincoln confers with General Ambrose E. Burnside at Aquia Creek, Virginia, over his prospective assault on Fredericksburg. The general wishes for a direct attack while the president argues for a multipronged approach. At length, the president's suggestion is rejected.

WEST: The retiring Confederate Army of Tennessee under General Braxton Bragg occupies the settlement at Murfreesboro, Tennessee. Having abandoned Kentucky to its fate, the general grimly determines to maintain a Confederate presence in central Tennessee.

NAVAL: The USS *Mount Vernon* captures the Confederate blockade-runner *Levi Rowe* off New Inlet, North Carolina.

The USS *Kittatinny* seizes the Confederate schooner *Diana* in the Gulf of Mexico.

November 28

SOUTH: Federal forces rout Southern counterparts in a heavy skirmish at Frankfort, Virginia, seizing 100 prisoners.

WEST: In a preemptive strike, Union general James G. Blunt and 5,000 men attack 2,000 Confederate cavalry under General John S. Marmaduke at Cane Hill, Arkansas. In a nine-hour running battle, the Southerners are driven into the Boston Mountains. Fortunately, they are covered by a skillful rearguard action by General Joseph O. Shelby's troopers and escape intact with 45 casualties to a Union tally of 41. Blunt declines to pursue for fear of being surrounded, but his presence, 100 miles from the nearest Union reinforcements, induces Confederate general Thomas C. Hindman to march overland and attack his isolated column.

November 29

NORTH: Winfield S. Hancock, George G. Meade, John F. Reynolds, John M. Schofield, and Daniel E. Sickles are appointed major generals, U.S. Army.

SOUTHWEST: General John B. Magruder arrives to take charge of the District of Texas, New Mexico, and Arizona. He makes the recapture of the port city of Galveston an immediate priority and begins to marshal the men and ships necessary for a surprise attack.

NAVAL: In an attempt to better facilitate distribution of coal among blockading vessels, Captain H. A. Adams gains appointment as coordinator of coal supply at Philadelphia, Pennsylvania. Fuel consumption in the South Atlantic Blockading Squadron alone is running at 950 tons a week.

General John B. Magruder orders the Confederate steamers *Bayou City* and *Neptune* outfitted with bales of cotton "armor" and transformed into "cottonclads." They will figure prominently in the upcoming attack on Galveston, Texas.

November 30

SOUTH: After incessant delays, pontoons and other bridging equipment requested by General Ambrose E. Burnside finally arrive at Falmouth, Virginia. The Army of the Potomac is now able to cross the Rappahannock River to Fredericksburg, but during this interval, General Robert E. Lee rushes 35,000 men under General James Longstreet to the heights on the city.

NAVAL: The Confederate raider CSS *Alabama* successfully eludes the pursuing warship USS *Vanderbilt* and captures the Union bark *Parker Cook* off the Leeward islands, Atlantic Ocean.

December 1

POLITICS: President Abraham Lincoln proffers a plan for compensated emancipation to the 37th Congress, but it elicits little enthusiasm. "In giving freedom to the slave, we assure freedom to the free," he insists. Lincoln also promises to help colonize those wishing to depart.

The third session, 37th Congress convenes.

SOUTH: General Thomas J. Jackson's corps occupies defensive positions on the right flank of General Robert E. Lee's army at Fredericksburg.

WEST: General Ulysses S. Grant dispatches the XIII Cavalry Corps, a cavalry force of four regiments under Colonel Theophilus L. Dickie, to pursue Confederates fleeing southward from his base at Oxford, Mississippi, across the Tallahatchie River.

NAVAL: Secretary of the Navy Gideon Welles makes his second annual report to President Abraham Lincoln. He announces that 427 ships are in commission, mounting an aggregate of 1,577 guns, while personnel have risen to 28,000 crew, with an additional 12,000 mechanics and laborers.

The USS *Sagamore* captures the British blockade-runner *By George* off Indian River, Florida.

The USS *Tioga* captures the Confederate schooner *Nonsuch* off the Bahama Banks.

December 2

NAVAL: Armed boats from the USS *Sachem* chase the Confederate steamer *Queen of the Bay* until it grounds on Padre Island, Texas. Ensign Alfred H. Reynolds is seriously wounded, however, and is forced to abandon his boats on Mustang Island. The sailors end up retreating 30 miles overland before rejoining their vessel at Aransas Bay.

December 3

WEST: The Union XIII Cavalry Corps under Colonel Theophilus L. Dickie skirmishes heavily with Confederate forces dug in along the Yocknapatalfa River, Mississippi. Dickie then tries skirting the resistance by extending his pursuit in the direction of Coffeeville.

Union troops under General Alvin P. Hovey occupy Grenada, Mississippi, after fleeing Confederates destroy 15 locomotives and 100 railroad cars to prevent their capture.

General Thomas C. Hindman marches his Confederate Army of the Trans-Mississippi, 11,000 strong, out from Van Buren, Arkansas, in bitter winter weather. His goal is to strike and destroy the isolated and outnumbered Union division of General James G. Blunt at Cane Hill. However, once Blunt is alerted to Hindman's approach, he appeals to General Francis J. Herron's division at Springfield, Missouri, 100 miles distant, for help.

NAVAL: The USS *Cambridge* captures the Confederate schooners *J. C. Roker* and *Emma Tuttle* off the North Carolina coast.

The USS *Daylight* apprehends the British blockade-runner *Brilliant* off Wilmington, North Carolina.

December 4

SOUTH: Union and Confederate outposts skirmish along the Rappahannock River.
WEST: Union forces capture Winchester, western Virginia, along with 145 Southern prisoners.

General Joseph E. Johnston arrives to coordinate the military operations of General John C. Pemberton at Vicksburg, Mississippi, and General Braxton Bragg at Nashville, Tennessee. This additional level of control further complicates an already Byzantine command structure.

NAVAL: The USS *Anacostia, Coeur de Lion, Cuttituck,* and *Jacob Bell* trade fire with Confederate batteries at Port Royal, Virginia, before withdrawing.

December 5

POLITICS: President Abraham Lincoln pardons the bulk of 303 Sioux tribesmen slated for execution for their role in a bloody uprising. The final number of condemned and hanged is 39.

WEST: The Union XIII Cavalry Corps, scouting in the vicinity of Coffeeville, Mississippi, engages superior Confederate forces under Generals Mansfield Lovell and Lloyd Tilghman. Harsh fighting ensues as the troopers are forced back by numbers, yet they skillfully withdraw with alternating defensive lines. Colonel Theophilus L. Dickey then breaks off the battle and rides back to Union lines, concluding his five-day pursuit of General Earl Van Dorn. For his effort, Dickey seizes 750 captives, 200 horses, and four wagons at a cost of 10 killed, 63 wounded, and 43 captured. Lovell reports his casualties as seven killed and 43 wounded.

NAVAL: Armed boats from the USS *Mahaska* and *General Putnam* capture the schooners *Seven Brothers* and *Galena* and destroy an additional schooner and two sloops in the Severn River, Maryland.

The USS *Baron de Kalb* captures the Confederate steamer *Lottie* near Memphis, Tennessee.

The Confederate raider CSS *Alabama* under Captain Raphael Semmes captures the Federal schooner *Union* off Haiti, releasing it on a bond.

December 6

West: General Joseph Wheeler attacks and captures part of a Federal wagon train at Mill Creek, Tennessee.

In one of the most amazing forced marches of the entire Civil War, two Union divisions from the Army of the Frontier under General Francis J. Herron slog from Springfield, Missouri, and speedily arrive at Fayetteville, Arkansas, to assist General James G. Blunt's force at Cane Hill. Herron, braving rough terrain and bitter cold, covers the distance in only three days—a remarkable accomplishment that literally preserves the Union war effort in Arkansas.

Naval: The USS *Diana* seizes the Confederate steamers *Southern Methodist* and *Naniope* on the Mississippi River near Vicksburg.

December 7

Politics: President Jefferson Davis, anxious for the fate of Vicksburg, Mississippi, contacts General John C. Pemberton and inquires: "Are you in communication with General J. E. Johnston? Hope you will be reinforced in time."

West: A force of 2,400 Confederate raiders under General John H. Morgan surprises and captures Hartsville, Tennessee, along with 1,800 Union captives under Colonel Absalom B. Moore. Morgan's losses in this hotly waged affair total 21 dead and 104 wounded, but he inflicts 58 killed and 204 wounded on the defenders.

Troops in the Confederate Department of Mississippi and East Louisiana are organized into two army groups under Generals Sterling Price and Earl Van Dorn.

General Thomas C. Hindman commences the Battle of Prairie Grove by dispatching a small Confederate cavalry force under Colonel J. C. Monroe to distract and occupy the attention of General James G. Blunt at Cane Hill. Meanwhile, Hindman advances on the footsore and recently arrived host of General Francis J. Herron at Prairie Grove, eight miles from Fayetteville. He possesses 11,000 men and badly outnumbers his opponent, but after achieving strategic surprise, he inexplicably assumes defensive positions. Fighting commences at 9:30 A.M. when the aggressive Herron attacks what he perceives to be a small Confederate force, unaware that Hindman's entire army is present. He is repelled badly in a series of charges while subsequent Confederate advances are likewise defeated by superior Union artillery. Neither side can end the impasse, although Hindman's fortunes dim considerably when Blunt, surmising that Monroe's cavalry is a feint, hurriedly marches to Prairie Grove with his fresh troops. Additional attacks and counterattacks ensue with little gain to either side until nightfall finally ends the contest.

Prairie Grove is a hard-fought and bloody draw, considering the numbers engaged. Union forces totaling 8,000 men sustain 175 dead, 813 wounded, and 263 captured (1,251) while 10,000 Confederates present suffer 164 killed, 817 wounded, and 336 missing (1,317). Moreover, Hindman, his army rapidly disintegrating through desertion, evacuates the field that night and heads back to Van Buren. His defeat signals the continuing Union domination of Missouri and northern Arkansas.

NAVAL: The Confederate raider CSS *Alabama* under Captain Raphael Semmes captures the steamer *Ariel* off Cuba, taking 700 captives, including 150 U.S. Marines under Commander Louis C. Sartori.

December 8

POLITICS: President Abraham Lincoln recommends Captain John L. Worden for a vote of thanks from the U.S. Congress for his role in commanding the USS *Monitor*.

NAVAL: The USS *Daylight* captures the Confederate sloop *Coquette* off New Topsail Inlet, North Carolina.

December 9

WEST: Confederate cavalry under General Joseph Wheeler attack a Union wagon train at La Vergne, Tennessee.

December 10

POLITICS: The U.S. House of Representatives approves a bill creating the new state of West Virginia on a vote of 96–55.

SOUTH: A Confederate attack on Plymouth, North Carolina, partially burns the town and damages Union shipping offshore.

NAVAL: The USS *Currituck* trades fire with a Confederate battery at Brandywine Hill, Virginia.

The ironclad USS *Southfield* takes artillery fire while supporting Federal troops off Plymouth, North Carolina.

The USS *Sagamore* captures the British blockade-runner *Alicia* in the Indian River, Florida.

December 11

SOUTH: John H. Morgan is promoted to brigadier general, C.S.A.

The Army of the Potomac under General Ambrose E. Burnside begins to bridge its way across the Rappahannock River, opposite Fredericksburg, Virginia. However, as the fog lifts, Burnside's engineers receive heavy and effective sniper fire from General William Barksdale's Mississippi brigade. Burnside then orders his artillery to bombard Fredericksburg in retaliation, which inflicts considerable damage but fails to dislodge the snipers. At length, several boatloads of volunteers row themselves across the river under fire and finally flush the Southerners from the town. The Army of the Potomac begins to ferry troops en masse at night, but Barksdale's tenacity brings General Robert E. Lee another 24 hours to strengthen and perfect his defensive works on the heights overlooking the city.

WEST: Confederate general Nathan B. Forrest rides with 2,500 troopers out of Columbia, Tennessee, intending to harass Union lines of communication. His goal is to wreck portions of the Mississippi Central Railroad and the Mobile and Ohio Railroad. Forrest's first objective, however, is the town of Lexington.

December 12

SOUTH: Vengeful troops of the Union Army of the Potomac are preoccupied in a looting binge at Fredericksburg, Virginia. Meanwhile, General Robert E. Lee, realizing that the enemy has crossed in strength for a major effort, hastily summons the corps of General Thomas J. Jackson from positions downstream, and he gradually occupies the right flank of Lee's line. By nightfall, General Ambrose E. Burnside masses 112,000 troops (16 divisions) below the Confederate positions and plans for an assault at dawn.

NAVAL: The USS *Delaware, Shawsheen, Lockwood,* and *Seymour* sail up the Neuse River, North Carolina, to support an army expedition against nearby Goldsboro. Low-water levels ultimately thwart their mission.

The Federal ironclad USS *Cairo* under Commander Thomas O. Selfridge strikes a Confederate "torpedo" (mine) on the Yazoo River, Mississippi, and sinks. This is the first of 40 Union vessels ultimately lost to submerged Southern ordnance.

WEST: General John C. Pemberton appoints the recently disgraced general Earl Van Dorn to assume command of a three-brigade division of Confederate cavalry. His command includes mounted units from Texas, Tennessee, Missouri, and Mississippi, totaling 3,500 troopers.

December 13

SOUTH: Patrick R. Cleburne is prompted to major general, C.S.A.

The Battle of Fredericksburg, Virginia, commences at 10:00 A.M. as a dense fog suddenly lifts and reveals to Southerners the awe-inspiring sight of serried ranks of blue-coated infantry advancing below them. The first thrust is hurled against General Robert E. Lee's lines on the Confederate right when General William B. Franklin commits divisions under Generals George G. Meade and John Gibbon to strike General Thomas J. Jackson. Advancing through heavy fire, Meade and Gibbon find a convenient gap midway through Jackson's erstwhile strong position and pour through. The Federals then surprise a brigade under General Maxcy Gregg, killing him and routing his South Carolinians, but Franklin fails to follow up this surprising breakthrough with reinforcements. Consequently, Jackson's riposte proves sharp and effective: He dispatches the divisions of Jubal A. Early and Daniel H. Hill to slash at both Union flanks, and the Federals flee down the hill with heavy losses. The only real chance for a Northern victory that day is squandered.

As Burnside's main attack develops, it is directed against Lee's left flank, along a steep hill called Marye's Heights. This is defended by General James Longstreet, who prides himself on his defensive expertise, and it ostensibly proves the strongest part of the Confederate line. Longstreet carefully arrays his men behind strong stone walls fronting the open fields that Union forces have to pass. Moreover, any advance also takes them into the teeth of interlocking fields of fire from Colonel Edward P. Alexander's artillery. The drama unfolds as the grand division of General Edwin V. Sumner and part of General Joseph Hooker's command, 60,000 strong, charge bravely uphill—with predictable slaughter. On and on they come in 16

Battle of Fredericksburg, Virginia December 13, 1862 Lithograph by Currier & Ives *(Library of Congress)*

waves, only to be blasted back with heavy losses. Despite Herculean courage and terrible sacrifice, no Federal soldier gets closer than 20 yards to Longstreet's line before succumbing to concentrated rifle and cannon fire. The one-sided slaughter continues well into the evening before Burnside finally calls off the attack. Undeterred by staggering losses, he intends to renew the struggle on the following day, but senior subordinates convince him to relent.

In a long string of Union defeats this year, Fredericksburg is the worst. Burnside's losses amount to 1,284 killed, 9,600 wounded, and 1,769 missing (12,653). The well-protected Confederates predictably sustain half as much carnage, 608 dead, 4,116 injured, and 653 missing (5,377). In reviewing mountains of bodies literally piled before Marye's Heights, Lee aptly remarks, "It is well that war is so terrible. We should grow too fond of it." Meanwhile President Abraham Lincoln, on hearing of Union losses, sullenly declares, "If there is a worse place than Hell I am in it." Northern morale and support for the war plunges to its lowest ebb.
WEST: President Jefferson Davis arrives at Murfreesboro, Tennessee, to review Confederate forces under General Braxton Bragg.

Confederate raiders under General Nathan B. Forrest pause at the Tennessee River near Clifton, Tennessee, to construct flatboats.

Federal troops defeat Confederate forces in a large skirmish at Tuscumbia, Alabama.

December 14

SOUTH: The Army of the Potomac under General Ambrose E. Burnside begins withdrawing back across the Rappahannock River as Confederate forces under General Robert E. Lee continue strengthening their defensive works. Lee summarily ignores General Thomas J. Jackson's urgings to counterattack decisively and possibly destroy the Union force.

General John G. Foster leads Union troops on a successful sortie from New Bern, North Carolina, that captures nearby Kinston.

The Confederate Department of the Gulf is assigned to General Simon B. Buckner.

WEST: General Ulysses S. Grant orders a Union cavalry force from Spring Dale, Mississippi, under Colonel Theophilus L. Dickie to cut the Mobile and Ohio Railroad.

Texas Rangers launch a surprise raid against Union pickets at Helena, Arkansas, capturing 23 soldiers.

December 15

SOUTH: The Army of the Potomac completes its withdrawal across the Rappahannock River, covered by darkness and heavy rainfall. Prior to retreating, General Ambrose E. Burnside sends a flag to General Robert E. Lee requesting a temporary truce to retrieve the Union dead—and those still alive after two days of exposure to the cold. Lee magnanimously grants his request.

WEST: General Nathan B. Forrest and his 2,500 troopers cross the Tennessee River at Clifton, Tennessee, sinking their flatboats in shallow water to retrieve them later.

NAVAL: Assistant Naval Secretary Gustavus V. Fox broaches a possible attack against Wilmington, North Carolina, to Admiral Stephen P. Lee. "Though the popular clamor centers upon Charleston," he notes, "I consider Wilmington a more important point in a military and political point of view."

December 16

SOUTH: The Army of the Potomac reoccupies Falmouth, Virginia, where General Ambrose E. Burnside issues a directive accepting full responsibility for the disaster at Fredericksburg.

General Benjamin F. Butler bids farewell to his command at New Orleans, Louisiana, and is formally succeeded by General Nathaniel P. Banks, who brings additional reinforcements for extended operations upriver.

WEST: A Union force of 700 men and two cannon under Colonel Robert G. Ingersoll, 11th Illinois Cavalry, is dispatched from Jackson, Tennessee. They trot 28 miles east to the town of Lexington with orders to obstruct and delay an impending Confederate raid under General Nathan B. Forrest. Unfortunately, only about 200 of Ingersoll's men are veterans, and the balance are hastily trained recruits.

December 17

POLITICS: Radical Republican senators precipitate a cabinet crisis for President Abraham Lincoln by demanding the resignation of Secretary of State William H. Seward and replacing him with the present treasury secretary, Salmon P. Chase.

Highly insulted, Seward tenders his resignation to the president, who summarily refuses to accept it.

SOUTH: Advancing Union forces reoccupy Baton Rouge, Louisiana.

WEST: General Nathan B. Forrest and 2,500 raiders make preparations to storm Lexington, Tennessee. The garrison commander, Colonel Robert G. Ingersoll, gives orders to destroy all crossings approaching the town, but his men somehow overlook a bridge on the Lower Road.

General Ulysses S. Grant issues General Order No. 11, expelling Jews from his theater of operations. "The Jews, as a class violating every regulation of trade established by the Treasury Department, and also department orders," it reads, "are hereby expelled from the department within twenty-four hours from the receipt of this order." Grant is pressured to rescind the directive in a few weeks.

A division of 3,500 Confederate cavalry under General Earl Van Dorn clatters out of Grenada, Mississippi, intent on raiding the main Federal supply depot at Holly Springs. To confuse Union military intelligence, he takes an indirect route and initially rides north toward Tennessee as far as Ripley before suddenly cutting west, splitting up his columns, and hitting his objective from three different directions.

December 18

WEST: General Nathan B. Forrest and 2,500 Confederates attack a Union cavalry detachment under Colonel Robert G. Ingersoll defending Lexington, Tennessee. The fighting actually begins at dawn when Union troopers raid a Confederate encampment, which is beaten off. Forrest then draws up his men in an elaborate feint, as if they intend to strike the Union left flank. Instead, the Confederates clatter across an unburned bridge on the Lower Road, enabling them to flank a portion of the defenders under Colonel Isaac R. Hawkins. Ingersoll tries desperately to realign his men and repels three headlong charges by Southern veterans, but eventually he is overrun and surrenders. Forrest sustains 35 casualties to a Federal total of 17 killed and injured, with an additional 170 captured.

Federal army units are reorganized in the Army of the Tennessee under General Ulysses S. Grant: General John A. McClernand, XIII Corps; William T. Sherman, XV Corps; Stephen A. Hurlbut, XVI Corps; and James B. McPherson, XVII Corps.

NAVAL: Admiral David G. Farragut strongly suggests reoccupying Baton Rouge, Louisiana, to General Nathaniel P. Banks, who is newly arrived, as a preliminary for the eventual campaign against Port Hudson on the Mississippi River.

December 19

WEST: Confederate cavalry under General Nathan B. Forrest skirmish heavily with Union forces at Spring Creek and Jackson, Tennessee.

General Ulysses S. Grant, alerted to the presence of a large Confederate raiding column in the vicinity of his main supply depot at Holly Springs, Mississippi, warns garrison commander Colonel Robert C. Murphy to prepare his defenses.

December 20

WEST: The XIII Corps, consisting of 32,000 Union troops in four divisions under General William T. Sherman, embarks aboard transports at Memphis, Tennessee, and sails down the Mississippi River. Sherman intends to flank Confederate defenses at Vicksburg, Mississippi, in concert with demonstrations farther inland by General Ulysses S. Grant. These maneuvers are calculated to pin Confederate reinforcements at Grenada and prevent them from reaching the city.

A lightning Confederate raid by General Nathan B. Forrest on Humbolt, Tennessee, results in 50 Union casualties.

In a spectacularly devastating move, Confederate cavalry under General Earl Van Dorn capture a primary Union stockpile at Holly Springs, Mississippi, worth $1.5 million, along with 1,500 prisoners. He does so by utilizing superb marching discipline en route, which keeps Union forces—and his own men—unsure as to his ultimate objective. Van Dorn is further abetted by garrison commander Colonel Robert C. Murphy who, while forewarned, takes no precautions to increase patrolling or prepare adequate defenses. Consequently, the Confederates swoop into town at dawn unopposed, except by a detachment of the 2nd Illinois Cavalry, which is quickly subdued. Van Dorn then orders the bulk of supplies burned, tracks torn up, and telegraph wires cut. This activity takes the raiders 10 hours to accomplish—a good indication of the mountain of stores captured. His mission complete, Van Dorn rides north to elude any Union pursuers. Holly Springs is one of the most devastating cavalry raids in U.S. military history and harbors dire consequences for General Ulysses S. Grant's upcoming Vicksburg campaign.

NAVAL: Commander David D. Porter and the USS *Black Hawk* join forces with the army under General William T. Sherman at Helena, Arkansas, in preparation for joint operations against Vicksburg, Mississippi.

December 21

WEST: General John H. Morgan departs Alexandria, Tennessee, with 3,100 Confederate cavalry, on his third Kentucky raid. His mission is to sever the Louisville and Nashville Railroad, thereby cutting General William S. Rosecrans's principal supply route back to Louisville.

Confederate cavalry under General Nathan B. Forrest capture Union City, Tennessee.

General Ulysses S. Grant, having lost his main supply base at Holly Springs, Mississippi, to rampaging Confederate cavalry under General Earl Van Dorn, evacuates Oxford and marches back to Memphis, Tennessee. This withdrawal terminates his first attempt to attack the Confederate citadel at Vicksburg. Defeated but undeterred, Grant intends to dispense with his dependency on railroads for supplies the next time, but because Confederate raiders have also cut available telegraph lines, Grant loses contact with General William T. Sherman, then poised to attack Vicksburg, Mississippi. He cannot inform him of his withdrawal.

December 22

NORTH: President Abraham Lincoln salutes the courage of the Army of the Potomac, downplays its recent defeat at Fredericksburg, and confers with General Ambrose E. Burnside.

SOUTH: General Robert C. Schenck replaces General John E. Wool as commander of the Middle Military Department, Virginia.

WEST: Confederate cavalry under General John H. Morgan ford the Cumberland River and gallop into Kentucky on another extended raid.

NAVAL: The USS *Huntsville* captures the Confederate schooner *Courier* off Tortugas, Florida.

December 23

POLITICS: President Jefferson Davis excoriates Union general Benjamin F. Butler for his treatment of civilians in New Orleans, Louisiana, and promises to hang him if captured.

SOUTH: General Simon B. Buckner becomes commander of the Confederate Department of the Gulf.

WEST: General Edmund Kirby-Smith resumes command of the Department of East Tennessee.

Texas Rangers stage a successful raid on Union pickets on St. Francis Road, Helena, Arkansas, capturing 18 soldiers.

December 24

SOUTH: The Union XVIII Corps is constituted as the Department of North Carolina under General John G. Foster.

NAVAL: The USS *Charlotte* captures the Confederate steamer *Bloomer* in Choctawhatchee River, Florida.

The army garrison at Columbus, Kentucky, is strengthened against possible Confederate attack by the arrival of the gunboat USS *New Era.*

December 25

NORTH: President and Mrs. Lincoln spend Christmas Day visiting Union wounded in various hospitals.

WEST: Confederate raiders under Colonel John H. Morgan fight Union troops at Bear Wallow, Kentucky, as the town of Glasgow is also captured.

December 26

NORTH: General John Sedgwick succeeds Darius N. Couch as commander of II Corps, Army of the Potomac.

SOUTH: General J. E. B. Stuart takes 1,800 Confederate cavalry on his latest raid behind Union lines by fording the Rappahannock River at Brandy Station, Virginia. This time, he is ordered to capture supply bases along Telegraph Road.

WEST: Union cavalry under General Samuel P. Carter depart Manchester, Kentucky, on an extended raid against Confederate railroad lines in the upper Tennessee Valley.

Confederate cavalry under Colonel John H. Morgan capture Nolin, Kentucky, to disrupt Union communications.

The 43,000-man Army of the Cumberland under General William S. Rosecrans begins to advance from Nashville, Tennessee, toward General Braxton Bragg's Confederates at Murfreesboro. However, his advance is dogged by cold, wet weather along with effective mounted resistance by Confederate cavalry under General Joseph Wheeler.

The XIII Corps under General William T. Sherman disembarks 32,000 men at Johnson's Plantation, at the mouth of the Yazoo River. This places his Union forces on the northern outskirts of Confederate defenses at Vicksburg, Mississippi, roughly six miles from the city itself. However, the defenders, numbering only 6,000 men, are being reinforced by troops from nearby Grenada to a strength of nearly 14,000. Furthermore, Sherman's approach is beset by intractable swampland that funnels any contemplated attack on Chickasaw Bluffs toward its center.

Federal authorities at Mankato, Minnesota, simultaneously hang 38 Santee (Sioux) warriors for their complicity in a bloody insurrection. This killing remains the largest mass execution in American history.

NAVAL: The Federal gunboat flotilla under Commodore David D. Porter, having escorted General William T. Sherman's expedition up the Yazoo River, begins to shell Confederate positions on nearby Haynes's Bluff to cover the landing.

December 27

SOUTH: General J. E. B. Stuart, intent on attacking a Union supply depot at Dumfries, Virginia, is thwarted after learning that the garrison is as large as his 1,800-man mounted column. Another force under Colonel Wade Hampton successfully scatters the 17th Pennsylvania Cavalry at Occoquan Creek, taking 19 captives.

WEST: Confederate cavalry under General John H. Morgan capture 600 Union prisoners in a surprise attack on Elizabethtown, Kentucky. He then begins to uproot tracks and trestles belonging to the Louisville and Nashville Railroad.

General Williams S. Rosecrans skirmishes with Confederate forces as he advances down Murfreesboro Pike, Tennessee.

Advancing Union forces under General William T. Sherman encounter increasing Confederate resistance north of Vicksburg, Mississippi, including the destruction of the Vicksburg and Shreveport Railroad. Worse, as they press southward, they traverse nearly impassable terrain, bayous, and swampland before reaching their objective at Chickasaw Bluffs. Once deployed, they advance under the cover of bombardment provided by gunboats under Commodore David D. Porter. Sherman gradually discovers only four practical approaches to the bluffs, all swept by well-sited Confederate batteries.

NAVAL: The USS *Roebuck* seizes the British schooner *Kate* at the mouth of the St. Mark's River, Florida.

The USS *Magnolia* captures the British schooner *Carmita* off the Marquesas Keys, Florida.

The USS *Cincinnati, Baron de Kalb, Louisville, Lexington, Marmora,* and the ram *Queen of the West* duel with a large Confederate battery on Drumgould's Bluff above the Yazoo River.

December 28

POLITICS: In an attempt to diffuse rising class tensions, the Confederate Congress strikes a clause in its Conscription Act that allows draftees to hire substitutes to take their place.

SOUTH: A column of Confederate cavalry under General J. E. B. Stuart successfully tangles with Federal cavalry near Selectman's Fort on Occoquan Creek, taking 100 prisoners. His subsequent pursuit captures an amply stocked Union camp. He then gallops on to Burke's Station, only 12 miles from Washington, D.C., and telegraphs a humorous message to Quartermaster General Montgomery C. Meigs about the poor quality of Union mules. The Confederates then spur their mounts across the Rappahannock River to safety.

WEST: Confederate raiders under Colonel John H. Morgan destroy the bridge at Muldraugh's Hill, Kentucky.

General Earl Van Dorn, commanding 3,500 Confederate cavalry, slips through Union lines, crosses the Tallahatchie River, and arrives safely back at Grenada, Mississippi. His spectacularly successful raid covers 500 miles in two weeks and completely cripples the developing Union attack against Vicksburg. Union cavalry under Colonel Benjamin Grierson ride hard to intercept the fleeing raiders, but to no avail.

Outside Chickasaw Bluffs, Mississippi, General Frederick Steele's 4th Division makes a preliminary probe of Confederate defenses near Blake's Levee, but he is halted by heavy artillery fire and defensive works erected in his path. Every indication of impenetrable defenses manifests before him, but General William T. Sherman is determined to attack in force. Thanks to telegraph wires that have been cut, he also remains uninformed about General Ulysses S. Grant's disaster at Holly Springs and that the Confederates have reinforced Chickasaw Bluffs to a strength of 14,000 men.

New Madrid, Missouri, is evacuated by Federal troops.

Union forces under General James G. Blunt successfully engage Confederate forces under General Thomas C. Hindman at Dripping Springs (Van Buren), Arkansas, taking 100 captives, 40 wagons, and numerous supplies. Five Confederate steamers are also sunk or burned to prevent capture. Hindman promptly falls back on Little Rock with his remaining 4,000 men.

NAVAL: The USS *Anacostia* captures the Confederate schooner *Exchange* in the Rappahannock River, Virginia.

The USS *Sagamore* captured the British blockade-runner *Elizabeth* off the coast of Florida.

December 29

WEST: General John H. Morgan and his Confederate cavalry seize Boston, Kentucky.

Union cavalry under General Samuel Carter secure numerous Confederate prisoners as he raids along the Blountsville Road, Tennessee.

Skirmishing continues at Lizzard, Tennessee, as General William S. Rosecrans continues advancing on Confederate-held Murfreesboro.

The 32,000 Union troops of XIII Corps under General William T. Sherman attack prepared Confederate positions along Chickasaw Bluffs, six miles north of Vicksburg, Mississippi. Opposing them are 14,000 defenders in carefully prepared defenses under General Stephen D. Lee. Sherman's plan requires a direct assault on the Confederate center in overwhelming force, assisted by supporting fire from Admiral David D. Porter's gunboats. Accordingly, the 3rd Division and 4th Division under Generals Frederick Steel and George W. Morgan skirt the swampland to their front and advance directly on Walnut Hills. Once at the base of the bluffs, they brave a maelstrom of Confederate artillery and rifle fire delivered from the heights and are driven back bloodily. Further attacks throughout the day achieve little beyond depleting Union ranks, and Sherman finally suspends the action at nightfall. Union losses in this lopsided affair amount to 208 killed, 1,005 wounded, and 563 missing (1,776). Confederates casualties are 63 dead, 134 wounded, and 10 missing (207). Defeat here ends the first Union campaign to capture Vicksburg; six months will elapse before efforts can resume.

NAVAL: The USS *Magnolia* captures the British blockade-runner *Flying Fish* off Tortugas, Florida.

Admiral David D. Porter's gunboat squadron renders close artillery support to the army of General William T. Sherman at Chickasaw Bluffs, Mississippi, and then covers their withdrawal.

December 30

WEST: Colonel John H. Morgan skirmishes with Union forces outside of New Haven, Kentucky.

Union troops under General Samuel P. Carter continue raiding Confederate positions in Tennessee, destroying several railroad bridges and capturing the towns of Union and Carter's Depot.

Confederate raiders under General Nathan B. Forrest encamp at Parker's Cross Roads (Red Mound), Tennessee, prior to refloating their sunken flatboats at Clifton and crossing the Tennessee River to safety. However, when his scout detects an approaching Union force, he decides to fight rather than run. As a precaution, he dispatches a scouting force under his brother William to watch the Confederate rear from the direction of Clarksville.

General William S. Rosecrans and 43,000 men of his Army of the Cumberland trudge into Murfreesboro, Tennessee, from Nashville, having taken three days to cover 30 miles in bad weather. He then establishes his line running roughly north to south behind Stone's River, across which sit 37,000 men of the Confederate Army of Tennessee under General Braxton Bragg. In a curious turn of events, both leaders are intending to attack the following day by hitting their opponent's right flank. However, Rosecrans inadvertently assists Bragg by ordering his left flank under General Alexander McCook to extend his line with false campfires to give an impression of greater strength. The ploy backfires when Bragg laboriously deploys and strengthens troops around McCook's real flank so that, when the attack kicks off at dawn, the Confederates enjoy better numbers than they otherwise might have possessed. But a curious play of chivalry also unfolds the evening before battle as military bands in the opposing camps serenade each with competing tunes—then strike up the sentimental "Home Sweet Home."

December 31

POLITICS: President Abraham Lincoln approves an act establishing West Virginia as the 35th state.

SOUTH: A cavalry column under General J. E. B. Stuart concludes its latest foray behind Union lines by riding into Culpeper Court House, Virginia. He has seized 200 captives and 20 wagons at a cost of a single trooper dead, 13 injured, and 13 missing.

WEST: General John H. Morgan's command skirmishes with Union forces at New Market, Kentucky.

At 6:00 A.M., the Confederate army of General Braxton Bragg launches an all-out assault against the Union Army of the Cumberland along Stone's River near Murfreesboro, Tennessee. This move, spearheaded by the corps of General William J. Hardee, catches Union forces off their guard and destroys the division of General Richard W. Johnson. Fleeing Federals withdraw nearly three miles before General Alexander McCook organizes new defensive lines on the right flank. Meanwhile, the corps of General Leonidas Polk assails the Union center, butting up against the well-handled brigades of Generals Philip H. Sheridan and Jefferson C. Davis. Once Confederate cavalry under General Joseph Wheeler spill over from the Union right and onto the Nashville Pike to their rear, however, Sheridan and Davis likewise retreat. General William S. Rosecrans, meanwhile, watching his army disintegrate around him, energetically visits threatened parts of his line, brings up new units, and consolidates his defenses. He has to maintain control of the Nashville Pike, which is his principal line of communication back to Nashville.

Fortunately for Rosecrans, Bragg remains far behind at headquarters, relying solely on reports to stay abreast of battlefield developments. For this reason, a fresh division of four brigades under General John C. Breckinridge remains uncommitted, when they might have proved decisive. Polk's assault then bogs down after he encounters, without reinforcements, a heavily wooded section called the Round Forest. This defensive point, known popularly as "Hell's Half Acre," witnesses some of the battle's most desperate fighting. But despite costly charges bravely delivered, Polk's graycoats fail to pry the defenders out. By this time, Rosecrans's entire line resembles the letter "V," with both flanks drawn sharply back from the center, capably defended by General George H. Thomas's division. Sheridan's troops, running low on ammunition, gradually fall back again just as Confederate attacks along the line peter out at 3:00 P.M. By the slimmest of margins, the Army of the Cumberland survives what comes perilously close to an embarrassing rout. Rosecrans also stubbornly refuses to retreat, despite the pleas of subordinates. Bragg, meanwhile, is convinced that he has won the contest and telegraphs word of his "victory" to the capital at Richmond. Moreover, he fully expects the Federals to abandon their positions before daylight.

General Nathan B. Forrest and 2,100 Confederate cavalry engage the 2nd Union brigade under Colonel Cyrus L. Dunham at Parker's Cross Roads, Tennessee. In preliminary fighting, Forrest manages to surround Dunham and hem him in on three sides. He then demands his surrender, as many Union soldiers are already flying white flags and coming forward in small groups. Dunham, however, refuses and Forrest prepares to decide the issue by a coup de main.

However, Confederate plans are suddenly overturned when Colonel John W. Fuller's 3rd Cavalry Brigade suddenly appears from the direction of Clarksville and attacks the Confederates from behind. Apparently, Forrest's brother William, tasked with patrolling the Confederate rear, took the wrong road and failed to detect their advance. Panic ensues as the Confederate troopers hastily abandon their captured wagons and cannon. Only quick thinking on Forrest's part saves his command: He speedily orders his remaining men to charge against both Dunham and Fuller. In the ensuing confusion, the Confederates ride through Union lines and find a narrow avenue of escape. Forrest's losses amount to 60 killed and wounded, along with 300 captured. Union casualties are given as 27 killed, 140 wounded, and a like number of prisoners. Parker's Cross Roads proves a rare setback for Forrest, and his sheer survival adds further luster to his mounting reputation. Furthermore, Confederate raiding further cripples the Union campaign against Vicksburg, Mississippi, for several months.

Confederate forces under General John S. Marmaduke advance from Lewisburg, Arkansas, into Missouri.

NAVAL: The famous ironclad USS *Monitor,* en route from Hampton Roads, Virginia, to Beaufort, North Carolina, sinks in a gale off Cape Hatteras while under tow. Sixteen crewmen perish, and 47 are rescued by the USS *Rhode Island.*

1863

January 1

POLITICS: "I do order and declare that all persons held as slaves within said designated states, and parts of states, are, and henceforward shall be free," President Abraham Lincoln declares. His Emancipation Proclamation becomes law, although it only affects African Americans in the Confederacy. Slaves in Union-held areas and the strategic border states of Maryland, Kentucky, and Missouri are exempt and remain in bondage for the time being. However, all blacks liberated by force remain eligible to be armed and trained for military service. As anticipated, Lincoln's ploy garners plaudits from France and Britain, further diminishing European sympathy for the South and, with it, the likelihood of intervention on its behalf.

NORTH: General Ambrose E. Burnside tenders his resignation to President Abraham Lincoln, who declines to accept. The general also expresses anxiety that none of his divisional commanders demonstrate faith in his capacity as either a strategist or a leader.

WEST: Combat at Murfreesboro, Tennessee, is suspended as both sides redress ranks and tend to their wounded. At daybreak, General Braxton Bragg is flummoxed to find that the Union Army of the Cumberland is standing its ground defiantly before him. In fact, General William S. Rosecrans, while abandoning the Round Forest salient that had anchored his line the day before, simply withdraws a short distance and establishes new lines farther back along Stone's River. Moreover, tonight he orders Colonel William Beatty's troops to cross the river to occupy the high ground immediately facing General John C. Breckinridge's division on the Confederate right. Both sides then begin to gird themselves for a resumption of combat on the following day.

Union forces skirmish with Confederate cavalry under General Nathan B. Forrest at Clifton, Tennessee.

General William T. Sherman commences to pull Federal troops out of the Yazoo region north of Vicksburg, Mississippi.

An attack by Texas Rangers against Union outposts in Helena, Arkansas, nets 30 prisoners.

SOUTHWEST: A surprise Confederate attack is mounted by General John B. Magruder on Galveston, Texas. In the predawn darkness, he quickly moves 1,500 men and several cannon onto Galveston Island and attacks a Union garrison consisting of 250 men of Colonel Isaac Burrell's 42nd Massachusetts. However, the Southerners are quickly detected and blasted back by accurate naval gunfire from the squadron offshore. By daylight, Magruder judges his attack a failure and withdraws while an intense naval battle unfolds in the harbor. The Confederates finally prevail, and the Union garrison surrenders. Once Galveston is secure, it remains in Southern hands for the rest of the war, serving as a major port.

NAVAL: The USS *Currituck* captures the Confederate sloop *Polter* off the Potomac River.

A sortie by Confederate "cottonclads" CSS *Bayou City* and *Neptune* under Major Leon Smith, C.S.A., pitches into a Union blockade force under Commander William B. Renshaw off Galveston, Texas. To facilitate the attack, the Confederate vessels carry 300 volunteer sharpshooters into battle. Renshaw's squadron, consisting of the USS *Harriet Lane, Owasco, Corypheus, Sachem, Clifton,* and *Westfield,* is caught flatfooted and scatters in the face of what they perceive to be heavily armed Confederate ironclads. Ships on both sides are rammed in the ensuing melee, and the *Westfield,* Renshaw's flagship, runs hard aground. The cutter *Harrier Lane* is also taken in a fierce hand-to-hand battle in which its captain dies, although the Southern steamer *Bayou City* sustains heavy damages and the *Neptune* sinks. Renshaw, seeing the battle lost, orders his squadron into open water, but rather than see the *Westfield* captured, he remains behind to set off charges to destroy it. He and 12 other sailors die when the explosives detonate prematurely. All told, the Confederate victory at Galveston is an impressive, hard-fought affair. Magruder's forces lose 26 killed and 117 wounded while Union losses are 21 dead, 36 injured, and 250 captured.

January 2

NORTH: General James S. Wadsworth assumes temporary command of the I Corps, Army of the Potomac.

WEST: In a manner reminiscent of General J. E. B. Stuart, 1,100 Confederate cavalry under General Joseph Wheeler ride twice around the Army of the Cumberland at Murfreesboro, Tennessee, destroying 1,000 wagons and taking hundreds of prisoners.

General Braxton Bragg, surveying the new line held by General William S. Rosecrans at Stone's River (Murfreesboro), elects to renew the struggle. However, he possesses relatively few intact formations with which to wage it. The largest is General John C. Breckinridge's Kentuckian division, and Bragg commits them against the Union left wing partially anchored on Stone's River. Breckinridge, perceiving the strength of the enemy position, protests the command but orders his men to a frontal assault at 3:00 P.M. The initial Southern charge sweeps two Union brigades from the ridge, forcing them to re-form at the water's edge. The 4,500 Kentuckians then fall on the survivors with a yell, forcing them back across Stone's

River. But Rosecrans, observing his left in danger of crumbling, directs Captain John Mendenhall, chief of artillery, to mass 57 cannon on the river's west bank. This position is significantly higher than the east bank and clearly sweeps the open ground before them.

At about 4:45 P.M. Breckinridge moves forward and charges directly into the teeth of concentrated artillery fire from across the river. His men are repulsed bloodily with 1,700 casualties and withdraw under cover. Suddenly, the Kentuckians are decisively assailed in the flank by fresh Union troops under General James S. Negley and driven back. Breckinridge's defeat signals the end of the battle, and many senior Confederates, including General Leonidas K. Polk, implore Bragg to retreat. He does so only reluctantly and that night puts his army in motion for Shelbyville and Tullahoma, 30 miles distant. Rosecrans, meanwhile, tends to his own shattered army and does not attempt a pursuit.

In proportion to actual numbers engaged, the clash outside Murfreesboro is among the war's bloodiest. There are few laurels to either side. Rosecrans held the field and claims a narrow tactical victory but at the cost of 1,730 dead, 7,802 wounded, and 3,717 missing (13,249) among 41,400 present. Confederate losses are slightly lower with 1,294 killed, 7,945 injured, and 1,027 missing (10,266) out of 34,739. But the already outnumbered Army of Tennessee can scarcely afford such attrition, and Bragg's leadership suffers from a rising tide of criticism. The door to Middle Tennessee is being forced open, but six months lapses before the Army of the Cumberland is rebuilt and resumes offensive operations.

Confederate cavalry under General Nathan B. Forrest recross the Tennessee River at Clifton, Tennessee.

General John H. Morgan's Confederate raiders ford the Cumberland River back into Tennessee. His latest effort culminates in 1,800 prisoners and $2 million in wrecked equipment and railroad tracks. Morgan sustains only 2 killed, 24 wounded, and 64 missing, and he is thanked by the Confederate Congress for his actions.

General John A. McClernand accepts command of the 32,000-strong Army of the Mississippi at Milliken's Bend, Louisiana. His independent command includes General George W. Morgan's I Corps and General William T. Sherman's II Corps.

New Madrid, Missouri, is reoccupied by Federal troops.

Union forces skirmish with Confederates under General John S. Marmaduke at White Spring, Arkansas.

January 3

WEST: General Braxton Bragg's rear guard tangles with Union forces at Burnsville, Tennessee, as the Confederates continue falling back toward Shelbyville and Tullahoma. Two Union brigades push forward in pursuit, although General William S. Rosecrans does not press vigorously.

NAVAL: The USS *Currituck* captures the Confederate sloop *Potter* between the Potomac and Rappahannock rivers.

January 4

NORTH: General John F. Reynolds is reinstated as commander of I Corps, Army of the Potomac.

General in Chief Henry W. Halleck orders General Ulysses S. Grant to rescind his controversial General Order No. 11, which expels all Jews from his department.

WEST: Ignoring prior authorization, General John A. McClernand moves 32,000 Federal troops of his Army of the Mississippi from Milliken's Bend, Louisiana, on an expedition into Arkansas. He embarks the corps of Generals George W. Morgan and William T. Sherman onto transports and sails up the Arkansas River, intending to capture the large Confederate outpost at Arkansas Post 50 miles upstream. This impressive, well-armed fortification, constructed on a high bluff overlooking the waterway, poses a menace to Union river traffic in that region.

NAVAL: The USS *Quaker City* seizes the Confederate sloop *Mercury* near Charleston, South Carolina. Confederate diplomatic dispatches are seized, containing reports on ironclads under construction in Britain for the Confederate navy.

Admiral David D. Porter's squadron, consisting of the gunboats USS *Baron de Kalb, Louisville, Cincinnati, Signal, Marmora, Lexington, New Era, Rattler, Glide,* and *Black Hawk,* escorts army troops up the White River, Arkansas, to seize Fort Hindman in conjunction with General John A. McClernand.

January 5

NORTH: General Ambrose E. Burnside, still tussling with subordinates over his proposed thrust across the Rappahannock, again tenders his resignation to President Abraham Lincoln "to relieve you from all embarrassment in my case." It is again declined.

WEST: Federal forces under General William S. Rosecrans occupy the city of Murfreesboro, Tennessee, as the Army of Tennessee under General Braxton Bragg continues withdrawing southward.

General William T. Sherman accepts command of II Corps, Army of the Mississippi, while en route on the expedition against Fort Hindman, Arkansas.

NAVAL: Armed boats from USS *Sagamore* capture the British blockade-runner *Avenger* in Jupiter Inlet, Florida.

January 6

WEST: Confederate forces under General John S. Marmaduke attack Beaver Station, Missouri, and burn Fort Lawrence.

NAVAL: The USS *Mahaska* and *Commodore Morris* escort a joint expedition up the Pamunkey River, Virginia, as far as White House and West Point, destroying small craft and stores en route.

The USS *Pocahontas* captures the Confederate blockade-runner *Antona* off Cape San Blas, Florida.

January 7

POLITICS: The Democratic-controlled Illinois state legislature roundly condemns President Abraham Lincoln's Emancipation Proclamation and excoriates the chief executive for turning the war into a crusade for liberating African-American slaves.

NORTH: General Henry W. Halleck accepts General Ambrose E. Burnside's proposed attack plan across the Rappahannock River, even though it is to be executed in the deep of winter.

WEST: Ozark, Missouri, is occupied by Confederate forces under Generals Sterling Price and John S. Marmaduke.

NAVAL: General Erasmus D. Keyes and Commander Foxhall A. Parker lead a joint army-navy expedition from Yorktown, Virginia, up the Pamunkey River to West Point and White House.

January 8

POLITICS: John P. Usher is appointed secretary of the interior.

WEST: General Joseph Wheeler leads Confederate cavalry on an extended raid into Tennessee, hitting the settlements of Mill Creek, Harpeth Shoals, and Ashland.

Confederates under General John S. Marmaduke launch an unsuccessful attack on Springfield, Missouri.

A Union ambush at Berryville, Arkansas, kills 10 Confederate bushwhackers.

NAVAL: The USS *Sagamore* captures the British blockade-runner *Julia* off Jupiter Inlet, Florida.

The USS *Tahoma* seizes the Confederate vessel *Silas Henry* after running it aground at Tampa Bay, Florida.

January 9

SOUTH: Confederate troops under General Roger A. Pryor are defeated by General Michael Corcoran outside Suffolk, Virginia.

WEST: General William S. Rosecrans reorganizes his Army of the Cumberland into the XIV Corps under General George H. Thomas, the XX Corps under General Alexander M. McCook, and the XXI Corps under General Thomas L. Crittenden.

General John S. Marmaduke captures the Union garrison at Hartville, Missouri.

NAVAL: Armed boats from USS *Ethan Allen* land and destroy a Confederate salt-works near St. Joseph, Florida.

The transport *Sparking Sea* strikes a reef near Key West, Florida, and sinks; its crew is rescued by the gunboat USS *Sagamore*.

January 10

NORTH: In a celebrated court-martial, General Fitz John Porter is cashiered and dropped from the army rolls for disobeying orders at the Battle of Second Manassas. Not only does this deprive the Union army of a highly capable leader, but also the verdict remains in contention for many years until it is finally overturned in 1879.

General Franz Sigel is appointed commander of the Grand Reserve Division, Army of the Potomac.

General Thomas W. Sherman is appointed commander of the New Orleans, Louisiana, garrison.

A combined expedition of 32,000 men under General John A. McClernand and Admiral David D. Porter continues sailing 50 miles up the Arkansas River to break up a Confederate concentration at Fort Arkansas (Arkansas Post). This formidable position is garrisoned by 5,000 men under General Thomas J. Churchill. Once landed, Union troops under Generals George W. Morgan and William T. Sherman are to envelop and isolate the post while heavy naval guns silence its batteries.

NAVAL: The USS *Octorara* seizes the British blockade-runner *Rising Dawn* in the North West Providence Channel, Bahamas.

Admiral David G. Farragut orders Commander Henry H. Bell to reconstitute the blockade of Galveston, Texas, as soon as practicable. Bell's USS *Brooklyn* consequently bombards Confederate defenses of that town.

The gunboat squadron of Admiral David D. Porter, consisting of USS *Baron de Kalb, Louisville, Cincinnati, Lexington, Rattler,* and *Black Hawk,* engages in a heavy exchange of fire with the 11-gun battery at Fort Hindman on the Arkansas River. After covering the landing of troops, the vessels shell Confederate positions but fail to run past the fort.

January 11

WEST: General James B. McPherson takes control of the XVII Corps in Tennessee.

A force of 32,000 Union troops under John A. McClernand and Admiral David D. Porter attacks Hindman (Arkansas Post) under General Thomas J. Churchill. The assault occurs in conjunction with a nearby squadron of Federal gunboats on the White River, whose accurate fire silences the Confederate batteries. However, the ground assault, when it develops at 3:00 P.M., is repelled roundly with losses. Churchill nonetheless realizes the hopelessness of his position and surrenders later that day. McClernand captures 4,791 Southerners, who also lose 28 dead and 81 wounded, along with 17 cannon, thousands of weapons, and tons of ammunition. Union losses are recorded as 134 dead, 898 wounded, and 29 missing. This victory not only restores Union control of the Arkansas River but also bolsters Northern morale.

Confederates under General John S. Marmaduke lose 150 men while skirmishing with Union forces under Colonel Lewis Merrill at Wood's Fork, Missouri. Federal casualties tally 35.

NAVAL: The USS *Matthew Vassar* captures the Confederate schooner *Florida* off Little River Inlet, Florida.

The paddle steamer USS *Hatteras,* cruising 30 miles off Galveston, Texas, is approached at night by a mysterious vessel. This turns out to be the Confederate raider CSS *Alabama* under Captain Raphael Semmes, which sinks the *Hatteras* in a fierce engagement of only 13 minutes. Semmes rescues the entire crew, after which Union ships redouble their efforts to track and corner this elusive foe.

Confederate guerrillas capture the Federal gunboat USS *Grampus No. 2* on the Mississippi River north of Memphis, Tennessee.

Federal gunboats under Admiral David D. Porter effectively shell the Confederate works of Fort Hindman, Arkansas (Arkansas Post), on the Arkansas River. Naval fire proves entirely effective in reducing both guns and fortifications, and Porter notes: "No fort ever received a worse battering, and the highest compliment I can pay to those engaged is to repeat what the rebels said: 'You can't expect men to stand up against the fire of those gunboats.'" His gunboats also managed to corner and sink the ram CSS *Pontchartrain* near Little Rock.

January 12

POLITICS: The third session of the 1st Confederate Congress convenes at Richmond, Virginia, where President Jefferson Davis addresses the legislators, stating that he still hopes eventual European recognition. Davis also vehemently castigates the Union's recent Emancipation Proclamation.

NORTH: The venerable general John E. Wool is appointed commander of the Department of the East.

WEST: Confederate cavalry under General Joseph Wheeler destroys the huge Union supply depot at Ashland, Tennessee, effectively immobilizing the Army of the Cumberland for nearly six months.

NAVAL: The USS *Currituck* destroys a Confederate saltworks at Dividing Creek, Virginia.

January 13

SOUTH: In South Carolina, Union colonel Thomas W. Higginson begins to recruit former African-American slaves for his 1st South Carolina Volunteer Infantry.

WEST: Federal troops under General John A. McClernand capture St. Charles and other settlements along the White River, Arkansas.

NAVAL: The USS *Currituck* captures the Confederate schooner *Hampton* in Dividing Creek, Virginia.

The steamer USS *Hastings* is captured on the Cumberland River by cavalry under General Joseph Wheeler. Wheeler also seizes three steamboats full of wounded troops; these he places on one vessel and allows them to move on. The remaining boats are burned.

A combined army-navy expedition is mounted along the Mississippi River from USS *General Bragg* against Confederate guerrillas known to be operating from Mound City, Arkansas. Several buildings consequently are burned.

January 14

SOUTH: Federal forces under General Godfrey Weitzel wage a successful battle against Confederates at Bayou Teche, Louisiana.

SOUTHWEST: General Edmund Kirby-Smith is appointed commander of the Confederate Army of the Southwest.

NAVAL: The USS *Columbia* grounds on the coast of North Carolina and two days later is burned by its crew to prevent capture.

Federal gunboats USS *Kinsman, Estrella, Calhoun,* and *Diana* attack and sink the Confederate gunboat CSS *Cotton* at Bayou Teche, Louisiana.

A joint expedition under Commander John G. Walker and General Willis A. Gorham steams up the White River, Arkansas, to St. Charles. There, troops from two transports seize the town while the USS *Baron de Kalb* continues upstream in search of CSS *Blue Wing.*

January 15

POLITICS: President Abraham Lincoln takes a break from his usual routine and visits the Washington Navy Yard to confer with Admiral John A. B. Dahlgren and to observe new weapons testing.

WEST: Union troops burn the town of Mound City, Arkansas, in retaliation for supporting guerrilla activities.

NAVAL: The USS *Octorara* captures the British sloop *Brave* in the North West Providence Channel, Bahamas.

January 16
SOUTH: General John Sedgwick assumes command of the IX Corps, Army of the Potomac, in Virginia.

NAVAL: Confederate raider CSS *Florida* under Lieutenant John N. Maffitt skillfully evades Union blockaders under the cover of darkness and slips out of Mobile Bay, Alabama. This celebrated raider eventually seizes 15 Union vessels.

The USS *Baron de Kalb* captures Devall's Bluff, Arkansas, while pursuing CSS *Blue Wing* up the White River.

January 17
POLITICS: President Abraham Lincoln signs legislation allowing for the immediate payment of military personnel. He also asks Congress for currency reforms to halt mounting inflation throughout the North.

SOUTH: Jubal A. Early gains appointment as a major general, C.S.A.

Frederick A. Hoke is promoted to brigadier general, C.S.A.

WEST: General Ulysses S. Grant, resenting General John A. McClernand's disregard for proper channels in mounting his recent expedition against Fort Hindman, Arkansas, summarily orders him to rejoin his main force at Milliken's Bend, Louisiana.

NAVAL: The USS *Baron de Kalb, Forest Rose,* and *Romeo* ply the White River and arrive off Des Arc, Arkansas, where Confederate supplies are seized.

January 18
SOUTH: Acting on the orders of General Henry Heth, the 64th North Carolina under Colonel James A. Keith sweeps through Shelton Laurel, western North Carolina, in search of Northern sympathizers operating there. At length, he nets 15 male captives, most of whom are not associated with bushwhacking operations, and marches them off to a mountain gorge. Ignoring pleas for mercy, they are lined up, shot, and buried in shallow graves. Word of the massacre outrages Confederate secretary of War James A. Seddon and North Carolina Governor Zebulon B. Vance, who demand an immediate inquiry. Confederate army officials drag their feet over the ensuing months, and none of the perpetrators are ever punished.

NAVAL: The USS *Zouave* captures the Confederate sloop *J. C. McCabe* on the James River, Virginia.

The USS *Wachusett,* under Captain Charles Wilkes, and the *Sonoma* capture the Confederate steamer *Virginia* off Mugeres Island, Mexico.

Admiral David D. Porter, concluding operations on the White River, Arkansas, renews his efforts against the Confederate citadel at Vicksburg, Mississippi, by ordering all available gunboats to Milliken's Bend on the Yazoo River.

January 19
SOUTH: In an attempt to redeem his reputation, General Ambrose E. Burnside orders two grand divisions under General Joseph Hooker and General William B. Franklin across the Rappahannock River at Bank's Ford, Virginia. This move places the Army of the Potomac within 10 miles of Fredericksburg and behind Robert E. Lee's Army of Northern Virginia. The winter weather has been excellent of late, but this quickly and dramatically changes.

General Carl Schurz assumes command of the XI Corps, Army of the Potomac.

NAVAL: The Confederate raider CSS *Florida* under Lieutenant John N. Maffitt captures the Union brig *Estelle* at sea.

January 20

SOUTH: Joseph Wheeler is promoted to major general, C.S.A.

The Army of the Potomac under General Ambrose E. Burnside begins its infamous "mud March." The general intends to bolster his flagging reputation by a surprise march around the Army of Northern Virginia's left flank and a rapid crossing of the Rappahannock to force it into battle in the open. But no sooner does his turning maneuver commence than inclement weather sets in, and troops, supplies, and the all-important pontoon bridges bog down on roads, churned to knee-deep mud.

General David Hunter resumes his post as commander of the Department of the South.

WEST: Confederates under General John S. Marmaduke seize Patterson, Missouri.

NAVAL: The Confederate raider CSS *Florida* under Lieutenant John N. Maffitt enters Havana, Cuba.

January 21

POLITICS: President Abraham Lincoln endorses revocation of the infamous "Jew Order" of General Ulysses S. Grant because it "proscribed an entire religious class, some of whom are fighting in our ranks."

President Jefferson Davis dispatches General Joseph E. Johnston to Manchester, Tennessee, to confer with General Braxton Bragg over his unexplained abandonment of Murfreesboro. He does so amid a demonstrated lack of confidence in Bragg's ability to lead from senior subordinates.

NORTH: President Abraham Lincoln approves the court-martial verdict against General Fitz John Porter, and he is formally cashiered and dismissed from the military.

SOUTH: The march of the Army of the Potomac under General Ambrose E. Burnside is stymied by heavy rain and inclement weather conditions during its attempted flank march to the Rappahannock River, Virginia. His columns are bedeviled by roads choked with mud that exhaust soldiers and beasts alike. The Confederates have since become aware of Burnside's move and harass the struggling Federals with jocular offers of assistance.

NAVAL: The USS *Daylight* destroys an unnamed blockade-runner off New Topsail Inlet, North Carolina.

The USS *Ottawa* captures the Confederate schooner *Etiwan* off Charleston, South Carolina.

The USS *Chocura* seizes the British blockade-runner *Pride* off Cape Romain, South Carolina.

A sudden sortie by Confederate cottonclads CSS *Josiah Bell* and *Uncle Ben* under Major Oscar M. Watkins, C.S.A., captures the steamers USS *Morning Light* and *Velocity* off Sabine Pass, Texas. This temporarily interrupts the Union blockade.

January 22
South: General Ambrose E. Burnside's offensive across the Rappahannock River into Virginia stumbles and ends because of heavy rain and mud-choked roads. The suffering troops, stiffened by rations of liquor, begin to brawl among themselves as morale continues to sink. After heated consultations with subordinates, Burnside concludes that his master stroke has failed and orders the men back into camp at Falmouth, Virginia. They thus endure another round of exhaustive marching in mud so thick that entire wagon trains sink to their axles.
West: General Ulysses S. Grant takes charge of Union forces in Arkansas while General John A. McClernand is punitively reduced to commander of the XIII Corps, Army of the Tennessee. Grant then begins construction of an ambitious canal at Swampy Toe Peninsula, opposite Vicksburg, Mississippi, to allow Union shipping to circumvent its defenses on the Mississippi River.

General Joseph Wheeler assumes command of all Confederate cavalry in Middle Tennessee.
Naval: The USS *Commodore Morris* captures the Confederate vessels *John C. Calhoun, Harriet,* and *Music* in Chuckatuck Creek, Virginia.

The Confederate raider CSS *Florida* under Lieutenant John N. Maffitt seizes and burns the Union brigs *Windward* and *Corris Ann* off Cuba.

January 23
North: A demoralized—and rather soggy—Army of the Potomac settles into winter quarters at Falmouth, Virginia, directly across from Fredericksburg. General Ambrose E. Burnside, agitated by the performance of several subordinates, issues General Order No. 8, which peremptorily strips Generals Joseph Hooker, Edwin V. Sumner, and William B. Franklin of their commands. The general then rides to Washington, D.C., to confer with President Abraham Lincoln and to defend his decision.
Naval: The USS *Cambridge* captures the Confederate schooner *Time* off Cape Fear, North Carolina.

January 24
Naval: Admiral David D. Porter arrives back at the Yazoo River and prepares to ascend that body as a way of outflanking the defenses of Vicksburg, Mississippi, from the north.

January 25
Politics: Massachusetts governor John A. Andrew authorizes recruitment of the 54th Massachusetts Infantry, which is composed entirely of African Americans and led by white officers.
North: General Ambrose E. Burnside is removed as commander of the Army of the Potomac and replaced by General Joseph "Fighting Joe" Hooker, a boisterous individual and one of Burnside's loudest critics. Generals William B. Franklin and Edwin V. Sumner, however, remain relieved of duties pending a court of inquiry.
South: The Virginia Partisan Rangers under Lieutenant John S. Mosby skirmish with Federal troops at Fairfax Court House, Virginia.

WEST: Confederates under General John S. Marmaduke end their raid into Missouri by arriving back at Batesville, Arkansas.

NAVAL: The USS *Currituck* captures the Confederate sloop *Queen of the Fleet* in Tapp's Creek, Virginia.

January 26

POLITICS: President Abraham Lincoln orders a major shakeup in the Army of the Potomac leadership with General Darius N. Couch assuming command of the Right Grand Division, General George G. Meade taking charge of the Central Grand Division, and General Oliver O. Howard leading the Left Grand Division. General Charles Griffin is also appointed to take temporary command of the V Corps. The president also congratulates General Joseph Hooker as commander of the Army of the Potomac, despite rumors that he feels a military dictatorship is necessary to win the war. "Only those generals who gain successes can set up dictators," Lincoln notes. "What I ask of you is military success, and I will risk the dictatorship."

NAVAL: The Confederate raider CSS *Alabama* under Captain Raphael Semmes seizes and burns the Union ship *Golden Rule* off Haiti.

January 27

POLITICS: Philadelphia newspaperman A. D. Boileau is arrested for allegedly publishing an anti-Union editorial in his *Journal*.

WEST: In response to Shoshone attacks on settlers and miners in the Great Basin region, Colonel Patrick E. Connor of the 1st California Cavalry leads 300 soldiers on an expedition against the encampment of Chief Bear Hunter on the Bear River, Idaho Territory. The site is well chosen by the Native Americans, who have mustered 300 warriors—it is located along the sides of a deep ravine. For this reason, Connor orchestrates a two-pronged assault that flanks the camp and allows soldiers to fire down from the heights. After a raging conflict of several hours, Bear Hunter and 224 warriors are cut down, and the soldiers take an additional 164 women and children prisoners. Federal losses are 21 dead and 46 wounded. The humbled Shoshone sign a treaty forfeiting their claims to the Great Basin region; Connor gains promotion to brigadier general.

NAVAL: The USS *Hope* seizes the British blockade-runner *Emma Tuttle* off Charleston, South Carolina.

The ironclad USS *Montauk* under Captain John L. Worden spearheads a Federal assault on Fort McAllister on the Ogeechee River, Georgia. This is a test run for the new vessels in preparation for an assault on the more formidable defenses of Charleston, South Carolina. Accompanied by USS *Seneca, Wissahickon, Dawn,* and mortar boat *C. P. Williams,* Worden engages Confederate batteries for four hours. Fighting proves inconclusive, and the squadron is withdrawn. The *Montauk* receives 14 hits, none of them serious. But Admiral Samuel F. Du Pont, who orders the attack, is disappointed by the results, especially the slow firing rate and inaccurate aim of his vessels. "If one ironclad cannot take eight guns," he ponders, "how are five to take 147 guns in Charleston Harbor."

The Confederate raider CSS *Alabama* under Captain Raphael Semmes captures and burns the Union brig *Chastelaine* in the Caribbean.

January 28
POLITICS: President Jefferson Davis warns General Theophilus Holmes of the dangers confronting his Trans-Mississippi Department. "The loss of either of the two positions—Vicksburg or Port Hudson—would destroy communication with the Trans-Mississippi Department," he writes, "and inflict upon the Confederacy an injury which I am sure you have not failed to appreciate."
SOUTH: John D. Imboden is appointed brigadier general, C.S.A.
NAVAL: The USS *Sagamore* sinks the British blockade-runner *Elizabeth* off Jupiter Inlet, Florida.

January 29
POLITICS: The Confederate Congress authorizes a loan of $15 million from French financiers.

A pensive president Jefferson Davis inquires of General John C. Pemberton at Vicksburg, Mississippi, "Has anything or can anything be done to obstruct the navigation from Yazoo Pass down?"
WEST: Colonel James H. Wilson, an engineer, is ordered to depart Helena, Arkansas, with specialists and equipment for an expedition down Yazoo Pass. This turns out to be a major drive to flank the Confederate defenses of Vicksburg from behind, although the region is known to be a tangled, swampy morass.
NAVAL: The USS *Unadilla* seizes the British blockade-runner *Princess Royal* near Charleston, South Carolina.

The USS *Brooklyn*, assisted by Federal gunboats *Scotia, Owasco,* and *Katahdin*, bombards Confederate positions at Galveston, Texas. Its captain notes with some trepidation that enemy shot sails easily over his squadron, at a range of two and a half miles.

The Federal gunboat USS *Lexington* is attacked by Confederate artillery while steaming down the Cumberland River between Cairo, Illinois, and Nashville, Tennessee, but accurate counterfire quickly disperses the antagonists.

January 30
WEST: General Ulysses S. Grant, officially placed in charge of western operations at Milliken's Bend, Louisiana, begins to formulate a new strategic campaign against Vicksburg, Mississippi.
NAVAL: A joint expedition sailing with the USS *Commodore Perry* lands armed parties near Hertford, North Carolina. Two bridges are destroyed and several small vessels sunk.

The Federal gunboat USS *Isaac Smith* is caught in a heavy crossfire while steaming up the Stono River, South Carolina, runs aground, and is captured.

Admiral David D. Porter instructs the USS *Linden* to cooperate with army forces under General Ulysses S. Grant while his men dig a canal to circumvent Confederate defenses at Vicksburg, Mississippi. He also orders the squadron to sweep the Yazoo River for supplies of cotton to deprive the Confederacy of this valuable commodity. Captured bales are also to be employed as additional armor for his ships.

January 31

WEST: Union and Confederate forces skirmish heavily in the wake of General Braxton Bragg's withdrawal from Murfreesboro, Tennessee. A heavy engagement at Dover results in 300 Southern captives for a Federal loss of five.

NAVAL: Obscured by a thick haze, Confederate steam rams CSS *Palmetto State* and *Chicora* under Commanders Duncan N. Ingraham and John R. Tucker sortie against the South Atlantic Blockading Squadron of Admiral Samuel F. Du Pont off Charleston, South Carolina. The converted merchantman *Mercedita,* rammed and riddled by cannon fire, surrenders; the USS *Keystone State* sustains heavy damage and is rescued by the *Memphis.* Union losses are 24 killed and 24 wounded, most by scalding. The Confederate vessels then withdraw back to Charleston, having dented the Union blockade but accomplishing little else.

The Confederate raider CSS *Retribution* seizes the Union schooner *Hanover* in the West Indies.

February 1

POLITICS: By this period in the war, inflation erodes the Confederate dollar such that it yields the purchasing power of only 20 cents.

SOUTH: General George Sykes temporarily takes command of the V Corps, Army of the Potomac.

WEST: Advancing Union forces capture the town of Franklin, Tennessee.

NAVAL: The ironclad USS *Montauk* under Captain John L. Worden, assisted by *Seneca, Wissahickon, Dawn,* and the mortar boat *C. P. Williams,* again attack Fort McAllister on the Ogeechee River, Georgia. This time, the vessels initiate action at much closer range and manage to inflict heavy damage. *Montauk* sustains 48 hits in the four-hour exchange, none of them serious.

The USS *Passaic* under Captain Percival Drayton, accompanied by the *Marblehead,* conducts a detailed reconnaissance up the Wilmington River, Georgia.

The USS *Tahoma* and *Hendrick Hudson* capture the British blockade-runner *Margaret* off St. Petersburg, Florida.

The USS *Two Sisters* seizes the Confederate sloop *Richards* off Boca Grande, Mexico.

February 2

NORTH: The Department of Washington, D.C., is constituted while its attendant garrison is designated XXII Corps.

WEST: Colonel James H. Wilson cuts into the Mississippi River levee, spilling water into the Yazoo Pass region and raising its level to support gunboats.

NAVAL: The USS *Mount Vernon* drives the Confederate schooner *Industry* aground at New Topsail Inlet, North Carolina. The vessel is subsequently burned.

The Federal ram USS *Queen of the West* under Colonel Charles R. Ellet runs past the batteries of Vicksburg, Mississippi, and is struck 12 times without sus-

Line engraving depicting the February 2, 1863, attack by U.S. ram *Queen of the West* on the Confederate steamer *City of Vicksburg* off Vicksburg, Mississippi, published in *Harper's Weekly*, 1863 *(Naval Historical Foundation)*

taining serious damage. It then attacks the Confederate vessel *City of Vicksburg* before proceeding farther up the Red River to destroy supply caches deposited there.

February 3
DIPLOMACY: Secretary of State William H. Seward receives an offer made through the French embassy to mediate the war.

POLITICS: The U.S. Congress votes Captain John L. Worden its thanks for service rendered as captain of the USS *Monitor*.

WEST: Confederate cavalry under General Nathan B. Forrest unsuccessfully attacks Union forces under Colonel Abner C. Harding, garrisoning Fort Donelson, Tennessee. Harding reports a loss of 12 dead and 30 injured; the Southerners lose over 100 killed, 400 wounded, and 300 prisoners.

General Joseph Wheeler's Confederate raiding column is repulsed at the Cumberland Iron works, Tennessee.

The levee at Yazoo Pass, Mississippi, is opened to allow access to Vicksburg from behind. A combined expedition consisting of 5,000 troops under General Leonard F. Ross then departs upstream.

Naval: The USS *Midnight* seizes the British blockade-runner *Defy* off the Georgia coast.

The USS *Sonoma* captures the British blockade-runner *Springbo* off the Bahamas.

The Confederate raider CSS *Alabama* under Captain Raphael Semmes seizes and burns the Union schooner *Palmetto* off Puerto Rico.

The USS *Lexington, Fairplay, St. Clair, Brilliant, Robb,* and *Silver Lake* provide supporting fire to army troops at Fort Donelson, Tennessee, repelling a Confederate attack by General Nathan B. Forrest.

A combined expedition under General Leonard F. Ross proceeds down the Yazoo River, accompanied by the gunboats USS *Baron de Kalb* and *Chillicothe.*

February 4
South: General John Sedgwick succeeds William F. Smith as commander of VI Corps, Army of the Potomac.

West: Confederate troops under General John S. Marmaduke are driven from Batesville, Arkansas, by pursuing Union forces.

Naval: The USS *New Era* captures the Confederate steamer *W. A. Knapp* near Island No. 10 in the Mississippi River.

February 5
Politics: Queen Victoria outlines to Parliament her government's reasons for refusing to pursue mediation efforts between the North and the South, namely, because there are few reasonable expectations for success.

North: General Joseph Hooker reorganizes the Army of the Potomac and dispenses with his predecessor's "grand divisions" scheme. A new nine corps structure is implemented under Generals John F. Reynolds (I), Darius N. Couch (II), Daniel E. Sickles (III), George G. Meade (V), John Sedgwick (VI), William F. Smith (IX), Franz Sigel (XI), Henry W. Slocum (XII), and George Stoneman (U.S. Cavalry Corps).

February 6
Diplomacy: Secretary of State William H. Seward unilaterally rejects a French offer to mediate hostilities.

South: The Union IX Corps under General William F. Smith relocates to Newport News, Virginia, to increase pressure on Richmond from the east.

February 7
North: Command of the Department of Washington, D.C., is delegated to General Samuel P. Heintzelman.

Naval: The new Confederate ironclads CSS *Tuscaloosa* and *Huntsville* are launched at Selma, Alabama, and then taken to Mobile to be outfitted.

The gunboat USS *Glide* is destroyed by fire at Cairo, Illinois.

The USS *Forest Rose* is damaged by low hanging trees while traversing Yazoo Pass, Mississippi.

February 8
Politics: Allegedly disloyal statements lead the *Chicago Times* to be suspended temporarily from publication.

NAVAL: At the behest of General John G. Foster, the Federal gunboat *Commodore McDonough* traverses the Stono River, South Carolina, looking for newly erected Confederate batteries. None are noted.

February 9
SOUTHWEST: The Confederate Army of the Southwest under General Edmund Kirby-Smith extends its authority to the entire Trans-Mississippi Department.
NAVAL: The USS *Coeur de Lion* captures the Confederate schooner *Emily Murray* near Machadoc Creek, Virginia.

February 10
NAVAL: The Federal ram USS *Queen of the West* steams farther down the Red River, Louisiana.

The Federal ram USS *Dick Fulton* sustains damage from Confederate forces at Cyrus Bend, Arkansas.

February 11
DIPLOMACY: In London, Confederate agent James M. Mason addresses the lord mayor's banquet and promotes the desirability of recognition for the Confederacy.

February 12
NAVAL: The Confederate raider CSS *Florida* under Lieutenant John N. Maffitt seizes and burns the Union clipper ship *Jacob Bell,* along with cargo estimated at $2 million.

The USS *Conestoga* captures the Confederate steamers *Rose Hambleton* and *Evansville* on the White River, Arkansas.

The USS *Queen of the West* steams up the Red and Atchafalaya rivers, Louisiana, destroying a Confederate wagon train.

February 13
NAVAL: The USS *New Era* captures the Confederate steamers *White Cloud* and *Rowena* near Island No. 10 on the Mississippi River.

The ironclad USS *Indianola* runs past Confederate batteries at Vicksburg, Mississippi, intending to join the *Queen of the West* at the mouth of the Red River as a blockading force.

A combined, light-draft expedition into Yazoo Pass, consisting of USS *Rattler, Romeo, Forest, Rose, Chillicothe, Baron de Kalb,* and *Matamora,* arrives off Helena, Arkansas.

February 14
NAVAL: The USS *Tioga* captures the British blockade-runner *Avon* off the Bahamas.

The USS *Forest Rose* captures the Confederate steamer *Chippewa Valley* at Island No. 63 on the Mississippi River.

The U.S. ram *Queen of the West* under Colonel Charles R. Ellet moves 15 miles up the Black River and captures the steamer CSS *New Era No. 5.* While returning back downstream, his vessel is bracketed by Confederate artillery, run aground, and captured intact. The Union crew, however, escapes by transferring to its prize and sailing off.

February 15
WEST: Confederate raiders under General John H. Morgan are repulsed by Union troops near Cainsville, Tennessee.
NAVAL: The USS *Sonoma* captures the Confederate brig *Atlantic* at sea.

February 16
POLITICS: The U.S. Congress authorizes the Conscription Act, making all men aged between 20 and 45 liable for military service to address the inadequacies of voluntary enlistment. However, substitutes can still be hired for $300.
WEST: General Stephen A. Hurlbut gains control of the XVI Corps, Army of the Mississippi.

February 17
POLITICS: The order suspending publication of the *Chicago Times* is rescinded by General Ulysses S. Grant.
WEST: Federal troops burn the town of Hopefield, Arkansas, in retaliation for Confederate attacks on shipping.
NAVAL: Confederate forces seize the Federal tug USS *Hercules* opposite Memphis, Tennessee.

The Federal ironclad USS *Indianola* arrives at the mouth of the Red River, having successfully run the Confederate gauntlet at Vicksburg, Mississippi. It stations itself there to maintain the Union blockade.

February 18
POLITICS: Union troops break up a convention by Democrats in Frankfort, Kentucky, which they construe as pro-Confederate.
SOUTH: General James Longstreet is ordered to transfer two divisions of his corps from the Army of Northern Virginia near Fredericksburg to bolster the defenses of Richmond, Virginia.
NAVAL: The USS *Victoria* captures the Confederate brig *Minna* off Shallotte Inlet, North Carolina.

Armed boats from the USS *Somerset* capture the blockade-runner *Hortense* at sea.

February 19
POLITICS: Federal troops convalescing in a hospital at Keokuk, Iowa, angered by antiwar sentiments expressed in the local newspaper *Constitution,* hobble over and ransack the news offices.
SOUTH: President Jefferson Davis contacts General Joseph E. Johnston, noting anxiously how little confidence General Braxton Bragg solicits from his senior subordinates. "It is scarcely possible in that state of the case for him to possess the requisite confidence of the troops," Davis notes. However, the president is not disposed toward removing his old friend and confidant from command.

WEST: Skirmishing between Federals and Confederates under General Nathan B. Forrest at Yazoo Pass north of Vicksburg, Mississippi.

NAVAL: The Confederate raider CSS *Retribution* captures the Federal brig *Emily* in the Caribbean.

February 20

WEST: Union troops under Colonel Alfred H. Terry skirmish with Santee (Sioux) outcasts in the Dakota Territory.

NAVAL: The USS *Crusader* captures the Confederate schooner *General Taylor* in Mobjack Bay, Virginia.

February 21

NAVAL: The USS *Thomas Freeborn* and *Dragon* trade fire with Confederate batteries below Fort Lowry, Virginia.

The USS *Dacotah* and *Monticello* exchange salvos with Confederate batteries at Fort Caswell, North Carolina.

The Confederate raider CSS *Alabama* under Captain Raphael Semmes seizes and burns the Federal ship *Golden Eagle* and bark *Olive Jane*.

February 22

WEST: Union cavalry surprise General Earl Van Dorn's supply column at Tuscumbia, Alabama, taking supplies and prisoners.

February 23

POLITICS: Pennsylvanian Simon Cameron, former secretary of war, resigns his post as minister to Russia.

NAVAL: The USS *Dacotah* and *Monticello* engage Confederate batteries at Fort Caswell, North Carolina.

The USS *Potomska* captures the British blockade-runner *Belle* off Sapelo Sound, Georgia. Armed boats from USS *Caswell* and *Arago* capture the Confederate blockade-runner *Glide* off Little Tybee Island, Georgia.

The USS *Kinsman* hits a snag and sinks in Berwick Bay, Louisiana, losing six crew members.

February 24

WEST: After three weeks of intense work, Union troops finally clear the Yazoo Pass of overhanging vegetation. General Leonard F. Ross reassembles an armada of transports and ironclads to venture downstream.

SOUTHWEST: The Arizona Territory is carved out of the New Mexico Territory by an act of Congress.

NAVAL: Armed boats from the USS *Mahaska* capture and sink the Confederate sloop *Mary Jane* and barge *Ben Bolt* in the York River, Virginia.

The USS *State of Georgia* captures the blockade-runner *Annie* off Cape Romain, South Carolina.

The USS *Tahoma* captures the Confederate schooner *Stonewall* off Key West, Florida.

A Confederate naval deserter informs Union blockaders of submarines and other "infernal machines" being assembled and tested at Mobile, Alabama.

The Confederate vessels CSS *William H. Webb* and *Beatty,* assisted by the newly acquired *Queen of the West,* repeatedly ram the ironclad USS *Indianola* of Commander George Brown below Warrenton, Mississippi. Outnumbered and outmaneuvered by speedier craft, *Indianola* sustains serious damage and partially sinks, so Brown surrenders. The Confederates, cognizant of their valuable prize, undertake immediate steps to raise and salvage it. This loss convinces Admiral David D. Porter to abandon efforts to blockade the Red River with single vessels detached from the main fleet.

February 25

POLITICS: The U.S. Congress approves a national banking system drawn up by Secretary of the Treasury Salmon P. Chase, whereby participating institutions reserve up to one-third of their capital in U.S. Securities. These, in turn, serve as a basis for issuing national bank notes (currency) to the public to facilitate long-term financing of the war effort. This system lasts with little modification until establishment of the Federal Reserve in 1913.

SOUTH: Confederate cavalry under General Fitzhugh Lee surprise a Union cavalry outpost at Hartwood Church, Virginia, taking 150 prisoners.

General Daniel H. Hill receives command of Confederate forces in North Carolina.

NAVAL: The USS *Conemaugh* runs the British blockade-runner *Queen of the Waves* aground at the mouth of the North Santee River, South Carolina.

The USS *Vanderbilt* captures the British merchant vessel *Peterhoff* off St. Thomas in the Caribbean, sparking a British diplomatic protest over the disposition of mail found on the vessel. Eventually, President Abraham Lincoln orders the craft and all confiscated mail returned to their owners.

A force of light-draft Federal gunboats enters the Yazoo Pass after army troops clear away trees and other obstructions from the riverbanks.

Confederates scuttle the newly acquired USS *Indianola* to prevent its recapture at the hands of a fast-approaching, formidable Union "warship"; actually, this is an old coal barge disguised as an ironclad with dummy stacks, guns, and superstructure, being floated downstream for that purpose by Admiral David D. Porter.

February 26

SOUTH: General James Longstreet becomes commander of Confederate forces in the Department of Virginia and North Carolina. At this time, his I Corps consists of divisions under Generals John B. Hood and George E. Pickett.

Confederate rangers under Captain John S. Mosby rout a Union detachment near Germantown, Virginia.

WEST: Confederate irregulars burn a Union train near Woodburn, Tennessee.

General Sterling Price is transferred formally back to the Confederate Trans-Mississippi Department.

SOUTHWEST: On further reflection, the National Council of Cherokee Indians abolishes slavery, renounces its prior alliance with the Confederacy, and rejoins the Union.

February 27

NAVAL: The Confederate raider CSS *Alabama* under Captain Raphael Semmes seizes the Union ship *Washington* in the mid-Atlantic and then releases it on bond.

February 28

NAVAL: The USS *Wynandank* captures the Confederate schooners *Vista* and *A. W. Thompson* off Piney Point, Virginia.

The ironclad USS *Montauk* under Captain John L. Worden, accompanied by *Seneca, Wissahocken,* and *Dawn,* sails up the Ogeechee River and sinks the blockade-runner CSS *Rattlesnake* (nee *Nashville*) near Fort McAllister, Georgia. However, *Montauk* strikes a torpedo and temporarily grounds itself on a mudbank to affect repairs.

The USS *New Era* seizes the Confederate steamer *Curlew* off Island No. 10 in the Mississippi River.

The Yazoo River expedition glides onto the Coldwater River several days ahead of army transports. They are joined by the rams USS *Fulton* and *Lioness* and the gunboat *Petrel.*

March 1

WEST: Confederate raiders under General Nathan B. Forrest skirmish with Union forces at Bradyville, Tennessee.

Union forces capture and occupy Bloomfield, Missouri.

March 2

NORTH: The U.S. Congress authorizes four major generals and nine brigadier generals for the U.S. Army, with an additional 40 major generals and 200 brigadier generals for the volunteers. Conversely, 33 ranking officers are dismissed from the service on a variety of charges.

SOUTHWEST: Federal troops depart New Orleans on an expedition to the mouth of the Rio Grande.

NAVAL: The Confederate raider CSS *Alabama* under Captain Raphael Semmes seizes and burns the Federal ship *John A. Parks.*

March 3

DIPLOMACY: The U.S. Congress passes a resolution condemning all offers of mediation as "foreign intervention."

POLITICS: President Abraham Lincoln signs the Enrollment or Federal Draft Act, whereby all able-bodied males between 20 and 46 years of age are eligible for military service. This is the first such legislation enacted by the Federal government.

The U.S. Congress approves a loan of $300 million for the year 1863. It also formally and finally suspends writs of habeas corpus as a wartime expedient.

Jay Cooke is named Federal agent tasked with promoting the sale of war bonds.

The U.S. Congress establishes the National Academy of Sciences.

The 37th U.S. Congress adjourns.

WEST: The Idaho Territory is formed by act of Congress, sliced from parts of the adjoining Washington and Dakota territories, and incorporates parts of present-day Montana and Wyoming.

NAVAL: An armed boat from the USS *Matthew Vassar* proceeds up the Little River Inlet, North Carolina, and burns a large vessel there, but on the return trip, the crew is captured by Confederates.

The ironclads USS *Passaic, Nahant,* and *Patapsco,* accompanied by gunboats *Seneca, Dawn,* and *Wissahocken* and three mortar boats, engage the batteries of Fort McAllister, Georgia, for six hours. Little damage is inflicted, but the attack gives Union boat crews practical training for their upcoming moves against Charleston, South Carolina.

March 4

WEST: Confederates under General Earl Van Dorn successfully surround and skirmish with Federal troops at Franklin, Tennessee. Union cavalry manage to ride to safety, but the infantry component of the expedition is forced to surrender.

NAVAL: The USS *James S. Chambers* captures the Spanish blockade-runner *Relampago* at sea and the Confederate schooner *Ida* after it runs ashore at Sanibel Island, Florida.

March 5

POLITICS: In Columbus, Ohio, rampaging Union troops gut the editorial offices of the newspaper *Crisis* for allegedly printing pro-Southern editorials.

WEST: General Earl Van Dorn advances with 6,000 Confederates against a Union position at Thompson's Station, Tennessee. The defenders consist of 2,857 Federal soldiers and cavalry supported by six cannon under Colonel John Coburn. Rather than retreat, Coburn elects to attack the enemy camp and is assailed in turn by cavalry under General Nathan B. Forrest. When these are driven off, the remaining Union infantry stubbornly defend two hills and beat back numerous Confederate charges. At length, a final attempt is mounted by Forrest that finally breaks Union resistance and Coburn surrenders. The Confederates sustain 357 casualties while capturing 1,221 Federals. Bad blood subsequently ensues when Van Dorn accuses Forrest of hoarding captured Union supplies for his own use, a charge Forrest vehemently denies. These two headstrong cavaliers nearly come to dueling before calmer heads prevail.

NAVAL: The USS *Lockwood* safely returns from an armed expedition up the Pungo River to destroy a bridge and break up enemy supply dumps.

The USS *Aroostook* chases the Confederate blockade-runner *Josephine* aground near Fort Morgan, Mobile Bay, Alabama, destroying it by gunfire.

March 6

NAVAL: The Confederate raider CSS *Florida* under Lieutenant John N. Maffitt captures and burns the Union ship *Star of Peace* at sea.

March 7

POLITICS: Federal troops in Baltimore, Maryland, confiscate all song sheets that are deemed "secession music."

SOUTH: A Federal expedition from New Bern, North Carolina, to Mattamuskeet ends in controversy when Colonel Charles C. Dodge, commanding, accuses the

103rd Pennsylvania Volunteers of unauthorized burning, plundering, and disre-spectful conduct toward local women.

WEST: Federal forces under General Nathaniel P. Banks advance from New Orleans toward Port Hudson, Louisiana, to campaign in concert with General Ulysses S. Grant at Vicksburg, Mississippi.

General Edmund Kirby-Smith arrives to assume command of all Confederate forces in the Trans-Mississippi Department.

NAVAL: Admiral Samuel P. Lee of the North Atlantic Blockading Squadron, having detached many officers and sailors as prize crews, requests reinforcements to make up manpower deficiencies.

March 8

SOUTH: A sudden raid by Captain John S. Mosby and his Confederate rangers captures General Edwin H. Stoughton in his headquarters at Fairfax County Court House, Virginia, along with 32 prisoners and 58 horses. The general was sleeping in bed at the time and rudely was awakened by a slap on his backside—delivered by Mosby himself. This was one of the most daring—if embarrassing—acts of the entire war.

General Daniel H. Hill's troops skirmish heavily with Union defenders outside Fort Anderson near New Bern, North Carolina.

WEST: Progress on the Yazoo River expedition, slow to begin with, is hindered fur-ther by trees felled along the way by retreating Confederates, as well as by the usual overhanging vegetation on the riverbanks. Two additional days are required to clear away all obstacles before additional progress can be made downstream.

NAVAL: The USS *Sagamore* captures the Confederate sloop *Enterprise* near Mosquito Inlet, Florida.

March 9

NAVAL: The USS *Quaker City* captures the British blockade-runner *Douro* near Wilmington, North Carolina.

The USS *Bienville* captures the Confederate schooner Lightning off Port Royal, South Carolina.

The 22-boat combined expedition to the Yazoo River under General Leonard F. Ross finally clears the Talluhatchie River and reaches the confluence of the Yalobusha and Tazoo rivers. There, they encounter a small Confederate fortifi-cation christened Fort Pemberton near Greenwood, Mississippi, and prepare to bombard it.

March 10

POLITICS: In the Prize Cases, the Supreme Court approves the legality of the Union naval blockade on a 5–4 vote. They do so by declaring the right of a sovereign state to conduct a blockade while simultaneously denying that the Confederate States of America actually exists. The Court also rules that while only Congress has the power to declare war, Lincoln, as commander in chief, has the authority to suppress a rebellion.

President Abraham Lincoln signs a general amnesty for all soldiers, presently absent without leave, to rejoin their units by April 1, 1863.

President Jefferson C. Davis ventures to Vicksburg, Mississippi, where he confers with General John C. Pemberton about affairs in the West.

SOUTH: Federal forces, including a large number of African-American soldiers, seize and occupy Jacksonville, Florida.

NAVAL: The USS *Gem of the Sea* sinks the Confederate sloop *Petee* off Indian River Inlet, Florida.

The USS *Norwich* and *Uncas* ships troops up the St. John's River, Florida, where armed parties land and recapture Jacksonville.

The USS *Chillicothe* destroys a bridge spanning the Tallahatchie River above Fort Pemberton, Mississippi. The Confederate steamer *Thirty-fifth Parallel* is also sunk to prevent capture.

March 11

NAVAL: A Federal gunboat expedition moving up the Tallahatchie River engages Confederate batteries under General William W. Loring at Fort Pemberton, Greenwood, Mississippi. In the course of battle, the ironclad USS *Chillicothe* receives repeated hits and withdraws in damaged condition.

March 12

NAVAL: The USS *Kittatinny* captures the Confederate vessel *D. Sargent* in the Gulf of Mexico.

Admiral David G. Farragut arrives at Baton Rouge, Louisiana, with his flagship USS *Hartford* and prepares to advance past Confederate defenses at Port Hudson on the Mississippi River.

March 13

SOUTH: A horrific explosion rocks the Confederate Ordnance Laboratory on Brown's Island, Richmond, Virginia, killing 70 workers, principally women. This accident highlights how far men have been supplanted as industrial workers due to wartime conditions in the South.

Confederate forces under General Daniel H. Hill launch a night attack against Fort Anderson on the Neuse River, North Carolina, which is repulsed by naval gunfire.

NAVAL: Federal gunboats USS *Hunchback, Hetzel, Ceres,* and *Shawsheen* render invaluable support fire during a surprise Confederate attack on Fort Anderson, North Carolina.

The USS *Huntsville* captures the British blockade-runner *Surprise* near Charlotte Harbor, Florida.

The USS *Octorara* captures the British blockade-runner *Florence Nightingale* in North East Providence Channel, Bahamas.

The Confederate raider CSS *Florida* under Lieutenant John N. Maffitt captures and burns the Union ship *Aldebaran* at sea.

The ironclad USS *Chillicothe*, accompanied by gunboats *Baron de Kalb* and *Matamora,* again engage Confederate batteries at Fort Pemberton at Greenwood, Mississippi. In two hours, the *Chillicothe* receives an additional 38 hits, and the flotilla withdraws back up the Tallahatchie River.

March 14

SOUTH: General Nathaniel P. Banks advances his Army of the Gulf on Port Hudson, Louisiana, with 30,000 men. He establishes several artillery batteries to assist the passage of Admiral David G. Farragut's fleet and then returns to Baton Rouge when the attempt fails. It is now painfully apparent to Union authorities that Port Hudson, a position second only in strength to Vicksburg, Mississippi, must be reduced by assault in the near future.

NAVAL: Admiral David G. Farragut's squadron of seven ships runs past Confederate batteries at Port Hudson, Louisiana, at 11:00 P.M. The admiral's flagship USS *Hartford*, lashed together alongside the *Albatross*, weathers a storm of shot and shells and makes the passage intact. The remaining vessels are supported by mortar fire from army units, but resistance proves fierce and they are driven back downstream. The *Mississippi* grounds, catches afire, and drifts helplessly until exploding with a loss of 64 lives. Moreover, Farragut is cut off from his surviving warships, *Monongahela* and *Richmond*, for several weeks.

Admiral David D. Porter pushes the gunboats USS *Louisville, Cincinnati, Carondelet, Pittsburgh,* and *Mound City,* four mortar boats, and four tugs up the Yazoo River to secure Steele's Bayou near Vicksburg, Mississippi. Over the next weeks, they pass successively upstream hoping to turn the city's defenses from the rear, but progress is slow due to the overgrown riverbanks.

March 15

NAVAL: The Confederate raider CSS *Alabama* under Captain Raphael Semmes captures the Union ship *Punjab* off the Brazilian coast and releases it on bond.

Armed boats from the USS *Cyane* seize the schooner and suspected Confederate blockade-runner *J. M. Chapman* in San Francisco Bay, California. Various military stores found in its cargo holds demonstrate its belligerent intent.

March 16

NORTH: Philip H. Sheridan is promoted to major general, U.S. Army.

WEST: Cavalry under Generals Earl Van Dorn and Joseph Wheeler are designated Confederate army corps within the Army of Tennessee.

General William T. Sherman arrives at Hill's Plantation, Mississippi, with the 2nd Division, XV Corps, to support a riverine advance to Steele's Bayou by Admiral David D. Porter.

NAVAL: The USS *Octorara* captures the Confederate sloop *Rosalie* and schooner *Five Brothers* off the east coast of Florida.

Federal gunboats of the Yazoo River expedition again engage Fort Pemberton, Greenwood, Mississippi, whereupon the ironclad USS *Chillicothe* receives eight more hits, suffers 22 casualties, and drifts helplessly. The attack finally is halted by General Leonard F. Ross, and he makes ready to withdraw downstream in defeat. Failure here terminates General Ulysses S. Grant's attempts to circumvent the Confederate defenses of Vicksburg, Mississippi, through the backdoor.

Admiral David D. Porter confers with General Ulysses S. Grant at Hill's Plantation at the head of Black Bayou, Mississippi, and then leads five of his ironclads up Deer Creek in an attempt to reach Steele's Bayou from the northeast.

March 17

SOUTH: General Ambrose E. Burnside is reassigned to command of the IX Corps, Army of the Potomac, although he subsequently shares this position with General John G. Parke.

A force of 2,100 Union cavalry and six guns under General William W. Averell advances from Morrisville, Virginia, and heads for the Rappahannock River intending to surprise Confederate cavalry stationed at Culpeper Court. While crossing at Kelley's Ford, Union troops are delayed by Confederate sentinels who alert General Fitzhugh Lee to their presence. The Confederates quickly take to their saddles and advance to meet the intruders with 800 men. Averell then lines up his five regiments abreast behind a stone wall, lets the Confederates gallop to within close range, and mows them down with intense artillery and carbine fire. Lee withdraws to a second position farther back and regroups as Union troopers advance in turn. A series of charges and countercharges ensue throughout the afternoon with little advantage to either side before Averell ends the contest at 5:30 P.M. and withdraws across the river in good order. As a parting jest, he leaves Lee, a former West Point roommate, a sack of coffee and a note inquiring if he enjoyed his visit. Union losses total 58 while the Confederates report 133 killed and wounded. Foremost among the fallen is the youthful Southern artillerist Major John Pelham, who is mortally struck by an artillery fragment. Kelley's Ford also puts Southern horsemen on notice of the proficiency their Union opposites have acquired with greater experience.

Captain John S. Mosby surprises and captures a 25-man picket at Herndon Station, Virginia.

NAVAL: The Yazoo River expedition, stymied by Fort Pemberton near Greenwood, Mississippi, steams back down the Tallahatchie River.

March 18

POLITICS: The Democratic-controlled state legislature of New Jersey passes a number of peace resolutions condemning all aspects of the war effort and demanding a negotiated ending. This prompts a sharp response from state regiments in the field, who pass resolutions of their own condemning the legislature's activities as "wicked" and "cowardly."

WEST: General Theophilus H. Holmes is appointed commander of the Confederate District of Arkansas.

NAVAL: The USS *Wissahickon* destroys the Confederate steamer *Georgiana* as it attempts to run the blockade off Charleston, South Carolina.

March 19

SOUTH: General William F. Smith transfers two divisions from his IX Corps at Newport News, Virginia, to the Department of the Ohio.

NAVAL: The USS *Octorara* captures the British blockade-runner *John Williams* off the Bahamas.

Admiral David G. Farragut continues northward by running his steam sloop USS *Hartford* and the ironclad *Albatross* past Confederate guns at Grand Gulf, south of Vicksburg, Mississippi. Despite heavy fire, he sustains only eight casualties and safely anchors the following day off Warrenton.

The Steele's Bayou expedition of Admiral David D. Porter continues up Deer Creek, Mississippi, and begins to encounter Confederate snipers from the shoreline. Porter disembarks 300 sailors to clear the banks of infantry and remove obstacles placed in the river by fleeing Southerners.

March 20
SOUTH: General Daniel H. Hill rings the Union garrison at Washington, North Carolina, with several batteries and deploys several brigades to obstruct possible reinforcements from New Bern. Washington itself is invested by a brigade under General Richard B. Garnett. The garrison commander, General John G. Foster, endures several days of bombardment before Federal gunboats in the nearby Pamlico River arrive to assist.
NAVAL: The USS *Ethan Allen* seizes the British blockade-runner *Gypsy* near St. Joseph's Bay, Florida.

The Steele's Bayou expedition of Admiral David D. Porter no sooner steams past Rolling Fork on Deer Creek, Mississippi, than Confederate forces begin to fell trees and other obstacles behind the fleet to trap it there. Three Southern regiments are then dispatched from Haynes's Bluff to attack and possibly capture the entire squadron.

March 21
NORTH: General Edwin V. Sumner dies of natural causes in Syracuse, New York.
WEST: General William T. Sherman's expedition to Steele's Bayou gropes along the tree-choked river banks, much harassed by snipers and man-made obstacles. Progress is steady but slow, but he increases the tempo to rescue Admiral David D. Porter's squadron, trapped by obstacles at Deer Creek. Protracted skirmishing erupts along the banks as Sherman tries to obstruct a force of 3,000 Confederates from attacking the gunboats in narrow waters.

The Yazoo River expedition of General Leonard F. Ross, now reinforced by troops under General Isaac F. Quinby on Moon Lake, turns around and steams back toward Fort Greenwood, Mississippi.
NAVAL: The USS *Victoria* and *William Bacon* seize the British blockade-runner *Nicolai I* off Cape Fear, North Carolina.

March 22
WEST: Confederate forces under General John Pegram embark on an extended raid into Kentucky.

Mount Sterling, Kentucky, is captured by Confederate troopers belonging to General John H. Morgan's command.
NAVAL: The USS *Tioga* captures British blockade-runners *Granite City* and *Brothers* off Abaco, Bahamas.

Admiral David D. Porter concedes that efforts to seize Steele's Bayou from the Yazoo River have failed, and he commences sailing back to Hill's Plantation, Mississippi, with General William T. Sherman's infantry onboard. Natural obstacles in the river and along the shoreline, complicated by trees felled by fleeing Confederates, thwart another attempt to outflank Vicksburg via inland waterways.

March 23

SOUTH: Virginia Partisan Rangers under Captain John S. Mosby defeat a Federal detachment at Little River Turnpike, Virginia, but then they are surprised and almost captured in turn by Union cavalry.

NAVAL: The USS *Arizona* captures the Confederate sloop *Aurelia* near Mosquito Inlet, Florida.

The Confederate raider CSS *Alabama* under Captain Raphael Semmes captures and burns the Union ship *Morning Star* and the whaler *Kingfisher* off the Brazilian coast.

Admiral David G. Farragut orders the USS *Hartford* and *Albatross* to bombard Confederate works off Warrenton, Mississippi.

March 24

WEST: Confederate forces under General John Pegram skirmish with Union forces at Danville, Kentucky.

Union cavalry under Colonel Benjamin H. Grierson fight a skirmish with pursuing Confederates near La Grange, Tennessee.

NAVAL: The USS *Mount Vernon* captures the British blockade-runner *Mary Jane* off New Inlet, North Carolina.

Admiral David D. Porter's ironclad squadron safely reaches Black Bayou, Mississippi, after almost being trapped on Deer Creek by Confederate infantry. His expedition sustains one engineer killed and four sailors wounded for the effort.

March 25

NORTH: General Ambrose E. Burnside transfers as commanding officer of the Department of the Ohio, succeeding General Horatio G. Wright, who reports back to the Army of the Potomac to command a division.

WEST: General Nathan B. Forrest and his Confederate cavalry column attack Union troops garrisoning in Brentwood, Tennessee. These consist of 520 men of the 22nd Wisconsin under Colonel Edward Bloodgood, with an additional 230 men of the 19th Michigan in a small stockade south of town. Forrest, who had cut all Union telegraph lines beforehand, approaches with two brigades and surrounds both detachments. Some skirmishing ensues, but both Union detachments surrender. But as the Confederate marauders withdraw along the Little Harpeth River, they are set on by a third party of Union cavalry under General Green C. Smith, who recaptures some wagons and supplies. Forrest, nevertheless, concludes another successful raid and escapes with 700 prisoners to Columbia, Tennessee.

NAVAL: The USS *State of Georgia* and *Mount Vernon* capture the Confederate schooner *Rising Dawn* off New Inlet, North Carolina.

The USS *Fort Henry* captures the Confederate schooner *Ranger* at Cedar Keys, Florida.

The USS *Kanawha* captures the Confederate schooner *Clara* off Mobile, Alabama.

The USS *Wachusett* takes the British blockade-runner *Dolphin* off St. Thomas in the Caribbean.

The Confederate raider CSS *Alabama* under Captain Raphael Semmes burns the Union ships *Charles Hill* and *Nora* off the Brazilian coast.

Confederate batteries at Vicksburg, Mississippi, engage rams USS *Lancaster* and *Switzerland* as they attempt to run past their position. The former, struck 30 times, sinks while the latter is so heavily damaged that a planned assault against Warrenton is postponed.

March 26

POLITICS: Voters in the new state of West Virginia approve the gradual emancipation of all slaves.

The Confederate Congress in Richmond, Virginia, approves the Impressment Act, authorizing government agents to seize slaves and foodstuffs to supply the Confederate military. Waste and abuse in its enforcement lead several state governments to condemn the practice.

March 27

POLITICS: President Abraham Lincoln entertains numerous American Indian leaders at the White House and implores them to take up agriculture. "I can see no way in which your race is to become as numerous and prosperous as the white race," he lectured, "except by living as they do, by the cultivation of the earth."

NAVAL: The USS *Pawnee* provides close support fire during an army expedition against Cole's Island, South Carolina.

The USS *Kendrick Hudson* captures the British schooner *Pacifique* off St. Mark's Florida.

The USS *Hartford* under Admiral David G. Farragut bombards Confederate defenses at Warrenton, Mississippi, below Vicksburg.

March 28

WEST: Confederates under General John Pegram skirmish with Union forces at Danville and Hickman's Bridge, Kentucky.

NAVAL: The USS *Stettin* captures the British steamer *Aries* off Bull's Bay, South Carolina.

The Confederate raider CSS *Florida* under Lieutenant John N. Maffitt captures the Union bark *Lapwing* and impresses it as a tender under the new name *Oreto*.

The Federal gunboat USS *Diana* under Captain Thomas L. Peterson sails up the Atchafalaya River, Louisiana, toward Pattersonville, with several companies from the 160th New York and 12th Connecticut onboard. En route, Peterson is ambushed by 500 Confederates on the riverbank, supported by cavalry and artillery. Accurate cannon fire rakes the *Diana,* killing Peterson and driving the infantry from its decks. After a running battle of three hours, *Diana* loses its steering mechanism, grounds, and finally surrenders with a loss of 33 Federals killed and 120 captured. This vessel, which previously had been seized by Union forces at New Orleans in April 1862, reenters Confederate service under General Richard Taylor at Bayou Teche.

March 29

SOUTH: General Carl Schurz is appointed to command the XI Corps, Army of the Potomac.

Southern forces fail to secure Fort Magruder at Williamsburg, Virginia, with a surprise attack.

WEST: General Ulysses S. Grant dispatches General John A. McClernand with troops to Milliken's Bend, Louisiana, on the west bank of the Mississippi River, with orders to march south to New Carthage. Grant now begins the process of divesting himself from supply bases at Memphis, Tennessee.

NAVAL: The USS *South Carolina* seizes the Confederate schooner *Nellie* at Port Royal, South Carolina.

Personnel from the USS *Norwich* evacuate Jacksonville, Florida, after razing most of the town.

The USS *Albatross* joins Admiral David G. Farragut's *Hartford* in a sustained bombardment of Confederate batteries at Warrenton, Mississippi.

March 30

POLITICS: President Abraham Lincoln announces that April 30, 1863, will be designated a national day of fasting and prayer.

SOUTH: Confederate forces under General Daniel H. Hill enact a siege of Union forces at Washington, North Carolina, the course of which is interrupted by Federal gunboats offshore.

NAVAL: The USS *Monticello* captures the British blockade-runner *Sue* near the Little River, North Carolina.

The Confederate raider CSS *Florida* under Lieutenant John N. Maffitt captures and burns the Union bark *M. J. Colcord* at sea.

March 31

NORTH: Oliver O. Howard is appointed major general, U.S. Army.

SOUTH: Captain John S. Mosby and his Virginia Partisan Rangers engage and defeat a Union cavalry detachment at Drainesville, Virginia, inflicting 60 casualties and prisoners.

NAVAL: The USS *Memphis* captures the British schooner *Antelope* off Charleston, South Carolina.

The USS *Two Sisters* captures the Confederate schooner *Agnes* off the Tortugas, Florida.

Admiral David G. Farragut sails USS *Hartford, Albatross,* and the recently repaired ram *Switzerland* past Confederate batteries at Grand Gulf, Mississippi. They continue to the Red River and establish a blockade there.

April 1

SOUTH: Captain John S. Mosby's 65 men are surprised in camp by 200 Union cavalry at Broad Run, Virginia, but they repulse their antagonists with 107 casualties.

WEST: General Francis J. Herron succeeds General John M. Schofield as commander of the Army of the Frontier in Missouri.

NAVAL: The USS *Commodore Morris* proceeds up the Ware River, Virginia, where it seizes Patterson Smith's Plantation and burns 22,000 bushels of grain. A body of Confederate cavalry attempting to interfere is driven off.

The USS *Tuscumbia* under Admiral David D. Porter hosts General Ulysses S. Grant and William T. Sherman on a grand reconnaissance of the Yazoo River as far as Haynes's Bluff. The sheer nature of the terrain and other obstacles convince Grant to abandon any advance on Vicksburg, Mississippi, from this direction. The general now turns his attention to operations below the city.

April 2

POLITICS: Richmond, Virginia, is the scene of an infamous "Bread Riot." This morning, a small crowd of women and boys announce that they are going to proceed from Capital Square to obtain bread. Numerous onlookers gradually join the procession, which swells to more than 1,000 and grows increasingly unruly. Full-scale rioting and looting then erupts with many businesses being ransacked. President Jefferson Davis, upon hearing of the outbreak, bravely races over, throws himself in the midst of the angry throng, and demands that they disperse or be fired on by the militia. His warning chills the participants, and they gradually disperse.

SOUTH: General Oliver O. Howard replaces General Carl Schurz as commander of the XI Corps, Army of the Potomac.

WEST: General Ulysses S. Grant meets with Admiral David D. Porter to promulgate a final plan of operations against Vicksburg, Mississippi. They decide that while forces under General William T. Sherman mount a large-scale diversion along Haynes's Bluff to the north, the main force under Grant will march south down the west bank of the Mississippi River. Porter likewise will sail south past the city to reunite with Grant at Hard Times, 30 miles south of Vicksburg. There the entire army will embark and be carried across to the Confederate shore.

NAVAL: Naval gunboats in the Pamlico River, North Carolina, race to the rescue of besieged Union forces at Washington under General John G. Foster. Heavy naval gunfire silences several Confederate guns on the shoreline, painfully demonstrating that Union lines of communication to the garrison remain functional.

Armed boats from the USS *Fort Henry* begin a week-long reconnaissance of Bayport, Florida.

April 3

NAVAL: The USS *New London* and *Cayuga* capture the British blockade-runner *Tampico* off Sabine Pass, Texas.

A Federal expedition consisting of the gunboats USS *Lexington, Brilliant, Robb, Silver Lake,* and *Springfield* bombard and destroy the town of Palmyra, Tennessee, in retaliation for recent Confederate attacks on Union shipping.

April 4

DIPLOMACY: American minister Charles F. Adams loudly protests the impending departure of the vessel *Alexandra*, destined for eventual service in the Confederate navy.

SOUTH: Union forces attack a Confederate battery at Rodman's Point, Washington, North Carolina, but are repulsed.

WEST: The Yazoo River expedition of Generals Leonard F. Ross and Isaac F. Quinby fails again to bombard Fort Pemberton, Greenwood, Mississippi, into submission, and steams back to the Mississippi River in defeat.

Naval: The Confederate raider CSS *Alabama* under Captain Raphael Semmes captures and eventually burns the Union ship *Louisa Hatch* off the Brazilian coast.

April 5

Politics: President Abraham Lincoln meets with General Joseph Hooker at Fredericksburg, Virginia, to discuss strategy. At this time, both leaders concur that the object of future military operations should center upon the destruction of General Robert E. Lee's army, with Richmond, Virginia, a secondary concern.

Naval: Admiral Samuel F. Du Pont marshals his ironclads and steams from North Edisto, South Carolina, intending to attack the harbor defenses of Charleston.

April 6

Diplomacy: The British government seizes the newly completed warship *Alexandra* to placate the U.S. government. However, the vessel eventually will be released to the Confederacy by the courts.

Naval: With the Stono bar safely buoyed, Admiral Samuel F. Du Pont leads his squadron of nine heavily armed ironclads into the outer fringes of Charleston Harbor, South Carolina, and anchors there for the night.

The USS *Huntsville* captures the Confederate sloop *Minnie* off Charlotte Harbor, Florida.

April 7

West: Confederate cavalry under General Joseph Wheeler hit the Louisville and Nashville and Nashville and Chattanooga railroads at Antioch Station, Tennessee.

Naval: Adverse tides keep Admiral Samuel F. Du Pont's ironclad squadron from deploying within range of Fort Moultrie and Sumter, Charleston Harbor, South Carolina, until nearly 3:00 P.M. He then finds the channels to the city not only lined with submerged obstacles but also filled with floating range markers to assist gunnery from the forts. Moreover, as the battle intensifies, Du Pont's slow-firing monitors are able to loose only 139 rounds while 77 well-handled Confederate cannon fire off 2,200 shells. The USS *Weehawken* is hardest hit, striking a mine and sustaining 53 hits in only 40 minutes before withdrawing. The remaining eight ironclads in the squadron likewise are battered by heavy and accurate shore fire. *Keokuk* alone suffers 90 hits, many near or below the waterline, which render it nearly uncontrollable.

Du Pont, who had anticipated the worst, finally suspends the action at nightfall and withdraws, thankful that it was "a failure instead of a disaster." The admiral seeks to renew the contest on the morrow but is dissuaded by his captains, who regard the attempt as suicidal. The rebuff off Charleston represents the U.S. Navy's biggest defeat in the Civil War and painfully underscores Du Pont's oft-expressed belief that the city simply is too strong to be taken by sea power alone.

The USS *Barataria* runs aground on Lake Maurepas, Louisiana, and is burned to prevent capture.

April 8

South: President Abraham Lincoln and General Joseph Hooker review the Army of the Potomac at Falmouth, Virginia, across the Rappahannock River from Fredericksburg.

NAVAL: The badly damaged ironclad USS *Keokuk* sinks outside of Charleston, South Carolina. However, its signal books eventually are recovered by the Confederates, who can now discern the squadron's communications.

The USS *Gem of the Sea* captures the British blockade-runner *Maggie Fulton* near the Indian River Inlet, Florida.

This night, Edward C. Gabaudan, secretary to Admiral David G. Farragut, joins his superior by sailing downstream past Vicksburg, Mississippi, in a small boat covered with branches. Its somewhat large size attracts Confederate sentinels, who, upon rowing closer, simply pronounce his vessel "a log" and return to shore.

April 9
NAVAL: Off the French coast, the former merchant vessel *Japan* secretly is commissioned into the Confederate navy as the commerce raider CSS *Georgia* under Commander William L. Maury. This vessel ultimately seizes nine Union ships on a cruise to the Cape of Good Hope, but its questionable sailing abilities result in an early decommissioning.

April 10
POLITICS: President Jefferson Davis exhorts his countrymen to forego the planting of cotton and tobacco in favor of foodstuffs that are desperately needed by Confederate forces. "Let fields be devoted exclusively to the production of corn, oats, beans, peas, potatoes, and other food for man and beasts," he lectured, "and let all your efforts be directed to the prompt supply of these articles in the districts where our armies are operating."

SOUTH: Confederate general Alfred Moulton arrives at Bisland, Louisiana, on the Teche River. There, he constructs Fort Bisland to obstruct the Union advance under General Nathaniel P. Banks. Moulton is joined there eventually by General Richard Taylor, bringing Confederate strength up to 4,000 men and two steamers.

WEST: General Earl Van Dorn attacks Union troops at Franklin, Tennessee, but he is repulsed by cavalry under General Gordon Granger, losing nearly 300 men.

NAVAL: A landing party from the USS *Kingfisher* surprises and captures Confederate pickets on Edisto Island, South Carolina.

Armed boats from the USS *New London,* while reconnoitering at Sabine City, Texas, accost a small Confederate sloop and seize Captain Charles Fowler of the CSS *Josiah Bell.*

Landing parties from the USS *Conestoga* scour the banks of Beulah Bend, Mississippi, destroying several guerrilla posts.

April 11
SOUTH: General James Longstreet leads 20,000 veteran soldiers on a loose "siege" of Suffolk, Virginia, south of the James River. There, he confronts 25,000 Federals of the IX Corps under General John J. Peck behind a series of elaborate fortifications.

General Henry A. Wise's Confederates again fail to surprise the Union garrison at Fort Magruder, Williamsburg, Virginia.

WEST: Colonel Abel D. Streight leads 1,700 Union cavalry on a raid into Georgia from Nashville, Tennessee. However, his force consists entirely of infantrymen who have been mounted on mules to negotiate the rough terrain anticipated in northern Alabama.

NAVAL: The USS *Flag* and *Huron* run the Confederate blockade-runner *Stonewall Jackson* aground near Charleston, South Carolina, destroying it with gunfire.

Admiral Samuel P. Lee of the North Atlantic Blockading Squadron dispatches several gunboats under Lieutenant William B. Cushman to assist in the defense of Suffolk, Virginia.

April 12

POLITICS: President Abraham Lincoln is informed by General Joseph Hooker that he wishes to swing around General Robert E. Lee's left flank and threaten Richmond, Virginia. The president reminds his general that the destruction of Lee's army remains paramount.

SOUTH: The XIX Corps of General Nathaniel P. Banks, numbering 16,000 men in three divisions, moves up the Teche River toward Irish Bend on Bayou Teche, Louisiana, hoping to engage 4,000 Confederates under General Richard Taylor. Banks marches two divisions overland while ordering 4,500 men of General Cuvier Grover's division to land north of the fort to cut their retreat. As Grovier comes ashore, his troops engage Fort Bisland in a three-hour artillery duel that ends with nightfall. Taylor then prepares to have General Henry H. Sibley's Texas Brigade attack Banks's left flank on the morrow to drive him back.

NAVAL: The Federal gunboats USS *Stepping Stones, Commodore Barney, Commodore Morris,* and *Crusader* take up stations along the Nansemond River, Virginia, to prevent Confederate troops from crossing.

A Confederate boat crew captures the Union steamer *Fox* at Pass l'Outre, Mississippi, and two days later, it runs the blockade outside Mobile, Alabama.

April 13

SOUTH: At Irish Bend, Louisiana, Confederate forces gird to deliver an early morning strike against superior forces under General Nathaniel P. Banks. Unfortunately, General Henry H. Sibley, the officer entrusted with that operation, is either inebriated or too ill to comply. The opportunity passes quickly, and the Federals, greatly outnumbering the defenders, push their earthworks to within 400 yards of Fort Bisland. General Richard Taylor, rather than be crushed between Banks and the Union division of General Cuvier Grover once it begins to press down from the north, resolves to abandon his position. His men skillfully skirt Union soldiers along the river and deploy to attack at dawn and to allow the garrison at Fort Bisland to escape.

WEST: General Ambrose E. Burnside, commanding the Department of the Ohio, suppresses Copperhead (Peace Democrat) activities with a general order instituting military tribunals—and the firing squad—for treasonable activities. Furthermore, any individuals displaying wanton sympathy for the South can expect prompt deportation to Confederate lines.

NAVAL: President Abraham Lincoln instructs Admiral Samuel F. Du Pont to maintain his position with Charleston Harbor and keep the Confederates apprehensive over another attack.

The USS *Annie* captures the Confederate schooner *Mattie* off the Florida coast.

The USS *Rachel Seaman* captures the Confederate schooner *Maria Alfred* off the Mermentau River, Louisiana.

April 14

SOUTH: Confederates under General Richard Taylor abandon Fort Bisland, Louisiana, in the face of strong Union forces. En route, his men attack and surprise Federal troops under General Cuvier Grover while the main force under General Nathaniel P. Banks, farther south, cautiously occupies the fort. Grover remains in camp and fails to pursue, so Taylor's small command escapes intact. Union casualties amount to about 600 men. Confederate losses are not known but are presumed lighter. However, Taylor is forced to scuttle the recently recaptured CSS *Diana.*

NAVAL: Accurate gunfire from Federal gunboats USS *Mount Washington, Steeping Stones,* and *Commodore Barney* thwarts Confederate efforts to surround the Union garrison at Suffolk, Virginia.

The USS *Huntsville* seizes the British blockade-runner *Ascension* off the Florida Gulf coast.

The USS *Sonoma* captures the Confederate schooner *Clyde* in the Gulf of Mexico.

A task force consisting of USS *Estrella, Arizona,* and *Calhoun* attacks and sinks the Confederate ram CSS *Queen of the West* in Grand Lake, Louisiana.

April 15

SOUTH: Union general John G. Foster sails down the Pamlico River from Washington, North Carolina, past Confederate shore batteries, and into New Bern for reinforcements. General Daniel H. Hill then abandons his siege and withdraws inland.

Advancing Union forces under General Nathaniel P. Banks occupy Franklin, Louisiana.

WEST: General Ulysses S. Grant assembles 45,000 troops at Milliken's Bend, Mississippi, 10 miles north of the Confederate bastion of Vicksburg. He next orders the corps of General James B. McPherson south down the left bank of the Mississippi River to New Carthage, to join the troops of General John A. McClernand already there. Meanwhile, General William T. Sherman's command begins to demonstrate before Chickasaw Bluffs as a feint.

A Federal expedition under General Grenville M. Dodge advances from Corinth, Mississippi, into Courtland, Alabama.

NAVAL: Union gunboats under Lieutenant William B. Cushing silence several Confederate batteries while operating on the Nansemond River near Suffolk, Virginia.

The USS *Monticello* captures the Confederate schooner *Odd Fellow* off Little River, North Carolina.

The USS *William G. Anderson* captures the Confederate schooner *Royal Yacht* on the Gulf of Mexico.

The Confederate raider CSS *Alabama* under Captain Raphael Semmes captures and burns the whalers *Kate Cory* and *Lafayette* off Fernando de Noronha, Brazil.

April 16

POLITICS: President Jefferson Davis signs legislation permitting minors under 18 to hold military commissions.

SOUTH: Federal forces advance from Washington, North Carolina, and briefly tangle with the Confederate rear guard under General Daniel H. Hill at nearby Kinston.

WEST: A gala ball held at Vicksburg, Mississippi, to celebrate the city's perceived impregnability is interrupted suddenly by defiantly heavy gunfire as the Union fleet once again sallies past on the Mississippi River.

NAVAL: The Federal gunboat USS *Mount Washington* is severely damaged by masked Confederate batteries while steaming along the Nansemond River, Virginia.

The USS *Hendrick Hudson* captures the British blockade-runner *Teresa* off the Florida coast.

The USS *Vanderbilt* seizes the British blockade-runner *Gertrude* off the Bahamas.

Admiral David D. Porter, from his flagship USS *Benton*, successfully passes 12 vessels southward past Confederate batteries on the Vicksburg bluffs, Mississippi. The action lasts two and a half hours, and despite a withering cannonade, Porter succeeds completely. Most of his vessels are struck, but only the transport *Henry Clay* sinks, and the gunboat *Forest Queen* is disabled. The squadron then berths off New Carthage, Mississippi, and prepares to transport the army of General Ulysses S. Grant.

April 17

WEST: Colonel Benjamin H. Grierson embarks on an ambitious, 16-day diversionary cavalry raid from La Grange, Tennessee, down through Mississippi and on to Baton Rouge, Louisiana. He is ordered to tear up tracks and telegraph wires and take prisoners, thereby deflecting attention away from General Ulysses S. Grant's impending move toward Vicksburg, Mississippi. To complete this 600-mile sojourn, Grierson commands 1,700 troopers of the 6th and 7th Illinois Cavalry, the 2nd Iowa, and a battery of horse artillery.

Confederate cavalry under General John S. Marmaduke departs Arkansas and commences a second raid into Missouri.

NAVAL: The USS *Wanderer* captures the Confederate schooner *Annie B.* near Egmont, Florida.

The Confederate raider *CSS Florida* under Lieutenant John N. Maffitt captures and burns the Union ship *Commonwealth* off the Brazilian coast.

April 18

POLITICS: The Confederate Congress authorizes a volunteer navy to encourage the outfitting of warships at private expense.

SOUTH: The Federal gunboat USS *Stepping Stones* under Lieutenant William B. Cushing, carrying 270 soldiers of the 8th Connecticut and 89th New York, suddenly appears before Confederate-held Fort Huger on the Nansemond River, Virginia. Before the garrison can react, the Federals push into the fort, seizing 137 prisoners and five cannon. Cushing then escapes unmolested while blame for the defeat is heaped upon the 55th North Carolina, entrusted with defending that post. Duels of honor are subsequently waged between several officers of General Evander M. Law's staff as to where blame lays.

WEST: Colonel Benjamin H. Grierson's Union cavalry column skirmishes on its line of march with Confederates at New Albany, Mississippi.

A force of 3,000 Confederates under General John S. Marmaduke is repulsed at Fayetteville, Arkansas, by a 2,000-man Union garrison.

NAVAL: The USS *Stettin* captures the Confederate steamer *St. John* off Cape Romain, South Carolina.

The USS *Gem of the Sea* sinks the British blockade-runner *Inez* at Indian River Inlet, Florida.

The USS *Susquehanna* captures the Confederate schooner *Alabama* off the Florida Gulf coast.

Armed boats from the USS *New London* and *Cayuga* are attacked and driven back to sea by Confederate forces at Sabine City, Texas.

April 19

SOUTH: President Abraham Lincoln, accompanied by General in Chief Henry W. Halleck and Secretary of War Edwin M. Stanton, visit Aquia Creek, Virginia, to ascertain military matters.

NAVAL: The USS *Housatonic* captures the Confederate sloop *Neptune* near Charleston, South Carolina.

The USS *Powhatan* seizes the Confederate schooner *Major E. Willis* off Charleston, South Carolina.

April 20

POLITICS: President Abraham Lincoln declares that the new state of West Virginia be established from the westernmost counties of Virginia as of June 20, 1863.

SOUTH: Opelousas and Washington, Louisiana, are occupied by Federal forces under General Nathaniel P. Banks.

WEST: General John D. Imboden departs Shenandoah Mountain, Virginia, with 3,365 men on a raid against the Baltimore and Ohio Railroad.

Confederate cavalry under General John S. Marmaduke skirmishes with Union troops at Patterson, Missouri.

NAVAL: A joint expedition captures a Confederate fortification at Hill's Point on the Nansemond River, Virginia, along with five cannon and 160 prisoners.

The USS *Lodona* captures the British blockade-runner *Minnie* off Bulls Bay, South Carolina.

The USS *Octorara* seizes the British blockade-runner *W. Y. Letch* off the Florida coast.

Landing parties from the USS *Port Royal* seize a large cache of cotton at Apalachicola, Florida.

The USS *Estrella, Clifton, Arizona,* and *Calhoun* bombard and capture Fort Burton, Butte á la Rose, Louisiana.

The Confederate raider CSS *Oreto* under Lieutenant Samuel W. Averett captures the Union ship *Kate Dyer* at sea, releasing it on bond.

The USS *Sterling Price* and *Tuscumbia* reconnoiter down the Mississippi River to Grand Gulf, soon to be the object of a Union assault.

April 21

WEST: General William E. Jones leads a large Confederate foray against the Baltimore and Ohio Railroad in West Virginia. He intends to rendezvous with General John D. Imboden near Oakton and Grafton.

Union cavalry under Colonel Benjamin H. Grierson skirmishes with Confederates at Palo Alto, Mississippi. Grierson, hotly pursued by Southern cavalry, cleverly splits his column in two by sending Colonel Edward Hatch of the 2nd Iowa Cavalry off to threaten the Mobile and Ohio Railroad, after which he is to beat a hasty retreat back to La Grange, Tennessee. The Confederates, as anticipated, mistakenly chase Hatch, leaving Grierson free to gallop through the heart of Mississippi virtually unopposed.

NAVAL: The USS *Octorara* captures the British blockade-runner *Handy* off the east coast of Florida.

The USS *Rachel Seaman* captures the Confederate schooner *Nymph* off Pass Cavallo, Texas.

The USS *Lafayette,* under Admiral David D. Porter's direction, bombards a Confederate battery under construction at Grand Gulf, Mississippi.

A convoy of army transports passes the batteries at Vicksburg, Mississippi, at night and under heavy fire. Of six vessels, the steamer *Tigress* sinks while *Empire City* and *Moderator* are badly damaged. The remainder join the main army under General Ulysses S. Grant at New Carthage, Mississippi, granting him the amphibious lift necessary to ferry across the Mississippi River en masse.

April 22

POLITICS: President Jefferson Davis, ever alarmed for the security of Vicksburg, Mississippi, suggests to General John C. Pemberton that he disrupt Federal activities on the Mississippi River by launching fire rafts.

WEST: Union forces under General Grenville M. Dodge battle with Confederate forces at Rock Cut, Alabama.

General John S. Marmaduke skirmishes with Union defenders at Fredericktown, Missouri.

NAVAL: The USS *Mount Vernon* captures the Confederate schooner *St. George* off New Inlet, North Carolina.

April 23

NAVAL: Confederate steamers *Merrimac, Charleston,* and *Margaret and Jessie* dart past the Union blockade and enter Wilmington, North Carolina.

The USS *Pembina* captures the Confederate sloop *Elias Beckwith* off Mobile, Alabama.

The USS *Tioga* captures the British blockade-runner *Justina* at sea.

The Confederate raider CSS *Florida* under Lieutenant John N. Maffitt captures and burns the Union bark *Henrietta* at sea.

April 24

POLITICS: President Abraham Lincoln authorizes General Order No. 100, the so-called Liber Code, an early attempt to codify and standardize laws pertaining to war.

To combat spiraling inflation, the Confederate Congress levies a 10 percent "tax kind" on all produce harvested throughout the South. This move is resented greatly by the agrarian sector, which is already subject to requisition by the Confederate commissary and quartermaster offices.

SOUTH: Union forces under General Grenville M. Dodge capture Tuscumbia, Alabama.

WEST: The Army of the Tennessee under General Ulysses S. Grant reaches Hard Times Plantation, Louisiana, on the left bank of the Mississippi River. There, he immediately prepares to ferry directly across to Bruinsville, Mississippi, and implement his strategy of encircling Vicksburg from below.

Colonel Benjamin H. Grierson's Union cavalry storms into Newton Station, Mississippi, seizing a newly arrived ammunition train and tearing up miles of valuable track belonging to the Southern Mississippi Railroad. This places Union raiders only 100 miles east of the Confederate bastion of Vicksburg, and General John C. Pemberton orders several infantry and artillery regiments from Jackson to intercept them.

Confederate cavalry under General John S. Marmaduke battle with Union forces at Mill Creek Bridge, Missouri.

NAVAL: The USS *Western World* and *Samuel Rotan* seize the Confederate schooners *Martha Ann* and *A. Carson* off Horn Harbor, Virginia.

The USS *De Soto*, obviously having a good day, captures the Confederate schooners *General Prim* and *Rapid*, along with sloops *Jane Adelie* and *Bright* in the Gulf of Mexico.

The USS *Pembina* seizes the Confederate schooner *Joe Flanner* at sea.

The Confederate raider CSS *Alabama* under Captain Raphael Semmes captures the Union whaler *Nye* off the Brazilian coast.

The Confederate raider CSS *Florida* under Lieutenant John N. Maffitt captures and sinks the Union ship *Oneida* at sea.

Admiral David D. Porter stations gunboats on the Mississippi River off the mouth of the Big Black River to isolate Confederate batteries at Grand Gulf, Mississippi.

April 25

WEST: General Dabney H. Maury assumes command of the Confederate Department of East Tennessee.

SOUTHWEST: Pro-Confederate Cherokees under Colonel Stand Watie skirmish with Union troops at Webber's Falls, Indian Territory.

Apache Indians attack Federal troops near Fort Bowie, Arizona Territory, and then withdraw.

NAVAL: The Confederate raider CSS *Georgia* under Lieutenant William L. Maury captures and sinks the Union ship *Dictator* off the Cape Verde Islands.

April 26

SOUTH: A suddenly sortie by Union troops under General Michael Corcoran surprises outposts belonging to General George E. Pickett outside of Suffolk, Virginia, but they are driven back to their lines.

West: Confederate cavalry under General John D. Imboden ride from Beverly, West Virginia, toward Buchannon, but newly arrived Union reinforcements in that area force them back to Beverly.

A column of mule-mounted Union infantry under Colonel Abel Streight rides south from Tuscumbia, Alabama, to Rome, Georgia, to wreck the Western and Atlantic Railroad.

Union forces under General John McNeil repel an attack by General John S. Marmaduke's Confederates at Cape Girardeau, Missouri, inflicting 40 dead and 200 wounded for a loss of six killed and six wounded.

Naval: The USS *Sagamore* captures the Confederate schooner *New Year* off Tortugas, Florida.

The USS *De Soto* captures the British blockade-runner *Clarita* in the Gulf of Mexico.

The Confederate raider CSS *Alabama* under Captain Raphael Semmes seizes and burns the Union ship *Dorcas Prince* east of Natal, Brazil.

April 27

South: At Falmouth, Virginia, the 134,000-strong Army of the Potomac is put in motion under General Joseph Hooker. Hooker takes 75,000 men down the banks of the Rappahannock River, intending to deploy them in the region known as the Wilderness, 10 miles behind Confederate lines. Meanwhile, an additional 40,000 troops under General John Sedgwick remain behind at Fredericksburg, Virginia, threatening the main Confederate force under General Robert E. Lee. No previous Union commander has enjoyed such a numerical preponderance over Southern forces.

West: General Simon B. Buckner replaces General Dabney H. Maury as commander of the Department of East Tennessee. Maury consequently transfers south to head the District of the Gulf in Louisiana.

Union forces surprise the Texas Legion of General Earl Van Dorn at Carter Creek Pike, Tennessee.

Naval: Armed boats from the USS *Monticello* and *Matthew Vassar* attack and sink the British blockade-runner *Golden Liner* in Murrell's Inlet, South Carolina.

The USS *Preble* is accidently destroyed by fire while at anchor off Pensacola, Florida.

April 28

South: General Joseph Hooker orders his Army of the Potomac across the Rappahannock River and into positions around Chancellorsville, Virginia, while General John Sedgwick remains with 40,000 men at Fredericksburg; hoping to distract and contain the Army of Northern Virginia under General Robert E. Lee.

West: Confederate general John S. Bowen, observing the large Union flotilla sailing toward Grand Gulf, Mississippi, hastily wires General John C. Pemberton at Vicksburg to dispatch all available reinforcements to his position. The brigades of Generals Edward D. Tracy and William E. Baldwin are put in motion that evening, racing south.

Naval: The tug *Lily* is rammed accidently by USS *Choctaw* on the Yazoo River, Mississippi, and sinks.

April 29

SOUTH: General John Stoneman's Union cavalry division crosses the Rappahannock River into Virginia and commences a major raid. He then dispatches General William W. Averell's brigade toward Gordonsville to tear up the Orange and Alexandria Railroad while he accompanies the main body under General John Buford against the Richmond, Fredericksburg and Potomac Railroad. Unfortunately, not only does this endeavor prove ineffectual, but it also strips the Army of the Potomac of its cavalry and thus its ability to scout and reconnoiter in dense terrain.

WEST: Confederate cavalry under General William E. Jones capture the Union depot at Buchannon, Virginia, taking 500 prisoners and 1,500 horses and burning several bridges.

NAVAL: The USS *Juanita* captures the Confederate schooner *Harvest* at sea north of the Bahamas.

A joint expedition consisting of the USS *Tyler, Choctaw, Baron de Kalb, Signal, Romeo, Linden, Petrel, Black Hawk,* three mortar boats, and 10 transports, wend their way up the Yazoo River in an elaborate feint toward Haynes's Bluff, Mississippi. This evolves to prevent Confederate reinforcements from shifting southward to Grand Gulf.

Admiral David D. Porter's gunboat squadron bombards Confederate batteries on the Mississippi River at Grand Gulf, Mississippi. After five hours of continuous combat, Southern cannon are silenced while the USS *Benton, Tuscumbia,* and *Pittsburgh* receive damage. That same evening, Porter's transports skirt the remaining batteries without incident as Federal forces bypass Grand Gulf altogether. Total Union losses are 18 killed and 57 wounded; the Confederates sustain three dead and 19 injured.

April 30

SOUTH: The Army of the Potomac under General Joseph Hooker marches 30 miles down the banks of the Rappahannock River and crosses 10 miles behind General Robert E. Lee's position at Fredericksburg, Virginia. Considering the size and complexity of his operation, Hooker executes it brilliantly and catches the Confederates off guard. But Lee reacts with typical boldness by once again dividing his army in the face of the enemy: Leaving 10,000 men under General Jubal A. Early to watch the Federals near Fredericksburg, he hastily marches with 50,000 men toward the crossroads at Chancellorsville.

WEST: General Ulysses S. Grant ferries the XIII Corps of General James A. McClernand and the XVII Corps of General James B. McPherson—23,000 men—across the Mississippi River at Bruinsburg, Mississippi. This critical maneuver establishes a Union bridgehead on the east bank of the river only 35 miles below the Confederate bastion of Vicksburg. "All the campaigns, labors, hardships, and exposures, from the month of December previous to this time, that had been made and endured, were for the accomplishment of this one object," Grant later reflects. Moreover, with Confederate attention fixed on General William T. Sherman's feint at Haynes's Bluff to the north and Colonel Benjamin H. Grierson's raid to the south, it is an opportune time to advance inland almost unopposed. By nightfall, Federal troops have pushed several miles inland to confront General John S. Bowen's division at Port Gibson.

NAVAL: The gunboat squadron and transports of Admiral David D. Porter cover and ferry the army of General Ulysses S. Grant across the Mississippi River at Bruinsburg, 10 miles below Grand Gulf, Mississippi. With a single, masterful stroke, Confederate defenses are neutralized, and Union forces are now able to approach the citadel of Vicksburg from the rear.

May 1

POLITICS: The third session, first Confederate Congress, adjourns. Previously, they authorized military tribunals to execute any white Union officers caught commanding African-American soldiers. Black soldiers seized in uniform, if not killed outright, are likewise to be sold into slavery.

Peace Democrat Clement L. Vallandigham gives a speech at Mount Vernon, Ohio, in which he denounces "this wicked, cruel, and unnecessary war." Such sentiments mark him for eventual arrest.

SOUTH: Advanced elements of the Army of Northern Virginia under General Thomas J. Jackson arrive near Chancellorsville, Virginia, and tangle with Union pickets nearby. However, their aggressive demeanor apparently unnerves General Joseph Hooker, who inexplicably orders his Army of the Potomac off clear terrain and into the woody morass known as the Wilderness. By this single expedient, he forfeits the strategic initiative to General Robert E. Lee, as well as neutralizes his advantages in artillery. Meanwhile, Confederate cavalry under General J. E. B. Stuart skillfully discern that the Union right flank is "in the air" and subject to be turned. Lee, sizing up his adversary's intentions, defies all tenets of military wisdom by dividing his forces a second time. He orders Jackson to take 30,000 men—the bulk of his army—on a circuitous, 14-mile end run around Hooker's right, there to deliver a crushing flank attack. Lee himself will hold Hooker's attention by aggressively posturing his remaining 20,000 men as skirmishers. Considering the sheer odds—Hooker fields 75,000 men—this is a dire expedient at best. Lee, however, is gambling on the Union leader's timidity.

General John Stoneman and his Union cavalry column skirmishes with Confederates at Rapidan Station, Virginia.

WEST: Advancing inland from Bruinsburg, Mississippi, General Ulysses S. Grant masses 23,000 men and attacks 8,000 Confederates under General John S. Bowen at Port Gibson. Grant arrays his two brigades to cover the Bruinsburg and Rodney roads, which run parallel atop a high ridge and are flanked by impassable ravines. The XIII Corps of General John A. McClernand, mustering 18,000 men, is assigned most of the fighting. The terrain, unfortunately, strongly favors the defense and Union troops wage a hard fight to evict General Martin E. Green's brigade from Rodney Road. At length, numbers prevail and Southerners gradually relinquish the field. Meanwhile, fighting along Bruinsburg Road proves equally fierce and occasions the death of Brigadier General Edward D. Tracy, but again the Confederates yield. Southern hopes are revived suddenly when Bowen receives last-minute reinforcements from Vicksburg and promptly counterattacks along Rodney Road. The Federals are unable to contain the surge until Grant personally brings up additional troops that finally turn the tide of battle. Having lost his strong defensive position, Bowen retreats rapidly beyond Bayou Pierre, burning the bridge behind him. The Union lodgement is now secure.

Port Gibson was a protracted contest, lasting from 6:00 A.M. to nearly sunset. Union losses are 131 dead, 719 wounded, and 25 missing to a Confederate tally of 68 killed, 380 wounded, and 384 missing. The Southerners perform extremely well, considering the odds, and tied up two entire Union divisions for a day. Nevertheless, Grant consolidates his beachhead as his offensive gathers momentum. The race to Vicksburg now begins in earnest. To facilitate his advance, Grant takes the bold expedient of cutting his own supply lines by carrying all essential impedimenta on his soldiers's backs and foraging off the land. Unconstrained by lines of communication, he now enjoys complete freedom of maneuver.

Confederates under General John S. Marmaduke end their latest raid into Missouri by fighting a final skirmish at Chalk Bluff along the St. Francis River, Arkansas.

Naval: Armed boats from the USS *Western World* and *Crusader* burn two Confederate schooners at Milford Haven, Virginia.

The USS *Kanawha* captures the Confederate schooner *Dart* at sea.

Union gunboats exchange fire with Confederate batteries along Haynes's Bluff, Mississippi. The USS *Choctaw* receives 53 hits, but none of the vessels are seriously impaired.

May 2

South: Proceeding all night with celerity and great marching discipline, 30,000 Confederates under General Thomas J. Jackson steal their way around the Army of the Potomac's right flank at Chancellorsville, Virginia. En route, he is observed by General Daniel E. Sickles, who sends troops off in pursuit. Jackson's move is also perceived by General Oliver O. Howard, commanding the largely German-speaking XI Corps, but he takes no precautions to guard his exposed flank. Jackson, meanwhile, competently arranges his troops into a two-mile long line across Howard's right, and at 6:00 P.M. he slashes into the Federals with a vengeance. The Germans, struck while preparing dinner, crumble under the Confederate onslaught, fleeing two miles. By then Federal resistance stiffens once they bump up against Hooker's center, and fighting bogs down in thick woods and fading light. Jackson, ignoring the mounting confusion around him, then rides forth on a personal reconnaissance mission and he is accidently shot by men of the 18th North Carolina. Nonetheless, Hooker is completely unnerved by this unexpected onslaught, and he retreats back farther into the woods, abandoning the strategic knoll called Hazel Grove without a fight. Confederate general Ambrose P. Hill assumes temporary control of II Corps after Jackson is hit, but he himself is subsequently wounded. Command then reverts to General J. E. B. Stuart.

Confederate forces under General James Longstreet abandon their siege of Suffolk, Virginia, and withdraw back to rejoin the Army of Northern Virginia.

WEST: Federal forces under General Ulysses S. Grant bridge Bayou Pierre outside Port Gibson, Mississippi, and fan out into the countryside. He next seeks to seize the town of Edwards Station, 16 miles east of Vicksburg, to cut the Vicksburg and Jackson Railroad and isolate the garrison.

Union cavalry raiders under Colonel Benjamin H. Grierson fight their final skirmish with Confederate forces at Robert's Ford on the Comite River, Louisiana, before clattering into Baton Rouge, Louisiana. Grierson concludes his spectacular raid with a loss of three dead, seven injured, nine missing, and five ill soldiers left behind for treatment. Confederates losses are estimated at 100 dead, 500 captured, 3,000 weapons taken, and more than 50 miles of railroad and telegraph lines destroyed. In light of his success, essential for masking General Ulysses S. Grant's movement across the Mississippi River, Grierson receives promotion to brigadier general.

NAVAL: The USS *Sacramento* captures the British blockade-runner *Wanderer* at Murrell's Inlet, North Carolina.

Armed boats from the USS *Roebuck* attack and seize the British blockade-runner *Emma Amelia* near St. Joseph's Bay, Florida.

The USS *Perry* captures the Confederate schooner *Alma* at sea.

The Federal gunboats USS *Cricket, Conestoga, Rattler,* and *General Bragg* commence escorting steamers to dissuade guerrilla attacks around Greenville, Mississippi.

May 3

SOUTH: At first light, the struggle renews around Chancellorsville, Virginia. General J. E. B. Stuart mounts 50 cannon atop Hazel Grove and bombards the Union forces of General Joseph Hooker. Hooker, though still outnumbering the Southerners by nearly two to one, will not relinquish his defensive posture, and terrible, confused fighting erupts in the thickly wooded Wilderness. Gradually, both Union flanks are perilously bent back. Then Hooker, suddenly stunned by a falling column, orders his army to retreat gradually toward the Rappahannock River—a move protested by many subordinates.

General Robert E. Lee arrives to take command, and he is greeted by delirious cheering from his troops. However, he has yet to make preparations to attack Hooker when intelligence is received that General John Sedgwick is advancing from Fredericksburg behind him. Convinced that Hooker is spent and lacks offensive spirit to attack, Lee unhesitatingly divides his force the third time in as many days, leaving 20,000 men to contain Hooker while he marches General Richard H. Anderson's division to meet the Union threat.

Combat at Chancellorsville occasions very heavy losses on both sides: Hooker suffers 1,606 dead, 9,762 injured, and 5,919 captured or missing (17,287) while Lee sustains 1,649 killed, 9,106 wounded, and 1,708 missing (12,463). In addition, Lee and the South are deprived of "Stonewall" Jackson, who dies shortly afterward. This loss irreparably shatters the most outstanding tactical duo of the Civil War, and the Army of Northern Virginia, while still formidable, is never quite as devastatingly effective.

General John Sedgwick's VI Corps, numbering 19,000 men, is ordered by General Joseph Hooker to storm the heights of Fredericksburg, Virginia, and then attack the Army of Northern Virginia from the west. Twice Union forces charge General Jubal A. Early's division along Marye's Heights and are as often repelled. On his third try, Sedgwick orders the men forward with unloaded muskets to settle the issue with cold steel alone. The change in tactics works stunningly, and Early is ejected from his field-works. Union losses are roughly 1,100 to 475 Southerners.

As Early's Confederates withdraw to the southwest, the VI Corps proceeds west toward Chancellorsville until it encounters General Cadmus M. Wilcox's brigade on a high ridge, on which sits Salem Church. Fighting develops further once additional Confederates under General Lafayette McLaws arrive to strengthen Wilcox. Sedgwick's men charge several times, but the Southerners, enjoying an advantage in elevation, invariably blast them back. Combat ceases once darkness settles. Sedgwick incurs 1,523 casualties while the Confederates sustain only 674.

Captain John S. Mosby surprises and defeats Union cavalry at Warrenton Junction, Virginia, and is then surprised by the 1st West Virginia Cavalry.

Union forces under General John J. Peck heavily probe Confederate lines outside of Suffolk, Virginia, eagerly ascertaining that their main body under General James

The Battle of Chancellorsville May 1–4, 1863 Lithograph by Currier & Ives *(Library of Congress)*

Longstreet has retired. Longstreet, meanwhile, leads the bulk of his command over the Blackwater River to safety. Casualties from operations around Suffolk amount to roughly 900 Confederates and 260 Federals.

WEST: Colonel Abel D. Streight surrenders 1,500 men of his "Mule Brigade" to General Nathan B. Forrest at Cedar Bluff, Alabama. Forrest, possessing only 600 men, surrounds his opponent and, by constantly parading them and a single battery of guns, bluffs Streight into believing he is actually outnumbered.

Confederate positions along Grand Gulf, Mississippi, are hastily abandoned as General Ulysses S. Grant pushes Union troops inland.

NAVAL: Confederate troops drive off armed boats from the USS *William G. Andrews* at St. Joseph's Island, Texas.

The Confederate CSS *Alabama* under Captain Raphael Semmes captures and burns the Union bark *Sea Lark* off Brazil, carrying a cargo estimated at $500,000.

The gunboat squadron of Admiral David D. Porter moves to engage Confederate batteries at Grand Gulf, Mississippi, and finds that the defenders have evacuated the post beforehand. "The Navy holds the door to Vicksburg," he writes General Ulysses S. Grant. Immediately afterward, Porter rendezvouses with Admiral David G. Farragut off the mouth of the Red River, Louisiana.

May 4

SOUTH: The Battle of Salem Church, Virginia, continues as General John Sedgwick renews his attack on Confederate positions. However, General Robert E. Lee, convinced that the main Union army at Chancellorsville is inert, boldly divides his army by dispatching General Robert Anderson's division to assist the defenders. Additional reinforcements under General Jubal A. Early also arrive and begin to press Sedgwick's men from three sides. Outnumbered and nearly outflanked, the Federals skillfully withdraw toward the Rappahannock River and entrench. After several Southern attacks are repulsed, Lee calls off the action and determines to destroy Sedgwick's force the following day. Union casualties for the day total 4,700; Confederate losses are unknown but probably as severe.

NAVAL: The USS *Chocura* and *Maratanza* capture the Confederate sloop *Express* off Charleston, South Carolina.

The USS *Kennebec* seizes the Confederate schooner *Juniper* at sea.

Admiral David D. Porter leads an expedition up the Red River consisting of USS *Benton, Lafayette, Pittsburgh, Sterling Price,* the ram *Switzerland,* and the tug *Ivy*. Meanwhile, Admiral David G. Farragut departs and sails downstream to New Orleans, Louisiana.

The USS *Albatross* and several gunboats steam up the Red River to engage Fort De Russy at Alexandria, Louisiana.

May 5

POLITICS: Having denounced the war as "wicked and cruel," Ohio senator Clement L. Vallandigham, a Northern Democrat and an outspoken Southern sympathizer, or "Copperhead," is arrested at his home by Union soldiers. As he is removed to the headquarters of General Ambrose E. Burnside at Cincinnati, Ohio, riots ensue and culminate in the burning of several pro-administration newspapers.

SOUTH: Over the protest of subordinates, General Joseph Hooker leads his recently humbled Army of the Potomac back over the Rappahannock River.

The Union VI Corps under General John Sedgwick, having been repulsed from Salem Church, Virginia, crosses the Rappahannock River at Bank's Ford to safety. This is the final action of the Chancellorsville campaign, and it occasions Union losses of 900 men to a Confederate tally of 1,200.

NAVAL: The USS *Tahoma* captures the Confederate schooner *Crazy* off Charlotte Harbor, Florida.

Federal gunboats under Admiral David D. Porter approach Fort De Russy on the Red River, Louisiana, finding it abandoned.

May 6

SOUTH: A recovering General Ambrose P. Hill succeeds General Thomas J. Jackson, who is mortally wounded, as commander of II Corps, Army of Northern Virginia.

WEST: A skirmish at Sherwood, Missouri, results in the death of 30 white and black Union soldiers. Vengeful Federals return the following day and burn the town.

NAVAL: The USS *Dragon* captures the Confederate schooner *Samuel First* off Potomac Creek, Virginia.

The USS *R. R. Cuyler* captures the Confederate steamer *Eugenie* at sea.

The Confederate raider CSS *Florida* under Lieutenant John N. Maffitt captures the Union brig *Clarence* off the Brazilian coast. The vessel is then impressed into Confederate service under Lieutenant Charles W. Read and commences raiding operations in the mid-Atlantic.

May 7

POLITICS: A pensive president Jefferson Davis wires General John C. Pemberton at Vicksburg, Mississippi, that he is "anxiously expecting further information of your active operations. . . . You may expect whatever it is in my power to do for your aid."

SOUTH: A Union cavalry column under General John Stoneman crosses Racoon Ford, Virginia, ending a less than spectacular "raid."

WEST: As General William T. Sherman begins to march his XV Corps overland from Milliken's Bend, Mississippi, the Army of the Tennessee under General Ulysses S. Grant begins a concerted drive on the state capital of Jackson.

Confederate general Earl Van Dorn is murdered in his tent at Spring Hill, Tennessee, by the angry husband of an alleged suitor.

NAVAL: Admiral David D. Porter steps ashore and accepts the surrender of Alexandria, Louisiana.

May 8

POLITICS: President Abraham Lincoln declares that all foreigners wishing to become citizens remain eligible for the draft.

SOUTH: General George Stoneman concludes his lackluster cavalry raid through northern Virginia by rejoining the Army of the Potomac, having lost only 17 killed and 75 wounded. Compared to Confederate efforts elsewhere, this effort fails to exert any impact on events at Chancellorsville and leads to Stoneman's transfer as cavalry corps commander.

WEST: General William T. Sherman's XV Corps joins General Ulysses S. Grant's main army in Mississippi.

NAVAL: The USS *Primrose* captures the Confederate schooner *Sarah Lavinia* off Corrotoman Creek, Virginia.

The USS *Canandaigua* captures the Confederate blockade-runner *Cherokee* near Charleston, South Carolina.

The USS *Flag* seizes the Confederate schooner *Amelia* off Charleston, South Carolina.

The USS *Richmond,* accompanied by several mortar boats, bombards Confederate fortifications at Port Hudson, Louisiana.

May 9

POLITICS: To oversee the new national bank, Congress appoints Hugh McCulloch to serve as comptroller of currency.

SOUTH: General Joseph E. Johnston is ordered to Mississippi to assume command of Confederate defenses there.

General Thomas W. Sherman's Federal soldiers proceed along the Amite River, Louisiana, capturing supplies and numerous prisoners.

WEST: Union oil facilities at Oiltown, West Virginia, are destroyed in a Confederate raid conducted by General William E. "Grumble" Jones.

Union forces under General Ulysses S. Grant continue advancing on Utica, Mississippi, skirmishing en route.

NAVAL: The USS *Aroostook* captures the Confederate schooner *Sea Lion* at sea.

May 10

SOUTH: General Thomas J. Jackson, known famously as "Stonewall" and admired by soldiers on both sides, dies of pneumonia at Guiney's Station, Virginia. His passing proves an irreparable loss to General Robert E. Lee and the Confederate war effort.

NAVAL: Armed boats from USS *Owasco* and *Katahdin* capture and sink the Confederate blockade-runner *Hanover* off Galveston, Texas.

The USS *Mound City* shells and destroys a Confederate battery at Warrenton, Mississippi.

May 11

POLITICS: Secretary of the Treasury Salmon P. Chase, after disputing an appointment, angrily offers to resign from President Abraham Lincoln's cabinet, but the president declines to accept.

WEST: General John C. Pemberton learns that Union forces under General Ulysses S. Grant are approaching Edwards Station rapidly, 16 miles east of Vicksburg, Mississippi, apparently to sever the Jackson and Vicksburg Railroad into the city. He therefore instructs the 4,000 men of General John Gregg's brigade to depart the capital of Jackson and contest the town of Raymond to slow their advance. Gregg arrives and accordingly sets up roadblocks, assumes defensive positions, and awaits Grant's approach.

Union cavalry under Colonel Benjamin H. Grierson cut the New Orleans and Jackson Railroad at Crystal Springs, Mississippi.

Confederate cavalry under General John S. Marmaduke skirmish with Union troops at Mount Vernon and Taylor's Creek, Arkansas.

May 12

WEST: At 9:00 A.M., General John A. Logan's 3rd Division of General James B. McPherson's XVII Corps advances on Raymond, Mississippi, encountering strong resistance from General John Gregg's Confederates. An intense firefight erupts at close range owing to the densely forested terrain, and neither side wields effective control over their units. The ground, together with intense smoke and dust, also keeps Gregg from perceiving how badly outnumbered he is. Nonetheless, he leads a charge that nearly routs the 23rd Indiana and 20th Ohio regiments until Logan personally rallies them and halts the Confederate onslaught. Additional Union forces arrive, and the long blue line surges back across the field, sweeping the rebels before them. McPherson then commits his entire corps, 12,000 strong, and cracks the Southern right wing. Gregg, finally realizing his predicament, orders a general disengagement and retreats in good order toward Jackson. McPherson spends the evening quietly bivouacked on the battlefield.

Raymond is a sharp little action lasting several hours and costs the Union 72 dead, 252 wounded, and 190 missing while the Confederates sustain 66 killed, 339 injured, and 37 missing. More significantly, the stoutness of Confederate defenses convinces General Ulysses S. Grant to alter his approach toward Vicksburg: Rather than be caught between the two fires of General John C. Pemberton in the west and General Joseph E. Johnston to the east, he seeks to overwhelm disparate Confederate forces piecemeal before they can unite.

NAVAL: The USS *Conemaugh* and *Monticello* shell and sink five Confederate schooners in Murrell's Inlet, South Carolina.

Federal gunboats ferry Union cavalry across the Tennessee River for an impending assault on Linden, Tennessee.

May 13

SOUTH: Governor Zebulon B. Vance of North Carolina complains about the high levels of Confederate deserters to President Jefferson Davis.

WEST: General Ulysses S. Grant resumes his advance toward Jackson, Mississippi, with the XV Corps of William T. Sherman and the XIII Corps of James B. McPherson moving rapidly up the Mississippi Springs Road while the XVII Corps of General John A. McClernand moves north in the direction of Clinton.

General Joseph E. Johnston arrives at Jackson, Mississippi, to find a small garrison of 6,000 men under General John Gregg and woefully predicts "I am too late." He realizes that two full Union corps presently are marching up the road toward the city, so Johnston gives the order to evacuate troops and other supplies immediately. He also instructs General John C. Pemberton to take 22,000 men from the Vicksburg garrison, march east, and catch the Federals between them. Meanwhile, Gregg makes preparations to cover Johnston's impending withdrawal.

NAVAL: Armed boats from the USS *Kingfisher* raid Edisto, South Carolina, destroying 800 bushels of cotton collected there.

The USS *Daffodil* seizes the British blockade-runner *Wonder* off Port Royal, South Carolina.

The USS *Huntsville* captures the Confederate schooner *A. J. Hodge* off the east coast of Florida.

The USS *De Soto* captures the Confederate schooner *Sea Bird* near Pensacola Bay, Florida.

The Confederate raider CSS *Florida* under Lieutenant John N. Maffitt captures and burns the Union ship *Crown Point* off the Brazilian coast.

Admiral David D. Porter, having deployed his gunboat fleet along the Red River, Louisiana, returns to Grand Gulf, Mississippi.

May 14

SOUTH: General Robert E. Lee attends a high-level strategy conference in Richmond, Virginia, where he advocates a risky but potentially rewarding scheme to invade Pennsylvania and defeat Northern forces on their own soil. Such a ploy would further discredit the Republican Party and possibly secure European intervention on the Confederacy's behalf.

General Nathaniel P. Banks begins to advance 30,000 Federal troops from Baton Rouge toward the Confederate bastion at Port Hudson, Louisiana. After Vicksburg, this is the only remaining Southern strong point on the Mississippi River; it is defended by 5,000 men under General Franklin Gardner.

WEST: At about 9:00 A.M., the advance guard of General James B. McPherson's XIII Corps makes contact with Confederate outposts before Jackson, Mississippi. However, Union movements from the west are suddenly hampered by heavy downpours, and McPherson is content simply to fire his artillery and skirmish. Meanwhile, the XV Corps of General William T. Sherman plunges ahead from the south, which forces Confederate general John Gregg to spread his 6,000 men in a thin line to contain both forces. Once the rain stops, McPherson, perceiving the fragility of Confederate defenses, suddenly orders a bayonet charge that quickly overruns Gregg's earthworks. Sherman also sends his men forward, and they seize several poorly guarded cannon. Gregg's remaining troops nevertheless fight doggedly until he receives word from General Joseph E. Johnston that army trains have evacuated the city. Gregg then expertly disengages and escapes north from the city.

Union losses at Jackson were 42 killed, 251 wounded, and seven missing whereas Confederates casualties are estimated at 200. General Ulysses S. Grant now obtains a strategic railroad junction east of Vicksburg, Mississippi, completing his stranglehold of the city. He next prepares to deal with Confederate forces under General John C. Pemberton approaching from the west.

NAVAL: Armed boats from the USS *Currituck* seize the Confederate schooner *Ladies' Delight* off Urbana, Virginia.

The USS *Fort Henry* captures the Confederate sloop *Isabella* on Waccasassa Bay, Florida.

May 15

POLITICS: Angry Federal troops storm the offices of the newspaper *Jeffersonian* at Richmond, Indiana, and ransack it on account of purported anti-Union sentiments.

WEST: General John C. Pemberton, ordered by General Joseph E. Johnston to march east from Edward's Station, Mississippi, with 22,000 men and trap General Ulysses S. Grant's Union army between them, disobeys orders. Instead, he marches south from Edwards Station toward Grand Gulf to cut the Union supply line—unaware that Grant has already done so and is living off the land.

Confederate guerrillas under William C. Quantrill skirmish with Union troops at Pleasant Hill, Missouri.

NAVAL: The USS *Canandaigua* captures the Confederate sloop *Secesh* off Charleston, South Carolina.

The USS *Kanawha* seizes the British blockade-runner *Comet* near Fort Morgan, Mobile Bay, Alabama.

Commodore James Palmer receives command of naval forces assisting in the reduction of Port Hudson, Louisiana.

May 16

WEST: General John C. Pemberton deploys his 22,000 men along a commanding elevation known locally as Champion's Hill, Mississippi, roughly halfway between Jackson and Vicksburg. He places General William W. Loring's division on his left with John S. Bowen holding the center and Carter L. Stevenson on the right. The three-mile field is dominated by thick woods and undulating fields favoring the defense, although less so at Steven's end. Pemberton also receives new orders from General Joseph E. Johnston that direct him to combine forces immediately outside Jackson, but it is too late. On comes the 32,000-strong Union army of General Ulysses S. Grant, who deploys the XIII Corps of General James B. McPherson on his right and the XVII Corps under General John A. McClernand on the left. General William T. Sherman's XV Corps is left as a garrison at Jackson to protect the Union rear.

Fighting commences at 10:00 A.M. as McPherson hits Stevenson's division on the left and a tremendous struggle ensues at close quarters. A Confederate counterattack almost pushes Union forces back into Grant's headquarters, but they are enfiladed by concentrated artillery fire and driven off in disorder. Champion's Hill changes hands no less than three times before Pemberton, running short of men, orders Loring to shift unengaged portions of his division to support the center and left. When the temperamental Loring refuses to comply, the unaided Confederates begin to collapse. By 5:30 P.M., Pemberton's army is in full flight across Baker's Creek, burning the bridge behind him. Loring's division is cut off from the main body, so he retreats to the northeast and eventually joins Johnston's forces east of Jackson.

Champion's Hill is the hardest-fought and most decisive engagement of the Vicksburg campaign. Through rapidity of movement, Grant prevents two disparate Confederate forces from uniting against him and defeats each piecemeal. Union losses are 410 dead, 1,844 wounded, and 187 missing (1,838) to a Confederate tally of 381 killed, 1,018 wounded, and 2,441 missing or captured (3,840). The Northerners also capture no less than 27 cannon. Grant finally is poised to move on Vicksburg itself.

NAVAL: The USS *Courier* captures the Confederate vessels *Angelina* and *Emeline* off the South Carolina coast.

The USS *Powhatan* captures the Confederate sloop *C. Routereau* off Charleston, South Carolina.

The USS *Two Sisters* captures the Confederate schooner *Oliver S. Breese* off the Anclote Keys. Florida.

May 17

SOUTH: A sudden Confederate cavalry raid against Union forces on the west bank of the Mississippi River secures numerous prisoners and cattle destined for the army of General Nathaniel P. Banks.

WEST: General John C. Pemberton, routed at Champion Hill the day before, prepares to defend a bridgehead along the west bank of the Big Black River 12 miles east of strategic Vicksburg, Mississippi. He places 5,000 men and 18 cannon under General John S. Bowen behind a hastily erected loop of entrenchments and cotton bales, with both flanks anchored on the Big Black. Better defensive positions are available in hills to the west, but Pemberton chose his position to reestablish contact with General William W. Loring's division, which had become separated from the main body. Unknown to Pemberton, Loring presently is marching off in the opposite direction to join General Joseph E. Johnston at Jackson.

At 5:00 A.M., the first elements of General John A. McClernand's XVII Corps encounter Bowen's pickets, and both sides gird for combat. General Eugene A. Carr sends the fresh brigade of General Michael Lawler forward to probe Confederate defenses, and he uncovers a small gap on their left. Lawler quickly orders the 21st and 23rd Indiana into the breech, with the 11th Wisconsin and 22nd Iowa in support. These units completely surprise and overpower Southerners in their sector and began to roll up their line. Bowen desperately tries shoring up his flagging formation, but additional Union units crash through his center and the entire perimeter collapses. By 10:00 A.M., Confederate forces are streaming back across the Big Black. Pemberton manages to fire the bridges over the river, but the Southerners do not stop running until they reach the outskirts of Vicksburg.

Big Black River is another debacle for the Confederates, who lose 1,751 killed, wounded, and missing, along with 18 artillery pieces. Union casualties amount to 279. In two weeks of dazzling campaigning, the road to Vicksburg is completely open to General Ulysses S. Grant.

NAVAL: The USS *Minnesota* captures the Confederate schooner *Almira Ann* on the Chickahominy River, Virginia.

The USS *Courier* seizes the Confederate schooner *Maria Bishop* off Cape Romain, South Carolina.

The USS *Kanawha* captures the Confederate schooner *Hunter* at sea.

The Confederate blockade-runner *Cuba* burns itself rather than be captured in the Gulf of Mexico by the USS *De Soto*.

May 18

DIPLOMACY: In yet another blow to Confederate aspirations, Foreign Secretary Lord Russell declares to the House of Lords that Great Britain harbors no intention of intervening in the American conflict.

WEST: General William T. Sherman leads a diversionary force up the Yazoo River, intending to storm Snyder's Bluff and Haynes's Bluff north of Vicksburg, Mississippi.

Union forces under General Ulysses S. Grant cross the Big Black River and take up storming positions outside the Confederate bastion of Vicksburg. The Confederate position appears outwardly hopeless, but General John C. Pemberton declares his intention to fight to the last. That same day, General Joseph E. Johnston wires the general and warns him against becoming trapped in the city. But for Pemberton, Vicksburg, and the Confederacy, it is all too late.

NAVAL: Armed boats from the USS *R. R. Cuyler* capture and sink the Confederate schooner *Isabel* near Fort Morgan, Mobile Bay, Alabama.

The USS *Octorara* seizes the British blockade-runner *Eagle* off the Bahamas.

The USS *Kanawha* captures the Confederate schooner *Ripple* at sea.

The USS *Shepherd Knapp* hits a reef near Cap Haitien, Haiti, and is scuttled.

Commander John Grimes leads Federal gunboats USS *Baron de Kalb, Choctaw, Linden, Romeo, Petrel,* and *Forest Rose* up the Yazoo River in concert with General William T. Sherman. The vessels subsequently shell the defenses of Vicksburg itself.

The gunboat USS *Linden,* accompanied by five army transports, attacks and destroys a Confederate battery on Island No. 82 in the Mississippi River.

May 19

POLITICS: To end divisive sentiments arising from the arrest and detainment of Congressman Clement L. Vallandigham (D-Ohio), who advocates peace, Secretary of War Edwin M. Stanton orders him released and deported to Confederate lines.

WEST: General Ulysses S. Grant, eager to attack Confederate defenses at Vicksburg, Mississippi, before they are consolidated, orders General William T. Sherman's XV Corps to attack the north fringes of the city. Despite commendable bravery and desperate fighting, the blue-clad infantry are flung back with heavy losses at the Stockade Redan. Other attacks around the city's perimeter by Generals John B. McPherson and John B. McClernand suffer similar defeat. Grant then suspends the action before trying again. Meanwhile, growing numbers of army and navy siege guns begin to play havoc on the city's inhabitants with a continuous bombardment that plays out for seven weeks.

NAVAL: The USS *Sopronia* captures the Confederate schooner *Mignnonette* off Piney Point, Virginia.

The USS *Huntsville* captures the Spanish blockade-runner *Union* off St. Petersburg, Florida.

The USS *De Soto* captures the Confederate schooner *Mississippian* in the Gulf of Mexico.

May 20

SOUTH: Union forces under General John G. Foster pursue retreating Confederates beyond Kinston, North Carolina, as Southern troops withdraw to support other threatened areas.

NAVAL: Armed boats from the USS *Louisiana* capture the Confederate schooner *R. T. Renshaw* at Tar River, North Carolina.

The USS *Amanda* is driven ashore on the Florida coast during a storm and is wrecked.

May 21

SOUTH: General Joseph E. Johnston orders General Franklin Gardner to abandon Port Hudson, Louisiana, and come to the aid of Vicksburg, Mississippi. Gardner, however, disobeys and remains strongly ensconced behind four and a half miles of earthworks and natural fortifications on a sharp bend along the Mississippi River. The following day, he is surrounded by 30,000 Federal troops under General Nathaniel P. Banks.

WEST: Confederate forces hastily abandon Yazoo City, Mississippi, in the face of an approaching Union flotilla, destroying a number of tooling shops and boat under construction.

NAVAL: The USS *Currituck, Anacostia,* and *Satellite* capture the Confederate schooner *Emily* off the mouth of the Rappahannock River.

The USS *Union* seizes the British blockade-runner *Linnet* off Charlotte Harbor, Florida.

Federal gunboats USS *Baron de Kalb, Choctaw, Forest Rose, Linden,* and *Petrel,* all directed by Commander John Grimes, steam up the Yazoo River from Haynes's Bluff, Mississippi, to Yazoo City. There they shell a Confederate navy yard and destroy three warships under construction—including one described as "a monster, 310 feet long and 70 beam . . . she would have given us much trouble."

May 22

POLITICS: The U.S. War Department establishes the Bureau of Colored Troops to better coordinate the recruitment of African Americans from all regions of the nation.

President Jefferson Davis implores General Braxton Bragg in Tennessee to come to the assistance of Vicksburg, Mississippi, if possible.

SOUTH: General Winfield S. Hancock assumes command of the II Corps, Army of the Potomac.

General Alfred Pleasonton is appointed commander of the Cavalry Corps, Army of the Potomac, replacing General George Stoneman.

WEST: General Ulysses S. Grant again launches a frontal assault on the defenses of Vicksburg, Mississippi, hitting a three-mile stretch of entrenched positions following a continuous and heavy bombardment. This time, both General William T. Sherman's XV Corps and James B. McPherson's XVII Corps are to attack simultaneously in an attempt to overpower the defenders. However, infantry movements are negated by deep, narrow ravines fronting the six strong points selected, which are also backed by a line of high breastworks. Hard fighting and heavy sacrifice avail little to the attackers, and Grant calls the action off. Of the 45,000 Union troops committed, they suffer 502 killed, 2,550 wounded, and 147 missing (3,199). Confederate casualties amount to fewer than 500. Grant then resigns himself to the formal siege operations he sought to avoid. Food shortages, intense summer heat, and unparalleled suffering by civilians are nonetheless taking their toll on the defenders.

NAVAL: The army steamer *Allison* sinks the Confederate schooner *Sea Bird* near New Bern, North Carolina.

Armed boats from USS *Fort Henry* capture the Confederate sloop *Isabella* in Waccasassa Bay, Florida.

The USS *Benton, Mound City, Carondelet,* and *Tuscumbia* resume their bombardment of Vicksburg, Mississippi. All are hit by return fire but are not seriously damaged.

May 23
POLITICS: Secretary of War John A. Seddon strongly suggests to President Jefferson Davis that Confederate forces in the Trans-Mississippi Department mount an offensive operation of some kind to relieve the pressure on Vicksburg, Mississippi. Specifically, he cites the recapture of Helena, Arkansas, as a possible objective, for it partially serves as a supply base for the army of General Ulysses S. Grant.
SOUTH: Richard S. Ewell is promoted to lieutenant general, C.S.A.
WEST: The Army of the Gulf under General Nathaniel P. Banks continues encircling Port Hudson, Louisiana, prior to making a general assault. Banks brings 30,000 men to bear against a Confederate garrison of 7,000 under General Franklin Gardner, a former New Jersey resident married into a prominent Southern family.

May 24
SOUTH: Ambrose P. Hill is appointed lieutenant general, C.S.A.

Henry Heth is appointed major general, C.S.A.
WEST: General John A. Schofield replaces General Samuel R. Curtis as commander of the Department of the Missouri.
NAVAL: Armed boats from the USS *Port Royal* capture the Confederate sloop *Fashion,* burn a repair dock at Devils's Elbow, Florida, and then move on to capture the Confederate sloop *Fashion* near Apalachicola.

Federal gunboats of the Yazoo River expedition begin to move up the adjoining Sunflower River to destroy stocks of grain gathered along its banks.

May 25
POLITICS: Peace Democrat Clement L. Vallandigham is released from prison prior to his deportation across Confederate lines at Murfreesboro, Tennessee.
WEST: An attempt by Federal forces to mine their way through Confederate defenses at Vicksburg, Mississippi, fails when a tunnel, crammed with 2,200 pounds of gunpowder is detonated, only to reveal additional enemy lines beyond.
NAVAL: Union forces skirmishing near Port Hudson, Louisiana, seize the Confederate steamers *Starlight* and *Red Chief* on the Mississippi River.

The Confederate raider CSS *Alabama* under Captain Raphael Semmes captures and burns the Union ship *Gildersleeve* off Bahía, Brazil.

May 26
POLITICS: Peace Democrat Clement L. Vallandigham is finally banished to the Confederacy for the duration of the war and is handed over at Murfreesboro, Tennessee.

SOUTH: General Nathaniel P. Banks assembles a council of war and decides to attack the formidable defenses of Port Hudson, Louisiana, directly. Banks settles on a heavy naval bombardment followed by a mass infantry assault at select points of the Confederate line. He originally intends to hit the Confederates simultaneously at several points, but coordinating the actions of subordinates proves nearly impossible over the rough terrain encountered.

NAVAL: The USS *Ceres, Shawsheen,* and *Brinker* steam up the Neuse River in support of army operations against Wilkinson's Point, North Carolina.

May 27

SOUTH: At 6:00 A.M., General Nathaniel P. Banks launches his long-anticipated attack on Confederate defenses at Port Hudson, Louisiana. The combined assaults on the northern breastworks by General Christopher Auger and Godfrey Wetzel become separated inadvertently in bad terrain and are driven off piecemeal. Once the Confederates repel their blue-clad assailants here, Gardner immediately shifts his garrison to cover other threatened portions of the line. Fighting rages for six straight hours, and Union forces gain a foothold on the embankment but are inevitably driven off. A subsequent advance by General Thomas W. Sherman also is repulsed, and Banks finally suspends the effort. Union losses are 293 dead, 1,545 wounded, and 157 missing (1,995) while the Confederates record 235 casualties.

The first attack on Port Hudson also occasions the first large-scale employment of African-American troops in battle. Mustering on the combat line are the 1st and 3rd Regiments of Louisiana Native Guards, with the former a French-speaking battalion raised among the Creole elite of New Orleans. The unit is distinguished further in its being commanded by black officers, while the newly recruited 3rd Regiment consists of former slaves led by whites. Their ill-fated charge against the 39th Mississippi at the northernmost fringes of the Confederate line is badly repulsed, but the Native Guards perform extremely well throughout their baptism of fire.

WEST: General William T. Sherman attacks Fort Hill on the Mississippi River and is repulsed.

NAVAL: The USS *Coeur de Lion* sinks the Confederate schooners *Gazelle* and *Flight* in the Yeocomico River, Virginia.

The CSS *Chattahoochee* is sunk accidently by a boiler explosion in the Chattahoochee River, Georgia, killing 18 sailors.

The USS *Brooklyn* captures the Confederate schooner *Blazer* at Pass Cavallo, Texas.

Admiral David G. Farragut's squadron, consisting of the USS *Hartford, Richmond, Genesee, Essex,* and *Monongahela,* remains actively engaged in the reduction of Port Hudson, Louisiana.

The Federal gunboat USS *Cincinnati* under Lieutenant George M. Bache is sunk by cannon fire at Fort Hill, near Vicksburg, Mississippi, suffering 25 killed and 15 missing. The vessel nonetheless goes down with it colors flying defiantly from the mast, eliciting praise from General William T. Sherman.

May 28

NORTH: The 54th Massachusetts Infantry, composed entirely of African Americans, parades through Boston under Colonel Robert G. Shaw, a wealthy Brahmin and devoted abolitionist. The unit then ships out to Hilton Head, South Carolina, for service in the siege of Charleston.

WEST: General George L. Hartsuff rises to command XXIII Corps, Army of the Tennessee.

NAVAL: The USS *Brooklyn* captures the Confederate sloop *Kate* off Point Isabel, Texas.

May 29

WEST: General Ambrose E. Burnside protests the release of Copperhead Clement L. Vallandigham from imprisonment and tenders his resignation to President Abraham Lincoln, who refuses it.

NAVAL: The USS *Cimarron* captures the Confederate blockade-runner *Evening Star* near Wassaw Sound, Georgia.

The Confederate raider CSS *Alabama* under Captain Raphael Semmes captures and burns the Union ship *Jabez Snow* in the South Atlantic.

May 30

SOUTH: General Robert E. Lee reorganizes his Army of Northern Virginia into four corps: General James Longstreet (I), General Richard S. Ewell (II), General Ambrose P. Hill (III), and General J. E. B. Stuart (Cavalry Corps).

Virginia Partisan Rangers under Captain John S. Mosby attack and burn a railroad train near Bealton, Virginia.

NAVAL: The USS *Forest Rose* and *Linden* capture and sink the Confederate vessels *Dew Drop* and *Emma Bett* on the Quiver River, Mississippi.

A Union boat expedition captures the Confederate schooner *Star* and the sloop *Victoria* at Brazos Santiago, Texas.

The USS *Rhode Island* runs the Confederate steamer *Margaret and Jessie* ashore at Eleuthera Island, Bahamas.

May 31

POLITICS: In a high-level strategy session at Richmond, Virginia, President Jefferson Davis openly expresses to General Robert E. Lee his dissatisfaction over General Joseph E. Johnston's failure to handle affairs outside Vicksburg, Mississippi, in a timely way. "Genl. Johnson did not, as you thought advisable, attack Grant promptly," he declares, "and I fear the result is that which you anticipated if time was given."

NAVAL: The USS *Pawnee* and *E. B. Hale* cover Federal troops embarkations on James Island, South Carolina.

In his latest display of interservice cooperation, Admiral David D. Porter offers General William T. Sherman two large naval guns for service ashore at Vicksburg, Mississippi, manned by naval personnel.

The USS *Carondelet* and *Forest Queen* assist Union troops to evacuate Perkins Landing on the Mississippi River, Louisiana, while keeping Confederate troops at bay with heavy support fire.

June 1

WEST: General Ambrose E. Burnside closes offices belonging to the *Chicago Times* over seemingly disloyal pronouncements, creating an uproar and another political headache for President Abraham Lincoln.

June 2

POLITICS: President Jefferson Davis orders Peace Democrat Clement L. Vallandigham transported to Wilmington, North Carolina, for detention there as an enemy alien.

NAVAL: The USS *Anacostia* and *Primrose* capture the Confederate sloop *Flying Cloud* at Tapp's Creek, Virginia.

The Confederate raider CSS *Alabama* under Captain Raphael Semmes captures and burns the Union bark *Amazonian* in the South Atlantic after an eight-hour chase.

June 3

NORTH: Benjamin H. Grierson is promoted to brigadier general, U.S. Army.

SOUTH: General Robert E. Lee begins his second invasion of the North by moving 75,000 men of the Army of Virginia from Fredericksburg, Virginia, toward the Shenandoah Valley. General Ambrose P. Hill's corps is detained temporarily near Fredericksburg until needed.

Union general Quincy A. Gilmore assumes temporary command of the Department of the South in South Carolina.

The African-American 54th Massachusetts Infantry under Colonel Robert G. Shaw disembarks at Port Royal, South Carolina. This is the first black unit raised in the North to be committed to combat operations.

WEST: Elements of the Union IX Corps under General John G. Parke begin to reinforce General Ulysses S. Grant outside Vicksburg, Mississippi.

NAVAL: The USS *Stars and Stripes* captures the Confederate sloop *Florida* at St. Mark's Bay, Florida.

The Federal ram USS *Switzerland* reconnoiters up the Atchafalaya River, Louisiana, as far as Simmesport, where it encounters heavy resistance and withdraws.

June 4

POLITICS: President Abraham Lincoln orders Secretary of War Edwin M. Stanton to revoke General Ambrose E. Burnside's suspension of the *Chicago Times*.

WEST: Skirmishing erupts between Confederates under General Braxton Bragg and General William S. Rosecrans's Union troops at Snow Hill, Tennessee.

NAVAL: The USS *Commodore McDonough, Island City,* and *Cossack* support Federal troop landings at Bluffton, South Carolina.

A naval force consisting of USS *Switzerland, Lafayette,* and *Pittsburgh* bombards Confederate positions at Simmesport, Louisiana, driving the defenders off.

June 5

SOUTH: Fighting erupts at Franklin's Crossing on the Rappahannock River as troops of General Ambrose P. Hill's command skirmish with the Union VI Corps under General John Sedgwick. Sedgwick has orders to test Confederate defenses across the river to determine whether they are still there in strength; if not, it is assumed that the Army of Northern Virginia under General Robert E. Lee has headed north to invade Maryland. Accordingly, Sedgwick's 26th New Jersey and 5th Vermont masses at Franklin's Crossing and wade across. They encounter severe sniper fire from Confederate sharpshooters along the riverbank and are driven back. Sedgwick then arrives to oversee personally the deployment of pontoon bridges across the Rappahannock, which are laid under fire. Additional Union troops then dash across, overrunning the Confederate rifle pits and taking 35 captives. Federal losses are six killed and 35 injured. The stiff resistance encountered convinces Sedgwick that the Southerners are still present in force, and he reports his findings to General Joseph Hooker. Hooker, unconvinced, next orders several cavalry forays into the countryside for further reconnaissance. Hill, meanwhile, lingers at Franklin's Crossing for another day before heading off to join Lee in Maryland.

WEST: General John G. Park arrives from North Carolina to assume command of the IX Corps near Vicksburg, Mississippi.

NAVAL: A combined expedition consisting of the USS *Commodore Morris* and *Commodore Jones,* the army gunboat *Smith Briggs,* and the transport *Winnissimet* ascend the Mattapony River, Virginia, to attack Confederate ordnance works at Walkerton. Confederate general Henry A. Wise characterizes the ensuing affair as "a daring and destructive raid."

The USS *Wissahickon* sinks an unidentified Confederate steamer off Charleston, South Carolina.

The Confederate raider CSS *Alabama* under Captain Raphael Semmes captures and burns the Union ship *Talisman* in the mid-Atlantic.

June 6

SOUTH: At Brandy Station, Virginia, General J. E. B. Stuart holds a grand review of 8,000 Confederate cavalry for a large assembly of political dignitaries and spectators gathered on railroad cars.

WEST: General Richard Taylor is ordered by Edmund Kirby-Smith to attack Union positions along Milliken's Bend, Louisiana, and relieve pressure on Vicksburg, Mississippi, across the river. Taylor musters 4,500 men for the effort, with the brigade of General Henry E. McCulloch advancing directly on the town while two others cover the northern and southern flanks. En route, the Confederate advance is detected by elements of the 10th Illinois Cavalry, who alert the commander at Milliken's Bend, Colonel Hermann Lieb. Union forces hastily make preparations to receive their visitors.

NAVAL: The USS *Tahoma* captures the grounded Confederate schooner *Statesman* near Gadsen's Point, Florida.

The Confederate raider CSS *Florida* under Lieutenant John N. Maffitt captures and burns the Union ship *Southern Cross* at sea.

The Confederate raider CSS *Clarence* under Lieutenant Charles Read, formerly a prize of CSS *Florida,* captures the Union bark *Whistling Wind* off Cape Romain, South Carolina.

The Federal gunboat USS *Tyler* seizes the Confederate steamer *Lady Walton* off the mouth of the White River, Arkansas.

June 7

SOUTH: Union forces burn Brierfield, President Jefferson Davis's plantation, as they advance below Vicksburg, Mississippi.

AT 5:30 A.M., 1,500 Confederate soldiers under General Henry E. McCulloch attack 1,061 Federals at Milliken's Bend, Louisiana, and push them back onto the river bank. Federal troops under Colonel Hermann Lieb then make a determined stand, aided by the 9th and 13th Louisiana, and 1st Mississippi, three regiments of newly recruited African Americans, who fight courageously. At length, the gunboats USS *Choctaw* and *Lexington* appear on the Mississippi River at about 7:00 A.M. and pound the attackers with heavy and accurate cannon fire. After three hours of intense fighting the Confederates withdraw. The African Americans, who suffer disproportionately high casualties, subsequently murder several Confederate prisoners after learning that they previously had killed black captives in their custody. Union losses in this affair tally 101 dead, 285 injured, and 266 missing while the Confederates sustain 44 killed, 131 wounded, and 10 missing.

SOUTHWEST: French forces occupy Mexico City at the behest of Emperor Napoleon III.

NAVAL: The Confederate raider CSS *Clarence* under Lieutenant Charles Read captures the Union schooner *Alfred H. Partridge* at sea, releasing it on a bond.

Good shooting by the Federal gunboat USS *Lexington* and ironclad *Choctaw* enfilades and helps defeat a strong Confederate thrust at Milliken's Bend, Louisiana.

June 8

SOUTH: The Army of Northern Virginia under General Robert E. Lee arrives at Culpeper Court House, Virginia, where General J. E. B. Stuart stages another elaborate cavalry review. Stuart, a jaunty, supremely confident gamecock, delights in displaying his finely honed troopers, but nonetheless he is slated to receive some rather unexpected—and very unwelcome—visitors.

At Falmouth, Virginia, General Alfred Pleasonton musters his Union cavalry corps, two infantry brigades, and six light batteries (11,000 men in all) for a reconnaissance in force across the Rappahannock River. His mission is to locate the main body of Confederates and ascertain if they are moving north on an offensive into Union territory.

NAVAL: Armed Confederate boats board and capture the Union steam tug *Boston* at Pass à l'Outre on the Mississippi River. The rebels then go on to take and burn the Union barks *Lenox* and *Texana* before boldly sailing the *Boston* past the blockading squadron and into Mobile Bay, Alabama.

The Confederate raider CSS *Georgia* seizes the Union ship *George Griswold*, releasing it on bond.

June 9

SOUTH: At 4:00 A.M., General John Buford's cavalry brigade splashes across the Rappahannock River at Beverly while, four miles downstream, a similar force under General David M. Gregg crosses at Kelly's Ford. General Alfred Pleasonton has thrown two columns against the known headquarters of General J. E. B. Stuart in an attempt to catch the wily trooper in a coordinated pincer attack. Buford, covered by a morning fog, pitches into the pickets of General William E. Jones's Confederate cavalry, rolls them back from the river, and seizes 150 prisoners. He then gallops ahead to Brandy Station, Virginia, in search of Stuart's main body.

Several of Jones's troopers frantically gallop back into Stuart's headquarters, informing him of Buford's approach. The general, with 9,500 veteran troopers scattered over a wide area, immediately dispatches riders out to reassemble the command at Brandy Station while he organizes defenses along Fleetwood Hill. Buford, meanwhile, wastes no time in driving Confederate cavalry back until they are reinforced by General Wade Hampton's brigade. A violent charge by the 12th Virginia Cavalry brings the Union advance to a halt, and combat degenerates into a series of spectacular charges and countercharges. Fleetwood Hill changes hands several times in a flurry of flashing sabers as both sides feed addition squadrons and artillery into the swirling fray, and a stalemate ensues.

At this juncture, Gregg's division surprises Stuart by making a sudden appearance south of the Confederate camp at about noon. Previously, Gregg weakened his force by detaching a column under Colonel Alfred N. Duffie on a circuitous march around the Southern position, but he remains nowhere in sight. The Union advance hesitates after encountering a single Confederate cannon, while Jackson brings up the remnants of Jones's brigade to confront this latest threat. Just then, Hampton's division finally drives Buford's tiring troopers off Fleetwood Hill while Duffie attacks Confederate outposts at Stevensburg, five miles away. Charges and countercharges continue at Brandy Station amid great displays of bravery from both sides until Pleasonton, perceiving dust clouds on the horizon, assumes that columns of Confederate infantry are approaching. He then signals his men to fall back, and the fighting dies down across the line. Union forces then draw off in good order and recross the Rappahannock.

Brandy Station is the largest mounted engagement of the war and a tactical victory for the Confederates, who held the field and inflict 936 Union casualties for the loss of 523. However, the 10-hour struggle underscores the excellent progress Union cavalry have achieved under capable leadership. Henceforth, they remain capable adversaries until the end of the war. Pleasonton also proves to General Joseph Hooker that the Army of Northern Virginia indeed is advancing northward. But most significant of all, Stuart, whose quick actions twice retrieve the day from brushes with disaster, is criticized sharply for allowing himself to be surprised. Thereafter, this dashing but sensitive leader seeks out some kind of spectacular accomplishment, worthy of praise, to retrieve his sullied reputation. The upcoming invasion of Pennsylvania promises him such an opportunity, although with fatal consequences for the South.

A total of 20 Federals are killed and another 14 wounded after a powder magazine accidentally explodes at Alexandria, Virginia.

NAVAL: The Confederate raider CSS *Clarence* under Lieutenant Charles Read captures and burns the Union brig *Mary Alvina* at sea.

A naval battery is landed under Commander Edward Terry to assist in the reduction of Port Hudson, Louisiana.

Union mortar boats resume their protracted bombardment of Vicksburg, Mississippi, attempting to cut off resupply efforts and undermine civilian morale. On average, they hurl 175 heavy explosive shells into the city every day while citizens cower in nearby caves.

June 10

NORTH: General Thomas H. Brooks assumes control of the Department of the Monongahela, Pennsylvania.

General Darius N. Couch becomes head of the Department of the Susquehanna, Pennsylvania.

SOUTH: The fateful Gettysburg campaign begins as the Confederate II Corps under General Richard S. Ewell departs Culpeper, Virginia, and tramps northward toward Maryland.

Partisans under Captain John S. Mosby surprise Union troops in camp at Seneca Mills, Maryland, and retire quickly across the Potomac River to Virginia.

WEST: The Confederate Army of Tennessee experiences something of a religious revival as General Braxton Bragg is confirmed in the Episcopalian Church.

NAVAL: Confederate prisoners overpower the Union steamer *Maple Leaf* and conduct themselves to Cape Henry, Virginia.

Admiral Samuel F. Du Pont, cognizant of the danger posed to his wooden vessels by the new Confederate ram CSS *Atlanta,* orders the ironclads USS *Weehawken* and *Nahant* to proceed immediately from Port Royal, South Carolina, to Wassaw Sound, Georgia.

June 11

POLITICS: In an act of defiance by Peace Democrats in Ohio, they nominate Clement L. Vallandigham as their gubernatorial candidate, despite the fact that the Confederate government shipped him off to Canada.

SOUTH: The African-American 54th Massachusetts Infantry participates in the burning of Darien, Georgia.

WEST: Confederate cavalry under General Nathan B. Forrest skirmish with Union troops at Triune, Tennessee.

NAVAL: The USS *Florida* captures the Confederate steamer *Calypso* trying to run the blockade off Wilmington, North Carolina.

The USS *Memphis, Stettin,* and *Ottawa* run the Confederate steamer *Havelock* aground on Folly Island in Charleston Harbor and then destroy it with gunfire.

June 12

NORTH: In light of approaching Confederate forces, Pennsylvania governor Andrew Curtin calls out the state militia.

SOUTH: The Confederate II Corps under General Richard S. Ewell crosses the Blue Ridge Mountains and descends into the Shenandoah Valley, Virginia.

Federal forces advance out of Suffolk, Virginia, and engage Confederate forces under General Daniel H. Hill at Blackwater.

General Quincy A. Gilmore formally replaces General David Hunter as commander of the Department of the South in South Carolina.

WEST: General Richard S. Ewell, advancing along the Blue Ridge Mountains of western Virginia, detaches General Richard E. Rodes's division and a cavalry brigade of General Albert G. Jenkins toward the town of Berryville. Once there, they are to drive out the 1,800-man Union garrison of Colonel Andrew T. McReynolds before marching on to Martinsburg. While en route, however, McReynolds is alerted to the Confederate approach, and he cleverly marches his unit out of town and off to Summit Point, where it will double back to the main garrison at Winchester. The garrison commander in that town, General Robert H. Milroy, had grown aware of enemy activity below him, but owing to cut telegraph wires, he never receives an order to fall back on Harper's Ferry.

NAVAL: The CSS *Clarence* under Lieutenant Charles Read captures the Union bark *Tacony* off Cape Hatteras, North Carolina, then transfers his crew and continues raiding in the new vessel. Two prizes, the schooner *Schindler* and the brig *Arabella*, are also caught and burned along with *Clarence*.

June 13

SOUTH: To counter recent Confederate moves, the Union Army of the Potomac under General Joseph Hooker repositions itself from behind the Rappahannock River to Centreville, Virginia.

Following a severe bombardment, General Nathaniel P. Banks summons General Franklin Gardner to surrender Port Hudson, Louisiana, but he steadfastly declines.

WEST: A brigade of Confederate cavalry under General Albert G. Jenkins fails to catch the retreating garrison of Colonel Andrew T. McReynolds at Berryville, Virginia, and after much riding can only engage his rear guard at Opequon Creek. The hard-marching McReynolds then joins General Robert H. Milroy's main force at Winchester that evening and prepares for defensive action there. Jenkins, meanwhile, continues to Martinsdale with the division of General Robert E. Rodes close behind in support.

General Richard S. Ewell's II Corps, meanwhile, occupies Berryville, Virginia, while planning an immediate strike against Winchester to drive out or possibly capture the Union garrison. To that end, he dispatches two divisions under General Jubal A. Early and Edward Johnson to encircle the town from three directions. The defenders are unaware of these preparations.

NAVAL: The USS *Sunflower* captures the Confederate schooner *Pushmahata* off the Tortugas, Florida.

The USS *Juniata* captures the Confederate schooner *Fashion* off the Cuban coast.

Federal gunboats resume their prolonged bombardment of Port Hudson, Louisiana, softening up that position for another Union assault on the following day.

The Confederate raider CSS *Georgia* under Lieutenant William L. Maury captures and burns the Union bark *Good Hope* at sea.

June 14

POLITICS: President Abraham Lincoln anxiously goads General Joseph Hooker into some kind of action to oppose this latest Confederate incursion. "If the head of Lee's army is at Martinsburg and the tail of it on the Plank road between Fredericksburg and Chancellorsville, the animal must be very slim somewhere. Could you not break him?"

NORTH: Hugh J. Kilpatrick is promoted to brigadier general of cavalry U.S. Army.

SOUTH: At 4:00 A.M., General Nathaniel P. Banks hurls another assault against Confederate defenses at Port Hudson, Louisiana. This time, an entire infantry division under General Halbert E. Payne charges against the strong point at Priest Cap and, despite brave efforts, recoils with heavy loss. Several hours of savage fighting ensue before Banks suspends the action and draws off with 203 killed, 1,401 wounded, and 188 missing (1,805). The well-protected Confederates lose 22 killed and 25 wounded. The Union siege then resumes, and because the fort's supply line remains cut, time is on Banks's side.

WEST: A Confederate cavalry brigade under General Albert G. Jenkins hastens on the town of Martinsburg, western Virginia, garrisoned by Colonel Benjamin F. Smith 1,500 Federal troops. Despite the odds, Smith aggressively deploys his artillery and skirmishers, halting Jenkins squarely in his tracks. As Confederates dither, Union troops strip the town of everything useful, place all materials on waiting trains, and cart them away. It is not until 5:00 P.M. that infantry under General Robert E. Rodes arrives and finally attacks the town, sweeping away a handful of remaining defenders and seizing 200 captives. But for the second time in two days, an outnumbered Union garrison eludes superior Confederate forces.

The Confederate II Corps of General Richard S. Ewell engages a Federal force under General Robert H. Milroy at Winchester, western Virginia. Milroy initially believes that Confederates to his front are simply a large raiding party, but by the time he realizes that the entire Army of Northern Virginia is bearing down on him, it is too late. He now has few options beyond sequestering his command in numerous forts as the divisions of Generals Jubal A. Early and Edward Johnson surround the town. At 6:00 P.M., 22 Confederate cannon open up on the Union works while the Louisiana brigade overruns the Star Fort, one of Milroy's key positions. The general then hastily convenes a war council that elects to spike its artillery, burn its baggage trains, and evacuate Winchester in the early morning. General Richard S. Ewell, who next appears with the remainder of the II Corps, anticipates such a withdrawal, so after nightfall, he instructs Johnson to reposition men along the Martinburg Turnpike at Stevenson's Depot and cut Milroy's retreat.

General Theophilus H. Holmes, commanding the Confederate District of Arkansas, receives orders from the Confederate War Department to mount an offensive against Helena, Arkansas. This move is perceived as the best possible way of relieving Union pressure on Vicksburg, Mississippi. But nearly three weeks elapse before the lethargic Holmes can scrape together sufficient manpower and supplies to comply.

Federal soldiers torch the town of Eunice, Arkansas, following attacks on the USS *Marmora*.

NAVAL: The USS *Lackawanna* captures the Confederate steamer *Neptune* at sea.

The Confederate raider CSS *Florida* under Lieutenant John N. Maffitt captures and burns the Union ship *Red Gauntlet* in the West Indies.

The Confederate raider CSS *Georgia* under Lieutenant William L. Maury captures the Union bark *J. W. Seaver,* releasing it on a bond.

June 15

POLITICS: President Abraham Lincoln calls for 100,000 militia to muster in Pennsylvania, Maryland, Ohio, and western Virginia to thwart recent Confederate advances northward.

NORTH: The approach of the Army of Northern Virginia on Pennsylvanian soil causes outbreaks of excitement and panic at Baltimore, Maryland.

WEST: Confederates under General Edward Johnson prepare to ambush the retiring forces of General Robert H. Milroy at Stevenson's Depot, four miles north of Winchester, Virginia. Milroy's garrison quietly departs at 1:00 A.M., taking the Martinburg Turnpike running north and then east—the most obvious route out of town. His 6,000 men continue groping along in the dark until 3:30 A.M. when they encounter General Edward Johnson's division in blocking positions. Desperate fighting erupts as Milroy attempts to outflank the Confederates, but only he and roughly 2,700 men cut their way to freedom. Among the huge haul subsequently captured by the Confederates are 2,500 prisoners, 300 wagons, 300 horses, and 23 cannon. Union combat losses add an additional 905 dead and 348 wounded to the tally while Ewell sustains 47 killed, 219 wounded, and three missing. This impressive victory removes Federal forces from the Shenandoah Valley, thereby clearing the way for General Robert E. Lee's invasion of Pennsylvania.

General Stephen A. Hurlbut orders 1,600 Union cavalry from his XVI Corps on a major sweep through northwestern Mississippi to gather supplies and disrupt the enemy.

Confederate general Joseph E. Johnston frantically wires General John C. Pemberton at Vicksburg, Mississippi, that his position is hopeless and that he must abandon the city immediately to save his army. However, Pemberton never receives the message owing to cut telegraph wires, and he remains trapped within his works by Federal forces under General Ulysses S. Grant.

NAVAL: The formidable new Confederate steam ram CSS *Atlanta* under Commander William Webb sails into the Wassaw Sound, Georgia, intending to engage Union blockaders. That evening, he positions his vessel to surprise the monitors at dawn.

The Confederate raider CSS *Tacony* under Lieutenant Charles Read captures and burns the Union brig *Umpire* off the Virginian coast.

The USS *Lackawanna* captures the Confederate steamer *Planter* in the Gulf of Mexico.

The USS *Juliet* captures the Confederate steamer *Fred Nolte* on the White River, Arkansas.

The USS *Marmora* and *Prairie Bird* land parties ashore that burn buildings and railroad equipment at Gaines Landing and Eunice, Arkansas.

The USS *General Sterling Price* and *Mound City* begin a three-day reconnaissance of the Mississippi River below Vicksburg, Mississippi, during the course of which 70 small Confederate boats are destroyed.

June 16

NORTH: General Robert E. Lee begins to ford the Potomac River at Point of Rocks, Maryland, and commences his second invasion of the North. Panic grows throughout Washington, D.C., from fear of a outright Confederate attack.

The new Confederate offensive leads to a furious spate of telegrams between General in Chief Henry W. Halleck and General Joseph Hooker as to General Robert E. Lee's intentions. Hooker wants to rush his troops north and confront Lee above Washington, D.C., while Halleck insists that he follow the Confederates and relieve the garrison at Harper's Ferry, West Virginia, en route.

SOUTH: Responding to the Southern invasion of Maryland, General Joseph Hooker begins to position the Army of the Potomac at Fairfax Court House, Virginia, to pursue.

NAVAL: The USS *Circassian* captures the Confederate sloop *John Wesley* off St. Mark's, Florida.

The Confederate raider CSS *Florida* under Lieutenant John N. Maffitt captures and burns the Union ship *B. F. Hoxie* in the West Indies.

The USS *New Era* sinks nine boats gathered by Confederates on an island north of Island No. 10 in the Mississippi River for an impending attack there.

June 17

SOUTH: As the Army of Northern Virginia under General Robert E. Lee advances north into Maryland, General J. E. B. Stuart is ordered to screen his right flank from prying Federal eyes. His Union opposite, General Alfred Pleasonton, is both determined to uncover Confederate intentions and come to grips with his grey-coated adversaries. Stuart previously had dispatched Colonel Thomas Munford, 5th Virginia Cavalry, to scout the vicinity of Aldie, Virginia, where he brushes against Union troopers under General Hugh J. Kilpatrick. An intense, four-hour fight for possession of the town ensues, with Kilpatrick getting the worst of it, but he is reinforced continually by General David M. Gregg. Simultaneously, another engagement erupts several miles away at Middleburg, when the 1st Rhode Island Cavalry of Colonel Alfred Duffie fights bravely but is overpowered by Stuart's main body. The Union troopers gradually surrender, but Duffie manages to escape with 35 men still in the saddle. Fighting then dies down for the evening; Union losses for the day total about 300 to a Confederate tally of 100.

NAVAL: The ironclads USS *Weehawken* under Captain John Rodgers, assisted by the *Nahant,* engage Commander William A. Webb and the formidable steam ram CSS *Atlanta* as it challenges the Union blockade in Wassaw Sound, Georgia. *Atlanta* grounds in the channel during its approach and subsequently is worked free, but its rudder is damaged and the ship steers erratically. *Weehawken* and *Nahant* then slip quickly into point-blank range and pound their armored adversary to good effect, dismounting two of *Atlanta's* guns and injuring crew members. When the lumbering giant grounds again, Webb finally surrenders along with 145 prisoners. This constitutes a major loss to the ever-shrinking Confederate navy.

Armed boats from the USS *Itasca* capture the Confederate blockade-runner *Miriam* off Brazos Santiago, Texas.

June 18

SOUTH: General Alfred Pleasonton, angered about losses to his cavalry command at Aldie and Middleburg, Virginia, on the previous day, makes arrangements to storm the latter town. The 16th Pennsylvania Cavalry under Colonel J. Irwin Gregg accomplishes that feat after hard fighting but then receives orders to ride quickly back to Aldie, and Middletown is abandoned and reoccupied by Southerners.

WEST: General Ulysses S. Grant summarily relieves General John A. McClernand from command of the XIII for continued insubordination and replaces him with General Edward O. C. Ord. The final straw comes when McClernand issues unauthorized laudatory statements to his men for their role in the failed assault on Vicksburg, in which he also denigrates the performance of other units.

NAVAL: The USS *Tahoma* captures the British blockade-runner *Harriet* off the Anclote Keys, Florida, and subsequently forces the British vessel *Mary James* ashore at Clearwater.

The USS *James C. Chambers* captures the Confederate schooner *Rebekah* near Tampa Bay, Florida.

The USS *Winona* breaks up a concentration of Confederate cavalry outside Plaquemine, Louisiana, thereby defeating a Confederate attempt to seize nearby Donaldsonville and cut off Union forces that are besieging Port Hudson.

June 19

NORTH: The Confederate II Corps under General Richard S. Ewell continue crossing the Potomac River into Maryland and approaches southern Pennsylvania as Generals Ambrose P. Hill and James Longstreet prepare to follow en masse.

SOUTH: In continuing actions to penetrate the Confederate cavalry screen, Colonel J. Irwin Gregg's 16th Pennsylvania retakes the town of Middleburg, Virginia, after hard fighting and 100 casualties.

NAVAL: The USS *Para* captures the Confederate schooner *Emma* off Mosquito Inlet, Florida.

A naval battery planted ashore engages and repulses Confederates forces near Cerro Gordo, Tennessee.

June 20

POLITICS: Financier Jay Cooke oversees creation of the first national bank in Philadelphia and helps spearhead the drive for Union war bonds.

NORTH: The city of Baltimore, Maryland, erects breastworks to preclude any Confederate raids there.

Skirmishing erupts between contending forces at Upperville and Haymarket, Maryland.

SOUTH: Union cavalry under General Alfred Pleasonton increases pressure on the mounted screen of General J. E. B. Stuart, now left unsupported east of the Blue Ridge Mountains. Accordingly, General David M. Gregg's division is ordered to attack General Wade Hampton's force at Goose Creek, Virginia, while another force under General John Buford threatens to flank the Confederates. Stuart, seeking to preserve his command, withdraws in good order to Upperville for the night.

WEST: West Virginia joins the Union as the 35th state and a stalwart Northern ally. Moreover, its constitution mandates the gradual elimination of slavery.

NAVAL: The USS *Primrose* captures the Confederate sloop *Richard* Vaux at Blakestone Island in the Potomac River.

The Confederate raider CSS *Alabama* under Captain Raphael Semmes captures and burns the Union bark *Conrad* at sea.

The Confederate raider CSS *Tacony* under Lieutenant Charles Read seizes the Union vessel *Isaac Webb* and releases it on a bond.

June 21

SOUTH: Union cavalry under General Hugh J. Kilpatrick skirmish with screening elements of the Army of Northern Virginia at Upperville, Virginia. The Confederate troopers of General J. E. B. Stuart, though pressured, withdraw in good order and form new defensive positions along Ashby's Gap. In light of four days of intense fighting, General Alfred Pleasonton informs General Joseph Hooker that the Confederates are definitely on the move, apparently into the Shenandoah Valley.

NAVAL: The USS *Florida* captures the Confederate schooner *Hattie* off Frying Pan Shoals, North Carolina.

The USS *Owasco* and *Cayuga* capture the Confederate sloop *Active* at Sabine Pass, Texas.

The Confederate raider CSS *Tacony* under Lieutenant Charles Read captures and burns the Union ship *Byzantium* off the New England coast.

The USS *Santiago de Cuba* captures the British blockade-runner *Victory* off Palmetto Point, Eleuthera Island, Bahamas.

June 22

NORTH: Alfred Pleasonton is appointed major general, of cavalry U.S. Army.

SOUTH: General J. E. B. Stuart receives discretionary and somewhat vague instructions from General Robert E. Lee ordering him alternately to raid Union supply lines and to guard the army's right flank as it advances northward into Pennsylvania.

WEST: General William S. Rosecrans prepares to launch his strategic flanking movement from Murfreesboro, Tennessee, toward Tullahoma to force General Braxton Bragg's Army of Tennessee behind the Tennessee River. He undertakes the offensive to preclude the chance of any Southern reinforcements reaching the besieged city of Vicksburg, Mississippi.

NAVAL: The USS *Shawsheen* captures the Confederate schooner *Henry Clay* in Spring Creek, Bay River, North Carolina.

The USS *Itasca* captures the British blockade-runner *Sea Drift* off Matagorda Island, Texas.

The Confederate raider CSS *Tacony* under Lieutenant Charles Read seizes five fishing schooners off the New England coast, burning four and releasing 75 prisoners of the fifth.

June 23

NORTH: The Army of Northern Virginia under General Robert E. Lee nears Chambersburg, Pennsylvania, with several disparate Northern columns groping along in pursuit.

SOUTH: General John A. Dix, commanding the Department of Virginia, spurs Union troops forward in an expedition from Yorktown, Virginia, to South Anna Bridge.

Confederate forces capture 1,000 Union troops at Brashear City, Louisiana.

WEST: The Army of the Cumberland under General William S. Rosecrans ends six months of inactivity at Murfreesboro, Tennessee, by advancing several columns toward Tullhoma. By moving east around General Braxton Bragg's flank, Rosecrans aspires to maneuver the enemy out of strong defensive positions and also prevent them from shipping reinforcements to aid in the defense of Vicksburg, Mississippi.

Union troops burn the town of Sibley, Missouri, after being fired on by Confederate bushwhackers.

NAVAL: Commander Pierce Crosby leads a naval expedition consisting of the Federal gunboats USS *Commodore Barney, Commodore Morris, Western World,* and *Morse* in a combined operation up the Pamunkey River, Virginia. They venture goes unmolested as far upriver as White House.

The USS *Flambeau* seizes the British blockade-runner *Bettie Cratzer* at Murrell's Inlet, South Carolina.

The USS *Pursuit* captures the Confederate sloop *Kate* at Indian River, Florida.

The Confederate raider CSS *Tacony* under Lieutenant Charles Read captures fishing schooners *Ada* and *Wanderer.*

June 24

NORTH: The I and III Corps of Generals James Longstreet and Ambrose P. Hill, respectively, reach the Potomac River and cross into Maryland en route to Pennsylvania. Skirmishing erupts in the vicinity of Antietam.

WEST: The Union Department of West Virginia is set up under the aegis of General Benjamin F. Kelley.

Elements of the Army of the Cumberland and the Army of Tennessee skirmish at Big Spring Branch, Tennessee. The flanking movement initiated by General William S. Rosecrans remains beset by inclement weather and heavy downpours, which hamper marching.

NAVAL: Admiral John A. B. Dahlgren is relieved of duties at the Washington Navy Yard and is ordered to succeed Admiral Samuel F. Du Pont as new commander of the South Atlantic Blockading Squadron.

The Confederate raider CSS *Tacony* under Lieutenant Charles W. Read captures the Union ship *Shatemuc* in New England waters and releases it on bond. At this juncture, Read decides to burn the *Tacony* and transfers his crew to a new capture, the schooner *Archer.*

The USS *Sumpter* collides with the steamer *General Meigs* in a dense fog off Hampton Roads, Virginia, and sinks.

The USS *Santiago de Cuba* captures the Confederate steamer *Britannia* off Palmetto Point, Eleuthera Island, Bahamas.

June 25

NORTH: Having briefly crossed the Potomac River into Maryland, Confederate cavalry under General J. E. B. Stuart capture 125 Union wagons and 400 prisoners at Rockville. Then, while approaching the town of Haymarket, Stuart bumps against troops of the II Corps under General Winfield S. Hancock. Stiff resistance induces him to continue circling farther east around the Union flank—and farther away from the Army of Northern Virginia.

SOUTH: General Joseph Hooker dispatches three corps under General John F. Reynolds to intercept the Army of Northern Virginia as it moves north, but the Federals depart too late and can only follow.

General J. E. B. Stuart leads three cavalry brigades north from Salem Depot, Virginia, to join the main Confederate army north of the Potomac River. However, Stuart's interpretation of his otherwise discretionary orders ultimately takes him away from the main theater of operations. Furthermore, they hinder Confederate intelligence-gathering abilities at a time when the whereabouts of pursuing Union forces are unknown.

WEST: Union forces besieging Vicksburg, Mississippi, explode 2,200 pounds of gunpowder that had been tunneled under the 3rd Louisiana redoubt. Two regiments then try to rush a gap in Confederate defenses but are stopped by additional fortifications farther back.

NAVAL: The USS *Crusader* lands armed parties, which burn several houses along Pepper Creek, Point Comfort, Virginia, in retaliation for being fired on.

The USS *Sagamore* captures the British blockade-runner *Frolic* near Crystal River, Florida.

The Confederate raider CSS *Georgia* under Lieutenant William L. Maury captures the Union ship *Constitution* at sea.

June 26

NORTH: General Jubal A. Early's division of Confederates presses on through Gettysburg, Pennsylvania, toward York.

SOUTH: Confederate cavalry under General J. E. B. Stuart continue detouring 23 miles around Union forces, heading toward Fairfax Court House, Virginia.

WEST: Large-scale fighting erupts between General William S. Rosecrans and General Braxton Bragg at Shelbyville, Tennessee. The Federals sustain 45 dead, 463 injured, and 13 missing while the Confederate tally amounts to 1,634, including many captured.

NAVAL: Admiral Andrew H. Foote dies in New York City of wounds received at the siege of Fort Donelson in February 1862.

The Confederate schooner CSS *Archer* under Lieutenant Charles W. Read boldly attacks and sinks the U.S. revenue cutter *Caleb Cushing* at Portland, Maine, but subsequently surrenders to the USS *Forest City* after expending its last ammunition. This concludes the naval career of Read who, in the span of only 19 days, captures 22 vessels, despite the 47 Union ships looking for him.

A gunboat squadron consisting of the USS *Commodore Barney, Commodore Morris, Western World,* and *Morse* covers the landing of army troops at White House on the Pamunkey River, Virginia.

Admiral David G. Farragut's vessels, including USS *Richmond, Genesee,* and *Essex* commence a heavy bombardment of Confederate positions at Port Hudson, Louisiana.

The American ship *Pembroke,* while navigating the Shimonoseki Straits of southern Japan, is fired on by coastal fortifications commanded by the local daimyo. No casualties or damage result, but the incident is reported to U.S. Navy authorities in Yokohama.

June 27

NORTH: President Abraham Lincoln appoints General George G. Meade to replace General Joseph Hooker as commander of the Army of the Potomac.

General Robert E. Lee begins to consolidate the Army of Northern Virginia around Chambersburg, Pennsylvania, with a view toward threatening the state capital of Harrisburg. The towns of Carlisle and York are occupied temporarily by Southern forces.

SOUTH: Confederate cavalry under General J. E. B. Stuart clash with Union forces at Fairfax Court House, Virginia, taking some prisoners. He approaches the town eager to secure supplies abandoned by General Joseph Hooker but is surprised and nearly captured in a sudden charge by 86 troopers of the 11th New York Cavalry. Fortunately, Stuart and his suite are quickly rescued by the 1st North Carolina Cavalry under Colonel Laurence S. Baker, who abruptly pushes the attackers back. The Confederate horsemen then easily occupy Fairfax Court House, dining on captured food, and helping themselves to ample supplies of boots and gloves. Stuart is apparently so pleased with himself that he intends to continue raiding the Union rear—instead of rejoining the Army of Northern Virginia as planned. His force crosses the Potomac River into Maryland that evening.

Confederate forces under General Thomas H. Taylor attack Donaldsonville, Louisiana, but they are repelled.

WEST: As Union forces under General William S. Rosecrans occupy Manchester, Tennessee, General Braxton Bragg decides to withdraw southward to stronger positions at Chattanooga.

NAVAL: The USS *Tioga* captures the British blockade-runner *Julia* near the Bahamas.

The Confederate raider CSS *Florida* under Lieutenant John N. Maffitt captures the Union whaler *V. H. Hill* near Bermuda and releases it on a bond.

June 28

NORTH: Confederate cavalry under General Albert G. Jenkins gallops to within four miles of Harrisburg, Pennsylvania, alarming the population.

General Robert E. Lee is startled to learn that Union forces are gathering at Frederick, Maryland, threatening his rear. Their exact intentions remain hazy as all of Lee's cavalry under General J. E. B. Stuart have departed on a raid deep into Union territory. The Confederates remain virtually blind for several days; therefore, Lee, as a precaution, orders his dispersed command to concentrate in the vicinity of Gettysburg, an important road junction in Pennsylvania.

The division of General Jubal A. Early enters York, Pennsylvania, demanding shoes, clothing, rations, and $100,000. He has to be content with some minor supplies and $28,000.

WEST: A column of Union infantry from the Army of the Cumberland captures Decherd, Tennessee, immediately following its evacuation by General Braxton Bragg's Confederates.

General John C. Pemberton, defending the vital Confederate bastion at Vicksburg, Mississippi, is petitioned by his soldiers to surrender rather than see the entire force starve to death. After a seven-week siege, the final curtain is about to fall.

General Benjamin M. Prentiss, commanding the Union garrison at Helena, Arkansas, is apprised of an impending attack by Confederate forces under General Theophilus H. Holmes. He immediately strengthens his position and solicits gunboat support from the navy.

NAVAL: Admiral Samuel P. Lee detaches vessels from the North Atlantic Blockading Squadron to assist in the defense of Baltimore and Annapolis, Maryland.

Armed boats from the USS *Fort Henry* capture the Confederate schooner *Anna Maria* in the Steinhatchee River, Florida.

The Confederate raider CSS *Georgia* under Lieutenant William L. Maury takes the Union ship *City of Bath* off the Brazilian coast.

June 29

NORTH: George A. Custer is promoted to brevet brigadier general, of cavalry U.S. Army.

The Army of the Potomac under General George G. Meade marches northward through Maryland to engage a marauding Confederate army.

General J. E. B. Stuart's cavalry, scouting for the Army of Northern Virginia, pause long enough at Halt's Woods, Maryland, to wreck tracks belonging to the Baltimore and Ohio Railroad. Then they gallop off to Westminster, brushing aside some Union skirmishers.

NAVAL: The USS *Susquehanna* and *Kanawha* capture the British blockade-runner *Ann* near Mobile Bay, Alabama.

June 30

POLITICS: President Abraham Lincoln ignores continuing pressure to reappoint General George B. McClellan as head of the Army of the Potomac.

NORTH: General John F. Reynolds is ordered by General George M. Meade to occupy the road junction at Gettysburg, Pennsylvania. Several Confederate columns are presently converging on that very point. The town is then occupied by a cavalry division under General John Buford, who, recognizing the value of the intersection, prepares his command to defend it. He briefly tangles with a Confederate brigade that withdraws in the waning daylight. Those soldiers form part of General Henry Heth's division, sent to Gettysburg to collect shoes, but when Heth reports the presence of Union forces to III Corps commander General Ambrose P. Hill, Hill blithely dismisses the notion, insisting that the Federals were still in Maryland.

Marauding Confederate cavalry under General J. E. B. Stuart skirmish with Union troops under General Elon Farnsworth at Hanover, Pennsylvania. A battle then unfolds as Union reinforcements arrive under Generals Hugh J. Kilpatrick and George Custer while the Confederates are assisted by General Fitzhugh Lee. During intense fighting in the streets of the town, Stuart exposes himself recklessly and a counactercharge by Kilpatrick nearly captures him. Stuart's gray-clad troopers momentarily fall back to the edge of town to regroup, at which point Custer sends dismounted troopers to attack Confederate artillery on Stuart's right and force them back. These troops then are driven off in turn, but Stuart is convinced that his force is imperiled so he breaks off contact by nightfall. Union losses are 19 dead, 73 injured, and 123 missing to a Confederate tally of nine killed, 50 wounded, and 58 missing. The fight at Hanover, while inconclusive, holds dire implications for the rapidly unfolding events at Gettysburg, 10 miles west. Rather than join the Army of Northern Virginia concentrating there, Stuart takes an even wider detour around pursuing Union forces and rests for the evening at Dover, Pennsylvania.

WEST: General Braxton Bragg's Army of Tennessee, outflanked by approaching Union forces, abandons Tullahoma, Tennessee, and begins to withdraw across the Tennessee River toward Chattanooga.

NAVAL: The USS *Ossipee* captures the Confederate schooner *Helena* off Mobile, Alabama.

July 1

POLITICS: The Missouri State Convention votes to end slavery on July 4, 1870.

NORTH: On this fateful morning, the Confederate division of General Henry Heth forages in the vicinity of Gettysburg, Pennsylvania, when they unexpectedly encounter dismounted Union cavalry under General John Buford. A sharp battle quickly develops as the Southerners impulsively charge and are repulsed by rapidly firing Spencer carbines. General William D. Pender's division then arrives to assist Heth just as the Union I Corps under General John F. Reynolds begins to deploy around Gettysburg. Reynolds is killed early on, and his celebrated Iron Brigade suffers severely as terrific fighting erupts along McPherson's Ridge. Gradually, Federal troops yield to the mounting Confederate onslaught and are driven back into the town. Combat intensifies further as Generals Oliver O. Howard and Abner Doubleday arrive with the XI and III Corps, respectively, as does the entire Confederate II Corps of General Richard S. Ewell. Quick maneuvering allows the rebels to roll up Howard's line, and soon union troops are also streaming through Gettysburg in confusion.

Disaster is averted when General Winfield S. Hancock comes galloping up at the head of his II Corps and occupies high ground immediately below Gettysburg along Cemetery Hill. He then rallies the shaken survivors of I and XI Corps, further strengthening the Union line. At this juncture, General Robert E. Lee rides up to supervise affairs and orders Ewell's corps to attack Union positions "if possible." Ewell, however, is concerned about the exhausted condition of his men and the strength of the craggy hills before him, so no attack ever develops. The absence of Thomas "Stonewall" Jackson at the head of the II Corps is never more keenly felt. Ewell's well-intentioned delay grants Union forces a badly needed respite and allows the bulk of the Army of the Potomac to occupy excellent defensive terrain around Gettysburg that evening. General George G. Meade arrives on the battlefield at midnight and, after reviewing his positions, determines to defend them on the morrow. Casualties for the day amount to 9,000 Federals and 6,800 Confederates. The Southerners obtain a fine tactical victory but inadvertently fumble their chances for a strategic one.

A Confederate staff rider finally locates the elusive cavalry of General J. E. B. Stuart and orders him to join General Robert E. Lee at Gettysburg, Pennsylvania, with all haste.

SOUTH: Elements of the IV and VII Corps, Army of the Potomac, under Generals George W. Getty and Erasmus D. Keyes, respectively, press ahead from White House, Virginia, in the direction of South Anna River and Bottom's Bridge.

General Daniel H. Hill gains temporary command of the Department of Richmond, Virginia, to help thwart recent Union advances.

WEST: General William S. Rosecrans climaxes his successful Tullahoma Campaign by bloodlessly occupying Chattanooga, Tennessee. This is one of the outstanding contests of maneuvering during the war, and he performs brilliantly.

General Joseph E. Johnston, commanding 32,000 men at Jackson, Mississippi, begins to push forward to assist the Confederate defenders of Vicksburg. En route, he finds his path blocked by the XV Corps of General William T. Sherman, strongly deployed behind the Big Black River.

July 2

POLITICS: Confederate vice president Alexander H. Stephens writes to President Abraham Lincoln about prisoner exchanges and potential discussions to end the war. Lincoln declares that he is not interested.

NORTH: At Gettysburg, Pennsylvania, 75,000 Confederates confront 85,000 Federals whose defensive line resembles a fish hook with its right anchored on Culp's Hill to the north and then running the length of Cemetery Ridge to a large hill called Little Round Top on its extreme left. General George G. Meade, an engineer by training, skillfully crams nearly the entire Army of the Potomac on the rugged, low-lying hills and carefully places his men and batteries to make the rough terrain work against the Confederates. The scenario is crystal clear to General James Longstreet, who remonstrates against attacking further and urges General Robert E. Lee to withdraw. Lee, however, determines to defeat the enemy where he finds them. Over Longstreet's continuing objections, he orders strong advances on both Union flanks. On the right, Ewell makes several futile and costly attempts to storm Culp's Hill, ably defended by General George S. Greene's New Yorkers, and finally earns a minor foothold on Cemetery Hill. This lodgment subsequently is lost to a sudden charge by the Union XII Corps at dawn the following day.

The bulk of fighting occurs at the Union left where Longstreet orchestrates a major drive of several divisions. The massed Confederates then suddenly encounter the Union III Corps of General Dan E. Sickles, who, against orders, pushes his command a mile ahead of the main defensive line while seeking better positions. The result creates an exposed salient that Generals John B. Hood and Lafayette McLaws charge and force themselves through, routing Sickles in the process and carrying the Peach Orchard, the Wheatfield, and Devil's Den after strenuous combat. At one point, the Southern advance actually carries them through the Union center, but a sharp countercharge by General Winfield S. Hancock seals the gap and pushes the Confederates back downhill. The crisis of the day develops on the extreme Union left at Little Round Top, which has been left ungarrisoned and on which the Confederates rapidly march. Southern artillery posted here could perilously command the entire Union left center but, at the last possible moment, General Gouverneur K. Warren rushes men and guns up on top of the hill to prevent a possible disaster.

The First Minnesota Infantry fighting at the Battle of Gettysburg, where it incurred the highest casualty rate of any unit in the Civil War *(The National Guard Heritage)*

A tremendous firefight then unfolds between Colonel Joshua Chamberlain's 20th Maine and an Alabama brigade sent to dislodge them. Chamberlain, his ammunition spent and with men falling fast around him, orders a last-ditch bayonet charge down the slopes of Little Round Top that routs the Confederates and saves Meade's left flank. Both sides subsequently draw off in the waning daylight to assess their losses and gird for another day of sacrifice. Meade, during a late night strategy session, then correctly predicts that Lee, foiled on either flank, will direct the bulk of his efforts at the Union center. This proves the most fortuitous intuition of the war—and, overnight, Meade rushes men and artillery to the threatened sector in advance.

Late in the afternoon, General J. E. B. Stuart stumbles into the headquarters of General Robert E. Lee at Gettysburg, Pennsylvania. An exasperated Lee, who entered the fight without accurate information for lack of proper reconnaissance, curtly declares, "Well, General Stuart, you are here at last."

WEST: Confederate cavalry under Colonel William L. Jackson and Union troopers led by General William W. Averill spar at Beverly, West Virginia.

General John H. Morgan leads 2,500 Confederate cavalry across the Cumberland River at Burkesville, Tennessee, on an extended foray through Kentucky, Indiana, and Ohio.

NAVAL: The USS *Samuel Rotan* seizes the Confederate schooner *Champion* off the Piantatank River, Virginia.

The USS *Cayuga* captures the Confederate sloop *Blue Bell* in the Mermentau River, Louisiana.

The USS *Covington* captures the Confederate steamer *Eureka* near Commerce, Mississippi.

The USS *Juanita* captures the British blockade-runner *Don Jose* at sea.

The Confederate raider CSS *Alabama* under Captain Raphael Semmes captures and burns the Union ship *Anna F. Schmidt* in the South Atlantic.

July 3

NORTH: Throughout the morning, General Robert E. Lee masses additional infantry and artillery along Missionary Ridge, intending to crush the Union center. Again he does so over the protests of General James Longstreet, who favors a wide turning movement around the Union left. But Lee prevails, and at 1:00 P.M., the 140 cannon of General Alexander E. Porter commence to bombard the Union line. The Federals fight back with 100 cannon of their own, initiating the largest artillery duel in American history. Most of the Southern ordnance fired overshoots the Union line, inflicting only minor damage, and after an hour, the Union cannon cease shooting to conserve ammunition. At 3:00 P.M., 15,000 Confederates from the divisions of Generals George E. Pickett, Johnston Pettigrew, and Isaac Trimble advance from the nearby wood lines in paradelike fashion. They traverse what amounts to an absolute killing ground, for the Union batteries are sited carefully to achieve mutual and interlocking fields of fire. Losing heavily at every step, the Southerners nonetheless close the distance and are greeted with concentrated rifle fire. Only a handful of surviving Confederates penetrate Meade's line and are quickly swallowed up or thrown back by Union reserves. Eventually, thousands of wounded and stunned survivors—about half the number committed—stream back across the field toward Seminary Ridge in abject defeat. Lee, surveying the carnage, is heard to murmur, "It's all my fault, my fault."

One act remained to play out. Confederate cavalry under General J. E. B. Stuart, conspicuously absent in the first two days of fighting, are now ordered to seek out and assail the Union rear. En route, Stuart encounters Union cavalry under General David M. Gregg, who fights the Southerners to a standstill in one of the biggest cavalry encounters of the war. The overworked brigade of General George A. Custer particularly distinguishes itself in repeated, headlong charges, after which Stuart draws back, his mission unfulfilled.

The debacle at Gettysburg represents the high tide of Confederate fortunes. Lee's ill-advised switch from a strategic to tactical offensive fails and proves prohibitively costly. Three days of ferocious combat against an enemy enjoying terrain advantages deprives the Army of Northern Virginia of 2,592 killed, 12,709 wounded, and 5,150 missing (20,451)—the actual loss may have been upward of 28,000—a horrific toll of irreplaceable, trained manpower. The Army of the Potomac opposing him, while victorious, is also savaged, sustaining 3,155 dead, 14,529 injured, and 5,365 missing (23,049). Magnifying the Union victory is the fact that the North can far more easily make up such losses. So with Gettysburg, along with events farther west at Vicksburg, a turning point is reached in the course of military events and fortunes. From this date forward, it is no longer a matter of if the Confederacy will lose its bid for independence but rather when.

SOUTH: Union forces abandon Suffolk, Virginia, and withdraw back to Norfolk.

WEST: Confederate cavalry under General John H. Morgan skirmish with Union troops at Columbia, Kentucky, and sustain considerable loss.

The Army of the Cumberland crosses the Elk River, Tennessee, at which point General William S. Rosecrans halts his pursuit of General Braxton Bragg. The Tullahoma campaign to maneuver his adversary out of strong defensive positions succeeds brilliantly, costing Union forces 560 casualties to a Confederate tally of 1,634, 11 cannon, and several tons of supplies captured.

General John C. Pemberton and General Ulysses S. Grant arrange an armistice and confer about surrender terms at Vicksburg, Mississippi. Grant bluntly informs his opposite: "You will be allowed to march out, the officers taking with them their side arms and clothing, and the field, staff, and cavalry officers one horse each. The rank and file will be allowed all their clothing but no other property."

General Theophilus H. Holmes, leading the Confederate District of Arkansas, assembles an army of 7,600 infantry and cavalry to attack Union positions at Helena, Arkansas. His opponent, General Benjamin M. Prentiss, is amply forewarned, diligent, and well prepared for battle.

NAVAL: Armed boats from the USS *Fort Henry* capture the Confederate sloop *Emma* off Sea Horse Key, Florida.

The onset of surrender negotiations at Vicksburg, Mississippi, signals an end to the ongoing bombardment there. Naval personnel fire 16,000 rounds from a variety of ships, gunboats, and mortar boats, in addition to 13 heavy naval guns hauled and handled ashore.

July 4

POLITICS: Confederate vice president Alexander H. Stephens rides the CSS *Torpedo* down the James River under a flag of truce and steams to Hampton Roads, Virginia. There he hopes to meets with Union officials in an attempt to spur dialogue between the two governments, but Federal authorities turn him back.

NORTH: Despite pleas and entreaties from President Abraham Lincoln, General George G. Meade declines to pursue or hound the fleeing Confederates. In light of the horrific casualties recently sustained by his Army of the Potomac, its many officer losses and depleted units, his reluctance is understandable.

The Army of Northern Virginia under General Robert E. Lee withdraws in good order from Gettysburg, Pennsylvania, and marches for Williamsport, Maryland, to recross the Potomac River back to Virginia. Progress is slow owing to incessant rain and a wagon train of wounded stretching 17 miles, but the Federals decline to push the Southerners hard.

WEST: General John H. Morgan's Confederate cavalry are rebuffed at Green River Bridge, Kentucky.

Vicksburg surrenders to General Ulysses S. Grant after a brutal, seven-week siege. Union losses for the entire campaign amount to roughly 800 killed, 3,900 injured, and 200 missing out of 77,000 committed. The Confederates suffer 900 dead, 2,500 wounded, 200 missing, and 29,491 captured. Surrender at Vicksburg also facilitated the capture of Port Hudson, downstream, four days later. The Confederacy now is cut completely in twain along the Mississippi River, with virtually no ability left to transfer desperately needed food, manpower, or munitions to either side. Thanks to Grant's offensive brilliance, tactical savvy, and ruthlessness to succeed, another tipping point has been reached in military affairs—henceforth, there is no turning back. "Grant is my man," an ebullient president Abraham Lincoln beams, "and I am his the rest of the war."

Union forces defending Helena, Arkansas, under General Benjamin M. Prentiss withstand a determined Confederate attack from Generals Theophilus H. Holmes and Sterling Price. At about 5:00 A.M., Price launches an early morning assault that manages to overrun Union Battery C, but that post then is bombarded thoroughly by surrounding batteries and the gunboat USS *Tyler* on the Mississippi River. Unable to make further headway and unwilling to withstand the a withering cannonade, Price concedes defeat and withdraws at about 11:00 A.M. Southern losses in this badly bungled venture are 380 killed, 1,100 wounded, and another 1,100 taken captive from 7,600 present. The 4,100 Federals lose only 239 killed, wounded, or missing.

Chief Little Crow, who initiated the Santee (Sioux) uprising in Minnesota almost a year earlier, is shot dead by farmers while picking berries.

NAVAL: Following Vicksburg's capitulation, Admiral David D. Porter's gunboat squadron hoists anchor and sails south to facilitate Port Hudson's reduction.

The Federal gunboat USS *Tyler* intervenes decisively in the defense of Helena, Arkansas, against large Confederate forces, and heavy fire prompts them to retreat.

July 5

NORTH: The retreating Army of Northern Virginia under General Robert E. Lee skirmishes with pursuing Union forces at Cunningham's Cross Roads, Pennsylvania.

SOUTH: General Henry W. Wessels leads a Union expedition from Plymouth, North Carolina, toward Confederate troop concentrations at nearby Williamston.

WEST: Confederate cavalry under General John H. Morgan skirmish with Union troops at Bardstown and Lebanon, Kentucky, taking 400 prisoners. Among the Confederates slain is Morgan's younger brother Thomas.

General William T. Sherman marches from Vicksburg, Mississippi, with 40,000 men in three corps (11 divisions) under Generals Frederick Steele, Edward O. C. Ord, and John G. Parke to recapture Jackson. His first mission is to drive General Joseph E. Johnston's army from behind the Big Black River. The contending forces skirmish along Birdsong Ferry before Union troops construct several bridges and begin to ford. Johnston then retires in good order back to Jackson as Sherman methodically pushes his army forward in pursuit.

July 6

NORTH: The battered Confederate Army of Northern Virginia tramps through Hagerstown, Maryland, unhurried and in excellent marching order. The column then halts at Williamsport to construct pontoon bridges, but the rain-swollen Potomac River remains unfordable for several days. In a desperate and heroic rearguard action, General John D. Imboden thwarts a surprise attack on the Confederate wagon train by General Hugh J. Kilpatrick and John Buford. Imboden skillfully resists until reinforcements under General J. E. B. Stuart arrive and force the Union troopers off.

WEST: The Knights of the Golden Circle, a violent Copperhead group, seize guns and ammunition from a Federal arsenal at Huntington, Indiana.

General William T. Sherman continues pursuing Confederate forces under General Joseph E. Johnston to the vicinity of Jackson, Mississippi.

NAVAL: Admiral John A. Dahlgren relieves Admiral Samuel F. Du Pont of command of the North Atlantic Blockading Squadron off Port Royal, South Carolina. Du Pont's removal is as much about mounting friction with Secretary of the Navy Gideon Welles as it is about his failure before Charleston.

The USS *De Soto* captures the Confederate blockade-runner *Lady Maria* off Clearwater, Florida.

The Confederate raider CSS *Alabama* under Captain Raphael Semmes captures and burns the Union ship *Express* off the Brazilian coast.

July 7

POLITICS: President Abraham Lincoln, buoyed by the news of Vicksburg's surrender, writes, "if General Meade can complete his work, so gloriously prosecuted thus far, by the literal or substantial destruction of Lee's army, the rebellion will be over."

NORTH: The Army of the Potomac under General George G. Meade reoccupies Maryland Heights, Maryland, while President Abraham Lincoln frets over the lack of a more vigorous pursuit.

WEST: Confederate cavalry under General John H. Morgan skirmish with Union troops at Shepherdsville, Kentucky.

General Joseph E. Johnston deploys 26,000 in earthworks in and around Jackson, Mississippi, awaiting an onslaught by superior Union forces under General William T. Sherman. He possesses the divisions of General William W. Loring, John C. Breckinridge, Samuel G. French, and William H. T. Walker, along with a cavalry division under William H. Jackson.

SOUTHWEST: Colonel Kit Carson recruits Ute and Zuni Indians in his continuing campaign against the Navajo.

NAVAL: Confederate raiders under Colonel John H. Morgan seize the steamers *John T. McCombs* and *Alice Dean* at Brandenburg, Kentucky.

The USS *Monongahela* and *New London* trade shots with Confederates batteries near Donaldsonville, Louisiana.

The Confederate raider CSS *Florida* under Lieutenant John N. Maffitt captures the Union ship *Sunrise,* releasing it on a bond.

July 8

North: General Andrew A. Humphreys is designated chief of staff, Army of the Potomac.

South: Generals Nathaniel P. Banks and Franklin Gardner negotiate for the surrender of Port Hudson, Louisiana. Gardner, while low on food, initially balks at capitulation until hearing of Vicksburg's demise.

West: General John H. Morgan crosses the Ohio River at Cumming's Ferry, Kentucky, and begins to raid Indiana and southern Ohio. There is some apprehension that Morgan's presence might rekindle pro-Confederate Copperhead activities in that region.

Naval: Armed boats from the USS *Restless* and *Rosalie* seize the Confederate schooner *Ann* in Horse Creek, Florida.

A Federal gunboat squadron sails 500 miles up the Ohio River to help thwart a Confederate cavalry raid mounted by Colonel John H. Morgan. En route, they recapture the steamers *John T. McCombs* and *Alice Dean.*

July 9

South: An accidental ordnance explosion at Fort Lyon, Virginia, kills 20 Union soldiers and wounds 14 more.

General Quincy A. Gillmore orders the landing of troops on James Island, west of Morris Island, Charleston Harbor, South Carolina, as a diversion prior to launching an all-out assault on Battery Wagner. The operation concludes without serious resistance.

After a heroic, 47-day siege, Confederate general Franklin Gardner surrenders Port Hudson, Louisiana, to the Army of the Gulf under General Nathaniel P. Banks. The Southerners lose roughly 146 killed, 447 wounded and 6,400 captured while Union losses top 708 dead, 3,336 injured, and 319 missing. Another 4,000 to 5,000 men are incapacitated by disease or heat stroke. But victory here removes the last Confederate obstruction on the Mississippi River, which can now be navigated freely as far north as St. Louis, Missouri.

West: General John H. Morgan's Confederate raiders skirmish with Union troops at Corydon, Indiana.

General William T. Sherman and three corps continue advancing on Jackson, Mississippi, skirmishing while approaching the town of Clinton. General Joseph E. Johnston, commanding the Confederate Department of the West, hastily makes preparations to resist his onslaught.

Naval: Armed boats from the USS *Tahoma* seize a large flatboat loaded with supplies near Manatee River, Florida.

July 10

North: Quincy A. Gillmore is promoted to major general, U.S. Army, replacing General David Hunter as commander of the Department of the South. He inherits a force of 11,000 soldiers, 350 cannon, and 400 engineers, along with orders to capture Charleston, South Carolina. This he prepares to do in earnest.

General Robert E. Lee begins to concentrate his forces around Williamsport, Maryland, while Union forces skirmish with his rear guard.

South: The siege of Charleston, South Carolina, begins as General Quincy A. Gillmore lands 3,700 Federal troops of General George C. Strong's brigade on Morris Island, overpowering Confederate forces stationed there. Gillmore next begins to prepare to carry Battery Wagner, a strategic point garrisoned by General William B. Taliaferro. This officer commands 900 men and several cannon in a stout, low-lying sand-and-palmetto fortification whose strength belies its nondescript appearance. Many Northerners also regard Charleston as the "cradle of the Confederacy," and its capture remains a political imperative. Initial operations here cost Union forces 15 dead and 91 injured; Confederate losses are 294 killed, wounded, and missing.

As a diversion for the impending assault against Battery Wagner, Gilmore dispatches Colonel Thomas W. Higginson on an expedition to burn a bridge on the South Edisto River below Morris Island. This consists of 250 men of his own 1st South Carolina Colored Infantry and the 1st Connecticut Battery, carried by a steamer, a tug, and a transport. Things quickly go awry when progress up the Edisto halts at the confluence of the Pon Pon River, where sharp timber spikes were thrown across the river's neck. While negotiating these obstacles, the tug *Governor Milton* and the transport *Enoch Dean* ground while being shelled by Confederate land batteries along Willstown Bluff. After several failed attempts to attack the bridge, Higgson orders the grounded ships burned, and he steams back to base.

West: Confederate raiders under General John H. Morgan skirmish with Union troops at Salem, Indiana.

A quick raid on Union City, Tennessee, by Confederate troops under Colonel J. B. Biffle nets 100 Federal prisoners.

Union forces under General William T. Sherman begin to invest the state capital of Jackson, Mississippi, intending to drive off Confederates under General Joseph E. Johnston.

Naval: The USS *Shenandoah* and *Ethan Allen* sortie from Boston Navy Yard, Massachusetts, to scour the seas for the Confederate raider CSS *Florida.*

Admiral John A. Dahlgren initiates a second naval siege of Charleston, South Carolina, by bombarding Confederate positions on Morris Island. The ironclads USS *Nahant, Weehawken, Catskill,* and *Montauk* subsequently are damaged by Confederate artillery fire, none seriously. This attack also signals another prolonged period of shelling at Charleston.

The USS *New London,* steaming from Donaldsonville, Louisiana, to New Orleans, is attacked en route by Confederate artillery and damaged.

July 11

Diplomacy: American minister to Britain Charles F. Adams strongly denounces the British practice of building ironclads and outfitting blockade-runners for the Confederacy. He makes clear to Foreign Secretary Earl John Russell that Northern patience is running out over such transgressions.

North: The implementation of the draft law stirs resentment among New York's lower classes, which are mostly Irish and highly resentful toward African Americans.

SOUTH: General Daniel H. Hill is appointed lieutenant general, C.S.A., over the objections of President Jefferson Davis, who resents Hill's criticism of his good friend and confidant General Braxton Bragg.

A Union assault on Battery Wagner, Charleston Harbor, South Carolina, is launched by General Quincy A. Gillmore. The force consists of several companies of the 7th Connecticut, backed up by additional men from the 9th Maine and 76th Pennsylvania. However, Gillmore seriously underestimates Southern defenses and is unaware that the garrison had been enlarged to 1,200 men recently. Owing to the island's peculiar geography, all attacks funneling along a narrow strip of beach are amply covered by the fort's heavy cannon. The ensuing assault is easily beaten back with a Union loss of 49 killed, 123 wounded, and 167 missing while the Confederates sustain only six dead and six wounded. The besiegers then bring up an assortment of 40-rifled cannon and mortars and maintain a relentless barrage until another attack can be mounted.

NAVAL: The USS *Yankee* captures the Confederate schooner *Cassandra* at Jones Point on the Rappahannock River.

July 12

NORTH: The Army of the Potomac under General George G. Meade advances to Williamsport, Maryland, to confront the Army of Northern Virginia under General Robert E. Lee. Once Meade beholds the array of Confederate earthworks stretching for several miles, however, he relents from attacking and builds fortifications of his own.

WEST: General John H. Morgan's raiding party reaches Vernon, Indiana.

Troops under Generals William T. Sherman and Joseph E. Johnston spar in the vicinity of Clinton, Mississippi. Union forces unleash a lengthy bombardment of Confederate fortifications, and suddenly a brigade under Colonel Isaac Pugh attacks Confederate redoubts defended by General John C. Breckinridge. Pugh does so unsupported and without authorization, losing 500 out of 800 men. Consequently, General Jacob G. Lauman, Pugh's divisional commander, is relieved of command.

NAVAL: The USS *Penobscot* forces the Confederate blockade-runner *Kate* ashore at Smith's Island, North Carolina, but fails to destroy it.

July 13

POLITICS: President Abraham Lincoln admonishes General John M. Schofield, commanding in Missouri, over his arrest of William McKee, editor of the *St. Louis Missouri Democrat,* for alleged antiwar activity.

NORTH: Violent antidraft riots erupt in New York shortly after the first names are drawn for induction. At length, a seething mob of 50,000 Irish émigrés attacks the draft office, burning it to the ground. During the next four days, violence escalates until Federal troops are brought in to restore order. More than 1,000 people, principally African Americans targeted by the Irish, are killed or injured.

At Williamsport, Maryland, General Robert E. Lee orders pontoon bridges thrown immediately across the Potomac River, as waters levels begin to subside. That same day, General George G. Meade orders a cavalry reconnaissance of Confederate positions at Williamsport for the following morning.

SOUTH: The Army of Northern Virginia under General Robert E. Lee begins to cross the Potomac River back into Virginia, ending his celebrated and costly second invasion of the North.

Major fighting erupts along Bayou La Fourche, Louisiana, as the Union brigades of Colonel Nathan A. M. Dudley and Joseph S. Morgan advance down both banks to dislodge a Confederate force under General Joseph Green. Green, however, decides to strike first and, with only 700 troops at his disposal, strikes Dudley on both flanks simultaneously. The Federal force quickly folds and falls back in confusion. On the east bank, Morgan's brigade advances to engage with a smaller party of 400 Confederates, but their commander inexplicably panics and withdraws. The emboldened Southerners then charge, routing their opponents. The disgraced Morgan retreats all the way back to Donaldsonville, Louisiana, where he is accused of inebriation and is discharged.

WEST: General John H. Morgan takes his Confederate cavalry into Ohio, and martial law is declared in Cincinnati.

Yazoo City and Natchez, Mississippi, fall to Union forces under General Francis J. Herron.

NAVAL: Commodore Hiram Paulding positions gunboats around New York City to help restore order during the draft riots there.

The USS *Katahdin* captures the British blockade-runner *Excelsior* at San Luis Pass, Texas.

The USS *Forest Rose* and *Petrel* capture the Confederate steamer *Elmira* on the Tensas River, Louisiana.

The USS *Rattler* and *Manitou* capture the Confederate steamer *Louisville* in the Little Red River, Louisiana.

A river squadron consisting of the USS *Baron de Kalb, Kenwood, Signal, New National,* and *Black Hawk* convoys 5,000 Union troops up the Yazoo River to attack Yazoo City, Mississippi. The town falls, and 17 Confederate vessels are scuttled, but the *Baron de Kalb* hits a mine and sinks.

Commander David S. McDougal of the USS *Wyoming,* apprised of the unprovoked attack on the American vessel *Pembroke* in the Shimonoseki Straits, Japan, weighs anchor at Yokohama and prepares to deal directly with the offenders.

July 14

POLITICS: President Abraham Lincoln, disillusioned by General George G. Meade's lax pursuit of retreating Confederates, indelicately informs him, "Your golden opportunity is gone and I am distressed immeasurably because of it."

NORTH: The Army of Northern Virginia steadily evacuates Willamsport, Maryland, after throwing pontoon bridges across the Potomac River and marching back into Virginia. The main force arrives in safety, leaving behind two divisions under General Henry Heth as a rear guard. However, at 7:00 A.M., General George A. Custer's cavalry brigade sweeps into nearby Falling Waters, rounding up several stragglers. General John Buford's division is also en route, but General Hugh J. Kilpatrick arrives first and orders two companies of the 6th Michigan Cavalry to charge two entire Confederate brigades. They sacrifice themselves heroically, and in the ensuing melee manage to mortally wound the capable Confederate general James J. Pettigrew, a popular and effective officer. Custer then throws the balance of his regiment forward as skirmishers, just as Buford's division deploys behind the Southerners. In brief fighting, the Federals capture 719 prisoners, three battle flags, and two cannon, but Confederate losses would have been far greater had Kilpatrick restrained himself until all his cavalry was up in force. This action concludes General Robert E. Lee's second invasion of the north.

SOUTH: Union forces capture Fort Powhatan on the James River, Virginia, which opens that waterway to naval forces as far as Drewry's Bluff.

WEST: General John H. Morgan's Confederate raiders skirmish with Union troops at Camp Dennison, outside Cincinnati, Ohio.

General Joseph E. Johnston, entrenched at Jackson, Mississippi, learns of a large Federal ammunition supply wagon headed from Vicksburg to reinforce the army of General William T. Sherman before him. He thereupon dispatches his entire cavalry force under General William H. Jackson to intercept these supplies and preclude Sherman's anticipated bombardment. After the effort fails, Johnston feels he has little recourse but to abandon the town in the face of overwhelming numbers.

NAVAL: The Federal gunboat squadron under Admiral Samuel P. Lee consisting of USS *Sagamon, Lehigh, Mahaska, Morse, Commodore Barry, Commodore Jones, Shokokon,* and *Seymour* capture Fort Powhatan on the James River, Virginia.

The USS *R. R. Cuyler* captures the Confederate steamer *Kate Dale* off the Tortugas, Florida.

The USS *Jasmine* seizes the Confederate sloop *Relampago* off the Florida Keys.

July 15

POLITICS: Stricken by news of Gettysburg, Vicksburg, and Port Hudson, a somber president Jefferson Davis intones, "The clouds are truly dark over us."

WEST: Confederate raiders under General John H. Morgan, stymied by stiffening Federal resistance, swing west of Cincinnati, preparing to recross the Ohio River. Union forces on both land and water are in hot pursuit and are closing the gap.

SOUTHWEST: After the Arkansas River becomes fordable, Union general James G. Blunt assembles 3,000 men (mostly Indians and African Americans) and two batteries for a preemptive strike against 6,000 Confederates gathering at Elk Creek, Indian Territory. He intends to disperse General Douglas H. Cooper's command before he is reinforced by 3,000 additional Confederates under General William L. Cabell. Should such a preponderance of numbers concentrate, they will force Federal troops to surrender Fort Gibson, Indiana Territory, thereby ceding control of the region to the South.

NAVAL: The USS *Yankee* captures the Confederate schooner *Nanjemoy* in the Coan River, Virginia.

Armed boats from the USS *Stars and Stripes* and *Somerset* destroy Confederate saltworks at Marsh's Island, Florida.

The USS *Santiago de Cuba* captures the Confederate steamer *Lizzie* off the Florida coast.

July 16

SOUTH: Union troops under General Alfred H. Terry repel a determined Confederate attack on James Island, South Carolina, despite heavy shelling from Grimball's Landing on the nearby Stono River.

WEST: General Joseph E. Johnston begins a nighttime evacuation of Jackson, Mississippi, rather than face envelopment by General William T. Sherman. He accordingly falls back across the Pearl River in the darkness and withdraws to Morton, 30 miles farther east. Confederate casualties in the "siege" of Jackson total about 600 while Sherman's losses are 1,122.

NAVAL: The steamer *Imperial* docks at New Orleans, Louisiana, from St. Louis, Missouri. It is the first vessel to travel the Mississippi River in uninterrupted fashion for more than two years.

The USS *Pawnee* and *Marblehead* are hit repeatedly during a Confederate assault on Union positions on James Island, South Carolina. They nonetheless respond with heavy supporting fire, and the attackers are driven off with loss.

Armed boats from the USS *Port Royal* seize a cotton shipment ready for departure through the blockade at Apalachicola, Florida.

The Confederate raider CSS *Georgia* under Lieutenant William L. Maury captures the Union ship *Prince of Wales* and releases it on a bond.

The USS *Wyoming* under Commander David S. McDougal is fired on by several Japanese shore batteries while passing Shimonoseki Straits, Japan. A flotilla of small junks and steamers then sorties to engage him. *Wyoming* counters by firing heavy guns at close range, completely gutting the Japanese vessels and silencing the batteries. American losses are four dead and seven wounded. The attack had been mounted by the daimyo of Chosu, who determines to embarrass the Tokugawa shogunate and possibly hasten its downfall.

Confederate naval agent James D. Bulloch contracts with the French firm of Lucien Arman to construct an ironclad warship that eventually emerges as CSS *Stonewall*.

July 17

SOUTH: Federal siege guns continue flailing away at Battery Wagner, Charleston Harbor, South Carolina, in preparation for a second assault. The 1,300 Confederate defenders remain safely ensconced in their bombproofs and, despite a deluge of ordnance pouring down on them, suffer only eight killed and 20 wounded in two days.

WEST: Jackson, Mississippi, falls a second time to Union forces under General William T. Sherman. He orders the division of General Frank P. Blair to protect the civilian population from looting, but the town is sacked nonetheless by vengeful Northerners.

SOUTHWEST: A force of 3,000 Union troops under General James G. Blunt attack General Douglas H. Cooper's 6,000 Confederate Choctaw, Cherokee, and Texans at Honey Springs, Indian Territory. Cooper enjoys larger numbers, but Blunt possesses more cannon and higher-quality ammunition. Following a protracted artillery duel, Blunt sends his 1st Kansas Colored Infantry and 2nd Indian Home Guard forward against the Confederate center. They are received hotly by the dismounted 20th and 29th Texas Cavalry, whose heavy fire routs the Federal Indians. This induces the Texans to charge

home against the 1st Colored, which bravely holds its ground and allows the scream-
ing rebels to approach closely before devastating them with point-blank volleys. The
Texans suddenly turn and run, taking a large part of Cooper's center with them.

Aggressive by nature, Blunt advances and outflanks Douglas twice before his
Indians mount a whooping counterattack that fails, but that buys them sufficient
time to cross the Elk River to safety. Union forces then charge into the Confederate
encampment at Elk Creek, burning tons of valuable supplies and safely withdrawing
before General William L. Cabell's division arrives. Blunt's prompt action saves the
Indian Territory for the Union. Honey Springs is also the largest encounter waged
in the Indian territory; Union losses are recorded as 13 dead and 47 captured to a
Confederate loss estimated at 134 killed and wounded, with 47 missing. Curiously,
this was the first time that Native Americans found themselves pitted against African Americans, who greatly distinguished themselves in combat.

NAVAL: The Federal ram USS *Monarch* assists Union troops in recapturing Hickman, Kentucky, from Confederate cavalry.

July 18

SOUTH: A second Federal assault on Battery Wagner, Charleston Harbor, South Carolina, devolves on two brigades of 6,000 men under Colonel H. S. Putnam and General Thomas G. Stevenson. The attack, which kicks off at 7:45 P.M., is courageously
spearheaded by Colonel Robert G. Shaw's African-American 54th Massachusetts,
which, ignoring heavy fire and losses, clambers up the Confederate parapet and
plants its flag. Consequently, Sergeant William H. Carney becomes the first African-American soldier to win the Medal of Honor in this conflict. Other Union columns also score minor lodgments elsewhere, but the roused Confederates quickly
contain or eject all of them. Extremely heavy losses ensue, including five out of six
regimental commanders, and General Quincy A. Gillmore calls off the attempt.
Union casualties total 246 dead, 880 wounded, and 389 missing (1,515), including
the heroic Colonel Shaw. Moreover, the exemplary conduct of his 54th Massachusetts Infantry affords dramatic proof that African Americans will and can fight well
if only given the chance. The Confederates, meanwhile, suffer only 36 killed, 133
wounded, and five missing. This latest repulse induces Gilmore to initiate formal
siege operations.

General Edward E. Potter leads a Federal expedition from New Bern, North
Carolina, against nearby Rocky Mount.

General John G. Foster takes command of the Department of Virginia and
North Carolina.

WEST: A skirmish at Pomeroy, Ohio, indicates that Federal troops are closing their
noose around Confederate raiders under General John H. Morgan.

NAVAL: Gunfire from the USS *Jacob Bell, Resolute,* and *Racer* drive off Confederate
infantry attempting to capture the Federal vessel *George Peabody,* which had run
aground at Matthias Point, Virginia.

Admiral John A. B. Dahlgren's ironclad squadron, consisting of the USS *Montauk, New Ironsides, Catskill, Nantucket, Weehawken,* and *Patapsco,* lends heavy supporting fire during the failed assault on Battery Wagner. Firing begins at 12:00 P.M.,
and the vessels close to within 300 yards of Confederate works, but the moment

The 54th Massachusetts Volunteer Infantry Regiment fighting on Morris Island, where their heroic actions in battle helped dispel skepticism in those who believed that blacks could not be good soldiers *(The National Guard Heritage)*

his vessels cease fire to allow for the Union infantry assault, the defenders suddenly reemerge and repulse them.

The USS *De Soto, Ossipee,* and *Kennebec* capture the Confederate steamers *James Battle* and *William Bagley* in the Gulf of Mexico.

Armed boats from the USS *Vincennes* and *Clifton* capture the Confederate barge *H. McGuin* on Bay St. Louis, Mississippi.

July 19
NORTH: New York merchants organize relief for African-American victims of the recent draft riots.

WEST: The Army of the Potomac crosses over the Potomac River into Harper's Ferry and down the Shenandoah Valley.

Federal troops under Generals Edward H. Hobson and James M. Shackleford heavily defeat General John H. Morgan's Confederate raiders at Buffington Island on the Ohio River; 800 captives are taken.

Confederate general Daniel H. Hill replaces General William J. Hardee as commander of the II Corps, Army of Tennessee.

NAVAL: The USS *Canandaigua* drives the Confederate steamer *Raccoon* aground in Charleston Harbor, South Carolina.

After traversing 500 miles in the past 10 days, Federal gunboats USS *Moose, Reindeer, Victory, Springfield, Naumkeag, Allegheny, Belle, Fairplay,* and *Silver Lake* outflank Buffington Island in the Ohio River, thereby cutting the retreat of Confederate raiders under Colonel John H. Morgan. Pursuing Union forces take 3,000 prisoners, along with all of Morgan's artillery.

July 20

SOUTH: General George W. Getty assumes command of VII Corps in the Union Department of Virginia and North Carolina.

WEST: The straggling survivors of General John H. Morgan's raid skirmish with Union troops near Hockingport and Coal Hill, Ohio, before riding north from the Ohio River.

NAVAL: The USS *Shawsheen* captures the Confederate schooners *Sally, Helen Jane, Elizabeth, Dolphin,* and *James Brice* off Cedar Island, Neuse River, North Carolina.

July 21

WEST: General John D. Imboden is appointed commander of the Confederate Valley District, Virginia.

NAVAL: Armed boats from the USS *Owasco* and *Cayuga* capture and sink the Confederate schooner *Revenge* off Sabine Pass, Texas.

The transport USS *Sallie Ward* runs aground at Island No. 82 on the Mississippi River and is subsequently destroyed by Confederate artillery fire.

July 22

NAVAL: The New York Chamber of Commerce releases figures stating Union losses to Confederate raiders at 150 vessels worth $12 million. This is stark testimony to the effectiveness of the oceanic raiders CSS *Alabama, Florida,* and *Georgia* and their wily commanders.

The U.S. Navy lands and crews a four-gun battery ashore at Morris Island, Charleston Harbor, South Carolina, to assist bombarding nearby Fort Sumter.

July 23

WEST: Federal forces occupy Manassas Gap, western Virginia, but prove unable to intercept the Army of Northern Virginia and prevent it from moving down the Luray Valley into the Shenandoah region. An advance on Wapping Heights by General William H. French's III Corps, Army of the Potomac, is rebuffed by Confederates under General Richard S. Ewell.

July 24

SOUTH: Federal troops under General Quincy A. Gilmore continue consolidating their hold on Morris Island and Battery Wagner, Charleston Harbor, South Carolina.

In response to perceived French hostility toward the United States, evinced by the occupation of Mexico City, General Nathaniel P. Banks is ordered to prepare troops at New Orleans, Louisiana, for an expedition to the Texas coast.

NAVAL: The USS *Iroquois* captures the Confederate blockade-runner *Merrimac* off the North Carolina coast.

The USS *Arago* seizes the Confederate steamer *Emma* near Wilmington, North Carolina.

Federal warships USS *New Ironsides, Weehawken, Patapsco, Montauk, Catskill, Nantucket, Paul Jones, Ottawa, Seneca,* and *Dai Ching* under Admiral John A. B. Dahlgren bombard Battery Wagner in Charleston Harbor, South Carolina, to support army operations.

July 25
SOUTH: Union forces scouting the region around Goose Creek, Virginia, are twice ambushed and badly mauled by Virginia Partisan Rangers under Major John S. Mosby and withdraw.

A Federal expedition from Portsmouth, Virginia, against Jackson, North Carolina, ends with the death of Confederate general Matt Whitaker.
WEST: Confederate cavalry under Colonel John S. Scott embark on a three-week raid into eastern Kentucky with a pitched battle at Williamsburg.

The Confederate Department of East Tennessee is absorbed into the Department of Tennessee under General Braxton Bragg.

A Federal expedition out of Natchez, Mississippi, burns cotton mills and other buildings at nearby Kingston, Liberty, and Woodville.

After wreaking havoc with Confederate rail lines, General William T. Sherman withdraws from Jackson, Mississippi, and marches back to Vicksburg.

July 26
POLITICS: Kentucky U.S. senator John J. Crittenden, author of the Crittenden Compromise of 1860, dies in Frankfort, Kentucky.
WEST: After a continuous running fight of several days, General John H. Morgan and his remaining 364 troopers surrender at Salineville, Ohio. He is slated for confinement at the Ohio State Penitentiary in Columbus.

Confederate cavalry under Colonel John S. Scott skirmish with Federal troops at Rogersville, Kentucky.
SOUTHWEST: Former Texas governor Sam Houston, who refused to take an oath of allegiance to the Confederacy, dies on his ranch at the age of 70.

July 27
NAVAL: The USS *Clifton,* supported by the *Estrella, Hollyhock,* and *Sachem,* trade shots with Confederate artillery along the Atchafalaya River, Louisiana.

The Confederate raider CSS *Florida* under Lieutenant John N. Maffitt sails from Bermuda with a full complement of coal and ammunition and makes for Brest, France, to effect a major overhaul.

July 28
POLITICS: President Jefferson Davis, taking stock over recent Confederate misfortunes, writes that, "If a victim would secure the success of our cause, I would freely offer myself."

SOUTH: At Aldie, Virginia, Major John S. Mosby and his partisan rangers seize several Union wagons but subsequently lose them to a sharp counterattack.

NAVAL: Armed boats from USS *Beauregard* and *Oleander* raid New Smyrna, Florida, backed by the guns of *Sagamore* and *Para*. Several schooners and a large supply of cotton, ready for export, were all put to the torch.

July 29

DIPLOMACY: Queen Victoria informs Parliament that she sees "No reason to depart from the strict neutrality which Her Majesty has observed from the beginning of the contest." This is the latest blow to Confederate hopes for European military intervention.

SOUTH: General Innis N. Palmer takes charge of the XVIII Corps in the Union Department of Virginia and North Carolina.

NAVAL: The USS *Niphon* captures the British blockade-runner *Banshee* at New Inlet, North Carolina.

The USS *Shawsheen* seizes the Confederate schooner *Telegraph* in Rose Bay, North Carolina.

The USS *Rosalie* captures the British blockade-runner *Georgie* on the Caloosahatchie River, Florida.

Admiral David G. Farragut is relieved of blockading duty along the Texas coast by Admiral Charles H. Bell and sets sail for New York in USS *Hartford*.

July 30

POLITICS: President Abraham Lincoln threatens to execute captured Confederate officers and to subject Southern soldiers to hard labor if captured Union officers are harmed in any manner for leading African-American troops or if former slaves are returned to bondage.

July 31

WEST: General John A. Logan and 1,700 Union cavalrymen skirmish with Confederates at St. Catharine's Creek, Mississippi.

NAVAL: The Confederate raider CSS *Tuscaloosa* under Lieutenant John Low captures the Union ship *Santee* at sea, releasing it on a bond.

August 1

POLITICS: To ameliorate mounting desertion problems, President Jefferson Davis offers an amnesty to all ranks who are present without leave, warning that they have no choice but "victory, or subjugation, slavery, and utter ruin of yourselves, your families, and your country."

The Union IV and VII Corps are broken up and absorbed by other commands.

SOUTH: Vengeful Union troops vigorously corner the partisan rangers of Major John S. Mosby, taking several prisoners at Warrenton Junction, Virginia.

WEST: Noted Confederate spy Belle Boyd is again arrested at Martinsburg, West Virginia, and sent to Washington, D.C., for imprisonment.

A gathering of an estimated 3,000 to 12,000 Democrats at Matton, Illinois, assembles to hear Peace Democrat John R. Eden denounce the administration of

President Abraham Lincoln. Coles County remains a hotbed of antiwar agitation for the rest of the war.

Confederate cavalry under Colonel John S. Scott skirmish with Union troops at Smith's Shoals on the Cumberland River, just prior to crossing back to Tennessee.

A Union cavalry division under General John W. Davidson begins a concerted drive against Confederates at Little Rock, Arkansas.

NAVAL: The USS *Yankee* captures the sloop *Clara Ann* off the Coan River, Virginia.

Federal gunboats attack the Confederate steamer *Chesterfield* in Charleston Harbor, which thoroughly alarms the defenders.

Admiral David D. Porter formally succeeds Admiral David G. Farragut as commander of all naval forces and operations along the Mississippi River.

August 2

SOUTH: General Quincy A. Gillmore, commanding Federals forces outside Charleston, South Carolina, orders the construction of a siege battery built upon the swampy ground of Morris Island in the harbor. This is the future site for on 8-inch rifle Parrot cannon firing 200-pound projectiles, which is quickly dubbed "Swamp Angel" by the troops.

August 3

POLITICS: To discourage continuing violence, New York governor Horatio Seymour asks President Abraham Lincoln to suspend conscription in his state. The president declines.

SOUTH: Wade Hampton and Fitzhugh Lee are appointed major general, C.S.A.

WEST: The Union IX Corps is transferred from Vicksburg, Mississippi, back to Kentucky.

NAVAL: A naval reconnaissance consisting of the USS *Sangamon, Cohasset,* and *Commodore Barney* steams up the James River, Virginia, in a naval squadron commanded by Captain Guert Gansevoort.

August 4

SOUTH: General John Buford and the 1st Cavalry Division, I Corps, fight with Confederate troops at Brandy Station, Virginia.

NAVAL: Armed Confederate boat crews from the CSS *Chicora* and *Palmetto State* capture a Union picket at Vincent's Creek, Morris, Island, Charleston.

August 5

WEST: Union cavalry under General William W. Averell begin a protracted raid from Winchester, Virginia, toward Franklin, West Virginia. He leads a force of 2,000 men, including four mounted regiments and two batteries, with orders to destroy Confederate saltpeter and gunpowder works there.

General Frederick Steele assumes command of Federal forces at Helena, Arkansas.

NAVAL: The USS *Commodore Barney* is damaged heavily by a Confederate electric mine off Dutch Gap, on the James River, Virginia. The vessel would have been completely destroyed save for the device's premature detonation.

The U.S. Marine detachment under Major Jacob Zeilin, augmented to 500 men, lands on Morris Island, Charleston Harbor, South Carolina.

The Confederate raider CSS *Alabama* under Captain Raphael Semmes captures the Union bark *Sea Bride* off Cape of Good Hope, South Africa; the prize is then sold to an English merchant.

August 6

POLITICS: President Jefferson Davis assures a jittery governor Milledge L. Bonham of South Carolina of his continuing support for the defense of Charleston, "which we pray will never be polluted by the footsteps of a lustful, relentless, inhuman foe."

SOUTH: Major John S. Mosby and his partisan rangers seize Union sutler's wagons near Fairfax Court House, Virginia.

NAVAL: The Federal gunboat expedition up the James River, Virginia, consisting of USS *Sagamon, Cohasset,* and *Commodore Barney* are fired on by Confederate artillery. The latter vessel is struck 30 times, including one shot through the boilers, which disables it.

An armed launch from CSS *Juno* captures a Federal launch from USS *Wabash* in Charleston Harbor, South Carolina.

The USS *Fort Henry* captures the Confederate sloop *Southern Star* off St. Martin's Reef, Florida.

The USS *Antonia* captures the British blockade-runner *Betsey* off Corpus Christi, Texas.

The USS *Paw Paw* hits a snag on the Mississippi River and sinks near Hardin's Point, Arkansas.

The Confederate raider CSS *Florida* under Lieutenant John N. Maffitt captures the Union vessel *Francis B. Cutting* and releases it on bond.

August 7

WEST: The Union XIII Corps under General Cadwallader C. Washburn is transferred from the Department of the Tennessee to the Department of the Gulf.

NAVAL: Naval gunfire from the USS *Mound City* breaks up a Confederate mounted attack near Lake Providence, Louisiana.

August 8

SOUTH: General Robert E. Lee tenders his resignation to President Jefferson Davis because of Lee's recent failure at Gettysburg, but the offer is declined.

NAVAL: The USS *Sagamore* captures the British blockade-runners *Clara Louise, Southern Rights,* and *Shot,* along with the Confederate schooner *Ann* off the Florida coast.

August 10

POLITICS: At a meeting with President Abraham Lincoln, abolitionist Frederick Douglass stridently protests the inequality of pay between white and black soldiers, despite assurances from recruiters that they would be paid the same.

SOUTH: Once the XIII Corps arrives at Carrollton, Louisiana, General Edward O. C. Ord is appointed the new commander.

WEST: General Frederick Steele leads Federal forces toward Little Rock, Arkansas, from Helena.

SOUTHWEST: Confederate regiments at Galveston, Texas, mutiny over a lack of rations and furloughs, but order is gradually restored.

NAVAL: Admiral David G. Farragut receives a tumultuous hero's welcome as the USS *Hartford* arrives at New York City.

The USS *Princess Royal* captures the Confederate vessel *Atlantic* off the Rio Grande, Texas. However, the vessel is recaptured by its crew and sails into Havana, Cuba.

The USS *Cayuga* seizes the Confederate schooner *J. T. Davis* off the Rio Grande, Texas.

August 11

SOUTH: A quick raid by Virginia Partisan Rangers under Major John S. Mosby nets 19 Union wagons at Annandale, Virginia.

Confederate cannon at Battery Wagner, Fort Sumter, and James Island unleash a sudden bombardment of Union positions on Morris Island, Charleston Harbor, South Carolina, forcing fatigue parties to scurry for cover.

August 12

NORTH: President Abraham Lincoln declines to reappoint General John A. McClernand to a new command, effectively ending his military career.

SOUTH: Federal artillerists initiate counterbattery fire with heavy Parrott rifles against Battery Wagner and Fort Sumter, Charleston Harbor, South Carolina. The brick walls of the latter post suffer considerable damage, and within hours, most of its guns are dismounted.

NAVAL: The USS *Princess Royal* captures the British blockade-runner *Flying Scud* off Brazos, Texas.

Admiral Charles H. Bell of the Pacific Squadron orders the USS *Narragansett* to patrol the waters between San Francisco and Acapulco, Mexico, to protect American mail steamers better.

The experimental submarine CSS *Hunley* heads for Charleston, South Carolina, to bolster the defenses of that beleaguered city against a Union flotilla offshore. A novelty, the submarine consists of an iron steam boiler that has been waterproofed and fitted with tapered bow and stern sections. The Hunley is 40 feet long and only 3.5 feet in diameter, being propelled by five men operating a crankshaft-driven propeller.

August 13

NAVAL: A Federal squadron consisting of the USS *Lexington, Cricket,* and *Marmora* steams up the White River, Arkansas, lands at Des Arc, and destroys a telegraph office and some wires. The next day, the Confederate steamers *Kaskakia* and *Thomas Sugg* are also captured en route back to the Red River.

August 14

NORTH: General George G. Meade takes leave of the Army of the Potomac to visit Washington, D.C., to discuss forthcoming strategy with President Abraham Lincoln and his cabinet.

SOUTH: Command of the Union XI Corps reverts to General John J. Peck.

WEST: A building housing the captured sisters of known Confederate guerrillas collapses in Kansas City, Missouri, killing five. This act enrages scattered bands of irregulars, who coalesce and begin to plot grim retaliation.

NAVAL: The USS *Bermuda* captures the British blockade-runners *Carmita* and *Artist* off the Texas coast.

August 15

SOUTH: A Union sweep of the region between Centreville and Aldie, Virginia, fails to snare Confederate raider Major John S. Mosby but acquires several prisoners belonging to his command.

NAVAL: The Confederate submarine CSS *Hunley* arrives at Charleston, South Carolina, from Mobile, Alabama, on two covered railroad cars. General Pierre G. T. Beauregard, commanding the city's defenses, is eager to impress the experimental device into active service.

August 16

SOUTH: General Gouverneur K. Warren assumes command of the II Corps, Army of the Potomac.

WEST: After considerable prodding from the government, General William S. Rosecrans pushes his Army of the Cumberland out of Tullahoma and south toward Chattanooga. He brings with him the XXI Corps of General Thomas L. Crittenden, General George H. Thomas's XIV Corps, and General Alexander M. McCook's XX Corps. Due to mountainous terrain before him, Rosecrans plans to spread the three columns widely to cover all three passes, a risky ploy that endangers his command with defeat in detail. Nonetheless, additional forces under General Ambrose E. Burnside also depart Camp Nelson, Lexington, Kentucky, and advance into East Tennessee. By dint of effective maneuvering, Rosecrans intends to catch General Braxton Bragg's Confederates between himself and Burnside's force.

NAVAL: The USS *Pawnee* narrowly escapes serious damage when an electric torpedo (mine) explodes under its stern at Stono Inlet, South Carolina. In response, Admiral John A. B. Dalhgren orders large nets stretched across the inlet to prevent additional mines from transiting to the fleet.

The USS *De Soto* captures the Confederate steamer *Alice Vivian* in the Gulf of Mexico.

The USS *Gertrude* seizes the Confederate steamer *Warrior* at sea.

The USS *Rhode Island* captures the British blockade-runner *Cronstadt* off Man of War Bay, Abaco, Bahamas.

August 17

SOUTH: General Quincy A. Gilmore orders 11 heavy gun on Morris Island, Charleston Harbor, South Carolina, to commence the first saturation bombardment of Fort Sumter. They fire 938 shots on the first day alone, shattering its remaining brick structures.

NAVAL: The USS *Satellite* captures the Confederate schooner *Three Brothers* in the Great Wicomico River, Maryland.

The USS *Crocus* runs aground at night on Bodlies Island, North Carolina, and subsequently is abandoned.

Admiral John A. B. Dahlgren's squadron takes up bombardment positions in a joint attack on Confederate defenses in Charleston, South Carolina. Present are the ironclads USS *Weehawken, Catskill, Nahant, Montauk, Passaic, Patapsco,* and *New Ironside,* assisted by the gunboats *Canandaigua, Mahaska, Cimarron, Ottawa, Wissahocken, Dai Ching, Seneca,* and *Lodona.* During the next five days, the fleet concentrates its fire on various defensive positions, including Fort Sumter, whose counterfire kills Captain J. W. Rodgers of the *Catskill.*

The USS *De Soto* captures the Confederate steamer *Nita* in Apalachicola Bay, Florida.

August 18
NORTH: Intrigued by new weapons, President Abraham Lincoln test-fires the new, rapid-fire Spencer carbine at Treasury Park, Washington, D.C. This weapon gives Federal units a decided edge in firepower over Confederate units that are still armed with muzzle-loading rifles.
SOUTH: The Union bombardment of Fort Sumter, Charleston Harbor, South Carolina, shows no letup, but the garrison still clings tenaciously behind its masonry ruins.
SOUTHWEST: Federal troops under Colonel Kit Carson skirmish with Pueblo Indians at Pueblo, Colorado.
NAVAL: The USS *Niphon* chases the Confederate steamer *Hebe* aground off Fort Fisher, Wilmington, North Carolina, destroying it by gunfire.

The CSS *Oconee* flounders in heavy seas off St. Catherine's Sound, Georgia.

August 19
NORTH: The military draft resumes in New York without further violence.
WEST: Union cavalry under General William W. Averell destroy Confederate saltpeter works at Franklin, West Virginia.
NAVAL: Landing parties from the USS *Norwich* and *Hale* raid Jacksonville, Florida, and destroy a Confederate signal station.

The USS *Restless* captures the Confederate schooner *Ernti* off the Florida Keys.

August 20
SOUTH: General William B. Franklin takes charge of the Union XXIX Corps in Louisiana.
WEST: Federal forces directed by General Ambrose E. Burnside reach the Tennessee River in East Tennessee.

Three hundred Confederate guerrillas under William C. Quantrill begin their raid into Kansas.
SOUTHWEST: Colonel Kit Carson commences his "scorched earth" policy against the Navajo Indians in the New Mexico Territory, assisted by Ute, Zuni, and Mescalero Apache tribe members. All captives taken then are transferred to a reservation at Bosque Redondo for resettlement.

August 21

SOUTH: The Union bombardment of Fort Sumter, Charleston Harbor, South Carolina, intensifies further as General Quincy A. Gillmore readies "Swamp Angel," a huge Parrott gun lobbing 200-pound incendiary projectiles. Digging an emplacement for this heavy piece and dragging it into position over the swampy ground of Morris Island has taken three weeks. Fully functional, it prepares to fire incendiary rounds at the Charleston waterfront, 7,900 yards distant.

WEST: General Robert B. Potter assumes command of the Union IX Corps in Kentucky.

General John G. Fosters returns to Tennessee to resume command of the Union XVIII Corps.

William C. Quantrill and 450 Confederate and Missouri irregulars storm into Lawrence, Kansas, a noted abolitionist center and hotbed for Union jayhawker activity. During the next four hours, they systematically round up and execute 180 men and boys and then burn 185 buildings before departing. It is the single largest atrocity of the Civil War, condemned by North and South alike.

NAVAL: The CSS *Torch*, a Confederate torpedo boat, attacks and fails to destroy the Federal ironclad USS *New Ironsides* in the channel off Morris Island, Charleston, South Carolina. Having approached to within 40 yards of its target at night, Pilot James Carlin cuts his engines and drifts toward his quarry, but prevailing currents pitch his vehicle alongside the larger navy vessel instead of into it. Carlin's engines then stall for several tense moments as *New Ironsides* labors to depress its cannon low enough to sink the intruder. When the *Torch*'s engine suddenly start, Carlin withdraws his ship back into the harbor, straddled by parting shots from his intended victim.

The Confederate raider CSS *Florida* under Commander John N. Maffitt captures and burns the Union ship *Anglo Saxon* off Brest, France.

August 22

SOUTH: Fort Sumter, Charleston Harbor, South Carolina, endures six days of heavy pounding from Union batteries on nearby Morris Island and sustains heavy damage, yet remains defiant. Meanwhile, the large Union cannon dubbed "Swamp Angel" is disabled while firing its 36th round and abandoned. Beforehand, it lobbed incendiary shells toward the city's waterfront, igniting several fires and panicking the populace.

WEST: Union cavalry under General William W. Averell skirmishes with Colonel William Jackson's Confederates at Huntervsille, Virginia, driving them toward Warm Springs.

General William S. Rosecrans dispatches Union forces from Tracy City, Tennessee, to the Tennessee River.

NAVAL: Armed boats from USS *Shohokon* capture and sink the Confederate schooner *Alexander Cooper* at New Topsail Inlet, North Carolina. The men then destroy a nearby saltworks.

The USS *Cayuga* captures the Confederate schooner *Wave* off Corpus Christi, Texas.

Following the latest round of intense bombardment, Admiral John A. B. Dahlgren moves his ironclad fleet, consisting of USS *Montauk, Weehawken, Nahant, Passaic,* and *Patapsco,* in closer to engage Confederate defenses at Fort Sumter, Charleston Harbor, South Carolina. However, when *Passaic* accidentally grounds near the fort, his attack is delayed in having to get the vessel refloated, and at daylight, the squadron hauls off, having accomplished little.

August 23

SOUTH: Union gunners, having fired 5,009 rounds into Fort Sumter, Charleston Harbor, South Carolina, reduce that post to rubble. But the garrison, with only one cannon still mounted, refuses to yield.

NAVAL: A Confederate expedition under Lieutenant John T. Wood takes four boats filled with 60 sailors and 30 sharpshooters and seizes the Union steamers USS *Reliance* and *Satellite* off Windmill Point on the Rappahannock River, Virginia. The captured vessels subsequently are scuttled a few days later for want of fuel and spare parts.

Admiral John A. B. Dahlgren leads the ironclads USS *New Ironsides, Weehawken, Montauk, Passaic,* and *Patapsco* back into Charleston Harbor, South Carolina, for another round of bombardment. Fort Sumter initially is targeted; then they shift their aim to Fort Moultrie before a thick fog descends and obstructs the gunners of both sides. At daybreak, Dahlgren signals for the squadron to haul off, and fighting ceases.

August 24

SOUTH: Union cavalry under General Hugh J. Kilpatrick skirmish with Confederates near George Court House, Virginia.

Major John S. Mosby begins a protracted raid against Union forces around Warrenton Junction and Alexandria, Virginia.

August 25

SOUTH: Union infantry attacks on Confederate rifle pits outside Battery Wagner, Charleston Harbor, South Carolina, are beaten back.

WEST: Union cavalry under General William W. Averill destroy additional Confederate saltpeter works along Jackson's River, West Virginia. Moving west toward White Sulphur Springs, his command engages a strong force of Confederates before settling in for the evening.

General Thomas Ewing, commanding the Union Border District, issues his controversial General Order No. 11. This edict forces all the inhabitants of Bates, Cass, Jackson, and parts of Vernon counties, Missouri, long suspected of collaborating with Confederate guerrillas, to abandon their homes. The houses then are peremptorily burned in retaliation for the Lawrence massacre. An estimated 20,000 people are displaced, causing enmity and hardship lasting several years beyond the war. Ewing, against his better judgment, drew up the orders on the insistence of General James Lane, a noted Union frontier jayhawker and a popular politician. Lane subsequently threatened to ruin's Ewing's military reputation if he fails to enforce all the measure's harshest provisions.

NAVAL: The newly acquired CSS *Satellite* under Lieutenant John T. Wood attacks and captures the Union schooners *Golden Rod, Coquette,* and *Two Brothers* at the mouth of the Rappahannock River, Virginia.

The USS *William G. Anderson* captures the Confederate schooner *Mack Canfield* off the Rio Grande, Texas.

August 26

POLITICS: In a letter to Unionists in Springfield, Illinois, President Abraham Lincoln writes, "I do not believe any compromise, embracing the maintenance of the Union is now possible. . . . Peace does not appear so distant as it did."

SOUTH: Confederate general John B. Floyd dies of natural causes near Abingdon, Virginia.

Federal troops finally storm the rifle pits fronting Battery Wagner on Morris Island, Charleston Harbor, South Carolina.

WEST: Union cavalry under General William W. Averell skirmish heavily with Confederate forces at White Sulphur Springs, West Virginia. His 2,000 troopers dash headlong into an equal number of Confederates under Colonel George S. Patton, sent there to stop the Union marauders. Averell dismounts, attacks repeatedly across densely wooded terrain, and is defeated. He then remounts and retires in the direction of Callaghan's Station. Union losses are 26 dead, 125 injured, and 67 captured while Patton records 20 killed, 129 wounded, and 13 missing.

SOUTHWEST: Union troops under General James G. Blunt defeat Colonel Stand Watie's Confederate Cherokee in a skirmish at Perryville, Indian Territory.

NAVAL: Armed boats from the USS *Beauregard* seize the Confederate schooner *Phoebe* near Jupiter Inlet, Florida.

August 27

NORTH: Confederate cavalry under General J. E. B. Stuart skirmish with Union forces at Edward's Ferry, Maryland.

WEST: Union cavalry under General William W. Averell trot into Beverly, West Virginia, ending his recent raid.

NAVAL: The USS *Sunflower* captures the Confederate schooner *General Worth* in the Straits of Florida.

The USS *Preble* is accidentally destroyed by fire at Pensacola, Florida.

The USS *William G. Anderson* captures the Confederate schooner *America* off the Texas coast.

The Confederate raiders CSS *Alabama* under Captain Raphael Semmes and CSS *Tuscaloosa* under Lieutenant John Low briefly rendezvous in the Bay of Angra Pequena off the West African coast. Semmes then orders the *Tuscaloosa* to cruise off the Brazilian coast.

August 29

WEST: As Union forces under General William S. Rosecrans flank the city of Chattanooga, Tennessee, Confederates under General Braxton Bragg must soon either fight or fall back.

Naval: The experimental submarine CSS *Hunley,* under Lieutenant John A. Payne, tragically sinks on a trial run in Charleston Harbor, South Carolina, killing six crew members. The vessel apparently founders in the wake of the steamer *Etiwan* while its hatches were opened for better ventilation.

The Federal gunboat USS *Estrella* is detached from the West Gulf Blockading Squadron and ordered up the Mississippi River to assist the ironclad *Essex* in anti-guerrilla patrols.

August 30

South: Union batteries on Morris Island, Charleston Harbor, South Carolina, continue their bombardment of Fort Sumter.

Naval: The Confederate steamer CSS *Sumter* is fired on and sunk by shore batteries on Sullivan's Island, Charleston, South Carolina, after mistaking it for a passing Union vessel.

The Confederate raider CSS *Georgia* under Lieutenant William L. Maury captures the Union ship *John Watts* in the mid-Atlantic, releasing it on bond.

A detachment of U.S. Marines assigned to the Mississippi River Squadron captures 35 prisoners, including three Confederate paymasters at Bolivar, Mississippi. They were transporting $2.2 million of Confederate currency at the time.

August 31

South: General Robert C. Schenck assumes command of the Union VIII Corps along with the Middle Department, Virginia.

General Alpheus S. Williams gains command of the Union XII Corps, Army of the Potomac.

Naval: The USS *Gem of the Sea* captures the Confederate sloop *Richard* at Peach Creek, Florida.

September 1

Politics: President Jefferson Davis assures Tennessee governor Isham G. Harris that troops and arms are being dispatched to General Braxton Bragg's forces in Tennessee.

South: Both Fort Sumter and Battery Wagner on Morris Island, Charleston Harbor, South Carolina, remain under continual bombardment from Union cannon, which lob another 627 rounds against their already battered position. Both garrisons, however, continue to resist.

West: After preliminary maneuvering, the Union Army of the Cumberland under General William S. Rosecrans finally crosses the Tennessee River and heads for Chattanooga, Tennessee.

Fort Smith, Arkansas, is evacuated by Confederates under General William L. Cabell and subsequently falls to advancing Union forces commanded by General Frederick Steele.

Naval: Admiral John A. B. Dahlgren leads his ironclad force in a five-hour night action against Fort Sumter, Charleston Harbor, South Carolina. The vessels steam to within 500 yards of their target before opening fire, and they receive 70 hits from shore batteries before action is suspended at daybreak.

September 2

POLITICS: To curtail mounting manpower shortages, the Alabama state legislature considers the use of slaves in the army.

SOUTH: Union forces establish trench works within 80 yards of Battery Wagner, Morris Island, South Carolina, forcing Confederate authorities to prepare an evacuation effort.

WEST: The Army of the Cumberland under General William S. Rosecrans begins to cross the Tennessee River in pursuit of retreating Confederates.

Union forces under General Ambrose E. Burnside occupy Knoxville, Tennessee, severing the sole remaining direct railhead between eastern and western portions of the Confederacy. Henceforth, the Confederates must employ a tenuous, roundabout route stretching from Virginia to Georgia and thence to Tennessee.

NAVAL: An armed expedition from the USS *Star of the Sea* reconnoiters Peace Creek, Florida, destroying several buildings and small craft.

September 4

SOUTH: Confederate cavalry under General J. E. B. Stuart try unsuccessfully to snare Union general Joseph J. Bartlett at New Baltimore, Virginia.

WEST: General Ulysses S. Grant is badly injured in a fall from his horse at New Orleans, Louisiana.

The Army of the Cumberland under General William S. Rosecrans continues crossing the Tennessee River at Bridgeport, Alabama, below Confederate positions at Chattanooga, Tennessee.

Confederate guerrillas raid the town of Quincy, Missouri, taking four prisoners from the 18th Iowa and subsequently executing them.

Federal forces ambush Confederate bushwhackers at Big Creek, Missouri, killing six guerrillas.

NAVAL: Admiral John H. Bell of the West Gulf Blockading Squadron begins to assemble ships for a joint amphibious expedition from New Orleans to Sabine Pass, Texas. This is undertaken to dissuade French occupation forces in Mexico from crossing the Rio Grande into Texas.

September 5

DIPLOMACY: After being warned by American ambassador Charles F. Adams, British foreign secretary Lord Russell confiscates the two "Laird Rams" before they can be delivered to Confederate agents in Britain. Adams previously advised the British that "it would be superfluous for me to point out to your Lordship that this is war." Government seizure of these dangerous vessels ends a prolonged diplomatic sore point between London and Washington.

POLITICS: A pensive president Jefferson Davis contacts General Braxton Bragg over seemingly flagging Confederate fortunes in Tennessee, asking: "What is your proposed plan of operation? Can you ascertain intention of enemy?"

SOUTH: Union forces tenaciously and methodically push their earthworks to within a few yards of Battery Wagner on Morris Island, South Carolina. Expectations for a final and presumably victorious Federal assault are rife.

WEST: General William S. Rosecrans, convinced that Confederates under General Braxton Bragg are fleeing Chattanooga, Tennessee, into Georgia, daringly divides his army into three parts to cover three, widely spaced mountain passes south of the city.

September 6

SOUTH: Battery Wagner and Battery Gregg, on Morris Island, Charleston Harbor, South Carolina, are evacuated secretly by General Pierre G. T. Beauregard. Barges manned by the crews of CSS *Chicora* and *Palmetto State* row to Cumming Point at night and lift the survivors off, although marauding Federal gunboats snare several prisoners by daylight. This final act concludes 60 days of nearly continuous bombardment by Union land and naval forces—one-third of the 900 defenders have been either killed or wounded. Casualties during the final phase of operations cost the Union 71 dead, 278 wounded, and nine missing while Taliaferro loses 38 dead and 150 wounded.

NAVAL: A landing party from the USS *Argosy* secures Confederate ammunition stores at Bruinsburg, Mississippi.

September 7

SOUTH: Union forces advance on Batteries Wagner and Gregg, Morris Island, South Carolina, finding them desolate and abandoned. Meanwhile Confederate forces under General William B. Taliaferro attack Union pickets on Battery Island, South Carolina, destroying the bridge and landing to nearby Horse Island.

WEST: Union forces reoccupy Cumberland Gap, Tennessee.

SOUTHWEST: A combined army-navy expedition under General William B. Franklin arrives off the bar at Sabine Pass, Texas.

NAVAL: Admiral John A. B. Dahlgren demands the surrender of Fort Sumter in Charleston Harbor, South Carolina, and when the defenders refuse, he conducts a reconnaissance in force with the ironclads USS *Weehawken* and *New Ironsides*. En route, *Weehawken* grounds in the channel, and *New Ironsides* interposes itself between Fort Moultrie and the stricken ship, receiving intense fire and 50 hits. The vessels then retire offshore by daylight to make repairs.

Federal gunboats USS *Clifton*, *Sachem*, *Arizona*, and *Granite City* arrive off Sabine Pass, Texas, to support a combined expedition under General William B. Franklin.

September 8

SOUTH: General Quincy A. Gillmore, encouraged by his final conquest of Battery Wagner, Charleston Harbor, South Carolina, prepares for an amphibious expedition against nearby Fort Sumter in conjunction with naval forces under Admiral John A. B. Dahlgren.

WEST: After initial hesitation, General Braxton Bragg abandons Chattanooga, Tennessee, and withdraws 65,000 men toward Lafayette, Georgia.

SOUTHWEST: A small Confederate battery of 42 men under 20-year-old Lieutenant Richard W. Dowling, 1st Texas Heavy Artillery, engages a 4,000-man amphibious expedition under Union general William B. Franklin. Franklin's goal is to seize

Hand-tinted copy of a line engraving by Smyth, depicting USS *New Ironsides* and two monitors in action at Charleston, South Carolina, ca. 1863 *(Naval Historical Foundation)*

the mouth of the Sabine River on the Texas-Louisiana border. Federal gunboats USS *Clifton, Sachem, Arizona,* and *Granite City,* along with several army transports, work themselves across the bar as Confederate gunners hunker down behind their defenses at Fort Griffin. Dowling allowed the vessels to approach to within close range before unleashing a destructive cannonade at 4:00 P.M. Previously, he carefully pre-positioned white poles in the river as range markers, and his six outdated, smoothbore cannon are handled with aplomb. Consequently, the *Sachem* is disabled by a direct shot through its boilers while the *Clifton* grounds directly beneath the Confederate guns and takes a pounding. Both gunboats promptly surrender, after which the expedition withdraws back over the bar and sets sail for New Orleans. Considering the sheer disparity of forces, this is a humiliating defeat for the North, which loses 19 dead, nine wounded, 37 missing, and 315 captured. Dowling suffers no casualties, and President Jefferson Davis hails his stand as "one of the most brilliant and heroic achievements in the history of warfare." Defeat here prompts General Nathaniel P. Banks to shift his attention to the Rio Grande region.

NAVAL: The small Confederate cottonclad CSS *Uncle Ben* assists in the repulse of Union forces at Sabine Pass, Texas.

September 9

DIPLOMACY: The British government formally initiates steps to prevent the two "Laird Rams" from entering into Confederate service.

SOUTH: General James Longstreet's I Corps of 15,000 men begins to embark on trains in Virginia for a nine-day trek to Lafayette, Georgia, to reinforce the Army of Tennessee.

WEST: Union forces under General Ambrose E. Burnside recapture the Cumberland Gap in eastern Tennessee.

The strategic city of Chattanooga, Tennessee, surrenders to the Army of the Cumberland under General William S. Rosecrans without a shot being fired. General Braxton Bragg then falls back 28 miles to Lafayette, Georgia, where he is to receive promised reinforcements.

The Union division of General James S. Negley (XIV Corps) arrives alone and unsupported at McLemore's Cove, Georgia, and General Braxton Bragg orders an assault by Generals Patrick R. Cleburne and Thomas C. Hindman to destroy it. However, Hindman, fretful over being attacked himself, refuses to budge, and Negley escapes intact the next day.

NAVAL: Admiral John A. B. Dahlgren launches a nighttime assault on Fort Sumter, Charleston Harbor, South Carolina, by 413 sailors and U.S. Marines under Commander Thomas H. Stevens. But the Southerners, having earlier recovered the code book from the sunken USS *Keokuk,* are able to decipher Union signals and anticipate the attack. Consequently, the Federals are rebuffed with 100 prisoners. A similar expedition planned by General Quincy A. Gillmore is also summarily cancelled. More significantly, Dahlgren requests additional monitor craft from Secretary of the Navy Gideon Welles; when he refused, the navy stopped its bombardment campaign, and operations against Charleston settle into a blockade.

September 10

SOUTH: Vindictive Georgia troops sack offices of the *North Carolina Standard* in Raleigh, North Carolina, for printing editorials favoring a negotiated settlement with the Union.

WEST: This day finds the Army of the Cumberland under General William S. Rosecrans widely dispersed over a broad area with General Alexander M. Cook (XXI Corps) at Alpine, Georgia, General George H. Thomas (XIV Corps) at McLemore's Cove, and General Thomas L. Crittenden at Chattanooga. He is unaware that General Braxton Bragg actually is regrouping and receiving reinforcements in northern Georgia.

Confederate forces under General Sterling Price evacuate Little Rock, Arkansas, for nearby Rockport, whereupon General Frederick Steele's Federals move in and establish a pro-Union administration. This is another grievous blow to a Confederacy already reeling from the loss of Vicksburg, and it seriously imperils the Trans-Mississippi Department under General Edmund Kirby-Smith. Confederate governor Harris Flanigan is forced to relocate to Washington, Arkansas, where he remains for the next two years.

NAVAL: The USS *Hastings* lends fire support to General Frederick Steele's troops at Devall's Bluff on the White River, Arkansas.

September 11

POLITICS: President Abraham Lincoln authorizes General Andrew Johnson, military governor of Tennessee, to form a civilian government. He also declines to accept General Ambrose E. Burnside's latest attempt to resign.

NAVAL: The USS *Seminole* captures the British blockade-runner *William Peel* off the Rio Grande, Texas.

September 12
WEST: Union and Confederate forces skirmish heavily below Chattanooga, Tennessee.

NAVAL: The USS *Eugenie* captures the Confederate steamer *Alabama* off the Chandeleur Islands, Louisiana.

The Confederate steamer *Fox* is scuttled by its own crew to prevent being captured by the USS *Genesee* at Pascagoula, Mississippi.

September 13
SOUTH: The Army of the Potomac under General George G. Meade occupies Culpeper Court House shortly after it is evacuated by Confederates under General Robert E. Lee. Lee, weakened by the detachment of General James Longstreet's corps to Georgia, falls back across the Rapidan River.

General Henry W. Slocum is restored as commander of the XII Corps, Army of the Potomac.

WEST: The War Department instructs General Ulysses S. Grant to transfer all available forces from Corinth, Mississippi, to Tuscumbia, Alabama, in support of General William S. Rosecrans at Chattanooga, Tennessee.

General Braxton Bragg orders General Leonidas K. Polk to attack and overwhelm the isolated Union XXI Corps of General Thomas L. Crittenden at Lee and Gordon's Mill, northern Georgia. But Polk dithers, demands reinforcements, and fails to move in a timely fashion. Hence, another part of the widely scattered Army of the Cumberland escapes annihilation. General William S. Rosecrans finally recognizes the danger his army faces and orders all three corps to begin to concentrate at Lee and Gordon's Mills along Chickamauga Creek. For the intervening week, both armies race north toward Chattanooga.

NAVAL: The USS *Cimarron* captures the British blockade-runner *Jupiter* near Wassaw Sound, Georgia.

The USS *De Soto* captures the steamer *Montgomery* in the Gulf of Mexico.

A rather unsporting raid by Confederate cavalry nets 20 crew members of the USS *Rattler* as they attend church services at Rodney, Mississippi.

September 14
SOUTH: Union forces under General George M. Meade cross the Rapidan River, Virginia, seeking to engage an elusive Army of Northern Virginia. Skirmishing erupts along the line at Somerville, Racoon, and Robertson's Fords.

September 15
SOUTH: An accidental magazine explosion at Battery Cheves, James Island, South Carolina, kills six Confederate soldiers.

General Edward O. C. Ord arrives to take command of the Union XIII Corps, Louisiana.

WEST: Skirmishing erupts at Catlett's Gap, Georgia, as the armies of Generals William S. Rosecrans and Braxton Bragg begin to concentrate for a final confrontation.

September 16
WEST: The Army of the Cumberland under General William S. Rosecrans continues concentrating along Chickamauga Creek, 12 miles below Chattanooga, Tennessee.

Naval: The USS *Coeur de Lion* captures the Confederate schooner *Robert Knowles* in the Potomac River.

The USS *San Jacinto* captures the Confederate steamer *Lizzie Davis* off the Florida west coast.

September 17

West: Union and Confederate forces skirmish at Owen's Ford, West Chickamauga Creek, whereby General Braxton Bragg misses yet another opportunity to attack the separated corps of General William S. Rosecrans's Army of the Cumberland. Both sides continue concentrating forces in anticipation of a major clash.

Naval: The USS *Adolph Hugel* impounds the sloop *Music* for blockade violations off Alexandria, Virginia.

September 18

West: The Army of the Cumberland and the Army of Tennessee confront each other across West Chickamauga Creek, Georgia. For once, the Confederates outnumber Federal forces, having massed 68,000 men to a Union tally of 58,000. General Braxton Bragg seeks to interpose his troops between General William S. Rosecrans and his main supply base at Chattanooga, Tennessee, but increasing skirmishes with Union cavalry along Reed's and Alexander's bridges delay movement a full day. Meanwhile, Rosecrans grows concerned that he is about to be outflanked and hastily summons General George H. Thomas's XIV Corps on a lengthy nighttime march—inadvertently across Bragg's line of march.

September 19

West: The Battle of Chickamauga begins once advance elements of General George H. Thomas's XIV Corps encounter Confederate cavalry under General Nathan B. Forrest on the Union left. As fighting escalates, both Generals Braxton Bragg and William S. Rosecrans cancel their respective plans for the day and continually feed additional units into the rapidly expanding fray. Various Union formations remain somewhat disjointed, and a frontal assault by Bragg's entire army might have rolled them up in detail, but that leader remains fixated by the piecemeal struggle to his immediate front. At length, large attacks launched by General Leonidas K. Polk are repulsed with loss. Then General Patrick R. Cleburne also charges Union positions before nightfall and is likewise rebuffed. The day's combat occasioned serious losses to both sides and little else. This evening, following the arrival of General James Longstreet's I Corps, Bragg appoints him to command his left wing while General Leonidas K. Polk directs the right.

Naval: A small group of Confederate sailors under Acting Masters John Y. Beall and Edward McGuire attack and capture the Union schooner *Alliance* in Chesapeake Bay, intending to stalk and seize other prizes by stealth.

September 20

South: John B. Hood is appointed a lieutenant general, C.S.A.

Union cavalry under Generals John Buford and Hugh J. Kilpatrick attack Confederate supply lines near Gordonsville, Virginia, capturing both wagons and cattle.

Major John S. Mosby skirmishes with Union forces at Upperville, Virginia.

WEST: General Braxton Bragg intends to renew combat at Chickamauga at dawn, but confusion and delays down his chain of command preclude any Confederate advance before 9:00 A.M. The pattern of fighting remains similar to the previous day, with General Leonidas K. Polk committing piecemeal attacks on an entrenched, unyielding Union line. The knotty, heavily forested nature of the terrain greatly complicates the movement and deployment of troops en masse, so a "soldier's battle" unfolds between small, determined bands of men. At 9:00 A.M., a forceful Southern charge at the Union center nearly reaches the Lafayette Road, but it is repelled by Federals holding either flank. Another bloody stalemate seems in the offing until fate intervenes.

At about 10:30 A.M., General William S. Rosecrans is mistakenly informed that a gap has developed in the center of his line—in fact there was none—so he orders General Thomas J. Wood's division to plug it. No sooner does Wood remove his troops than General James Longstreet's veterans come pouring through, six brigades deep. The unexpected onslaught completely sweeps away the Union center and right, carrying Rosecrans and several ranking leaders along in a tumultuous retreat.

All that remains to stave off disaster is the XIV Corps of General George H. Thomas, which assumes strong defensive positions along Snodgrass Hill. Longstreet and other Confederate leaders repeatedly assail Thomas's position but are invariably beaten back with losses. Union prospects improve significantly when General Gordon Granger disobeys Rosecrans and rushes his Reserve Corps forward to support Thomas. Granger himself is in the very thick of intense fighting, holding aloft the flag of the 115th Illinois throughout the contest. Clinging to Snodgrass Hill with heroic determination, the beleaguered yet imperturbably calm Thomas gains the moniker "Rock of Chickamauga" by preserving the Army of the Cumberland from otherwise certain destruction. Fighting ceases along the line by nightfall, and Thomas skillfully extricates his command through McFarland's Gap in good order. To accomplish this, Granger orders his 21st and 89th Ohio and 22nd Michigan, whose ammunition is exhausted, to hold the ridge above the pass with bayonets alone. Only after the last of Thomas's column passes through do they finally surrender.

Chickamauga is the bloodiest battle waged in the western theater, with both sides suffering loss rates approaching 28 percent. For the Union, this entails 1,656 dead, 9,749 injured, and 4,774 missing (16,179) while the Confederates lose 2,389 killed, 13,412 wounded, and 2,003 missing (17,804). Among the fatally wounded is Confederate general Ben Hardin Helm, President Abraham Lincoln's brother-in-law, who is mourned by both the president and his wife. General Daniel H. Hill, after scrutinizing the casualty lists, characterizes Chickamauga as "a barren victory." The Army of Tennessee could not sustain such attrition for long, but Bragg compounded his problems by failing to pursue the beaten enemy aggressively. This lackluster leadership causes further rifts in an already fractious chain of command and sullied his already faltering reputation. Rosecrans, his erstwhile sterling persona destroyed, likewise suffers repercussions for his mismanagement of affairs during—and after—the battle.

Confederate forces under General Samuel Jones skirmish with Federal troops at Zollicoffer, Tennessee, and they pursue the defeated troops as far as the villages of Blountsville and Carter's Depot. The former is an important railroad junction through which the Tennessee and Virginia Railroad passes. General Ambrose E. Burnside, wishing to appropriate that rail for his own use, warns Jones to evacuate citizens from the village as he intends to take it back.

September 21

POLITICS: President Abraham Lincoln repeatedly orders General Ambrose E. Burnside at Knoxville, Tennessee, to reinforce General William S. Rosecrans's shattered army at Chattanooga, but the general refuses to budge.

WEST: Five Union divisions under General George H. Thomas abandon their position at Rossville Gap and reach Chattanooga in good order. The Confederate pursuit, when it finally materializes, remains strangely lax in execution.

NAVAL: Confederate raiders on the commandeered vessel *Alliance* seize the Union schooner *J. J. Houseman* in Chesapeake Bay.

September 22

WEST: Union cavalry forces under Colonel John W. Foster charge into Blountsville, Tennessee, to dislodge the 1st Tennessee Cavalry under Colonel James E. Carter. They head directly into prepared Confederate positions, and a four-hour fight erupts after which the bluecoats finally prevail and capture the town. Foster's losses are six dead and 14 injured, and he reports the seizure of 50 Confederates.

General William S. Rosecrans continues rallying the Army of the Cumberland in Chattanooga, Tennessee, while General Ulysses S. Grant dispatches three divisions of the XV Corps from Vicksburg, Mississippi, under General William T. Sherman to assist him. Meanwhile, the Confederate Army of Tennessee leisurely occupies the high ground around the city to commence a siege.

General Joseph O. Shelby takes his "Iron Brigade" of Confederate cavalry out of Arkadelphia, Arkansas, on an extended raid throughout Missouri.

NAVAL: Confederate raiders in the commandeered schooner *Alliance* seize the Union schooners *Samuel Pearsall* and *Alexandria* in Chesapeake Bay.

The USS *Connecticut* captures the British blockade-runner *Juno* off Wilmington, North Carolina.

Landing parties from the USS *Seneca* destroy Confederate saltworks near Darien, Georgia.

The USS *De Soto* recaptures the Federal army tug *Leviathan* in the Gulf of Mexico after its prior seizure by Confederate raiders at South West Pass, Mississippi River.

September 23

NORTH: Secretary of War Edwin M. Stanton begins to orchestrate skillfully the transfer of 20,000 men of the XI and XII Corps from the Army of the Potomac to Chattanooga, Tennessee. They will be shuttled quickly and efficiently along 1,233 miles of railroad track in the biggest transfer of military personnel prior to the Franco-Prussian War.

SOUTH: General George E. Pickett is transferred to the Confederate Department of North Carolina.

NAVAL: The USS *Thomas Freeborn* chases the commandeered schooner *Alliance* until it grounds at Milford Haven, Virginia, and is burned.

September 24
DIPLOMACY: The Confederate government appoints Ambrose D. Mann as its special agent to the Papal States in Rome.

WEST: Rather than defend Missionary Ridge and Lookout Mountain, both natural strong points, General William S. Rosecrans moves all his forces into Chattanooga, Tennessee. This timid display induces General Braxton Bragg to initiate a siege by occupying all high ground surrounding the city without Union interference.

General Joseph Hooker accepts command of the Union XI and XII Corps, then en route to Chattanooga, Tennessee, by rail.

NAVAL: A total of eight Russian warships arrive individually in New York City. They are seeking safety in American ports as Great Britain and France are threatening war over the Polish insurrection, although the move is widely interpreted in the North as a sign of diplomatic support. Another fleet of six vessels eventually anchors in San Francisco, California, and the Russians are warmly received by the political establishments of both cities.

September 25
POLITICS: President Abraham Lincoln castigates General Ambrose E. Burnside at Knoxville, Tennessee, for not reinforcing Union forces besieged at Chattanooga. Having struggled, he wrote, "to get you to assist General Rosecrans, and you have repeatedly declared you would do it, and yet you steadily move the contrary way." On further reflection, the letter is not sent.

WEST: Confederate cavalry under General John D. Imboden launch a successful attack on Cheat River, West Virginia.

General Mahlon D. Manson assumes command of the XXIII Army Corps, Army of the Tennessee.

NAVAL: The USS *Tioga* captures the Confederate steamer *Herald* off the Bahamas.

September 26
SOUTH: General Henry C. Whiting is assigned to command the Confederate District of Cape Fear and the defenses of Wilmington, North Carolina.

SOUTHWEST: General Edmund Kirby-Smith, trying to rally flagging morale in his Confederate Trans-Mississippi Department, declared to fellow citizens: "Your homes are in peril. Vigorous efforts on your part can alone save portions of your state from invasion. You should contest the advance of the enemy, thicket, gully, and stream; harass his rear and cut off his supplies."

September 27
NORTH: President Abraham Lincoln again implores General Ambrose E. Burnside at Knoxville, Tennessee, to forward reinforcements to assist General William S. Rosecrans at Chattanooga. "My order to you meant simply that you should save Rose-

crans from being crushed out, believing if he lost his position, you could not hold East Tennessee in any event."

WEST: General Braxton Bragg determines to starve out the Army of the Cumberland from Chattanooga, Tennessee, and orders General Joseph Wheeler's cavalry to raid tenuous Union lines of communication throughout 60-mile-long Sequatchie Valley. Wheeler, who has little experience as a raider, openly doubts his prospects for success, yet declares to subordinates, "I have my orders, gentlemen, and I will attempt the work."

General Joseph O. Shelby's Confederate cavalry skirmishes with Union troops at Moffat's Station, Arkansas.

NAVAL: The USS *Clyde* captures the Confederate schooner *Amaranth* off the Florida Keys.

September 28
WEST: General William S. Rosecrans accuses subordinates, Generals Alexander McCook and Thomas L. Crittenden, of failing to obey his orders at Chickamauga, and both are relieved of command pending a court of inquiry.

September 29
WEST: General John S. Williams and his 1,700 Confederate cavalry drive Union troops from Jonesborough, Tennessee, where they hold their position.

NAVAL: The Federal gunboats USS *Lafayette* and *Kenwood* arrive at Morganza, Louisiana (on Bayou Fordoche), to support General Napoleon J. T. Dana's beleaguered command. His troops had been attacked previously by Confederate forces, losing 400 prisoners, and are now reduced to 1,500 men. The presence of gunboats, however, deters General Thomas Green from renewing his assault.

The USS *St. Louis* under Commander George H. Preble drops anchor at Lisbon, Portugal, after a fruitless 100-day search for Confederate raiders.

September 30
NAVAL: The USS *Rosalie* captures the British blockade-runner *Director* on the Sanibel River, Florida.

October 1
POLITICS: President Abraham Lincoln instructs General John M. Schofield, commanding Union forces in Missouri, to place increasing emphasis on civilian rule and domestic tranquility. "Your immediate duty, in regard to Missouri, now is to advance the efficiency of that establishment and to so use it, as far as practicable, to compel the excited people there to leave one another alone."

SOUTH: General J. E. B. Stuart's Confederate troopers surprise a Union outpost on the north side of Robertson's River, Virginia, taking several prisoners.

WEST: General Robert Ransom arrives at Jonesboro, Tennessee, and orders General John S. Williams to take 1,700 Confederate cavalry on an expedition to seize the Cumberland Gap. Williams, however, exceeds his orders and rides eight miles past Greenville.

Union general Joseph Hooker arrives at Nashville, Tennessee, slightly ahead of his XI and XII Corps.

General Joseph Wheeler leads 4,000 Confederate cavalry in skirmishes with Colonel George Crook's 4th Ohio Cavalry at Smith's Cross Roads, Tennessee, as he clamps down on Northern supply lines. A large Federal wagon train is also captured by the marauding Southerners.

Confederate guerrillas under William C. Quantrill begin to leave Kansas and ride for the relative safety of the Indian Territory to evade Union patrols.

October 2

WEST: Final elements of the Union XI and XII Corps under General Joseph Hooker reach Bridgeport, Alabama, after an impressive journey of 1,159 miles by rail.

Confederate cavalry under General Joseph Wheeler accosts a Union supply train in the Sequatchie Valley, Tennessee, capturing 800 wagons, 1,200 prisoners, and 4,000 mules.

Due to the activities of Confederate cavalry, the Army of the Cumberland, besieged in Chattanooga, is experiencing acute food shortages.

NAVAL: The USS *Bermuda* captures the British blockade-runner *Florrie* off Matagorda, Texas.

October 3

POLITICS: President Abraham Lincoln designates the last Thursday in November Thanksgiving Day.

Secretary of War Edwin M. Stanton authorizes liberated African-American slaves to enlist in Maryland, Tennessee, and Missouri.

SOUTH: Union batteries on Morris Island, Charleston Harbor, South Carolina, cease firing on Fort Sumter after throwing an additional 560 shells at that beleaguered fortification.

WEST: Confederate cavalry under General John S. Williams clash with General Samuel P. Carter's Union troops outside Greenville, Tennessee. After a prolonged skirmish, the Federals withdraw.

The town of McMinnville, Tennessee, is captured by 2,500 Confederate cavalry under General John A. Wharton, who seizes 585 prisoners.

General William B. Franklin leads 19,500 Union troops of his XIX Corps from Fort Bisland, Louisiana, and marches westward from Berwick Bay. His objective is to march up to Bayou Teche as far as Lafayette and then to proceed directly into Texas. Simultaneously, General Cadwallader C. Washburn conducts the XIII Corps from Berwick to Bayou Carrion Crow for the same reason. Both columns are opposed by 8,000 Confederates under General Richard Taylor.

October 4

WEST: General James R. Chalmers leads Confederate cavalry on an extended raid into western Tennessee and northern Mississippi.

Confederate cavalry under General Joseph O. Shelby skirmishes with Union forces at Neosho, Missouri.

October 5

WEST: Union cavalry under General Samuel P. Carter stage a night attack on the Confederate camp at Greenville, Tennessee. However, General John S. Williams mounts a staunch defense, and the Federals eventually withdraw.

The Army of the Cumberland, besieged at Chattanooga, Tennessee, is reinforced by the arrival of the XI and XII Corps under General Joseph Hooker, along with portions of the XV Corps from Vicksburg, Mississippi.

Confederate cavalry under General Joseph Wheeler score a major blow by destroying the Stone's River Railroad bridge at Murfreesboro, Tennessee. However, their rear guard is subsequently scattered by the charge of General Robert B. Mitchell's 2nd Union Cavalry Division.

General Joseph O. Shelby's Confederate raiders skirmish with Union troops at Stockton, Missouri.

NAVAL: The CSS *David,* a torpedo boat with an especially low silhouette and equipped with an exploding spar, steams out of Charleston Harbor, South Carolina, at night intending to jab at the waterline of USS *New Ironsides.* Its approach goes nearly undetected until Federal sentinels open fire with small arms, which is immediately followed by the detonation of the Confederate device. The *New Ironsides* sustains heavy damage while *David,* its own boilers extinguished by the explosion, drifts helplessly alongside its victim for several minutes. Commander W. T. Glassell and a sailor are consequently captured, but the two remaining crew members relight the boilers and steam off to safety. A concerned admiral John A. B. Dahlgren anticipates future attacks. "How far the enemy may seem encouraged I do not know," he wrote the navy secretary, "but I think it will be well to be prepared against a considerable issue of these small craft."

Armed boats from the USS *Granite City* capture the British blockade-runner *Concordia* at Calcasieu Pass, Louisiana.

October 6

WEST: General Joseph Wheeler's Confederate cavalry column is handled roughly by the 2nd Cavalry Division under General Robert B. Mitchell, and nearly driven into the Duck River before escaping.

General James R. Chalmer's Confederate cavalry skirmish along the Coldwater River, Mississippi.

General Joseph O. Shelby's Confederate raiders hit Union positions at Humansville, Missouri.

Confederate guerrillas under William C. Quantrill attack what they think is an isolated Union outpost at Baxter Springs, Kansas. The garrison, consisting of 90 men of the 2nd Kansas Colored Infantry and 3rd Wisconsin Cavalry, are nearly overwhelmed but gradually repel the guerrillas through effective use of a howitzer. Meanwhile, a second column commanded by Quantrill encounters the retinue of General James G. Blunt, then shifting his headquarters from Fort Scott to Fort Smith, Arkansas. The guerrillas, clad in captured blue uniforms, trot right up to the column of 100 men and several wagons before shooting. Only Blunt and a third of his men manage to escape; the rest are captured and murdered in cold blood;

among those slain is the son of General Samuel R. Curtis. This affair leads to Blunt's dismissal for negligence.

NAVAL: The USS *Beauregard* captures the Confederate sloop *Last Trial* off Key West, Florida.

The USS *Virginia* captures the British blockade-runner *Jenny* off the Texas coast.

October 7

SOUTH: Confederate cavalry under General J. E. B. Stuart successfully raid Union pickets at Utz's Ford on the Rapidan River, Virginia.

Union reconnaissance parties report unusual Confederate activity south of the Rapidan River. In fact, General Robert E. Lee, aware that the Army of the Potomac has been weakened by the transfers of two corps to the West, prepares to strike at its right flank.

WEST: Union and Confederate cavalry under Generals Samuel P. Carter and John S. Willliams, respectively, skirmish again outside Greenville, Tennessee.

NAVAL: Landing parties from the USS *Cayuga* destroy the grounded Confederate blockade-runner *Pushmahata* off the Calcasieu River, Louisiana.

A bold overland expedition launched from the USS *Osage* from the Mississippi to the Red River results in the destruction of the Confederate steamers *Robert Fulton* and *Argus*.

October 9

POLITICS: President Jefferson Davis stops in Atlanta, Georgia, en route to Tennessee and harangues the populace to thunderous applause.

SOUTH: General Robert E. Lee advances against the right flank of General George G. Meade's Army of the Potomac by crossing the Rapidan River and marching north toward Washington, D.C. With one corps detached in Tennessee, Lee musters the II Corps of General Richard S. Ewell, the III Corps of newly elevated general Ambrose P. Hill, and the cavalry corps under General J. E. B. Stuart.

WEST: General Joseph Wheeler ends his spectacularly successful strike against Union supply lines by recrossing the Tennessee River at Muscle Shoals, Alabama. In a week, he inflicts 2,000 Union casualties, captures more than 1,000 wagons, burns five bridges, tears up miles of track, and ruins millions of dollars in equipment. This proves one of the most destructive raids of the entire war and nearly throttles the Army of the Cumberland, already on half rations at Chattanooga, Tennessee. However, Wheeler's own losses exceed 2,000 and raise questions as to his abilities as a raider.

NAVAL: The Confederate raider CSS *Georgia* under Lieutenant William L. Maury captures and burns the Union ship *Bold Hunter* off the coast of West Africa.

October 10

NORTH: The War Department requests additional gunboat support for the army of General William T. Sherman at Eastport, Tennessee.

SOUTH: General Robert E. Lee, apprised that the Army of the Potomac has dispatched the VI and VII Corps to assist Union forces at Chattanooga, Tennessee, opts for offensive operations and moves toward the Army of the Potomac. Meanwhile, General George M. Meade informs a disappointed President Abraham Lincoln that he is falling back behind the Rappahannock to thwart Confederate moves to turn his right flank and interpose themselves between him and Washington, D.C.

Confederate authorities are forced to dispatch 1,000 soldiers to suppress mounting Union sentiment in and around Elizabeth City and Edenton, North Carolina. The troops are also there to help enforce local conscription efforts.

WEST: In Tennessee the Union XX and XXI Corps are consolidated into the new IV Corps under General Gordon Granger.

General Ambrose E. Burnside directs a cavalry brigade and an infantry division at Blue Springs, Tennessee, where 1,700 Confederates under General John S. Williams are lurking. The Federals advance in force across broken, heavily wooded terrain and nearly break the Confederate line when they are suddenly bombarded by masked batteries. Burnside, having lost 100 men killed and wounded, orders a withdrawal back to Knoxville. Williams, who also falls back through the Cumberland Gap, records his losses at 261.

President Jefferson Davis arrives at Chattanooga, Tennessee, to confer with General Braxton Bragg over military strategy. He is also there to quell seething unrest between Bragg and his senior subordinates.

October 11

SOUTH: Heavy skirmishing erupts around the Rapidan and Rappahannock rivers as Confederate forces occupy Culpeper, Virginia, and maneuver for advantage in the still-evolving Bristoe Campaign. General Robert E. Lee, wishing to emulate his earlier success at Second Manassas, sends the III Corps under General Ambrose P. Hill on a circuitous march around the Union right while the II Corps of General Richard S. Ewell advances along the Orange and Alexandria Railroad.

WEST: Confederate cavalry under General Joseph O. Shelby capture Boonville, Missouri, on the Missouri River.

NAVAL: The USS *Nansemond* shells the Confederate steamer *Douro* after driving it aground at New Inlet, North Carolina, wrecking it. This vessel previously had been captured on March 9, 1863, and sold, but somehow it ended up back in Confederate hands.

The USS *Madgie* sinks in rough seas while being towed off Frying Pan Shoals, North Carolina.

The USS *Union* captures the Confederate steamer *Spaulding* near St. Andrew Sound, Georgia.

October 12

NAVAL: The USS *Kanawha* and *Eugenie*, while chasing a Confederate steamer into Mobile Bay, Alabama, receive heavy fire from nearby Fort Morgan and draw off.

October 13

POLITICS: The Republican governors prevail during elections held in Indiana, Iowa, and Ohio. Foremost among the victors are Andrew Curtin, Pennsylvania's prowar governor and staunch ally of President Abraham Lincoln. By contrast, Peace Democrat Clement L. Vallandigham, who ran for the Ohio governorship while exiled in Canada, is defeated soundly by a proadministration Republican.

SOUTH: While scouting ahead of the main Confederate army, General J. E. B. Stuart suddenly finds himself surrounded by two Union brigades belonging to the II Corps, which encamp for the evening on either side of Catlett's Station, Virginia. He orders his men sequestered in the nearby woods and silently waits for dawn.

A Federal attempt to snare Confederate guerrilla leader Silas F. Gregory fails at Indiantown, North Carolina.

WEST: President Jefferson Davis, after conferring with General Braxton Bragg in northern Georgia, authorizes that officer to transfer the contentious general Daniel H. Hill from his command.

General Joseph O. Shelby meets with a rare rebuff while attacking the Union garrison at Arrow Rock, Missouri.

NAVAL: An armed boat from the USS *Braziliera* captures the Confederate schooner *Mary* off St. Simon's, Georgia.

October 14

NORTH: General Samuel P. Heintzelman is replaced by General Christopher C. Augur as head of the Department of Washington, D.C., and its attendant XXII Corps.

SOUTH: General Ambrose P. Hill, marching through Warrenton, Virginia, perceives the rear guard of General George G. Meade strung out and fording the Broad Run at Bristoe Station. Hill, anxious to inflict damage, immediately decides to attack. However, he does so impetuously without proper reconnaissance and commits only two brigades of General Henry Heth's division to the assault. Hill's target is the V Corps of General George Sykes, but, unknown to him, the entire II Corps of General Gouveneur K. Warren lays in wait behind a railroad embankment at right angles to his advance. No sooner do the North Carolina brigades of General John R. Cooke and William W. Kirkland charge than they are enfiladed immediately by a hail of artillery and musketry. Hit continuously from the front and the side, Heth's attack crumbles after 40 minutes of one-sided slaughter, and he withdraws. By day's end, the Confederates sustain 1,361 casualties, including Cooke and Kirkland wounded, while Union losses are 548. The following day, while traversing the field still strewn with Confederate dead, Hill attempts to explain his embarrassing predicament to General Robert E. Lee, who curtly replies, "Bury these poor men and let us say no more about it."

Confederate cavalry under General J. E. B. Stuart, surrounded by Union forces at Catlett's Station, Virginia, suddenly charge through the enemy camp in a dense fog. The Southerners are repulsed by troops under General Joshua Owen and Colonel Thomas Smyth, but the bulk of Stuart's cavalry escape in the confusion. The Federals lose 11 killed and 42 wounded while taking 28 prisoners. The only Confederate fatality is Colonel Thomas Ruffin of the 1st North Carolina Cavalry. Once again, Stuart's bold resourcefulness in the face of steep odds voids a potential disaster.

WEST: Union cavalry under General William W. Averell skirmish with Confederates at Salt Lick Bridge, West Virginia.

Naval: The USS *Queen City* departs from Helena, Arkansas, and lends close-fire support to army troops engaged at Friar's Point, Mississippi. The expedition nets more than 200 bales of cotton.

October 15
West: Union forces capture all 37 men of a Confederate raiding party who were trying to burn the bridge at Hedgesville, West Virginia.
Naval: The day before it is to be committed to combat, the experimental Confederate submarine CSS *Hunley* disastrously founders a second time in Charleston Harbor, South Carolina, killing all seven crew members with the craft's inventor, Horace L. Hunley, among them. General Pierre G. T. Beauregard, still impressed with the potential of the craft, orders it raised from a watery grave and pressed back into service.

The USS *Honduras* captures the British blockade-runner *Mail* off St. Petersburg, Florida.

The USS *Commodore* and *Corypheus* destroy a Confederate tannery at Bay St. Louis, Mississippi.

October 16
Politics: President Abraham Lincoln, acting through the offices of General in Chief Henry W. Halleck, urges General George G. Meade to attack General Robert E. Lee's forces, but Meade continues resisting such prodding. Lee, meanwhile, falls back and assumes strong defensive positions behind the Rappahannock line.
West: General Ulysses S. Grant assumes control of the new Military Division of the Mississippi, which unites the old departments of the Ohio, the Cumberland, and the Tennessee under a single tent. This effectively places him in control of Federal military operations from the Appalachians to the Mississippi River. Grant himself has been summoned to Cairo, Illinois, for a conference with Secretary of War Edwin M. Stanton, although the two will encounter each other accidently at Indianapolis, Indiana.
Naval: Landing parties from the USS *Adela* and *Tahoma* march 14 miles overland up the Hillsboro River, Florida, to launch a night attack on known Confederate blockade-runners *Scottish Chief* and *Kate Dale*. Both vessels are burned, but the Federal sailors suffer five killed, 10 wounded, and five captured.

The USS *Tennessee* captures the British blockade-runner *Friendship* near Rio Brazos, Texas, and also drives the Confederate schooner *Jane* ashore.

October 17
Politics: President Abraham Lincoln requests the services of 300,000 more volunteers.
South: General Robert E. Lee disengages the Army of Northern Virginia and marches away from Bull Run, Virginia. To help mask this maneuver, General J. E. B. Stuart divides his cavalry command, sending General Wade Hampton's brigade through Gainesville and Haymarket while General Fitzhugh Lee directs his brigade toward Manassas Junction and Bristoe Station.

WEST: General William S. Rosecrans is relieved formally from the Army of the Cumberland and succeeded by General George H. Thomas. The new commander calmly reviews the perilous situation of his army at Chattanooga, Tennessee, and declares, "We will hold the town till we starve."

NAVAL: Armed boats from the USS *Ward* burn the Confederate schooner *Rover* at Murrell's Inlet, North Carolina.

October 18

SOUTH: Confederate cavalry under General J. E. B. Stuart, approaching Groveton, Virginia, suddenly encounter General Hugh J. Kilpatrick's Union cavalry. Stuart withdraws in the direction of Gainesville and then holds his position until nightfall, awaiting the arrival of his second brigade under General Fitzhugh Lee. Once present, Lee then suggests that on the following morning Stuart should feign retreat and withdraw slowly toward Warrenton. This will enable Lee's troopers to assail Kilpatrick's left flank and rear the moment they cross Broad Run. Stuart agrees to the stratagem and makes dispositions to implement it.

A quick strike by the Virginia Partisan Rangers under Major John S. Mosby leads to the capture of 100 horses, prisoners, and valuable equipment near Annandale, Virginia.

WEST: Confederate forces under General John D. Imboden surround and capture 250 men of the 9th Maryland at Charles Town, West Virginia.

NAVAL: Confederate divers relocate the hull of the submarine CSS *Hunley* in nine fathoms of water and begin recovery operations.

October 19

SOUTH: As anticipated, Confederate cavalry under General J. E. B. Stuart are attacked by General Hugh J. Kirkpatrick's Union troopers at Warrenton, Virginia. Stuart, with the brigade of General Fitzhugh Lee secretly deployed on the Union flank, falls back to Buckland Mills on Broad Run, enticing the impetuous Kilpatrick forward. Kilpatrick willingly obliges, and he sends General George A. Custer's Michigan brigade to commence the affair. Just as the fighting begins, Lee's brigade suddenly strikes Custer's flank and rear with his 2nd Virginia Cavalry. Stuart, observing the trap sprung, instantly orders the 1st North Carolina forward at the charge. Custer's men are predictably routed and flee directly into General Henry E. Davis's brigade as it canters up in support. Chaos reigns as the startled troops try to extricate themselves, and Kilpatrick orders a retreat with vengeful Confederates pursuing hotly. Stuart gradually reins in his men after a five-mile chase from Buckland back to Warrenton, securing 150 prisoners and eight wagons for a loss of 30 casualties. Thereafter, this embarrassing affair becomes jocularly known among Southern horsemen as the "Buckland Races."

Having failed to lure General George G. Meade into battle, the Army of Northern Virginia of General Robert E. Lee settles into defensive positions along the Rappahannock River, with bridgeheads at Rappahannock Station and Kelly's Ford. His aborted Bristoe Campaign cost the Confederacy 205 killed and 1,176 wounded (1,381) to a Federal tally of 136 dead, 733 wounded, and 1,423 missing (2,292).

Nonetheless, Union forces have been pushed back 40 miles in another brilliant offensive maneuver.

October 20
SOUTH: General Cadwallader C. Washburn assumes command of the XIII Corps in Mississippi.

WEST: Confederate cavalry under Colonel George C. Dibrell attack a Union wagon train at Philadelphia, Tennessee, inflicting 479 casualties.

NAVAL: A party from the USS *T. A. Ward* lands at Murrell's Inlet, North Carolina, looking for freshwater, but it is surprised by Confederate cavalry and loses 10 men captured.

The USS *Annie* captures the British blockade-runner *Martha Jane* off Bayport, Florida.

October 21
SOUTH: Union forces under General William B. Franklin occupy Opelousas, Louisiana, the farthest they reach during the so-called Bayou Teche operation.

NAVAL: The USS *Currituck* captures the Confederate steamer *Three Brothers* in the Rappahannock River, Virginia.

The USS *Nansemond* chases the Confederate steamer *Venus* aground near Cape Fear, North Carolina, where it is burned to prevent capture.

The USS *J. P. Jackson* captures the Confederate schooner *Syrena* off Deer Island, Mississippi.

October 22
SOUTH: Pursuing Federal forces attack and overrun a detachment belonging to Major John S. Mosby's partisan rangers near Annandale, Virginia.

NAVAL: The unescorted Union steamer *Mist* is boarded and destroyed by Confederate guerrillas at Ship Island, Mississippi. Hereafter, Admiral David D. Porter advises General William T. Sherman that "steamers should not be allowed to land anywhere but at a military port, or at a place guarded by a gunboat."

October 23
SOUTH: President Jefferson Davis relieves General Leonidas Polk as corps commander in the Army of Tennessee to end tensions with his superior, General Braxton Bragg. He is replaced by General William J. Hardee.

WEST: General Ulysses S. Grant arrives at Chattanooga, Tennessee, and assumes command of the Army of the Cumberland. Accompanied by General George H. Thomas, they advance to within gunshot range of Confederate lines below Lookout Mountain for a peek at enemy positions. Satisfied, Grant next orders a new supply route established from Bridgeport to the beleaguered garrison, the so-called Cracker Line. He also begins to plan an immediate counterstrike against General Braxton Bragg on the heights overlooking the city. Union fortunes are bolstered further by the forthcoming arrival of the XI and XII Corps under General Joseph Hooker, and the XV Corps of General William T. Sherman.

NAVAL: The USS *Norfolk Packet* captures the Confederate schooner *Ocean Bird* near St. Augustine Inlet, Florida.

October 24

WEST: Acting on the advice of Chattanooga's chief engineer, General William F. Smith, General Ulysses S. Grant authorizes a strategy to open up a new supply route on the Tennessee River below Confederate-held Racoon Mountain. This stratagem is necessary to supplant the awkward 60-mile route for supplies from northern Alabama through the Sequatchie Valley, which is also subject to interdiction by Confederate cavalry.

General William T. Sherman is appointed commander of the Army of the Tennessee once it finally arrives at Chattanooga, Tennessee, from Vicksburg, Mississippi.

NAVAL: The USS *Calypso* captures the British blockade-runner *Herald* off Frying Pan Shoals, North Carolina.

The Federal gunboats USS *Hastings* and *Key West* arrive at Eastport, Mississippi, in support of army operations along the Tennessee River under General William T. Sherman.

The USS *Conestoga* captures the Confederate steamer *Lille Martin* and the tug *Sweden* off Napoleon, Mississippi.

October 25

WEST: Confederate forces under General John S. Marmaduke attack and temporarily occupy Pine Bluff, Arkansas.

NAVAL: The USS *Kittatinny* captures the Confederate schooner *Reserve* off Pass Cavallo, Texas.

October 26

SOUTH: Major John S. Mosby's partisans attack a Union wagon train near New Baltimore, Virginia, seizing 145 horses before Union cavalry arrives to chase them off.

Union batteries recommence their second, intensive bombardment of Fort Sumter, Charleston Harbor, South Carolina. They fire 625 heavy shot into the crumbling works on the first day.

General William B. Franklin abandons his proposed offensive into East Texas through the bayou country and halts at Opelousas. He finds the foreboding, swampy terrain, made worse by incessant rainfall, impassible and retraces his steps back to New Iberia. The retreating Federals are followed closely by Confederate forces under ever-aggressive General Richard Taylor, who awaits an opportunity to strike.

WEST: As General Joseph Hooker approaches Chattanooga, Tennessee, with the XI and XII Corps, General William B. Hazen of IV Corps orchestrates laying a pontoon bridge across the Tennessee River at Brown's Ferry, opposite Confederate-held Racoon Mountain, to open up a riverine supply line to the beleaguered city. A brigade under General John B. Turchin then crosses over, defeats a determined charge by the 15th Alabama on the west bank, and secures a bridgehead. Union bases in northern Alabama are now capable of funneling aid directly to the garrison without resorting to the torturous trail running north through the mountains.

NAVAL: The ironclad fleet under Admiral John A. B. Dahlgren commences another intensive, two-week bombardment of Fort Sumter, Charleston Harbor, South Carolina. Despite a terrific pounding, the Confederate garrison holds on.

October 27

WEST: General Joseph Hooker commences operations to reopen the Tennessee River and facilitate the flow of Union supplies to Chattanooga, Tennessee. He advances the XI and XII Corps under his command from Bridgeport, Alabama, toward Brown's Ferry on the Tennessee River, crosses over, and clears Confederates from nearby Racoon Mountain. This move forces General Evander M. Law's division to withdraw to the west side of Lookout Mountain. Hooker also positions a force under General John W. Geary, XII Corps, at Wauhatchie Station to guard his line of communications from possible attack.

General William T. Sherman advances from Vicksburg, Mississippi, toward Chattanooga, Tennessee, having been directed previously by General in Chief Henry W. Halleck to repair Union rail lines en route. General Ulysses S. Grant, however, summarily cancels his instructions and orders him forward to Chattanooga with all speed.

NAVAL: A convoy of Federal troops under General Nathaniel P. Banks departs New Orleans, Louisiana, escorted by the USS *Monongahela*, *Virginia*, and *Owasco*. They are tasked with capturing Brazos, Santiago, and the mouth of the Rio Grande, Texas. It is anticipated that success here will deter French troops from crossing the river from Mexico.

The USS *Granite City* captures the Confederate schooner *Anita* at Pass Cavallo, Texas.

October 28

WEST: General Braxton Bragg orders General James Longstreet to mount an attack on the Union bridgehead at Brown's Ferry. Instead, Longstreet instructs the division of General Micah Jenkins to hit the Union rear guard at Wauhatchie Station at night. Although the attack is scheduled to kick off at 10:00 P.M., the four Southern brigades became lost in the dark and can only grope their way toward Union positions. Longstreet then cancels the operation and returns to camp, but his messenger never reaches Jenkins in time. At about midnight, the first Union sentries are encountered and eliminated, but General John W. Geary is alert and mounts a strong defense with two brigades.

General John M. Palmer assumes command of the XIV Corps in Tennessee.

NAVAL: The Confederate raider CSS *Georgia* under Lieutenant William L. Maury concludes a seven-month cruise against Union commerce by dropping anchor at Cherbourg, France.

October 29

SOUTH: President Jefferson Davis, continuing on his morale-raising tour of the Deep South, stops at Atlanta, Georgia.

The latest round of Union bombardment at Fort Sumter, Charleston Harbor, South Carolina, amounts to 2,691 shells and 33 slain Confederates, but the defenders still refuse to yield.

WEST: President Jefferson Davis grants a petition by General Nathan B. Forrest to be detached from the Army of Tennessee on the grounds that he has feuded seriously with General Braxton Bragg. The renowned "Wizard of the Saddle" is then granted an independent command based in northern Mississippi.

An early morning Confederate attack unfolds against Union positions at Wauhatchie Station, Tennessee. General Micah Jenkin's division of four brigades hits the Union camp hard in the darkness, but Federal troops under General John W. Geary, firing at muzzle flashes, resist stoutly. The Confederates charge the 'V' shaped Union line repeatedly, but fail to break it, and at 3:00 A.M., Jenkins retreats back to Lookout Mountain. Fighting dies down along the line as General Joseph Hooker dispatches General Carl Schurz's division to Geary's aid, but they became lost and fail to arrive. Confederate losses are 34 killed, 305 wounded, and 69 missing to a Union tally of 78 killed, 327 wounded, and 15 missing. The tenuous union supply line remains secure.

Union cavalry belonging to General George H. Thomas attack and rout a detachment of Confederates at Centerville, Tennessee, taking 90 captives.

General Frank P. Blair assumes command of the XV Corps in Tennessee.

October 30

POLITICS: A gathering of Unionists convenes at Fort Smith, Arkansas, to elect a representative to the U.S. Congress.

NORTH: James H. Wilson is appointed brigadier general, U.S. Army.

WEST: The Federal transport *Chattanooga* arrives up the Tennessee River and docks at Chattanooga, Tennessee, bringing much needed sustenance to the beleaguered Army of the Cumberland.

NAVAL: The USS *Annie* captures the British blockade-runner *Meteor* at Bayport, Florida.

The USS *Vanderbilt* captures the Confederate bark *Saxon* at Angra Pequena, Africa.

Federal gunboats USS *Lexington, Hastings, Key West, Cricket, Tobb, Romeo,* and *Peosta* relocate by steaming from the Mississippi to the Tennessee River in support of General William T. Sherman.

October 31

SOUTH: Union batteries continue with the latest round of shelling at Fort Sumter, Charleston Harbor, South Carolina.

NAVAL: Instruction begins for 52 midshipmen at the Confederate Naval Academy housed aboard the CSS *Patrick Henry* at Drewry's Bluff, James River, Virginia.

November 1

SOUTH: Federal gunners dump another 768 rounds on the shattered remnants of Fort Sumter, South Carolina, but the garrison, holed up in bombproofs, grimly hangs on.

Union forces under General William B. Franklin withdraw from Opelousas, Louisiana, back to New Iberia. This concludes the latest Union attempt to reach Sabine Pass, Texas, via Bayou Teche.

WEST: A force 5,000 Union cavalry and mounted infantry under General William W. Averell clatters out from Beverly, West Virginia, and into the Allegheny Mountains on an extended raid toward Lewisburg. Averell's orders are to destroy the East Tennessee and Virginia Railroad in concert with another column commanded by General Alfred N. Duffie.

Union steamers continue landing supplies at Brown's Ferry on the Tennessee River, signaling the end of General Braxton Bragg's siege of Chattanooga, Tennessee. Because General George H. Thomas's hungry defenders eagerly await the new influx of hardtack, the new route is christened the "Cracker Line."

November 2

POLITICS: A Pennsylvania committee, tasked with organizing festivities surrounding the dedication of a Union cemetery for soldiers fallen at the Battle of Gettysburg, invites President Abraham Lincoln to attend the ceremony, slated for November 19. To their surprise and delight, the chief executive accepts and begins to work on a speech in which to express his justification of the war effort.

SOUTH: President Jefferson Davis is on hand to witness Union artillerists fire another 793 rounds against Fort Sumter, Charleston Harbor, South Carolina. Nonetheless, he "did not believe that Charleston would ever be taken."

November 3

SOUTH: Union gunners pour an additional 661 rounds on the ruins of Fort Sumter, Charleston Harbor, South Carolina, apparently to no effect.

Major John S. Mosby defeats a detachment of Union cavalry at Catlett's Station, Virginia.

Union and Confederate force skirmish heavily along the Bayou Borbeau, Louisiana. Three Federal divisions under General William B. Franklin's XIX Corps encamp carelessly and beyond mutual supporting distance. General Richard Taylor, though outnumbered two to one, masses his Confederates for a sudden attack on General Stephen G. Burbridge's exposed division. Security proves lax, and when Southern cavalry under General Thomas Green suddenly emerge out of a ravine, the Yankees scatter in camp. Burbridge, unable to reform his line, calls the retreat and is hounded all the way back to the camp of General George F. McGinnis, three miles distant. Losses in this sharp and embarrassing affair are 25 Union dead, 129 wounded, and 562 captured, along with one cannon.

WEST: A force 1,700 Union cavalry under General Alfred N. Duffie gallops out from Charleston, West Virginia, on a converted drive against Confederate positions at Lewisburg. Once present, he is to destroy the East Tennessee and Virginia Railroad in concert with a column led by General William W. Averell.

Confederate cavalry under General John R. Chalmers unsuccessfully attack the Union garrison at Collierville, Tennessee, losing 95 men.

General John McNeil assumes command of the Union District of the Frontier.

NAVAL: The USS *Kenwood* captures the Confederate steamer *Black Hawk* off Port Hudson, Louisiana.

Federal gunboats *Monongahela*, *Owasco*, and *Virginia* support troop landings under General Nathaniel P. Banks as they capture Brazos Island, Texas. The Union finally acquires a toehold in the Lone Star State.

November 4

WEST: General Braxton Bragg directs General James Longstreet to march 15,000 men against Union positions at Knoxville, Tennessee. The actual decision originates with President Jefferson Davis, partially to tie down Union assets in the eastern portion of the state and partially to lessen tensions between two headstrong leaders by separating them. Longstreet takes with him the divisions of General Micah Jenkins, General Lafayette McLaws, two artillery battalions under General Edward P. Alexander, and the cavalry of General Joseph Wheeler. The move itself is a bold expedient, which, if successful, will reopen direct communications with Virginia. Bragg, however, is seriously weakening his own defensive lines just as General Ulysses S. Grant prepares to attack below Chattanooga.

SOUTHWEST: Brownsville, Texas, is formally occupied by Union forces under Generals Napoleon J. T. Dana and Nathaniel P. Banks.

NAVAL: The USS *Virginia* captures the British blockade-runner *Matamoras* off the mouth of the Rio Grande, Texas.

The USS *Monongahela, Virginia,* and *Owasco* assist the army troops of General Napoleon J. T. Dana to seize Brownsville, Texas.

November 5

POLITICS: President Abraham Lincoln rebukes General Nathaniel P. Banks for his tardy efforts at reestablishing a constitutional government in Louisiana, which, he insists, must assure African Americans "on the question of their permanent freedom."

SOUTH: In several operations Major John S. Mosby reports that he has captured 75 prisoners and more than 100 mules and horses in the region Union forces deem "Mosby's Confederacy."

WEST: In light of General James Longstreet's offensive against Knoxville, Tennessee, General Ulysses S. Grant pensively awaits reinforcements under General William T. Sherman so that he finally can break the Confederate stranglehold on Chattanooga. For Grant, it is imperative to strike General Braxton Bragg before Longstreet attacks and possibly defeats General Ambrose E. Burnside's IX Corps at Knoxville.

NAVAL: The USS *Nansemond, Keystone State,* and *Howquah* chase and capture the Confederate vessel *Margaret and Jessie* off Myrtle Beach, South Carolina. This is one of the more enterprising blockade-runners extant, having completed 15 successful trips.

The cannonading of Fort Sumter, South Carolina, continues unabated, and Admiral John A. B. Dahlgren notes: "The only original feature left is the northeast face, the rest is a pile of rubbish."

The USS *Beauregard* seizes the British blockade-runner *Volante* near Cape Canaveral, Florida.

The USS *Virginia* and *Owasco* capture the British blockade-runners *Science* and *Dashing Wave* at the mouth of the Rio Grande, Texas.

November 6

POLITICS: President Jefferson Davis pays a morale-raising visit to Wilmington, North Carolina.

WEST: General William W. Averell encounters a Confederate brigade of 1,700 men and six cannon under General John Echols at Droop Mountain, West Virginia. Averell quickly plans to send his infantry skirting around the enemy left while his own artillery and cavalry demonstrate against Echol's center. At 3:00 P.M., the Confederate line, threatened from two directions, collapses and flees down the mountainside. Averell, having captured a battle flag and a cannon, declines to pursue.

Confederate cavalry under General William E. Jones captures Rogersville, Tennessee, netting 775 prisoners, 32 wagons, and 1,000 horses.

SOUTHWEST: General Nathaniel P. Banks lands and consolidates Union positions at Brownsville and Point Isabelle, Texas.

NAVAL: The Confederate raider CSS *Alabama* under Captain Raphael Semmes captures and burns the Union bark *Amanda* in the Dutch East Indies.

November 7

SOUTH: The Army of the Potomac pushes two brigades over the Rappahannock and into stiff fights at Kelly's Ford and Rappahannock Station. General Robert E. Lee has maintained a bridgehead on the north bank of the Rappahannock River, not really expecting General George G. Meade to attack in force, but when he does, the defenders are caught unawares. General William H. French, commanding the I, II, and II Corps, is ordered to cross the Rappahannock River at Kelly's Ford, then guarded by General Robert Rodes' division. At the onset, the 2nd and 30th North Carolina are overwhelmed in a surprise attack, and many are captured; 349 are casualties. Union forces now are established firmly on the south bank of the Rappahannock.

Five miles upstream, General John Sedgwick moves his V and VI Corps rapidly against Rappahannock Station, defended by the celebrated "Louisiana Tigers" of Colonel Harry T. Hays and a division under General Robert Hoke. Fighting rages throughout the day as Federal troops work their way around the Confederate flanks, but they fail to press their attack home. Combat stops with nightfall, and General Lee somewhat naturally assumes the enemy would not attack further that night, so he declines to reinforce the bridgehead. He intends to counterattack the following day, but Sedgwick preempts him. That evening, through a driving downpour, he leads the 6th Maine in a bayonet charge that startles the "Tigers" and drives them from their rifle pits. The 5th Wisconsin also comes up in support and makes good progress until the coup finally is delivered by a brigade under Colonel Emory Upton. The Confederate bridgehead is crushed, and 1,600 prisoners are taken, including Colonel Archibald C. Godwin. Total Confederate casualties number 2,023, principally captured, while the Federals lose 370. Lee, somewhat embarrassed to find his defensive positions suddenly compromised, rapidly withdraws south toward Culpeper Court House.

WEST: Union cavalry columns under General William W. Averell and Alfred N. A. Duffie unite in Lewisburg, West Virginia, where they destroy numerous Confederate supplies. But finding their path to Dublin blocked by felled trees and other obstacles, both leaders decide to abandon their raid.

NAVAL: Armed boats from the USS *Sagamore* capture the British blockade-runner *Paul* near Bayport, Florida.

Confederate guerrillas capture and burn the steamer *Allen Collier* at Whitworth's Landing, Mississippi, after it left the protection of the Federal gunboat USS *Eastport*.

November 8

WEST: John C. Breckinridge replaces General Daniel H. Hill as commander of the II Corps, Army of Tennessee, because of tensions with commanding General Braxton Bragg.

NAVAL: The USS *James Adger* and *Niphon* capture the Confederate steamer *Cornubia* near New Inlet, North Carolina.

November 9

POLITICS: President Abraham Lincoln attends the theater in Washington, D.C., ironically observing actor John Wilkes Booth perform in *The Marble Heart*.

President Jefferson Davis's train finally chugs into Richmond, Virginia, slowed somewhat by a snowstorm.

NAVAL: Admiral David D. Porter suggests to Secretary of the Navy Gideon Welles that the Coast Survey be employed in making detailed maps of the various creeks and tributaries emanating from the Mississippi River, "where navigation is made up of innumerable lakes and bayous not known to any but the most experienced pilots."

The USS *James Adger* finally seizes the Confederate vessel *Robert E. Lee* off Cape Lookout Shoals, North Carolina. This is another successful blockade-runner with 20 completed trips on its ledgers.

The USS *Niphon* captures the Confederate vessel *Ella and Annie* near Masonboro Inlet, North Carolina.

November 10

SOUTH: The Army of Northern Virginia, falling back, settles into defensive positions behind the Rapidan River to await developments.

For the past three days Union gunners deliver 1,753 artillery rounds against the ruins of Fort Sumter, Charleston Harbor, South Carolina, without prompting a Confederate surrender.

NAVAL: The USS *Howquah* captures the Confederate steamer *Ella* off Wilmington, North Carolina.

After two weeks of concentrated bombardment, the ironclad squadron of Admiral John A. B. Dahlgren reports having fired 9,036 projectiles at Fort Sumter, Charleston Harbor, South Carolina. The post is reduced to rubble yet refuses to yield.

The Confederate raider CSS *Alabama* under Captain Raphael Semmes captures and burns the Union clipper ship *Winged Racer* in the Straits of Sunda off Java.

November 11

POLITICS: President Jefferson Davis, ever concerned about the situation before Chattanooga, Tennessee, warns General Braxton Bragg to "not allow the enemy to get up all his reinforcements before striking him, if it can be avoided."

SOUTH: The politically well-connected general Benjamin F. Butler supersedes General John G. Foster as commander of the Union Department of Virginia and North

Carolina. He immediately orders troops to arrest any civilians using "opprobrious or threatening language" against them.

NAVAL: The Confederate raider CSS *Alabama* under Captain Raphael Semmes burns the Union clipper *Contest* in the Gaspar Straits.

November 12

SOUTH: Union batteries on Morris Island, Charleston Harbor, South Carolina, commence another prolonged bombardment of the still defiant Fort Sumter.

WEST: Generals James Longstreet and Joseph Wheeler mass their respective commands at Loudon, Tennessee, prior to advancing on nearby Knoxville. The weather and marching conditions up to this point have been horrid and greatly impede their progress.

November 14

WEST: General Nathan B. Forrest is assigned to the Confederate command of West Tennessee.

At Chattanooga, General William T. Sherman begins a personal reconnaissance of the northern end of Missionary Ridge, constituting the right wing of General Braxton Bragg's Army of Tennessee.

General James Longstreet's 15,000 Confederates begin to cross the Tennessee River at Loudon, Tennessee, having covered only 60 miles in eight days of hard marching. He then makes a tactical mistake by dispatching the bulk of his cavalry under General Joseph Wheeler on a raid toward the Holston River south of Knoxville. This deprives him of his best fighting troops just as a series of small-scale engagements starts to erupt. Prior to Longstreet's arrival, General Ambrose E. Burnside gallops into Loudon to supervise the evacuation of 5,000 Union troops there personally, and he shepherds them back to Knoxville. This effort turns out to be Burnside's best performance of the entire war, and a curious parallel race then unfolds as the two forces—almost within gunshot of each other—slog through ankle-deep mud vying to reach Knoxville first.

NAVAL: Union forces apprehend Confederate navy master John Y. Beall on the Virginia coast before he and his select band of 14 sailors are able to steal a steamer.

The USS *Dai Ching* captures the Confederate schooner *George Chisholm* at the Santee River, South Carolina.

The USS *Bermuda* recaptures the Union schooner *Mary Campbell* from Confederate forces near Pensacola, Florida.

November 15

SOUTH: Union gunners fire off an additional 2,328 rounds at Fort Sumter, Charleston Harbor, South Carolina, during the past three days without eliciting Confederate capitulation.

WEST: Having reached the Holston River, Confederate cavalry under General Joseph Wheeler arrive on the heights across from Knoxville, Tennessee. Wheeler decides that Union positions are too strong to attack, and so he withdraws.

The army of General James Longstreet and a division of Union troops commanded by General Ambrose E. Burnside slog through a driving rain and mud to reach Knoxville, Tennessee, first. Throughout their ordeal, the contestants are separated only by one mile and a bend in the Tennessee River. Burnside, anxious to avoid being trapped outside the city, redoubles efforts to reach Campbell's Station ahead of the enemy. Longsteet, meanwhile, dispatches General Lafayette McLaw's division to capture the crossroads ahead of him. Both sides encamp in the vicinity of Lenoir for the evening.

Having traversed 675 miles by boat, rail, and road, General William T. Sherman finally arrives at Bridgeport, Alabama, with four divisions, totaling 17,000 men, intended for the relief of Chattanooga, Tennessee. The general rides ahead to confer with General Ulysses S. Grant about his impending offensive.

Union authorities begin to crack down on illicit trade with either the enemy and or by war profiteers throughout western Tennessee and northern Mississippi.

NAVAL: The USS *Lodona* captures the British blockade-runner *Arctic* off Frying Pan Shoals, North Carolina.

The USS *Leigh* grounds under the guns of Fort Moultrie, Charleston Harbor, South Carolina, and has to be rescued and towed by the ironclad *Nahant*. Three of the *Leigh's* crew members win the Congressional Medal of Honor for carrying a line from their crippled vessel to *Nahant* under heavy enemy fire.

November 16

WEST: Confederate cavalry under General John D. Imboden attack a Union supply train near Burlington, West Virginia, taking 25 captives and 245 horses.

The Confederate corps of General James Longstreet and a retiring Union column under General Ambrose Burnside depart Lenoir, Tennessee, in the early morning darkness. Both sides detach mounted forces ahead of their infantry to capture Campbell's Station, 10 miles distant, first. Burnside, feeling he is losing the race, also burns his baggage and wagons to increase his speed. Continual skirmishing erupts as the Union column fortuitously reach the crossroads just 15 minutes ahead of the Confederates and deploys to give battle. Longstreet then dispatches the brigade of General Evander M. Law around the Union position to strike it from behind while the division of General Lafayette McLaws hits the Union right. Burnside, perceiving this turning movement, falls back a half mile after his main line repulses an attack by McLaws. Law then makes a tardy appearance along the front of the readjusted Union line instead of its rear, and he is likewise beaten back. Fighting ceases at night, and Longstreet concedes both the race and Campbell's Station to the Yankees. Burnside, who conducted his movements with alacrity under trying conditions, suffers 318 casualties to a Confederate tally of 174. Union forces now proceed promptly into Knoxville and prepare for a siege.

SOUTHWEST: Union forces under General Nathaniel P. Banks occupy Corpus Christi, Texas.

November 17

WEST: General William W. Averell concludes his successful Union cavalry raid by returning to New Creek, West Virginia.

General James Longstreet begins to position his corps to besiege Knoxville, Tennessee.

Southwest: Union forces under General Nathaniel P. Banks storm a Confederate battery on Mustang Island, Aransas Pass, Texas.

Naval: The USS *Mystic* captures the Confederate schooner *Emma D.* off Yorktown, Virginia.

The USS *Monongahela* covers the landing of Federal forces under General Nathaniel P. Banks on Mustang Island, Aransas Pass, Texas. Several crew members come ashore to man some howitzers, which bombard the Confederate garrison into surrendering.

November 18

North: President Abraham Lincoln, somewhat depressed over the illness of his son Tad, boards a special train that takes him to Gettysburg, Pennsylvania, for the purpose of dedicating a military cemetery.

South: Union and Confederate cavalry under Generals George A. Custer and Wade Hampton clash at Germanna Ford, Virginia.

West: A Union sweep of the region between Vienna, Virginia, and the Blue Ridge Mountains results in the capture of several of Major John S. Mosby's partisan rangers.

Naval: The USS *Granite City* captures the Confederate schooner *Amelia Ann* and the Spanish bark *Teresita* off Aransas Pass, Texas.

Federal gunboats USS *Choctaw, Franklin,* and *Carondelet* bombard Confederate batteries along the Mississippi River at Hog Point, Louisiana.

The Federal schooner *Joseph L. Garrity* is seized by Confederate sympathizers lurking onboard and taken to British Honduras, where it is converted into the blockade-runner *Eureka.*

November 19

North: A gathering of 15,000 citizens at Gettysburg, Pennsylvania, is harangued with stirring oratory for two hours by Edward Everett. Onlookers are next greeted by the spectacle of a gaunt, towering president Abraham Lincoln striding to the podium. In only two minutes, he delivers his "Gettysburg Address," one of the most seminal political speeches in all history. "Four score and seven years ago our fathers brought forth, upon this continent, a new nation, conceived in liberty, and dedicated to the proposition that all men are created equal," it began. The audience listens in raptured silence, applauding lightly and not fully comprehending the import of what they are hearing. But in only 272 words, Lincoln codifies the ideals of the American republic and the absolute, essential necessity for preserving it: "That this nation, under God, shall have a new birth of freedom," he intones, "and that government of the people, by the people, for the people, shall not perish from the earth." This display of timeless eloquence resonates down to the present.

South: Fort Sumter is hit by an additional 694 shells thrown by a ring of Union siege guns at Charleston Harbor, South Carolina.

West: After Union forces under General Ambrose E. Burnside occupy and fortify the city of Knoxville, Tennessee, he orders a cavalry brigade of 700 men under General William P. Sanders to dismount and contest the advance of Confederates under General James Longstreet. Sanders mounts a tenacious defense and contains his antagonists for several hours before being killed, the only Southern-born general in Northern employ to die in combat. Burnside subsequently renames Fort Loudon, on the extreme northwest of the city, Fort Sanders in his honor.

November 20

POLITICS: Considering his recent address at Gettysburg a disappointment, President Abraham Lincoln contacts Edward Everett saying, "I am pleased to know that, in your opinion, the little I did say was not entirely a failure."

SOUTH: Union siege guns fire a further 1,344 rounds at Fort Sumter, Charleston Harbor, South Carolina, killing three defenders and wounding 11.

November 21

SOUTH: A Union sweep of the region between Bealeton and Thoroughfare Gap, Virginia, results in the capture of several partisans belonging to Major John S. Mosby's command.

Virginia Partisan Rangers under Major John S. Mosby attack and capture several Union wagons at Liberty, Virginia.

WEST: Union reinforcements under General William T. Sherman begin to cross the Tennessee River at Brown's Ferry before marching against General Braxton Bragg's right flank along Missionary Ridge. Additional forces under General Joseph Hooker also begin to deploy to storm the Confederate left near the Chattanooga Valley, Tennessee. Union movements are complicated further by a difficult landscape and driving rain, which delays their progress.

NAVAL: The USS *Grand Gulf* and the army transport *Fulton* seize the British steamer *Banshee* off Salter Path, North Carolina.

November 22

WEST: General Braxton Bragg detaches additional troops under General Patrick R. Cleburne from his Army of Tennessee to assist in the siege of Knoxville. Meanwhile, General Ulysses S. Grant orders his men into offensive positions for a major attack against Confederate troops around Chattanooga, Tennessee.

SOUTHWEST: Federal troops under General Nathaniel P. Banks besiege Fort Esperanza, Matagorda Island, Texas.

NAVAL: The USS *Jacob Bell* provides supporting fire for troop landings on St. George's Island, Maryland.

The USS *Aroostook* captures the Confederate schooner *Eureka* near Galveston, Texas.

November 23

WEST: General Ulysses S. Grant, prior to assaulting the main Confederate defenses of Braxton Bragg along Missionary Ridge, orchestrates a clever reconnaissance in force near the enemy's center. He orders General George H. Thomas to parade the IV Corps in full view of enemy positions along Orchard Knob, Tennessee, a long, low mound that would allow Union troops deploying out of Chattanooga to enjoy greater maneuvering room. At a given signal—and without artillery support—the divisions of Generals Thomas J. Woods and Philip H. Sheridan suddenly charge the unsuspecting defenders. What happens next is a minor miracle. At 12:30 P.M.,

Southerners of the 24th and 28th Alabama gathered about Orchard Knob to observe the military movement gradually drift away when they perceive a parade in progress. When a signal gun fires at precisely 1:30 P.M., the Union troops lurch forward, completely dispersing and overrunning their astonished opponents. This easy success enables Union troops to deploy at the very foot of Lookout Mountain and causes Grant to modify further his battle plans for the morrow. Union losses in this minor coup prove light, and 200 Confederates are also taken captive. Orchard Knob also serves as Grant's headquarters for the remainder of the campaign.

Confederate general Carter L. Stevenson, commanding an emaciated division on nearby Lookout Mountain, wires General Braxton Bragg that he lacks sufficient strength to hold his position against a determined Union assault. Stevenson sent his message in the prescribed code, unaware that Federal intelligence could decipher it, and General Ulysses S. Grant now realizes now vulnerable this important facet of the Confederate line is. He quickly instructs General Joseph Hooker to proceed immediately with three divisions to Lookout Mountain, on the Confederate left, and to seize Rossville Gap toward its rear. A redoubtable Union blow is assuming definite form.

General Patrick R. Cleburne's division, previously dispatched to Knoxville to assist General James Longstreet, is recalled hurriedly by General Braxton Bragg back to Chattanooga, Tennessee, and posted on the extreme right along Missionary Ridge.

SOUTHWEST: Federal forces under General Nathaniel P. Banks begin an overland campaign from the Texas coast to Rio Grande City.

November 24

SOUTH: Fort Sumter, Charleston Harbor, South Carolina, is pelted with another 270 Union rounds that leave three killed and two wounded.

WEST: At 8:00 A.M., General Joseph Hooker marches his three divisions—12,000 men—to the foot of Lookout Mountain, Tennessee, and begins to scale the 1,100-foot summit. Their advance is masked conveniently by a dense layer of fog blanketing the slope and blinding the defenders. Confederates under General Carter L. Stevenson, who scarcely can muster 2,693 men to oppose them, resist tenaciously but give ground before the Federal juggernaut. Hooker's attack, spearheaded by General John W. Geary's division, makes good progress, steadily driving the defenders up the slope. Resistance, including artillery fire, stiffens on a plateau halfway up the mountain, and Hooker stops to reorganize and bring up ammunition. Stevenson, having repeatedly requested General Braxton Bragg for reinforcements without response, suddenly is instructed to withdraw and reposition his command on the far right of the line at 2:30 P.M. The fleeing Confederates then burn a bridge behind them and withdraw in the night.

Meanwhile, anxious Union leaders gaze up on the mountain, shrouded with impenetrable, low-laying fog, and wonder how the battle is proceeding. By 8:00 P.M., Hooker has reached all his objectives, and the following morning, when the fog finally disperses, all are immediately relieved to behold the Stars and Stripes flying boldly from the summit. For this reason, the clash at Missionary Ridge becomes popularly known as "the Battle above the Clouds." Casualties are unrecorded by either side but appear to have been light. Furthermore, Hooker is poised to operate against the left and rear of the Confederate defenses by pressing on to Rossville Gap.

At the other end of Bragg's line, troops under General William T. Sherman advance to seize what he thinks is the north end of Missionary Ridge. Instead, the strip of land he captures is separated from the ridge by a wide ravine, thereby tipping off General Braxton Bragg that an assault is imminent.

NAVAL: The USS *Pawnee* and *Marblehead* cover army troops as they sink piles and other obstructions in the Stono River above Legareville, South Carolina.

November 25

SOUTH: Union gunners fire off 517 rounds into the crumbling defenses of Fort Sumter, Charleston Harbor, South Carolina, with little effect.

WEST: At Chattanooga, the final struggle between Generals Ulysses S. Grant, with 64,000 troops, and Braxton Bragg, commanding 46,000, is at hand. At 10:00 A.M., General William T. Sherman, with 16,000 men, begins a concerted drive against the Confederate right anchored on Missionary Ridge. The terrain encountered is rough, favoring the defense, and is manned ably by the 4,000 veterans of General Patrick R. Cleburne's division. Sherman consequently attacks Tunnel Hill all morning and into the afternoon with little to show beyond lengthening casualty lists. This is primarily because Union attacks are delivered piecemeal rather than by means of one crushing blow; hence, Cleburne remains able to shift his troops constantly to each threatened point. Just as the Confederates, whose ammunition is almost exhausted, seem on the verge of being overwhelmed, Cleburne orders a sharp bayonet charge downhill that scatters the tiring bluecoats. Sherman's alarming lack of progress also forces General Ulysses S. Grant to mount diversions elsewhere to prevent General Braxton Bragg from shifting reinforcements over to his right.

General Joseph Hooker's command is then ordered to attack Rossville Gap from Lookout Mountain on Bragg's left, which threatens the Confederate rear. Hooker's progress, however, is delayed because of the necessity to rebuild a bridge over Chickamauga Creek, so Grant next instructs General George H. Thomas, presently holding the Union center, to seize the rifle pits fronting the main Confederate position across Missionary Ridge. Grant simply intends this maneuver as a diversion to tie down Confederate troops until the flank attacks succeed.

At 3:00 P.M., Thomas dutifully masses 20,000 men below Orchard Knob and leads them forward. Cheering Federals under General Thomas J. Wood and Philip H. Sheridan quickly overrun lightly held Confederate positions and then—without orders—continue charging up the slopes of Missionary Ridge. Gathering impetus as they advance and seeking to avenge their humiliation at Chickamauga two months earlier, the surging blue tide drives Confederates from position after position until they stand victorious along the crest of the ridge. General John C. Breckinridge, commanding the Southern center, lacks the manpower necessary to establish a reserve, so the Union advance continues unchecked while

U.S. gunboat *Fort Hindman,* part of the Mississippi River fleet   *(Library of Congress)*

the defenders scramble down the opposite slope. This extraordinary "Miracle of Missionary Ridge" suddenly ruptures Bragg's center, and he has no recourse but to order his remaining troops on either flank to withdrawn quickly to Dalton, Georgia.

The Confederate stranglehold on Chattanooga is both decisively—and dramatically—ended through Grant's bold stroke. Union casualties are 684 dead, 4,329 injured, and 322 missing (5,335), only marginally lighter than a Confederate loss of 361 dead, 2,180 injured, and 4,146 missing—mostly captured (6,687). In addition to securing Tennessee for the Union, the victory wields two other benefits of immense import to the conduct of subsequent military events: The road to Georgia is now open and Ulysses S. Grant is slated to receive his well-deserved promotion to lieutenant general.

NAVAL: The USS *Fort Hindman* captures the Confederate steamer *Volunteer* off Natchez Island, Mississippi.

Confederate agents sail the unfinished CSS *Rappahannock* from Britain to preclude its probable seizure by the government. The vessel makes for France.

November 26

SOUTH: Five corps of the Army of the Potomac under General George G. Meade successfully cross the Rapidan River, covered by a fog. Meade is now relying on the speed and stealth of his 85,000 men to crush the dispersed right wing of the Army of Northern Virginia before it can concentrate and oppose him. However, events go quickly awry as the marching order breaks down, units became entangled with each other, and valuable time is lost. The confusion alerts General Robert E. Lee that something is afoot, and he begins to marshal his men to confront the enemy head-on.

WEST: Generals William T. Sherman and George H. Thomas mount a pursuit of fleeing Confederates at Rossville Gap. They continue withdrawing until General Patrick R. Cleburne is ordered to constitute a rear guard at Ringgold Gap and Chickamauga Station, Georgia.

General Washington L. Elliott is ordered to use all available cavalry from the Army of the Cumberland to assist Union forces besieged at Knoxville, Tennessee.

NAVAL: The USS *James Adger* captures the British blockade-runner *Ella* off Masonboro Inlet, North Carolina.

The USS *Antonia* captures the Confederate schooner *Mary Ann* near Corpus Christi, Texas.

November 27

SOUTH: No sooner is the Army of the Potomac successfully across the Rapidan River than the III Corps of General William H. French, leading the advance, takes the wrong road and spends several hours countermarching about. The delays allow the Army of Northern Virginia to deploy General Edward Johnson's division at Payne's Farm, Virginia, directly in his path, and heavy fighting erupts. Johnson first repels the Union division of General Joseph B. Carr and then pitches into them, driving the Federals back onto difficult terrain that slows the Confederate advance. The Southerners subsequently are halted in their tracks and fall back. Meanwhile, elements of General Ambrose P. Hill's III Corps and Jubal A. Early's II Corps arrive in support, at which point Meade suspends the action. Confederate losses are 545 while Union losses, not recorded, are probably as light. The fact that Meade lost the element of surprise fatally compromises his ensuing Mine Run campaign.

Union gunners fire an additional 280 rounds into Fort Sumter, Charleston Harbor, South Carolina.

WEST: General John H. Morgan and several Confederate officers stage a daring escape from the State Penitentiary in Columbus, Ohio.

Confederates under General Patrick R. Cleburne mount an effective rear-guard action at Ringgold Gap, Georgia, as the Army of Tennessee under General Braxton Bragg falls back on Dalton. At 8:00 A.M., Cleburne, mustering only 4,157 muskets, confronts a force twice his size under General Joseph Hooker. That officer, without bothering to reconnoiter, marches one brigade directly into the gap where the Southerners are lying behind ledges and outcrops. The Federals immediately are blasted back with heavy losses while additional Union troops are dispatched to ascend the mountain on Cleburne's flank. These too stumble into a clever ambush and are sent scampering down the slope. Strong Union moves against the Confederate left then are stopped by artillery fire, and renewed attacks develop into a costly stalemate. At 12:00 P.M., Cleburne is ordered by General Joseph Hardee to withdraw from his position, and he disengages. His stiffly fought action bought the Army of Tennessee four precious hours and inflicts 507 Union casualties. The Confederates sustain 20 dead, 190 wounded, and 11 missing.

General William T. Sherman is ordered to provide relief for the Union garrison besieged at Knoxville, Tennessee. He dispatches two divisions from the IV Corps under General Gordon Granger.

NAVAL: The USS *Two Sisters* captures the Confederate schooner *Maria Alberta* off Bayport, Florida.

November 28

SOUTH: General Robert E. Lee continues thwarting a possible attack from the Army of the Potomac under General George M. Meade by assuming strong defensive positions along Mine Run Creek. Astute Confederate moves, such as the construction of extensive trenchworks and field fortifications, doom the Union offensive before it can unfold.

WEST: General Braxton Bragg, hated by his subordinates and humiliated before Chattanooga, formerly submits his resignation to President Jefferson Davis.

Confederate cavalry under General Nathan B. Forrest depart for operations against the Memphis and Charleston Railroad in West Tennessee.

General William T. Sherman marches to the relief of General Ambrose E. Burnside at Knoxville, Tennessee, with parts of the Union XI, XIV, and XV Corps.

General James Longstreet orders an attack on Fort Sanders in an attempt to capture Knoxville, Tennessee. This evening, a heavy fog forces him to cancel the assault, but he nonetheless sends his sharpshooters forward to cover the impending advance. Their presence outside Union lines alerts the defenders, who are strongly ensconced behind a deep, impassable ditch fronting their parapet.

NAVAL: The USS *Chippewa,* while convoying Federal troops up Skull Creek, North Carolina, on reconnaissance duty, engages entrenched Confederate infantry and prevents them from thwarting the mission.

November 29

POLITICS: President Abraham Lincoln recovers from a mild case of smallpox.

WEST: The Confederate attack on Fort Sanders in Knoxville, Tennessee, goes forward at 6:00 A.M., despite frightfully cold winter weather. Prior reconnaissance has been poor, and the attackers have no idea of what was is in store for them. Three brigades of infantry charge forward but, lacking ladders, prove unable to surmount the deep, ice-filled ditch surrounding the works. They also encounter telegraph wire strung out between trees at knee-level as an obstruction—a primitive form of barbed wire. As their momentum fails, Union infantry and artillery on the parapet rake them with murderous fire for 20 minutes. Only a handful of Confederates finally mount the fort's wall before being dispatched, and the rest retreat in disorder. General James Longstreet is willing to launch another attack, but his subordinates dissuade him from doing so. Confederate losses reach 129 killed, 458 wounded, and

226 missing, while the Union sustains five dead and eight wounded. Longstreet's debacle at Fort Sanders signals the end of his "siege" of Knoxville and, on receiving word of Braxton Bragg's rout at Chattanooga, he prepares to withdraw.

SOUTHWEST: Confederate forces evacuate Fort Esperanza on Matagorda Island, Texas.

NAVAL: The USS *Kanawha* captures the schooner *Wenoa* near Mobile, Alabama.

A naval gun crew operates a howitzer battery in support of army operations against Pass Cavallo, Texas.

November 30

SOUTH: General George G. Meade prepares his army for a massive blow on prepared Confederate positions along Mine Run, but he is dissuaded from doing so by General Gouverneur K. Warren.

WEST: President Jefferson Davis grants General Braxton Bragg's request to be relieved of command of the Army of Tennessee at Dalton, Georgia, and he is succeeded temporarily by General William J. Hardee.

SOUTHWEST: Union forces occupy Fort Esperanza on Matagorda Island, Texas.

December 1

POLITICS: Notorious Southern spy Bell Boyd, suffering from typhoid fever, again is released from a Federal prison in Washington, D.C., and warned to steer clear of Union territory.

SOUTH: General George M. Meade begins to wind down his Mine Run campaign by crossing the Army of the Potomac back over the Rapidan River, Virginia, and into winter quarters. General Robert E. Lee starts to position the Army of Northern Virginia for an offensive of its own by dispatching Generals Richard H. Anderson's and Cadmus M. Wilcox's divisions forward to assail Meade's left flank.

WEST: Confederate forces under General Samuel Jones capture $700,000 worth of Union stores at Mount Sterling, Kentucky, along with 250 horses and 100 prisoners without a single loss to his command.

Charging Union cavalry surprise General Joseph Wheeler's command at Jonesville, Virginia, near Cumberland Gap, taking several prisoners.

General James B. McPherson, commanding the Union XVII Corps, attacks and dislodges General Wirt Adams' Confederates from Camp Cotton, Mississippi.

December 2

SOUTH: General George G. Meade concludes his unsuccessful Mine Run Campaign and successfully withdraws Union forces north of the Rapidan River. General Robert E. Lee, rousing his own men for a quick counterstrike, advances on Union positions only to find them deserted. "I am too old to command this army," he opines. "We should have never permitted those people to get away." The Mine Run operation costs the Confederates 601 casualties, the Union sustains 1,653. Furthermore, Lee becomes impressed by the power of entrenchments and intends to employ them in defensive situations whenever possible.

WEST: In an emotional ceremony, General Braxton Bragg surrenders command of the Army of Tennessee to General William J. Hardee at Dalton, Georgia.

NAVAL: Armed boats from the USS *Restless* destroy Confederate saltworks along Lake Ocala, Florida.

December 3
WEST: The I Corps of General James Longstreet abandons Knoxville, Tennessee, and enters into winter quarters at nearby Greenville. From this position, he is at liberty to remain in the theater or march to rejoin General Robert E. Lee in Virginia. General Ambrose E. Burnside, meanwhile, fails to pursue the Confederates vigorously, which forces General Ulysses S. Grant to maintain sizable Union forces in Tennessee until the following spring.
NAVAL: The USS *New London* captures the Confederate schooner *Del Nile* off Padre Pass Island, Texas.

December 4
SOUTH: Nathan B. Forrest is promoted to major general, C.S.A.

The latest round of concentrated bombardment increases at Charleston Harbor, South Carolina, to more than 1,300 rounds in the past seven days.
WEST: General James Longstreet continues to withdraw his 15,000 Confederates northeast of Knoxville, Tennessee, inching toward the Virginia border. General John G. Parke finally initiates a tepid pursuit of Southerners with 4,000 cavalry under General James M. Shackleford.

December 5
SOUTH: General Henry H. Lockwood assumes command of the Union VIII Corps and Middle Department in Virginia.
NAVAL: A boat crew dispatched from the USS *Perry* in search of blockade-runners is captured in Murrell's Inlet, South Carolina. "These blunders are very annoying," Admiral John A. B. Dahlgren concedes, "and yet I do not like to discourage enterprise and dash on the part of our officers and men. Better to suffer from the excess than the deficiencies of these qualities."

December 6
WEST: General William T. Sherman and his staff arrive at the command tent of General Ambrose E. Burnside in Knoxville, Tennessee.
NAVAL: The ironclad USS *Weehawken,* overloaded with ammunition, founders in an ebb tide and sinks outside Charleston Harbor, South Carolina, with a loss of 24 officers and men.

The USS *Violet* and *Aries* capture the British steamer *Ceres* off the mouth of the Cape Fear River, North Carolina.

December 7
POLITICS: The first session of the 38th Congress convenes in Washington, D.C.

The fourth session of the 1st Confederate Congress gathers in Richmond, Virginia. President Jefferson Davis acknowledges the failures of the previous years but declares: "The patriotism of the people has proven equal to every sacrifice demanded by their country's need."
NAVAL: Secretary Gideon Welles makes his third annual report, declaring U.S. Navy strength to be 34,000 seamen and 588 warships, displacing 467,967 tons and carrying

4,443 guns. Moreover, these vessels have accounted for the capture or destruction of more than 1,000 Southern and foreign vessels attempting to run the Union blockade.

A party of 15 Confederate sympathizers under John C. Braine board the Union steamer *Chesapeake* at New York, seize that vessel on its run to Portland, Maine, and conduct it to Nova Scotia, Canada.

December 8

POLITICS: To exacerbate the growing rift in Southern politics, President Abraham Lincoln addresses the opening of the 38th Congress and proffers his Proclamation of Amnesty and Reconstruction to all Southerners who take a loyalty oath. In it, he offers to recognize the sitting government of any seceded state provided that at least 10 percent of voters submit to the oath and abolish slavery. The amnesty does not apply to high-ranking Confederate officials or former military men who resigned to join the Confederacy, but Radical Republicans still find the offer too conciliatory.

WEST: A Union cavalry column under General William W. Averell departs New Creek, West Virginia, on a raid against the Virginia and Tennessee Railroad at Salem, Virginia. Simultaneously, additional cavalry under General Eliakim P. Scammon ride from Charleston toward Lewisburg in support.

NAVAL: The USS *Braziliera* runs the British blockade-runner *Antoinette* aground on Cumberland Island, Georgia, and then burns it.

The USS *Neosho* and *Signal* bombard and destroy a Confederate battery at Morganza, Louisiana, thereby rescuing the merchant steamer *Henry Von Phul*.

December 9

SOUTH: Major John S. Mosby leads an attack on Union camps at Lewinsville, Virginia.

A mutiny by African-American troops at Fort Jackson, Louisiana, is suppressed by white officers. Two transgressors subsequently receive punishment by whipping.

WEST: General John G. Foster succeeds General Ambrose E. Burnside as commander of the Department of the Ohio, principally over his lackadaisical conduct throughout the Chattanooga campaign. Recriminations also follow on the Confederate side as General James Longstreet draws up charges against several of his own staff officers.

NAVAL: The USS *Circassian* captures the British blockade-runner *Minna* off Cape Romain, South Carolina.

The USS *Kennebec* captures the Confederate schooner *Marshall Smith* near Mobile, Alabama.

December 10

NAVAL: The USS *Bloomer* and *Restless* destroy a saltworks and several Confederate schooners at St. Andrews, Florida.

Confederate raiders capture and burn the merchant schooner *Josephine Truxillo* and barge *Stephany* on Bayou Lacomb, Louisiana.

December 11

SOUTH: Union shelling of Fort Sumter, Charleston Harbor, South Carolina, scores a direct hit on an ammunition magazine, killing 11 and wounding 41 Confederates. Despite a veritable hurricane of shot and shell, the defenders pluckily refuse to surrender.

WEST: General John A. Logan replaces General Frank P. Blair as commander of the Union XV Corps in Tennessee.

NAVAL: While attempting to raise the sunken USS *Indianola* from its Mississippi River berth, the Federal ironclad *Carondelet* exchanges fire with Confederate forces along the shoreline, driving them off.

December 12

POLITICS: Henceforth, the Confederate government refuses to accept any supplies sent from the North to Union captives.

SOUTH: A quick raid by Union forces nets 90 Southern prisoners at Charles City Court House, Virginia.

WEST: General Samuel D. Sturgis is assigned to command all Union cavalry in the Department of the Ohio.

December 13

SOUTH: Virginian Partisan Rangers under Major John S. Mosby attack a sleeping Union camp at Germantown, Virginia, killing two soldiers and making off with several horses.

WEST: A force of 4,000 Union cavalry under General James M. Shackleford occupies Bean's Station, Tennessee, while pursuing Confederates under General James Longstreet. Longstreet, observing Shackleford outdistance his infantry support, suddenly turns and enacts a three-pronged attack to catch the Federals in a vise and destroy them. That night, he dispatches four cavalry brigades under General William T. Martin on a circuitous route around the Holston River to assail the Union flank, while an additional two cavalry brigades under General William E. Jones undertake an even longer march to hit Shackleford from behind. Longstreet himself marches with General Bushrod R. Johnson's infantry division to meet the Yankees head on at Bean's Station.

December 14

POLITICS: President Abraham Lincoln grants Mrs Mary Todd's Lincoln's half-sister a general amnesty after she visits the White House and takes a loyalty oath.

WEST: General James Longstreet attacks Bean's Station, Tennessee, at 2:00 A.M., startling but not dislodging Union cavalry under General James M. Shackleford. The Federals post their artillery on a nearby hill overlooking their position and closely engage Longstreet's infantry. This contest is supposed to absorb Shackleford's attention while Confederate cavalry columns strike their flank and rear, but neither General William T. Martin nor William E. Jones appear in time. At length, Shackleford conducts an orderly retreat through Bean's Gap to Blain's Cross Roads and digs in behind a rail breastwork. Pursuing Confederate forces decline attacking him there and withdraw. Fighting in terrible winter weather inflicts roughly 200 casualties on both sides. Bean's Station is the last action of the otherwise dreary Knoxville campaign, which cost the Confederates 182 dead, 768 wounded, and 142 missing (1,142), to a Union tally of 92 killed, 394 wounded, and 207 captured (693).

December 15

SOUTH: Joseph O. Shelby is promoted to major general, C.S.A.

General Jubal A. Early is appointed to command of the Confederate Valley District, Virginia.

WEST: Confederates under General Jubal A. Early sortie from Hanover Junction, Virginia, to cut off Union cavalry under General William W. Averell at nearby Millborough.

General John C. Breckinridge relinquishes command of the II Corps, Army of Tennessee, to General Thomas C. Hindman.

December 16

NORTH: General John Buford dies of tuberculosis in Washington, D.C.

SOUTH: President Jefferson Davis, forgoing past difficulties, appoints General Joseph E. Johnston to supersede General William J. Hardee as commander of the Army of Tennessee. General Leonidas K. Polk also is appointed to head the Army of Mississippi.

WEST: General William W. Averell's cavalry column surprises the inhabitants of Salem, Virginia, as he occupies the town and begins to destroy the depot and railroad bridges found there.

NAVAL: The USS *Huron* captures the Confederate vessel *Chatham* near Doboy Sound, Georgia.

The USS *Ariel* seizes the Confederate sloop *Magnolia* near the west coast of Florida.

December 17

POLITICS: President Abraham Lincoln promulgates plans for a Federal Bureau of Emancipation to assist liberated African Americans. Congress, however, fails to enact it until March 1865.

NAVAL: The USS *Ella and Annie* apprehends the recently commandeered steamer *Chesapeake* in Sambro Harbor, Nova Scotia. A Vice Admiralty Court in Halifax subsequently releases the vessel back to its original owners.

The USS *Roebuck* captures the British blockade-runner *Ringdove* near the Indian River, Florida.

Landing parties from the USS *Moose* report capturing and destroying a distillery operated by Confederate irregulars on Seven Miles Island, Tennessee.

December 18

POLITICS: President Abraham Lincoln, displeased with General John M. Schofield's handling of civilian affairs in Missouri, suggests to Secretary of War Edwin M. Stanton that he simultaneously be sacked and promoted to major general, thereby avoiding any ruffled feathers.

SOUTH: The latest Union sweep between Vienna and Middleburg, Virginia, nets several partisans belonging to Major John S. Mosby's command.

December 19

NAVAL: An expedition consisting of USS *Restless, Bloomer,* and *Caroline* scours St. Andrews Bay, Florida, eliminating 290 saltworks and 268 buildings in a 10-day period.

December 20

NAVAL: The USS *Governor Buckingham* captures the Confederate blockade-runner *Antonica* after it is grounded near Frying Pan Shoals, North Carolina.

The USS *Fox* seizes the Confederate steamer *Powerful* at the mouth of the Suwannee River, Florida.

The USS *Sunflower* takes the Confederates blockade-runner *Hancock* in Tampa Bay, Florida.

The USS *Antona* captures the Confederate schooner *Exchange* off Velasco, Texas.

December 21

WEST: General Jacob D. Cox receives command of the Union XXIII Corps at Knoxville, Tennessee.

December 22

SOUTH: General Leonidas K. Polk is formally transferred as commander of the Confederate Department of Mississippi and Louisiana.

December 23

NAVAL: Admiral David G. Farragut, eager to resume active duty, informs Secretary of the Navy Gideon Welles that his USS *Hartford* is ready to depart save for some crew shortages.

December 24

WEST: General William W. Averell concludes his Union cavalry's third raid for the year by reaching Beverly, West Virginia. The inability of General Samuel Jones to intercept him with superior numbers of Confederates leads to his eventual dismissal as commander of the Western Department.

Cavalry under Generals Benjamin H. Grierson and Nathan B. Forrest clash outside of Estenaula and Jack's Creek, Tennessee.

NAVAL: The USS *Fox* captures the British blockade-runner *Edward* near the mouth of the Suwannee River, Florida.

The USS *Sunflower* captures the Confederate vessel *Hancock* in Tampa Bay, Florida.

The Confederate raider CSS *Alabama* under Captain Raphael Semmes seizes and burns the Union bark *Texan Star* in the Strait of Malacca, Dutch East Indies.

December 25

SOUTH: Federal forces raiding Leesburg, Virginia, capture several men belonging to Major John S. Mosby's partisan rangers.

WEST: Union cavalry under General William W. Averell return to Beverly, West Virginia, concluding a three-week raid against the Virginia and Tennessee Railroad.

NAVAL: Landing parties from the USS *Daylight* and *Howquah* destroy four saltworks at Bear Inlet, North Carolina.

In a surprise bombardment, the USS *Marblehead* receives 20 hits from Confederate batteries off Legareville, Stono River, South Carolina, but landing parties from accompanying vessels *Pawnee* and *C. P. Williams* drive them off.

The Federal gunboat USS *Tahoma* bombards Fort Brooke in Tampa Bay, Florida, for two hours but decides against landing an armed party to seize it.

December 26
WEST: Cavalry under Generals Benjamin H. Grierson and Nathan B. Forrest spar at New Castle and Somerville, Tennessee.

NAVAL: The USS *Reindeer* and army steamer *Silver Lake No. 2* conduct a detailed reconnaissance of the Cumberland River from Nashville, Tennessee, to Creelsboro, Kentucky. During the next five days, they are fired upon but are not seriously damaged.

The Confederate raider CSS *Alabama* under Captain Raphael Semmes captures and burns the Union ships *Sonorà* and *Highlander* in the Straits of Malacca.

December 27
NORTH: President Abraham Lincoln and Secretary of War Edwin M. Stanton pay a goodwill visit to Confederate prisoners at Point Lookout, Maryland.

WEST: General Joseph E. Johnston arrives at Dalton, Georgia, to take charge of the Confederate Department of Tennessee with its attendant—and somewhat battered—army.

December 28
POLITICS: The Confederate Congress in Richmond, Virginia, abolishes the practice of hiring draft substitutions and also modifies the detested tax in kind.

Confederate cavalry under General Joseph Wheeler attack a supply train belonging to General George H. Thomas at Charleston, Tennessee.

December 29
SOUTH: General Winfield S. Hancock, seriously wounded at Gettysburg five months earlier, resumes command of the Union II Corps, Army of the Potomac.

NAVAL: A squadron consisting of the USS *Nipsic, Sanford, Geranium, Daffodil,* and *Ethan Allen* steam into Murrel's Inlet, South Carolina, to search for blockade-runners and break up enemy troop concentrations that had attacked Union gunboats.

Armed boats from the USS *Stars and Stripes* burn the Confederate blockade-runner *Caroline Gertrude* at the mouth of the Ocklockonee River, Florida.

December 30
NAVAL: Armed boats from the USS *Pursuit* destroy two Confederate saltworks at St. Joseph's Bay, Florida.

December 31
POLITICS: President Jefferson Davis names North Carolina senator George Davis in an interim appointment to replace outgoing Wade Keyes as Confederate attorney general.

NAVAL: A naval squadron consisting of the USS *Sciota, Granite City, Monongahela, Penobscot,* and *Estrella* attempt to land Federal troops on the Matagorda Peninsula, Texas, but the maneuver is aborted in the face of heavy seas. In the course of sporadic fighting, the Confederate gunboat *John F. Carr* is run ashore and burned.

The USS *Kennebec* seizes the Confederate blockade-runner *Grey Jacket* at sea.

Looking over events of the past year, Navy secretary Gideon Welles is pleased to state: "The war has been waged with success, although there have been in some instances errors and misfortunes. But the heart of the nation is sounder and its hopes higher."

1864

January 1

SOUTH: Major John S. Mosby tangles with Union forces outside Rectortown, Virginia.

WEST: The Department of Kansas is reestablished.

NAVAL: The USS *Huron* intercepts and sinks the British blockade-runner *Sylvanus* in Doboy Sound, Georgia.

January 2

POLITICS: General Patrick L. Cleburne and other officers petition for the possible use of African Americans in the Confederate army to address endemic manpower shortages. Not only does President Jefferson Davis ignore the recommendation, but he ultimately denies Cleburne a well-deserved promotion to lieutenant general because of it.

Senator George Davis of North Carolina formally replaces Wade Keys as Confederate attorney general.

WEST: Federal troops occupy Santa Catalina Island, off the California coast.

January 3

SOUTH: Confederate cavalry under General William E. Jones surprises and defeats General Orlando B. Wilcox at Jonesville, Virginia, taking 383 prisoners, 27 wagons, and three cannon.

WEST: General Fitzhugh Lee's cavalry defeat Union forces in Hardy County, West Virginia, seizing a large supply train belonging to General Benjamin F. Kelley. Among his trophies are 250 head of cattle.

SOUTHWEST: General Francis J. Herron assumes command of Union forces along the Rio Grande, Texas.

NAVAL: Gunfire from the USS *Fort Jackson, Iron Age, Montgomery, Daylight,* and *Fahkee* destroys the beached Confederate steamer *Bendigo* at Lockwood's Folly Inlet, South Carolina.

January 4

POLITICS: President Jefferson Davis instructs General Robert E. Lee to begin to requisition food from civilians as becomes necessary.

WEST: General Edmund Kirby-Smith warns General Richard Taylor of a possible invasion of western Louisiana, insisting, "I still think Red and Washita Rivers, especially the former, are the true lines of operation for an invading column, and that we may expect an attempt to be made by the enemy in force before the rivers fall."

January 5

POLITICS: More than 1,000 African-American citizens of New Orleans, Louisiana, including a handful of War of 1812 veterans, petition for the right to vote and send it to President Abraham, Lincoln.

SOUTHWEST: Federal troops, aided by Apache warriors, rout a large detachment of Navaho along the Pecos River, New Mexico Territory, killing and capturing several in freezing weather.

January 6

SOUTH: General Joseph J. Reynolds is appointed commander of Federal forces at New Orleans, Louisiana.

WEST: The Department of Arkansas is officially constituted.

SOUTHWEST: Colonel Christopher "Kit" Carson begins a protracted winter campaign against hostile Navajo in the Canon de Chelly region of the New Mexico Territory. General James H. Carleton, commanding that department, anxiously wires that his numerous Navajo prisoners are suffering from want of winter clothing and requisitions supplies from the Indian Department.

NAVAL: Confederate guerrillas attack and disable the Federal steamer *Delta* on the Mississippi River.

January 7

POLITICS: President Abraham Lincoln, beset by a rash of army desertions, invariably commutes the death sentence of offenders, insisting, "I am trying to evade the butchering business, lately."

President Jefferson Davis appoints William Preston as envoy to Mexico.

SOUTH: Confederate cavalry under Major John S. Mosby rout a larger Union detachment at Warrenton, Virginia, taking 30 captives and 40 horses.

A detachment of the 21st Georgia Cavalry captures 25 Union prisoners at Waccamaw Neck, South Carolina.

NAVAL: Admiral John A. B. Dahlgren, informed of Confederate submarine technology being tested at Charleston, South Carolina, warns ships of his South Atlantic Blockading Squadron to guard against attacks.

The USS *Montgomery* and *Aries* run the Confederate steamer *Dare* aground at North Inlet, South Carolina; then parties board and burn it.

The USS *San Jacinto* captures the Confederate schooner *Roebuck* at sea.

January 8

SOUTH: General John H. Morgan, recently escaped from the Ohio State Penitentiary, is feted in Richmond, Virginia.

WEST: Seventeen-year-old David O. Dodd is hanged as a Confederate spy in Little Rock, Arkansas.

NAVAL: The USS *Kennebec* captures the Confederate blockade-runner *John Scott* after an eight-hour chase off Mobile, Alabama.

January 9

SOUTH: General Gouverneur K. Warren is appointed commander of the II Corps, Army of the Potomac.

NAVAL: James O. Putnam, U.S. Consul at Le Havre, France, notifies Captain John Winslow of the USS *Kearsarge* that Confederate vessels CSS *Georgia, Florida,* and *Rappahannock* are planning to attack and overwhelm him once he departs from Brest.

January 10
SOUTH: Major John S. Mosby surprises a Union detachment in its camp at Loudoun Heights, Virginia, only to be driven off when the defenders unexpectedly rally.

NAVAL: The USS *Iron Age* is sunk by Confederate artillery after running aground at Lockwood's Folly Inlet, South Carolina.

The USS *Keystone State, Quaker City,* and *Tuscarora* run the Confederate steamer *Vera* ashore off Little River Inlet, South Carolina, whereupon it is burned by its crew.

Armed boats from the USS *Roebuck* seize the Confederate sloop *Maria Louise* near Jupiter Inlet, Florida.

January 11
POLITICS: U.S. senator John B. Henderson of Missouri proposes a joint resolution for the abolishment of slavery, which ultimately manifests as the 13th Amendment to the Constitution.

NAVAL: The USS *Minnesota, Daylight, Aries,* and *Governor Buckingham* intercept the Confederate blockade-runner *Ranger* and force it aground off Lockwood's Folly Inlet, South Carolina, destroying it with gunfire.

The USS *Honeysuckle* captures the British blockade-runner *Fly* off Jupiter Inlet, Florida.

Armed boats from the USS *Roebuck* seize the British blockade-runner *Susan* in Jupiter Inlet, Florida.

January 12
NAVAL: A naval squadron consisting of the USS *Yankee, Currituck, Anacostia, Tulip,* and *Jacob Bell* supports Union cavalry under General Gilman Marston on an expedition between the Potomac and Rappahannock rivers, Virginia.

January 13
POLITICS: President Abraham Lincoln instructs Generals Quincy A. Gilmore in Florida and Nathaniel P. Banks in Louisiana to begin to reconstitute civil authority and free governments, "with all possible dispatch."

President Jefferson Davis advises General Joseph E. Johnston against falling back from his present strong position at Dalton, Georgia, declaring, "I trust you will not deem it necessary to adopt such a measure."

NAVAL: Armed boats from the USS *Two Sisters* capture the Confederate schooner *William* off the Suwannee River, Florida.

January 14
NAVAL: Armed boats from the USS *Roebuck* force the British blockade-runner *Young Racer* aground at Jupiter Inlet, Florida.

The USS *Union* captures the Confederate steamer *Mayflower* off Tampa Bay, Florida.

The Confederate raider CSS *Alabama* under Captain Raphael Semmes captures and burns the Union vessel *Emma Jane* off the coast of Malabar, India.

January 15

NAVAL: Confederate secretary of the navy Stephen R. Mallory assigns Commander James W. Cooke to command the steam ram CSS *Albemarle,* then under construction at Halifax, North Carolina.

The USS *Beauregard* captures the British blockade-runner *Minnie* off Mosquito Inlet, Florida.

January 16

WEST: General Samuel R. Curtis resumes command of the Union Department of Kansas.

Confederate cavalry attached to General James Longstreet's I Corps defeat their Union opposites under General Samuel D. Sturgis in a heavy skirmish at Dandridge, Tennessee.

NAVAL: Armed boats from the USS *Fernandina* capture the Confederate sloop *Annie Thompson* in St. Catherine's Sound, Georgia.

The USS *Gertrude* captures the Confederate schooner *Ellen* off Mobile Bay, Alabama.

January 17

WEST: General Orlando B. Wilcox succeeds General Robert B. Potter to the command of the Union IX Corps at Knoxville, Tennessee.

January 18

NAVAL: Armed boats from the USS *Roebuck* seize the Confederate sloop *Caroline* off Jupiter Inlet, Florida.

The USS *Stars and Stripes* captures the Confederate steamer *Laura* off the Ocklockonee River, Florida.

Admiral David G. Farragut arrives at Mobile Bay, Alabama, onboard the USS *Hartford* and proceeds to inspect the Confederate defenses. He is especially concerned about the large Confederate steam ram CSS *Tennessee* and begins to enact plans to destroy it.

January 19

WEST: The pro-Union Arkansas constitutional convention embraces antislavery provisions in its new document.

NAVAL: Navy secretary Gideon Welles alerts Admiral David D. Porter as to the possible introduction of Confederate "coal torpedoes"—cast-iron bombs made to resemble pieces of coal and designed to exploded in a ship's boiler. Crews must be alert to prevent enemy agents from placing such devices in Union coal depots. If any are caught, he has "given orders to commanders of vessels not to be very particular about the treatment of any of these desperados if caught—only summary punishment will be effective."

Armed boats from the USS *Roebuck* capture the British blockade-runner *Eliza* and Confederate sloop *Mary* at Jupiter Inlet, Florida.

January 20
POLITICS: President Abraham Lincoln advises General Frederick Steele, commanding the District of Arkansas, to schedule free elections as soon as possible to reestablish a free civilian government.
NAVAL: Federal warships begin to reconnoiter Forts Morgan and Grimes at the mouth of Mobile Bay, Alabama, at the behest of Admiral David G. Farragut.

January 21
POLITICS: A gathering of pro-Union citizens in Nashville, Tennessee, proposes a constitutional convention bent on abolishing slavery.
SOUTHWEST: Federal forces begin a reconnaissance mission on the Matagorda Peninsula, Texas.
NAVAL: The USS *Sciota* and *Granite City* cover disembarking troops at Smith's Landing, Texas, and protect their rear as they advance down the Matagorda Peninsula.

January 22
POLITICS: Isaac Murphy becomes governor of the free-state portions of Arkansas after a vote by the State Convention.
WEST: General William S. Rosecrans is assigned commander of the Federal Department of the Missouri, replacing General John M. Schofield.
Union forces capture 28 Confederate forage wagons near Wilsonville, Tennessee.
NAVAL: The USS *Restless* captures the Confederate blockade-runner *William A. Kain* in St. Andrew's Bay, Florida.

January 23
POLITICS: President Abraham Lincoln approves a policy whereby plantation owners must recognize freedom for all former slaves and hire them on the basis of contract law.

January 25
SOUTH: Union forces resume their bombardment of Fort Sumter, Charleston Harbor, South Carolina.
WEST: Federal troops abandon Corinth, Mississippi, in a move to consolidate defenses better.

January 26
DIPLOMACY: William L. Drayton, U.S. minister to France, expresses embarrassment about the presence of several Confederate cruisers in French waters and the government's inability to detail a few naval vessels to deal with them.
WEST: General John G. Parke resumes command of the IX Corps at Knoxville, Tennessee, and commences operations to dislodge General James Longstreet's Confederates from Russellville, Tennessee. To facilitate this, he dispatches Union cavalry under General Samuel D. Sturgis south of the French Broad River to harass his communications. That same day, Confederate cavalry under General William

T. Martin engages Sturgis near Fairgrove, Tennessee. Martin, supported by artillery, manages to drive the Federals back toward Sevierville after heavy skirmishing. Sturgis, meanwhile, regroups and prepares to renew the conflict on the morrow.

January 27

POLITICS: President Jefferson Davis summons General Braxton Bragg to Richmond, Virginia, for consultation as long as his "health permits."

WEST: Continuous skirmishing ensues between major forces under General James Longstreet and John G. Parke near Dandridge, Tennessee. General Samuel D. Sturgis's Union cavalry advance on Confederate positions in the vicinity of Fair Gardens, Tennessee, with three regiments and the 18th Indiana Battery. An entire day of charges and countercharges ensues until the 2nd and 4th Indiana Cavalry finally sweep down the Fair Gardens Road, netting 2 cannon and 112 Southern prisoners. Total Confederate losses are around 200 while Sturgis sustains 60 to 70 killed and wounded. Confederate general William T. Martin subsequently falls back to Swann's Island on the French Broad River to await reinforcements.

January 28

WEST: General Jubal A. Early directs Generals Edward L. Thomas and Thomas L. Rossiter on a combined infantry/cavalry raiding force from New Market, Virginia, toward Union positions in the Allegheny Mountains. Their goal is to secure forage for the horses and steal cattle for the men.

General John M. Schofield gains appointment as commander of the Department of the Ohio, while General George Stoneman is designated to lead the XXIII Corps.

After defeating General William T. Martin's Confederates in several skirmishes around Fair Gardens, Tennessee, General Samuel D. Sturgis is beset by strong Confederate infantry forces under General Bushrod R. Johnson. Heavy skirmishing results, and Union troopers fall back to their original positions near Sevierville. General William T. Martin then repositions his Confederate cavalry near Fair Gardens and awaits developments.

General Leonidas K. Polk receives command of the newly designated Confederate Department of Alabama, Mississippi, and East Louisiana.

NAVAL: The USS *Beauregard* captures the British blockade-runner *Racer* off Cape Canaveral, Florida.

The army steamer *Western Metropolis* captures the Confederate steamer *Rosita* off Key West, Florida.

January 29

WEST: Confederate raiders under Generals Edward L. Thomas and Thomas L. Rossiter advance on Moorefield, West Virginia, brushing aside Union detachments blocking the road. While pursuing in the direction of nearby Medley, the 12th Virginia Cavalry stumbles on a Federal wagon train under escort. Rossiter quickly brings up his three remaining regiments, who dismount and pitch into the Federals. A mounted charge by the 35th Battalion of Virginia Cavalry also breaks the Union center as other units turn their flank and the Northerners flee, abandoning 95 wagons. At a cost of 25 casualties, the victorious Rossiter takes 80 captives along with 1,200 cattle and 500 sheep.

January 30

WEST: Confederate raiders under General Thomas L. Rossiter advance from Medley, West Virginia, to nearby Petersburg, where they abscond with Union additional supplies and ammunition. However, alert to the approach of Federal reinforcements, they fall back on General Edward L. Thomas's infantry brigade and gradually ride back into the Shenandoah Valley, concluding a highly successful raid.

Men of the 54th Illinois kill a Democrat who refuses to take a loyalty oath in Mattoon, Illinois.

Recently disgraced general William S. Rosecrans is appointed commander of the Department of the Missouri.

General Frederick Steele becomes commander of the Department of Arkansas.

NAVAL: The Confederate ironclad CSS *Charleston* is launched at Charleston, South Carolina.

Confederate guerrillas fire on the Union steamer *Sir William Wallace* on the Mississippi River.

January 31

POLITICS: President Abraham Lincoln again urges General Nathaniel P. Banks at New Orleans, Louisiana, to begin to institute civilian authority, leaving him, "at liberty to adopt any rule which shall admit to vote any unquestionably loyal free state men and none others. And yet I do wish they would all take the oath."

SOUTH: General George E. Pickett arrives outside New Bern, North Carolina, with orders to capture the city from Union forces, He commands 13,000 troops in three brigades under General Robert F. Hoke, 14 cannon, and a complement of cavalry. Pickett also enjoys the assistance of Commander John T. Wood, an audacious Confederate naval commander. The Southerners conceive a three-pronged attack to catch Union defenders under General Innis N. Palmer in a pincer from both flanks and the center.

WEST: General William T. Sherman instructs General Nathaniel P. Banks to cooperate closely with the gunboats of Admiral David D. Porter in the upcoming Red River campaign, Louisiana.

NAVAL: Commander Charles W. Flusser, accompanied by 40 sailors, 240 soldiers, and a 12-pound howitzer, sails down the Roanoke River and captures the town of Windsor, North Carolina, meeting no resistance.

February 1

POLITICS: President Abraham Lincoln authorizes a draft of 500,000 men to serve three years or until the duration of the war.

The U.S. House of Representative creates the rank of lieutenant general, U.S. Army, with Ulysses S. Grant in mind.

SOUTH: General George E. Pickett attacks Union forces under General Innis N. Palmer at Batchelder's Creek, North Carolina, inflicting 326 casualties and forcing the Northerners back onto New Bern. However, two Confederate columns under

General Seth M. Barton and Colonel James Dearing perceive Federal defenses at Fort Anderson as too formidable, and the attack founders. By nightfall, Pickett cancels his offensive and delays the scheduled advance of General Robert F. Hoke's division.

WEST: General William T. Sherman orders a Union cavalry column under General William Sooy Smith to depart Colliersville, Tennessee, raid southward along the Memphis and Ohio Railroad, and unite with his own main column outside Meridian, Mississippi, no later than February 10.

NAVAL: The USS *Commodore Morris* and *Minnesota* support army landings at Smithfield, Virginia. The attack is repelled in a heavy fog and the force withdraws with the loss of the army transport *Smith Briggs.*

The USS *Sassacus* captures the Confederate blockade-runner *Wild Dayrell* at Stump Inlet, North Carolina, and burns it.

Armed boats from the USS *Braziliera* captures the Confederate sloop *Buffalo* off Brunswick, Georgia.

February 2

SOUTH: General George E. Pickett, frustrated by the doughty defense of New Bern, North Carolina, withdraws General Robert F. Hoke's division back to Kinston. Though a fiasco, his raid gains a measure of notoriety when 22 former Confederate soldiers are caught wearing Union uniforms. They subsequently are all hanged for desertion following a controversial drumhead trial.

WEST: In Chattanooga, Tennessee, 129 Confederate deserters take a loyalty oath to the United States.

NAVAL: In a bold endeavor, the Federal sidewheel steamer USS *Underwriter* suddenly falls to Confederate boats under Commander John T. Wood in the Neuse River near New Bern, North Carolina. However, when the vessel proves unable to get its steam back up, Wood burns his quarry to prevent recapture. This daring act gains him the thanks of the Confederate Congress.

The Federal tug USS *Geranium* captures eight sailors belonging to the Confederate Torpedo Corps near Fort Moultrie, Charleston, South Carolina.

Federal ironclads USS *Leigh, Nahant,* and *Pasaic* bombard the grounded Confederate steamer *Presto* in Charleston Harbor, South Carolina.

Admiral John A. B. Dahlgren conducts the USS *Ottawa, Norwich, Mahaska, Dai Ching,* and *Water Witch* up the St. John's River, Florida, in support of army moves against Jacksonville under General Quincy A. Gillmore.

February 3

POLITICS: To suppress espionage, desertion, and disloyalty better, President Jefferson Davis recommends suspending writs of habeas corpus for cases involving spying and desertion.

WEST: General William T. Sherman departs Vicksburg, Mississippi, with 26,800 men of the XVI (General Stephen A. Hurlbut) and XVII Corps (General James B. McPherson), while a separate column of 8,000 cavalry under General William Sooy Smith is supposed to depart from Colliersville, Tennessee. Together, they intend to clear Confederate forces out of northern Mississippi as far as the town of Meridian, 120 miles to the east, and devastate the region to deny Southerners railroads, cotton, wheat, and other foodstuffs. This, in effect, is a dress rehearsal for Sherman's notorious "March to the Sea."

NAVAL: The USS *Midnight* captures the Confederate schooner *Defy* near Doboy Light, Georgia.

Federal gunboats USS *Petrel, Marmora, Exchange,* and *Romeo* steam up the Yazoo River to knock out a Confederate battery at Liverpool, Mississippi, to assist the Union expedition against Meridian. In response, Southerners burn the steamer *Sharp* to prevent its capture.

February 4

WEST: Union forces under General James B. McPherson link up with General William T. Sherman at Champion's Hill, Mississippi, prior to the final drive on Meridian.

Union forces depart Helena, Arkansas, and begin to push up the White River.

NAVAL: The USS *Sassacus* forces the Confederate steamer *Nutfield* aground off New River Inlet, North Carolina, and then burns it.

Armed boats from the USS *Beauregard* capture the Confederate boat *Lydia* off Jupiter Narrows, Florida.

February 5

SOUTH: Federal troops repel Major John S. Mosby's attack on their rear guard and capture several Confederates. Among them is William E. Ormsby, a Union deserter who joined the Southerners; he is summarily tried by a drumhead court-martial and executed.

Union forces under General Truman Seymour embark at Hilton Head, South Carolina, and sail for Jacksonville, Florida.

WEST: General William T. Sherman's troops approach Jackson, Mississippi, after skirmishing with Confederate forces under General Wirt Adams.

NAVAL: Commander John R. Tucker informs superiors that the boilers aboard the CSS *Chicora* are nonfunctional and that the vessel now can be employed only as a stationary, floating battery.

The USS *De Soto* captures the British blockade-runner *Cumberland* off Santa Rosa Island, Gulf of Mexico.

February 6

POLITICS: The Confederate Congress outlaws the importation of luxuries or the possession of U.S. paper money. It also mandates that half of tobacco and food exports must be surrendered to government agents before ships are allowed to clear ports.

SOUTH: Union forces under General George G. Meade make an aborted crossing of the Rapidan River at Morton's Ford, but they are recalled after heavy fighting.

General Benjamin F. Butler orders a Union expedition from Yorktown, Virginia, against Richmond, but the move is defeated by Confederates under General Eppa Hunton at Baltimore Store.

WEST: General William T. Sherman occupies Jackson, Mississippi, before resuming his drive against the rail junction at Meridian.

NAVAL: The USS *Cambridge* bombards the grounded Confederate steamer *Dee* near Masonboro, North Carolina.

February 7
DIPLOMACY: William Preston becomes the Confederate envoy to French-controlled Mexico. The Confederacy supports Napoleon III's occupation of that country and its puppet the ruler, Emperor Maximilian, in the hope of gaining diplomatic recognition and possibly military intervention.

SOUTH: Federal forces under General Truman Seymour occupy Jacksonville, Florida, and prepare to move west toward the Suwannee River. By invading the center of the state, they hope to deprive the Confederacy of much-needed cattle, grain, and other valuable commodities, as well as accelerate the reintegration of Florida into the Union.

WEST: General Leonidas K. Polk abandons Brandon, Mississippi, as Union forces under General William T. Sherman advance from the state capital at Jackson.

NAVAL: The USS *Norwich* traps the Confederate steamer *St. Mary's* in McGirt's Creek, Florida, where it is scuttled.

February 8
SOUTH: General Truman Seymour advances inland from Jacksonville, Florida, and skirmishes with Confederate forces at Ten-Mile Run.

WEST: The divisions of Generals Stephen D. Lee and William W. Loring unite at Morton, Mississippi, and commence to fall back toward Meridian before the army of General William T. Sherman.

February 9
POLITICS: President Abraham Lincoln sits through a photographic session; one portrait is subsequently utilized on the U.S. five-dollar bill.

SOUTH: 109 Union officers under Colonel Thomas E. Rose tunnel themselves free from Libby Prison in Richmond, Virginia, with 59 ultimately reaching Union lines. Rose and 48 others are recaptured while two die from drowning.

Federal forces seize John's Island in Charleston Harbor, South Carolina.

WEST: General John M. Schofield replaces General John G. Foster as commander of the Federal Department of the Ohio.

Federal forces under General William T. Sherman reoccupy Yazoo City, Mississippi, without resistance.

NAVAL: An armed cutter from the USS *Patapsco* captures the Confederate schooner *Swift* off Cabbage Island, Georgia.

February 10
SOUTH: Union troops continue advancing from Jacksonville, Florida, toward Lake City.

WEST: General William Sooy Smith finally receives the Union cavalry brigade of Colonel George E. Waring and prepares to depart Coliersville, Tennessee, belatedly for Meridian, Mississippi.

NAVAL: The USS *Florida* sinks the Confederate blockade-runners *Fanny and Jenny* and *Emily* once they ground off Masonboro Inlet, North Carolina.

The Confederate raider CSS *Florida* under Lieutenant Charles M. Morris slips out of Brest, France, after seven months of undergoing repairs. Under the cover of a thick fog and rain, he slips past the USS *Kearsarge* and escapes.

February 11
SOUTH: General Joseph Finnegan assembles 600 men at Lake City, Florida, as Confederate defenses coalesce to stop a Union advance commanded by General Truman Seymour.
WEST: A Union train belonging to the Baltimore and Ohio Railroad is thrown off the tracks at Kearneysville, West Virginia, by Confederate guerrillas under Major M. H. Gilmore. The crew and passengers are then robbed of valuables, and the raiders depart.

Ten days late, 8,000 Union cavalry under General William Sooy Smith finally clatter out of Collierville, Tennessee, en route to a rendezvous with General William T. Sherman. Progress is slow owing to rains and swampy terrain. As they advance, more than 1,000 African-American slaves join the column seeking freedom and protection.
NAVAL: The USS *Queen* captures the Confederate schooner *Louisa* at the mouth of the Brazos River, Texas.

February 12
NORTH: President Abraham Lincoln enjoins General Hugh J. Kilpatrick at the White House, whereupon the latter discusses plans for a possible raid against Richmond, Virginia, to free Union prisoners kept there. The president listens intently to the blustery cavalryman and at length grants his approval.
WEST: General William T. Sherman continues his Meridian, Mississippi, campaign by advancing from the west while General William Sooy Smith rides down from the north. Skirmishing ensues but does not hinder either column.

February 13
NAVAL: The USS *Morse,* while conducting a reconnaissance mission up Potopotank Creek, Virginia, captures the Confederate sloop *Margaret Ann.*

The USS *Forrest Rose* helps defeat three Confederate attacks on Waterproof, Louisiana.

February 14
SOUTH: Advancing Federal troops under General Quincy A. Gillmore occupy Gainesville, Florida, without resistance.
WEST: Meridian, Mississippi, falls without resistance to Union forces under General William T. Sherman, who covers 150 miles in 11 days. He then begins systematically to destroy all buildings, supplies, and railroads in his earliest application of what will become known as "Total War." Sherman notes: "For five days, 10,000 men worked hard and with a will in that work of destruction." Ultimately, 115 miles of track, 61 bridges, and 20 locomotives are laid to waste. Confederate general Leonidas K. Polk, too weak to intervene, remains a hapless spectator to the destruction but did remove the bulk of supplies and rolling stock stored there to Demopolis, Alabama. Sherman, meanwhile, awaits the arrival of General William Sooy Smith's cavalry column, now overdue by several days.

February 15

POLITICS: The Confederate Congress appropriates $5 million for a sabotage campaign based in Canada. It is to be orchestrated by Confederate veteran Thomas C. Hines, who intends to meet and coordinate his actions with those of Peace Democrats from the North. Meanwhile, President Jefferson Davis evinces concern that General William T. Sherman might march from Meridian, Mississippi, directly on Montgomery, Alabama.

WEST: Federal troopships land the African-American 12th Louisiana Infantry at Grand Gulf, Mississippi, for the purpose of confiscating cotton stores. No resistance is encountered.

NAVAL: The USS *Forest Rose* lends valuable gunfire support to Union forces under attack at Waterproof, Louisiana.

The USS *Virginia* captures the British blockade-runner *Mary Douglas* off San Luis Pass, Texas.

February 16

SOUTH: Federal troops, attacking Fairfield, North Carolina, in a severe snowstorm, capture an entire company of Confederates in their camp.

WEST: An altercation erupts between soldiers of the 54th Illinois and local Democrats in Paris, Edgar County, Illinois.

Federal troops begin a major campaign against hostile Indians in the vicinity of Fort Walla Walla, Washington Territory.

NAVAL: The USS *Montgomery* captures the British blockade-runner *Pet* near Lockwood's Folly, South Carolina.

The USS *Para* supports an army advance up the St. John's River, Florida, engaging several Confederate batteries en route.

The USS *Octorara* and *J. P. Jackson*, accompanied by six mortar schooners, begin to bombard Fort Powell, Mobile Bay, Alabama.

The USS *St. Clair* and the army steamer *Hope* collide on the Mississippi River during a gale, and the latter sinks.

February 17

POLITICS: The Confederate Congress suspends writs of habeas corpus as it relates to arrests made by authority of the president or the secretary of war. They also expand the draft to include all white males between the ages of 17 and 50. Another act allows the employment of African-American slaves as army laborers. The fourth session, first Confederate Congress then adjourns.

Confederate Vice President Alexander H. Stephen continues protesting the suspension of habeas corpus, insisting it is "Far better that our country be overrun by the enemy, our cities sacked and burned, and our land laid desolate, than that the people should suffer the citadel of their liberties to be entered and taken by professed friends." In light of his opposition, the Georgia legislature counters with a resolution reaffirming the state's support for the war and all measures this may entail.

SOUTH: General William H. French assumes command of the III Corps, Army of the Potomac.

Sepia wash drawing by R. G. Skerrett, 1902, after a painting then held by the Confederate Memorial Literary Society Museum, Richmond, Virginia *(Naval Historical Foundation)*

A surprise attack by Federal troops nets 13 of Major John S. Mosby's partisan rangers at Piedmont, Virginia.

NAVAL: The submarine CSS *Hunley* under Lieutenant George E. Dixon attacks and sinks the 1,934-ton Union screw sloop USS *Housatonic* under Captain Charles W. Pickering in Charleston Harbor, South Carolina. Despite precautions, the attackers are sighted at 8:45 P.M. only 100 yards away, and the Union ship immediately slips its cable and begins to back off. *Hunley* still manages to ram its spar torpedo under the *Housatonic*'s starboard side, which explodes and fatally damages it. Fortunately only five sailors drown, with the rest saved by clinging to the masts as *Housatonic* settles in shallow water. *Hunley* apparently survives the explosion intact and remains topside long enough to signal by lantern that it was returning; then it inexplicably sinks a third time with all hands. Nevertheless, *Housatonic* enjoys the melancholy distinction of being the first warship in history lost to a submarine attack.

The USS *Tahoma* destroys a Confederate saltworks at St. Marks, Florida.

February 18

POLITICS: President Abraham Lincoln declares the port of Brownsville, Texas, open for trade and ends the Federal blockade there.

February 20

SOUTH: Union troops celebrate Confederate raider John S. Mosby's promotion to lieutenant colonel by raiding his headquarters at Front Royal, Virginia; the rebels quickly recover and drive their attackers off.

The Battle of Olustee transpires between General Truman Seymour and Joseph Finnegan, with both sides numbering about 5,000 men apiece. The Northerners encounter Finnegan's force safely dug in behind entrenchments, but Seymour nonetheless orders an advance. First to engage the Confederates is Colonel Joseph Hawley's brigade, consisting of the 7th New Hampshire and the 8th U.S. Colored Infantry, which advances bravely but is decimated by heavy musket fire. As they withdraw in confusion, a battle-hardened Georgia brigade under General Alfred H. Colquett leaps from their entrenchments and charges Colonel William Barton's brigade in the Union center, roughly handling it and taking several cannon. The Confederates then find themselves out of ammunition, their advance falters, and both sides scramble to redress their lines.

Seymour, thoroughly bested, brings his final brigade under Colonel James Montgomery to act as a rear guard. Finnegan then orders an all-out charge against the retreating Federals, but the Confederates are delayed for several minutes by the desperate stand of African-Americans of the 35th U.S. Colored Infantry and the celebrated 54th Massachusetts. Seymour then skillfully extricates his troops and averts a general disaster, principally because Finnegan bungles use of his cavalry and fails to pursue effectively. Casualties at Olustee proportionately equaled or exceeded those of any other Civil War engagement. Seymour sustains a bruising 203 dead, 1,152 wounded, and 506 missing (1,861)—a staggering loss rate of 34 percent, while Finnegan loses 93 killed and 841 injured (946), or 20 percent. More important, the Union's defeat here ensures that Florida remains a vital source of cattle, grain, and other valuable supplies for Confederate armies until the end of hostilities.

WEST: General William Sooy Smith encounters a Confederate cavalry brigade under Colonel Jeffrey E. Forrest at Prairie Station, Mississippi, and begins to skirmish. An extended fire fight erupts as the Northerners lurch toward the town of West Point while Southerners continue gathering in strength.

General William T. Sherman, tired of waiting for General William Sooy Smith's cavalry to reinforce him, abandons Meridian, Mississippi, and retrogrades back to Vicksburg. However, he takes a circuitous northern route attempting to establish contact with his missing cavalry. To date, Union losses are 21 killed, 68 wounded, and 81 missing (170).

NAVAL: Admiral John A. B. Dahlgren, greatly alarmed by the loss of the USS *Housatonic* to a Confederate torpedo attack, suggests to Navy secretary Gideon Welles that the government offer a $20–$30,000 reward for the capture or destruction of any such craft. "They are worth more to us than that," he concludes.

February 21

SOUTH: Partisan rangers under Colonel John S. Mosby disperse a Union raiding party at Dranesville, Virginia, killing 15 and taking 70 captives for a cost of one dead and four wounded.

WEST: Colonel Jeffrey E. Forrest continues skirmishing heavily with Union cavalry at West Point, Mississippi, as his elder brother, General Nathan B. Forrest, arrives with reinforcements. In fact, he is trying to lure Smith into an elaborate ambush staged by the elder Forrest. But General William Sooy Smith, with twice the man-power, is convinced that he is heavily outnumbered and ignominiously withdraws. Smith's retrograde movement ends all attempts to unite with General William T. Sherman at Meridian.

NAVAL: The USS *Para* captures the Confederate steamer *Hard Times* on the St. John's River, Florida.

February 22

POLITICS: Senator Samuel Pomeroy of Kansas, viewing President Abraham Lincoln as unelectable, begins a covert attempt to have Secretary of the Treasury Salmon P. Chase nominated as the Republican Party's standard bearer. However, once his "Pomeroy Circular" is printed, it creates an uproar and a backlash against Chase, who ends his candidacy for the presidency. He also offers to resign over the matter, but Lincoln declines to accept.

Michael Hahn is elected governor of the free-state portions of Louisiana.

WEST: A riot between soldiers and Democrats in Paris, Edgar County, Illinois, results in one civilian death and two wounded soldiers.

General George H. Thomas conducts a large reconnaissance in force of Confederate defenses at Dalton, Georgia, to ascertain if General Joseph E. Johnston has weakened his forces by sending detachments to either General Leonidas Polk in Mississippi or General James Longstreet in Tennessee. To that end, several divisions from General John M. Palmer's XIV Corps proceed through Ringgold Gap and onto the plains near Tunnel Hill.

Confederate cavalry under General Nathan B. Forrest attack and defeat a larger Union rear guard under General William Sooy Smith near Okolona, Mississippi. However, resistance stiffens as the Southerners engage the main Union body, and several Confederate charges are bloodily repelled. The most notable casualty is Colonel Jeffrey E. Forrest, the general's younger brother. Two Union countercharges likewise fail with the loss of six cannon, and Smith then retreats in the direction of Pontotoc. Forrest, whose men are exhausted and low on ammunition, allows them to depart; he records 27 dead and 97 wounded Southerners while claiming 162 prisoners and three stands of colors.

NAVAL: The USS *Whitehead* shells and destroys a corn mill at Rainbow Bluff, North Carolina.

The USS *Virginia* captures the British blockade-runner Henry Colthirst near San Luis Pass, Texas.

The USS *Linden* hits a snag in the Arkansas River and sinks.

February 23

POLITICS: Secretary of the Treasury Salmon P. Chase absents himself from cabinet meetings in light of disclosures surrounding the recent Pomeroy Circular.

SOUTH: General John A. McClernand receives command of the XIII Corps in Louisiana.

The battered column of General Truman Seymour trudges back into Jacksonville, Florida, concluding that state's only major campaign.

WEST: Confederate cavalry under General Stephen D. Lee unite with General Nathan B. Forrest near West Point, Mississippi, but too late to play a role in defeating Union troopers under General William Sooy Smith.

Skirmishes increase between Union troops under General John M. Palmer's XIV Corps and the Army of Tennessee under General Joseph E. Johnston outside Dalton, Georgia. Despite the strength of the Confederate position, Palmer brings up additional forces and continually presses the Southerners back up higher ground.

NAVAL: The USS *Lancaster,* anchored at Acapulco, Mexico, helps repel an attack by hostile Native Americans.

February 24

POLITICS: President Abraham Lincoln signs legislation to compensate slave owners in Union-controlled regions by paying them $300 when their slaves join the Union army.

The U.S. Senate, following the House's lead, votes to create the rank of lieutenant general.

SOUTH: General Braxton Bragg gains appointment as chief of operations, Confederate army, at Richmond, Virginia. He now serves as President Jefferson Davis's de facto chief of staff.

WEST: Forces under General John M. Palmer's XIV Corps continue skirmishing with Confederate troops at Tunnel Hill, Georgia, testing the strength of their defenses. The division of General Richard W. Johnson begins to ascend the rocky face of the position while under heavy fire from General Alexander P. Stewart's Confederates. The Southerners then fall back in good order and take up strong positions along Tunnel Hill (Buzzard's Roost) to await the Union advance, but nightfall closes the contest.

NAVAL: The USS *Nita* forces the Confederate blockade-runner *Nan Nan* aground in the East Pass of the Suwannee River, Florida.

February 25

WEST: General John C. Breckinridge replaces General Samuel Jones as commander of the Confederate Western Department of Virginia.

General John M. Palmer and his XVI Corps continue probing Confederate positions at Buzzard Roost Gap, Georgia, but they encounter heavy resistance. The division of General Absalom Baird works its way up steep slopes under heavy fire, making steady progress but also taking considerable casualties. After a flanking move by General Jefferson C. Davis stalls along the west side of the imposing ridge, Palmer calls off the effort and withdraws that evening. Union losses are 289 casualties to 140 Confederates, but General George H. Thomas confirms that General Joseph E. Johnston is very strongly entrenched around Dalton. He then divines the strategy, implemented three months later, of sending Union troops through Snake Gap Creek, 15 miles behind Confederate lines, to outflank the defenders. More important, his steady pressure on Johnson necessitates that the corps of General Thomas J. Hardee, recently dispatched to assist General Leonidas Polk in Mississippi, be recalled back to the Army of the Tennessee.

General Oliver O. Howard is reappointed commander of the XI Corps in Tennessee.

NAVAL: The USS *Roebuck* captures the British blockade-runner *Two Brothers* in the Indian River, Florida.

February 26
POLITICS: President Abraham Lincoln reaffirms his faith in General Benjamin F. Butler and also commutes all death sentences for desertion to imprisonment for the duration.
SOUTH: Edward P. Alexander is appointed brigadier general, C.S.A.
WEST: Confederate cavalry under Colonel John M. Hughes capture Washington, Tennessee, and they inflict 75 Union casualties.

Union cavalry under General William Sooy Smith straggle back toward Colliersville, Tennessee, following their ill-fated Meridian expedition. Smith claims to have liberated 3,000 slaves, taken 200 captives, and burned 2,000 bales of cotton at a cost of 47 killed, 157 wounded, and 120 missing. Realistically, this is another lackluster effort, and General William T. Sherman laconically dismisses it as "unsatisfactory."
NAVAL: A boat from the USS *Nipsic* is captured while on picket duty in Charleston Harbor, South Carolina, by the Confederate cutter CSS *Palmetto State*.

February 27
SOUTH: Andersonville Prison, near Americus, Georgia, a sixteen-and-one-half-acre log stockade, receives its first Union captives. Crowded and squalid from the onset, it gradually gains infamy as the worst prison site in the South.
WEST: General George H. Thomas concludes his probing actions outside Dalton, Georgia, and withdraws back into Tennessee.
NAVAL: Armed boats from the USS *Tahoma* land and destroy Confederate saltworks along Goose Creek, Florida.

The USS *Roebuck* captures the British blockade-runner *Nina* and the Confederate schooner *Rebel* off the Indian River Inlet, Florida.

February 28
SOUTH: A force 3,500 Union cavalry under General Hugh J. Kilpatrick prepares for an extended raid toward Richmond, Virginia, in a bid to free Union prisoners held at notorious Libby Prison. The effort has been sanctioned personally by both President Abraham Lincoln and Secretary of War Edwin M. Stanton after they learned of horrendous conditions experienced by Northern prisoners. One of Kilpatrick's principal subordinates is Colonel Ulric Dahlgren, son of Admiral John A. B. Dahlgren, whose participation harbors considerable controversy. The troopers leave camp in high spirits this evening and ford the Rapidan River at Ely's Ford.

To assist the raid on Richmond, General George A. Custer takes his brigade of 1,500 troopers on a raid through Albemarle County, Virginia, while General John Sedgwick's VI Corps creates another diversion in the direction of Madison Court House.
WEST: General John B. Hood gains appointment as commander of the II Corps, Army of Tennessee.
NAVAL: The USS *Penobscot* captures the British blockade-runner *Lilly* off Velasco, Texas.

February 29

POLITICS: The U.S. Congress formally revives the rank of lieutenant general at the behest of President Abraham Lincoln.

SOUTH: General Hugh J. Kilpatrick leads 3,500 Federal cavalry across the Rapidan River and gallops toward Richmond, Virginia. On reaching Spotsylvania, he dispatches a column of 500 men under Colonel Ulric Dahlgren toward Goochland Court House to attack Richmond from the south as he hit it from the north. The troopers forge ahead despite inclement weather.

WEST: Union forces begin to reconnoiter the Red River region of Louisiana in preparation for a major offensive there.

NAVAL: Armed boats under Lieutenant William B. Cushing of the USS *Monticello* raid Smithville, North Carolina, in a bold attempt to capture Confederate general Louis Hebert. However, Hebert had departed for Wilmington earlier that day and is not in his tent when Cushing suddenly storms it—being within 50 yards of a Confederate barracks.

Admiral David D. Porter dispatches Commander Frank Ramsey up the Black and Ouachita rivers, Louisiana, with the gunboats USS *Osage, Ouachita, Lexington, Conestoga, Cricket,* and *Fort Hindman.* This move in undertaken in conjunction with and preparation for the much large Red River expedition.

The USS *Penobscot* captures the Confederate schooners *Stingray* and *John Douglas* near Velasco, Texas.

The USS *Virginia* captures the Confederate schooner *Camilla* at Galveston, Texas, and then attacks and burns the sloop *Catherine Holt* off San Luis Pass.

March 1

POLITICS: President Abraham Lincoln nominates General Ulysses S. Grant for the rank of lieutenant general.

SOUTH: General Hugh J. Kilpatrick, meeting resistance as his cavalry column approaches the Confederate capital of Richmond, Virginia (then only lightly defended by invalids and civilians), suddenly cancels his raid, veers away, and recrosses the Chickahominy River. En route, he is pursued sharply by Confederate cavalry under General Wade Hampton, which successfully attack and drive the troopers off in confusion. Colonel Ulric Dahlgren, meanwhile, finding the James River swollen and impassible, decides to shift his attack from the east instead of from the south. He also hangs an African-American guide for mistakenly leading his column astray. But Dahlgren, having approached to within two-and-a-half miles of the city, encounters heavy resistance and becomes separated from his main column with only 100 men. He then calls off the raid and attempts to circle back to rejoin Kilpatrick.

NAVAL: The USS *Connecticut* captures the British blockade-runner *Scotia* off Cape Fear, North Carolina.

The USS *Southfield* and *Whitehead* rescue of the army gunboat *Bombshell,* on the Chowan River, North Carolina, once that vessel is cut off by Confederate batteries.

The USS *Roebuck* captures the British blockade-runner *Lauretta* at Indian River Inlet, Florida.

The Confederate raider CSS *Florida* under Lieutenant Charles M. Morris escapes from Funchal, Madeira, with the USS *St. Louis* in hot pursuit.

March 2

POLITICS: The U.S. Senate confers the rank of lieutenant general on Ulysses S. Grant.

SOUTH: A detachment of 100 Union cavalry under Colonel Ulric Dahlgren is ambushed at Mantapike Hill, King and Queen County, Virginia, and he is killed while 92 of his men are captured. The Confederates then recover papers allegedly suggesting a plot to burn Richmond and to assassinate President Jefferson Davis; both the Union government and General George G. Meade promptly and vehemently deny any complicity. This ill-fated endeavor also costs the North 340 killed, wounded, and captured, in addition to 583 horses lost.

General George A. Custer successfully concludes his own raid through Albemarle County, Virginia, and reaches the safety of Union lines.

NAVAL: Admiral David D. Porter arrives off the mouth of the Red River, Louisiana, with his Mississippi Squadron for the planned expedition against Shreveport and east Texas. He is increasingly concerned by declining water levels on the river but nonetheless resolves to proceed apace.

A naval reconnaissance up the Black River, Louisiana, under Commander Frank Ramsay stops to engage Confederate artillery below Harrisonburg. Ramsay's flagship, USS *Fort Hindman,* is struck 27 times and retires with one engine severely damaged.

March 3

POLITICS: General Ulysses S. Grant is ordered to Washington, D.C., where he is to be promoted to lieutenant general.

NAVAL: The USS *Dan Smith* captures the British blockade-runner *Sophia* off the Altamaha Sound, Georgia. The prize ultimately is abandoned in a gale shortly afterward.

March 4

POLITICS: The U.S. Senate confirms Andrew Johnson to serve as governor of Tennessee.

Pro-Union governor Michael Hahn is sworn into office at New Orleans, Louisiana.

SOUTH: A Confederate advance on Portsmouth, Virginia, is repulsed by Union forces under General David B. Birney and cavalry led by General Hugh J. Kilpatrick.

General James P. Anderson assumes command of the Confederate District of Florida.

WEST: Advanced elements of General William T. Sherman's army reach Vicksburg, Mississippi, escorted by 5,000 slaves and 3,000 captured draft animals. He has covered 360 miles through enemy territory and inflicted great materiel damage on the enemy, while suffering only 113 killed, 385 wounded, and 414 missing (912). Strategically, his Meridian campaign fails to destroy Confederate rail lines or reduce enemy troop levels in northern Mississippi effectively, as both are gradually restored. But the effort convinces Sherman of the intrinsic effectiveness of scorched-earth tactics, and his willful devastation presaged what would be conducted on a far vaster scale through Georgia. The concept of total war against an entire enemy population begins to congeal in his mind. In effect, the Meridian campaign is a dress rehearsal for the destructive policies under which he gains considerable notoriety.

NAVAL: The USS *Pequot* captures the British blockade-runner *Don* off Wilmington, North Carolina.

March 5

POLITICS: Confederate authorities issue new regulations mandating that all Southern vessels donate half their cargo capacity to government shipments. This is undertaken as much to reduce wartime profiteering as to alleviate mounting supply shortages.

WEST: Confederate cavalry under General Joseph Wheeler surprises General Absalom Baird's camp at Leet's Tan-yard, Georgia, capturing his camp, wagons, and numerous prisoners.

NAVAL: A Confederate boarding party under daring commander John T. Wood captures a Union telegraph station at Cherry Point, Virginia. They then attack and capture the Union army transports *Aeolus* and *Titan,* docked nearby. Two days later, Wood scuttles the latter vessel on the Piankatank River.

A naval reconnaissance effort under Commander Frank Ramsay steams down the Black River, Louisiana, reaching the mouth of the Red River.

Federal gunboats USS *Petrel* and *Marmora* lend gunfire ashore to Union troops defending Yazoo City, Mississippi, from a Confederate attack.

March 6

WEST: Federal troops pull out of Yazoo City, Mississippi, under Confederate pressure.

General William T. Sherman appoints General Andrew J. Smith to command lead elements of the Red River expedition, Louisiana, and carefully instructs him to work closely with the gunboat flotilla under Admiral David D. Porter.

NAVAL: The USS *Grand Gulf* captures the British blockade-runner *Mary Ann* off Wilmington, North Carolina.

The USS *Peterhoff* collides with the *Monticello* off New Inlet, North Carolina, and sinks.

A Confederate torpedo boat successfully rams the USS *Memphis* twice in the North Edisto River, South Carolina, but the Union vessel escapes owing to a faulty spar torpedo that fails to detonate. Had it exploded eight feet below the waterline as intended, *Memphis* would undoubtedly have been destroyed.

March 7

WEST: President Jefferson Davis urges General James Longstreet to resume offensive operations in either Kentucky or Tennessee.

March 8

NORTH: General Ulysses S. Grant formally accepts his commission as lieutenant general at a ceremony in the White House and then meets and confers with President Abraham Lincoln for the first time. Grant thus becomes the first American military leader to hold such lofty rank since George Washington.

WEST: General Franz Sigel is appointed commander of the Department of West Virginia, with orders to clear Confederates out of the strategic Shenandoah Valley.

A Union expedition under General Grenville M. Dodge seizes Courtland and Moulton, Alabama, along with valuable supplies, ammunition, and provisions.

NAVAL: The USS *Conestoga* under Commander Thomas O. Selfridge accidentally is rammed by the *General Price* off Grand Gulf, Mississippi, and sinks with the loss of two dead. Ironically, both of Selfridge's previous commands, the *Cumberland* and *Cairo,* were also lost to ramming.

The USS *Virginia* captures the Confederate sloop *Randall* at San Luis Pass, Texas.

March 9

NORTH: General Ulysses S. Grant succeeds General Henry W. Halleck as general in chief, with the latter being demoted to his chief of staff. Grant then ventures to Brandy Station, Virginia, headquarters of the Army of the Potomac. To maintain good relations with officers of that force, General George G. Meade technically remains the commanding officer under Grant.

SOUTH: Union cavalry under General Hugh J. Kilpatrick burn a grain mill and other property in the vicinity of Carlton's Store, King and Queen County, Virginia, to punish the inhabitants for the recent ambush slaying of Colonel Ulric Dahlgren.

NAVAL: The USS *Yankee* conducts a reconnaissance down the Rappahannock River as far as Urbanna, Virginia.

The USS *Shokokon* and General Putnam escort an army expedition under General Isaac J. Wistar up the York and Mattapony rivers, Virginia, as far as Sheppard's Landing.

Admiral David D. Porter assembles his gunboat squadron at the mouth of the Red River, Louisiana, prior to the advance against Shreveport.

March 10

SOUTH: After conferring with General George G. Meade, commander of the Army of the Potomac, General Ulysses S. Grant departs by rail for Nashville, Tennessee, for additional meetings with General William T. Sherman.

Colonel John S. Mosby is bested in a skirmish with superior Federal forces at Charlestown and Kabletown, Virginia.

General Nathaniel P. Banks begins to concentrate troops at New Orleans, Louisiana, in preparation for his Red River expedition to the heartland of the Confederate Trans-Mississippi Department. The bulk of his forces consist of 10,000 men under General Andrew J. Smith, on loan from General William T. Sherman at Vicksburg. Concurrently, a Union column under General Frederick Steele also is slated to leave Little Rick, Arkansas, and advance on Shreveport from the west. This campaign, the brainchild of General Henry W. Halleck, is designed to clear an opening into East Texas. However, it is undertaken over the objections of Generals Ulysses S. Grant and William T. Sherman, who feel that Mobile, Alabama, is a more significant target. Banks, meanwhile, wishes to seize as much Confederate cotton as possible from this highly productive region for that commodity remains highly overpriced in Northern markets and promises to fetch him windfall profits on the open market.

WEST: General Franz Sigel replaces General Benjamin F. Kelley as commander of the Union Department of West Virginia.

NAVAL: The USS *Virginia* captures the Confederate schooner *Sylphide* off San Luis Pass, Texas.

Federal gunboats and ironclads escort army transports carrying General Andrew J. Smith's division down the Mississippi River from Vicksburg, Mississippi, to the mouth of the Red River, Louisiana. Once at the confluence of both rivers, their first objective is Fort De Russy, 30 miles to the west.

March 11

NAVAL: Armed boats from the USS *Beauregard* and *Norfolk Packet* capture the British blockade-runners *Linda* and *Hannah* off Mosquito Inlet, Florida.

The USS *San Jacinto* seizes the Confederate schooner *Lealtad* off Mobile, Alabama.

The USS *Aroostook* captures the British blockade-runner *Mary P. Burton* off Velasco, Texas.

March 12

NORTH: Sweeping leadership changes are finalized in the Union army with General Ulysses S. Grant in overall command of military operations; General Henry W. Halleck serving as his chief of staff; General William T. Sherman leading the Military Division of the Mississippi, including the Departments of the Arkansas, the Cumberland, the Ohio, and the Tennessee; and General James B. McPherson heading both the Department and Army of the Tennessee.

SOUTH: General Nathaniel P. Banks begins to orchestrate his move up the Red River, Louisiana, with a view toward seizing Shreveport. His ultimate goal is to gain a lodgment in the Texas interior and sever the flow of supplies eastward. Advanced forces under General Andrew J. Smith are convoyed up the Red River to Alexandria, Louisiana, their first objective. Banks himself is detained two more weeks at New Orleans to help the struggling civilian administration of Governor Michael Hahn get established.

NAVAL: The USS *Massachusetts* captures the Confederate sloop *Persis* in Wassaw Sound, Georgia.

The USS *Columbine* supports army movements up the St. John's River, Florida, culminating in an attack on Confederate positions at Pilatka.

The USS *Aroostook* captures the Confederate schooner *Marion* off Velasco, Texas.

Admiral David D. Porter leads an armada of 13 ironclads, four tinclads, and four wooden gunboats up the Red River, Louisiana, in concert with the Shreveport expedition of General Nathaniel P. Banks. The USS *Essex, Lafayette, Choctaw, Ozark, Osage, Neosho, Fort Hindman,* and *Cricket* pause to help bombard Fort De Russy, Louisiana, into submission. Meanwhile, army transports convey the 3rd Division, XVI Corps of General Andrew J. Smith up as an advanced force.

March 13

POLITICS: President Abraham Lincoln, after receiving a signed petition from African Americans in Louisiana, encourages Governor Michael Hahn of Louisiana to consider drafting a new state constitution that allows minorities to vote. Curiously, of the 1,000 blacks signing the document, no less than 27 had previously served under General Andrew Jackson in the War of 1812 with a promise of freedom that was subsequently retracted.

NAVAL: Federal gunboats USS *Benton, Chillicothe, Louisville, Pittsburgh, Mound City, Ouachita, Lexington,* and *Gazelle* steam up the Atchafalaya River, Louisiana, and cover troop landings at Simmesport. Meanwhile, the *Eastport* and *Neosho* remain behind to assist in the reduction of Fort De Russy.

March 14

SOUTH: Union forces under General Andrew J. Smith seize Fort De Russy on the Red River, Louisiana, along with 325 prisoners and 12 cannon. This remains the only tactical success of the ensuing campaign.

WEST: General John G. Parke and his IX Corps begin to transfer from eastern Tennessee to Annapolis, Maryland.

March 15

POLITICS: Michael Hahn, newly elected governor of Louisiana, receives powers previously reserved for the military government as civil authority is transferred slowly back to politicians. This proves a forerunner of what ultimately unfolds during Reconstruction.

NAVAL: The USS *Eastport, Lexington,* and *Ouachita* unsuccessfully intercept Confederate vessels fleeing over the Alexandria Rapids, Louisiana. The Southern steamer *Countess* grounds in the process and is destroyed by its crew to prevent capture. The bulk of Admiral David D. Porter's squadron continues working its way toward Alexandria as long as water levels permit.

The USS *Nyanza* captures the Confederate schooner *J. W. Wilder* on the Atchafalaya River, Louisiana.

March 16

SOUTH: Union forces under General Andrew J. Smith occupy Alexandria, Louisiana, supported by nine Federal gunboats.

WEST: General Nathan B. Forrest begins a protracted cavalry raid into West Tennessee and Kentucky.

Confederate cavalry under Colonel John M. Hughs attack the Nashville and Chattanooga Railroad near Tullahoma, Tennessee, destroying a train, taking 60 Union captives, and killing 20 African Americans.

General Sterling Price succeeds General Theophilus H. Holmes as commander of the Confederate District of Arkansas.

NAVAL: Landing parties under Commander Thomas O. Selfridge of the USS *Osage* occupy Alexandria, Louisiana, ahead of General Andrew J. Smith's army troops.

The USS *Neptune* and *Galatea* are ordered into the Caribbean to escort California steamers carrying shipments of gold.

The Confederate raider CSS *Alabama* under Captain Raphael Semmes drops anchor at Capetown, South Africa, to take on supplies.

March 17
SOUTH: General Nathaniel P. Banks, detained at New Orleans, Louisiana, for political reasons, misses his scheduled rendezvous with General Andrew J. Smith at Alexandria.
WEST: Generals Ulysses S. Grant and William T. Sherman meet at Nashville, Tennessee, to coordinate their strategy closely. They then board trains for Cincinnati, Ohio, after Grant declares, "Headquarters will be in the field and, until further orders, will be with the Army of the Potomac."

March 18
POLITICS: Pro-Union Arkansas voters ratify a new constitution mandating the abolishment of slavery.
WEST: General William T. Sherman formally gains appointment as commander of the Military Division of the Mississippi.
NAVAL: General Edmund Kirby-Smith orders the steamer *New Falls City* scuttled at Scopern's Cut-off, below Shreveport on the Red River, Louisiana, as an obstacle. He also instructs that no less than 30 torpedoes be placed below Grand Ecore to further hobble Union advances upstream.

March 19
POLITICS: The Georgia state legislature grants President Jefferson Davis a vote of confidence and, following the next significant Confederate victory, desires that peace talks be conducted with Washington, D.C., but solely on the basis of Southern independence.
SOUTH: Colonel John S. Mosby ambushes and defeats a larger Union detachment at Salem and Orleans, Virginia.

March 20
NAVAL: The USS *Honeysuckle* captures the Confederate sloop *Florida* in the Gulf of Mexico.

The USS *Tioga* captures the Confederate sloop *Swallow* at sea.

March 21
POLITICS: President Abraham Lincoln approves legislation allowing the Nevada and Colorado territories to become states.
SOUTH: Union cavalry under General Joseph A. Mower defeat Confederate troops at Henderson's Hill, Louisiana, taking 250 prisoners, 200 horses, and four cannon. Such losses temporarily cripple General Richard Taylor's ability to conduct adequate scouting and reconnaissance.
NAVAL: The USS *Hendrick Hudson* rams and sinks the Confederate blockade-runner *Wild Pigeon* at sea.

Confederates scuttle the CSS *Clifton* at Sabine Pass, Texas, after it runs aground and cannot be refloated.

March 22

NORTH: General Lew Wallace replaces General Henry H. Lockwood as commander of the Middle Department, headquartered at Baltimore, Maryland.

WEST: General Nathan Kimball succeeds General Frederick Steele as commander of the Union Department of Arkansas once the latter departs Little Rock on an expedition toward the Red River, Louisiana.

March 23

POLITICS: General Ulysses S. Grant hurriedly arrives back in Washington, D.C., eager to put in motion a simultaneous advance from four different armies across the entire South.

SOUTH: The Union I Corps is discontinued, and its troops are reabsorbed by the V Corps, Army of the Potomac under General Gouverneur K. Warren, who has himself replaced General George Sykes.

WEST: General Frederick Steele, ordered into the field by the War Department despite chronic supply shortages, reluctantly leads 10,400 Union troops out of Little Rock, Arkansas. His mission is to proceed east and link up with the Red River expedition of General Nathaniel P. Banks. Steele initially objected to the move as roads, such as they exist, are poor and his flanks remain vulnerable to attack by hard-riding Confederate cavalry. More important, Steele's efforts are dogged by lack of adequate food and fodder for troops and pack animals alike.

NAVAL: A Union naval party seizes an unnamed Confederate steamer on the Santee River, South Carolina, and burns it at the wharf.

March 24

SOUTH: Although never fully recovered from wounds received at Gettysburg, General Winfield S. Hancock resumes command of the II Corps, Army of the Potomac.

The Union III Corps is disbanded, and its troops are distributed among the II and VI Corps, Army of the Potomac.

WEST: A surprise raid by General Nathan B. Forrest captures Union City, Tennessee.

General Nathaniel P. Butler finally arrives at Alexandria, Louisiana, and a week behind schedule before commanding the Union drive up the Red River toward Shreveport. However, he is disconcerted to learn that General Andrew J. Smith's 10,000 troops must revert back to General William T. Sherman no later than April 25 in order to join the advance through Georgia. Banks receives additional bad news in the form of declining levels of water on the Red River itself, which jeopardizes continuing naval support from Admiral David D. Porter's gunboats. Undeterred, Banks orders the campaign to continue.

NAVAL: The USS *Britannia* sails from Beaufort, North Carolina, with 200 soldiers and 50 sailors, in an aborted raid against Swansboro. The expedition is frustrated by unexpectedly heavy seas.

The USS *Stonewall* captures the Confederate sloop *Josephine* off Sarasota Sound, Florida.

March 25

SOUTH: General David M. Gregg replaces General Alfred M. Pleasonton as commander of cavalry forces, Army of the Potomac.

WEST: General Nathan B. Forrest attacks and captures the town of Paducah, Kentucky, with his force of 2,800 cavalry. However, Colonel Stephen G. Hicks, the garrison commander, refuses to surrender and withdraws his 665 into the safety of nearby Fort Anderson. Forrest, espying the strength of his position, has no intention of attacking, but Colonel Albert P. Thompson nonetheless charges at the head of his 3rd and 7th Kentucky Cavalry. The Confederates are repulsed bloodily with losses of 10 killed (including Thompson) and 40 wounded, while Hicks records 14 killed and 46 wounded. Forrest withdraws with 50 captives and 400 horses, several of which are confiscated from civilians.

NAVAL: Armed boats from the USS *Winona* capture the Confederate blockade-runner *Little Ada* in the South Santee River, South Carolina, but are driven off by Southern artillery batteries, abandoning their prize.

Cannon fire from the gunboats USS *Peosta* and *Paw Paw* help repel Confederate raiders at Paducah, Kentucky, along the Tennessee River.

March 26
WEST: The approach of large Union cavalry forces toward Paducah, Kentucky, induces General Nathan B. Forrest to retire in the direction of Fort Pillow, Tennessee, on the Mississippi River.

March 27
SOUTH: General Ulysses S. Grant rejoins the Army of the Potomac, now headquartered at Culpeper Court House, Virginia.

Union prisoners begin to arrive en masse at Camp Sumter in Andersonville, Georgia. Once filled to capacity, it becomes the most squalid and infamous prison camp of the South.

March 28
SOUTH: General Nathaniel P. Banks continues his advance from Alexandria, Louisiana, toward Shreveport.

WEST: Charleston, Illinois, is the scene of violent antiwar rioting, aimed at Union soldiers on furlough. Throngs of Democrats gather to hear antiwar congressional candidate John R. Eden speak, as hundreds of soldiers mill around nearby. Once liquor starts to flow, shots are exchanged suddenly between the two parties, and Democrats under Sheriff John O'Hare begin to retrieve hidden weapons from nearby wagons. Six men are killed and 20 injured by Knights of the Golden Circle (Copperheads) before the violence is suppressed by reinforcements. An additional 50 Democrats are arrested, with 29 held indefinitely by military authorities at Springfield, until a clemency order by President Abraham Lincoln releases them.

General Richard Taylor begins to mass 16,000 men to resist a Union advance down the Red River toward Shreveport, Louisiana, an important cotton-producing center.

Union troops under Colonel Powell Clayton, having marched from Pine Bluff, Arkansas, defeat a small Confederate force at Mount Elba.

NAVAL: The USS *Shokokon* successfully engages a force of Confederate cavalry at Day's Point, Virginia.

The USS *Kingfisher* runs aground off St. Helena Sound, South Carolina, and is scuttled by its crew.

Armed boats from the USS *Sagamore* destroy two unnamed blockade-runners near Cedar Keys, Florida.

Secretary of the Navy Gideon Welles alerts Commander John C. Carter to have the USS *Michigan* ready to sail once the ice breaks on Lake Erie. He has received rumors that Confederates are planning to launch a raid from nearby Canada.

March 29

POLITICS: President Abraham Lincoln prevails on General George G. Meade to forsake a court of inquiry pertaining to his performance at the Battle of Gettysburg. For some time, the general has weathered attacks on his leadership by the Northern press and seeks vindication.

WEST: Union forces under General Nathaniel P. Banks reach Natchitoches, Louisiana, where the general renders a fateful decision: Rather than continue on a road skirting the banks of Red River, protected by the guns of Admiral David D. Porter's gunboats, Banks now veers inland along a more direct route toward his primary objective at Shreveport. Federal troops must now traverse a wilderness region along a single road wide enough for only one wagon. Meanwhile, Confederates under General Richard Taylor burn 10 miles of cotton fields in the Union army's path to deny them that valuable commodity. Taylor then assumes defensive positions at Mansfield, interposing his force between Banks and Shreveport.

A Union column under General Frederick Steele slogs into Arkadelphia, Arkansas, to rest and await reinforcements in the form of two cavalry brigades under General John M. Thayer.

Colonel Powell Clayton, advancing from Mount Elba, Arkansas, rides south and again surprises a Confederate supply train at Long View on the Sabine River. He captures 35 wagons and 260 prisoners.

NAVAL: Armed boats from the USS *Commodore Barney* and *Minnesota* ascend the Chuckatuck Creek and land parties ashore. A quick raid of Confederate headquarters at Cherry Grove, Virginia, nets 20 captives.

Admiral David D. Porter's attempts to get his gunboats over the Alexandria rapids is frustrated by unusually low levels of water on the Red River. The USS *Eastport* is hoisted carefully over the rocks, but the hospital ship *Woodford* strikes a snag and sinks.

The Confederate raider CSS *Florida* under Lieutenant Charles M. Morris captures the Union vessel *Avon* at sea and burns it.

March 30

WEST: Having consolidated his position at Mount Elba, Arkansas, Colonel Powell Clayton opens up a supply route toward Camden to assist the approaching Union column of General Frederick Steele.

March 31

NAVAL: Armed boats from the USS *Sagamore* destroy the Confederate schooner *Etta* and another unnamed vessel near Cedar Keys, Florida.

April 1

WEST: General Frederick Steele, having waited in vain for cavalry reinforcements under General John M. Thayer, departs Arkadelphia, Arkansas, and marches toward the Red River, Louisiana. Dwindling supplies also force him to place the men and pack animals under his command on half rations. Meanwhile, his progress is dogged by Confederate cavalry under Generals Joseph O. Shelby and John S. Marmaduke.

NAVAL: The Federal army transport *Maple Leaf* strikes a Confederate torpedo in the St. John's River, Florida, and sinks off Mandarin Point.

April 2

WEST: Confederate cavalry under General Joseph O. Shelby attack and overturn a Union rear guard at Okolona, Arkansas, taking 160 prisoners.

April 3

SOUTH: General Nathaniel P. Banks and his army reach Grand Ecore, Louisiana, encountering heightened Confederate resistance. He also receives reinforcements in the form of several army transports.

NAVAL: The USS *Eastport, Cricket, Mound City, Chillicothe, Pittsburg, Ozark, Neosho, Osage, Lexington, Fort Hindman,* and *Louisville* escort General Andrew J. Smith's corps up the Red River to Grand Ecore, Louisiana. The troops then slog overland from Natchitoches for an attack on Shreveport with the main force under General Nathaniel P. Banks. However, dwindling water levels remain a concern as Admiral David D. Porter's 13 gunboats and 30 transports barely make it over the Alexandria Rapids.

April 4

DIPLOMACY: In light of French aggression toward Mexico, the U.S. House of Representatives unanimously passes a resolution protesting the policies of Napoleon III. It reaffirms American resolve never to recognize a monarchical regime set up in the Western Hemisphere at the behest of any European power. Meanwhile, the government extends it support of rebel forces under President Benito Juárez.

SOUTH: The Union XI and XII Corps are consolidated into the new XX Corps under General Joseph Hooker; General Jacob D. Dox takes charge of the XXIII Corps and, in a major shift of leadership, the aggressive general Philip H. Sheridan replaces General David M. Gregg as cavalry commander, Army of the Potomac.

WEST: General John M. Schofield becomes commander of the XXIII Corps, Army of the Tennessee.

NAVAL: The USS *Sciota* captures the Confederate schooner *Mary Sorly* (nee U.S. revenue cutter *Dodge*) at Galveston, Texas.

April 6

POLITICS: The Convention of Louisiana, meeting at New Orleans, adopts a new state constitution abolishing slavery.

NORTH: The Union Department of the Monongahela merges with the Department of the Susquehanna in Pennsylvania.

WEST: The army of General Nathaniel P. Banks continues advancing from abandons the banks of the Red River along a narrow road toward Shreveport, Louisiana.

Thus, his force, as it approaches General Richard Taylor's Confederates at Mansfield, becomes literally strung out for miles through the bayou wilderness.

NAVAL: The USS *Estrella* captures the Confederate mail schooner *Julia A. Hodges* in Matagorda Bay, Texas.

April 7

WEST: The Confederate I Corps under General James Longstreet is ordered from Greeneville, Tennessee, and back to the Army of Northern Virginia.

NAVAL: The USS *Beauregard* captures the British blockade-runner *Spunky* off Cape Canaveral, Florida.

Admiral David D. Porter conducts the Federal gunboats USS *Cricket, Fort Hindman, Lexington, Osage, Neosho,* and *Chillicothe* up the Red River to support army troops at Shreveport, Louisiana.

April 8

POLITICS: The U.S. Congress approves the 13th Amendment to the Constitution by a vote of 38 to six. Slavery is now formally abolished in all territories controlled by the United States.

SOUTH: Richard Taylor is appointed lieutenant general, C.S.A.

The Union army of 18,000 men under General Nathaniel Banks moves in single file toward Mansfield, Louisiana, where it confronts General Richard Taylor's 8,000 Confederates at Sabine Crossroads. The Southerners are dug in comfortably behind extensive fieldworks awaiting a Union attack. But once Taylor notices how dispersed the Federals have allowed themselves to become—Banks's wagon train alone is three miles long, which prevents reinforcements from coming up—he orders his men forward. General Alfred Mouton's division attacks the Union left with a cheer but is badly cut up by musketry. Mouton is killed, but his survivors rally under General Camille J. Polignac and press forward, assisted by Texans under General John G. Walker to their right. The Confederates then crash through two Union lines, overrunning Banks's artillery and wagon train, which they immediately stop to plunder. This delay grants Federals under General William H. Emory sufficient time to form a third line; it, too, is attacked heavily but repulses the Southerners. Emory's stand also enables the bulk of Banks's forces to retreat toward Pleasant Hill, 15 miles east, as fighting gradually winds down.

Mansfield proves to be the decisive encounter of the Red River campaign and the largest waged in the Trans-Mississippi theater. Banks is stopped in his tracks and is thrashed soundly due to slovenly deployments. Union losses are also severe considering the numbers engaged and amount to 113 dead, 581 injured, and 1,541 missing (2,235). The victorious Taylor, who captures 20 cannon, 200 wagons, and 1,000 draft animals, suffers more than 1,000 casualties. The Confederates are reinforced tonight by General Thomas J. Churchill's division and immediately pursue the defeated bluecoats downriver.

April 9

NORTH: Union strategy for an all-out push against the Confederacy is finalized into five major components: General Nathaniel P. Banks is to capture Mobile, Alabama;

General William T. Sherman is to drive into Georgia from Tennessee and seize Atlanta; General Franz Sigel is to advance down the Shenandoah Valley, breadbasket of the Confederacy, and General Benjamin F. Butler is to descend on Richmond, Virginia, from the south bank of the James River. But most important, General George G. Meade's Army of the Potomac is to rivet their attention on General Robert E. Lee and the Army of Northern Virginia. "Wherever Lee goes, there you will go also," Grant declares.

SOUTH: General Nathaniel P. Banks consolidates 18,000 men of his shaken army, now reinforced by two veteran divisions from General Andrew J. Smith's XVI Corps, along Pleasant Hill, Louisiana. The Northerners are posted strongly and are ready by the time Confederates under General Richard Taylor appear on the battlefield at 9:00 A.M. However, Taylor's 12,000 men are exhausted by all-night marching, and his attack is delayed by several hours. It is not until 4:30 P.M. that Confederate artillery open up and Churchill's division sweeps forward in a flanking movement around Banks's left. As this transpires, Taylor also commits General Thomas Green's cavalry and a Texas division under General John G. Walker to assail the Union center. These movements are repelled bloodily, although Churchill makes good progress initially and routs two Federal brigades. Suddenly, Churchill is himself assailed in the right flank by a deft counterattack organized by Smith, and he reels backward. Additional charges against the Union line result in nothing but further losses, so Taylor orders combat to cease by nightfall.

Pleasant Hill is a major tactical victory for Banks, who rescues his army from the previous day's humiliation at Mansfield. Union losses are 152 killed, 859 wounded, and 495 captured (1,506) to a Confederate tally of 1,621. However, Union forces continue falling back on Grand Ecore, spelling an end of the Red River campaign. The aggressive Taylor wishes to pursue further, but his superior, General Edmund Kirby-Smith, orders the bulk of his army back into Arkansas to contain a Federal offensive there.

WEST: General George Stoneman transfers from Virginia to the Department of the Ohio as head of all Union cavalry.

General Frederick Steele is reinforced by cavalry under General John M. Thayer at Elkin's Ferry, Arkansas, although this does nothing to alleviate chronic supply shortages. The Union column also is beset persistently by Confederate guerrillas and cavalry.

NAVAL: At 2:00 A.M., the USS *Minnesota* is damaged by a spar torpedo handled by the Confederate torpedo boat CSS *Squib* under Lieutenant Hunter Davidson off Newport News, Virginia. The intruder was detected at 150 yards' distance, but the *Minnesota*'s guns could not be depressed in time. Davidson manages to place his charge in his target's port quarter, but fortunately for the Union vessel, the damage incurred proves slight. *Squib* then steams off to safety under heavy musket fire, thoroughly alarming Union vessels in the area.

April 10

SOUTH: The Red River campaign grounds to an ignominious close as General Nathaniel P. Banks withdraws back to Grand Ecore, Louisiana, General Frederick

Steele stalls in Arkansas. A victorious General Richard Taylor is ordered back to Mansfield by General Edmund Kirby-Smith.

WEST: General Oliver O. Howard replaces General Gordon Granger as commander of the IV Corps, Army of the Tennessee.

Union forces under General Frederick Steele encounter stiff Confederate resistance under General Sterling Price at Prairie D'Ane, Arkansas, and a continuing fight develops during the next four days. With the Red River campaign under General Nathaniel P. Banks concluded, Steele now finds himself marooned deep behind enemy lines with few supplies and no prospect of reinforcements. Nonetheless, he continues advancing toward better positions at Camden to await developments.

NAVAL: Admiral David D. Porter's Mississippi Squadron steams up the Red River and escorts army transports as far as Springfield Landing, Louisiana, 30 miles below Shreveport. Further progress is blocked by the Confederate steamer *New Falls City,* which is sunk in midstream as an obstacle. The vessels are beset further by falling water levels and news of General Nathaniel P. Banks's recent defeat at Sabine Cross Roads.

April 11

POLITICS: The pro-Union administration of Dr. Isaac Murphy is inaugurated at Little Rock, Arkansas.

NAVAL: The USS *Nita* captures the Confederate vessel *Three Brothers* near the mouth of the Homosassa River, Florida.

The USS *Virginia* captures the Confederate blockade-runner *Juanita* at San Luis Pass, Texas.

Admiral David D. Porter's gunboat flotilla slowly begins to work its vessels over the Alexandria rapids while under fire from Confederate artillery and snipers. However, the water level is dipping so low that the majority of his fleet becomes trapped upstream.

April 12

SOUTH: Confederate forces pursuing after the Battle of Pleasant Hill encounter General Thomas K. Smith's division, XVI Corps at Blair's Landing, Louisiana. These troops are covered by several Union gunboats in the adjacent Red River. General Thomas Green nonetheless dismounts his cavalry and artillery to engage them. The aggressive Green, somewhat inebriated, leads a foolish charge against the waiting flotilla and is pummeled by heavy shells fired from the riverfront; he is among the very first killed. The Southerners sustain 300 casualties to a Union tally of only 57.

WEST: General Simon B. Buckner is appointed commander of the Confederate Department of East Tennessee.

A force of 1,500 Confederate cavalry under General James R. Chambers invests Fort Pillow, Tennessee, on the Mississippi River, then defended by 557 Union soldiers, including 262 African Americans, under Major Lionel F. Booth. The fort, a wretchedly designed open earthwork, is partially stormed by Chambers, whose first charge seizes the outer works and renders the Union cannon useless. From

Confederate batteries fire on Union transport ships during the Red River Campaign, March–May 1864. Engraving, *Harper's Weekly*

there, Confederate snipers also fire down into the garrison, killing Major Booth. His successor, Major William F. Bradford, grimly awaits promised reinforcements from downstream and holds on. At 10:00 A.M., General Nathan B. Forrest arrives and, after several more hours of fighting, concludes that the fort cannot be defended. At 3:30 P.M., a flag of truce goes forward demanding Bradford's surrender, but he refuses. Forrest then orders an all-out assault on the last ring of defense, which falls easily. Surviving Federals then either flee over the bluffs and dive into the Mississippi River or try surrendering, but the enraged Confederates apparently go on a rampage. Many Union soldiers, largely African Americans, are apparently murdered in cold blood. The fort is abandoned soon after, and Forrest departs for Jackson, Tennessee. Confederate losses at Fort Pillow are 14 killed and 86 wounded, a pittance compared to Union casualties of 231 dead, 100 wounded, and 226 captured—only 58 African Americans are taken alive. The extent of the slaughter results in charges of massacre being leveled against Forrest, who denies any complicity. But thereafter "Remember Fort Pillow!" becomes a rallying cry for black soldiers.

NAVAL: Armed boats from the USS *South Carolina* and *T. A. Ward* seize the British blockade-runner *Alliance* after it runs aground on Daufuskie Island, South Carolina.

The USS *Estrella,* escorting two army steamers, helps General Fitz H. Warren land troops in Matagorda Bay, Texas, and subsequently captures two small vessels.

The Federal gunboat USS *New Era* assists in the defense of Fort Pillow, Tennessee, but after the fort falls and captured cannon are turned on the vessel, it withdraws upriver.

Admiral David D. Porter's Mississippi Squadron and several army transports begin their trek back down the Red River, Louisiana, engaging enemy troops at Blair's Landing, Louisiana. Heavy and accurate fire from the USS *Neosho, Lexington, Hindman,* and *Osage* drives off Confederate dismounted cavalry and cannon from the riverbanks, killing General Thomas Green in the process. The *Osage* also makes naval history in this engagement by employing for the first time jerry-rigged periscopes to direct naval gunfire.

April 13

NAVAL: A naval expedition consisting of the USS *Stepping Stones, Commodore Morris, Commodore Perry, Commodore Barney, Shokokon,* and *Minnesota* unsuccessfully tries to trap the Confederate torpedo vessel CSS *Squib* on the Nansemond River, Virginia.

The USS *Rachel Seaman* captures the British blockade-runner *Maria Alfred* on the Mermentau River, Louisiana.

The USS *Nyanza* captures the Confederate schooner *Mandoline* at Atchafalaya Bay, Louisiana.

April 14

SOUTH: General John Sedgwick assumes command of the VI Corps, Army of the Potomac.

General Ambrose E. Burnside takes charge of the IX Corps, Army of the Potomac.

WEST: Confederate cavalry under General Abraham Buford, informed by local newspapers that General Nathan B. Forrest's recent raid missed capturing 140 army horses concealed in a foundry at Paducah, Kentucky, suddenly reappear in force. The Union garrison under Colonel Stephen C. Hicks simply withdraws once again into nearby Fort Anderson, and the Southerners make off with valuable new mounts.

NAVAL: The USS *New Era, Platte Valley,* and *Silver Cloud* approach Fort Pillow, Tennessee, and, finding it vacant, fire shells at nearby Confederate forces.

The USS *Peosta, Key West, Fairplay,* and *Victory* approach Paducah, Kentucky, on the Ohio River and drive off Confederate forces gathering along the bank.

The USS *Moose, Hastings,* and *Fairy* engage Confederate cavalry at Columbus, Kentucky, on the Mississippi River.

April 15

POLITICS: Governor Andrew Johnson of Tennessee delivers a speech in Knoxville endorsing the principles of emancipation.

SOUTH: Colonel John S. Mosby ambushes and defeats a large Union contingent at Waterford, Virginia.

WEST: Union cavalry directed by General John M. Schofield surprise Confederates at Greeneville, Tennessee, taking 25 captives.

General Frederick Steele occupies Camden, Arkansas, to gather supplies and rest his hungry men. Meanwhile, Confederates under General Sterling Price continue arriving to threaten his flank and rear.

NAVAL: The USS *Virginia* forces the Confederate sloop *Rosina* aground near San Luis Pass, Texas, destroying it.

The Federal gunboat USS *Eastport* strikes a Confederate torpedo on the Red River below Grand Ecore, Louisiana, and grounds itself in shoal waters to carry out repairs.

April 16

NORTH: An official report by the U.S. government lists 146,634 Confederate prisoners of war.

NAVAL: The army transport *General Hunter* strikes a torpedo and sinks in the St. John's River, Florida.

April 17

NORTH: General Ulysses S. Grant suspends all prisoner exchanges until the Confederates release identical numbers of Union captives—an impossible demand, given their restricted manpower. To this end, Grant also insists: "No distinction whatever will be made in the exchange between white and colored prisoners." Confederate authorities strongly disagree with his dictates, and the practice of prisoner exchanges halts, resulting in longer retention of captives in already overcrowded facilities. Grant's ploy also seriously impairs the South's ability to regain trained manpower.

SOUTH: General Robert F. Hoke gathers up 7,000 men and attacks the Union garrison at Plymouth, North Carolina. His objective is the 2,834 Union infantry, cavalry, and artillery commanded by General Henry W. Wessells, who are supported further by an offshore gunboat squadron.

WEST: To alleviate mounting supply shortages, General Frederick Steele dispatches a foraging expedition from Camden, Arkansas, to confiscate stores of Southern corn. Colonel James M. Williams then marches from camp with 695 men, mostly from the 1st Kansas Colored Volunteers, two cannon, and 198 wagons. En route, he receives additional reinforcements, bringing his numbers up to 1,170 men.

NAVAL: The Federal gunboats USS *Southfield*, *Ceres*, and *Miami*, accompanied by the army steamer *Bombshell*, assist in the defense of Plymouth, North Carolina. Confederate attackers are driven off, but the *Bombshell* sustains serious damage and sinks.

The USS *Owasco* captures the British blockade-runner *Lilly* off Velasco, Texas.

April 18

SOUTH: General Pierre G. T. Beauregard arrives to replace General Samuel Jones as commander of the Department of North Carolina and Southern Virginia.

General Robert F. Hoke continues his campaign against the Union garrison at Plymouth, North Carolina, by shelling enemy positions and capturing Fort Wessels with several determined charges. However, Federal troops cling stubbornly to nearby Fort Williams, and now Hoke's success hinges on the appearance of the Confederate ram CSS *Albemarle*.

WEST: Confederate cavalry under General John S. Marmaduke detect a party of 1,170 Union soldiers near Poison Springs, Arkansas, and prepare to give battle with 1,700 troopers. He then is joined by General Samuel B. Maxey's command, which brings Confederate numbers up to 3,335. Maxey, although nominally outranking Marmaduke, allows him to take tactical control of the battle. The Confederates then advance, meeting staunch resistance from African Americans of the 1st Kansas Colored Volunteers and are thrown back repeatedly. But Southern numbers gradually assert themselves and the Union troopers suddenly gave way, creating a gap in the Union lines. Colonel James M. Williams strives to close ranks as the Confederates charge again, and he is in the act of covering his wagon train when Marmaduke's masked cannons open fire. The Federal column now is caught in a crossfire and crumbles quickly as survivors flee for the safety of Camden, 10 miles distant. Union losses would have been far higher save for Maxey's decision to overrule Marmaduke and eschew the pursuit in order to secure the wagon train.

Poison Springs is a significant Union defeat for it forces General Frederick Steele's army at Camden on the defensive, where it languishes on half rations. The victorious Marmaduke also captures all 198 wagons and four cannon, and he inflicts 204 killed and missing, along with 97 wounded. Confederate losses are pegged at 13 killed, 81 wounded, and one missing. Sadly, most of the Union dead are African Americans captured in battle and then slaughtered without mercy by Missourians, Arkansans, and Confederate Choctaw.

NAVAL: The USS *Commodore Read* engages and destroys a Confederate supply base at Circus Point on the Rappahannock River, Virginia.

The Confederate ram CSS *Albemarle* departs Hamilton, North Carolina, under Commander James W. Cooke and sails down the Roanoke River. The vessel's appearance is greatly anticipated by Confederate forces currently besieging Plymouth. But while steaming en route, the vessel experiences engine and steering malfunctions and is forced to anchor above the town that evening.

Armed boats from the USS *Beauregard* capture the British blockade-runner *Oramoneta* near Matanzas Inlet, Florida.

The USS *Fox* captures and burns the Confederate schooner *Good Hope* off the Homosassa River, Florida.

April 19

POLITICS: The U.S. Congress passes legislation authorizing the admittance of Nebraska as a state.

SOUTH: Colonel John S. Mosby raids a Union wedding ceremony at Leesburg, Virginia, and then conveys his greetings to Federal troops and Union-leaning inhabitants of the area.

NAVAL: The huge Confederate steam ram CSS *Albemarle* under Commander James W. Cooke attacks the Federal squadron consisting of the USS *Miami, Ceres,* and *Southfield* off Plymouth, North Carolina. Arriving at 3:30 A.M., *Albemarle* strikes and sinks the USS *Southfield,* killing Commander C. W. Flusser. The surviving Union vessels draw off, leaving the Federal garrison ashore unsupported and with Confederate forces commanding all water approaches to Plymouth.

A Confederate torpedo boat makes a failed attempt to strike and sink the USS *Wabash* off Charleston harbor, South Carolina. The attack is detected, and the intended victim manages to raise steam and get underway, but the attackers are finally discouraged by heavy swells.

The USS *Owsaco* captures the British blockade-runner *Laura* in the Gulf of Mexico.

The USS *Virginia* captures the Mexican blockade-runner *Alma* off the Texas coast.

April 20

NORTH: The government reduces rations accorded to Southern prisoners of war in retaliation for mistreatment of Union captives.

SOUTH: General Robert F. Hoke attacks and captures 2,800 Union prisoners and a large quantity of supplies at Plymouth, North Carolina, after a three-day siege. Key to his success is the arrival of the Confederate ram CSS *Albemarle,* which bombards the defenders from offshore. For his success, Hoke receives promotion to major general. Confederate losses are 163 killed and 554 wounded.

WEST: General Edmund Kirby-Smith arrives outside Camden, Arkansas, with three divisions to confront the 13,500 Union troops of General Frederick Steele. The Confederates then begin to maneuver to come between Steele and the capital at Little Rock. Steele, meanwhile, gratefully receives a Union supply train from Pine Bluff, which partially ameliorates his otherwise tenuous supply situation.

April 21

POLITICS: President Abraham Lincoln confers with the governors of Ohio, Indiana, Illinois, and Iowa.

SOUTH: General Nathaniel P. Banks withdraws his army from Grand Ecore, Louisiana, and back to Cloutiersville while closely pursued by Confederate cavalry.

NAVAL: The USS *Eureka* trades fire with a concealed Confederate battery on the Potomac River near Urbanna, Virginia.

Armed boats from the USS *Howquah, Fort Jackson,* and *Niphon* land and destroy Confederate saltworks at Masonboro Sound, North Carolina, taking 160 captives.

Armed boats from the USS *Ethan Allen* attack and destroy a Confederate saltworks at Murrell's Inlet, South Carolina.

Landing parties from the USS *Cimarron* destroy a rice mill and 5,000 bushels of rice at Winyah Bay, South Carolina.

Armed boats from the USS *Sagamore* destroy 400 bales of cotton at Clay Landing, Florida.

The Federal gunboats USS *Petrel* and *Prairie Bird* lend supporting fire to Union forces attacking Yazoo City, Mississippi. However, once *Petrel* steams past Confederate batteries, it proves unable to turn around in the confining waters downstream.

The Federal gunboat USS *Eastport* is refloated after striking a torpedo and limps down the Red River. During the next five days, the damaged vessel grounds itself eight times to effect repairs and covers only 60 miles.

April 22

POLITICS: The first U.S. coins with the inscription "In God We Trust" are minted as per an act of Congress.

President Jefferson Davis writes General Leonidas K. Polk concerning African-American prisoners. "If the negroes are escaped slaves, they should be held safely for recovery by their owners," he states. "If otherwise, inform me."

SOUTH: Fitzhugh Lee is appointed major general, C.S.A.

WEST: To gather additional supplies for his starving forces, General Frederick Steele dispatches 240 wagons on an expedition to Pine Bluff, Arkansas. They are accompanied by Colonel Francis M. Drake, commanding 1,200 infantry and 240 cavalry as an escort.

NAVAL: The Confederate steam ram CSS *Neuse* grounds on its maiden voyage from Kinston, North Carolina, and cannot be refloated. It then is destroyed to prevent capture.

The USS *Petrel* again engages Confederate batteries during a Union assault on Yazoo City, Mississippi. *Petrel* comes off poorly in the exchange, grounds, and is captured by General Wirt Adams with a loss of 10 killed.

The USS *Monticello* boards the British schooner *James Douglas* at sea, only to find it abandoned.

April 23

SOUTH: As the army of General Nathaniel P. Banks retreats from Grand Ecore, Louisiana, a body of Confederate cavalry under General Hamilton P. Bee seizes Monet's Ferry at Cane River Crossing. Because this was the only fordable point in the vicinity, Union troops under General William H. Emory counterattack to regain control of the ferry. Colonel Francis Fessenden dislodges Southerners from behind the high bank they occupy, and Bee withdraws safely to a nearby hillside. Union troops then construct a pontoon bridge on the river, over which Banks's army passes the following day. General Richard Taylor waxes critical over Bee's inept performance and for allowing the Federals to escape. Union losses are estimated at 300; the Confederates sustain about 50 casualties.

WEST: General Frank P. Blair assumes command of the Union XVII Corps in Tennessee.

General James F. Fagan, after learning of the Union wagon train dispatched by General Frederick Steele to Pine Bluff, Arkansas, dispatches 4,000 Confederate cavalry under Generals William L. Cabell and Joseph O. Shelby to intercept the wagon train on the Warren Road.

April 24

WEST: A large Union wagon train wends its way back to Pine Bluff, Arkansas, including 500 Iowa cavalry and 300 former African-American slaves seeking freedom. They proceed down the Warren Road unaware that sizable Confederate forces lurk nearby, preparing to strike.

April 25

SOUTH: Confederate raiders under Colonel John S. Mosby storm a Union outpost at Hunter's Mills, Virginia, capturing men and horses.

General Nathaniel P. Banks's men begin to straggle into Alexandria, Louisiana, concluding their ill-fated campaign up the Red River.

General Robert Ransom is assigned to take charge of the Confederate Department of Richmond.

WEST: A force of 4,000 Confederate cavalry under General William L. Cabell surprises a Union wagon train at Mark's Mills, Arkansas, catching the armed escort of Colonel Francis M. Drake in a pincer. Advanced elements tangle at 8:00 A.M., after which impetuous Southerners drive the Federals back into their wagons. Drake falls seriously wounded before Union defenses can sort themselves out. A final charge from the north delivered by General Joseph O. Shelby clinches the victory, and the Northerners surrender en masse. Cabell seizes 240 wagons and 1,700 prisoners while only 300 Federals escape back to their main force at Camden. Confederate losses are given as 41 killed, 108 wounded, and 144 missing. Moreover, enraged Southerners also murder 150 African-American slaves who had attached themselves to the column. This defeat also impels General Frederick Steele to abandon Camden, Arkansas, in the face of superior numbers and dwindling supplies.

NAVAL: The Confederate raider CSS *Alabama* under Captain Raphael Semmes captures the Federal ship *Rockingham* west of the Cape Verde Islands and sinks it with cannon fire.

April 26

SOUTH: General Ulysses S. Grant orders Union troops to evacuate Washington, North Carolina, following the recent loss of Plymouth. He also orders the town of New Bern held at all costs and has its defenses strengthened.

The battered Union army of General Nathaniel P. Banks continues filtering through Alexandria, Louisiana, and remains two days awaiting the gunboat fleet of Admiral David D. Porter.

WEST: Outnumbered and nearly surrounded by Confederates under Generals Edmund Kirby-Smith and Sterling Price, General Frederick Steele abandons Camden, Arkansas, and marches back to Little Rock. He methodically begins to evacuate that night and skillfully slips past Confederate outposts without detection.

NAVAL: Armed boats from the USS *Ottawa* and *Pawnee* accompany several army transports up the St. John's River in defense of Fort Gates and St. Augustine, Florida.

The Mississippi Squadron under Admiral David D. Porter wages a running fight while passing Confederate batteries near Alexandria on the Red River, Louisiana. In this first round of fighting, the USS *Cricket* sustains heavy damage while the pump steamer *Champion No. 3* is crippled, drifts, and is captured. The wooden gunboat *Juliet* also receives several hits but is fortunately towed out of harm's way by *Champion No. 5*.

The Federal gunboat USS *Eastport,* having grounded six times due to damage from striking a mine, is scuttled on the Red River, Louisiana.

April 27

POLITICS: President Jefferson Davis dispatches a special commissioner to Canada to help to negotiate a possible truce with the United States.

NORTH: In Washington, D.C., General in Chief Ulysses S. Grant begins to issue detailed orders to unleash his multipronged assault on the South.

WEST: General Frederick Steele, having skillfully evacuated Camden, Arkansas, with 13,500 men, begins a laborious slog back to Little Rock. He eludes Confederate vigilance for several hours, but his situation, 70 miles behind enemy lines, low on supplies, and substantially outnumbered, is a perilous one. General Edmund Kirby-Smith then tardily throws a pontoon bridge over the Ouachita River, a feat delaying him several hours, and commences to pursue. The progress of both sides is greatly encumbered by mud and driving rain.

NAVAL: Admiral David D. Porter makes a second attempt to run past Confederate batteries along the Red River near Alexandria, Louisiana. The USS *Fort Hindman* and *Juliet* receive some damage while the pump steamer *Champion No. 5* burns and sinks. The heavy ironclad USS *Neosho* also arrives from downstream to lend assistance. Porter reassembles his surviving craft at Alexandria.

The Confederate raider CSS *Alabama* under Captain Raphael Semmes captures and burns the Federal bark *Tycoon* east of Salvador, Brazil.

April 28

SOUTH: Union batteries in Charleston Harbor, South Carolina, commence to bombard Fort Sumter, throwing an addition 510 rounds throughout the ensuing week.

WEST: General Egbert B. Brown orders Union forces in Johnson County, Missouri, to pursue Confederate guerrilla William C. Quantrill.

NAVAL: Admiral David D. Porter's flotilla remains trapped on the Red River by receding water levels. The admiral himself is resigned to the necessity of scuttling his entire squadron to prevent its capture, and he advises Navy secretary Gideon Welles that, "you may judge my feelings at having to perform so painful a duty."

April 29

POLITICS: The U.S. Congress increases all duties by 50 percent to fund the war effort better.

WEST: General George Crook leads 6,155 men into the Allegheny Mountains, Virginia, for the purpose of cutting the Virginia and Tennessee Railroad. From the onset, his progress is hampered by harsh terrain and drenching rain.

The Union column of General Frederick Steele reaches the rain-swollen banks of the Saline River at Jenkin's Ferry and makes preparations to cross a rickety pontoon bridge. However, the close proximity of pursuing Confederate units necessitates the deployment of a strong rear guard of 4,000 men under General Samuel Rice, VII Corps.

NAVAL: Federal gunboats USS *Yankee, Fuchsia, Thomas Freeborn,* and *Tulip* steam up Carter's Creek, Virginia, to destroy a Confederate base camp.

The USS *Honeysuckle* captures the British blockade-runner *Miriam* off Key West, Florida.

Admiral David D. Porter's gunboat flotilla sits almost completely stranded on the Red River near Alexandria, Louisiana, by declining water levels. Fortunately, succor arrives when army engineer Colonel Joseph Bailey proposes building a series of dams to raise the water. Once the depth reaches seven feet, chutes can be opened to allow the vessels to slip through. "This proposition looked like madness," Porter concedes, "and the best engineers ridiculed it, but Colonel Bailey was so sanguine of success that I requested General Banks to have it done." The result proves to be one of the most remarkable improvisations of the entire war.

April 30

SOUTH: President Jefferson Davis issues orders to return all captured slaves found fighting in Union ranks back to their rightful owners "on proof and payment of charges."

Five-year-old Joe Davis, son of President Jefferson Davis, dies of injuries received in a fall at the Confederate White House in Richmond, Virginia.

WEST: General Franz Sigel leads 6,500 Union troops down the Shenandoah Valley toward Staunton, where he can cut the strategic Virginia Central Railroad.

The Battle of Jenkin's Ferry, Arkansas, develops as Confederate cavalry under John S. Marmaduke approach a Union rear guard under General Samuel Rice. Rice deploys his 4,000 men in a position with strongly secured flanks, which require the Confederates, fielding twice as many men, to attack frontally across a swampy morass. In rapid succession, the brigades of Generals Thomas J. Churchill, Mosby M. Parsons, and John G. Walker all advance and hurl themselves against Rice's position, being invariably driven back with losses. At length, General Frederick Steele passes the bulk of his army over the Sabine River and dutifully extricates his remaining men. General Edmund Kirby-Smith thus loses his final chance to destroy Federal forces in Arkansas completely. Union casualties are 63 dead, 413 wounded, and 45 missing (521), including the skillful general Rice, who is mortally wounded. Confederate losses are 86 killed and 356 wounded (442). As an afternote, men of the U.S. 2nd Colored Infantry murder several Southern prisoners in retaliation for atrocities inflicted on African Americans at Poison Springs the previous April.

NAVAL: The USS *Vicksburg* captures the British blockade-runner *Indian* off Charleston, South Carolina.

The USS *Conemaugh* captures the Confederate schooner *Judson* off Mobile, Alabama.

Confederate blockade-runners *Harriet Lane* and *Alice* slip past the USS *Katahdin* in a heavy rainstorm and evade the Union blockade off Galveston, Texas.

To reserve the Mississippi Squadron of Admiral David D. Porter, Colonel Joseph Bailey begins to construct a dam of logs across the Red River. Through this engineering expedient, the water levels are expected to rise sufficiently to allow Porter's vessels to pass over the Alexandria rapids. "Two or three regiments of Maine men were set to work felling trees," Porter notes, "Everyman seemed to be working with a vigor seldom seen equaled." Their efforts relieve Porter of having to scuttle his squadron to avoid being captured.

May 1

SOUTH: General John P. Hatch is tapped to succeed General Quincy A. Gillmore as commander of the Department of the South.

WEST: Colonel John S. Mosby captures eight wagons belong to General Franz Sigel's army at Bunker Hill, West Virginia.

NAVAL: The USS *Morse, General Putnam,* and *Shawsheen* escort an army expedition up the York River to West Point, Virginia. The vessels subsequently move up the Pamunkey and Mattaponi rivers to patrol for enemy forces.

The USS *Fox* captures the Confederate sloop *Oscar* off St. Marks, Florida.

May 2

POLITICS: The first session, second Confederate Congress convenes in Richmond, Virginia.

President Jefferson Davis addresses the opening session of the second Confederate Congress, accusing Northerners of "barbarism" through their "Plunder and devastation of the property of noncombatants, destruction of private dwellings, and even of edifices devoted to the worship of God."

SOUTH: General William H. Emory replaces General William B. Franklin as commander of the Union XIX Corps, Louisiana.

WEST: General Franz Sigel leads 6,500 Union troops out of Winchester Virginia, and down the Shenandoah Valley Pike toward New Market. His goal is to deny the Confederacy access to any food or cattle grown in this highly productive region.

General William W. Averell leads 2,000 Union cavalry out from Logan's Court House, Virginia, for a diversionary attack against Saltville. He moves in conjunction with another large raid by General George Crook in western Virginia.

May 3

POLITICS: President Abraham Lincoln and his cabinet discuss the recent murder of African-American prisoners at Fort Pillow, Tennessee.

SOUTH: General Ulysses S. Grant orders the the Army of the Potomac, 122,000 strong, to begin to cross the Rapidan River and to move on Richmond, Virginia. General George G. Meade, however, disputes this strategy and argues against traversing the Wilderness to hit the Confederate left flank, but Grant seeks to cut General Robert E. Lee off from Richmond. As the imposing Federal host starts to lurch toward its objective, Lee reacts by moving 66,000 men of the Army of Northern Virginia up from Orange Court House. He anticipates that the harsh terrain will negate Grant's superiority in numbers, ensuring a fairer fight. The ensuing fray promises to be a clash of titans.

WEST: General Frederick Steele's disgruntled Union troops wearily trudge into Little Rock, Arkansas, after their unsuccessful campaign to reach the Red River, Louisiana. His losses amount to 2,750 killed, wounded, and captured, along with nine cannon and 640 wagons lost. Fortunately, deft maneuvering in the face of superior Confederate numbers keeps his army intact and allows the Union to maintain partial control of the Trans-Mississippi Confederacy.

NAVAL: The USS *Chocura* captures the British blockade-runner *Agnes* at the mouth of the Brazos River, Texas, and then snares the Prussian schooner *Frederick the Second* in the same area.

The USS *Virginia* captures and sinks the Confederate schooner *Experiment* in the Gulf of Mexico.

May 4

POLITICS: The U.S. House of Representatives passes the punitively worded Wade-Davis Reconstruction Bill 73 to 59 over President Abraham Lincoln's objections. Curiously, Radical Republican politicians such as Thaddeus Stevens find the measure too conciliatory.

SOUTH: General Ulysses S. Grant and General George G. Meade direct the Army of the Potomac across the Rapidan River, Virginia, toward the heavily forested area known as the Wilderness. They lead a veteran force of 122,000 men, divided into four commands: General Winfield S. Hancock's II Corps, the V Corps under Gouverneur K. Warren, General John Sedgwick's VI Corps, and General Ambrose E. Burnside's IX Corps. Warren and Sedgwick cross the Germanna Ford east of Fredericksburg, Virginia, while Hancock does the same at Ely's Ford, six miles to the east. From there, they march directly into a thick, pine scrub forest of the Wilderness.

General Robert E. Lee, meanwhile, seeking to negate Grant's preponderance in numbers, advances to engage him in the Wilderness, where the rough terrain and thick foliage work to his advantage. He has at his disposal 66,000 veteran troops divided up into General James Longstreet's I Corps, General Richard S. Ewell's II Corps, and General Ambrose P. Hill's III Corps. Longstreet is not in the immediate vicinity and receives orders to march there at once.

General Benjamin F. Butler leads his Army of the James in transports from Fortress Monroe, Virginia, and then down the James River toward Richmond, Virginia.

WEST: General William T. Sherman advances his force of 110,000 men from Chattanooga, Tennessee, against Confederate forces under General Joseph E. Johnston. The Union goal is Atlanta, Georgia, an important communications hub.

NAVAL: The USS *Sunflower, Honduras,* and *J. L. Davis* assist General Daniel Woodbury's soldiers in the seizure of Tampa, Florida. The naval landing party is allowed to hoist the Stars and Stripes over the town.

May 5

SOUTH: The Battle of the Wilderness erupts when General Gouverneur K. Warren's V Corps encounters General Richard S. Ewell's II Corps along the Orange Turnpike Road. Warren is well positioned to sweep the Southerners before him, but his insurmountable delays in attacking grant Ewell time to rush up reinforcements. At 1:00 P.M., a tremendous seesaw struggle erupts in the woods with both sides taking and inflicting heavy casualties but neither side proving able to dislodge the other. General John Sedgwick's VI Corps then deploys and attempts to turn Ewell's left flank but is repulsed. Fighting in this sector dies down at nightfall.

Two miles south, General Winfield S. Hancock's II Corps engages General Ambrose P. Hill's III Corps in fierce fighting. An all-out Confederate advance surges ahead initially, but Hill is halted by General George W. Getty's division, VI Corps, which stands long enough for Hancock to make his greater numbers felt. Hill then is driven back gradually with heavy losses, and Hancock prepares to overwhelm his weakened opponent on the following day.

The Army of the James under General Benjamin F. Butler lands 39,000 men of Generals Quincy A. Gillmore's X Corps and William F. Smith's XVIII Corps at Bermuda Hundred, Virginia. This places Union forces within marching distance of the Confederate capital at Richmond, then lightly defended.

A Confederate assault on New Bern, North Carolina, by General Robert F. Hoke is rebuffed once the CSS *Albemarle* fails to penetrate Union naval defenses. The Southerners then abandon the siege and begin to withdraw.

WEST: Virginian Partisan Rangers under Captain John H. McNeill seize Piedmont, West Virginia, along with several trains, cars, and 104 prisoners.

The 2nd Cavalry Division under General William W. Averell clatters out of Logan Court, Virginia, and advances toward Wyoming Court House. The division skirmishes with the 8th Virginia Cavalry near Saltville.

NAVAL: The ironclad ram CSS *Albemarle* under Commander James W. Cooke, escorted by the smaller *Bombshell,* and *Cotton Plant,* enters Albemarle Sound off Plymouth, North Carolina, to engage Federal warships stationed there. The Union armada under Captain Melancthon Smith mounts 60 cannon to Cooke's two banded Brooke rifles, but the latter's ship is armored heavily and nearly is impervious to cannon fire. Broadsides are exchanged, and the wooden Union vessels sustain damage until Smith orders USS *Sassacus* to charge the *Albemarle* at full steam. The ensuing collision damages both vessels, and once *Albemarle* puts a point-blank cannon shot through *Sassacus*'s boilers, it drifts helplessly out of the fight. Union side-wheelers *Mattabesett* and *Wyalusing* then hurry up to assist and keep the Southerners under a steady bombardment. With *Albemarle* maneuvering badly and *Bombshell* captured, Cooke orders his vessel and *Cotton Plant* back up the Roanoke River. His withdrawal leaves Confederate forces without naval support, and their ongoing attack on New Bern falters.

The Federal gunboats USS *Covington* and *Signal* and the transport *Warner* are sunk near Dunn's Bayou on the Red River, Louisiana, after being attacked by Confederate troops and artillery.

May 6
SOUTH: Stand Watie, a Cherokee chief, is appointed a brigadier general, C.S.A.

The Battle of the Wilderness continues as General Winfield S. Hancock's II Corps, advancing down the Orange Plank Road, smashes into General Ambrose P. Hill's III Corps, nearly breaking it. General Ambrose E. Burnside's IX Corps, which arrives late, is also thrown into the fray, although he blunders into Hill's reserves and is stopped. At that precise moment, General James Longstreet makes his own sudden, if belated, appearance with the veteran I Corps and hits Hancock's left and rear. A hard-fought slugging match at close range ensues until four Confederate brigades discover a secret path around the Union left and attack. Longstreet hammers Hancock back across the line and pushes the Federals onto Brock Road. The hard-charging leader then is wounded seriously by friendly fire while General Micah Jenkins, riding alongside him, is killed. Ironically, Longstreet falls at almost the same spot where "Stonewall" Jackson was wounded fatally a year earlier. Command delays ensue, and the Confederates are unable to resume advancing before

4:00 P.M., which gives Hancock ample time to prepare defenses. When the Confederates finally attack, they encounter entrenched Federals backed by artillery and are repulsed.

Two miles away, General John Sedgwick's VI Corps renews its struggle with General Richard S. Ewell's II Corps along the Orange Turnpike. Ewell strikes first at 4:30 A.M. and is repulsed, as are subsequent Union attacks. The fresh Confederate division under General John B. Gordon then manages to work its way around the Union right and charges, severely disrupting Warren's line. The onset of nightfall dampens further fighting, and both sides settle behind entrenched lines. Worse, the dry vegetation and undergrowth are set ablaze by the fighting, and hundreds of wounded soldiers, unable to crawl to safety, perish horribly in the flames.

The Wilderness is an unequivocal tactical victory for the South as General Lee tackled an opponent twice his size—in an area where he was least expected—and handles him roughly. Grant, who endures the ignominy of having both flanks turned, suffers staggering losses: 2,246 men dead, 12,037 injured, and 3,383 missing (17,666); Confederate casualties, though not recorded, are probably in the vicinity of 8,000. But Grant, unlike Union commanders before him, ignores the setback and, by dint of single-minded determination, completely alters the war's strategic equation. He fully intends to maintain the initiative by sidestepping around Lee's left flank, and inch ever closer to Richmond, Virginia. Lee is thus reduced to following close at hand. "Whatever happens," Grant tells President Abraham Lincoln, "there will be no turning back." This newfound doggedness, missing in the first three years of combat, marks a turning point in the Civil War, whereupon the tide begins to turn inexorably in favor of the North.

The Army of the James under General Benjamin F. Butler slowly advances 39,000 men toward lightly manned Confederate defenses under General George E. Pickett, but he fails to press its advantage. Pickett, commanding only 10,000 men at Petersburg, stands his ground, and Butler timidly starts to entrench. His only offensive action is to order 1,000 troops from the XVIII Corps under General Charles A. Heckman to cut the Richmond and Petersburg railroad, and this is repulsed by Colonel Charles Graham and 600 Confederates.

A Federal expedition from Key West occupies Tampa, Florida.

NAVAL: The side-wheeler USS *Commodore Jones* detonates a 2,000-pound Confederate torpedo and sinks in the James River, Virginia, with a loss of 40 lives. Ironically, the vessel then was dragging the river for mines in concert with the *Mackinaw* and *Commodore Morris*.

Armed boats from the USS *Dawn* support an army attack on Wilson's Wharf, Virginia, and help burn a signal station.

The USS *Eutaw, Osceola, Pequot, Shokokon,* and *Putnam* support landing operations of General Benjamin F. Butler's Army of the James at Bermuda Hundred, Virginia, and subsequently move inland as far as is practicable.

A sortie by the ironclad ram CSS *Raleigh* at New Inlet, North Carolina, forces the USS *Britannia* and *Nansemond* to withdraw, allowing an unnamed blockade-runner to escape.

The USS *Grand Gulf* captures the British blockade-runner *Young Republic* east of Savannah, Georgia.

The Federal steamer USS *Granite City* and the tinclad *Wave* are shelled by Confederate batteries on the Calcasieu River, Louisiana, and are forced to surrender. Union losses total 174; the Confederates report 21 casualties.

May 7

NORTH: Edward R. S. Canby is promoted to major general, U.S. Army.

SOUTH: Richard H. Anderson replaces the critically wounded James Longstreet as commander of the Confederate I Corps, Army of Northern Virginia.

The struggle of the Wilderness concludes as General Ulysses S. Grant maintains the initiative by attempting to slip around the Confederate right and march 12 miles southeast toward Spotsylvania Court House. Possession of this crucial crossroads would grant Union forces an open road to Richmond, Virginia. General Gouverneur K. Warren's VI Corps is then detailed to seize the junction while Federal cavalry under General Philip H. Sheridan move to seize and clear the Brock Road. He has only the division of General Wesley Merritt available, but this is sent trotting down the road toward Spotsylvania.

Sheridan's advanced brigade under General George A. Custer then rides directly into General Fitzhugh Lee's dismounted Confederate troopers at Todd's Tavern, and intense fighting erupts in the underbrush. Additional Union and Confederate cavalry arrive under Generals Wesley Merritt and Wade Hampton, respectively, but the Southerners, though hard pressed, keep their lines intact. To break the impasse, Sheridan directs the cavalry of General David M. Gregg to circle east along the Catharpin Road and catch Lee in a pincer attack. Lee, however, shifts his line accordingly to meet the new threat, and the Union movement bogs down. At nightfall, Sheridan abandons efforts to clear the Brock Road and returns to camp. Union casualties are in the vicinity of 250, with Confederates probably sustaining as many. Consequently, Confederates under General Richard H. Anderson secure Spotsylvania Court House ahead of Union forces.

General Benjamin F. Butler details 8,000 men under General William Brooks to seize the Richmond and Petersburg railroad, and they push back General Bushrod Johnson's 2,700 Confederates from Port Walthall Junction to Swift Creek. Nonetheless, some Union soldiers contemptuously refer to Butler's dilatory campaign as a "stationary advance."

WEST: The Military Division of West Mississippi is created under General Edward R. S. Canby.

The Atlanta campaign begins. General William T. Sherman, commanding the Armies of the Cumberland (General George H. Thomas), the Ohio (General John M. Schofield), and the Tennessee (General James B. McPherson), totaling more than 100,000 men, swiftly advances on Dalton, Georgia. There, he confronts the Army of Tennessee under General Joseph E. Johnston and his 62,000 Confederates. These are organized into two corps under Generals John B. Hood and William J. Hardee, while a third corps under General Leonidas Polk is en route from Mississippi. Southern Confederate cavalry are led by the highly capable general Joseph Wheeler. The contenders are equally matched from a leadership standpoint, and the ensuing campaign comes to resemble a chess match played over impassable terrain.

The Federals begin by marching 25 miles south and applying pressure on Confederates at Rocky Face Ridge, pushing them back as far as Buzzard's Roost Pass. Meanwhile, McPherson's Army of the Tennessee is dispatched below Confederate positions to Snake Gap Creek, 15 miles distant, where he can cut Johnson's rail line decisively and possibly bag his entire force.

NAVAL: The Federal steamer USS *Shawsheen* is attacked by Confederate forces while dragging for torpedoes along the James River, Virginia, and is captured off Chaffin's Bluff. The vessel subsequently is burned and sunk.

The USS *Howquah, Nansemond, Mount Vernon,* and *Kansas* engage the CSS *Raleigh* off New Inlet, North Carolina. The Confederate vessel then grounds at the mouth of the Cape Fear River and is scuttled.

May 8

SOUTH: Thousands of soldiers from both sides file into positions along a three-mile front at Spotsylvania Court House, Virginia. Both General Gouverneur K. Warren's V Corps and General John Sedgwick's VI Corps then charge and attempt to dislodge Confederates from their earthworks, but they are repelled heavily. Moreover, General Robert E. Lee instructs his men to fell trees, dig trenches, and strengthen all defensive lines with earthworks. The most conspicuous feature to arise is a mile-long, half-mile-deep salient dubbed the "Mule Shoe" owing to its protruding shape. General Ulysses S. Grant, undeterred by the growing strength of Lee's position, still probes for Southern weaknesses. Lee's position then gradually assumes a more definite form with General Richard H. Anderson's I Corps on the left, General Richard S. Ewell's II Corps in the center, and General Jubal A. Early's III Corps on the right. All are entrenched heavily with ample reserves to prevent breakthroughs in any given sector.

General Jubal A. Early temporarily replaces the ailing General Ambrose P. Hill as commander of the III Corps, Army of Northern Virginia.

WEST: Union forces under General John Newton, IV Corps, continue pressing against Confederate defenders at Mill Creek Gap, Georgia. The Southerners give ground slowly, falling back and up stronger defensive terrain. At length, General John W. Geary's XX Corps launches three uphill attacks against Dug Gap to flank Buzzard's Roost and is repelled, resulting in 350 casualties.

May 9

SOUTH: The Army of the Potomac deploys on an arc outside Confederate lines erected around Spotsylvania Court House. The far right is occupied by General Winfield S. Hancock's II Corps, followed by General Gouverneur K. Warren's V Corps, General John Sedgwick's VI Corps, and General Ambrose E. Burnside's IX Corps finally anchoring the left. All told, 100,000 Federals confront 60,000 Confederates across the three-mile line that is strongly fortified and skillfully manned.

General John Sedgwick of the VI Corps is killed by a sniper's bullet at Spotsylvania, Virginia, after declaring "They couldn't hit an elephant at this distance." Command then reverts to General Horatio G. Wright.

General Philip H. Sheridan takes seven cavalry brigades, totaling almost 10,000 troopers, on a raid against Richmond, Virginia. He does so in the hopes of luring Confederate cavalry under General J. E. B. Stuart into the open and crushing them with superior numbers. However, this move deprives the Army of the Potomac of its ability to reconnoiter Confederate positions adequately, a deficiency that costs General Ulysses S. Grant dearly.

After a few more half-hearted advances toward Petersburg, General Benjamin F. Butler dispatches General William F. Smith's XVIII Corps toward Petersburg, where they encounter Confederates under General Bushrod Johnson at Swift Creek. Johnson attacks prematurely at Arrowhead Church and is repulsed with losses, but Butler withdraws his Army of the James from Fort Clifton, Virginia, and back to City Point. Several of his generals strongly suggest throwing a pontoon bridge across the Appomattox River for a better approach to the city, but Butler rejects this sagacious advice in favor of throwing up defensive works across Bermuda Neck.

General Stephen D. Lee accepts command of the Confederate Department of Alabama, Mississippi, and East Louisiana.

WEST: General George Crook, riding at the head of 6,155 Union troops, advances into southwestern Virginia, to destroy a portion of the Virginia and Tennessee Railroad. En route, he engages 2,400 Confederates and 10 cannon under General Albert G. Jenkins at Cloyd's Mountain, Virginia. Jenkins, badly outnumbered and commanding a mixed force of tough veterans and local home guards, carefully chooses good defensive positions on a high, wooded bluff and awaits Crook's attack. That general, having surveyed the strength of this deployment, resolves to send Colonel Carr B. White's brigade around the Confederate right. Crook then leads his two remaining brigades against Jenkins's center and traverses an open meadow under heavy fire. As the Federals close in, a brigade of Ohio troops under Colonel Rutherford B. Hayes (a future president) is directed to hit the Confederate right and center.

The ensuing fight proves tenacious and costly to both sides as they form and battle around a rail breastworks. A bloody impasse continues for several hours until White's column suddenly appears on the Confederate left and begins to roll up their line. Resistance collapses and Jenkins, seriously wounded, falls captive along with his cannon. Surviving Confederates subsequently rally under General John McCausland, who forms a successful cavalry rear guard and withdraws. The victorious Crook suffers 688 men to a Confederate tally of 538. He goes on to burn the New River Bridge, thereby cutting the Virginia and Tennessee Railroad, and then rapidly pulls back after receiving word of the Union defeat at the Wilderness.

The Union IV, XIV, and XX Corps renew their attacks on Buzzard's Roost, Georgia, encountering tough resistance from General Alexander P. Stewart's division. Skirmishes and demonstrations also erupt along Rocky Face Ridge where Union cavalry under General Edward M. McCook dispute ground with General Joseph Wheeler's Confederate troopers. Meanwhile, farther south, General James B. McPherson's Army of the Tennessee successfully penetrates Snake Gap Creek, placing him behind General Joseph E. Johnston's main force. But McPherson, perceiving what he thought were impervious Confederate defenses at nearby Resaca, inexplicably retreats. Snake Gap Creek, however, is held by a single brigade of 1,400 infantry under General James Cantey and Union forces squander a golden opportunity to capture General Joseph E. Johnston's entire army.

Naval: Admiral David G. Farragut, stationed off Mobile Bay, Alabama, urgently requests the Navy Department to augment his flotilla with Union ironclads and thus neutralize the large Confederate steam ram CSS *Tennessee*. His impending attack on that port depends up on it.

The USS *Connecticut* captures the British blockade-runner *Minnie* at sea.

On the Red River near Alexandria, Louisiana, a log dam constructed by Colonel Joseph Bailey suddenly collapses. This mishap causes a viable chute to form inadvertently over the falls at Alexandria, so Admiral David D. Porter orders ironclads USS *Osage* and *Neosho* and steamers *Fort Hindman* and *Lexington* to run it. Amazingly, all four vessels easily float over the obstacles as 30,000 soldiers and sailors cheer from the riverbanks. Encouraged by success, Bailey commences a new dam to rescue the remaining vessels of Porter's marooned squadron.

May 10

South: Determined to test Confederate defenses, General Ulysses S. Grant begins to organize large-scale thrust against Spotsylvania Court House, Virginia. He believes that General Robert E. Lee has weakened his center sufficiently by reinforcing his flanks and orders a strong assault against the "Mule Shoe" in consequence. During the afternoon, General Winfield S. Hancock's II Corps manages briefly to work its way around the Confederate left, but the onset of night cancels operations in that sector. But the day's accolades go to Colonel Emory Upton, who arrayed his 12 regiments in a densely packed assault column. At 6:00 p.m., Upton's force charges and penetrates the Mule Shoe's left flank, overturning General Richard Rodes's division and taking 1,000 prisoners. The Union lodgment, unfortunately, is not supported, and General Robert E. Lee directs a strong counterattack that drives Upton's force back to their lines. Grant is nonetheless singularly impressed by Upton's innovation and vows to try the same experiment on a larger scale. He then shifts Hancock's corps to the right of the Union line and prepares to renew the contest.

Three brigades of Confederate troopers under General J. E. B. Stuart arrive at Beaver Dam Station, Virginia, hotly trailing General Philip H. Sheridan's cavalry column. Though outnumbered, Stuart dispatches a brigade under General John B. Gordon to harass the Union rear while deploying Generals William C. Wickham and Lunsford L. Lomax into blocking positions at the junction of Yellow Tavern, six miles north of Richmond. Sheridan's column previously had passed through Beaver Dam Station that morning, burning an estimated 915,000 meat rations and 504,000 bread rations—losses the food-strapped Army of Northern Virginia could scarcely afford. Stuart is determined to stop them from doing more harm.

As General Benjamin F. Butler continues dithering at Bermuda Hundred, General Pierre G. T. Beauregard arrives from Weldon, North Carolina, to take command of the Petersburg, Virginia, defenses. He begins by rushing six Confederate brigades into strong positions along Drewry's Bluff.

West: Confederate raiders under Colonel John S. Mosby storms a Union cavalry outpost at Front Royal, Virginia, seizing prisoners and horses.

The Battle of Spotsylvania Court House May 7–20, 1864 Painting by Lewis Prang *(Library of Congress)*

General William W. Averell's cavalry division encounters Confederates under Generals John Morgan and William E. Jones at Wytheville, Virginia. He battles them for four hours, sustaining 114 casualties before withdrawing toward Dublin.

Generals Benjamin F. Kelley and John D. Imboden clash heavily at Lost River Gap, West Virginia.

General James B. McPherson declines pushing ahead through Snake Creek Gap, Georgia, and commences to fortify his position. Unknown at the time, he is opposed by only a single cavalry brigade under General James Cantey. McPherson, however, is unsupported, wary of his left flank, and fearful that General Joseph E. Johnston might throw the weight of his entire army against him. He digs in and awaits developments. "Such an opportunity does not occur twice in a single life!" an exasperated General William T. Sherman declares. Johnston's line of retreat consequently remains intact and, when apprised of the danger to his army, he immediately prepares to occupy safer ground.

NAVAL: Army transport *Harriet A. Weed* strikes a Confederate torpedo in the St. John's River, Florida, and sinks.

The USS *Connecticut* captures the British blockade-runner *Greyhound* at sea.

Back on the Red River, the dam constructed by Colonel Joseph Bailey to raise water levels is breeched deliberately and the ironclads USS *Mound City, Pittsburgh,* and *Carondelet* successfully shoot over the rapids. Admiral David D. Porter informs Secretary of the Navy Gideon Welles: "The passage of these vessels was a beautiful sight, only to be realized when seen."

May 11

SOUTH: Ignoring heavy losses, General Ulysses S. Grant renews the struggle at Spotsylvania Court House by hitting the Confederate center again. Only this time, he orders the entire II Corps of General Winfield S. Hancock drawn up into dense assault columns to spearhead the assault. Based on events of the previous day, Grant fully expects to overpower Southern forces that are manning the entrenchments at the "Mule Shoe." Meanwhile, General Robert E. Lee carefully monitors reports of Union movement and concludes that Grant is readying to slip around his left flank again. Lee determines to foil him in the act and orders artillery removed from the Mule Shoe, which renders it vulnerable to attack.

At 11:00 A.M., a tremendous cavalry fight ensues as 4,500 Confederates under General J. E. B. Stuart are attacked by twice their number under General Philip H. Sheridan at Yellow Tavern, Virginia. This places a marauding Union cavalry column only six miles north of the Confederate capital at Richmond. Stuart, having deployed his two brigades in a "V" formation, calmly awaits the Union onslaught at the road junction and initially repels moves against his left and center. At 4:00 o'clock, however, the brigade of General George A. Custer masses for a charge on the Confederate left, scatters General Lunsford L. Lomax's brigade, and seizes two cannon. Then Stuart, leading the 1st Virginia Cavalry on a sharp counterattack, successfully drives Custer back to his own lines but is shot mortally in the abdomen and evacuated. The Confederates, badly shaken, repulse additional attacks by Sheridan, and Union forces gradually withdraw eastward down the Chickahominy River. Union losses are estimated at 704 casualties while the Confederates sustain more than 300—including the dashing, irreplaceable Stuart, who dies the following day.

WEST: Confederate cavalry under General John D. Imboden surprise a Union outpost at Port Royal, Virginia, seizing 464 prisoners. This does little to stop General Franz Sigel's leisurely but seemingly inexorable drive down the Shenandoah Valley.

General Edward R. S. Canby is appointed commander of the Federal Military Division of West Mississippi.

May 12

SOUTH: The struggle at Spotsylvania, Virginia, continues as General Ulysses S. Grant launches a crushing assault on the center of General Robert E. Lee's defensive lines. The attack kicks off at 4:35 A.M. as General Winfield S. Hancock's II Corps, arrayed into dense columns, springs forward. The blue wave slams irresistibly into Southern defenses and overwhelms General Edward Johnson's "Stonewall Division," capturing him, 3,000 men, and 20 cannon. Hancock then loses control of his men as they pour through the salient as uncoordinated knots of soldiers. At this crisis, General

Robert E. Lee orders General John B. Gordon's division forward to stop them, which drives Hancock's men back outside the works. The ensuing eight hours witness a vicious, point-blank musketry duel that degenerates into hand-to-hand fighting, bayonet clashing, and rock throwing. In light of the terrible carnage, this sector is christened "Bloody Angle" by the survivors.

As the drama unfolds in Lee's center, Grant launches additional attacks on the Confederate line with General Horatio G. Wright's VI Corps. Wright is beaten back with losses, but the Southerners, losing men heavily, establish new defense lines along the base of the salient and withdraw by 4:00 P.M. Fighting gradually sputters out in a gathering rainstorm, and both sides relent. This latest Union repulse affords stark testimony to the tremendous defensive power of Confederate fieldworks, which have elevated the lowly spade to that of cannon and rifled muskets in tactical significance. Casualties during the two-day period are horrendous: Grant loses 2,725 killed, 13,416 wounded, and 2,258 missing (18,339) men to an estimated Confederate tally of 10,000—including 3,000 captured. General Robert E. Lee triumphs once again over a more numerous adversary, but the vaunted Army of Northern Virginia is being bled white by Grant's determination to fight and his willingness to absorb higher losses.

The Army of the James under General Benjamin F. Butler finally sorties from its defensive works and advances against Confederate lines at Drewry's Bluff, Virginia, with 15,000 men.

WEST: Colonel John S. Mosby captures a large Union wagon train near Strasburg, Virginia.

General John C. Breckinridge arrives at Staunton, Virginia, with 5,500 soldiers, militia, and a contingent of cadets from the Virginia Military Institute.

General Joseph E. Johnston expertly abandons his strong defenses at Dalton, Georgia, and falls back on new positions at Resaca. This pattern of advance and retreat will be repeated continuously over the intervening weeks.

NAVAL: Admiral Samuel P. Lee, alarmed by the recent loss of several warships, establishes an antitorpedo (mine) squadron on the James River, consisting of the USS *Stepping Stones, Delaware,* and *Tritonia.* They are ordered to patrol the waterways constantly for enemy activity and to remain always underway to prevent them from being surprised at night.

The USS *Beauregard* captures the Confederate sloop *Resolute* off the Indian River, Florida.

Armed boats from the USS *Somerset* capture a boatload of Confederate sailors near Apalachicola, Florida, who were themselves intending to capture the USS *Adela.*

May 13

SOUTH: General Philip H. Sheridan withdraws his cavalry column from the Richmond area.

Confederate defenses under General Robert F. Hoke at Drewry's Bluff, Virginia, are seized partially by 15,000 men from the Army of the James under General Benjamin F. Butler. That officer then suspends his attack to form new defense lines of his own. Such vacillation is a good indication of Butler's tactical ineptitude and prompts General Pierre G. T. Beauregard, commanding at Richmond, to counterattack and drive him back into Bermuda Hundred.

Union forces commence a four-day bombardment of Fort Sumter, Charleston Harbor, South Carolina, hurling an additional 1,140 rounds at the derelict but as of yet still defiant fortress.

General Andrew J. Smith's Union troops evacuate Alexandria, Louisiana, completely laying waste to the town and adjoining regions. Reputedly, after the fires recede, only two houses remain standing.

WEST: Union forces finally pour through Snake Creek Gap, Georgia, and occupy Dalton, too late to trap the army of General Joseph E. Johnston, which now lays safely ensconced 13 miles south at Resaca.

Confederate cavalry under General Joseph O. Shelby commences a raid north of the Arkansas River, Arkansas.

NAVAL: The USS *Ceres*, accompanied by the army transport *Rockland,* raids the Alligator River, North Carolina, seizes the Confederate schooner *Ann S. Davenport* and destroys a nearby corn mill.

The USS *Louisville, Chillicote,* and *Ozark,* the last of Admiral David D. Porter's gunboats, dash over a wing dam on the Red River, Louisiana, and float on to safety. The ingenuity of army engineers under Colonel Joseph Bailey, performing their work entirely under fire, saved the squadron from certain destruction after two weeks of intensive exertion. "Words are inadequate to express the admiration I feel for the abilities of Lieutenant Colonel Bailey," Porter wrote, "This is without doubt the best engineering feat ever performed."

May 14

SOUTH: General Pierre G. T. Beauregard begins to marshal forces for a counterattack on the Union Army of the James outside Drewry's Bluff, Virginia. He has available the divisions of Generals Robert F. Hoke and Robert Hanson.

WEST: General John D. Imboden continues skirmishing against the advance of General Franz Sigel as it reaches Mount Jackson, Virginia, seven miles north of New Market.

The armies of Generals William T. Sherman and Joseph E. Johnston confront each other in full battle array at Resaca, Georgia. The Federals muster 100,000 men and the Confederates, recently joined by General Leonidas K. Polk from Mississippi, number 60,000. Sherman begins the battle by launching General John M. Schofield's XXIII Corps in a headlong assault at the intersection of where Generals John B. Hood's and William J. Hardee's corps meet. Schofield charges hard and long all day but is repelled with heavy losses. Fighting then moves down the line to the Confederate right, where General John Logan's XV Corps engages Polk's infantry. The Federals manage to storm a line of earthworks along Camp Creek, situated on some low-lying hills, a significant gain allowing them to mount artillery pieces to shell and possibly destroy the remaining Confederate army. Polk tries repeatedly to dislodge the Federals and fails, but Sherman is slow to recognize the advantage within his grasp, and fighting in this sector dies down.

The day's toughest struggle occurs on the Union left, where the aggressive Hood successfully strikes along the Dalton-Resaca wagon road. However, a division dispatched by General George H. Thomas then halts the Confederate drive and sends them scampering back to their starting point. Resaca concludes with few measurable gains by either side, and more hard fighting is anticipated the following day.

May 15

SOUTH: Outside Richmond, Virginia, General Pierre G. T. Beauregard masses 10 infantry brigades into two divisions commanded by General Robert F. Hoke and Robert Ransom, while holding two brigades in reserve under General Alfred Colquitt. He intends to strike heavily at the right flank of General Benjamin F. Butler's Army of the James on the morrow and hopefully drive it headlong back into the Bermuda Hundred Peninsula.

WEST: General Franz Sigel resumes advancing with 6,500 men toward New Market, Virginia, as 5,500 Confederates under General John C. Breckinridge occupy strong defensive positions. A prolonged artillery duel ensues at long range at which point Breckinridge, tired of waiting for Sigel to charge, orders his own men forward. Two infantry brigades, linked by a force of dismounted cavalry between them, easily clear Sigel's forces from the town amid a cheering populace. However, a large Union battery posted on a hillside directly out of town badly cuts up Breckinridge's men as they clear New Market. A gap opens up in his ranks, and Breckinridge, lacking reserves, reluctantly orders 264 cadets (or "Katydids") from the Virginia Military Institute to fill it. "Put the boys in," he orders, and they advance strongly despite mounting casualties and a heavy downpour. At 3:00 P.M., the Confederates crown the heights and seize two cannon while defeated Federals stream across the Shenandoah River to Strasburg and safety. Union losses are 96 dead, 520 wounded, and 225 missing (841) to a Confederate tally of 43 killed, 474 injured, and three captured (520). The VMI Cadets lose 10 killed and 47 wounded, without wavering, a loss rate of 20 percent.

General William W. Averell concludes another fruitless raid by linking up with Union forces under General George Crook at Union, Virginia.

The Battle of Resaca resumes as Union troops under General Joseph Hooker engage the Confederates of General John B. Hood on the Union left. A confusing, costly battle, fought from ravines and entanglements, ensues with heavy losses to both sides. Meanwhile, General William T. Sherman orders a division of the XVI Corps over the Oostanaula River to seize a strategic railroad bridge in the Confederate rear. General Joseph E. Johnston, his lines of communication now threatened, expertly disengages, throws a pontoon bridge across the river, and withdraws to safety in the predawn darkness. Losses in the two-day struggle amount to 6,000 Federals and 5,000 Confederates, yet Sherman continues pushing ever deeper into Georgia.

The retreating army of General Nathaniel P. Banks skirmishes with Confederate cavalry under General Arthur P. Bagby at Avoyelles, Louisiana, and then continues withdrawing to Marksville.

NAVAL: The USS *Kansas* captures the British blockade-runner *Tristram Shandy* off Fort Fisher, North Carolina.

The Federal gunboat USS *St. Clair,* moving down the Red River, engages and defeats a Confederate battery near Eunice's Bluff, Louisiana.

May 16

SOUTH: A force of 18,000 Confederates under General Pierre G. T. Beauregard launches a sharp attack on the Union Army of the James near Drewry's Bluff, Virginia. Previously, General Benjamin F. Butler drew his 15,000 troops into a defensive line with General Quincy A. Gillmore's X Corps on the left and General William F. Smith's XVIII Corps on the right. But Beauregard, availing himself of a heavy ground fog, directs General Robert Ransom's division to turn Smith's right, which is accomplished skillfully. Ransom then charges and captures General Charles A. Heckman and 400 prisoners before his ammunition fails and brings him to a halt. Meanwhile, Confederate forces under General Robert F. Hoke hit the Union center, but, confused and partially lost in the fog, his attack flounders. Gillmore then counterattacks through a gap in the Southern line, forcing them back. The Confederates of General William H. C. Whiting mass and make one final dash at the Union center and are rebuffed. As fighting dies down, Butler withdraws back behind fortifications along Bermuda Hundred. Confederate losses are 355 dead, 1,941 wounded, and 210 missing (2,506) while the Union sustains 290 killed, 2,380 wounded, and 1,390 missing (4,160). Moreover, Beauregard now completely bottles up his adversary on the peninsula, and Butler remains unable to assist future Union drives on Richmond or Petersburg.

General Nathaniel P. Banks retreats to Mansura, Louisiana, encountering Confederate forces under General Camille A. Polignac. Heavy skirmishing forces the Southerners back, and the Federals continue withdrawing.

WEST: General Joseph E. Johnston begins to abandon positions at Resaca, Georgia, and withdraws toward Calhoun and Adamsville.

NAVAL: The Mississippi Squadron of Admiral David D. Porter finally reenters the Mississippi River after two months of dramatic but unsuccessful campaigning along the Red River, Louisiana.

May 17

SOUTH: Colonel John S. Mosby tangles with Federal cavalry at Waterford, Virginia, inflicting nine casualties.

General Ulysses S. Grant remains eager to resume offensive operations at Spotsylvania Court House, Virginia. Certain that General Robert E. Lee has weakened his left flank by placing the shattered corps of General Richard S. Ewell there, he orders General Winfield S. Hancock's II Corps and General Gouverneur K. Warren's VI Corps to prepare for an assault on the morrow.

General Pierre G. T. Beauregard pushes his Confederates force to just opposite Union defensive lines at Bermuda Hundred, Virginia. This effectively seals the Army of the James on a peninsula, neutralizing it as a threat to either Richmond or Petersburg.

WEST: General Joseph O. Shelby's Confederate cavalry seize Dardanelle, Arkansas.

General William T. Sherman threatens both of General Joseph E. Johnston's flanks near Adamsville, so he retrogrades again toward the Cassville-Kingston region.

May 18

SOUTH: General Ulysses S. Grant attacks Spotsylvania Court House one last time looking for Confederate weaknesses. He feels that recent troop shifts have weakened their left flank, so he directs the V and VI Corps to attempt breaking through. However, General Richard S. Ewell, bolstered by 29 cannon, easily shatters the Federals as they charge across open ground. Grant's forces once again are thrown back, suffering 500 casualties to Ewell's 30. He finally concludes that General Robert E. Lee's position is impregnable and issues orders to sidestep his left flank entirely and march southeast toward Richmond, Virginia.

As General Nathaniel P. Banks's army approaches the Atchafalaya River, it encounters strong Confederate forces at Yellow Bayou, Louisiana. General Andrew J. Smith then dispatches a brigade under General Joseph A. Mower to drive off the rebels, lest they interfere with river-crossing operations. Mower's 4,500 men perform exactly as ordered and pitch into a thick belt of Confederate skirmishers, driving them back onto the main body under General John Wharton. Wharton, in turn, counterattacks as the Union troops become mired in thick underbrush and forces them off in turn. Mower subsequently halts the new Southern assault, and both sides separate once the dense undergrowth catches fire. The ongoing struggle does not interfere with bridging operations across the Atchafalaya River. By the time the battle subsides, Union losses are 350 while the Confederate tally stands at 608. Banks proceeds to move his men across the waterway to safety.

WEST: As General William T. Sherman begins to pursue fleeing Confederates toward Kingston, Georgia, his columns become widely separated and vulnerable to attack. General John B. Hood receives orders to attack the following day, but he uncharacteristically reacts with caution.

Union cavalry under General Kenner Garrard capture Rome, Georgia, after dislodging Confederates there under General Samuel G. French.

NAVAL: Admiral James Buchanan, after much exertion, finally floats the large steam ram CSS *Tennessee* over the Dog River bar and into Mobile Bay, Alabama.

A landing party from the USS *Stockdale* is attacked by Confederate cavalry near the mouth of the Tchefuncta River, Louisiana.

The Confederate raider CSS *Florida* under Lieutenant Charles M. Morris captures and burns the Union schooner *George Latimer* at sea.

May 19

NORTH: Literary circles are saddened by the death of noted New England writer and novelist Nathaniel Hawthorne at Plymouth, New Hampshire.

SOUTH: The Confederate II Corps of General Richard S. Ewell mounts a sudden counterattack at Spotsylvania Court House, hoping to catch Union forces in marching order. However, Federal troops are prepared and hurl back the Southerners with 900 casualties to a Union tally of 1,500. This final burst of activity concludes the bloodshed at Spotsylvania, scene of the Civil War's most vicious fighting.

The army of General Nathaniel P. Banks finally crosses the Atchafalaya River, Louisiana, as the Red River campaign draws to an ignominious conclusion.

West: Union cavalry under Generals William W. Averell and George Crook take Meadow Bluff, West Virginia, thereby ending their raid against the Virginia and Tennessee Railroad.

General Joseph E. Johnston orders General John B. Hood to counterattack the scattered Union XXIII Corps but then countermands his instructions and falls back across the Etowah River toward Allatoona Pass, Georgia. He does so over the protests of Generals William J. Hardee and Leonidas K. Polk, who prefer to stand and fight.

Naval: The USS *General Price* opens fire on a Confederate battery at Tunica Bend, Louisiana, on the Mississippi River and rescues the transport steamer *Superior*. An armed party lands and then pursues the attackers, burning their headquarters.

The USS *De Soto* captures the Confederate schooner *Mississippian* in the Gulf of Mexico.

May 20

South: General Ulysses S. Grant directs the Army of the Potomac south and east in an attempt to outflank the Confederates along the Mattaponi River, Virginia. His objective is Hannover Station, 24 miles north of Richmond, where the Virginia Central Rail Road intersects with the Richmond, Fredericksburg, and Potomac Railroad, a major Southern supply artery.

General Pierre G. T. Beauregard, intending to bottle up General Benjamin F. Butler's Army of the James further at Bermuda Hundred Peninsula, launches a heavy attack on Federal defensive positions held by General Quincy A. Gillmore's X Corps at Ware Bottom Church, Virginia. Initially, the divisions of Generals Alfred H. Terry and Adelbert Ames are hard pressed and driven back. Quincy is forced to spend several hours sorting his command out before finally launching a counterattack that afternoon, which nearly drives the Confederates back to their starting positions. A Southern counterattack also is repulsed bloodily, resulting in the capture of General William S. Walker before Beauregard cancels further assaults. Union losses are roughly 800 to 700 for the Confederates, but Beauregard could now shorten his lines before Bermuda Hundred, and Butler remains effectively hemmed in and unable to assist the ongoing Richmond, Virginia campaign.

The army of General Nathaniel P. Banks completes crossing the 600-yard-wide Atchafalaya River, ending his ill-fated Red River campaign in western Louisiana.

West: Colonel John S. Mosby attacks a Union wagon train near Strasburg, West Virginia, and is repulsed.

Naval: The Mississippi Squadron of Admiral David D. Porter covers the withdrawal of General Nathaniel P. Banks's army across the Atchafalaya River, Louisiana, signaling the end of the Red River campaign.

May 21

Diplomacy: Secretary of State William H. Seward instructs U.S. minister to France John Bigelow that, while he is to remonstrate against French actions in Mexico, he must avoid outright belligerence until after the Civil War has ended.

South: Bested by Southern fortifications around Spotsylvania, General Ulysses S. Grant begins to probe Confederate lines near Milford Station, Virginia. He is surprised by the lack of strong resistance and prepares to sidestep around the Confederate left flank to appear in force across the North Anna River. Grant thus exercises strategic initiative over his opponent, forcing General Robert E. Lee to react and follow.

WEST: General Franz Sigel, having lost the Battle of New Market, is relieved of command in the Shenandoah Valley and replaced by General David Hunter.

NAVAL: The USS *Atlanta* and *Dawn* shell Confederate cavalry attacking Fort Powhatan on the James River, Virginia.

May 22

SOUTH: The Army of Northern Virginia under General Robert E. Lee assumes defensive positions along the North Anna River, slightly ahead of General Ulysses S. Grant. To that end, he deploys General Richard S. Ewell's II Corps on his right, General James Longstreet's I Corps on his center, and General Ambrose P. Hill's III Corps on his left.

WEST: General William T. Sherman again outflanks Confederate defenders under General Joseph E. Johnston and bypasses them at Allatoona, Georgia. Johnson then predictably falls back to new positions at Dallas.

NAVAL: The USS *Crusader* captures the Confederate schooner *Isaac L. Adkins* on the Severn River, Maryland.

May 23

SOUTH: The Union II Corps of General William S. Hancock deploys on the northern bank of the North Anna River at Chesterfield Ford while the IX Corps under General Ambrose E. Burnside lands at Jericho Mills. Meanwhile, the V and VI Corps under Generals Gouverneur K. Warren and Horatio G. Wright, respectively, operate to the west of Jericho Mills. A hasty attack by General Cadmus M. Wilcox's division against Jericho Mills is rebuffed with 642 casualties, and Federal troops commence to dig in.

WEST: General William T. Sherman continues advancing his army from Cassville, Georgia, toward Dallas, where he intends to cross the Etowah River.

General John H. Morgan gallops into Kentucky on another extended raid.

NAVAL: The Federal side-wheeler USS *Columbine* is captured by men of the Confederate 2nd Florida Cavalry at Horse Landing, Palatka, Florida, after grounding on a mud bank. The vessel sustains 20 casualties before capitulating, whereupon the Southerners burn it.

May 24

SOUTH: General Ulysses S. Grant throws pontoon bridges across the North Anna River and continues crossing his Army of the Potomac. Grant also is supported by newly arrived Union cavalry under General Philip H. Sheridan, back from his raid near Richmond, Virginia. General Ambrose E. Burnside's IX Corps next begins to probe Confederate lines at Ox Ford cautiously and finds them too strong to be carried. General Robert E. Lee, again anticipating Union moves, ingeniously deploys the Army of Northern Virginia into an inverted "V" formation, to lure the unsuspecting Federals into a trap. Grant inadvertently nearly obliges him—having scattered his command across the North Anna River and inviting crushing blows in piecemeal—but Lee is suddenly taken ill, and no attack goes forward. Once Grant perceives the danger to his army, he withdraws back across the North Anna River.

Two African-American regiments repel an attack by Confederate cavalry under General Fitzhugh Lee at Wilson's Wharf, Virginia.

WEST: General Joseph E. Johnston orders his Confederates to fall back on new defensive positions at Dallas, Georgia.

Confederate cavalry under General Joseph Wheeler attack Union supply lines at Burnt Hickory, Georgia.

NAVAL: The USS *Dawn* bombards Confederate forces attacking army troops at Wilson's Wharf on the James River, Virginia.

Confederate forces capture and burn the Federal steamer *Lebanon* at Ford's landing, Arkansas.

May 25

SOUTH: The Army of the Potomac under General Ulysses S. Grant, having probed Confederate lines along the North Anna River, Virginia, to no avail, prepares to shift suddenly by marching east toward Cold Harbor. Fortunately, General Robert E. Lee is too ill to order a crushing assault on his widely scattered formations, and the Federals redeploy without interference.

WEST: General David Hunter receives orders to advance down the Shenandoah Valley and capture Lynchburg, Virginia, an important railroad junction. From there, he is to continue south and possibly threaten Charlottesville. It is anticipated that General Robert E. Lee will be forced to dispatch reinforcements to that theater, thereby weakening the defenses of Richmond.

The XX Corps under General Joseph Hooker, advancing on New Hope Church, Georgia, collides head on with General John B. Hood's Confederates. The Federals initially are repulsed until Hooker masses two entire divisions and charges the troops of General Alexander P. Stewart. Stewart, however, clings tenaciously to his ground and, at length, Hooker retires with 1,600 casualties. This encounter places Union forces only 25 miles northeast of Atlanta.

NAVAL: A armed boat from the USS *Mattabesett* unsuccessfully tries to sink the Confederate steam ram CSS *Albemarle* in the Roanoke River, North Carolina. They carefully tow two 100-pound torpedoes up the Middle River, North Carolina, jump overboard, and then swim to within a few yards of their quarry when a sentry detects their approach. The swimmers manage to escape capture, with each ultimately receiving the Congressional Medal of Honor.

The USS *McDonough, E. B. Hale, Dai Ching,* and *Vixen* accompany a combined expedition up the Ashepoo and South Edisto rivers, South Carolina. They advance as far as the town of Williston but, after failing to establish contact with army troops, withdraw back downstream. While moving downstream, the transport *Boston* grounds and is scuttled.

May 26

DIPLOMACY: Robert H. Pruyn, U.S. minister to Japan, requests that the USS *Jamestown* be dispatched to Kanagawa in a preemptive show of force. Japanese authorities are threatening to close that port to all foreign commerce.

POLITICS: The Montana Territory is carved from the eastern portion of the Idaho and Dakota territories.

SOUTH: The Army of the Potomac suddenly pivots east after crossing the North Anna River and heads for the Pamunkey River, turning General Robert E. Lee's right flank. Previous operations in this vicinity result in 2,623 Union casualties and 2,517 Confederate.

General John G. Foster accepts command of the Department of the South.

WEST: A force of 10,000 Union troops under General David Hunter departs Strasburg, Virginia, and commences marching down the Shenandoah Valley toward Staunton. However, 3,000 Confederate cavalry under General John D. Imboden fell trees and other obstacles in Hunter's path, impeding his advance.

Union forces under General James B. McPherson occupy Dallas, Georgia, while General John M. Schofield approaches New Hope Church.

May 27
SOUTH: The Army of Northern Virginia under General Robert E. Lee begin to shift its defensive lines from the North Anna River. Meanwhile, Union cavalry under General George A. Custer cross the Pamunkey River and capture Hanovertown, Virginia. The mounted divisions of Generals Alfred T. A. Torbert and David M. Gregg quickly gallop over and begin to probe westward for Confederates.

WEST: General William T. Sherman conducts several heavy probes of the right flank of Confederate lines along the New Hope–Dallas line, Georgia. An attack mounted by General Oliver O. Howard's IV Corps at Pickett's Mills is repulsed by General Patrick R. Cleburne's Confederates with 1,500 casualties. Encouraged by this tactical success, General Joseph E. Johnston orders General John B. Hood to attack the Union left flank on the following morning.

General Joseph O. Shelby assumes command of all Confederate troops north of the Arkansas River, Arkansas.

NAVAL: The USS *Ariel* captures and burns the Confederate sloop *General Finegan* near Chassahowitzka Bay, Florida.

The USS *Admiral* captures the Confederate steamer *Isabel* off Galveston after a six-hour chase.

May 28
POLITICS: Puppet emperor Maximilian of Austria lands at Vera Cruz, Mexico, in order to assume his throne. A political neophyte, he is backed by the machinations of the French emperor Napoleon III and opposed by Mexican politician-turned-guerrilla Benito Juárez. The United States considers his presence a violation of the long-stated Monroe Doctrine, but Washington is too preoccupied with civil war to do anything beyond diplomatic protests.

SOUTH: General Robert E. Lee shifts his headquarters to Atlee's Station, Virginia, to observe Union army movements toward Richmond better. He then deploys General Ambrose P. Hill's III Corps to guard the Virginia Central Railroad, while the I and II Corps under Generals Richard A. Anderson and Jubal A. Early settle in behind Totopotomo Creek. The Army of the Potomac, meanwhile, continues marching southeast down the north bank of the Pamunkey River, seeking an opening along Lee' right flank.

Union cavalry under General David M. Gregg encounter General Wade Hampton's Confederate troopers at Haw's Shop, Virginia, and a large mounted action ensues. Hampton's South Carolinians, equipped with long-range Enfield rifles, bloodily repulse Gregg's initial charge, and a protracted dismounted fight develops. Confederate numbers prevail as the Union cavalrymen are forced back, but at 2:00 P.M., General George A. Custer's Michigan brigade suddenly dashes onto the field. The "Wolverines" quickly dismount and engage the Southerners with rapid-fire Spencer carbines, forcing Hampton to retreat in turn. After seven hours of fighting, the Confederates withdraw and inform General Robert E. Lee that Union forces are firmly established over the Pamunkey River.

WEST: General John B. Hood, on reconnoitering Union lines, reports that Federal troops are strongly entrenched, so General Joseph E. Johnston cancels his impending assault.

A reconnaissance in force by General William J. Hardee is repulsed at Dallas, Georgia, by General James B. McPherson. The attack was made by General William B. Bates division, which goes forward unsupported and sustains heavy losses from Union defenders.

NAVAL: The USS *Admiral* captures the Confederate steamer *Isabel* off Galveston, Texas, following a six-hour chase. Significantly, this vessel completed 20 successful runs before finally being snared.

May 29

SOUTH: General Ulysses S. Grant, having crossed the Army of the Potomac over the Pamunkey River, Virginia, resumes marching southwest toward the Confederate capital of Richmond, unaware that General Robert E. Lee already is moving troops in the direction of Cold Harbor.

General Jubal A. Early is formally appointed to lead the Confederate II Corps, Army of Northern Virginia—"Stonewall" Jackson's old command.

NAVAL: The USS *Cowslip* captures the Confederate sloop *Last Push* off the Mississippi coast.

May 30

SOUTH: General Ulysses S. Grant's Army of the Potomac, moving along the Totopotomoy Creek, suddenly swings toward Cold Harbor, Virginia, possession of which would place his force within 10 miles of Richmond. Meanwhile, General Robert E. Lee, perceiving that the Union V Corps under General Gouverneur K. Warren is isolated, launches an attack at Bethesda Church to destroy it. The Confederate II Corps under General Jubal A. Early maneuvers around Warren's left flank and charges, routing the Pennsylvania Reserves, but the Federals reform and throw him back. Further attacks under General Stephen D. Ramseur also fail to dislodge the defenders, and the Confederates withdraw to new defenses at Cold Harbor.

WEST: Union cavalry under General George Crook gallop from Meadow Bluff, West Virginia, to join General David Hunter's main Union army in the Shenandoah Valley.

General John H. Morgan begins his final raid against Union lines of communication by entering Kentucky.

NAVAL: The USS *Keystone State* and *Massachusetts* capture the British blockade-runner *Caledonia* off Cape Fear, North Carolina, following a three-hour chase.

May 31

POLITICS: Radical Republicans, dissatisfied with President Abraham Lincoln, nominate former general John C. Frémont in Cleveland, Ohio, as their party candidate for chief executive. They also select General John Cochrane of New York to be vice president. Among Frémont's strongest supporters is African-American abolitionist Frederick Douglass, who feels that Lincoln is far too lenient toward Southerners in his plans for Reconstruction.

SOUTH: General Ulysses S. Grant's Overland Campaign to Richmond, Virginia, while a tactical failure, thus far proves a brilliant strategic success. In one very bloody month, he forces the redoubtable Army of Northern Virginia from positions along the Rapidan River to the gates of the Confederate capital.

General Philip H. Sheridan is ordered to ride and occupy the crossroads at Cold Harbor, Virginia. In the process, he encounters Confederate troopers under General Fitzhugh Lee and drives them off with rapid-fire Spencer carbines.

Richard H. Anderson and Jubal A. Early are promoted to lieutenant general, C.S.A.

NAVAL: The USS *Commodore Perry* trades shot with a Confederate battery on the James River, Virginia, taking six hits over two hours.

June 1

NORTH: Joshua L. Chamberlain is appointed a brigadier general, U.S. Army.

SOUTH: Union cavalry under General Philip H. Sheridan repel a determined attack by General Richard H. Anderson's Confederates at Old Cold Harbor, Virginia, largely through the use of new, rapid-fire Spencer carbines. In the course of the day, Sheridan is relieved by VI and XVIII Corps, who drive the Southerners back until a strong counterattack restores their line. General Ulysses S. Grant, believing that the Confederates are exhausted and their line weakly held, orders General Winfield S. Hancock's II Corps to march all night toward Cold Harbor and prepare for a daylight assault in the morning. Union losses for the day amount to 2,650 while the Confederate casualties are probably as heavy.

WEST: Confederate cavalry under General John H. Morgan attack Union supply lines at Pound Gap, Kentucky.

General Samuel D. Sturgis departs Memphis, Tennessee, at the head of 8,100 men to prevent Confederate raiders under General Nathan B. Forrest from cutting the all-important Nashville and Chattanooga Railroad. He commands a cavalry brigade under General Benjamin H. Grierson and an infantry brigade under Colonel William L. McMillan, along with 22 cannon and 250 supply wagons. From the onset, the column is hampered by heavy rain and progress is slow.

Union cavalry under General George Stoneman seizes Allatoona Pass, Georgia, securing an important railhead. Meanwhile, General William T. Sherman, begins to look for other avenues to outmaneuver the tenacious General Joseph E. Johnston.

Dead being reburied after the Battle of Cold Harbor *(U.S. Army Military History Institute)*

NAVAL: The wooden paddle wheeler USS *Exchange* is damaged by Confederate batteries on the Mississippi River near Columbia, Arkansas.

June 2

SOUTH: At Cold Harbor, Virginia, General Ulysses S. Grant prepares his men for a frontal assault against what he perceives as weak Confederate lines. However, he cancels the action after General Winfield S. Hancock's II Corps, delayed by fatigue and hot weather, arrives in poor condition. Grant reluctantly postpones his attack another day, which grants General Robert E. Lee additional time to dig in and strengthen his lines. In that respect, Cold Harbor is probably the best defensive position that his Army of Northern Virginia ever held. Lee is about to hand Grant another abject lesson in the power of defensive fieldworks.

WEST: Heavy skirmishing develops between 10,000 Union troops under Generals David Hunter and 3,000 Confederates of General John D. Imboden at Coventry, Virginia. The Southerners suffer the worst of it and withdraw.

Naval: The USS *Victoria* destroys the Confederate steamer *Georgianna McCaw* after running it aground near Wilmington, North Carolina.

The USS *Wamsutta* chases the British blockade-runner *Rose* aground at Pawley's Island, South Carolina, sinking it.

Armed boats from the USS *Cowslip* conduct a destructive foray up Biloxi Bay, Mississippi, destroying several small craft shops and saltworks.

June 3

South: The Battle of Cold Harbor unfolds across a continuous, seven-mile front, inundated with earthen fortifications and interlocking fields of fire. The Southern position, manned by 59,000 men, consists of General Jubal A. Early's II Corps on the left, General Richard H. Anderson's I Corps in the center, and General Ambrose P. Hill anchoring the right. Arrayed against them are 108,000 Federal troops of the XI Corps under General Ambrose E. Burnside on the left, followed by the XVIII Corps of General William F. Smith, the VI of General Horatio G. Wright, and General Winfield S. Hancock's II Corps on the right. General Ulysses S. Grant's strategy is simple: Assault the entire Confederate position and, once a weak spot develops, call up reserves to pour through it. But Grant, unaware of the extent of Southern entrenchments before him, is setting the stage for a tragedy.

The Union assault kicks off at 4:30 a.m., as 40,000 Federal troops charge across the open fields in dense columns. The defenders allow them to close, and then they unleash withering torrents of bullets and canister that tear apart formations, cutting men down in droves. Only General Francis Barlow's brigade briefly penetrates Confederate lines on the left before recoiling under heavy fire. Within 30 minutes, the conflict at Cold Harbor ends as suddenly as it began. No less than 7,000 Federals have been killed or wounded, while Southern losses are slightly under 1,500. It is the biggest military blunder of Grant's career, and the Northern press starts assailing him as a "butcher." As he later wrote, "I regret this assault more than any I have ever ordered," and he never again launched frontal attacks against prepared works.

General Robert E. Lee has won his final open field battle, for Cold Harbor marks an end to the mobile phase of Grant's Overland campaign to Richmond. Both sides have endured staggering losses since the beginning of May, with Union casualties exceeding 50,000. The Southern toll amounts to 32,000, which, while lower, is severe. But body counts do not tell the entire story: At the strategic level, Lee's losses actually constitute a higher percentage of his army, 46 to 41 percent. Grant, moreover, receives a constant and steady flow of reinforcements, whereas Confederate manpower resources are dwindling rapidly. But this could scarcely be accomplished, let alone sustained, without equal determination on the political front. President Abraham Lincoln's willingness to both embrace and endure a contest of attrition, with all the heartbreak it entails, ultimately breaks the South's ability to resist and wins the war.

West: Union cavalry under General William W. Averell trots out of Bunger's Mills, West Virginia, en route to join the main force under General David Hunter near Lynchburg, Virginia.

Union forces under General William T. Sherman march northwest of the New Hope, Dallas line, and General Joseph E. Johnston begin to abandon his position at New Hope, Georgia.

General Edward R. S. Canby offers to assist Admiral David D. Porter by providing troops for periodic sweeps along the banks of the Mississippi River to prevent further guerrilla-style attacks on shipping.

NAVAL: The USS *Water Witch* is captured by 130 Confederate troops in boats under Lieutenant Thomas P. Pelot in Ossabaw Sound, Georgia. The raiders strike at 2:00 A.M. and were almost on their victim when detected; the ship nonetheless is carried after a wild, hand-to-hand melee. Pelot is one of five Confederates killed while another 17 are injured.

June 4

WEST: General William E. Jones arrives from Bristol, Virginia, to receive command of Confederate forces in the Shenandoah Valley from General John D. Imboden. He brings reinforcements that increase Southern strength up to 5,600 men.

Union cavalry under General Samuel D. Sturgis advance from Memphis, Tennessee, toward Ripley, Mississippi, in search of General Nathan B. Forrest.

The Army of Tennessee under General Joseph E. Johnston departs New Hope Church, Georgia, and begins to occupy ready-made defensive lines around Marietta.

General Andrew J. Smith and 10,000 men of the Union XVI and XVII Corps embark at Vicksburg, Mississippi, and steam north on the Mississippi River to Sunnyside Landing, Arkansas. Once ashore, he is to begin antiguerrilla operations against General John S. Marmaduke.

NAVAL: The USS *Ticonderoga* is assigned patrol duties in the Gulf of St. Lawrence to guard against Confederate raids in New England waters.

The USS *Fort Jackson* captures the Confederate steamer *Thistle* off Charleston, South Carolina.

June 5

SOUTH: General Ulysses S. Grant orders General Philip H. Sheridan, on a mounted raid toward Charlottesville, Virginia, to tear up the Virginia Central Railroad before pressing onward to join General David Hunter in the Shenandoah Valley. Grant anticipates that a raid of this magnitude will distract Confederate attention as he slips his Army of the Potomac over the James River and closer to Richmond.

WEST: A force of 15,000 Union troops under General David Hunter, having advanced down the Shenandoah Valley as far as Harrisonburg before turning east, engages 5,600 Confederates under General William E. Jones at Piedmont, Virginia. The Federals repel Southern skirmishers before encountering their main body under Jones. Hunter then brings up artillery and commences to bombard at 9:00 A.M. before attacking the Confederate left with troops under Colonel Augustus Moor. Moor makes good progress initially but is finally slowed and repelled. Jones then counterattacks until being halted by new troops under Colonel Joseph Thoburn. Moor, meanwhile, rallies his men and, assisted by a cavalry brigade under General Julius Stahel, renews his advance on Jones's right. Charging through a gap in the Southern line, the Federals capture all of Jones's artillery, and his line buckles and shatters. The outnumbered, exhausted Confederates run wildly, and Jones is killed while trying to rally them. Union losses are 780 while the Southerners incur nearly 1,600. Hunter's victory finally clears the way for a Northern invasion of the Shenandoah Valley.

General Andrew J. Smith disembarks on the Mississippi River and lands 10,000 Union troops at Sunnyside Landing, Arkansas. Proceeding inland, they encounter the 3rd Missouri Cavalry under Colonel Colton Greene at Ditch Bayou and run him off after a protracted skirmishing.

NAVAL: The USS *Keystone State* captures the British blockade-runner *Siren* off Beaufort Harbor, North Carolina.

June 6

WEST: The Union Army under General David Hunter occupies Staunton, Virginia, unopposed, and begins to raze both the town and its adjoining countryside.

Union general Joseph A. Mower marches from Sunnyside Landing, Arkansas, with 4,000 troops to evict Colonel Colton Greene's 3rd Missouri Cavalry from Ditch Bayou. Intense skirmishing erupts amid dense undergrowth and swampy land as the Federals push forward and the Southerners yield ground slowly. At length, Greene introduces a handful of cannon whose fire throws Mower's men into confusion as Union artillery become helplessly mired in mud. After seven hours of fighting—in which they held off seven times their number—Greene's troopers fall back beyond Lake Chicot and safety. Union losses in this embarrassing affair total 250; the Confederates admit to only 37.

NAVAL: The USS *Metacomet* captures the Confederate steamer *Donegal* off Mobile, Alabama.

The USS *Louisville* covers the embarkation of 8,000 Federal troops under General Andrew J. Smith near Sunnydale, Arkansas, on the Mississippi River. This activity follows a brief campaign along Bayou Macon to suppress Confederate guerrilla activity.

June 7

POLITICS: The Republican Party convenes at Baltimore, Maryland, to nominate its presidential and vice presidential candidates. With the assistance of several prowar Democrats, they are able to portray themselves as the "National Union Convention."

NORTH: John Gibbon is appointed major general, U.S. Army.

SOUTH: General Philip H. Sheridan rides off from New Castle Ferry, Virginia, with 6,000 troopers under Generals Alfred T. A. Tolbert and David M. Gregg. His mission is to raid the Virginia Central Railroad before proceeding into the Shenandoah Valley to link up with General David Hunter. They assume a line of march northwest toward Trevilian Station to begin their destructive work.

WEST: Union cavalry under Generals William W. Averell and George Crook join the main Union force under General David Hunter near Staunton, Virginia.

A large Union column under General Samuel D. Sturgis trudges into Ripley, Mississippi, having taken a full week to traverse 50 miles. However, General Nathan B. Forrest, fully apprised of Union movements and intentions, begins to lay an elaborate snare for the intruders at Brice's Cross Roads.

NAVAL: Union batteries on Morris Island, Charleston, South Carolina, bombard the Confederate steam transport *Etiwan,* sinking it off Fort Johnson.

Armed boats from the USS *Clyde* and Sagamore ascend the Suwannee River, Florida, and seize 100 bales of cotton near Clay Landing.

June 8

POLITICS: A Republican convention held in Baltimore, Maryland, renominates Abraham Lincoln to run for the presidency. However, Vice President Hannibal Hamlin is dropped in favor of Tennessee governor Andrew Johnson, a Southern war Democrat, whose presence should broaden the ticket's appeal. Their platform calls for a military end to the rebellion and ratification of the 13th Amendment to abolish slavery.

SOUTH: Alert Confederate scouts inform cavalry leader General Wade Hampton of General Philip H. Sheridan's departure from New Castle Ferry, Virginia. Because the Federals ride northwest, he correctly deduces that Sheridan is headed for Trevilian Station and gallops off with 4,700 cavalry and three batteries to intercept him.

WEST: Confederate raiders under General John H. Morgan capture the town of Mount Sterling, Kentucky, and rob a bank of $18,000.

General William T. Sherman gathers his men for an advance on Marietta, Georgia, and resumes his flanking tactics. However, General Nathan B. Forrest's activities force him to detach increasing numbers of men to protect rapidly lengthening lines of communication with Tennessee, thereby weakening available field forces.

NAVAL: Federal gunboats USS *Chillicothe, Neosho,* and *Fort Hindman* steam up the Atchafalaya River, Louisiana, and successfully engage a Confederate battery above Simmesport.

June 9

POLITICS: President Abraham Lincoln suggests a constitutional amendment to outlaw slavery.

WEST: Union forces drive General John H. Morgan's raiders out of Mount Sterling, Kentucky, and he withdraws toward Winchester.

NAVAL: The USS *New Bern* runs the Confederate steamer *Pevensey* aground off Beaufort, North Carolina.

The USS *Rosalie* captures the Confederate steamer *Emma* on Marco Pass, Florida.

The USS *Proteus* captures the British blockade-runner *R. S. Hood* north of the Little Bahama Bank.

June 10

POLITICS: In light of a growing manpower crisis, the Confederate Congress authorizes military service for all males aged between 17 and 50 years of age.

SOUTH: General Richard Taylor is relieved of commanding the District of West Louisiana and replaced by Texas general John G. Walker.

WEST: Confederate cavalry under General John H. Morgan enter Lexington, Kentucky, seize several hundred horses, and push on to the capital at Frankfort.

In a stunning display of tactical virtuosity, General Nathan B. Forrest and 3,500 Confederate cavalry rout a Union force twice its size at Brice's Cross Roads, Mississippi. Forrest anticipates that General Samuel D. Sturgis will commit his cavalry to battle first, followed by his infantry, and he determines to defeat each in detail as they come up. At 5:30 A.M., a force of 3,300 Union cavalry approaches the crossroads under General Benjamin H. Grierson, and a protracted fight between dismounted troopers commences in earnest. The Confederates, holding high ground and protected by densely wooded terrain, manage to keep Grierson at a standstill while his men are exhausted steadily by the day's intense heat. Around noon, the first elements of Union infantry under Colonel William L. McMillen, also fatigued by a five-mile jog to the battlefield, begin to arrive.

Forrest, eager to maintain the battlefield initiative, begins to launch counterattacks at selected positions along the Union line, all of which are repulsed. However, the effort further tires his opponents. Judging the moment right, at 5:00 P.M., he unleashes a simultaneous attack against the Union left, right, and center while a small force maneuvers around Sturgis's rear. The tiring Federals, hit from all sides, suddenly bolt from the field and career headlong into their extensive wagon and artillery train, overturning both. They are hotly pursued overnight by the Confederates, and the Union retreat degenerates into a rout. Forrest, outnumbered two to one, thus clinches the greatest victory of his already remarkable career: For a loss of 96 dead Confederates and 396 wounded (492), he inflicts 223 killed, 394 wounded, and 1,623 captured (2,240). A further 16 cannon, 1,500 stands of arms, and 192 wagons are also seized. But despite his remarkable success, Forrest remains unable to cut General William T. Sherman's supply line into Georgia.

NAVAL: Colonel Jacob Zeilin becomes the seventh commandant, U.S. Marine Corps.

The USS *Union* captures the Confederate sloop *Caroline* at Jupiter Inlet, Florida.

The USS *Elk* captures the Confederate sloop *Yankee Doodle* at the mouth of the Pearl River, Mississippi Sound.

June 11

SOUTH: General Robert E. Lee dispatches General Jubal A. Early into the Shenandoah Valley to stop Union depredations there under General David Hunter. If successful, he is then at liberty to march up the valley to threaten Washington, D.C., thereby forcing General Ulysses S. Grant to divert reinforcements from the Richmond, Virginia, front. Early's force also receives a new designation, Army of the Valley.

Generals Philip H. Sheridan rides into Trevilian Station, Virginia, where he confronts the division of General Wade Hampton waiting for him in the woods. Sheridan quickly dispatches the Michigan brigade of General George A. Custer to turn Hampton's right flank and slash at his rear, which he does with aplomb. Before the stunned Confederates realize what hits them, Custer dashes in between Hampton and General Fitzhugh Lee's division, capturing 50 wagons, 800 prisoners, and 1,500 horses. Lee is tardy sorting his command out but then begins to pressure the unsupported Custer hard, striking him from front and behind. The Michiganders are hard pressed for several hours, losing their own wagons, and almost overrun before Custer forms a triangular defensive box and beats back Lee's attacks. At the last minute, Sheridan gallops up with reinforcements and scatters the Southerners, taking 500 prisoners as fighting winds down for the evening.

WEST: Vengeful Union forces under General David Hunter burn the Virginia Military Institute at Lexington, Virginia. Hunter then pauses several days to rest and reorganize his newly constituted Army of West Virginia, a mistake that allows hard-pressed Confederates to rush reinforcements toward the important rail junction at Lynchburg.

Confederate cavalry under General John H. Morgan capture Cynthiana, Kentucky, seizing 300 prisoners and threatening the capital at Frankfort.

General Nathan B. Forrest hotly pursues defeated Union cavalry under General Samuel D. Sturgis, skirmishing with them at Ripley, Mississippi.

The Union XIII Corps is disbanded in the Department of Missouri.

NAVAL: The Confederate raider CSS *Alabama* under Captain Raphael Semmes docks at Cherbourg, France, to carry out badly needed repairs. His arrival does not escape the attention of the American vice consul in residence, who notifies Captain John A. Winslow of the USS *Kearsarge* at Dover, England, of his presence.

June 12

SOUTH: General Ulysses S. Grant begins to shift his Army of the Potomac strategically from Cold Harbor, Virginia, south toward Petersburg—50 miles distant. Union engineers already operating on the James River construct a pontoon bridge 2,100 feet long in only eight hours: One of the greatest engineering triumphs of the war, its existence remains entirely unknown to General Robert E. Lee. Simultaneously, the XVIII Corps of General William F. Smith boards transports down the Pamunkey River and sails for Bermuda Hundred on the south bank of the James River.

General Philip A. Sheridan's cavalry renew their clash with Generals Wade Hampton and Fitzhugh Lee at Trevilian Station, Virginia. General Alfred T. A. Torbert's division is tasked with charging dismounted Confederates at Mallory's Cross Roads while General David M. Gregg's troopers tear up tracks belonging to the Central Virginia Railroad at Louisa Court House. However, Hampton's well-situated soldiers repel seven Union charges, at which point Sheridan concludes his raid and withdraws back to Union lines outside Petersburg. Trevilian Station is one of the largest all-cavalry battles of the Civil War and among the most costly: Sheridan admits to 735 killed, wounded, and missing while Confederate losses are estimated at 1,000. Moreover, Hampton's tactically adroit leadership foils a major Union raid and prevents the Federals from reinforcing the Shenandoah Valley.

WEST: Union forces under General Stephen G. Burdrige evict General John H. Morgan's 1,300 Confederate raiders from Cynthiana, Kentucky, killing or capturing half. The surviving rebels gallop off in the direction of Abdington, Virginia, and safety.

NAVAL: Gale winds force the USS *Lavender* onto Lookout Shoal, North Carolina, and it sinks with the loss of nine crewmen. The survivors are rescued two days later by the army steamer *John Farron.*

The USS *Flag* captures the Confederate sloop *Cyclops* off Charleston, South Carolina.

June 13

SOUTH: The campaign for Richmond, Virginia, begins as General Robert E. Lee mistakenly marches troops southward to confront what he believes is the latest Union advance toward the Confederate capital via Malvern Hill and White Oaks Swamp. Meanwhile, General Ulysses S. Grant continues advancing unopposed toward the James River and Petersburg.

To counter recent Union advances in the Shenandoah Valley, General Jubal A. Early's II Corps detaches from the Army of Northern Virginia at Petersburg and moves westward by rail to Lynchburg.

General Richard S. Ewell is appointed commander of the Department of Richmond, Virginia.

WEST: A Union cavalry column under General Samuel D. Sturgis skirmishes with Confederate pursuers at Collierville, Tennessee, ending its mismanaged campaign against General Nathan B. Forrest. Consequently, the inept Sturgis spends the balance of the war at Memphis, "awaiting orders."

NAVAL: The USS *Kearsarge* under Captain John A. Winslow departs Dover, England, en route to Cherbourg, France, and a fateful confrontation with the CSS *Alabama.*

June 14

POLITICS: The first session, second Confederate Congress, adjourns.

SOUTH: Union troops of the XVIII Corps under General William F. Smith disembark at Bermuda Hundred to reinforce General Benjamin F. Butler's Army of the James.

WEST: General Joseph E. Johnston calls a staff conference at his headquarters near the summit of Pine Mountain, Marietta, Georgia. Nearby Union forces fire several rounds from their heavy Parrott cannons, and a shell strikes and kills General Leonidas K. Polk. General Alexander P. Stewart succeeds him as corps commander.

NAVAL: The USS *Courier* runs aground and is wrecked on Abaco Island, Bahamas.

The USS *Kearsarge* under Captain John A. Winslow positions itself in international waters off Cherbourg, France, awaiting the departure of the CSS *Alabama.*

June 15

POLITICS: The 13th Amendment to the U.S. Constitution fails to be ratified in the House of Representatives, falling 13 votes short (95 to 66) of the two-thirds majority needed.

The U.S. Congress passes legislation granting equal pay to African-American soldiers. For many months, black personnel have refused to accept less pay than their white counterparts in protest.

Former congressman and Peace Democrat Clement L. Vallandigham arrives in Ohio following his Canadian exile. He thereupon resumes work for securing a negotiated peace with the Confederacy.

SOUTH: General William F. Smith and 12,500 men of his XVIII Corps make a stumbling approach on the half-manned defenses of Petersburg, Virginia, then poorly held by the 2,200 Confederates of General Henry A. Wise. Smith is reinforced that evening by General Winfield S. Hancock's II Corps, but he elects not to storm the city under a moonlit night. This vacillation permits General Pierre G. T. Beauregard to consolidate Petersburg's defenses rapidly by funneling in additional troops.

General Alfred H. Terry assumes command of the Union X Corps, Army of the Potomac.

WEST: Union forces under General William T. Sherman begin to close with Confederate forces arrayed near Marietta, Georgia.

SOUTHWEST: Confederate Cherokees under General Stand Watie shell and capture the Union steamer *J. R. Williams* at Pleasant Bluffs on the Arkansas River. It is carrying ample rations for the Union garrison at Fort Gibson, Indian Territory, recently burdened by 5,000 Unionist Indian refugees.

NAVAL: Crews from the Federal gunboats USS *Lexington* and *Tyler* detain three northern steamers off Beulah's Landing, Mississippi, that were caught trading with the enemy.

The USS *General Bragg, Winnebago,* and *Naiad* engage a Confederate battery at Como Landing, Louisiana, on the Mississippi River. General Bragg is hit and temporarily disabled by enemy fire.

June 16

POLITICS: President Abraham Lincoln, addressing the Sanitation Fair in Philadelphia, Pennsylvania, declares, "War, at best, is terrible, and this war of ours, in its magnitude and duration, is one of the most terrible." But he continues to assure his audience, stating, "We accepted this war for an object, a worthy object, and the war will end when that object is obtained."

SOUTH: General Pierre G. T. Beauregard masses 14,000 men at Petersburg, Virginia, to stop an unexpected Union advance on the city. Nonetheless, General William F. Smith's XVIII Corps manages to capture several redans and a mile of Confederate trenches on the city's outer perimeter. However, Smith declines to press home his numerical superiority, and his hesitancy is one of the most costly Union mistakes of the war. It prolongs the fighting by nearly a year.

Unknown to the Confederates, General George G. Meade's entire Army of the Potomac silently slips across the James River and steadily advances on Petersburg, Virginia. It is a masterstroke capable of ending the war.

WEST: The Confederate II Corps of General Jubal A. Early reaches Charlottesville, Virginia, although delays in rail service mean that only half of his 8,000 men reach Lynchburg in time to aid its defense.

General Joseph E. Johnston retires to new positions near Mud Creek, Georgia.

NAVAL: The USS *Commodore Perry,* at the behest of General Benjamin F. Butler, bombards Fort Clifton on the James River, Virginia.

A joint Union expedition consisting of the USS *Lockwood, Louisiana,* and army transport *Ella May* begins to operate up the Pamlico and Pungo rivers, North Carolina. They capture and burn the Confederate schooners *Iowa, Mary Emma,* and *Jenny Lind* before returning downstream.

Captain Raphael Semmes, eager to try conclusions with the USS *Kearsarge* offshore, begins to take on supplies of coal and munitions for the CSS *Alabama* at Cherbourg, France.

June 17

NORTH: An explosion rocks part of the Washington Arsenal, killing 18 and injuring 20.

SOUTH: General William F. Smith's XVIII Corps finally launches strong attacks on the newly strengthened defenses of Petersburg, Virginia, and is repulsed by Confederates under General Bushrod R. Johnson.

WEST: Confederate forces under General John C. Breckinridge and John D. Imboden defend Lynchburg, Virginia, against General David Hunter's Union troops. The initial Union drive, delivered by General George Crook, pushes aside Confederate outposts while cavalry under General Alfred N. Duffie advance from the west. Southern resistance then suddenly stiffens following the arrival of General Jubal A. Early, who directs the division of General Stephen Ramseur into the front lines. Hunter elects not to press the conflict further and encamps for the night.

General William T. Sherman begins to probe Confederate positions at Mud Creek, Georgia, seeking a weak spot.

NAVAL: The CSS *Florida* captures and burns the Union brig *W. C. Clarke* at sea.

June 18

SOUTH: The siege of Petersburg, Virginia, begins in earnest once General Robert E. Lee arrives with the Army of Northern Virginia. Lee, commanding 50,000 bedraggled and hungry men, defends a line 26 miles long while simultaneously guarding the four railroads out of the city that constitute his lifeline. Ulysses S. Grant leads 110,000 well-equipped soldiers, backed by a steady stream of replacements that the Confederates cannot match. Yet, to underscore the strength of Southern defenses, a heavy probe by II Corps under General David B. Birney is repulsed. The past four days of fighting in the city's outskirts cost the Union 10,586 casualties while better-protected Southerners sustain about 4,000.

General David B. Birney replaces the ailing General Winfield S. Hancock as commander of the II Corps, Army of the Potomac.

General Thomas W. Sherman takes charge of Union forces in the vicinity of New Orleans, Louisiana.

WEST: General David Hunter's 18,000 Union soldiers renew their attack on Lynchburg, Virginia. However, newly arrived Confederates under General Jubal A. Early boost the defenders to 14,000 men, who resist tenaciously. Hunter is especially foiled by excellent Confederate artillery fire that smothers his own inexperienced gunners. At length, the Union columns under Generals George Crook, William W. Averell, and Jeremiah Sullivan fail to turn Early's position or to score any significant penetrations despite heavy fighting. Hunter concludes that the Confederates have been reinforced heavily overnight and actually outnumber him. He therefore ignominiously halts the engagement and withdraws up the Shenandoah Valley toward Liberty. This timidity emboldens Early, and he regains the strategic initiative by energetically pursuing his larger adversary. Casualties at Lynchburg are not recorded but are believed to be relatively light for both sides.

General Joseph E. Johnston abandons his line at Pine Mountain, Georgia, and falls back to even stronger positions along Kennesaw Mountain, two miles west of Marietta. This elevated ridge line probably constitutes the best defensive terrain his army will hold during the entire Atlanta campaign.

June 19

WEST: Union forces under General David Hunter withdraw from the Shenandoah Valley completely and escape into the Kanawha Valley of West Virginia. Confederates under General Jubal A. Early hotly pursue from behind.

Union forces rout a detachment of Texas Rangers at Hahn's Farm, Arkansas.

NAVAL: The USS *Kearsarge* under Captain John A. Winslow engages the CSS *Alabama* under Captain Raphael Semmes off Cherbourg, France. The Union vessel enjoys a slightly larger crew and marginally heavier armament, but a decided advantage in ordnance since the *Alabama*'s ammunition has deteriorated from lengthy exposure to salt air. Moreover, Winslow takes the precaution of wrapping vulnerable parts of his ship with heavy chains that function as armor. At 11:00 A.M., the antagonists meet seven

Engagement between the CSS *Alabama* and the USS *Kearsarge* June 19, 1864 Painting by Xanthus R. Smith (*Naval Historical Foundation*)

miles offshore and begin to circle at 900 yards distance while 15,000 spectators throng the beach. Semmes commences firing at a mile's distance while Winslow, enjoying superior speed, gradually narrows the range and holds his fire until within a half mile. Both vessels handle their guns well; *Kearsarge* receives 28 hits, including a potentially disastrous strike by a 100-pound shell that fails to explode. But Union gunnery is superb and inflicts tremendous damage on the unprotected *Alabama,* puncturing its hull repeatedly. Within an hour, the celebrated raider begins to list, and Semmes, unable to dash for the French coast, abandons ship. *Alabama* settles beneath the waves stern first as the English yacht *Deerhound* sails in to rescue the wallowing Confederates, including Semmes. Casualties are three Union wounded to 26 Confederate killed, 21 wounded, and 64 captured. This action terminates the Confederacy's most celebrated commerce raider: Since its commissioning in 1862, *Alabama* has sailed 75,000 miles and seized 63 Union ships worth $4.5 million. Winslow subsequently receives a well-deserved promotion to commodore for his lopsided triumph.

June 20

SOUTH: A Union cavalry detachment is routed by Colonel John S. Mosby at Centreville, Virginia, losing 39 captives.

Union forces launch a major expedition from Batchelder's Creek, North Carolina, against nearby Kinston. Some prisoners and horses are taken.

WEST: General William T. Sherman's army moves up against a new Confederate defensive line in the Kennesaw Mountains.

NAVAL: The USS *Morse* and *Cactus* bombard Confederate batteries near White House, Virginia, which have been harassing army supply trains.

The USS *Calypso* and *Nansemond* escort an army expedition up the New River, North Carolina, in an attempt to sever the Wilmington and Weldon Railroad.

June 21

POLITICS: President Abraham Lincoln visits Union troops in the siege lines at Peterburg, Virginia, making a conspicuous target for snipers in his tall, stovepipe hat.

Confederate secretary of the treasury Christopher G. Meminger resigns over criticism of his handling of monetary affairs.

SOUTH: As General Ulysses S. Grant attempts extending Confederate siege lines to the breaking point by moving troops to the south and west of Petersburg, Virginia. However, stiff resistance halts the Federal drive short of the Weldon Railroad. Grant then prepares to hurl two corps and a cavalry division against that vital Confederate supply line.

WEST: General Joseph Hooker's XX Corps reaches Kolb's Farm on the extreme left flank of Confederate positions along Kennesaw Mountain. General Joseph E. Johnston, fearing he will be flanked and ejected from fine defensive terrain, orders the corps of General John B. Hood to march from his right flank over to the endangered point on the left.

NAVAL: Gunfire from the USS *Shokokon* rescues the army transport *Eliza Hancox* from a Confederate attack near Cumberland Point, Virginia.

A Confederate squadron consisting of the CSS *Virginia II, Fredericksburg,* and *Hampton,* backed by land batteries, engages the Union James River squadron at

Trent's and the Varina Reaches. Little damage results to either side and the Confederates withdraw back upstream.

June 22

SOUTH: General Ulysses S. Grant, confronting strong Southern defenses before him at Petersburg, Virginia, tries his time-honored tactic of shifting troops around the Confederate flank in a bid to extend and weaken their lines by cutting the Weldon Railroad. General David B. Birney's II Corps and General Horatio G. Wright's VI Corps, supported by a cavalry division under General James H. Wilson, advance through dense woods to reach their objective. Due to the nature of the terrain, a sizable gap develops between the two forces, a fact which Confederate general Ambrose P. Hill quickly exploits. General Cadmus M. Wilcox's division is ordered to engage Wright's VI Corps as a diversion while Generals William Mahone and Bushrod R. Johnson assail Birney's flank. The assault is delivered savagely and routs the veteran division of General John Gibbon, taking 1,600 prisoners. Further fighting results in a stalemate by nightfall, and the Union leaders fall back to regroup and try again.

Generals James H. Wilson and August V. Kautz take 3,300 Union troopers on a major cavalry raid from Lee's Mill, Virginia, and against the South Side and Danville Railroad.

WEST: General John H. Morgan receives command of the Department of Western Virginia and East Tennessee.

Colonel John S. Mosby captures Duffield's Depot, West Virginia, along with 50 Union prisoners.

General John B. Hood exceeds his orders to extend the Confederate left flank at Kennesaw Mountain by launching an unauthorized assault with 11,000 men against Union positions at Kolb's Farm, Georgia. General Joseph Hooker, commanding 14,000 troops and 40 cannon, is forewarned of Hood's approach and makes careful preparations to receive him in strength. Concentrated musketry and canister fire at close range mows charging Confederates down, and Hood draws off with 1,500 casualties to a Union tally of 250.

NAVAL: The Federal gunboat USS *Lexington* attacks and drives off a body of Confederates from White River Station, Arkansas.

June 23

SOUTH: Union generals David B. Birney and Horatio G. Wright repeat their attack on Confederate defenses along the Weldon Railroad, Petersburg, with their II and VI Corps, respectively. A good initial advance recovers all ground lost on the previous day but a stubborn defense mounted by General William Mahone blocks them from cutting the railroad. At dusk, the Federals again withdraw below the Jerusalem Plank Road with 2,962 casualties. Eight weeks elapse before General Ulysses S. Grant mounts a major effort in this vital sector again.

WEST: General Jubal A. Early energetically conducts 14,000 Confederate troops northward up the Shenandoah Valley in pursuit of General David Hunter. Hunter, retreating rapidly westward, escapes Early's grasp but leaves Washington, D.C., exposed to attack.

NAVAL: The heavy ironclad USS *Tecumseh* is ordered out of the James River, Virginia, and steams off to join the West Gulf Blockading Squadron off Mobile, Alabama.

Lieutenant William B. Cushing rows a small reconnaissance party from the USS *Monticello* up the Cape Fear River and endeavors to obtain the location of the CSS *Raleigh*. They are unaware that this vessel has been scuttled on May 6, but the mission provides Union forces with additional intelligence. Moreover, three seamen, David Warren, William Wright, and John Sullivan, all receive the Congressional Medal of Honor for their participation.

June 24

POLITICS: The Maryland Convention gathers and votes to abolish slavery.
SOUTH: Union cavalry under General Philip H. Sheridan are rebuffed at Samaria Church, Virginia, while returning from their aborted raid toward Lynchburg.
NAVAL: The wooden paddle-wheeler USS *Queen City* is attacked and captured by Confederate forces of General Joseph O. Shelby at Claredon on the White River, Arkansas. The USS *Tyler, Fawn,* and *Naumkeag* arrive on the scene shortly after, disperse the attackers, and recapture several Union sailors. However, *Queen City* is sunk by Confederates to prevent its recapture.

June 25

SOUTH: Colonel Henry Pleasant's 48th Pennsylvania, composed mostly of miners from Schuykill County, begin to tunnel beneath Confederate defenses at Petersburg, Virginia. The plan is initially approved by General Ambrose E. Burnside, IX Corps commander, while General Ulysses S. Grant also gives his grudging acceptance. The miners intend to burrow 511 feet long under a South Carolinian battery positioned at Elliott's Salient. Once finished, they will stock 8,000 pounds of gunpowder beneath it and light a fuse. During the next month, Burnside specially trains the African-American division of General Edward Ferrero to spearhead the assault once the changes have been detonated.

General Philip H. Sheridan's cavalry column, thwarted in its drive to Lynchburg, Virginia, ferries across the James River and rejoins the main Union army outside Petersburg.

General James H. Wilson's cavalry raid stumbles at the Staunton River Bridge near Roanoke Station, Virginia, thanks to dogged resistance by 900 Confederate infantry.

SOUTHWEST: Texas Rangers attack and disperse a small Union force at Rancho Las Rinas, Texas, killing 20 men.

June 26

WEST: A force of 14,000 Confederates under General Jubal A. Early occupies Staunton, Virginia, without opposition and then continues marching northward toward Winchester.

The Army of the Ohio under General John M. Schofield, having been ordered to make a "demonstration" against the Confederate position at Kennesaw Mountain, Georgia, sends three brigades across Olley's Creek to secure a foothold on the southern bank. Resistance proves surprisingly light, and he easily accomplishes his mission. However, General William T. Sherman ignores these important gains, calculating that General Joseph E. Johnston's main army is spread dangerously thin along the heights of Kennesaw Mountain. He intends to test his theory by attacking in force on the morrow.

NAVAL: The USS *Norfolk Packet* captures the Confederate sloop *Sarah Mary* off Mosquito Inlet, Florida.

June 27

POLITICS: President Abraham Lincoln formally accepts the Union (Republican) Party's nomination for the presidency.

SOUTH: General William S. Hancock resumes command of the II Corps, Army of the Potomac, following a brief illness.

WEST: General William T. Sherman wages the Battle of Kennesaw Mountain, Georgia, against General Joseph E. Johnston. He impatiently abandons his slow but successful flanking tactics because heavy rains turn the roads into quagmires, which precludes any such maneuvering. He also believes that Johnston, strung along a ridge line seven miles long, is stretched perilously thin. In fact, the Confederates are arrayed skillfully along high ground strewn with large boulders and trees—affording a perfect killing ground to troops advancing from below. Nevertheless, Sherman decides to make several feints on Johnston's flanks before striking him directly in the center—where he is strongest.

The first wave comprises two divisions from General John A. Logan's XV Corps, Army of the Tennessee, which charge uphill and rapidly clear Confederate defenders from their first line of entrenchments. However, as his 5,500 men clamber up the hillside, General William W. Loring's troops respond with intense musketry and artillery fire, dropping Federals in bloody clumps. The attack, suffering heavy losses, is called off after two hours.

The main thrust against Johnston's line occurs farther south along Cheatham's Hill, stoutly held by General William J. Hardee's corps. Up the slopes go 8,000 men from the divisions of Generals Jefferson C. Davis and John Newton, XIV Corps, which quickly overrun the line of defenders in rifle pits. But after pushing beyond the trenches, both commanders are raked by unerring sheets of fire from above that cut down soldiers in droves. Renewed and costly charges ensue, but the second Confederate line under Generals Patrick R. Cleburne and Benjamin F. Cheatham never is imperiled seriously. By the time this advance is suspended, Federals are crumpling within 15 yards of Confederate lines.

Losing heavily by the minute, Sherman finally calls off the assault. His losses range upward of 3,000, including two generals killed, while Johnston incurs about 750 casualties. Kennesaw Mountain proves the most costly mistake of the Atlanta campaign, and Sherman has little recourse but to continue maneuvering once the soggy ground dries out.

NAVAL: The USS *Nipsic* captures the Confederate sloop *Julia* at Sapelo Sound, Georgia.

The USS *Proteus* captures the British blockade-runner *Jupiter* off Man-of-War Cay, Bahamas.

June 28

POLITICS: President Abraham Lincoln signs legislation repealing the fugitive slave acts.

SOUTH: General James H. Wilson's cavalry force pauses at Stoney Creek Station, Virginia, where they are chased by Confederate troopers under General Wade Hampton. The Northerners then are attacked in force and roughly handled, abandoning their artillery, wagons, and wounded.

June 29

WEST: A quick raid by Colonel John S. Mosby on Charlestown and Duffield's Station, West Virginia, nets 25 captives. Numerous storehouses are burned, and telegraph wires are cut.

NAVAL: The USS *Hunchback* and *Saugus* shell Confederate batteries at Deep Bottom, along the James River, Virginia.

June 30

POLITICS: The U.S. Congress approves the Internal Revenue Act to help finance the war. The Morriff Tariff Act of 1861 is also modified to increase the duties levied.

Secretary of the Treasury Salmon P. Chase tenders his resignation to President Abraham Lincoln who, much to his surprise, accepts it. "You and I have reached a point of mutual embarrassment in our official relation which it seems cannot be overcome," Lincoln writes, "or longer sustained, consistently with public service."

WEST: General Jubal A. Early continues his Shenandoah offensive by advancing on New Market, Virginia.

NAVAL: An armed boat from the USS *Roebuck* captures the Confederate sloop *Last Resort* at Indian River Inlet, Florida.

The USS *Glasgow* forces the Confederate steamer *Ivanhoe* to run aground near Fort Morgan, Mobile Bay, Alabama. Four boatloads of sailors from the *Metacomet* and *Kennebec* accost the stricken vessel that night and burn it under the very guns of Fort Morgan.

July 1

POLITICS: President Abraham Lincoln appoints William P. Fessenden as the new secretary of the treasury.

The U.S. Senates passes the Wade-Davis Reconstruction Bill, 26 to 3, with 20 abstaining.

SOUTH: The 3rd Division of U.S. Cavalry under General James H. Wilson staggers back into Peterburg, Virginia, following a disappointing raid against the Petersburg and Weldon Railroad.

WEST: General Irvin McDowell is appointed commander of the Department of the Pacific.

Having abandoned frontal assault tactics, General William T. Sherman initiates a new flanking movement around Kennesaw Mountain and moves in the direction of Marietta, Georgia.

NAVAL: The USS *Merrimac* captures the Confederate sloop *Henrietta* at sea off Tampa, Florida.

The Confederate raider CSS *Florida* under Lieutenant Charles M. Morris captures and burns the Union bark *Harriet Stevens* at sea south of Bermuda.

July 2

SOUTH: Union troops land and gain a lodgment on Johnson Island, Charleston Harbor, South Carolina.

WEST: Confederates under General Jubal A. Early occupy Winchester, Virginia, before commencing their drive on Harper's Ferry, West Virginia.

General Joseph E. Johnston, reacting to the latest Union maneuver, begins to evacuate his position along Kennesaw Mountain, Georgia, and occupies prepared lines below Marietta at Smyrna.

NAVAL: The USS *Keystone State* captures the British blockade-runner *Rouen* near Wilmington, North Carolina.

Federal monitors USS *Leigh* and *Montauk* accompany and support army operations up the Stono River, South Carolina, in an attempt to cut the Charleston-Savannah Railroad.

July 3

SOUTH: Union forces launch attacks on Fort Johnson, Charleston, South Carolina, and are repulsed with 140 prisoners.

WEST: Confederate forces under General Jubal A. Early advance in the region of Buckton, Virginia, driving 5,000 Union troops under General Franz Sigel across the Potomac River at Maryland Heights. Early, declining to assault such a strong position, moves up to cross the river at Shepherdstown.

General George Crook is appointed commander of the Department of West Virginia.

The Army of Tennessee under General Joseph E. Johnston occupies new defensive works near Smyrna, Georgia, astride the Western and Atlantic Railroad. He thereby stands firm north of the Chattahoochee River, a move that General William T. Sherman failed to anticipate.

July 4

POLITICS: President Abraham Lincoln signs legislation modifying certain aspects of the Enrollment Act of 1863, striking the clause allowing substitutes to be purchased for $300.

The president also clashes with Radical Republicans over the tenor of reconstruction by refusing to sign the Wade-Davis Bill, which would have placed conditions for Reconstruction solely in the hands of Congress. He specifically objects to provisions requiring loyalty oaths by 50 percent of each state's 1860 voters.

The first session, 38th Congress adjourns.

WEST: General Jubal A. Early prepares to cross the Potomac River at Patterson's Creek Bridge, West Virginia, and into Maryland.

Union forces under General William T. Sherman stage demonstrations at Nickajack Creek and Turner's Ferry, Georgia, while scouting for a route across the Chattahoochee River. To that end, he sends Generals Oliver O. Howard (IV Corps) and Grenville M. Dodge (XVI Corps) to attack Confederate positions once across the river. Howard moves down on the Western and Atlantic Railroad as ordered, enjoying good progress until he reaches Vining's Station. There, Confederates under General William J. Hardee resist stoutly from a line of entrenchments. Rather than incur heavy casualties, Howard abruptly stops and digs in himself. Dodge, meanwhile, throws a pontoon bridge across Nickajack Creek near Ruff's Mills and pushes inland for nearly a mile before encountering Confederate cavalry and Georgia militia under generals Gustavus W. Smith and William H. Jackson. The Federals are unable to evict the Southerners in hard fighting, so they fall back and consolidate their bridgehead. General Joseph E. Johnston, anticipating that he is about to be flanked again, repositions the Army of Tennessee north of the Chattahoochee and heavily fortifies all bridges and crossings.

A sharp Union counterattack scatters the command of General Joseph O. Shelby in Searcy County, Arkansas.

NAVAL: The USS *Magnolia* captures three small boats laden with supplies several hundred miles east of Florida. That such craft even are dispatched on the open seas is a good indication of the torpid state of the Confederate economy.

The USS *Hastings* trades shots with Confederate sharpshooters along the White River above St. Charles, Arkansas.

July 5

POLITICS: New York journalist Horace Greeley receives peace feelers from the Confederate government and contacts President Abraham Lincoln. Lincoln authorizes Greeley to meet with said individuals at Niagara Falls, New York.

NORTH: General Jubal A. Early sidesteps Harper's Ferry and crosses the Potomac River to Shepherdstown, Maryland, with 12,000 men. His approach triggers an alarm in Washington, D.C., and cries for 24,000 volunteers are raised. The first officer to respond is General Lew Wallace, commander of the Middle Department at Baltimore, who rapidly moves 3,000 troops in the direction of Monocacy Junction, two miles east of Frederick.

SOUTH: General Andrew J. Smith leads a Union force of 14,000 men and 24 cannon from La Grange, Tennessee, toward Tupelo, Mississippi, intending to capture or destroy the army of General Nathan B. Forrest. He is ordered by General William T. Sherman to "bring Forrest to bay and whip him if possible."

WEST: General William T. Sherman brushes against Confederate defenses along the Chattahoochee River, Georgia. Finding General Joseph E. Johnston strongly dug in behind formidable fieldworks, he instructs General George H. Thomas and his Army of the Cumberland to demonstrate before their lines while General James B. McPherson's Army of the Tennessee feints a river crossing at Turner's Ferry, 12 miles downstream. General John M. Schofield also marches the Army of the Ohio across the Chattahoochee to outflank the defenders along Soap Creek.

July 6

NORTH: Confederates under General Jubal A. Early occupy Hagerstown, Maryland, demanding $200,000 for depredations committed earlier by Union forces in the Shenandoah Valley. Meanwhile, Union defenses at Monocacy Junction are bolstered by the arrival of the 8th Illinois Cavalry.

The 3rd Division, VI Corps, begins to move from Virginia to Baltimore, Maryland, to aid in the defense of the city.

July 7

NORTH: General Ulysses S. Grant, realizing the seriousness of Confederate thrusts in Maryland, rushes General James B. Rickett's division (VI Corps) to Baltimore, where it arrives that night, and marches for Monocacy Junction. There, it will join General Lew Wallace, holding the intersection with 3,000 men. Meanwhile, General Jubal A. Early's Confederates commence a leisurely advance on Middletown.

SOUTH: Union troops are forced off James Island, Charleston Harbor, South Carolina, sustaining 330 casualties to a Southern tally of 163. The most recent round of bombardment also drops another 784 rounds on the ruins of Fort Sumter.

NAVAL: The USS *Ariel, Sea Bird, Stonewall,* and *Rosalie* accompany Federal troops on a raid against Brookville and Bayport, Florida. They seize a quantity of cotton and burn a customs house before returning to the Anclote Keys.

July 8

POLITICS: President Abraham Lincoln pocket vetoes the Wade-Davis Reconstruction Act by refusing to sign it. This earns him the ire of Radical Republicans, who redouble their efforts to have Lincoln dropped as the party's standard-bearer in the fall presidential election.

NORTH: A hodgepodge of Union forces under General Lew Wallace assumes defensive positions behind the Monocacy River near Frederick, Maryland, to defend the national capital against General Jubal A. Early's advancing Confederates. On the day before battle, he cobbles together 6,000 men from various sources.

WEST: General Albion P. Howe succeeds Franz Sigel as commander at Harper's Ferry, West Virginia.

Union troops under General John M. Schofield cross the Chattahoochee River, Georgia, at Phillips' Ferry, near the mouth of Soap Creek, Georgia, thereby flanking General Joseph E. Johnston's defensive positions. Here, General Oliver O. Howard throws a pontoon bridge across Powell's Ferry while other troops establish lodgments along Pace's Ferry. Facing three hostile bridgeheads, Johnston orders an immediate withdrawal from the Chattahoochee line and heads for the defenses of Atlanta, only eight miles distant.

NAVAL: The USS *Fort Jackson* captures the British blockade-runner *Boston* off the South Carolina coast.

The USS *Sonoma* captures the Confederate steamer *Ida* near the Stono River, South Carolina.

The USS *Azalea* and *Sweet Briar* seize the Confederate schooner *Pocahontas* near Charleston, South Carolina.

The USS *Kanawha* forces the Confederate blockade-runner *Matagorda* aground near Galveston, where it is destroyed by cannon fire from the Penguin and Aroostook.

The Confederate raider CSS *Florida* under Charles M. Morris seizes and burns the Union whaler *Golconda* southwest of Bermuda.

July 9

POLITICS: The Fabian tactics of General Joseph E. Johnston, which have so infuriated General William T. Sherman, unfortunately draw the ire of President Jefferson Davis. Seeking a possible pretext to relieve Johnston, whom he personally dislikes, Davis dispatches General Braxton Bragg to his headquarters on a "fact-finding" mission. Johnston, meanwhile, withdraws from the Chattahoochee River to Peachtree Creek, only three miles north of Atlanta, Georgia.

NORTH: General Jubal A. Early repeats demands that the city of Hagerstown, Maryland, turn over $200,000 to compensate prior Union abuses in the Shenandoah Valley. He then proceeds to join the Battle of Monocacy, then in its initial stages.

General Lew Wallace and 6,000 Union troops confront 14,000 Confederates under General Jubal A. Early at Monocacy, Maryland. Early intends to turn the Union left flank from the onset and orders his cavalry under General John McCausland to find a ford across the Monocacy River. That accomplished, the corps of John C. Breckinridge crosses over to do battle with General James B. Rickett's division. Rickett's veterans easily repulse two Confederate charges by General John B. Gordon as the Southerners gradually work their way around the Union left. A final charge by General William R. Terry's Virginia brigade dislodges the Federals, and they break in disorder at 4:30 P.M. Wallace then orders his entire line withdrawn up the Baltimore Pike, which is accomplished in reasonably good order; Early declines to pursue. Union losses are 98 killed, 594 wounded, and 1,188 captured (1,880) while the Confederates suffer about 700 lost. The road to Washington, D.C. is now open, but Wallace's stand at Monocacy delays Early's advance an entire day, granting the capital additional time to strengthen its defenses.

WEST: A Union column of 14,000 men under General Andrew J. Smith crosses the Tallahatchie River at New Albany, Mississippi, and continues marching south toward Pontotoc.

The Confederate Army of Tennessee under General Joseph E. Johnston abandons the Chattahoochee River line, the last remaining natural barrier between Union forces and Atlanta, Georgia, and filters into the city's outer chain of defenses. Johnston, cannily outflanked again, had no alternative, but his latest withdrawal distresses the Confederate high command.

NAVAL: The Confederate raider CSS *Florida* under Lieutenant Charles M. Morris captures and burns the Union bark *Greenland* and the schooner *Margaret Y. Davis* off Cape Henry, Virginia.

The USS *Gettysburg* captures the Confederate steamer *Little Ada* off Cape Romain, South Carolina.

July 10

NORTH: Confederates under General Jubal A. Early pass through Rockville, Maryland, to confront Union defenders at Fort Stevens, outside Washington, D.C. The post is held only lightly by 209 inexperienced artillerists, but President Abraham Lincoln blithely exclaims, "Let us be vigilant but keep cool. I hope neither Baltimore nor Washington will be sacked." Fortunately, Union reinforcements are being rushed to the capital from several directions before the Confederates can mount an attack.

WEST: General Lovell H. Rosseau, commanding the District of Tennessee, receives orders from General William T. Sherman to lead a Union raid from Decatur, Alabama, against the Montgomery and West Point Railroad and do "all possible mischief." En route, he is pursued closely by General Stephen D. Lee, commander of the Department of Alabama, Mississippi, and East Louisiana.

NAVAL: The USS *Roebuck* captures the British blockade-runner *Terrapin* at Jupiter Inlet, Florida.

The USS *Monongahela, Lackawanna, Galena,* and *Sebago* attack the Confederate steamer *Virgin* off Fort Morgan, Mobile Bay, Alabama, forcing it aground. Southern cannon fire from the fort keeps the Union vessel at bay while the *Virgin* is subsequently refloated and towed into the bay.

The CSS *Florida* under Lieutenant Charles M. Morris captures and burns the Union bark *General Berry* 35 miles off the Maryland coast. It then proceeds to seize the schooner *Howard,* the bark *Zelinda,* and the steamer *Electric Spark* in the same vicinity. Such depredation alarms government and civilian officials.

The USS *Mount Vernon* and *Monticello* are detached from the South Atlantic Blockading Squadron to search for the CSS *Florida.* The USS *Ino* is disguised further as a merchantman in an attempt to lure the Confederate raider into battle.

July 11

NORTH: General Robert E. Rode's Confederate division marches to within gunshot of Fort Stevens, District of Columbia, then manned by only 209 gunners. Fortunately, General Jubal A. Early's command is exhausted by a combination of intensely hot weather and hard marching and elects not to attack. Had he done so the Confederates might have easily pushed on to Washington, D.C., itself. This fortuitous delay allows Federal defenses to congeal under the direction of General Christopher Augur, who throws skirmishers forward to engage the Southerners. Meanwhile, the 1st and 2nd Divisions of General Horatio G. Wright's VI Corps, joined by elements of General Quincy A. Gilmore's XIX Corps, arrive to bolster the city's defenses. Even President Abraham Lincoln himself shows up as an onlooker and to give encouragement to the outnumbered garrison. That evening, Early decides to attack Fort Stevens on the morrow and then reverses himself after learning of Union reinforcements.

SOUTH: General Edward O. C. Ord assumes command of the VIII Corps and the Union Middle Department, Virginia.

WEST: General Andrew J. Smith's column of 14,000 men reaches Pontotoc, Mississippi, while Confederates under General Nathan B. Forrest begin to mass at nearby Okolona, intending to lure him into a large ambush.

NAVAL: Armed boats from the USS *James L. Davis* land at Tampa, Florida, to destroy a large Confederate saltworks.

July 12

NORTH: Confederates under General Jubal A. Early withdraw from the Washington, D.C., region, cautiously pursued by General Horatio G. Wright's Federal troops. The division of General Richard E. Rodes is somewhat roughly handled in the ensuing chase, but it escapes intact. For a few tense moments, President Abraham Lincoln, visiting the parapets, is under enemy fire, and a young army officer, Oliver Wendell Holmes (a future Supreme Court justice) inadvertently shouts, "Get down, you fool!" While retreating, the Southerners burn down the house of Postmaster General Montgomery Blair.

NAVAL: The USS *Whitehead* and *Ceres,* accompanied by the steamer transport *Ella May,* venture up the Scuppernong River as far as Columbia, North Carolina. There, they destroy a bridge and some grain stores before withdrawing.

The USS *Penobscot* captures the Confederate blockade-runner *James Williams* off Galveston, Texas.

A combined Union expedition against Bayport, Florida, safely returns to the Anclote Keys, having burned several hundred bales of cotton and a customshouse.

July 13

NORTH: General Horatio G. Wright assumes command of Union defenses in and around Washington, D.C., as Confederates under General Jubal A. Early withdraw toward Leesburg to recross the Potomac River.

SOUTH: General Braxton Bragg, sent to General Joseph E. Johnston's headquarters in Georgia to assess matters, files a predictably negative report of that commander to President Jefferson Davis. "It is a sad alternative, but the case seems hopeless in present hands," Bragg writes. "The means are surely adequate if properly employed, especially the cavalry is ample." Davis then prepares to make a dramatic change in commanders.

WEST: General Andrew J. Smith's column, heading south, suddenly veers east to Tupelo, Mississippi, ostensibly to sever the Mobile and Ohio Railroad. Smith actually is concerned that General Nathan B. Forrest is waiting to entrap him in the prairie region around nearby Okolona. Confederate cavalry begin to nip at Smith's rear and flanks, but they are largely deflected. Forrest remains eager to attack but still awaits the arrival of his superior, General Stephen D. Lee, and 2,000 reinforcements.

General William T. Sherman finishes moving the bulk of his forces across the Chattahootchee River, Georgia.

General Napoleon B. Buford leads a column of Union cavalry in pursuit of Confederate raiders under General Joseph O. Shelby in western Tennessee.

NAVAL: Armed boats from the USS *Vicksburg* destroy all bridges over the South River to preclude large-scale Confederate raids near Annapolis, Maryland.

July 14

WEST: General Jubal A. Early crosses the Potomac River at White's Ferry and arrives back in Leesburg, Virginia. Union forces under General Horatio G. Wright decline to pursue.

A force of 7,500 Confederates under Generals Stephen D. Lee and Nathan B. Forrest gathers to attack Union positions outside Tupelo, Mississippi. General Andrew J. Smith has positioned his 14,000 troops expertly along a low ridge with secure flanks and a clear field of fire, awaiting their approach. The Confederate attack launches at 7:00 A.M. and continues for three hours. They make repeated and heroic charges against the waiting Federals, only to be decimated by concentrated musketry and artillery fire. By 1:00 P.M., Lee calls off the action and orders a withdrawal. Smith, enjoying a two-to one advantage in numbers, could have counterattacked and easily smashed the battered Confederates, but he likewise prepares to retreat. The Battle of Tupelo is a surprising tactical victory for the North, but it leaves Forrest's command intact and still functioning. Union losses are 77 killed, 559 wounded, and 39 missing (674) to a Confederate tally of 210 dead and 1,116 injured (1,326).

NAVAL: The USS *Pequot* and *Commodore Morris* bombard Confederate batteries at Malvern Hill, Virginia, in an action lasting four hours.

The USS *Paul Jones* is captured in the Ossabaw Sound, Georgia, while hunting the CSS *Water Witch*.

July 15

NORTH: Union forces under General Horatio K. Wright remain poised north of the Potomac River opposite Leesburg, Virginia, but they do not cross. General Jubal A. Early's Confederates continue loitering in and around that town to rest and recuperate.

WEST: General Andrew J. Smith's Union column files through Tupelo, Mississippi, en route to Tennessee. Confederates under General Nathan B. Forrest, still smarting from their earlier reverse, hound his rear guard incessantly until their leader is painfully wounded.

July 16

POLITICS: A pensive president Jefferson Davis cables General Joseph E. Johnston at Atlanta, Georgia, "I wish to hear from you as to present situation and your plan of operations so specifically as will enable me to anticipate events." Johnston matter of factly replies, "As the enemy is double our number, we must be on the defensive. My plan of operations must therefore depend upon that of the enemy."

SOUTH: While General Joseph E. Johnston continues strengthening the defenses of Atlanta, Georgia, Union forces under General James B. McPherson begin an enveloping movement through Decatur.

WEST: General Jubal A. Early's Confederates reenter the Shenandoah Valley, unencumbered by a Union pursuit, and push on toward Berryville.

NAVAL: Confederate artillery along the James River, Virginia, engage the USS *Mendota, Pequot,* and *Commodore Morris* at Four Mile Creek. *Mendota* is struck several times and sustains damage; thereafter, enemy activity temporarily closes navigation on the James River.

July 17

WEST: General Jubal A. Early reaches Strasburg, Virginia, having brushed aside General David Hunter's force at Snicker's Ferry.

General Joseph E. Johnston is preparing to pounce on the isolated Army of the Cumberland under General George H. Thomas at Peachtree Creek, Georgia. Suddenly, a telegraph from President Jefferson Davis arrives at his headquarters, outlining his replacement by General John B. Hood, an impetuous, aggressive fighter. "As you failed to arrest the advance of the enemy to the vicinity of Atlanta," it read, "far in the interior of Georgia, and express no confidence that you can defeat or repel him, your are hereby relieved from the command of the Army and Department of Tennessee." Davis's meddling and personal antipathy for the irritable yet highly capable Johnston marks a dramatic turning point in the course of events. As General William T. Sherman declares, Confederate authorities "rendered us most valuable service."

General William T. Sherman's army crosses the Chattahoochee River, only eight miles from Atlanta, Georgia, and approaches the city and its environs.

July 18
POLITICS: President Abraham Lincoln renews his call for 500,000 volunteers and draftees, an unpopular move that militates against his reelection chances.

President Jefferson Davis appoints George A. Trenholm of South Carolina as the new Confederate secretary of the treasury.

With the Union army nearing the gates of Atlanta, Georgia, Mayor Thomas Calhoun and the city council convene for the last time, thereby concluding the rule of municipal government.

SOUTH: John B. Hood is promoted to lieutenant general, C.S.A., the last such officer appointed, and he succeeds General Joseph E. Johnston.

Union forces under General George H. Thomas push Confederate cavalry across Peachtree Creek, Georgia, prior to crossing three miles north of Atlanta. Capitalizing on plans drawn up by the recently relieved General Joseph E. Johnston, General John B. Hood intends to catch Federal troops in the act of crossing and possibly defeat them piecemeal.

WEST: Confederates under General Jubal A. Early repulse a Union attack on them at Cool Spring, Virginia.

July 19
WEST: Superior Union forces press General Jubal A. Early's Confederates at Berry's Ford and Ashby's Gap, Virginia, as they fall back toward Winchester.

As Union troops under General James B. McPherson push through Decatur, Georgia, the Army of the Cumberland under General George H. Thomas occupies Peachtree Creek to the north. General John B. Hood also begins to marshal Confederate forces for a massive strike against Thomas.

July 20
WEST: Union cavalry under General William W. Averell surprise a brigade from General Stephen D. Ramseur's division at Stephenson's Depot, West Virginia. Confederate losses are 73 dead, 130 wounded, and 267 captured, along with four cannon. Meanwhile, General Jubal A. Early continues withdrawing up the Shenandoah Valley and finally settles in at Strasburg.

No sooner does the 20,000-man Army of the Cumberland under General George H. Thomas cross Peachtree Creek, Georgia, three miles north of Atlanta, than it is heavily attacked by 19,000 Confederates under the newly appointed general John B. Hood. For this purpose, Hood arrays General Alexander P. Stewart's corps on the left, General William J. Hardee's line in the center, and General Benjamin F. Cheatham's corps on the right. However, Cheatham proves slow in getting into position, and the Confederate attack does not materialize until 4:00 P.M., giving the Federals ample time to prepare defenses. Fighting begins on the Union left, where two of Cheatham's divisions charge General John Newton's division, IV Corps. Despite turning Newton's left and taking some headway, the Southerners are repulsed gradually by heavy artillery fire. In the center, Stewart directs General Einfield S. Featherston's division into a gap between the Union divisions of General John W. Geary and William T. Ward. Fighting proves fierce, and the 26th Wisconsin, surrounded on a hillside, scavenges ammunition from Confederate fallen to hold their position. Eventually, a Union countercharge across the line throws Featherston back to his original positions.

The hardest fighting of the day occurs on the right where General Edward C. Walthall's Confederates penetrate the division of Generals Alpheus S. Williams and John W. Geary, XX Corps. Infiltrating along numerous ravines, they manage to surround Geary on three sides and press him hard for three hours. The 61st Ohio, which loses half its strength, shoots down charging Confederates within 10 feet of its line, but holds fast. A Southern breakthrough briefly threatening the flank and rear of General Joseph F. Knipe's division also is repelled by artillery fire. His gambit having failed, Hood suspends the action at 7:00 P.M. and orders a retreat.

Peachtree Creek is the first of Hood's highly audacious but ultimately futile attempts to save Atlanta, and it costs him 2,500 men to a Union tally of 1,779 killed, wounded, and missing. Nonetheless, he prepares to regain lost ground as soon as circumstances favor the offensive.

As the Army of the Tennessee under General James B. McPherson closes in on Atlanta, Georgia, from the east, his troops receive enfilade fire from a position known as Bald Hill. General Walter Q. Gresham is wounded, his 4th Division is galled by Confederate artillery, and McPherson orders troops under General Mortimer D. Leggett to storm the strong point on the morrow.

The Union column under General Andrew J. Smith returns to La Grange, Tennessee, and boards trains for Memphis. His campaign against General Nathan B. Forrest is cancelled, ostensibly for want of supplies, and disappoints the Union high command. However, it did keep the supply lines of General William T. Sherman open for several critical weeks as Confederate raiders are forced to regroup.

July 21

WEST: General George Crook's force of 8,500 men occupies Winchester, Virginia, and he dispatches cavalry under General William W. Averell to divine Confederate intentions farther up the Shenandoah Valley.

General James B. McPherson's Union attack Confederate defenders under General Patrick R. Cleburne at Bald Hill outside Atlanta, Georgia. General Mortimer D. Leggett's men go forward covered by intense Union artillery fire and charge up the slopes. Both sides lose about 350 casualties before the Federals stand victorious on the hillcrest, and Cleburne withdraws. The Union now enjoys a vantage point from which artillery fire can rain down on the city.

Unbeknownst to McPherson, General John B. Hood is preparing a massive strike against his Army of the Tennessee. To that end, he orders the corps of General

William J. Hardee to slip carefully out from behind its fortifications in Atlanta, execute a 15-mile night march to Decatur, and place his troops behind the Union flank and rear. Hood is counting on McPherson's lack of a cavalry screen to render Hardee's approach undetectable.

NAVAL: The USS *Prairie Bird* captures the steamer *Union* on the Mississippi River for trading with the enemy.

July 22

POLITICS: President Jefferson Davis orders General Edmund Kirby-Smith to assist the Army of Tennessee under General John B. Hood. In light of the fact that Federal gunboats patrol the Mississippi River, this proves an impossible order to fulfill.

SOUTH: General Edward O. C. Ord officially is made commander of the XVIII Corps, Army of the Potomac.

WEST: General Horatio K. Wright and his VI Corps are withdrawn from the Shenandoah region, and command devolves on General George Crook at Kernstown, Virginia. General Jubal A. Early, with Confederate forces concentrated behind Cedar Creek near Strasburg, welcomes the news and prepares to advance and attack scattered Union forces.

General Lovell H. Rosseau concludes his successful raid into northern Alabama, having destroyed miles of track belonging to the Montgomery and West Point Railroad. His losses are 12 killed and 30 wounded.

General John B. Hood initiates the Battle of Atlanta by ordering General William J. Hardee's corps to strike at the Army of the Tennessee under General James B. McPherson. The Southerners slightly outnumber their opponents by 36,000 to 30,000. However, Hardee errs by not pushing troops far enough to the east, and instead of turning McPherson's left flank, he strikes it head on. The Confederate divisions of Generals William H. T. Walker and William B. Bate then charge the Federals ferociously but are repelled in bloody fighting by the XVI Corps of General Grenville M. Dodge. Tragedy then strikes Union forces as McPherson, reconnoitering ahead of his troops, encounters a Confederate picket and is shot dead. General James A. Logan succeeds him in command just as the veteran divisions of Generals Patrick R. Cleburne and George E. Manley lace into General Francis M. Blair's XVII Corps on the Union right. Fighting is intense and deadly as Southerners exploit a gap in the Federal line, but the bluecoats hold firm until a reserve brigade arrives and forces their assailants back.

The final act to play out occurs at the Union center, when Hood commits General Benjamin F. Cheatham's corps and General Gustavus W. Smith's Georgia militia against Logan's own XV Corps. Charging Confederates briefly penetrate Union lines as far as the Georgia Railroad and then stall in the face of stiffening resistance. Reinforced Federals then storm across the field in turn, driving the graycoats before them and retaking their position. Repulsed across the line, Hood concedes defeat and withdraws.

Hood's second sortie from Atlanta proves another failure that costs him 8,000 casualties. Union losses are 430 killed, 1,559 wounded, and 1,733 missing (3,722). The foremost fatality is the popular and capable McPherson, a close friend and confident of his fellow Ohioan, General William T. Sherman.

NAVAL: An armed landing party from the USS *Oneida* captures a Confederate cavalry patrol near Fort Morgan, Mobile Bay, Alabama.

July 23

POLITICS: The Louisiana State Convention adopts a new constitution that outlaws slavery.

SOUTH: General Robert E. Lee, wary of a Union thrust north of the James River, orders General Joseph B. Kershaw to move his division to the vicinity of Darbytown, Virginia, and await developments.

General David B. Birney takes charge of the X Corps, Army of the Potomac.

WEST: Union cavalry under General Alfred N. Duffie skirmish with Confederate troopers two miles south of Winchester, Virginia, amid telling signs of a Southern resurgence in the Shenandoah Valley. In fact, General Jubal A. Early is close at hand with 14,000 men and intends to strike the 8,500-man garrison of General George Crook's VIII Corps at Kernstown. That commander, alerted as to Confederate intentions, assumes defensive positions below the town.

NAVAL: The USS *Prairie Bird* rescues 350 survivors from the sinking army transport *B. M. Bunyan* after it hits a snag off Shipworth's Landing, Mississippi.

July 24

WEST: General Jubal A. Early's 14,000 Confederates engage the smaller Union VIII Corps under General George Crook at Kernstown, Virginia. Early, who deploys his army before the town, orders General John C. Breckinridge to outflank the Federals position on their left as Generals John B. Gordon and Gabriel C. Wharton engage them frontally. Crook's 8,500 men initially withstand several charges until they are finally flanked by Breckinridge while struck frontally by Gordon. They bolt from the field and flee up the Valley Pike toward Bunker Hill, West Virginia, 12 miles distant. Crook's defeat would have been much costlier, but Early mishandles his cavalry, and he escapes intact. Union losses are 1,185, including 479 captured; Confederate casualties are unknown but presumably lighter. This easy triumph further emboldens the aggressive Early, who prepares his command for a new invasion of Pennsylvania. Unfortunately for the South, his success also convinces the political establishment in Washington, D.C., that vigorous new leadership is necessary to secure the Shenandoah region.

NAVAL: Confederate raiders capture and burn the steamer *Kingston* after it grounds near Windmill Point on the Virginia shore.

July 25

WEST: Confederates under General Jubal A. Early pursue the defeated Federals of General George Crook to Bunker Hill, West Virginia. Heavy rain impedes marching on both sides.

General William T. Sherman orders the cavalry division of General George Stoneman to prepare for an extended raid into the Georgia countryside for the purpose of cutting the Macon and Western Railroad into Atlanta. He also shifts the axis of his approach toward that city from north and east to west, and orders the Army of the Tennessee, now under General John A. Logan, to march from the right wing to the left. Howard's objective is the town of East Point, Georgia, where the Macon and Western and Atlanta and West Point railroads converge. These tracks represent General John B. Hood's last line of supply to and from Atlanta.

General John Pope, commanding the Department of the Northwest, orders a new expedition against hostile Lakota (Sioux).

NAVAL: Acting master's mate John Woodman leads a daring night reconnaissance effort up the Roanoke River to Plymouth, North Carolina, to ascertain the condition of the Confederate ram CSS *Albemarle*. This imposing warship has remained an object of Union consternation for several months and restricts them from committing offensive operations in and around Plymouth.

The USS *Undine* strikes a snag in the Tennessee River near Clifton, Tennessee, and sinks. Beforehand, acting master John L. Bryant removes several cannon and plants them in the city to defend it from marauding Confederates.

July 26

SOUTH: General Ulysses S. Grant orders Generals Winfield S. Hancock and Philip H. Sheridan to mount a large-scale diversionary attack north of the James River to assist the upcoming assault on Petersburg, slated for July 30. He anticipates that the move will force General Robert E. Lee to shift his men northward, thereby weakening the city's defenses in time for Grant's main attack. Furthermore, should the diversion succeed, Sheridan is to take his troopers on a raid against either Richmond, Virginia, or the Virginia Central Railroad.

General Dabney H. Maury is assigned commander of the Confederate Department of Alabama, Mississippi, and East Louisiana.

WEST: General Oliver O. Howard formally succeeds to command the Army of the Tennessee, replacing the slain James B. McPherson. General David S. Stanley then replaces him as head of the IV Corps.

Union cavalry under General George A. Stoneman depart the Atlanta, Georgia, region on a major raid toward Macon. He is ordered to feint east toward Augusta before turning southwest toward his objective at Lovejoy's Station. There, Stoneman will also link up with another mounted division under General Edward M. McCook.

NAVAL: A landing party from the USS *Shokokon* is attacked at Turkey Bend, Virginia, forcing that vessel to come up and lend supporting fire.

July 27

NORTH: General Henry W. Halleck, chief of staff, assumes new responsibilities as head of the Union Middle Department, and the Departments of Washington, West Virginia, and the Susquehanna.

SOUTH: General Winfield S. Hancock moves his II Corps over the James River, closely followed by General Philip H. Sheridan's cavalry division. Advancing on New Market, Virginia, as far as Deep Bottom Run, their column encounters unexpectedly heavy resistance from Confederates under General Cadmus M. Wilcox. Sheridan, meanwhile, shifts troopers northward around Hancock's right flank and begins to probe down the Darbytown Road before running headlong into General

Henry Heth's division. General Ulysses S. Grant subsequently arrives on the scene to supervise Union operations north of the James River.

WEST: Rather than storm the heavily fortified defenses of Atlanta, Georgia, General William T. Sherman resolves on partial siege while dispatching cavalry raids against railroads and other supply lines into the city.

General Joseph Hooker resigns as commander of the XX Corps in a snit and is replaced by General Alpheus S. Williams.

General George Stoneman disregards orders to ride toward Lovejoy's Station, Georgia, and gallops due south, leaving General Kenner Garrard and 2,000 troopers to hold Flat Rock. Stoneman hopes to score a spectacular coup by liberating thousands of Union prisoners held at Macon and Andersonville.

SOUTHWEST: Confederate Cherokees under General Stand Watie and Texas cavalry under Colonel Richard M. Gano capture a small Union outpost near Fort Smith, Arkansas.

NAVAL: The Federal tugs *Belle, Martin,* and *Hoyt* are fitted with spar torpedoes off New Bern, North Carolina, which are intended for use against any Confederate ironclads in that vicinity.

Union boat crews secretly slip into Mobile Bay, Alabama, at night, and begin to mark Confederate torpedo fields with buoys.

July 28

SOUTH: As Union forces under General Winfield S. Hancock and Philip H. Sheridan continue probing Confederate lines along the Darbytown Road, Virginia, General Joseph B. Kershaw's Confederates surprise and charge the Union troopers. Sheridan's force dismounts and repulses the attack, and they seize 300 prisoners and two battle flags. General Ulysses S. Grant, however, views Southern defenses in the vicinity as impenetrable, and he orders Hancock and Sheridan withdrawn back to the Petersburg lines. Three days of fighting cost the Union 334 casualties.

WEST: General Jubal A. Early dispatches 2,500 cavalry under General John McCausland with orders to seize Chambersburg, Pennsylvania. He is then to demand money and gold from the inhabitants or burn the village to the ground.

General Oliver O. Howard and the Army of the Tennessee advance on East Point, Georgia, determined to sever the last remaining rail lines into Atlanta. But Confederate general John B. Hood divines Howard's intent and tries to stay an elaborate ambush by dispatching the corps of Generals Stephen D. Lee and Alexander P. Stewart to hit the Union left flank near Ezra Church and roll it up. The Southerners advance as ordered, but instead of hitting Howard's flank, they mistakenly veer into the front of General John A. Logan's VX Corps. The tactically astute Logan barricades his men at right angles to Howard's line and is strongly positioned to resist an attack. Lee nonetheless commits his men to charge and is beaten off bloodily three times. Stewart then adds his command to the fray and likewise is defeated. By the time the Confederates depart Ezra Church, they have lost upward of 5,000 men to a Union tally of only 562. The battle did stop Union forces from severing Atlanta's supply line, but it so depletes the Army of Tennessee that General John B. Hood is hereafter forced on the defensive.

Confederate cavalry under General Joseph Wheeler attack and defeat Union troopers under General Kenner Garrard at Flatshoals, Georgia, forcing him to withdraw north.

General Alfred Sully engages a large number of hostile Teton Lakota (Sioux) Indians in their camp at Killdeer Mountain (North Dakota). Sully is looking for remnants of the Santee (Eastern Sioux) warriors who had instigated a bloody uprising in Minnesota two years earlier, especially their notorious chief Inkpaduta. He sought refuge among his Teton brethren, who prepare to give battle rather than surrender him. Sully takes the unusual measure of deploying his 3,000 men in a hollow square and advancing in this formation toward the camp. This walking wall of firepower gradually evicts the Teton from their campsite, and they flee, losing an estimated 150 warriors. Sully sustains five killed and 10 wounded.

SOUTHWEST: Confederate Cherokee under General Stand Watie and Texas cavalry under Colonel Richard M. Gano attack and destroy Union haying operations at Blackburn's Prairie, Indian Territory.

NAVAL: The USS *Agwam* and *Mendota* bombard Confederate artillery at Four Mile Creek on the James River, Virginia.

July 29
NORTH: Confederate cavalry under General John McCausland cross the Potomac River at Cave Spring, west of Williamsport, Maryland, causing a local panic. His progress is somewhat delayed by a small body of Federal troops, whose determined stand enables trains to depart Chambersburg, Pennsylvania, with valuable supplies and equipment.

SOUTH: With an explosive-laden tunnel successfully completed beneath Confederate lines outside Petersburg, Virginia, General Ambrose E. Burnside prepares General Edward Ferrero's division of African Americans to charge into the breech following its detonation. Burnside, however, is stopped by Generals Ulysses S. Grant and George Gordon Meade, who feel they might be accused of sacrificing black troops if the scheme backfires. Burnside thereupon orders one of his three untrained, white divisions into line. Lots are drawn, and it falls on General James H. Ledlie to spearhead the assault.

WEST: Union cavalry under General Edward M. McCook seize Jonesboro, Georgia, and begin to tear up track and demolish rolling stock.

NAVAL: The USS *Whitehead* escorts army steamers *Thomas Coyler* and *Massasoit* up the Chowan River, North Carolina, capturing the Confederate steamer *Arrow* en route.

July 30
NORTH: A force of 2,500 Confederate cavalry under General John McCausland occupies Chambersburg, Pennsylvania, at 5:30 A.M. McCausland then rouses the inhabitants out of bed and demands either $100,000 in gold or $500,00 in cash to compensate for houses previously burned in the Shenandoah Valley. When the residents fail to produce the amount demanded, Southerners, somewhat abetted by liquor, systematically begin to fire the town. By early afternoon, 550 houses smolder

in ruins, with 3,000 people homeless. McCausland then gallops off toward McConnellsburg. The damage inflicted amounts to $1.6 million.

South: At 3:30 A.M., the "Battle of the Crater" unfolds as fuses to an explosive-laden tunnel dug beneath Confederate lines at Petersburg are lit. They fail to explode as planned, so volunteers are sent back down the shaft to relight them. At 4:45 A.M., the ground beneath Elliott's Salient erupts furiously, destroying an artillery emplacement and killing 278 South Carolinian troops. The Union forces, equally stunned, pause for 15 minutes before charging into the smoking crater, measuring 170 feet long, 80 feet wide, and 30 feet deep. But General James H. Ledlie absents himself from the proceedings, and his advance stalls at the bottom of the pit. Confederate forces, recovering from the shock, quickly rush reinforcements to the threatened point and shoot downward into the milling, leaderless Federals. General Edward Ferrero's African-American division is then committed to the fray and is repelled bloodily at the crater's rim by Confederates under General William Mahone. By 1:00 P.M., the attack, a disastrous failure, is called off. Union losses amount to 504 killed, 1,881 wounded, and 1,413 missing (3,798), while the Southerners suffer 361 killed, 727 injured, and 403 missing (1,491). Grant himself calls it "the saddest affair I ever witnessed in the war."

West: General Henry W. Slocum becomes commander of the Union XX Corps in Georgia.

Union cavalry under General Edward M. McCook are defeated by General Joseph Wheeler's troopers at Newman, Georgia. Surrounded by five enemy brigades, McCook orders his men to cut their way through enemy lines and regroup north of the Chattahoochee River. This desperate maneuver succeeds, although Union losses include 500 men, their pack train, and two cannon.

General George Stoneman's cavalry engage 2,500 Confederates and Georgia militia outside Macon, Georgia. The Kentucky troopers under his command charge the rebel barricades and are repulsed. But no further attacks are mounted as the enlistment period for these volunteers is about to expire and they are far more interested in surviving than fighting. Disgusted, Stoneman has little recourse but to abandon plans to liberate Union prisoners at Andersonville and spurs his command south toward Pensacola, Florida.

Southwest: Confederate forces reoccupy Brownstown, Texas.

Confederate Cherokee under General Stand Watie and Texas cavalry under Colonel Richard M. Gano sack and destroy a Fort Smith commissary post, absconding with $130,000 worth of food and clothing.

Naval: A landing party from the USS *Potomska* captures and wrecks two Confederate saltworks on the Black River, Georgia. However, the men are hotly pursued by Confederates, and only the presence of their rapid-fire Spencer carbines prevents their capture.

July 31

North: General John McCausland's Confederate cavalry occupy Hancock, Maryland, from which he demands $30,000 and cooked rations. The men then ride onto Bevansville for the evening.

West: General George Stoneman's cavalry column departs the outskirts of Macon, Georgia, and attempts circling around the city to cross the Ocmulgee River. He advances as far as Hillsboro before being set upon by General Alfred Iverson and three brigades of Confederate troopers near Sunshine Church. Stoneman tries fighting his way out of encirclement but ultimately surrenders with 700 men. However, brigades under Colonels Horace Capron and Silas Adams cut themselves free and gallop off with Colonel's William C. P. Breckinridge's Confederates giving chase. Stoneman's ambitious raid is the biggest cavalry fiasco of the war and nearly paralyzes General William T. Sherman's mounted arm for several weeks.

Naval: With the assistance of the pump steamer *Little Champion*, the USS *Undine* is refloated on the Tennessee River, repaired, and gradually pressed back into service.

August 1

North: General Philip H. Sheridan is chosen to head the Army of the Shenandoah with the specific goal of defeating Confederate forces under General Jubal A. Early.

Confederate cavalry under General John McCausland ride through Cumberland, Maryland, skirmish with Union forces under General Benjamin F. Kelley en route, and then settle in near Old Town for the evening.

West: Fighting continues between the mounted forces of Generals Napoleon B. Buford and Joseph O. Shelby at Bardstown and New Haven, Kentucky.

Union artillery commences a protracted bombardment of Atlanta, Georgia.

A Union cavalry column under Colonels Horace Capron and Silas Adams advances toward Athens, Georgia, intending to take the town by storm, but they abandon the attempt after being misled by a guide. The two columns then separate and ride on, hotly pursued by Colonel William C. P. Breckinridge's Confederate troopers.

Union cavalry under General Alfred Pleasonton overrun several guerrilla camps near Independence, Missouri.

August 2

North: General John McCausland's Confederate cavalry column disperses a Union artillery detachment and captures Old Town, Maryland, astride the Potomac River. They then cross the river and set up an encampment at Springfield, West Virginia.

South: Union forces under General Edward R. S. Canby begin a concerted advance on Mobile, Alabama, while General Gordon Granger commands troops landing in Mobile Bay.

Southwest: Confederate Cherokee under General Stand Watie and Texas cavalry under Colonel Richard M. Gano briefly shell Fort Smith, Arkansas.

Naval: A landing party of 115 Union sailors under Commander George M. Colvocoresses of the USS *Saratoga* raids a Confederate coastal guard meeting at McIntosh Court House, Georgia, and returns with 26 captives and 22 horses.

Confederate agents abandon attempts to sail the CSS *Rappahannock* out of French waters as the government will allow only a 35-man crew.

August 3

North: General Jubal A. Early's Confederates withdraw from Maryland and back into West Virginia.

General David Hunter dispatches 1,500 Union cavalry under General William W. Averell from West Virginia into Maryland to find and defeat Confederate raiders under General John McCausland.

A Union cavalry column under Colonel Horace Capron encamps at Jug Tavern, Georgia, where it is suddenly attacked at dawn by Confederate troopers under Colonel William C. P. Breckinridge. The routed Federals hastily scamper across a nearby bridge until it collapses into Mulberry Creek, drowning scores of men and horses. Union losses are estimated at 250.

SOUTH: General Gordon Granger lands 1,300 Union troops on Dauphin Island, Alabama, but fails to storm Fort Gaines at the entrance of Mobile Bay. He spends the next two days building artillery emplacements for a siege.

WEST: General Andrew J. Smith is dispatched on another expedition to Columbus, Mississippi, against the ever-troublesome General Nathan B. Forrest.

NAVAL: The USS *Miami* bombards Confederate artillery positions at Wilcox's Landing, Virginia.

Armed Union boats make a final nighttime foray into Mobile Bay, Alabama, marking Confederate torpedo fields with buoys and disabling them when practical.

August 4

WEST: Confederate cavalry under General John McCausland attack part of the Baltimore and Ohio Railroad at New Creek, West Virginia, but they are repulsed. They then ride to a new encampment at nearby Moorefield to rest their mounts.

General William T. Sherman, pursuant to a strategy of circling Atlanta, Georgia, from the west, orders General John M. Schofield's Army of the Ohio, reinforced by General John M. Palmers XIV Corps, Army of the Tennessee, to storm Confederate earthworks near Utoy Creek. Success here places him within two miles of the strategic railroad junction at East Point.

General Sterling Price receives permission from Confederate authorities to prepare an invasion of Missouri for the early fall.

NAVAL: The USS *Miami* and *Osceola* attack and disperse Confederate artillery gathered near Harrison's Landing on the James River, Virginia.

August 5

POLITICS: Radical Republicans Benjamin Wade and Henry W. Davis denounce President Abraham Lincoln for vetoing the bill they have sponsored and openly campaign to depose him. "The authority of Congress is paramount and must be respected," they insist.

NORTH: Union cavalry under General William W. Averell is apprised of recent Confederate activity at New Creek, West Virginia, and stealthily begin to approach their encampment at Moorefield.

SOUTH: Confederate forces abandon Fort Powell, Mobile Bay, Alabama, once Federal warships slip past and begin to bombard it from behind.

WEST: General John M. Schofield maneuvers the Army of the Ohio to assault Confederate defenses at Utoy Creek, Georgia, but a command dispute with General John M. Palmer, XIV Corps, delays his projected assault until the following day. During the impasse, General William B. Bate's Confederate division strengthens his position with abatis and earthworks.

NAVAL: At 6:00 A.M., Admiral David G. Farragut launches an all-out attack to capture Mobile Bay, Alabama. He approaches his objective with the ironclad monitors USS *Tecumseh, Manhattan, Winnebago,* and *Chickasaw* in the van while his remaining 14 wooden warships are lashed together in pairs, with smaller vessels tied on the outside and away from Confederate defenses. The armada then approaches the bay, and heavy cannon at Fort Morgan commence to shell them as they pass by. Disaster then suddenly strikes when *Tecumseh* detonates a torpedo and sinks 30 seconds later with the loss of 90 crewmen. *Brooklyn,* the next lead vessel, suddenly reverses its engine and backs up, causing the squadron to jam up dangerously. An anxious Farragut, lashed to the rigging of his screw sloop *Hartford,* inquires what the problem is, and *Brooklyn*'s captain responds "torpedoes!" "Damn the torpedoes, full speed ahead!" is Farragut's immortal (and apocryphal) reply, so *Hartford* plunges directly into the Confederate minefield. The fleet immediately closes up and steams ahead while, miraculously, no other vessels are lost.

Having overcome one major obstacle, Farragut next confronts the large Confederate ram CSS *Tennessee* under Admiral James Buchanan. *Tennessee* sorties against the entire Union fleet, escorted by smaller warships *Selma, Morgan,* and *Gaines,* and tries ramming the *Hartford.* Farragut easily dodges his slower adversary while all 17 ships of the squadron pummel it with intense cannon fire. In short order, the *Gaines* sinks, *Selma* surrenders, and *Morgan* beaches itself. This leaves *Tennessee* alone to face the entire Union fleet, and Buchanan orders it under the protection of Fort Morgan's guns to effect repairs.

Battle of Mobile Bay August 5, 1864 Painting by Xanthus Smith, 1890 *(U.S. Naval Academy Museum)*

By 9:00 A.M., Buchanan judges the battle lost but refuses to surrender. He then leads the *Tennessee* out on a suicide mission against Farragut's squadron in the bay. Faster Union vessels quickly surround the lumbering ram as it fails to strike several targets, while rifled cannon fire blasts away its smokestack and steering chains. His ship now adrift and armor plates buckling under the weight of Union ordnance, the seriously wounded Buchanan finally lowers his flag at 10:00 A.M. By dint of daring and expert seamanship, Farragut wins his second decisive gamble of the Civil War and closes the Confederacy's last remaining port on the Gulf Coast. Union losses are 145 killed and 170 wounded while the defeated Southerners report 12 dead and 20 injured.

August 6

SOUTH: Responding to pleas from General Jubal A. Early in the Shenandoah Valley, General Robert E. Lee dispatches the infantry division of Joseph B. Kershaw and the cavalry division of General Fitzhugh Lee from Richmond, Virginia, as reinforcements. With them, Lee hopes that Early may blunt the new Federal offensive developing against him.

WEST: General Philip H. Sheridan arrives at Harper's Ferry, West Virginia, to assume command of the Army of the Shenandoah. This consists of the VI Corps under General Horatio G. Wright, the VIII Corps under General George Crook, and the XIX Corps under General William H. Emory, and three cavalry divisions under General Alfred T. A. Torbert—a total of 43,000 men.

General William W. Averell passes through Romney, West Virginia, en route to Confederate encampments near Moorefield, taking great precautions to seize all outlaying pickets first. Once positioned, he intends to attack the main camp directly while sending a detachment to strike from the east. Averell rests his horses for several hours and then begins to advance on his quarry, covered by early morning darkness.

General John M. Schofield attacks Utoy Creek, Georgia, to seize the nearby railroad junction at East Point. He dispatches two brigades under Generals Jacob B. Cox and Milo Hascall at 10:00 A.M., but the former is pinned down by enemy fire from across Sandtown Road. Cox then rallies and charges three times but is repulsed with heavy losses. On his right, Hascall enjoys better success driving the Southerners back, but fighting ceases after nightfall and a heavy rain.

General Frederick Steele launches a campaign from Little Rock, Arkansas, intending to defeat General Joseph O. Shelby near the Little Red River.

NAVAL: The Confederate raider CSS *Tallahassee* under Lieutenant John T. Wood slips out of Wilmington, North Carolina, commencing a three-week cruise that nets 33 Union vessels.

The much-feared Confederate ram CSS *Albemarle* departs Plymouth, North Carolina, and steams down the Roanoke River, anchoring near its mouth.

The ironclad monitor USS *Chickasaw* commences to bombard Fort Powell, Mobile Bay, Alabama, forcing the garrison under Colonel James M. Williams to evacuate the post. The rest of the Union fleet unleashes a tremendous bombardment against nearby Fort Gaines, which remains defiant. This is despite the fact that Union monitors sail to within point-blank range of its walls, firing 100-pound shells.

August 7

NORTH: General Ulysses S. Grant's choice of 33-year-old General Philip H. Sheridan to lead the newly designated Army of the Shenandoah causes concern for President Abraham Lincoln and Secretary of War Edwin M. Stanton. Both fear that the youthful Sheridan is too inexperienced for so delicate a mission, but Grant reiterates his desire to have this aggressive, headstrong firebrand at the helm.

SOUTH: Having weathered a terrific bombardment from land and sea forces, Colonel Charles D. Anderson receives a flag of truce sent by Admiral David G. Farragut and agrees to surrender Fort Gaines, Mobile Bay, Alabama, on the morrow.

WEST: Union cavalry under General William W. Averell surprise General Bradley T. Johnson's Confederate troopers at Moorefield, West Virginia. The brigade of Major Thomas Gibson gallops through their camp before dawn, routing them and then pursues fleeing survivors of the 8th Virginia Cavalry into the Potomac River. Averell's second brigade under Colonel William H. Powell shortly after strikes General John McCausland's camp in identical fashion, overcomes determined resistance from the 21st Virginia Cavalry, and routs the Southerners. Averell reports taking 420 captives, 400 horses, three flags, and four cannon. Union losses are nine killed and 32 wounded. Johnson subsequently accuses McCausland of neglect of duty, although an inquiry is never held. The defeat also reinforces General Jubal A. Early's perception that his mounted arm is of limited use.

General John M. Schofield moves his Army of the Ohio forward from Utoy Creek to the important rail junction at East Point, Georgia, and beholds extensive Confederate fortifications there. He then declines attacking and orders his men to fortify positions along Sandtown Road. Fighting in the vicinity costs the Union 306 casualties while the Confederates incur less than 100.

August 8

SOUTH: Colonel Charles D. Anderson formally surrenders Fort Gaines, Mobile Bay, Alabama, following a prolonged naval bombardment. The victorious Union fleet then replenishes its ammunition and assumes bombardment positions off Fort Morgan, the final domino to fall.

NAVAL: The USS *Violet* ran aground on a bar off Cape Fear River, North Carolina, and is burned by its crew.

August 9

SOUTH: General Jefferson C. Davis assumes command of the Union XIV Corps in Georgia.

Colonel John S. Mosby routs a larger Union detachment at Fairfax Station, Virginia.

Confederate saboteurs detonate a 12-pound torpedo on a large Union transport at City Point, Virginia. The ensuing explosion ignites chain reactions of stored ordnance throughout the city, showering General Ulysses S. Grant with debris. Casualties total 43 killed and 126 injured.

Federal troops begin formally investing Fort Morgan, Mobile Bay, Alabama, ringing it with cannon and warships, but General Richard L. Page, a former shipmate of Admiral David G. Farragut, refuses to surrender.

WEST: General Philip H. Sheridan marshals his forces for a push from Halltown and Harper's Ferry, West Virginia, down the Shenandoah Valley. His objective is the camp of General Jubal A. Early's Army of the Valley, encamped at Bunker Hill, West Virginia, only 12 miles distant.

General William T. Sherman, having dragged several large Parrott rifles and siege guns up to Bald Hill, Georgia, orders them to begin to bombard Atlanta and its environs. For the next two weeks Union cannon rain down 5,000 shots a day on the beleaguered inhabitants, as much to undermine their morale as to cause damage.

NAVAL: The USS *Catskill* attacks and sinks the Confederate blockade-runner *Prince Albert* off Fort Moultrie, South Carolina.

Admiral David G. Farragut's squadron intensely bombards Fort Morgan, Mobile Bay, Alabama, after General Richard L. Page refuses to surrender. The newly captured CSS *Tennessee* is also towed into position by the USS *Port Royal*, now manned by Union gunners. The fleet is assisted further by 3,000 infantry under General Gordon Granger, who contribute land artillery and sniper fire to the barrage.

August 10

WEST: General Philip H. Sheridan leads Union forces out of Harper's Ferry and into the Shenandoah Valley as General Jubal A. Early falls back on Winchester, Virginia.

Unable to overcome Union superiority in numbers, General John B. Hood dispatches 4,500 crack cavalry under General Joseph Wheeler from Covington, Georgia. There he is to disrupt General William T. Sherman's supply lines north of Atlanta, Georgia, and then wreak havoc throughout eastern Tennessee. Hood anticipates that by sabotaging the critical Macon and Western Railroad, Federal forces will be obliged to either fall back or face starvation.

NAVAL: The Confederate raider CSS *Tallahassee* under Commander John T. Wood takes and burns six Union prizes within 80 miles of Sandy Hook, New Jersey.

The transport steamer *Empress* is attacked by a Confederate battery on the Mississippi River at Gaines Landing, Arkansas. The Federal gunboat USS *Romeo* eventually arrives, silences the Confederates, and tows the hapless vessel to safety. The Southerners are defeated, but both vessels incur serious damage. *Empress* alone sustains 63 hits.

August 11

WEST: Confederates under General Jubal A. Early fall back on Cedar Creek, Virginia, as invigorated Union forces under General Philip H. Sheridan pursue.

NAVAL: Confederate batteries at Gaines's Landing, Arkansas, engage the Federal gunboats USS *Prairie Bird* and *Romeo* in a lengthy exchange before being silenced.

August 12

WEST: Continual skirmishing erupts between the armies of Generals Philip H. Sheridan and Jubal A. Early along Cedar Creek, as neither side feels sufficiently strong to initiative offensive action.

NAVAL: The Confederate raider CSS *Tallahassee* under Commander John T. Wood takes and burns six more prizes off the New York coast.

August 13
SOUTH: On learning that large Southern reinforcements are being transferred to the Shenandoah theater from Deep Bottom Run, Virginia, General Ulysses S. Grant orders General Winfield S. Hancock's II Corps, the X Corps of General David B. Birney, and the 2nd Cavalry Division under General David M. Gregg to strike Confederate defenses there. If successful, Union troops can break through 10 miles southeast of Richmond.

The 43rd Virginia Cavalry under Colonel John S. Mosby captures Berryville, Virginia, along with a Union supply train, 500 horses, 200 head of cattle, and several prisoners.

General John G. Parke is appointed commander of the IX Corps, Army of the Potomac.

WEST: Skirmishing commences between the cavalry forces of General Joseph A. Mower and Nathan B. Forrest at Hurricane Creek, Mississippi.

General Alfred Pleasonton conducts large-scale antiguerrilla actions against William C. Quantrill's raiders in La Fayette, Saline, and Howard counties, Missouri.

NAVAL: The Confederate raider CSS *Tallahassee* under Commander John T. Wood takes and burns the Union schooner *Lammont Du Pont* and the bark *Glenavon* a few miles from New York City, and a greatly alarmed commercial sector appeals to Secretary of the Navy Gideon Welles for navy ships to destroy "the pirate."

The USS *Agwam* trades fire with several Confederate batteries along Forty Mile Creek on the James River.

A Confederate squadron consisting of CSS *Virginia II, Richmond, Fredericksburg, Hampton, Drewry,* and *Nansemond* shells Union army positions at Dutch Gap, Virginia, for 12 hours before withdrawing back up the James River. The damage inflicted is slight.

August 14
SOUTH: General Winfield S. Hancock moves his II Corps, General David B. Birney's X Corps, and the 2nd Cavalry Division over the James River toward Deep Bottom Run, Virginia. However, his initial probes are repulsed with 500 casualties, indicating that Confederate defenses are still fully manned.

WEST: General Richard H. Anderson arrives at Fort Royal, Virginia, with a Confederate infantry and cavalry division, prior to entering the Shenandoah Valley. General Philip H. Sheridan's lines of communication now possibly are threatened, so he orders General Wesley Merritt's cavalry division to reconnoiter Fort Royal and ascertain enemy strength and intentions. Meanwhile, the bulk of Union forces withdraw north of Halltown in the direction of Harper's Ferry, West Virginia.

Confederate cavalry under General Joseph Wheeler attack and destroy tracks belonging to the Western and Atlantic Railroad south of Dalton, Georgia. However, he is unable to overpower the town's Union garrison, so then he gallops north into Tennessee for similar work.

NAVAL: The Confederate raider CSS *Tallahassee* under Commander John T. Wood captures and sinks the Union ship *James Littlefield* in the Atlantic.

August 15
SOUTH: General David B. Birney maneuvers his X Corps down the Charles City Road, intending to attack Fussell's Mills, Virginia, on the following day. General Gouverneur K. Warren also marches his V Corps from the Union right flank to the left for an eventual strike against the strategic Weldon Railroad.

The army of General William T. Sherman continues advancing southwest of Atlanta, Georgia.

Union forces under General John P. Hatch raid the Florida Railroad near Gainesville, Florida.

General Richard Taylor is appointed commander of the Confederate Department of Alabama, Mississippi, and East Louisiana.

WEST: Union and Confederate forces skirmish at Cedar Creek, Virginia, and once General Philip H. Sheridan withdraws toward Winchester, General Jubal A. Early follows. Sheridan is instructed by General Ulysses S. Grant to act cautiously, as the Confederates opposite him are believed to number 40,000 and, furthermore, given President Abraham Lincoln's precarious political future, an embarrassing defeat must be avoided at all costs. Early, however, misinterprets this behavior as timidity on Sheridan's part, a miscalculation for which he pays dearly.

NAVAL: The Confederate raider CSS *Tallahassee* under Commander John T. Wood captures and scuttles six more Union schooners off the New England coast.

The USS *Niagara* seizes the British steamer *Georgia* off the coast of Portugal. That vessel, previously serving the Confederacy as CSS *Georgia,* had been sold to British merchants and is now confiscated on account of its prior activity. A prize court in Boston subsequently condemns the vessel.

August 16
SOUTH: General David B. Birney's X Corps attacks Confederate positions along the Darbytown Road and achieves a minor breakthrough at Fussell's Mills. However, he lacks manpower to exploit his success, and a swift Southern counterattack by General Charles W. Field seals the breach. Union casualties amount to 2,000, the Confederates half that amount.

WEST: Union cavalry under General Wesley Merritt engage General Richard H. Anderson's Confederate division at Front Royal, Virginia. A swirling saber melee erupts between the Southern troopers of General William C. Wickham and Union cavalry under General Thomas C. Devlin once Confederates ford the Shenandoah River. A decisive charge by Devlin sends them scampering back across after he seizes two flags and 139 prisoners. At nearby Guard Hill, a Confederate brigade under General William T. Wofford receives a dismounted attack by General George A. Custer's cavalry brigade. The bluecoats, armed with rapid-fire Spencer carbines, gradually outgun and drive the defenders from the hillside, and they break and run across the river in a panic. Merritt thus confirms the presence of strong Confederate forces at Front Royal, a fact inducing General Philip H. Sheridan to continue retreating in the direction of Harper's Ferry, West Virginia.

Colonel John S. Mosby surprises and defeats a Union force at Kernstown and Charlestown, West Virginia.

NAVAL: The Confederate raider CSS *Tallahassee* under Commander John T. Wood captures and burns four more prizes off the New England coast.

The USS *Mount Washington, Delaware, Mackinaw,* and *Canonicus* of the James River Squadron support Federal troops as they advance from Dutch Gap, Virginia.

An armed party from the *USS Saratoga* again raids McIntosh County, Georgia, destroying a bridge and a saltworks and seizing 100 prisoners.

August 17

WEST: General Jubal A. Early attacks the Union rear guard at Winchester, Virginia, as General Philip H. Sheridan continues to retrograde toward Berryville.

NAVAL: The Confederate raider CSS *Tallahassee* under Commander John T. Wood arrives at Halifax, Nova Scotia, to take on a supply of coal. Mortimer M. Jackson, the U.S. consul present, protests its arrival and alerts Commander George A. Steven of the USS *Pontoosuc* at Eastport, Maine.

August 18

NORTH: General Ulysses S. Grant again refuses Confederate requests to resume prisoner exchanges. This deprives the South of critically needed manpower, but it also prolongs the hardships of Union captives languishing in poorly maintained Confederate prisons. In truth, the South can barely feed its own soldiers, let alone thousands of prisoners.

SOUTH: Confederate forces attack General Winfield S. Hancock's II Corps at Deep Bottom Run, Virginia, and are repelled with losses. But General Ulysses S. Grant remains convinced that Confederates defenses north of the James River have not been depleted, and he recalls Hancock's expedition back across the river to Petersburg. Operations in this vicinity cost the Union 2,901 killed, wounded, and captured, to a Southern tally of about 1,500. The seven-day foray does, however, prevent General Robert E. Lee from dispatching additional reinforcements into the Shenandoah Valley.

At 4:00 A.M., General Gouverneur K. Warren's V Corps attacks and captures Globe Tavern and portions of Weldon Railroad outside Petersburg, Virginia. This move threatens to extend Union siege lines around the city and force the Confederates to defend more ground with fewer troops. But General Pierre G. T. Beauregard, commanding at Petersburg, quickly dispatches General Henry Heth's division to slash at Warren's left flank. Heth accordingly attacks out of dense woods around 2:00 P.M., driving the division of General Romeyn B. Ayres before him. Timely Union reinforcements from Generals Samuel W. Crawford and Lysander Cutler's divisions suddenly arrive and drive the Confederates back. Ayres loses about 900 men in heavy fighting. During the night, both sides consolidate their positions and muster additional troops. But General Robert E. Lee cannot allow the Weldon line to be cut, and he prepares to take it back by force.

WEST: General Jubal A. Early harasses General Philip H. Sheridan's withdrawal to Harper's Ferry, West Virginia, by striking at Opequon Creek, Virginia.

A force of 4,000 Union cavalry under General Hugh J. Kilpatrick is dispatched by General William T. Sherman to raid the Atlanta and West Point Railroad at Fairburn, Georgia. That done, he is to spur his command toward Lovejoy's Station for similar work against the Macon and Western Railroad, 20 miles southeast of Atlanta.

August 19

SOUTH: General Gouverneur K. Warren's V Corps at Weldon Station is reinforced by three divisions of the IX Corps, plus General Gershom Mott's division from II Corps. These arrive and deploy in time to meet a large Confederate assault of several brigades orchestrated by General Ambrose P. Hill, maneuvering to recapture the Weldon Railroad at all costs. Due to the thickness of the woods, Confederates under General William Mahone steal to within a few yards of the Union right, then rush fiercely, and nearly collapse it. General Samuel W. Crawford and many of his men fall captive before men of the XI Corps arrive, counterattack, and force Mahone back into the woods. At the center, General Romeyn B. Ayres spars with General Henry Heth inconclusively until the Southerners finally withdraw. By nightfall, Warren's position has been heavily jostled in several places, but he retains control of the Weldon Railroad. Union losses total 198 killed, 1,105 wounded, and 3,152 missing (4,455); Confederate casualties are estimated at 1,600.

WEST: The armies of General Philip H. Sheridan and Jubal A. Early continue skirmishing in the vicinity of Winchester, West Virginia.

Union cavalry under General Hugh J. Kilpatrick arrive at Jonesboro, Georgia, a major supply depot, and burn quantities of stores and equipment before pushing on to their next major objective at Lovejoy's Station.

NAVAL: The Confederate raider CSS *Tallahassee* under Commander John T. Wood departs Halifax, Nova Scotia, and sets sail for Wilmington, North Carolina.

August 20

SOUTH: Fighting dies down along the Weldon Railroad as the V Corps of General Gouverneur K. Warren entrenches and strengthens its position against possible Confederate attacks.

Federal forces operating near Charleston, South Carolina, burn the town of Legareville.

WEST: General Hugh J. Kilpatrick's cavalry column gallops into Lovejoy's Station, Georgia, but has only begun to tear up tracks belonging to the Macon and Western Railroad when it is attacked by Confederate cavalry under General William H. Jackson. Stiff fighting ensues, after which the Union troops break through and escape to rejoin William T. Sherman's main army near Atlanta.

NAVAL: The USS *Pontoosuc* sorties from Eastport, Maine, to Halifax, Nova Scotia, but it arrives seven hours too late to stop the Confederate raider CSS *Tallahassee*. Commander John T. Wood, meanwhile, captures and burns the Union brig *Roan* in the North Atlantic.

August 21

SOUTH: General Robert E. Lee abandons the Weldon Railroad outside Petersburg, Virginia, after renewed attacks by General Ambrose P. Hill fail to dislodge Union defenders from Globe Tavern.

General Richard L. Page, commanding Fort Morgan, Mobile Bay, Alabama, destroys his powder supply to preclude any chance hit by Union shells. By this time, no less than 25 army cannon, 16 mortars, and the guns of Admiral David G. Farragut's entire squadron are playing upon his position.

WEST: Union forces under General Philip H. Sheridan successfully withdraw up and out of the Shenandoah Valley to Harper's Ferry, West Virginia. A planned attack by generals Jubal A. Early and Richard H. Anderson miscarries for want of close cooperation.

A surprise raid by 2,000 Confederate cavalry under General Nathan B. Forrest captures Memphis, Tennessee, and the local Union commander, General Cadwallader C. Washburn, only narrowly escapes in his nightclothes. Forrest then resumes raiding Federal supply lines with almost total impunity during the next two months. His success even elicits backhanded praise from Sherman, who refers to him as "that Devil Forrest."

August 22

SOUTH: The weary II Corps of General Winfield S. Hancock is transferred from the front lines at Petersburg to Reams's Station, a quiet sector, to undertake fatigue duties along the Weldon Railroad. The force consists of infantry divisions under General John Gibbon and Nelson A. Miles, and a cavalry division under General David M. Gregg—tough, veteran troops but completely spent by constant fighting.

WEST: Skirmishing continues at Charlestown, West Virginia, as Confederates under General Jubal A. Early continue pressing General Philip H. Sheridan near Harper's Ferry.

NAVAL: An armed party from the USS *Potomsk* raids the Satilla and White rivers, Georgia, taking numerous prisoners and burning supplies.

August 23

POLITICS: President Abraham Lincoln expresses pessimism over his reelection chances, noting "It will be my duty to co-operate with the President elect, as to save the Union between the election and the inauguration, as he will have secured his election on such ground that he cannot possibly save it afterwards."

SOUTH: General Richard I. Page surrenders Fort Morgan, Mobile Bay, Alabama, after two weeks of intensive bombardment; Federal forces now completely control all adjoining waters. Wilmington, North Carolina, remains the only functioning Confederate port.

WEST: Union cavalry under General Hugh J. Kilpatrick, bested by strong Confederates defenses at Lovejoy's Station, rejoin General William T. Sherman's main force outside Decatur, Georgia. Despite grandiose claims, his recent raid against Southern rail lines is another failure.

NAVAL: Armed boats from the USS *Saratoga*, *T. A. Ward*, and *Braziliera* conduct an unsuccessful raid up the Turtle River, Georgia. As they approach their objective, the army encampment at Bethel fires at them from the shoreline and forces the vessels back downstream.

August 24

SOUTH: General Ambrose P. Hill sorties the Confederate III Corps out of it trenches, intending to strike Union positions at Reams's Station, Virginia.

WEST: Heavy skirmishing continues between the forces of General Frederick Steele and Joseph O. Shelby at Devall's Bluff, Arkansas.

SOUTHWEST: A party of 420 troopers of the 2nd Kansas Cavalry is attacked in camp by 800 Confederate Cherokee under General Stand Watie and 1,200 Texas cavalry under Colonel Richard M. Gano at Gunter's Prairie, Indian Territory. The defenders lose 20 men. Southerners and Indians then ride northwest of Fort Gibson and strike at a 125-man Union force at Flat Rock Ford, killing 40 more.

NAVAL: The USS *Keystone State* and *Gettysburg* capture the Confederate steamer *Lilian* off Wilmington, North Carolina. The vessel subsequently is acquired by the navy and is assigned to the blockading squadron.

The USS *Narcissus* captures the Confederate schooner *Oregon* in Biloxi Bay, Mississippi Sound.

August 25

SOUTH: At 5:00 P.M., Confederates under General Ambrose P. Hill savagely assault the Union II Corps of General Winfield S. Hancock at Reams' Station, Virginia. Hill's 10,000 men initially rebound off divisions commanded by Generals Nelson A. Miles and David M. Gregg, until parts of the former suddenly buckle. Southerners under Generals Henry Heth and Cadmus M. Wilcox then pour through the breech, capturing several cannon and hundreds of prisoners. Worse, when General John Gibbon's division, exhausted from fatigue work, is ordered up to plug the gap, it stumbles badly and likewise runs. Hancock then withdraws from the area covered by elements of General Orlando Wilcox's IX Corps. Union losses in this embarrassing affair totaled 2,372, the vast majority of whom are prisoners. The Confederates, who suffer only 700 casualties, also seize nine cannon, 3,100 small arms, and several horses.

WEST: General Jubal A. Early, confronting entrenched Union forces at Harper's Ferry, West Virginia, bypasses them with a small holding force in place and moves on to Shepherdstown. From there, he intends another invasion of Maryland.

General William T. Sherman, unwilling to storm the defenses of Atlanta, Georgia, and with the whole of his cavalry having failed to cut Confederate supply lines, resolves to throw the weight of his entire army against the Macon and Western Railroad. This is the sole remaining supply route into the city. He then orders six army corps on a circuitous route to Rough and Ready and Jonesboro where they can best sever this strategic link. As a precaution, Sherman also orders the XX Corps to guard his own railroad bridges spanning the Chattahoochee River.

NAVAL: The Confederate raider CSS *Tallahassee* under Commander John T. Wood successfully runs the Union blockade and reaches Wilmington, North Carolina, having seized 31 prizes.

August 26

POLITICS: A convention of African Americans in Philadelphia, Pennsylvania, advance resolutions calling for the commissioning of black military officers.

NORTH: General Jubal A. Early's Confederate army crosses the Potomac into Maryland for a third time and skirmishes with Union forces at Williamsport.

SOUTH: General Edward O. C. Ord assumes temporary control of the Army of the James outside of Richmond, Virginia.

August 27

SOUTH: Near Atlanta, Georgia, General William T. Sherman dispatches Generals Oliver O. Howard and Hugh J. Kilpatrick on a direct march against General John B. Hood's rail lines at Jonesboro. Hood counters by marching the corps of Generals William J. Hardee and Stephen D. Lee to defeat the Union columns before the Macon and Western Railroad can be interdicted.

NAVAL: The USS *Niphon* and *Monticello* run up Masonboro Inlet, North Carolina, destroy a Confederate battery, and they capture numerous arms and supplies.

Ill-health forces Admiral David G. Farragut to request sick leave from the West Gulf Blockading Squadron inside Mobile Bay, Alabama. "I have now been down in this Gulf and the Caribbean Sea nearly five years out of six," he explains, "with the exception of the short time at home last fall, and the last six months have been a severe drain on me, and I want rest, if it is to be had."

August 28

WEST: General Philip H. Sheridan advances from Harper's Ferry, West Virginia, back toward the Shenandoah Valley without opposition.

General William T. Sherman pushes the Army of the Cumberland under General George H. Thomas onto the Montgomery and Atlanta Railroad while General Oliver O. Howard and his Army of the Tennessee advance on Fairburn, Georgia. Meanwhile, the Army of the Ohio under General John M. Schofield moves up to Mount Gilead Church as General Henry W. Slocum's XX Corps defends Union lines around Atlanta. If successful, these movements threaten General John B. Hood's final rail link out of the city, trapping him inside.

General Sterling Price assumes command of divisions under Generals John S. Marmaduke and James F. Fagan at Camden, Arkansas, prior to marching them across the Arkansas River back into Missouri.

August 29

POLITICS: The Democratic National Convention convenes in Chicago, Illinois, where Copperhead Clement L. Vallandigham delivers the keynote address.

WEST: General Philip H. Sheridan orders his men into action at Smithfield Crossing along the Opequon River, brushing aside a small Confederate detachment.

General Sterling Price continues gathering forces at Princeton, Arkansas, for his final attempt at conquering Missouri for the South.

NAVAL: A Confederate torpedo (mine) explodes in Mobile Bay, Alabama, killing five Union sailors and wounding another nine. Admiral David G. Farragut resolves to eliminate all these potential ship-killing weapons before departing.

August 30

POLITICS: The Democratic National Party Convention in Chicago, Illinois, adopts a peace platform demanding an immediate end to hostilities with the South. The

Democratic Party's political platform is virtually the exact mirror opposite of President Abraham Lincoln and the Republicans.

WEST: General George Crook replaces General David Hunter as commander of the Department of West Virginia.

General Oliver O. Howard, commanding the XV, XVI, XVII Corps and Hugh J. Kilpatrick's cavalry division, crosses the Flint River and marches to within one mile of Jonesboro, Georgia. There, he perceives Confederate forces under General William J. Hardee approaching to engage him. In fact, General John B. Hood has ordered Hardee to strike the Union column in concert with General Stephen D. Lee and drive them back across the Flint.

NAVAL: The USS *Fawn* convoys army transports on an unsuccessful expedition up the White River, Arkansas, in search of Confederate raiders under General Joseph O. Shelby.

August 31

POLITICS: The Democratic National Convention at Chicago, Illinois, nominates former general George B. McClellan as its candidate for the presidency and George H. Pendleton of Ohio for vice president.

SOUTH: A force of 20,000 Confederates under General William J. Hardee attack 20,000 Union soldiers of General Oliver O. Howard at Jonesboro, Georgia. The Federals are strongly posted in a semicircle on high ground and enjoy clear fields of fire. Moreover, Hardee experiences considerable difficulty coordinating the action of subordinates, and his battlefield strategy miscarries. Interminable delays ensue before General Patrick R. Cleburne drives toward Northern positions at 3:00 P.M. under a withering fire. General Stephen D. Lee's columns receive similar treatment and are also thrown back. Hardee's piecemeal attacks disintegrate in the face of determined resistance, and he finally withdraws with 2,000 casualties. Howard loses a mere 178.

The Army of the Ohio under General John M. Schofield severs the Macon and Western Railroad between Jonesboro and Atlanta, Georgia, cutting General John B. Hood's final supply line. The city is now doomed.

NAVAL: The British blockade-runner *Mary Bowers* runs aground near Rattlesnake Shoals, Long Island, South Carolina, and is completely wrecked.

September 1

WEST: The Army of the Shenandoah under General Philip H. Sheridan threatens Winchester, Virginia, as skirmishing flares up along Opequon Creek.

General John B. Hood begins to evacuate Atlanta, Georgia, once Union forces cut the Macon and Western Railroad, and he withdraws down the McDonough Road to Lovejoy's Station. There, he is to unite with General William J. Hardee's battered corps. A large ammunition depot unable to be moved in time is also burned and its detonation resonates at General William T. Sherman's headquarters, 15 miles distant.

Confederates under General William J. Hardee are attacked by superior Union forces as the struggle at Jonesboro, Georgia, continues. General William T. Sherman designs an elaborate movement by several corps to ensnare and possibly capture

General William J. Hardee's corps. General Jefferson C. Davis's XIV Corps advances to engage, only to find the Southerners strongly posted behind impassable terrain. Union attacks are then committed on a piecemeal basis, and the Federals sustain considerable losses, but Davis finally penetrates their thin defenses, taking hundreds of prisoners from General Daniel C. Govan's brigade. Hardee promptly counterattacks with General Benjamin Chetham's division, after which the Union advance grounds to a halt. Davis then passively defends his gains as the Confederates, after nightfall, limp safely to Lovejoy's Station. Union losses are 1,274 out of 20,460 present; the Confederates suffer 911 among the 12,661 engaged. Hardee's determined stand grants General John B. Hood's forces sufficient time to slip out from Sherman's ever-constricting noose.

September 2
POLITICS: To offset critical manpower shortages, General Robert E. Lee advises President Jefferson Davis of the need to replace white laborers with African-American slaves, thereby freeing the former for military service.

SOUTH: General Robert E. Lee, severely pressed in the trenches of Petersburg, Virginia, pressures General Jubal A. Early to return the division of General Richard H. Anderson on loan to him.

"So Atlanta is ours and fairly won," General William T. Sherman telegraphs President Abraham Lincoln, as the city surrenders to the XX Corps of General Henry W. Slocum. This single act immediately rekindles Lincoln's sagging election prospects while exerting a distressing effect throughout the South. During the past four months Union forces have sustained 4,423 dead and 22,822 wounded while the Confederates endure 3,044 killed and 18,952 injured. A further 17,335 from both sides have either been captured or simply lost through desertion.

NAVAL: Secretary of the Navy Gideon Welles receives permission to mount a large amphibious assault against Fort Fisher, Wilmington, North Carolina. Success here will close the Confederacy's sole remaining port.

The USS *Naiad* silences a Confederate battery at Rowe's Landing, Louisiana.

September 3
POLITICS: President Abraham Lincoln, in honor of recent victories at Mobile, Alabama, and Atlanta, Georgia, declares the upcoming September 5 to be a day of national celebration and prayer as such events, "call for devout acknowledgment to the Supreme Being in whose hands are the destinies of nations."

WEST: General Philip A. Sheridan, heavily reinforced, advances again on General Richard H. Anderson's division at Berryville, Virginia, defeating the Confederates as they retreat back to their main force at Winchester.

NAVAL: President Abraham Lincoln orders a 100-gun salute at the Washington Navy Yard in honor of Union successes in Mobile Bay, Alabama.

September 4
SOUTH: The latest 60-day bombardment of Fort Sumter, Charleston Harbor, South Carolina, ends after 14,666 rounds are fired. The Confederate flag still wafts defiantly from the rubble.

WEST: General John H. Morgan is killed by Union forces under General Alvan C. Gillem at Greeneville, Tennessee. An additional 100 Confederates die while 75 are captured.

September 5
POLITICS: Voters in Louisiana ratify a new constitution abolishing slavery.
SOUTH: Confederate sergeant and scout George D. Shadburne informs General Wade Hampton of a weakly held Union corral holding 3,000 cattle at Coggins Point, Virginia. Given critical food shortages in the Army of Northern Virginia, this is an opportunity too good to pass on, so Hampton draws up plans to both raid and rustle the herd.
WEST: Skirmishing continues along Opequon Creek, West Virginia, between Union and Confederate forces.
NAVAL: Admiral David D. Porter replaces Admiral Samuel P. Lee as commander of the North Atlantic Blockading Squadron.

The USS *Keystone State* and *Quaker City* capture the British blockade-runner *Elsie* off Wilmington, North Carolina.

September 6
SOUTH: General Richard Taylor is appointed commander of the Confederate Department of Alabama, Mississippi, and East Louisiana.
WEST: A Confederate force numbering 12,000 men under General Sterling Price finally crosses the Arkansas River at Dardanelle, Arkansas, en route to the Missouri state line. When the Union garrison at Little Rock under General Frederick Steele makes no attempt to intercept or impede his march, moves are undertaken in Washington, D.C., to replace him.
NAVAL: The USS *Proteus* captures the British blockade-runner *Ann Louisa* in the Gulf of Mexico.

September 7
SOUTH: General Benjamin F. Butler resumes command of the Army of the James outside of Richmond, Virginia.

Union gunners at Charleston, South Carolina, fire an additional 573 rounds at Fort Sumter without eliciting its surrender.

General William T. Sherman issues Special Field Order No. 67 to the inhabitants of Atlanta, Georgia, requiring 1,600 families to begin to evacuate the city. "War is cruelty and you cannot refine it," he declares to the city's mayor, "When peace does come you may call on me for anything. Then I will share with you the last cracker."
WEST: General Philip H. Sheridan and Jubal A. Early continue jockeying for position as they skirmish near Winchester, West Virginia.

September 8
POLITICS: George B. McClellan accepts the Democratic Party nomination but rejects a peace platform, declaring, "The Union is the one condition of peace—we ask for no more." He nonetheless continues railing against President Abraham Lincoln's handling of the war as a failure.

NAVAL: The USS *Tritonia, Rodolph,* and *Stockdale* escort an army transport against a large Confederate saltworks on the Bonsecours River near Mobile, Alabama. This factory is so extensive that destroying it consumes nearly an entire day.

September 9
SOUTH: To help break the stalemate before Richmond, Virginia, General Ulysses S. Grant urges the newly victorious general William T. Sherman to resume offensive operations as soon as practicable.

WEST: General Joseph Wheeler, having completed his raid against Union supply lines in Tennessee, concludes his mission by crossing the Tennessee River at Florence, Alabama. In fact, his endeavors achieve very little because Union repair crews quickly restore damaged sections of the railways attacked. The net result of Wheeler's raid is actually to deprive General John B. Hood of cavalry during critical phases of the Atlanta campaign.

NAVAL: The USS *Kanawha* reconstitutes the Federal blockade of Brownsville, Texas, eight months after it had been suspended by President Abraham Lincoln. This is due to the recent evacuation of Union forces from the city.

September 10
NAVAL: A landing party from the USS *Wyalusing* raids Elizabeth City on the Pasquotank River, North Carolina, and takes 29 citizens for interrogation concerning the recent burning of the Federal mail steamer *Fawn* in their vicinity. They then learn that the raid had been conducted by crew members of the CSS *Albemarle.*

The USS *Santiago de Cuba* captures the Confederate steamer *A. D. Vance* off Wilmington, North Carolina.

The USS *Augusta Dinsmore* captures the Confederate schooner *John* near Velasco, Texas.

The USS *Magnolia* seizes the Confederate steamer *Matagorda* off Cape San Antonio, Cuba.

September 11
WEST: General William T. Sherman and John B. Hood conclude a 10-day truce to facilitate evacuating civilians and their belongings from Atlanta, Georgia. When petitioned by the inhabitants to reconsider, Sherman declares, "You might as well appeal against the thunderstorm as against these terrible hardships of war." The age of total war manifests with a vengeance.

NAVAL: A naval expedition consisting of the USS *Rodolph, Stockdale,* and army transport *Planter* ascends the Fish River at Mobile Bay, Alabama, for the purpose of seizing a Confederate sawmill. On the return leg of the voyage, the vessels receive fire by sharpshooters lining the riverbanks, but no injuries result.

September 12
NORTH: President Abraham Lincoln and General Ulysses S. Grant express anxiety to General Philip H. Sheridan about the apparent stalemate in the Shenandoah Valley. Lincoln goes so far as to suggest quietly that Sheridan should be reinforced, thus allowing him to strike with overwhelming force.

WEST: General Sterling Price's Confederates cross the White River, Arkansas, and march to Pocahontas to unite with General Joseph O. Shelby's cavalry division. The

Ruins of a train depot, blown up on Sherman's departure from Atlanta, Georgia *(Library of Congress)*

Army of Missouri is then reorganized into three divisions under Shelby, James F. Fagan, and John S. Marmaduke. Price commands 12,000 men and 14 cannon, but only half his force is armed or trained adequately. The Confederates hope to supply themselves with captured Union weapons as they proceed across Missouri in three distinct columns.

September 13
WEST: More skirmishing takes place between outposts at Bunker Hill and Opequon Creek, West Virginia.

September 14

SOUTH: General Wade Hampton and 4,000 Confederate cavalry, guided by Sergeant George D. Shadburne, embark on a major raid to secure Union cattle corralled at Coggins Point, Virginia. To confuse the Federals, they gallop southwest, then southeast, before veering northeast to the Rowanty Creek.

WEST: General Richard H. Anderson again marches his Confederate division out of the Shenandoah Valley to reinforce the defenses of Richmond, Virginia. This transfer manifestly weakens General Jubal A. Early's army, and his withdrawal is observed by Union spy Rebecca Wright.

September 15

SOUTH: General Wade Hampton and 4,000 Confederate cavalry take a circuitous route for 18 miles until they arrive unseen at Blackwater Creek, Virginia, pausing there until nightfall before advancing on Union pickets at Sycamore Church.

WEST: General Ulysses S. Grant rides north from Petersburg to discuss strategy with General Philip H. Sheridan in the Shenandoah Valley.

September 16

SOUTH: At dawn General Wade Hampton's cavalry charge a Union force at Coggin's Point, Virginia, completely dispersing elements of the 1st D.C. Cavalry and the 13th Pennsylvania Cavalry. They then abscond with 2,486 head of cattle—along with 300 prisoners—in a line stretching seven miles long. Hampton, having sustained only 61 casualties, arrives back behind Confederate lines the following day. This is the largest incidence of cattle rustling in history.

WEST: Rebecca West, a Union spy in Winchester, Virginia, observes the departure of General Joseph Kershaw's Confederate cavalry division and 12 cannon from the army of General Jubal A. Early. She immediately relays the intelligence back to General Philip H. Sheridan, then conferring with General Ulysses S. Grant about strategy at Charlestown, West Virginia. News of this transfer of forces back to Richmond induces Sheridan to attack immediately. Grant fully concurs, laconically stating, "Go in," and then departs.

General Nathan B. Forrest leads 4,500 cavalry out of Verona, Mississippi, on another extended raid against General William T. Sherman's communications in middle Tennessee and northern Alabama.

NAVAL: Armed boats from the USS *Ariel* capture 4,000 pounds of cotton near Tampa Bay, Florida.

September 17

POLITICS: Former general John C. Frémont withdraws his name from the election contest and urges a united Republican effort. The former general and explorer fears that a Democratic victory might lead to either recognition of the Confederacy or the resumption of slavery.

WEST: General Jubal A. Early, though outnumbered three to one by nearby Union forces, advances 12,000 men toward Martinsburg, Virginia, to cut the Baltimore and Ohio Railroad.

September 18

WEST: General Jubal A. Early arrays his 12,000 men defensively at Winchester, Virginia. However, his men are scattered with the divisions of Generals Robert E. Rodes and John B. Gordon sent to Martinsburg, whereas General Stephen D. Ramseur's men straddle the Berryville Pike. Early does so out of a misplaced conviction that General Philip H. Sheridan is cautious and dares not attack. But his disjointed, widely dispersed deployment does not go unnoticed and convinces Sheridan to strike in force the following day.

General John M. Schofield orders a cavalry column under General Stephen O. Burbridge to depart Mount Sterling, Kentucky, and mount a diversion against Saltville on the Virginia border. This is undertaken to mask an even larger raid conducted by General Alvan C. Gillem, who intends to strike into southwestern Virginia from east Tennessee.

September 19

POLITICS: President Jefferson Davis advises the governors of South Carolina, North Carolina, Alabama, Georgia, Virginia, and Florida that recent proclamations requiring aliens to either serve in the army or leave are depriving the Confederacy of many skilled workers. Moreover, he insists that "harmony of action between the States and Confederate authorities is essential to the public welfare."

WEST: At 2:00 P.M., General Philip H. Sheridan's army, numbering 35,000 men, attacks the 12,000 Confederates of General Jubal A. Early at Winchester, Virginia. Sheridan hopes to surprise and annihilate the isolated division of Stephen D. Ramseur, but he errs in pushing General William H. Emory's XIX Corps through the defile at Berryville Canyon. This action not only funnels the Union thrust over a narrow front and alerts Ramseur, but it also enables divisions under Generals Robert E. Rodes and John B. Gordon to arrive in support. Heavy fighting forces Ramseur to give way; then Rodes and Gordon strike back in a vicious counterattack stunning the XIX Corps. Worse, as the newly arriving VI Corps of General Horatio G. Wright begins to deploy, a gap develops between the Union formations, and the Southerners force their way between them. Rodes is killed in the struggle as the Union lines surge back, while Early consolidates his outnumbered force along better lines.

The crisis occurs when Sheridan, judging the moment right, unleashes the VIII Corps under General George Crook. This infusion of new force staggers the weary Confederates, who break and re-form new lines farther back under General John C. Breckinridge. A desperate cavalry charge by General Fitzhugh Lee fails to stop the approach of Union troopers under Generals Wesley Merritt and William W. Averell, and resistance completely crumbles at about 5:00 P.M. Early labors mightily to keep his withdrawal from becoming a rout and gradually assumes new defensive positions at Fisher's Hill, 20 miles south. Significantly, this is the first time that the Confederate II Corps, "Stonewall" Jackson's old command, yields the palm of victory. Early's losses total 276 killed, 1,827 wounded, and 1,818 missing (3,611). The victorious Sheridan incurs 697 dead, 3,983 injured, and 338 missing (5,018).

SOUTHWEST: General John M. Thayer, commanding the District of the Frontier at Fort Smith, Arkansas, dispatches a supply train of 306 wagons and an escort of 610 soldiers to the relief of Fort Gibson. En route, they are attacked by Confederate Indians under General Stand Watie and Texas cavalry under Colonel Richard M. Gano at Cabin Creek, Indian Territory, who eject the defenders from their flimsy stockade, scattering them. The raiders then steal away with 202 wagons and 1,253 mules.

NAVAL: Confederate agents under Master John Y. Beall overpower the crew of the steamer *Philo Parsons* on Lake Erie and conduct it to Johnson's Island to free several prisoners. En route, they also seize and burn the steamer *Island Queen,* but they are thwarted by the timely appearance of the USS *Michigan.* The Confederates then sail *Philo Parsons* to Canada and safety.

Armed boats from the USS *Niphon* land at Masonboro Inlet, North Carolina, to reconnoiter the defenses of nearby Wilmington.

September 20

POLITICS: President Jefferson Davis departs Richmond, Virginia, for Georgia in an attempt to bolster Southern morale there.

SOUTH: Simon B. Buckner is promoted to lieutenant general, C.S.A.

WEST: General Jubal A. Early regroups his scattered forces at Fisher's Hill, Virginia, as Union cavalry pursue them sharply. This is a strong natural position, but Early lacks adequate manpower to man it sufficiently. Meanwhile, rearguard actions erupt at Strasburg, Middletown, and Cedarville as Federal forces under General Philip H. Sheridan approach.

General Stephen O. Burbridge leads 3,500 Union cavalry out of Mount Sterling, Kentucky, and rides toward Saltville, Virginia.

General Sterling Price captures Keytesville, Missouri, as he advances on St. Louis.

September 21

NORTH: General Philip H. Sheridan is appointed permanent commander of the Middle Military District, which encompasses the Shenandoah Valley.

WEST: The Army of the Shenandoah under General Philip H. Sheridan gathers its strength at Strasburg, Virginia, before plunging in full strength at Confederate positions along Fisher's Hill. After surveying General Jubal A. Early's deployment, Sheridan orders the VIII Corps of General George Crook on a wide encircling movement around the Confederate left while detaining divisions of Generals Horatio G. Wright and William H. Emory to his front. As Crook carefully departs this evening, taking every possible precaution not to be observed, the cavalry division of General Alfred T. A. Torbert is also sent clattering into the Luray Valley to swing around Early at New Market Gap and cut his retreat.

Confederate cavalry under General Nathan B. Forrest cross the Tennessee River and move against Athens, Tennessee.

September 22

POLITICS: President Jefferson Davis arrives by train at Macon, Georgia, and assures compatriots that "Our cause is not lost."

WEST: The Battle of Fisher's Hill begins this afternoon when 28,000 Union troops under General Philip H. Sheridan start to make feints and probes along the Confederate line. General Jubal A. Early, who possesses only 9,000 men, suspects that a ruse of some kind is in play and prepares to retreat. Suddenly, the two hidden divisions of the VIII Corps under General George Crook scream down the hillside on the Confederate left, sweeping aside the dismounted cavalry of General Lunsford L. Lomax. One brigade is headed by Colonel Rutherford B. Hayes, a future president of the United States. General Stephen D. Ramseur, whose Confederate division holds the left, tries realigning his men to halt the onslaught, but they are routed by the surging tide. Sheridan then orders Generals Horatio G. Wright and William H. Emory to charge the enemy in front, yelling, "Forward! Forward everything!" The excited Federals then pitch into the enemy, and Early's army crumbles around him. The onset of darkness permits the bulk of his men to retreat, a fact made possible by General Alfred T. A. Torbert's inability to traverse the Luray Valley in time.

Early's Confederates are thrashed thoroughly, although his losses total only 30 killed, 210 injured, and 995 missing (1,235), along with 14 cannon. Considering the natural strength of Fisher's Hill, especially its steep, imposing bluff, Sheridan suffers only 36 killed, 414 wounded, and six missing (456). He then declines to pursue his defeated enemy vigorously, preferring instead to hold back and commence implementing a "scorched earth" policy to devastate the fertile Shenandoah.

September 23

DIPLOMACY: Under European and U.S. pressure the Japanese shogun Tokugawa agrees to keep Yokohama and other ports open to Western vessels.

POLITICS: President Abraham Lincoln requests the resignation of Postmaster General Montgomery Blair as a concession for Radical Republican support in the upcoming election.

SOUTH: General Stephen A. Hurlburt assumes command of the Union Department of the Gulf.

WEST: General Jubal A. Early continues withdrawing back to Woodstock, Virginia, 25 miles from Fisher's Hill as General Philip H. Sheridan's Union forces linger in place while burning crops and farms throughout the Shenandoah Valley.

NAVAL: The side-wheeler USS *Antelope* strikes a snag and sinks in the Mississippi River off New Orleans.

September 24

POLITICS: President Abraham Lincoln appoints William Dennison the new postmaster general to replace the outgoing Montgomery Blair.

WEST: General Philip A. Sheridan moves down the Shenandoah Valley, but instead of pursuing the defeated Confederates, he burns farms and crops to eliminate the Confederacy's breadbasket. He does so with the complete approbation of General Ulysses S. Grant, who advises, "If the war is to last another year we want the Shenandoah Valley to remain a barren waste." Sheridan does not disappoint his superior.

The town of Athens, Tennessee, falls to Confederate cavalry under General Nathan B. Forrest.

NAVAL: The USS *Fuschia*, *Thomas Freeborn*, and *Mercury* raid a boatworks on Stutt's Creek, Virginia. They capture five small boats and destroy a fishery before returning safely.

September 25

SOUTH: President Jefferson Davis arrives at Palmetto, Georgia, to confer with General John B. Hood over strategy. Because of personality clashes, Hood has requested a replacement for ornery General William J. Hardee, which is done. Davis also approves of Hood's strategy for invading Tennessee to strike at Union supply lines, thereby forcing General William T. Sherman's Union army to evacuate Georgia.

WEST: Union forces under General Philip H. Sheridan reach Harrisonburg, Virginia, and continue devastating the surrounding countryside.

General Jubal A. Early's shattered Army of the Valley pulls into Port Republic, Virginia, to rest and regroup. He also is expecting reinforcements from the Army of Northern Virginia to ameliorate earlier losses.

The Confederate army of General Sterling Price enters Fredericktown, Missouri. As the divisions of Generals James F. Fagan and John S. Marmaduke proceed to attack Ironton, cavalry under General Joseph O. Shelby become tasked with cutting rail lines between that town and St. Louis.

NAVAL: The USS *Howquah, Niphon,* and *Governor Buckingham* trade fire with Confederate batteries at Wilmington, North Carolina, and also manage to run the blockade-runner *Lynx* aground, destroying it with cannon fire.

September 26

WEST: Union and Confederate cavalry skirmish at Brown's Gap, Virginia.

Confederate cavalry under General Nathan B. Forrest hit a Union garrison at Pulaski, Tennessee.

A force of 8,000 Confederates under General Sterling Price attacks General Thomas Ewing's 1,450-man Union garrison at Fort Davidson, Pilot Knob, Missouri. This post, though small, is well defended, and Price, declining to employ his artillery train, commits troops to a series of uncoordinated frontal assaults. These are invariably repulsed with upward of 1,000 casualties, but given the stark disparity in numbers, Ewing realizes he cannot hold much longer.

Notorious partisan William "Bloody Bill" Anderson gathers 200 veteran guerrillas four miles south of Centralia, Missouri, 120 miles northwest of St. Louis.

NAVAL: The Confederate raider CSS *Florida* under Lieutenant Charles M. Morris captures and burns the Union bark *Mondamin* off the South American coast.

September 27

WEST: At 2:30 A.M., General Thomas Ewing skillfully evacuates Fort Davidson at Pilot Knob, Missouri, and silently steals through Confederate lines to escape in the darkness. The garrison also detonates all their ammunition and spikes their cannon, so the Confederates gain very little for their sacrifice. By morning, General Sterling Price orders an immediate pursuit, but Ewing covers 66 miles in the next 39 hours and receives reinforcements at Leasburg, south of St. Louis.

Thirty Confederate guerrillas under William "Bloody Bill" Anderson ride into Centralia, Missouri, and systematically rob the town and plunder its inhabitants. What started as brigandage ends up as murder when a train suddenly pulls into town and Anderson apprehends 23 unarmed Union soldiers. These are summarily executed save for Sergeant Thomas Goodman, whom he hopes to exchange for a captive guerrilla. The bushwhackers then ride off back to Singleton's Farm, four miles distant, where Goodman eventually is released unharmed.

Tragedy at Centralia continues when Major A. V. E. Johnson next arrives with 158 men of his newly recruited 39th Missouri Infantry, mounted on mules. Ignoring pleas to refrain from pursuing the guerrillas, he leaves half his command in town and takes the rest directly into a deadly ambush. Johnson and his men all die, and then the guerrillas return to Centralia to kill any remaining soldiers. By the time "Bloody Bill" completes his black deed, 116 soldiers are dead, two are wounded, and six remain missing. This is one of the most reprehensible acts in the violent undercurrents of civil war in Missouri.

NAVAL: Landing parties conduct a second reconnaissance up Masonboro Inlet, North Carolina, for additional intelligence about the defenses of Wilmington.

The USS *Arkansas* captures the Confederate schooner *Watchful* on Barataria Bay, Louisiana.

Admiral David D. Porter bids the men and officers of his Mississippi River Squadron farewell as he departs to assume command of the North Atlantic Blockading Squadron off Wilmington, North Carolina.

September 28

SOUTH: General Ulysses S. Grant begins to probe the defenses of Richmond and Petersburg, Virginia, for weaknesses. He orders General George G. Meade to attack a section of the Confederate line four miles southwest of Petersburg in the vicinity of Poplar Springs Church. Meade accordingly assigns 20,000 men from General Gouverneur K. Warren's V Corps and General John G. Parke's IX Corps to the task. Grant anticipates that this ploy will prevent General Robert E. Lee from shifting men to the defense of Richmond, where another major drive is pending. Lee, however, begins to move General Richard H. Anderson's troops across to the north bank of the James River as a precaution.

General Benjamin F. Butler's Army of the James dispatches General Edward O. C. Ord's XVIII Corps and General David B. Birney's X Corps across the James River for a three-pronged assault on Richmond's outer perimeter. The intended targets are Fort Harrison and New Market Heights, to be struck simultaneously the following day.

WEST: General Jubal A. Early herds his surviving soldiers into Waynesboro, Virginia, to rest and receive reinforcements.

General William J. Hardee is relieved of command in the Army of Tennessee for his inability to coexist with General John B. Hood. He is subsequently dispatched to command the Confederate Department of South Carolina, Georgia, and Florida.

September 29

SOUTH: Two divisions of the V Corps under General Gouverneur K. Warren strike Confederate positions along the Squirrel Level Road near Poplar Springs Church, Virginia. The defenders and their position are quickly overrun, but delays on behalf of General John G. Parke's IX Corps enable General Ambrose P. Hill to rush up reinforcements and counterattack. Struck in the flank by Generals Henry Heth and

Cadmus M. Wilcox, Parke abandons his gains and falls back among Warren's troops at Peeble's Farm. Subsequent Confederate assaults in the vicinity are repulsed by artillery fire.

General Benjamin F. Butler next directs the Union X and XVIII Corps on a two-pronged attack against the defenses of Richmond, Virginia. General David B. Birney's X Corps of 18,000 men attacks up the slopes of New Market Heights, spearheaded by General Charles A. Paine's African-American division. The black troops encounter heavy fire and dogged resistance, losing 800 men in less than an hour, but they tenaciously forge ahead and storm the earthworks in a tremendous display of courage and sacrifice. The Southerners finally are driven off the heights after three costly assaults. Significantly, of 16 Congressional Medals of Honor awarded to African Americans during the war, no less than 14 originate here.

Simultaneously, General Edward O. C. Ord's XVIII Corps surges ahead against Fort Harrison, then garrisoned by 800 inexperienced artillerymen. The Federals have little problem storming their objective and also beat off an attack by Confederates retreating from New Market Heights. Ord then gathers up his men to attack Fort Gilmer atop Chaffin's Bluff, which falters when he falls severely wounded. A body of Union cavalry under General August V. Kautz also probes in strength down the Darbytown Road, only to be rebuffed by heavy artillery fire. The Union troops begin to entrench and strengthen their lines for an inevitable Southern counterattack on the following day.

WEST: Skirmishing resumes between the forces of General Philip H. Sheridan and Jubal A. Early at Waynesborough, Virginia.

General John B. Hood crosses the Army of Tennessee over the Chattahochee River, intending to cut the Western and Atlantic Railroad, a major Union supply artery.

Advanced elements of General Sterling Price's Confederate army clash with Union forces outside Leasburg and Cuba, Missouri. Price since has abandoned the notion of capturing St. Louis, now defended by General Andrew J. Smith's XVI Corps, so he continues westward along the Missouri River.

NAVAL: The USS *Niphon* forces the British blockade-runner *Night Hawk* aground near Fort Fisher, North Carolina, and destroys it.

Confederate sympathizer John C. Braine and his followers seize the Union steamer *Roanoke* off the Cuban coast and bring that vessel to Bermuda. After failing to smuggle coal and other supplies from the island, he burns his vessel and is detained temporarily by British authorities.

September 30

SOUTH: Eager to prevent Union troops from lengthening his trench lines, General Robert E. Lee arrives at Richmond, Virginia, with eight infantry brigades to recapture Fort Harrison. He launches the divisions of Generals Robert F. Hoke and Charles Field in a bid to overwhelm the defenders, but entrenched Federals easily repel four determined charges. Union general George J. Stannard displays conspicuous skill in defending his works, and he falls critically wounded after defeating their final lunge. Lee, finally thwarted, sullenly withdraws to construct new lines of entrenchments closer to the capital. Union losses for the past two days top 3,300 while the Confederates suffer approximately 2,000.

WEST: Union cavalry under General Stephen O. Burbridge skirmish with General Henry L. Giltner's Confederate troopers at Cedar Bluff, Virginia.

NAVAL: Ships of the Confederate James River Squadron under Commodore James K. Mitchell lend naval support fire to the unsuccessful attack on Fort Harrison, Virginia. They also prevent Union troops from occupying strategic Chaffin's Bluff afterward.

October 1

SOUTH: General John G. Parke's IX Corps advances on Confederate siege lines near Poplar Springs Church again but does not attack. Instead, his men dig entrenchments of their own, extending them out to connect with Union lines around Globe Tavern on the Weldon Railroad.

WEST: General John B. Hood moves his surviving forces south around Atlanta to assail General William T. Sherman's railroad lines at Salt Springs, Georgia.

General Nathan B. Forrest's cavalry skirmish with Union garrisons at Athens and Huntsville, Alabama.

General Stephen O. Burbridge's 3,500 cavalry engage and drive back a Confederate rear guard under General Henry L. Giltner at Clinch Mountain, Virginia. The heavily outnumbered Giltner falls back on improvised defenses at nearby Saltville. There Burbridge engages a mixed force of 2,800 soldiers, bushwhackers, and militia under General John S. William, losing heavily with every charge. By the time Federal troopers finally storm Southern defenses, their ammunition is nearly expended and Burbridge orders a retreat back to Kentucky this evening. Union losses are 329 killed, wounded, or missing; the Confederates sustain about 190 casualties.

Advancing Southerners under General Sterling Price engage Federal troops at Franklin and Lake Springs, Missouri.

NAVAL: The USS *Niphon* runs the British blockade-runner *Condor* aground at Port Fisher, North Carolina, and Confederate spy Rose O'Neal Greenhow drowns when the small boat she escapes in capsizes. Greenhow is found with $2,000 in British gold in a bag around her neck. Intense fire from the fort also prevents the Union vessel from destroying the steamer.

October 2

SOUTH: President Jefferson Davis appoints General Pierre G. T. Beauregard commander of the Division of the West to help coordinate the operations of Generals John B. Hood and Richard Taylor. In truth, Davis dislikes Beauregard and resents both his tendency to meddle and his endless penchant for grandiose schemes.

Confederate forces under General Ambrose P. Hill attack Union entrenchments manned by General John G. Parke's IX Corps along Poplar Springs Church but are repulsed. Fighting in this vicinity has depleted Union forces by 2,800 men while the Southerners sustain around 1,300 casualties. Consequently, General Robert E. Lee is obliged to stretch his dwindling manpower resources even thinner to cover the lost ground.

WEST: General John B. Hood begins to cut General William T. Sherman's supply lines between Atlanta and Chattanooga by tearing up tracks belonging to the Western and Atlantic Railroad.

Confederate forces at Saltville, Virginia, most notably guerrillas under Champ Ferguson and a Tennessean brigade under Felix H. Robertson, roam the recent battlefield and execute upward of 100 wounded African-American soldiers of the 5th U.S. Colored Cavalry found alive. Several white Union soldiers are also murdered in cold blood.

General Sterling Price's Confederates occupy Washington, Missouri, on the Missouri River. This action places his force 50 miles from St. Louis.

October 3

POLITICS: President Jefferson Davis, while passing through Columbia, South Carolina, exhorts his fellow citizens to persevere and predicts the defeat of General William T. Sherman.

WEST: General George H. Thomas is dispatched back to Nashville, Tennessee, with orders to curtail any further mischief caused by General John B. Hood to Union lines of communication.

General Alexander P. Stewart's Confederate corps hits Union positions at Big Shanty, Georgia, seizing 175 captives.

Confederates under General Sterling Price engage Union forces at Hermann and Miller's Station, Missouri, outside St. Louis. His success prompts the rerouting of General Andrew J. Smith's corps to that town instead of reinforcing General George H. Thomas's army at Nashville, Tennessee.

NAVAL: Captain Raphael Semmes departs England aboard the English steamer *Tasmanian* and begins to work his way back to the Confederacy.

October 4

POLITICS: Postmaster General William Dennison joins President Abraham Lincoln's cabinet.

Syracuse, New York, is the scene of the "National Convention of Colored Citizens of the United States," with 144 delegates drawn from 18 states. They promulgate the National Equal Rights League, headed by John M. Langston of Ohio.

SOUTH: General William T. Sherman repositions his forces along Kennesaw Mountain for a possible strike at General John B. Hood's army as it marches westward.

WEST: Confederate forces operating against the Western and Atlantic Railroad attack Union positions at Ackworth, Georgia, seizing 250 prisoners.

General Sterling Price, wary of Union reinforcements arriving at St. Louis, Missouri, veers away from the town and heads west.

NAVAL: The Confederate raider CSS *Florida* under Lieutenant Charles M. Morris drops anchor at Bahía, Brazil, closely watched by the USS *Wachusett*.

October 5

POLITICS: President Jefferson Davis appears before cheering crowds at Augusta, Georgia, and lauds them with ringing oratory predicting a complete Confederate victory. "Never before was I so confident that energy, harmony, and determination would rid the country of its enemy," he declares, "and give to the women of the land that peace their good deeds have so well deserved."

SOUTH: A division of Confederates under General Samuel G. French, numbering 3,276 men, becomes tasked with capturing a major Union supply depot at Allatoona Pass, Georgia. That post is defended by 2,025 Union soldiers under the recently arrived General John M. Corse, who counts both rugged terrain and rapid-fire Henry repeating rifles in his favor. For several hours, the Southerners attack from the west and the south, at one point driving the defenders back into their mountaintop fort, but Corse invariably rallies and sweeps his antagonists back down the slopes. French concludes that the position cannot be carried and marches off to join the main army under General John B. Hood. Union losses are 706 while the Confederates sustain 897. This stalwart defense also inspires the noted hymn, "Hold the Fort, For We Are Coming."

General William J. Hardee assumes command of the Department of South Carolina, Georgia, and Florida to separate him from General John B. Hood.

WEST: The Confederate column under General Sterling Price marches west along the Missouri River, occupying the town of Heiman. His rear guard is harassed by Federal cavalry under General Alfred Pleasonton, which induces him to bypass Jefferson City and continue onto Boonville.

NAVAL: A boat expedition from the USS *Restless* enters St. Andrew's Bay, Florida, and destroys a large saltworks along with 150 buildings.

The USS *Mobile* captures the British blockade-runner *Annie Virdon* off Velasco, Texas.

At Bahía, Brazil, the USS *Wachusett* arrives and challenges the smaller CSS *Florida* to a duel in international waters, and the latter respectfully declines. Local authorities extract promises from both captains that Brazilian neutrality will be respected.

October 6

POLITICS: The *Richmond Enquirer* breaks new ground by printing an essay promoting the use of African-American soldiers for the Confederacy. The idea gradually is receiving greater currency, although President Jefferson Davis is never reconciled to it.

WEST: General Philip A. Sheridan, considering the Shenandoah Valley campaign closed, begins to withdraw his army north, destroying everything in its path. General Jubal A. Early, ensconced at Blue Gap, welcomes this turn of events and orders General Thomas L. Rosser's cavalry division to harass withdrawing Federals at every step.

Confederate cavalry under General Nathan B. Forrest harry Union forces at Florence, Alabama.

NAVAL: The USS *Wamsutta* chases the Confederate steamer *Constance* aground on Long Island in Charleston harbor, South Carolina.

October 7

SOUTH: General Robert E. Lee again determines to recapture Fort Harrison, Virginia, in an attempt to restore his siege lines outside Richmond, Virginia. He orders two divisions under General Robert F. Hoke and Charles W. Field, assisted by a cavalry brigade under General Martin W. Gary, to drive Union forces from the Darbytown Road. At dawn these three columns simultaneously fall on 1,700 Union cavalry under General August V. Kautz, driving them back in confusion. Pushing forward, the Confederates encounter stiffer resistance from General Alfred H. Terry's division, X Corps, at Johnson's Farm. Terry uses delays in Field's advance to bring up artillery reinforcements, and at 10:00 A.M., he repulses several piecemeal charges, killing General John Gregg of the famed Texas brigade. Hoke also makes a tardy appearance but fails to advance, at which point Lee calls off the attack and withdraws. Confederate casualties are 1,350 to a Union tally of 399. Defeat here further convinces Lee to begin to dig new lines of trenches closer to Richmond.

WEST: The army of General Philip H. Sheridan continues its policy of burning crops and confiscating livestock at Woodstock, Virginia. To date, his men have destroyed 2,000 barns, 70 flour mills, driven off 4,000 head of cattle, and killed 3,000 sheep. Sheridan vows that when he is finished, the region around Staunton "will have little in it for man or beast." Meanwhile, Confederate cavalry under General Thomas L. Rosser skirmish with the Union rear guard commanded by Generals Wesley Merritt and George A. Custer at Brook's Gap.

NAVAL: The USS *Aster,* while chasing a blockade-runner toward Fort Fisher, North Carolina, runs aground and is destroyed to prevent capture. The crew is rescued by the *Niphon,* which also tows the *Berberry* to safety once it is also disabled while trying to tow the *Aster* off the bar.

The USS *Wachusett* under Commander Napoleon Collins decides to attack and capture the Confederate raider CSS *Florida* at Bahía, Brazil, after learning that Lieutenant Charles M. Morris and most of his crew are ashore. At 3:00 A.M., Collins slips his cable, sneaks past a Brazilian gunboat, and rams his quarry. The *Florida* surrenders after a brief struggle, having previously accounted for 37 Union prizes. However, the nature of its seizure, a blatant violation of Brazilian neutrality, raises acute diplomatic ramifications.

October 8

WEST: General Thomas L. Rosser and his Confederate troopers continue dogging the Union rear guard under Generals Wesley Merritt and George A. Custer. However, their commanding officer, General Alfred T. A. Torbert, denies them permission to engage their opponent. When word of his reluctance reaches General Philip H. Sheridan's ears, he angrily informs Torbert to "start out at daylight and whip the Rebel cavalry or get whipped!" Sheridan further promises to observe the dust up from nearby Round Top Mountain.

Opposing cavalry under General Sterling Price and Alfred Pleasonton skirmish at Jefferson City, Missouri.

NAVAL: The Federal vessel *Steam Picket Boat No. 2* is burned to prevent capture after its crew is captured ashore at Wicomico Bay, Virginia.

The British steamer *Sea King* departs England for Madeira where it will be commissioned as the Confederate raider CSS *Shenandoah.*

October 9

WEST: Union cavalry brigades under Generals George A. Custer and Wesley Merritt engage the Confederate cavalry division of General Thomas L. Rosser at Tom's Brook,

Virginia. As Custer leads 2,500 troopers against Rosser's 3,500 men, he recognizes his adversary as an old West Point roommate and doffs his hat before engaging. Meanwhile, Merrit gallops down the Valley Pike to engage the 1,500 troopers of General Lunsford L. Lomax's division. As Custer and Rosser spar, Merritt crashes headlong into his opponent, routing him. Custer, however, is forced to maneuver around the Confederate left flank to evict the Southerners from their strong position. As Rosser obligingly falls back to Tom's Brook, Custer charges his former acquaintance head-on, routing him, and chases the scampering Southerners 20 miles. Merritt enjoys similar success and pursues Lomax for 26 miles. This is one of the biggest triumphs of the Union mounted arm over its vaunted adversary and is celebrated as "The Woodstock Races." Union losses are nine killed and 48 wounded to a Confederate tally of 350 killed, wounded, or captured, along with 11 cannon and many wagons seized.

General Sterling Price captures Boonsboro, Missouri, while moving steadily northwest away from St. Louis. There, he adds in 2,000 new recruits to his army, which remains chronically short of weapons.

NAVAL: The USS *Sebago* trades fire with Confederate batteries at Freeman's Wharf, Mobile Bay, Alabama, suffering five casualties.

October 10

SOUTH: General John B. Hood skirmishes with Union forces around Rome, Georgia.

WEST: General Philip H. Sheridan moves north and occupies a strong position along Cedar Creek, Virginia, 15 miles south of Winchester, enticing Confederates under General Jubal A. Early to follow.

General Nathan B. Forrest easily disperses a Union boat-borne expedition against him at Eastport, Mississippi.

NAVAL: The USS *Montgomery* captures the British blockade-runner *Bat* off Wilmington, North Carolina.

The Federal gunboats USS *Key West* and *Undine,* escorting the transports *City of Peking, Kenton,* and *Aurora* on an expedition against Eastport, Mississippi, are interdicted on the Tennessee River by Confederate artillery under General Nathan B. Forrest. After a severe exchange, the vessels withdraw down the river.

October 11

POLITICS: The recent round of elections in Pennsylvania, Ohio, and Indiana demonstrates continuing support for President Abraham Lincoln.

WEST: General William T. Sherman concentrates his army at Rome, Georgia, in preparation for attacking Confederates under General John B. Hood as they march west.

General Sterling Price continues lurching northwest through Missouri, skirmishing with Union forces at Boonville and Brunswick.

October 12

POLITICS: U.S. Supreme Court chief justice Roger B. Taney, titular head of that body since 1835, dies in Washington, D.C. He wrote the majority opinion for the infamous *Dred Scott* decision of 1857, which reaffirmed the status of African-American slaves as property, thereby exacerbating sectional tensions.

SOUTH: Continual skirmishing erupts between Union and Confederate forces at Resaca, Georgia, as General John B. Hood marches toward Alabama.

NAVAL: Admiral David D. Porter assumes control of the North Atlantic Blockading Squadron off Wilmington, North Carolina, from Admiral Samuel P. Lee. "It will be almost useless to enjoin on all officers the importance of their being vigilant at all times," he declared. "We have an active enemy to deal with, and every officer and man must be on the alert."

The USS *Chocura* captures the British blockade-runner *Louisa* off Aransas Pass, Texas.

October 13

POLITICS: Maryland narrowly approves a new constitution mandating the abolition of slavery. The tally is 30,174 to 29,799, a margin of only 374 votes.

SOUTH: A drive by General Alfred Terry's X Corps down Darbytown Road, Virginia, is checked by heavy resistance from General Richard H. Anderson's troops.

WEST: General Jubal A. Early advances his greatly reduced Confederate army back to their old position at Fisher's Hill, Virginia.

Confederate raiders under Colonel John S. Mosby capture and burn a train belonging to the Baltimore and Ohio Railroad near Kearneysville, West Virginia, absconding with $173,000 from a Union paymaster.

General John B. Hood's Confederates seize the railroad north of Resaca, Georgia, to cut General William T. Sherman's supply lines back to Tennessee.

NAVAL: Landing parties from the USS *Braziliera* and *Mary Sanford* skirmish with Confederate cavalry at Yellow Bluff, White Oak Creek, Georgia. After freeing several slaves from a nearby plantation, they embark and return downstream.

October 14

WEST: Skirmishing flares anew between Union and Confederate forces in the vicinity of Cedar Creek, Virginia.

General Sterling Price issues an appeal to the people of Missouri to flock to the Confederate banner. His will is largely unheeded.

A force of 2,500 Confederates under General John B. Clark crosses the Missouri River at Arrow Rock and advances on the nearby settlement of Glasgow, Missouri, where a large cache of Union arms reputedly is stored.

October 15

SOUTH: General Braxton Bragg is detached from service at Richmond, Virginia, and sent to Wilmington, North Carolina, to coordinate defenses there.

WEST: Confederate general John B. Clark besieges the town of Glasgow, Missouri, with 2,500 men. The garrison consists of 750 state militia and a handful of Federal troops under Colonel Chester Harding. Harding resists stoutly for several hours until the Southerners capture several buildings on the northeast part of town. Clark then immediately demands his surrender, threatening to unleash guerrilla forces if he resists further. Harding, low on ammunition, complies and is paroled. Union losses are 11 dead and 32 wounded, but they still inflict around 100 casualties on the Confederates.

Worse, the Federals manage to destroy all weapons in their possession, defeating the purpose of the attack.

Paris, Missouri, falls to Confederate forces under General Sterling Price.

October 16

West: General Philip H. Sheridan leaves his army at Cedar Creek, Virginia, 15 miles south of Winchester, and makes for a high-level strategy conference with Secretary of War Edwin M. Stanton and General Henry W. Halleck in Washington, D.C. General Horatio G. Wright remains in charge during his absence.

General Sterling Price's army seizes Ridgely, Missouri, as it moves westward along the Missouri River.

General James G. Blunt crosses the Missouri state line from Kansas with 15,000 troops, although his militia refuses to advance any farther than Big Blue River. Blunt nonetheless reaches Lexington with 2,000 soldiers and assumes blocking positions around the town.

October 17

South: General James Longstreet resumes command of the I Corps, Army of Northern Virginia, following a lengthy convalescence.

West: General John B. Gordon and Captain Jedediah Hotchkiss, a topographical engineer, steal on the Union army encamped at Cedar Creek, Virginia, ascend Massanutten Mountain, and examine the Northern encampment closely. They discern that their left is entirely "in the air" and subject to a sudden flanking assault. This intelligence is relayed immediately to General Jubal A. Early.

General Pierre G. T. Beauregard assumes command of the Confederate Military Division of the West to promote better harmony between feuding commanders.

General John B. Hood relents from attacks on Union forces in the vicinity of Gadsden, Alabama, and continues westward in the mistaken belief that General William T. Sherman will follow to protect his line of communications with Tennessee.

Confederates under General Sterling Price occupy Carrollton, Missouri, and commence a drive on Lexington. However, Union forces under General Samuel R. Curtis are approaching from the west, General Andrew J. Smith is marching from the east, and Federal cavalry under General Alfred Pleasonton closely trail the Southerners from behind.

October 18

West: Indomitable general Jubal A. Early, learning that General Philip H. Sheridan is absent from his army, plans to attack the Union encampment at Cedar Creek. Acting on General John B. Gordon's advice, he sends three divisions along differing paths that ultimately converge behind the exposed VIII Corp of General George Crook on the left. This march, carried out under extreme secrecy, is one of the most audacious turning movements of the entire war.

October 19

North: Lieutenant Bennet H. Young and his band of 20 Confederate Kentuckians slip across the Canadian border and attack three banks in St. Albans, Vermont, 15 miles from the border. Two citizens are shot, one fatally. After absconding with

$20,000, the Southerners set fire to several buildings and try to recross the border. But as word of the attack spreads, a nearby Union officer forms a posse and chases after the marauders. They catch the raiders on Canadian soil and then turn them over to authorities there for processing and extradition. St. Albans is the northernmost "engagement" of the Civil War.

WEST: At 5:00 A.M., the Battle of Cedar Creek erupts as the Confederate divisions of Generals Clement A. Evans, Stephen Ramseur, and John Pegram plunge out of an early morning fog and into the Union camp at Cedar Creek. The Federal VIII and IX Corps, flanked and completely surprised, simply crumble before the Confederate onslaught. The only real resistance mounted comes from General George W. Getty's division, VI Corps, which resists pluckily and convinces General Jubal A. Early to dislodge the division first before pursuing the beaten troops. Gordon and other leaders advise against the distraction, but at length Getty gradually is pushed back. A break in the fighting develops as the hungry, ragged Confederates pause to loot the Union camp thoroughly. Early, though outnumbered two to one, achieves a striking tactical victory, capturing 1,300 prisoners and 18 cannon. The remnants of three Union corps are reduced to a leaderless throng milling about three miles from camp.

Fortunately, General Philip H. Sheridan is returning from his strategy conference in Washington, D.C., and encounters numerous refugees as he approaches Cedar Creek. Sheridan then spurs his horse for 12 miles and rallies his shaken command. Sheridan's presence is electric, and soon the revitalized Federals regroup and counterattack the exhausted, disorganized Confederates, hitting their left flank at 4:00 P.M. This equally sudden onslaught, spearheaded by General George A. Custer's cavalry, proves too much for Early's men. They bolt from the field, and a vengeful Union pursuit chases them all the way past Fisher's Hill. It a remarkable change in fortunes for Sheridan, who snatches victory from the jaws of defeat. As Early bitterly remonstrates, "The Yankees got whipped and we got scared." Confederate losses are 320 dead, including the talented general Stephen D. Ramseur, 1,540 wounded, and 1,050 missing (2,810) while the Union suffers 644 killed, 3,430 injured, and 1,591 missing (5,671). Sheridan also captures 43 cannon and 300 wagons. More important, Cedar Creek is the straw that finally breaks Southern resistance in the strategic Shenandoah Valley. That this region remains solidly in Union hands for the remainder of the war portends ill for the Confederacy's survival.

General Nathan B. Forrest leads his cavalry out of Corinth, Mississippi, and rides east intending to cooperate with General John B. Hood in Alabama after raiding around Johnsonville, Tennessee.

General Sterling Price's Confederates occupy Lexington, Missouri, ejecting the advance troops of General James G. Blunt. Price, realizing he nearly is surrounded by two converging Federal columns, marches south between his antagonists and determines to defeat each one separately.

NAVAL: The USS *Mobile* captures the Confederate schooner *Emily* at San Luis Pass, Texas.

The English steamer *Sea King* arrives in the Madeira Islands where it is converted into the Confederate raider CSS *Shenandoah* and is commissioned under Lieutenant James I. Waddell.

October 20

POLITICS: President Abraham Lincoln decrees that the last Wednesday of every November will be celebrated as "a day of Thanksgiving and Praise to Almighty God the beneficent Creator and Ruler of the Universe."

WEST: Union cavalry pursue defeated remnants of General Jubal A. Early's army down the Shenandoah Valley. The shattered Confederates continue falling back on New Market.

NAVAL: Armed boats from the USS *Stars and Stripes* ascend the Ocklocknee River, Florida, and destroy a Confederate fishery on Marsh's Island.

October 21

NORTH: General George Crook is appointed a major general, U.S. Army.

WEST: General William T. Sherman halts his pursuit of General John B. Hood at Gaylesville, Alabama, once his Confederate column reaches Gadsden.

A skirmish with Federal cavalry along the Little Blue River alerts General Sterling Price that General James R. Blunt's Army of the Frontier remains within striking distance. Confederate forces experience little difficulty driving off 400 dismounted troopers and two cannon, yet they are rebuffed when they try to pursue across the river. Price's superiority in numbers eventually threatens to run both Union flanks, so Blunt falls back and joins General Samuel R. Curtis's main force at Big Blue River.

NAVAL: The USS *Fort Jackson* captures the Confederate steamer *Wando* off Cape Romain, South Carolina.

The USS *Sea Bird* captures the British blockade-runner *Lucy* off Anclote Keys, Florida.

October 22

WEST: General Sterling Price commits a brigade under Joseph O. Shelby to feint against the main Union line at Big Blue River, Missouri, while launching two brigades under General Sidney D. Jackman against their center. However, General Samuel R. Curtis's command holds firm and forces the Confederates back. Meanwhile, a Southern regiment under Colonel Alonzo Slayback discovers an unprotected ford upstream and crosses to threaten the exposed Union right flank. The fighting gradually dissipates by nightfall, and Curtis falls back in the direction of Westport to regroup.

Simultaneously, General Alfred Pleasonton begins to move up behind the Confederates on the Little Blue River. A Confederate brigade under General William L. Cabell fails to halt the Federal onslaught, losing 400 prisoners and two cannon. The surviving Southerners under General John S. Marmaduke fall back across the river in good order, alerting Price to the danger. The general then girds his command for a fighting withdrawal southward.

NAVAL: Confederate secretary of the navy Stephen R. Mallory writes to President Jefferson Davis, defending his strategy to deploy the CSS *Tallahassee* and *Chickamauga* as commerce raiders rather than detaining them at Wilmington, North Carolina, as part of the city's defenses. "A cruise by the *Chickamauga* and *Tallahassee* against the northern coasts and commerce would at once draw a fleet of fast steamers from the blockading squadron off Wilmington in pursuit of them," he reasons, "and this alone would render such a cruise expedient."

A boat expedition from the USS *Tacony* embarks on a reconnaissance mission up the Roanoke River, North Carolina, where it is fired on by Confederate forces. The Northerners are forced to take cover in a swamp to evade pursuers where they build a makeshift raft to reach the mouth of the river and safety.

The USS *Wamsutta*, *Geranium*, and *Mingoe* run the British blockade-runner *Flora* aground at Charleston, South Carolina, and it is destroyed by cannon fire from nearby Morris Island the following day.

October 23

WEST: The Battle of Westport, Missouri, erupts between Generals Sterling Price and surrounding Union forces. General James G. Blunt advances against General Joseph O. Shelby across Brush Creek and recoils. However, the Confederates cannot spare the reserves to pursue him because General Alfred Pleasonton's force looms across the Big Blue River, pressing on their rear. At length, General Samuel R. Curtis reinforces Blunt, and he pushes back over Brush Creek just as Pleasonton's column works its way across the river. The Confederates under General John S. Marmaduke resist strongly, but they are ejected from their commanding bluff and a rout ensues. Surrounded and outnumbered, Price's army flees in confusion to the southwest. However, at this juncture the Union leaders begin to squabble among themselves over what to do next, and the Southerners escape with their supply train. Casualties are estimated at 1,500 men for both sides in this action, the last major engagement of the Trans-Mississippi region.
NAVAL: Vessels of the South Atlantic Blockading Squadron sink the grounded blockade-runner *Flamingo* off Sullivan's Island, South Carolina.

October 24

WEST: General Sterling Price concedes defeat and moves his Confederates southward down the border between Kansas and Missouri. His movements are slowed by an enormous baggage train loaded with plunder with which the soldiers are reluctant to part.
NAVAL: The USS *Nita* seizes the abandoned blockade-runner *Unknown* off Clearwater Harbor, Florida, while the *Rosalie* captures an unnamed Confederate sloop off Little Marco down the coast.

October 25

WEST: Confederates under General Sterling Price are attacked by Union cavalry General Alfred Pleasonton at Marais de Cynges River, 60 miles south of Westport on the Kansas border. Though outnumbering their opponents, the demoralized Southerners rapidly give ground, and Price loses one-third of his baggage train. General John S. Marmaduke is also taken prisoner.
NAVAL: An armed party from the USS *Don* lands at Fleet's Point, Great Wicomoco River, Virginia, and burns several barracks.

Admiral George F. Pearson assumes command of the Pacific Squadron from Admiral Charles H. Bell.

October 26

SOUTH: General Ulysses S. Grant wishes to cut the South Side Railroad by launching a small offensive north of the James River. To achieve this, he orders General Benjamin F. Butler to take several divisions of the X and XVIII Corps and advance against Fair Oaks, outside of Richmond, Virginia. Meanwhile, the II, V, and IX Corps are likewise to march toward the Boydton Plank Road, another vital supply route.

WEST: General John B. Hood brushes against a large Union garrison at Decatur, Alabama, sidesteps it, and moves off farther west. He expects to unite with Confederate cavalry under General Nathan B. Forrest soon, but that leader is delayed in Tennessee by independent operations and fails to rendezvous.

Confederate outlaw William "Bloody Bill" Anderson is killed in a Union ambush near Richmond, Missouri.

NAVAL: The USS *Adolph Hugel* captures the Confederate schooner *Coquette* in Wade's Bay on the Potomac River.

Lieutenant William B. Cushing leaves the blockading squadron and arrives in the Roanoke River intending to destroy the CSS *Albemarle* at its moorings. However, his ships ground at the river's mouth, and the attack is postponed until the following evening.

October 27

SOUTH: An advance by 43,000 Union troops commences against the South Side Railroad, south of Petersburg, Virginia, in the early morning rain. Operations entrusted to the Army of the James consist of throwing General Alfred Terry and the X Corps against Charles City while General Godfrey Weitzel leads the XVIII Corps against Fair Oaks. Terry's movement is unimpeded, but General James Longstreet, commanding the defenses of Richmond, Virginia, concludes that Weitzel's maneuver is dangerous and marshals forces to oppose him. As the XVIII Corps moves down the Williamsburg Road, it suddenly confronts the divisions of Generals Robert F. Hoke and Charles W. Field. Weitzel's main thrust is blunted, but an African-American brigade under General John Holman then slips around the Southern flank and charges. Holman's progress is also stopped by dogged resistance from General William Mahone's Confederates, and Weitzel, seeing further gains impractical, orders his men withdrawn. Union losses are 1,103 to a Confederate tally of 451.

Meanwhile even larger operations unfold near Hatcher's Run. The II Corps under General Winfield S. Hancock, the V Corps under General Gouverneur K. Warren, and the IX Corps under General John G. Parke—43,000 men in all—march seven miles southwest of Petersburg through autumn rain. Parke's command meets heavy resistance from General Cadmus M. Wilcox's command and stops. Warren and Hancock nevertheless press forward until they finally reach Boydton Plank Road. There, General Wade Hampton's Confederate cavalry suddenly assails Hancock's left while General Ambrose P. Hill pushes the divisions under Generals Henry Heth against his center and William Mahone strikes his right and rear. The three Confederate forces converge suddenly on the II Corps, causing great confusion, but Hancock calmly sorts out his men and beats back determined Southern assaults. Nightfall closes the engagement at Hatcher's Run, and the Federals fall back to their lines. Hancock suffers 166 dead, 1,028 wounded, and 564 missing, whereas Confederate losses are estimated at about 1,000. General Ulysses S. Grant subsequently concludes offensive operations for the year and settles into winter quarters. The thin gray line prevails again, but its serried ranks grow thinner with every skirmish.

NAVAL: The imposing Confederate ram CSS *Albemarle* is sunk by a spar torpedo operated by 21-year-old Lieutenant William B. Cushing at Plymouth on the Roanoke River, North Carolina. Cushing utilized two 30-foot steam launches, each outfitted with a 14-foot spar torpedo, and a crew of 15. He has the good fortune of passing within 20 feet of the Confederate picket ship *Southfield* without detection and is almost atop the *Albemarle* when sentries observe him in the dark. Cushing then overruns floating log booms placed as protection, strikes his quarry under its port quarter while receiving heavy fire, and detonates the charge. The *Albemarle,* fatally damaged, quickly sinks as does Cushing's own vessel. He then swims to shore alone. At daybreak, the enterprising officer commandeers a small boat and rows eight miles down the Roanoke River to Albemarle Sound, and he is rescued by the USS *Valley City.* Only Cushing and one other member of the expedition make it back; the remaining 13 are captured.

October 28

WEST: In a rare defeat, the 8th Illinois Cavalry routs Confederates under Colonel John S. Mosby, killing eight rangers and capturing nine.

Confederate cavalry under General Nathan B. Forrest arrive at Paris Landing, Tennessee, on the Tennessee River, where they immediately begin to raise obstacles along the waterway to interdict Union water traffic.

General William T. Sherman abandons his own lines of communication at Ladiga, Alabama, and moves westward back toward Atlanta, Georgia. General John B. Hood being beyond his grasp, he next turns his attention to Savannah, Georgia, on the coast.

General James G. Blunt's division surprises and attacks General Sterling Price's retreating army at Newtonia, Missouri. However, quick reactions from General Joseph O. Shelby and his "Iron Brigade" allow the bulk of the Confederates to withdraw intact. After two hours, Blunt nearly runs out of ammunition as Shelby begins to press his left flank, but the timely arrival of General John B. Sanborn and three more Union brigades staves off defeat. Shelby then disengages and slips away. Both sides claim victory, but the Union forfeits its only real chance to destroy Price.

NAVAL: The Confederate raider CSS *Chickamauga* under Lieutenant John Wilkinson slips past the Union blockade off Wilmington, North Carolina.

The USS *Calypso* and *Eolus* capture the British blockade-runner *Lady Sterling* off Wilmington, North Carolina.

The USS *General Thomas* and the army gunboat *Stone River* successfully engage a Confederate battery on the Tennessee River near Decatur, Alabama.

October 29

WEST: In a controversial decision, Department of the Missouri commander General William S. Rosecrans calls all forces under his command back to their respective stations. This leaves General Samuel R. Curtis with only 3,500 cavalry to pursue General Sterling Price's larger Confederate force.

NAVAL: With the fearsome CSS *Albemarle* sunk, a Federal naval squadron consisting of the USS *Valley City, Commodore Hall, Tacony, Shamrock, Otsego, Wyalusing,* and *Whitehead* attack Confederate defenses at Plymouth on the Albemarle River, North Carolina.

October 30

WEST: The Army of Tennessee under General John B. Hood occupies Tuscumbia, Alabama, prior to crossing the Tennessee River. His progress prompts Federal troops to begin to concentrate at Pulsaski, Tennessee.

Confederate cavalry under General Nathan B. Forrest capture the transport *Mazeppa* on the Tennessee River, including its cargo of 9,000 pairs of shoes.

NAVAL: The Confederate raider CSS *Shenandoah* under Lieutenant James I. Waddell captures and sinks the Union bark *Alina* off the Azores.

The Confederate raider CSS *Olustee* (nee *Tallahassee*) under Lieutenant William H. Ward, evades the Union blockade off Wilmington, North Carolina, and begins an Atlantic cruise.

The USS *Undine* and army transports *Venus* and *Cheeseman* are captured by Confederate cavalry under General Nathan B. Forrest on the Tennessee River near Johnsonville, Tennessee. The vessels resist for three hours until *Undine's* ammunition gives out, and the vessel is beached. Forrest then forms a slapdash Confederate "navy" on the river bend, backed by shore artillery, to interrupt Union river communications.

October 31

POLITICS: Nevada becomes the nation's 36th state. Its two Republican-leaning U.S. senators provide the exact margin necessary to approve the 13th Amendment to the Constitution. The state is also expected to contribute three electoral votes to Lincoln's reelection bid.

WEST: General John B. Hood arrives at Tuscumbia, Alabama, and marches his army northward into Tennessee, still laboring under the mistaken belief that General William T. Sherman will follow.

NAVAL: A Federal navy squadron of seven warships bombards Confederate defenders at Plymouth, North Carolina, until a large magazine is detonated and they evacuate that post. Armed landing parties seize Fort Williams, along with 37 captives and 22 cannon.

The USS *Wilderness* and *Niphon* capture the British blockade-runner *Annie* off New Inlet, North Carolina.

The USS *Katahdin* captures the British blockade-runner *Albert Edward* near Galveston, Texas.

The Confederate raider CSS *Chickamauga* under Lieutenant John Wilkinson captures and sinks the Union ships *Emma L. Hall* and *Shooting Star* off the New England coast.

November 1
POLITICS: The new Maryland state constitution, abolishing slavery, is enacted.
WEST: General Nathan B. Forrest advances his cavalry and captured boats down the Tennessee River as far as Johnsonville, Tennessee, where he places artillery on the riverbank and lays in wait for Union river traffic.

General Andrew J. Smith's XVI Corps departs Missouri and heads for Nashville to reinforce the army under General George H. Thomas.
NAVAL: The Confederate raider CSS *Chickamauga* under Lieutenant John Wilkinson seizes and burns the Union schooners *Goodspeed* and *Otter Rock* in the North Atlantic.

Admiral Samuel P. Lee becomes commander of the Mississippi Squadron at Mound City, Illinois.

November 2
NORTH: Secretary of State William H. Seward informs the major of New York that Confederate agents arriving from Canada are planning to burn the city down by election day.
NAVAL: The USS *Santiago de Cuba* captures the Confederate steamer *Lucy* off Charleston, South Carolina.

General Nathan B. Forrest proceeds downstream on the Tennessee River with *Venus* and *Undine*, two captured naval vessels. En route, they encounter the Union paddle wheelers USS *Key West* and *Tawah*, whereupon a protracted battle ensues. Eventually *Venus* is driven ashore near Johnsonville, Tennessee, and recaptured while *Undine* remains in Confederate hands and escapes downstream.

The Confederate raider CSS *Chickamauga* under Lieutenant John Wilkinson captures the Union bark *Speedwell* off New Jersey and releases it on a bond.

November 3
WEST: The Union IV Corps arrives at Pulaski, Tennessee, to help obstruct the advance of General John B. Hood's Confederates.

November 4
WEST: General John C. Breckinridge leads a small Confederate army from western Virginia into eastern Tennessee. There, he encounters an equally small Federal force at Strawberry Plains, Tennessee, and drives them off.
NAVAL: Artillery under General Nathan B. Forrest attack and sink the Union paddle wheelers USS *Key West*, *Tawah*, and *Elfin* on the Tennessee River near Johnsonville, Tennessee. But reinforcements arrive in the form of steamers *Moose*, *Brilliant*, *Victory*, *Curlew*, *Fairy*, and *Paw Paw*, which force the Confederates to beach and burn CSS *Undine*. Forrest also bombards a large Union depot across the river at Johnsonville, inflicting considerable devastation. His latest raid disrupts the flow of Union supplies and results in considerable damage: Four gunboats, 14 steamers, 17 barges, 33 cannon,

150 captives, and 75,000 tons of supplies ruined. Total loses to the Union exceed $6.7 million.

November 5
WEST: General Nathan B. Forrest, flushed with success, rides south from Johnsonville, Tennessee, toward Corinth, Mississippi, there to join the main Confederate army under General John B. Hood.

NAVAL: The USS *Patapsco* drives an unidentified sloop aground off Fort Moultrie, Charleston harbor, South Carolina, and burns it.

The USS *Fort Morgan* captures the Confederate blockade-runner *John A. Hazard* in the Gulf of Mexico.

The Confederate raider CSS *Shenandoah* under Lieutenant James I. Waddell captures and burns the Union schooner *Charter Oak* off the Cape Verde Islands.

November 6
WEST: More than 100 Copperheads and Confederate sympathizers are arrested by Colonel Benjamin Sweet in Chicago, Illinois. They allegedly were plotting to seize the polls on election day, stuff the ballots, and then burn the city down. None of those arrested are ever prosecuted.

General Sterling Price's men fight a rearguard action at Cane Hill, Arkansas, having evacuated Missouri for the last time.

NAVAL: Armed boats from the USS *Adela* capture the Confederate schooner *Badger* at St. George's Sound, Florida.

The USS *Fort Morgan* captures the Confederate schooner *Lone* off Brazos Pass, Texas.

November 7
POLITICS: The second session of the 2nd Confederate Congress convenes in Richmond, Virginia. President Jefferson Davis declares that the Confederacy still desires a negotiated settlement with the North, but only on the basis of independence. Despite the recent fall of Atlanta, Davis assures Congress, "There are no vital points on the preservation of which the continued existence of the Confederacy depends."

November 8
POLITICS: The Republican ticket of President Abraham Lincoln and Vice President Andrew Johnson decisively wins reelection by 2,330,552 votes to 1,835,985 votes for General George B. McClellan. This translates into 212 Republican electoral votes to 21 for the Democrats; McClellan carries only the states of New Jersey, Delaware, and Kentucky. The margin of 55 percent proves so large that the 81 electoral votes of seceded states would not have altered the outcome. Moreover, Lincoln receives his highest percentage of support from soldiers and sailors fighting in the ranks.

NAVAL: The CSS *Shenandoah* under Lieutenant James I. Waddell captures and burns the Union bark *Godfrey* southwest of the Cape Verde Islands.

November 9

WEST: The army of General William T. Sherman organizes itself into two wings under Generals Oliver O. Howard (XV, XVII Corps) and Henry W. Slocum (XIV, XX Corps) prior to marching on Savannah, Georgia.

Sherman then declares: "The army will forage liberally on the country during the march." All ranks are expected to refrain from destroying private property, if possible, but this is still the first mass application of total war against all segments of society.
NAVAL: The USS *Stepping Stones* seizes the Confederate sloops *Reliance* and *Little Elmer* at Mobjack Bay, Virginia.

November 10

POLITICS: At a party celebrating his election victory, President Abraham Lincoln implores his fellow citizens to remain steadfast in the pursuit of final victory and to reunite the country.
WEST: General Jubal A. Early, while defeated, gives ground slowly and harasses Union advances down the Shenandoah Valley.

General William T. Sherman marches his men from Kingston, Georgia, back to Atlanta, prior to advancing on Savannah.
NAVAL: The Confederate raider CSS *Shenandoah* under Lieutenant James I. Waddell captures and scuttles the Union brig *Susan* southwest of the Cape Verde Islands.

November 11

WEST: Union troops begin to raze the ground in and around Rome, Georgia, leveling bridges, shops, mills, and all useful property as they wend their way back to Atlanta.

General George H. Thomas briefly clashes with Confederates under General John C. Breckinridge at Bull's Gap, eastern Tennessee.
NAVAL: The Federal tug USS *Tulip* sinks in the Potomac River after a boiler explosion that kills 49 members of its crew.

The USS *Lancaster* accosts the steamer *Salvador* and removes Confederate raiders led by Thomas E. Hogg, then en route from Panama to California. The agents were planning to seize the steamer and convert it into a commerce raider.

November 12

WEST: At Rome, Georgia, General William T. Sherman gathers up 60,000 infantry and 5,500 artillery for his proposed "March to the Sea."
NAVAL: Commander Napoleon Collins and the USS *Wachusett* arrive at Norfolk, Virginia, with the captured CSS *Florida* in tow. However, Secretary of State William H. Seward, angered by Collins's overt breach of Brazilian neutrality, orders the vessel returned to Brazil. Collins is also tried by court-martial and is dismissed from the service, but Secretary of the Navy Gideon Welles arranges his reinstatement.

Landing parties from the USS *Hendrick Hudson* and *Nita* attack Confederate saltworks near Tampa, Florida, but they are driven back by enemy cavalry.

The Confederate raider CSS *Shenandoah* under Lieutenant James I. Waddell captures the Union clipper ship *Kate Prince* and the brig *Adelaide,* near the equator, releasing both on a bond.

Sherman's March to the Sea November 1864 Painting by F. O. C. Darley *(Library of Congress)*

November 13

WEST: General Jubal A. Early is ordered back to New Market, Virginia, there to dispatch part of his army from the Shenandoah Valley to the defenses of Richmond and Petersburg, Virginia. This act concludes his celebrated Shenandoah Valley campaign, which involved 1,670 miles of marching and 75 encounters of various sizes.

NAVAL: The Confederate raider CSS *Shenandoah* under Commander James I. Waddell captures and burns the Union schooner *Lizzie M. Stacey* near the equator.

November 14

POLITICS: President Abraham Lincoln accepts General George B. McClellan's resignation from the U.S. Army.

NORTH: Philip H. Sheridan is promoted to major general, U.S. Army.

WEST: Union forces under General William T. Sherman continue pulling up railroads and burning crops and buildings around Atlanta, Georgia. Meanwhile, General Henry W. Slocum leads the XV and XVII Corps out of the city and begins to head off for Savannah.

General John M. Schofield arrives at Pulaski, Tennessee, and assumes command of Union forces concentrating there.

November 15

WEST: General William T. Sherman departs a thoroughly devastated Atlanta, Georgia, and rolls toward Savannah and the sea with 62,000 men. To maximize foraging, his force deploys in two wings of four columns. The right wing is led by General Oliver O. Howard (XIV and XX Corps), his left is under General Henry W. Slocum (XV and XVII Corps), while two cavalry divisions are commanded by General Hugh J. Kilpatrick. Sherman also defies conventional military practice by severing his own lines of communication and living off the land. Most notoriously, he also embarks on a 60-mile-wide swath of destruction across the state, destroying anything of use to the Confederacy. His unequivocal object is to "make Georgia howl," and within 21 days, Sherman's "bummers" inflict damage on the South approaching $100 million, leaving a twisted, blackened landscape in their wake. The age of "total war" has arrived.

November 16

WEST: Union forces under General Hugh J. Kilpatrick brush aside Confederate cavalry under General Joseph Wheeler at Lovejoy Station, Georgia. The principal attack is made by the dismounted 8th Indiana Cavalry, which dislodges the Southerners and drives them in the direction of Beaver Creek. Kilpatrick captures 50 prisoners and two cannon.

General Nathan B. Forrest's cavalry forces finally augment the Confederate Army of Tennessee at Shoal Creek, Tennessee. His arrival signals a general advance by General John B. Hood into Tennessee and the final Confederate offensive of the war.

November 17

POLITICS: President Jefferson Davis dismisses outright any notion proposed by Georgia state senators to conclude a separate peace treaty with the U.S. government.

WEST: General John C. Breckinridge concludes his brief offensive into Tennessee by withdrawing back into western Virginia.

NAVAL: The Federal side-wheelers USS *Otsego* and *Ceres* steam up the Roanoke River, North Carolina, on an extended reconnaissance mission.

November 18

SOUTH: President Jefferson Davis instructs General Howell Cobb to mobilize the state's entire militia force and oppose the advance of General William T. Sherman. He then places the entire force under the command of General William J. Hardee.

WEST: Despite the recent eclipse of Confederate fortunes, guerrilla bands skirmish with Union forces at Fayette, Missouri.

November 19

POLITICS: President Abraham Lincoln lifts the blockades from Norfolk, Virginia, and Pensacola, Florida, declaring them open for business.

SOUTH: Georgia governor Joseph E. Brown orders all men between the ages of 16 and 55 to join the militia to oppose General William T. Sherman, but few actually step forward.

NAVAL: The Confederate raider CSS *Chickamauga* under Lieutenant John Wilkinson runs the Union blockade off Wilmington, North Carolina, covered by a fog, and anchors under the guns of Fort Fisher. The crew then calmly waits for high tide to lift the vessel over the bar and into the Cape Fear River. The USS *Kansas, Wilderness, Cherokee,* and *Clematis* fire on the vessel once the mist lifts, but *Chickamauga* safely escapes upstream.

November 20

WEST: Union forces under General William T. Sherman skirmish with Confederate defenders at Walnut Creek, East Macon, and Griswoldville, Georgia, as they proceed inexorably toward the coast.

NAVAL: Admiral David D. Porter, acting on the behest of General Benjamin F. Butler, orders the Union steamer USS *Louisiana* sent to Beaufort, North Carolina, crammed with explosives. With it, Butler hopes to damage seriously the Confederate defenses of Fort Fisher, Wilmington, North Carolina.

November 21

WEST: The Army of Tennessee under General John B. Hood advances 31,000 men and 8,000 cavalry out of Florence, Alabama, and toward Nashville, Tennessee, threatening Union lines of communication. He commands three infantry corps under Generals Benjamin F. Cheatham, Stephen D. Lee, Alexander P. Stewart, with a cavalry corps under the redoubtable Nathan B. Forrest. However, his timetable has been delayed three weeks by Forrest's absence, and during that interval, General George H. Thomas strengthens the defenses of Nashville.

General William J. Hardee makes a stand at Macon, Georgia, with a motley assortment of militia and veteran cavalry under General Joseph Wheeler. Union forces do not make an appearance as anticipated. Concluding that Macon is not their objective, Hardee then orders Wheeler to begin to slash attacks on the rear of the enemy columns.

Georgia militiamen under General Gustavus W. Smith ride trains from Macon to Augusta and begin to march toward Griswoldville, Georgia, to impede approaching Union forces.

NAVAL: The USS *Iosco* captures the Confederate schooner *Sybil* off the North Carolina coast.

Armed boats from the USS *Avenger* capture Confederate supplies on the Mississippi River near Bruinsburg, Mississippi.

November 22

SOUTH: General Henry W. Slocum's Union troops approach the state capital of Milledgeville, Georgia, forcing the legislature to flee in panic.

WEST: General John B. Hood rapidly approaches Columbia, Tennessee, intending to cut off Union forces under General John M. Schofield at nearby Pulaski. However, Schofield divines Hood's intentions at the last possible moment and hurriedly maneuvers northward to escape.

General Gustavus W. Smith's division of Georgia militia attacks dismounted Union cavalry under General Hugh J. Kilpatrick at Griswoldville, Georgia. The levies bravely charge several times before being repulsed with 600 casualties; Kilpatrick sustains around 100 casualties.

November 23

SOUTH: Union forces brush aside Confederate defenders at Milledgeville, Georgia, easily occupying the state capital.

WEST: General Edward R. S. Canby departs Vicksburg, Mississippi, and marches toward Jackson to capture supplies destined for General John B. Hood's army in Tennessee.

SOUTHWEST: The surviving Confederates of General Sterling Price's column enter Bonham, Texas.

November 24

WEST: Union cavalry under General John M. Schofield attack and drive off Confederate defenders under General Nathan B. Forrest near Columbia, Tennessee. The Federals then dig in behind the Duck River and await the Army of Tennessee under General John B. Hood.

General William T. Sherman departs Milledgeville, Georgia, and continues his trek toward Savannah. To confuse the Confederates, he orders General Hugh J. Kilpatrick to make a feint 30 miles northwest toward Augusta and then to ride east to sever the Augusta and Savannah Railroad.

SOUTHWEST: An expedition of 300 soldiers and Ute/Apache Indians under Colonel Christopher "Kit" Carson, patrolling the Canadian River in the Texas Panhandle for hostile Commanche and Kiowa bands, detects a large Indian encampment near the ruins of an abandoned trading post called Adobe Walls. Carson secures his own wagon train, conducts a 15-mile night march, and prepares to attack the unsuspecting Indians at dawn.

NAVAL: The USS *Chocura* chases the Confederate schooner *Louisa* onto a bar near the San Bernard River, Texas. A sudden gale subsequently destroys the stricken vessel.

November 25

NORTH: Confederate agents dispatched from Canada set fire to 10 New York hotels in an unsuccessful attempt to burn down the city. One Southern perpetrator is caught and eventually hanged.

SOUTH: General Joseph Wheeler's Confederate cavalry harass General John M. Schofield's Union column near Sandersville, Georgia.

SOUTHWEST: Colonel Christopher "Kit" Carson leads 200 charging cavalry through a hostile Kiowa encampment near Adobe Walls, Texas. Simultaneously, his Ute and Apache steal the warriors's horses. However, the survivors flee into nearby Comanche lodges with pleas for help, and soon hundreds, if not thousands, of angry warriors begin to mass to attack the intruders. Carson, suddenly confronted by the largest aggregation of Native Americans he ever beheld, quickly ducks into the ruins of Adobe Walls. Fortunately for him, the fire of hostile two 12-pound mountain howitzers keeps the Indians at bay. Several hours of shooting at long range ensue, and Carson prepares to withdraw under the cover of darkness. Smoke from a plains fire set by the Kiowa also cloaks his movement. The Americans and their Native-American consorts ride quickly back to the safety of New Mexico. Carson suffers two dead and 10 wounded; Kiowa/Comanche losses are between 50 and 150, due mainly to artillery fire. In point of sheer numbers engaged, Adobe Walls is also the largest Indian battle waged in Texas.

November 26

SOUTH: Advancing Union forces under General William T. Sherman skirmish with Confederates at Sanderson, Georgia.

WEST: General Thomas L. Rosser departs the Shenandoah Valley with two Confederate cavalry brigades, intending to raid the Union depot at New Creek, West Virginia.

The Confederate Army of Tennessee arrives outside Columbia, Tennessee, and finds Federal troops under General John M. Schofield entrenched and ready to receive him.

General Joseph Wheeler encounters the 8th Indiana and 2nd U.S. Cavalry in camp at Sylvian Grove, Georgia, and drives them toward the main Union column at Briar Creek.

November 27

SOUTH: Union troops under General John W. Davidson depart Baton Rouge, Louisiana, intending to cut the Mobile and Ohio Railroad, which is guarded by Confederate forces under General Dabney H. Maury.

WEST: Confederate cavalry under General Thomas L. Rosser engage and defeat a Union detachment sent from New Creek, West Virginia. The Federal commander at New Creek, Colonel George R. Latham, however, takes no special precautions against attack.

General John M. Schofield, confronting a larger Confederate force outside Columbia, Tennessee, begins to pull his men north of the Duck River. He believes that the attack, when mounted, will come from south of the city.

Confederate cavalry lash out at General William T. Sherman's army outside of Waynesboro, Georgia, in a vain effort to slow Union forces down.

A Union cavalry column under General Hugh J. Kilpatrick encamps for the night at Buck Head Creek, Georgia, unaware that Confederate troopers under General Joseph Wheeler are within striking distance.

NAVAL: The Union steamer *Greyhound,* serving as the headquarters ship of General Benjamin F. Butler, explodes and sinks in the James River, Virginia, with a high-ranking conference in attendance. Fortunately, Butler, General Robert Schenck, and Admiral David D. Porter escape unharmed. This was probably the work of a notorious Confederate "coal torpedo" that had been shoveled accidentally or deliberately into the *Greyhound*'s boiler.

Armed boats with Union sailors capture the British blockade-runner *Beatrice* off Charleston, South Carolina.

The USS *Princess Royal* captures the British blockade-runner *Flash* off Brazos Santiago, Texas, and subsequently seizes the schooner *Neptune* later in the day.

The USS *Metacomet* captures the Confederate steamer *Susanna* off Campeche Banks, Mexico.

The Federal ram USS *Vindicator* and stern-wheeler *Prairie Bird* transport and cover the landing of Union cavalry as they destroy railroad tracks and a bridge over the Big Black River near Vicksburg, Mississippi.

November 28

SOUTH: Confederate partisans under Colonel John S. Mosby are bested in a skirmish at Goresville, Virginia, by men of the Independent Battalion of Virginia Cavalry, a Unionist formation.

Union general John G. Foster marches 5,500 men from Hilton Head, South Carolina, to troop transports waiting offshore and sails down the Broad River. He intends to land near Boyd's Neck, stride overland, and cut the Savannah and Charleston Railroad.

WEST: Confederate cavalry under General Thomas L. Rosser stage a surprise attack on Fort Kelley at New Creek, West Virginia. In a swift 30-minute action, they capture the fort and 700 Federals, the majority of whom are cooking lunch. Colonel George R. Lantham fails to prepare the garrison despite ample reports of enemy activity at nearby Moorefield, and he is discharged dishonorably from the service.

General John B. Hood deploys part of his force under General Stephen D. Lee south of Columbia, Tennessee, to give the impression of an attack from south of the city. Hood, however, secretly shifts the bulk of his forces east to cross the Duck River above the town and so cut off any Union retreat. Meanwhile, General Nathan B. Forrest defeats a body of Union cavalry under General James H. Wilson at Spring Hill and drives them in the direction of Franklin. General John M. Schofield then decides to withdraw his army across the Duck River before the trap is sprung. He advances toward Spring Hill.

General Joseph Wheeler orders his Confederate cavalry to attack Union troopers bivouacked along Buck Head Creek, Georgia. Their commander, General Hugh J. Kilpatrick, having unwisely pitched his tent outside the camp, nearly falls captive, while men of the 5th Ohio Cavalry repel the Southerners with rapid-fire carbines. Kilpatrick then forms a new battle line at Reynold's Plantation, repulsing two more Confederate charges. Wheeler finally reins in his men, who regroup, while Kilpatrick escapes intact toward Louisville.

The Union District of Mississippi is constituted with General Napoleon J. T. Dana as commanding officer.

November 29

SOUTH: General John P. Hatch forms a brigade of infantry, a brigade of sailors, and eight cannon to march from Boyd's Neck, South Carolina, toward Grahamville and there to sever an important railroad depot linking Charleston to Savannah, Georgia. However, the Federals, misled by poor maps, march and countermarch aimlessly for several hours, allowing Confederate troops and militia to arrive.

WEST: General John M. Schofield, threatened by Generals John B. Hood and Nathan B. Forrest at Spring Hill, Tennessee, skillfully extricates his forces. He does so after Hood commits three infantry divisions to the attack and fighting breaks down into skirmishing across the line. Tonight, Union forces slip through the very fingers of the Confederates and begin a hard slog toward Franklin, 12 miles distant. That town has been secured earlier by the VI Corps of General David S. Stanley.

Colorado militia and howitzers under Colonel John M. Chivington attack a peaceful Cheyenne camp at Sand Creek, Colorado. The Native Americans under

Chief Black Kettle have been directed there by military authorities with the under- standing that they will be safe. Nonetheless, vengeful militiamen attack the sleeping camp at dawn with artillery fire and then charge, killing everyone they encounter. Black Kettle, in an act of desperation, raises an American flag over his tent as a peace gesture but to no avail. "It may perhaps be unnecessary for me to state that I cap- tured no prisoners," Chivington gloats. As many as 149 Native Americans, including women and children, are cut down and scalped, an act that General Nelson A. Miles condemned as "the foulest and most unjustified crime in the annals of America." Militia losses are nine dead and 40 wounded. Chivington is feted subsequently as a hero in Denver, but a congressional inquiry denounces the massacre and ends his military career. The surviving Native Americans go on a rampage lasting several months, but the U.S. government eventually pays the survivors an indemnity.

NAVAL: The monitors USS *Onondaga* and *Mahopac* trade shots inconclusively with a Confederate battery on the James River for three hours.

Commander George H. Preble's 450-man naval brigade, drawn from the South Atlantic Blockading Squadron, disembarks at Boyd's Landing on the Broad River, South Carolina. His mission is to act in concert with nearby army troops and help establish contact with the army of General William T. Sherman.

November 30

SOUTH: General John P. Hatch leads a Union expedition of 4,000 men against Con- federate defenses at Honey Hill, South Carolina. There 2,000 Georgia militia under General Gustavus W. Smith are posted strongly along the crest of high ground bor- dered by streams. Hatch launches three frontal assaults, all of which are repelled by Southern artillery fire. At length, the Federals withdraw with 746 casualties; Smith's losses are about 100. It is an impressive performance by the state levies.

WEST: General John M. Schofield arrives at Franklin, Tennessee, with 15,000 men of his IV and XXII Corps and immediately strengthens existing defensive works. Within hours, he is joined by 23,000 men of the Confederate Army of Tennessee under General John B. Hood, which assumes offensive positions south of town. The corps of General Stephen D. Lee has yet to arrive with the bulk of Confederate artillery, but after surveying Union Lines, the aggressive Hood decides to assault it frontally using the divisions of Generals Patrick R. Cleburne, John Brown, and William Bate. He does so over the objections of General Nathan B. Forrest and Benjamin F. Cheatham. Accordingly, at 4:00 P.M., a tide of graycoats surge forward across two miles of open fields. Hood's initial charge catches two Union brigades under General George D. Wagner out in the open, sweeps them from the ground, and chases them back toward the Federal trenches. The main Union line is there- fore obliged to hold its fire until cheering Southerners are nearly on top of them. They then unleash a concentrated fusillade toppling men by the hundreds. Still, the impetus of the Southern attack is so great that Confederates crash through the first line of barricades and enter the town. Colonel Emerson Opdyke's Federal brigade then comes tearing from the reserves, flings itself on the disorganized enemy, and violently ejects them from the trenches. Hood's men, now compressed into a dense mass, resist violently but are cut down from concentrated artillery fire on either flank. Fighting finally ceases about 9:00 P.M. as shattered Southern ranks withdraw from the town. The disputed ground, for all intents and purposes, resembles a slaughter pen.

The Battle of Franklin is a grievous miscalculation by the offensive-minded Hood. No less than six of his generals are killed, including the highly accomplished Cleburne, with another six seriously wounded. Moreover, the Army of Tennessee loses 1,750 dead, 3,800 wounded, and 702 missing (6,252) in another feckless frontal attack. Union losses by comparison are 189 killed, 1,033 injured, and 1,104 missing (2,326), but Schofield resumes withdrawing until reaching Nashville on the following day. Hood then lopes off in pursuit, setting the stage for an even bigger Southern tragedy.

General Andrew J. Smith's XVI Corps arrives at Nashville, Tennessee, to reinforce Union defenders under General George H. Thomas.

NAVAL: Commander George H. Preble leads a naval brigade of 150 marines and 350 sailors from the South Atlantic Blockading Squadron in an army attack on Honey Hill, Grahamville, South Carolina. This action is undertaken to cut the Charleston and Savannah Railroad, as well as to establish contacts with the army of General William T. Sherman. The sailors perform well despite a Northern defeat.

A naval expedition of five boats and 100 Union sailors from the USS *Ethan Allen* and *Dai Ching* sweeps up the South Altamaha River, South Carolina, to find escaped Union prisoners reputedly hiding there.

An armed party from the USS *Midnight* raids and destroys a Confederate saltworks at St. Andrew's Bay, Florida.

The USS *Itasca* captures the British blockade-runner *Carrie Mair* off Pass Cavallo, Texas.

December 1

POLITICS: President Abraham Lincoln appoints Kentuckian James Speed to replace outgoing Edward Bates as attorney general.

WEST: In order to deceive the Confederates as to his real intentions, General William T. Sherman dispatches Union cavalry under General Hugh J. Kilpatrick toward Augustus, Georgia, to give the impression his main force is heading in that direction.

The Union XXIII Corps under General John M. Schofield withdraws to new defensive positions at Nashville, Tennessee, forming part of greater defenses there under General George H. Thomas. The Confederate Army of Tennessee under General John B. Hood also resumes its advance toward the city.

NAVAL: The USS *Rhode Island* captures the British blockade-runner *Vixen* off Cape Fear, North Carolina.

Admiral Samuel P. Lee strengthens his Mississippi River Squadron with the addition of the heavy ironclads USS *Neosho* and *Carondelet*. This is in response to a major Confederate advance across the Tennessee River.

December 2

WEST: Confederate general Thomas L. Rosser, concluding his successful raid against New Creek, West Virginia, returns to camp in the lower Shenandoah Valley.

General John B. Hood arrives before Nashville, Tennessee, with approximately 24,000 men in the corps of Generals Stephen D. Lee, Alexander P. Stewart, and Benjamin F. Cheatham. A sizable force of veteran Confederate cavalry is also present under redoubtable General Nathan B. Forrest, which is soon detached and exerts little influence on events. Hood immediately commences fortifying his position southeast of the city by building several redoubts. Lacking the manpower to attack the Union position outright, he hopes to lure the federals into hitting him instead. He soon will be granted his wish as General George H. Thomas occupies Nashville with 55,000 men, including the VI Corps under General Thomas J. Wood, the XVI Corps under General Andrew J. Smith, and the XXIII Corps under General John M. Schofield. The Union cavalry corps of General James H. Wilson, detached from the city, is also nearby, resting and refitting.

General Thomas J. Wood replaces the wounded general David S. Stanley as commander of the Union IV Corps, Nashville, Tennessee.

General Sterling Price trudges into Laynesport, Arkansas, at the head of his defeated, exhausted column. This concludes Price's final effort to capture Missouri for the Confederacy; he covered 1,488 miles, fought 43 engagements, and lost 4,000 men, chiefly deserters, during his campaign.

General Grenville M. Dodge replaces General William S. Rosecrans as commander of the Department of the Missouri.

NAVAL: The USS *Chicopee* escorts a combined expedition up the Chowan River to Pitch Landing, North Carolina, where Confederate supply caches are found and burned.

The Federal troop transports *Prairie State, Prima Donna,* and *Magnet* are captured by Confederate forces on the Cumberland River, Tennessee, near Bell's Mill.

December 3

WEST: Union forces under General William T. Sherman reach Millen, Georgia. Meanwhile, Confederate cavalry under General Joseph Wheeler strike Union positions between Millen and Augusta, whereupon Sherman orders cavalry under General Hugh J. Kilpatrick to hunt down the elusive Southerners.

General George H. Thomas is urged by both President Abraham Lincoln and General Ulysses S. Grant to attack General John B. Hood's army immediately outside Nashville, Tennessee. Instead, Thomas meticulously and unhurriedly begins to strengthen his defenses while awaiting additional reinforcements.

NAVAL: The USS *Emma* forces the Confederate steamer *Ella* aground at Bald Head Point, North Carolina, and a boarding party subsequently burns it.

The USS *Mackinaw* captures the Confederate schooner *Mary* off Charleston, South Carolina.

Armed parties from the USS *Nita, Stars and Stripes, Hendrick Hudson, Ariel,* and *Two Sisters* attack and destroy a large Confederate saltworks at Rocky Point, Tampa Bay, Florida.

December 4

SOUTH: Heavy skirmishing at Waynesboro, Georgia, between cavalry forces of Generals Joseph Wheeler and Hugh J. Kilpatrick. The Union troopers discover the

Southerners behind a series of barricades, which are reduced by horse artillery and flanking attacks by the 9th Michigan and 10th Ohio cavalry. The Confederates then retreat to an even longer line of defenses that cannot be flanked easily, so Kilpatrick orders them stormed by frontal assault. Accordingly, the 9th Pennsylvania, 2nd, 3rd, and 5th Kentucky Cavalry, supported by the dismounted 8th Indiana, charge forward and drive the defenders off. Wheeler then extricates his men across Briar Creek and escapes toward Augusta, having sustained 250 casualties to Kilpatrick's 170.

NAVAL: The USS *R. R. Cuyler, Mackinaw,* and *Gettysburg* capture the Confederate steamer *Armstrong* east of Charleston, South Carolina.

The USS *Pursuit* captures the Confederate vessel *Peep O'Day* off the Indian River, Florida.

The USS *Chocura* captures the Confederate schooner *Lowood* off Velasco, Texas.

The USS *Pembina* captures the Dutch blockade-runner *Geziena Hilligonda* off Brazos Santiago, Texas.

The Confederate raider CSS *Shenandoah* under Lieutenant James I. Waddell captures and burns the Union bark *Edward* off Tristan da Cunha in the South Atlantic.

A naval squadron consisting of the USS *Moose, Carondelet, Fairplay, Reindeer,* and *Silver Lake* attacks Confederate batteries at Bell's Mill on the Cumberland River, Tennessee. Confederate defenders under General John B. Hood and Nathan B. Forrest fail to stop the gunboats, which recapture the three transports *Prairie State, Prima Donna,* and *Magnet,* seized a day earlier along with many Union prisoners.

December 5

POLITICS: The second session, 38th U.S. Congress convenes in Washington, D.C.

WEST: Confederate cavalry under General Nathan B. Forrest trots off to capture Murfreesboro, Tennessee, from Union forces under General L. H. Rosseau.

NAVAL: Secretary of the Navy Gideon Welles submits his fourth annual report to President Abraham Lincoln, stating navy strength at 671 ships, including 62 ironclads, which mount 4,600 cannon and have seized 1,400 Confederate vessels since the war began. "The blockade of a coastline," he declares, "greater in extent than the whole coast of Europe from Cape Trafalgar to Cape North, is an undertaking without precedent in history."

The Federal monitors USS *Saugus, Onondaga, Mahopac,* and *Canonicus* trade shots with Confederate batteries at Howlett's Landing, James River, Virginia.

The Federal tug *Lizzie Freeman* is captured by Confederate forces while anchoring at Smithfield, Virginia.

The naval brigade of Commander George H. Preble lands up the Tulifinny River and supports army operations at Tulifinny Crossroads, Georgia. Confederate resistance proves fierce and Union forces are unable to sever the Savannah-Charleston Railroad.

The USS *Chocura* captured the British blockade-runner *Julia* off Velasco, Texas.

December 6

POLITICS: President Abraham Lincoln, in a conciliatory move, appoints Radical Republican and former secretary of the treasury Salmon P. Chase as the fifth

Chief Justice of the U.S. Supreme Court, succeeding the recently deceased Roger B. Taney.

WEST: General George H. Thomas again is ordered by General Ulysses S. Grant to attack Confederate forces under General John B. Hood at Nashville "and wait no longer for remount of your cavalry." Nonetheless, when Thomas dithers awaiting additional horses, Grant prepares to remove him from command.

Confederate cavalry under General Hylan B. Lyon depart Paris, Tennessee, for an extended raid against Hopkinsville, Kentucky.

NAVAL: Federal monitors USS *Saugus, Onondaga, Mahopac,* and *Canonicus* continue trading fire with Confederate batteries at Howlett's Landing, James River, Virginia.

The USS *Sunflower* captures the Confederate sloop *Pickwick* off St. George's Sound, Florida.

The USS *Chocura* captures the British blockade-runner *Lady Hurley* off Velasco, Texas.

The USS *Princess Royal* forces the Confederate schooner *Alabama* aground at San Luis Pass, Texas, and captures it.

The Federal ironclad USS *Neosho,* along with the steamers *Fairplay, Silver Lake,* and *Moose,* escorts several army transports down the Cumberland River from Nashville. Approaching Bell's Mills, Tennessee, they are beset by heavy fire from Confederate batteries ashore, which is answered by the heavily armored *Neosho.* The Union flag is then shot from its mast and falls onto the deck. Quartermaster John Ditzenback calmly braves a storm of Southern shot, walks on the deck, and reattaches it to the only remaining mast. He obtains the Congressional Medal of Honor. The all-day contest finally concludes at nightfall with *Neosho* having been struck more than 100 times, sustaining minor damage.

December 7

SOUTH: General Benjamin F. Butler begins to mass his forces at Fortress Monroe, Virginia, in anticipation of a large expedition against Wilmington, North Carolina. General Godfrey Wentzel originally had been slated to command the effort, but Butler uses his still considerable political influence to take control.

WEST: Union cavalry under General Robert L. Milroy attack and defeat General Nathan B. Forrest outside Murfreesboro, Tennessee, taking 200 captives and 14 cannon.

NAVAL: Union vessels force the blockade-runner *Stormy Petrel* ashore at Wilmington, North Carolina, and then destroy it with gunfire.

The USS *Narcissus* strikes a torpedo in Mobile Bay, Alabama, and sinks in a heavy storm, although without loss of life.

December 8

NORTH: General Ulysses S. Grant, perplexed over General George H. Thomas's inactivity at Nashville, Tennessee, contacts General Henry W. Halleck and writes, "If Thomas has not struck yet, he ought to be ordered to hand over his command to Schofield."

SOUTH: General Benjamin F. Butler ferries 6,500 men from his Army of the James down the James River to Fortress Monroe, Virginia. There they embark on ships intending to attack Fort Fisher, Wilmington, North Carolina.

NAVAL: The USS *Cherokee* captures the British blockade-runner *Emma Henry* off the North Carolina coast.

The USS *J. P. Jackson* and *Stockdale* capture the Confederate schooner *Medora* in the Mississippi Sound.

The USS *Itasca* runs the Confederate sloop *Mary Ann* ashore at Pass Cavallo, Texas, and then destroys it with cannon fire.

December 9

NORTH: General Ulysses S. Grant, frustrated by the perceived lack of aggressiveness from General George H. Thomas, orders General John M. Schofield to succeed him. The directive is then suspended when Thomas informs Grant that his intended attack is cancelled because of a winter storm. While the cold weather inconveniences Thomas, it causes the poorly clad and sheltered Confederates under General John B. Hood to shiver in their trenches. The fast-frozen ground also proves impossible to dig through for strengthening field works.

NAVAL: The USS *Otsego* strikes two Confederate torpedoes and sinks on the Roanoke River near Jamesville, North Carolina. The Federal tug USS *Bazely,* in the act of rescuing survivors, also strikes a device and sinks.

December 10

POLITICS: President Abraham Lincoln appoints General William F. Smith and Henry Stanberry special commissioners to report on civil and military matters west of the Mississippi River.

WEST: General William T. Sherman's Union army of 60,000 men reaches the outskirts of Savannah, Georgia. The 18,000 defenders under General William J. Hardee flood the rice fields, forcing prospective Federal attacks to be committed over a very narrow front, so Sherman mounts siege operations instead.

General George Stoneman leads 1,500 Union horsemen on an expedition out of Knoxville, Tennessee, to destroy Confederate salt and lead factories in southwestern Virginia.

NAVAL: The CSS *Macon, Sampson,* and *Resolute* steam down the Savannah River to engage Union batteries at Tweedside, Georgia. *Resolute* is struck repeatedly, abandoned, and ultimately captured while the remaining vessels flee upstream back to Augusta.

The USS *O. H. Lee* captures the British blockade-runner *Sort* near the Anclote Keys, Florida.

December 11

WEST: General George H. Thomas, having delayed his planned attack, again is urged by General Ulysses S. Grant to strike John B. Hood's Confederates outside Nashville, Tennessee. Thomas replies that he will attack once the weather, which is dreadful, improves.

December 12

WEST: General William T. Sherman's army, now stationary, can no longer victual itself, so he orders General Oliver O. Howard to capture Fort McAlister on the Ogeechee River. This move will open a line of supply to the Union fleet offshore.

General George H. Thomas again assures chief of staff General Henry W. Halleck that he will attack Confederates gathered outside Nashville, Tennessee, once weather conditions permit.

December 13

DIPLOMACY: Charles Coursel, a Montreal police magistrate, declares he has no authority to detain Lieutenant Bennet Young and his 20 compatriots for their role in the raid on St. Albans, Vermont, and releases them on bond. A political uproar ensues, and Secretary of State William H. Seward notifies the British government that Washington will nullify the Rush-Bagot Agreement of 1817 in one-year's time. Under this act, the U.S.-Canadian border was demilitarized following the War of 1812.

NORTH: A sorely vexed General Ulysses S. Grant orders General John A. Logan from Virginia to Tennessee to replace General George H. Thomas for failing to take offensive action. Grant also prepares to visit Nashville and supervise matters personally.

WEST: Union cavalry under General George Stoneman defeat General Basil W. Duke's Confederates at Kingsport, Tennessee.

Fort McAllister on the Ogeechee River, Georgia, is attacked by the 2nd Division, XV Corps, under General William B. Hazen. The fort, though formidably armed and constructed, is garrisoned by only 150 Confederates under Major George W. Anderson. Hazen, by comparison, marshals 1,500 picked troops to spearhead the assault, which begins at 4:45 P.M. The Federals quickly clear the ditch and abattis, taking some losses from buried land torpedoes, and the fort falls after hand-to-hand fighting. Union losses are 24 dead and 110 wounded to a Confederate tally of 17 killed and 31 injured. Consequently, General William T. Sherman establishes communication with the South Atlantic Blockading Squadron in Ossabaw Sound, and food supplies are soon steaming their way up the Ogeechee River.

The 13th Colored U.S. Infantry conducts a destructive foray from Barrancas, Florida, to Pollard, Alabama, destroying all public property that cannot be brought off.

NAVAL: An ailing and fatigued admiral David G. Farragut arrives in New York City with the USS *Hartford,* receiving his second hero's welcome.

A large Union expedition under General Benjamin F. Butler departs Fortress Monroe, Virginia, and steams south to attack Fort Fisher, Wilmington, North Carolina. The USS *Sassacus* is detailed to tow the hulk *Louisiana,* laden with explosives, into position off the fort.

December 14

SOUTH: General Edward O. C. Ord is picked to command the Army of the James outside Richmond, Virginia.

WEST: A prompt attack on Bristol, Tennessee, by Union cavalry under General George Stoneman defeats General John C. Vaughn's Confederates and nets 300 Confederate prisoners.

The weather near Nashville, Tennessee, has moderated, and General George H. Thomas wires anxious superiors that he intends to attack General John B. Hood's Confederate army on the following day. True to form, Thomas methodically and unhurriedly arranges his men for the task.

NAVAL: A naval squadron consisting of the USS *Winona, Sonoma,* and several gunboats is assigned to support the Union advance on Savannah, Georgia, by bombarding Forts Beaulieu and Rosedew in Ossabaw Sound.

Seven Union gunboats of the Mississippi River Squadron slip down the Cumberland River from Nashville, Tennessee, and position themselves opposite the main Confederate battery on the Confederate army's left flank.

December 15

SOUTH: The combined expedition of General Benjamin F. Butler arrives off the North Carolina coast, after missing a rendezvous with the fleet under Admiral David D. Porter.

WEST: A Union cavalry column under General George Stoneman crosses into western Virginia and occupies the town of Abingdon, burning a number of buildings.

General Pierre G. T. Beauregard, commanding the Military Division of the West, instructs General William J. Hardee to save his army rather than be bottled up and captured at Savannah, Georgia.

The Battle of Nashville commences as General George H. Thomas unleashes the XVI and IV Corps against the Confederate left under General Benjamin F. Cheatham. Simultaneously, a large diversionary attack by General James B. Steedman's African-American troops sustains heavy losses but pins down the Confederate right. All the while, General John B. Hood is shifting men furiously to support his overextended line, but it crumbles beforehand. The Southerners, stunned and startled by the weight of Thomas's sledgehammer blows, fall back to a new, more compact position a mile and a half distant. Hood, badly outnumbered, should have retreated tonight, but he defiantly elects to make another stand.

NAVAL: A quick raid up the Coan River, Virginia, by the USS *Coeur de Lion* and *Mercury* destroys 30 small Confederate craft.

Federal gunboats under Commander Le Roy Fitch, especially the heavy monitors *Neosho* and *Carondelet,* actively participate in the Battle of Nashville by bombarding Confederate formations along the shore line. Their heavy fire helps drive the Southern left flank from the field.

December 16

WEST: The Battle of Nashville continues as General George H. Thomas, startled that General John B. Hood's Confederates have not retreated, renews his drive against their re-formed left wing. The attack rolls forward at 3:30 P.M. with General James H. Wilson's cavalry turning the Southern left flank and racing ahead to cut their retreat. This is followed 30 minutes later by a massive attack on the Confederate left-center, which completely overpowers the defenders. Hood's men score better results at the fortified position of Overton Hill on the right, where a major Union thrust is repelled, but the tide of fugitives fleeing down the turnpike becomes irresistible. In the ensuing rout, the Federals capture General Edward Johnson and nearly all of Hood's artillery. Only the onset of darkness and the timely arrival of General Nathan B. Forrest's cavalry prevent his army from being completely annihilated.

Nashville is a decisive Confederate defeat that terminates virtually all organized resistance in the western theater. Hood's losses included 1,500 killed or wounded, along with 4,462 captured (5,962). Thomas, a methodical, if plodding, pugilist, incurs far fewer casualties: 387 dead, 2,558 wounded, and 12 missing (3,057). Nashville is also the only instance in the Civil War when an entire Southern army dissolves in abject panic from the field of battle.

NAVAL: The USS *Mount Vernon* and *New Berne* capture and sink the Confederate schooner *G. O. Bigelow* at Bear Inlet, North Carolina.

December 17

SOUTH: President Jefferson Davis glumly informs General William J. Hardee that he cannot reinforce the Confederate defenders of Savannah, Georgia, with troops drawn from the Army of Northern Virginia.

WEST: Skirmishing erupts between Union cavalry under General George Stoneman and Confederates under General John C. Breckinridge at Wytheville, Virginia. The Southerners are forced back, losing 200 prisoners and eight cannon.

Confederates mount a tenacious rearguard action allowing the army of General John B. Hood to escape. Pursuing Union cavalry under General James H. Wilson prove relentless, however.

General William T. Sherman sends a flag of truce into Confederate lines and formally demands the surrender of Savannah, Georgia.

December 18

POLITICS: President Abraham Lincoln pleads for an additional 300,000 volunteers to bolster the Union army's battered ranks.

WEST: Confederates under General John C. Breckinridge stand at Marion, Virginia, against General George Stoneman's Union cavalry, and they are outflanked. They subsequently retire toward the mountains of North Carolina.

General William J. Hardee refuses General William T. Sherman's demand for surrender at Savannah, Georgia, and prepares to abandon the city.

NAVAL: The USS *Louisiana,* heavily laden with 200 tons of gunpowder for an impending attack on Fort Fisher, Wilmington, North Carolina, is briefly towed out of Charleston Harbor, South Carolina, then returned owning to heavy seas.

December 19

WEST: General George A. Custer's cavalry conduct a destructive romp from Kernstown, Virginia, to Lacey Springs, burning property and disrupting enemy communications. However, his attempt to cut the Virginia Central Railroad proceeds only as far as Harrisonburg before resistance stiffens.

A force of 8,000 Union cavalry under General Alfred T. A. Torbert ranges over portions of the Shenandoah Valley from Winchester to Gordonsville, Virginia, torching crops, farm buildings, and anything of value to the enemy.

Union troops from the XX Corps reach the South Carolina shore outside Savannah, Georgia, thereby threatening the only remaining escape route for General William J. Hardee's Confederates. He orders the city evacuated that evening.

NAVAL: The CSS *Waterwitch,* a former Union vessel, is burned by Confederates on the Vernon River near Savannah, Georgia, to prevent its recapture.

The USS *Princess Royal* captures the Confederate schooner *Cora* off Galveston, Texas.

December 20

SOUTH: Savannah Georgia is evacuated successfully by Confederate forces under General William J. Hardee, which cross the Savannah River on a pontoon bridge constructed from rice boats. However, the defenders are forced to abandon 250 heavy cannon.

WEST: Union cavalry under General George Stoneman storm into Saltville, Virginia, destroying numerous saltworks over the next two days.

NAVAL: Admiral David G. Farragut lowers his flag from the USS *Hartford* in the New York Navy Yard and concludes his naval career.

A boat expedition launched from the USS *Chicopee, Valley City,* and *Wyalusing* against Rainbow Bluff, North Carolina, is rebuffed by Confederate torpedoes and artillery fire along the Roanoke River.

December 21

SOUTH: Savannah, Georgia, falls to Union forces under General William T. Sherman, thereby completing his 285-mile "March to the Sea." He telegrams President Abraham Lincoln, "I beg to present to you as a Christmas gift the city of Savannah with 150 heavy guns and also about 25,000 bales of cotton."

WEST: General Benjamin H. Grierson leads a mounted expedition from Memphis, Tennessee, against the Mobile and Ohio Railroad in northern Alabama and Mississippi.

NAVAL: The Confederate blockade-runner *Owl* slips past Union vessels off Wilmington, North Carolina, and makes for the open sea.

Armed boats from the USS *Ethan Allen* venture up the Altamaha River, South Carolina, on an intelligence-gathering mission.

Confederate sailors scuttle the CSS *Savannah, Isondiga, Firefly,* and the floating battery *Georgia* at Savannah, Georgia, preventing their capture by Union forces.

December 22

WEST: General George Stoneman concludes his raid into western Virginia, departs Saltville, and rides back to Knoxville, Tennessee. In 12 days, he covers 460 miles, taking 900 captives and 19 cannon.

General Joseph J. Reynolds replaces General Frederick Steele as commander of the Department of Arkansas.

December 23

POLITICS: President Abraham Lincoln approves congressional legislation creating the rank of vice admiral; David G. Farragut becomes the first American naval officer so honored, granting him the equivalent rank of lieutenant general.

NAVAL: A belated, combined expedition of 65,000 men under General Benjamin F. Butler and five warships under Admiral David D. Porter arrives off Fort Fisher,

Wilmington, North Carolina. This is possibly the most formidable coastal fortification in the entire Confederacy, being an earthenwork 480 yards long, 60 feet high, and mounting 50 heavy cannon. It currently houses a garrison of 1,500 men under Colonel William Lamb.

The USS *Acacia* captures the British blockade-runner *Julia* near Alligator Creek, South Carolina.

December 24

NAVAL: The USS *Louisiana,* packed with explosives and intended to be detonated under the guns of Fort Fisher, Wilmington, North Carolina, accidently explodes 250 yards away from its objective. When this fails to damage the defenses, 60 Union warships under Admiral David D. Porter begin a concerted bombardment, which strikes the fort at a rate of 115 shells a minute. The pyrotechnics are awe-inspiring but produce relatively little damage.

Federal gunboats under Admiral Samuel D. Lee move down the Tennessee River in a failed attempt to interdict General John B. Hood at Chickasaw, Alabama. The vessels are thwarted by declining water levels below Great Mussel Shoals and withdraw.

December 25

SOUTH: An attack on Fort Fisher, Wilmington, North Carolina, by the Army of the James under General Benjamin F. Butler, transpires. He lands 2,200 men at 2:00 A.M. and advances inland, thinking that the defenses of the fort have been silenced. Suddenly, Confederate gunners unleash a torrent of shot and shell that keeps the attackers 50 yards from their walls. Butler is so nonplussed by stout resistance that he summarily cancels the entire operation and withdraws back to the fleet offshore. Moreover, this retreat is conducted so hastily that 700 Union soldiers remain trapped on the beach for the next two days. Confederate reinforcements under General Robert F. Hoke subsequently arrive to bolster Wilmington's defenses.

December 26

WEST: General John B. Hood begins to ferry the remnants of his army over the Tennessee River at Bainbridge, Tennessee, and heads for Tupelo, Mississippi. This concludes his ill-fated Nashville campaign, the latest nail in the Confederacy's coffin.

The Confederate blockade-runner *Chameleon* (nee *Tallahassee*) successfully evades Union vessels and slips out of Wilmington, North Carolina, after the attack on Fort Fisher.

December 27

SOUTH: General Benjamin F. Butler returns with his expedition to Fortress Monroe, Virginia, where news of his rebuff at Wilmington, North Carolina, enrages the normally detached Ulysses S. Grant.

NAVAL: At midnight an armed boat from the USS *Virginia* cuts out the Confederate schooner *Belle* in Galveston harbor, Texas, only yards away from a Southern guard boat.

December 28

NORTH: General Ulysses S. Grant admits to President Abraham Lincoln that operations against Fort Fisher, North Carolina, are a complete fiasco. Furthermore, he insists that General Benjamin F. Butler be sacked for "gross and culpable failure."

NAVAL: Commander George H. Preble's 500-man naval brigade returns to the South Atlantic Blockading Squadron after four weeks of campaigning ashore.

The USS *Kanawha* destroys an unnamed Confederate sloop at Caney Creek, Texas.

The Confederate raider CSS *Shenandoah* under Lieutenant James I. Waddell captures and burns the Union bark *Delphine* in the Indian Ocean.

December 29

WEST: The Union cavalry column under General George Stoneman finishes its recent raid into western Virginia by galloping into Knoxville, Tennessee.

December 30

POLITICS: Maryland politician Francis P. Blair contacts President Jefferson Davis and suggests meeting with him in Richmond, Virginia, as a peace overture and to "explain the view I entertain in reference to the state of affairs of our Country."

NORTH: President Abraham Lincoln, less vulnerable politically after his landslide election, relieves General Benjamin F. Butler as commander of the Army of the James.

NAVAL: Strong winds drive the USS *Rattler* against a snag, and it sinks near Grand Gulf, Mississippi.

December 31

SOUTH: Union forces settle comfortably into their siege lines outside Petersburg and Richmond, Virginia, constantly reinforced to a strength of 110,000 men and capably led by General Ulysses S. Grant. By contrast, the once-formidable Army of Northern Virginia of General Robert E. Lee, undersupplied and underfed, dwindles steadily through illness, desertion, and combat. His 66,000 gaunt, ragged soldiers remain determined and capable, but they continue perishing in the cold and mud that is the reality of trench warfare. Furthermore, over the succeeding months Lee must contain possible Union breakthroughs at any point along a 35-mile long defensive perimeter. The efficacy of Grant's war-winning strategy—to pin Lee inside his fortifications and bleed him through sheer attrition—is never more apparent. Consequently, the prospects of complete Union victory seldom have appeared brighter.

NAVAL: An exhausted and ailing admiral David G. Farragut is feted by New York City merchants, who present him with a $50,000 government bond.

Armed boats from the USS *Wabash* and *Pawnee* run aground in Charleston Harbor, South Carolina, and 27 Union sailors fall captive.

The USS *Metacomet* captures the Confederate schooner *Sea Witch* off Galveston, Texas.

1865

January 1

South: Army engineers ignite 12,000 pounds of gunpowder at Dutch Gap, Virginia, to assist a canal excavation. When the dirt tossed by the explosion simply falls back into place, General Benjamin F. Butler abandons efforts to build a detour for Union vessels on the James River, Virginia.

West: The 11th U.S. Colored Infantry conducts antiguerrilla sweeps in Arkansas with a heavy skirmish at Bentonville.

Federal troops skirmish fiercely with Snake warriors along the Canyon City Road, Oregon.

Naval: The USS *San Jacinto,* progenitor of the notorious *Trent* affair of 1861, is wrecked on No Name Key, Bahamas.

January 2

South: General Samuel W. Crawford gains temporary command of the V Corps, Army of the Potomac, Virginia.

West: Union forces under General Benjamin H. Grierson engage Confederate forces at Franklin and Lexington, Mississippi, as they destroy sections of the Mobile and Ohio Railroad.

Naval: Secretary of the Navy Gideon Welles contacts Secretary of War Edwin M. Stanton and expresses the dire necessity for capturing and closing Wilmington, North Carolina, "the only port by which any supplies whatever reach the rebels."

January 3

South: General Alfred H. Terry receives command of the forthcoming joint expedition against Fort Fisher, Wilmington, North Carolina. At this stage of the war, even General Benjamin F. Butler's political allies cannot salvage his waning fortunes.

General Oliver O. Howard moves the bulk of the Army of the Tennessee from Savannah, Georgia, toward Beaufort on the South Carolina border.

West: General Benjamin H. Grierson continues raiding along the Mobile and Ohio Railroad near Mechanicsburg, Mississippi.

Naval: The USS *Harvest Moon* transports a detachment of Union troops from Savannah, Georgia, to Beaufort, South Carolina.

The USS *Kanawha* captures the Confederate schooner *Mary Ellen* in the Gulf of Mexico.

January 4

South: General Alfred H. Terry embarks 8,000 Federal troops at Bermuda Landing, Virginia, as part of the renewed expedition against Fort Fisher, Wilmington, North Carolina.

West: General Benjamin H. Grierson concludes his raid against the Mobile and Ohio Railroad with a skirmish at Ponds, Mississippi. To date, he has destroyed 20,000 feet of bridges and other roadways, 20 miles of telegraph wire, 14 locomotives, 95 rail cars, and 300 army wagons.

A Union expedition up the White River culminates in the seizure of 407 head of cattle at Augusta, Arkansas.

NAVAL: Admiral David D. Porter begins to lay down his strategy for the reduction of Fort Fisher, Wilmington, North Carolina. He intends to use a naval infantry brigade of sailors and U.S. Marines to hit the fort frontally while army troops storm the rear.

Armed boats from the USS *Don* seize several Confederate torpedoes on the right bank of the Rappahannock River, Virginia.

January 5
POLITICS: President Abraham Lincoln authorizes James Singleton to pass through Union lines and enter the Confederacy; his mission is to encourage peace negotiations unofficially.

NAVAL: Boats from the USS *Winnebago* land and seize copper kettles, small boats, and other impedimenta at Bon Secours, Alabama.

The Federal ironclad USS *Indianola* is raised from its muddy berth in the Mississippi River after being sunk by enemy action on May 24, 1863.

January 6
POLITICS: Representative J. M. Ashley of Ohio renews the political drive to approve the 13th Amendment to the Constitution. "If slavery is wrong and criminal, as the great body of Christian men admit," he declares, "it is certainly our duty to abolish it."

President Jefferson Davis pens a caustic letter to Vice President Alexander H. Stephens in which he claims that his whispering campaign against him is undermining Confederate morale. "I assure you that it would be to me a source of the sincerest pleasure to see you devoting your great and animated ability exclusively to upholding the confidence and animating the spirit of the people to unconquerable resistance against their foes," he declares.

January 7
SOUTH: General Edward O. C. Ord replaces General Benjamin F. Butler as commander of the Department of Virginia and North Carolina. This is largely done at the behest of General Ulysses S. Grant, who feels that Butler manifestly is incapable of commanding a large force such as the Army of the James. Moreover, by sheer seniority of rank, Butler is next in line to succeed Grant as overall commander in his absence.

WEST: Elements of the Union XIX Corps are transferred from the Shenandoah Valley to Savannah, Georgia.

A large body of around 1,000 Cheyenne and Sioux warriors, still resenting the Sand Creek Massacre, attack frontier settlements at Julesburg and Valley Station, Colorado Territory. The Native Americans send a small detachment forward to lure the garrison out and a party of the 7th Iowa Cavalry under Captain Nicholas J. O'Brien obliges them. However, the intended ambush miscarries when it is sprung too early, and the cavalrymen scamper back into the fort. The frustrated warriors, unable to breach such strong defenses, subsequently loot and burn the town.

NAVAL: Admiral David D. Farragut pays a courtesy call on the White House to discuss current events with President Abraham Lincoln and Secretary of the Navy Gideon Welles.

The French-built ironclad *Sphinx,* sold to Denmark and then relinquished after the Schleswig-Holstein War, is resold secretly to the Confederacy by French emperor Napoleon III. This vessel, soon to be christened CSS *Stonewall,* is potentially the most powerful Confederate warship of the war. Captain Thomas J. Paige then sails it from Copenhagen to Spain on its maiden voyage.

January 8
SOUTH: General Edward O. C. Ord, commanding the Army of the James, also takes control of the Department of Virginia and North Carolina.
WEST: To alleviate near-starvation among his troops, General Thomas L. Rosser leads 300 Confederate cavalry from Staunton, West Virginia, on a raid against well-stocked Union encampments at Beverly. To accomplish this, the Southerners brave high snow drifts and howling winter winds for 75 miles.

General John A. Logan resumes command of the Union XV Corps in Tennessee.
NAVAL: Transports carrying the army of General Alfred H. Terry rendezvous with the naval squadron of Admiral David D. Porter off Beaufort, North Carolina. The two leaders then finalize plans for the impending assault on Fort Fisher, Wilmington, North Carolina.

January 9
POLITICS: President Abraham Lincoln dispatches Secretary of War Edwin M. Stanton to Savannah, Georgia, for discussions with General William T. Sherman. Among the issues raised is Sherman's alleged mistreatment of African-American refugees.

Representative Moses Odell, a New York Democrat, endorses the proposed constitutional amendments to outlaw slavery, insisting: "The South by rebellion has absolved the Democratic party at the North from all obligation to stand up longer for the defense of its 'cornerstone.'"

The Tennessee constitutional convention approves an amendment abolishing slavery and readies the amendment for a popular vote.
SOUTH: General William T. Sherman entertains Secretary of War Edwin M. Stanton at his headquarters in Savannah, Georgia.
WEST: General John B. Hood straggles into Tupelo, Mississippi, with remnants of his once-proud Army of Tennessee. President Jefferson Davis intends to transfer the bulk of the survivors eastward to contest the advance of General William T. Sherman in the Carolinas.
NAVAL: The USS *Wyalusing* captures the Confederate schooner *Triumph* off the mouth of the Perquimans River, North Carolina.

January 10
POLITICS: Heated debate in the U.S. House of Representatives continues as to a constitutional amendment to abolish slavery. Representative Fernando Wood of New York insists its passage negates any chance for peaceful reconciliation with the South.
WEST: A body of 300 Confederate cavalry under General Thomas L. Rosser reaches the Philippi Turnpike north of Beverly, West Virginia, and prepares to storm nearby Union positions at dawn.

NAVAL: The USS *Valley City* seizes the Confederate steamer *Philadelphia* in the Chowan River, Virginia.

January 11

POLITICS: The Missouri constitutional convention approves an ordinance abolishing slavery.

WEST: Despite freezing weather, 300 Confederate cavalrymen under General Thomas L. Rosser attack Union encampments at Beverly, West Virginia. The defenders, comprising detachments from the 8th and 34th Ohio Cavalry, are caught by surprise and overwhelmed before serious resistance is mounted. Rosser secures 583 captives, 100 horses, 600 rifles, and, above all, 10,000 rations to feed his hungry men.

January 12

POLITICS: Secretary of War Edwin M. Stanton confers with African-American leaders in Washington, D.C., about how to best assimilate freed slaves into society. Garrison Frazier, the group's spokesman, suggests that blacks continue farming the land until they are able to purchase it. And, despite allegations of callous indifference by General William T. Sherman toward "contrabands," Frazier states, "We have confidence in General Sherman, and think that what concerns us could not be in better hands."

Senior Maryland politician Francis P. Blair confers with President Jefferson Davis in Richmond, Virginia, sounding out possible overtures for peace. To facilitate a possible rapprochement, Blair suggests mounting a joint military expedition against the French in Mexico. Davis dismisses the scheme as quixotic, but he acquiesces in sending Confederate representatives to a conference with President Abraham Lincoln in February.

SOUTH: General John G. Parke resumes command of the IX Corps, Army of the Potomac, Virginia.

WEST: General Richard Taylor is instructed by President Jefferson Davis to transfer troops from the Army of Tennessee at Tupelo, Mississippi, to bolster Confederate defenses in the Carolinas. "Sherman's campaign has produced bad effect on our people, success against his future operations is needful to reanimate public confidence," he contends, "Hardee requires more aid than Lee can give him, and Hood's army is the only source to which we can now look."

NAVAL: Admiral David D. Porter arrives off Wilmington, North Carolina, with a fleet of 59 warships and 8,000 men commanded by General Alfred H. Terry. This is the largest Union armada and combined expedition of the entire war.

The new and formidable ram CSS *Columbia* grounds in Charleston harbor on its maiden voyage and efforts to refloat it fail.

January 13

SOUTH: General Alfred H. Terry lands four brigades of white troops and one of African Americans, totaling 8,000 men, outside Fort Fisher, Wilmington, North Carolina. As the whites take up assault positions, the black soldiers dig strong fortifications across the peninsula to forestall the arrival of Confederate reinforcements from General Robert F. Hoke's division.

General John B. Hood resigns from the Army of Tennessee at Tupelo, Mississippi, and he is succeeded temporarily by General Pierre G. T. Beauregard.

Naval: Admiral David D. Porter's fleet begins a protracted bombardment of the Confederate defenses at Fort Fisher, Wilmington, North Carolina. During the next two days, his fleet pours an estimated 1.6 million pounds of explosive ordnance on the Southern garrison, commanded by Colonel William Lamb.

Commander Stephen B. Luce takes the USS *Pontiac* 40 miles up the Savannah River to confer with General William T. Sherman. Luce's experience with the general indelibly impresses on him the need to educate navy officers in the principles of warfare and eventually inspires him to found the U.S. Naval War College in Newport, Rhode Island.

January 14

South: Union troops under General Alfred H. Terry resist General Braxton Bragg's efforts to reinforce the Confederate garrison at Fort Fisher, Wilmington, North Carolina. Nonetheless, 350 make it through under General William H. C. Whiting, bringing garrison strength up to roughly 2,000 men.

Naval: The armada of Admiral David D. Porter, mounting 627 heavy cannon, continues its concentrated bombardment of Confederate defenses at Fort Fisher, Wilmington, North Carolina. Porter moves his ships to within 1,000 yards and delivers a meticulously aimed fire that strikes Fort Fisher's defenses at a rate of 100 shells per minute. Within hours, most of the fort's heavy cannon have been rendered useless.

The USS *Seminole* captures the Confederate schooner *Josephine* off the Texas coast.

The Confederate blockade-runner *Leila* founders off the mouth of the Mersey River, England, killing Commander Arthur Sinclair, C.S.N.

January 15

Politics: Edward Everett, a former U.S. congressman from Massachusetts, dies in Boston at the age of 71.

South: General John Gibbon assumes control of the XXIV Corps, Army of the James. This transfer signals that his formally cordial relationship with General Winfield S. Hancock has ended.

General Alfred H. Terry commences an all-out assault on Fort Fisher, Wilmington, North Carolina, with three brigades commanded by Generals Newton M. Curtis, Galusha Pennypacker, and Louis H. Bell. The attack is launched in concert with a large naval brigade that advances against the fort's northeastern salient. Meanwhile, the army troops move inland around the rear of Confederate defenses and storm numerous lines of entrenchments and parapets. Resistance is fierce, and all three Union brigadiers are either killed or wounded in fierce, hand-to hand fighting that lasts eight hours. General William H. C. Whiting and Colonel William Lamb make repeated entreaties for reinforcements, but General Braxton Bragg, with 6,000 men under General Robert F. Hoke nearby, makes no attempt to interfere. At length, Porter sails in closer with concentrated firepower against the defenders while Terry commits his final brigade under General Joseph C. Abbott. The remaining Confederates are overpowered by 10:00 P.M. and surrender.

The Union Assault on Fort Fisher January 15, 1865 Painting by Lewis Prang *(Library of Congress)*

The fall of Fort Fisher is a major victory and demonstrates the Union's skill at massive, combined operations. Terry's and Porter's combined losses are 266 killed, 1,018 wounded, and 57 missing (1,341) with Colonels Pennypacker and Curtis receiving the Congressional Medal of Honor. Confederate losses total around 500 with an additional 1,500 captured. Both General Whiting and Colonel Lamb are wounded, the former mortally. Federal forces finally have slammed the door shut on the South's sole remaining open port, and Confederate vice president Alexander H. Stephens regards its fall as "one of the greatest disasters that had befallen our cause from the beginning of the war."

WEST: General John M. Schofield's XXIII Corps begins to embark on army transports at Clifton, Tennessee to Cincinnati, Ohio, en route to Washington, D.C., and eventual deployment in North Carolina.

NAVAL: Admiral David D. Porter orders the monitors USS *New Ironsides, Saugus, Canonicus, Monadnock,* and *Mahopac* to within 1,000 yards of Fort Fisher, Wilmington, North Carolina, and unleashes a withering, point-blank bombardment. Several hours of cannonading silence virtually all of the forts heavy cannon, at which point firing ceases and a naval brigade of 1,600 sailors and 400 U.S. Marines lands ashore under Commander K. Randolph Breese. This force is tasked with launching diversionary attacks while army troops work their way around to the rear of Confederate defenses. Three desperate charges are launched and repelled with the loss of 309 casualties, but the defenders are successfully distracted. For their role in the victory, no less than 35 sailors and marines win the Congressional Medal of Honor.

Admiral John A. B. Dahlgren agrees to provide a diversion at Charleston, South Carolina, to draw Confederate attention away from General William T. Sherman's army marching up from Savannah, Georgia. Prior to this decision, several naval vessels are dispatched to find and mark numerous obstacles blocking the harbor. In the course of such activity, the ironclad USS *Patapsco* strikes a torpedo near the entrance of Charleston harbor, South Carolina, sinking 15 seconds later with the loss of 62 officers and men.

January 16

POLITICS: Maryland politician Francis P. Blair conveys a letter from President Jefferson Davis to President Abraham Lincoln suggesting peace negotiations "between the two nations." Lincoln, like Davis, dismisses any notion of a joint military expedition to expel the French from Mexico, but he agrees to attend a peace conference slated for February.

The Confederate Congress, lacking confidence in President Jefferson Davis's conduct of affairs, passes a resolution 14 to 2 to appoint General Robert E. Lee as general in chief and also restore General Joseph E. Johnston to commander of the Army of Tennessee.

NORTH: Alfred H. Terry is promoted to major general, U.S. Army.

SOUTH: Two drunken U.S. sailors accidentally ignite 13,000 pounds of gunpowder at Fort Fisher, Wilmington, North Carolina, killing 25 Federals, injuring 66, and leaving an additional 13 missing.

General Braxton Bragg abandons Smithville and Reeves Point, North Carolina, blowing up Fort Caswell and other defensive works at the mouth of the Cape Fear River.

General William T. Sherman directs his army north from Savannah, Georgia, and toward South Carolina. He also issues Special Field Order No. 15, which confiscates land on the Georgia coast for the express purpose of settling African-American refugees. He later insists this is nothing more than a temporary expedient until the refugees can be settled inland on a more permanent basis.

NAVAL: Confederate secretary of the navy Stephen R. Mallory urges the James River Squadron under Commander John K. Mitchell to sortie southward and attack a large Union supply depot at City Point, Virginia. This major installation is General Ulysses S. Grant's base of operations. "If we can block the river at or below City Point," he reasons, "Grant might be compelled to evacuate his position."

January 17

SOUTH: General George W. Getty takes charge of the VI Corps, Army of the Potomac, Virginia.

NAVAL: Admiral David D. Porter, surveying the size and strength of Fort Fisher, Wilmington, North Carolina, marvels over its construction yet concludes that "no *Alabamas, Floridas, Chickamaugas,* or *Tallahassees* will ever fit out again from this port, and our merchant vessels very soon, I hope, will be enabled to pursue in safety their avocation." Porter also orders Wilmington's signal lights lit and those of his warships dimmed, to lure any unsuspecting blockade-runners into his grasp.

Boat crews from the USS *Honeysuckle* seize the English blockade-runner *Augusta* in the Suwannee River, Florida.

A combined expedition mounted from the Mississippi Squadron lands at Somerville, Alabama, seizing 90 captives and several horses.

January 18

POLITICS: President Abraham Lincoln hands Francis P. Blair a letter to President Jefferson Davis, demonstrating his willingness to negotiate peace for the inhabitants "of our one common country."

SOUTH: Command of the Savannah, Georgia, region falls to on General John G. Foster and the Department of the South.

WEST: Confederate cavalry under General Thomas L. Rosser surprise Union outposts near Lovettsville, Virginia, and then evade a hasty Federal pursuit.

NAVAL: Lieutenant William B. Cushing of the USS *Monticello* lands at Fort Caswell, North Carolina, and raises the Stars and Stripes.

Confederate blockade-runners *Granite City* and *Wave* successfully evade the Union blockade at Calcasieu Pass, Louisiana.

January 19

POLITICS: President Abraham Lincoln inquires of General Ulysses S. Grant about the possibility of finding Robert Lincoln, his eldest son, a staff position. Grant subsequently appoints him assistance adjutant general with a rank of captain.

President Jefferson Davis, intent on shoring up support for his flagging reputation as a war leader, convinces General Robert E. Lee to serve as general in chief of Confederate forces. Lee reluctantly agrees but cautions, "I must state that with the addition of the immediate command of the army, I do not think I could accomplish any good."

SOUTH: General William T. Sherman orders his army to begin to march north toward the South Carolina border. A two-pronged drive toward Columbia, the state capital, is developing.

January 20

POLITICS: Secretary of War Edwin M. Stanton, recently arrived from Savannah, Georgia, confers with President Abraham Lincoln as to recent conversations held with General William T. Sherman.

SOUTH: General William T. Sherman's army marches north, encountering strong Confederate resistance at Pocotaligo and along the Salkehatchie River, South Carolina.

WEST: Federal troops fight off an attack by hostile Cheyenne and Arapaho at Fort Learned, Kansas.

The Arizona Territory is joined to the Department of the Pacific.

NAVAL: A somewhat surprised admiral David D. Porter, aboard the USS *Malvern*, watches as Confederate blockade-runners *Stag* and *Charlotte* inadvertently anchor near his vessel in Wilmington harbor and are captured. They are unaware of Fort Fisher's recent capture.

Confederate blockade-runner *City of Richmond* drops anchor at Quiberon Bay, France, and awaits the arrival of the CSS *Stonewall* to transfer men and supplies aboard.

January 21

SOUTH: General William T. Sherman begins to relocate his headquarters from Savannah, Georgia, to Beaufort, South Carolina. Overall, Union movements are delayed two weeks by incessant rains.

WEST: General John M. Schofield's XXIII Corps disembarks from transports at Cincinnati, Ohio, following a five-day journey from Clifton, Tennessee. Here, they entrain for Washington, D.C., and eventual service in North Carolina.

NAVAL: Confederate secretary of the navy Stephen R. Mallory again urges Commander John K. Mitchell of the James River Squadron to strike Union supply depots at City Point, Virginia. "You have an opportunity, I am convinced, rarely presented to a naval operations officer," Mallory insists, "and one which may lead to the most glorious results to your country."

The USS *Penguin* runs the Confederate blockade-runner *Granite City* aground off Velasco, Texas, and destroys it with gunfire.

January 22

NAVAL: An armed boat from the USS *Chocura* captures and burns the Confederate schooner *Delphina* in Calcasieu Pass, Louisiana.

Lieutenant John Low, C.S.N., sails the steamer CSS *Ajax* from Dublin, Ireland, and makes for Nassau to receive its armament. However, adroit diplomacy by American minister Charles F. Adams dissuades the British from allowing any guns to be shipped there.

January 23

POLITICS: President Jefferson Davis, reacting to pressure from the Confederate Congress, signs the General-in-Chief Act, which renders General Robert E. Lee supreme military commander.

WEST: Command of the much-depleted Army of Tennessee formally reverts to General Richard Taylor at Tupelo, Mississippi, where he commands 18,000 men. More than 4,000 soldiers have been transferred to South Carolina to reinforce General William J. Hardee.

NAVAL: Commodore John K. Mitchell sorties down the James River past Richmond, Virginia, to attack a Union supply depot at City Point. Sailing with him are the CSS *Virginia II, Fredericksburg, Drewry, Torpedo, Richmond, Scorpion, Wasp,* and *Hornet.* Mitchell's progress halts once the *Virginia II* and *Richmond* run aground on Union obstacles placed at Trent's Reach. However, Union commander W. A. Parker is criticized severely for declining to engage the Southerners and withdrawing his own ironclad squadron to deeper water.

The USS *Fox* captures the British blockade-runner *Fannie McRae* in the Gulf of Mexico.

January 24

NORTH: Reversing himself, General Ulysses S. Grant now approves of renewed prisoner of war exchanges. The Southerners' arrival home will only exacerbate Confederate food shortages.

SOUTH: General Orlando B. Wilcox takes temporary command of the IX Corps, Army of the Potomac, Virginia.

WEST: General Nathan B. Forrest assumes control of the Confederate District of Mississippi, East Louisiana, and West Tennessee.

NAVAL: The CSS *Drewry* is hit by Union artillery fire on the James River and explodes. Then the USS *Onondaga* and *Massasoit* under Commander W. A. Parker steam up the James River to engage Confederate vessels under Commodore John K. Mitchell, but the Southerners retire upstream.

The Confederate ironclad CSS *Stonewall* anchors at Quiberon Bay, France, to receive a full complement of crew from the blockade-runner *City of Richmond*.

January 25

NAVAL: The USS *Tristram Shandy* captures the Confederate steamer *Blenheim* off New Inlet, North Carolina.

As the army of General William T. Sherman advances from Savannah, Georgia, ships of Admiral John A. B. Dahlgren's South Atlantic Blockading Squadron dip into nearby rivers to provide naval support whenever possible.

The Confederate raider CSS *Shenandoah* under Lieutenant James I. Waddell drops anchor off Melbourne, Australia, to take on supplies and carry out repairs.

January 26

SOUTH: To mask his forthcoming advance on Columbia, South Carolina, General William T. Sherman dispatches a column toward Charleston as a diversion.

NAVAL: The tug USS *Clover* captures the Confederate blockade-runner *Coquette* in the Combahee River, South Carolina. Meanwhile, the *Dai Ching*, which grounds in the same river, is scuttled and abandoned.

January 27

POLITICS: President Jefferson Davis begins to choose a commission to conduct informal peace talks as suggested by Francis P. Blair. This ultimately consists of Vice President Alexander H. Stephens, Senate president Robert Hunter, and Assistant Secretary of War John A. Campbell. They are authorized to discuss possible political moves leading to an armistice.

SOUTH: General Gouverneur K. Warren resumes command of the V Corps, Army of the Potomac, Virginia.

WEST: Command of the Confederate District of Mississippi, East Louisiana, and West Tennessee reverts to General Nathan B. Forrest.

General Robert E. Lee advises President Jefferson Davis of potentially ruinous desertion rates in the Army of Northern Virginia. He ascribes the unrest to a constant lack of food and suggests that the Commissary Department do better.

NAVAL: The USS *Eutaw* steams up the James River, Virginia, and captures the torpedo boat CSS *Scorpion*.

The USS *Ariel* captures an unnamed boat near the Manatee River, Florida.

January 28

SOUTH: Skirmishing occurs as Union forces under General William T. Sherman pass along the Combahee River, South Carolina.

WEST: Union forces repel a Confederate attack on Athens, Tennessee, losing 20 men in the process.

NAVAL: General Ulysses S. Grant arrives onboard the USS *Malvern* to confer with Admiral David D. Porter. Grant then persuades the admiral to provide naval support for an offensive up the Cape Fear River against Fort Anderson, North Carolina.

The USS *Valley City* steams down the Chowan River and helps repel a Confederate night attack against a Union encampment at Colerain, North Carolina.

The Torpedo boat CSS *St. Patrick* successfully strikes the USS *Octorara* at night off Mobile Bay, Alabama, but its spar torpedo fails to detonate. The Confederate vessel then flees undamaged into the darkness.

The Confederate ironclad CSS *Stonewall* departs Quiberon Bay, France, and steams for El Ferrol, Spain, to take on additional coal.

January 30

SOUTH: Advance elements from the Army of Tennessee arrive at Augusta, Georgia, to join Confederate forces under General William J. Hardee.

WEST: The Military Division of the Missouri is set up and includes the Departments of Missouri and the Northwest; General John Pope is appointed commanding officer.

NAVAL: A boat crew from the USS *Henry Brinker,* scouting King's Creek, Virginia, uncovers two 150-pound Confederate torpedoes and the galvanic batteries necessary to detonate them from the shore.

The USS *Cherokee* bombards Confederate troops at Half Moon Battery, North Carolina.

January 31

POLITICS: The U.S. House of Representatives finally musters the two-thirds (119 to 56) majority necessary to approve the 13th Amendment to the Constitution, which abolishes slavery. This legislation had been passed previously by the U.S. Senate on April 8, 1864, and now is handed off to the states for ratification.

SOUTH: General Robert E. Lee is appointed general in chief of Confederate forces in light of continuing dissatisfaction concerning President Jefferson Davis's handling of military affairs.

The Department of North Carolina is created with General John M. Schofield as commanding officer.

General David S. Stanley takes charge of the IV Corps in East Tennessee and North Alabama.

February 1

POLITICS: Illinois becomes the first state to ratify the 13th Amendment to the Constitution, formally abolishing slavery.

John Rock, an African-American attorney from Boston Massachusetts, becomes the first minority lawyer to practice before the U.S. Supreme Court.

Confederate secretary of war James A. Seddon resigns from office due to political pressure.

SOUTH: General William T. Sherman departs Savannah, Georgia, with 62,000 men and heads toward the South Carolina border. His command consists of two wings under Generals Oliver O. Howard's Army of the Tennessee (XV, XVII Corps) and Henry W. Slocum's Army of Georgia (XV and XX Corps), aided by a cavalry division of General Hugh J. Kilpatrick. The Northerners are eager to wreak havoc in the heart of secessionism, and their penchant for destruction—while officially against orders—exceeds anything inflicted on Georgia.

WEST: General John B, Magruder is appointed head of the District of Arkansas.

NAVAL: Boat crews from the USS *Midnight* land and destroy a large saltworks at St. Andrew's Bay, Florida.

February 2

POLITICS: President Abraham Lincoln departs Washington, D.C., to meet with Confederate peace commissioners at Hampton Roads, Virginia.

Rhode Island and Michigan are the second and third states to ratify the 13th Amendment.

SOUTH: General John G. Parke resumes command of the IX Corps, Army of the Potomac, Virginia.

Skirmishing breaks out at Whippy Swamp, South Carolina, between forces under Generals William T. Sherman and William J. Hardee. The approach of Federal troops also induces Confederate authorities to prepare to evacuate Charleston.

WEST: Marauding Cheyenne and Sioux pay a second visit to Julesburg, Colorado, chasing the inhabitants into the nearby fort and burning whatever buildings they find standing.

NAVAL: The USS *Pinola* captures the Confederate schooner *Ben Willis* in the Gulf of Mexico.

February 3

POLITICS: President Jefferson Davis dispatches Confederate vice president Alexander H. Stephens, John A. Campbell, and Robert M. T. Hunter to confer with President Abraham Lincoln and Secretary of State William H. Seward aboard a ship off Hampton Roads, Virginia. The meeting deadlocks since the Southerners insist on independence for the Confederacy as a precondition for peace, whereas Lincoln will accept only their unconditional surrender.

Maryland, New York, and West Virginia ratify the 13th Amendment, for a total of six states.

SOUTH: Federal troops battle with Confederates at Rivers's Bridge, South Carolina, as the army under General William T. Sherman grinds inexorably forward.

WEST: The Confederate District of North Mississippi and West Tennessee is set up under General Marcus J. Wright.

The Confederate District of South Mississippi and East Tennessee is created under General Wirt W. Adams.

Naval: The CSS *Macon* and *Sampson,* berthed on the Savannah River, Georgia, are ordered to turn over all powder and ammunition supplies to Confederate army units operating in the vicinity of Augusta.

The USS *Matthew Vassar* seizes the Confederate blockade-runner *John Hale* off the Florida coast following a chase of four hours.

February 4

Politics: President Abraham Lincoln returns to Washington, D.C., somewhat distraught that little has been accomplished through peace negotiations. He then assures General Ulysses S. Grant, "Nothing transpired, or transpiring, with the three gentlemen from Richmond is to cause any change, hindrance, or delay of your military plans or operations."

South: General Ulysses S. Grant, determined to stretch Confederate defenses at Petersburg, Virginia, to the breaking point, orders Union forces to cut off Southern wagon trains near Hatcher's Run along Boydton Plank Road. The II Corps under General Andrew A. Humphreys, the V Corps of General Gouverneur K. Warren, and a cavalry division led by General John M. Gregg draw the assignment.

Fighting erupts at Angley's Post Office and Buford's Bridge, South Carolina, as General William T. Sherman surges farther into the state.

Naval: The USS *Wamsutta* and *Potomska* run an unidentified blockade-runner ashore at Breach Inlet, South Carolina.

Armed boats from the USS *Midnight* land and destroy a saltworks at West Bay, Florida.

February 5

Politics: President Abraham Lincoln floats the idea of offering $400 million to slave states if they will surrender by April 1. His cabinet uniformly rejects the suggestion, however, so Lincoln abandons it.

South: General Ulysses S. Grant launches a renewed offensive along the Boydton Plank Road near Hatcher's Run (Dabney's Mill), Virginia. Union cavalry under General David M. Gregg arrive at Dinwiddie Court House, find only a few Confederate wagons and no troops, and subsequently encamp nearby. Meanwhile, General Gouverneur K. Warren's V Corps also moves up to Hatcher's Run while the II Corps of General Andrew A. Humphreys occupies the nearby Vaughan Road. Throughout the course of the day, Confederates launch several strong attacks but are repulsed. Humphreys is then reinforced overnight by Gregg's cavalry, and fighting dies down across the line.

Naval: A joint expedition from the USS *Roanoke* up the Pagan and Jones creeks, Virginia, leads to the capture of an unnamed Confederate torpedo boat.

Lieutenant William B. Cushing leads an armed expedition up the Little River, South Carolina, to seize cotton supplies and prisoners.

The Confederate blockade-runner *Chameleon* tries and fails to run the Union blockade off Charleston, South Carolina, then turns and departs for Nassau.

The USS *Niagara* under Commodore Thomas T. Craven, learning of the CSS *Stonewall*'s departure, sails from Dover, England, possibly to intercept it off the coast of Spain.

February 6

POLITICS: In reporting to the Confederate Congress on the recent conference held at Hampton Roads, President Jefferson Davis denounces President Abraham Lincoln for insisting on unconditional surrender as the basis for peace. He declares this unacceptable and vows that the struggle for Southern independence will go on.

General John C. Breckinridge is appointed Confederate secretary of war to replace outgoing James A. Seddon.

SOUTH: Heavy fighting resumes along Hatcher's Run, Virginia, as Confederate forces under General John B. Gordon's division slam into the exposed V Corps of General Gouverneur K. Warren. In the course of fighting, Confederate general John Pegram is killed attacking Union lines. However, a sharp thrust by additional Southerners under General Clement A. Evans contests the Federals along the Boydton Plank Road until nightfall ends the action.

General Robert E. Lee formally is designated general in chief of Confederate armies, although at this stage of the struggle this assignment is merely symbolic.

General Edward O. C. Ord becomes commander of the Department of Virginia.

February 7

POLITICS: Maine and Kansas ratify the 13th Amendment; the Delaware legislature fails to muster a two-thirds majority.

SOUTH: Fighting continues at Hatcher's Run, Virginia, as Union forces successfully extend their siege lines. The Federals sustain 170 dead, 1,100 injured, and 182 missing (1,512). Confederate losses are not known but are presumed to be nearly as heavy. Worse, General Robert E. Lee's defensive perimeter is now stretched to 37 miles in length, increasingly hard for his 46,000 men to hold against superior numbers. This action momentarily concludes General Ulysses S. Grant's efforts to shift forces leftward.

Union troops under General William T. Sherman capture the Edisto River Bridge, South Carolina, and cut the Augusta and Charleston Railroad at Blackville, but progress is slowed by swamps and swollen rivers.

NAVAL: Armed boats from the USS *Bienville* enter Galveston harbor, Texas, and capture the British blockade-runners *Annie Sophie* and *Pet.* However, they fail to apprehend the Confederate blockade-runner *Wren.*

February 8

POLITICS: President Abraham Lincoln signs a U.S. House resolution declaring that 11 states of the soon-to-be-defunct Confederacy should not enjoy representation in the electoral college.

SOUTH: Elements of General John M. Schofield's XXIII Corps trickle into Fort Fisher, Wilmington, North Carolina, following their rapid transfer from the Tennessee interior.

General William T. Sherman responds to a letter from General Joseph Wheeler complaining that Union troops are destroying private homes and property. "Vacant houses being of no use to anybody, I care little about," he writes, "I don't want them destroyed, but do not take much care to preserve them."

WEST: General Grenville M. Dodge assumes command of the Department of Kansas.

February 9

POLITICS: On the recommendation of General Robert E. Lee, now general in chief, President Jefferson Davis enacts a pardon for all Confederate deserters who report back to their units within 30 days.

Unionists in Virginia ratify the 13th Amendment outlawing slavery.

SOUTH: General Quincy A. Gilmore replaces General John G. Foster as commander of the Department of the South.

The Division of Northern Louisiana is formed with General Francis J. Herron as commanding officer.

The Division of Southern Louisiana, centered at New Orleans, is set up under General Thomas W. Sherman.

The XXIII Corps fully deploys at Fort Fisher, Wilmington, North Carolina, under General John M. Schofield, who also commands the Department of North Carolina. His orders are to forge inland, take Wilmington, and affect a new supply route for General William T. Sherman as the latter advances up from South Carolina.

NAVAL: The USS *Pawnee, Sonoma,* and *Daffodil* bombard Confederate batteries in Togodo Creek, North Edisto, North Carolina. This action is undertaken in support of General William T. Sherman's army, then moving north near the coast.

February 10

WEST: The Department of Kentucky is created under General John M. Palmer.

The Department of the Cumberland is created with General George H. Thomas as commanding officer.

NAVAL: Captain Raphael Semmes is promoted to rear admiral, C.S.N., for his conduct as commander of the CSS *Alabama,* and he is instructed to take command of the James River Squadron, Virginia.

The USS *Shawmut* and *Huron* bombard Confederate batteries and Fort Anderson on the Cape Fear River, North Carolina.

The ironclad USS *Lehigh,* assisted by several gunboats, cruises the Stono and Folly rivers, South Carolina, in support of army movements and occasionally engages Confederate land batteries.

The USS *Princess Royal* captures and burns the Confederate steamer *Will o' Wisp* off Galveston, Texas.

February 11

SOUTH: The army of General William T. Sherman severs the Augusta and Charleston Railroad, which prevents Charleston, South Carolina, from receiving reinforcements. General William J. Hardee becomes convinced, mistakenly, that the city is Sherman's ultimate objective.

The XXIII Corps under General John M. Schofield makes preparations to steam up the Cape Fear River in transports provided by Admiral David D. Porter, and outflank the defenders of Fort Anderson, North Carolina.

NAVAL: A party of 100 Confederate sailors under Lieutenant Charles W. Read marches from Drewry's Bluff, Virginia, toward City Point on the James River. There, they are to capture several Union vessels, outfit them with spar torpedoes, and then attack and sink any Union ironclads in the area. Success here would leave remaining Federal ships at the mercy of Confederate ironclads waiting upstream. Southern control of the James River could severely compromise the Union army's ability to supply itself at Petersburg.

The USS *Keystone State, Aries, Montgomery, Howquah, Emma,* and *Vicksburg* bombard Half Moon Battery on Cape Fear River, six miles above Fort Fisher, North Carolina.

The USS *Penobscot* captures the British blockade-runner *Matilda* in the Gulf of Mexico.

The USS *Niagara* arrives off La Coruña, Spain, to shadow the CSS *Stonewall* anchored at nearby El Ferrol.

February 12
POLITICS: The Electoral College meets and confirms President Abraham Lincoln's election victory on a vote of 212 to 21.

SOUTH: Union forces under General William T. Sherman advance into Branchville, South Carolina. His soldiers are particularly vengeful during this phase of the march, knowing that the movement for secession commenced here. Sherman's presence forces Confederates under General Pierre G. T. Beauregard across the Edisto River, from whence they begin to concentrate at Cheraw. In effect, Beauregard abandons the central reaches of the state to preserve his army.

WEST: A party of 100 Union soldiers surrounds and attacks the home of noted Confederate guerrilla captain Jeff Williams in Lewisburg, Arkansas, killing him.

General Samuel R. Curtis assumes command of the Department of the Northwest.

NAVAL: A daring Confederate naval expedition conducted by Lieutenant Charles W. Read is cancelled on account of worsening weather and fears of a Union army ambush. He then marches back to Richmond, Virginia, where almost all of his 100 volunteers require medical attention due to exposure.

Confederate blockade-runners *Carolina, Dream, Chicora, Chamelon,* and *Owl* sortie from Nassau and try to run the Union blockade off Charleston, South Carolina, from a variety of directions.

February 13
DIPLOMACY: Lord John Russell informs American diplomats in London of the government's unease over the recent American naval buildup in the Great Lakes region, which negates the 1817 Rush-Bagot Agreement. The British are summarily told that any buildup is in direct response to the Confederate raid on St. Albans, Vermont, on October 19, 1864, which originated from Canada.

POLITICS: Reacting to complaints from west Tennessee politicians, President Abraham Lincoln admonishes military authorities there, insisting that, "the object of the war being to restore and maintain the blessings of peace and good government, I desire you to help, and not hinder, every advance in that direction."

SOUTH: The projected movement of General Jacob D. Cox's division, XXII Corps, to outflank Fort Anderson, North Carolina, is hampered by heavy rain and muddy conditions.

NAVAL: The crews of the Confederate vessels CSS *Chicora, Palmetto State,* and *Charleston,* 300 men and officers in all, are marched from Charleston, South Carolina, under Commander John R. Tucker. They are instructed to assist in the defense of Wilmington, North Carolina.

February 14

SOUTH: Wade Hampton is appointed lieutenant general, C.S.A.

General John M. Schofield, citing heavy rain and poor marching conditions, temporarily halts his planned flanking movement by General Jacob D. Cox's division against Fort Anderson, North Carolina.

General William T. Sherman departs Orangeburg, South Carolina, directs Union forces across the Congaree River, and begins to advance on Columbia with both wings of his army. General Pierre G. T. Beauregard makes preparations to flee and also orders the garrison of Charleston under General William J. Hardee to escape possible encirclement.

WEST: General George Stoneman takes charge of the District of East Tennessee.

NAVAL: The Confederate blockade-runner *Celt* runs aground while attempting to enter Charleston harbor, South Carolina.

February 15

SOUTH: The army of General William T. Sherman halts just south of Columbia, South Carolina, as Confederates continue evacuating the state capital. To mask this move, they bombard the Union encampments from across the Congaree River.

General Alexander Asboth becomes commander of the District of West Florida.

WEST: General Mosby M. Parsons takes command of the Confederate Department of Arkansas.

NAVAL: The Union steamer *Knickerbocker* runs hard aground at Smith's Point, Virginia, where it is burned by Confederate forces.

The USS *Merrimac* founders and is allowed to sink off the Florida coast; the crew is rescued by the steamer *Morning Star.*

February 16

POLITICS: The 13th Amendment is ratified by Indiana, Nevada, and Louisiana.

SOUTH: The division of General Jacob D. Cox, XXII Corps, ferries up the Cape Fear River in transports toward Smithville, North Carolina. This movement is part of General John M. Schofield's campaign to evict Confederate defenders from Wilmington.

Federal artillery begin to shell Columbia, South Carolina, while troops under General Oliver O. Howard throw a pontoon bridge across the Broad River north of the city. Meanwhile, the defenders under Generals Pierre G. T. Beauregard and Wade Hampton complete the evacuation of their troops. Farther east, General William J. Hardee is also preparing to flee Charleston rather then become pinned within it.

WEST: Confederate cavalry under General John Crawford capture Union garrisons at Athens and Sweet Water, Tennessee.

NAVAL: Gunboats and transports under Admiral David D. Porter ferry the XXIII Corps of General John M. Schofield from Fort Fisher, North Carolina, to Smithville on the Cape Fear River.

February 17
POLITICS: The U.S. Congress repudiates all debts accrued by various Confederate governments.

SOUTH: General Jacob D. Cox leads 8,000 Federal troops ashore at Smithville on the Cape Fear River, prior to attacking Fort Anderson, North Carolina. Once reinforced by the division of General Adelbert Ames, X Corps, he pushes inland to cut off the Confederate garrison.

Union forces under General William T. Sherman accept the surrender of Columbia, capital of South Carolina, from city officials. Meanwhile, General Wade Hampton's cavalry burn enormous stores of cotton bales prior to retreating, sparks from which ignite several uncontrollable fires. The Federals, flushed with victory and revenge, also enjoy free access to liquor, and discipline begins to dissolve. Fires break out all evening and destroy two-thirds of the city. Southerners are convinced that Columbia has been torched on Sherman's orders, and they mark it as a defining atrocity of the war. Sherman denies any culpability and claims the fire was caused by the sparks that spread from burning cotton bales.

Charleston, South Carolina, is evacuated by Confederate forces under General William J. Hardee, ending an epic siege lasting 567 days. The defenders, who abandon 250 heavy cannon, begin to move north in the direction of Cheraw.

NAVAL: Federal warships under Admiral David D. Porter bombard Fort Anderson, North Carolina. To draw Confederate fire, the Union ships tow "Old Bogey," a fake ironclad assembled from a scow, limber, and canvas, to the head of their line. As expected, it draws the most fire and spares the fleet considerable damage.

Armed boats from the USS *Pawnee, Sonoma, Ottawa, Winona, Potomska, Wando,* and *J. S. Chambers* launch a major diversionary landing at Bull's Bay, South Carolina, to assist the army under General William T. Sherman. Part of this force then unites with the division of General Edward E. Potter and continues driving Confederate forces inland.

The USS *Mahaska* captures the Confederate schooner *Delia* near Bayport, Florida.

February 18
POLITICS: General Robert E. Lee agrees in principle to the notion of arming slaves to fight for Southern independence, but he feels they must be employed as free men to be effective.

SOUTH: General Jacob D. Cox's division begins to maneuver to attack Fort Anderson, Wilmington, North Carolina, closely supported by naval vessels.

General William T. Sherman orders all factories, supply houses, and railroad facilities found in Columbia, South Carolina, burned to deny their use to the Confederacy.

Charleston, South Carolina, is occupied by Union forces under General Alexander Schimmelfenning. For many Federals, capture of this "fire-eater" capital is sweet revenge.

WEST: Men of the 12th U.S. Colored Artillery defeat a Confederate attack on Fort Jones, Colesburg, Kentucky.

The Union XIII under General Gordon Granger and XVI Corps under General Andrew J. Smith are created for service in Mississippi and Missouri, respectively.

NAVAL: The ironclads CSS *Chicora, Palmetto,* and *Charleston* are scuttled by Confederate authorities at Charleston, South Carolina, to prevent their capture by Admiral John A. B. Dahlgren.

The USS *Catskill* seizes the Confederate blockade-runner *Deer* during the Southern evacuation of Charleston, South Carolina.

The USS *Gladiola* captures the Confederate steamer *Syren* near Charleston, South Carolina.

The USS *Pinola* captures and sinks the Confederate schooner *Anna Dale* off Pass Cavallo, Texas.

The USS *Forest Rose* disperses a gathering of Confederates at Cole's Creek, Mississippi.

The Confederate raider CSS *Shenandoah* under Lieutenant James I. Waddell hoists anchor and sails from Port Philip Bay, Melbourne, Australia. During this three-week visit to affect repairs, word of his arrival reaches the Union whaling fleet, which promptly clears out of the South Pacific region.

February 19

SOUTH: Union forces under General William T. Sherman continue wreaking havoc against foundries, railroads, machine shops, and arsenals in Columbia, South Carolina.

As Union troops intensify their drive on Wilimington, North Carolina, General Jacob D. Cox's command begins to load into boats to outflank Fort Anderson along the Cape Fear River. However, General Johnson Hagood evacuates his post this evening, and the garrison escapes to Town Creek, eight miles north.

NAVAL: The Confederate truce vessel *A. H. Schultz,* used for prisoner exchanges, strikes a torpedo on the James River near Chaffin's Bluff and sinks.

The USS *Gertrude* seizes the Mexican brig *Eco* as it attempts to run the blockade off Galveston, Texas.

February 20

POLITICS: The Confederate House of Representatives approves the use of African-American slaves as soldiers.

SOUTH: Union troops under General Jacob D. Cox pursue fleeing Confederates from Fort Anderson, North Carolina, and corner them at Town Creek. The ensuing Federal attack carries their position, and the Southerners withdraw with a loss of 350 casualties. Union losses are recorded as 60.

Having finished their work of destruction at Columbia, South Carolina, the army of General William T. Sherman stakes out a new objective at Goldsborough, North Carolina.

A force of 500 Confederate infantry and cavalry under Major William Footman besieges the Union garrison at Fort Myers, southern Florida. The post is defended by 275 men of the 110th New York, 2nd Florida Cavalry, and the 2nd U.S. Colored Infantry under Captain James Doyle. No assaults are launched, and the contenders engage in an artillery duel at long range for most of the day. At length, Footman moves off with an estimated 40 casualties, while Doyle sustains four wounded and four missing. Thus Union forces prevail in this, the southernmost battle waged in the Civil War.

WEST: General John H. Morgan assumes command of the District of Arizona.

NAVAL: Confederate defenders of Fort Strong, North Carolina, release 200 free-ranging torpedoes down the Cape Fear River at night. Fortunately, most are caught in the nets of rowboats detailed for that purpose and no vessels are lost.

February 21

POLITICS: Citing intense opposition, the Confederate Congress postpones final consideration of a bill authorizing the use of African-American slaves as soldiers.

SOUTH: General Robert E. Lee alerts Confederate secretary of war John C. Breckinridge that, if absolutely necessary, he will abandon Richmond, Virginia, and make all haste for Burkeville to maintain communication with Confederate forces in the Carolinas. He also requests that General Joseph E. Johnston be returned speedily to active duty as the health of General Pierre G. T. Beauregard appears tenuous.

Union forces under General Jacob D. Cox reach the southwestern side of Wilmington, North Carolina. General Braxton Bragg then orders the Confederate division of Robert F. Hoke to evacuate from that city.

WEST: A swift raid by Confederate partisan rangers under Captain Jesse McNeill against Cumberland, Maryland, captures an embarrassed General George Crook and Benjamin F. Kelley in their residence.

Captain Gurnsey W. Davis and 50 men of his 13th Illinois Cavalry float down the Arkansas River from Pine Bluff, Arkansas, and set up a base camp at Douglas Landing. He is aware of a Confederate presence about three miles downriver, but heavy rainfall dissuades him from attacking.

SOUTHWEST: General Douglas H. Cooper takes charge of the Confederate District of the Indian Territory.

NAVAL: The gunboat squadron of Admiral David D. Porter again rings Fort Strong, North Carolina, and pours in concentrated fire as army troops advance up along the banks of Cape Fear River.

February 22

POLITICS: Tennessee voters approve a new state constitution that abolishes slavery while Kentucky rejects the 13th Amendment.

SOUTH: General Robert E. Lee appoints General Joseph E. Johnston commander of the Departments of South Carolina, Georgia, and Florida.

Union forces under General John M. Schofield occupy Wilmington, North Carolina, formerly the last remaining open port of the Confederacy. The Federals are now poised to conduct military operations toward the interior of the state, and to facilitate this, Schofield orders all railroad tracks in the vicinity repaired. When this proves impractical, he shifts his efforts toward converting New Bern into a major staging area.

Confederate forces evacuate Fort Strong, on the Cape Fear River, North Carolina.

General William T. Sherman's Union army approaches Rocky Mount, South Carolina, after intense skirmishing at Camden. He continues giving the impression that his goal is Charlotte, North Carolina, when it is actually Goldsborough, where he can effect a union with General John M. Schofield.

WEST: General John McNeil takes charge of the Union District of Central Missouri.

Confederate guerrillas attack the camp of Captain Gurnsey W. Davis early in the morning, wounding four men. Davis, who prepared for their assault in advance, moves his men back to the Arkansas River to embark and return to Pine Bluff. His experience underscores the dangers that small groups of Federals face while operating in the Arkansas back country.

NAVAL: Admiral David D. Porter personally runs up the Stars and Stripes at Fort Strong, Cape Fear River, North Carolina.

Admiral John A. B. Dahlgren dispatches a squadron of warships to capture Georgetown, South Carolina, thereby establishing lines of communication with General William T. Sherman's advancing army.

February 23

POLITICS: The 13th Amendment is ratified by Minnesota.

SOUTH: General William T. Sherman's XX Corps crosses the Catawba River, South Carolina, while approaching the North Carolina state line.

General John Newton embarks a small force consisting of the 2nd U.S. Florida Cavalry and the 2nd and 99th U.S. Colored Infantry on ships of the East Gulf Coast Blockading Squadron at Key West, Florida. He then sails for St. Marks, intending to close that port to blockade-running.

February 24

SOUTH: General William T. Sherman vigorously protests to General Wade Hampton the alleged murder of several Union soldiers on a foraging expedition. Hampton replies that his government authorizes him to execute any Union soldiers caught burning private property. Moreover, "This order shall remain in force so long as you disgrace the profession of arms by allowing your men to destroy private dwellings."

NAVAL: Secretary of the Navy Gideon Welles instructs Admirals John A. B. Dahlgren and John K. Thatcher, of the South Atlantic Blockading Squadron and West Gulf Squadron, respectively, to detach their least efficient vessels from active duty and send them north in be placed.

February 25

SOUTH: General Joseph E. Johnston arrives at Charlotte, North Carolina, to resume command of the Army of Tennessee and all Confederate forces in South Carolina, Georgia, and Florida. In reality, he leads a skeleton force of roughly 25,000 hungry, ragged men, and "In my opinion, these troops form an army far too weak to cope with Sherman."

General John M. Schofield orders General Innis N. Palmer, commanding Union forces at New Bern, North Carolina, to commence to rebuild all railroad tracks in the direction of Goldsborough.

General Frederick Steele assumes command of Union troops at Pensacola Bay in anticipation of a concerted Union drive against nearby Mobile, Alabama.

NAVAL: Confederates scuttle the CSS *Chickamauga* on the Cape Fear River, North Carolina.

Armed boats from the USS *Catalpa* and *Ningoe* battle with Confederate cavalry at Georgetown, South Carolina, and seize the town.

The USS *Marigold* captures the British blockade-runner *Salvadora* in the Straits of Florida.

The USS *Chenango* captures the Confederate sloop *Elvira* at sea.

February 26
SOUTH: The Union XX Corps of General William T. Sherman approach Hanging Rock, South Carolina, although progress remains somewhat hampered by heavy rains.

WEST: General Winfield S. Hancock assumes command of the Department of West Virginia.

February 27
WEST: Generals Philip H. Sheridan and Wesley Merritt take 10,000 cavalry down the Shenandoah Valley toward Lynchburg, Virginia, intending to sever the Virginia Central Railroad and the James River Canal. His command consists of the 1st Cavalry Division under General Thomas C. Devlin and the 3rd Cavalry Division under General George A. Custer.

NAVAL: Commodore John R. Tucker, heading 350 Confederate sailors and officers, arrives at Fayetteville, North Carolina. From here, he is to march to Richmond, Virginia, and form the nucleus of a naval brigade.

The USS *Proteus* captures the Confederate steamer *Ruby* in the Gulf of Mexico.

The USS *Penobscot* captures and burns the Confederate schooners *Mary Anges* and *Louisa* off Aransas Pass, Texas.

February 28
SOUTH: Nathan B. Forrest is promoted to lieutenant general, C.S.A.

General William T. Sherman's army skirmishes heavily at Rocky Mount and Cheraw, South Carolina, as it nears the North Carolina border.

NAVAL: The USS *Honeysuckle* runs the British blockade-runner *Sort* onto the coast of Florida, capturing it.

The USS *Arizona* is destroyed by a fire and explosion on the Mississippi River below New Orleans.

March 1
POLITICS: The 13th Amendment is ratified by Wisconsin but rejected by New Jersey.

SOUTH: General Ulysses S. Grant begins to marshal the Army of the Potomac for a massive strike against Confederate defensive lines around Richmond and Petersburg, Virginia.

WEST: Union forces under General George A. Custer skirmish with General Thomas L. Rosser's Confederates at Mount Crawford, Virginia. Rosser, possessing only a few hundred men to oppose nearly 5,000 Union troopers, sets fire to the bridge spanning the Middle Fork of the Shenandoah River to delay the blue-coated juggernaut. Before heavy damage results, Custer unexpectedly charges across the bridge in strength, scattering his opponents.

NAVAL: The side-paddle steamer USS *Harvest Moon* strikes a Confederate torpedo off Georgetown, South Carolina, sinking in five minutes. Admiral John A. B. Dahlgren is aboard at the time but escapes unharmed.

March 2

SOUTH: General Robert E. Lee requests a conference with General Ulysses S. Grant although the latter demurs, declaring that he lacks any authority to convene one.

The XX Corps of General William T. Sherman's army occupies Chesterfield, South Carolina.

WEST: The cavalry division of General George A. Custer clatters up to Waynesboro, Virginia, where it observes the 2,000 Confederates of General Gabriel C. Wharton's division on a ridge line, supported by a few hundred cavalry under General Thomas L. Rosser. This force constitutes the pitiful remnant of General Jubal A. Early's much-feared army, which had ravaged the Shendandoah Valley throughout the previous summer and fall. At a glance, Custer perceives that Rosser lacks the manpower to cover both of his flanks and dispatches three dismounted regiments to encircle the Confederate left without detection. At 3:00 P.M., with his troopers in place, he sounds the charge, and his flankers burst from the wood's on Wharton's left. Custer simultaneously leads his two remaining brigades on a thundering advance through the Confederate center. The Southerners simply dissolve under the onslaught and flee. Quick movements by Union cavalry cut off the majority's escape although Early and his staff gallop off the field.

The Union victory at Waynesboro, while small, finally ends four years of Confederate resistance in the Shenandoah Valley. Custer takes 1,600 prisoners, 17 flags, 11 cannon, and 200 wagons for a loss of nine dead or wounded. The main body under General Philip H. Sheridan arrives shortly after, and Union forces spend the next three weeks laying waste the countryside with scant opposition.

General Benjamin H. Grierson assumes command of all Federal cavalry in the Military Division of West Mississippi.

NAVAL: The U.S. Congress establishes the Office of Solicitor and Naval Judge Advocate General.

The USS *Pontiac* captures the Confederate steamer *Amazon* off Savannah, Georgia.

The USS *Fox* forces the Confederate schooner *Rob Roy* to be scuttled in Deadman's Bay, Florida.

March 3

POLITICS: President Abraham Lincoln, through Secretary of War Edwin M. Stanton, instructs General Ulysses S. Grant to ignore General Robert E. Lee's intimations toward peace unless he surrenders first.

Congress institutes the Bureau for the Relief of Freedmen and Refugees (Freedmen's Bureau) to assist former African-American slaves to find work, education, and land. This organization, in effect, functions as the nation's first social welfare agency and is tasked with assisting 4 million former slaves adjust to freedom.

To regulate finances better, the U.S. Congress levies a 10-percent tax on state bank notes to drive them out of circulation. These are then replaced by Federal bank notes drawn from institutions belonging to the national banking system. It is a move calculated to improve centralized financing for the war effort.

The second session, 38th Congress adjourns its final session.

SOUTH: General William T. Sherman's army occupies Cheraw, South Carolina, forcing Confederate units across the Pee Dee River.

WEST: Union forces under General Philip H. Sheridan occupy Charlottesville, Virginia, prior to moving onto Petersburg.

A joint expedition is launched against St. Marks Fort near Tallahassee, Florida, under Commander Robert W. Schufeld and General John Newton.

The USS *Honeysuckle* captures the Confederate blockade-runner *Phantom* off the Florida coast.

The USS *Glide* captures the Confederate schooner *Malta-of-Belize* in Vermilion Bayou, Louisiana.

March 4

POLITICS: President Abraham Lincoln is inaugurated for a second term in Washington, D.C. Despite the carnage and acrimony of the past four years, he strikes a conciliatory tone with his adversaries. "With malice toward none; with charity for all, with firmness in the right, as God gives us to see the right, let us strive to finish the work we are in," he declares, "to bind up the nation's wounds, to care for him who shall have borne the battle, and for his widow and his orphan—to do all which may achieve and cherish a just and lasting peace, among ourselves, and with all nations." In contrast to Lincoln's eloquence, newly elected vice president Andrew Johnson delivers a rambling, incoherent speech that offends many in the audience.

Unionist William G. Brownlow is elected governor of Tennessee to replace Andrew Johnson.

SOUTH: The expedition of General John Newton lands at St. Marks, Florida, after delays caused by ship groundings. He then proceeds overland to the nearby town of Newport.

NAVAL: Acting on a request from General Ulysses S. Grant, Secretary of the Navy Gideon Welles dispatches several heavy monitors up the James River, then riding high, to City Point, Virginia. Grant wishes to deter any possible Confederate attacks on his main supply base at this critical juncture of operations against Richmond.

The Union transport *Thorn* strikes a torpedo in the Cape Fear River, North Carolina, and sinks.

General Edward R. S. Canby requests Admiral Samuel P. Lee for additional mortar craft to support his upcoming attack on Mobile, Alabama.

Federal gunboats USS *General Burnside* and *General Thomas* steam down the Tennessee River and bombard the encampment of General Philip D. Roddey at Mussel Shoals, Alabama. Shore parties subsequently land and capture the position.

March 5

POLITICS: Comptroller of Currency Hugh McCulloch is appointed secretary of the treasury, replacing William Fessenden, who resigns after winning reelection as U.S. senator from Maine.

SOUTH: Union troops under General John Newton skirmish with Confederates as they attempt to cross the St. Marks River, Florida, to capture St. Marks. However, finding the enemy strongly dug in along the riverbank and at nearby Newport, he posts a holding force and sends the bulk of his troops north to a position known locally as Natural Bridge.

NAVAL: Armed boats from the USS *Don* skirmish with Colonel John S. Mosby's partisan rangers in Passpatansy Creek, Maryland, capturing a large boat.

March 6

SOUTH: General Joseph E. Johnston formally takes charge of all Confederate forces in North Carolina.

The army of General William T. Sherman crosses the Pee Dee River, South Carolina, and begins to approach Fayetteville, North Carolina. Meanwhile, General Hugh J. Kilpatrick leads 4,000 Union cavalry to cover the left flank of Sherman's advance.

The 600-man expedition of General John Newton encounters strong Confederate defenses under General William Miller at Natural Bridge, Florida. The Federals make repeated attempts to outflank them but find Southern positions too strong to assail. Reinforcements also bring Miller's strength up to about 1,000 men, so Newton falls back and entrenches on an open pine barren. The Confederates subsequently pursue and attack rashly, but they are repulsed. Union forces then withdraw back to the coast unhindered. Newton's losses are 148 men from all causes while the Confederates sustain six dead and between 20 and 30 wounded. This minor Southern victory prevents the state capital at Tallahassee from being attacked.

WEST: General Alexander M. McCook takes command of the District of Eastern Arkansas.

NAVAL: The USS *Commodore Read, Yankee, Delaware,* and *Heliotrope* accompany a joint expedition to Hamilton's Crossing, Virginia, capturing prisoners and supplies and wrecking an important railroad bridge.

The USS *Jonquil* is damaged by a Confederate torpedo while in the act of clearing the Ashley River, South Carolina.

March 7

POLITICS: Admiral David D. Porter testifies before Congress, proffering some salty commentary as to the military abilities of General Benjamin F. Butler and Nathaniel P. Banks.

SOUTH: General Jacob D. Cox and 13,000 Federal troops begin to skirmish outside Fayetteville, North Carolina, while New Bern is converted into a major Federal supply base. Cox's superior, General John M. Schofield, also directs him to repair railroad lines toward Goldsborough prior to uniting with the army of General William T. Sherman. However, progress stalls at Southwest Creek, just short of Kinston, where 6,500 Confederates under Generals Braxton Bragg and Robert F. Hoke have massed. Both sides then engage in a day-long artillery duel at long range as Bragg awaits reinforcements from the Army of Tennessee.

NAVAL: The USS *Chenango* conducts a reconnaissance mission from Georgetown, South Carolina, and 45 miles up the Black River. No serious resistance is encountered.

March 8

POLITICS: The Confederate Senate authorizes African-American slaves to bear arms for military service on a vote of 9-8.

SOUTH: General Braxton Bragg, recently reinforced with 2,000 Confederates from the Army of Tennessee, attacks General Jacob D. Cox's Union forces in the vicinity of Kinston, North Carolina. The main body under General Robert F. Hoke easily crashes through Colonel Charles Upham's advance brigade, but progress stalls as resistance stiffens. Meanwhile, Bragg dispatches General Daniel H. Hill on a wide movement around the Union rear instead of directly supporting Hoke, which accomplishes little. Fighting dies down with nightfall as both side bring up additional forces.

The Union army under General William T. Sherman crosses the state line into North Carolina and begins to ford the Lumber River.

Union cavalry under General Hugh J. Kilpatrick overrun a small Confederate rear guard belonging to General William J. Hardee's army. They then learn that General Wade Hampton's cavalry division is marching right behind, so Kilpatrick devises an elaborate snare to entrap them. He accordingly spreads out his three brigades across the swampy ground near Monroe's Cross Roads, North Carolina, intending to catch his quarry from whatever direction he approaches. In truth, Kilpatrick's overly dispersed deployment nearly causes his own destruction.

WEST: A large cavalry column under General Philip H. Sheridan canters east from the Shenandoah Valley toward Duguidsville, Virginia, en route to joining the main Union force outside Petersburg.

Confederate general Edmund Kirby-Smith, sensitive about letters criticizing him in Southern newspapers, offers to resign from command of the Trans-Mississippi Department. President Jefferson Davis declines to accept.

NAVAL: The USS *Chenango* steams up the Black River and trades fire with Confederate cavalry at Brown's Ferry, South Carolina.

March 9

POLITICS: President Abraham Lincoln accepts the resignation of John P. Usher as secretary of the interior and appoints Assistant Secretary William Otto to succeed him.

Vermont ratifies the 13th Amendment to the Constitution.

South: General Robert E. Lee warns Confederate secretary of war John C. Breckinridge about endemic supply shortages. "Unless the men and animals can be subsisted, the army cannot be kept together, and our present lines must be abandoned," he states.

The Battle of Kinston, North Carolina, resumes, as General Braxton Bragg renews his attack on General Jacob D. Cox's XXII Corps. He dispatches General Robert F. Hoke on another flank attack that dislodges Federals under General Samuel P. Carter while General Daniel H. Hill makes similar gains against Cox's right. But neither commander can dislodge a second line of defenders under General Thomas H. Ruger and the Confederate onslaught stumbles. Bragg, unable to destroy the XXII Corps, then orders his men across the Neuse River and back into Kinston. Union losses are 57 killed, 264 wounded, and 935 captured (1,257) while the Confederates lose 11 dead, 107 wounded, and 16 captured (134).

As General Wade Hampton's Confederate cavalry ride north toward Monroe's Cross Roads, North Carolina, a Union officer from the 5th Kentucky Cavalry unknowingly blunders into his pickets and is captured along with 16 troopers. From him, Hampton learns that General Hugh J. Kilpatrick awaits in ambush—and in a very dispersed deployment. Hampton is also apprised that Colonel George E. Spencer's Union brigade posted no pickets to avoid being detected. He resolves to attack from that direction on the morrow and turn the tables on his antagonist; the two sides are evenly matched with roughly 4,000 veteran troopers apiece.

March 10

South: Having failed to destroy the Union army of General Jacob D. Cox, Confederates under General Braxton Bragg begin to withdraw toward Goldsborough, North Carolina, for an eventual linkup with General Joseph E. Johnston's forces.

Under cover of an early-morning fog, Confederate cavalry under Generals Wade Hampton and Joseph Wheeler successfully attack the Union troopers of General Hugh J. Kilpatrick at Monroe's Cross Roads. Kilpatrick, clad only in his undershirt, narrowly escapes capture as General Matthew Butler's Southerners gallop through his camp, sweeping up all in their path. Suddenly, the rebels stop to plunder Union stores while Wheeler's thrust stumbles while traversing swampy ground. Kilpatrick uses the delay to rally the brigades of Colonels Thomas J. Jordan and Smith D. Atkins and then counterattacks with horse artillery and rapid-fire carbines. The Federals gradually recapture their bivouac as Hampton withdraws in good order toward Fayetteville. Losses are not recorded accurately, but the Southerners claim having inflicted upward of 500 casualties. Kilpatrick insists his losses are no greater than 190 while killing 80 Confederates and taking 30 captives. Thereafter, this affair is jocularly referred to on both sides as the "Battle of Kilpatrick's Pants."

March 11

Politics: President Abraham Lincoln declares an amnesty for all army and navy deserters returning to their units within two months. Failure to do so carries the loss of citizenship.

South: Union cavalry under General Philip H. Sheridan advance to Goochland Court House en route to Petersburg, Virginia.

General William T. Sherman's army occupies Fayetteville, North Carolina, where he grants his army a five-day resting spell. The first Union troops to arrive, a company of 67 cavalrymen under Captain William R. Duncan, trot into town unopposed until they encounter a Confederate rear guard under General Wade Hampton. The Southerners immediately charge and rout their antagonists, killing 11 and capturing 12, including Duncan. Shortly after, the 4th Division, XVII Corps, of General Giles A. Smith marches up and forces Hampton back over the Cape Fear River. Mayor Archibald McLean then surrenders his town to the Federals.

SOUTHWEST: General Lew Wallace meets with Confederate general James Slaughter and Colonel John Ford to arrange an unofficial truce in the Rio Grande region of Texas.

NAVAL: A naval force consisting of the USS *Eolus, Maratanza, Lenapee,* and *Nyjack* sails up the Cape Fear River toward Fayetteville, North Carolina, to assist army troops under General Alfred H. Terry.

The USS *Monroe* is seized and then released by Confederate guerrillas on the Big Black River, Mississippi.

The Confederate steamer CSS *Ajax* under Lieutenant John Low anchors at Nassau, being inspected closely by British authorities for arms or armament.

March 12

SOUTH: A Federal sweep through Loudoun County, Virginia, fails to apprehend Colonel John S Mosby's Confederate Partisan Rangers.

While recuperating at Fayetteville, the army of General William T. Sherman keeps busy by torching all railroad, factory, and storage facilities within their grasp. Among the machinery destroyed are gun-making tools and dies first seized at Harper's Ferry, West Virginia, in 1861.

NAVAL: The USS *Quaker City* captures the British blockade-runner *R. H. Vermilyea* in the Gulf of Mexico.

The tug USS *Althea* strikes a Confederate torpedo in the Blakely River, Alabama, and sinks.

March 13

POLITICS: Desperate to secure additional manpower, President Jefferson Davis signs the "Negro Soldier Law," allowing African Americans to serve in the Confederate army. The legislation implies that slaves who serve may be manumitted at a later date with the permission of their owner and state legislatures. Had such pragmatic measures been approved earlier, they may have mitigated Confederate personnel deficiencies and yielded a positive impact on the Southern war effort.

SOUTH: Union cavalry under General Philip H. Sheridan skirmish with Confederate forces at Beaver Dam Station, Virginia, en route to joining up with the main Federal force outside Petersburg.

NAVAL: A naval force consisting of the USS *Morse, Commodore Read, Delaware,* and *Mosswood* steams up the Rappahannock River to assist army operations near Fort Lowry, Virginia. There they sink eight boats, destroy a bridge, and silence a battery without loss.

March 14

DIPLOMACY: Despite Southern overtures toward emancipation, Lord Palmerston declares to Confederate envoys James M. Mason and Duncan F. Kenner that English diplomatic recognition is now a foregone possibility, seeing how the war will in all likelihood end in a matter of weeks.

SOUTH: Federal troops under General Jacob D. Cox occupy Kinston, North Carolina, prior to advancing on Goldsborough.

NAVAL: The USS *Wyandank* captures the Confederate schooner *Champanero* at St. Inigoes Creek, Maryland.

The USS *Shawmut* and *Commodore Morris* are dispatched up the York and Pamunkey rivers, Virginia, to keep the waterways free of enemy interference.

Armed boats from the USS *Lodona* land at Broro Neck, Georgia, and destroy a large saltwork operating there.

March 15

SOUTH: Union cavalry under General Philip H. Sheridan reach Hanover Court House, Virginia, en route to Petersburg.

General William T. Sherman orders his army out from Fayetteville, North Carolina, and toward Goldsborough, after totally destroying all property of use to the Confederacy, including the city's former U.S. Arsenal. Then Sherman, to keep Confederates confused as to his real intentions, orders the left wing under General Henry W. Slocum to feint in the direction of Raleigh. Meanwhile, Union cavalry under General Hugh J. Kilpatrick advance to Averasboro where they run headlong into General William J. Hardee's division of 6,000 men, strongly posted with a swamp on the right and the Black River to their left. Hardee, ordered to ascertain Union strength for General Joseph E. Johnston, is full of fight and repels Kilpatrick's probes.

March 16

SOUTH: General Pierre G. T. Beauregard becomes second in command of Confederate forces in North Carolina under General Joseph E. Johnston.

General Alexander P. Stewart takes charge of all infantry and artillery forces in the Army of Tennessee.

The Battle of Averasboro, North Carolina, erupts as Union cavalry under General Hugh J. Kilpatrick pushes his 8th Indiana Cavalry forward. These forces drive back the skirmishers of Colonel Alfred Rhett's advance brigade, but they are stopped cold by the main body of Confederates under General Lafayette McLaws. The Southerners gradually work their way around Kilpatrick's flank, forcing him back until additional Federal reinforcements arrive. All four divisions of the Union XX Corps under General Henry W. Slocum then deploy on the field and drive the Confederates back into their strong field fortifications. Fighting continues as Federal troops try and fail to flank McLaw's works, and fighting gradually winds down with nightfall. General William J. Hardee subsequently orders the Confederates to fall back on Smithville, which is accomplished without incident. Union losses total 95 dead, 53 wounded, and 54 missing (202), while the Confederates record 682 from all causes. The result of this insignificant encounter is to delay General

William T. Sherman's left wing significantly, further separating it from the rapidly advancing right wing.

NAVAL: The USS *Pursuit* captures the British blockade-runner *Mary* on the Indian River, Florida.

Admiral Henry K. Thatcher, newly arrived on the scene, offers General Edward R. S. Canby the use of several light draft gunboats to support army operations against Mobile, Alabama.

The USS *Quaker City* captures the Confederate blockade-runner *Telemico* in the Gulf of Mexico.

March 17

SOUTH: General Edward R. S. Canby begins his drive against Mobile, Alabama, with 32,000 men of the XVI and XII Corps; his opponent, General Dabney H. Maury, musters only 2,000. Canby intends to capture the city by means of a pincer's movement, with one column under General Frederick Steele proceeding out of Pensacola to the east as he leads another force from the west along the right shore of Mobile Bay. However, progress by the XIII and XVI Corps proves slow due to muddy conditions and the need to corduroy the roads to allow heavy siege artillery to accompany the march.

NAVAL: The Coastal Survey steamer *Bibb* strikes a Confederate torpedo in Charleston harbor, South Carolina, and is damaged heavily but survives.

The USS *Quaker City* captures the Confederate schooner *George Burkhart* in the Gulf of Mexico.

March 18

POLITICS: The 2nd session, second Confederate Congress adjourns, although in a pique over President Jefferson Davis's insinuations of obstructionism.

SOUTH: Union forces under General John M. Schofield skirmish at the Neuse River Bridge during their advance on Goldsborough, North Carolina.

General Henry W. Slocum's troops skirmish heavily with General Wade Hampton's cavalry as he approaches Bentonville, North Carolina. Meanwhile, General Joseph E. Johnston begins to concentrate troops nearby to attack and possibly destroy the Federal left wing. At the very least, he wants to seriously delay Union forces from concentrating in overwhelming strength near Goldsborough. Johnston then arrays his 21,000 men in an arc across the Goldsboro Road, with General Braxton Bragg on the left, General William J. Hardee in the center, and General Alexander P. Stewart on the right.

NAVAL: A naval force consisting of the USS *Don, Stepping Stones, Heliotrope,* and *Resolute* sails up the Rappahannock River, Virginia, and destroys a Confederate supply base at Montrose that had supported guerrilla operations. A naval party, landed ashore, then scatters a party of Southern cavalry.

March 19

SOUTH: Union cavalry under General Philip H. Sheridan reach White House on the Pamunkey River, Virginia, prior to linking up with the main Federal force at Petersburg.

The Battle of Bentonville, North Carolina, commences as General Henry W. Slocum orders William P. Carlin's division, XX Corps, down the Goldsboro Road toward Cole's Plantation. En route, Carlin encounters large numbers of heavily entrenched Confederates and halts. This is the signal for General Joseph E. Johnston to attack, and he pushes Carlin's division back in confusion until the Federals are reinforced by fresh troops under General William Cogswell. Desperate fighting breaks out along the line as hard-charging Southerners prove unable to break through Union lines. General Braxton Bragg then tardily orders General Robert F. Hoke's division into action, allowing Slocum to strengthen his line. Also, as General William B. Taliaferro's Southerners advance, they are outflanked by Federal troops and forced back with losses. Conflict ceases at nightfall, and both sides rush up reinforcements

General Frederick Steele continues leading 13,000 Federal troops out of Pensacola, Florida, and marches west toward Mobile, Alabama. His first objective is the reduction of Fort Blakely, but progress over the soggy ground remains slow.

General Thomas K. Smith is appointed commander of the District of South Alabama.

NAVAL: The USS *Massachusetts* brushes up against a Confederate torpedo in Charleston harbor, South Carolina, which fortunately fails to explode. The incident occurs only 50 yards from where the ironclad *Patapsco* sank on January 15, 1865.

March 20

SOUTH: The right wing of General William T. Sherman's army under General Oliver O. Howard marches toward Bentonville, North Carolina, to reinforce the left wing under General Henry W. Slocum. His arrival gives him a total of 60,000 veteran troops—three times the size of his Southern opponent. Confederates under General Joseph E. Johnston, meanwhile, take no offensive measures and instead strengthen their fortifications. They are especially eager to protect Mill Creek Bridge, their only escape route, from being seized. Considering the odds, Johnston hopes to wage a defensive battle to his advantage and possibly to inflict crippling losses on the Union army, should they attack.

WEST: A force of 6,000 Union cavalry under General George Stoneman departs Jonesborough, Tennessee, on a wrecking expedition through North Carolina. His primary objective is to destroy tracks and bridges belonging to the Tennessee and Virginia Railroad.

NAVAL: The former Confederate ram *Albemarle* is raised from its muddy berth on the Roanoke River, North Carolina.

March 21

SOUTH: The Battle of Bentonville resumes as General William T. Sherman dispatches General Joseph A. Mower's division to turn the Confederate left and rear while the main Union force demonstrates to their front. Mower makes surprisingly good progress and nearly reaches Mill Creek Bridge before being struck violently on both flanks and driven back. However, Johnston simply lacks the manpower to follow up decisively so he disengages and withdraws across Mill Creek Bridge northwest toward Smithville.

Bentonville is the last conventional clash of the Civil War, and both sides perform exceedingly well under fire. Union casualties are 191 killed, 1,168 wounded, and 287 missing (1,646) to a Confederate tally of 239 killed, 1,694 injured, and 673 missing (2,606). Johnston, unfortunately, is unable to make up his losses and never challenges Sherman again in the field.

General Innis N. Palmer assumes command of the District of Beaufort, South Carolina.

General Edward R. S. Canby lands troops at Dannelly's Mills on the Fish River, Alabama, and proceeds overland toward Spanish Fort as a part of his overall strategy against Mobile. He takes with him the XVI Corps under General Andrew J. Smith, the XIII Corps of General Gordon Granger, and a division of African Americans under General John P. Hawkins.

NAVAL: Commander Arthur R. Yates, commanding the USS *J. P. Jackson*, orders rations issued to the starving inhabitants of Biloxi, Mississippi.

The CSS *Stonewall* under Captain Thomas J. Paige attempts to sail from El Ferrol, Spain, but is detained two days owing to stormy weather.

March 22
SOUTH: After a brief pursuit of General Joseph E. Johnston, the army of General William T. Sherman begins to concentrate in the vicinity of Goldsborough, North Carolina, where he waits for Union reinforcements and supplies advancing from the coast.

General James H. Wilson, at the head of 13,500 Union cavalry, crosses the Tennessee River from Gravelly Springs, Tennessee, into northern Alabama. His objective is to seize the Confederate munitions center at Selma and advances the crack divisions of Generals Edward M. McCook, Eli Long, and Emory Upton; this is the largest cavalry force ever fielded in American history. Moreover, thanks to his rigorous training regime, all ranks are exceptionally well disciplined and armed with the latest repeating rifles. Then Wilson, to confuse the defenders en route, divides his force and moves along three divergent trails. Each column is ordered to remain in mutual supporting distance of the others in the event of Confederate resistance.

March 23
POLITICS: President Abraham Lincoln and his son Tad depart Washington, D.C., for City Point, outside Petersburg, Virginia, to consult with General William T. Sherman and General Ulysses S. Grant.

SOUTH: The combined armies of Generals William T. Sherman and John M. Schofield, numbering in excess of 100,000 men, unite at Goldsborough, North Carolina. Sherman has covered 425 miles from Savannah, Georgia, in only 50 days and without a major mishap. It is an organizational and logistical triumph and far exceeding his better known "March to the Sea" in complexity and difficulty. General Joseph E. Johnston, heavily outnumbered, concedes to General Robert E. Lee that "I can do no more than annoy him."

March 24
POLITICS: President Abraham Lincoln arrives at Fortress Monroe, Virginia, prior to meeting with General Ulysses S. Grant at City Point.

South: General Robert E. Lee, in light of his slowly eroding defenses in and around Petersburg, conceives his last tactical offensive of the war. He orders General John B. Gordon to take elements of several Confederate corps and seize a portion of nearby Union lines. A breakthrough here will undoubtedly force General Ulysses S. Grant to concentrate his forces near the break, thereby allowing other portions of the Army of Northern Virginia to slip out of Petersburg and join General Joseph E. Johnston in North Carolina. Gordon, an excellent commander, selects Fort Stedman, only 150 yards from Confederate lines and garrisoned by men of the IX Corps under General Orlando B. Wilcox.

Naval: The USS *Republic* lands several armed parties ashore up the Cape Fear River, North Carolina, to halt raiding activities by General Joseph Wheeler's cavalry.

The USS *Quaker City* captures the Confederate blockade-runner *Cora* off the Texas coast.

The French-built ironclad ram CSS *Stonewall* departs El Ferrol, Spain, for Havana, Cuba, while the wooden vessels USS *Niagara* and *Sacramento* under Commodore Thomas T. Craven hover at a distance, declining to engage. "At this time the odds in her favor were too great and too certain, in my humble judgement, to admit of the slightest hope of being able to inflict upon her even the most trifling injury," he explains, "whereas, if we had gone out, the *Niagara* would most undoubtedly have been easily and promptly destroyed." Craven, however, subsequently is court-martialed and convicted for failing to engage the enemy, but his verdict is suspended by Secretary of the Navy Gideon Welles.

March 25

Politics: President Abraham Lincoln arrives at City Point, Virginia, to confer with General Ulysses S. Grant.

South: At 4:00 A.M., the Battle of Fort Stedman, Virginia, erupts as Confederate pioneer companies silence outlaying Union pickets and remove their abattis. Then 11,000 Confederates unexpectedly pour into Union trenches near Fort Stedman, surprising the defenders and capturing the fort and Batteries X, XI, and XII. However, as Confederates fan out intending to exploit their breakthrough, resistance intensifies from nearby Fort Haskell and Battery IX, which mires their impetus. Gordon then digs in along a lightly manned perimeter as Federal troops regroup for a major counterattack. At about 7:45 A.M., General John F. Hartranft leads 4,000 men back toward the trenches near Fort Stedman, driving Gordon's veterans back. As the gray masses withdraw across the field, they sustain a particularly withering crossfire from Union batteries posted on either flank. Several thousand Confederates unexpectedly surrender rather then be killed.

Fort Stedman is the last tactical gambit of the Army of Northern Virginia and a heavy defeat for General Robert E. Lee. Lacking the necessary manpower to exploit Gordon's initial surprise, the Southerners lose about 3,500 men, including 1,500 captured. Union casualties amount to 72 killed, 450 wounded, and 522 missing (1,044). Lee now has little recourse but to prepare for the immediate evacuation of Petersburg.

The first Federal supply train from the coast reaches General William T. Sherman's army at Goldsborough, North Carolina.

NAVAL: In light of Confederate military activity, Admiral David D. Porter orders several gunboats up the Appomattox River to guard Union pontoon bridges in and around City Point.

March 26
SOUTH: A force 9,000 Federal cavalry under General Philip H. Sheridan crosses the James River and unites with the main Union force under General Ulysses S. Grant, bringing Union numbers up to 122,000 men—twice the strength of Confederate defenders.

General Robert E. Lee, wary of General William T. Sherman's army catching him from behind while General Ulysses S. Grant pins him frontally, warns President Jefferson Davis to prepare for the inevitable. He tells Davis, "I fear now it will be impossible to prevent a junction between Grant and Sherman, nor do I deem it prudent that this army should maintain its position until the latter shall approach too near."

NAVAL: Armed sailors from the USS *Benton* join an expedition under General Benjamin G. Farrar that captures Trinity, Louisiana, along with numerous prisoners and stores.

March 27
SOUTH: General Alfred H. Terry assumes command of the X Corps in North Carolina.

A force of 32,000 Union troops under General Edward R. S. Canby besieges Spanish Fort, Alabama, by planting 50 siege cannon and 30 field pieces in its vicinity. But the 2,000-man garrison of General Randall L. Gibson proves defiant, and a prolonged artillery duel ensues for the next 13 days.

NAVAL: Secretary of the Navy Gideon Welles orders the USS *Wyoming* to find and destroy the elusive Confederate raider CSS *Shenandoah*.

Admiral Henry K. Thatcher orders several tinclads and gunboats up the Blakely River to support army operations against Spanish Fort. This proves a perilous operation, for the waters have been strewn thickly with Confederate torpedoes.

The CSS *Stonewall* under Captain Thomas J. Paige puts into Lisbon, Portugal, closely followed by the USS *Niagara* and *Sacramento*.

March 28
POLITICS: President Abraham Lincoln, Generals Ulysses S. Grant and William T. Sherman, and Admiral David D. Porter confer on the steamship *River Queen* to discuss postwar policy toward former Confederates. Lincoln, fearful of continuing guerrilla activity, instructs his officers to offer generous terms to their soon-to-be-repatriated countrymen.

WEST: The District of the Plains is formed by combining the Districts of Utah, Colorado, and Nebraska and assigned to General Patrick E. Connor.

NAVAL: The gunboat USS *Milwaukee* strikes a Confederate torpedo and sinks in the Blakely River, Alabama; no lives are lost.

Secretary of the Navy Gideon Welles picks Commodore Sylvanus W. Godon to head up the newly reconstituted Brazil Squadron.

The USS *Niagara*, while sailing up a river to the city of Lisbon, Portugal, is suddenly fired on by guns from a fort and Commodore Thomas T. Craven steams downstream. The Portuguese government subsequently apologizes for the incident.

March 29

SOUTH: The Appomattox campaign begins as 19,000 Confederates under Generals Fitzhugh Lee and George E. Pickett are directed by General Robert E. Lee to outflank Union forces at Lewis Farm, near Gravelly Run, Virginia. General Ulysses S. Grant simultaneously dispatches 13,000 cavalry under General Philip H. Sheridan, supported by 30,000 men of the II Corps and V Corps under Generals General Andrew A. Humphrey and Gouverneur K. Warren, respectively, to turn the extreme far right of Lee's defensive line, southwest of Petersburg, Virginia. Union troops encounter Pickett's skirmish line along the Boydton and Quaker roads and gradually push it back. Warren's V Corps also engages Confederates under General Bushrod Johnson and forces them into new positions along White Oak Road. Fighting dies amid heavy rainfall that evening.

General James H. Wilson's cavalry column passes through Elyton, Alabama, where 1,100 cavalrymen under General John T. Croxton are detached to raid Tuscaloosa and burn all public property.

WEST: General George Stoneman's Union cavalry clash with Confederates at Wilkesborough, North Carolina.

NAVAL: The monitor USS *Osage* strikes a Confederate torpedo in the Blakely River, Alabama, and sinks with a loss of four killed and eight wounded.

March 30

POLITICS: In light of the Confederacy's fading fortunes, President Jefferson Davis confides to a friend: "Faction has done much to cloud our prospects and impair my power to serve the country."

SOUTH: General Philip H. Sheridan concentrates troops at Dinwiddie Court House, southwest of Petersburg, Virginia, and renews his march north in a driving rain. He is repelled gradually in heavy fighting by General Fitzhugh Lee's Confederate cavalry. Meanwhile, the II Corps under General Andrew A. Humphreys and the V Corps under General Gouverneur K. Warren slowly press forward toward Gravelly Run, threatening Confederate positions and the vital Southside Railroad.

General Nathan B. Forrest's cavalry arrive at Scottsville, Alabama, from Tupelo, Mississippi, intending to intercept the roving columns of General James H. Wilson at Elyton.

NAVAL: Lieutenant Charles W. Read takes command of the CSS *William H. Webb* on the Red River, Louisiana. Despite the fact the vessel is unarmed, undermanned, and lacks fuel, he prepares for a dash down the Mississippi River to the open sea—300 miles distant.

March 31

SOUTH: Union forces under General Philip H. Sheridan continue turning the Confederate right flank at Dinwiddie Court House, Virginia. He suddenly is assailed in the left flank by General George E. Pickett's division and shoved back violently. The V Corps under General Gouverneur K. Warren also advances along the White Oak Road, encountering heavy Confederate resistance. In the course of fighting, Warren's 2nd Division is driven off in confusion by General Bushrod Johnson, but a prompt counterstroke by his 3rd Division recaptures all lost ground. Considering that nearly 50,000 Federals prove unable to dislodge 10,000 defenders, the South wins a decided tactical victory. Then Pickett, cognizant of how dangerously thin his force is stretched, withdraws to Five Forks under cover of darkness. There, General Robert E. Lee, fearing the precariousness of his entire perimeter, solemnly instructs Pickett to "Hold Five Forks at all hazards."

The Union cavalry column of General Emory Upton skirmishes with General Nathan B. Forrest's troopers at Montevallo, Alabama. Forrest manages to hit the Union force from behind, temporarily driving them from the field, but they rally and counterattack. A large-scale saber-and-pistol duel erupts as the Confederates gradually retreat toward Ebenezer Church. Federal scouts then capture a Southern courier carrying Forrest's plans, and the information is relayed immediately to Wilson. He dispatches the brigade of General Edward M. McCook to seize and destroy the bridge at Centerville, over which Forrest expects 3,000 men under General William H. Jackson to arrive.

NAVAL: Armed Confederates seizes the Union schooner *St. Mary's* off the Patuxent River, Chesapeake Bay. The vessel then is commandeered to Nassau.

The USS *Iuka* captures the British blockade-runner *Comus* off the Florida coast.

April 1

POLITICS: President Abraham Lincoln returns to Washington, D.C., from the *River Queen.*

Confederate Florida governor John Milton commits suicide at his home.

NORTH: Wesley Merritt is promoted to major general, U.S. Army.

SOUTH: The Battle of Five Forks commences as General Philip H. Sheridan orders cavalry under Generals George A. Custer and Thomas C. Devlin to slash at the Confederate right flank while his remaining forces pin them down frontally. The lynchpin of his attack devolves on General Gouverneur K. Warren's V Corps, which is slated to work its way around the Confederate left and crush it with three divisions. Inexplicably, senior Confederate generals George E. Pickett and Fitzhugh Lee are not present as the struggle develops, being at a fish bake several miles to the rear. Warren, meanwhile, is misled by faulty maps and his turning movement is delayed by several hours. It is not until 4:00 P.M. that General Romeyn B. Ayers's division finally crashes through the wafer-thin Southern defenses. Sheridan then orders his cavalry to charge the entire Confederate line, and it shatters. Thousands of Southerners, finding themselves cut off by Colonel Randall S. Mackenzie's troopers, lay down their arms en masse. The result is a complete and decisive Union victory, though somewhat soured by Sheridan's decision to arbitrarily sack Warren as commander of V Corps. Pickett is also relieved by General Robert E. Lee.

Five Forks cost the Union around 124 killed, 706 injured, and 54 missing (986) while the Confederates lose 450 dead, 750 wounded, and 3,244 captured (4,444) in addition to 11 flags and four cannon. More important, General Robert E. Lee's defensive line is compromised entirely and the South Side Railroad—his final supply line into Petersburg—virtually cut. Lee has no recourse but to abandon Richmond immediately to save his army from imminent capture.

Union cavalry under Generals Eli Long and Emory Upton continue pressing General Nathan B. Forrest at Ebenezer Church, Alabama, where he awaits the arrival of General James R. Chalmer's division. Forrest then deploys three brigades of 1,500 men under Generals Philip D. Roddey and Daniel W. Adams, and Colonel Edward Crossland in a thin line across the Selma Highway. At 4:00 P.M., the first Union wave under Long gallops forward, crashes into the Confederate center, and is repulsed. Forrest is engaged closely in desperate hand-to-hand fighting, receives a severe saber slash before shooting down his antagonist. Upton's command then moves up, dismounts, and charges Adams's troops on the Southern right. The Confederates again prevail in a tough scrap, throwing the Federal troopers back. However, when another part of Upton's men hit Forrest's center-left, held by Alabama militia, they bolt and the entire line collapses. The Confederates then flee pell-mell for Selma, with vengeful Union cavalry pursuing closely. Federal loses amount to 12 dead and 40 wounded to a Confederate tally of 300, mostly captured.

Colonel Andrew B. Spurling's Union cavalry, XIII Corps, engages and defeats the 46th Mississippi Cavalry in a hot action at Sibley's Mills, five miles outside of Fort Blakely, Alabama. The Federals, reinforced by African Americans from General John B. Hawkins's division, trounce the Southerners, capturing a flag and inflicting 74 casualties for a loss of two wounded. Shortly afterward, the 13,000 men of General Frederick Steel's column arrive and besiege the fort.

NAVAL: The tinclad USS *Rodolph* strikes a Confederate torpedo in the Blakely River, Alabama, and sinks with a loss of four killed, 11 wounded, and three missing. Ironically, it was towing an apparatus intended to help raise the *Milwaukee,* sunk by mines four days previously.

The Confederate raider CSS *Shenandoah* under Lieutenant James I. Waddell anchors at Lea Harbor, Ascension Island, in the Eastern Carolines. There it seizes the Union whalers *Pearl, Harvest, Hector,* and *Edward Carey,* which are then stripped of supplies and burned.

April 2

POLITICS: As Confederate defenses around Richmond, Virginia, collapse, a greatly relieved president Abraham Lincoln telegraphs General Ulysses S. Grant, "Allow me to tender to you, and all with you, the nation's grateful thanks for this additional and magnificent success."

SOUTH: General Ulysses S. Grant decisively orders an all-out assault on the crumbling Confederate defenses ringing Petersburg, Virginia. At 4:30 A.M., General Horatio G. Wright's VI Corps storms the Southern right at Fort Fisher as far as Hatcher's Run, fatally rupturing General Robert E. Lee's lines. The XXIV Corps also charges down Boydton Plank Road, routing the defenders while the redoubtable general

Ambrose P. Hill falls while rallying his men. If General Robert E. Lee is to evacuate safely the Army of Northern Virginia to Amelia Court House, he needs additional time to remove them; fortunately, he acquires it once the surging Union tide laps up against Fort Gregg.

Fort Gregg is garrisoned by barely 500 survivors from Generals Nathaniel G. Harris's and Cadmus M. Wilcox's divisions. Around noontime, they are beset by two entire Union divisions under Generals Robert S. Foster and John W. Turner, but the embattled Confederates manage to repel three attacking waves. Federal troops subsequently find an unguarded trench leading into the fort and storm it. Undeterred, the defenders resist fiercely in hand-to-hand fighting before being overwhelmed. Confederate casualties are 57 killed and 129 wounded, and 30 captured to a Union tally of 714.

As the conflict at Fort Gregg rages, the II Corps of General Andrew A. Humphreys inches farther west, seizes the Crow Salient, and pushes up Claiborne Road. General Nelson A. Miles's division, II Corps, is approaching Sutherland's Station when it stumbles on General Henry Heth's Confederates. Miles is ordered personally to exploit Humphrey's initial breakthrough, and he charges the milling Southerners before they can regroup. Heth's men quickly are swept aside and routed, losing 1,000 prisoners and two cannon. Moreover, the South Side Railroad is now firmly in Union hands. But the delays incurred here and at Fort Gregg permit General Robert E. Lee to extricate his remaining troops by nightfall.

General Robert E. Lee begins to evacuate Petersburg, Virginia, and advises President Jefferson Davis to relocate the seat of the Confederate government from Richmond. His 18,500 Confederates no longer can stem a concerted drive by 63,000 Federals, who capture the Petersburg lines at a cost of 625 dead, 3,189 wounded, and 326 missing (4,140); Southern losses are unknown but are considered equally heavy. Lee, however, skillfully shuttles his command over the Appomattox River without Union interference and departs for Amelia Court House, 39 miles southwest of Richmond, and thence begins an overland slog down the Richmond and Danville Railroad to Danville. He intends, or at least hopes, to link up with General Joseph E. Johnston somewhere in North Carolina. Thus, the siege of Petersburg, which commenced on June 15, 1864, successfully terminates with Union losses of 5,100 killed, 24,800 wounded, and 17,500 captured or missing; Confederate casualties are variously estimated at between 28,000 and 38,000.

Meanwhile, General Richard S. Ewell, commanding Southern forces in Richmond, issues orders to burn all military supplies and equipment that cannot be moved. As flames shoot out into the sky, looters take to the streets, adding to the general sense of mayhem. This evening, Ewell removes the last remaining Confederate soldiers from the capital, and he marches them across the Mayo Bridge on the James River. The bridge is burned behind him to prevent a pursuit.

General Joseph A. Mower takes charge of the XX Corps, North Carolina.

General James H. Wilson arrives before Selma, Alabama, a heavily fortified city guarded by 5,000 men under General Nathan B. Forrest. Fortunately for the Federals, they seize the British civil engineer responsible for constructing an elaborate series of fieldworks, redans, palisades, and ditches; he freely informs his captors of the layout. Wilson then dispatches General Eli Long to attack the Confederate right while dismounted; the troopers cross 600 yards of open space, taking heavy losses. Long is wounded, but his men spill over the redoubts as General Emory Upton's dismounted division also threads its way through a swamp on the Confederate left. Wilson then decides the issue with a thundering charge down the Selma Road, which unnerves and finally routs the defenders. By nightfall, the city is secured, and Union forces begin to burn factories, storage facilities, railyards, and anything of use to the Confederacy. Forrest's losses are 2,700 captured and 102 cannon seized; Wilson sustains 46 dead, 300 wounded, and 13 missing.

WEST: General George Stoneman's Union cavalry column crosses into Virginia and divides into three parts to burn bridges at Wytheville, the New River Valley, and the Roanoke River valley.

NAVAL: Confederate secretary of the navy Stephen R. Mallory orders the James River Squadron, consisting of CSS *Virginia II, Richmond, Fredericksburg, Nansemond, Hampton, Roanoke, Torpedo, Shrapnel,* and *Patrick Henry,* scuttled to prevent capture. "The spectacle," Admiral Raphael Semmes writes, "was grand beyond description." All naval remaining personnel are ordered to pick up rifles and serve as an infantry brigade.

A naval expedition consisting of the USS *Shamrock, Wyoming, Hunchback, Valley City,* and *Whitehead* departs Plymouth, North Carolina, and steams up the Roanoke River as far as Stumpy Reach in support of General William T. Sherman's army.

April 3

POLITICS: President Jefferson Davis and his cabinet arrive by special train in Danville, Virginia.

SOUTH: Union forces under General Godfrey Weitzel, commander of the African-American XXV Corps, prepare to occupy Richmond, Virginia. At 5:30 A.M., Weitzel sends a small party under Major Atherton H. Stevens, which is received by the civil authorities at city hall. Richmond then surrenders to Union forces, who promptly raise the Stars and Stripes over the state capitol. Weitzel himself arrives three hours later and orders all fires extinguished, looters arrested, and order restored. An eerie calm settles over the former Confederate capital as President Jefferson Davis's residence is occupied and transformed into a military headquarters.

President Abraham Lincoln, visiting General Ulysses S. Grant in Petersburg, declares, "Thank God I have lived to see this. It seems to me that I have been dreaming a horrid dream for four years, and now the nightmare is gone."

The Army of Northern Virginia disengages and slips out of the Richmond-Petersburg trenches and moves westward to make for Amelia Court House. General James Longstreet takes the point, while General John B. Gordon forms the rear guard. Additional forces join the lengthening column, with General William Mahone marching behind from Bermuda Hundred. Moreover, General Richard S. Ewell is expected to join them from Richmond on the morrow. General Robert E. Lee now commands 30,000 ragged, hungry, and worn out men—aptly pursued by a well-supplied, well-fed force three times their size.

After decisively breaking through at Five Forks, Virginia, General Philip H. Sheridan orders his cavalry on a "Hell for leather" pursuit of fleeing Confederates. General Wesley Merritt's division then canters off in the direction of Amelia Court House, intending to cut off the enemy's retreat. Spearheading this movement is General George A. Custer, a recklessly daring cavalier. Custer, galloping ahead of his column, suddenly perceives a Confederate rear guard at Namozine Creek under General William P. Roberts. He quickly deploys horse artillery to distract the defenders while the 1st Vermont Cavalry crosses farther upstream to turn their flank. The Southerners, quickly perceiving this threat, abandon their position and fall back.

Custer subsequently presses ahead for another five miles toward Namozine Church, where a Confederate cavalry division under General Rufus Barringer is collected. A quick reconnaissance by the 8th New York Cavalry reveals the extent of Southern defenses and Custer orders them around the Southern left flank. En route, they suddenly crash into the 1st North Carolina Cavalry, and an intense melee erupts. Meanwhile, Custer leads the 1st Vermont and 15th New York on a thundering charge toward the Confederate center, routing them. The general's younger brother, Lieutenant Thomas W. Custer, helps capture the colors of the 2nd South Carolina Cavalry and 15 prisoners, winning a Congressional Medal of Honor. Union losses in this sharp encounter are unknown, but they secure 350 captives, 100 horses, and a cannon.

General David S. Stanley leads his IV Corps on an expedition to Asheville, North Carolina.

Fort Blakely, Alabama, is invested by 13,000 Federal troops under General Frederick Steele. It is defended by 4,000 Confederates led by General St. John R. Liddell. The progress of Union siege lines is hampered by enfilading fire from the CSS *Nashville* at the mouth of the Raft River.

NAVAL: A force of 50 midshipmen from the Confederate Naval Academy are chosen to escort the archives and treasury of the government from Richmond, Virginia, to Danville.

The naval brigade of Commodore John R. Tucker departs Drewry's Bluff, Virginia, now attached to the Confederate division of General George W. "Custis" Lee.

As Confederate forces withdraw from Richmond, Virginia, Admiral David D. Porter instructs his fleet to begin extensive antitorpedo sweeps up numerous rivers, creeks, and estuaries.

April 4
POLITICS: President Abraham Lincoln ventures up the James River to Richmond, Virginia, aboard the USS *Malvern*. Once ashore, he is escorted by Admiral David D. Porter and 10 sailors to the Confederate White House, being greeted by throngs of former African-American slaves. Many of these reach out and touch Lincoln's person to convince themselves that he is not an apparition.

President Jefferson Davis, pausing momentarily at Danville, Virginia, calls on fellow Southerners not to lose hope, for ultimate victory is certain to come from "our own unquenchable resolve."

SOUTH: The Army of Northern Virginia, having achieved a day's head start out of Richmond, Virginia, arrives at Amelia Court House to discover that promised rations for the starving troops have failed to arrive. Instead, ordnance supplies have been dispatched by mistake, and General Robert E. Lee orders his men to forage for themselves. Meanwhile, pursuing Union forces quickly close the gap.

Union cavalry under General Philip H. Sheridan advance to Jetersville, Virginia, cutting off the Army of Northern Virginia's retreat. General George G. Meade and the II and V Corps, Army of the Potomac, also arrive. The two commanders then dig in and wait for the Confederates to attack them.

General John T. Croxton's Union cavalry column occupies Tuscaloosa, Alabama, capturing three cannon and burning various public stores.

SOUTHWEST: General John B. Magruder is appointed head of the Confederate District of Texas, New Mexico, and Arizona.

NAVAL: Admiral David G. Farragut and his entourage arrive in Richmond, Virginia, to inspect the city.

Admiral Henry K. Thatcher agrees to supply General Edward R. S. Canby with rowboats and sailors capable of assisting in the assault on Forts Tracey and Huger.

A naval battery consisting of three 30-pound Parrott rifles is landed on the banks of the Blakely River to participate in the reduction of Spanish Fort, Alabama.

April 5

POLITICS: As President Abraham Lincoln delights in sitting in Jefferson Davis's chair, he is approached by Confederate assistant secretary of war John A. Campbell, himself a former U.S. Supreme Court justice, who requests that the president help maintain the rule of law in Virginia.

Secretary of State William H. Seward is severely injured in a carriage accident in Washington, D.C.

SOUTH: Union troopers under General George Crook encounter a Confederate wagon train outside Jetersville, Virginia, and Crook orders the 1st Pennsylvania Cavalry forward. They capture 200 wagons, 11 flags and 320 prisoners. The Confederates react sharply by dispatching General Fitzhugh Lee's cavalry in pursuit, which harry the Federals as far as Amelia Springs before encountering reinforcements under General J. Irvin Gregg. Northern losses are reported as 20 killed and 96 wounded.

General Robert E. Lee, preparing to depart Amelia Court House, is now joined by the troops of General Richard S. Ewell, bringing his strength up to 58,000. Lee now determines to attack Union forces under Generals Philip H. Sheridan and George G. Meade presently entrenching at Jetersville. Three divisions under General James Longstreet are readied to march, but Lee cancels the move after learning that more Federal troops are approaching. To avoid encirclement, he orders a night march around the Union left flank followed by a quick dash to Farmville in the hopes of finding supplies there. Meade, the senior Union commander, declines attacking as the VI Corps has yet to appear. Federal troops continue milling around their fortifications until 10:30 P.M., when General Ulysses S. Grant arrives and personally directs the pursuit.

NAVAL: The Union steamer *Harriet DeFord* is seized by Confederate partisans as it sails up the St. Mary's River, Maryland. The vessel subsequently is taken to Dimer's Creek, Virginia, and burned.

April 6

SOUTH: The Battle of Sayler's Creek unfolds as the Army of Northern Virginia, retreating from Amelia Court House to Farmville, Virginia, inadvertently separates into three parts. Closely pursuing Union forces are thus able to exploit gaps between the commands of Generals Richard S. Ewell, Richard H. Anderson, and John B. Gordon with disastrous effect. Trouble begins when Anderson halts his long wagon train to fend off some Union cavalry, but he fails to inform the lead division under General James Longstreet, which continues marching off. General Horatio G. Wright's Federal troops then assail Ewell's isolated detachment near Harper's Farm near Little Sayler's Creek, supported by 20 cannon. The Confederates initially repulse the Union advance as they pour over the flooded creek, but the division of General George W. Getty effectively flanks the defenders. Ewell's entire line then is double-enveloped promptly, and 3,400 troops surrender.

Another drama develops to Ewell's right and rear, where a Union cavalry division under General Wesley Merritt attacks General Anderson's corps. Here, the weak formations of General George E. Pickett and Bushrod Johnson collapse before a determined onslaught by Generals George A. Custer and Thomas C. Devlin. As Southern defenses crumble, Anderson's survivors flee into the woods while victorious Federals round up another 2,600 captives, 300 wagons, and 15 cannon.

The final act to play out occurs on the Confederate left, where 17,000 men of General Andrew A. Humphrey's II Corps engage General Gordon's rear guard, numbering 7,000. Gordon is protecting a Confederate wagon train bogged down in the mud. The Federals attack, and after heavy fighting proves inconsequential, Humphreys sends a column around the Southern left. Gordon, now nearly outflanked, hastily withdraws from the creek with the loss of 1,700 men.

Sayler's Creek proves disastrous to the Army of Northern Virginia, which loses 7,700 men and eight generals—one fifth of its overall strength. Union losses amount to only 166 killed and 982 wounded. This is one of the largest number of American soldiers captured in a single action prior to Bataan in 1942. General Robert E. Lee, who accompanied Longstreet in the van, rode back to observe the fighting and aptly exclaims, "My God! Has the army been dissolved?" Sayler's Creek thus proves both a black day for the vaunted Army of Northern Virginia and its final encounter with the tenacious Army of the Potomac.

Meanwhile, Confederates under General James Longstreet continue withdrawing toward High Bridge, an important trestle over the Appomattox River. En route, Longstreet perceives that a Union force of three infantry regiments has been detached toward High Bridge by General Edward O. C. Ord to burn it. Longstreet reacts quickly by dispatching two cavalry divisions under Generals Thomas L. Munford and Thomas L. Rosser to stop them. Intense hand-to-hand fighting erupts at the southeast end of the bridge where Union forces are overwhelmed and General

Theodore Read killed. The victorious Southerners capture 800 prisoners while saving the strategic bridge.

Union cavalry under General James H. Wilson spar with General Nathan B. Forrest's troopers at Lanier's Mills, Sipsey Creek, and King's Store, Alabama.

General John T. Croxton's cavalry column skirmishes with pursuing Confederates under General William W. Adams at Eutaw, Alabama, losing 34 men and two ambulances.

WEST: Confederate Partisan Rangers under Colonel John S. Mosby surprise and attack the Unionist Loudoun Country Rangers near Charles Town, West Virginia. This is Mosby's final military action of the war and, typically, a success.

April 7

DIPLOMACY: The U.S. government, having lost millions of dollars in shipping to the English-built CSS *Alabama,* begins litigation to recoup damages.

POLITICS: An anxious president Abraham Lincoln, on hearing that General Robert E. Lee might capitulate if cornered, orders General Ulysses S. Grant to "Let the thing be pressed."

Tennessee ratifies the 13th Amendment while William G. Brownlow, an unabashed Unionist, is inaugurated as governor.

SOUTH: After the Confederate division of General John B. Gordon crosses High Bridge, Virginia, General Andrew A. Humphrey's II Corps shows up in pursuit. The Southerners set fire to the bridge behind them, but Federal troops rush forward to extinguish its flames. Humphrey then hurriedly crosses over to the north bank of the Appomattox River, tangling with a Confederate rear guard under General William Mahone. The Northerners succeed in pushing the Southerners back, and by noon, the entire II Corps forces its way across.

This development proves particularly distressing for General Robert E. Lee, who now abandons his plan for marching to Farmville in favor of moving 38 miles farther west to Appomattox Court House. Union cavalry under General Philip H. Sheridan then suddenly appear and force the Confederates to give battle at Cumberland Church. Humphrey's II Corps also arrives and adds to the general confusion. The Southerners manage to beat off numerous attacks, capturing General J. Irvin Gregg in the process, but Lee leads his weary, hungry troops on their final night march. He is also forced to order two trains, laden with rations for his hungry troops, to depart immediately for Lynchburg and safety.

General Ulysses S. Grant, arriving at Farmville at the head of 80,000 men, suggests to General Robert E. Lee that he surrender and avoid the useless effusion of blood. "The result of the last week must convince you of the hopelessness of further resistance on the part of the Army of Northern Virginia in this struggle," he states, "I feel that it is so, and regard it as my duty to shift from myself the responsibility of any further effusion of blood." Lee initially dismisses the notion and determines to fight on.

April 8

POLITICS: President Abraham Lincoln returns to the White House after an eventful stay at Richmond, Virginia.

South: Rather than surrender, General Robert E. Lee seeks to break through Union forces blocking his path at Appomattox Court House. But that night, hearts sink as the campfires of 80,000 Union soldiers light up the evening sky in the distance. Federal cavalry under Philip H. Sheridan also arrive at Appomattox, west of Lee's camp, again blocking his withdrawal. At a council of war held late that night, Lee and his generals agree to attack Sheridan in the morning, dislodge his forces, and then press on to Lynchburg. Previously, Sheridan's cavalry capture several trainloads of food intended for the starving Army of Northern Virginia at Pamplin's Station.

At Spanish Fort, Alabama, a charge by the 8th Iowa gains a lodgment in the Confederate defenses. That evening, General Randall L. Gibson evacuates his garrison on a hidden walkway and through the nearby marshes. The Southerners sustain 93 killed and 350 wounded in a two-week period. General Edward R. S. Canby also captures 500 prisoners and 50 cannon.

Naval: The party of Confederate midshipmen escorting the archives and treasury of state to Charlotte, North Carolina, is threatened by Union cavalry and veers southward. They also convince Confederate first lady Varina Davis to accompany them for safety's sake.

April 9

South: Palm Sunday. General Robert E. Lee directs Generals John B. Gordon and Fitzhugh Lee to attack General Philip H. Sheridan's cavalry at Appomattox Court House, Virginia. The Federal troopers are dislodged gradually from their position and Lee discerns that General Edward O. C. Ord's Army of the James is waiting in strength directly behind them. Lee finally acknowledges the hopelessness of his position and parlays with Union authorities to discuss surrender terms. "There is nothing left for me to do but to go and see General Grant," he states, "and I would rather die a thousand deaths."

At 1:30 P.M., General Robert E. Lee, accompanied only by his secretary, meets with General Ulysses S. Grant and formally surrenders the Army of Northern Virginia at Appomattox, Virginia. They convene at the house of Wilbur McLean—an act of significant irony. Previously, McLean lived at Bull Run where, in July 1861, his house served as a hospital for victorious Confederate forces. He thereupon relocated to Appomattox to escape the tumult of war. The terms Grant proffers are quite generous, whereby all of Lee's 30,000 men are paroled and allowed to return home, officers are permitted to retain side arms, and all horses and mules are to remain with their rightful owners. Lee then addresses his men, declaring, "Go to your homes and resume your occupations. Obey the laws and become good citizens as you were soldiers." As a final gesture, Union forces issue 25,000 rations to the half-starved Confederates. The bloody, bitter Civil War reaches a dignified and humane denouement.

General Thomas A. Smyth dies of wounds received two days earlier at Farmville, Virginia, becoming the last Union general fatality.

Fort Blakely, Mobile, Alabama, is besieged by 45,000 Federal troops once General Frederick Steele receives 32,000 reinforcements under General Edward R. S. Canby. An assault force of 16,000 men then attacks the Confederate defenses at

This painting depicts the surrender of Robert E. Lee and his army at Appomattox Court House, Virginia, to General Ulysses S. Grant. *(Library of Congress)*

noon, covered by the fire of 37 field pieces and 75 siege guns. The Federals charge headlong into torpedo-laced fields, taking special care to avoid the visible trip wires, and vault directly into the Confederate works. Their success prompts General St. John R. Liddell to surrender after 20 minutes of fighting. Union losses are 113 killed and 516 wounded (629) while 3,423 Confederates are captured along with 40 cannon. Fort Blakely is also the last, significant pitched engagement of the Civil War.

WEST: The cavalry column of General George Stoneman reunites in western Virginia before raiding Winston-Salem, North Carolina. After destroying all public property, the column gallops off to nearby Salisbury, where a sizable number of Union prisoners are confined.

NAVAL: The Confederate blockade-runner *Chameleon* docks at Liverpool, England, unaware the Civil War is drawing rapidly to a conclusion.

CSS *Nashville* under Lieutenant John W. Bennett sails close to shore and tries to rescue as many Confederates from Fort Blakely as possible before being driven off by Union sharpshooters.

April 10

POLITICS: President Abraham Lincoln is accosted by happy crowds in Washington, D.C., and then asks a military band to strike up "Dixie," "one of the best tunes I have ever heard."

President Jefferson Davis, on learning of General Robert E. Lee's capitulation, departs Danville with his cabinet and makes for Greensborough, North Carolina.

NORTH: News of General Robert E. Lee's capitulation triggers wild celebrations in Northern cities.

SOUTH: General Robert E. Lee issues Order No. 9, bidding a formal farewell to the men and officers of the Army of Northern Virginia. "With an increasing admiration of your constancy and devotion to your country," Lee writes, "and a grateful remembrance of your kind and generous consideration of myself, I bid you an affectionate farewell."

General William T. Sherman departs Goldsborough, North Carolina, and advances on Raleigh to engage remaining Confederate forces under General Joseph E. Johnston. Word of Lee's capitulation reaches Johnston, meanwhile, and he begins to angle for a formal surrender.

As Union siege artillery continue playing on Forts Huger and Tracy in Mobile, Alabama, General Dabney H. Maury makes preparations to abandon the city and retreat.

April 11

POLITICS: President Abraham Lincoln delivers his final public address to enthusiastic crowds gathered about the White House. He again preaches magnanimity and peaceful reconciliation with the inhabitants of former secessionist states.

SOUTH: General William T. Sherman's army advances on Raleigh, North Carolina.

The Confederate government train pulls into Greensborough, North Carolina, carrying President Jefferson Davis and his cabinet.

Union cavalry under General James H. Wilson cross the Alabama River and ride off to attack Montgomery.

General Dabney H. Maury formally abandons Forts Hugar and Tracy at Mobile, Alabama, escaping with 4,500 men and 27 cannon.

NAVAL: The USS *Sea Bird* captures the Confederate sloops *Florida* and *Annie* near the Crystal River, Florida, sinking both.

April 12

SOUTH: The Army of Northern Virginia formally capitulates at Appomattox Court House to General Joshua L. Chamberlain. Confederates under General John B. Gordon then lead a weathered column of Southern troops along the Richmond Stage Road, completely lined by Union forces. As the solemn procession passes, Chamberlain orders his men to present arms in salute, which is promptly returned by the Southerners. Roughly 28,000 Confederates sullenly file down the road, stack arms, roll up their flags, and prepare to return home.

President Jefferson Davis, readying to flee from Greensborough, North Carolina, confers with General Joseph E. Johnston about the potential surrender of Confederate forces. He then authorizes Johnson to meet with General William T. Sherman and ask for terms.

General William T. Sherman's army skirmishes with Confederate forces outside Raleigh, capital of North Carolina.

Mayor R. H. Slough of Mobile, Alabama, formally surrenders to General Gordon Granger.

WEST: A Union cavalry column under General George Stoneman encounters a motley defense force of 800 men under General William M. Gardner at Salisbury,

North Carolina. Fighting in the ranks is former lieutenant general and defender of Vicksburg John C. Pemberton, now functioning as an ordnance inspector. When Stoneman finds his approach to Salisbury blocked by an unplanked bridge and strong Confederate fieldworks across Grants Creek, he dispatches the 12th Kentucky Cavalry to demonstrate in front while the 11th Kentucky and 13th Tennessee Cavalry ford farther upstream to catch the enemy from behind. This action causes the enemy flanks to crumble, at which point Stoneman directs the 6th Tennessee Cavalry to capture Gardner's artillery in a stirring charge. The bridge over Grant's Creek is also repaired under fire, over which General John K. Miller's cavalry surge, routing the Confederates. Stoneman, however, proves unable to rescue any Union captives held in town as they had previously been moved to Charlotte. After his men then burn all public property, Stoneman spurs his command back toward Tennessee.

Montgomery, Alabama, is captured by cavalry under General James H. Wilson, burning all public stores.

Union forces under General Edward R. S. Canby finally occupy Mobile, Alabama, after sustaining losses of 232 dead, 1,303 injured, and 43 missing (1,578).

NAVAL: Fleeing Confederate forces scuttle the CSS *Huntsville* and *Tuscaloosa* at Mobile, Alabama, to prevent capture while the *Nashville, Baltic,* and *Morgan* steam up the Tombigbee River to escape.

April 13

POLITICS: Secretary of War Edwin M. Stanton orders the military draft suspended and also reduces supply requisitions.

SOUTH: Union forces under General William T. Sherman enter Raleigh, North Carolina, and continue to Greensborough.

NAVAL: The tug USS *Ida* strikes a Confederate torpedo near Choctaw Pass, Mobile Bay, Alabama, and sinks. This is the fifth U.S. Navy vessel lost in five weeks.

April 14

POLITICS: In his final cabinet meeting, President Abraham Lincoln reiterates his call for reconciliation with the South.

NORTH: At 10:15 P.M., President Abraham Lincoln, while attending a performance of *Our American Cousin* at Ford's Theater in Washington, D.C., is suddenly shot from behind by actor John Wilkes Booth. Secretary of State William H. Seward, recovering at home from injuries received in a carriage crash, also survives an assassination attempt by Lewis Powell. Secretary of War Edwin M. Stanton declares martial law in the District of Columbia and initiates a massive dragnet to snare the assassins.

SOUTH: General William T. Sherman agrees to enter into surrender negotiations with General Joseph E. Johnston at Durham Station, North Carolina.

General Robert Anderson hoists the American flag over the remnants of Fort Sumter, Charleston Harbor, South Carolina. It is the identical standard lowered by him on April 14, 1861.

NAVAL: The gunboat USS *Sciota* strikes a Confederate torpedo and sinks in Mobile Bay, Alabama. A nearby launch from the USS *Cincinnati* also blows up after brushing against a torpedo, losing three killed.

The Confederate raider CSS *Shenandoah* under Lieutenant James I. Waddell hoists anchor for the East Carolines and sails north toward the Kuriles.

April 15

POLITICS: President Abraham Lincoln dies at 7:22 A.M., leaving Secretary of War Edwin M. Stanton to declare, "Now he belongs to the ages." Vice President Andrew Johnson is then sworn in as the nation's 17th chief executive by Chief Justice Salmon P. Chase; Johnson's first request is to ask members of Lincoln's cabinet to remain in their offices.

President Jefferson Davis departs Greensborough, North Carolina, on horseback and rides all night toward Lexington.

NORTH: George A. Custer is promoted to major general, U.S. Army.

April 16

SOUTH: General James H. Wilson's army occupies Columbus, Georgia, after brushing aside a hodgepodge collection of Confederates and militia and taking 1,200 captives and 52 cannon. The victorious troopers then commence to burn several factories, 100,000 cotton bales, 15 locomotives, and 200 railcars. Meanwhile, another column under General Edward M. McCook seizes West Point, destroying an additional 19 locomotives and 200 railcars.

NAVAL: Confederate forces capture and burn the USS *St. Paul* in the Hatchee River, Tennessee.

April 17

POLITICS: John Wilkes Booth, who injured his leg after assassinating President Abraham Lincoln, hides himself near Port Tobacco, Maryland. He then waits for transportation over the Potomac River to continue his escape.

The body of President Abraham Lincoln lies in state in the East Room of the White House, Washington, D.C.

President Jefferson Davis and his entourage arrive at Salisbury, North Carolina.

SOUTH: General William T. Sherman and Joseph E. Johnston confer at the Bennet House, Durham Station, North Carolina, to draw up surrender terms.

NAVAL: The ironclad CSS *Jackson* (nee *Muscogee*) is destroyed on the Chattahoochee River near Columbus, Georgia, by Union cavalry surging through the town.

The naval escort guarding Confederate archives and treasury arrives safely at Washington, Georgia. First Lady Varina Davis is left behind as the party continues to Augusta.

The USS *Maria A. Wood* clears Confederate obstructions on the Blakely River channel, Mobile Bay, Alabama. The vessel then enters the city of Mobile.

April 18

SOUTH: General Joseph E. Johnston agrees to surrender his 37,000 men to General William T. Sherman at Durham Station, North Carolina. However, terms of their "Memorandum or Basis of Agreement" are viewed as overly generous, and they are disavowed by the government. Sherman is accused of overstepping his authority and is ordered to renegotiate the pact, offering the same terms used at Appomattox.

April 19

POLITICS: Funeral services are held for President Abraham Lincoln in Washington, D.C., and huge crowds throng the proceedings.

President Jefferson Davis and his remaining cabinet flee to Charlotte, North Carolina.

SOUTH: General Henry W. Halleck assumes command of the newly instituted Military of the James, Virginia.

WEST: General Simon B. Buckner receives command of the newly created District of Arkansas and West Louisiana.

General John Pope recommends the surrender of all Confederate forces west of the Mississippi River to General Edmund Kirby-Smith, on the same terms offered to General Robert E. Lee.

NAVAL: The Federal gunboat USS *Lexington* steams up the Red River, Louisiana, bearing terms of surrender for General Edmund Kirby-Smith.

April 20

POLITICS: Arkansas ratifies the 13th Amendment.

SOUTH: General Robert E. Lee writes to President Jefferson Davis, voicing opposition to the latter's plan to wage extended guerrilla warfare throughout the South.

Federal troops under General James H. Wilson occupy Macon, Georgia, without resistance, although skirmishes are still reported in the countryside. Here, Wilson learns of the war's end. His raid is one of the most successful of the war, covering 525 miles in only 28 days, capturing 6,820 prisoners, 23 flags, 288 cannon, and cutting a swath of destruction across Alabama and Georgia. Despite this litany of achievements, Wilson's losses are light and amount to 99 killed, 598 wounded, and 28 missing.

April 21

POLITICS: A train bearing the casket that holds the body of President Abraham Lincoln departs Washington, D.C., for Springfield, Illinois, as immense crowds of mourners gather along the tracks en route.

SOUTH: Colonel John S. Mosby, "the vaunted Gray Ghost," refuses to surrender his 43rd Virginia Cavalry battalion and instead simply disbands them at Millwood, Virginia.

NAVAL: The Union steamer *Sultana* departs New Orleans with 100 passengers and sails up the Mississippi River to Vicksburg, Mississippi. Boiler problems are brought to the attention of Captain J. Cass Mason en route, and he resolves to remedy them at Vicksburg.

The USS *Cornubia* captures an unnamed British schooner off Galveston, Texas.

April 22

POLITICS: John Wilkes Booth and his accomplice David E. Herold escape in a small rowboat from Maryland to Virginia.

SOUTH: Union cavalry under General John T. Croxton occupy Talladega, Alabama, dispersing 500 militia and burning several factories and ironworks.

General Benjamin F. Butler briefly resumes his command of the Department of the Gulf, Louisiana.

NAVAL: The side-wheel steamer USS *Black Hawk* catches fire and explodes on the Ohio River near Mound City, Illinois.

April 23

SOUTH: A Union expedition under General Horatio G. Wright, VI Corps, and General Wesley Merritt's cavalry, takes 500 Southern prisoners at Danville and South Boston, Virginia. General James Dearing dies of wounds at Lynchburg, Virginia, the last ranking Southerner to perish.

NAVAL: Lieutenant Charles W. Read enacts his daring plan to dash down the Mississippi River in CSS *Webb* and make for the open sea past New Orleans. The ironclads USS *Manhattan* and *Fort Hindman* briefly engage Read as he emerges from the Red River, but his vessel proves faster than its plodding pursuers and escapes downstream.

April 24

POLITICS: President Andrew Johnson formally rejects the surrender agreement reached between General William T. Sherman and General Joseph E. Johnston. Sherman is informed by General Ulysses S. Grant himself, who arrives at Raleigh, North Carolina, to do so.

Political assassins John Wilkes Booth and Davis Herold make their way to Port Conway, Virginia.

NAVAL: Admiral Samuel P. Lee urges special vigilance along the Mississippi River "to prevent the carrying across of plunder and property in the hands of Jefferson Davis and his Cabinet, and also to seize their persons."

The Union steamer *Sultana* departs Vicksburg, Mississippi, loaded with 2,100 newly released Union prisoners and 200 civilians—six times its legal carrying capacity. The reason for the overload is that the Federal government is paying steamers to transport prisoners north at a rate of five dollars per soldier and 10 dollars per officer. However, Captain J. Cass Mason decides against having his faulty boilers overhauled and, instead, simply patches them up until he reaches St. Louis, Missouri.

The CSS *Webb* under Lieutenant Charles W. Read passes through New Orleans, Louisiana, at flank speed, easily thwarting slower pursuers. As he passes the city, Federal gunboats score several direct hits, but his vessel proceeds unimpeded toward the sea. However, having reached 25 miles below the city, the USS *Richmond* intercepts the Confederates by moving upstream. Read, trapped between two fires, finally beaches the *Webb* and surrenders.

April 25

POLITICS: Union troops chase political assassins John Wilkes Booth and David E. Herold to Bowling Green, Virginia, just south of the Rappahannock River. The two fugitives then take refuge in the barn of farmer Richard H. Garrett.

April 26

POLITICS: John Wilkes Booth is cornered in a barn near Bowling Green, Virginia, while attempting to escape from Virginia and dies from gunshot wounds. David E. Herold is captured.

President Jefferson Davis departs Charlotte, North Carolina, and ventures to the Trans-Mississippi region, vowing there to carry on a guerrilla struggle for Southern rights and independence.

SOUTH: General Joseph E. Johnston and General William T. Sherman meet again at Durham Station, North Carolina, and renegotiate a surrender agreement with terms similar to those at Appomattox.

April 27

NAVAL: The body of John Wilkes Booth arrives aboard the monitor USS *Montauk* in the Anacostia River outside Washington, D.C., where an autopsy is performed. David E. Herold is also kept in chains in the ship's hold.

Commodore William Radford of the James River Flotilla and the USS *Tristram Shandy* are alerted to watch for the approaching ironclad CSS *Stonewall.*

At 2:00 A.M., boilers on the Union steamer *Sultana* explode with a deafening roar, hurling crew and passengers alike into the frigid waters of the Mississippi River. By the time help finally arrives from Memphis, Tennessee, two hours later, more than 1,700 people perish through burns and hypothermia; only 600 survivors are fished from the waters. *Sultana* remains the single biggest disaster in U.S. maritime history and eclipses the more famous *Titanic,* 47 years later.

April 28

POLITICS: The train bearing President Abraham Lincoln's casket passes through Cleveland, Ohio, where it is viewed by 50,000 citizens.

President Jefferson Davis accepts the resignation of Confederate treasury secretary George A. Trenholm from his cabinet.

April 29

POLITICS: President Andrew Johnson issues an Executive Order lifting commercial restrictions against all Southern states except Texas.

President Jefferson Davis and his entourage reach Yorksville, South Carolina.

NAVAL: The USS *Donegal* is ordered from Bull's Bay, South Carolina, to the Savannah River, Georgia, to search for the CSS *Stonewall.*

An armed party from the USS *Moose* attacks and scatters a Confederate raiding party of the Cumberland River, Tennessee, inflicting 20 casualties, and taking six captives.

April 30

SOUTH: General Edward R. S. Canby holds preliminary talks with General Richard Taylor at Mobile, Alabama, as to the latter's forthcoming surrender. Afterward, Taylor ventures back to his headquarters at Meridian, Mississippi, and makes preparations.

May 1

POLITICS: President Andrew Johnson calls for a board of nine army officers to try eight individuals implicated in President Abraham Lincoln's death. The accused are now subject to military justice rather than civil proceedings.

President Jefferson Davis reaches Cokesbury, South Carolina, en route to the Florida coast. There, he and his party hope to catch a ship and sail to Texas.

SOUTH: The cavalry column of General John T. Croxton arrives at Macon, Georgia, covering 650 miles in 30 days and eluding superior numbers of Confederate pursuers.

WEST: Recently disgraced general Gouverneur K. Warren replaces General Napoleon J. T. Dana as head of the Department of Mississippi.

May 2

POLITICS: President Andrew Johnson accuses a fugitive Jefferson Davis of complicity in the assassination of President Abraham Lincoln and offers $100,000 for his capture.

President Jefferson Davis arrives at Abbeville, South Carolina, and heads for Washington, Georgia, escorted by four brigades of cavalry under General Basil W. Duke. Members of his cabinet begin to object to his intention to renew the struggle through guerrilla warfare.

Confederate secretary of the navy Stephen R. Mallory tenders his resignation to President Jefferson Davis at Washington, Georgia.

NAVAL: Commander Matthew F. Maury departs Britain with $40,000 worth of electrical equipment to manufacture torpedoes at Galveston, Texas. During his sojourn abroad, the talented Maury perfects a controlled mine system whereby torpedoes, planted on a grid pattern and corresponding to a chart, can be selectively detonated when enemy vessels reach their proximity.

May 3

POLITICS: The funeral train bearing the body of President Abraham Lincoln pulls into Springfield, Illinois.

Confederate secretary of state Judah B. Benjamin resigns from office and eventually flees to Britain.

NORTH: The funeral train of President Abraham Lincoln pulls into Springfield, Illinois.

SOUTH: The Army of Tennessee under General Joseph E. Johnston formally lays down its arms near Durham Station, North Carolina. This concludes the Civil War in the East.

Confederate president Jefferson Davis and his cabinet arrive at Washington, Georgia.

May 4

POLITICS: The remains of President Abraham Lincoln are interred at Springfield, Illinois.

SOUTH: General Richard Taylor surrenders all Confederate forces east of the Mississippi River to General Edward R. S. Canby at Citronelle, Alabama. He receives the identical terms proffered to General Robert E. Lee and is further allowed to utilize trains and steamers to send his men home.

Naval: Commodore Ebenezer Farrand surrenders Confederate naval forces on the Tombigbee River to Admiral Henry K. Thatcher, including CSS *Morgan, Balti, Black Diamond,* and *Nashville.*

The CSS *Ajax* drops anchor at St. George's, Bermuda, hoping to pick up its armament from Havana, Cuba. However, British governor W. G. Hamley obstructs any such moves.

May 5

Politics: President Jefferson Davis and his dwindling party of followers arrive at Sandersville, Georgia.

Connecticut ratifies the 13th Amendment abolishing slavery.

May 6

Politics: President Andrew Johnson appoints General David Hunter to head the military commission tasked with trying those accused of assassinating President Abraham Lincoln. The accused are prosecuted by Joseph Holt, judge advocate general of the U.S. Army.

North: James H. Wilson is promoted to major general, U.S. Army.

West: General Thomas L. Rosser surrenders his Confederate cavalry at Lexington, Virginia.

May 8

West: General Edward R. S. Canby formally accepts the paroles of General Richard Taylor's forces in Mississippi, Alabama, and East Louisiana.

Naval: The USS *Insonomia* captures the British blockade-runner *George Douthwaite* near the Warrior River, Florida.

May 9

Politics: President Andrew Johnson declares the naval blockade to remain in place for two more weeks to impede any escape by fugitive Confederate leaders.

Francis H. Pierpont receives official recognition as governor of Virginia; previously he headed Unionist Virginians in Federal-held territory.

The trial of eight suspected conspirators begins in Washington, D.C.

President Jefferson Davis is reunited with his wife Varina at Dublin, Georgia.

West: General Nathan B. Forrest disbands his men rather than surrender.

May 10

Politics: President Andrew Johnson declares armed resistance "virtually at an end," although skirmishing persists in rural parts of the South.

President Jefferson Davis and his wife are captured near Abbeville, Georgia, by men of the 1st Wisconsin and 4th Michigan Cavalry under Lieutenant Colonel Benjamin Pritchard—part of General James H. Wilson's command. His detention signals the end of the Confederate government.

General Samuel Jones surrenders Confederate forces at Tallahassee, Florida.

West: Dreaded Confederate guerrilla William C. Quantrill is mortally wounded and captured near Taylorsville, Kentucky.

May 11

WEST: General Jeff Thompson surrenders at Chalk Bluff, Arkansas.

SOUTHWEST: Colonel Theodore H. Barrett, 62nd U.S. Colored Infantry, disregards the unofficial truce along the Rio Grande region of Texas by mustering 250 men of his regiment and 50 troopers of the 2nd Texas Cavalry to attack a Confederate outpost at White's Ranch on the road to Brownstown. The column is commanded by Colonel David Branson, who leads them over the rain-swollen Boca Chica River toward their objective. Finding this position abandoned, Branson rests his men in a thicket for the night.

NAVAL: Captain Thomas J. Paige and the CSS *Stonewall* docks at Havana, Cuba.

May 12

POLITICS: President Andrew Johnson appoints General Oliver O. Howard to head the Freedmen's Bureau.

SOUTH: General Adelbert Ames becomes commander of the X Corps, Florida.

SOUTHWEST: Colonel David Branson's Union column defeats a force of 300 Confederate cavalry at Palmito Ranch, Texas, on the road to Brownsville. After regrouping, the Southerners counterattack and drive the Federal forces back to White's Ranch. Overnight, both sides continue receiving reinforcements.

May 13

WEST: General Edmund Kirby-Smith confers with the Confederate governors of Arkansas, Louisiana, and Missouri in Marshall, Texas. Smith intends to surrender his forces, but General Joseph O. Shelby threatens to arrest him if he tries.

SOUTHWEST: Colonel Theodore H. Barrett arrives to take command of Union troops under Colonel David Branson and leads them back into combat at Palmito Ranch, Texas. They engage a force of Confederate cavalry under Colonel John S. Ford, who deftly outflanks the overconfident Federals. Barrett promptly falls back, hotly pursued by the Southerners, who chase him for 17 miles. The fighting then stops once Barrett reaches his original starting point at White's Ranch. Union losses are estimated at around 130 killed, wounded, or captured; the Confederates suffer far less. While small, Palmito Ranch is also the last pitched encounter of the Civil War. Once Ford interrogates his prisoners and learns that the war is over, he begins to disband Confederate forces along the Rio Grande.

May 16

POLITICS: President Jefferson Davis, his family, and several ranking Confederate officials are placed on steamers and sent down the Savannah River, Georgia, to Port Royal, South Carolina.

May 17

SOUTH: General Philip H. Sheridan becomes commander of all Federal troops west of the Mississippi and south of the Arkansas rivers, where scattered Confederate resistance continues.

General Edward R. S. Canby relieves General Benjamin F. Butler as head of the newly enlarged Department of the Gulf, whose jurisdiction now encompasses Louisiana, Mississippi, Alabama, and Florida.

May 19

NAVAL: Captain Thomas J. Page hands over the CSS *Stonewall* to the captain general of Cuba for $16,000, with which he pays off his crew. The vessel ultimately is sold to Japan.

The USS *Grosbeak* receives the surrender of the 2nd Arkansas at Laconia, Arkansas.

May 20

WEST: Federal soldiers repel an attack by hostile Sioux on Deer Creek, Dakota Territory, killing and wounding around 50.

NAVAL: Secretary of the Navy Gideon Welles appoints a naval board headed by Admiral David G. Farragut to investigate the present affairs of the displaced U.S. Naval Institute and to make recommendations for the future.

Federal authorities arrest former Confederate secretary of the navy Stephen R. Mallory at LaGrange, Georgia.

May 21

NAVAL: The far-ranging CSS *Shenandoah* under Lieutenant James I. Waddell enters the Sea of Okhotsk in search of Union whaling vessels.

May 22

POLITICS: President Andrew Johnson opens all Southern seaports as of July 1 with the exception of four facilities in Texas: Galveston, La Salle, Brazos Santiago, and Brownsville.

President Jefferson Davis arrives in chains at Fortress Monroe, Virginia, and will remain confined there until May 13, 1867.

NAVAL: *Picket Boat No. 5* seizes the Confederate steamers *Skirwan, Cotton Plant, Fisher,* and *Egypt Mills* in the Roanoke River, North Carolina.

Commander Matthew F. Maury arrives at Havana, Cuba, with thousands of dollars of electrical equipment for building and detonating torpedoes. However, on hearing of the Confederacy's demise, he abandons his attempt to reach Galveston, Texas.

May 23

POLITICS: The Piedmont government, a collection of Unionist politicians from Virginia, occupies the state capital at Richmond.

NORTH: The Grand Armies of the Republic parade in a mass review at Washington, D.C., and flags are permitted to fly at full mast for the first time in four years. Curiously, not one of the 166 African-American regiments raised during the war is present at the festivities.

NAVAL: The USS *Azalea* captures the British blockade-runner *Sarah M. Newhall* off Savannah, Georgia.

May 24

NORTH: The army of General William T. Sherman, sporting a much looser appearance than the spit-and-polish Army of the Potomac, victoriously tramps through Washington, D.C. Sherman also refuses to shake hands with Secretary of War Edwin M. Stanton over their recent imbroglio concerning the surrender of General Joseph E. Johnston.

Naval: The USS *Cornubia* and *Princess Royal* sink the Confederate blockade-runner *Denbigh* and the schooner *Le Compt* off Galveston, Texas.

May 25

South: An accidental explosion of 20 tons of Confederate gunpowder occurs in Mobile, Alabama, wrecking facilities and inflicting 300 casualties. Quartermaster John Cooper, having dashed into the fires and rescued a wounded man on his back, receives his second Congressional Medal of Honor.

Naval: The USS *Vanderbilt* tows the captured Confederate ram CSS *Columbia* to Hampton Roads, Virginia.

Admiral Henry K. Thatcher notes that Confederate defenses at Sabine Pass, Texas, have been disbanded and the Stars and Stripes is hoisted over them by men of the USS *Owasco*.

Commander Matthew F. Maury, fearing that his prior work on torpedoes makes him ineligible for a parole, sails from Havana, Cuba, to Mexico.

May 26

South: General Simon B. Buckner, representing general Edmund Kirby-Smith, surrenders to General Edward R. S. Canby's deputy general Peter J. Osterhaus at New Orleans, Louisiana. This act formally dissolves all remaining Confederate forces west of the Mississippi River. General Joseph O. Shelby, however, defiantly leads 1,000 followers south into Mexico to found a military colony.

May 27

Politics: President Andrew Johnson empties the prisons of almost all Southerners held under military jurisdiction.

North: Benjamin H. Grierson is appointed major general, U.S. Army.

Naval: Acting on instructions from Admiral John A. B. Dahlgren, the USS *Pontiac* deposits several Confederate torpedoes for examination at the U.S. Naval Academy.

The CSS *Spray* surrenders to Union forces in the St. Mark's River, Florida.

The Confederate raider CSS *Shenandoah* under Lieutenant James I. Waddell captures and burns the Union whaler *Abigail* in the Sea of Okhotsk.

May 29

Diplomacy: In a detailed letter, American minister to Britain Charles F. Adams outlines to Foreign Minister Lord John Russell that British-built Confederate warships are responsible for the destruction of 110,000 tons of American shipping—and compensation is in order. This damage is so extensive that the United States forfeits its prior position as the world's largest maritime carrier.

Politics: President Andrew Johnson proclaims an amnesty and pardon to any former Confederates submitting to a loyalty oath. He also extends recognition to four new state governments established by his predecessor along with plans for readmitting Southern states into the Union. Johnson's continuation of moderate reconstruction or, as he deems it, "restoration," spells certain trouble at the hands of Radical Republicans.

William H. Holden gains appointment as provisional governor of North Carolina.

June 1

NAVAL: Army troops conveyed by USS *Itasca* occupy Apalachicola, Florida.

The USS *Ouachita* and seven gunboats convoy 4,000 troops under General Francis J. Herron, up the Red River, Louisiana, to secure Confederate forts and posts. In this manner, the large ironclad CSS *Missouri* is secured at Alexandria.

June 2

DIPLOMACY: The government of Great Britain officially rescinds belligerent status for the Confederacy.

POLITICS: President Andrew Johnson pardons Lambdin P. Milligan, a notorious "Copperhead" agitator sentenced to hang.

SOUTHWEST: General Edmund Kirby-Smith formally surrenders Confederate forces at Galveston, Texas, to General Edmund J. Davis. The articles of capitulation are signed aboard the USS *Fort Jackson*.

NAVAL: Secretary of the Navy Gideon Welles begins a downsizing and economizing policy by ordering the Mississippi Squadron of Admiral Samuel P. Lee reduced to 15 ships.

June 3

NAVAL: The CSS *Missouri* surrenders to U.S. naval forces on the Red River, Louisiana.

Admiral Louis M. Goldsborough receives command of the reconstituted European Squadron.

June 5

NAVAL: Captain Benjamin F. Sands directs landing parties from the USS *Cornubia* and *Preston* to occupy Galveston, Texas, and raise the Stars and Stripes.

June 6

POLITICS: President Andrew Johnson orders all remaining Confederate prisoners of war released.

Voters in Missouri ratify a new constitution abolishing slavery.

WEST: Confederate guerrilla William C. Quantrill dies of wounds at Louisville, Kentucky.

NAVAL: Commander Matthew F. Maury, C.S.N., arrives at Veracruz, Mexico, and proceeds to Mexico City to present his credentials to Emperor Maximilian. The receipt of several letters from family members strongly advising him not to return home convinces him that this is the right course to pursue.

June 7

NAVAL: The USS *Ouachita* seizes the CSS *Cotton* and removes it to the mouth of the Red River.

June 8
NORTH: A tardy Union VI Corps parades through Washington, D.C.

June 9
NAVAL: Per order of Secretary of the Navy Gideon Welles, the East and West Gulf squadrons are united under the leadership of Admiral Henry K. Thatcher. The North and South Atlantic squadrons likewise are consolidated under Admiral John A. B. Dahlgren.

The CSS *Ajax* under Lieutenant John Low arrives back at Liverpool, England, where it is interned by authorities. Low himself decides to remain abroad rather than return home.

June 13
POLITICS: President Andrew Johnson appoints William L. Sharkey provisional governor of Mississippi, continuing his policy of restoring civilian authority as quickly as possible.

June 17
POLITICS: President Andrew Johnson appoints James Johnson and Andrew J. Hamilton provisional governors of Georgia and Texas, respectively.

June 21
POLITICS: President Andrew Johnson appoints Lewis E. Parsons provisional governor of Alabama.

June 22
NAVAL: The Confederate raider CSS *Shenandoah* under Lieutenant James I. Waddell fires the last naval shots of the war by capturing the Union whalers *William Thompson, Euphrates, Milo, Sophia Thornton,* and *Jerah Swift* in the Bering Sea. Waddell hears rumors that the war has ended from his captives but disbelieves them for lack of evidence.

June 23
POLITICS: President Andrew Johnson declares the Union naval blockade of all Southern states officially over.
SOUTHWEST: General Stand Watie surrenders his Confederate Cherokee at Doaksville, Indian Territory. He is the last Confederate general to capitulate.
NAVAL: Admiral Samuel F. Du Pont dies unexpectedly at Philadelphia, Pennsylvania, aged 61 years.

The Confederate raider CSS *Shenandoah* under Lieutenant James I. Waddell captures and burns the Union whaler *General Williams* in the Bering Sea.

June 24
POLITICS: President Andrew Johnson lifts all commercial restrictions from states and territories west of the Mississippi River.

June 26
NAVAL: The Confederate raider CSS *Shenandoah* under Lieutenant James I. Waddell seizes and burns the Union whalers *Nimrod, William C. Nye, Catherine, General Pike, Isabella,* and *Gipsey* in the Bering Sea.

June 27

NAVAL: Commander Matthew F. Maury, C.S.N., finally has his audience with Emperor Maximilian in Mexico City, Mexico.

June 28

NAVAL: The Confederate raider CSS *Shenandoah* seizes Union whalers *Brunswick, Favorite, James Murray, Nile, Hillman, Nassau, Isaac Howland, Waverly, Martha, Favorite, Covington,* and *Congress,* bonding a handful and burning the rest. In a voyage traversing 58,000 miles, this is Waddell's most enterprising day.

June 30

POLITICS: A military commission finds all eight conspirators implicated in the assassination of President Abraham Lincoln guilty. David E. Herold, Lewis Payne, George A. Atzerodt, and Mary E. Surratt are sentenced to hang while Dr. Samuel Mudd, Samuel Arnold, and Michael O'Laughlin receive life imprisonment; Edward Spangler receives six-years' imprisonment.

July 1

POLITICS: President Andrew Johnson declares all Southern ports open to foreign commerce and shipping.

New Hampshire ratifies the 13th Amendment.

NAVAL: The Confederate raider CSS *Shenandoah* under Lieutenant James I. Waddell, threatened by ice floes in the Bering Sea, sails south looking for additional victims.

July 3

WEST: General Patrick E. Conner arrives at Fort Laramie, Wyoming, to orchestrate military activity against ongoing Arapaho raids.

July 7

POLITICS: Four individuals implicated in the assassination of President Abraham Lincoln go to the gallows in Washington, D.C. Four others are relocated to serve their sentences in the Dry Tortugas islands, Florida.

July 13

POLITICS: President Andrew Johnson appoints William Marvin provisional governor of Florida.

July 14

NAVAL: The Confederate blockade-runner *Owl* under Commander John N. Maffitt steams into the Mersey River and drops anchor at Liverpool. He then disbands his crew and turns the vessel over to an English shipping firm.

July 15

NAVAL: The Confederate raider CSS *Shenandoah* under Lieutenant James I. Waddell finally clears the Bering Sea and steers south intending to attack San Francisco, California.

July 16

NAVAL: With the encouragement of Emperor Maximilian, Commander Matthew F. Maury draws up a detailed plan for Confederate immigration to Mexico.

July 18
NAVAL: The USS *Colorado* arrives at Vlissingen, Netherlands, where Admiral Louis M. Goldsborough takes command of the newly reconstituted European Squadron.

July 19
POLITICS: Governor J. Madison Wells implores the inhabitants of Louisiana to take the oath of allegiance or lose their right to vote.

July 20
NAVAL: The army transport *Quinnebaug* strikes a reef outside Beaufort, North Carolina, and sinks with the loss of 25 lives. The survivors are rescued eventually by boats from the USS *Anemone* and *Corwin*.

July 31
NAVAL: The Potomac Flotilla is disbanded.

The East Indian squadron is established under Commodore Henry H. Bell, commanding the USS *Wachusett, Hartford,* and *Wyoming*. His mission is to patrol waters from the Strait of Sunda to the Sea of Japan.

August 2
NAVAL: Lieutenant James I. Waddell of the CSS *Shenandoah* learns from the British vessel *Barracouta* that the Civil War has in fact ended. Fearing that he and his crew will be charged with piracy and ignoring protests from his crew, he orders the vessel to make for Britain via Cape Horn.

August 12
NAVAL: The Brazil Squadron arrives at Bahía, Brazil, with the USS *Susquehanna, Monadnock, Chippewa, Monticello, Canonicus, Shawmut, Fahkee,* and *Wasp* to protect American interests in the South Atlantic.

August 14
NAVAL: The once-imposing Mississippi Squadron of 80 warships is disbanded by Admiral Samuel P. Lee; henceforth, U.S. Navy presence on the western waterways is reduced to five vessels.

August 21
POLITICS: The Mississippi state legislature negates its secessionist ordinance and also abolishes slavery.

August 23
NAVAL: The USS *Commodore McDonough* sinks while under tow from Port Royal, South Carolina, to New York.

August 24
SOUTH: Clara Barton and Captain James M. Moore conclude their activities to identify and register Union dead at Andersonville Prison, Georgia.

August 28
NAVAL: Admiral David D. Porter is appointed the sixth superintendent of the U.S. Naval Academy and orchestrates its transfer from Newport, Rhode Island, back to Annapolis, Maryland. Porter serves four years, rising there to vice admiral.

September 1
SOUTH: Former general Robert E. Lee becomes president of Washington College, Virginia.

September 3
WEST: A detachment of Federal troops from General Patrick E. Connor's command engages a combined party of Arapaho, Comanche, and Sioux warriors at the Battle of Powder River, Idaho Territory.

September 4
WEST: Roughly 2,000 hostile Indians continue to attack a Federal detachment at Powder River, Montana Territory, killing two soldiers and losing 13 warriors.

September 5
POLITICS: The South Carolina legislature repeals its ordinance of secession, declaring it null and void.

September 11
NAVAL: Emperor Maximilian approves of Commander Matthew F. Maury's plans to encourage Confederate immigration to Mexico.

September 14
WEST: Representatives of nine Native American tribes (Cherokee, Creek, Choctaw, Chickasaw, Osage, Seminole, Seneca, Shawnee, and Quapaw) gather at Fort Smith, Arkansas, and sign a treaty of loyalty to the United States.

September 16
NAVAL: The Confederate raider CSS *Shenandoah* under Lieutenant James I. Waddell rounds Cape Horn and enters the Atlantic Ocean en route to Liverpool, England.

September 18
NAVAL: Emperor Maximilian of Mexico appoints Commander Matthew F. Maury an "Honorary Counselor of the State" and "Director of the National Observatory."

September 23
WEST: Native Americans attack an army encampment in the Harney Lake valley, Oregon Territory; this is the last recorded engagement of the Civil War period.

October 2
SOUTH: Former general Robert E. Lee takes his oath of allegiance to the United States and receives a full pardon.
NAVAL: Commodore John Rodgers leads the USS *Vanderbilt, Tuscarora, Powhatan,* and *Monadnock* round Cape Horn and into the Pacific Ocean to reinforce the Pacific Squadron.

October 11
POLITICS: Former Confederate vice president Alexander H. Stephens and several high-ranking cabinet officers are paroled by President Andrew Johnson.

October 12
POLITICS: President Andrew Johnson declares an end to martial law in Kentucky.

October 20
NAVAL: The steam tug USS *Nettle* sinks after colliding with an ironclad.

November 3
NAVAL: Secretary of the Navy Gideon Welles instructs all U.S. Navy vessels to render proper honors on entering English ports. This diplomatic nicety is resumed once the British government retracts belligerent status from the now-defunct Confederacy.

November 5
NAVAL: Lieutenant James I. Waddell docks the CSS *Shenandoah* at Liverpool, England, after covering 58,000 miles and seizing 38 prizes without loss of life.

November 6
NAVAL: Lieutenant James I. Waddell surrenders the CSS *Shenandoah* to British authorities. His is the final Confederate flag struck. After a few days in confinement, the crew is released by British authorities. *Shenandoah* subsequently is turned over to U.S. minister Charles F. Adams, who sells the vessel to the Sultan of Zanzibar. Waddell, meanwhile, is reviled by the American government as the "Anglo-American Pirate Captain," which induces him to remain in England until 1875.

The USS *Jacob Bell* sinks while being towed to New York.

The USS *Anna* is wrecked on the Florida coast.

The USS *Itasca* strikes a Confederate mine in Mobile Bay, Alabama, and sinks.

The tug USS *Rose* strikes a Confederate mine in Mobile Bay, Alabama, and sinks.

November 9
POLITICS: The North Carolina legislature overturns its 1861 secession ordinance, outlaws slavery, and elects new members to Congress.

November 10
SOUTH: Captain Henry Wirz is hanged by Union authorities for his role as commandant of notorious Andersonville Prison, Georgia. He is the only former Confederate so punished.

November 13
POLITICS: The South Carolina state legislature ratifies the 13th Amendment.

November 23
NAVAL: The former Confederate ironclad CSS *Stonewall* is escorted by the USS *Rhode Island* and *Hornet* to the Washington Navy Yard, following its purchase from the governor-general of Cuba. The vessel ultimately is sold to Japan.

November 24
POLITICS: The state legislature of Mississippi passes laws concerning vagrancy, labor service, and other "black codes" intending to regulate African Americans and define

their roles in the greater society. Henceforth, blacks are not allowed to serve on juries, cannot testify against white persons in a court of law, cannot bear arms, and cannot gather in large numbers. Collectively, this is the first manifestation of what becomes known as "Jim Crow" laws during the 20th century.

December 1

POLITICS: The government revokes wartime suspension of the writ of habeas corpus, except in states of the former Confederacy, the District of Columbia, and the New Mexico and Arizona territories.

December 2

POLITICS: The Alabama state legislature ratifies the 13th Amendment, fulfilling the requisite three-fourths approval by the states.

December 4

POLITICS: The 39th U.S. Congress convenes and institutes the Joint Committee on Reconstruction to oppose President Andrew Johnson. Known as the "Committee of Fifteen," it consists of nine Republicans and six Democrats, and votes repeatedly along party lines. Among its first actions is to dispute the credentials of newly elected senators and representatives from states of the former Confederacy, hence denying them seats in Congress.

The 13th Amendment is ratified by North Carolina but it fails in Mississippi.
NAVAL: Secretary of the Navy Gideon Welles reconstitutes the West India Squadron under Commodore James S. Palmer of the USS *Rhode Island*. His command includes the *De Soto, Swatara, Monongahela, Florida, Augusta, Shamrock, Ashuelot,* and *Monocacy.*

December 5

DIPLOMACY: Secretary of State William H. Seward instructs U.S. minister to France John Bigelow to enunciate to Emperor Napoleon III, in no uncertain terms, American displeasure with the French occupation of Mexico.
POLITICS: The 13th Amendment is ratified by Georgia.

December 6

POLITICS: In his first annual message to Congress, President Andrew Johnson declares, with "gratitude to God in the name of the people for the preservation of the United States," that the Union has been restored.

December 11

POLITICS: The 13th Amendment is ratified by Oregon.

December 14

POLITICS: Representative Thaddeus Stevens of Pennsylvania, an outspoken Radical Republican, assumes the mantle of leadership within the Committee of Fifteen.

December 18

POLITICS: Secretary of State William H. Seward declares the 13th Amendment to the Constitution, approved by 27 states, as adopted. After nearly two and a half contentious centuries, the incubus of slavery is expunged from the American polity and psyche alike.

December 24

POLITICS: The Ku Klux Klan is founded in Tennessee as a secret society intent on terrorizing African Americans. Former Confederate general Nathan B. Forrest is installed as the first Grand Wizard.

December 27

NAVAL: Secretary of the Navy Gideon Welles makes his annual report to the president, declaring navy strength at nearly 700 warships, a far cry from the 42 vessels in commission at the onset of hostilities. Personnel during this period also mushroomed from 7,600 to 51,000 rank and file. "After the capture of Fort Hatteras and Clark in August 1861," he beams, "port after port was wrested from the insurgents, until the flag of the Union was again restored in every harbor and along our entire coast, and the rebellion wholly suppressed." While less dramatic than events on land, the persistent naval blockade played a major role in the economic and strategic collapse of the Confederacy.

Former Confederate admiral Raphael Semmes is arrested and brought to Washington, D.C., for allegedly violating parole conditions. He remains in custody until April 1866 and is never brought to trial.

Alexander, Edward P. (1835–1910)

Confederate general

Edward Porter Alexander was born in Washington, Georgia, on May 26, 1835, the son of affluent parents. He gained admittance to the U.S. Military Academy, West Point, in 1835 and graduated third in his class by 1839; at the time of his attendance, Robert E. LEE was military superintendent. Alexander also displayed considerable promise as an instructor and taught at West Point until October 1858, when he rose to first lieutenant and accompanied Colonel Albert S. JOHNSTON west as a member of his Mormon expedition. Alexander returned to the academy in 1859 where, in concert with Major Albert J. Myer, he helped perfect the "wigwam" (semaphore) system of signaling with flags or lanterns. This permitted armies in the field to communicate vital information over greater distances. He subsequently transferred back to the frontier as part of the garrison at Fort Steilacom, Washington Territory. Though Southern-born, Alexander did not readily embrace secession, but once the process began in the spring of 1861, he resigned his commission and offered his service to the Confederacy.

On March 16, 1861, Alexander joined the staff of General Pierre G. T. BEAUREGARD as a captain in the signal service. He performed valuable service at the Battle of Bull Run on July 21, 1861, by transmitting information of a Union flanking movement back to headquarters, which enabled Beauregard to parry the blow. During the Peninsula campaign of 1861, Alexander became one of the first Confederate officers employed in balloon

Confederate general Edward P. Alexander *(Massachusetts Commandery Military Order of the Loyal Legion and the U.S. Army Military History Institute)*

reconnaissance at the Battle of Gaines's Mill on June 27, 1862. But as a young officer, he was particularly drawn to the artillery service, and it was here that he made his greatest contributions. General Robert E. Lee, now head of the Army of Northern Virginia, sought out Porter to replace the incompetent general William N. Pendleton as his chief of artillery. Alexander accordingly gained promotion to lieutenant colonel as of July 1862 and became indelibly associated with the "long arm of Lee" thereafter. He displayed great talent in sighting his field pieces at the Battle of Fredericksburg on December 13, 1862, transforming parts of that field into a killing ground. Lee was so pleased by his performance that he arranged Alexander's promotion to colonel in charge of an artillery battalion with General James Longstreet's I Corps. In this capacity, he accompanied General Thomas J. Jackson on his famous flank march at Chancellorsville, Virginia, in May 1863. He proved instrumental in massing 30 cannon at Hazel Grove on May 4, 1863, which drove off the Union army of General Joseph Hooker.

On July 3, 1863, Alexander performed his most noted deed of the war. At this, the climactic third day of Gettysburg, he massed more than 140 cannons, hub-to-hub, for a sustained bombardment of Union positions. These dueled with 100 Union cannon on the opposite heights, which ceased fire to conserve their ammunition. Confederate gunners kept up a tremendous cannonade, which, owing to the excellent defensive dispositions of General George G. Meade, mostly passed harmlessly overhead. Following the bloody repulse of General George E. Pickett, Alexander provided covering fire for the retreating Confederates. In the fall of 1863, he next accompanied General Longstreet west to reinforce the Army of Tennessee under General Braxton Bragg. Alexander missed the bloody fight at Chickamauga on September 20, 1863, but he did render useful service during the ill-fated siege of Knoxville that December. Bragg's successor, General Joseph E. Johnston, was so impressed with Alexander's abilities that he requested his transfer to the Army

of Tennessee—but General Lee flatly refused to release him.

On March 1, 1864, Alexander rose to brigadier general and resumed his activities as Longstreet's chief of ordnance with the I Corps. He and his cannon were conspicuous in the bloody encounters of the Wilderness and Spotsylvania in May 1864, where a new adversary, General Ulysses S. Grant, kept maneuvering the Confederates back to their capital of Richmond, Virginia. Alexander next distinguished himself in the bloody fighting at Cold Harbor and Petersburg that summer, in which massed Union attacks invariably were repelled with slaughter. Prior to the July 30, 1864, Battle of the Crater, outside Petersburg, Alexander accurately predicted that the Federals might attempt mining beneath Confederate defensive works and urged his superiors to begin countermining operations. Alexander then was wounded by a sniper and sent to the rear to recuperate before the attack transpired. He rejoined the army just as General Lee was about to abandon the Richmond-Petersburg area, and he subsequently urged his superior against surrendering at Appomattox. Alexander finally laid down his arms on April 9, 1865, with the rest of the Army of Northern Virginia.

In the postwar period, Alexander again distinguished himself as a mathematics and engineering professor at the University of South Carolina, Columbia, where he also penned numerous and well-received treatises about railroad management. In 1885, President Grover Cleveland appointed the former artillerist director of the Union Pacific Railroad, and he subsequently used his surveying skills to settle a boundary dispute between Nicaragua and Costa Rica. Alexander use published numerous memoirs and essays on the Civil War and was one of a handful of officers willing to criticize the military leadership of Robert E. Lee. Alexander died in Savannah, Georgia, on April 28, 1910, the Confederacy's leading artillerist.

Further Reading

Boggs, Marion A., ed. *The Alexander Letters, 1787–1900.* Athens: University of Georgia Press, 1980.

Cole, Philip M. *Civil War Artillery at Gettysburg: Organization, Equipment, Ammunition, and Tactics.* Cambridge, Mass.: Da Capo Press, 2002.

Gallagher, Gary W., ed. *Fighting for the Confederacy: The Personal Recollections of General Edward Porter Alexander.* Chapel Hill: University of North Carolina Press, 1989.

Golay, Michael. *To Gettysburg and Beyond: The Parallel Lives of Joshua Lawrence and Edward Porter Alexander.* New York: Crown, 1994.

Hazlet, James C., Edwin Olmstead, and M. Hume Parks. *Field Artillery Weapons of the Civil War.* Urbana: University of Illinois Press, 2004.

Murray, R. L. E. P. *Alexander and the Artillery Action in the Peach Orchard.* Wolcott, N.Y.: Benedum Books, 2000.

Naisawald, Louis V. *Cannon Blasts: Civil War Artillery in the Eastern Armies.* Shippensburg, Pa.: White Mane Books, 2004.

Anderson, Richard H. (1821–1879)

Confederate general

Richard Heron Anderson was born in Statesburg, South Carolina, on October 7, 1821, the grandson of a Revolutionary War officer. In 1838, he was admitted to the U.S. Military Academy and graduated four years later, 40th in his class. As a second lieutenant, Anderson passed through the Cavalry School at Carlisle, Pennsylvania, and served in the 1st U.S. Dragoons at Little Rock, Arkansas Territory. In 1847, he accompanied General Winfield SCOTT's invasion of Mexico at Veracruz, fought with distinction at St. Augustin on August 17, 1847, and received a brevet promotion to first lieutenant. After the war, Anderson transferred back to Pennsylvania and stayed as a cavalry instructor until 1852. That year, he rose to captain and shipped west to serve in a number of outposts in Texas, New Mexico, and Kansas. In 1858, Anderson was selected to accompany Colonel Albert S. JOHNSTON on his noted Mormon expedition, and the following year, he was posted to Fort Kearney, Nebraska Territory. It was while on this duty that the first rumblings of secession were heard. Anderson, who did not support slavery, felt tremendous pressure from his family to join the

Confederate general Richard H. Anderson *(Massachusetts Commandery Military Order of the Loyal Legion and the U.S. Army Military History Institute)*

Confederacy after South Carolina left the Union in December 1860. Therefore, he reluctantly resigned his commission in February 1861 and offered his services as colonel of the 1st South Carolina Regiment.

Anderson initially served under General Pierre G. T. BEAUREGARD during the fateful bombardment of Fort Sumter, Charleston, on April 12–14, 1861, and subsequently succeeded him as city commander. On July 19, 1861, Anderson advanced to brigadier general and was attached to the army of General Braxton BRAGG at Pensacola, Florida. On October 9, 1861, he first saw combat by organizing and leading a successful overnight raid against Union forces on Santa Rosa Island, and in February 1862, he was transferred to Virginia to command a brigade in General James LONGSTREET's division. Anderson fought exceedingly well throughout the Peninsula campaign of that spring, winning laurels from superiors for aggressive fighting at Williamsburg, Seven Pines, and the Seven Days' battles. He then rose to major general on July 14, 1862, under General Benjamin HUGER. Anderson was in the thick of fighting at Second Bull Run on August 30, 1862, and later accompanied General Thomas J. JACKSON in maneuvers culminating in the capture of Harper's Ferry on September 15, 1862. Two days later, he helped decisively reinforce General Robert E. LEE at Antietam, receiving severe injuries in combat. Anderson recovered in time to participate at Fredericksburg, February 13, 1862, but was only lightly engaged, but by dint of his fearlessness under fire and eagerness to engage the enemy, he acquired a popular reputation as "Fighting Dick."

During the Chancellorsville campaign of May 1863, Anderson commanded one of three brigades entrusted with holding back the far larger army of General Joseph HOOKER while Jackson launched his famous flank attack. On May 4, 1863, he proved instrumental in helping defeat the VI Corps of General John Sedgwick at Salem Church, Virginia. After the death of Jackson, Anderson's division transferred to General Ambrose P. HILL's III Corps, and he accompanied him throughout the Gettysburg campaign. Anderson was closely engaged on the second day of combat, and he helped sweep General Daniel SICKLES III Corps from their positions at the Peach Orchard. The following day, his division marched in support of General George E. PICKETT's memorable charge against the Union center and withdrew with the main army back to Virginia. Anderson temporarily succeeded Longstreet as commander of I Corps once the latter was wounded at the Wilderness on May 6, 1864. That evening, he performed his most famous deed by force-marching to the strategic road junction at Spotsylvania Court House, arriving there only minutes ahead of Union forces, and repelling numerous attacks by General Gouverneur K. Warren. His prompt actions allowed the Army of Northern Virginia under General Lee to erect defensive positions around Spotsylvania, which blunted another determined Union drive on Richmond. Consequently, he received promotion to

lieutenant general on May 31, 1864. When Longstreet returned to the field that October, Anderson resumed his duties as a divisional commander. He served capably throughout the siege of Richmond and Petersburg, Virginia, and he helped conduct the army out of that area when Lee abandoned the capital on April 2, 1865. Four days later, Anderson suffered his only defeat at Sayler's Creek, whereby his command nearly was annihilated by Union forces under General Philip H. SHERIDAN. He was then relieved of command and sent home.

After the war, Anderson eked out a marginal existence as a laborer with the South Carolina Railroad for many years, rising to agent. He lived in poverty until 1875 when the position of state phosphate inspector was proffered. Anderson, one of the Confederacy's finest divisional-level leaders, died in relative obscurity at Beaufort, South Carolina, on June 26, 1879.

Further Reading

Elliott, Joseph C. *Lieutenant General Richard Heron Anderson: Lee's Noble Soldier.* Dayton, Ohio: Morningside House, 1985.

Gallagher, Gary W., ed. *The Second Day at Gettysburg: Essays on Confederate and Union Military Leadership.* Kent, Ohio: Kent State University Press, 2001.

Grimsley, Mark. *And Keep Moving On: The Virginia Campaign, May–June, 1864.* Lincoln: University of Nebraska Press, 2002.

Marvel, William. *Lee's Last Retreat: The Flight to Appomattox.* Chapel Hill: University of North Carolina Press, 2002.

Pfanz, Harry W. *Gettysburg—Culp's Hill and Cemetery Ridge.* Chapel Hill: University of North Carolina Press, 1993.

Smith, Derek. *Lee's Last Stand: Sailor's Creek, Virginia, 1865.* Shippensburg, Pa.: White Mane Books, 2002.

Anderson, Robert (1805–1871)

Union general

Robert Anderson was born near Louisville, Kentucky, on June 14, 1805, into a family with deep Southern roots. He graduated from the U.S. Military Academy in 1825 and joined the 3rd U.S. Artillery as a second lieutenant. As such, Anderson fought in the Black Hawk War of 1832, gaining brevet promotion to captain for gallantry, and also served in Florida's Second Seminole War (1836–38). Anderson next participated in General Winfield SCOTT's invasion of Mexico in 1847, winning a second brevet to major for gallantry at Molino del Rey, in which he was also wounded. Thereafter, he spent the next several years serving with various artillery boards and also translated French military texts for army use. Anderson, a proslavery, Southern-born officer, seemed a natural choice to Secretary of War John B. FLOYD to head the Federal garrison at Charleston, South Carolina, in November 1860. That state was being buffeted violently by the winds of secession, and it was hoped that Anderson, by dint of his Southern sensibilities, might diffuse tensions there.

After arriving in Charleston, Anderson remained polite, even deferential, to city authorities but also adamant toward fulfilling his duties. His position worsened considerably after December 20, 1861, when South Carolina passed a secession ordinance and tensions with the federal government—and its troops—increased. At that time, Anderson commanded 137 men at Fort Moultrie, a wretched fortification in Charleston proper that was indefensible from the land side. Fearing for the safety of his men—and without prior authorization from the War Department—Anderson acted decisively. On the evening of December 26, 1860, he quietly and efficiently transferred the garrison from Fort Moultrie to Fort Sumter on an island in the harbor. Once there, he cabled superiors as to his predicament and awaited further instructions. Predictably, the secessionist-leaning secretary Floyd was livid over the unauthorized transfer and demanded it be countermanded, but President James Buchanan refused and settled for the status quo. He was counting on Anderson's well-grounded reputation for tact and intelligence, along with his unswerving loyalty to the Union, to forestall any outbreak of violence.

Charleston authorities naturally were incensed that the U.S. garrison had slipped from their grasp

and demanded Anderson's surrender. That officer politely but firmly refused. To underscore his pledge of neutrality, he took no action on January 9, 1861, when Southern batteries fired the first unofficial shots of the Civil War by driving off the supply ship *Star of the West*. However, Confederate leaders, seeking diplomatic recognition for their national sovereignty, simply could not tolerate the presence of Federal troops in one of their largest seaports. General Pierre G. T. BEAUREGARD, the local military commander, was then ordered to bombard the insolent Yankees into submission if they failed to depart. As previously, Anderson politely declined and Southerners began to line the shoreline with heavy cannon. Anderson also informed both Beauregard and President Abraham LINCOLN that his garrison was nearly out of victuals and would have to capitulate within days if not

Union general Robert Anderson *(Massachusetts Commandery Military Order of the Loyal Legion and the U.S. Army Military History Institute)*

resupplied. The crisis mounted when Lincoln announced his decision to send a ship with food—not reinforcements—to the beleaguered garrison. This proved one contingency that Confederate authorities could not allow, and so again, on April 11, 1861, they informed Anderson that either he must surrender immediately or they would open fire. When the stalwart officer again refused to abandon his duty, the slide toward civil war became inevitable.

Confederate batteries opened fire at 4:30 A.M. on the morning of April 12, 1861, and bombarded Fort Sumter continuously for the next 34 hours. Anderson gave Captain Abner DOUBLEDAY the honor of firing the first Union shot of the war, but in the end, he was simply overpowered and capitulated at noontime on April 14. His men then were trundled off by the Confederates and allowed to depart by boat. Anderson's heroic stand rendered him the first Northern hero of the Civil War, but privately, he remained grief-stricken over his inability to prevent the outbreak of war. Anderson gained promotion to brigadier general on May 15, 1861, and appointment as commander of the Department of Kentucky (later the Department of the Cumberland) from May to October 1861. His calm presence helped shore up Unionist sympathies in this, his native state. However, Anderson remained dogged by ill health and retired from active service in October 1863 after being replaced by General William T. SHERMAN. Anderson briefly donned his general's uniform on April 14, 1865, when he personally raised the same American flag over Fort Sumter that had been lowered four years earlier. Anderson, a quiet, efficient professional soldier, died while vacationing in Nice, France, on October 26, 1871.

Further Reading

Detzer, David. *Allegiance: Fort Sumter, Charleston, and the Beginning of the Civil War.* New York: Harcourt, 2002.

Garrison, Webb S. *Lincoln's Little War.* Nashville, Tenn.: Rutledge Hill Press, 1997.

Hendrickson, Robert. *Sumter, the First Day of the Civil War.* Chelsea, Mich.: Scarborough, 1997.

Klein, Maury. *Days of Defiance: Sumter, Secession, and the Coming of the Civil War.* New York: Vintage Books, 1999.

McGinty, Brian. "Robert Anderson: Reluctant Hero." *Civil War Times Illustrated* 31, no. 2 (1992): 44–47, 58, 68.

Ramsey, David M. "Robert Anderson in the Civil War." Unpublished master's thesis, Florida State University, 1974.

Wait, Eugene M. *Opening of the Civil War.* Commack, N.Y.: Nova Science Pub., 1999.

Anderson, William (ca. 1837–1864)
Confederate guerrilla

William Anderson probably was born in Kentucky around 1837 and relocated with his family to Council Grove, Kansas Territory, in 1854. The frontier then was reeling from the effects of the Kansas-Nebraska Act of that year, which allowed new states in the union on the basis of "popular sovereignty." This well-intentioned legislation triggered an onslaught of lawlessness as pro- and antislavery groups violently competed for political supremacy. For good measure, criminal elements frequently sided with either group if it suited their own agenda. The ensuing mayhem and murder bequeathed to the territory an uncomely reputation as "Bleeding Kansas." Tensions between the two groups were exacerbated further following the onset of secessionism in 1861. Anderson's own father, a somewhat shady figure, was gunned down in a confrontation with pro-Union settlers in March 1862. With the Civil War now in full swing, the warring factions coalesced into violent groupings favoring either the South ("Bushwhackers") or the North ("Jayhawkers"). Both sides were utterly ruthless in dealing with the other and frequently committed atrocities against civilians, law enforcement figures, and anyone else who got in their way.

By 1862, Anderson had matured into a tall, willowy youth with a penchant for horse theft. He initially favored the pro-Northern faction and generally helped himself to the plunder they accrued. Following the death of his father, however, he relocated to western Missouri and promptly switched sides. The catalyst for his reversion to barbarism occurred on August 13, 1863, when his two sisters, under arrest for alleged Confederate activities, died when the jail confining them collapsed. Anderson consequently joined a gang of frontier desperados under Captain William C. QUANTRILL and began to wreak his own personal brand of vengeance against Unionists. On August 21, 1863, he waged a full measure of activities at Lawrence, Kansas, which was seized by Quantrill's guerrillas. These ruffians, who included Frank and Jesse James, Cole Younger, and a host of future outlaws, systematically rounded up and murdered 200 men and boys before burning the town to the ground. On October 6, Anderson, wearing Union garb, also helped ambush the military escort of General James G. Blunt at Baxter Springs, Kansas, capturing and killing 110 prisoners. Shortly afterward, Anderson was promoted to lieutenant and wintered with the guerrillas in Texas. He subsequently broke with the violent Quantrill after one of his own men was executed and went on to form his own gang of outlaw marauders. By this time, Anderson has also earned, and apparently reveled in, his grim sobriquet of "Bloody Bill."

Commencing in the spring of 1864, Anderson's gang of 50 guerrillas swept the plains of western and central Missouri, robbing and gunning down soldiers and civilians alike. His career climaxed on September 27, 1864, when he captured the town of Centralia, Missouri, robbing the residents and torching the town. At this point, a train pulled into the station bearing 24 unarmed Union soldiers, of whom 23 were bound and executed in cold blood. Union reinforcements arrived shortly after and pursued the guerrillas, but Anderson led them directly into an ambush, killing an additional 100 prisoners. Despite his notoriety, General Sterling PRICE openly employed Anderson and his men as scouts during his final invasion of Missouri, which came to grief at Westport on October 23, 1864. Four days later, Anderson was patrolling outside the town of Orrick when he

stumbled directly into a Jayhawk ambush. He was killed in the ensuing fight, and his body was propped up for public display by vengeful settlers. Anderson's remains then were interred in an unmarked grave after being dragged through the street by horses. He left a bloody legacy whose tradition of violence was perpetuated in the postwar period by the James brothers and other former and notorious subordinates.

Further Reading
Bird, Roy. *Civil War in Kansas*. Gretna, La.: Pelican Publishing, 2004.
Gilmore, Donald L. *Civil War on the Missouri-Kansas Border*. Gretna, La.: Pelican Publishing, 2006.
Mackey, Robert R. *The Uncivil War: Irregular Warfare in the Upper South, 1861–1865*. Norman: University of Oklahoma Press, 2004.
Nichols, Bruce. *Guerrilla Warfare in Civil War Missouri, 1863*. Jefferson, N.C.: McFarland, 2006.
Stiles, T. J. *Jesse James: Last Rebel Guerrilla of the Civil War*. New York: Alfred A. Knopf, 2002.
Wood, Larry. *The Civil War Story of Bloody Bill Anderson*. Austin, Tex.: Eakin Press, 2003.

Ashby, Turner (1828–1862)
Confederate general
Turner Ashby was born in Fauquier County, Virginia, on October 23, 1828, grandson of a Revolutionary War hero. He entered business as an adult and gained local renown for his striking appearance and abilities as a horseman. In 1859, Ashby had his first brush with military matters when he raised a company of volunteer cavalry to help combat the abolitionist John Brown at Harper's Ferry. His services were not then needed, but he maintained his company and continually patrolled the reaches of western Virginia, searching for abolitionist activity. After the Civil War erupted in April 1861, he and John D. IMBODEN originated a plan to seize the Federal arsenal and valuable gun-making machinery at Harper's Ferry, although they were thwarted when the garrison burned their outpost to the ground. Ashby also reached a personal turning point in June 1861 when his younger brother was killed in a skirmish with sol-

diers of the 11th Indiana Infantry under Colonel Lew WALLACE. He immediately swore to avenge his loss and nursed a growing hatred for the Unionists. His energetic services came to the attention of Colonel Thomas J. JACKSON, who then prevailed on General Joseph E. JOHNSTON to commission Ashby into the Confederate service. Accordingly, on July 23, 1861, Ashby was inducted as a lieutenant colonel of the 7th Virginia Cavalry.

Ashby quickly emerged as one of the first Southern cavalry leaders of note and an exceptionally enterprising leader. On one occasion, he disguised himself as a doctor and rode for miles behind Union lines to ascertain their strength and intentions. His men also constantly patrolled the lower Shenandoah Valley against Federal incursions and raids. Ashby acquitted himself well, rising to colonel of the 7th Virginia Cavalry that November. However, his regiment had ballooned in size to 27 companies—far too large from an administrative standpoint. He was also somewhat lax in matters of discipline, and his men acquired a reputation for plundering on the battlefield. Such behavior repelled the spit-and-polish Jackson, who threatened to disband Ashby's command and distribute it among other units if he failed to instill a proper military regimen. The enraged cavalier promptly stormed into his superior's tent and threatened in turn to resign from the army. Jackson relented—on condition that he properly instruct his men. Ashby agreed, and on May 23, 1862, he gained promotion to brigadier general in time to participate in the famous Shenandoah Valley campaign of that year.

During the ensuing two months, Ashby performed scouting, screening, and combat activities for Jackson, frequently against superior numbers but usually victorious. His only real error occurred on May 23, 1862, while reconnoitering in the vicinity of Kernstown, when he inadvertently reported that the town was occupied by a handful of Union troops. On the basis of this report, Jackson then advanced to Kernstown—and headlong into General James Shield's division, which largely had been concealed in the nearby woods. The

ensuing repulse was the only blot on Jackson's otherwise illustrious campaign. Ashby subsequently performed well in the Confederate victory at Winchester two days later, but he failed to intercept the retreat of General Nathaniel P. BANKS successfully when his men again reverted to plundering captured enemy wagons.

At length, Jackson began an orderly withdrawal from the Shenandoah Valley in the face of superior numbers, and Ashby provided the rear guard. As the Confederates withdrew toward Port Republic, Union forces under General John C. Frémont pushed troops forward to engage them. Ashby repulsed one determined charge at Chestnut Ridge on June 6, 1862, when the enemy brought up fresh infantry in support. Ashby did likewise and dismounted to encourage his troops. He then led a charge on foot, shouting, "Forward my brave men!" and was shot down and killed. Jackson, who appreciated his talent as a scout, deeply regretted his passing. "As a partisan officer I never knew his superior," Stonewall confided, "His daring was proverbial; his powers of endurance almost incredible; his tone of character heroic; and his sagacity almost intuitive in divining the purposes and movements of the enemy." Ashby, revered by his men as the "White Knight of the Valley," was interred at Winchester, Virginia, having died before achieving his full potential as a combat officer.

Further Reading

Anderson, Paul C. *Blood Image: Turner Ashby in the Civil War and the Southern Mind*. Baton Rouge: Louisiana State University Press, 2002.

Bushong, Millard K. *General Turner Ashby and Stonewall's Valley Campaign*. Verona, Va.: McClure, 1980.

Cochran, Darrell. "First of the Cavaliers: General Turner Ashby's Brief Glory." *Civil War Times Illustrated* 25, no. 10 (1987): 22–28.

Ecelbarger, Gary L. *We Are in for It! The First Battle of Kernstown*. Shippensburg, Pa.: White Mane Books, 1997.

O'Toole, John T. "The Revenge of Turner Ashby." *Civil War* 58 (August 1996): 40–44.

Paterson, Richard. "Schemes and Treachery." *Civil War Times Illustrated* 28, no. 2 (1989): 38–45.

B

Banks, Nathaniel P. (1816–1894)

Union general

Nathaniel Prentiss Banks was born in Waltham, Massachusetts, on January 16, 1816, the son of a textile foreman. He initially worked in the mills, but, disliking physical labor, he studied law in his spare time and was admitted to the state bar in 1839. He then became active within the Democratic Party, rising steadily through the ranks and winning a seat in the state House of Representatives in 1849. Political success whetted Banks's appetite, and in 1853, he successfully stood for a seat in the U.S. House of Representatives, maneuvering himself into the speakership a year later. But Banks grew disillusioned with the Democratic Party's stance on slavery, so in 1856, he joined the newly formed Republican Party. He then quit Congress and successfully ran for the Massachusetts governorship in 1857, being reelected consecutively two more times. In 1860, Banks resigned from politics altogether to replace George B. MCCLELLAN as president of the Illinois Central Railroad. He still enjoyed deep political roots in the Republican Party and, as a New Englander, a high national profile. Therefore, when President Abraham LINCOLN put in a call for volunteers in April 1861, Banks gained appointment as major general of volunteers to shore up political support from New England. This was done strictly for geopolitical reasons, for Banks, though a skilled administrator, lacked any prior experience in the art of war.

Following the Union debacle at Bull Run on July 21, 1861, Banks was tapped to succeed the disgraced general Robert Patterson as commander of Federal troops in the strategic Shenandoah Valley. The following spring, he received orders to clear the valley of Confederate forces, and he was trounced soundly by General Thomas J. JACKSON at Winchester on May 25, 1862. Union forces abandoned so many valuable supplies in their flight across the Potomac River that victorious Confederates denegraded him as "Commissary Banks." The following June, Banks's force was reorganized in the II Corps in the Army of Virginia under General John POPE. On August 9, 1862, he again tangled with General Ambrose P. HILL at Cedar Mountain, Virginia, being badly defeated and driven from the field. By this time, complaints about Banks's lackluster leadership reached the ears of the Joint Committee on the Conduct of the War, but Lincoln, who needed the general for political reasons, refused to dismiss him outright. Therefore, in November 1862, he was sent to New Orleans, Louisiana, to replace another controversial "political general," Benjamin F. BUTLER.

Once in charge, Banks moderated Butler's harsh policies toward Southerners, released political prisoners, and opened churches to worship. He also organized new elections under the old state constitution and attempted to enfranchise African Americans. But whatever goodwill these moves

Union general Nathaniel P. Banks *(Massachusetts Commandery Military Order of the Loyal Legion and the U.S. Army Military History Institute)*

generated was irretrievably lost once Banks authorized recruitment of former slaves as the Corps d'Afrique. In the spring of 1863, Banks returned to the field by acting in concert with Union forces under General Ulysses S. GRANT at Vicksburg, Mississippi. His objective was to reduce the fortified enclave at Port Hudson, Louisiana, possession of which would clear navigation along the Mississippi River. But Banks again stumbled badly; despite clear numerical superiority, he proved unable to defeat the garrison of General Franklin Gardner, and he was repulsed bloodily in three major attacks on May 27, June 11, and June 14, 1862. It was not until word of Vicksburg's fall

arrived that Gardner finally capitulated on July 9 after Banks sustained 3,000 casualties. For the rest of the year, he remained occupied with several fruitless expeditions along the Texas coast, which achieved nothing.

Despite open grumbling about ineptitude, Banks received his most important military assignment in the spring of 1864 when General Henry W. HALLECK ordered him to mount a joint expedition up the Red River and into east Texas. As usual, Banks was lackadaisical in his leadership and commenced operations several weeks behind schedule. After bloodlessly seizing Alexandria, Louisiana, he proceeded overland by a narrow road toward his next objective at Shreveport. His tardy deployment induced Confederates under General Richard TAYLOR to attack him at Sabine Cross Roads on April 9, 1864, where Union troops were defeated heavily. The following day, Banks fought Taylor to a draw at Pleasant Hill; nonetheless, he continued his retreat back to New Orleans. En route, the accompanying gunboat squadron of Admiral David D. PORTER nearly was lost on the Red River due to falling water levels, and only the intercession of Colonel Joseph Baily, an engineer, saved the gunboats. Shortly after arriving at New Orleans in June, Banks finally was supplanted by General Edward R. S. CANBY. He never again held a field command and resigned his commission in August 1865.

After the war, Banks resumed his political activities with considerable success, returning to Congress repeatedly. Always eager to gain an advantage, he constantly switched allegiances from Republican to Democratic and back again as suited his needs. Banks died at Waltham, Massachusetts, on September 1, 1894, having been one of the more dismal political appointees of the Civil War.

Further Reading

Ayers, Thomas. *Dark and Bloody Ground: The Battle of Mansfield and the Forgotten Civil War in Louisiana.* Dallas: Taylor Trade, 2001.
Bounds, Steve, and Curtis Milbourn. "The Battle of Mansfield." *North & South* 6, no. 2 (2003): 26–41.

Dawson, Joseph G. "Lincoln's Political Generals." Unpublished Ph.D. diss., Texas A & M University, 2004.

Forsyth, Michael J. *The Red River Campaign of 1864 and the Loss by the Confederacy of the Civil War.* Jefferson, N.C.: McFarland, 2002.

Gallagher, Gary W. *The Shenandoah Valley Campaign of 1862.* Chapel Hill: University of North Carolina Press, 2003.

Goss, Thomas J. *The War within the Union High Command: Politics and Generalship during the Civil War.* Lawrence: University Press of Kansas, 2003.

Joiner, Gary D. *Through the Howling Wilderness: the 1864 Red River Campaign of Union Failure in the West.* Knoxville: University of Tennessee Press, 2006.

Persons, Benjamin S. *From This Valley They Say You Are Leaving: The Union Red River Campaign, March 1864 to May 1865.* Bloomington, Ind.: 1st Books Library, 2003.

Beauregard, Pierre G. T. (1818–1893)

Confederate general

Pierre Gustave Toutant Beauregard was born in St. Bernard Parish, Louisiana, on May 28, 1818, the son of French parents. Throughout life, his somewhat short stature seemed offset by a towering ego. In 1834, he gained admittance to the U.S. Military Academy and, studious disciple of Napoleon that he was, graduated second in his class four years later. Among his friends and classmates was Irvin McDowell, a future Union general. Beauregard, now a second lieutenant in the elite Corps of Engineers, subsequently held a number of important construction positions along the East Coast. He served for a decade, acquitting himself well in numerous assignments, and in 1847, General Winfield Scott appointed him a staff engineer. Beauregard fought with distinction during the Mexican War, being wounded twice and winning two brevet promotions for bravery at Veracruz, Cerro Gordo, and Contreras. Privately—and consistent with his tempestuous disposition—Beauregard fumed over not receiving greater recognition for his talents. After the war, he resumed his construction and engineering activities, which culminated in the prestigious appointment as superintendent of cadets at West Point on January 23, 1861.

Unfortunately, secession was in the wind, and when Beauregard made some impolitic remarks about Southern rights, he was dismissed from office four days later. He lingered on in the military until Louisiana left the Union in February 1861 and then resigned his commission and offered his service to the Confederate States of America.

On March 1, 1861, President Jefferson DAVIS appointed Beauregard a brigadier general in the Confederate army and appointed him commander of Southern forces at Charleston, South Carolina. This placed him at the very center of secessionist activities, for Confederate authorities remained flummoxed over what to do with the Federal garrison ensconced at Fort Sumter. On April 12, 1861, Beauregard received orders to bombard Major Robert ANDERSON into submission, an act precipitating the bloodiest conflict in U.S. history. For his role, Beauregard became lionized throughout the South as a Confederate hero. He was next appointed

Confederate general Pierre G. T. Beauregard *(National Archives)*

to command Confederate forces assembled for the defense of Virginia. He was technically second in command to General Joseph E. JOHNSTON, but the latter was diplomatic enough to allow him to conduct the battle and secure the Southern victory over General McDowell at Bull Run on July 21, 1861. However, success exacerbated tensions with President Davis, for Beauregard strongly felt that the defeated Federals should have been pursued to the very gates of Washington, D.C., and his tactless and public remarks about the president led to their permanent estrangement. Nevertheless, on August 13, 1861, the banty leader received promotion to lieutenant general and was sent west to serve with the Army of Mississippi under General Albert S. JOHNSTON. On a lighter note, Beauregard also found the time to design the famous "Stars and Bars" Confederate battle flag, which has symbolized the South ever since.

Beauregard helped formulate the overly complicated plan for the April 6, 1861, Battle of Shiloh, which nearly destroyed the army of General Ulysses S. GRANT. After Johnston was killed in action, Beauregard continued leading the army until an influx of Union reinforcements drove him from the field on April 7. He then skillfully extricated his command but further sullied his reputation with Davis by trying to portray the encounter as a victory. A month later, Beauregard was forced to yield the strategic railroad junction of Corinth, Mississippi, to General Henry W. HALLECK, which did little to endear him to Confederate authorities. Then, reeling from chronic throat pain, Beauregard took an unauthorized medical leave, which handed the president a pretext for relieving him of command—permanently. His fateful replacement was General Braxton BRAGG, a Davis sycophant and a decidedly uneven military leader. After recuperating, Beauregard ventured back east to accept command of the Department of South Carolina, Georgia, and Florida, headquartered at Charleston. His most successful accomplishment was repelling the April 1863 naval assault by Admiral Samuel F. DU PONT, along with lesser attacks mounted by his successor, Admiral John A. B. DAHLGREN. His per-

formance was impressive enough for General Robert E. LEE to invite him to serve with the Army of Northern Virginia, but Beauregard remained coy and held out for an independent command. Accordingly, on April 23, 1864, he was appointed head of the newly renamed Department of North Carolina and Southern Virginia.

Beauregard performed his finest work in the defense of Petersburg, Virginia, which brought the Confederate war effort several additional months of life. On May 16, 1864, he drove back larger Union forces under General Benjamin F. BUTLER from Drewry's Heights, Virginia, effectively sealing his Army of the James in the peninsula of Bermuda Hundred. But Beauregard also took it upon himself to bombard Confederate headquarters with myriads of hopelessly Napoleonic schemes for winning the war, which drove President Davis to distraction. Eager to rid himself of this irksome leader, Davis once again transferred Beauregard to command of the Department of the West, an administrative position created to coordinate all Confederate forces in Mississippi, Alabama, Georgia, and the Carolinas. When his best efforts failed to contain the army of General William T. SHERMAN from taking Atlanta and Savannah, Georgia, Beauregard returned east again to command Southern forces in South Carolina. He and General Joe Johnston both surrendered to Sherman on April 18, 1865, closing a controversial military career.

Back in civilian life, Beauregard served as president of the Jackson and Mississippi Railroad and also managed to direct the Louisiana State Lottery Commission. He also engaged in a heated, no-holds-barred publishing war with Johnston and Davis over who, precisely, lost the Confederacy. The contentious, capable Beauregard, popularly known as "Napoleon in Gray," died at New Orleans on February 21, 1893.

Further Reading
Arnold, James R. *Shiloh, 1862: The Death of Innocence.* Westport, Conn.: Praeger, 2004.
Beauregard, Pierre G. T. *A Commentary on the Campaign and Battle of Manassas.* New York: G. P. Putnam's Sons, 1891.

Detzer, David. *Donnybrook: The Battle of Bull Run.* San Diego: Harcourt, 2004.

Echelberry, Earl. "War Cloud Lowering." *Military Heritage* 3, no. 1 (2001): 48–46, 58–59, 98.

Engel, Stephen D. *Struggle for the Heartland: The Campaign from Fort Henry to Corinth.* Lincoln: University of Nebraska Press, 2001.

Gallagher, Gary W., and Joseph T. Glatthaar, eds. *Leaders of the Lost Cause: New Perspectives on the Confederate High Command.* Mechanicsburg, Pa.: Stackpole Books, 2004.

Jones, Wilmer L. *Generals in Blue and Gray.* 2 vols. Westport, Conn.: Praeger, 2004.

Martin, David G. *The Shiloh Campaign, March–April 1862.* Cambridge, Mass.: Da Capo Press, 2003.

Rafuse, Ethan S. *A Single Grand Victory: The First Campaign and Battle of Manassas.* Wilmington, Del.: Scholarly Resources, 2002.

Bragg, Braxton (1817–1876)

Confederate general

Braxton Bragg was born in Warrenton, North Carolina, on March 22, 1817, the son of a wealthy planter. Well educated at a local military academy, he entered the U.S. Military Academy in 1833 and graduated four years later, fifth in his class. Bragg then received a lieutenant's commission in the 3rd U.S. Artillery and fought competently in the Second Seminole War despite repeated bouts with fever. By this time, he had acquired a reputation as a stern, competent officer, but one combative and garrulously disposed. Bragg also began to exhibit what today might be considered a persecution complex, for he continually complained about being ignored and neglected. None of this interfered with his performance in the Mexican War (1846–48), which proved exemplary. Bragg received three brevet promotions while serving under General Zachary Taylor, and his handling of cannon at the Battle of Buena Vista undoubtedly saved the American army from defeat. After the war, Bragg returned to his usual routine of frontier garrison duty, with its concomitant slow promotions, and he angrily brooded over his lack of official recognition. Fed up with an indifferent military bureaucracy, he resigned his commission

Confederate general Braxton Bragg *(Library of Congress)*

in March 1855 and retired to Louisiana to run a sugar plantation.

As the Civil War approached in the spring of 1861, Bragg, on paper at least, appeared to be one of the more promising Confederate officers. Commissioned a brigadier general on February 23, 1861, he gained appointment as commander of coastal defenses between Pensacola, Florida, and Mobile, Alabama, winning plaudits for military administration and his ability to train raw recruits. Consequently, he rose to major general in January 1862 and received the II Corps in the then-forming Army of Mississippi under General Albert S. JOHNSTON. In this capacity, he distinguished himself at the Battle of Shiloh (April 6–7, 1862) until Union reinforcements prompted a Confederate withdrawal. The following June, General Pierre G. T. BEAUREGARD departed the theater on sick leave, and President Jefferson DAVIS, Bragg's longtime confidant, appointed him head of the Army of Mississippi. Bragg immediately took to the offensive and, in a fine display of administrative mettle, expertly shuttled his troops by rail from Mississippi to the gates of Kentucky. His ensuing invasion kept Union forces off balance for several weeks despite only sullen cooperation from General Edmund KIRBY-SMITH. Bragg was well positioned to capture the strategic Union base at Louisville, but he allowed himself to become caught up in the politics of creating a Confederate government at Frankfort. This distraction allowed Federals under General Don C. BUELL to occupy Louisville, receive reinforcements, and finally confront the Confederates at Perryville, Kentucky, on October 8, 1862. The result was a bloody standoff that ended Bragg's invasion, and he fell back through the Cumberland Gap into Tennessee. The following month, his force was renamed the Army of Tennessee, which faced a new adversary in General William S. ROSECRANS. After retreating before superior Union forces, Bragg suddenly turned and pounced on Rosecrans at the Battle of Murfreesboro (Stone's River) (December 30, 1862–January 3, 1863), another bloody encounter. Both sides suffered heavy losses, and the Confederates came close to driving Rosecrans from the field, but in the end, Bragg was forced to retreat again. Heavy casualties among Kentuckian troops also led to accusations of abuse by their commander, General John C. BRECKINRIDGE. Bragg's inability to win, coupled with a recalcitrant disposition that alienated superiors and subordinates alike, prompted calls for his dismissal. President Davis, unfortunately, remained loyal to his old friend, and no action was taken.

Confederate fortunes in the West continued declining throughout 1863. During the summer months, Rosecrans's Army of the Cumberland brilliantly outmaneuvered Bragg near Tullahoma, Tennessee, forcing the Southerners to abandon the city without a shot. Bragg simply fell back to the mountains of northern Georgia where he was reinforced by General James LONGSTREET's I Corps before suddenly and violently attacking Rosecrans at Chickamauga on September 19–20, 1863. The Confederates finally prevailed in this bloody slugfest, although their casualties were heavier due to Bragg's repeated use of frontal assaults. Worse, he failed to promptly pursue and destroy Rosecrans's shattered army, now holed up at Chattanooga, Tennessee, which Bragg was content to simply besiege. Discontent with his leadership was rife, and General Nathan B. FORREST became so angered by Bragg's lethargy that they nearly dueled, and he requested a transfer elsewhere. Continuing disagreement with General Longstreet also resulted in the latter's assignment to besiege Knoxville just as Union forces under General Ulysses S. GRANT were building up strength for a counterattack. The hammer fell on Bragg on November 23, 1863, when the Army of Tennessee was routed from heights ringing Chattanooga and he withdrew back to Dalton, Georgia. Bragg, his own confidence severely depleted, requested to be relieved of command, and he was replaced by General Joseph E. JOHNSTON on December 1, 1863.

By the spring of 1864, Bragg was back in Richmond, Virginia, acting as a senior military adviser to his old friend President Davis. In this capacity, one of the most fateful tasks he performed was recommending that General Johnston be replaced by General John B. HOOD. That October, Bragg shifted to North Carolina to assist in the defense of Fort Fisher at Wilmington. When that fort fell to Union forces on January 15, 1865, he was criticized severely for failing to rush badly needed reinforcements to its defense. For the next four months, he functioned as a divisional commander under General Johnston and finally surrendered with him on April 18, 1865. After the war, Bragg found work in Alabama as superintendent of public works and then relocated to Galveston, Texas, where he worked as chief engineer of the Gulf, Colorado, and Santa Fe Railroad. He died in Galveston on September 27, 1876, a good fighter and a talented soldier but temperamentally unsuited for the demanding nuances of high command.

Further Reading

Bradley, Michael R. *Tullahoma: The 1863 Campaign for the Control of Middle Tennessee.* Shippensburg, Pa.: Burd Street Press, 2000.

Broadwater, Robert P. *The Battle of Perryville, 1862: Culmination of the Failed Kentucky Campaign.* Jefferson, N.C.: McFarland, 2006.

Daniel, Larry J. *Cannoneers in Gray: The Field Artillery of the Army of Tennessee, 1861–1865.* Tuscaloosa: University of Alabama Press, 2005.

Gallagher, Gary W., and Joseph T. Glatthaar, eds. *Leaders of the Lost Cause: New Perspectives on the Confederate High Command.* Mechanicsburg, Pa.: Stackpole Books, 2004.

Haughton, Andrew. *Training, Tactics and Leadership in the Confederate Army of Tennessee: Seeds of Failure.* Portland, Ore.: Frank Cass, 2000.

Hess, Earl J. *Banners to the Breeze: The Kentucky Campaign, Corinth, and Stones River.* Lincoln: University of Nebraska Press, 2000.

Lepa, Jack H. *The Civil War in Tennessee, 1862–1863.* Jefferson, N.C.: McFarland, 2007.

McCaslin, Richard B. *The Last Stronghold: The Campaign for Fort Fisher.* Abilene, Tex.: McWhiney Foundation Press, 2003.

Spruill, Mat. *Storming the Heights: A Guide to the Battle of Chattanooga.* Knoxville: University of Tennessee Press, 2003.

Breckinridge, John C. (1821–1875)

Confederate general

John Cabell Breckinridge was born near Lexington, Kentucky, on January 16, 1821, into one of that state's most prominent political families. He was educated at Centre College, the College of New Jersey, and Transylvania College with degrees in law, being carefully groomed to continue the family's tradition of public service. Shortly after opening his law practice in Kentucky, Breckinridge obtained a major's commission in the 3rd Kentucky Regiment and briefly served in the Mexican War (1846–48). He failed to see combat but did act as a legal adviser to General Gideon J. Pillow in his dispute with General Winfield Scott. Once back home, Breckinridge's drive, intellect, and family name catapulted him into the political arena with a seat in the state house of representatives. In 1856, and much to his surprise, the promising young politician was nominated as James Buchanan's vice presidential candidate and won.

At age 35, he thus became the youngest individual ever to occupy that office. Breckinridge was largely ignored by the Buchanan administration as the president's attention was increasingly preoccupied by mounting sectional tensions over the issue of slavery and secession. Though a slave owner himself, Breckinridge felt that the institution was doomed, and he also worked tirelessly against secession among firebrand Southerners. When the Democratic Party split along regional lines in 1860, these same extremists nominated him as their presidential candidate, despite his open disdain for their position. He nonetheless proffered himself as a moderate alternative to Abraham Lincoln, who went on to win the election. Breckinridge was then appointed to serve in the U.S. Senate by the Kentucky state legislature, commencing in January 1861.

Confederate general John C. Breckinridge *(Massachusetts Commandery Military Order of the Loyal Legion and the U.S. Army Military History Institute)*

In the Senate, Breckinridge defended the right of Southern states to secede, although he invariably cautioned against it. The Civil War commenced in April 1861, and five months later a Federal court in Kentucky ordered Breckinridge arrested for treason. He then fled to the Confederacy, received a brigadier general's commission the following November, and set about organizing the famous "Orphan Brigade" for Kentucky expatriates like himself. Despite his lack of formal military training, Breckinridge performed ably under General Albert S. JOHNSTON at the April 6–7, 1862, Battle of Shiloh, where he commanded the reserves. He rose to major general in June 1862 and, on August 5, 1862, led an ill-fated attack against Union troops at Baton Rouge, Louisiana, that nearly succeeded. He then marched north to serve under General William J. HARDEE's corps in the Army of Tennessee. Breckinridge again distinguished himself in combat at Murfreesboro (December 31, 1862–January 3, 1863), although his brigade sustained heavy losses from Union artillery fire. He consequently quarreled with commanding General Braxton BRAGG over the mistreatment of his men and was urged by many subordinates to duel with him. Breckinridge, fortunately, transferred south again before personal resentments culminated in tragedy.

Breckinridge subsequently joined the army of General Joseph E. JOHNSTON and fought in the defense of Jackson, Mississippi. He then transferred back to the Army of Tennessee as part of General Daniel H. HILL's division, performing well at the bloody Battle of Chickamauga, September 19–20, 1863. His good performance resulted in command of an understrength corps during the Battle of Chattanooga, November 25, 1863, another heavy Confederate defeat. To prevent another collision with Bragg, who accused Breckinridge of being drunk, President Jefferson DAVIS interceded by transferring the disgruntled Kentuckian east to replace General John H. MORGAN as head of the Department of Southwest Virginia. Breckinridge was now responsible for the defense of the Shenandoah Valley, the "breadbasket of the Confederacy," and on May 15, 1864, he defeated a larger Union force under General Franz SIGEL at New Market. This engagement witnessed the deployment of 247 youthful cadets (or "Katydids") from the nearby Virginia Military Institute, whose outstanding behavior that bloody day entered Southern folklore. Breckinridge then transferred again to the Army of Northern Virginia under General Robert E. LEE, where he rendered useful service in fighting at Cold Harbor on June 3, 1864. That summer, he accompanied General Jubal A. EARLY back to the Shenandoah Valley, where he again fought valorously and futilely against superior numbers under General Philip H. SHERIDAN. Breckinridge then returned west once more to the Army of Tennessee, this time under General John B. HOOD and saw active service at the defeat at Nashville, Tennessee, on December 15–16, 1864. In February 1865 President Davis appointed Breckinridge to be his final secretary of war. His most significant contribution was in convincing the president to end the war honorably and not besmirch the Confederacy's name by resorting to guerrilla warfare. "This has been a magnificent epic," he maintained, "In God's name let it not terminate in a farce."

After the fall of Richmond in April 1865, Breckinridge rejoined Johnston in North Carolina, where he served as a negotiator in surrender negotiations with General William T. SHERMAN. Fearing arrest, he then fled to Cuba and Britain, remaining abroad for three years. Breckinridge, under a general amnesty in 1868, finally returned to Kentucky, where he resumed his legal activities. Thereafter, he also served as a spokesman for national reconciliation and formally denounced the infamous Ku Klux Klan for violence against African Americans. Breckinridge died of physical exhaustion in Lexington, Kentucky, on May 17, 1875, aged but 54 years. On balance, he was probably the most gifted "political general" of either side.

Further Reading

Davis, William C. *Honorable Defeat: The Last Days of the Confederate Government.* New York: Harcourt, 2001.

Haines, J. D. *Put the Boys In: The Story of the Virginia Military Institute Cadets at the Battle of New Market.* Austin, Tex.: Eakin Press, 2003.

Heenhan, Jim. "Final Attack at Stones River." *Military Heritage* 5, no. 2 (2003): 52–59.

Hess, Earl J. *Banners to the Breeze: The Kentucky Campaign, Corinth, and Stones River.* Lincoln: University of Nebraska Press, 2000.

Jones, Wilmer L. *Generals in Blue and Gray.* 2 vols. Westport, Conn.: Praeger, 2004.

Lepa, Jack H. *The Shenandoah Valley Campaign of 1864.* Jefferson, N.C.: McFarland, 2003.

Naisawald, L. Van Loan, and James I. Robertson. *The Battle of Lynchburg: Seize Lynchburg–If Only for a Single Day.* Lynchburg, Va.: Warwick House Pub., 2004.

Buchanan, Franklin (1800–1874)

Confederate admiral

Franklin Buchanan was born in Baltimore, Maryland, on September 17, 1800, and he commenced his long association with naval affairs by becoming a midshipman on January 28, 1815. He first sailed with Commodore Oliver H. Perry onboard the frigate USS *Java* and spent the next two decades performing routine work with a variety of squadrons. Buchanan invariably acquitted himself well, rising to lieutenant in January 1825 and commander in September 1841. After he commanded the steam frigate *Mississippi* and the sloop *Vincennes,* Secretary of the Navy George Bancroft tasked him with drafting plans for a new naval academy to be constructed at Annapolis, Maryland. Buchanan's scheme proved so thorough that Bancroft appointed him to serve as the first superintendent in 1845. In this capacity, he grafted his own sense for high academics and no-nonsense discipline onto the curriculum and gave that institution its successful start. Buchanan then petitioned for active duty once the war with Mexico erupted in 1846, and in March 1847 he received command of the sloop *Germantown*. He then accompanied the squadrons of commodores David C. Conner and Matthew C. Perry in various actions around the Gulf of Mexico, winning high praise for competence and bravery. In 1853

Confederate admiral Franklin Buchanan *(U.S. Navy)*

Buchanan was selected to command Perry's flagship *Susquehanna* on its fateful voyage to establish diplomatic relations with Japan. He remained in Asia for two years before returning home to administer the Washington Navy Yard as a captain in 1855.

As a Southerner, Buchanan mistakenly believed that his native state of Maryland was about to secede, and he tendered his resignation on April 22, 1861. Maryland, however, stayed loyal to the Union, but when Buchanan petitioned to withdraw his resignation, Secretary of the Navy Gideon Welles summarily refused it. For many weeks thereafter, Buchanan hovered between the two feuding camps, but in September 1861 he joined the Confederate navy as a captain posted with the Bureau of Orders and Details. He functioned well, but Buchanan, a strident man of action, chafed as a bureaucrat and agitated for a more active role. In February 1862 he then received command of the

James River Squadron and spent several weeks supervising conversion of the captured steam frigate *Merrimac* into the armored ram CSS *Virginia*. On March 8, 1862, Buchanan forever altered the nature of naval warfare by steaming off to engage the Union blockading squadron at Hampton Roads, Virginia. In a fierce, one-sided action, he quickly sank the wooden frigate *Cumberland* and drove another wooden vessel, the *Congress*, aground. Ironically, his younger brother was an officer on board this vessel. This action also marked the immediate ascendancy of iron warships. Buchanan, who exposed himself fearlessly in the battle, was struck by a bullet fired from the shoreline and severely injured. Consequently, he missed the legendary duel with the Union ironclad *Monitor* on the following day. In light of his performance at the helm of *Virginia*, he became the Confederacy's first admiral on August 21, 1862.

For the next two years, Buchanan applied his considerable skills at improving the defenses of Mobile, Alabama, a significant Confederate port. He also oversaw construction of four new ironclads, of which only one, the *Tennessee*, was in service when Union forces attacked on August 5, 1864. That memorable day, Admiral David G. FARRAGUT braved Confederate guns and minefields and ran his squadron directly into the bay, sweeping aside feeble Southern opposition. Buchanan, badly outnumbered, might have enjoyed better success employing his armored ships as floating batteries, but he unhesitatingly threw *Tennessee* against the entire Union squadron and tried repeatedly to ram the *Hartford*, Farragut's flagship. Wounded again and his vessel badly damaged, Buchanan struck his flag and surrendered. He remained a prisoner until March 1865, when he was paroled and returned to Mobile. He surrendered there a second time the following May and left the Confederate service. After the war, Buchanan served as president of the University of Maryland before dying in Talbot County, Maryland, on May 11, 1874. He was among the Confederacy's bravest and most accomplished naval leaders.

Further Reading

Campbell, R. Thomas. *Confederate Phoenix: The CSS Virginia*. Shippensburg, Pa.: Burd Street Press, 2001.

———. *Iron Courage: Confederate Ironclads in the War Between the States*. Shippensburg, Pa.: Burd Street Press, 2002.

Friend, Jack. *West Wind, Flood Tide: The Battle of Mobile Bay*. Annapolis, Md.: Naval Institute Press, 2003.

Garcia, Pedro. "Through a Gate of Fire." *Military Heritage* 4, no. 3 (2002): 62–75.

Park, Carl D. *Ironclad Down: The USS Merrimack-CSS Virginia from Construction to Destruction*. Annapolis, Md.: Naval Institute Press, 2007.

Silverstone, Paul H. *Civil War Navies, 1855–1883*. Annapolis, Md.: Naval Institute Press, 2001.

Symonds, Craig L. "Rank and Rancor in the Confederate Navy." *MHQ* 14, no. 2 (2002): 14–19.

Buell, Don C. (1818–1898)

Union general

Don Carlos Buell was born near Marietta, Ohio, on March 23, 1818, the son of a businessman. He attended the U.S. Military Academy in 1837 and graduated four years later in the lower half of his class. Buell then received his lieutenant's commission in the 3rd U.S. Infantry, with whom he initially fought in the closing stages of Florida's Second Seminole War. He subsequently transferred to General Zachary Taylor's Army of Texas to fight in the Mexican War (1846–48). Buell distinguished himself in combat at Monterrey, Contreras, and Churubusco, winning two brevet promotions and becoming badly wounded. Now a captain, he next fulfilled a variety of outpost duties along the frontier before transferring to the adjutant general's office in the Department of the Pacific. In 1859 he was briefly attached to the secretary of war's office and then returned east just as the Civil War seemed imminent. Recalled to Washington, Buell became a brigadier general on May 17, 1861, and helped organize Washington, D.C.'s defenses before receiving a division in General George B. McCLELLAN's Army of the Potomac. Holding a well-deserved reputation for efficiency, administration, and strategy, he was considered one of the Union army's most promising officers, and much was expected of him.

In November 1861 Buell transferred west once more, replacing General William T. SHERMAN as head of the Department of the Ohio. He then received orders to secure Nashville, Tennessee, but vacillated until General Ulysses S. GRANT first secured Forts Henry and Donelson in February 1862. Buell was nonetheless promoted to major general of volunteers and ordered to continue advancing down the Tennessee River in support of Grant. On the evening of April 6, 1862, his army reached Pittsburg Landing after the first day of costly fighting at the Battle of Shiloh, and on the following morning, Buell attacked and drove off Confederates under General Pierre G. T. BEAURE-GARD. That May, under the jurisdiction of General Henry W. HALLECK, he participated in the glacial campaign against Corinth, Mississippi. On June 10, 1862, Buell commanded four divisions in an attempt to repair the Memphis and Charleston Railroad leading to Chattanooga, Tennessee. This proved tedious work, and his efforts were greatly vexed by Confederate raiding activities under General John H. MORGAN. Consequently, Chattanooga was occupied by the Confederate Army of Tennessee under General Braxton BRAGG, who then prepared to invade Union-held territory farther north.

The turning point in Buell's fortunes occurred in August 1862 when Confederate armies under Generals Bragg and Edmund KIRBY-SMITH invaded Kentucky. With his base at Louisville now threatened, Buell hastily marched north to Louisville and managed to secure it while Bragg was at Frankfort installing a Confederate government. Once reinforced and resupplied, Buell prepared for a military showdown with Bragg. The War Department, however, had tired of what they considered Buell's lethargic leadership and ordered him to turn command of the Army of the Ohio over to General George H. THOMAS. But Thomas, a loyal subordinate, declined the appointment seeing that Buell was nearly ready to attack, and the latter retained his command. On October 8, 1862,

he encountered Bragg at Perryville, Kentucky, and a bloody battle raged. Buell enjoyed numerical superiority of 55,000 to 15,000—roughly three to one—but Bragg nearly managed to drive the Federals from the field before finally retreating. Buell, however, manifestly failed to pursue the defeated Southerners, and they leisurely withdrew through the Cumberland Gap and back into Tennessee. For this reason, he was relieved of command by the War Department on October 24, 1862, and was replaced by General William S. ROSECRANS.

Buell angrily contested his dismissal, claiming he was short on supplies, and demanded a court of inquiry. His claims were then investigated for several months, but the military commission issued a report without recommendation. Buell thus remained "awaiting orders" for the next two years until his term as general of volunteers expired. On June 1, 1864, Buell also resigned his

Don Carlos Buell *(Massachusetts Commandery Military Order of the Loyal Legion and the U.S. Army Military History Institute)*

regular army commission and left the service altogether. He then retired to Louisville as president of the Green River Iron Works until his death there on November 19, 1898. Buell retains the reputation as a talented disciplinarian and administrator but an essentially uninspired and plodding performer.

Further Reading

Broadwater, Robert P. *The Battle of Perryville, 1862: Culmination of the Failed Kentucky Campaign.* Jefferson, N.C.: McFarland, 2006.

Engle, Stephen D. *Don Carlos Buell: Most Promising of All.* Chapel Hill: University of North Carolina Press, 1999.

Hess, Earl J. *Banners to the Breeze: The Kentucky Campaign, Corinth, and Stones River.* Lincoln: University of Nebraska Press, 2000.

Noe, Kenneth. *Perryville: This Grand Havoc of Battle.* Lexington: University Press of Kentucky, 2001.

Prokopowicz, Gerald J. *All for the Regiment: The Army of the Ohio, 1861–1862.* Chapel Hill: University of North Carolina Press, 2001.

Ross, Charles D. *Civil War Acoustic Shadows.* Shippensburg, Pa.: White Mane Books, 2001.

Union general John Buford *(Library of Congress)*

Buford, John (1826–1863)

Union general

John Buford was born in Woodford, Kentucky, on March 4, 1826, and he relocated with his family to Rock Island, Illinois. From there he gained admittance to the U.S. Military Academy in 1844 and graduated four years later as a second lieutenant in the 2nd U.S. Dragoons. Buford then proceeded to the frontier, where he performed routine service in Texas, New Mexico, and Kansas for several years. In 1855 he rose to regimental quartermaster and that year accompanied General William S. Harney in a war against the Sioux. Buford fought well at the Battle of Ash Hollow, September 3, 1855, in which Little Thunder's band was defeated, and he won commendations from Colonel Philip St. George Cooke. Two years later, Buford accompanied Colonel Albert S. JOHNSTON in his Mormon Expedition of 1857–58, expertly handling quartermaster functions across a grueling, 1,000

mile, midwinter march. Buford rose to captain on March 9, 1859, and was serving with the regiment in Utah when the Civil War erupted in April 1861. To underscore his expertise in handling cavalry, he marched the 2nd Dragoons 1,500 miles to Washington, D.C., in only 60 days. Despite his consistently excellent performance, Buford remained unable to secure an independent command and spent the first year of the war as a major on the Inspector General's staff.

In July 1862 General John POPE arrived in the East to command of the newly constituted Army of Virginia and was appalled to find Buford, one of the military's most experienced cavalry officers, behind a desk. He thereupon appointed him a brigade commander with a rank of brigadier general. In this capacity, Buford defeated Confederate cavalry at Verdiersville, Virginia, on August 17, 1862, capturing the plumed hat of General J. E. B. STUART and signed orders from General Robert E. LEE. He fought equally well against superior Confederate numbers at Thoroughfare Gap on August 28–29 before being brushed aside by General James LONGSTREET's I Corps. In the process, Buford alerted Pope of Longstreet's arrival on his left flank, but the general failed to act on this valuable intelligence, and his army was nearly destroyed. On August 30 Buford received a severe wound while covering the Army of Virginia's retreat, but his good performance resulted in an appointment as chief of cavalry in the Army of the Potomac under General Joseph HOOKER. He next bore a conspicuous role in General George Stoneman's raid during the Chancellorsville campaign of May 1863 and again covered the Union retreat. On June 9 Buford gained additional laurels by turning in a fine performance at Brandy Station, June 9, 1863, under General Alfred PLEASONTON, affording additional proof that Union troopers had closed the qualitative gap with their Southern counterparts.

The war in the East took a new direction when General Lee struck north into Union territory and invaded Pennsylvania. Buford, having skirmished intermittently with Stuart's troopers at Aldie, Gap, Upperville, Middleburg, and Ashby's Gap, Virginia, covered the left flank of the I Corps under General John REYNOLDS. On arriving at the strategic road junction at Gettysburg, Buford encountered and drove off Confederate infantry in the area. He then promptly alerted superiors, dismounted his troopers, and prepared for combat along McPherson's Ridge. On July 1, elements of General Henry HETH's Confederate division stumbled headlong into Buford's position while foraging for shoes and were heavily repelled by his rapid-fire Spencer carbines. As more and more combatants were thrown in from both sides, Buford dutifully clung to the crossroads until he was relieved by Reynolds. He then shifted his forces to oppose the approaching corps of General Richard S. EWELL, delaying them several hours. His tenacious conduct allowed the main Union force under General George MEADE to occupy the high ground overlooking Gettysburg, a major factor in the ensuing Confederate defeat.

After Gettysburg, Buford skirmished intermittently with the Confederate rear guard and fought in a heavy action near Williamsport, Maryland on July 6, 1863. The following November, his fortunes crested with an appointment as cavalry commander in the Army of the Cumberland. Buford, unfortunately, was stricken with typhoid and obtained a badly needed medical leave. He died in the house of General Stoneman on December 16, 1863, just hours after President Abraham LINCOLN promoted him to major general. His death was a serious loss to the Army of the Potomac, particularly its mounted arm.

Further Reading

Longacre, Edward G. General John Buford: A Military Biography. Cambridge, Mass.: Da Capo Press, 2003.

McKinney, Joseph W. Brandy Station, Virginia, June 9, 1863: The Largest Cavalry Battle of the Civil War. Jefferson, N.C.: McFarland, 2006.

Newton, Steven H. McPherson's Ridge: The First Battle for the High Ground, July 1, 1863. Cambridge, Mass.: Da Capo Press, 2002.

Phipps, Michael. "The Devil's to Pay": General John Buford, United States Army. Gettysburg, Pa.: Farnsworth House Military Impressions, 1995.

Wittenberg, Eric J. The Union Cavalry Comes of Age: Hartwood's Church to Brandy Station, 1863. Dulles, Va.: Brassey's, 2005.

Burnside, Ambrose E. (1824–1881)

Union general

Ambrose Everett Burnside was born in Liberty, Indiana, on May 23, 1824, the son of a former South Carolinian who had emancipated his slaves. After working as a tailor several years, he was admitted to the U.S. Military Academy in 1843 and graduated four years later as a second lieutenant in the 3rd U.S. Artillery. Burnside arrived in Mexico during final phases of the 1846–48 war there, seeing no combat. He subsequently fulfilled routine garrison duties along the western frontier and was slightly wounded in a skirmish with Apaches. His experience in the field convinced him that cavalrymen needed better weapons than the standard-issue Hall carbine, so in 1853 he resigned his commission and established a gun factory in Bristol, Rhode Island. Burnside then designed and manufactured a functional, rapid-fire carbine for military use, but he went bankrupt when anticipated government contracts failed to materialize. Fortunately, his good friend George B. McClellan offered help in 1858 by appointing him treasurer of the Illinois Central Railroad. Burnside worked there until the Civil War broke out in April 1861. That month, he returned east to become colonel of the 1st Rhode Island Volunteers and subsequently led a brigade at Bull Run the following July. He also befriended President Abraham Lincoln, who arranged his promotion to brigadier general of volunteers on August 6, 1861.

Union general Ambrose E. Burnside *(Library of Congress)*

In October 1861 Burnside received an important assignment: He was to accompany the fleet of Commodore Louis M. Goldsborough to the North Carolina coast, establish a base, and recruit from what were believed to be thousands of Southern Unionists. He performed well at the seizure of Roanoke Island and New Bern in the spring of 1862, capturing 2,500 prisoners and 32 cannon while also closing the Albemarle and Pamlico inlets to blockade-runners. This success made him a national hero, and Lincoln rewarded him with a promotion to major general and command of the IX Corps in the Army of the Potomac under General McClellan. He had previously, perhaps conscious of his own limitations as a leader, declined Lincoln's offer to serve as the army's leader. Lincoln again proffered command of the Army of the Potomac in the wake of General John Pope's debacle at Second Manassas that August, and again Burnside demurred. He next fought at the Battle of Antietam on September 17, 1862, where he commanded both his IX Corps and General Joseph L. Hooker's I Corps. However, Burnside's performed sluggishly and, by failing to cross the Rohrbach Bridge in time, lost an opportunity to crush the Confederate left flank.

After McClellan was dismissed on November 7, 1861, Lincoln offered Burnside command of the Army of the Potomac a third time, and he reluctantly accepted. He immediately concocted an elaborate scheme to slip behind the Confederates by bridging the Rappahannock River at Fredericksburg, Virginia, and making a sudden dash on Richmond. Burnside anticipated that this maneuver would force General Robert E. Lee's army out into the open where it could be engaged to his advantage. However, pontoons and other bridging equipment were slow in arriving, and Lee had ample time to occupy and fortify Fredericksburg ahead of Union forces. On December 13 Burnside nonetheless put his plan in motion and hurled 122,000 men against Confederate fieldworks with disastrous effects: Union forces were bloodily repulsed with more than 12,000 casualties. In January 1863 Burnside further sullied his reputation by proposing a midwinter march around the Confederates, which, following the onset of heavy rain, quickly degenerated into the infamous "mud march." Lincoln, with few regrets, finally dismissed Burnside from the Army of the Potomac on January 26, 1863, and replaced him with Hooker.

In March 1863 Burnside transferred to the Department of the Ohio, where he again displayed some of his previous energy. He moved quickly to subdue "Copperhead" activities of former congressman Clement L. Vallandigham, arresting him for treason. He then promulgated General Order No. 38, which shut down two newspapers and promised swift imprisonment for any individual suspected of pro-Confederate sympathies. Ultimately, Lincoln repudiated Burnside's measures, but they proved popular with local Unionists. He then orchestrated military movements culminating in the defeat and capture of General John H. MORGAN's raiding party in Ohio. In September 1863 Burnside marshaled his forces, advanced through the Cumberland Gap, and captured Knoxville, Tennessee. Two months later, he artfully withstood a determined siege by General James LONGSTREET's veteran I Corps, thereby prevented him from rushing reinforcements to beleaguered Confederate forces at Chattanooga. For these effective actions, he received the thanks of Congress. Burnside had partially rehabilitated his reputation, so Lincoln also directed him to return to the Army of the Potomac where he resumed command of his old IX Corps under General Ulysses S. GRANT.

In the spring and summer of 1864, Burnside accompanied Grant's overland campaign against Richmond, Virginia. He fought competently at the bloody encounters of Wilderness, Spotsylvania Court House, and in the trenches of Petersburg. His downfall occurred on July 4, 1864, when he failed to support Union troops from his corps adequately as they waged the infamous Battle of the Crater, a stinging Union defeat. A court of inquiry conducted by General George G. MEADE found him at fault, although there was plenty of blame to go around, and Burnside was relieved from active duty. The fact that Meade had removed

a large contingent of specially trained African-American troops from Burnside's command prior to the battle—contributing materially to the debacle—went unmentioned. Burnside finally resigned his commission on April 15, 1865, and reentered the civilian sector.

Burnside subsequently returned to Rhode Island where he enjoyed a highly successful political career. He won three consecutive terms as governor (1866–68) before being elected to the U.S. Senate in 1874. That year, he also served as national commander of the Grand Army of the Republic, a noted veteran's organization. Burnside died in Bristol, Rhode Island, on September 13, 1881, a capable commander promoted beyond his abilities. Ironically, he is best remembered for his bushy facial whiskers, which have since entered popular lexicon as "sideburns."

Further Reading

Brooks, Victor. *The Fredericksburg Campaign: October 1862–January 1863.* Conshohocken, Pa.: Combined Publishing, 2000.

Cannan, John. *Burnside's Bridge, Antietam.* Conshohocken, Pa.: Combined Publishing, 2001.

———. *The Crater: Burnside's Assault on the Confederate Trenches, July 30, 1864.* London: Leo Cooper, 2003.

O'Reilly, Francis A. *The Fredericksburg Campaign: Winter War on the Rappahannock.* Baton Rouge: Louisiana State University Press, 2003.

Pfanz, Donald C. *War So Terrible: A Popular History of the Battle of Fredericksburg.* Richmond, Va.: Page One History Publications, 2003.

Rable, George. *Fredericksburg! Fredericksburg!* Chapel Hill: University of North Carolina Press, 2002.

Taaffe, Stephen R. *Commanding the Army of Potomac.* Lawrence: University Press of Kansas, 2006.

Wert, Jeffrey D. *The Sword of Lincoln: The Army of the Potomac.* New York: Simon and Schuster, 2005.

Butler, Benjamin F. (1818–1893)

Union general

Benjamin Franklin Butler was born in Deerfield, New Hampshire, on November 5, 1818, and, in 1838, he graduated from Waterville (Colby) College, Maine, with a law degree. He eventually

Union general Benjamin F. Butler *(Library of Congress)*

established a practice in Massachusetts but gradually forsook it in favor of a career in politics. Here, Butler demonstrated a knack for canvassing people's sympathies and was repeatedly elected to the state legislature as a Democrat. Butler also served as a major general of state militia. In 1859 he made an unsuccessful run for the governorship, and the following year, he arrived in Charleston, South Carolina, to vote for Jefferson DAVIS as the party's presidential candidate. Staunchly pro-Southern, he threw his support behind John C. BRECKINRIDGE at the breakaway convention held at Baltimore. However, once Southern states began to secede after Abraham LINCOLN's electoral victory that November, Butler quickly professed his loyalty to the Union and received a brigadier general's commission in the state militia. In this capacity, he performed critically important work in the early days of the war by taking the 8th Massachusetts Regiment into Baltimore, Maryland, suppressing pro-Confederate rioters, and then restoring rail lines and other communications to Washington, D.C. A grateful President Lincoln then appointed him the first major general of volunteers and placed him in charge of Union forces at Fortress Monroe, Virginia.

Controversy was never far from Butler's door. While at Fortress Monroe, he electrified the North and antagonized the South by refusing to return three African-American slaves who reached his camp. Declaring them "contraband of war," he allowed them to work for the army. Such a stance made him the darling of Radical Republicans, whose ranks Butler joined to enhance his standing with the government. However, Butler's indelible ineptitude manifested itself on June 10, 1861, when troops under his command badly bungled a skirmish with General John B. MAGRUDER's Confederates at Big Bethel, Virginia. Lincoln, unwilling or unable to remove such a politically valuable asset, then appointed Butler to accompany Commodore Silas H. Strigham on a six-ship expedition to Cape Hatteras, North Carolina. On August 27, 1861, Butler's 800 men helped capture Pamlico Sound, two forts, and 615 prisoners—the first Union victory after the debacle at Bull Run in July. Lincoln then granted him a leave of absence to recruit soldiers in New England while even more ambitious plans for him were developing.

In April 1862, Butler accompanied Commodore David G. FARRAGUT on an ambitious, combined expedition against New Orleans, Louisiana. On May 1, 1862, Farragut successfully ran his fleet past Southern forts and compelled the city to surrender, whereupon Butler acted as military governor. His seven-month tenure proved both controversial and acrimonious. Butler treated Southern defiance harshly. In one instance, he hanged Louisianan William Mumford for lowering an American flag. He also thwarted invective heaped on his troops by Creole ladies through his infamous Order No. 28, the much reviled "Woman Order," which required all disrespectful females to be treated as prostitutes. The Southern press was enraged by Butler's cavalier attitude and dubbed him "Beast Butler." Confederate president Jefferson DAVIS went so far as to brand him an outlaw and to be "immediately executed if captured." On the brighter side, Butler worked conscientiously to improve city sanitation, assist the poor, and actively recruit African-American slaves into the Union army. However, when he and several subordinates became embroiled in financial improprieties, he became more of a liability than an asset. In December 1862, President Lincoln felt emboldened enough to remove Butler from command and replace him with the equally inept general Nathaniel P. BANKS.

Butler remained inactive through 1863 while political allies pressured the president for his reinstatement. In December, he gained appointment as commanding officer of the Department of Virginia and North Carolina, and with it the Union XVIII Corps. In the spring, his command was expanded to include the X Corps and redesignated the Army of the James. With these 40,000 men Butler was supposed to work closely with General Ulysses S. GRANT in coordinating attacks against the Richmond–Petersburg line. However, in May 1864, Butler moved sluggishly against Petersburg, then lightly defended, and he was stopped in his tracks by General Pierre G. T. BEAUREGARD at the Battle of Drewry's Bluff, May 12–16. Thereafter, the Army of the James was effectively "bottled up" on the peninsula of Bermuda Hundred and was unable to participate in the struggle for Richmond. Grant wanted him removed for squandering these military assets, but Lincoln waited until his successful reelection bid in November 1864 before relieving Butler and sending him back to Massachusetts. Butler, however, still possessed powerful allies in the Republican Party, so in December 1864, he was teamed with Admiral David D. PORTER for a joint expedition against Fort Fisher outside of Wilmington, North Carolina. On December 23, Butler launched an ill-fated attempt to destroy the fort with an old vessel crammed with explosives, which this resulted in nothing but spectacular pyrotechnics. He landed his troops on December 25—and then promptly reembarked them after pronounc-

ing Fort Fisher unassailable. Such display of wanton incompetence finally prompted Grant to petition Lincoln for Butler's immediate removal, which finally materialized on January 7, 1865. Eight days later, Fort Fisher was forcefully carried by Admiral Porter and the same force under General Alfred H. TERRY. Butler remained unemployed for the remainder of the war and finally resigned his commission on November 30, 1865.

Back in civilian life, Butler resumed his successful career in politics. He was elected five times to the U.S. House of Representatives as a Radical Republican and also served one term as governor of Massachusetts in 1882. While in Congress, he helped spearhead the impeachment drive against President Andrew Johnson for his alleged lenient treatment of former Confederates. In 1884, Butler, ambitious as ever, also made an unsuccessful bid for the presidency at the head of the Greenback Party. He died in Washington, D.C., on January 1, 1893, one of the most incompetent "political generals" of the Civil War.

Further Reading

Butler, Benjamin F. *Butler's Book: Autobiography and Personal Reminiscences of Major General Benjamin F. Butler.* Boston: A. M. Thayer, 1892.

Dawson, Joseph G. "Lincoln's Political Generals." Unpublished Ph.D. diss., Texas A & M University, 2004.

Goss, Thomas J. *The War within the Union High Command: Politics and Generalship during the Civil War.* Lawrence: University Press of Kansas, 2003.

McCaslin, Richard B. *The Last Stronghold: The Campaign for Fort Fisher.* Abilene, Tex.: McWhiney Foundation Press, 2003.

Morgan, Michael. "The Beast at His Best." *Civil War Times* 42, no. 6 (2004): 24–31.

Pena, Christopher. *General Butler: Beast or Patriot: New Orleans Occupation, May–December, 1862.* Bloomington, Ind.: 1st Books, 2003.

Smith, Michael T. "The Beast Unleashed: Benjamin F. Butler and Conceptions of Masculinity in the Civil War North." *New England Quarterly* 79, no. 2 (2006): 248–276.

C

Canby, Edward R. S. (1817–1873)

Union general

Edward Richard Sprigg Canby was born at Piatt's Landing, Kentucky, on November 9, 1817, and raised in Crawfordsville, Indiana. He graduated from the U.S. Military Academy near the bottom of his class in 1839 and received a second lieutenant's commission in the 2nd U.S. Infantry. Canby then fought in Florida's Second Seminole War between 1839 and 1842 before rotating west for a stint of routine garrison duty. Promoted to captain in 1846, he accompanied General Winfield SCOTT's army the following year in the Mexican War (1846–48), winning two brevet promotions for bravery at Cerro Gordo and Churubusco. After the war, he joined the adjutant general's department of the 10th Military District in California until March 1855, when the rank of major, 10th U.S. Infantry was proffered. In this capacity, Canby marched with Colonel Albert S. JOHNSTON during the famous Mormon expedition of 1857–58 before resuming mundane garrison duties and minor campaigning against the Navajo in 1860–61.

The onset of the Civil War in April 1861 found Canby serving as commander of Fort Defiance, New Mexico Territory, and within months, he rose to colonel of the newly raised 19th U.S. Infantry. In light of his talent for military administration, he gained appointment as commander of the Department of New Mexico, headquartered at Fort Craig. His intense efforts at recruiting, training, and equipping soldiers throughout this desolate region paid dividends in the spring of 1862 when a Confederate column under General Henry H. SIBLEY invaded New Mexico from Texas. Canby unsuccessfully resisted Sibley at a hard-fought encounter near Valverde on February 21, 1862, at which point he resorted to Fabian tactics and lured his opponent farther from supply lines. Once reinforced by Colorado Volunteers under Colonel John M. Chivington, Canby resumed the offensive, attacking Sibley's scattered detachments at Glorieta Pass on March 28, 1862. When the Confederates lost their entire baggage train to a surprise Union assault, Sibley had no recourse but to fall back to Texas. Canby then shadowed the Confederates closely, skirmishing intensely at Peralta on April 15, and then allowing them to withdraw back to El Paso unmolested. His solid, if unspectacular, leadership preserved the New Mexico Territory for the Union and stopped the Confederate drive on California.

Shortly afterward, Canby was reinforced by the California column under Colonel James CARLETON and received a well-deserved promoted to brigadier general on March 31, 1862. The following September, he departed and transferred to the War Department in Washington, D.C., to serve as Secretary of War Edwin M. Stanton's assistant. Canby performed well, and in March 1863, he temporarily assumed control of troops tasked with restoring order in New York City after violent antidraft riots. On May 11, 1864, he advanced to major general and gained appointment as commander of the Military Division of West Mississippi, eventually replacing the inept general Nathaniel P. BANKS. On November 6, 1864, Canby was severely wounded in a Confederate guerrilla attack while steaming up the White River, Arkansas, but he recovered in time to orchestrate a campaign against Mobile, Alabama. In concert with troops under General Frederick Steele and a Union fleet commanded by Admiral Henry K. Thatcher, Canby conducted a methodical campaign that gradually reduced Confederate fortifications and drove the city to capitulate on April 12, 1865. After Southern resistance collapsed, Canby was called on to receive the surrender of General Richard TAYLOR's forces on May 4, 1865, followed by that of General Simon B. Buckner (representing Edmund KIRBY-SMITH) on May 26. These were the final Confederate field armies east of the Mississippi River to lay down their arms.

Canby enjoyed a highly active postwar career commencing in 1866 when he received promotion to brigadier general in the regular army. He also headed on Reconstruction efforts in Virginia and the Carolinas, becoming the only military figure to lead more than one department. In August 1870, Canby became commander of the Department of Columbia, which included the Washington, Idaho, and Alaska territories. Three years later, he accepted responsibility for the Military Division of the Pacific. In March 1873, tensions with the Modoc tribe of northern California exploded into open warfare, and Canby was called to restore the peace. He earnestly tried to achieve a settlement by negotiating directly with aggrieved Modoc leaders in face-to-face talks at Siskiyou. On April 11, 1873, while conversing with Modoc chief Captain Jack, he was suddenly shot and killed. He is the only high-ranking military officer killed at the hands of Native Americans.

Further Reading

Alberts, Don E. *The Battle of Glorieta: Union Victory in the West.* College Station: Texas A & M University Press, 1998.

Edrington, Thomas S. *The Battle of Glorieta Pass: A Gettysburg in the West, March 26–28, 1862.* Albuquerque: University of New Mexico Press, 1998.

Heyman, Max L. *Prudent Soldier: A Biography of Major General E. R. S. Canby.* Glendale, Calif.: Arthur H. Clark, 1959.

O'Brien, Sean M. *Mobile, 1865: Last Stand of the Confederacy.* Westport, Conn.: Praeger, 2001.

Waugh, John C. *Last Stand at Mobile.* Abilene, Tex.: McWhiney Foundation, 2001.

Whitlock, Flint. *Distant Bugles, Distant Drums: The Union Response to the Confederate Invasion of New Mexico.* Boulder, Colo.: University Press of Colorado, 2006.

Carleton, James H. (1814–1873)
Union general

James Henry Carleton was born in Lubec, Maine, on December 27, 1814, and as a young man he aspired to be a writer. To that end, he corresponded with noted novelist Charles Dickens, but Carleton reached a turning point in his life during the so-called Aroostook War between Maine and New Brunswick. He served as a militia lieutenant and took an immediate liking to military service, so Carleton sought out a regular army commission. In 1839 he was commissioned a second lieutenant in the 1st U.S. Dragoons and two years later reported for duty at Fort Gibson, Indian Territory (Oklahoma). During the next few years, Carleton performed routine garrison service at various frontier posts and also accompanied numerous dragoon expedition into the hinterlands. In 1844 Carleton rode with Colonel Stephen W. Kearney, the noted explorer, along the Oregon Trail to South Pass and, consistent with his literary bent, published a colorful account for the frontier newspaper *Spirit of the Times.* When the Mexican War commenced in 1846, Carleton served as aide-de-camp to General John E. Wool and the following year received a brevet promotion to captain at the Battle of Buena Vista. Protracted illness precluded further wartime service, and Carleton resumed garrison duty at posts throughout the Old Southwest. In 1852 he served as commander of Fort Union, New Mexico Territory, and conducted numerous forays against hostile Jicarilla Apache with the noted scout Christopher "Kit" Carson. By the advent of the Civil War in April 1861, Carleton enjoyed a well-deserved reputation as an efficient, if humorless, frontier administrator.

In August 1861, Carleton, then stationed in California, was promoted to colonel of the 1st California Infantry. The following spring, General George Wright, commanding the Department of the Pacific, chose this veteran frontier fighter to lead 2,000 men eastward across the deserts and assist the Union war effort in New Mexico. Carleton did so with commendable efficiency and shepherded the so-called California column into Tucson, Arizona Territory, in May 1862. His approach induced Confederate forces under General Henry H. SIBLEY to abandon the New Mexico Territory altogether and slip back into Texas. Carleton, a brigadier general as of April 28, 1862, next succeeded General Edward R. S. CANBY as head of the Department of New Mexico and immediately subjected the unruly outlands to martial law. Confederate sympathizers such as Sylvester Mowry were promptly arrested and detained while Carleton sparred constantly with Judge Joseph Knapp over the legality of various detentions.

However, the biggest challenge facing Carleton's quest for frontier order came from the Navajo and Mescalero Apache. He summarily ordered both tribes into close confinement on reservations and, when they refused to obliged, conducted a scorched-earth war against them. Carleton then ordered Kit Carson and other scouts to execute any male Native Americans found in arms, but they wisely ignored such punitive measures and simply burned their crops to force them into submission. After the Navajo submitted, Carleton rounded up 9,000 tribe members and marched them 300 miles to reservations at Bosque Redondo in what has become reviled as the "Long Walk." His harshness toward both whites and Native Americans proved unpopular and draconian, but he maintained order throughout a precarious time in frontier history. For his efforts, he gained brevet promotion to major general in 1865

and transferred to a new command in Texas the following year. Two years later, the government reversed Carleton's policies and allowed the Navaho to return home.

In October 1866, Carleton became lieutenant colonel of the 4th U.S. Infantry, then stationed at San Antonio. He remained there seven years before dying of pneumonia on January 7, 1873, a harsh but effective frontier administrator.

Further Reading

Dunlay, Thomas W. *Kit Carson and the Indians.* Lincoln: University of Nebraska Press, 2000.

Hunt, Aurora. *Major General James Henry Carleton, Western Frontier Dragoon.* Glendale, Calif.: Arthur Clark, 1958.

Hutton, Paul A., ed. *Soldiers West: Biographies from the Military Frontier.* Lincoln: University of Nebraska Press, 1987.

Masich, Andrew E. *The Civil War in Arizona: The Story of the California Volunteers.* Norman: University of Oklahoma Press, 2006.

Miller, Darlis. *The California Column in New Mexico.* Albuquerque: University of New Mexico Press, 1982.

Pelzer, Louis, ed. *The Prairie Logbooks: Dragoon Campaigns to the Pawnee Villages in 1844 and to the Rocky Mountains in 1845.* Lincoln: University of Nebraska Press, 1983.

Cleburne, Patrick R. (1828–1864)

Confederate general

Patrick Ronayne Cleburne was born in County Cork, Ireland, on March 16, 1828, the son of a noted physician. He aspired to follow his father by pursuing pharmacology at the University of Dublin, but he failed the entrance exam. Deeply ashamed, Cleburne next joined the British army by enlisting in the 49th Foot in 1846, serving three years. He eventually purchased his release in 1849 and emigrated to the United States. After settling in Helena, Arkansas, in 1850 he worked as a druggist, studied law, and opened a successful law practice in 1855, the same year he became a naturalized citizen. By 1860, with the storm clouds of secession gathering, Cleburne joined the Yell Rifles as a private and eventually was elected captain. This unit subsequently joined nine other companies to form the 1st Arkansas Infantry, in which Cleburne became colonel as of May 14, 1861. As the Civil War unfolded, Cleburne's unit was amalgamated into a division commanded by General William J. HARDEE, and the two leaders became fast friends. During the next three years, their military activities invariably were intermingled.

In the fall of 1861, Cleburne accepted command of a brigade under General Albert S. JOHNSTON's command at Bowling Green, Kentucky, and they accompanied that leader as he fell back to Tennessee. Cleburne, now a brigadier general, first saw action at the Battle of Shiloh on April 6, 1862, where he formed the extreme left wing of the Confederate advance and drove Union forces up against the Tennessee River. The next day, a determined Union counterattack forced Confederates from the field, but Cleburne's brigade formed a successful rear guard preventing the retreat from becoming a rout. Cleburne subsequently accompanied the invasion of Kentucky under General Braxton BRAGG that summer, being severely wounded at the Battle of Richmond on August 30, 1862. Fortunately, he recovered in time to distinguish himself at the Battle of Perryville on October 8, 1862, suffering two additional wounds. Cleburne then fought capably again at the Battle of Stone's River (Murfreesboro) (December 31, 1862–January 3, 1863), where his ruthless attack ran the Union right wing back four miles. Afterward, he accompanied Bragg's army back to Shelbyville and, like many subordinates, came to despise his commanding officer. Nonetheless, he was promoted to major general as of November 1862, becoming the Confederacy's ranking officer of foreign birth.

Cleburne next accompanied the Army of Tennessee throughout the Tullahoma campaign, which afforded no real fighting and resulted in another Confederate retreat. However, Bragg then suddenly turned and struck at the Army of the Cumberland under General William S. ROSE-CRANS at Chickamauga on September 19–20, and Cleburne was in his element. He so ferociously assailed the Union position that Rosecrans shifted his men away from the center—just as General James LONGSTREET came crashing through the center. Cleburne performed equally well during his dogged defense at the Battle of Missionary Ridge, November 25, 1863, and repulsed several determined attacks by General William T. SHERMAN. Bragg then retreated again, and Cleburne's division, assisted by General Joseph WHEELER's cavalry, remained behind at Ringgold Gap as a rear guard. On November 27, 1863, he expertly repelled several attempts by General Joseph L. HOOKER to force the pass, ensuring a safe Confederate withdrawal. For all his skill in combat, Cleburne twice received the thanks of the Confederate Congress, and he was popularly heralded as the "Stonewall of the West."

Confederate general Patrick R. Cleburne *(Library of Congress)*

Cleburne seemed slated for higher command, but in the winter of 1863–64, his prospects for promotion suddenly waned. Irish by birth and never having owned slaves, he circulated a petition calling on the Confederate government to enlist African Americans into the army in exchange for freedom. Such a move might tap into a half-million willing recruits and, furthermore, also induce the hesitant governments of Britain and France to bestow diplomatic recognition. But Confederate authorities were stunned by his proposal, and President Jefferson Davis, who took steps to have Cleburne's suggestion quashed, also withheld his well-deserved promotion to lieutenant general. He nevertheless continued functioning as a divisional leader with fine performances under General Joseph E. Johnston at Kennesaw Mountain and Bald Hill on June 27 and July 22, 1864. Cleburne performed his final duties to the Confederacy while accompanying General John B. Hood's ill-fated offensive into Tennessee that fall. On November 30, 1864, he led his men in a desperate charge on the entrenched Union forces of General John M. Schofield at Franklin. Cleburne lost two horses under him, yet he rallied his men and charged on foot—only to be shot dead within 50 yards of Federal lines. He was one of six Southern generals slain that day, and his remains eventually were interred at Helena, Arkansas. Cleburne's natural aggressiveness and tactical finesse renders him the most accomplished Confederate officer of his grade, and he was possibly the finest divisional commander of the entire war.

Further Reading

Brennan, Patrick. "The Battle of Franklin." *North & South* 8, no. 1 (2005): 26–46.

Evans, E. Raymond. *Cleburne's Defense of Ringgold Gap.* Signal Mountain, Tenn.: Mountain Press, 1998.

Farley, M. Foster. "The Battle of Franklin." *Military Heritage* 1, no. 5 (2000): 60–67.

Joslyn, Mauriel L. "The Youth and Irish Military Service of Patrick Cleburne (1828–1864)." *Irish Sword* 23, no. 19 (2002): 87–98.

Joslyn, Mauriel L., ed. *A Meteor Shining Brightly: Essays on the Life an Career of Major General Patrick R. Cleburne.* Macon, Ga.: Mercer University Press, 2000.

Logsdon, David R. *Eyewitnesses at the Battle of Franklin.* Nashville, Tenn.: Kettle Mills Press, 2000.

Crittenden, George B. (1812–1880)

Confederate general

George Bib Crittenden was born in Russellville, Kentucky, on March 20, 1812, the son of a prominent state politician and future governor. He attended the U.S. Military Academy in 1827 and graduated four years later, midway in a class of 45. Crittenden subsequently served as an infantry lieutenant during the Black Hawk War of 1832 and then performed several years of routine garrison work in Alabama and Georgia. However, he resigned his commission in April 1833 to study law at Transylvania University. He was admitted to the bar but then abandoned his profession for military adventurism in the Republic of Texas. In December 1842 Crittenden volunteered to accompany a 250-man expedition against Ciudad Merir, Mexico, under Colonel William S. Fisher. When the entire company was captured, he and his messmates endured harsh captivity in a filthy Mexico City prison. The inmates staged a failed escape attempt, at which point their captors decided to execute every 10th man on the draw of a black bean. Crittenden pulled a white bean, handed it to a friend who had a family, and then drew another white bean and luckily escaped the firing squad. He spent nearly a year in prison before Secretary of State Daniel Webster managed to arrange his release. In 1846 Crittenden resumed his military activities as a captain of mounted Kentucky riflemen, and he received a brevet promotion for bravery at the battles of Contreras and Churubusco. After the war, he reentered the U.S. Army with a rank of major, but his career was jeopardized by frequent dissipation. Nonetheless, Crittenden rose to lieutenant colonel and was a ranking officer in the New Mexico Territory when the Civil War erupted in April 1861.

Back in Kentucky, Crittenden's father, John J. Crittenden, father of the "Crittenden Compromise" to avert war, begged his son not to join the Confederacy. His own younger brother, Thomas

L. Crittenden, joined the Union army as a high-ranking officer. But Crittenden, for reasons of his own, sided with the South and resigned his commission. By June 1861, he was a Confederate brigadier general commanding forces at Knoxville, Tennessee. A popular figure, Crittenden rose to major general the following November, and he was ordered to assume command of Southern forces from Generals Felix K. Zollicoffer and William H. Carroll. That November—and without authorization—Zollicoffer took 4,000 men and entrenched them on the north bank of the Cumberland River near Beech Grove, Kentucky. He did this despite the fact that the state legislature had declared its neutrality and wished combatants from either side to remove their forces.

By January 1862, Zollicoffer's isolated detachment had attracted the attention of Union forces under General George H. Thomas, and Crittenden marched to reinforce him. Thomas, meanwhile, decided to dislodge the Confederates, then foolishly deployed with a flooded river to their back, and he advanced with 7,000 men. Crittenden, however, resolved to strike first, and he hastily gathered up his small force before Thomas could combine with other Federals. On January 19, 1862, he fiercely assailed the Union camp near Mills Springs (Logan's Crossroads), Kentucky. The Confederates enjoyed success initially until General Zollicoffer became separated from his troops in a fog, blundered into Union lines, and was shot dead. Thomas then adroitly dispersed Crittenden's renewed assaults with a deadly enfilade fire. The battered Southerners withdrew with heavy losses while Thomas pursued them leisurely. Crittenden managed to evacuate Beech Grove and get the bulk of his forces across the rain-swollen Cumberland River, although forced to abandon his baggage and artillery. Mills Springs, though small in scope, harbored huge consequences for it peeled back the first line of Confederate defenses in Kentucky, exposing Forts Henry and Donelson to attack by General Ulysses S. Grant the following month.

No sooner did Crittenden's command wearily trudge into Murfreesboro, Tennessee, than he faced accusations of being drunk in battle. He strenuously rebuked the charges, whereupon General Albert S. Johnston appointed him to command his reserve at Iuka in northern Mississippi. Crittenden thus received a second chance to rehabilitate his reputation, but on April 1, 1862, General William J. Hardee arrived at his camp on inspection and found it in disarray. Crittenden was arrested and court-martialed for drunkenness, and he resigned his commission in October 1862. He spent the balance of the war acting as a volunteer aide on the staff of General John S. Williams. Crittenden returned to Frankfort, Kentucky, after the war, where, thanks to family connections, he was installed as the state librarian in 1867. He died in obscurity at Danville on November 27, 1880, one of the least efficient Confederate commanders of the western theater.

Further Reading

Dalton, David C. "Zollicoffer, Crittenden, and the Mill Springs Campaign." *Filson Club Historical Quarterly* 60 (1986): 463–471.

Hafendorfer, Kenneth A. *Mill Springs: Campaign and Battle of Mill Springs, Kentucky.* Louisville, Ky.: KH Press, 2001.

Hess, Earl J. *Banners to the Breeze: The Kentucky Campaigns, Corinth, and Stone's River.* Lincoln: University of Nebraska Press, 2000.

Mason, Kevin G. "Black Sabbath: The Battle of Mill Springs." Unpublished master's thesis, University of Tennessee, 1997.

Myers, Raymond E. *General Felix Zollicoffer and the Battle of Mill Springs.* Louisville, Ky.: Filson Club Historical Society, 1998.

Stevens, Peter F. "The Black Bean Draw." *American History* 32, no. 4 (1997): 36–40, 63–64.

Crook, George (1829–1890)

Union general

George Crook was born near Dayton, Ohio, on September 23, 1829, the son of farmers. After passing through the U.S. Military Academy in 1852, he served as a second lieutenant with the 4th U.S. Infantry at various posts in California and Oregon. Crook partook of innumerable skirmishes

Union general George Crook *(Library of Congress)*

with hostile Native Americans and in 1857 was struck by an arrow, a wound that he carried for life. But Crook, unlike most contemporaries, studied the native tribes closely to learn more about them and thus avail himself more innovative tactics against them. In time, he came to empathize with them and frequently railed against the civilian bureaucrats in Washington, D.C., who exploited them. By 1861, Crook was a lowly infantry captain, and that May he transferred east with expectations for fighting in the then-unfolding Civil War. That September, he was made colonel of the 36th Ohio Infantry and spent a year rendering useful service in westernmost Virginia. Crook then rose to brigadier general of volunteers in August 1862 and acquitted himself well in heavy fighting at South Mountain and Antietam that fall. He subsequently transferred west, commanding a cavalry division in General William S. Rosecrans's Army of the Cumberland. Crook bore a full measure of campaigning at Tullahoma and distinguished himself at the bloody encounter at

Chickamauga on September 19–20, 1863. After Rosecrans fell back to Chattanooga, Tennessee, Crook was entrusted with keeping Union supply lines open, and, on October 6, 1863, he defeated Confederate raiders under General Joseph Wheeler at Farmington and drove them across the Tennessee River. He then rose by brevet to regular colonel shortly afterward.

In the spring of 1864 Crook was back east again as commander of the Department of West Virginia. As such, he conducted several successful raids against Confederate communications throughout the Kanawha District. On July 23–24, he was surprised and heavily defeated at Kernstown, Virginia, by resurgent Confederates under General Jubal A. Early. In August 1864 Crook nonetheless succeeded the inept general David Hunter as commander of the Department of West Virginia. He also joined General Philip H. Sheridan's Army of the Shenandoah, commanding the VIII Corps, and he was conspicuously engaged in several pitched battles against Early's hard-charging Confederates. These included the Union victories at Winchester, Fisher's Hill, and, last, Cedar Creek on October 19, 1864, where he was initially surprised by Early but then rallied his men and helped win the day. Crook then suddenly fell captive to Confederate partisans led by Captain John H. McNeil and spent several weeks in confinement at Richmond's notorious Libby Prison. He was exchanged and returned to service in time to serve in the final phases of the Richmond–Petersburg campaign. On April 1, 1865, Crook's cavalry was heavily employed at the decisive victory at Five Forks, Virginia, and contributed greatly to the boxing in of General Robert E. Lee at Appomattox. Crook closed the war with the final ranks of brevet major general of volunteers and brevet major general, U.S. Army.

After the war, Crook reverted back to his regular rank of lieutenant colonel, 32nd U.S. Infantry, and returned to the western frontier. He soon emerged as one of America's greatest Indian fighters, commencing with a successful campaign to subdue the Paiutes of Oregon in 1868. Three years later, President Ulysses S. GRANT dispatched him to Arizona, where he helped suppress an Apache uprising led by Cochise. Disregarding army dogma, he pioneered the use of pack-mules for supplies and friendly Apache scouts to track down hostile natives. Moreover, his respect and affection for Native Americans earned him the moniker "Gray Fox" from the people he subdued. In 1876 Crook participated in the great uprising in the Black Hills of the Dakotas, and he was defeated by Chief Crazy Horse at the Rose Bud on March 17, 1876, which indirectly led to the death of Colonel George A. CUSTER one week later. Crook rebounded by attacking and destroying the village of Chief American Horse at Slim Buttes on September 9, 1876. With the Sioux and Cheyenne finally brought under control, Crook made it his personal policy to protect Native Americans from grasping Indian agents and meandering frontiersmen to forestall future outbreaks of violence.

In 1882 frontier violence flared up when the Apache rose under the leadership of Geronimo. Crook pursued the wily chief with a single company of cavalry and 200 friendly Apaches deep into Mexican territory, and he convinced him to surrender. Geronimo again escaped from the reservation in 1885, but Crook's lenient policies had run their course with the government, and he was eventually replaced by General Nelson A. Miles. Ultimately, Miles was forced to employ Apache scouts in similar fashion to bring Geronimo to bay. Crook subsequently took charge of the Division of the Missouri in May 1888, headquartered at Chicago, Illinois, where he directed final phases of the Indian wars. Though far removed from the frontier, he nonetheless remained a strident spokesman on behalf on Native American rights until his death there on March 21, 1890. He was also one of the Union's most capable divisional commanders.

Further Reading

Aleshire, Peter. *The Fox and the Whirlwind: General George Crook and Geronimo: A Paired Biography.* New York: Wiley, 2000.

Alexander, Robert. *Five Forks: Waterloo of the Confederacy.* East Lansing: Michigan State University Press, 2003.

Coffey, David. *Sheridan's Lieutenants: Philip Sheridan, His Generals, and the Final Years of the Civil War.* Wilmington, Del.: Rowman and Littlefield, 2005.

Lepa, Jack H. *The Shenandoah Valley Campaign of 1864.* Jefferson, N.C.: McFarland, 2003.

Longacre, Edward G. *The Cavalry at Appomattox: A Tactical Study of Mounted Operations during the Civil War's Climactic Campaign, March 27–April 9, 1865.* Mechanicsburg, Pa.: Stackpole Books, 2003.

O'Beirne, Kevin. "Crook's Devils." *Military Heritage* 1, no. 4 (2000): 62–75.

Robinson, Charles M. *General Crook and the Western Frontier.* Norman: University of Oklahoma Press, 2001.

Schmitt, Martin F., ed. *General George Crook: His Autobiography.* Norman: University of Oklahoma Press, 1986.

Curtis, Samuel R. (1805–1866)

Union general

Samuel Ryan Curtis was born in Champlain, New York, on February 3, 1805, and raised in Licking County, Ohio. He passed through the U.S. Military Academy in 1831 and was posted as a second lieutenant with the 7th U.S. Infantry. Curtis performed garrison duty at Fort Gibson, Indian Territory, for only a year before resigning his commission. He then successively served as an engineer on the National Road and chief engineer on the Muskingum River before studying law in 1841. During the War with Mexico (1846–48), he became colonel of the 3rd Ohio Infantry, but mostly he performed as adjutant general under General John E. Wool. Curtis also briefly functioned as military governor of Matamoros, Camargo, Monterrey, and Saltillo. Afterward, he relocated to Keokuk, Iowa, as a chief engineer on several river projects and then in St. Louis, Missouri, for the same reason. Curtis then entered politics as a Republican in 1856, serving first as major of Keokuk and then in the U.S. House of Representatives where he ceaselessly advocated creation of a transcontinental railroad. Curtis, a droll, uncharismatic figure, was nonetheless respected for his personal integrity, and he gained reelection to Congress in 1858 and 1860. In 1861 he attended the Peace Conference in Washington, D. C., to possibly avert secession and the violence that would accompany it. After the Civil War commenced in April 1861, he returned to Iowa and helped raise that state's first volunteer regiments; Curtis himself was elected unanimously colonel of the 2nd Iowa Infantry. Moreover, on the recommendation of General in Chief Winfield SCOTT, he was elevated to brigadier general the following May.

After resigning from Congress, Curtis accepted his first command at St. Louis, Missouri, which he rapidly helped bring under order. His principal activity was in helping to arrange the relief and replacement of the inept general John C. Frémont from command of the Department of the Missouri in November 1861. His successor, General Henry W. HALLECK, placed Curtis in charge of the District of Southwest Missouri with orders to eliminate a threat posed by Confederates under General Sterling PRICE. He performed admirably with the scanty resources allotted him and pushed the Southerners deep into Arkansas. There, Price was unexpectedly reinforced by General Earl VAN DORN, who then turned to attack Curtis's Army of the Southwest at Pea Ridge (Elkhorn Tavern) on March 7–8, 1862. Van Dorn staged an elaborate flanking movement that placed his army behind the Federals, but Curtis simply ordered his entire force to about-face, and assisted by artillery under General Franz SIGEL, he decimated several determined, if piecemeal, attacks. The Confederates eventually were driven off in confusion, Missouri was saved for the Union, and Curtis won a promotion to major general.

In September 1862 Curtis succeeded Halleck as head of the Department of the Missouri and quickly ran afoul of internecine politics and personalities. He failed to get along with either General John M. SCHOFIELD, his principal subordinate, or Governor H. R. Gamble. Curtis also proved unable to stem systemic outbreaks of guerrilla warfare, and his often draconian responses, such

as imposing levies upon suspected Confederate sympathizers, drove people into the enemy ranks. In May 1863 President Abraham LINCOLN removed Curtis from St. Louis and reassigned him to lead the Department of Kansas, a command requiring less political finesse and more administrative skill. Curtis functioned competently until the fall of 1864, when General Price launched a final bid to conquer Missouri for the Confederacy. Curtis quickly raised a force of 4,000 soldiers and confronted twice his numbers at Big Blue River on October 21, 1864. He was driven back but made a tenacious stand at Westport, Missouri, two days later. Here the cavalry of General Alfred PLEASONTON hit the Southerners from behind, and Price hastily fell back toward Arkansas. Curtis pursued him doggedly, mauling several Confederate rear guards, but he quarreled with Pleasonton, and the Confederates escaped. In January 1865 he was reassigned to the Department of the Northwest to conduct several peace treaty talks with the Sioux, the Crow, and other neighboring tribes. Curtis finally was discharged from the military in April 1866.

Back in civilian life, Curtis continued advocating his lifelong passion, the transcontinental railroad. In 1866 President Andrew Johnson appointed him to a three-man commission to explore its possible development. Curtis died suddenly at Council Bluffs, Iowa, on December 26, 1866, a brusque but otherwise useful officer of the western theater.

Further Reading
Beckenbaugh, Terry L. "The War of Politics: Samuel Ryan Curtis, Race, and the Political/Military Establishment." Unpublished Ph.D. diss., University of Arkansas, Fayetteville, 2001.
Bird, Roy. *Civil War in Kansas.* Gretna, La.: Pelican Publishing, 2004.
DeBlack, Thomas R. *With Fire and Sword: Arkansas, 1861–1874.* Fayetteville: University of Arkansas Press, 2003.
Gerteis, Louis S. *Civil War St. Louis.* Lawrence: University Press of Kansas, 2001.
Ham, Sharon. "End of Innocence." *Iowa Heritage Illustrated* 85, nos. 2–3 (2004): 64–79.

Johnson, Mark W. *That Body of Brave Men: The U.S. Regular Infantry and the Civil War in the West, 1861–1865.* Cambridge, Mass.: Da Capo Press, 2003.

Shea, William L., and Grady McWhiney. *War in the West: Pea Ridge and Prairie Grove.* Abilene, Tex.: McWhiney Foundation, 2001.

Custer, George A. (1839–1876)

Union general

George Armstrong Custer was born in New Rumley, Ohio, on December 5, 1839, and he taught briefly at an academy in Monroe, Michigan. In 1857 he gained admittance to the U.S. Military Academy and graduated four years later at the bottom of his class. As a cadet, Custer proved sullen, inattentive, and ill-disposed toward discipline. However, after graduating in 1861, he received his lieutenant's commission, 2nd U.S. Cavalry, just as the Civil War erupted, and he compiled one of the most meteoric rises in American military history. During the Battle of Bull Run, he caught the eye of General George B. McClellan, who appointed him an aide-de-camp. Custer performed heroically throughout the Peninsula campaign of 1862 and subsequently requested a combat command. He next served under General Alfred Pleasonton at the Battle of Aldie, June 17, 1863, with such distinction that he received, on Pleasonton's strongest recommendation, promotion to brevet brigadier general. Aged but 23 years, Custer was now the youngest general in the Union army, and his Michigan cavalry brigade, which he dubbed "The Wolverines," became renowned for their dash and discipline—and for donning the flashy red necktie of their commander. The following month, he fought with exceptional valor at Gettysburg, where, on July 3, 1863, his brigade prevented Confederate cavalry under General J. E. B. Stuart from attacking the Union rear.

In 1864 Custer transferred to the division of General Hugh J. Kilpatrick, and he was closely engaged in several severe engagements in General Ulysses S. Grant's overland drive to Richmond. His most noted encounter was at Yellow Tavern on May 11, 1864, in which he conducted the action that fatally wounded General Stuart. That summer, he joined General Philip H. Sheridan's Army of the Shenandoah to command an entire division. Always at the forefront of the action, Custer struck savagely at Confederate armies in Union victories at Winchester, Fisher's Hill, and Cedar Creek, invariably with decisive effect. He then received brevet promotion to major general at the age of 24 and assumed command of the 3rd Cavalry Division from General James H. Wilson. With it, he literally destroyed General Jubal A. Early's army at Waynesboro, Virginia, on March 2, 1865, and the following month added further luster to his name by charging equally hard at Dinwiddie Court House and the decisive Union victory at Five Forks on April 1, 1865. Custer's hard-riding troopers then proved instrumental in pursuing the Confederate army of Northern Virginia to Appomattox, Virginia, and bringing it to

Union general George A. Custer *(Library of Congress)*

bay. On April 9, 1865, when General Robert E. LEE sent forward a white flag to the Union lines, it was received by Custer. In the course of four years of combat, Custer had 11 horses killed underneath him, yet he was only wounded once. War's end found him the darling of the mounted arm and the national press, both totally captivated by his long, blonde hair, indifference to danger, and ravenous appetite for glory.

Custer was retained in the postwar service but reduced in rank to his regular grade of captain as of March 1866. Four months, later the 7th U.S. Cavalry was organized, and he became its lieutenant colonel. Custer next reported for duty in Kansas where he first experienced Indian fighting under General Winfield S. HANCOCK. Dissatisfied and perplexed by Native American tactics, he took an unauthorized leave of absence, was court-martialed, and was suspended for a year. In 1868 General Sheridan managed to have him reinstated and, on November 27, Custer committed a memorable atrocity by attacking the peaceful village of Chief Black Kettle on the Washita River. Despite official disapproval of this ill-advised action, no disciplinary action resulted, and Custer remained on active duty in Kansas. In 1873 he experienced his first brush with Sioux while protecting miners in the Black Hills region of South Dakota. Three years later, tensions exploded into open warfare, and Custer was assigned to an army column under General Alfred H. TERRY. Another force under General George CROOK was supposed to be advancing from the east but met defeat at the Rose Bud River and was forced to withdraw. Meanwhile, Custer recklessly forged ahead, and on June 25, 1876, the 7th Cavalry happened upon a large Native-American encampment at Little Big Horn. Despite the fact that the camp was inhabited by thousands of warriors, Custer divided his command and attacked. He was quickly overwhelmed by Chiefs Crazy Hose and Gall and killed along with 261 men of the 7th Cavalry. Six companies of the regiment under Major Marcus A. Reno and Captain Frederick W. Benteen managed to entrench themselves on a hillside and beat off attacks for two days until Terry arrived with the main column. "Custer's Last Stand," as Little Big Horn came to be known, was not the largest defeat suffered at the hands of Native Americans, but it certainly was the most sensationalized. It virtually assured that Custer's larger-than-life persona would remain an essential part of American frontier mythology.

Further Reading

Barnett, Louisek. *Touched by Fire: The Life, Death, & Mythic After Life of George Armstrong Custer.* Lincoln: University of Nebraska Press, 2006.

Coffey, David. *Sheridan's Lieutenants: Phil Sheridan, His Generals, and the Final Year of the Civil War.* Wilmington, Del.: Rowman and Littlefield, 2005.

Hatch, Tom. *The Cavalry of Appomattox: A Tactical Study of Mounted Operations during the Civil War's Climactic Campaign, March 27–April 9, 1865.* Mechanicsburg, Pa.: Stackpole Books, 2003.

Ovies, Adolfo. *Crossed Sabers: General George Armstrong Custer and the Shenandoah Campaign.* Bloomington, Ind.: Author House, 2004.

Robbins, James. *Last in Their Class: Custer, Pickett, and the Goats of West Point.* New York: Encounter Books, 2006.

Walker, Paul D. *The Battle that Saved the Union: Custer vs Stuart at Gettysburg.* Gretna, La.: Pelican Publishing, 2002.

D

Dahlgren, John A. B. (1809–1870)

Union admiral

John Adolphus Bernard Dahlgren was born in Philadelphia, Pennsylvania, on November 13, 1809, the son of a Swedish consul. He attempted to join the U.S. Navy in 1825 but was rejected as too young. However, after accompanying a merchant vessel for a year, he gained an appointment as acting midshipman in March 1826. For the next decade, Dahlgren served on a variety of ships and in several squadrons, and his abilities at mathematics resulted in a posting with the U.S. Coastal Survey. He acquitted himself well in most capacities, but in 1837 he was sidelined with vision problems and received a four-year furlough. While seeking treatment in Europe, he also studied the primitive rocket technology of the day. Dahlgren resumed his naval career as a lieutenant in 1842, and four years later, he requested sea duty during the Mexican War but, in light of his technical expertise, was assigned to the Washington Navy Yard instead. There, he helped found the U.S. Navy Ordnance Department and functioned as assistant inspector. During the next 15 years, Dahlgren became closely identified with the latest developments in naval weaponry. He is best remembered for designing and constructing the famous Dahlgren cannon in 1851, based on his understanding that explosive forces in a cannon are greater at the rear end than at the muzzle. Consequently, his cannons were thicker in back

than in front, and their distinct teardrop shape earned them the moniker "soda bottles." In practice, the 11- and 15-inch diameter Dahlgrens possessed superior muzzle velocity, range, and accuracy than contemporary European designs. He also designed a light-weight howitzer suitable for small boats and landing parties. Dahlgren furthered his reputation as an ordnance authority by writing and publishing several texts on the subject, which were professionally well received.

As the Civil War approached in the spring of 1861, Dahlgren's superior, Captain Franklin BUCHANAN, resigned as head of the Washington Navy Yard to join the South. Dahlgren then took energetic measures to fortify and defend the navy yard against possible Confederate attack. President Abraham LINCOLN so appreciated his performance that he arranged Dahlgren's appointment as director of the Bureau of Ordnance in July 1862 and promotion to captain through a special act of Congress the following August. In the ensuing months, he was actively employed in designing, testing, and mounting stronger weapons for new classes of ironclad warships. Dahlgren performed his tasks capably, and in February 1863, he advanced to rear admiral. The following July, he was ordered to succeed the unfortunate Admiral Samuel F. DU PONT as head of the South Atlantic Blockading Squadron.

On station, Dahlgren's immediate object was the reduction and capture of Charleston, South

Union admiral John A. B. Dahlgren *(Library of Congress)*

Carolina. He sailed his heavy ironclads into the harbor and bombarded the city's defenses on several occasions, but aside from demolishing some old forts, he failed to subdue the port. In the course of several months, he also lost several monitor vessels to the Confederate "torpedoes" (mines). Thereafter, he maintained an iron blockade of Charleston and authorized occasional raids upriver to keep the defenders off balance. In December 1864, Dahlgren played an important role in the capture of Savannah, Georgia, by supplying the army of General William T. SHERMAN with food and supplies. His heavy cannon, meanwhile, enjoyed success equally at sea and on land. Several naval batteries were landed ashore to assist General Ulysses S. GRANT during the July 1863 siege of Vicksburg, Mississippi, where their heavy firepower smothered Confederate defenses. In August 1864, the large-bore Dahlgrens employed on Admiral David G. FARRAGUT's monitors USS *Manhattan* and *Chickasaw* helped damage and

subdue the Confederate ram CSS *Tennessee* under now Admiral Buchanan at Mobile Bay. Dahlgren himself occupied the evacuated city of Charleston in February 1865 and relinquished control of the squadron by war's end. Sadly, his son, Colonel Ulric Dahlgren, had been killed in General Hugh J. KILPATRICK's cavalry raid against Richmond, Virginia, on March 2, 1864.

Dahlgren resumed his technical research in Washington, D.C., as bureau chief, but in 1866, he assumed command of the South Pacific Squadron. In July 1868 he returned to the navy yard, rose to commandant the following year, and died there in that capacity on July 12, 1870. His famous cannon, though rendered obsolete by advances in rifled artillery, saw continued service with the U.S. Navy until the early 1890s.

Further Reading

Browning, Robert M. *Success Is All That Was Expected: The South Atlantic Blockading Squadron during the Civil War.* Washington, D.C.: Brassey's, 2002.

Canfield, Eugene B. "Guns for the Monitors." *Naval History* 14, no. 4 (2000): 48–55.

Fuller, Howard. *Navies and Naval Operations of the Civil War, 1861–65.* London: Conway Marine, 2005.

Phelps, W. Chris. *The Bombardment of Charleston, 1863–1865.* Gretna, La.: Pelican Publishing, 2002.

Roberts, William H. *Now the Contest: Coastal and Oceanic Naval Operations in the Civil War.* Lincoln: University of Nebraska Press, 2004.

Schneller, Robert J. *A Quest for Glory: A Biography of Rear Admiral John A. Dahlgren.* Annapolis, Md.: Naval Institute Press, 1995.

Davis, Charles H. (1807–1887)

Union admiral

Charles Henry Davis was born in Boston, Massachusetts, on January 16, 1807, was well educated, and attended Harvard University in 1824. However, he quit school two years later to join the U.S. Navy as a midshipman and spent a decade cruising the Pacific Ocean and Mediterranean Sea. Davis received his lieutenant's commission in March 1834, and in 1842 he returned to Harvard to complete his degree. In light of his mathematical prowess, he found steady employment with the U.S. Coast Survey, and he published numerous scientific papers on the effects of tides. Davis advanced to commander in June 1854 and three years later assumed control of the Pacific Squadron. In this capacity, he arranged the rescue of American renegade adventurer William Walker from Nicaragua in May 1857. Two years later, he reported to the offices of the Nautical Almanac Office at Harvard, and he continued publishing scientific tracts as they related to naval and maritime service.

When the Civil War erupted in April 1861, Davis initially was assigned to the Bureau of Detail in Washington, D.C. It was his responsibility to provide accurate charts, proper organization, and efficient logistics for a sustained blockade of the lengthy Confederate coastline. He also assisted in planning intricate combined army-navy expeditions against the Confederate coast, most notably Cape Hatteras in August 1861. Three months later, he accompanied Admiral Samuel F. Du Pont on a campaign against Port Royal, South Carolina, and bore a conspicuous role in the victory of November 7, 1861. Success here planted the first Union lodgment on South Carolinian soil since the fall of Fort Sumter the previous April, and he received promotion to captain. Davis also pioneered the use of "stone fleets," namely, old wooden vessels filled with rock and sunk off Confederate harbors to obstruct them.

In the spring of 1862, Davis was tapped to succeed the ailing captain Andrew H. Foote as commander of the Mississippi Squadron. On June 5, 1862, once reinforced by several army rams under Colonel Charles Ellet, Davis fought and won the Battle of Plum Run Bend against a small but determined Confederate squadron. That same afternoon, he landed at Memphis, Tennessee, and received the city's surrender. Promoted to commodore, he next sailed south to Vicksburg, Mississippi, and joined forces with the fleet of Admiral David G. Farragut. There, in concert with army units, he energetically conducted a series of raids along the Mississippi River that kept Confederate forces from crossing the river and reinforcing the garrison. His string of luck ended on July 15, 1862, when the large Confederate ram CSS *Arkansas* sortied from the Yazoo River and passed directly through Davis's squadron. The Union vessels, badly outgunned, came off poorly in the engagement, which prompted Secretary of the Navy Gideon Welles to replace the scholarly Davis with a more aggressive officer. On October 1, 1862, Commander David D. Porter was chosen as his successor, and Davis reported back to Washington, D.C., to resume his scientific inquiries. As a sop to any hurt feelings on the matter, Davis also received a promotion to rear admiral as of February 1863.

Davis effectively managed the Bureau of Navigation, under whose aegis fell the navy's scientific

Union admiral Charles H. Davis *(U.S. Navy)*

office and its academy, until the war concluded in 1865. He was also responsible for creating the new Hydrographic Office to facilitate chart making and navigational aids. Davis also strongly suggested creation of a National Academy of Science, which was founded in 1863. At the conclusion of hostilities, he transferred from the Navy Department to the Naval Observatory as superintendent. He then took to sea in 1867 to command the Brazilian Squadron, remaining at sea for three years. In 1870 Davis came ashore for the last time as commandant of the Norfolk Navy Yard, Virginia, where simmering resentment against Northerners made his tenure decidedly unpleasant. He then resumed his work at the National Observatory, dying there on February 18, 1887. Although not exactly a combat officer of the first rank, Davis made indelible contributions to naval science as one of the most accomplished researchers of his day.

Further Reading

Campbell, R. Thomas. *Confederate Naval Forces on Western Waters: The Defense of the Mississippi River and Its Tributaries.* Jefferson, N.C.: McFarland, 2005.

Davis, Charles H. *Life of Charles Henry Davis, Rear Admiral, 1807–1877.* Boston: Houghton Mifflin, 1899.

Hearn, Chester G. *Ellet's Brigade: The Strangest Outfit of All.* Baton Rouge: Louisiana State University Press, 2000.

Joiner, Gary D. *Mr. Lincoln's Brown Water Navy: The Mississippi Squadron.* Lanham, Md.: Rowman & Littlefield, 2007.

Konstam, Angus. *Mississippi River Gunboats of the American Civil War, 1861–1865.* Oxford, U.K.: Osprey, 2002.

Silverstone, Paul H. *Civil War Navies, 1855–1883.* Annapolis, Md.: Naval Institute Press, 2001.

Davis, Jefferson (1808–1889)

President, Confederate States of America

Jefferson Davis was born in Christian County, Kentucky, on June 3, 1808, and raised in Mississippi. After briefly attending Transylvania University, he opted to apply to the U.S. Military Academy in 1825 and graduated four years later in the middle of his class. As a second lieutenant in the 1st U.S. Infantry, he fought briefly in the Black Hawk War of 1832 under General Zachary Taylor, and he conducted Sauk chief Black Hawk into confinement at Jefferson Barracks, Missouri. In May 1834 he transferred to the 1st U.S. Dragoons while also courting Sarah Knox Taylor, the general's daughter. They were married over his objections, and he resigned his commission to run a plantation in Mississippi. Tragically, Davis lost his young bride to malaria six months later, and he suffered intermittent bouts of illness for the rest of his life. Davis withdrew into seclusion for nearly a decade and finally emerged in 1844 to run for Congress. That year, he successfully stood for a seat in the U.S. House of Representatives and resigned two years later to participate in the war with Mexico that he had so strenuously advocated.

In 1846 Davis was commissioned colonel of the 1st Mississippi Rifle Regiment, and he joined his ex-father-in-law General Taylor at the mouth of the Rio Grande. He fought well at the Battle of Monterrey, where his men distinguished themselves in house-to-house fighting. Afterward, most of Taylor's regular troops were transferred to the army of General Winfield Scott, and Taylor, now mustering mostly militia, was attacked by General Antonio López de Santa Anna at Buena Vista on February 22, 1847. Once again, Davis was in the thick of the fray and bravely repulsed a Mexican cavalry charge that threatened artillery commanded by captains Braxton Bragg and George H. Thomas. He sustained a foot wound for the effort and returned to Mississippi a hero. He subsequently won appointment to complete an unfinished term in the U.S. Senate. In the wake of the Mexican War, sectional tensions between the North and South magnified exponentially over the issue of expanding slavery into newly acquired territories. Davis, while an articulate defender of Southern rights and slavery, left the Senate in 1851 to run unsuccessfully for the governor's office in his home state. He avoided the public arena for two years until 1853 when President Franklin Pierce appointed him secretary of war. In this

Jefferson Davis, president of the Confederate States of America *(National Archives)*

capacity, Davis displayed considerable foresight and innovation. He introduced badly needed administrative reforms, sought out the newest rifled weapons for the infantry, replaced wooden cannon carriages with metal ones, and at one point even introduced camels into the arid southwest on an experimental basis. By the time he left office in 1857, he was considered one of the War Department's most efficient bureaucrats.

In the spring of 1857, Davis was easily reelected to the Senate, where he forcefully and eloquently championed states rights and slavery. However, unlike many Southern "firebrands," he sought accommodation with the North to preserve the Union. When the Democratic Party split during the election year of 1860, he threw his support behind John C. BRECKINRIDGE and was aghast that Abraham LINCOLN, who opposed the expansion of slavery, won the election. Southern states then began to secede from the Union in December 1860,

and Davis reluctantly but determinedly sided with Mississippi. On January 21, 1861, he delivered an anguish-ridden farewell speech to the Senate before departing to tender his services to the emerging Confederate States of America. Once home, Davis fully expected to become a major general of state forces, but on February 9, 1861, he was genuinely surprised to learn that the secessionist congress, meeting in Montgomery, Alabama, nominated him to serve as president of this new Southern entity. He was inaugurated nine days later in Montgomery and then transferred the seat of Confederate governance to Richmond, Virginia, to shore up support from that state. In July 1861 the initial victory of General Pierre G. T. BEAUREGARD over General Irwin McDOWELL at Bull Run caused elation throughout the South and a premature sense of relief, but victory here belied severe and long-term deficiencies that dogged the Confederacy throughout its brief existence. The North's superior manpower and larger industrial base, coupled with Davis's own inability to secure cooperation between individual states within the Confederacy, doomed the fledgling state as both a political and a military entity. The celebrated prowess of Southern armies notwithstanding, multiplicity of the problems Davis encountered as chief executive simply proved insurmountable.

Davis firmly believed in his cause, stridently defended it, and remained fixated upon an ultimate Confederate victory to the bitter end. However, as chief executive, he had a tendency to meddle with his generals and interfere with military matters. He also was blinded to the incompetence of his friends Braxton BRAGG and Leonidas POLK, and he refused to remove them from power despite repeated displays of ineptitude. Moreover, Davis clashed repeatedly with talented yet headstrong leaders such as Beauregard and Joseph E. JOHNSTON, and periodically relieved them at inopportune times. Fortunately for the South, he commiserated well with his most successful field commander, General Robert E. LEE, and he worked closely with him. The eastern theater thus received the greater part of the administration's attention while events in the West, where the war would be lost, remained a consistent lower priority.

As Confederate fortunes waned, Davis lacked the authority to shift manpower decisively from one theater to the next owing to resistance from state governments. He thus was forced to invoke measures such as conscription, taxation, and confiscation to strengthen the overall Confederate position. These policies struck at the very heart of states's rights—the philosophical underpinning of his regime—and led to a chorus of condemnation from Southern politicians. He further compounded his problems by refusing to entertain the notion of employing African-American slaves in the military in exchange for freedom. This recalcitrance negated a pool of manpower numbering 2 million—at a period when the North ultimately added 180,000 black soldiers to their own roster. By the time such pragmatic measures were forced on him by the Confederate Congress in the spring of 1865, they arrived far too late to alter the outcome of events. After the fall of Richmond in April 1865, Davis and his cabinet hastily fled south, intending to reach the trans-Mississippi region and carry on the struggle for Southern independence through guerrilla warfare. When he and his entourage were seized by General James H. WILSON's cavalry at Irwinville, Georgia, on May 10, 1865, the Confederate States of America had reached its climactic denouement.

Davis was incarcerated in chains at Fortress Monroe, Virginia, although public outcry mitigated his harsh conditions. He remained confined for two years before being released and, though indicted for treason, was never brought to trial. Davis subsequently returned to a life of poverty in Mississippi with his faithful wife Varina, where he penned an extensive apologia for the war. In it, he vehemently blamed men such as Beauregard and Johnston for defeat while minimizing his own role in the debacle. Davis, who never applied for a pardon and never renewed his citizenship, died at Beauvior, Mississippi, on December 6, 1889. For many decades thereafter, in the minds of many fellow Southerners, he remained the embodiment and symbol of the Confederacy's proud and defiant "Lost Cause."

Further Reading

Cashin, Joan E. *Never at Peace: Varina Howell Davis and the Civil War.* Boston: Houghton Mifflin, 2005.

Collins, Donald E. *The Death and Resurrection of Jefferson Davis.* Lanham, Md.: Rowman and Littlefield, 2005.

Davis, Jefferson. *The Rise and Fall of the Confederate Government.* 2 vols. New York: D. Appleton, 1881.

Detzer, David. *Dissonance: Between Fort Sumter and Bull Run in the Turbulent First Days of the Civil War.* Orlando, Fla.: Harcourt, 2006.

Eicher, David J. *Dixie Betrayed: How the South Really Lost the Civil War.* New York: Little Brown, 2006.

Escott, Paul D. *Military Necessity: Civil-Military Relations in the Confederacy* Westport, Conn.: Praeger Security International, 2006.

Hattaway, Herman, and Richard E. Berlinger. *Jefferson Davis, Confederate President.* Lawrence: University Press of Kansas, 2002.

Jones, Wilmer L. *Generals in Blue and Gray.* 2 vols. Westport, Conn.: Praeger, 2004.

Monroe, Haskell W., and James T. McIntosh, eds. *The Papers of Jefferson Davis.* 10 vols. Baton Rouge: Louisiana State University Press, 1971–1999.

Doubleday, Abner (1819–1893)

Union general

Abner Doubleday was born in Ballston Spa, New York, on June 26, 1819, and attended school in nearby Cooperstown. He enjoyed a close association with athletics as a youth and undoubtedly played baseball there, but the polite fiction surrounding his originating the game has been discredited by historians. Doubleday was admitted to the U.S. Military Academy in 1838 and graduated four years later midway in his class. He was then commissioned a second lieutenant in the 3rd U.S. Artillery and performed several tours of routine garrison work along the Atlantic coast before transferring to the Army of Texas under General Zachary Taylor in 1846. He subsequently fought at the Battle of Monterrey that year, acquitting himself well and gaining promotion to first lieutenant in March 1847. After the war Doubleday reported for duty along the frontier, where he rose to captain in 1855 and fought in Florida's Third Seminole War. In December 1860 he accompanied Major Robert ANDERSON when his company was sent to garrison Fort Moultrie in Charleston, South Carolina. Anderson feared for the safety of his men following that state's secession on December 20, 1861, and he ordered them transferred to the incomplete works of Fort Sumter in Charleston harbor. Doubleday commanded the first company to reach the fort and began to strengthen the works and mount cannon. On April 12, 1861, Confederate forces under General Pierre G. T. BEAUREGARD commenced bombarding Fort Sumter, and Anderson allowed Doubleday the honor of firing the first Union shots of the Civil War in response. The garrison surrendered two days later, and Doubleday departed by boat for the North.

As the Civil War unfolded, Doubleday gained promotion to major and command of the 17th U.S. Infantry. With them, he campaigned in the Shenandoah Valley before advancing to brigadier general in February 1862. He then transferred to the Army of the Potomac under General John POPE and performed well in severe fighting at Groveton and Second Bull Run in August 1862. Doubleday then rose to command a division, was actively engaged at Stone Mountain, Antietam, and Fredericksburg that fall, and received promotion to major general as of November 1862. He next saw action at Chancellorsville in May 1863. Doubleday by now had acquired the reputation of a tenacious fighter but one who moved with such deliberation that his troops nicknamed him "Old Forty-Eight Hours."

During initial stages of the Gettysburg campaign, Doubleday commanded a division in General John F. REYNOLDS's I Corps. In this capacity, he arrived with Reynolds in the late morning of July 1, 1863, to reinforce Union cavalry under General John BUFORD, and he succeeded Reynolds to the command after he was killed. Gettysburg was Doubleday's finest hour. Outnumbered

and outmaneuvered by General Richard S. EWELL's Confederates, he relinquished control of the town slowly until the bulk of his forces were safely ensconced on nearby heights. He acquitted himself well, considering the confused events of the first day, but General George G. MEADE, commanding the Army of the Potomac, disapproved of Doubleday's tendency toward lethargic movements. He therefore appointed General John Newton, an officer with less seniority, to command the I Corps for the remainder of the engagement. Doubleday was appreciably incensed by the slight but returned to his division and performed well during the next two days. His men bore a prominent role in repulsing the climactic charge by General George E. PICKETT on July 3, 1863, but Doubleday, smarting from Meade's treatment, withdrew from active duties two days later.

Doubleday spent the remainder of the war performing administrative duties in Washington,

Union general Abner Doubleday *(Library of Congress)*

D.C. He also testified vindictively against General Meade during an official congressional inquiry in 1864, the strident tenor of which only besmirched his own reputation. His only other active service during the war was commanding a small part of Washington's defenses during General Jubal A. EARLY's raid of July 1864. After the war, Doubleday reverted back to his lineal rank of lieutenant colonel, 23th U.S. Infantry, and accompanied his men to San Francisco, California. He then rose to colonel in 1867, transferred to the African-American 24th U.S. Infantry in Texas, and served competently until his retirement in December 1873. Never one to let go of a grudge, he also published several tracts on Gettysburg that excoriated General Meade and exaggerated his own role. Doubleday died at Mendham, New Jersey, on January 26, 1893, better remembered for allegedly inventing baseball than for his conscientious service during the Civil War.

Further Reading

Doubleday, Abner. *Chancellorsville and Gettysburg.* New York: Da Capo Press, 1994.

———. *Reminiscences of Fort Sumter and Moultrie, 1860–1861.* Baltimore: Nautical and Aviation Publishing, 1998.

Newton, Steven H. *McPherson's Ridge: The First Battle for the High Ground, July 1, 1863.* Cambridge, Mass.: Da Capo Press, 2002.

Pfanz, Harry W. *Gettysburg—The First Day.* Chapel Hill: University of North Carolina Press, 2001.

Ramsey, David M. "The 'Old Sumter Hero': A Biography of Major General Abner Doubleday." Unpublished Ph.D. diss., Florida State University, 1980.

Du Pont, Samuel F. (1803–1865)

Union admiral

Samuel Francis Du Pont was born in Bergen Point, New Jersey, on September 25, 1803, the scion of a prominent Delaware family. His father, politically connected to former president Thomas Jefferson, prevailed on his old friend to have Du Pont receive a midshipman's commission in 1815. Two years later, he commenced a series of cruises

Union admiral Samuel F. Du Pont *(U.S. Navy)*

in the Mediterranean and South American squadrons, rising to lieutenant in 1826 and commander by 1843. When the Mexican War erupted in 1846, Du Pont commanded the sloop USS *Cyane* in the Pacific, and with it, he transported the troops of Major John C. Frémont from San Francisco to San Diego, California. He then proceeded to clear enemy forces from the towns of Guaymas, Mazatlán, and La Paz, and later he assisted Commander William B. Shubrick in the capture of San Jose. In this last engagement, Du Pont accompanied a landing party ashore and rescued a party of U.S. Marines besieged in a church. He returned to Washington, D.C., in 1848 and served on a number of important boards, including one recommending creation of a naval academy. He rose to captain in 1855 and stirred considerable acrimony that year as a member of the Efficiency Board, which discharged 201 incompetent officers from active service. He also recommended modernization by advocating wholesale adoption of steam propulsion and better weapons for naval vessels. In 1856 Du Pont commanded the *Minnesota* to China, where he witnessed and carefully analyzed the latest Anglo-French amphibious tactics in operations against Chinese forts. He returned home in 1860 and received command of the Washington Navy Yard, his final peacetime assignment.

Once the Civil War broke out in April 1861, Du Pont sat as senior member on the vitally important Blockade Board, a body tasked with drawing up operational strategy and tactics for use against the Confederate coastline and military installations found there. On September 18, 1861, he received command of the strategic South Atlantic Blockading Squadron. Two months later, on November 7, 1861, Du Pont attacked and captured Port Royal, South Carolina, in concert with General Benjamin F. BUTLER. This constituted the first Federal lodgment on South Carolinian soil since the fall of Fort Sumter in April. Du Pont then continued with a string of minor successes by seizing Tybee Island and Fort Pulaski off Savannah, Georgia, along with numerous points on the coast of Florida the following spring. In recognition of his success, Du Pont received both the thanks of Congress and promotion to rear admiral in July 1862.

By the spring of 1863, Northern politicians were agitating for some kind of punitive action against Charleston, South Carolina, long viewed as the seat of secessionism. In light of Du Pont's seemingly effortless victories against other points along the coast, pressure mounted on him to launch an all-out attack on the city. Du Pont, however, demurred. His new and highly touted monitor craft, while heavily armored, possessed few cannon for offensive purposes and would be outgunned badly in any engagement against Charleston's intricate defenses. To prove his point, he staged a test run of tactics on Fort McAllister, Georgia, on March 3, 1863. Here, the monitors *Passaic, Patapsco,* and *Nahant* under Commander John L. WORDEN attacked and bombarded the enemy post, taking heavy fire in return and accomplishing little. Moreover, the cramped waters of Charleston harbor singularly militated against the successful circling and bombarding tactics employed elsewhere, and Du Pont further warned civilian authorities that the city could be taken only in concert with army troops. Secretary of the Navy Gideon Welles nonetheless caved in to political pressure and ordered Du Pont to attack the city. The admiral sullenly complied, fully expecting to be defeated. On April 7, 1863, Du Pont led seven monitors and one armored steamer into Charleston harbor in a lopsided, two-hour duel with numerous shore batteries directed by General Pierre G. T. BEAUREGARD. His ships were all struck repeatedly, and one monitor, the *Keokuk,* sank the next day. A storm of public and private criticism then arose against the admiral, who tendered his resignation. Du Pont still managed to remain on station for three more months, during which time one of his ships under Commander John RODGERS captured the Confederate vessel CSS *Atlanta.* Du Pont was then replaced by Admiral John A. B. DAHLGREN on July 6, 1863, who, like his predecessor, failed to capture Charleston by a coup de main.

Du Pont returned to his home at Wilmington, Delaware, a bitter, disillusioned man and for several months engaged Secretary Welles in a heated public diatribe over responsibility for the Charleston debacle. He died suddenly in Philadelphia, Pennsylvania, on June 23, 1865, a distinguished officer whose career was ended by the very action he strongly opposed.

Further Reading
Browning, Robert M. *Success Is All that Was Expected: The South Atlantic Blockading Squadron during the Civil War.* Washington, D.C.: Brassey's, 2002.

Coombe, Jack D. *Gunsmoke over the Atlantic: First Naval Actions of the Civil War.* New York: Bantam Books, 2002.

Fuller, Howard. *Navies and Naval Operations of the Civil War, 1861–65.* London: Conway Marine, 2005.

Phelps, W. Chris. *The Bombardment of Charleston, 1863–1865.* Gretna, La.: Pelican Publishing, 2002.

Roberts, William H. *Now for the Contest: Coastal and Oceanic Naval Operations in the Civil War.* Lincoln: University of Nebraska Press, 2004.

Weddle, Kevin J. *Lincoln's Tragic Admiral: The Life of Samuel Francis Du Pont.* Charlottesville: University of Virginia Press, 2005.

E

Early, Jubal A. (1816–1894)
Confederate general

Jubal Anderson Early was born in Franklin County, Virginia, on November 3, 1816, and well educated at local academies. He entered the U.S. Military Academy in 1833 and graduated four years later midway in his class. Early initially saw service as a second lieutenant in the 3rd U.S. Artillery and fought briefly in Florida's Second Seminole War. He then lost interest in military matters and resigned his commission in 1839 to study law. Two years later, Early gained election to the Virginia House of Delegates and also served intermittently as state attorney. Once the Mexican War broke out in 1846, he donned a uniform to serve with the 1st Virginia Volunteers under General Zachary Taylor, but he performed little beyond garrison duty. Unfortunately, Early contracted severe rheumatism in Mexico, which rendered him stooped and gangly beyond his years. He then returned home to resume his successful political career and, in April 1861, was elected to attend the state secessionist convention. Here, Early argued strenuously against secession, but once Virginia left the Union on April 17, 1861, he offered his services to his home state as colonel of the 24th Virginia Infantry. In this capacity, he commanded a brigade at Bull Run on July 21, 1861, acquitting himself well and winning promotion to brigadier general the following month.

During the next three years, Early, a coarse, hard-drinking, and rather profane individual, found himself catapulted into the front ranks of Confederate generalship. He performed capably under General Joseph E. JOHNSTON through the Peninsula campaign and was badly wounded at Williamsburg on May 5, 1862. He recovered in time to fight again at Malvern Hill the following July and subsequently served in General Richard S. EWELL's division of General Thomas J. JACKSON's II Corps. Fighting valorously at Second Bull Run, Antietam, and Fredericksburg, he earned praise from both Jackson and General Robert E. LEE, who affectionately referred to his crusty subordinate as "My Bad Old Man." Early advanced to major general in April 1863 and was selected by Lee to contain General John Sedgwick's Union force at Fredericksburg, while he went on to win a stunning offensive victory at Chancellorsville on May 2–3, 1863. He consequently rose to major general and further distinguished himself in hard fighting at Gettysburg, July 1–3, 1863. In May 1864 Early was tapped to succeed General Ambrose P. HILL temporarily as commander of the III Corps at the Wilderness and Spotsylvania, performing well at that level of command. Then, promoted to lieutenant general as of May 31, he succeeded Ewell as commander of the III Corps in June 1864, whereupon General Lee detached him from the Army of Northern Virginia on a special mission.

In June 1864 Early loped into the Shenandoah Valley with orders to clear that strategic region of Union forces. On June 18, 1864, he defeated General David Hunter at Lynchburg, Virginia, and pursued him vigorously out of the area. He then undertook the bold gambit of raiding the Union capital of Washington, D.C., brushing aside a small Union force under General Lew WALLACE at Monocacy on July 9, 1864. His sudden appearance on the outskirts of the District of Columbia forced General Ulysses S. GRANT to siphon off badly needed manpower from his Richmond campaign to defend the seat of government. Ultimately, the VI and XIX Corps were dispatched. Early had toyed with the idea of attacking Fort Stevens on July 11, but he ultimately withdrew back into the

Confederate general Jubal A. Early *(Massachusetts Commandery Military Order of the Loyal Legion and the U.S. Army Military History Institute)*

Shenandoah. Union forces under General Horatio G. Wright pursued him warily and then pulled back with the bulk of his forces. A force under General George CROOK remained behind at Kernstown, where, on July 24, Early suddenly turned on his pursuers, scattering them. He then deployed several cavalry columns northward, one of which burned the town of Chambersburg, Pennsylvania, on July 13, 1864. Confederate success here greatly embarrassed the government and prompted Grant to take drastic measures to end diversions in this theater once and for all.

In September 1864, General Philip H. SHERIDAN entered the Shenandoah with 40,000 men and orders to pursue and crush Early's army of 18,000 veterans. In quick succession, Sheridan defeated the Confederates at Winchester, September 19,1864, and Fisher's Hill two days later. Early was forced to retreat farther down the valley until Sheridan stopped advancing and left to attend a strategy conference in Washington. Then Early, assisted by Generals John C. BRECKINRIDGE and John B. GORDON, unexpectedly struck at Cedar Creek on October 19, 1864, nearly routing the Federals before Sheridan arrived to rally his men and launch a devastating counterattack. This defeat marked the end of Early's celebrated Shenandoah Valley campaign, and he fell back to Waynesboro, Virginia, to recoup the survivors. On March 2, 1865, General George A. CUSTER suddenly attacked the Confederates, finally smashing the remnants of Early's army. General Lee never held Early personally accountable for the debacle, but the Southern press blamed him for losing this strategic region, and he lost his command shortly before hostilities ceased.

After the war ended, Early fled to Mexico and Canada, where he composed his memoirs. He subsequently returned to Virginia in 1867 and played a significant role in the postwar period by championing the "Lost Cause" theory of the Civil War. He enjoyed a wide-ranging, popular audience, since many hard-core Confederates simply refused to accept defeat gracefully. Early also resumed his successful legal practice and served as the first president of the Southern Historical Association, which extolled the virtues of General Lee and blamed the loss of the war on subordinates such as General James LONGSTREET. Early, who never petitioned to have his citizenship restored, died at Lynchburg, Virginia, on March 2, 1894—an "unreconstructed" Confederate to the bitter end.

Further Reading

Cooling, Frank B. "The Campaign That Could Have Changed the War—and Did: Jubal Early's 1864 Raid on Washington, D.C." *Blue & Gray* 7, no. 5 (2004): 12–23.

Early, Jubal A. *A Memoir of the Last Year of the War for Independence in the Confederate States of America.* Columbia: University of South Carolina Press, 2001.

Gallagher, Gary W., ed. *The Shenandoah Campaign of 1864.* Chapel Hill: University of North Carolina Press, 2006.

Jones, Wilmer L. *Generals in Blue and Gray.* 2 vols. Westport, Conn.: Praeger, 2004.

Lepka, Jack H. *The Shenandoah Valley Campaign of 1864.* Jefferson, N.C.: McFarland, 2003.

Naisawald, L. VanLoan, and James I. Robertson. *The Battle of Lynchburg: Seize Lynchburg—If Only for a Single Day!* Lynchburg, Va.: Warwick House Pub., 2004.

Patchan, Scott C. *Shenandoah Summer: The 1864 Valley Campaign.* Lincoln: University of Nebraska Press, 2007.

Evans, Nathan G. (1824–1868)

Confederate general

Nathan George Evans was born in Marion County, South Carolina, on February 3, 1824, and he studied at Randolph-Macon College. In 1844, on the recommendation of John C. Calhoun, Evans gained admittance to the U.S. Military Academy. Uninspired as a cadet, he acquired the lifelong moniker "Shanks" owing to his spindly legs. After graduating in 1848, Evans joined the 1st U.S. Dragoons as a second lieutenant and commenced a wide-ranging tour of frontier posts. In 1855 he transferred to the newly raised 2nd U.S. Cavalry, in which many future Confederate generals rode.

Now a captain, Evans gained a reputation for fearlessness in battle, and on one occasion, he slew two Comanche chiefs at the Battle of Wachita Village, October 1, 1858. The South Carolina state legislature voted him an elaborate sword in consequence. Evans remained on the frontier until his native state seceded from the Union in December 1860, whereupon he resigned his commission in February 1861 and joined the South Carolina cavalry as a major.

Throughout the bombardment of Fort Sumter, April 12–14, 1861, Evans served as an adjutant general for state forces. Two months later, he gained promotion to lieutenant colonel of the 4th South Carolina Infantry and subsequently commanded a brigade under General Pierre G. T. BEAUREGARD in Virginia. While deployed at Manassas Junction on July 21, 1861, it was Evans who first detected the massive Union turning movement of General Irwin McDOWELL, consisting of 17,000 men. Evans, commanding only 5,000 soldiers, ably defended the Stone Bridge and obstructed their passage until superior numbers forced him back. He was then reinforced by General Barnard E. Bee and Colonel Wade HAMPTON, who were also driven off, but Evans's delaying tactics allowed General Beauregard to react decisively and win the day. For his efforts he gained promotion to colonel, becoming one of South Carolina's earliest wartime heroes. On October 21, 1861, Evans subsequently intercepted a column of Union troops under Colonel Edward D. Baker at Ball's Bluff, Virginia, routing them with a loss of 214 casualties and 714 captives. This little disaster portended very large consequences for it induced Senator Benjamin F. Wade, a Radical Republican, to found the Joint Congressional Committee on the Conduct of the War. The committee operated as a political oversight board and was legally empowered to scrutinize, subpoena, or arrest any Union leader for alleged misbehavior. Evans, meanwhile, received both the thanks of the Confederate Congress and promotion to brigadier general.

Evans acquired such notoriety that his command, popularly known as the "Tramp Brigade," functioned virtually as an autonomous unit. He then marched it back to South Carolina in December 1861 to take command of the 3rd Military District. There, Evans gained additional laurels for defeating several small Union incursions along the coastline. In the summer of 1862, he marched back to Virginia as part of General James LONG-STREET's corps and performed well at Second Bull Run that August. Evans then took temporary command of an entire division during the invasion of Maryland, fighting tenaciously at the battles of South Mountain and Antietam. He then led the "Tramp Brigade" back to North Carolina where, on December 13, 1862, he fiercely resisted General John G. Foster's drive on Kinston. By this time, Evans, a known heavy drinker, was under investigation for dissipation on the battlefield and General Beauregard relieved him of command pending the outcome. Cleared of all charges, he resumed command of the brigade by summer.

In June 1863 Evans was posted to Vicksburg, Mississippi, as part of General William W. LORING's division. In this capacity, he fought under General Joseph E. JOHNSTON at the unsuccessful defense of Jackson, Mississippi, on July 9–16, 1863, and then transferred back east to Savannah, Georgia, for garrison duty. Beauregard, still commanding the district, refused to grant him serious responsibilities, but once he transferred north, Evans became commander of South Carolina's 1st Military District. Shortly after assuming control, he fell off his horse and sustained serious injuries that incapacitated him for the rest of the war. He was in Richmond, Virginia, when it fell to Union forces on April 3, 1865, and fled west with Confederate president Jefferson DAVIS. After the war, Evans relocated to Midway, Alabama, to serve as a school principal. He died there in that capacity on November 30, 1868, a brave officer compromised by his addiction to alcohol.

Further Reading
Conrad, James L. "From Glory to Contention: The Sad History of 'Shanks' Evans." *Civil War Times Illustrated* 22, no. 9 (1983): 32–38.
Detzer, David. *Donnybrook: The Battle of Bull Run*. San Diego: Harcourt, 2004.
Howard, William F. *The Battle of Ball's Bluff: The Leesburg Affair, October 21, 1861*. Lynchburg, Va.: A. E. Howard, 1994.
Priest, John M. *Before Antietam: The Battle of South Mountain*. Shippensburg, Pa.: White Mane Books, 1992.
Silverman, Jason H., Samuel N. Thomas, and Beverly D. Evans. *Shanks: The Life and Wars of Nathan George Evans*. Cambridge, Mass.: Da Capo Press, 2002.
Stone, DeWitt B., ed. *Wandering to Glory: Confederate Veterans Remember Evans Brigade*. Columbia: University of South Carolina Press, 2001.

Ewell, Richard S. (1817–1872)
Confederate general

Richard Stoddert Ewell was born in Washington, D.C., on February 8, 1817, the son of a physician, and was raised in Prince William County, Virginia. In 1836 he matriculated at the U.S. Military Academy and graduated four years later as a second lieutenant in the 1st U.S. Dragoons. Significantly, Ewell rode with his regiment for 20 years. In 1845 he accompanied the dragoon expeditions of Colonel Philip St. George Cooke and Stephen W. Kearny along the Santa Fe and Oregon trails. In the Mexican War (1846–48), he joined General Winfield SCOTT's army and won a brevet promotion to captain for bravery at the battles of Contreras and Churubusco in August 1847. In the latter engagement, he escorted his wounded commander, Captain Philip KEARNY, to the rear and then led his company with distinction. Afterward, he resumed garrison duty along the western frontier and skirmished several times with the Apache under Cochise (1855–57). Two years later, he accompanied noted explorer Colonel Benjamin Bonneville and helped survey the newly acquired lands of the Gadsden Purchase. Ewell next commanded Fort Buchanan, Arizona Territory, in 1860 before illness necessitated a sick leave back to Virginia. Though personally opposed to secession, he resigned his commission and joined the Confederacy once Virginia left the Union in April 1861. Ewell then received a lieutenant colonel's commission in the infantry.

On June 1, 1861, Ewell was slightly injured in a skirmish outside Fairfax, Virginia, becoming in all likelihood the first Southern field officer wounded in action. He was then promoted to brigadier general on June 17, 1861, and commanded troops at Bull Run on July 21, 1861. There, General Pierre G. T. Beauregard directed him to attack Union forces at Centreville, Virginia, but the orders were lost in transit, and he failed to distinguish himself. Nevertheless, on January 24, 1862, Ewell advanced in rank to major general and assumed command of the division formerly led by General Edmund Kirby-Smith. He then joined General Thomas J. Jackson's II Corps and bore conspicuous roles in the spectacular Shenandoah Valley campaign of that spring. Jackson and Ewell worked well in tandem, and they scored victories over General Nathaniel P. Banks at Winchester, Virginia, on May 25, 1861, and General John C. Frémont at Cross Keys on June 8. Jackson's corps then shifted to Virginia's peninsula to join the Army of Northern Virginia under General Robert E. Lee. During the Second Bull Run campaign against General John Pope, Ewell was heavily engaged at Groveton on August 28, 1862, and lost his left leg. He convalesced for nine months and returned to the field a lieutenant general as of May 23, 1863.

After the smashing Confederate victory at Chancellorsville (May 5–6, 1862), Ewell was chosen to replace the mortally wounded Jackson as commander of II Corps. He then helped spearhead Lee's invasion of Pennsylvania with a brilliant victory over Union forces at Winchester, Virginia (June 13–15, 1863), taking nearly 4,000 prisoners. Ewell was preparing to march against Harrisburg, Pennsylvania, when Lee suddenly ordered him to assist General Ambrose P. Hill's III Corps at the strategic road junction called Gettysburg. On July 1, 1863, after a hard slog, Ewell nursed his footsore command into the town and drove out the Union XI Corps of General Oliver O. Howard. Then, in one of the war's most controversial decisions, he elected not to storm the

Confederate general Richard S. Ewell *(Massachusetts Commandery Military Order of the Loyal Legion and the U.S. Army Military History Institute)*

lightly defended heights of Cemetery Hill nearby. At the time, Ewell was acting under discretionary orders from Lee to attack, "If possible." However, this hesitation enabled Union forces under General George G. Meade to consolidate their defenses on highly favorable terrain, which cost the Confederates heavily during the next two days. Ewell justified his actions as pursuant to Lee's instructions, but thereafter he was highly criticized for potentially losing the battle. On July 2 and 3, his corps mounted numerous attacks against Culp's Hill in the rear of Union positions but was invariably driven back downhill. Ewell subsequently fell back with the main army to Virginia. From May 5–12, 1864, his command again was engaged actively in the bloody battles of the Wilderness and Spotsylvania, suffering heavy losses. Ewell was then severely injured by a fall from his horse and Lee replaced him with General Jubal A. EARLY. While recovering, Lee ordered him to take charge of Richmond's defenses. His most notable service occurred on September 29, 1864, when he rushed reinforcements to Fort Harrison and repelled a serious Union probe of the city's defenses. Ewell capably defended the city until April 3, 1865, when Richmond was evacuated by Confederate forces. While marching west, Ewell's corps was cornered at Sayler's Creek, Virginia, by General Philip H. SHERIDAN and nearly was annihilated on April 7, 1865. He was taken prisoner and endured a brief spell of captivity at Fort Sewall, Massachusetts, before being released. After the war, Ewell retired to a farm in Maury County, Tennessee, where he died of pneumonia on January 25, 1872. "Old Bald Head," as he was affectionately known, was a talented commander with many favorable attributes, but in terms of decisiveness and alacrity of movement, he proved no replacement for "Stonewall."

Further Reading

Casdorph, Paul D. *Confederate General R. S. Ewell: Robert E. Lee's Hesitant Commander*. Lexington: University Press of Kentucky, 2004.

Cox, John D. *Culp's Hill: The Attack and Defense of the Union Flank, July 2, 1863*. Cambridge, Mass.: Da Capo Press, 2003.

Jones, Wilmer L. *Generals in Blue and Gray*. Westport, Conn.: Praeger, 2004.

Newton, Steven H. *McPherson's Ridge: The First Battle for the High Ground, July 1, 1863*. Cambridge, Mass.: Da Capo Press, 2002.

Pfanz, Donald. *Richard S. Ewell: A Soldier's Life*. Chapel Hill: University of North Carolina Press, 1998.

Pfanz, Harry W. *Gettysburg—the First Day*. Chapel Hill: University of North Carolina Press, 2001.

Smith, Derek. *Lee's Last Stand: Sailor's Creek, Virginia, 1865*. Shippensburg, Pa.: White Mane Books, 2002.

Tumilty, Victor. "Filling Jackson's Shoes." *Civil War Times* 42, no. 2 (2003): 24–31.

F

Farragut, David G. (1801–1870)

Union admiral

James Glasgow Farragut was born in Campbell's Station, Tennessee, on July 5, 1801, the son of a U.S. Navy sailing master. He relocated to New Orleans, Louisiana, with his family, and after losing both parents to disease, he was adopted by Captain David Porter in 1808. Porter subsequently arranged for Farragut to receive a midshipman's commission, and during the War of 1812, he accompanied his adopted father on the famous Pacific cruise of the USS *Essex*. Many British whaling vessels were captured, and at one point Farragut, aged but 12 years, served as prize master onboard the *Alexander Barclay*. He became a prisoner when the *Essex* was in turn taken by HMS *Phoebe* and *Cherub* on February 18, 1814, and sailed home. Captain Porter publicly lauded his adopted son for bravery in battle, and Farragut honored his adopted father by changing his name to David. During the next 45 years, Farragut fulfilled a wide-ranging variety of missions both at home and abroad. He then rejoined in father as part of the Caribbean "Mosquito Squadron" to suppress piracy in 1822. Farragut rose to lieutenant three years later and, in 1828, while commanding the sloop *Erie,* witnessed the French and British fleets bombard and capture the Mexican castle of San Juan de Ulloa. This incident underscored to Farragut the vulnerability of fortifications to plunging artillery fire. He next fulfilled an uneventful stint of blockade duty during the Mexican War (1846–48); returned to Washington, D.C., to publish a number of technical treatises; and in 1854 directed construction of naval facilities at Mare Island, San Francisco. By the time Farragut became a captain in 1855, he was regarded as a competent but relatively undistinguished career officer. He was also a longtime resident of Norfolk, Virginia, but after the Civil War commenced in April 1861, his pro-Union sympathies required him to move to New York. He quickly tendered his services to the U.S. government, but the Navy Department, suspicious of his Southern roots, restricted his activities to supervising a retirement board.

After many months of officially imposed inactivity, fate intervened on Farragut's behalf when President Abraham LINCOLN sanctioned an amphibious attack on his home port of New Orleans. It was only after the intercession of his adopted brother, Commander David D. PORTER, that Secretary of the Navy Gideon Welles delegated the mission to Farragut. He now headed the West Gulf Blockading Squadron and for two months meticulously gathered a fleet of 24 wooden warships and 19 mortar gunboats off Ship Island, Mississippi. On April 18, 1862, after carefully plotting his approach to the city, Farragut directed Porter's gunboats to bombard Forts Jackson and St. Philip, on the Mississippi River, into submission. A week elapsed without the desired results, however, and the famously impatient Farragut ordered his fleet to pass the forts at night and take the city by storm. On the night of April 24, 1862, he audaciously accomplished exactly that, sweeping aside a small Confederate flotilla at the cost of one vessel sunk. The river was then running high, and with his guns pointed over the levees toward the city, New Orleans surrendered on April 25 and was occupied by troops under General Benjamin F. BUTLER. This was a major Union victory with significant military consequences: The South lost its biggest port while the Union acquired a strategic base controlling both the Mississippi River and the Gulf of Mexico. A grateful Congress voted Farragut their thanks and promoted him to rear admiral on July 16, 1862; he is the first American naval officer accorded such high rank.

Farragut followed up his success by running the fleet up the Mississippi River and operating for a time off the Confederate bastion at Vicksburg, Mississippi. He tried to capture that vital city with

Union admiral David G. Farragut *(Library of Congress)*

naval power alone but was thwarted by an inability to bombard the high bluffs on which it sat. He was eventually joined by the Mississippi River Squadron of Captain Charles H. DAVIS, whose lack of aggressiveness led to his eventual replacement by Porter. Farragut then sailed back downstream to assist General Nathaniel P. BANKS in the reduction of Port Hudson, Louisiana, on July 8, 1863, which constituted part of General Ulysses S. GRANT's efforts at Vicksburg. Control of the entire Mississippi River from St. Louis to New Orleans then reverted back to Union hands for the remainder of the war. Farragut next began to plan an ambitious assault on the significant port of Mobile, Alabama, but ill health necessitated his return to New York for convalescence. It was not until the spring of 1864 that he felt strong enough to resume duties with the West Gulf Blockading Squadron. He then spent several months assembling his ships, charting the waters in and around Mobile Bay, and marking torpedo (mine) fields as necessary. At dawn on August 5, 1864, Farragut led his squadron of four armored monitors and 14 wooden vessels past the guns of Fort Morgan. En route, the ironclad *Tecumseh* struck a mine and sank quickly, causing the entire squadron to back up. Farragut, lashed to the mainmast of the *Hartford* to better observe events, inquired as to the problem and barked back, "Damn the torpedoes! Full speed ahead!" The Union fleet then crashed into Mobile Bay sinking a small Confederate squadron before tangling with and subduing the ram CSS *Tennessee* under redoubtable Admiral Franklin BUCHANAN. Fort Morgan managed to hold out until August 23, 1864, after which the second-largest Confederate port was firmly in Union hands. In recognition of his second splendid achievement, Congress elevated him to the rank of vice admiral on December 23, 1864.

Farragut returned to New York shortly after to recuperate his health, and he missed the major naval effort at Fort Fisher, Wilmington, North Carolina. He then partook of minor operations along the James River, Virginia, in the spring of 1865 when the war ended. On July 26, 1866, Congress again promoted him to full admiral, and he assumed command of the European Squadron on an extended goodwill tour through 1867. Farragut died in Portsmouth, New Hampshire, on August 14, 1870, one of the boldest exponents of naval power in American history. His contributions to the Union victory were essential.

Further Reading

Duffy, James P. *Lincoln's Admiral: The Civil War Campaigns of David Farragut.* New York: Wiley, 1997.

Friend, Jack. *West Wind, Flood Tide: The Battle of Mobile Bay.* Annapolis, Md.: Naval Institute Press, 2003.

Fuller, Howard. *Navies and Naval Operations of the Civil War, 1861–65.* London: Conway Maritime, 2005.

Garcia, Pedro. "Losing the Big Easy." *Civil War Times Illustrated* 41, no. 2 (2002): 46–53, 64–65.

Harris, William C. "Damn *These* Torpedoes, too!" *Civil War Times Illustrated* 39, no. 1 (2000): 36–42.

Hearn, Chester G. *Admiral David Glasgow Farragut: The Civil War Years.* Annapolis, Md.: Naval Institute Press, 1998.

Schneller, Robert J. *Farragut: America's First Admiral.* Washington, D.C.: Brassey's, 2002.

Sweetman, Jack, ed. *The Great Admirals: Command at Sea, 1587–1945.* Annapolis, Md.: Naval Institute Press, 1997.

———. *Great American Naval Battles.* Annapolis, Md.: Naval Institute Press, 1998.

Suhr, Robert. "A Run for New Orleans." *Military Heritage* 2, no. 1 (2000): 52–59, 86–87.

Floyd, John B. (1806–1863)

Confederate general

John Buchanan Floyd was born in Smithfield, Virginia, on June 1, 1806, the son of a planter. He passed through South Carolina College in 1829 with a law degree and commenced a successful practice at home. In 1847 he parleyed his skills into politics by successfully standing for a seat in the House of Delegates and a year later served as governor of Virginia. As a politician, Floyd fully embraced slavery and states's rights, but he proved ambivalent toward secession. In 1856 he strongly supported the presidential candidacy of James Buchanan and received the appointment of secretary of war in return. Floyd, lacking any practical military experience, enjoyed a stormy tenure in office amid rising claims of corruption and cronyism. The bulk of accusations arose from his apparent mishandling of Indian trust funds and the alleged channeling of profits into the hands of friends and relatives. Floyd deepened his reputation for controversy in 1860 by appointing Joseph E. JOHNSTON, his brother in law, to be quartermaster general, over the heads of more experienced individuals such as Colonel Robert E. LEE. Once the nation was buffeted by the rising tide of secessionism, Floyd's actions were viewed in a more treasonable light. At one point, he arranged for the transfer of 125,00 small arms to arsenals throughout the South, a move greeted with suspicion by many Northerners. Floyd simply countered that he was making room for new stocks of rifled weapons that were expected soon. A congressional committee investigated Floyd and cleared him of any improprieties in February 1861, but by then the issue was moot. Floyd, angered by what he considered the illegal transfer of Federal troops from Fort Moultrie, Charleston, South Carolina, to Fort Sumter in the harbor, demanded that President Buchanan countermand the move. When Buchanan refused to order Major Robert ANDERSON into compliance, Floyd resigned from office on December 29, 1860, and returned to Virginia.

On May 23, 1861, Floyd became a brigadier general in the Confederate army. The following August, he assumed control of the Army of the Kanawha in western Virginia and was tasked with protecting the Allegheny Mountains from Union attacks. He waged a number of ineffective skirmishes at Cross Lanes and Carnifex Ferry that September, losing valuable ground. However, the following December, he transferred his brigade to the army of General Albert S. JOHNSTON in Kentucky, where he was assigned to command Forts Henry and Donelson. These strategic posts, on the Cumberland and Tennessee rivers, respectively, constituted the first line of Southern defenses in the middle sector, and they were vital to the Confederate cause. For this reason, in the spring of

1862, they became the objects of a concerted Union offensive under General Ulysses S. GRANT and Captain Andrew H. FOOTE. On February 6, 1862, Foote managed to capture Fort Henry with gunboats alone while Grant prepared to march overland to besiege the remaining post.

For several days Floyd, in concert with Generals Gideon J. PILLOW and Simon B. Buckner, deliberated about what to do. On February 6, 1862, Fort Donelson's gunners drove off Foote's gunboats, but Floyd believed that his position was hopeless. The Confederates then sortied in strength against Grant's besieging army the following day, and they nearly broke through, but indecisiveness at the last minute allowed a Union counterattack to shut the defenders back into their fort. That evening, Floyd and Pillow made a fateful decision to escape with part of the garrison while Buckner remained behind to surrender. On February 16, 1862, Floyd and Pillow departed before Grant accepted the surrender of Fort Donelson—a major blow to the Confederacy. The entire affairs so disgusted Major Nathan B. FORREST that he disregarded orders and likewise cut his way to safety. Floyd then made his way to Nashville, where Johnston placed him in charge of evacuation efforts. However, once Confederate president Jefferson DAVIS learned of the circumstances by which Floyd abandoned his command, he relieved him on March 11, 1862. This act should have ended his military career, but Floyd's political connections ran deep, and in April 1862, the Virginia legislature promoted him to major general of militia. He then spent the balance of the year garrisoning saltmines and railroads in the southwestern portion of the state before dying at Abingdon on August 26, 1863. All told, Floyd's flirtation with military command bore disastrous consequences for the Confederacy that he sought so earnestly to serve.

Further Reading

Engle, Stephen D. *Struggle for the Heartland: The Campaign from Fort Henry to Corinth.* Lincoln: University of Nebraska Press, 2001.

Gott, Kendall D. *Where the South Lost the War: An Analysis of the Fort Henry–Fort Donelson Campaign, February 1862.* Mechanicsburg, Pa.: Stackpole Books, 2003.

McKnight, Brian D. *Contested Borderland: The Civil War in Appalachian Kentucky and Virginia.* Lexington: University Press of Kentucky, 2006.

Pinnegar, Charles. *Brand of Infamy: A Biography of John Buchanan Floyd.* Westport, Conn.: Greenwood Press, 2002.

Symonds, Craig, et al. "Who Were the Worst Ten Generals?" *North & South* 7, no. 3 (2004): 12–25.

Tucker, Spencer C. *"Unconditional Surrender": The Captures of Forts Henry and Donelson.* Abilene, Tex.: McWhiney Foundation Press, 2001.

Foote, Andrew H. (1806–1863)
Union admiral

Andrew Hull Foote was born in New Haven, Connecticut, on September 12, 1806, and raised in a strict, religious household. In 1822 he gained admittance to the U.S. Military Academy, but he matriculated only six months before receiving his midshipman's commission in the U.S. Navy. During the next two decades, he held a wide variety of billets both on land and on sea, rising to lieutenant in 1831. Ten years later, he assumed command of the frigate USS *Cumberland* and, consistent with his deeply held religious beliefs, made history by organizing the first shipwide temperance society. Foote subsequently launched a drive to ban alcoholic rations on navy vessels, which finally became official policy in 1862. He also agitated against flogging and zealously pursued antislavery activities off the coast of Africa. Ashore, Foote was active in abolitionist activities, and in 1854, he published an account of his activities entitled *Africa and the American Flag.* In 1856 he advanced to command and took the sloop *Portsmouth* on a tour of Asia, where he witnessed British naval operations during the so-called Arrow War against China. On November 21, 1856, Chinese gunners at Canton mistakenly fired on his vessel, so Foote promptly landed 300 sailors and marines ashore, stormed four barrier forts, and killed an estimated 250 defenders at a cost of 29 killed and wounded. He

Union admiral Andrew H. Foote *(National Archives)*

sailed home in 1858 and received command of the Brooklyn Navy Yard, a post he held when the Civil War commenced.

In June 1861 Foote was ordered to replace Commander John RODGERS as head of the embryonic Mississippi River Squadron, headquartered at St. Louis, Missouri. He assisted engineer James B. Eads in constructing several armored gunboats for use on the western waters. These 12 small vessels, mounting 143 heavy cannon, quickly proved invaluable assets for exploiting riverine warfare against the Confederacy. Foote also struck up cordial relations with the local military commander, General Ulysses S. GRANT, who shared his strate-

gic vision for offensive operations. Their first objective was Fort Henry on the Cumberland River, which Foote bombarded into submission on February 6, 1862, without army assistance. He next sailed on to engage the much stronger position of Fort Donelson on the Tennessee River while Grant marched overland to besiege it. On February 14 Foote engaged the Confederate batteries, situated on a high bluff, which subjected his armada to a plunging fire. He was rebuffed with severe losses and sustained a foot injury but refused to relinquish command. Hobbling on crutches, Foote next deployed his craft in concert with General John POPE's forces at Island No. 10 in the Mississippi River. After several days of ineffectual bombardment, he slipped the ironclad *Carondelet* past Confederate defenses on the night of April 4, 1862, cutting the garrison off and prompting its surrender three days later. The upper Mississippi River was now entirely clear of a Confederate presence, but Foote's declining health necessitated his replacement by Commander Charles H. DAVIS in June 1862.

In light of his exceptional service, Foote received both the thanks of Congress and promotion to rear admiral as of June 16, 1862. He remained actively employed in New York as chief of the Bureau of Equipment and Recruiting, although he chafed in the role of a bureaucrat. Foote then lobbied for an active command, and in June 1863, he succeeded Admiral Samuel F. DU PONT as head of the South Atlantic Blockading Squadron. He never lived to accept command, dying suddenly in New York on June 26, 1863. Foote made invaluable contributions to the Union war effort through his expertise with gunboats and his demonstrated willingness to work closely with army commanders.

Further Reading

Coombe, Jack D. *Thunder along the Mississippi: The River Battles That Split the Confederacy.* New York: Sarpedon, 1996.

Forlenza, Gerald A. "A Navy Life: The Pre-Civil War Career of Rear Admiral Andrew Hull Foote." Unpublished Ph.D. diss., Claremont Graduate School, 1991.

Gott, Kendall D. "Gateway to the Heartland." *North &
South* 7, no. 2 (2004): 46–59.

Jackson, Rex T. *James B. Eads: The Civil War Ironclads on
His Mississippi.* Bowie, Md.: Heritage Books, 2004.

Konstam, Angus. *Mississippi River Gunboats of the American Civil War.* Oxford: Osprey, 2002.

Tucker, Spencer C. *Andrew Foote: Civil War Admiral
on Western Waters.* Annapolis, Md.: Naval Institute
Press, 2000.

Forrest, Nathan B. (1821–1877)

Confederate general

Nathan Bedford Forrest was born in Chapel Hill,
Tennessee, on July 13, 1821, the son of an impov-
erished blacksmith. He accompanied his family to
Mississippi where his father died in 1837 and left
him, at the age of 16, responsible for feeding a
large family. Forrest never attended school and
remained semiliterate throughout his entire life,
but he proved himself a singularly driven man.
After working as a day laborer, he learned to trade
in cattle and slaves and eventually established a
prosperous plantation. Forrest proved so adept at
selling cotton that he became a self-made million-
aire by the time the Civil War began in April 1861.
He initially joined the 7th Tennessee Cavalry as a
private and then received permission to raise and
equip a regiment at his own expense as its lieutenant colonel. In February 1862 he fought well at the
defense of Forts Henry and Donelson, and on the
night of the 16th, he escaped rather than surrender. Such initiative brought him promotion to
colonel, and he gained additional laurels at the
Battle of Shiloh (April 6–7, 1862), capturing a
Union battery and advancing to brigadier general.
In July 1862 Forrest was assigned to the army of
General Braxton BRAGG, a man for whom he
expressed strong antipathy. He nonetheless performed well as an independent raider, and on July
13, 1862, he bluffed the Union garrison at Murfreesboro, Tennessee, into surrendering. Bragg,
who viewed Forrest as more of a nuisance than an
asset, subsequently stripped him of command and
ordered him south to raise a new force. Forrest
readily complied, and from December 1862 to
January 1863, he accompanied General Earl VAN
DORN on several effective raids against General
Ulysses S. GRANT's supply lines. When Van Dorn
later accused Forrest of hoarding captured Union
supplies for his own use—a charge Forrest vehemently denied—the two headstrong cavaliers
nearly came to blows.

The secret of Forrest's success was his ability to
move suddenly, strike unexpectedly, and withdraw quickly along prearranged escape routes. His
oft-quoted mantra of "Get there first with the
most men" was germane to his success but also a
luxury he seldom enjoyed. In fact, Forrest exhibited an uncanny knack for engaging and defeating
forces much larger than his own. For example, in
April 1863, he surrounded and bluffed the 2,000-
man column of Colonel Abel D. Streight into surrendering to his 500 men at Rome, Georgia.

Confederate general Nathan B. Forrest *(Massachusetts
Commandery Military Order of the Loyal Legion and the U.S.
Army Military History Institute)*

Forrest subsequently rejoined the Army of Tennessee under General Bragg that summer and fought well at the bloody battle of Chickamauga on September 18–20, 1863. However, Forrest became so outraged by Bragg's unwillingness to pursue General William S. ROSECRANS's defeated army that a duel seemed in the offing. He then requested an immediate transfer, and President Jefferson DAVIS allowed him to set up an independent command in nearby Mississippi with a rank of major general as of December 4, 1863. From here, Forrest was at liberty to slash at Union supply routes in Tennessee and northern Alabama while also parrying the occasional Federal thrust against him. The only serious blot on his military reputation was the capture of Fort Pillow, Tennessee, on April 12, 1864, whereby he apparently allowed his men to lose control and massacre part of the African-American garrison. On June 10, 1864, Forrest scored his biggest tactical success by attacking and routing General Samuel G. Sturgis's 10,000 Union soldiers at Brice's Cross Roads, Mississippi. However, he suffered a heavy defeat while operating under General Samuel D. Lee at Tupelo on July 13–15, 1864, and returned to raiding. He scored a spectacular success at Johnston, Tennessee, nearly crippling General William T. SHERMAN's supply lines on his march to Georgia. Sherman grew so exasperated that he declared that Forrest must be destroyed "if it costs ten thousand lives and breaks the treasury." He subsequently served under General John B. HOOD during his ill-fated advance on Nashville, Tennessee, and he skillfully covered the Confederate withdrawal throughout December 1864.

Forrest rose to lieutenant general in February 1865 but his shrinking command confronted insurmountably steep odds. On April 2, 1865, General James H. WILSON's cavalry corps drove Forrest and his troopers out of Selma, Alabama, his last and largest defeat. He finally surrendered to Union authorities at Gainesville, Alabama, on May 9, 1865, and returned home to his ruined plantation. After the war, Forrest tried to recoup his fortune but enjoyed little success. He spent the balance of his remaining years in Memphis, Tennessee, as president of a railroad company. Forrest also acquired considerable notoriety by founding the infamous Ku Klux Klan in 1867, serving as its first and only Grand Wizard. He subsequently disbanded the group in 1869 after failing to curb its violent excesses against African Americans. Forrest died in Memphis on October 29, 1877, at the age of 56. His greatest leadership trait, a single-minded determination to succeed, probably makes him the Confederacy's most accomplished cavalry leader and a partisan raider of the first order. Like Wade HAMPTON and Richard TAYLOR, he is one of only three Confederates who were elevated to lieutenant general without prior military training.

Further Reading

Ashdown, Paul. *The Myth of Nathaniel Bedford Forrest.* Lanham, Md.: Rowman and Littlefield, 2005.

Black, Robert W. *Cavalry Raids of the Civil War.* Mechanicsburg, Pa.: Stackpole Books, 2004.

Bradley, Michael R. *Nathan Bedford Forrest's Escort and Staff.* Gretna, La.: Pelican Pub. Co., 2006.

Browning, Robert M. *Forrest: The Confederacy's Relentless Warrior.* Washington, D.C.: Brassey's, 2004.

Cimprich, John. *Fort Pillow, a Civil War Massacre, and Public Memory.* Baton Rouge: Louisiana State University Press, 2005.

Davidson, Eddy. *Nathan Bedford Forrest: In Search of the Empire.* Gretna, La.: Pelican Pub. Co., 2006.

Keithly, David. "Pay the Devil Asymmetrically: Nathan Bedford Forrest in the American Civil War." *Civil Wars* 5, no. 4 (2002): 77–102.

Russell, Michael B. "Fort Pillow: Press, Propaganda, and Public Perception During the American Civil War." Unpublished master's thesis, University of Arkansas, Fayetteville, 2002.

G

Gibbon, John (1827–1896)

Union general

John Gibbon was born in Holmesburg, Pennsylvania, on April 20, 1827, the son of a physician. He relocated with his family to Charlotte, North Carolina, as a child and was admitted from there to the U.S. Military Academy in 1842. Gibbon graduated five years later, having been held back a year owing to difficulties with an English course. Now a second lieutenant of the 4th U.S. Artillery, he accompanied his gun crew to Mexico in 1847 but saw no action. He next served in Florida by assisting Seminole Indians in their move to the Indian Territory (Oklahoma), from which he acquired lasting sympathy for Native Americans. By 1855, Gibbon was promoted captain and back at West Point as an artillery instructor where, in 1859, he published his seminal *The Artillerist's Manual*. This text is significant in being the first American book on the subject, for prior to its appearance the army simply utilized the latest French manuals. Gibbon was stationed in Utah Territory when the secession crisis erupted in 1861 and his Southern origins caused a degree of suspicion among fellow officers. Nonetheless, and despite the fact that his three brothers served the Confederacy, he remained loyal to the Union.

Gibbon first saw service by commanding a battery in the newly raised Army of the Potomac, and, on November 8, 1861, he joined General Irwin McDowell's division as chief of artillery. A hard-edged professional and an excellent disciplinarian, he rose to brigadier general on May 2, 1862, and led a brigade in General Rufus King's division. In this respect, Gibbon differed from many of his West Point contemporaries by not despising volunteer soldiers. Instead, he paid them due respect, carefully trained them, and cultivated their loyalty. His command consisted of four regiments from Wisconsin and one from Illinois, which he outfitted with white pants and tall black hats to improve esprit de corps. The "Black Hat Brigade," as they were initially known, experienced its baptism of fire at Groveton, Virginia, on August 28, 1862, where it was ambushed by Confederates under General Thomas J. JACKSON. Gibbon calmly led his men into a battle in which they suffered 40 percent casualties but held their ground dutifully. He next distinguished himself in bloody fighting at South Mountain and Antietam, where General Joseph HOOKER pronounced his troops the "Iron Brigade"—and the moniker stuck. Gibbon subsequently led a division in General John F. REYNOLDS I Corps at Fredericksburg on December 13, 1862, where he was severely wounded. After recovering, he was assigned to divisional command in the II Corps of General Winfield S. HANCOCK, and he fought actively in the ill-fated Chancellorsville campaign.

During the first day of Gettysburg, July 1, 1863, the Iron Brigade was one of the first infantry units to reinforce Union cavalry under General

Union general John Gibbon *(Library of Congress)*

capacity, he helped pursue the Army of Northern Virginia from Richmond in April 1865 and was one of three commissioners selected to arrange the surrender of General Robert E. LEE at Appomattox on April 9.

Gibbon was retained in the peacetime establishment with a rank of colonel of the 36th and then the 7th U.S. Infantry, and he was posted back on the frontier. In this capacity, his unit formed part of General George CROOK's column and was the first to reach the survivors of General George A. CUSTER's 7th Cavalry at Little Big Horn. The following year, he played a prominent role in the Nez Perce War against Chief Joseph and was repulsed by the tribe's warriors at the Battle of Big Hole, Montana, on August 9, 1877. Gibbon, who sustained his third and final wound in this fight, afterward befriended the chief. In 1885 he accepted command of the Department of Columbia and the following year took charge of the Department of the Pacific at San Francisco. Gibbon retired from the army in 1891 and eventually settled in Baltimore, Maryland, where he served as commander of the Military Order of the Loyal Legion. He died there on February 6, 1896, a loyal Southerner and an outstanding combat commander.

John BUFORD. Gibbon led it into the thick of combat under General John F. REYNOLDS, where it suffered horrific casualties but again acquitted itself well. On July 3, 1863, Gibbon's command absorbed the main Confederate charge by General George E. PICKETT on Cemetery Hill, driving the Southerners off with heavy losses. At the height of the engagement, Gibbon received a second serious wound and was borne from the battlefield. After months of convalescence, he rejoined Hancock's II Corps in time for General Ulysses S. GRANT's Overland campaign against Richmond, Virginia, in May 1864. Gibbon then fought capably at the bloody battles of the Wilderness, Spotsylvania, and Cold Harbor before settling into the long siege at Petersburg. He rose to major general in June 1864, but his formally cordial relations with Hancock soured, and Gibbon was transferred to command the XXIV Corps, Army of the James. In this

Further Reading

Berkoff, Todd S. "'Our Boys Mowed Their Ranks Like Grass': The Iron Brigade at Brawner's Farm." *Military Heritage* 2, no. 4 (2001): 64–71, 98.

Herdegen, Lance J. *The Men Stood Like Iron: How the Iron Brigade Won Its Name.* Bloomington: Indiana University Press, 1997.

Lavery, Donald S. *Iron Brigade General: John Gibbon, A Rebel in Blue.* Westport, Conn.: Greenwood Press, 1993.

Newton, Steven H. *McPherson's Ridge: The First Fight for the High Ground, July 1, 1863.* Cambridge, Mass.: Da Capo Press, 2002.

Nolan, Alan T., and Sharon E. Vipond. *Giants in Their Tall Hats: Essays on the Iron Brigade.* Bloomington: Indiana University Press, 1998.

Wert, Jeffrey D. *A Brotherhood of Valor: The Common Soldiers of the Stonewall Brigade, C.S.A., and the Iron Brigade, U.S.A.* New York: Simon and Schuster, 1999.

Gordon, John B. (1832–1904)

Confederate general

John Brown Gordon was born in Upson County, Georgia, on February 6, 1832, and he studied at the University of Georgia. However, he quit school briefly to study law and subsequently managed a mine in northwestern Georgia. Gordon was also passionately pro-secessionist, so when the Civil War erupted in April 1861, he joined a company of mountain men called the "Racoon Roughs" and functioned as their captain. When Georgia authorities declined to accept their services, he marched them across the state line to become part of the 6th Alabama Infantry. Gordon, despite his lack of professional military training, adjusted well to mili-

Confederate general John B. Gordon *(National Archives)*

tary life, and in April 1862, he advanced to colonel. He then fought in the Peninsula campaign of 1862 under General Richard Rodes, seeing combat at Seven Pines and Malvern Hill. In the latter engagement, Gordon assumed command of the brigade when Rodes fell wounded. That fall, Gordon helped spearhead the Confederate advance into Maryland, and he saw active duty at the battles of South Mountain and Antietam as part of General Daniel H. Hill's division. On September 17, 1862, Gordon's brigade held the Sunken Road in the center of General Robert E. Lee's position, where it beat off repeated attacks by superior numbers of Union troops. In the course of combat, Gordon was hit no less than five times, with the last bullet smashing into his left cheek, knocking him unconscious. In light of his sterling behavior, he received promotion to brigadier general, although he required several months for recuperation.

In the spring of 1863, Gordon commanded a brigade of Georgia troops in General Jubal A. Early's division. He fought well at Chancellorsville and Gettysburg that year and performed exceptionally well during the 1864 Overland campaign against General Ulysses S. Grant. At the Battle of Spotsylvania on May 12, 1864, Federals under General Winfield S. Hancock overran the Confederate salient at the "Mule Shoe" and threatened to break their line when Gordon promptly counterattacked and drove them back. Consequently, he gained promotion to major general and accompanied Early's II Corps throughout the famous Shenandoah campaign of the summer and fall of 1864. As such, he bore conspicuous roles in fighting at Lynchburg, Monocacy, and Kernstown during the initial Confederate resurgence and then at the losing battles of Winchester, Fisher's Hill, and Cedar Creek against General Philip H. Sheridan. Afterward, Early's army was broken up, and the survivors returned to the Army of Northern Virginia outside Petersburg, Virginia. Gordon had yet to be promoted to lieutenant general, but he was nevertheless tasked with conducting the final Confederate offensive of the war against Fort Stedman on

March 25, 1865. Defeat here signaled the eventual collapse of Southern defenses, and Gordon conducted a tenacious rearguard action that allowed the Army of Northern Virginia to escape intact. He next fought at Sayler's Creek on April 6, 1865, where most of the II Corps was captured or destroyed, and he briefly succeeded General Richard S. Ewell as commander. Lee then appointed Gordon to draw up documents outlining his surrender to General Grant on April 12, 1865. He also received the special distinction of being allowed to lead the bedraggled Confederates out of camp, past Union troops lining the roads at Appomattox. When General Joshua L. Chamberlain unexpectedly ordered his men to present arms as a token of respect, Gordon had his men do the same, thereby returning "honor for honor."

After the war, Gordon enjoyed a lengthy and successful political career. He gained election to the U.S. Senate in 1873 as a Democrat, becoming the first former Confederate to preside over that body. He also served as a leading voice for national reconciliation and urged Southerners to work wholeheartedly for reunification. He also prevailed on Northern politicians to end the period of Reconstruction and allow self-rule in former states of the Confederacy. As a spokesperson for the "New South," Gordon was also a proponent of modernization and industrialization to assist his region in breaking from its long agrarian tradition. In 1886 Gordon was elected governor of Georgia, and two years later, he served again in the U.S. Senate. In a throwback to his earlier life, when the United Confederate Veterans was established in 1890, Gordon was elected its first commander in chief. He held the post at the time of his death in Miami, Florida, on January 9, 1904. He was among the Confederacy's most successful divisional commanders and the only corps-level leader without professional military instruction.

Further Reading
Bates, Thomas. "One of the Best: John Brown Gordon's Rise in the Army of Northern Virginia." Unpublished master's thesis, James Madison University, 2001.
Eckert, Ralph L. *John Brown Gordon: Soldier, Southerner, American.* Baton Rouge: Louisiana State University Press, 1989.
Lepa, Jack H. *The Shenandoah Campaign of 1864.* Jefferson, N.C.: McFarland, 2003.
Lowry, Joseph E. "Lee's Last Throw of the Dice." *Military Heritage* 6, no. 3 (2004): 62–69.
Gordon, John B. *Reminiscences of the Civil War.* New York: C. Scribner's Sons, 1903.
Smith, Derek. *Lee's Last Stand: Sailor's Creek, Virginia, 1865.* Shippensburg, Pa.: White Mane Books, 2002.

Gorgas, Josiah (1818–1883)
Confederate general

Josiah Gorgas was born in Running Pumps, Pennsylvania, on July 1, 1818, the son of poor farmers, and he was forced to quit school in order to help support his large family. After enduring a hardscrabble existence, he gained admittance to the U.S. Military Academy in 1837 and graduated four years later, sixth in a class of 52. Gorgas was then posted as a second lieutenant in the Ordnance Corps, for which he showed considerable promise. He remained at the Watervliet Arsenal, New York, for many years and in 1845 spent a year in Europe to study foreign ordnance. He returned home in time to fight in the Mexican War (1846–48), with the army under General Winfield Scott. Gorgas acquitted himself well while sighting cannon at the siege of Veracruz, and Scott appointed him head of the ordnance depot there. After the war, Gorgas resumed his routine activities at a number of Federal arsenals around the country. However, while stationed at Mount Vernon, Alabama, in 1853, he married the daughter of a former governor. After this time, he increasingly identified his personal interests with those of the South. Gorgas, who had lost a brevet promotion to internal army politics, finally rose to captain in 1855 and was commanding the Franklin Arsenal in Philadelphia, Pennsylvania, when the Civil War commenced in April 1861. After some initial wavering, his wife and her family prevailed on him to throw his lot in with the South, and he resigned his commission to join the Confederate army.

Gorgas was initially posted as a major within the Confederate Ordnance Corps, but President Jefferson Davis, acting on the advice of General Pierre G. T. Beauregard, appointed him chief of Confederate ordnance on April 8, 1861. Thus situated, he was now responsible for procuring, constructing, and repairing all available weapons for Southern armies. On paper, Gorgas faced nearly insurmountable obstacles, for the Confederacy generally lacked an industrial base and possessed but a single cannon foundry in Richmond, Virginia. However, this heretofore unknown ordnance officer demonstrated outright genius at organization and improvisation, and he soon established himself as one of the Confederacy's greatest assets. To augment existing stocks, Gorgas instituted a systematized policy of thoroughly scavenging Union weapons and supplies captured on the battlefield. He next undertook a drastic expansion of existing factories and the addition of new ones, along with the concomitant gunpowder mills, foundries, and arsenals to manufacture rifles, pistols, swords, and cannon. Gorgas also founded the Confederate Nitre and Mineral Bureau to manage the utilization of all natural resources effectively. Realizing that the South could never match Northern industrial output, he dispatched numerous agents abroad to Europe to buy or barter for the requisite weapons, tools, and machinery. These items would then be transported home on a fleet of blockade-runners employed by the Ordnance Department. The system he originated proved highly efficient, and during the next four years, the Confederacy acquired 600,000 weapons, 2 million pounds of saltpeter, and 1.5 million pounds of lead.

Gorgas carried the process a step further through an ingenious system of decentralized distribution to offset the Confederacy's decided lack of railroads. It was administered by capable subordinates handpicked by Gorgas himself, and it worked surprisingly well considering the difficulties under which the South labored. Consequently, he almost singlehandedly kept Confederate field armies relatively well armed and equipped for the duration of the war. The Southern war effort could not have lasted as long as it did without his supervision, and on November 10, 1864, he gained promotion to brigadier general. His supply system remained in play until the very last days of the war, and Gorgas himself surrendered to Union authorities at Washington, North Carolina, on May 14, 1865.

In the postwar period, Gorgas tried his hand at administering an ironworks in Alabama, and after it failed, he turned to education in 1872 in becoming vice president of the University of the South at Sewanee, Tennessee. After a stormy tenure there, he transferred to the University of Alabama as its president in 1878. Poor health soon necessitated his retirement, and Gorgas spent the rest of his life as the university librarian. He died in Tuscaloosa, Alabama, on May 15, 1883, the most accomplished ordnance officer in American history—Union or Confederate.

Further Reading

Bragg, C. L. *Never for Want of Powder: The Confederate Powder Works in Augusta, Georgia.* Columbia: University of South Carolina Press, 2007.

Collins, Steven G. "From Pikes to Gunpowder: Josiah Gorgas and the Arming of an Agrarian Nation." Unpublished master's thesis, Southwest Texas State University, 1992.

Moore, Michael J. "Josiah Gorgas and the Richmond Ordnance Industry: The Arsenal of the Confederacy." Unpublished master's thesis, Old Dominion University, 1996.

Wiggins, Sarah W. *Love and Duty: Amelia and Josiah Gorgas and Their Family.* Tuscaloosa: University of Alabama Press, 2005.

Wiggins, Sarah W., ed. *The Journal of Josiah Gorgas, 1857–1878.* Tuscaloosa: University of Alabama Press, 1995.

Woodward, Steven E., et al. "Who Were the Top Ten Generals?" *North & South* 6, no. 4 (2003): 12–22.

Grant, Ulysses S. (1822–1885)
Union general

Hiram Ulysses Grant was born in Point Pleasant, Ohio, on April 27, 1822, the son of farmers. Listless and idle as a youth, his father managed to secure him an appointment to the U.S. Military Academy in 1839. While in attendance, his name was mistakenly recorded as Ulysses Simpson Grant, which he formally adopted. Grant proved a lackluster student, displaying aptitude for horsemanship and little else, but he graduated midway in his class by 1843 and was commissioned a second lieutenant in the 4th U.S. Infantry. He served briefly at the Jefferson Barracks, Missouri, before joining General Zachary Taylor's Army of Texas in 1846. When the Mexican War broke out, Grant was in the thick of fighting at Palo Alto, Resaca de la Palma, and Monterrey, and he subsequently transferred to the army of General Winfield SCOTT in 1847. During the advance on Mexico City he won two brevet promotions for bravery at the battles of Molino del Rey and Chapultepec. On a personal level, Grant opposed the conflict as an act of aggression against a neighboring country. After the war, he transferred to the western frontier for a long stint of routine garrison duty, rising to captain in 1853. However, the isolation and boredom took a heavy toll on Grant who, like many contemporaries, sought relief through excessive drinking. After officially being reprimanded, he resigned his commission in 1854 and rejoined his family at Galena, Illinois. For six years, Grant tried various business ventures, all of which conspicuously failed, and he ended up clerking in his father's tannery. Only the onset of civil war in 1861 fostered a dramatic turn in his personal fortunes.

Grant initially offered his service to the government and was ignored. After he worked several months for the state adjutant general, Congressman Elihu Washburne secured him an appointment as colonel of the 21st Illinois Volunteers in June 1861. Two months later, he received promotion to brigadier general and command of the District of Southeast Missouri. Early on, Grant revealed his predilection for offensive operations by seizing Paducah, Kentucky, on September 6, 1861, to keep it out of Confederate hands. On November 7, 1861, he attacked Southern forces at

Union general Ulysses S. Grant *(Library of Congress)*

Belmont, Missouri, drove General Gideon PILLOW's Confederates out of camp, and then lost control of his men, who engaged in plunder. A sharp counterattack by General Leonidas K. POLK sent the Federals fleeing back to their riverboats, and Grant luckily evaded capture. Consequently, Grant spent the next few months drilling and disciplining his men while badgering the theater commander, General Henry W. HALLECK, permission to attack Forts Henry and Donelson on the Cumberland and Tennessee rivers, respectively. When Halleck finally acquiesced, Grant energetically attacked and took both fortifications with timely assistance from Captain Andrew H. FOOTE and his gunboats. On February 15, 1862, Union forces experienced a close call when a Confederate sortie out of Fort Donelson surprised the bluecoats in their trenches, and the Southerners nearly escaped, but a prompt counterattack by Grant shut the defenders up in their works. Generals John B. FLOYD and Gideon J. Pillow then ignominiously chose to flee rather than surrender and accorded General Simon B. Buckner that melancholy task. Significantly, when Buckner formally asked Grant, an old acquaintance, for terms, he brusquely demanded and received unconditional surrender on February 16, 1862. Thereafter, the Union press lauded him as "Unconditional Surrender Grant."

Grant, seeking to maintain the strategic initiative, struck south along the Tennessee River and made a lodgment at Pittsburg Landing, Tennessee, better known as Shiloh. On the morning of April 6, 1862, his men were rudely surprised in camp by an entire Confederate army under General Albert S. JOHNSTON, driven to the river, and nearly defeated. That evening, Grant luckily obtained reinforcements from Generals Don C. BUELL and Lew WALLACE, which enabled him to counterattack General Pierre G. T. BEAUREGARD on the following day and regain lost ground. The resulting heavy casualties raised a storm of criticism against Grant in the press, and he consequently was superseded by the tottering Halleck for several weeks. After a glacial campaign against Corinth, Mississippi, Halleck transferred to Washington, D.C., as general in chief, and Grant was restored to command. He then orchestrated an offensive strategy against the Confederate bastion at Vicksburg, Mississippi, so as to cut the South in two. Through the winter and into the spring of 1863, he made no less than four direct and indirect approaches to the city from the north, frequently in concert with General William T. SHERMAN and naval vessels under Commander David D. PORTER, but to no avail. But on the evening of March 20, 1863, he brilliantly broke the impasse by marching down the left bank of the Mississippi

River and, with Porter's help, ferried his troops across below Confederate defenses. Striking inland with 25,000 men, he also launched General Benjamin H. GRIERSON on an extended raid to Baton Rouge, Louisiana, to mask his movements. Grant then cut his own supply lines and foraged off the land as Confederates under General Joseph E. JOHNSTON and John C. PEMBERTON tried frantically to stop him. Federal forces aggressively beat the divided Southerners in four pitched battles, driving off Johnston and trapping Pemberton within Vicksburg. Grant then launched two frontal assaults on the city that were bloodily repelled before settling into a protracted siege of 46 days. When Vicksburg finally surrendered to Grant on July 4, 1863, the Confederacy had been fatally split, and he received promotion to major general and command of the Division of the Mississippi.

Grant next turned his attention to Tennessee, where the Army of the Cumberland under General William S. ROSECRANS was besieged at Chattanooga by General Braxton BRAGG's Confederates. Moving quickly, Grant sacked Rosecrans in favor of General George H. THOMAS, reestablished a reliable supply route (the so-called Cracker Line), and ordered up four divisions under General Sherman. Bragg had unwillingly played into Union hands by dispatching General James LONGSTREET's veteran I Corps to besiege Knoxville, at which point, Grant fell on his diminished forces like a thunderbolt on November 25, 1863, in the twin battles of Lookout Mountain and Missionary Ridge. The Confederates were shattered and reeled back in defeat to Georgia. This unbroken string of victories now propelled Grant to the forefront of Union military leadership, and President Abraham LINCOLN arranged for his promotion to lieutenant general in March 1864. He also summoned his general to Washington to replace Halleck as general-in-chief and formulate an all-encompassing strategy to crush the tottering but as yet defiant Confederacy and end the Civil War. This marks Grant's greatest contribution to the war effort: promulgating a comprehensive, multipronged offensive that brought the full weight of superior Union manpower and resources on the South. In the western theater, General Sherman was to depart Tennessee and march for Atlanta, Georgia, and thence to Savannah and the sea. In the Deep South, General Nathaniel BANKS would lead an offensive up the Red River into western Louisiana as far as Texas to cut off any flow of supplies. In Virginia, the Army of the James under General Benjamin F. BUTLER was to attack along the south banks of the James River to threaten Petersburg. However, the main blow would be delivered by Grant himself to be aimed solely at the redoubtable Army of Northern Virginia under General Robert E. LEE. The contest, when it unfolded, would be a clash of giants.

In the late spring of 1864, Grant directed the Army of the Potomac under General George M. MEADE to begin the advance on Richmond. Lee countered by attacking at the Wilderness, May 5–6, where he repulsed Grant with heavy loses to both sides. But herein marked a paradigm shift in Union strategy: Though defeated, Grant did not withdraw; rather, he simply sidestepped to the left and continued inching toward Richmond. Lee followed and met him at Spotsylvania Court House, May 7–20, in another inconclusive bloody standoff. Absorbing casualties stoically, Grant sidestepped Lee again, forcing him on a march to the North Anna River. The Confederates moved adroitly and blocked him, so, for the only time in the campaign, Grant elected on a frontal attack at Cold Harbor on June 3, 1864, to smash through Lee's defenses. The resulting disaster cost Union forces 6,000 men in an hour and led to renewed accusations of Grant as a "butcher." Since the opening of the campaign, the Army of the Potomac had in fact suffered 50,000 casualties, nearly one-half its strength. Lee, in contrast, sustained an estimated 30,000 to 32,000 casualties, roughly half that amount. But whereas Grant received a steady influx of replacements to keep his manpower levels more or less constant, the Army of Northern Virginia was slowly hemorrhaging to death. Grant's strategy of movement and attrition was slowly paying decisive dividends. Later in June, he

stole a march on Lee, slipped across the James River on June 12–17, 1864, and advanced on a lightly guarded Petersburg. However, Union bungling and a furious reaction from Lee stalled his offensive, and a protracted nine-month siege ensued. Grant's most memorable attack, the so-called Battle of the Crater (July 30, 1864), was another costly fiasco owing to General Ambrose E. BURNSIDE's indecision. But, again, Lee's finely tuned offensive army was immobilized in trenches as Union forces maintained both the strategic and the tactical initiative over their adversaries.

By the fall of 1864, the new Union strategy hastened the Confederacy's downfall. While Grant pinned down Lee in Virginia, Sherman seized Atlanta and approached Savannah with a view toward moving up the Carolinas. Also, a new force under General Philip H. SHERIDAN had cleared Confederates out of the strategic Shenandoah Valley, robbing them of their most important breadbasket. Sheridan then delivered the fatal blow on April 1, 1865, when he finally broke Lee's defenses at Five Forks. Grant, judging the moment right, struck the Petersburg defenses with his entire army, and Confederate resistance crumbled. Lee managed to extricate his army and march westward, where it was surrounded at Appomattox Court House on April 9, 1865. Then, in a solemn ceremony, Lee met Grant and formally surrendered under the latter's very generous terms. Thus, a third Confederate force passed into the hands of "Unconditional Surrender" Grant, closing the bloodiest chapter in American history.

After the war, Grant was retained in the peacetime establishment, and Congress honored him with a rank of four-star general in 1866. Hailed as the savior of his country, he then successfully ran for the presidency in 1868 and 1872, winning easily. However, his tenure in office was marred by scandals that surrounded many of his appointees. No blame was ever attached to Grant who, through it all, remained personally untarnished. He then returned to private life and tried his hand at business, failed miserably, and went bankrupt. The old warrior, stricken by throat cancer, accepted his friend Mark Twain's advice and published his military memoirs, which proved surprisingly successful and rescued his family from insolvency. Grant died at Mount McGregor, New York, on July 23, 1885. With the possible exception of President Lincoln, no individual was more responsible for preserving the United States at a critical moment in its history. Grant's strategic vision and tactical tenacity were the driving forces behind Union victory.

Further Reading

Ballard, Michael B. *U.S. Grant: The Making of a General, 1861–1863*. Lanham, Md.: Rowman and Littlefield, 2005.

Bonekemper, Edward H. *A Victor, Not a Butcher: Ulysses S. Grant's Overlooked Military Genius*. Washington, D.C.: Regnery Pub., 2004.

Flood, Charles B. *Grant and Sherman: The Friendship That Won the Civil War*. New York: Farrar, Straus and Giroux, 2005.

Gott, Kendall D. *Where the South Lost the War: An Analysis of the Fort Henry–Fort Donelson Campaign, February 1862*. Mechanicsburg, Pa.: Stackpole Books, 2003.

Grant, Ulysses S. *The Civil War Memoirs of Ulysses S. Grant*. New York: Forge, 2002.

Hess, Earl J. *Trench Warfare under Grant and Lee: Field Fortifications in the Overland Campaign*. Chapel Hill: University of North Carolina Press, 2007.

Kionka, T. K. *Key Command: Ulysses S. Grant: District of Cairo*. Columbia: University Press of Missouri, 2006.

Longacre, Edward G. *General Ulysses S. Grant: the Soldier and the Man*. Cambridge, Mass.: Da Capo Press, 2006.

Mosier, John. *Grant*. New York: Palgrave Macmillan, 2006.

Taaffe, Stephen R. *Commanding the Army of the Potomac*. Lawrence: University Press of Kansas, 2006.

Walsh, George. *"Whip the Rebellion": Ulysses S. Grant's Rise to Command*. New York: Tom Doherty Associates, 2005.

Grierson, Benjamin H. (1826–1911)

Union general

Benjamin Henry Grierson was born in Pittsburgh, Pennsylvania, on July 8, 1826, and eventually set-

tled in Jacksonville, Illinois. He taught music for many years before entering the mercantile business and watching it fail in the Panic of 1857. When the Civil War commenced in April 1861, Grierson joined an Illinois militia regiment as a private and fought Confederate guerrillas in neighboring Missouri. He impressed his superiors with his bravery and skill, and on October 24, 1861, Grierson became a major in the 6th Illinois Cavalry. The appointment is curious since Grierson, who had been kicked in the face and permanently disfigured by a horse, thoroughly detested the beasts. He then rose by merit to colonel on April 12, 1862, and subsequently distinguished himself by vigorously pursuing Confederate raiders under General Earl VAN DORN in December of that year. His skill and aggressiveness brought him to the attention of General Ulysses S. GRANT, then planning ambitious moves against Vicksburg, Mississippi. Grierson was to play an integral role in his strategy.

On April 17, 1862, Grierson departed La Grange, Tennessee, with the 6th and 7th Illinois Cavalry, the 2nd Iowa Cavalry, and Battery K of the Illinois Light Artillery, totaling 1,700 men. His mission was to drive south through Mississippi and on to Union-held Baton Rouge, Louisiana, and tear up railroad tracks and telegraph wires en route. In this manner, he would create a strategic diversion, masking Grant's impending moves across the Mississippi River. During the next 16 days Grierson galloped hard, eluded numerous pursuers, and completely confounded the Confederate high command at Vicksburg. General John C. PEMBERTON consequently ordered all available units to try to intercept the elusive troopers, thereby committing his strategic reserve just as Grant prepared to strike. By the time Grierson successfully accomplished his mission, he had traversed 600 miles through enemy territory, captured 500 prisoners, and tore up 50 miles of track and telegraph wire. In light of his exceptional behavior, he gained promotion to brigadier general in June 1862 and was retained in the army of General Nathaniel P. BANKS during the successful siege of Port Hudson. Grierson ended the year transferring back to Tennessee, where he commanded a cavalry division in the XVI Corps of General Andrew J. Smith. In this capacity, he accompanied the ill-fated foray against General Nathan B. FORREST at Brice's Cross Roads on June 10, 1864, and was nearly routed. The following month, he was engaged closely under General Smith at the Battle of Tupelo (July 14, 1864), at which Forrest sustained a heavy defeat.

In November 1864 Grierson accepted command of the 4th Cavalry Division in the Military Division of Mississippi, but the following month, he was replaced by General James H. WILSON. He

Union general Benjamin H. Grierson *(Massachusetts Commandery Military Order of the Loyal Legion and the U.S. Army Military History Institute)*

then operated against General John B. HOOD's lines of communication during the Nashville campaign in December and, in February 1865, received promotion to major general. Grierson then joined General Edward R. S. CANBY's Military Division of West Mississippi, where he conducted numerous raids and forays deep into Alabama and Georgia. By war's end, he commanded 4,000 troopers and was widely respected as one of the Union's most adept cavalry leaders.

Grierson was retained in the peacetime establishment as colonel of the newly created 10th U.S. Cavalry, one of four units comprised solely of African Americans and white officers. During the next 25 years, he led his so-called Buffalo Soldiers across the Old Southwest, fighting innumerable skirmishes with Native Americans while also erecting miles of roads and telegraph wire. He also founded and directed construction of Fort Sill, Indian Territory (Oklahoma), which served as a major frontier outpost. Throughout the final phases of the Indian wars on the Southern Plains (1878–81), Grierson's 10th distinguished itself in combat against the Apache under Chief Victorio by eliminating them as a raiding force in West Texas. He was also unique in championing the cause of African-American soldiers at a time when many West Point–trained officers held them in disdain. Moreover, Grierson strove to deal honestly with Native Americans, a policy that brought him into conflict with his superior, General Philip H. SHERIDAN. In November 1866 Grierson assumed control of the District of New Mexico, and two years later, he left his beloved 10th Cavalry to succeed General Nelson A. Miles as commander of the Department of Arizona. Grierson finally resigned from the military in July 1890 and spent the rest of his life at his home in Jacksonville, Illinois. He died while vacationing at Omena, Michigan, on August 31, 1911, being only one of a handful of non-West Point graduates to attain the grade of brigadier general in the regular army. His unstinting defense of Native Americans and African-American soldiers sadly deprived him of well-deserved military promotions for almost 24 years.

Further Reading

Black, Robert W. *Cavalry Raids of the Civil War.* Mechanicsburg, Pa.: Stackpole Books, 2004.

Hutton, Paul A., ed. *Soldiers West: Biographies from the Military Frontier.* Lincoln: University of Nebraska Press, 1987.

Leckie, William H. *Unlikely Warriors: General Benjamin H. Grierson and His Family.* Norman: University of Oklahoma Press, 1984.

———. *The Buffalo Soldiers: A Narrative of the Black Cavalry in the West.* Norman: University of Oklahoma Press, 2003.

York, Neil L. *Fiction as Fact: The Horse Soldiers and Popular Memory.* Kent, Ohio: Kent State University Press, 2001.

H

Halleck, Henry W. (1815–1872)

Union general

Henry Wager Halleck was born in Westernville, New York, on January 16, 1815, the son of farmers. He ran away from home to escape the drudgery of agrarian life, and in 1837, he gained admittance to the U.S. Military Academy. Halleck, a gifted student, graduated third in his class in 1839 and was commissioned a second lieutenant in the elite Corps of Engineers. After strengthening the defenses of New York harbor, he ventured to Europe in 1844 on a grand tour of foreign fortifications. He returned home a year later to deliver in Boston, Massachusetts, a series of lectures on warfare that were subsequently published as *Elements of Military Art & Science* (1846). This was one of the first expressions of American military professionalism and was widely read by soldiers and militia officers alike. When the Mexican War erupted in 1846, Halleck sailed to the West Coast with Commander William B. Shubrick, where he built fortifications and participated in minor military actions. Halleck became a captain in 1847 and spent the next eight years in California as secretary of state in the military administration of General Bennett Riley, where he helped draw up the state constitution. He then resigned from the military in 1854 to pursue law and amassed a small fortune as an attorney and president of the Atlantic and Pacific Railroad. In 1861 Halleck furthered his reputation for scholarship by composing *International Law*, another widely read and highly praised work.

When the Civil War commenced in April 1861, Halleck sought out a regular commission, and General in Chief Winfield SCOTT prevailed on President Abraham LINCOLN to appoint him a major general. Halleck was then assigned to the Department of the Missouri, headquartered at St. Louis, to replace General John C. Frémont and to rectify his organizational chaos. A superb administrator, Halleck quickly reduced corruption and inefficiency, improved military discipline and morale, and suppressed Confederate guerrillas by posting garrisons around the state. By the winter of 1861, the Missouri Valley was firmly in Union hands, and he turned to cracking the first line of Southern defenses in Kentucky and Tennessee. In February 1862 Halleck authorized General Ulysses S. GRANT's Army of the Tennessee to attack Forts Henry and Donelson, which was done effectively. The following March, he helped orchestrate the fall of Island No. 10 with General John POPE's Army of the Mississippi while General Samuel R. CURTIS's Army of the Southwest won the Battle of Pea Ridge in Arkansas. He then allowed a concerted drive down the Tennessee River by Generals Grant, Don C. BUELL, and Lew WALLACE, which culminated in the bloody victory at Shiloh (April 6–7, 1862). Halleck, alarmed by rumors that Grant had been drinking heavily, subsequently arrived at his headquarters to take command in the field. His

Union general Henry W. Halleck *(Library of Congress)*

"Old Brains." From his office, he efficiently orchestrated a concerted mass effort to recruit, train, and equip thousands of soldiers over a vast area, thereby placing the Union army on a sounder wartime footing. This proved a very tall order in an army of volunteers, but Halleck managed to graft a veneer of military professionalism on an otherwise unruly lot. His principal failing was as a grand strategist, being overly cautious by nature and too concerned with the possession of strategic points. In an age of modern war, destruction of the enemy's forces had become paramount, a concept that Lincoln the novice fully embraced. Halleck was also something of an aloof individual, who allowed grand strategy to drift over the next two years by failing to challenge commanders in the field. He also quarreled with General Joseph HOOKER over how to handle General Robert E. LEE's invasion of Pennsylvania and ultimately replaced him with General George G. MEADE. In March 1864, Union strategy received a major boost when Grant replaced him as general in chief and Halleck was graciously "kicked upstairs" to serve as chief of staff. Thereafter, his impact on military affairs was minimal, and he contented himself in working as a highly efficient military bureaucrat. In July 1864 he left his office briefly to command Washington's defenses during the celebrated raid of General Jubal A. EARLY. Toward the end of the conflict, Halleck was transferred from the capital to placate Radical Republicans and was placed in charge of the Division of the James at Richmond, Virginia. There, he quarreled with General William T. SHERMAN about surrender terms accorded General Joseph E. JOHNSTON. The two men, previously close friends, were never reconciled from this dispute.

After the war, the government unceremoniously transferred Halleck to the Division of the Pacific, where he remained until 1869. That year, he assumed command of the Division of the South, which he held until his death at Louisville, Kentucky, on January 9, 1872. In terms of overall ability and potential, Halleck was the North's most gifted, yet least successful, soldier.

next objective, the strategic railroad junction at Corinth, Mississippi, fell on May 29, 1862, but only after a glacial campaign of three weeks against smaller Confederate forces under General Pierre G. T. BEAUREGARD. Halleck's plodding, uninspiring performance induced Lincoln to restore Grant to command in the western theater. Halleck subsequently was recalled to Washington, D.C., to serve as general in chief. It was hoped his demonstrated talent for military administration would lend greater coordination to the Union war effort.

As Lincoln predicted, Halleck excelled in the role as head military administrator, earning the unflattering but basically accurate moniker of

Further Reading

Engle, Stephen D. *Struggle for the Heartland: The Campaign from Fort Henry to Corinth.* Lincoln: University of Nebraska Press, 2001.

Marszalek, John F. *Commander of All Lincoln's Armies: A Life of General Henry W. Halleck.* Cambridge, Mass.: Belknap Press of Harvard University Press, 2004.

———. "Henry W. Halleck: The Early Seeds of Failure." *North and South* 8, no. 1 (2005): 78–86.

Rafuse, Ethan S. "McClellan and Halleck at War: The Struggle for Control of the Union War Effort in the West, November 1861–March 1862." *Civil War History* 49, no. 1 (2003): 32–51.

Ritter, Charles F., and Jon L. Wakelyn, eds. *Leaders of the American Civil War.* Westport, Conn.: Greenwood Press, 1998.

Smith, Timothy B. "A Siege from the Start: The Spring 1862 Campaign against Corinth, Mississippi." *Journal of Mississippi History* 66, no. 4 (2004): 403–424.

Hampton, Wade (1818–1902)

Confederate general

Wade Hampton was born in Charleston, South Carolina, on March 28, 1818, a scion of one of that state's most distinguished families. Well-educated at academies, he passed through South Carolina College in 1836 with a law degree but declined to practice. Instead, he managed his family's large plantation and estates, and he did this so deftly that he achieved great wealth. In 1852 Hampton parleyed his success into politics by winning a seat in the state legislature, where he functioned as a voice of moderation against a rising tide of secessionism. Curiously, Hampton, though a slave owner, openly questioned the continuing viability of the "peculiar institution" and opposed reopening the slave trade, and while he felt the secession by Southern states was legally and morally justified, Hampton insisted that it should not be attempted until all political and constitutional remedies had been exhausted. However, once South Carolina seceded from the Union in December 1860, he offered his services to the new Confederate States of America. The following April, Governor Francis Pickens authorized him to raise his own legion, a mixed force of cavalry, infantry, and artillery, at his own expense. Hampton obliged and served as its colonel, despite his lack of prior military training. The Hampton Legion first distinguished themselves at Bull Run on July 27, 1861, where Hampton was slightly wounded. On May 23, 1862, he advanced to brigadier general and served under General Thomas J. JACKSON throughout the noted Peninsula campaign of that year. Hampton was wounded again at Seven Pines on May 31, 1862, and the following July, he was transferred to the cavalry corps of General J. E. B. STUART, attached to the Army of Northern Virginia.

Hampton proved himself to be an outstanding leader of mounted troops. He accompanied Jackson throughout the Antietam campaign of September 1862, conducted several successful raids over the winter, and subsequently fought at Brandy Station (June 9, 1863) where his younger brother was killed, and Gettysburg (July 1–3, 1863), receiving three wounds. Hampton, however, came to

Confederate general Wade Hampton *(Massachusetts Commandery Military Order of the Loyal Legion and the U.S. Army Military History Institute)*

resent Stuart's tendency toward grandstanding as well as his reluctance to accord honors to anybody but his own Virginia cavalry. Nonetheless, he rose to major general as of September 3, 1863, and, following Stuart's death in May 1864, succeeded him as chief of the cavalry corps. Hampton's greatest accomplishment in this capacity was the June 11–12, 1864, Battle of Trevilian Station, where he stopped a larger Union force under General Philip H. SHERIDAN from reaching Lynchburg, Virginia. Hampton then assisted in the defeat of General Winfield S. HANCOCK's II Corps at Ream's Station on August 25, 1864. The following month, he led what amounted to the largest rustling operation in history by raiding behind Union lines and absconding with 2,500 head of cattle from Coggin's Point, Virginia. His troopers were then employed as makeshift cowboys as they herded their spoils back to Confederate lines.

By the spring of 1865, horses were becoming a scarce commodity in the Army of Northern Virginia, so Hampton began to drill his men to fight as foot soldiers. General Robert E. LEE then detached his command from the Petersburg area and transferred it to South Carolina to forage for mounts. On February 15, 1865, he was also promoted to lieutenant general. Hampton then transferred to the Army of Tennessee of General Joseph E. JOHNSTON in an attempt to halt Federal troops under General William T. SHERMAN from marching up the Carolinas. When the state capital of Columbia was nearly destroyed by fire, Hampton entered into an angry correspondence with Sherman about responsibility for the act, which the latter firmly denied. He also incurred a measure of notoriety by deliberately executing any Union stragglers found plundering private homes. With the collapse of the Confederacy in April 1865, Hampton made a futile attempt to escort President Jefferson DAVIS across the Mississippi River becoming one of the last high-ranking Confederates to surrender.

Hampton resumed his political career after the war and generally supported President Andrew Johnson's attempt at reconstruction. He also took the unprecedented step of endorsing limited civil rights for newly freed African-American slaves. Hampton, however, came to deplore the excesses of the Radical Republicans and eventually aligned himself with traditional Democratic interests and embraced a racially tinged agenda. He was elected governor in 1876 and also served a term in the U.S. Senate (1879–81) before becoming the commissioner of Pacific Railways (1893–97). Hampton died in Columbia, South Carolina, on April 11, 1902. A gifted, physically impressive individual, he, like Nathan B. FORREST and Richard TAYLOR, was one of three Confederates to become lieutenant general without a professional military background.

Further Reading
Ackerman, Robert K. *Wade Hampton III.* Columbia: University of South Carolina Press, 2007.
Cisco, Walter B. *Wade Hampton: Confederate Warrior, Conservative Statesman.* Washington, D.C.: Brassey's, 2004.
Longacre, Edward G. *Gentleman and Soldier: A Biography of Wade Hampton III.* Nashville: Rutledge Hill Press, 2003.
Simms, William G. *A City Laid Waste: The Capture, Sack, and Destruction of the City of Columbia.* Columbia: University of South Carolina Press, 2005.
Wittenberg, Eric J. *Glory Enough for All: Sheridan's Second Raid and the Battle of Trevilian Station.* London: Brassey's, 2002.
———. *The Battle of Monroe's Crossroads: And the Civil War's Final Campaign.* New York: Savas Beatie, 2006.

Hancock, Winfield S. (1824–1886)
Union general

Winfield Scott Hancock was born in Montgomery Square, Pennsylvania, on February 14, 1824, the son of a schoolteacher with deep roots in the Democratic Party. Hancock used his father's connections to secure an appointment to the U.S. Military Academy in 1840, from which he graduated midway in his class four years later. Now a second lieutenant in the 6th U.S. Infantry, he served three years on the western frontier as a recruiting officer before joining General Winfield SCOTT's army in Mexico. In short order, Hancock distinguished himself in fighting at Contreras and Churubusco, winning a brevet promotion for bravery. He rose to captain in 1855 and saw additional service against the Seminoles in Florida and in Kansas during the period of abolitionist troubles there. Hancock then transferred to southern California in May 1859, where he functioned as quartermaster. Despite his strong pro-Southern sympathies, he deplored secession and after April 1861 took measures to protect Federal property. He also agitated for a combat command and transferred east to become a brigadier general in General George B. McCLELLAN's Army of the Potomac.

Hancock fought steadily through the Peninsula campaign of 1861. Tall, commanding, and impressive in the saddle, he emerged as one of the Union's best commanders at the divisional and corps levels. At Williamsburg on May 4–5, 1862, his brigade outflanked Confederate forces, routing them. McClellan, who had witnessed the event, pronounced his performance "superb"—and the nickname stuck. Good combat leadership at South Mountain and Antietam in September 1862 culminated in command of a division in the II Corps with the rank of major general of volunteers. Hancock next fought at the bloody debacle at Fredericksburg on December 13, 1862, where his formation sustained 50 percent losses yet never wavered. He further distinguished himself at the heavy Union defeat at Chancellorsville, May 2–3, 1863, and mounted a steady rearguard action that allowed the battered forces of General Joseph HOOKER to escape destruction. In consequence of his excellent performance, President Abraham LINCOLN appointed Hancock head of the II Corps in June 1863.

Hancock made his most essential contribution at the three-day ordeal of Gettysburg, Pennsylvania, under General George G. MEADE. On July 1, 1863, he rushed his II Corps to the assistance of General John F. REYNOLDS I Corps, assumed command of Union forces from General Abner DOUBLEDAY, and completely stabilized Union positions

Union general Winfield S. Hancock *(Library of Congress)*

along Cemetery Hill Ridge and Culp's Hill. On July 2, while commanding the Union center, he repaired the damage incurred by General Daniel SICKLES insubordinate deployment of the III Corps and artfully shifted troops to the left to negate General James LONGSTREET's turning movement. On July 3 the locus of combat reverted back to the Union center, and Hancock's II Corps absorbed and bloodily repelled the determined charge by 15,000 Confederates under General George E. PICKETT. In the last few moments of battle, Hancock received a severe leg wound, yet refused assistance until victory was assured. Sadly and ironically, General Lewis A. Armistead, one of Hancock's best friends of the antebellum period, was mortally wounded urging on Southern troops against his position.

Several months of recuperation passed before Hancock rejoined the II Corps, now operating under the aegis of General Ulysses S. GRANT. Though still confined to an ambulance, he fought well in the bloody May 5, 1863, encounter at the Wilderness, driving General Ambrose P. HILL back several miles. At Spotsylvania (May 12, 1863), his II Corps successfully stormed Confederate defenses at the "Mule Shoe" until driven back by a determined charge by General John C. BRECKIN-RIDGE. However, his men suffered inordinate losses at Cold Harbor (June 3, 1864) and entered the siege of Petersburg with decimated ranks. Hancock was also feeling the effects of exhaustion and his old wound, and on June 15, 1864, he passed up an opportunity to storm lightly guarded Petersburg, Virginia. He was then roughly handled by Generals Hill and Wade HAMPTON at Ream's Station on August 25, 1864, and Grant, cognizant of his declining health, removed him from the line. Hancock next assumed new duties commanding the defenses of Washington, D.C., where he also recruited the Veteran Volunteer Corps for garrison purposes.

In 1866 Hancock gained promotion to major general, and the following year, he took charge of the Department of the Missouri. Here, he conducted operations against hostile bands of Cheyenne and Kiowa and also arranged for the court-martial of General George A. CUSTER for being absent without leave. In 1867 President Andrew Johnson transferred him from the frontier and assigned him duties as head of the Fifth Military District (Texas and Louisiana) during Reconstruction. He replaced the testy general Philip H. SHERIDAN as military governor, and his casual friendliness toward Southerners earned him the ire of many Radical Republicans. In keeping with his beliefs, Hancock issued orders to keep recently freed African-American slaves off juries and voter registration lists. General in Chief Grant angrily removed him for refusing to assert military prerogatives over civilian wishes, a stance endearing him to former Confederates, and he was exiled to the distant Department of Dakota. His row with the Republicans caught the eye of fellow Democrats, who needed a national standard-bearer, and

in 1880, he ran an unsuccessful campaign for president against Chester A. Arthur. He then resumed his duties as head of the Department of the East with headquarters on Governor's Island, New York. "Hancock, the Superb" died at that post on February 9, 1886, one of the greatest corps-level commanders on either side.

Further Reading

Cannon, John. *Bloody Angle: Hancock's Assault on the Mule Shoe Salient, May 12, 1864.* Cambridge, Mass.: Da Capo Press, 2002.

Constant, George W. "The Men Who Made Hancock 'Superb.'" *Civil War Times Illustrated* 40, no. 1 (2001): 38–44, 53–55.

Deppen, John. "Hancock the Superb." *Military Heritage* 5, no. 5 (2004): 40–49.

Gambore, A. M. *Hancock at Gettysburg and Beyond.* Baltimore: Butternut and Blue, 2002.

Grimsely, Mark. *And Keep on Moving: The Virginia Campaign, May–June, 1864.* Lincoln: University of Nebraska Press, 2002.

Jamieson, Perry D. *Winfield Scott Hancock: Gettysburg Hero.* Abilene, Tex.: McWhiney Foundation Press, 2003.

Kreisler, Lawrence A. "From Volunteers to Veterans: A Social and Military History of the II Corps, Army of the Potomac, 1861–1865." Unpublished Ph.D. diss., University of Alabama, 2001.

Newton, Steven H. *McPherson's Ridge: The First Battle for the High Ground, July 1, 1863.* Cambridge, Mass.: Da Capo Press, 2002.

Pfanz, Harry W. *Gettysburg—the First Day.* Chapel Hill: University of North Carolina Press, 2001.

Wert, Jeffrey D. *Gettysburg: Day Three.* New York: Simon and Schuster, 2001.

Hardee, William J. (1815–1873)
Confederate general

William Joseph Hardee was born in Little Saltilla, Georgia, on October 12, 1815, the son of a wealthy planter. He matriculated through the U.S. Military Academy and graduated in 1838 as a second lieutenant of the 2nd U.S. Dragoons. Hardee saw fighting in Florida's Second Seminole War but subsequently went to France in 1840 to study for two years at the Royal Cavalry School at Saumur.

In 1844 he joined General Zachary Taylor's Army of Occupation as a captain and patrolled the Texas frontier along the Rio Grande. Ownership of this stretch of land was disputed with Mexico, and during a patrol on April 25, 1846, Hardee was ambushed and captured. Exchanged the following month, he fought under Taylor at Monterrey that September and then joined the army of General Winfield SCOTT during its march on Mexico City. Hardee won two brevet promotions for bravery before the war ended in 1848, and afterward, he resumed routine military activities along the frontier. In 1853 Secretary of War Jefferson DAVIS ordered him to compile a new drill manual, and he wrote *Rifle and Light Infantry Tactics* (1855), which served as a standard text for both Union and Confederate armies during the Civil War. It differed from General Scott's *Infantry Tactics,* first published in 1815, by recognizing the increased range and lethality of rifled weapons and calling for faster marching rates, dispersed formations, and increased reliance on skirmishers. In 1855 Hardee was posted with the newly organized 2nd U.S. Cavalry, in whose ranks rode future luminaries Albert S. JOHNSTON, Robert E. LEE, George H. THOMAS, Earl VAN DORN, Edmund KIRBY-SMITH, and John B. HOOD. This regiment proved so outstanding in containing Comanche attacks in Texas—and was so overstaffed by Southerners—that it was popularly called "Jeff Davis's Own." In 1856 Hardee transferred from the frontier as a lieutenant colonel and served as commandant of cadets at West Point. After four years of useful service, he returned to Georgia on vacation, resigned his commission once his native state seceded on January 19, 1861, and joined the Confederate army as a colonel.

In June 1861 Hardee advanced to brigadier and proceeded to Arkansas to recruit a brigade. He joined General Johnston's Army of Mississippi commanding the III Corps and fought with distinction at Shiloh on April 6–7, 1862. Promoted to major general, he then accompanied General Braxton BRAGG during the ill-fated invasion of Kentucky. Hardee acquitted himself well at the bloody Battle of Perryville on October 8, 1862, inflicting heavy losses on General Don C. BUELL's Army of the Cumberland and winning promotion to lieutenant general. He then performed impressively at the Battle of Murfreesboro (Stone's River) on December 31, 1862–January 3, 1863, where his clever flanking tactics drove the right flank of General William S. ROSECRANS back three miles. However, Hardee greatly resented Bragg's vacillating leadership, quarreled with him, and transferred out of the Army of Tennessee to train troops in Mississippi. He then rejoined Bragg in time to command his right wing at Missionary Ridge on November 24, 1863, where his valiant stand prevented the Confederate army from being destroyed. When Bragg retired from command, President Davis offered Hardee command of the Army of Tennessee, but he declined and served instead under General Joseph E. JOHNSTON.

Throughout the ensuing Atlanta campaign, Hardee fought well but futilely against superior Union forces under General William T. SHERMAN.

Confederate general William J. Hardee *(Library of Congress)*

When Davis sacked Johnston and replaced him with General John B. Hood on July 17, 1864, he greatly resented being passed over. Moreover, he did not work well with the overly aggressive Hood, who decimated Hardee's command in a series of ill-advised offensives against Sherman. On July 22, 1864, Hardee surprised the army of General James B. McPherson at Peachtree Creek, killing him, but once Atlanta fell on September 2, 1864, he felt he could no longer function under Hood and requested a transfer. Hardee then received reassignment to the Department of South Carolina, Georgia, and Florida, where he continued opposing Sherman's march to the sea. He was forced to abandon Savannah to superior numbers on December 21, 1864, along with Charleston, South Carolina, in February 1865. Reunited with Johnston in North Carolina, he fought bravely at the battles of Averasboro and Bentonville on March 15–20, 1865, with his only son dying in the latter engagement. Hardee finally surrendered with Johnston at Durham's Station on April 21, 1865. After the war, he became a planter in Alabama, and he also served as president of the Selma and Meridian Railroad. Hardee, who acquired the nickname of "Old Reliable" on account of his steady leadership, died at Wytheville, Virginia, on November 6, 1873, a superior corps commander.

Further Reading

Arnold, James R. *Jeff Davis's Own: Cavalry. Comanches, and the Battle for the Texas Frontier.* New York: Wiley, 2000.

Bradley, Mark L., and David E. Roth. *Old Reliable's Finest Hour: The Battle of Averasboro, North Carolina, March 15–16, 1865.* Columbus, Ohio: Blue and Gray Enterprises, 2002.

Broadwater, Robert P. *Battle of Despair: Bentonville and the North Carolina Campaign.* Macon, Ga.: Mercer University Press, 2004.

Davis, Stephen. *Atlanta Will Fall: Sherman, Joe Johnston, and the Yankee Heavy Battalions.* Wilmington, Del.: Scholarly Resources, 2001.

Furqueron, James R. "The Finest Opportunity Lost: The Battle of Jonesborough, August 31–September 1, 1864." *North & South* 6, no. 6 (2003): 48–63.

Lepa, Jack H. *Breaking the Confederacy: The Georgia and Tennessee Campaigns of 1864.* Jefferson, N.C.: McFarland, 2005.

Noe, Kenneth. *Perryville: This Grand Havoc of Battle.* Lexington: University Press of Kentucky, 2001.

Heth, Henry (1825–1899)

Confederate general

Henry Heth was born in Blackheath, Virginia, on December 16, 1825, the son of a navy midshipman. In 1843 he entered the U.S. Military Academy and graduated four years later at the very bottom of his class. Now a lieutenant in the 1st U.S. Infantry, Heth ventured to Mexico in the final phases of the Mexican War and saw no combat. He then spent the next 12 years performing routine garrison duty at various posts along the western frontier. Heth rose to captain of the 10th U.S. Infantry in 1855 and finally fought against the Brule Sioux at Blue Water, Nebraska, performing competently. Two years later, he penned a manual entitled *A System of Target Practice*, which became a standard military treatise. In 1858 Heth accompanied Colonel Albert S. Johnston on his Mormon expedition, again eliciting praise from superiors. He was not particularly interested in politics and did not favor secession, but when Virginia left the Union in April 1861, he resigned his commission and offered his service to the Confederacy.

By August 1861 Heth was a lieutenant colonel in the quartermaster service under General John B. Floyd in western Virginia and commanded the 45th Virginia at Carnifex Ferry on September 10, 1861. President Jefferson Davis sought to have Heth become commander of Confederate forces in Missouri, but Southern commanders there resented his West Point background and politically negated the transfer. Heth nonetheless rose to brigadier general in February 1861 and won appointment as commander of the Lewisburg Military District. In this capacity, he fought and won several skirmishes against Union forces, but on May 9, 1862, he was himself defeated by Colonel George Crook and his 36th Ohio at

Lewisburg. Afterward, he relocated to Kentucky to serve under General Edmund KIRBY-SMITH, but he smarted over being in what he considered a military backwater. Heth began to agitate for another transfer back east, and in the spring of 1863, he was appointed a brigade commander in General Ambrose P. HILL's noted "Light Division." His subsequently tenure with General Robert E. LEE's Army of Northern Virginia was accomplished but fraught with peril for the South. In May 1862 Heth fought under General Thomas J. JACKSON's II Corps during the Chancellorsville campaign. He accompanied Jackson on his masterful turning movement of General Joseph HOOKER's right flank, being slightly wounded. Later that month, his good behavior resulted in promotion to major general and command of his own division. Personally brave but displaying a tendency toward rashness and a disdain for proper reconnaissance, Heth was now positioned to adversely influence upcoming military events.

During General Lee's invasion of Pennsylvania, Heth's Light Division formed part of Hill's III Corps. On July 1, 1863, he was foraging for shoes near the vital road junction of Gettysburg when his skirmishers encountered dismounted cavalry under General John BUFORD. At that time, he was under Lee's strict orders not to precipitate an action until the rest of the army arrived, but nonetheless, he committed a brigade under General James J. Pettigrew to attack. When his men were pushed back by Buford's rapid-firing carbines, Heth brought up additional forces and renewed the struggle. The sound of battle attracted men from both sides, and an unscheduled engagement unfolded. By nightfall, the Southerners had gained the upper hand, winning a solid tactical victory. But the hillsides of Gettysburg were not where Lee had planned to fight, and for the next two days, he waged a bloody battle with Union forces on ground of their own choosing. Heth, by dint of his rashness, was responsible for this, and his behavior engendered dire consequences for the Confederacy. His division had incurred heavy losses while he himself sustained a serious head wound—surviving only because he had stuffed his new hat with paper to make it fit better. He recovered in time to cover the army's retreat, although, at Falling Waters, Maryland, on July 14, 1863, his division was roughly handled by Union cavalry under General Hugh J. KILPATRICK.

Despite his mishandling of affairs at Gettysburg, Heth remained a popular commander with his troops. His division again was savaged by Union troops at Bristoe Station on October 14, 1863, and he subsequently rendered useful service at the Wilderness, Cold Harbor, and in the trenches of Petersburg in 1864. On August 24, 1864, Heth scored a surprising victory over General Winfield S. HANCOCK's II Corps at Ream's Station, Virginia, taking 2,000 prisoners. He then remained with the army until the bitter end and finally surrendered with Lee at Appomattox on April 9, 1865. After the war, Heth settled in Richmond as a businessman, although he eventually found employment with the federal government. He was also active in veteran's affairs, giving speeches, and he also penned an extensive memoir about the war years. Heth died in Washington, D.C., on September 27, 1899, a capable division commander when not given to rashness.

Further Reading
Gragg, Rod. *Covered with Glory: The 26th North Carolina Infantry at Gettysburg.* New York: HarperCollins, 2000.

Horn, John. *The Destruction of the Weldon Railroad, Deep Bottom, Globe Tavern, and Ream's Station, August 14–25, 1864.* Lynchburg, Va.: H. E. Howard, 1991.

Morrison, James L., ed. *The Memoirs of Henry Heth.* Westport, Conn.: Greenwood Press, 1974.

Newton, Steven H. *McPherson's Ridge: The First Battle for the High Ground, July 1, 1863.* Cambridge, Mass.: Da Capo Press, 2002.

Pfanz, Harry W. *Gettysburg—The First Day.* Chapel Hill: University of North Carolina Press, 2001.

Robbins, James S. *Last in Their Class: Custer, Pickett, and the Goats of West Point.* New York: Encounter Books, 2006.

Hill, Ambrose P. (1825–1865)

Confederate general

Ambrose Powell Hill was born in Culpeper County, Virginia, on November 9, 1825, and well educated at home. He entered the U.S. Military Academy in 1842 and, after missing a year due to illness, graduated in 1847 as a second lieutenant in the 1st U.S. Artillery. Hill, known as "Little Powell" on account of his short stature, accompanied his regiment south during closing phases of the Mexican War, saw no combat, and spent the postwar period pulling garrison duty in Texas. Between 1850 and 1855, he served in Florida during difficulties with the Seminoles there and subsequently transferred as a captain with the U.S. Coastal Survey. Though a Southerner, Hill opposed slavery on moral grounds, but he also supported the notion of states' rights. Accordingly, he resigned his commission in March 1861 and offered his services to the Confederacy as colonel of the 13th Virginia Infantry. He commanded a brigade at Bull Run in July 1861, but he saw no serious fighting. However, in light of his skill at training and disciplining soldiers, Hill rose to brigadier general in February 1862. It was during the Peninsula campaign of that year that he emerged as one of the finest divisional commanders in the Confederate service.

Confederate general Ambrose P. Hill *(National Archives)*

Hill initially served under General James LONGSTREET, an officer whom he came to dislike intensely. On May 5, 1862, he delivered a crushing blow to Union forces at Williamsburg, Virginia, winning promotion to major general and command of a six-brigade division—the largest in the Confederate army. Under Hill's expert eye and intense training regimen, it promptly became known as the "Light Division" on account of its rapidity of movement. He continued distinguishing himself throughout the internecine fighting of the Seven Days' battles, invariably taking heavy losses but always driving the enemy back. But, as his relations with Longstreet were at the breaking point, General Robert E. LEE arranged his transfer to the II Corps of General Thomas J. JACKSON to forestall a possible duel. The banty Hill, a flamboyant figure who disdained regular uniforms and who always went into combat bedecked in a bright red shirt, also failed to befriend the pious, spit-and-polish Jackson. The two men nonetheless worked well together on the battlefield at Cedar Mountain and Second Manassas in August 1862, and Hill received the honor of spearheading the Confederate drive into Maryland. Jackson, however, became incensed by Hill's lack of protocol and his slovenly marching order, and he had him arrested. Hill made the requisite adjustments in discipline and went on to to capture the Union garrison at Harper's Ferry, personally receiving its surrender. He then performed his greatest military feat at Antietam against General George B. MCCLELLAN on September 17, 1862, by hurriedly forwarding the Light Division and rescuing Lee's left flank from certain destruction. This proved to be one of the greatest forced marches of the war.

Hill subsequently performed well at Fredericksburg against General Ambrose E. BURNSIDE on December 13, 1862, and he accompanied Jackson's flank attack at Chancellorsville on May 2–3, which rolled up the army of General Joseph HOOKER. Following the death of Jackson, he was promoted to lieutenant general on May 24, 1863, and appointed head of the newly formed III Corps. But Hill, suffering from intermittent kidney problems, was increasingly ill, and his performance became uneven. His behavior at the crucial first day of Gettysburg on July 1, 1863, proved uninspired, and he allowed General Henry HETH's division to precipitate the battle before the rest of the army came up in support. His troops did manage to drive General John F. REYNOLD's I Corps and General Oliver O. HOWARD's IX Corps out of the town, but then they failed to seize the heights above. On October 14, 1863, Hill subsequently stumbled into a well-defended Union position, commanded by General Gouverneur K. Warren, without proper reconnaissance, and he lost two brigades in heavy fighting. On May 5–6, 1864, Hill's corps nearly was overwhelmed by General Winfield S. HANCOCK's command, and he dropped out of active duty from fatigue and illness. He resumed active duty by June and fought in the defense of Petersburg, Virginia, expertly driving off repeated Union attempts to severe Confederate communications. Illness again necessitated a medical furlough of several months, but just as he was returning on April 2, 1865, General Ulysses S. GRANT ordered a massive onslaught that penetrated Southern defenses. Hill was shot down trying to rally his command. Irascible and basically promoted beyond his abilities, he still enjoyed a sterling reputation among fellow Confederates; reputedly both Lee and Jackson called for him on their deathbeds.

Further Reading

Cross, David F. *A Melancholy Affair at the Weldon Railroad: The Vermont Brigade, June 23, 1864.* Shippensburg, Pa.: White Mane Books, 2003.

Jones, Wilmer L. *Generals in Blue and Gray.* 2 vols. Westport, Conn.: Praeger, 2004.

Newton, Steven W. *McPherson's Ridge: The First Battle for the High Ground, July 1, 1863.* Cambridge, Mass.: Da Capo Press, 2002.

Pfanz, Harry W. *Gettysburg—The First Day.* Chapel Hill: University of North Carolina Press, 2001.

Sears, Stephen. *Landscape Turned Red: The Battle of Antietam.* Boston: Houghton Mifflin, 2003.

Smith, Derek. *The Gallant Dead: Union and Confederate Generals Killed in the Civil War.* Mechanicsburg, Pa.: Stackpole Books, 2005.

Welsh, William E. "Little Powell's Big Fight." *Military Heritage* 6, no. 6 (2005): 50–57, 182.

Hill, Daniel H. (1821–1889)

Confederate general

Daniel Harvey Hill was born in the York District, South Carolina, on July 12, 1821, the son of farmers. His father died when he was a child, and Hill was raised by his stern Presbyterian mother, who indelibly influenced his social bearings. He also suffered from intermittent pain arising from a congenital spinal defect. Hill nonetheless managed to enter the U.S. Military Academy in 1838 and graduated four years later in the middle of his class. As a second lieutenant in the 1st U.S. Artillery, he fulfilled a long stint of garrison duty in the Southwest before heading south to fight in the Mexican War (1846–48). A lion in combat, Hill marched with the army under General Winfield SCOTT and garnered brevet promotions for gallantry at the battles of Contreras, Churbusco, and Chapultepec. The South Carolina legislature also voted him an ornate sword as a token of their esteem. But Hill terminated his promising career in February 1849 by resigning his commission to work as a mathematics instructor at Washington College, Virginia. He performed much useful work and also arranged for Thomas J. JACKSON to teach at the nearby Virginia Military Institute; Hill subsequently married Jackson's sister. In 1854 he transferred to Davidson College, North Carolina, where his fine grasp of administration rescued that institution from insolvency. Hill departed Davidson in 1859 to perform similar work at the newly created North Carolina Military Institute. When North Carolina seceded from the Union on May 20, 1861, Hill gained an appointment as colonel of the 1st North Carolina Volunteers.

On June 10, 1861, Hill, assisted by Colonel John B. MAGRUDER, fought and won the Civil War's first sizable encounter at Big Bethel, Virginia, by defeating Federal troops under General Benjamin F. BUTLER. This garnered him immediate promotion to brigadier general the following August along with command of the Pamlico District of North Carolina. In the spring of 1862, Hill advanced to major general and commanded a division under General Joseph E. JOHNSTON during initial phases of the Peninsula campaign. He next distinguished himself in the Seven Days' battles under General Robert E. LEE, especially at the very bloody engagement at Malvern Hill on July 1, 1862. However, Hill's outspoken, irascible disposition militated against him when he openly criticized Lee's leadership for the costly repulse there,

declaring, "It wasn't war, it was murder." He then engendered another controversy in September during the invasion of Maryland when a copy of Lee's secret instructions (Special Order 191) was dispatched to Hill wrapped around some cigars—and ended up in the hands of General George B. MCCLELLAN. As Union forces then converged on the scattered Confederates, Hill greatly distinguished himself at Crampton's Gap (South Mountain) on September 13, 1862, delaying McClellan's advance by four hours and allowing Lee to assemble behind Antietam Creek. He subsequently fought well defending the sunken lane against great odds four days later. However, Lee, still smarting from Hill's inopportune remarks, declined recommending him for promotion to lieutenant general. Hill was so angered by the snub that he threatened to resign, but he was dissuaded from doing so by his brother-in-law, "Stonewall Jackson."

Hill was transferred back to North Carolina in February 1863 and then performed useful work defending Richmond, Virginia, during the Gettysburg campaign. President Jefferson DAVIS was so impressed by his performance that he recommended him for a lieutenant generalship, and he transferred him to the western theater as a corps commander. Hill fought well at the bloody battle of Chickamauga on September 19, 1863, but he was impolitic in criticizing the leadership of General Braxton BRAGG. When Bragg, one of President Davis's closest friends, complained about Hill's behavior, Davis scuttled his forthcoming promotion. In the end, both men were removed from command, and Hill spent several months employed as a volunteer aide to General Pierre G. T. BEAUREGARD at Petersburg, Virginia. It was not until the spring of 1865 that he resumed field operations by commanding a division in General Stephen D. Lee's corps, and he fought at Bentonville, North Carolina, on March 19–21, 1865. Hill finally surrendered with General Johnston at Durham's Station the following April.

After the war, Hill resumed his activities as a highly skilled academic administrator at Arkansas Industrial University (now the University of

Confederate general Daniel H. Hill *(Library of Congress)*

Arkansas). He also actively edited and published several Confederate-oriented magazines for Southern consumption, wherein he criticized General Lee's generalship. In 1885 he transferred as president of the Middle Georgia Military and Agricultural College before dying at Charlotte, North Carolina, on September 24, 1889. Hill was among the South's best and most hard-hitting divisional commanders, whose career was perpetually thwarted by his otherwise tactless demeanor.

Further Reading

Bridges, Hal. *Lee's Maverick General, Daniel Harvey Hill.* Lincoln: University of Nebraska Press, 1991.

Burton, Brian K. *Extraordinary Circumstances: The Seven Days Battles.* Bloomington: Indiana University Press, 2001.

Hughes, Nathaniel C., and Timothy D. Johnson, eds. *A Fighter from Way Back: The Mexican War Diary of Lieutenant Daniel Harvey Hill, 4th Artillery, U.S.A.* Kent, Ohio: Kent State University Press, 2002.

Isenbarger, Dennis L. "Perpetual Stubbornness: The Relationship of President Jefferson Davis and Major General Daniel Harvey Hill." Unpublished master's thesis, Western Carolina University, 1997.

Jones, Wilmer L. *Generals in Blue and Gray.* 2 vols. Westport, Conn.: Praeger, 2004.

Sears, Stephen W. "The Twisted Tale of the Lost Order." *North & South* 5, no. 7 (2002): 54–65.

Hindman, Thomas C. (1828–1868)

Confederate general

Thomas Carmichael Hindman was born in Nashville, Tennessee, on January 28, 1828, and relocated with his family to Ripley, Mississippi, where his father served as an Indian agent. He was educated by tutors and at several private schools near Princeton, New Jersey, before joining the 2nd Mississippi Infantry in 1846. He then served in the Mexican War as a captain without seeing combat and returned home in 1848 to study law. After joining the bar in 1851, Hindman expressed an interest in politics, and he ran for office as a states' rights Democrat. That year, he also supported Jefferson Davis's gubernatorial candidacy and displayed real ability as a fiery rabble-rousing orator.

In 1853 Hindman himself won a seat in the Mississippi state legislature, where he remained for three years before relocating to Helena, Arkansas. A short, aggressive man who never minced his words, he made few friends among the political establishment, but his message of defiance toward the national government resonated with the voters, who sent him to Congress as a representative in 1858. There, Hindman functioned as a radical secessionist, and in 1860, he backed the presidential candidacy of John C. Breckinridge. Hindman then resigned his seat in order to serve as colonel of the newly formed 2nd Arkansas Infantry.

Given his ambition and political connections, Hindman's climb up the Confederate chain of command proved rapid. He advanced to brigadier general as of September 28, 1861, and had risen to major general by the spring of 1862. Hindman now commanded a division in General William J. Hardee's corps and acquitted himself well at the bloody Battle of Shiloh (April 6–7, 1862) by repeatedly attacking the so-called Hornet's Nest. He then repaired back to Arkansas as the newly installed commander of the Trans-Mississippi Department. Determined to transform this military backwater into a garrison state, Hindman strongly enforced conscription laws with prescribed punishments for failing to comply, and he raised 18,000 additional soldiers from scratch. However, his tactless and seemingly arbitrary methods incurred considerable resentment, and at length he was replaced by the more accommodating general Theophilus H. Holmes. The elderly Holmes diplomatically kept most of Hindman's methods in place and allowed him to carry out military functions. Consequently, Arkansas was well prepared to receive a Union invasion in the fall of 1862. Eager to engage the enemy, Hindman secretly marched 10,000 men against the divides forces of Generals James G. Blunt and Francis J. Herron at Prairie Grove on December 7, 1862. Having skillfully driven a wedge between the two forces, he inexplicably went on the defensive and gradually squandered his strategic surprise in piecemeal attacks. Thereafter, he requested a transfer out of Arkansas and into the Army of Tennessee.

Hindman remained without a command for several months, and his principal activity involved overseeing the court of inquiry investigating General Mansfield LOVELL for the loss of New Orleans, Louisiana. In July 1862 he was assigned a division under General Leonidas K. POLK at Chattanooga, Tennessee. Hindman subsequently fought well at the bloody encounter at Chickamauga on September 19–20, 1863, being seriously wounded. However, General Braxton BRAGG was displeased by Hindman's performance and relieved him of command. In January 1864 he further complicated his position with the Confederate government by endorsing General Patrick R. CLEBURNE's suggestion to offer African-American slaves freedom in exchange for military service. Hindman finally took charge of a division under General Joseph E. JOHNSTON and fought well during the opening phases of the Atlanta campaign before an eye injury necessitated his removal. He spent the final months of the war at his home in Helena.

After the war, Hindman initially fled to Mexico to escape prosecution, but he returned to Arkansas in 1867 to resume his political career. He remained an outspoken opponent of Radical Reconstruction and railed against what he considered "carpetbagger" rule by outsiders. On September 27, 1868, Hindman was suddenly murdered in his home, probably for political reasons; his death was never solved.

Further Reading

Bailey, Anne J., and Daniel E. Sutherland, eds. *Civil War Arkansas: Beyond Battles and Leaders.* Fayetteville: University of Arkansas Press, 2000.

Collins, Robert. *General James G. Blunt: Tarnished Glory.* Gretna, La.: Pelican Publishing, 2005.

Cozzens, Peter. "Hindman's Grand Delusion." *Civil War Times Illustrated* 39, no. 5 (2000): 28–35, 66–69.

DeBlack, Thomas R. *With Fire and Sword: Arkansas, 1861–1874.* Fayetteville: University of Arkansas Press, 2003.

Frazier, Rodney R. *Broken Swords: The Lives, Times, and Deaths of Eight Former Confederate Generals Mur-*dered After the Smoke of Battle Had Cleared. New York: Vantage Press, 2003.

Shea, William J., and Grady McWhiney. *War in the West: Pea Ridge and Prairie Grove.* Abilene, Tex.: McWhiney Foundation Press, 2001.

Hoke, Robert F. (1837–1912)
Confederate general

Robert Frederick Hoke was born in Lincolnton, North Carolina, on May 27, 1837, the son of a politician. He was 17 years old and attending the Kentucky Military Institute when his father died, prompting him to quit school and manage the family cotton mill and iron foundry. After North Carolina seceded on May 20, 1861, Hoke joined the 1st North Carolina Infantry under Colonel Daniel H. HILL as a second lieutenant. He then fought with distinction at the Battle of Big Bethel on June 10, 1861, one of the Civil War's first sizable clashes and a Confederate victory. Hoke, by dint of superior performance, continued rising in rank, and by the time he returned home in the spring of 1862, he was lieutenant colonel of the 33rd North Carolina. He again fought well at the defeat of New Bern on March 14, 1862, becoming the only Southern officer there to garner official praise. Hoke's regiment then shuttled back to the Army of Northern Virginia under General Robert E. LEE, where he acquitted himself well and captured an enemy battery at Glendale on June 30, 1862. After conspicuous bravery at Second Manassas in August and Antietam that September, he became colonel of the 21st North Carolina and part of General Jubal A. EARLY's division. In this capacity, he commanded an entire brigade at the December 13, 1862, Battle of Fredericksburg, badly repulsing a determined attack by General George G. MEADE. Against all expectations, Hoke ordered his Tar Heel troops to charge, and they did so ferociously, netting 300 Federal prisoners. Consequently, he rose to brigadier general as of January 19, 1863, at the age of 26.

In the spring of 1863, Hoke arrived in the Piedmont district of his home state to conduct both anti-Unionist operations and round up deserters who had been terrorizing the countryside. He then returned to Virginia and was severely wounded during opening phases of the Battle of Chancellorsville on May 3, 1863, while defending Marye's Heights against General John Sedgwick. Hoke consequently missed Gettysburg and was sent back home to recruit troops and collect deserters. In January 1864 he joined General George E. PICKETT's division in the failed siege of New Bern. Fortunately, he received an independent command and instructions to besiege and capture the Union lodgment at Plymouth, North Carolina, garrisoned by 3,000 Union troops under General Henry W. Wessels. Hoke methodically surrounded the Federal position and, assisted by the powerful Confederate ram CSS *Albemarle* offshore, drove the defenders from a series of fortifications. On April 20, 1864, Wessels surrendered in one of the few Confederate victories on North Carolina soil. Consequently, Hoke received the thanks of the Confederate Congress while President Jefferson DAVIS personally promoted him to major general, the Confederacy's youngest. When Hoke rejoined the Army of Northern Virginia again that summer, much was expected of this accomplished young warrior.

Unfortunately, Hoke had been advanced beyond his abilities. He fought well enough under General Pierre G. T. BEAUREGARD at Drewry's Bluff on May 10, 1864, which sealed General Benjamin F. BUTLER on the peninsula of Bermuda Hundred. But in a series of battles commencing with Cold Harbor on June 3, 1864, Hoke apparently lost his earlier dash and seemed incapable of coordinating his movement with other leaders. On June 24, 1864, his attack near Petersburg recoiled with heavy losses, and the following September, he failed, after three charges, to capture Union-held Fort Harrison. His division was then pulled from the line and sent to bolster the defenses of Fort Fisher, Wilmington, North Carolina, under General Braxton BRAGG. On January 15, Bragg forbade him from launching an attack on Federal troops that may have prevented the fort from falling to General Alfred H. TERRY. Hoke then transferred to the Army of Tennessee under General Joseph E. JOHNSTON, seeing active duty at the Battle of Bentonville (March 19–21, 1865). He finally surrendered his sword to Union forces at Durham Station the following April.

After the war, Hoke resumed his commercial activities and also served as director of the North Carolina Railroad. Despite his wartime celebrity, he avoided publicity and died in near obscurity in Raleigh on July 3, 1912. Hoke County, North Carolina, subsequently was created in honor of his memory.

Further Reading

Barefoot, Daniel W. General Robert F. *Hoke: Lee's Modest Warrior.* Salem, N.C.: John F. Blair, 1996.

Broadwater, Robert P. *Battle of Despair: Bentonville and the North Carolina Campaign.* Macon, Ga.: Mercer University Press, 2004.

Brooks, Victor. *The Fredericksburg Campaign.* Conshohocken, Pa.: Combined Publishing, 2000.

Joyner, Clinton. "Major General Robert Frederick Hoke and the Civil War in North Carolina." Unpublished master's thesis, East Carolina University, 1974.

McCaslin, Richard B. *The Last Stronghold: The Campaign for Fort Fisher.* Abilene, Tex.: McWhiney Foundation Press, 2003.

Moss, Juanita P. *Battle of Plymouth, North Carolina (April 17–20, 1864): The Last Confederate Victory.* Bowie, Md.: Willow Bend Books, 2004.

Hood, John B. (1831–1879)
Confederate general

John Bell Hood was born in Owingsville, Kentucky, on June 1, 1831, the son of a physician. He was admitted to the U.S. Military Academy in 1849, proved something of a sullen, undistinguished student, and graduated four years later as a second lieutenant in the 4th U.S. Infantry. Hood reported for duty in California, but in 1855, he transferred to the newly created 2nd U.S. Cavalry under Colonel Albert S. JOHNSTON. Hood rode with him for several years in Texas, waged numerous skirmishes with the Comanche, and was

Confederate general John B. Hood *(Library of Congress)*

well-deserved reputation as a "fighting general." At the Battle of Gaines's Mill, June 27, 1863, his Texans crashed through Union lines, took several cannon, and forced General Fitz John PORTER to retreat. The following August, Hood distinguished himself in combat at Second Manassas as part of General James LONGSTREET's I Corps, where he delivered a flank attack that sent the Union army of General John POPE reeling. In September, his Texans successfully fended off the attacks of two Union Corps at Antietam, sparing General Robert E. LEE's center—while nearly being annihilated in the process. He consequently rose to the rank of the major general the following October. His next big engagement was at Gettysburg, July 2, 1863, where he drove the advance troops of General Daniel SICKLES from Devil's Den before sustaining a crippling arm wound. He next spent several week recuperating before accompanying Longstreet to reinforce the Army of Tennessee under General Braxton BRAGG. On September 20, 1863, in the bloody battle of Chickamauga, he delivered a crushing assault that nearly destroyed the Army of the Cumberland under General William S. ROSECRANS, losing his left leg in the process. Thereafter, the aggressive Kentuckian had to be strapped into his saddle while campaigning. He then rose to lieutenant general as of February 1864 and to command of a corps under General Joseph E. JOHNSTON in the Atlanta campaign.

Hood, a devotee of massed assaults, did not work well with Johnston, a master of set-piece defensive tactics, and the Army of Tennessee was forced to yield before the superior numbers of General William T. SHERMAN. On July 17, President Jefferson DAVIS, discouraged by Johnston's inability to halt the Union advance, suddenly replaced him with Hood. Predictably, Confederate strategy switched to the offensive, and Hood was heavily repulsed at Peachtree Creek, Atlanta, and Ezra Church on July 20, 22, and 28, 1864. At length, the Confederates were forced to abandon Atlanta to Sherman on September 1, 1864, and General William J. HARDEE, expressing no confi-

wounded on one occasion. When the Civil War broke out in April 1861, Hood had no reservations about resigning his commission to fight for the South. However, because his native state of Kentucky remained neutral, he entered Confederate service from his adopted state of Texas. Hood spent several months in Virginia where he functioned as a cavalry instructor under General John B. MAGRUDER at Yorktown, Virginia, winning plaudits from superiors, but in October 1861, he switched back to the infantry as a colonel of the 4th Texas, and in February 1862, Hood advanced to brigadier general commanding the famous "Texas Brigade." Leading by example from the front and imposing an iron hand on his unruly recruits, he transformed them into the shock troops of the Confederacy.

Hood fought with great gallantry through the 1862 Peninsula campaign, acquiring the dence in Hood's ability to lead, requested a transfer. When Sherman subsequently marched from Atlanta to Savannah and the sea, Hood saw a strategic opportunity to lure him back. He collected the Army of Tennessee and rapidly marched westward in Alabama to attack Union lines of communication. When that ploy failed to distract Sherman, Hood redirected his line of march north into Tennessee and a possible drive to the Ohio River. On November 29, 1864, he failed to trap a portion of the Union army under John M. SCHOFIELD at Spring Hill and then pursued them to Franklin. There, on November 30, 1864—and despite the protests of his subordinates—Hood launched a series of frontal assaults on prepared Union positions that were bloodily and predictably shattered. Six Confederate generals, including the irreplaceable Patrick R. CLEBURNE, fell that day. Hood then followed Schofield until he fell back on General George H. THOMAS's Union army at Nashville. Though severely depleted in numbers and lacking sufficient artillery, the stubborn Kentuckian entrenched his men around the city, daring Thomas to attack him. On December 15–16, 1864, the unhurried Thomas obliged him, completely shattering the Confederates. The once mighty Army of Tennessee dissolved into a mass of refugees, and Hood was relieved of command at his own request on January 23, 1865. He was succeeded by General Richard TAYLOR and, in Mississippi, he finally surrendered to Union authorities at Natchez on May 31, 1865.

Hood retired to New Orleans, Louisiana, to work in the insurance industry, and he also penned an excellent, if vitriolic, set of memoirs which matter of factly blamed Bragg and Johnston for losing the war. Not surprisingly, he studiously downplayed his own role in the western disasters. After surviving poverty for many years, Hood died of yellow fever on August 30, 1879, at the age of 48. Unquestionably one of the Civil War's bravest, most aggressive, and most tenacious division-level fighters, he was simply out of his depth at higher command—with disastrous results for the South.

Further Reading

Bagby, Milton. "Advance and Retreat." *American History* 37, no. 4 (2002): 38–46.

Bailey, Anne J. *The Chessboard of War: Sherman and Hood in the Autumn Campaigns of 1864.* Lincoln: University of Nebraska Press, 2000.

Daniel, Larry J. *Cannoneers in Gray: The Field Artillery of the Army of Tennessee, 1861–1865.* Tuscaloosa: University of Alabama Press, 2005.

Gallagher, Gary W., and Joseph T. Glatthaar, eds. *Leaders of the Lost Cause: New Perspectives on the Confederate High Command.* Mechanicsburg, Pa.: Stackpole Books, 2004.

Haughton, Andrew. *Training, Tactics, and Leadership in the Confederate Army of Tennessee: Seeds of Failure.* Portland, Ore.: Frank Cass, 2000.

Hood, John B. *Advance and Retreat: Personal Experiences in the United States and Confederate Armies.* Lincoln: University of Nebraska Press, 1996.

Jacobsen, Eric A., and Richard A. Rupp. *For Cause & Country: A Study of the Affair at Spring Hill & the Battle of Franklin.* Franklin, Tenn.: O'More Publishing, 2006.

Lepa, Jack H. *Breaking the Confederacy: The Georgia and Tennessee Campaigns of 1864.* Jefferson, N.C.: McFarland, 2005.

McDonough, James L. *Nashville: The Western Confederacy's Final Gamble.* Knoxville: University of Tennessee Press, 2004.

Hooker, Joseph (1814–1879)

Union general

Joseph Hooker was born in Hadley, Massachusetts, on November 13, 1814, the son of a businessman. Declining to follow his father's profession, he gained admission to the U.S. Military Academy in 1837 and graduated four years later as a second lieutenant of artillery. Hooker initially saw active duty in Florida's Second Seminole War, where he rose to first lieutenant, and he subsequently returned to West Point to serve as adjutant. During the Mexican War (1846–48), he served as a staff officer under General Zachary Taylor and Winfield SCOTT, but he managed to see extensive combat and won three consecutive brevet promotions in fighting at Monterrey, National Bridge, and Chapultepec. During the trial of General Gideon PILLOW, he testified favorably on his behalf and gained the lasting enmity of Scott. After the war, Hooker was reassigned to the Division of the Pacific in California where, dissatisfied with slow promotions, he resigned his commission in 1853. Hooker then pursued farming and also served as a colonel in the militia until the Civil War erupted in April 1861. He immediately tendered his services to the army, but he was not offered a commission—possibly because of the obstruction of Scott, now general in chief. Hooker then traveled to Washington, D.C., where he finally landed a brigadier general's commission on May 17, 1861, and assignment to the capital's defenses. He performed well and was chosen by General George B. McCLELLAN to command a division in the newly formed Army of the Potomac.

Hooker first saw fighting in the Peninsula campaign of 1862, with General Samuel P. Heint-

Union general Joseph Hooker *(Library of Congress)*

zelman's III Corps, and he was closely engaged with General James LONGSTREET in the hard-fought encounter at Williamsburg on May 5, 1862. His bravery proved so conspicuous that he won both promotion to major general and the nickname "Fighting Joe." After more distinguished service under General John POPE at Second Manassas the following August, Hooker was closely engaged at South Mountain and Antietam, Maryland, in September 1862. During the latter contest, he orchestrated a heavy attack against General Robert E. LEE's left wing and might have prevailed had he been properly supported. General Ambrose BURNSIDE subsequently appointed him to command a grand division of two corps at Fredericksburg on December 13, 1862, where he was one of few Union officers to garner any distinction. Hooker, loud and indiscrete, openly complained about Burnside's leadership. President Abraham LINCOLN appointed him the new commander of the Army of the Potomac in January 1863. Hooker also gained a measure of notoriety in political circles by stating that both the army and the nation needed a dictator to win the war. "Only those generals who gain success can set up dictators," Lincoln advised him. "What I ask of you is military success and I will risk the dictatorship."

Hooker displayed considerable skill reorganizing and reinvigorating the much abused Army of the Potomac, and by May 1862, he possessed a splendidly trained and equipped force of 132,000 men—twice the size of General Robert E. Lee's Army of Northern Virginia. He then embarked on a bold strategy to slide around Lee's left flank through a rapid crossing of the Rapidan and Rappahannock rivers. Hooker's ploy worked brilliantly, and on May 1, 1863, his army was massed in a densely wooded area known as the Wilderness, only 10 miles from the unsuspecting Confederates. However, Lee took the even bolder expedient of dividing his army in the face of the enemy and dispatching the II Corps of General Thomas J. JACKSON to swing around and hit Hooker's own exposed right. Hooker, inexplicably, then lost his nerve and went on the defense, forfeiting all tactical initiative to the Confederates. He had also dispatched the bulk of his cavalry under General George Stoneman on a lengthy raid, thereby depriving himself of reconnaissance abilities that may have detected the enemy's approach. On May 2, Jackson launched his masterful flank attack, which routed the XI Corps of General Oliver O. HOWARD. Hooker then ordered his army, largely intact, strongly posted, and full of fight, to retreat over the protests of his generals. This closed the ill-fated Chancellorsville campaign, which ruined Hooker's reputation and cost the Union 17,000 men. Lincoln and General in Chief Henry W. HALLECK apparently also lost confidence in him and so interfered with his initial moves during the Gettysburg campaign that Hooker resigned three days before that fateful encounter transpired. He was hurriedly replaced by General George G. MEADE.

In the fall of 1863, Hooker transferred to the western theater to serve under General Ulysses S. GRANT, where he commanded the XI and XII Corps. In this capacity, he won a striking victory at Lookout Mountain on November 24, 1863, winning a major general's brevet in the regular army. Three days later, he sparred heavily with General Patrick R. CLEBURNE at Ringgold Gap, Georgia, and was unable to push back the Southern rearguard. Nevertheless, the following spring, he led the new XX Corps under General William T. SHERMAN in the Atlanta campaign, again distinguishing himself in several hard-fought battles. However, when General James B. McPHERSON was killed outside Atlanta on July 22, 1864, Sherman appointed General Howard—an officer of far less seniority—to succeeded him as commander of the Army of Tennessee. Hooker, enraged by the snub, promptly submitted his resignation in protest. He spent the balance of the war heading the Northern Department, a quiet sector.

After the war, Hooker led the Department of the East and the Department of the Lakes before resigning in 1868. He then lived in quiet seclusion until his death at Garden City, New York, on October 31, 1879, one of the Union's best corps commanders, an aggressive tactician who invariably inflicted more damage than he received. Unfortunately, his headstrong nature, sharp tongue, and indiscrete behavior alienated many around him and militated against his advancement.

Further Reading

Cubbison, Douglas R. "Tactical Genius above the Clouds: 'Fighting Joe' Hooker and John White Geary at the Battle of Lookout Mountain, November 24, 1863." *Tennessee Historical Quarterly* 61, no. 4 (2002): 266–289.

Dubbs, Carol K. *Defend This Old Town: Williamsburg during the Civil War.* Baton Rouge: Louisiana State University Press, 2002.

Longacre, Edward G. *The Commanders of Chancellorsville: The Gentleman vs the Rogue.* Nashville, Tenn.: Rutledge Hill Press, 2005.

Smith, Carl. *Chancellorsville, 1863: Jackson's Lightning Strike.* Westport, Conn.: Praeger, 2004.

Spruill, Mat. *Storming the Heights: A Guide to the Battle of Chattanooga.* Knoxville: University of Tennessee Press, 2003.

Taaffe, Stephen R. *Commanding the Army of the Potomac.* Lawrence: University Press of Kansas, 2006.

Wert, Jeffrey D. *The Sword of Lincoln: The Army of the Potomac.* New York: Simon and Schuster, 2005.

Howard, Oliver O. (1830–1909)

Union general

Oliver Otis Howard was born in Leeds, Maine, on November 8, 1830, the son of farmers. He graduated from Bowdoin College in 1850 and then entered the U.S. Military Academy. Howard graduated four years later, fourth in his class, and was commissioned a second lieutenant in the Ordnance Corps. After serving briefly in Florida's Third Seminole War, he transferred back to West Point to serve as a mathematics instructor. Howard by this time had undergone a profound religious conversion and seriously considered ordination to the ministry, but the onset of the Civil War induced him to become colonel of the 3rd Maine Infantry in June 1861. He then commanded a brigade at Bull Run the following July, which stampeded like the rest of General Irwin

Union general Oliver O. Howard *(Library of Congress)*

McDowell's army, but Howard performed well enough under fire to merit promotion to brigadier general in September. As part of General George B. McClellan's Army of the Potomac, he fought well in the Peninsula campaign and lost his right arm at the Battle of Fair Oaks on May 31, 1862. After recovering, Howard rejoined the army in time to fight well at Antietam, succeed a wounded general John Sedgwick to command a division, and then advance to major general that November. In the spring of 1863, he replaced the bumbling general Franz Sigel as commander of the XI Corps, which was a largely German-speaking unit. Howard's inadequacies for high command became quickly manifest at Chancellorsville on May 2, 1864, when General Thomas J. Jackson outflanked the XI Corps, routing it. On July 1, 1863, Howard arrived at Gettysburg shortly after the death of General John F. Reynolds and assumed command from General Abner Doubleday. Again, his XI Corps was pummeled heavily by an influx of Confederates under General Richard S. Ewell and driven off McPherson Ridge. Howard, luckily, had stationed his reserves along the high ground of Cemetery Ridge, and the Union line, now bolstered by additional troops under General Winfield S. Hancock, held firm. He subsequently received the thanks of Congress for this act. However, the commanding general, George M. Meade, remained unimpressed with his performance and did not resist when the XI Corps was transferred west to fight under General George H. Thomas in the Army of the Cumberland. On November 24–25, 1863, Howard fought capably at the Union victory of Chattanooga, and he subsequently received command of the new IV Corps under General William T. Sherman.

In the spring of 1864, Howard accompanied Sherman on his famous campaign against Atlanta, performing adequately. Moreover, when General James B. McPherson was killed outside Atlanta on July 22, 1864, Sherman elected Howard to lead the Army of the Tennessee over General Joseph Hooker—a move prompting the latter's resignation. Howard then accompanied Sherman on the march to Savannah and the subsequent campaign north into the Carolinas, again acquitting himself well. By war's end, he held a rank of brevet major general of volunteers.

In the immediate postwar period, Howard was chosen by President Andrew Johnson to head the newly created Freedmen's Bureau to assist liberated African-American slaves. He readily accepted the task, given his religious and abolitionist impulses, but he proved a lax administrator who refused to investigate the activities of subordinates. In 1867 the all-black Howard University was established at his behest, and he served as its first president (1869–72). In 1873 President Ulysses S. Grant dispatched Howard to the western frontier to quell an Apache uprising, and Howard, by dint of sincerity and personal honesty, convinced Chief Cochise to return to the reservation without bloodshed. By 1877 he commanded the Department of Columbia and successfully campaigned against Chief Joseph of the Nez Percé in concert with Generals John GIBBON and Nelson Miles. On October 5, 1877, he received the chief's surrender at Eagle Rock, Montana, ending his famous flight. In January 1881 Howard returned to West Point as superintendent for a year, and then he successively took charge of the Division of the Platte and the East. In 1893 Congress awarded him a Congressional Medal of Honor for his services at Fair Oaks in 1862. Howard retired from the army in 1894 and penned several lucid memoirs about his military experiences. He died in Burlington, Vermont, on October 26, 1909, an earnest, if mediocre, leader.

Further Reading

Howard, Oliver O. *Autobiography of Oliver Otis Howard, Major General, U.S. Army*. New York: Baker and Taylor, 1907.

Newton, Steven H. *McPherson's Ridge: The First Battle for the High Ground, July 1, 1863*. Cambridge, Mass.: Da Capo Press, 2002.

Pfanz, Harry W. *Gettysburg—The First Day*. Chapel Hill: University of North Carolina Press, 2001.

Valuska, David L., and Christian B. Keller. *Damn Dutch: Pennsylvania Germans at Gettysburg*. Mechanicsburg, Pa.: Stackpole Books, 2004.

Weland, Gerald. *O. O. Howard, Union General*. Jefferson, N.C.: McFarland, 1995.

Woodworth, Steven E. *Nothing but Victory: The Army of the Tennessee, 1861–1865*. New York: Alfred A. Knopf, 2005.

Huger, Benjamin (1805–1877)

Confederate general

Benjamin Huger was born in Charleston, South Carolina, on November 22, 1805, into a distinguished family of Huguenot descent. His father had served as aide-de-camp to General James Wilkinson during the War of 1812, while his mother was the daughter of General Thomas Pinckney of the American Revolution. Given this martial background, Huger attended the U.S. Military Academy in 1821 and graduated four years later at the top of his class. He was then commissioned second lieutenant in the 3rd U.S. Artillery and performed topographical duties until 1828,

when he left on a sabbatical to study artillery in Europe. Huger then joined the Ordnance Department, rising to captain in 1832. He commanded Fortress Monroe, Virginia, for 12 years while also sitting on various ordnance boards. During the Mexican War, he served in the army of General Winfield SCOTT as commander of the artillery train. His placement of field pieces at the siege of Veracruz proved masterful and resulted in brevet promotion to major. Huger subsequently was breveted two more times for bravery at Molino del Rey and Chapultepec, ending the war a lieutenant colonel. Afterward, he resumed his duties with the Ordnance Department, helped develop a new artillery system, and commanded a successive series of Federal arsenals from Harper's Ferry, Virginia, to Pikesville, Maryland. Huger's service was so esteemed by his home state that the South Carolina legislature voted him a ceremonial sword. The old soldier did not immediately tender his resignation when his native state seceded in December 1860; he waited until after the bombardment of Fort Sumter in April 1861. Prior to the outbreak of fighting, Huger had been dispatched to the fort to confer with fellow Southerner Major Robert ANDERSON, but the latter had already resolved to remain loyal to the Union, and their discussions came to naught.

The elderly soldier rose rapidly through the Confederate ranks, being commissioned a brigadier general in June 1861 and major general the following October. As such, he was entrusted with command of the Department of Southern Virginia and North Carolina, headquartered at Norfolk. Huger administered his grossly undermanned charge well until February 8, 1862, when a Union fleet under Admiral Louis M. Goldsborough anchored offshore and landed a Union army under General Ambrose E. BURNSIDE. When Huger failed to dispatch reinforcements, Burnside experienced little difficulty capturing the island from General Henry Wise. This proved an embarrassing loss to the South, and the Confederate Congress conducted an investigation into Huger's behavior. Meanwhile, the imposing Army of the

Potomac under General George B. McCLELLAN began to push up Virginia's Peninsula district toward Richmond. Huger, greatly outnumbered, hastily abandoned Norfolk to the Federals, scuttling the famous CSS *Virginia* in the process. He then joined Generals James LONGSTREET and Daniel H. HILL to command a division in the army under General Joseph E. JOHNSTON. Huger retreated with the main body until May 31, 1862, when Johnston turned and attacked the isolated corps of General Erasmus D. Keyes at Seven Pines (Fair Oaks). Unfortunately, Huger's deployment proved hopelessly inept, and his division became ensnared with Longstreet's men while marching down the same road. His subsequent lethargic movements allowed the Union troops to escape unscathed. Johnston was then replaced by the aggressive general Robert E. LEE, who counterattacked across the line in the Seven Day's battles. Again, Huger performed sluggishly, and furthermore, a congressional committee found him culpable for the loss of Roanoke. He thereupon was relieved of duty on July 12, 1862, and sent west in the less demanding role as inspector of ordnance and artillery. He functioned capably in this office until 1863, when he rose to chief of ordnance in the Trans-Mississippi Department until the end of the war. Afterward, Huger migrated to Fauquier County, Virginia, to farm. He died in Charleston, South Carolina, on December 7, 1877, a soldier of demonstrated technical competence, but too past his prime for the rigors of war.

Further Reading

Burton, Brian K. *Extraordinary Circumstances: The Seven Days Battles.* Bloomington: Indiana University Press, 2001.

Gallagher, Gary W., ed. *The Richmond Campaign of 1862: The Peninsula and the Seven Days.* Chapel Hill: University of North Carolina Press, 2000.

Newton, Steven H. *The Battle of Seven Pines, May 31–June 1, 1862.* Lynchburg, Va.: H. E. Howard, 1993.

Rhoades, Jeffrey L. *Scapegoat General: The Story of Major General Benjamin Huger.* Hamden, Conn.: Archon Books, 1985.

Sauers, Richard. "The Confederate Congress and the Loss of Roanoke Island." *Civil War History* 40, no. 2 (1994): 134–150.

Van Velzer, William R. "Benjamin Huger and the Arming of America, 1825–1861." Unpublished master's thesis, Virginia Polytechnic University, 1994.

I

Imboden, John D. (1823–1895)

Confederate general

John Daniel Imboden was born in Augusta County, Virginia, on February 16, 1823, and he matriculated at nearby Washington College (1841–42). He then studied law and opened up a successful practice at Staunton while also developing a taste for politics. Imboden was twice elected to the House of Delegates where he served as a staunch secessionist, but he proved unable to win a seat in the state secessionist convention. Concurrent with this, he joined the local militia and helped organize the Staunton artillery. Once Virginia seceded from the Union, Imboden accompanied Turner ASHBY and helped to seize the Federal arsenal at Harper's Ferry on April 19, 1861. He then advanced to colonel and served under General Pierre G. T. BEAUREGARD at the Battle of Bull Run (July 21, 1861). Imboden was conspicuously engaged at the defense of Henry House Hill, where he supported the command of General Bernard E. Bee. He next switched from artillery to cavalry by organizing the 1st Partisan Rangers in the spring of 1862. He led his scouts throughout General Thomas J. JACKSON's brilliant Shenandaoh campaign, and he fought conspicuously at the battles of Cross Keys and Port Republic that June. He subsequently joined the Army of Northern Virginia under General Robert E. LEE in time for the invasion of Maryland that fall, and he assisted in the capture of Harper's Ferry on September 15, 1862.

Imboden's good performance resulted in his promotion to brigadier general on January 28, 1863, and command of the Northwestern Brigade of the Department of Northern Virginia. Two months later, he performed his most impressive military deed by organizing a large mounted raid against the Baltimore and Ohio Railroad. On April 20, 1863, Imboden led 3,200 troopers into the hills of West Virginia while acting in concert with a force of similar size under General William E. "Grumble" Jones. For the next 37 days, the two cavaliers tore up 170 miles of track and absconded with scores of badly needed horses and livestock. Both forces then united to eliminate the petroleum fields at Oiltown, destroying 150,000 barrels of oil. By the time Imboden and Jones concluded their successful foray, they had seized more than 5,000 cattle and 1,200 horses, burned 24 bridges, acquired 1,000 small arms, and inflicted 800 Federal casualties. This was one of the greatest cavalry raids of the Civil War, and it was accomplished at little cost to the Confederacy.

By summer, Imboden's command had been reassigned to the Army of Northern Virginia as it advanced into Pennsylvania. He successfully screened Lee's left flank but arrived at Gettysburg on July 3, 1863, just as the Confederates were withdrawing. He then assisted the exhausted, battered survivors by acting as their rear guard. On July 6, 1863, the Army of Northern Virginia was pressed up against the flooded Potomac River

Confederate general John D. Imboden *(Massachusetts Commandery Military Order of the Loyal Legion and the U.S. Army Military History Institute)*

while Union cavalry nipped at its heels. Imboden, tasked with escorting the army's supply train and thousands of wounded soldiers, suddenly found himself set upon by Federal troopers under Generals Hugh J. Kilpatrick and John Buford near Williamsport, Maryland. However, having scrapped together all available manpower, including the walking wounded, he managed to hold the marauders back until generals Fitzhugh Lee and Wade Hampton arrived to reinforce him. By the fall, Imboden was active again in the Shenandoah Valley, and he captured the entire 9th Maryland at Charles Town in October. Highly commended by Lee, he next served under General John C. Breckinridge at New Market, Virginia, on May 15, 1864, where he helped defeat Federal forces under General Franz Sigel. He accompanied General Jubal A. Early's famous sortie into the Shenandoah Valley in the summer and fall before being driven out by General Philip H. Sheridan. As the year ended, Imboden contracted typhoid fever, and he was transferred to prison duties at Aiken, South Carolina, until hostilities ceased. Imboden revived his legal career after the war in Washington County, Virginia, and he was also active in Confederate veterans' affairs. He also vocally advocated developing the coal and iron resources of his native state. Imboden, one of the Civil War's most intrepid partisan fighters, died in Damascus, Virginia, on August 15, 1895.

Further Reading

Brown, Kent M. *Retreat from Gettysburg: Lee, Logistics, and the Pennsylvania Campaign.* Chapel Hill: University of North Carolina Press, 2005.

French, Stephen. *The Jones-Imboden Raid against the B & O Railroad at Roalesburg, Virginia, April 1863.* Saline, Mich.: McNaughton and Gunn for the Blue and Gray Education Society, 2001.

Gallagher, Gary W., ed. *The Third Day at Gettysburg and Beyond.* Chapel Hill: University of North Carolina Press, 1994.

Lepa, Jack H. *The Shenandoah Valley Campaign of 1864.* Jefferson, N.C.: McFarland, 2003.

Patchan, Scott C. "Piedmont: The Forgotten Battle." *North & South* 6, no. 3 (2003): 62–75.

Tucker, Spencer C. *Brigadier General John D. Imboden: Confederate Commander in the Shenandoah.* Lexington: University Press of Kentucky, 2003.

J

Jackson, Thomas J. (1824–1863)
Confederate general

Thomas Jonathan Jackson was born in Clarksburg, Virginia (West Virginia) and orphaned at an early age. Raised by an uncle, he possessed only rudimentary educational and social skills on being accepted to the U.S. Military Academy in 1842. Jackson, however, proved himself a willful individual, and by dint of hard work and perseverance, he graduated 17th out of a class of 59 four years later. He then joined the army of General Winfield SCOTT in Mexico, winning consecutive brevet promotions for bravery at Veracruz, Cerro Gordo, and Chapultepec. After the war, Jackson did routine garrison work in Florida and New York, but he resigned his commission in 1851 after his brother-in-law, Daniel H. HILL, managed to secure him a teaching appointment at the Virginia Military Institute (VMI) in Lexington. A boring instructor, he struggled with tactics and natural philosophy for a decade and was decidedly unpopular with students. Furthermore, Jackson's predilection for observing the strict nuances of Calvinism reinforced his reputation as a religious fanatic. He nonetheless lived quietly and shunned the public eye until 1859, when he commanded the VMI cadets during the capture of abolitionist John Brown at Harper's Ferry. Jackson was also staunchly Unionist in outlook, and it was not until Virginia seceded in April 1861 that he offered his sword to the Confederacy. Little known outside of Lexington, he could secure only the rank of colonel.

Jackson spent several weeks drilling his cadets for military service, and in June 1861, he was assigned to the army of General Joseph E. JOHNSTON in his native Shenandoah Valley. Shortly after, his troops were shunted by rail to assist General Pierre G. T. BEAUREGARD at Manassas Junction, Virginia, and they fought well in the Battle of Bull Run (July 21, 1861). Tasked with defending Henry House Hill, he did so with aplomb, whereupon General Bernard Bee declared, "There is Jackson standing like a stonewall." The sobriquet stuck and a legend was born. On October 7, 1861, Jackson advanced to major general, and he returned to the Shenandoah Valley to conduct one of the most brilliant campaigns in military history. He started off on the wrong foot in February 1862 by marching his command through freezing snow and was highly criticized by General William W. LORING. When Loring went over Jackson's head and complained to authorities, he nearly resigned from the service but was persuaded to remain. The following March, he was ordered to keep Union forces out of the Shenandoah Valley and prevent them from reinforcing General George B. McCLELLAN in his drive on Richmond. Jackson, with 17,000 men facing three Union armies totaling 64,000, immediately seized and kept the initiative by adroit offensive maneuvering. He was initially rebuffed by General James Shields at Kernstown on March 23, 1862, but his aggressiveness caused Union leaders to detain forces in the valley. He then marched rapidly and defeated General Nathaniel P. BANKS at Front Royal and Winchester, May 23 and 25, 1862, while dispatching the division of General Richard S. EWELL to dislodge General John C. Frémont at Cross Keys on June 8, 1862. Jackson himself lunged at Shields again at Port Republic on June 9, driving his superior numbers from the field. In only 48 days, his fast-marching forces, celebrated as "Jackson's foot cavalry," traversed 350 miles, inflicted 7,000 Federal casualties, and captured tons of badly needed supplies and equipment. In terms of rapidity of movement and economy of force, his 1862 Shenandoah campaign remains a singular military accomplishment, and it rendered him a hero throughout the South.

Confederate general Thomas J. Jackson *(Library of Congress)*

Having dispensed with opponents in the valley, Jackson hurried to join General Robert E. LEE's Army of Northern Virginia in time for the fast unfolding Peninsula campaign. His performance here was somewhat erratic owing to mental fatigue and unfamiliarity with local terrain, so his contributions were minimal. Jackson operated more successfully the following August, when he defeated General Banks again at Cedar Mountain on August 9, undertook a secret two day march that covered 51 miles, and captured General John POPE's supply base on the 27th. He next fought off a large Union counterattack at Groveton on the 28th and successfully defended Lee's left flank at Second Manassas on August 29–30. Jackson then spearheaded a Confederate advance back into the Shenandoah Valley by capturing Harper's Ferry on September 15, 1862, along with 12,000 Federals, before rapidly reinforcing Lee's depleted army at Antietam on September 17. There, he successfully fended off numerous Union attacks and won both promotion to lieutenant general and command of the newly organized II Corps. Jackson again commanded the left wing of the army at Fredericksburg (December 13, 1862), tenaciously defending his part of the line against determined Northern attacks by General Ambrose BURNSIDE. On many a far-flung field, the tactical rapport between Lee and Jackson proved an unbeatable combination.

Jackson reached his operational zenith during the Chancellorsville campaign of May 1862. No sooner had General Joseph HOOKER crossed the Rapidan River with 132,000 men than Lee decided to divide his force in the face of the enemy and send Jackson on a circuitous 12-mile march around the Union right flank. On May 2, 1863, "Stonewall" launched a crushing blow against General Oliver O. HOWARD's XI Corps, and he almost rolled up the Union line before darkness and caused the fighting to stop. Advancing ahead to reconnoiter at dusk, Jackson suddenly was shot and wounded by his own men. He lost his left arm in consequence and lingered for eight days before dying of pneumonia at Guinea Station, Virginia, on May 8, 1863. His death represented a cata-strophic loss to the Confederacy and Lee, in his own estimation, declared, "I have lost my right arm." Never again would the Army of Northern Virginia possess a commander with such an intui-tive grasp of Lee's orders. Moreover, his untimely demise undoubtedly hastened the Confederacy's downfall.

Further Reading

Alexander, Bevin. *Lost Victories: The Military Genius of Stonewall Jackson.* New York: Hippocrene Books, 2004.

Davis, Don. *Stonewall Jackson.* New York: Palgrave Mac-millan, 2007.

Gallagher, Gary W. *The Shenandoah Valley Campaign of 1862.* Chapel Hill: University of North Carolina Press, 2003.

Green, Jennifer. "From West Point to the Virginia Mili-tary Institute: The Educational Life of Stonewall Jackson." *Virginia Cavalcade* 49, no. 3 (2000): 134–143.

Hall, Kenneth. *Stonewall Jackson and Religious Faith in Military Command.* Jefferson, N.C.: McFarland, 2005.

Krick, Robert K. *Conquering the Valley: Stonewall Jack-son at Port Republic.* Baton Rouge: Louisiana State University Press, 2002.

Martin, David G. *Jackson's Valley Campaign: November 1861–June 1862.* Cambridge, Mass.: Da Capo Press, 2003.

Robertson, James I. "The Christian Soldier: General Thomas J. 'Stonewall' Jackson." *History Today* 53, no. 2 (2003): 29–35.

Smith, Derek. *The Gallant Dead: Union and Confederate Generals Killed in the Civil War.* Mechanicsburg, Pa.: Stackpole Books, 2005.

Wilkins, J. Steven. *All Things for Good: The Steadfast Fidelity of Stonewall Jackson.* Nashville, Tenn.: Cum-berland House, 2004.

Johnston, Albert S. (1803–1862)

Confederate general

Albert Sidney Johnston was born in Washington, Kentucky, on February 2, 1803, and educated at Transylvania University. There, he met and befriended Jefferson DAVIS, the future Confeder-ate president, before attending the U.S. Military Academy in 1826. Four years later, he graduated as a second lieutenant in the 2nd U.S. Infantry, and he performed garrison duty in the Black Hawk War. However, he resigned two years later to attend to his dying wife and subsequently migrated to Texas to fight in its war for indepen-dence. Johnston, a large, strapping individual exuding a commanding persona, enlisted as a pri-vate in the Texas army and within a year had risen to brigadier general. His headstrong antics angered many contemporaries, and in 1837, he was injured seriously in a duel. He then relin-quished his commission to serve as secretary of war for the new Texas Republic until 1840, when a disagreement with President Sam Houston resulted in his resignation. Johnston then farmed for many before serving as a colonel of the 1st Texas Rifles in the Mexican War (1846–48), fought well under Generals Zachary Taylor and William O. Butler, and won plaudits for his behavior in the September 1846 Battle of Monter-rey. He returned to his plantation after the war, but the following year, his fellow Kentuckian Tay-lor, now president, commissioned him major and paymaster of U.S. troops stationed in Texas. In 1855 Davis, now secretary of war, chose Johnston to head the newly formed and elite 2nd U.S. Cav-alry with Robert E. LEE as his lieutenant colonel and George H. THOMAS and William J. HARDEE his majors. In 1857 Johnston replaced Colonel William S. Harney as head of the Department of Texas, and in 1858 he conducted his famous Mor-mon expedition to restore Federal authority to the Utah Territory. By 1860 he functioned as brigadier general commanding the Department of the Pacific until the cusp of the Civil War. Though offered a position as second in command of Union forces in the Civil War by General Win-field SCOTT, Johnston resigned his commission once his adopted state of Texas seceded in Febru-ary 1861.

Johnston traveled three months from Califor-nia to reach Richmond, Virginia, to confer with his old friend Davis. Consequently, he was installed as a full general in the Confederate service and second only to General Samuel Cooper in seniority. He then accepted command of Department No. 2, which encompassed the western frontier from the Appalachian Mountains to the Indian Territory (Oklahoma). Given the vast expanse he was expected to defend, Johnston labored under many disadvantages as the Federals enjoyed superiority in numbers, equipment and, above all, ironclad river boats. Johnston nonetheless pushed his line far north into Kentucky, anchoring it on Forts Henry and Donelson on the Cumberland and Tennessee rivers, respectively. But on January 19, 1862, General George B. CRITTENDEN fumbled an attack at Mill Springs, Kentucky, losing heavily. In February 1862, further mismanagement by Generals Gideon J. PILLOW and John B. FLOYD resulted in the capture of both posts by General Ulysses S. GRANT. Johnston consequently ordered his Kentucky positions abandoned, and after Nashville fell to General Don C. BUELL in late February, he withdrew down to northern Alabama. The easy conquest of valuable land proved disheartening to Southern leaders, but Johnston simply lacked the wherewithal to confront larger Union armies. He then began to mass his forces at Corinth, Mississippi, assisted by reinforcements under General Pierre G. T. BEAUREGARD, and at length cobbled together a force numbering 40,000 men. This force he labeled the Army of Mississippi, which consisted of corps led by Generals Braxton BRAGG, Leonidas K. POLK, John C. BRECKINRIDGE, and his former major Hardee. Furthermore, Johnston decided against retreating another inch.

Once Grant resumed his advance down the Tennessee River by establishing a lodgment at Pittsburg Landing (Shiloh), Tennessee, Johnston sought to strike at him before reinforcements from General Buell's Army of the Ohio arrived. He then led his army from Corinth for several days in driving rain and arrived outside Grant's camp on April 5, 1862. On the following day, his massed corps completely surprised the Union pickets and charged directly into the Federal camp. The Northerners were nearly swept back to the river before Grant reestablished his defensive perimeter, and Johnston turned to mopping up scattered pockets of resistance. One of these, the so-called Peach Orchard, had repelled several Confederate attacks, and Johnston led the next one in person. There, he was struck in the leg by a bullet and bled to death before medical aid could be rendered. Command then reverted to Beauregard, who halted the battle and withdrew the next day. Johnston was thus the highest-ranking Confederate fatality of the Civil War and was mourned greatly. President Davis especially felt the loss and subsequently recorded that his death was "the turning point in our fate." Johnston's remains initially were interred at New Orleans, Louisiana, and then were transferred to their final resting place in his adopted state of Texas.

Further Reading

Arnold, James R. *Jeff Davis's Own: Cavalry, Comanches, and the Battle for the Texas Frontier*. New York: Wiley, 2000.

———. *Shiloh, 1862: The Death of Innocence*. Westport, Conn.: Praeger, 2004.

Eicher, John H., and David J. Eicher. *Civil War High Commands*. Stanford, Calif.: Stanford University Press, 2001.

Engle, Stephen D. *Struggle for the Heartland: The Campaign from Fort Henry to Corinth*. Lincoln: University of Nebraska Press, 2001.

Gallagher, Gary W., and Joseph T. Glatthaar, eds. *Leaders of the Lost Cause: New Perspectives on the Confederate High Command*. Mechanicsburg, Pa.: Stackpole Books, 2004.

Gott, Kendall D. *Where the South Lost the War: An Analysis of the Fort Henry–Fort Donelson Campaign, February, 1862*. Mechanicsburg, Pa.: Stackpole Books, 2003.

Hanson, Victor D. *Ripples of Battle: How Wars of the Past Still Determine How We Fight, How We Live, and How We Think*. New York: Doubleday, 2003.

Smith, Derek. *The Gallant Dead: Union and Confederate Generals Killed in the Civil War*. Mechanicsburg, Pa.: Stackpole Books, 2005.

Smith, Timothy B. *The Untold Story of Shiloh: The Battle and the Battlefield*. Knoxville: University of Tennessee Press, 2006.

Johnston, Joseph E. (1803–1891)

Confederate general

Joseph Eggleston Johnston was born in Prince Edward County, Virginia, on February 3, 1803, the son of a Revolutionary War veteran. In 1824 he matriculated at the U.S. Military Academy and graduated four years later in the upper third of his class. Johnston then served as a second lieutenant in the 4th U.S. Artillery in the Black Hawk War of 1832 and on the staff of General Winfield SCOTT during initial phases of Florida's Second Seminole War (1836). Johnston quit the military to work as a civilian engineer and then returned in 1837 to serve with the Topographical Engineer Corps. He rose to captain in 1846 and rejoined General Scott for the march on Mexico City in 1847. That year, he distinguished himself in combat at Cerro Gordo and Chapultepec, being wounded five times and receiving three brevet promotions. Johnston resumed his engineering work in Texas, where, in 1855, he became lieutenant colonel of the 1st U.S. Cavalry. Two years later, he accompanied Colonel Albert S. JOHNSTON during his Mormon expedition to Utah, and in 1860 his brother-in-law, Secretary of War John B. FLOYD, appointed him brigadier general and quartermaster of the army. Many questioned this appointment as an example of Floyd's penchant for nepotism. Johnston, however, remained at this post for less than a year, resigning his commission after the Civil War commenced in April 1861.

Johnston initially was employed as a brigadier general, commanding the Army of the Shenandoah, then considered something of a backwater. But in July 1861, he ordered the cavalry of Colonel J. E. B. STUART to confound nearby Union forces while he rushed his army by rail to Manassas Junction, Virginia, to assist General Pierre G. T. BEAUREGARD at the Battle of Bull Run. Johnston's appearance proved decisive and contributed greatly to the Southern victory there. The following August, he won promotion to full general, but controversy arose when Johnston angrily disputed his position as fourth in seniority behind Generals Samuel Cooper, Albert S. Johnston, and Robert E.

Confederate general Joseph Johnston *(National Archives)*

LEE. His quarrelsome disposition also alienated President Jefferson DAVIS and fueled the growing rift between them. Davis's antipathy for Johnston mounted during the 1862 Peninsula campaign when the latter, heavily outnumbered by General George B. MCCLELLAN's Army of the Potomac, continually gave ground and retreated toward Richmond. Johnston finally turned and pounced on a portion of the Federal army at Seven Pines (Fair Oaks) on May 31–June 1, 1862, in which he was severely wounded. He was then replaced permanently by Lee for the rest of the war.

Johnston remained unemployed for several months until May 1863, when Davis reluctantly appointed him to head up the Department of the West to coordinate efforts between Generals John C. PEMBERTON, Braxton BRAGG, and Edmund KIRBY-SMITH. Johnston, however, continually complained—with some validity—that the existing command structure was untenable and that this vast department was undermanned and underequipped. These deficiencies became readily apparent during General Ulysses S. GRANT's Vicksburg campaign: Johnston ordered Pemberton to withdraw from the city to save his army, but Davis countermanded his instructions. On May 14, 1863, Federal forces under General William T. SHERMAN drove Johnston away from his main base at Jackson, Mississippi, and when Vicksburg surrendered on July 4, Davis held him responsible for the debacle. He was again relieved of command and assigned minor duties in Alabama for six months until the next crisis arrived.

In December 1863 Johnston was tapped to replace General Braxton Bragg as head of the much-battered Army of Tennessee. The general, rather than heed Davis's preferences for an immediate offensive, spent the next few months at Dalton, Georgia, drilling, training, and reequipping his charge to counter more effectively Sherman's forthcoming campaign against Atlanta. That May, Sherman advanced with 100,000 troops against Johnston's 60,000, and an elaborate military dance unfolded. Johnston, a master of defensive tactics, continually thwarted Sherman's attempts to destroy him and repeatedly fell back to prepared positions. The Union commander grew so exasperated by these Fabian tactics that Union troops were committed to a frontal assault at Kennesaw Mountain on June 27, 1864, suffering heavy losses. Johnston again withdrew and kept his army intact until he was nearly at the gates of Atlanta. But his willingness to trade space for time angered Davis, who replaced Johnston with the more aggressive John B. HOOD on July 17, 1864. Johnston thus remained marooned without a command for six more months until February 1865 when, on the insistence of General Lee and the Confederate Congress, Davis restored him to lead remnants of the Army of Tennessee in North Carolina. Outnumbered three to one, he waged another futile attempt to halt Sherman's advance despite a bloody battle at Bentonville on March 19–21, 1865. Johnston finally surrendered his sword at Durham's Station

on April 18, 1865, although, when the U.S. government rejected Sherman's overly generous terms, he surrendered again on April 25.

After the war, Johnston sold insurance in Virginia and was elected to Congress as a representative in 1879. Six years later, President Grover Cleveland appointed him railroad commissioner, and while living in Washington, D.C., he befriended his former antagonist, Sherman. Johnston also penned a detailed and highly vitriolic set of memoirs in which he blamed Davis and Hood for losing the war. The pugnacious, combative Johnston, popularly regarded by his troops as "Fighting Joe," died in Washington of pneumonia on March 21, 1891; ironically, he contracted the malady while attending Sherman's funeral as a pallbearer.

Further Reading

Bradley, Mark L. *This Astonishing Close: The Road to Bennett Place.* Chapel Hill: University of North Carolina Press, 2000.

Broadwater, Robert P. *Battle of Despair: Bentonville and the North Carolina Campaign.* Macon, Ga.: Mercer University Press, 2004.

Daniel, Larry J. *Cannoneers in Gray: The Field Artillery of the Army of Tennessee, 1861–1865.* Tuscaloosa: University of Alabama Press, 2005.

Gallagher, Gary W., and Joseph T. Glatthaar, eds. *Leaders of the Lost Cause: New Perspectives on the Confederate High Command.* Mechanicsburg, Pa.: Stackpole Books, 2004.

Haughton, Andrew. *Training, Tactics, and Leadership in the Confederate Army of Tennessee: Seeds of Failure.* Portland, Ore.: Frank Cass, 2000.

Johnston, Joseph E. *Narrative of Military Operations during the Civil War.* New York: Da Capo Press, 1990.

Lepa, Jack H. *Breaking the Confederacy: The Georgia and Tennessee Campaigns of 1864.* Jefferson, N.C.: McFarland, 2005.

Longacre, Edward G. *Worthy Opponents: William T. Sherman, USA, Joseph E. Johnston, CSA.* Nashville, Tenn.: Rutledge Hill Press, 2006.

Symonds, Craig L. "Johnston's Toughest Fight." *MHQ* 16 (winter 2004): 56–61.

Towles, Louis P. "Dalton and the Rebirth of the Army of Tennessee." *Proceedings of the South Carolina Historical Association* (2002): 87–1000.

K

Kearny, Philip (1814–1862)

Union general

Philip Kearny was born in New York City on June 1, 1814, and orphaned at an early age. He was raised by a wealthy grandfather and pressured to attend Columbia College for a law degree in 1833. When his stepfather died three years later, he inherited a small fortune and fulfilled his lifelong ambition by joining the military. Kearny was then commissioned a second lieutenant in the 1st U.S. Dragoons and served along the western frontier alongside his famous uncle, Colonel Stephen W. Kearny, the explorer. After two years of service, he was sent to study cavalry tactics at the Royal Cavalry School in Saumur, France, and he subsequently served with the noted Chasseurs d'Afrique in Algiers. Kearny fought well in the successful campaign against noted rebel Abdel Kader and published an account of his experiences. In 1840 he returned to the United States and was tasked with writing a new cavalry manual for the army. Kearney retired briefly from the army in 1846, but he speedily rejoined following the onset of the Mexican War that year. Attached to General Winfield SCOTT's army, he conducted a gallant charge at Churubusco on August 20, 1847, losing his left arm and gaining brevet promotion to major. Kearney then remained on the frontier and retired again in 1851 to marry and enjoy his riches in New Jersey. Listless as ever, he rejoined the French army in 1859 as part of Emperor Napoleon III's

Imperial Guard, and he acquitted himself with distinction against the Austrians in the battles of Magenta and Solferino that year. His excellent service resulted in receipt of the cross of the Légion d'honneur, becoming the first American officer so honored. Kearny remained in Paris until the outbreak of the Civil War in 1861, whenupon he hurriedly returned to New Jersey and joined the army.

Given his reputation, Kearny had no trouble securing a brigadier generalship of New Jersey troops in the division of William B. Franklin's division. Mounted on a beautiful charger, he always led from the front and became known throughout both armies as the "One-armed Devil." In the course of General George B. McCLELLAN's 1862 Peninsula campaign, Kearny fought with distinction at Williamsburg on May 4–5, 1862, delivering a successful charge that rescued the division of General Joseph HOOKER. He also recklessly exposed himself in major fighting at Fair Oaks on June 1, 1862, where his favorite horse was killed and he grieved openly. Kearny then fought doggedly at the Battle of Glendale during McClellan's retreat, thereby preserving a Union withdrawal to Harrison's Landing. The following month, he advanced to major general and received command of a division in General Samuel P. Heintzelman's III Corps. Intent on improving the esprit de corps of his men, he also instituted the so-called Kearny Patch, a forerunner of the corps badge system adopted by the Union army. He then conducted himself exceedingly well under General John POPE at the Battle of Second Manassas on August 29–30, 1862, delivering the most successful Union charge of the day. On September 1, 1862, Kearny found himself arrayed against the redoubtable General Thomas J. JACKSON at Chantilly, and after severe fighting, he stopped a determined Confederate pursuit. In the midst of battle, Kearny recklessly—and typically—spurred his horse forward to reconnoiter and stumbled into a Confederate picket line. He was shot down trying to escape, but General Robert E. LEE sent his body, his horse, and his sword back across Union lines as a token of respect. Kearny's fall was a serious loss to the Army of the Potomac; in his memory, the men of his division instituted their own decoration, the Kearny Cross. The town of Kearny, New Jersey, was also renamed in his honor.

Further Reading

Gottfried, Bradley M. *Kearny's Own: The History of the First New Jersey Brigade in the Civil War*. New Brunswick, N.J.: Rutgers University Press, 2005.

Pindell, Richard. "Phil Kearny—the One-Armed Devil." *Civil War Times Illustrated* 27, no. 3 (1988): 16–21, 44–46.

Styple, William B., ed. *Letters from the Peninsula: The Civil War Letters of General Philip Kearny*. Kearny, N.J.: Belle Grove Publishing, 1988.

Smith, Derek. *The Gallant Dead: Union and Confederate Generals Killed in the Civil War*. Mechanicsburg, Pa.: Stackpole Books, 2005.

Taylor, Paul. *He Hath Loosed the Fateful Lightning: The Battle of Ox Hill (Chantilly), September 1, 1862*. Shippensburg, Pa.: White Mane Books, 2003.

Welker, David A. *Tempest at Ox Hill: The Battle of Chantilly*. Conshohocken, Pa.: Combined Publishing, 2001.

Kilpatrick, Hugh J. (1836–1881)

Union general

Hugh Judson Kilpatrick was born in Deckertown, New Jersey, on January 14, 1836, the son of a militia officer. He entered the U.S. Military Academy in 1857 and, showing some ability, graduated 19th in his class of 45 four years later. He was then commissioned a second lieutenant in the 1st U.S. Artillery but switched to captain in the 5th New York Infantry after the Civil War commenced in April 1861. In this capacity, he fought at Big Bethel, Virginia, on June 10, 1861, and was severely injured. While recovering, he used his political connections—and an uncanny knack for self-promotion—to transfer again to the 2nd New York Cavalry. Kilpatrick remained with the mounted arm for the rest of the war, and in 1862, he performed capably throughout General George B. MCCLELLAN's Peninsula campaign. The following August, he fought with distinction at Thoroughfare Gap and Second Manassas, rising to colonel as of December 1862 and brigadier general in June 1863. Kilpatrick fought well at the huge cavalry

Union general Hugh J. Kilpatrick *(Massachusetts Commandery Military Order of the Loyal Legion and the U.S. Army Military History Institute)*

clash at Brandy Station on June 9, 1863, under General Alfred PLEASONTON, and he actively skirmished with the Confederate cavalry of General J. E. B. STUART throughout the approach to Gettysburg that July. In concert with General George A. CUSTER, he managed to delay Stuart at Hanover, Pennsylvania, and prevented him from reaching the battlefield in time. On July 3, 1863, however, Kilpatrick enhanced his reputation for recklessness by ordering the brigade of General Elon J. Farnsworth to charge Confederate infantry head on. This indiscretion cost Farnsworth his life and garnered Kilpatrick the unflattering sobriquet of "Kill-cavalry."

In February 1864 Kilpatrick sought to rehabilitate his reputation by planning an ambitious raid against the Confederate capital at Richmond, Virginia, and liberate thousands of Union captives detained at the infamous Libby Prison. President Abraham LINCOLN reviewed the plan and enthusiastically endorsed it. On February 28, 1864, Kilpatrick galloped off with 4,000 troopers and crossed the Rapidan River. En route, he dispatched a small column of 500 men under Colonel Ulric Dahlgren, son of Admiral John A. D. DAHLGREN, to attack the city from the south. After hard riding in heavy rain and sleet, Kilpatrick arrived before Richmond—guarded by only 500 old men and boys—then suddenly lost his nerve. Some preliminary skirmishing convinced him to suspend the enterprise, and he withdrew. When Confederate cavalry attacked him in his camp that night, he abandoned the expedition altogether. Dahlgren, meanwhile, attacked the southern outskirts of the city and was rebuffed. As he fell back to Union lines, his column was ambushed, and Dahlgren was killed. Papers subsequently found on his body suggested that he was authorized to burn the city down and assassinate President Jefferson DAVIS, if possible, which led to a public uproar throughout the South. General George G. MEADE was forced to disavow publicly any knowledge of the matter, which did little to enhance Kilpatrick's reputation.

In the spring of 1864, Kilpatrick's cavalry division transferred west to the Army of the Cumberland under General George H. THOMAS. He then accompanied General William T. SHERMAN's campaign against Atlanta, Georgia, being heavily engaged in several skirmishes. On May 16, 1864, he fell severely wounded at Resaca and spent several weeks convalescing. Kilpatrick nonetheless accompanied his men in an ambulance as they burned their way across Georgia, sparring constantly with his old West Point rival General Joseph WHEELER. On August 22, 1865, he conducted a devastating raid against Jonesboro, Georgia, partaking fully of Sherman's order to burn or destroy anything of possible use to the Confederacy. Kilpatrick formally returned to the saddle as a brevet major general in 1865 and fought at the capture of Fayetteville, North Carolina. By war's end, he had risen to major general of volunteers and was generally acknowledged as one of the Union army's bravest—and most reckless—cavalry leaders.

After the war, Kilpatrick resigned his commission to serve as U.S. minister to Chile (1865–68). After President Ulysses S. GRANT recalled him, he entered politics by endorsing Horace Greeley for the presidency in 1872, and he also unsuccessfully stood for a congressional seat in 1880. The following year President James Garfield reappointed him minister to Chile, where he died in Santiago on December 4, 1881.

Further Reading

Black, Robert W. *Cavalry Raids of the Civil War.* Mechanicsburg, Pa.: Stackpole Books, 2004.

Mckinney, Joseph W. *Brandy Station, Virginia, June 9, 1863: The Longest Cavalry Battle of the Civil War.* Jefferson, N.C.: McFarland, 2006.

Pritchard, Russ A. *Raiders of the Civil War: Untold Stories of Actions Behind the Lines.* Guilford, Conn.: Lyons Press, 2005.

Rummel, George A. *Cavalry on the Road to Gettysburg: Kilpatrick at Hanover and Hunterstown.* Shippensburg, Pa.: White Mane Books, 2000.

Wittenberg, Eric J. *The Union Cavalry Comes of Age: Hartwood's Church to Brandy Station, 1863.* Dulles, Va.: Brassey's, 2005.

———. *The Battle of Monroe's Crossroads: And the Civil War's Final Campaign.* New York, Savas Beatic, 2006.

Kirby-Smith, Edmund (1824–1893)

Confederate general

Edmund Kirby-Smith was born in St. Augustine, Florida, on May 16, 1824, the son of a distinguished War of 1812 officer, Colonel Joseph Lee Smith. Later in life, he appended his mother's maiden name to his own and referred to himself as Kirby-Smith. He attended a private military academy in Virginia before attending the U.S. Military Academy in 1841, where he proved to be a mediocre student. Kirby-Smith nearly washed out due to nearsightedness, but in 1845 he received his second lieutenant's commission in the 5th U.S. Infantry. He then deployed with General Zachary Taylor as part of the Army of Occupation in Texas, and in 1847 he accompanied General Winfield SCOTT's advance on Mexico City. Kirby-Smith demonstrated prowess in battle by winning consecutive brevet promotions at Cerro Gordo and Contreras. He then performed routine garrison duty in the Southwest until serving as a mathematics instructor at West Point in 1849. Three years later, he shuttled back to the frontier, and in 1855, Kirby-Smith joined the newly raised 2nd U.S. Cavalry under Colonel Albert S. JOHNSTON. He spent the next five years skirmishing with hostile Comanche throughout Texas, acquitting himself well. He then rose to major in 1860 but resigned his commission to become a cavalry colonel in the Confederate service once Florida seceded in March 1861.

Kirby-Smith was initially posted in the Shenandoah Valley as chief of staff under General Joseph E. JOHNSTON and gradually rose to brigadier general. On July 21, 1861, he accompanied Johnston by train to the battlefield of Bull Run where he launched a crushing attack and was severely wounded. In October 1862 Kirby-Smith was promoted to major general and assigned to General Pierre G. T. BEAUREGARD's army in Mississippi. The following spring, he assumed command of the Department of Eastern Tennessee and prepared a small army to drive out Union forces from the Cumberland Gap. In August 1862 Kirby-Smith spearheaded the Confederate invasion of Ken-

Confederate general Edmund Kirby-Smith *(Library of Congress)*

tucky in concert with General Braxton BRAGG. On August 30 he crushed a smaller Union army under General William Nelson at Richmond, taking 4,000 captives, and subsequently occupied the capital of Lexington. However, neither Kirby-Smith nor Bragg coordinated their movements well, and both fell back before General Don C. BUELL's Army of the Ohio. Kirby-Smith fought well in the bloody engagements of Perryville in October and Murfreesboro in December–January, but he grew disenchanted with Bragg's lethargic leadership and requested a transfer.

Kirby-Smith, a lieutenant general as of October 1862, next received command of the Trans-Mississippi Department, encompassing Arkansas, Texas, West Louisiana, and the Indian Territory. The fall of Vicksburg, Mississippi, on July 4, 1863, cut the Confederacy in half, and Kirby-Smith was authorized by President Jefferson DAVIS to conduct his affairs with near autonomy. He now displayed a near genius for administration and, by running the Union blockade off Galveston, Texas, and bartering for weapons with cotton, he rendered his command nearly self-sufficient. In fact, he handled affairs so adroitly that his charge became celebrated as "Kirby-Smithdom." He consequently gained promotion to full general as of February 1864 and took active measures to thwart two Union drives against his department. That spring, he orchestrated the defeat of General Frederick Steele's offensive in Arkansas with generals Sterling Price and Joseph O. Shelby, while his talented subordinate, General Richard Taylor, defeated General Nathaniel Banks along the Red River. He then withdrew the bulk of Taylor's force to finish off Steele, which allowed the fleet of Admiral David D. Porter to escape and caused a rancorous response from his subordinate. But the Trans-Mississippi Department remained undisturbed for the reminder of the war, and on May 26, 1865, Kirby-Smith surrendered to General Edward R. S. Canby at Galveston. He was the last senior Confederate commander to do so.

After the war, Kirby-Smith fled to Cuba, but he returned two years later to serve as president of an insurance and telegraph company. In 1870 he joined the faculty of the University of Nashville and then the University of the South as a mathematics instructor, where he taught for the rest of his life. Kirby-Smith died in Suwanee, Tennessee, on March 28, 1893, the longest-surviving full general of the Confederacy.

Further Reading

Broadwater, Robert P. *The Battle of Perryville, 1862: Culmination of the Failed Kentucky Campaign.* Jefferson, N.C.: McFarland, 2006.

Forsyth, Michael J. *The Camden Expedition of 1864 and the Opportunity Lost by the Confederacy to Change the Civil War.* Jefferson, N.C.: McFarland, 2003.

Gallagher, Gary W., and Joseph T. Glatthaar, eds. *Leaders of the Lost Cause: New Perspectives on the Confederate High Command.* Mechanicsburg, Pa.: Stackpole Books, 2004.

Hafendorfer, Kenneth A. *Battle of Richmond, Kentucky, August 30, 1862.* Louisville, Ky.: KH Press, 2006.

Lagvanec, Cyril M. "Chevalier Bayard of the Confederacy: The Life and Career of Edmund Kirby Smith." Unpublished Ph.D. diss., Texas A & M University, 1999.

Prushankin, Jeffrey S. *A Crisis in Confederate Command: Edmund Kirby Smith, Robert Taylor, and the Army of the Trans-Mississippi.* Baton Rouge: Louisiana State University Press, 2005.

L

Lee, Fitzhugh (1835–1905)

Confederate general

Fitzhugh Lee was born in Clermont, Virginia, on November 19, 1835, a grandson of American Revolutionary War hero "Light Horse" Harry Lee. He attended the U.S. Military Academy in 1852, earning mediocre grades and so many disciplinary infractions that Superintendent Robert E. LEE, his uncle, nearly expelled him. Lee nevertheless graduated in 1856 near the bottom of his class and received his second lieutenant's commission. After a brief stint as instructor at the Cavalry School at Carlisle, Pennsylvania, he transferred to the 2nd U.S. Cavalry under Colonel Albert S. JOHNSTON and was posted on the Texas frontier. Lee distinguished himself in combat against the Comanche, and on May 19, 1859, he was severely injured. He recuperated at West Point as an assistant instructor before resigning his commission in April 1861 to offer his sword to the Confederacy.

Lee was initially posted with General Joseph E. JOHNSTON in the Shenandoah Valley, where he served as a staff officer. He then fought well at Bull Run on July 21, 1861, and rose to lieutenant colonel of the noted 1st Virginia Cavalry. Lee's career became indelibly bound up with that of his commander, General J. E. B. STUART, and in the spring of 1862, he participated in the ride around General George B. McCLELLAN's army, rising to brigadier general the following July. He next fought at Second Manassas the following August, where his tardy movements allowed the army of General John POPE to escape destruction, and he subsequently performed well at Antietam in September. On March 17, 1863, General William W. Averell nearly surprised Lee in camp at Kelly's Ford, Virginia, but he fought back tenaciously and gradually drove off superior Union forces. In May he performed his most significant task, that of uncovering the exposed flank of General Oliver O. HOWARD's XI Corps at Chancellorsville, which enabled a swift and crushing Confederate riposte. Lee then fought alongside Stuart at Brandy Station in June and Gettysburg in July, acquitting himself well and rising to major general commanding a division.

The waning fortunes of the Confederacy served to intensify Lee's battlefield performances. On May 7, 1864, his troopers reached strategic Spotsylvania Crossroads ahead of Union forces, and he skillfully withstood repeated attacks until reinforced by General Richard H. ANDERSON. After Stuart's death at Yellow Tavern, he served under another valiant trooper, General Wade HAMPTON. Lee then made a late appearance at Trevilian Station on June 11, 1864, but he managed to stop a concerted advance by General George A. CUSTER. A month later, Lee's division supported General Jubal A. EARLY's drive up the Shenandoah Valley. He participated in all the major battles against General Philip H. SHERIDAN and was critically injured at Third Winchester on September 19,

1864. Lee spent the next three months recuperating, and in March 1865, he succeeded Hampton as cavalry commander in the Army of Northern Virginia. The most notorious incident in his distinguished career occurred at Five Forks, Virginia, on April 1, 1865. Lee was absent from his command along with General George E. PICKETT, and both men were enjoying a shad bake far to the rear when Sheridan struck suddenly and overran Southern positions. On April 9, 1865, Lee conducted the very last Confederate cavalry charge of the war at Farmville, the same day his famous uncle surrendered at Appomattox.

Back in Virginia, Lee developed a taste for politics, and in 1885, he was elected governor as a Democrat. He subsequently lost a bid for the U.S. Senate, but in 1896, President Grover Cleveland appointed him the U.S. consul in Havana, Cuba. Here he displayed overt sympathies toward freedom-seeking Cuban rebels and advised the government to dispatch the battleship USS *Maine* to protect American interests. When the Spanish-American War broke out in 1898, President William McKinley commissioned him one of three former Confederates to hold the rank of brigadier general of volunteers. Lee then took control of the VII Corps but saw no fighting and later served as military governor of Havana. He then collaborated with fellow ex-Confederate general Joseph WHEELER in penning a book, *Cuba's Struggle against Spain* (1898). After a brief stint commanding the Department of the Missouri, Lee retired from the army in March 1901. He died in Washington, D.C., on April 28, 1905, a skilled leader of mounted troops.

Further Reading

Alexander, Robert. *Five Forks: Waterloo of the Confederacy: A Civil War Narrative.* East Lansing: Michigan State University Press, 2003.

Arnold, James R. *Jeff Davis's Own: Cavalry. Comanches, and the Battle for the Texas Frontier.* New York: Wiley, 2000.

Crawford, Mark. *Confederate Courage on Other Fields: Four Lesser Known Accounts of the War between the States.* Jefferson, N.C.: McFarland, 2000.

Longacre, Edward G. *Fitz Lee: A Military Biography of Major General Fitz Hugh Lee, C.S.A.* Cambridge, Mass.: Da Capo Press, 2005.

Morris, Roy, Jr. "Sweltering Summer Collision." *Military History* 9, no. 6 (1993): 42–49.

Nichols, James A. *General Fitzhugh Lee, a Biography.* Lynchburg, Va.: H. E. Howard, 1989.

Confederate general Fitzhugh Lee *(Massachusetts Commandery Military Order of the Loyal Legion and the U.S. Army Military History Institute)*

Lee, Robert E. (1807–1870)

Confederate general

Robert Edward Lee was born at Stratford, Westmoreland County, Virginia, on January 19, 1807, a son of famed Revolutionary War hero "Light Horse Harry" Lee. After being well educated locally, he entered the U.S. Military Academy in

Confederate general Robert E. Lee *(Library of Congress)*

1825 and graduated four years later second in his class—without a single demerit. Lee then received his second lieutenant's commission in the elite Corps of Engineers and acquired distinction in a variety of difficult tasks along the Mississippi River. He rose to captain in 1838 and joined the staff of General Winfield Scott during the Mexican War (1846–48). Lee fought with distinction at Cerro Gordo, made a daring reconnaissance of enemy positions, and subsequently performed well at the battles of Churubusco and Chapultepec. He ended the war as a brevet lieutenant colonel and between 1852 and 1855 also served as superintendent of cadets at West Point. In this post, he revitalized the curriculum and nearly expelled his nephew, Fitzhugh Lee, on account of poor grades and disciplinary infractions. In 1855 Lee was tapped to serve as lieutenant colonel of the newly raised 2nd U.S. Cavalry under Colonel Albert S. Johnston, a unit renowned for training

a number of future Confederate generals. He served in Texas until 1859 and then, during a furlough at home, commanded a detachment of U.S. Marines that captured abolitionist John Brown at Harper's Ferry, Virginia. In 1860 Lee received his first line command as colonel of the 1st U.S. Cavalry, and he also headed up the Department of Texas. By then the gathering war clouds induced General in Chief Scott to tender Lee a ranking position within the Federal army to crush the rebellion, but he respectfully declined. Lee, in fact, supported neither secession nor slavery, but he felt obliged to support his native state when it seceded on April 17, 1861. He subsequently accepted the post of major general of state forces.

In May 1861 Lee became a full general of Confederate forces at the behest of President Jefferson Davis, and third in seniority behind Generals Samuel Cooper and Albert S. Johnston. He then proceeded to bungle his first assignment in western Virginia, thanks largely to uncooperative subordinates such as General John B. Floyd, and he acquired the uncomely moniker of "Granny." Davis maintained his faith in Lee, fortunately, and reassigned him to strengthen defenses along the South Atlantic coast. By March 1862 Lee was back at Richmond acting in the capacity of senior military adviser to Davis. His most important work here was encouraging a Confederate offensive up the Shenandoah Valley by General Thomas J. Jackson to relieve pressure on the Confederate capital. In the spring of 1862, the huge Army of the Potomac under General George B. McClellan was advancing up the Virginia Peninsula as the main Confederate force under General Joseph E. Johnston continued giving ground. Fate intervened at the Battle of Seven Pines on June 1, 1862, when Johnston was severely wounded and was replaced by Lee. Lee then launched an audacious series of hard-pounding attacks on the surprised Unionists—the Seven Days' battles—which drove McClellan back from the gates of Richmond. Confederate losses were heavy, and he failed to destroy the corps of General Fitz John Porter, but Lee's offensive completely unnerved his adversary and brought the South a badly needed respite. He then completely overhauled his command, renaming it the Army of Northern Virginia, with two corps under Generals Jackson and James LONGSTREET. The new force successfully met its first test that summer when the Union Army of Virginia under General John POPE was nearly routed with 16,000 casualties at Second Manassas on August 29–30, 1862. Lee's losses, though considerable, were only 9,000.

Having seized the strategic initiative, Lee audaciously gambled on an invasion of Union territory and carried the war directly into Maryland. The result was another hard-fought clash with McClellan at Antietam on September 17, 1862, which nearly proved disastrous until Lee was rescued by the sudden appearance of General Ambrose P. HILL's division. This was the single bloodiest day of the Civil War with 12,400 Union and 13,700 Confederate casualties and a strategic defeat for Lee, who withdrew back to Virginia. Shortly afterward, the Army of the Potomac again was knocking at Virginia's door under a new leader, General Ambrose E. BURNSIDE, who attacked Lee as he sat entrenched behind strong field fortifications at Fredericksburg on December 13, 1862. The result was a lopsided slaughter with 13,000 Federal losses to a Confederate tally of 5,300. The second year of the war thus ended on a high note for Lee—in only six months he had risen from obscurity to an object of veneration, both among his men and among fellow Southerners.

In the spring of 1863, General Joseph HOOKER led a reconstituted Army of the Potomac across the Rapidan River in an attempt to outflank the wily Confederates. On May 2–3, 1863, Lee countered with the dangerous expedient of dividing his force in the face of the enemy and sending Jackson on a lengthy flank march around the Union right at Chancellorsville. The ensuing attack crushed Hooker's flank and induced him to retreat. Lee then boldly divided his force a third time and drove off an approaching force under General John Sedgwick. Chancellorsville is perhaps the best example of Lee's daring tactical virtuosity; he

had suffered 12,000 casualties, inflicted 17,000, and drove an army twice his size back into Union territory. However, the Confederate war effort received a mortal blow when the ever-perceptive Jackson was fatally wounded by friendly fire. Lee, for the remainder of the conflict, depended on subordinates who were equally brave but ultimately less capable.

In the summer of 1863, Lee sought to maintain the strategic initiative by reinvading Northern territory. His plan quickly went awry when General J. E. B. STUART led his cavalry on a spectacular ride into Pennsylvania, which deprived the Army of Northern Virginia of its reconnaissance capabilities. Consequently, when Lee collided with Union forces under General George G. MEADE at Gettysburg, Pennsylvania, on July 1, 1863, he was completely misled as to enemy strength and intentions. For the next two days the Confederates hurled their strength against strong Union positions and were repulsed with losses, culminating in the disastrous attack by General George E. PICKETT on July 3, 1863. Lee's defeat marked the high tide of Confederate military fortunes and, coupled with the surrender of Vicksburg, Mississippi, on July 4, a tipping point had been reached in the course of military events. Union losses of 23,000 nearly matched those of the 25,000 Southern casualties incurred, but the North, enjoying a larger population pool, readily made up such deficiencies.

Lee's next contest of strength occurred in the late spring of 1864, only this time against a new and completely different adversary. General Ulysses S. GRANT, the conqueror of Vicksburg, mustered 120,000 well-trained soldiers against 60,000 Confederates. Significantly, Grant determined to make the destruction of the Army of Northern Virginia his primary goal. He intended to accomplish this by maneuvering incessantly toward Richmond, Virginia, predicting that Lee had no recourse but to follow. A series of bloody encounters ensued at the Wilderness, Spotsylvania Court House, and Cold Harbor, in which Union casualties totaled 50,000 men—but Grant did not retreat. When confronted by insurmountable

Confederate resistance, he simply sidestepped to the left and inched closer toward Richmond. Lee, as anticipated, followed closely and by summer had become pinned within the earthworks of Petersburg, Virginia. With the once formidable Army of Northern Virginia bled white and neutralized from field operations, General William T. SHERMAN was able to break through to Atlanta and Savannah, Georgia, and gradually approach Richmond from behind. Meanwhile, to relieve Union pressure on his dwindling army, Lee dispatched General Jubal A. EARLY on his famous sweep through the Shenandoah Valley, which caused considerable alarm in Washington, D.C., and forced Grant to transfer numerous reinforcements to that theater. But Early's defeat at the hands of General Philip H. SHERIDAN in the fall of 1864 and the loss of the valley's resources that this represented signaled the coming collapse of the Confederacy.

Lee maintained his hungry, understrength forces in the trench works of Richmond and Petersburg for nearly a year as Grant continually received fresh reinforcements. As a sop toward the Confederate Congress, he also accepted the titular assignment as general in chief of all Southern armies in February 1865, but by then the Confederacy was in its death throes. The end came on April 1, 1865, when General Sheridan broke through General Fitzhugh Lee's defenses at Five Forks, Virginia, and Grant ordered a simultaneous assault across the line. Southern defenses crumbled under the repeated blows, and Lee, his position untenable, ordered the capital abandoned. He then extricated his surviving forces and made a run for North Carolina to join General Johnston, only to be halted at Appomattox Court House by Sheridan's cavalry. With superior Union forces closing in from all sides, Lee finally concluded that the game was up and surrendered to Grant with great dignity on April 9, 1865. Defeat had no dampening effect on the soldiers' overt affection for Lee, whom they affectionately called "Marse Robert."

After the war, Lee spurned lucrative offers of employment to work as president of Washington College in Lexington, Virginia. He accepted defeat with grace and urged former compatriots to work for unity and national reconciliation. Lee died at Lexington on October 12, 1870, an iconic figure of the Civil War and one of the most beloved, effective military leaders in American military history.

Further Reading

Cahart, Tom. *Lost Triumph: Lee's Real Plan at Gettysburg—and Why It Failed.* New York: G. P. Putnam's Sons, 2005.
Carmichael, Peter S. *Audacity Personified: The Generalship of Robert E. Lee.* Baton Rouge: Louisiana State University Press, 2004.
Fellman, Michael. *The Making of Robert E. Lee.* Baltimore: Johns Hopkins University Press, 2003.
Gallagher, Gary W., and Joseph T. Glatthaar, eds. *Leaders of the Lost Cause: New Perspectives on the Confederate High Command.* Mechanicsburg, Pa.: Stackpole Books, 2004.
Hess, Earl J. *Trench Warfare under Grant and Lee: Field Fortifications in the Overland Campaign.* Chapel Hill: University of North Carolina Press, 2007.
Jermann, Donald R. *Antietam: The Lost Order.* Gretna, La: Pelican Pub., 2006.
Katcher, Philip R. N. *Robert E. Lee.* London: Brassey's, 2004.
Longacre, Edward G. *The Commanders of Chancellorsville: The Gentleman vs the Rogue.* Nashville: Rutledge Hill Press, 2005.
Reid, Brian H. *Robert E. Lee: Icon for a Nation.* London: Weidenfeld and Nicolson, 2005.
Walsh, George. *Damage Them All You Can: Robert E. Lee's Army of Northern Virginia.* New York: Forge, 2002.

Lincoln, Abraham (1809–1865)
President, United States

Abraham Lincoln was born near Hodgenville, Kentucky, on February 12, 1809, the son of a backwoods family. He endured childhood poverty for many years while living on the frontiers of Indiana, becoming essentially self-taught. Lincoln eventually settled on a career in law in Springfield, Illinois, and briefly served as a militia captain during the brief Black Hawk War of 1832. The future commander in chief saw no combat save for, in his own words, "many bloody battles with mosquitoes." Lincoln subsequently acquired a taste for politics, joined the Whig Party, and in 1847 won a seat in the U.S. House of Representatives. In this capacity, he stridently opposed both the Mexican War and any expansion of slavery into newly acquired territories. In 1858 Lincoln ran unsuccessfully as a Republican for the U.S. Senate against Democrat Stephen A. Douglas, and he captured national attention through a series of lively debates. Consequently, the gaunt and gangly attorney saw his political capital soar, and in 1860 he handily won the party's nomination for the presidency. He ran—and won—on a platform dedicated to halting the expansion of slavery, not its abolition. However, Lincoln's ascension was construed as a direct threat to the South's "peculiar institution," and in December 1860 South Carolina voted to secede from the Union. This act induced other states to follow, and a new entity, the Confederate States of America, was already extant by the time Lincoln took his inaugural oath of office.

No neophyte chief executive ever confronted a more daunting, dangerous situation that did Lincoln in the spring of 1861, with a small standing army and the Southern third of the nation up in arms against the federal government. He nevertheless remained adamant that the Union would be preserved at any cost. Surprisingly, Lincoln proved himself a forceful and capable commander in chief who was unafraid of taking risks. To solidify his Northern political base, he overruled General In Chief Winfield SCOTT and authorized a relief expedition to resupply the Union garrison trapped at Fort Sumter, South Carolina. For political consumption, he underscored the fact that this was a humanitarian mission to deliver food, not reinforcements. It was a ploy calculated to force the hand of his Confederate counterpart, Jefferson DAVIS, who, as the head of a self-proclaimed sovereign nation, could not tolerate an American garrison residing in a major Southern harbor. On April 12, 1861, Confederate forces under General Pierre G. T. BEAUREGARD commenced bombard-

ing the fort, forcing Major Robert ANDERSON to surrender two days later. The Northern populace, waxing indifferent up until now, viewed this act as overt aggression against the United States and began to mobilize for war. Lincoln then moved with characteristic decisiveness by summoning 75,000 three-month volunteers, suspending writs of habeas corpus in threatened regions, and—most important—declaring the Southern coastline under a naval blockade.

Despite his prior lack of military training, Lincoln displayed an astonishing grasp of strategy based on the North's overwhelming preponderance in terms of manpower and industry. He therefore sought to implement a broad-based offensive to apply maximum pressure against the insurrectionists from as many directions as possible. Moreover,

President of the United States Abraham Lincoln (*National Archives*)

the commander in chief inculcated the very modern view that the destruction of enemy armies, and not the mere acquisition of territory, was tantamount to victory itself. He also agreed in principle to the overarching strategy enunciated by General Scott, whose so-called Anaconda Plan entailed dividing the Confederacy down the Mississippi River and slowly strangling the whole to death. In time this proved a war-winning strategy. Unfortunately for Lincoln, conduct of military operations was entrusted to a series of leaders who eschewed his strategic vision and proved incapable of defeating Southern armies in the field. Worst of all, the steady drum beat of politicians forced the president and his generals into combat long before their raw recruits were ready for it.

Commencing in July 1861, when the barely trained levies of General Irvin McDowell were routed at Bull Run, the Federal war effort remained beset by a succession of hesitant, if not outright blundering leaders: Generals George B. McClellan, John Pope, Ambrose E. Burnside, and Joseph Hooker all tried and failed to defeat the Army of Northern Virginia under the dazzling General Robert E. Lee; other appointees such as General Benjamin F. Butler, Nathaniel C. Banks, and Franz Sigel proved likewise incompetent but had to be retained out of pressing political concerns. Nor did Lincoln receive much cogent advice from General in Chief Henry W. Halleck, a splendid administrator but a lackluster strategist. For the first two years of the war, the only real Union success came from the steadily expanding blockade and capture of Southern ports at the hands of such professionals as Admirals Samuel F. Du Pont and David G. Farragut. Their endeavors restricted the flow of Confederate cotton to European markets and throttled the flow of weapons and raw materials returning through an extensive net of Southern blockade-runners. The impasse continued until July 1863 when General George G. Meade defeated Lee at Gettysburg while another figure, General Ulysses S. Grant, captured Vicksburg on the Mississippi River, severing the Confederacy in two. Lincoln finally saw in Grant that commodity the lack of which had so hobbled the war effort to date—an aggressive, relentless fighter who fully embraced the president's broad offensive scheme. Once Lincoln appointed Grant general in chief in the spring of 1864, the fate of the Confederacy was sealed.

Throughout the spring and early summer of 1864, the redoubtable Grant singularly failed to humble Lee's stubborn graycoats in the field. A series of bloody encounters at the Wilderness, Spotsylvania Court House, and Cold Harbor led to increasingly long casualty lists and open questioning as to Lincoln's very survival in the fall elections. Defeat and heavy losses took a heavy toll on the president, as did the death of his son Todd, but he willingly bore the burdens to provide Grant with whatever support he needed. The shift occurred by late summer and early fall. Once Grant had finally pinned Lee to the defense of Richmond, Virginia, the army of General William T. Sherman had captured Atlanta, Georgia, while forces under General Philip H. Sheridan swept the strategic Shenandoah Valley free of Confederates. This string of important victories dramatically resuscitated Lincoln's political fortunes, and in November he handily crushed his Democratic opponent, General McClellan. Six months later, the Confederacy lay in ruins: outnumbered, out of supplies, and flagging in spirit. Lee then surrendered to Grant at Appomattox on April 9, 1865, effectively ending military operations in the East. All the while, Lincoln took to the podium and pleaded for leniency toward the former Confederates and national unification without vindictiveness. The president never lived to see the country reunited: On April 14, 1865, he was cut down by John Wilkes Booth at Ford's Theater in Washington, D.C. Lincoln, the awkward, sad-looking leader who had labored so long and successfully to keep the nation whole, became the first chief executive assassinated in office. But because of his triumph at preserving the Union throughout the worse crisis in its history, Lincoln is frequently cited as America's greatest chief executive.

In addition to saving the United States, Lincoln ushered in a social revolution by finally vanquishing the centuries-old incubus of human bondage. This was a highly emotional issue to both North and South, and the chief executive nuanced the matter with great delicacy. Lincoln himself, while personally against slavery, was quite willing to accommodate it where it already existed. Once the South rejected this stance, he weathered the dire necessity of keeping strategic and slaveholding border states such as Maryland, Kentucky, and Missouri in the Union camp. He thereby completely ignored the demands of abolitionists and Radical Republicans to outlaw slavery altogether. A more incremental approach, one cued closely to the military course of the war, was ultimately preferable. In the fall of 1862, after the Union victory at Antietam, Lincoln issued his famous "Emancipation Proclamation," which only freed slaves in areas still under Confederate control. Furthermore, he consistently negated all attempts by Union commanders to free slaves so as not to lose continuing support from slaveholding Unionists. Despite his caution, these moves reveal much about Lincoln's grasp of foreign affairs: By firmly placing the American government on the side of emancipation, he minimized the risk of European intervention on behalf of the Confederacy. The British government, in particular, would certainly not enter an armed conflict to preserve Southern slavery. Lincoln also initially looked askance at the use of African-American troops until 1863, when shortages of white volunteers had to be remedied. Public opinion may have been mixed, and developments certainly infuriated Confederate sensibilities, but upward of 180,000 black troops flocked to the colors, fought magnificently, and further tipped the manpower scales in favor of the North. Toward the close of the war, Lincoln also embraced creation of the Freedmen's Bureau to help manumitted slaves readjust to living, working, and voting as free citizens. The president died before his dream of peacefully reintegrating former slaves and Confederates into society was realized. The chore consequently fell to individuals of lesser ability and conviction, with decidedly mixed and frequently unfortunate results. Had Lincoln lived as the guiding spirit behind postwar Reconstruction, the tumult of 20th-century civil rights movements may have been obviated altogether.

Further Reading

Cox, Hank H. *Lincoln and the Sioux Uprising of 1862.* Nashville, Tenn.: Cumberland House, 2005.

Detzer, David. *Dissonance: Between Fort Sumter and Bull Run in the Turbulent First Days of the Civil War.* Orlando, Fla.: Harcourt, 2006.

Griffin, John C. *Abraham Lincoln's Execution.* Gretna, La: Pelican Pub. Co. 2006.

Goodwin, Doris K. *Team of Rivals: The Political Genius of Abraham Lincoln.* New York: Simon and Schuster, 2005.

Harris, William C. *Lincoln's Last Months.* Cambridge, Mass.: Belknap Press of Harvard University Press, 2004.

Mansch, Larry D. *Abraham Lincoln, President-elect: The Four Critical Months from Election to Inauguration.* Jefferson, N.C.: McFarland, 2005.

Marcott, Frank B. *Six Days in April: Lincoln and the Union in Peril.* New York: Algora Publishing, 2005.

Marvel, William. Mr. *Lincoln Goes to War.* Boston: Houghton Mifflin, 2006.

Perret, Geoffrey. *Lincoln's War: The Untold Story of America's Greatest President as Commander in Chief.* New York: Random House, 2004.

Wheeler, Tom. *Mr. Lincoln's T-mails: The Untold Story of How Abraham Lincoln used the Telegraph to win the Civil War.* New York: Collins, 2006.

Longstreet, James (1821–1904)
Confederate general

James Longstreet was born in Edgehill, South Carolina, on January 8, 1821, the son of planters. He gained admittance to the U.S. Military Academy in 1838, compiling a mediocre academic record before graduating near the bottom of his class in 1842. He then served as a second lieutenant in the 4th and 8th U.S. Infantries while performing garrison duty at various posts along the Louisiana and Texas frontiers. When the Mexican War commenced in 1846, Longstreet joined the army of General Zachary Taylor, and he distin-

Confederate general James Longstreet *(Massachusetts Commandery Military Order of the Loyal Legion and the U.S. Army Military History Institute)*

guished himself at the battle of Monterrey. The following year, he accompanied General Winfield Scott on his march to Mexico City, winning a brevet promotion to major for gallantry and suffering severe wounds at Chapultepec. After the war, Longstreet returned to the frontier to serve as payroll master for many years. Once the Civil War broke out in April 1861, he resigned his commission and became a brigadier general in the Confederate army of General Pierre G. T. Beauregard. Longstreet proved himself a tremendous fighter, commencing at Blackburn's Ford on July 18, 1861, where he repulsed the advance guard of General Irvin McDowell. Three days later, he fought with distinction at Bull Run and pursued

fleeing Federal forces nearly to the gates of Washington, D.C.

Longstreet's fine performance resulted in his promotion to major general and command of a division in General Joseph E. Johnston's army. In this capacity, he conducted a fine rear-guard action against General Samuel P. Heintzelman's III Corps at Williamsburg on May 5, 1862, and he nearly routed a division under General Joseph Hooker. However, he bungled his next assignment at Seven Pines the following May 31, leading to a Confederate repulse. Longstreet then rebounded under General Robert E. Lee during his Seven Days' battles and subsequently received command of nearly half of Lee's infantry. He then decisively contributed to the overwhelming Confederate victory over General John Pope at Second Manassas on August 29–30, 1862, in concert with General Thomas J. Jackson. Longstreet's tendency toward caution then manifested itself when he strongly opposed Lee's invasion of Maryland that fall, but he fought exceedingly well at South Mountain and Antietam in September. The following month, Lee, who affectionately referred to Longstreet as his "Old War Horse," promoted him to lieutenant general with command of the newly organized I Corps. With the stodgy general, he capably defended Marye's Heights at the Battle of Fredericksburg on December 13, 1862, against General Ambrose Burnside.

In February 1863 Longstreet was detached on an independent command around Suffolk, Virginia, where he failed to distinguish himself. His lethargic movements also deprived him of participating in the decisive Confederate victory at Chancellorsville (May 2–3, 1863), but following the death of Jackson, he emerged as Lee's senior corps commander and his closest confidant. As a strategist, Longstreet embraced Lee's renewed northern offensive, but only in concert with a tactical defense once a battle situation developed. He therefore was somewhat aghast on July 2, 1863, when Lee decided to attack the strongly posted army of General George G. Meade at Gettysburg for the next two days. Longstreet sullenly complied with orders to hit the Union center along Cemetery Ridge, where a division under General John B. Hood dislodged the III Corps of General Daniel Sickles from the Peach Orchard but failed to turn the Union left at Little Round Top. In fact, Longstreet moved so tardily that it was not until 4:30 P.M. that his attack—scheduled for the morning—got underway. On July 3 he also vehemently remonstrated against Lee's plan to assault the Union center. He contributed only the division of General George E. Pickett to the ensuing debacle, and as he predicted, the Confederates were turned back with staggering losses. In the fall of 1863, the I Corps temporarily transferred west to bolster the Army of Tennessee under General Braxton Bragg. Longstreet bore a critical role in the Southern victory at Chickamauga (September 20, 1863), where his men smashed though an inadvertent gap caused by General William S. Rosecrans. However, deteriorating relations with Bragg resulted in Longstreet's assignment to besiege Knoxville, Tennessee, where he and General Joseph Wheeler failed to overcome Federal troops under General Burnside. The ensuing defeat of Bragg at Chattanooga on November 25, 1863, and the subsequent approach of General William T. Sherman with reinforcements induced Longstreet to abandon Knoxville for the winter.

Longstreet rejoined Lee in the spring of 1864 in time to oppose the Overland campaign of General Ulysses S. Grant. His timely appearance at the Wilderness on May 6, 1864, reinforced General Ambrose P. Hill's corps and drove off Federals under General Winfield S. Hancock. Unfortunately, Longstreet was accidently wounded by his own men at the height of the struggle, and he could not resume active duty until the following October. Command of the I Corps reverted to General Richard H. Anderson in his absence. Longstreet next commanded the defenses of Richmond, Virginia, until the Union breakthrough of April 2–3, 1865, and he retreated with Lee to Appomattox Court House. He remained in the field beside Lee until the latter's surrender to superior Union forces on April 9, 1865.

After the war, Longstreet entered business and gained the undying enmity of former friends by joining the Republican Party. President Grant, a West Point classmate, then appointed him surveyor of New Orleans in 1869 and postmaster in 1873. Commencing in 1880, he also served as minister to Turkey, U.S. marshal for Georgia, and U.S. railroad commissioner. Throughout this period, Longstreet embraced the vitriolic literary campaign ascribing blame for the loss of the war. He was one of few senior commanders willing to criticize Lee's leadership openly and was, in turn, bitterly assailed by former generals Jubal A. Early and Fitzhugh Lee for slowness and insubordination at Gettysburg—in effect, losing the battle. Longstreet, revered and reviled by many as "Old Pete," died at his home in Gainesville, Georgia, on January 2, 1904, an outstanding corps commander but undistinguished in an independent role.

Further Reading

Bloomberg, Arnold. "On They Came Like an Angry Flood." *Military Heritage* 4, no. 6 (2003): 72–80.

Dinardo, Richard L. "Southern by the Grace of God but Prussian by Common Sense: James Longstreet and the Exercise of Command in the U.S. Civil War." *Journal of Military History* 66, no. 4 (2002): 1011–1032.

Dinardo, Richard L., and Albert A. Nofi. *James Longstreet: The Man, the Soldier, the Controversy.* Conshohocken, Pa.: Combined Publishing, 1998.

Franks, Edward C. "In Defense of Braxton Bragg: The Detachment of Longstreet Considered." *North & South* 5, no. 5 (2002): 28–38.

Hastings, Earl C. *A Pitiless Rain: The Battle of Williamsburg.* Shippensburg, Pa.: White Mane Books, 1997.

Longstreet, James. *From Manassas to Appomattox: Memoirs of the Civil War in America.* Philadelphia: J. B. Lippincott, 1896.

Mendoza, Alexander. "Struggle in Command: General James Longstreet and the First Corps in the West, 1863–1864." Unpublished Ph.D. diss., Texas Tech University, 2002.

Rhea, Gordon C. *The Battle of the Wilderness, May 5–6, 1864.* Baton Rouge: Louisiana State University Press, 2004.

Loring, William W. (1818–1886)

Confederate general

William Wing Loring was born in Wilmington, North Carolina, raised in Florida, and served in the militia during the Second Seminole War (1835–42), rising to lieutenant. He then studied law at Georgetown College, gained admittance to the state bar, and won a seat in the state legislature, but when the Mexican War commenced in 1846, he joined the U.S. Army as a captain in the elite 2nd Mounted Riflemen. In this capacity, Loring accompanied the army of General Winfield SCOTT on its march to Mexico City, winning two brevet promotions for bravery at Contreras and Chapultepec. In the latter engagement, Loring lost his left arm. He ended the war a brevet lieutenant colonel

Confederate general William W. Loring *(Florida State Archives)*

and marched his regiment to Fort Leavenworth, Kansas, in anticipation of the famous gold rush to California. He then escorted settlers 2,500 miles to Oregon and back with a train of 600 wagons. Loring discharged his duties well under difficult conditions and consequently received command of the Department of Oregon in 1851. His regiment subsequently transferred to Texas and New Mexico, seeing constant action against hostile Comanche and Kiowa. In December 1856 Loring became the army's youngest colonel and also assumed control of Fort Union, New Mexico. Two years later, he accompanied Colonel Albert S. JOHNSTON on the noted Mormon expedition to Utah and the following year took a leave of absence to study in Europe. He returned in 1860 as commander of the Department of New Mexico. Loring, while a Southerner, did not embrace secession strongly, but after Florida left the Union in January 1861, he tendered his resignation and turned Fort Union over to Colonel Edward R. S. CANBY, another frontier stalwart.

In May 1861 Loring gained appointment as a brigadier general, and the following July he succeeded the slain general Robert B. Garnett as commander of the Northwestern Army in the Shenandoah Valley. This brought him under the aegis of General Robert E. LEE, Loring's junior in prewar days, and the two men failed to get along amicably. Following the Cheat Mountain expedition in September 1861, Lee was transferred to another sector and replaced by General Thomas J. JACKSON. On January 1, 1862, Jackson launched a midwinter offensive to capture the town of Romney, Virginia, and Loring's men suffered terribly from exposure to the elements. Jackson ordered him to remain behind in place, exposed to attack, so Loring violated the chain of command by complaining to friends in the Confederate War Department. When Secretary of War Judah P. Benjamin consequently ordered Jackson to remove Loring's command from Romney, the latter angrily threatened to resign his commission. Loring was then tactfully transferred from the valley on February 9, 1862, and reassigned to Norfolk as a major general.

In December 1862 Loring was again transferred, this time to the Army of the Mississippi under John C. Pemberton, whom he also outranked in the prewar army. The two men held each other in thinly veiled contempt and barely cooperated. Nonetheless, on March 11, 1863, Loring's gallant stand at Fort Pemberton, Greenwood, Mississippi, turned back a combined Union expedition along the Tallahatchie River. Mounting the parapet, he paraded back and forth under fire and encouraged his command to "Give them blizzards, boys!" Thereafter, he became jocularly known as "Old Blizzards." Loring's victory spared Vicksburg's defenses from being turned and forced General Ulysses S. Grant to campaign overland from below the city. On May 16, 1863, Grant caught up to Pemberton at Champion's Hill, Mississippi, driving the Southerners from the field and forcing Loring to break away from the main force. With Pemberton now shut up in Vicksburg, Loring marched to join General Joseph E. Johnston's army at Jackson. Months later, Pemberton vindictively accused Loring of insubordination and blamed him for the city's fall.

By the spring of 1864, Loring had transferred to the corps of General Leonidas K. Polk, and he fought with him against General William T. Sherman's advance into Georgia. Once Polk was killed on June 14, 1864, he assumed command of his corps until replaced by General Alexander P. Stewart—a good indication of Johnston's distrust of his abilities. Loring went on to fight well at the battles of Peachtree Creek and Ezra Church under General John B. Hood in July 1864, and then he accompanied Hood during the ill-fated advance into Tennessee. He again fought conspicuously at the defeats of Franklin and Nashville that fall and afterward took his surviving men back into North Carolina to rejoin Johnston. Loring performed well at Bentonville (March 19–21, 1865) before finally surrendering to Sherman at Greensboro on May 2, 1865.

For a former Confederate, Loring enjoyed an active and varied career throughout the postwar period. After serving as a banker in New York City, he departed for Egypt in 1869 and joined the army of Khedive Ismail I as a *lewan pasha* (brigadier general). He commanded the garrison of Alexandria for five years, led an expedition into the Sudan, and won the Battle of Kaya-Khor in 1874. Loring consequently enjoying the title of *pasha* and command of a division. He returned to the United States in 1879 to write about his experiences. Loring died in New York City on December 30, 1886, a talented, colorful, and stubborn military leader.

Further Reading

Loring, William W. *A Confederate Soldier in Egypt.* New York: Dodd, Mead, 1884.

Oliva, Leo E. *Fort Union and the Frontier Army in the South West.* Santa Fe, N.Mex.: Division of History, National Park Service, 1993.

Raab, James. *W. W. Loring—Florida's Forgotten General.* Manhattan, Kans.: Sunflower Press, 1996.

Rankin, Thomas M. *Stonewall Jackson's Romney Campaign, January 1–February 20, 1862.* Lynchburg, Va.: H. E. Holland, 1994.

Smith, Timothy B. *Champion Hill: Decisive Battle for Vicksburg.* New York: Savas Beatie, 2004.

Wessels, William L. *Born to Be a Soldier: The Military Career of William Wing Loring of St. Augustine, Florida.* Fort Worth, Tex.: Texas Christian University Press, 1971.

Lovell, Mansfield (1822–1884)
Confederate general

Mansfield Lovell was born in Washington, D.C., on October 20, 1822, a son of army surgeon-general Joseph Lovell. Orphaned by the death of his parents, he entered the U.S. Military Academy in 1838 and graduated four years later near the top of his class. Lovell then served as a second lieutenant in the 4th U.S. Artillery, performing garrison duty in Texas under General Zachary Taylor. When the Mexican War broke out, he accompanied Taylor's army and fought with distinction at Monterrey (September 18–21, 1846), being wounded and winning a brevet promotion. After serving as aide-de-camp to General John A. Quitman, he transferred to the army of General Winfield Scott in

1847 as it advanced on Mexico City. Lovell fought well at the storming of Chapultepec on September 14, 1847, receiving a second brevet to captain. Afterward, he performed several more tours of garrison duty along the frontier before resigning his commission in 1854. He then worked at an ironworks in New Jersey for four years until 1858, when he relocated to New York City as the city's first superintendent of street improvement. There, he met and befriended Gustavus W. Smith, a future Confederate general. Once the Civil War commenced in April 1861, Smith departed immediately for the South, but Lovell lingered in the city for several months before finally offering his service to the Confederacy that September. His tardiness at joining always produced an undercurrent of suspicion as to his actual loyalties.

On October 7, 1861, Lovell—thanks largely to the intercession of his friend Smith—became a major general in the Confederate army and head of Department No. 1, the city of New Orleans. Though the South's largest city and main port, he inherited a small garrison, few cannon, and inadequate naval resources. He spent the next several months strengthening Forts Jackson and St. Philip, 70 miles below the city on the Mississippi River, which any invading squadron would have to pass. Lovell performed well, considering his material deficiencies, but he proved much given to drink and bragging. Moreover, he stated repeatedly to the Southern press that New Orleans could be easily defended under present conditions. On April 18, 1862, a combined Union fleet of ships and mortar boats under Captains David G. Farragut and David D. Porter threaded its way up the Mississippi. As anticipated, Forts St. Philip and Jackson held the fleet at bay for a week until Farragut executed a brilliant night passage on April 24, 1862. Once the fleet pulled up alongside the helpless city and landed the army of General Benjamin F. Butler, Lovell had little recourse but to evacuate his army to safety. For this, he was immediately condemned in newspapers throughout the South,

even though leaders such as General Robert E. Lee sanctioned the appropriateness of his withdrawal. A court of inquiry also vindicated Lovell, but his subsequent career remained hobbled by a whispering campaign about alleged disloyalty. His own troops added to the hubbub by singing "The New Ballad of Lord Lovell," which satirized the loss of New Orleans and the most obvious consequence of heavy drinking—his conspicuous red nose.

In the fall of 1862, Lovell had succeeded to the command of the I Corps in the army of General Earl Van Dorn, in which he also served as second in command. On October 3–4, 1862, Van Dorn ordered a desperate attempt to retake the strategic railroad junction at Corinth, Mississippi, from Union forces under General William S. Rosecrans. Lovell performed well on the first day of fighting, which occasioned heavy Confederate losses, but on the second day, Van Dorn ordered his division to assault strongly entrenched Federal troops. Lovell, unwilling to sacrifice his command in a futile attack, only sent skirmishers forward while two other Southern divisions went forward, unsupported, and were mauled. Van Dorn then charged Lovell with insubordination, but he partially redeemed his reputation by conducting a splendid rear-guard action at Coffeeville, Mississippi, on October 5, 1862. Shortly after, Lovell was relieved, and he spent the balance of the war as a volunteer staff officer under General Joseph E. Johnston. Despite repeated entreaties for a new command, Lovell passed the remainder of the war in relative obscurity. In March 1865 General Lee requested that he receive the command of a corps, and the government finally relented, but the war ended before Lovell could reach his headquarters.

After the war, Lovell relocated to Georgia to work as a rice farmer, but in 1869 he lost his estate in a flood. He then returned to New York to hold down various positions as a surveyor and an engineer. Lovell died there on June 1, 1884, a talented officer but seldom employed by a government that never really trusted him.

Further Reading

Cozzens, Peter. *The Darkest Days of the War: Iuka and Corinth.* Chapel Hill: University of North Carolina Press, 1997.

Garcia, Pedro. "Losing the Big Easy." *Civil War Times Illustrated* 41, no. 2 (2002): 46–53, 64–65.

Hearn, Chester G. *The Capture of New Orleans.* Baton Rouge: Louisiana State University Press, 1995.

Heleniak, Roman J., and Lawrence L. Hewitt, eds. *The 1989 Deep Delta Civil War Symposium: Leadership during the Civil War.* Shippensburg, Pa.: White Mane Books, 1992.

Smith, Brier R. *Major General Mansfield Lovell and the Fall of New Orleans: The Downfall of a Career.* Memphis, Tenn.: Memphis Pink Palace Museum, 1973.

Sutherland, Daniel L. "Mansfield Lovell's Quest for Justice: Another Look at the Fall of New Orleans." *Louisiana History* 24, no. 3 (1987): 233–259.

Lyon, Nathaniel (1818–1861)

Union general

Nathaniel Lyon was born in Ashford, Connecticut, on July 14, 1818, the son of farmers. He entered the U.S. Military Academy in 1837 and graduated four years later a second lieutenant in the 2nd U.S. Infantry. Lyon next fought in Florida's Second Seminole War and performed garrison duty at Sacket's Harbor, New York, before accompanying General Winfield SCOTT's army in the Mexican War. Lyon, endowed with flaming red hair and a disposition to match, fought bravely at Contreras and Churubusco in 1847, winning a brevet promotion to captain. He next performed a stint of frontier duties and Indian fighting before being assigned to Fort Riley, Kansas, during the period known as "Bleeding Kansas." Lyon's encounter with slavery affected him profoundly, and he joined the Republican Party as an avid abolitionist. In February 1861, on the cusp of open hostilities, he was installed as commander of the U.S. Arsenal at St. Louis, Missouri. It proved to be a singularly fortuitous appointment for the North.

Throughout the spring of 1861, Missouri was split along Northern and Southern lines with Governor Claiborne F. Jackson firmly in the Confederate camp. Lyon, determined to hold St. Louis for the Union, began to recruit a Unionist militia known as the Home Guard from thousands of German-speaking immigrants. This move prompted Jackson to call out his own Confederate militia, the State Guard, that Lyon feared would be used to capture the St. Louis arsenal. With typical audacity and dispatch, he surrounded and captured many Confederate sympathizers at Camp Jackson on May 10, 1861, and then paraded them through the streets of the city. Riots broke out in consequence, and when the Home Guard fired into the crowd, killing 28 men, thousands fled the city and joined the Confederate side. Lyon's rash action may have bolstered Jackson's hand for the time being, but it also kept the arsenal out of Confederate hands and possibly saved Missouri for the Union. Lyon also conspired with Congressman Francis P. Blair, a Radical Republican, to remove the Southern-leaning general William S. Harney as commander of the Department of the West. Lyon then advanced to brigadier general of volunteers to succeed him and moved quickly to secure the Potosi lead mines for the Union. Then, to avoid further bloodshed, he conferred with Governor Jackson and State Guard commander Sterling PRICE at a hotel in St. Louis on June 11, 1861. Negotiations came to nothing and Lyon angrily stalked out declaring, "This means war!" He began to mobilize his troops to neutralize the Confederate threat once and for all.

Lyon, true to form, moved swiftly. On June 15, 1861, his troops captured the state capital of Jefferson City, forcing Governor Jackson to flee. Two days later, his Home Guard attacked state troops at Boonville, Missouri, defeating them. He then moved against the major city of Springfield, which fell on July 13, 1861. On August 2, 1861, Lyon engaged and defeated another Southern force at Dug Springs. There, he learned that a large Confederate force consisting of State Guard troops under Price and Texas forces under General Ben McCULLOCH were advancing on him with 11,000 men. Lyon, who possessed only 5,500, should have withdrawn, but, instead, he chose to attack over the objections of his second in command, Major

John M. SCHOFIELD. On August 10, 1861, he surprised the Confederates at Wilson's Creek by driving them from their camp and occupying a nearby ridge line. While Price's men counterattacked, a second Union column under Colonel Franz SIGEL marched to the rear of the Confederate camp and nearly routed the defenders before being defeated in turn. The Confederates, flushed with victory, were gathering for a final assault when Lyon launched his fourth charge of the day and fell mortally wounded. His army then safely extricated itself and withdrew, leaving the field to victorious but disorganized Southerners.

Lyon was the first Union officer of general rank to fall in combat and was enshrined among the North's first martyrs. His headstrong behavior undoubtedly contributed to his demise, but by acting promptly and aggressively in the early days of the crisis, he probably preserved Missouri for the Union. In December 1861 the slain officer posthumously received the thanks of Congress.

Further Reading

Brookshear, William R. *Bloody Hill: The Civil War Battle of Wilson's Creek.* Washington, D.C.: Brassey's, 2000.

Gerteis, Louis S. *Civil War St. Louis.* Lawrence: University Press of Kansas, 2001.

Johnson, Mark W. *That Brave Body of Men: The U.S. Regular Infantry and the Civil War in the West, 1861–1865.* Cambridge, Mass.: Da Capo Press, 2003.

Phillips, Christopher. *Damned Yankee: The Life of General Nathaniel Lyon.* Baton Rouge: Louisiana State University Press, 1990.

Piston, William G., and Richard W. Hatcher. *Wilson's Creek: The Second Battle of the Civil War and the Men Who Fought It.* Chapel Hill: University of North Carolina Press, 2000.

Smith, Derek. *The Gallant Dead: Union and Confederate Generals Killed in the Civil War.* Mechanicsburg, Pa.: Stackpole Books, 2005.

M

McClellan, George B. (1826–1885)

Union general

George Brinton McClellan was born in Philadelphia, Pennsylvania, on December 13, 1826, a member of an established and influential family. After briefly studying at the University of Pennsylvania, he was admitted to the U.S. Military Academy in 1842—aged only 16 years—and graduated four years later, second in his class. He then served as a second lieutenant in the elite Corps of Engineers, joining General Winfield Scott's army in time to serve in the Mexican War. McClellan distinguished himself in combat, winning two brevet promotions for bravery at Contreras, Churubusco, and Chapultepec. Afterward, he served as an instructor at West Point until 1851, and he was called on to design and construct Fort Delaware, undertake harbor clearing, and conduct railroad surveys. In 1855 McClellan rose to captain and journeyed to Europe to observe the ongoing Crimean War. He also studied cavalry tactics in Prussia and Austria and designed the so-called McClellan saddle, which remained in use for several decades. However, McClellan ended his promising military career by resigning his commission in 1857 to work as chief engineer of the Illinois Central Railroad. A superb administrator, he had risen to president of the Ohio and Mississippi Railroad by 1860.

When the Civil War began in April 1861, McClellan served as a major general of volunteers, commanding the Department of the Ohio. In this capacity, he helped plan and orchestrate several minor victories over Confederate forces in present-day West Virginia, especially the Battle of Rich Mountain (July 11, 1861). Success here brought him to the attention of President Abraham Lincoln, then desperately seeking to replace General Irvin McDowell as commander of Union forces. In July 1861 McClellan, who, while short in stature, cut an impressive military figure on horseback, gained appointment as head of the newly organized Army of the Potomac. That November, he also maneuvered to have himself appointed general in chief at the expense of his old mentor, General Scott. McClellan proved himself to be a superb disciplinarian and a first-class military organizer. Within months, he transformed his charge from an unruly mob into a finely honed military machine, eager for combat. The men came to revere their commander, in turn, christening him "Little Mac." Lincoln, however, grew frustrated by McClellan's lack of aggressiveness or, as he put it, his case of "the slows." McClellan ignored continual prodding by the government to attack, and on January 27, 1862, the president issued General War Order No. 1 mandating a general offensive. When McClellan still refused to budge, he was removed as general in chief and replaced by General Henry W. Halleck.

It was not until March 1862 that McClellan began his offensive with 118,000 men. He did so

Union general George B. McClellan *(National Archives)*

by transporting his huge army down the Potomac River to the Yorktown Peninsula, thus bypassing the strong fortifications of Richmond, Virginia. But McClellan, while possessing twice as many troops as General Joseph E. JOHNSTON, behaved cautiously and only inched his way inland. He was easily deceived by a smaller force under General John B. MAGRUDER at Yorktown, which he stopped to besiege and thereby squandered a month in preparations. McClellan next easily parried Johnston's careless thrust at Seven Oaks on May 31–June 1, 1862, but he then confronted the infinitely more aggressive general Robert E. LEE. Lee, taking advantage of his opponent's ingrained caution, launched the Seven Days' battles for the next week to intimidate him. McClellan, although besting the Confederates and inflicting heavier

losses, believed himself badly outnumbered and fell back to the James River. Lincoln became so angered by this display of timidity that he removed "Little Mac" in August and had the Army of the Potomac broken up and distributed among the new Army of Virginia under General John POPE. McClellan bitterly complained that his failure resulted from the lack of promised reinforcements, especially the 30,000 men General McDowell's I Corps that had been detained for the defense of Washington, D.C.

Pope's tenure as senior Union commander proved disastrous and came to grief at Second Manassas on August 29–30, 1862. Lee then crossed into Union territory by invading Maryland, and a desperate Lincoln restored McClellan to command. As before, he energetically reinvigorated the Army of the Potomac and was further bolstered by receipt of a copy of General Lee's secret orders. The orders revealed that Confederate forces were badly divided, but McClellan, true to form, reacted slowly. After winning a small victory at South Mountain on September 14, 1862, he confronted Lee's entire army at Antietam three days later. The Confederates were outnumbered badly 90,000 to 55,000 men, but McClellan attacked cautiously, failed to commit his entire army to the fray, and allowed Lee to escape a close brush with destruction. When the Southerners withdrew back to Virginia, McClellan failed to pursue them vigorously and instead called for reinforcements. Confederate cavalry under General J. E. B. STUART then conducted their second celebrated ride around the Army of the Potomac, and Lincoln again relieved McClellan in favor of General Ambrose E. BURNSIDE. Following a tearful farewell from his soldiers, he left the field, never to command again.

After waiting two years for orders that never came, McClellan accepted the Democratic Party's nomination for the presidency in 1864. He disavowed his party's peace platform and calls for a negotiated settlement with the South, but he nonetheless waxed critical of Lincoln's performance as commander in chief. The war weariness of the North coupled with high casualty rates from General Ulysses S. GRANT's Overland campaign to Richmond seemed to dampen Lincoln's political future. The soldiers, however, overwhelmingly rejected their former commander, and the president easily gained reelection with 212 electoral votes to 21. McClellan then resigned from the army altogether and toured Europe for three years. Back home, he became chief engineer for the New York City Department of Docks, and from 1878 to 1881, he served as governor of New Jersey. McClellan died in Orange, New Jersey, on October 29, 1885. He was among the most talented of Civil War leaders yet was simply unwilling to risk the splendid army he had so painstakingly created.

Further Reading

Beatie, Russell H. *Army of the Potomac, Vol. 1: Birth of Command, November 1860–September 1861*. New York: Da Capo Press, 2002.

Bonekemper, Edward H. *McClellan and Failure: A Study of Civil War Fear, Incompetence, and Worse*. Jefferson, N.C.: McFarland, 2007.

Dougherty, Kevin, and J. Michael Moore. *The Peninsula Campaign of 1862: A Military Analysis*. Jackson: University Press of Mississippi, 2005.

Jermann, Donald R. *Antietam: The Lost Order*. Gretna, La.: Pelican Publishing, 2006.

McClellan, George B. *McClellan's Own Story: The War for the Union*. New York: C. L. Webster, 1887.

McPherson, James M. *Crossroads of Freedom: Antietam*. New York: Oxford University Press, 2002.

Rafuse, Ethan S. *McClellan's War: The Failure of Moderation in the Struggle for the Union*. Bloomington: Indiana University Press, 2005.

Taaffe, Stephen R. *Commanding the Army of the Potomac*. Lawrence: University Press of Kansas, 2006.

Wert, Jeffrey D. *The Sword of Lincoln: The Army of the Potomac*. New York: Simon and Schuster, 2005.

McCulloch, Ben (1811–1862)

Confederate general

Ben McCulloch was born in Rutherford, Tennessee, on November 11, 1811, the son of a War of 1812 soldier from that state. He was raised on the frontier, befriended legendary scout Davy Crockett, and accompanied him to Texas in 1836. McCulloch missed dying at the Alamo on account of measles but subsequently distinguished himself at the decisive victory at San Jacinto. He then settled in Texas as a surveyor and also became one of the founding members of the noted Texas Rangers, organized for frontier defense. This ad hoc group of rough-hewn scouts fought well at the August 1840 Battle of Plum Creek in which he defeated the Great Comanche Raid of that year, and despite a reputation for brutality toward Indians and Mexicans, McCulloch became a popular figure in the southwestern press and won a seat in the Texas Congress. When the Mexican War erupted in 1846, he volunteered his services as a scout under General Zachary Taylor and further distinguished himself in the Battle of Monterrey. In February 1847 McCulloch performed particularly valuable service by detecting the approach of General Antonio de Santa Anna's army prior to the Battle of Buena Vista. Consequently, McCulloch received brevet promotion to major of U.S. Volunteers. After the war, he migrated to California at the height of the gold rush and then returned to Texas in 1852 to serve as a federal marshal. In 1858 he accompanied the Mormon expedition of Colonel Albert S. JOHNSTON and remained behind as a peace commissioner.

Once Texas seceded from the Union on February 1, 1861, McCulloch became a colonel of state troops. In that capacity, he received the surrender of U.S. forces under General David E. Twiggs at San Antonio. On May 11, 1861, he was appointed brigadier general at the behest of Confederate president Jefferson DAVIS and was assigned to command the Southwest Division, with troops in Texas, Louisiana, and Arkansas. He also was responsible for military matters in the nearby Indian Territory and arranged the commissioning of Cherokee Stand WATIE to brigadier general. As a military figure, McCulloch cultivated his larger-than-life image by remaining contemptuous of military protocol and regulations. As such, he invariably discarded his Confederate uniform in favor of a trademark black velvet outfit. His first military endeavor of consequence was to march troops into southwestern Missouri and reinforce the Confederate State Guard under General Sterling PRICE. On August 10, 1861, both men were surprised in camp by Union troops under General Nathaniel LYON and nearly routed. However, McCulloch managed to defeat a flanking force under Colonel Franz SIGEL and personally led a charge by Louisiana infantry that captured five cannon. Lyon was killed in the ensuing fracas, and the Confederates were left holding the field.

Victory did little to promote good relations between the headstrong McCulloch and the equally obstinate Price. In January 1862 Confederate authorities responded by creating the new Trans-Mississippi Department under General Earl VAN DORN to keep both in line. Heavy losses and internal disorganization stalled a Southern resurgence in the region for several months, and it was not until the spring that Van Dorn, Price, and McCulloch finally confronted a new threat posed by General Samuel R. CURTIS. Gathering 16,000 men, Van Dorn advanced on the Federals at Pea Ridge, Arkansas, on March 7, 1862. That morning, McCulloch rode ahead of the main body to reconnoiter the Union position, conspicuously decked out in his black uniform. He was then singled out by a sharpshooter and killed. Deprived of his sound judgment, Van Dorn waged a reckless and piecemeal action that forfeited control of northern Arkansas to the North. McCulloch had enjoyed renown as one of the first and greatest of the Texas Rangers, and his passing was greatly lamented. At the time of his death, he was also the second-most senior brigadier in Confederate service.

Further Reading

Brice, Donaly E. *The Great Comanche Raid: Boldest Indian Attack of the Texas Republic.* Austin, Tex.: Eakin Press, 1987.

Cutrer, Thomas W. *Ben McCulloch and the Frontier Military Tradition.* Chapel Hill: University of North Carolina Press, 1993.

DeBlack, Thomas R. *With Fire and Sword: Arkansas, 1861–1874.* Fayetteville: University of Arkansas Press, 2003.

Maberry, Robert T. "Texans and the Defense of the Confederate Northwest, April 1861–April 1862." Unpublished Ph.D. diss., Texas Christian University, 1992.

Piston, William G., and Richard W. Hatcher. *Wilson's Creek: The Second Battle of the Civil War and the Men Who Fought It.* Chapel Hill: University of North Carolina Press, 2000.

Shea, William L., and Grady McWhiney. *War in the West: Pea Ridge and Prairie Grove.* Abilene, Tex.: McWhiney Foundation Press, 2001.

McDowell, Irvin (1818–1885)

Union general

Irvin McDowell was born in Columbus, Ohio, on October 15, 1818, and he attended the Collège de Troyes in France before being admitted to the U.S. Military Academy in 1834. He graduated four years later midway in his class and served as a second lieutenant in the 1st U.S. Artillery during garrison stints along the Canadian border. In 1841 he transferred back to West Point as an instructor, rising there to first lieutenant, and in 1845 he joined the staff of General John E. Wool in Texas as a staff officer. In this capacity, McDowell fought in the Mexican War (1846–48), winning a brevet promotion to captain for gallantry at the Battle of Buena Vista in February 1847. He subsequently arrived at Washington, D.C., and was posted within the adjutant general's department. For the next 12 years, he performed well in staff assignments, rising to major and frequently serving as aide-de-camp to General Winfield SCOTT. After the Civil War commenced, McDowell used political connections through Scott and Secretary of the Treasury Salmon P. Chase to advance three grades to brigadier general as of May 11, 1861. He then accepted command of the Department of Northeastern Virginia and began to cobble together a force composed mainly of 90-day volunteers and poorly trained militia. Despite his lack of experience in handling large numbers of troops, McDowell discharged his duties with energy and dispatch, and, by July, he possessed a scratch force of 50,000 enthusiastic citizen soldiers. Given sufficient time, he would have undoubtedly welded this polyglot assemblage into a finely honed army—but this proved to be a luxury he could not afford. Moreover, his blunt, reserved personality won few admirers or friends among the soldiers and politicians with whom he had to contend.

Ever since the bombardment of Fort Sumter on April 12, 1861, the administration of President Abraham LINCOLN fell under increasing pressure to mount a major offensive against the Confederate capital of Richmond, Virginia, and crush the rebellion in one fell swoop. McDowell, as the commanding general in the theater, also felt the heat and was goaded into committing his troops to combat before they were ready. He nonetheless proffered an excellent plan for outflanking Confederate forces deployed at Manassas Junction under General Pierre G. T. BEAUREGARD. It was anticipated that a crushing victory here would severe Richmond's supply lines and end the rebellion without further bloodshed. On July 16, 1861, McDowell led his overconfident amateurs southward down the Warrenton Turnpike to thunderous cheers of "On to Richmond!" Two days later, he paused at Centreville to reorganize and to leisurely reconnoiter Confederate positions. On July 18 a Union force was bested at Blackburn's Ford by Confederates under General James LONGSTREET, which further reinforced McDowell's caution. His three-day delay also enabled Beauregard to summon 10,000 reinforcements under the highly capable general Joseph E. JOHNSTON, who boarded trains in the Shenandoah Valley. Union forces in the region under elderly general Robert Patterson were supposed to have assisted McDowell by pinning Johnston in place to prevent such a move, but they failed to do so.

The fateful encounter at Bull Run, on July 21, 1861, was ostensibly lost to the Union before the first gun was fired. When McDowell finally attacked, he did so slowly and by piecemeal, allowing the Southerners to feed additional units to the threatened sector and hold the Northerners off. Exhausted by a day of fighting in intense heat, McDowell's levies finally wilted in the face of

Johnston's reinforcements and departed the battlefield in an embarrassing stampede. The Southerners, equally disorganized by success, proved unable to mount an effective pursuit. In sum, McDowell originated a fine battle plan but one that proved beyond the ability of raw troops and officers to execute properly. Held as a scapegoat for defeat, he was replaced the following August by General George B. McCLELLAN.

When the Army of the Potomac was organized in August 1861, McDowell received com-

Union general Irvin McDowell *(National Archives)*

mand of the I Corps along with promotion to major general as of March 1862. But he played no role in McClellan's ambitious Peninsula campaign because the activities of General Thomas J. JACKSON in the Shenandoah Valley convinced President Lincoln that Washington was threatened. Hence, McDowell's I Corps remained in reserve, guarding the capital, and it saw little fighting: McClellan vocally cited his inaction as a major cause of his defeat at the hands of General Robert E. LEE. McDowell subsequently commanded the III Corps in the Army of Virginia under General John POPE. Like Pope, he received blame for the defeat at Second Manassas on August 29–30, 1862, and he was relieved from field command for the duration of the war. McDowell angrily demanded and received a court of inquiry that exonerated his behavior, but his wartime service concluded. It was not until July 1864 that he received command of the distant Department of the Pacific, followed by the Department of California in 1865.

After the war, McDowell gradually resuscitated his reputation as a fine military administrator. He commanded the Department of the East in 1868, rising to major general in 1872. He next fulfilled four years as head of the Department of the South before returning to the Department of the Pacific in 1876. McDowell finally retired in 1882 and died at San Francisco on May 4, 1885. While a capable staff officer and administrator, he could never live down the stigma of losing the Civil War's first large engagement.

Further Reading
Beatie, Russell H. *Army of the Potomac, Vol. 1: Birth of Command, November 1860–September 1861.* New York: Da Capo Press, 2002.
Davis, William C. *Battle at Bull Run: A History of the First Major Campaign of the Civil War.* Baton Rouge: Louisiana State University Press, 1995.
Detzer, David. *Donnybrook: The Battle of Bull Run, 1861.* San Diego: Harcourt, 2004.
Hennessy, John J. *Return to Bull Run: The Campaign and Battle of Second Manassas.* Norman: University of Oklahoma Press, 1993.
Jones, Wilmer L. *Generals in Blue and Gray.* 2 vols. Westport, Conn.: Praeger, 2004.
Rafuse, Ethan S. *A Single Grand Victory: The First Campaign and Battle of Manassas.* Wilmington, Del.: Scholarly Resources, 2002.

McPherson, James B. (1828–1864)
Union general

James Birdseye McPherson was born near Clyde, Ohio, on November 14, 1828, the son of farmers. He overcame a life of poverty to enter the U.S. Military Academy in 1849 and graduated four years later, first in his class. Posted as a second lieutenant within the elite Corps of Engineers, McPherson remained at the academy as an instructor until 1854, when he performed engineering work at New York and San Francisco. He rose to first lieutenant as of December 1858 and, as a strong Unionist, helped raise a volunteer company once the Civil War commenced in April 1861. Though promoted to captain and desiring a field command, McPherson was ordered to Boston to supervise harbor defenses. He then appealed to his former commander, now General Henry W. HALLECK, for help, and Halleck ordered him to St. Louis, Missouri, as his aide-de-camp with a rank of lieutenant colonel. In the winter of 1861, McPherson transferred to General Ulysses S. GRANT's staff as his engineering officer and capably discharged his duties at Forts Henry and Donelson in February 1862. He performed equally well in the Shiloh campaign that spring and was entrusted with supervising military railroads in Mississippi as a brigadier general of volunteers. In October 1862 he further distinguished himself by rushing reinforcements to General William S. ROSECRANS, then besieged at Corinth, Mississippi, and so effectively pursued Confederates under General Earl VAN DORN that he received both promotion to major general of volunteers and command of a division in the XIII Corps. McPherson next fought throughout the ensuing Vicksburg campaign, commanding the XVII Corps, and he bore prominent roles in the victories at Port Gibson, Jackson, and Champion's Hill in May 1863.

Union general James B. McPherson *(Massachusetts Commandery Military Order of the Loyal Legion and the U.S. Army Military History Institute)*

He then actively partook of the siege operations at Vicksburg and, following its capitulation on July 4, 1863, won appointment as its governor.

On recommendations from both Halleck and Grant, McPherson advanced to brigadier general in the regular army as of August 1863. He participated in General William T. SHERMAN's Meridian offensive in January 1864 and subsequently succeeded Sherman as commander of the Army of the Tennessee during the march to Atlanta. As expected, McPherson performed well in a difficult campaign of maneuver and only faltered once. In May 1864 Sherman dispatched him on a 40-mile march below Dalton, Georgia, where the army of General Joseph E. JOHNSTON was strongly entrenched. He advanced into Snake Gap Creek as ordered and was well positioned to cut off Johnston's entire army, but he suddenly and uncharacteristically grew cautious and retreated. This proved the most unfortunate mistake of his entire military career, for the pass was then guarded by three weak Confederate brigades, and his hesitation allowed Johnston to escape encirclement speedily. Nonetheless, McPherson's XVII Corps continued marching and fighting competently at Resaca, Dallas, and Kennesaw Mountain on the approach to Atlanta, and he helped to maneuver Johnston out of strong defensive positions.

Johnston's inability to stem Sherman's approach resulted in his replacement with the ever-aggressive general John B. HOOD, a former West Point roommate of McPherson. That officer, cognizant of Hood's well-deserved reputation for offensive tactics, immediately deployed his troops to meet what he anticipated would be an all-out assault. On July 22, 1864, Hood struck violently at Union forces outside Atlanta, and Confederates under General William J. HARDEE hit the Army of the Tennessee hard. After a raging battle of several hours, they were repulsed, thanks to McPherson's excellent dispositions. However, as McPherson was reconnoitering a gap between several of his units, he stumbled into a Confederate picket line and was shot dead at the age of 35. "The country has lost one of its best soldiers," General Grant lamented, "and I have lost one of my best friends." McPherson's death was a serious loss to the Union army, and had he lived, he may have been one of the towering figures of the postwar period.

Further Reading

Block, William. "The Pride of Clyde: James B. McPherson." *Northwest Ohio Quarterly* 74, no. 2 (2002): 50–62.

Cubbison, Douglas. *The Entering Wedge: The Battle of Port Gibson, 1 May 1863: A Scholarly Monograph.* Saline, Mich.: McNaughton and Gunn, 2002.

Melia, Tamara M. "James B. McPherson and the Ideals of the Old Army." Unpublished Ph.D., diss., Southern Illinois University, 1987.

Smith, Derek. *The Gallant Dead: Union and Confederate Generals Killed in the Civil War.* Mechanicsburg, Pa.: Stackpole Books, 2005.

Smith, Timothy B. *Champion's Hill: Decisive Battle for Vicksburg.* New York: Savas Beattie, 2005.

Woodworth, Steven E. *Nothing But Victory: The Army of the Tennessee, 1861–1865.* New York: Alfred A. Knopf, 2005.

Woodworth, Steven E., ed. *Grant's Lieutenants.* 2 vols. Lawrence: University Press of Kansas, 2001.

Magruder, John B. (1807–1871)
Confederate general

John Bankhead Magruder was born in Port Royal, Virginia, on May 1, 1807, the son of an attorney. He entered the U.S. Military Academy in 1826 and graduated in the middle of his class four years later as a second lieutenant in the 7th U.S. Infantry. As a student, Magruder was much given to heavy drinking and nearly was expelled for demerits. In 1831 he transferred to the 1st U.S. Infantry and performed useful service in Florida's Second Seminole War (1836–42). Magruder was next billeted in Texas as part of the Army of Occupation under General Zachary Taylor. He fought conspicuously in the Mexican War, commanding an artillery battery under General Gideon Pillow at Cerro Gordo in 1847 and winning brevet promotions to major and lieutenant colonel. After the war, Magruder resumed a long stint of garrison duty along the frontier and the East Coast, gaining notoriety for his lavish partying, elaborate attire, and a projected sense of superiority that manifested in the sobriquet "Prince John." In 1859 Magruder returned west again to serve as commander of Fort Leavenworth, Kansas, and he also toured as an artillery inspector. He was never overtly sympathetic toward secession, but after Virginia left the Union in April 1861, he resigned his commission and tended his service to the Confederacy as a colonel of infantry.

Magruder's flair for theatrics never deserted him in combat. On June 10, 1861, he led a small detachment of Confederates at Big Bethel, Virginia, defeating an equally small detachment of Federals under General Benjamin F. Butler. The Southern press immediately magnified his victory and lionized him to the point where he gained promotion to brigadier general in June and major general the following October. In the spring of 1862, he performed his best work by completely hoodwinking the vast army of General George B. McClellan at Yorktown into believing that his force of 15,000 men was much larger. Consequently, Union forces squandered an entire month, April 4–May 4, 1862, preparing for an unnecessary siege. However, General Joseph E. Johnston remained less impressed with his deportment, and after quarreling with him, Magruder sought a transfer to the Trans-Mississippi Department. While this transpired, Magruder fought capably at the Battle of Seven Pines (June 1, 1862), and he resumed his bluffing activities against McClellan during General Robert E. Lee's Seven Days' offensive. But after this point, his battlefield performance lessened through either lack of sleep or excessive drinking, and he fumbled assignments at Savage's Station on June 29, 1862, and at Malvern Hill on July 1, 1862. Lee was angered by his dilatoriness and was preparing charges against him when Magruder was transferred to the District of Texas, New Mexico, and Arizona.

Magruder's subsequent activities were competent, if anticlimactic. On January 1, 1863, he orchestrated a surprise attack on Union forces garrisoning the port of Galveston, Texas, capturing them and the revenue cutter *Harriet Lane* and driving off the blockading squadron. This proved a significant victory as Galveston remained a port of considerable blockade-running activity for the rest of the war. In 1864 he also coordinated his efforts with General Richard Taylor in West Louisiana, and his assistance helped defeat the Red River expedition of General Nathaniel C. Banks. Magruder then briefly commanded the District of Arkansas in the fall of 1864 before returning to Texas. He surrendered there to Union authorities on June 2, 1865. Like many disaffected Confederates, Magruder chose to emigrate to Mexico rather than return home. He served Emperor Maximilian as head of the Land Office of Colonization to encourage Southern immigration there. However, in November 1866 he sailed to Havana, Cuba, and then to New York City to practice law before finally settling down in San Antonio, Texas.

"Prince John" died there on February 18, 1871, a colorful, if marginal, military leader.

Further Reading

Casdorph, Paul D. *Prince John Magruder: His Life and Campaigns.* New York: Wiley and Sons, 1991.

Cotham, Edward T. *Battle on the Bay: The Civil War Struggle for Galveston.* Austin: University of Texas Press, 1998.

Moore, J. Michael. "The Damn Failure: The Battles of Lee's Mill and Damn No. 1." *North & South* 5, no. 5 (2002): 62–71.

Schroeder, Glenn B. *A Rebel and a Yankee: Cousins at War.* Greeley, Colo.: Immigrant Press, 2000.

Stever, Rex H. "Magruder's Scorched Earth Policy." *Journal of South Texas* 16, no. 1 (2003): 34–44.

Townsend, Stephen A. *The Yankee Invasion of Texas.* College Station: Texas A & M University Press, 2005.

Meade, George G. (1815–1872)

Union general

George Gordon Meade was born in Cadiz, Spain, on December 31, 1815, the son of a naval agent. The premature death of his father forced him to quit school to support his family, but, in 1831, he gained admittance to the U.S. Military Academy. Meade graduated four years later as a second lieutenant in the 3rd U.S. Artillery, where he fought in Florida's Second Seminole War before contracting a fever. He briefly served at the U.S. Arsenal in Watertown, Massachusetts, and then resigned his commission to work as a surveyor. In 1842 Meade rejoined the service as a lieutenant in the Topographical Engineers, and he performed boundary work in Maine and construction work in Philadelphia. He next accompanied General Zachary Taylor's army during the Mexican War, winning a brevet promotion for valor at the Battle of Monterrey (September 20–24, 1846). After a tour under General Winfield SCOTT in the advance against Mexico City the following year, Meade resumed his surveying work in Philadelphia, Florida, and along the Canadian border, rising to captain as of May 1856. The onset of the Civil War in April 1861 led to a commission as a brigadier general in the Pennsylvania Reserves, and he

spent several months manning the defenses of Washington, D.C.

Meade commenced to campaign actively by leading a brigade in the 1862 Peninsula campaign under General George B. MCCLELLAN. He fought conspicuously at Mechanicsville, Gaines's Mill, White Oak Swamp, and especially at Frayser's Farm (Glendale) on June 20, 1862, where he was wounded yet refused to quit the field. He had only partially recovered in time to see additional service under General John POPE at Second Manassas (August 29–30, 1862), and he commanded a division at Antietam on September 17, 1862. When the commander of I Corps, General Joseph HOOKER, fell wounded, Meade replaced him in

Union general George Meade *(Library of Congress)*

battle, performing capably. He consequently rose to major general the following November under General Ambrose E. BURNSIDE, and on December 17, 1862, during the disastrous Battle of Fredericksburg, he scored one of the few Union successes of the day with a minor breakthrough at General Thomas J. JACKSON's position. When command of the Army of the Potomac reverted to Hooker in the spring of 1863, Meade was entrusted with the command of V Corps, which was only slightly engaged at the disastrous defeat of Chancellorsville on May 2, 1863. Shortly after, the Army of Northern Virginia under General Robert E. LEE began its second incursion into Union territory by invading Pennsylvania. Hooker was then relieved of command, and when General John F. REYNOLDS declined to take up the mantle, Meade accepted it on June 28, 1863. He was somewhat taken aback by the appointment and not entirely pleased, but it proved most fortuitous for the country.

On July 1, 1863, Union and Confederate forces collided in an engagement at Gettysburg, Pennsylvania. Generals John BUFORD, Abner DOUBLEDAY, Oliver O. HOWARD, and Winfield S. HANCOCK waged a valiant fight, but they were driven out of town and up the slopes of nearby hills. Meade arrived on the battlefield at midnight, sorted through his jumbled units, and assumed a masterfully defensive position. With his surveyor's eye, he judiciously placed brigades and divisions along Cemetery Ridge, Little Round Top, and Culp's Hill in such a manner as to make the broken, heavily wooded terrain work for him and against the Confederates. Consequently, throughout July 2, 1863, Union forces ably repelled determined attacks by General James LONGSTREET along the critical left flank. The slovenly deployment of General Daniel E. SICKLES and his III Corps caused many anxious moments and heavy casualties, but otherwise Meade's line held firm. At a council of war that evening, Meade decided on a dawn attack to eliminate small Southern gains at the foot of Culp's Hill and cleverly anticipated that Lee, hav-

ing failed against both flanks, would most likely strike the Union center next. Throughout the evening, men and artillery shifted into position to meet the new threat. On July 3, 1863, Confederate artillery under Colonel Edward P. ALEXANDER heavily bombarded Cemetery Ridge for several hours, followed up by an assault by 15,000 infantry under General George E. PICKETT. This was repulsed bloodily by concentrated Union firepower, and Lee retreated back to Virginia after suffering losses of as many as 28,000 men. Meade's own casualties were considerable—at 23,000—so he declined to pursue actively.

Lincoln was gravely disappointed that the victor of Gettysburg failed to destroy Lee's army, but the general nonetheless received the thanks of Congress and promotion to regular brigadier general. General Ulysses S. GRANT arrived at Meade's headquarters the following spring as general in chief, but Meade was allowed to remain titular commander of the Army of the Potomac. Despite an awkward command arrangement, the two men worked well together, and Meade acquitted himself ably in bloody battles at the Wilderness and Spotsylvania Court House. On June 3, 1864, he proved instrumental in dissuading Grant from additional attacks at Cold Harbor, Virginia, which occasioned horrific losses. With Grant's approval, he rose to major general, U.S. Army, in August 1864. Meade continued fighting well throughout the Petersburg campaign and helped direct the final movements at Appomattox Court House with General Philip H. SHERIDAN which finally trapped Lee's army on April 9, 1865.

After the war, Meade remained in the service commanding the Department of the East, and, in 1868, he also performed reconstruction duties in Georgia, Alabama, and Florida. In 1869 he took charge of the Division of the Atlantic, where his final years proved uneventful save for a vitriolic and long-running dispute with Sickles concerning their respective roles at Gettysburg. Meade died in Philadelphia on November 6, 1872, of complications arising from his old wound. A more competent than brilliant leader, his skill at handling troops and effectively utilizing terrain won the Civil War's most decisive battle for the North.

Further Reading

Callihan, David L. "Passing the Test: George G. Meade's Initiation as Army Commander." *Gettysburg Magazine* 30 (July 2004): 30–48.

Hall, Jeffrey C. *The Stand of the United States Army at Gettysburg.* Bloomington: Indiana University Press, 2003.

Hyde, Bill. *The Union Generals Speak: The Meade Hearings on the Battle of Gettysburg.* Baton Rouge: Louisiana State University Press, 2003.

Meade, George W. *Life and Letters of General George G. Meade, Major General, United States Army.* 2 vols. New York: Charles Scribner's Sons, 1913.

Rafuse, Ethan S. *George Gordon Meade and the War in the East.* Abilene, Tex.: McWhiney Foundation Press, 2003.

Sauers, Richard A. *Meade: Victor of Gettysburg.* Washington, D.C.: Brassey's, 2003.

Sears, Stephen W. *Gettysburg.* Boston: Houghton Mifflin, 2003.

Taaffe, Stephen R. *Commanding the Army of the Potomac.* Lawrence: University Press of Kansas, 2006.

Trudeau, Andre N. *Gettysburg: A Testing of Courage.* New York: HarperCollins, 2002.

Wert, Jeffrey D. *The Sword of Lincoln: The Army of the Potomac.* New York: Simon and Schuster, 2005.

Meigs, Montgomery C. (1816–1892)

Union general

Montgomery Cunningham Meigs was born in Augusta, Georgia, on May 3, 1816, the son of a physician. He relocated to Philadelphia, Pennsylvania, with his family and briefly attended college there before transferring to the U.S. Military Academy in 1832. Meigs graduated near the top of his class four years later and was assigned to the elite Corps of Engineers. For the next 16 years, he distinguished himself in a variety of capacities, including a stint in service along the Mississippi River under Captain Robert E. LEE. He faced his biggest challenge in 1853 after being promoted to captain and assigned as chief engineer of the Washington Aqueduct Project, destined to bring supplies of freshwater to the capital, year round.

Union general Montgomery C. Meigs *(Library of Congress)*

Meigs successfully completed this daunting task eight years later by constructing the world's largest masonry arch over the Cabin John Branch, a tributary of the Potomac River. Throughout this same period, he was also responsible for designing and constructing new wings and domes for the Capitol Building. However, in 1860 he ran afoul of Secretary of War John B. FLOYD over the issue of contracts and was punitively reassigned to construction work in the Dry Tortugas off Florida. Meigs was recalled to Washington shortly after Floyd quit the government, and he attended the inauguration of President Abraham LINCOLN in February 1861. He the resumed routine engineering duties until the Civil War commenced the following April.

No sooner had hostilities erupted at Fort Sumter, South Carolina, than Meigs conferred with Commander David D. PORTER and Secretary of State William H. Seward about the necessity of reinforcing Fort Pickens off the coast of Pensacola, Florida. He then helped organize a successful relief expedition to that distant post, winning promotion to colonel, 11th U.S. Infantry in May 1861. But Meigs, disdaining a field command, requested succeeding Colonel Joseph E. JOHNSTON as quartermaster general of the army. Though never trained as a logistician, he was destined to make significant contributions to that field. Meigs inherited a small, chaotic department, totally unsuited to the task of arming and equipping a rapidly expanding army. Fortunately, he rapidly transformed it into a smoothly functioning instrument of war that met the ongoing needs of nearly 1 million soldiers. As quartermaster, Meigs bore responsibilities for acquiring and distributing food, clothing, and equipment for the various Union commands, along with the necessary transportation. He was also instrumental in promoting and paying for ironclad gunboats so essential to riverine warfare in the West. Unfortunately, an overreliance on civilian contractors engendered notoriously corrupt practices, including kickbacks and influence-peddling at every level. Meigs countered such abuse with his own brand of scrupulous honesty and accountability, and, by war's end, his department had distributed over $1.5 billion in materiel. In light of his superb performance, no Union army was ever defeated for want of supplies.

Meigs also demonstrated his bureaucratic prowess in the field by directing and supervising logistical operations in support of General Ulysses S. GRANT's overland campaign to Richmond, Virginia, in 1864. In July, when Confederates under General Jubal A. EARLY threatened Washington, D.C., he briefly commanded a division of War Department employees in the capital's defense. He also organized a complicated convoy of supply ships to assist General William T. SHERMAN's march from Savannah, Georgia, up to coast to Raleigh, North Carolina. Meigs endured a personal tragedy in October 1864 when his son was allegedly murdered by Confederate partisans. His son's commanding officer, General Philip H. SHERIDAN, was so outraged by the act that he literally burned every farm and building within five miles of the incident. Meigs's loss only spurred him on to greater efforts,

and for handling the complex business of army logistics seamlessly, he ended the war a brevet brigadier general. His antipathy for former colleague General Robert E. LEE proved to be so great that he designed and built Arlington National Cemetery on land previously owned by Lee's family.

Meigs resumed his engineering activities in the postwar period by supervising plans for a new War Department building and part of the new Smithsonian Institution. In 1876 he was tapped to visit Europe to observe military affairs and also served on a commission tasked with considering military reforms. He retired from active service in 1882, but he still found time to design the Pension Office Building, to serve as a Smithsonian regent, to join the American Philosophical Society, and to help found the American Academy of Science. The multitalented Meigs died in Washington, D.C., on January 2, 1892. He remains one of the most peerless bureaucrats of American military history and a major contributor to the ultimate Union victory.

Further Reading

Dickinson, William C., Dean A. Herrin, and Donald R. Kennon, eds. *Montgomery C. Meigs and the Building of the Nation's Capitol.* Athens: University of Ohio Press, 2001.

Hagerman, Edward. *The American Civil War and the Origins of Modern Warfare: Ideas, Organizations, and Field Command.* Bloomington: Indiana University Press, 1988.

Miller, David. *Second Only to Grant: Quartermaster General Montgomery C. Meigs: A Biography.* Shippensburg, Pa.: White Mane Books, 2000.

Risch, Erna. *Quartermaster Support for the Army: A History of the Corps, 1775–1939.* Washington, D.C.: Office of the Quartermaster General, 1962.

Stevens, Joseph E. "The North's Secret Weapon." *American History* 37, no. 1 (2002): 42–48.

Woodworth, Steve E., et al. "Who Were the Top Ten Generals?" *North & South* 6, no. 4 (2003): 12–22.

Morgan, John H. (1825–1864)

Confederate general

John Hunt Morgan was born in Huntsville, Alabama, on June 1, 1825, the son of a merchant and planter. He relocated to Lexington, Kentucky, with his family and briefly attended Transylvania University before being expelled for dueling. During the Mexican War, he joined the 1st Kentucky Cavalry as a lieutenant and performed useful service under General Zachary Taylor, especially at the Battle of Buena Vista (1847). Afterward, he returned to Kentucky to become a successful hemp manufacturer. He also maintained his militia contacts and in 1857 founded and led his own company, the Lexington Rifles. Morgan was openly sympathetic to the Confederacy and defiantly flew their flag over his factory throughout the period of Kentucky neutrality. But once the legislature finally declared for the Union in the fall of 1861, he moved to Tennessee and joined the Confederate army as a cavalry captain.

Morgan, handsome, dashing, and more than six feet tall, came to personify the romantic ideals of a cavalry raider. He rose to colonel after good behavior at the Battle of Shiloh in April 1862, and he was subsequently attached to General Joseph WHEELER's cavalry as part of General Braxton BRAGG's Army of Tennessee. In this capacity, he began to launch numerous and devastatingly effective raids against Union installations and lines of communication throughout Kentucky and Tennessee. On July 4, 1862, he commenced a 900-mile raid that netted 1,000 captives, cut railroad and telegraph lines, and delayed the advance of General Don C. BUELL's army by several weeks. On August 21, 1862, he confronted General Richard W. Johnson and 700 pursuing Union troopers; in the ensuing scrape, Johnson was captured and his command scattered. The following October, he advanced with 1,800 men and briefly seized his home town of Lexington for several hours. On December 7, 1862, Morgan launched another lightning foray that stormed into Hartsville, Tennessee, taking 1,700 Union prisoners. He then gained promotion to brigadier general, and President Abraham LINCOLN, frustrated as to the apparent ease of Morgan's movements, angrily wired General Henry W. HALLECK, declaring "They are having a stampede in Kentucky. Please look at it."

Consequently, more than 20,000 Federal troops were detached from field service to guard communication and supply lines. Morgan's daring success induced President Jefferson DAVIS to push through the Partisan Ranger Act on April 21, 1863, which raised mounted units specifically for raiding purposes.

In June 1863 Morgan initiated his most audacious raid by riding northward into Indiana and Ohio on a 24-day ride. He did so against the wishes of General Bragg, who sought a more conventional use for his 2,400 troopers. Morgan nonetheless ferried across the Ohio River and galloped 1,100 miles through the two states with Federal troops and a squadron of gunboats in hot pursuit. Morgan drove his men 50 miles in the saddle per day and at one point wildly galloped

Confederate general John H. Morgan (*Massachusetts Commandery Military Order of the Loyal Legion and the U.S. Army Military History Institute*)

through the suburbs of downtown Cincinnati. However, the bulk of his force was cornered at Buffington Island in the Ohio River and was captured, while Morgan himself managed to elude his pursuers until July 26. Thereafter, he was incarcerated in the Ohio State Penitentiary, Columbus, and was treated like a common brigand. But it was never safe to underestimate Morgan in times of adversity, and, on November 26, 1863, he affected a daring escape.

Morgan returned to the Confederacy with a hero's welcome and won assignment as commander of the Department of Southwestern Virginia. He then resumed his raiding activities, although with less success owing to the loss of skilled leaders and rising indiscipline among his troopers. When his forays began to resemble large-scale plundering expeditions, he was investigated by Confederate authorities and nearly was removed from command. But Morgan, determined to silence his critics, counted on one final raid against Nashville to exonerate his reputation. En route, he encamped at Greeneville, Tennessee, a region known for Unionist sympathies, and the inhabitants tipped off a nearby Federal garrison. On September 4, 1864, they surprised Morgan in camp, killing him. At the time of his death, his activities were of declining military value to the Confederacy and more likely a source of embarrassment, but for many months, Morgan was a formidable Confederate partisan and a hero throughout the South.

Further Reading

Black, Robert W. *Cavalry Raids of the Civil War.* Mechanicsburg, Pa.: Stackpole Books, 2004.

Ervin, Robert E. *The John Hunt Morgan Raid of 1863.* Jackson, Ohio: Jackson County Historical Society, 2003.

Foster, John M. "A Futile Resistance: The Response to Morgan's Raid in Indiana, July 8–13, 1863." Unpublished master's thesis, University of Indianapolis, 2003.

Gorin, Betty J. *"Morgan is Coming!": Confederate Raiders in the Heart of Kentucky.* Louisville, Ky.: Harmony House Publishers, 2006.

Sanders, Stuart W. "A Little Fight between Friends and Family." *Civil War Times Illustrated* 40, no. 5 (2001): 40–44, 66.

Smith, Derek. *The Gallant Dead: Union and Confederate Generals Killed in the Civil War.* Mechanicsburg, Pa.: Stackpole Books, 2005.

Mosby, John S. (1833–1916)

Confederate partisan

John Singleton Mosby was born in Edgemont, Virginia, on December 6, 1833, the son of farmers. He enrolled at the University of Virginia at 15, had an altercation with a bully, and shot him. After serving six months in jail, he studied law and was eventually admitted to the bar in Bristol County, Virginia. When the Civil War broke out in April 1861, Mosby joined the 1st Virginia Cavalry as a private. He fought at Bull Run that July before joining General J. E. B. STUART as a scout and originated the strategy of "riding around" the army of General George B. McCLELLAN during the 1862 Peninsula campaign. Mosby advanced to lieutenant that December and pushed hard for an independent command of rangers to harry Union detachments throughout Loudoun County. Permission was granted in February 1863, and Mosby commenced his soon to be legendary operations with only nine men.

A talented raider, Mosby quickly established himself as the bane of Union rear areas with his sudden attacks and equally quick escapes. He accomplished this by hand-picking his officers, strictly disciplining all ranks, and refraining from the cruel practices usually associated with other Southern partisans. Great emphasis was placed on rapidity of movement, followed by quick dispersion to prearranged regrouping sites. The men were also self-sufficient, bringing their own clothing and weapons, and always divided up captured spoils between them. Mosby's command was thus highly cohesive and tightly knit, and his men deemed no target too daunting for their small-scale, hit-and-run tactics. He underscored this fact on March 9, 1863, when, with only 29 men, he stole past Union sentries at Fair-

Confederate partisan John S. Mosby *(Library of Congress)*

fax Court House, awakened General Edwin H. Stoughton with a slap to his backside, and seized him along with 33 men and 58 horses. Mosby then rose to captain and major following another successful action near Chantilly. Throughout the Gettysburg campaign of July 1863, his men fed General Robert E. LEE a steady stream of accurate military intelligence, while his band of irregulars were incorporated into the Confederate army as Company A, 43rd Battalion, Partisan Rangers. Mosby then continued raiding Union outposts with near impunity, rising to lieutenant colonel in February 1864. His endeavors proved so galling to Union authorities that General George A. CUSTER hanged several partisans as brigands. Mosby countered by hanging several of Custer's men in retaliation, at which point the practice ceased on both sides.

By the fall of 1864, Mosby's rangers constituted the only organized resistance to Union forces in northern Virginia. With such speed and ease did he continue his slashing operations throughout Londoun and Fauquier counties that the region became known informally as "Mosby's Confederacy." In November 1864 an exasperated general Philip H. SHERIDAN dispatched Captain Richard Blazer and 100 Union scouts, armed with the latest Spencer repeating rifles, to eliminate the threat. However, Mosby easily ambushed and captured Blazer's detachment at Kabletown, Virginia, on November 18, 1864. It is estimated that no less than 30,000 Union soldiers became tied down hunting for the elusive raiders. General Ulysses S. GRANT vowed to hang Mosby without trial if he were caught. However, Mosby evaded capture, rose to colonel in December 1864, and continued harassing Union troops successfully until the end of the war. Rather than surrender his command, now numbering 1,900 men, the "Gray Ghost" simply disbanded them and they went home.

Mosby returned to his home a war hero, and he resumed his legal practice in Salem, Virginia. However, he became an anathema to former Confederates by joining the Republican Party and campaigning for President Grant. The admiration between Grant and Mosby proved mutual, and Grant elevated his former adversary to several posts within the government. In 1878 President Rutherford B. Hayes, another Civil War veteran, appointed Mosby U.S. consul to Hong Kong, where he remained until 1885. From 1904 to 1910, he served as assistant general in the State Department before dying at Warrenton, Virginia, on May 30, 1916. In terms of results, Mosby is probably the most successful partisan fighter in American history.

Further Reading

Ashdown, Paul. *The Mosby Myth: A Confederate Hero in Life and Legend.* Wilmington, Del.: Scholarly Resources, 2002.

Black, Robert W. *Cavalry Raids of the Civil War.* Mechanicsburg, Pa.: Stackpole Books, 2004.

Brown, Peter A. *Mosby's Fighting Parson: The Life and Times of Sam Chapman.* Westminster, Md.: Willow Bend Books, 2001.

Mackey, Robert R. *The Uncivil War: Irregular Warfare in the Upper South, 1861–1865.* Norman: University of Oklahoma Press, 2004.

Mosby, John S. *Take Sides with the Truth: The Postwar Letters of John Singleton Mosby to Samuel F. Chapman.* Lexington University Press of Kentucky, 2007.

Ramage, James A. *Gray Ghost: The Life of Colonel John Singleton Mosby.* Lexington: University Press of Kentucky, 1999.

P

Pemberton, John C. (1814–1881)

Confederate general

John Clifford Pemberton was born in Philadelphia, Pennsylvania, on August 10, 1814, the son of a successful businessman. He was well educated by tutors and briefly attended the University of Pennsylvania before transferring to the U.S. Military Academy in 1833. Pemberton graduated four years later as a second lieutenant in the 4th U.S. Infantry, and he saw service in Florida's Second Seminole War up through 1839. That year, he commenced a wide-ranging tour of garrison duty along the coast and frontiers. In 1846 he joined General Zachary Taylor's Army of Occupation and served as an aide to General William J. Worth during initial phases of the Mexican War. The following year, Pemberton transferred to General Winfield Scott's army, winning brevet promotions to captain and major for gallantry at Churubusco, Molino del Rey, and Chapultepec. After the war, he was stationed at Fortress Monroe, Virginia, and he married into a prominent family. Thereafter, his personal and political orientation became wedded to the South. He resumed garrison duties on the western frontier, rose to captain, and in 1858 accompanied Colonel Albert S. Johnston's Mormon expedition. Pemberton was serving at Fort Ridgely, Minnesota, in the spring of 1861 when the rising tide of secession—and family ties—convinced him to resign his commission and proffer his services to the Confederacy. This decision was roundly condemned by his family in Philadelphia, and two younger brothers joined the Union army.

Pemberton held various regimental grades until June 1861, when he advanced to brigadier general and was assigned to the defenses of Norfolk, Virginia. The following February 1862, he transferred to the Department of South Carolina, Georgia, and Florida as a major general to replace General Robert E. Lee. Pemberton proved himself to be a hard worker and a skilled engineer, and he constructed Battery Wagner, which proved so essential to the defense of Charleston, South Carolina. However, he was impolitic for suggesting that Fort Sumter, where secessionism began, be considered next to useless. He also went on record as stating that he would abandon his department rather than allow his small army to be captured. A firestorm of criticism erupted in the press, and at length President Jefferson Davis, mindful of Pemberton's status as a Northerner, removed him from command. But later that year, the tactless leader gained promotion to lieutenant general and he was entrusted with the Department of Mississippi and East Louisiana. Here, Pemberton's overriding concern was keeping the bastions of Vicksburg, Mississippi, and Port Hudson, Louisiana, in Southern hands.

Pemberton arrived in Vicksburg in November 1862, displacing General Earl Van Dorn, and he immediately set about strengthening its defenses.

An energetic leader, he also dispatched General William W. LORING along the Tallahatchie River to construct Fort Pemberton and help cover backwater approaches to the city. In December 1862 Pemberton ordered Confederate cavalry under General Earl VAN DORN to raid Union supplies at Holly Springs, Mississippi; the resulting destruction forced General Ulysses S. GRANT to postpone his impending Vicksburg campaign by several months. Pemberton also took measures to defend the city's northern approaches along Chickasaw Bluffs, and he bloodily repelled determined attacks by General William T. SHERMAN. His impressive success seemed to underscore Vicksburg's reputation for being unassailable.

Confederate fortunes declined precipitously in the spring of 1863 when Grant finally launched an attack by passing gunboats under Admiral David D. PORTER below the city, while he marched his army down the west bank of the Mississippi River and crossed it. He had also ordered Union cavalry under Colonel Benjamin H. GRIERSON to conduct a large-scale diversionary raid from Tennessee to Baton Rouge, Louisiana, to confuse the defenders. As anticipated, Pemberton was distracted by Grierson and failed to sortie against Grant in the field. Once General Joseph E. JOHNSTON had been driven from the capital of Jackson, Grant swerved west and attacked Pemberton at Champion's Hill and Big Black River on May 16–17, 1863, routing him. All the while Pemberton was also saddled with conflicting orders: Johnston ordered him to quit the city and save his army while President Davis insisted that he stay and fight. When Pemberton chose the latter course, he was shut up quickly by Grant's besieging forces. His Confederates turned back two strong Union assaults but then endured six weeks of close confinement and heavy bombardment. Faced with starvation, he finally surrendered Vicksburg and 30,000 soldiers unconditionally to Grant on July 4, 1863. He thus became an object of intense loathing in the Southern press despite the fact that, on balance, Pemberton had performed well against steep odds.

Once exchanged, Pemberton never again received a field command, ostensibly because Southern troops, more suspicious than ever of his Northern roots, threatened to mutiny rather than serve under him. He therefore resigned his general's commission and spent the remainder of the war as a lieutenant colonel and ordnance inspector in Richmond. He performed well in this capacity before surrendering with Johnston's army in April 1865. Afterward, Pemberton tried his luck at farming in Virginia and failed, so in 1876 he relocated his family back to Philadelphia. He died in Penllyn, Pennsylvania, on July 13, 1881, a talented and well-meaning military leader, transformed by bad luck into one of the most reviled figures of Confederate history.

Further Reading

Ballard, Michael B. *Vicksburg: The Campaign That Opened the Mississippi.* Chapel Hill: University of North Carolina Press, 2004.

Cotton, Gordon A., and Jeff T. Giambrone. *Vicksburg and the War.* Gretna, La.: Pelican Publishing, 2004.

Heathcote, T. A. *Vicksburg.* London: Brassey's, 2004.

Isbell, Timothy T. *Vicksburg: Sentinels of Stone.* Jackson: University Press of Mississippi, 2006.

Shea, William L., and Terrence J. Winschel. *Vicksburg Is the Key: The Struggle for the Mississippi.* Lincoln: University of Nebraska Press, 2003.

Smith, Timothy B. *Champion Hill: Decisive Battle for Vicksburg.* New York: Savas Beatie, 2005.

Winschel, Terrence J. *Triumph and Defeat: The Vicksburg Campaign.* New York: Savas Beatie, 2004.

Pickett, George E. (1825–1875)

Confederate general

George Edward Pickett was born in Richmond, Virginia, on January 25, 1825, the son of prosperous planters. He briefly read law before gaining admittance to the U.S. Military Academy in 1842. Pickett demonstrated slovenly academics and graduated at the very bottom of his famous class in 1846, alongside future luminaries such as George B. McCLELLAN and Thomas J. JACKSON. Thereafter, he served as a second lieutenant in the 8th U.S. Infantry in the army of General Winfield SCOTT during the advance on Mexico City. Pickett conducted himself bravely at the siege of Veracruz and the battles of Contreras and Churubusco, winning brevet promotions to lieutenant and captain. After performing garrison duty in Texas (1849–56), he shipped off for similar work in Washington Territory. In 1859 Pickett singlehandedly confronted three British warships contesting American possession of San Juan Island with only his company of infantry. War was averted through diplomacy, but he emerged as a national hero and was placed in charge of American forces on the island through 1861. When the Civil War erupted that April, he resigned his commission and returned to Virginia as a colonel in the Confederate service.

For many months into the war, Pickett was employed securing the defenses of the Rappahannock region, and, in January 1862, he rose to brigadier general. He then joined General James LONGSTREET's division in time for the Peninsula campaign. Pickett bravely conducted his "Gamecock brigade" at Williamsburg, Fair Oaks, and Gaines's Mill, where he fell severely wounded. Several months of recuperation ensued, but at the instigation of Longstreet, he rose to major general in October 1862. In this capacity, he commanded a division in Longstreet's I Corps at Fredericksburg, acquitting himself well during the bloody business of December 13, 1862. In the spring of 1863, he accompanied Longstreet on his failed campaign in Suffolk, Virginia, and he thus missed the decisive events at Chancellorsville that May. He then advanced with General Robert E. LEE into Pennsylvania in time to fight at Gettysburg. Pickett arrived on the battlefield on the evening of July 2, 1863, and his fresh troops were chosen to spearhead a massive Confederate charge against General George G. MEADE's center along Cemetery Ridge. Southern artillery under General Edward P. ALEXANDER bombarded the Union lines for several hours, unfortunately with little effect, and then Pickett's division advanced alongside that of General James J. Pettigrew and two brigades under General William D. Pender, a total of 15,000 veteran troops. As the men in parade-like fashion crossed a mile-long clearing, they fell under concentrated artillery and rifle fire from General Winfield S. HANCOCK's men, who simply cut them down in droves. A few determined survivors managed to penetrate Union lines briefly before being swept back, and Pickett withdrew with 10,000 casualties. His defeat, commonly regarded as "Pickett's Charge," is generally acknowledged as the high tide of Confederate military fortunes.

Defeat did not diminish Pickett's reputation as a fighting commander, and in the spring of 1864, he assumed command of the Department of Virginia and North Carolina. Thus disposed, he made a failed attempt to capture New Bern, North Carolina, from Union forces. He also gained considerable notoriety by summarily hanging 22 Southern deserters captured in Union uniforms. Thereafter

Confederate general George E. Pickett *(Library of Congress)*

Pickett returned to Virginia, and he helped bottle up the Union Army of the James under General Benjamin F. BUTLER at Bermuda Hundred in May 1864. He then apparently suffered from a spell of what would be diagnosed today as combat fatigue and was replaced by General Pierre G. T. BEAUREGARD. After recovering, Pickett was posted on the extreme right of the Confederate siege lines at Petersburg, where, on March 31, 1865, he masterfully repulsed a determined attack by Federal cavalry under General Philip H. SHERIDAN at Dinwiddie Court House. The next day, April 1, 1865, however, he singularly erred by attending a shad bake several miles to the rear with General Fitzhugh LEE, just as Sheridan renewed his assault at Five Forks. Deprived of leadership, Confederate defenses buckled, and Lee was forced to abandon Richmond hastily to escape encirclement. Pickett saw additional fighting at Sayler's Creek on April 6, 1865; then Lee finally relieved him of command. He surrendered at Appomattox Court House with the main army three days later.

Pickett fled to Canada after the war to avoid prosecution for executing the Confederate deserters. Declining an invitation to serve in the armies of the khedive of Egypt, he returned to Virginia under a general amnesty and entered the insurance industry. Pickett also engaged in a lengthy written battle to clear his reputation and openly blamed General Lee for the destruction of his division at Gettysburg. He died in Norfolk, Virginia, on October 25, 1875, an unquestionably brave officer, yet indelibly associated with two of the worst defeats in Confederate military history.

Further Reading

Alexander, Robert. *Five Forks: Waterloo of the Confederacy: A Civil War Narrative.* East Lansing: Michigan State University Press, 2003.

Gordon, Lesley J. *General George Pickett in Life and Legend.* Chapel Hill: University of North Carolina Press, 1998.

Hess, Earl J. *Pickett's Charge—The Last Attack at Gettysburg.* Chapel Hill: University of North Carolina Press, 2001.

Robbins, James S. *Last in Their Class: Custer, Pickett, and the Goats of West Point.* New York: Encounter Books, 2006.

Rollins, Richard, ed. *Pickett's Charge: Eyewitness Accounts at Gettysburg.* Mechanicsburg, Pa.: Stackpole Books, 2005.

Wert, Jeffrey D. *Gettysburg: Day Three.* New York: Simon and Schuster, 2001.

Pillow, Gideon J. (1806–1878)
Confederate general

Gideon Johnson Pillow was born in Williamson, Tennessee, on June 8, 1806, into a family of planters. After graduating from the University of Tennessee in 1827, he studied law and was admitted to the state bar three years later. Pillow, adept as an attorney and a Democratic Party operative, also developed an interest in politics and struck up a successful partnership with fellow lawyer James K. Polk. He played a direct role in securing the party nomination for Polk in 1844, and, two years later, President Polk appointed Pillow a brigadier general of volunteers for the ongoing Mexican War. He initially served as part of General Zachary Taylor's army in Texas, but the general declined to employ his troops. Pillow then transferred to General Winfield SCOTT's army during the campaign to Mexico City, where he composed several letters criticizing his Whig commander for the president's consideration. In fact, Pillow regarded himself as Polk's personal representative. Scott disliked Pillow in kind, especially after he botched his first combat assignment at Cerro Gordo on April 17, 1847. He nonetheless used political connections to secure promotion to major general and turned in respectable performances at Contreras, Churubusco, and Chapultepec, where he was wounded. However, Pillow used poor judgment by anonymously publishing critical essays about Scott in the *New Orleans Daily Delta,* whereupon he was arrested and court-martialed for insubordination. Pillow, ably defended by John C. BRECKINRIDGE, was eventually cleared of all charges, but the affair sullied his reputation. After the war, he returned to Tennessee to resume delving into politics.

A staunch Democratic, Pillow did not favor secession and worked to moderate calls for separation. He remained loyal to the Union until Tennessee seceded in the spring of 1861, whereupon Governor Isham G. Harris appointed him a major general of state forces. President Jefferson DAVIS, never previously impressed by Pillow's ability as a soldier, allowed him to become a brigadier general in the Confederate service the following July. In this capacity, he reported for service under General Leonidas POLK in the western part of the state. There, Pillow eagerly sought to invade nearby Kentucky and seize it for the Confederacy, which he accomplished on September 4, 1861, by occupying and fortifying Columbus. The move was roundly condemned by the Kentucky state legislature, heretofore neutral, which then threw its support behind the Union. On November 7, 1861, Pillow next fought under Polk at the Battle of Belmont, Missouri, in which Federal troops under General Ulysses S. GRANT were defeated and forced back to Illinois. His performance here seemed to enhance his military reputation, and in February 1862, Pillow received command of strategic Fort Donelson on the Cumberland River.

In the spring of 1862, the aggressive Grant set his sights on Forts Henry and Donelson to open up a waterborne invasion of the Confederate heartland. On February 6, 1862, a Union gunboat flotilla under Captain Andrew H. FOOTE cowed Fort Henry into submission as Grant prepared to march overland to Pillow's position at Fort Donelson. Grant knew Pillow from their Mexican War days and thoroughly despised him. Worse, on February 13, 1862, Pillow also was superseded by General John B. FLOYD just as the fort was being surrounded by Grant's forces. The two Confederate leaders bickered about what to do next, and Pillow prevailed on both Floyd and General Simon B. Buckner to cut their way through Union siege lines and escape. On February 15, 1862, the Confederates accomplished exactly that and were on the verge of escaping when Pillow inexplicably lost his nerve and ordered the men back to the fort! Grant then promptly sealed the defenders off

within their works. At a council of war held that evening, both Pillow and Floyd elected to abandon their command and leave Buckner to surrender the fort. Colonel Nathan B. FORREST was so disgusted by such wanton cowardice that he galloped his cavalry regiment through Union lines and escaped. On December 16, 1862, Buckner surrendered 15,000 badly needed troops to Grant, opening up an invasion route that ultimately spelled doom for the Confederacy.

President Davis was appreciably livid when he was apprised of what Pillow and Floyd had done, and both were summarily relieved. A court of inquiry found the former guilty of "grave errors of judgment," but he was eventually restored to command a brigade in the division of his old friend General Breckinridge. He then fought at the bloody Battle of Murfreesboro on January 2, 1863, performing adequately. The government next reassigned him as superintendent of the Conscript Bureau for Alabama, Mississippi, and Tennessee. Pillow ran his department with an iron fist and ruthlessly rounded up thousands of new soldiers. In March 1864 he requested command of a cavalry force to protect the iron and coal regions of central Alabama from marauding Union raiders, but he mishandled several encounters that summer and was relieved a second time. Pillow ended the war as commissary general of prisoners, and he surrendered to Union authorities at Montgomery on May 5, 1865.

The postwar period found Pillow a ruined man, and despite resumption of his successful law career in Memphis, he was overwhelmed by debts in 1876 and relocated to Lee County, Arkansas, to escape them. He lived there for several years as a subsistence farmer until his death in Helena on October 8, 1878. Pillow's command of Confederate forces had been rather brief, overall, but his tenure manifested disastrous consequences for the South.

Further Reading

Cooling, Benjamin F. "Lew Wallace and Gideon Pillow: Enigmas and Variations on an American Theme." *Lincoln Herald* 84 (1981): 651–658.

Gott, Kendall D. *Where the South Lost the War: An Analysis of the Fort Henry–Fort Donelson Campaign, February 1862.* Mechanicsburg, Pa.: Stackpole Books, 2003.

Hughes, Nathaniel C., and Roy P. Stonesifer. *The Life and Wars of Gideon J. Pillow.* Chapel Hill: University of North Carolina Press, 1993.

Roberts, Donald J. "Belmont: Grant's First Battle." *Military Heritage* 2, no. 6 (2001): 40–49.

Symonds, Craig, et al. "Who Were the Worst Ten Generals?" *North & South* 7, no. 3 (2004): 12–25.

Tucker, Spencer C. *"Unconditional Surrender": The Captures of Forts Henry and Donelson.* Abilene, Tex.: McWhiney Foundation, 2001.

Pleasonton, Alfred (1824–1897)

Union general

Alfred Pleasonton was born in Washington, D.C., on June 7, 1824, the son of President James Monroe's personal secretary. He matriculated at the U.S. Military Academy in 1840 and graduated near the top of his class four years later. Pleasonton then served as a second lieutenant in the 2nd U.S. Dragoons and served a number of frontier and garrison assignments. During the Mexican War, he accompanied the army of General Zachary Taylor and won a brevet promotion for gallantry at the battles of Palo Alto and Resaca de la Palma in 1846. Afterward, he remained with his regiment in the New Mexico Territory, rising there to adjutant. He advanced to captain in 1855 and served under General William S. Harney through a number of Indian conflicts in Florida, Kansas, Oregon, and Washington Territory. Following the onset of the Civil War in April 1861, he helped conduct his regiment, renamed the 2nd U.S. Cavalry, from Utah to Washington, D.C. Pleasonton became a major in the spring of 1862, fought capably in General George B. McLellan's Peninsula campaign, and won promotion to brigadier general of volunteers as of July. In this capacity, he rendered additional useful services at Second Manassas, South Mountain, and Antietam; while an aggressive leader, he proved less successful at gathering military intelligence.

On May 2, 1863, Pleasonton garnered additional distinction at the Union debacle of Chan-

Union general Alfred Pleasanton *(Library of Congress)*

cellorsville, where he successfully contested the advance of General Thomas J. Jackson's Confederates and rescued the remnants of General Oliver O. Howard's IX Corps. Shortly afterward, General Joseph Hooker appointed him chief of cavalry in the Army of the Potomac to replace the indifferent general George Stoneman. When General Robert E. Lee commenced his second invasion of the North that June, Pleasonton was dispatched to locate his whereabouts and report. On June 9, 1863, his troopers under Generals John Buford and Hugh J. Kilpatrick surprised the vaunted Confederate cavalry of General J. E. B. Stuart in camp at Brandy Station and nearly defeated them. Union forces ultimately relinquished the field, but the action served notice that Pleasonton's vigorous leadership had rendered his cavalry a force to reckon with. On June 22, 1863, he advanced to major general of volunteers and next performed valuable services throughout the three-day engagement at Gettysburg (July 1–3, 1863). Pleasonton again aggressively engaged his Southern counterparts but generally failed to distinguish himself in an intelligence-gathering capacity.

As an officer, Pleasonton was personally fearless, outspoken, and possessed a unique flair for self-promotion in the news media. His career entered a new phase after March 1864 when he publicly criticized the conduct of General George G. MEADE before the Joint Congressional Committee on the Conduct of the War—and he immediately found himself transferred to the nether regions. Pleasonton landed in the remote Department of Missouri as cavalry commander under General William S. ROSECRANS. He arrived in time to contest a large Confederate offensive under General Sterling PRICE, and he kept Price from capturing the capital of Jefferson City (October 8–22). Pleasonton then worked closely with Union forces under General Samuel R. CURTIS to corner Price at Westport, Missouri, where, in a series of battles along the Little Blue, Big Blue, and Marais des Cygnes rivers, the Southerners were defeated soundly and driven back to Arkansas. More damage might have been inflicted on Price had Pleasonton and Curtis not quarreled over the victory and mounted an effective pursuit. He nevertheless received additional brevets to brigadier and major general in the regular army for his fine service.

In the postwar period, Pleasonton reverted back to his lineal rank of lieutenant colonel in the 20th U.S. Infantry, where he resented serving under officers whom he had previously commanded. He resigned his commission in January 1868 and accepted several low-level positions within the federal government. In 1870 he briefly served as commissioner of Internal Revenue, and from 1872 to 1874, he served as president of the Cincinnati and Terre Haute Railroad. Pleasonton died in Washington, D.C., on February 17, 1897, a capable combat leader and the individual most responsible for improving the performance and morale of the cavalry in the Army of the Potomac.

Under his tenure, Federal troopers were able to meet Confederate cavalry on equal terms for the first time in the war.

Further Reading

Crouch, Richard E. *Brandy Station: A Battle Like No Other.* Westminster, Md.: Willow Bend Books, 2002.

Longacre, Edward G. "The Knight of Romance." *Civil War Times Illustrated* 13, no. 8 (1974): 10–23.

———. *Lincoln's Cavalrymen: A History of the Mounted Forces of the Army of the Potomac, 1861–1865.* Mechanicsburg, Pa.: Stackpole Books, 2000.

McKinney, Joseph W. *Brandy Station, Virginia, June 9, 1863: The Largest Cavalry Battle of the Civil War.* Jefferson, N.C.: McFarland, 2006.

Monnett, Howard N. *Action before Westport, 1864.* Niwot: University Press of Colorado, 1994.

Wittenberg, Eric J. *The Union Cavalry Comes of Age: Hartwood Church to Brandy Station, 1863.* Dulles, Va.: Brassey's, 2005.

Polk, Leonidas (1806–1864)

Confederate general

Leonidas Polk was born in Raleigh, North Carolina, on April 10, 1806, the son of affluent planters. After briefly attending the University of North Carolina, he transferred to the U.S. Military Academy in 1823, where he met and befriended future Confederate leaders Jefferson DAVIS, Joseph E. JOHNSTON, and Albert S. JOHNSTON. While in attendance, Polk came under the sway of the academy chaplain and acquired a profound sense of religiosity. He graduated near the top of his class in 1827 as a second lieutenant of artillery but resigned within a year to pursue religious studies. He next attended the Virginia Theological Seminary and was ordained an Episcopal minister in April 1830. After several years of preaching in Richmond, Polk gained an appointment as bishop of the Southwest, with a circuit that included Louisiana, Alabama, Mississippi, and Arkansas. Charismatic and convivial, he enjoyed considerable success spreading the Episcopal message in this thinly populated region, and, in 1841, he became the first bishop of Louisiana. By this time,

Polk, who had married into a wealthy, slave-owning family, had matured into a fiery Southern nationalist. Polk felt strongly that the South needed its own university to expunge itself of various "Yankee" beliefs and influences. During the years, he therefore collected $500,000 and received a 9,500-acre land grant in Sewanee, Tennessee. On October 9, 1860, he personally laid the cornerstone for what emerged as the University of the South, which finally opened its doors in 1868.

As the secession crisis mounted in the spring of 1861, Polk tendered his services to President Davis, who commissioned him a major general in the Confederate service. He was entrusted with Department No. 2, encompassing western Tennessee, eastern Arkansas, and the Mississippi River throughout that region. But Polk, though ambitious, was neither strategic-minded nor politically astute. On September 4, 1861, he erred grievously by dispatching General Gideon J. PILLOW to seize the heights of Columbus, Kentucky, and deny it to Union forces. This move not only angered the Kentucky government, which up until then had been studiously neutral but also forced them to declare their allegiance to the Federal government. This, in turn, facilitated Union moves to secure the headwaters of the Cumberland and Tennessee rivers, which constituted major invasion routes into the Southern heartland. Such subtleties were totally lost on Polk, who went on to attack and defeat a small Union thrust under General Ulysses S. GRANT at Belmont, Missouri, on November 7, 1861.

After the fall of Forts Henry and Donelson in the spring of 1862, Polk withdrew from Kentucky and joined his former West Point roommate, General Albert S. Johnston, at Corinth, Mississippi. There, he assumed command of the I Corps, Army of Mississippi and bravely conducted affairs on the Southern right wing throughout the bloody encounter of Shiloh in April 1862. He then served under Johnston's successor, General Braxton BRAGG, in the same capacity. However, Polk disliked Bragg intensely, and he soon headed the anti-Bragg faction within the western high command. Nonetheless, on October 8, 1862, Polk behaved competently in the Battle of Perryville, winning promotion to lieutenant general. He next fought at the Confederate defeat of Murfreesboro (December 3, 1862–January 3, 1863), earning scorn from Bragg for allegedly delaying his orders to attack. He fought bravely, however, and at one point mistakenly rode up to the 22nd Indiana Infantry. Polk rather dramatically convinced them that he was actually a Union general; then he spurred his horse and escaped. But command relations with Bragg finally ruptured following the costly Southern victory at Chickamauga on September 19–20, 1863, when Polk was court-martialed for failing to attack as ordered. Polk, meanwhile, used his influence with Davis to undercut Bragg and agitated to have him removed as head of the Army of Tennessee. To maintain peace among his feuding commanders, Davis appointed Polk to succeed General Joseph E. Johnston as head of the Department of Alabama, Mississippi, and East Louisiana.

In January 1864, Polk's Army of Mississippi proved unable to contain a Union offensive by General William T. SHERMAN, which captured Meridian, Mississippi. He then marched east to unite with Johnston's Army of Tennessee in time to oppose the Union march on Atlanta. Polk fought bravely in the various battles that failed to stem the Union advance, and he remained a popular figure with his troops. On June 14, 1864, while reconnoitering Federals positions near Pine Mountain, Georgia, he was struck by a Union cannon shell and killed. Polk, though hailed by his soldiers as the "Fighting Bishop," was at best a marginally competent commander who owed his high rank more to political connections than to ability.

Further Reading

Jones, Wilmer L. *Generals in Blue and Gray.* 2 vols. Westport, Conn.: Praeger, 2004.

Noe, Kenneth. *Perryville: This Grand Havoc of Battle.* Lexington: University Press of Kentucky, 2001.

Roberts, Donald J. "Belmont: Grant's First Battle." *Military Heritage* 2, no. 6 (2001): 40–49.

Robins, Glenn. *The Bishop of the Old South: The Ministry and Civil War Legacy of Leonidas Polk.* Macon, Ga: Mercer University Press, 2006.

Smith, Derek. *The Gallant Dead: Union and Confederate Generals Killed in the Civil War.* Mechanicsburg, Pa.: Stackpole Books, 2005.

Woodworth, Steven E. *No Band of Brothers: Problems in the Rebel High Command.* Columbia: University of Missouri Press, 1999.

Pope, John (1822–1892)

Union general

John Pope was born in Louisville, Kentucky, on March 16, 1822, the son of a judge. He entered the U.S. Military Academy in 1838 and graduated four years later as a second lieutenant in the Topographical Engineers. Pope then conducted survey work along the Canadian border and in Florida before joining the army of General Zachary Taylor in Texas. He subsequently fought well in the Mexican War, winning brevet promotions for bravery at the battles of Monterrey and Buena Vista. He then resumed his survey work on the western frontier, rising to captain in 1856 and serving as chief engineer of the Department of New Mexico. When the Civil War broke out in April 1861, he was performing light-house duty and became one of four army officers chosen to escort President Abraham LINCOLN from Springfield, Illinois, to Washington, D.C. In May 1861 Pope was elevated to the rank of brigadier general of volunteers and assigned to the Department of Missouri. An aggressive officer, he trounced Confederates under General Sterling PRICE at Blackwater on December 18, 1861, seizing 1,200 prisoners. Pope also worked behind the scenes to have the inept general John C. Frémont removed as commander of Missouri. In the spring of 1862, newly arrived general Henry W. HALLECK appointed Pope commander of the Army of the Mississippi with orders to clear Confederate forces out of the region. He then methodically besieged New Madrid, Missouri, taking it on March 14, 1862, before moving on to heavily defended Island No. 10 in the Mississippi River. Here, he worked closely with a gunboat flotilla under Captain Andrew H. FOOTE and cut a canal to allow armed vessels to pass below the island and sever it from the mainland. Consequently. Island No. 10 surrendered along with 3,500 prisoners on April 7, 1862. This victory cleared the upper reaches of the Mississippi to Union navigation as far south as Memphis, Tennessee, and Pope received a well-deserved promotion to major general. His Army of the Mississippi then joined General Ulysses S. GRANT's Army of the Tennessee and General Don C. BUELL's Army of the Ohio in Halleck's campaign against Corinth, Mississippi. Pope's good conduct also caught the attention of President Lincoln, who was anxious to replace the lethargic general George B. McCLELLAN as commander of Union forces in the East. In June 1862 he arrived in the Shenandoah Valley to assume command of the newly created Army of Virginia, succeeding his old nemesis Frémont. But rather then cement cordial relations with officers

Union general John Pope *(National Archives)*

in the Army of the Potomac, he alienated them by bombastically bragging about his victories in the West.

In August 1861, Pope commanded 70,000 men and began a cautious campaign against Richmond, Virginia. His advance was supposed to be supported by McClellan, still smarting over his recent removal from command and whose cooperation proved sullen. General Robert E. LEE used their unsynchronized movements to his advantage by dispatching half of his force under General Thomas J. JACKSON on a raid around Pope's right flank. On August 27, 1862, Jackson stormed into Pope's supply base at Manchester, Virginia, and then dug in and awaited the Union riposte. Pope, thinking that he had Jackson trapped, moved most of his army up to the old Manassas battlefield and began to attack his outnumbered adversary. He was unaware that Lee had dispatched the other half of his army under General James LONGSTREET through Thoroughfare Gap, which completely flanked the Union position. On August 29–30, 1862, while Pope contented himself with piecemeal attacks against Jackson's line, Longstreet suddenly lunged and began to roll up the Union line. Pope's forces recovered from their initial surprise and fell back in good order, heavily repelling an attack by Jackson at Chantilly on September 1, 1862. But another Union army had been humbled by Lee, and President Lincoln was forced to relieve Pope from command. Before leaving, he fixed the blame for his defeat squarely on General Fitz John PORTER, a McClellan ally, and likewise had him removed from command and cashiered. The Army of Virginia was then dissolved and command reverted back to General McClellan.

Thoroughly disgraced, Pope was reassigned to the Department of the Northwest, where he helped suppress an uprising by the Santee Sioux under Little Crow. In January 1865 he assumed command of the Department of the Mississippi while the rank of major general was conferred two months later. Pope subsequently served a stint in reconstruction duty in Alabama, Georgia, and Florida, where he championed civil rights for for-

mer African-American slaves. He then returned to the western frontier where, during the next two decades, he gradually rehabilitated his military reputation as an outstanding administrator. In this capacity, Pope, like Generals George CROOK, Benjamin H. GRIERSON, and Oliver O. HOWARD argued for better treatment of Native Americans to keep the peace and excoriated the graft and corruption of the Indian Bureau. He retired as commander of the Department of California in March 1886 and died at Sandusky, Ohio, on September 23, 1892. Pope was an effective military figure whose skill at bureaucracy always outdistanced his combat abilities.

Further Reading
Cozzens, Peter. *General John Pope: A Life for the Nation.* Urbana: University of Illinois Press, 2000.
———. "Roadblock on the Mississippi." *Civil War Times Illustrated* 41, no. 1 (2002): 40–49.
Cozzens, Peter, and Robert I. Girardi, eds. *The Military Memoirs of General John Pope.* Chapel Hill: University of North Carolina Press, 1998.
Langellier, John P. *Second Manassas, 1862: Robert E. Lee's Greatest Victory.* Westport, Conn.: Praeger, 2004.
Martin, David G. *The Second Bull Run Campaign, July–August 1862.* Cambridge, Mass.: Da Capo Press, 2001.
Shur, Robert C. "Cracking the Nut of Island No. 10." *Military Heritage* 7, no. 1 (2005): 64–71, 77.

Porter, David D. (1813–1891)
Union admiral

David Dixon Porter was born in Chester, Pennsylvania, on June 8, 1813, a son of Commodore David Porter, a naval hero of the War of 1812. His eminent family included foster brother David G. FARRAGUT, the future admiral, while his cousin Fitz John PORTER was a noted general. Porter went to sea at an early age with his father and was educated indifferently. He followed his father into the Mexican navy in 1826, being wounded and captured by Spanish forces. In 1829 he finally joined the U.S. Navy as a midshipman and completed several Mediterranean cruises. Promotion was slow, however, and Porter was only a lieutenant when the Mexican War broke out in 1846. He nonetheless distinguished himself onboard the steamer *Spitfire* and led a naval detachment that captured the town of Tabasco in June 1847. He remained barely employed during the postwar period and nearly quit the service to engage in merchant ship enterprises. Porter was reinstated to active status in 1855 and commanded the USS *Supply* to bring camels to Texas at the behest of Secretary of War Jefferson DAVIS. After 1857, he served as commandant of the Portsmouth, New Hampshire, Navy Yard, remaining there until 1861. After serving almost two decades as a lieutenant, Porter was ready to leave the navy altogether until the onset of the Civil War in April convinced him to remain in the service.

No sooner had the firing commenced than Porter, a highly aggressive, enterprising personality with considerable skill at self-promotion, advanced a bold scheme for the relief of Fort Pickens, Florida. When President Abraham LINCOLN personally approved of the plan, Porter, accompanied by Captain Montgomery C. MEIGS, sailed with the USS *Powhatan* and successfully reinforced the garrison there. En route, he ignored recall signals from Secretary of the Navy Gideon Welles, who had not been privy to the planning, and thereafter he distrusted Porter intensely. Nonetheless Porter rose to commander as of August 1861, and now part of the West Gulf Coast Blockading Squadron, he threw himself energetically into planning the capture of New Orleans, Louisiana. Moreover, he played a crucial role in convincing the government to assign his Southern-born foster brother, Farragut, to orchestrate the campaign. In April 1862 Porter led 20 mortar boats that helped bombard Forts St. Philip and Jackson into submission two days after New Orleans fell to Farragut. After receiving the thanks of Congress, Porter accompanied his brother up the Mississippi River to Vicksburg, Mississippi, which would occupy his attention for more than a year. In October 1862 he also succeeded Admiral Charles H. DAVIS as head of the Mississippi River Squadron, and he was pro-

Union admiral David D. Porter *(Library of Congress)*

moted acting rear admiral over the heads of 80 more senior officers. The headstrong Porter also worked closely with two other forceful personalities, Generals William T. SHERMAN and Ulysses S. GRANT, in the campaigns that followed, establishing a splendid precedent for combined operations in the war.

In January 1863 Porter gave naval support to General John A. McClernand's campaign against Fort Hindman, Arkansas, in another display of joint operations. But his greatest contribution came on April 16, 1863, when he ran his squadron past the batteries of Vicksburg and subsequently transported Grant's army across the Mississippi River to Bruinsburg, effectively sealing that city's fate. The following May, he pushed his gunboats up the narrow confines of the Yazoo River onto Steele's Bayou, forcing the Confederates to abandon several forts and scuttle three unfinished ironclads. Returning to the Mississippi, he next took up bombardment positions around Vicksburg, then besieged by Grant, and contributed to its discomfiture. General John C. PEMBERTON finally surrendered the city on July 4, 1863, and Porter received the thanks of Congress and official promotion to rear admiral.

In the spring of 1864, Porter accompanied General Nathaniel C. BANKS on his ill-fated Red River expedition into western Louisiana. His fleet was continually compromised by Bank's blundering and by declining water levels that nearly grounded all shipping. Only the timely intercession of Colonel Joseph Bailey, who constructed wing dams across the river, enabled Porter's command to run the Alexandria Rapids and escape intact. That fall, he assumed command of the North Atlantic Blockading Squadron and was tasked with capturing Fort Fisher, Wilmington, North Carolina. He had marshalled the largest naval squadron ever assembled in American history—120 vessels—but was thwarted when General Benjamin F. BUTLER ineptly handled the landing and withdrew in December 1864. Porter angrily persuaded superiors to grant him a second attempt, this time in concert with the infinitely more capable General Alfred H. TERRY. On January 15, 1865, Porter pushed his vessels in close support and covered Terry's troops as they successfully overran Fort Fisher, shutting the Confederacy's sole remaining port. Porter spent the final weeks of the war directing the Potomac River flotilla in concert with General Grant, and he forced Admiral Raphael SEMMES to scuttle his vessels. He was also on hand to greet President Lincoln while he toured Richmond shortly before the war ended in April 1865.

Porter was retained in the postwar establishment, and in August 1865 he became superintendent of the U.S. Naval Academy at Annapolis, Maryland. His tenure there was highly constructive, and he modernized the curricula and increased the emphasis on professionalism. He rose to vice admiral in July 1866, and as special adviser to the secretary of war under President Grant, he virtually ran the entire navy. Porter was promoted to full admiral following the death of

Farragut in 1870, becoming senior officer and only the second individual to hold that rank. He spent the next two decades actively employed on various boards until his death in Washington, D.C., on February 13, 1891. Brash, abrasive, and somewhat prone to political plotting, Porter was the most significant naval officer of the Civil War after Farragut.

Further Reading

Fonvielle, Chris E. *The Wilmington Campaign: Last Departing Rays of Hope.* Mechanicsburg, Pa.: Stackpole Books, 2001.

Fuller, Howard. *Navies and Naval Operations of the Civil War, 1861–65.* London: Conway Marine, 2005.

Hearn, Chester. *David Dixon Porter: The Civil War Years.* Annapolis, Md.: Naval Institute Press, 1998.

Joiner, Gary D. *Mr. Lincoln's Brown Water Navy: The Mississippi Squadron.* Lanham, Md.: Rowman & Littlefield, 2007.

McCaslin, Richard B. *The Last Stronghold: The Campaign for Fort Fisher.* Abilene, Tex.: McWhiney Foundation, 2003.

Porter, David D. *Incidents and Anecdotes of the Civil War.* New York: D. Appleton, 1885.

Roberts, William H. *Now for the Contest: Coastal and Oceanic Naval Operations in the Civil War.* Lincoln: University of Nebraska Press, 2004.

Stokes, David M. "Wherever the Sand Is Damp: Union Naval Operations in the Red River Campaign, 12 March–22 May 1864." *North Louisiana History* 34, no. 1 (2003): 45–65.

Porter, Fitz John (1822–1901)

Union general

Fitz John Porter was born in Portsmouth, New Hampshire, on August 31, 1822, the son of a U.S. Navy officer and cousin of the future admiral David D. PORTER. He passed through the prestigious Exeter Academy before gaining admission to the U.S. Military Academy in 1841, and he graduated near the top of his class four years later. Porter then served as a second lieutenant in the 4th U.S. Artillery at various posts along the western frontier before joining the army of General Winfield SCOTT during the Mexican War. He fought exceedingly well at Molino del Rey and Chapultepec in 1847, winning two brevet promotions to captain. Afterward, he returned to West Point as an instructor while also serving as adjutant to Superintendent Robert E. LEE. Porter subsequently transferred to Fort Leavenworth, Kansas, to serve as adjutant general in the Department of the West, and in 1859 he accompanied the Mormon expedition of Colonel Albert S. JOHNSTON. In early 1861, when secession and civil war seemed inevitable, Porter accepted a secret mission to remove Federal troops and stores from Texas, and he relocated five artillery batteries in the process. He then gained promotion to colonel of the 15th U.S. Infantry in May 1861, rising to brigadier general of volunteers a few days later. Porter also rendered impressive service in the Department of Pennsylvania, where he quickly raised, trained, and equipped 30 regiments for active service in short order. His excellent performance brought him to the attention of General George B. MCCLELLAN, who granted him command of a division in General Samuel P. Heintzelman's III Corps. Porter reciprocated by becoming an intensely partisan supporter of McClellan in the charged political atmosphere surrounding the Union high command.

McClellan commenced his long awaited Peninsula campaign in the spring of 1862, and Porter efficiently directed the siege of Yorktown. He then assumed command of the V Corps during the ill-fated drive on Richmond, Virginia. After some awkward maneuvering by McClellan, the V Corps was left stranded on the north bank of the rain-swollen Chickahominy River and thus became the object of General Robert E. LEE's new offensive. On June 26–27, 1862, Porter was attacked by larger numbers of Confederates at Mechanicsville and Gaines's Mill, but he nevertheless pummeled his opponents with heavy losses and withdrew in good order. After joining McClellan's main force, he conducted the tactical defense at Malvern Hill on July 1, 1862, whereby Lee was repulsed with horrific casualties and the Union army safely fell back to Harrison's Landing. For his stirring battlefield performance, Porter received promotion to

major general of volunteers and brigadier general in the regular army.

McClellan's lack of aggressive leadership resulted in his replacement by General John POPE in July 1862. Porter, as a firm supporter of his former commander, came to despise Pope as a braggart and impolitically criticized him in public. Pope returned such disdain in kind toward all McClellan supporters, which undermined unity of command in the newly organized Army of Virginia. On August 28, 1862, Porter found himself arrayed against General Thomas J. JACKSON's Confederates on the old battlefield of Bull Run. From his position on the far left of the Union line, he was ordered by Pope to turn Jackson's flank and attack his rear, but Porter became alarmed at the approach of Southern reinforcements under General James LONGSTREET. He thereby disobeyed orders and held his ground, keeping Longstreet in check for the time being. On August 30, 1862, Porter again received direct orders from Pope to

Union general Fitz John Porter *(Library of Congress)*

attack Jackson—which he promptly obeyed—and then the entire Union army collapsed when Longstreet finally advanced. Pope had no recourse but to withdraw, and he blamed his defeat on officers still loyal to McClellan. He specifically charged Porter with insubordination in the face of the enemy, and a court-martial was summoned. Porter countered by stating that, by holding Longstreet at bay as long as he did, he saved the entire army from destruction.

Porter remained with V Corps for the next three months after McClellan was restored to command, although he was lightly engaged. In November 1862 he was formally relieved of command and arrested. Porter's trial commenced on January 21, 1863, during which he was convicted by a board of Radical Republican officers closely aligned with Pope. Porter was then summarily cashiered from the service, and the Army of the Potomac lost, through political infighting, one of its finest combat officers. Porter spent the next 16 years of his life seeking official vindication, and in 1878, a board headed by General John M. SCHOFIELD finally recommended exoneration. It was not until 1882 that President Chester A. Arthur remitted the dishonorable part of Porter's sentence, and four years later, an act of Congress reinstated him as a colonel on the retired list. Porter, meanwhile, had flourished in a variety of civilian positions in New York and New Jersey. At one point, the khedive of Egypt offered him command of his entire army, but he declined. Porter died in Morristown, New Jersey, on May 21, 1901. He was a capable soldier whose indiscrete behavior cost him what might have been an outstanding Civil War career.

Further Reading

Anders, Curt. *Injustice of Trial: Second Bull Run. General Fitz John Porter's Courtmartial and the Schofield Board Investigation That Restored His Good Name.* Zionsville, Ind.: Guild Press/Emmis, 2002.

Haydock, Michael D. "The Court-Martial of Fitz John Porter." *American History* 33, no. 6 (1999): 48–57.

Langellier, John P. *Second Manassas, 1862: Robert E. Lee's Greatest Victory.* Westport, Conn.: Praeger, 2004.

Martin, David G. *The Second Bull Run Campaign, July–August, 1862.* Cambridge, Mass.: Da Capo Press, 2001.

Porter, Fitz John. *General Fitz John Porter's Statement of Services of the Fifth Army Corps, in 1862, in Northern Virginia.* New York: Evening Post Steam Presses, 1878.

Sears, Stephen W. "The Case of Fitz John Porter." *MHQ* 5, no. 3 (1993): 70–79.

Price, Sterling (1809–1867)
Confederate general

Sterling Price was born in Prince Edward County, Virginia, on September 20, 1809, the son of wealthy, slave-owning planters. He attended Hampton Sidney College before accompanying his family to Missouri, where he established himself as a wealthy tobacco planter and merchant. Success whetted Price's appetite for politics, and he served several terms in the state legislature before successfully standing for a congressional seat in 1844. He resigned in 1846 to fight in the Mexican War as colonel of the 2nd Missouri Infantry, which formed part of General Stephen W. Kearny's column. Price performed well in various duties and effectively subdued a revolt by Pueblo Indians in New Mexico in 1847. The following year, he led an expedition into northern Mexico, capturing the town of Chihuahua and winning promotion to brigadier general. His men, to whom Price paid particular attention, christened him "Old Pap." Back home, Price parleyed his wartime popularity into political success by being elected governor (1853–57). As the storm clouds of secession grew in 1860, he served as president of a state convention tasked with addressing this divisive issue. Price opposed secession, and he helped defeat the measure by a 69 to 1 vote. The dynamic events changed dramatically when pro-Union officer captain Nathaniel LYON seized pro-Southern militia at Camp Jackson on May 10, 1861, whereupon Price and thousands of Missourians declared for the Confederacy. Governor Claiborne F. Jackson subsequently appointed Price a major general commanding the militia, or

Confederate general Sterling Price *(Library of Congress)*

State Guard, and both men negotiated a peace pact with General William S. Harney on May 21, 1861, to keep Union forces out of Missouri. When Lyon and Congressman Francis P. Blair subsequently arranged for Haney's dismissal, Price and Claiborne met with them in St. Louis to forestall further violence on June 11, 1861, but Lyon angrily stormed out of the meeting, vowing to crush the rebellion.

Lyon quickly chased Price's ill-armed militia out of Jefferson City, and he was pursued by General Franz SIGEL, whom he repulsed at Carthage, Missouri, on July 5, 1861. Price continued falling back into northern Arkansas until reinforced by Confederates forces under General Ben McCULLOCH and marched back. Lyon, though outnumbered, attacked the secessionist forces at Wilson's Creek on August 10, 1861, and he was killed. Price followed up this victory by seizing a Union garrison at nearby Lexington, Missouri, on September 20, 1861, taking 3,000 prisoners and a large store of supplies. But a popular uprising failed to materialize, and Price gradually gave ground before a larger army under General John C. Frémont and returned to Arkansas. It was not until the spring of 1862 that he joined forces with McCulloch and General Earl VAN DORN and attacked the smaller army of General Samuel R. CURTIS at Pea Ridge/Elkhorn Tavern, on March 6–7. Federal troops prevailed, McCulloch was killed, and Price was wounded, leaving southern Missouri and northern Arkansas under Union control. In April 1862 Price rose to major general in the Confederate service and led a division of Missourians to assist General Pierre G. T. BEAUREGARD in Mississippi. Price then waged an inclusive battle against General William S. ROSECRANS at Iuka on September 19, 1862, and he was bested again at Corinth on October 3–4, 1862. Price, disgusted with Van Dorn, then ventured to Richmond, Virginia, to confer with President Jefferson DAVIS. There, he prevailed on Davis, who always suspected his loyalty, to allow him to return to the Trans-Mississippi Department and retake Missouri for the Confederacy.

In the summer of 1863, Price served in the Department of Arkansas under aged general Theophilus Holmes. Together, they waged an ill-considered attack on General Benjamin M. Prentiss at Helena on July 4, 1863, and they were badly repulsed. Price's attempt to hold Pine Bluff was also defeated on October 25, 1863. The following year, he found himself yielding ground before a large Union force under General Frederick Steele, then marching to join the Red River expedition of General Nathaniel C. BANKS. Once reinforced by the Confederates of General Edmund KIRBY-SMITH, Price halted Steele at Camden, Arkansas, pursued him as far as Jenkin's Ferry, and attacked his rear guard unsuccessfully on April 30, 1864. However, the western theater was being depleted of Union troops to support war efforts farther east, and Kirby-Smith dispatched Price on his long-sought invasion of Missouri.

Price, assisted by General Joseph O. SHELBY, assembled a force of 12,000 volunteers in September 1864 and crossed the state line into Missouri. However, nearly one-third of his men were unarmed, and most of them were poorly trained. Worse, the thousands of Missourians he expected to flock to his colors failed to materialize. Price then marched his ragtag ensemble and waged a costly encounter at Pilot's Knob on September 27, 1864, failing to capture either the Union garrison or its arms. Losses here compelled him to bypass St. Louis altogether, and on October 8, 1864, he halted outside Jefferson City before a large garrison under General Alfred PLEASONTON. Price's column was finally brought to bay on October 23, 1864, at Westport, Missouri, which the combined forces of Curtis and Pleasonton nearly destroyed. He then executed a hasty withdrawal through Kansas and back into Arkansas, covered by Shelby's cavalry. Price's dreams for conquering his home state for the Confederacy vanished, and after the war ended, he fled to Mexico.

In April 1865 Price offered his services to Emperor Maximilian and sought to encourage a Confederate colony. Illness and the collapse of the Mexican regime forced him back to St. Louis two years later, where he eked out a marginal existence. Price died there on September 29, 1867, a major and largely ineffective player in the Civil War's western theater.

Further Reading

Adams, George R. *General William S. Harney: Prince of Dragoons.* Lincoln: University of Nebraska Press, 2001.

DeBlack, Thomas R. *With Fire and Sword: Arkansas, 1861–1874.* Fayetteville: University of Arkansas Press, 2003.

Eakin, Joanne C. *The Battle of Independence, 11 August, 1862.* Independence, Mo.: Two Trails Pub., 2000.

Forsyth, Michael J. *The Camden Expedition of 1864 and the Opportunity Lost by the Confederacy to Change the War.* Jefferson, N.C.: McFarland, 2003.

Gerteis, Louis S. *Civil War St. Louis.* Lawrence: University Press of Kansas, 2001.

Hatcher, Richard W. *Wilson's Creek: The Second Battle of the Civil War and the Men Who Fought It.* Chapel Hill: University of North Carolina Press, 2000.

Monnett, Howard N. *Action before Westport, 1864.* Niwot: University Press of Colorado, 1995.

Quantrill, William C. (1837–1865)

Confederate guerrilla

William Clarke Quantrill was born in Dover, Ohio, on July 31, 1837, the son of a schoolteacher. Intelligent and well educated, he taught school for many years before relocating to the frontiers of Kansas around 1857. There, he degenerated into a life of debauchery under the assumed name of "Charlie Hart" and became adept at horse theft, gambling, and drinking. These activities blended into the turmoil of "Bloody Kansas," where pro- and antislavery factions staged numerous and invariably bloody confrontations. Quantrill initially joined a group of antislavery "Jayhawkers," and he plundered several proslavery camps and households until he was accused of stealing from his own men. He thereupon changed sides and became a Southern "bushwhacker" as an outlet for his sociopathic behavior. When the Civil War broke out in April 1861, it ushered in a period of intense lawlessness throughout Kansas and neighboring Missouri. Quantrill wasted no time aligning with the Confederacy, and his bandit gang assisted General Sterling PRICE in the capture of Lexington, Missouri, on September 20, 1861. Then he and many frontier ruffians resumed their killing and robbing spree, which induced General Henry W. HALLECK to issue General Order No. 32, stipulating that all parties caught engaging in such activity could expect summary execution. Such decrees provided little more than amusement to men of Quantrill's ilk; as exponents of hit-and-run tactics, most were never caught.

In August 1862 Quantrill was commissioned a captain in the Confederate service through the Partisan Ranger Act, despite unease over his unsavory reputation. In time, his command grew to 450 men, which included William "Bloody Bill" ANDERSON, Cole Younger, and Frank and Jesse James. As the ruthlessness of these men grew, Federal authorities responded in kind by arresting entire communities of suspected sympathizers and burning their homes. At one point, a derelict prison housing several prisoners—including Anderson's sister—collapsed, killing several inmates. Quantrill used the incident as a convenient pretext to extract gruesome revenge. On August 21, 1863, he led his men on a raid against Lawrence, Kansas, a known abolitionist center. Rounding up of men and boys, he executed 200 prisoners in cold blood, robbed the bank, and burned the entire town. This single act helped define Quantrill as the Civil War's most infamous guerrilla. "No fiend in human shape could have acted with more barbarity," an exasperated governor Thomas Carney exclaimed. General Thomas E. Ewing, under intense political pressure from Jayhawkers and Radical Republicans, then issued General Order No. 11, which led to the evacuation of four entire counties suspected of aiding the rebels.

On October 6, 1863, Quantrill again struck terror into his opponents by ambushing General James G. Blunt's mounted escort at Baxter Springs, Kansas, killing more than 100 Union soldiers and noncombatants in cold blood. But fate then intervened when his group, apparently dissatisfied by Quantrill's leadership, splintered into several small groups. Quantrill himself maintained a low profile for nearly a year until the fall of 1864, when he recruited a new band and began to raid in Kentucky. Union general John M. Palmer then recruited the noted Jayhawker, Captain Edward Terrill, to track down and eliminate the elusive raider. On May 10, 1865, Terrill accomplished exactly that, wounding and capturing Quantrill in a surprise raid at Taylorsville, Kentucky. The former guerrilla lingered for nearly a month in prison at Louisville before dying on June 6, 1865. Thus perished an individual universally reviled as the "bloodiest man in American history." Ironically, his legacy of brutality lived on in the postwar period in the actions of several outlaws who learned their bloody trade on the frontiers of Civil War Missouri.

Further Reading

Bird, Roy. *Civil War in Kansas*. Gretna, La.: Pelican Publishing, 2004.

Gilmore, Donald L. *Civil War on the Missouri-Kansas Border*. Gretna, La.: Pelican Publishing, 2005.

Mackey, Robert R. *The Uncivil War: Irregular Warfare in the Upper South, 1861–1865*. Norman: University of Oklahoma Press, 2004.

Nichols, Bruce. *Guerrilla Warfare in Civil War Missouri, 1863*. Jefferson, N.C.: McFarland, 2006.

Petersen, Paul R. *Quantrill of Missouri: The Making of a Guerrilla Warrior*. Nashville, Tenn.: Cumberland House, 2003.

Woodiel, Loftin C. "William C. Quantrill, Deviant or Hero?" Unpublished Ph.D. diss., St. Louis University, 2000.

R

Reynolds, John F. (1820–1863)

Union general

John Fulton Reynolds was born in Lancaster, Pennsylvania, on September 20, 1820, the son of a newspaper editor. After attending local academies, he gained admittance to the U.S. Military Academy in 1837 and graduated near the middle of his class four years later. He then served many years as a second lieutenant in the 3rd U.S. Artillery during a long stint of garrison duty in Texas. Reynolds accompanied the army of General Zachary Taylor during the Mexican War and won two brevets for bravery at Monterrey in 1846 and Buena Vista in 1847. After the war, he began a series of staff and command assignments that occasioned his rise to major. In 1856 Reynolds distinguished himself in combat against Native Americans of the Rogue River tribe of Oregon, and the following year, he marched with Colonel Albert S. JOHNSTON in the Mormon expedition. After fulfilling another tour of duty at Fort Vancouver, Washington Territory, Reynolds reported back to West Point in 1860, where he served as commandant of cadets and tactics instructor.

When the Civil War began, Reynolds was commissioned lieutenant colonel of the 14th U.S. Infantry on May 14, 1861, and two days later, he gained appointment as brigadier general of volunteers in Pennsylvania. He then garrisoned the defenses of Washington, D.C., for several months before serving as military governor of Fredericks-burg, Virginia, in May 1862, where he impressed the occupants with his fair and judicious behavior. The following June, he fought in General George B. McCLELLAN's Peninsula campaign at the head of a brigade of Pennsylvania volunteers. In this capacity, he fought exceedingly well at the battles of Mechanicsburg and Gaines's Mill (June 26 and 27, 1862), being captured in the latter struggle. News of his captivity at Richmond's Libby Prison induced citizens of Fredericksburg to petition Confederate authorities for his release, and he was exchanged the following August. Reynolds next led the Pennsylvania Reserve Division at the disastrous Battle of Second Manassas, one of few commanders to win praise from General John POPE. Once General Robert E. LEE invaded Maryland that September, Pennsylvania governor Andrew G. Curtin left the army to serve as commander of Pennsylvania state militia throughout the crisis. Reynolds then advanced to major general as of November 29, 1863, and he succeeded General Joseph HOOKER to command of the I Corps, Army of the Potomac. On December 13, 1862, a division of his men under General George G. MEADE made the only headway against Confederate defenses. In May 1862 Reynolds was present at the disastrous Battle of Chancellorsville, although lightly engaged. Nonetheless, he repeatedly urged General Hooker to attack the Confederate left in strength, which might have turned the tide of battle for the Union.

After Chancellorsville, President Abraham LINCOLN sought a new leader to replace the now disgraced Hooker as commander of the Army of the Potomac. Accordingly, he summoned Reynolds to the White House on May 31, 1863, to sound out his views. Reynolds, however, declined all offers after the president could not promise to restrain political influences on the high command and allow him to maneuver freely. The position therefore went to his old subordinate Meade, only three days prior to the fateful encounter at Gettysburg. At that time, Reynolds commanded the left wing of the army, consisting of the I Corps under General Abner DOUBLEDAY, the III Corps of General Daniel SICKLES, and the IX Corps of General Oliver O. HOWARD. On July 1, 1863, Meade ordered him to hold the vital crossroads at Gettysburg, and he arrived ahead of his troops to find Union cavalry under General John BUFORD heavily pressed by Confederate numbers. He then hastened back to urge his own command forward and was boldly deploying the 2nd Wisconsin Infantry to the front lines when a sniper's bullet killed him. Reynold's sacrifice was not in vain as his remaining troops bought additional precious time for Meade to bring up the rest of the army. Considering his latent ability as a fighting commander, his death was a serious loss to the Union army.

Further Reading

Hoffsommer, Robert D., ed. "Sergeant Charles Veil's Memoir: On the Death of Reynolds." *Civil War Times Illustrated* 21, no. 4 (1982): 16–25.

Jones, Wilmer L. *Generals in Blue and Gray*. 2 vols. Westport, Conn.: Praeger, 2004.

Longacre, Edward G. "John F. Reynolds." *Civil War Times Illustrated* 11, no. 5 (1972): 26, 35–43.

Newton, Steven H. *McPherson's Ridge: The First Battle for the High Ground, July 1, 1863*. Cambridge, Mass.: Da Capo Press, 2002.

Pfanz, Harry W. *Gettysburg—the First Day*. Chapel Hill: University of North Carolina Press, 2001.

Riley, Michael M. *"For God's Sake, Forward": General John F. Reynolds, United States Army*. Gettysburg, Pa.: Farnsworth House Military Impressions, 1995.

Rodgers, John (1812–1882)

Union naval officer

John Rodgers was born near Havre de Grace, Maryland, on August 8, 1812, a son of Commodore John Rodgers, a naval hero from the War of 1812. He went to sea as a midshipman in April 1828 and completed routine service aboard a succession of various squadrons before advancing to passed midshipman in June 1834. He then studied briefly at the University of Virginia and sailed with the Brazilian Squadron (1836–39) before serving in Florida's Second Seminole War. Rodgers rose to lieutenant in January 1840, completed more tours of duty abroad, and then reported for duty with the U.S. Coastal Survey. Having successfully fulfilled his tasks, Rodgers received his first command, the sloop USS *John Hancock*, in October 1852, as part of the North Pacific exploring and surveying expedition. He succeeded the seriously ill commodore Cadwalader Ringgold as expedition leader in 1854 and pushed his vessels farther north into the Bering Sea than any other individual to that time. After returning to Washington, D.C., in 1855 Rodgers advanced to commander and commenced to write a lengthy report of his endeavors. He was awaiting orders in this capacity when the Civil War broke out in April 1861.

Rodgers formed part of the botched Union attempt to destroy the Navy Yard at Norfolk, Virginia, where he was captured and then released by Virginian authorities. In May 1861 his services were requested by Major George B. MCCLELLAN at Cincinnati, Ohio, for the purpose of constructing and outfitting a squadron of armored gunboats for use on western waters. Rodgers then worked closely with engineer Samuel Pook to design and build the so-called Pook Turtles. However, his acerbic temperament led to friction with army personnel, so he was replaced by the more amicable Andrew H. FOOTE, and he was transferred to the converted steamer *Flag* as part of Commodore Samuel F. DU PONT's South Atlantic Blockading Squadron. Eager for action, Rodgers fought well in the November 7, 1861, seizure of Port Royal,

South Carolina, and he personally captured and occupied Fort Walker. Du Pont was so pleased with his performance that Rodgers subsequently hoisted the first American flag over enemy soil since the bombardment of Fort Sumter in April. The following November, he led expeditions that captured Tybee Island off the coast of Georgia and Fernandina Island, Florida, in March 1862. On May 15, 1862, Rodgers conducted the new and experimental ironclad monitor *Galena* up the James River to Drewry's Bluff, Virginia. There, he engaged in a lopsided duel with Confederate batteries on the cliffs and came off a poor second, sustaining 40 hits and 33 casualties. Despite this reverse, he advanced to captain in July 1862 and rejoined Du Pont the following November.

Rodgers next commanded the new, improved monitor *Weehawken*, which was better armored and more seaworthy than its predecessors. To put

Union naval officer John Rodgers *(Library of Congress)*

any doubts to rest, he led his vessel through several storms to confirm its survivability. Thus prepared, the *Weehawken* spearheaded Du Pont's ill-fated attack on Charleston Harbor on April 7, 1863, receiving 53 hits by the time the action was called off. Throughout the engagement, his vessel also pushed an antitorpedo (mine) device, known as a "boot-jack," to deflect and detonate the weapons. Rodgers then made suitable repairs and unhesitatingly engaged the formidable Confederate ram CSS *Atlanta* in Wassaw Sound, Georgia, on June 17, 1862, driving it ashore and capturing it in only 15 minutes. For this display of outstanding seamanship, he received the thanks of Congress and advanced to commodore. He then succeeded to the command of the newly designed monitors *Canonicus* and *Dictator,* which, unfortunately, proved so plagued with technical difficulties that he spent the rest of the war rendering them operational.

Rodgers was retained in the postwar service, and he commanded a small Pacific Squadron and the Boston Navy Yard. He rose to rear admiral in 1869 and the following year took control of the Asiatic Squadron to promote American interests in Korea, the self-styled "Hermit Kingdom." On June 9, 1871, Rodgers, carrying U.S. minister Frederick F. Low onboard, was suddenly fired on by a Korean fort. When no explanation or apology was forthcoming, he landed a detachment of sailors and marines, stormed the offending battery, and killed 243 Korean soldiers. This marked America's first armed intervention in northeast Asia, and after the Korean king refused all diplomatic overtures, Rodgers sailed home. He then finished his career by completing several tours of duty ashore before dying at the Naval Observatory in Washington on May 5, 1882. At the time of his passing, Rodgers was the navy's most senior officer of his grade.

Further Reading

Bradford, James C., ed. *Captains of the Old Steam Navy: Makers of the American Naval Tradition, 1840–1880.* Annapolis, Md.: Naval Institute Press, 1986.

Browning, Robert M. *Success Is All That Was Expected: The South Atlantic Blockading Squadron during the Civil War.* Washington, D.C.: Brassey's, 2002.

Chang, Gordon H. "Whose 'Barbarism'? Whose 'Treachery?' Race and Civilization in the Unknown United States–Korea War of 1871. *Journal of American History* 89, no. 4 (2003): 1331–1365.

Hackemer, Kurt. "The Other Ironclad: The USS *Galena* and the Critical Summer of 1862." *Civil War History* 40, no. 3 (1994): 226–247.

Quarstein, John V. *A History of Ironclads: The Power of Iron Over Wood.* Charleston, S.C.: The History Press, 2006.

Silverstone, Paul H. *Civil War Navies, 1855–1883.* Annapolis, Md.: Naval Institute Press, 2001.

Rosecrans, William S. (1819–1898)

Union general

William Starke Rosecrans was born in Kingston, Ohio, on September 6, 1819, the son of farmers. After his father died, he was forced to quit school and help support his family, and through dint of hard work, he received an appointment to the U.S. Military Academy in 1838. An excellent student, Rosecrans graduated fifth in his class four years later and was commissioned into the elite Corps of Engineers as a second lieutenant. In 1842 he commenced routine construction activities at Hampton Roads, Virginia, and Newport, Rhode Island, and he also served as an instructor at West Point (1843–47). However, Rosecrans grew disillusioned with low pay and slow promotion, so he resigned from the army in 1854 to pursue a career in business. For the next seven years, he worked as a civil engineer in Ohio and also operated his own kerosene distillery. Following the onset of hostilities in April 1861, Rosecrans quickly responded by serving as a volunteer aide-de-camp to Major George B. McClellan. He shortly after rose to lieutenant colonel of the 23rd Ohio Volunteers in June, and then President Abraham Lincoln appointed him a brigadier general in the regular army. In this capacity, he served under McClellan in western Virginia, gaining small but significant victories over Confederate forces at Richmond Mountain on July 11, 1861. McClellan, who received overall

Union general William S. Rosecrans *(Massachusetts Commandery Military Order of the Loyal Legion and the U.S. Army Military History Institute)*

credit for success here, was summoned east, and Rosecrans succeeded him as head of the Department of Western Virginia. His most important accomplishment was defeating General John B. Floyd at Carnifex Ferry on September 10, 1861, which helped clear West Virginia of Confederates.

In the spring of 1862, Rosecrans was succeeded by General John C. Frémont while he transferred west to join the Army of the Mississippi under General John Pope. In this capacity, he commanded the left wing of Pope's force during General Henry W. Halleck's Corinth campaign, and he succeeded him in command of the Army of the Mississippi in June 1862. This placed Rosecrans under the aegis of General Ulysses S. Grant, who regarded him as a marginally talented, plodding performer. As if to underscore this perception, Rosecrans defeated General Sterling Price at Iuka on September 19, 1862, then repelled General Earl VAN DORN at Corinth (October 3–4, 1862), but he fumbled the pursuit and allowed his foes to escape. He nevertheless received promotion to major general that fall and succeeded General Don C. BUELL as head of the Army of the Ohio, which he renamed the Army of the Cumberland. Rosecrans spent several weeks shadowing the Army of Tennessee under General Braxton BRAGG until he suddenly turned at Murfreesboro (Stones River) and fought from December 31, 1862 to January 3, 1863. A bloody standoff ensued as both sides pummeled each other's right flank, and Rosecrans nearly abandoned the contest before the Southerners were compelled by losses to withdraw. For his efforts here, he also received the thanks of Congress.

Typically, Rosecrans spent the next several months methodically training and preparing his army, a pace that vexed impatient superiors. It took considerable prodding, but he finally moved against Bragg in June 1863 during the so-called Tullahoma campaign, in which the Confederates were completely outmaneuvered and abandoned Chattanooga, Tennessee, without a shot being fired. It was, in truth, a brilliant achievement for which praise was deserved. However, Rosecrans grew careless by pursuing the Confederates into northern Georgia with his army widely dispersed. Bragg, now reinforced by General James LONGSTREET's corps from Virginia, predictably turned and struck back at Chickamauga on September 19–20. Rosecrans handled his troops well initially, until he inadvertently shifted a division and created a gap in his line just as Longstreet attacked. His army was completely shattered save for the magnificent stand of General George H. THOMAS, and he fell back in haste to Chattanooga. When

Rosecrans inexplicably allowed Bragg to occupy the high ground surrounding the city and besieged him, Grant arrived on October 19, 1863, and relieved him from command.

Rosecrans subsequently received command of the Department of the Missouri, where he quarreled with Generals Samuel R. CURTIS and Alfred PLEASONTON throughout General Sterling PRICE's invasion of that state. In December 1864 he reported to Cincinnati for orders, which never came, and finally he resigned in disgust in March 1867. Rosecrans served as minister to Mexico until being sacked a second time by President Grant in 1869. He then relocated to California, purchased a ranch, and dabbled in mining. In 1881 he won election to the U.S. House of Representatives, and he vindictively voted against back pay for Grant, then dying of throat cancer. Rosecrans served as register of the U.S. Treasury from 1885 to 1893 before dying at Redondo Beach, California, on March 11, 1898. He was a talented but essentially luckless commander who displayed flashes of brilliance alongside consistent sluggishness in the field.

Further Reading

Bowers, John. *Chickamauga and Chattanooga: The Battles That Doomed the Confederacy.* New York: Post Road Press, 2000.

Castel, Albert. "Victorious Loser: William S. Rosecrans." *Timeline* 19, no. 4–5 (2002): 32–41, 22–37.

———. "West Virginia, 1861: A Tale of a Goose, a Dog, and a Fox." *North & South* 7, no. 7 (2004): 44–55.

Daniel, Larry J. *Days of Glory: The Army of the Cumberland, 1861–1865.* Baton Rouge: Louisiana State University Press, 2004.

Lepa, Jack H. *The Civil War in Tennessee, 1862–1863.* Jefferson, N.C.: McFarland, 2007.

Ross, Charles D. *Civil War Acoustic Shadows.* Shippensburg, Pa.: White Mane Books, 2001.

S

Schofield, John M. (1831–1906)
Union general

John McAllister Schofield was born in Gerry, New York, on September 29, 1831, the son of a Baptist minister. He relocated to Illinois with his family as a child and in 1849 gained an appointment to the U.S. Military Academy. He graduated near the top of his class in 1853 and served as a second lieutenant with the 1st U.S. Artillery in Florida before returning to West Point as an instructor. In 1860 he obtained a leave of absence to teach physics at Washington University, St. Louis, Missouri, but he responded to President Abraham LINCOLN's call for volunteers the following spring. Schofield then became a major in the 1st Missouri Artillery and chief of staff under General Nathaniel LYON. In this capacity, he fought bravely at the defeat of Wilson's Creek on August 10, 1861, eventually winning the Congressional Medal of Honor for exemplary behavior. Prior to the battle, Schofield urged the badly outnumbered Lyon not to attack and also balked at Colonel Franz SIGEL's secret flanking march to the Confederate rear. That November, he became a brigadier general of Missouri militia, and head of the District of St. Louis and enjoyed some success rooting out Confederate guerrillas under William C. QUANTRILL. In November 1862 Schofield gained command of the Army of the Frontier, which was primarily concerned with antiguerrilla activities, but his nomination to major general was held up in Congress by political enemies. His promotion finally was approved in May 1863, at which point he assumed control of the Department of the Missouri. Schofield, however, was ambitious and used his good relationship with President Lincoln to agitate for a combat command. Accordingly, in February 1864, he assumed command of the Department of the Ohio and its constituent army, the XXIII Corps.

Throughout the spring and summer of 1864, Schofield formed part of General William T. SHERMAN's army as it marched to Atlanta, Georgia. He performed capably in the complex maneuvering that turned General Joseph E. JOHNSTON's Confederates out of several fortified positions. However, when Johnston's successor, General John B. HOOD, marched into Tennessee to cut Sherman's supply lines, Schofield was detached from the main army to slow him while General George H. THOMAS assembled a new army for the defense of Nashville. On November 28, 1864, Schofield skillfully extricated his command from a trap laid by Hood at Spring Hill, and then he occupied defensive positions around the city of Franklin. Hood attacked vigorously on November 30, 1864, and was vigorously repulsed with six generals killed and thousands of casualties. Schofield slipped away again, skillfully covered by General James H. WILSON's cavalry, and he rejoined Thomas at Nashville. On December 15–16, his XXIII Corps figured prominently in the rout of Hood and the near annihilation of his Army of Tennessee.

Schofield rose to major general of volunteers and performed an impressive movement of forces from Tennessee by riverboat, train, and ship to North Carolina. There, he helped orchestrate the capture of Wilmington before advancing inland to Goldsborough to link up with Sherman that March. In April 1865 Schofield participated in negotiations to end hostilities and was on hand to accept Johnston's surrender at Durham Station. He ended the war commanding the Department of North Carolina. Shortly afterward, President Andrew Johnson appointed him special envoy to France, where he compellingly convinced the government of Emperor Napoleon III to withdraw its forces from Mexico. He served as acting secretary of war under Johnston and also performed Reconstruction work. President Ulysses S. GRANT appointed him head of the Department of the Missouri in 1869. He later transferred to the Division of the Pacific, and in 1872, he ventured to Hawaii with the recommendation that the United States obtain Pearl Harbor as a naval base. In 1876 Schofield returned to West Point as commandant

and two years later headed a board of inquiry that overturned the court-martial verdict of General Fitz John PORTER.

Schofield's most daunting task occurred in 1888 when, following the death of General Philip H. SHERIDAN, he was elevated to commanding general of the army. Throughout his seven-year tenure, he oversaw improvements in the lot of the common soldiers while also fostering greater professionalism among the officer corps. He also broke precedent by urging that Native Americans be allowed to join the military as regular soldiers while the government helped assume for the care and feeding of their families. Perhaps Schofield's greatest contribution to the U.S. Army was his call for a German-style general staff system, which was adopted at the turn of the 20th century. He resigned from the army in 1895 as a lieutenant general before dying at St. Augustine, Florida, on March 4, 1906. In addition to being an outstanding combat officer, Schofield is widely regarded as among the army's finest peacetime administrators and reformers.

Further Reading

Connelly, Donald B. *John M. Schofield of the Politics of Governorship.* Chapel Hill: University of North Carolina Press, 2006.

Fonvielle, Chris E. *The Wilmington Campaign: Last Departing Rays of Hope.* Mechanicsburg, Pa.: Stackpole Books, 2001.

Lepa, Jack H. *Breaking the Confederacy: The Georgia and Tennessee Campaigns of 1864.* Jefferson, N.C.: McFarland, 2005.

McDonough, James L. *Nashville: The Western Confederacy's Final Gamble.* Knoxville: University of Tennessee Press, 2004.

Nichols, Bruce. *Guerrilla Warfare in Civil War Missouri, 1863.* Jefferson, N.C.: McFarland, 2006.

Schofield, John M. *Forty-Six Years in the Army.* Norman: University of Oklahoma Press, 1998.

Union general John M. Schofield *(Library of Congress)*

Scott, Winfield (1786–1866)
Union general

Winfield Scott was born near Petersburg, Virginia, on June 13, 1786, and he briefly attended William and Mary College. After studying law for several

Union general Winfield Scott *(National Archives)*

months, Scott joined the U.S. Army as a captain of artillery in 1808, commencing a distinguished military career that lasted more than a half-century. He gained national attention during the War of 1812, particularly at the bloody encounters of Chippewa and Lundy's Lane in July 1814, which demonstrated the ability of American troops to withstand professional British adversaries in the field. He ended the war a brevet major general, the nation's youngest. Throughout the postwar period, Scott functioned as the embodiment of military professionalism and composed the first infantry manuals employed since the American Revolution. By dint of superior skills, he became the army's commanding general in 1841, and he held that position for the next 20 years. Scott was also renowned for his towering stature, standing more than six-and-a-half-feet tall, and his equally commanding ego. In fact, his strict insistence on following the various nuances of military etiquette garnered him the nick-

name "Old Fuss and Feathers." Scott demonstrated his abilities as a commander during the Mexican War in 1847, when he conducted a near-flawless advance on Mexico City that constituted a textbook example of military planning and maneuver. Moreover, his example of success and the methods he employed influenced nearly 100 junior officers serving under him, who, over a decade later, rose to be generals in the Civil War. In 1852 he made a clumsy run for the presidency as a Whig and lost decisively to Democrat Franklin Pierce.

The 75-year-old Scott, though himself a Southerner, opposed secession as it unfolded in the fall of 1860. He tried to convince President James Buchanan to reinforce and strengthen army garrisons throughout the South, but his advice was ignored by Secretary of War John B. FLOYD. Once the new chief executive, Abraham LINCOLN, was in power, he advised him to abandon Fort Sumter, South Carolina, on the basis of it being militarily indefensible. Lincoln chose to ignore his advice and instead requested him to proffer a military strategy for subduing the rebellious South. The elderly Scott then articulated a comprehensive plan calling for a tight blockade of the Confederate coastline from Norfolk, Virginia, to Galveston, Texas, followed by a military offensive down the Mississippi Valley that utilized the various waterways as avenues of invasion. Furthermore, he predicted a three-year conflict requiring the service of 300,000 three-year soldiers—a far cry from the 75,000 three-month volunteers initially requested by Lincoln. It was his strategic vision that the South, cut off from trade with Europe and slowly dismembered through control of the Mississippi, would gradually but irrevocably succumb to superior Union numbers and resources. His solution failed to meet quicksilver political expectations for an immediate and decisive victory over the secessionists, so his strategy, ridiculed as the "Anaconda Plan," was initially discarded.

The wizened warrior also urged the administration against precipitously committing raw, barely trained troops to combat operations. Again, politicians scoffed at his caution, and he was strong-armed into approving a hasty offensive under General Irvin McDowell. This operation came to grief at Bull Run on July 21, 1861, as he predicted. Political and military leaders, now taking stock of Scott's advanced age and declining health, openly began to question his relevance to the military matters at hand. Scott undoubtedly hastened his own removal by appointing the young, brash general George B. McClellan who routinely disregarded the old soldier's advice and elbowed himself into the role of Lincoln's de facto military adviser, as head of the Army of the Potomac. Scott, old, ill, and feeling ignored, finally resigned his commission on October 31, 1861. He retired to the U.S. Military Academy, West Point, to write his memoirs. He also lived long enough to see his "Anaconda Plan" vindicated, for the basic outline was eventually adopted with successful results to the Union. Scott died at West Point on May 29, 1866, being both literally and figuratively a towering figure of American military history.

Further Reading

Eisenhower, John S. D. *Agent of Destiny: The Life and Times of General Winfield Scott.* New York: Free Press, 1997.

Johnson, Timothy D. *Winfield Scott: The Quest for Military Glory.* Lawrence: University Press of Kansas, 1998.

MacDonnell, Francis. "The Confederate Spin on Winfield Scott and George Thomas." *Civil War History* 44, no. 4 (1998): 255–266.

Perret, Geoffrey. "Anaconda: The Plan That Never Was." *North & South* 6, no. 4 (2003): 36–43.

Peskin, Allan. *Winfield Scott and the Profession of Arms.* Kent, Ohio: Kent State University Press, 2003.

Rafuse, Ethan S. "Former Whigs in Conflict: Winfield Scott, Abraham Lincoln, and the Secession Crisis Revisited." *Lincoln Herald* 103, no. 1 (2001): 8–22.

Semmes, Raphael (1809–1877)

Confederate admiral

Raphael Semmes was born in Charles County, Maryland, on September 27, 1809, and was orphaned at an early age. Raised by uncles, he joined the navy as a midshipman in 1826 and performed routine duties aboard a succession of vessels. In his spare time, Semmes also studied law and gained admittance to the bar in 1834. He rose to lieutenant in February 1837 and served in that capacity during the Mexican War. In October 1846 he commanded the brig USS *Somers* in the Gulf of Mexico until losing his ship and 40 crew members to a sudden squall. Exonerated by a court of inquiry, Semmes subsequently helped supervise the landing of General Winfield Scott at Veracruz in 1847 and campaigned alongside army troops during the advance on Mexico City. After the war, Semmes settled in Montgomery, Alabama, awaiting orders and practicing law. He rose to commander in 1855 and assumed responsibilities as lighthouse inspector for the Gulf region. Once Alabama seceded from the Union in February 1861, Semmes resigned his commission and joined the newly formed Confederate navy as a commander. His first assignment was to visit New York to purchase naval supplies before the onset of actual hostilities. On his return visit, Semmes stopped in Washington, D.C., to observe the inauguration of President Abraham Lincoln.

Before taking to sea, Semmes held lengthy discussions with Confederate secretary of the navy Stephen R. Mallory as to the probable course of naval events. Given the South's limited assets, both men agreed to pursue a *guerre de course,* namely, the outfitting of commerce destroyers to attack Northern shipping and sap Union economic vitality. On June 30, 1861, he took the converted steamer *Havana,* now armed and outfitted as the commerce raider CSS *Sumter,* out from Pass a L'Outre, Mississippi, and into open ocean. His was the first vessel to display the Confederate flag abroad, and over the course of the next few months Semmes steamed as far north as Maine, taking 18 prizes. His success forced Navy secretary Gideon Welles to dispatch several warships in pursuit, which finally cornered him at Gibraltar in April 1862. Semmes, noting the dilapidated condition of his vessel, decommissioned it and escaped to Nassau. He there awaited delivery of a new and more powerful vessel, the 200-foot steam sloop

CSS *Alabama,* which had been constructed clandestinely in England. In August 1862 Semmes, now a captain, outfitted his new vessel at Terceira in the Azores and sailed off into history. During the next two years, he attacked Union shipping at locales as far away as Singapore, ultimately seizing and burning 66 prizes. One victim, the Union warship USS *Hatteras,* was surprised at night off Galveston, Texas, and sunk in only 15 minutes. Semmes's haul made him the most successful privateer captain in naval history and forced the American government, which branded him a pirate, to redouble efforts to catch him.

After an exhausting cruise of 22 months, Semmes finally put in to Cherbourg, France, for some badly needed repairs. While there, he was blockaded in port by the *Kearsarge,* commanded by Captain John A. Winslow, a former acquaintance. In a rashly based decision, Semmes decided that his ship was more than a match for his opponent, and on June 19, 1864, he left Cherbourg to engage it. The *Kearsarge,* well armed, armored, and trained, proceeded to disable the *Alabama* systematically with accurate gunnery while the Confederate gunners aimed high. Semmes abandoned ship after a 45-minute contest and was rescued from capture by an English yacht—a violation of international law. He returned to the South as a hero, and in February 1865, he was made an admiral. For the final months of the war, Semmes commanded the James River Squadron of three ironclads and three gunboats, but he saw no serious action. He scuttled his ships before Richmond fell to the armies of General Ulysses S. GRANT on April 2, 1865, and he massed his sailors into a naval brigade. Semmes then served as a brigadier general in the army of General Joseph E. JOHNSTON and surrendered at Durham Station with that officer on April 26, 1865.

In December 1865 Semmes was arrested by government authorities and charged with piracy, but he was ultimately released. He then returned to Mobile, Alabama, to teach, edit a newspaper, and practice maritime law. Semmes died at Point Clear, Alabama, on August 30, 1877, but his success in war led to a major diplomatic fracas with England over the so-called Alabama Claims. Because the *Alabama* was built in England for hostile purposes against the United States, the courts viewed it as a breach of international neutrality. In 1872 the British government finally admitted culpability and paid $15.5 million in compensation to Semmes's numerous victims.

Further Reading
Bowcock, Andrew. *CSS Alabama: Anatomy of a Confederate Raider.* London: Chatham, 2002.

Gindlesperger, James. *Fire on the Water: The USS Kearsarge and CSS Alabama.* Shippensburg, Pa.: Burd Street Press, 2004.

Hollet, D. *The Alabama Affair: The British Shipyards Conspiracy in the American Civil War.* Wirral, U.K.: Avid Publications, 2003.

Merli, Frank J. *The Alabama, British Neutrality, and the American Civil War.* Bloomington: Indiana University Press, 2004.

Taylor, John M. *Semmes: Rebel Raider.* Washington, D.C.: Brassey's, 2004.

Tucker, Spencer. *Blue and Gray Navies: The Civil War Afloat.* Annapolis, Md.: Naval Institute Press, 2006.

Shelby, Joseph O. (1830–1897)
Confederate general

Joseph Orville Shelby was born in Lexington, Kentucky, on December 12, 1830, and he attended the University of Transylvania (1845–48). After a year in Pennsylvania to study rope manufacturing, he relocated with his family to Waverly, Missouri, to grow hemp and enter business. As a slaveholder, Shelby opposed abolitionists during the Kansas-Missouri border disputes, and he raised cavalry companies to raid his opponents. When the Civil War erupted in April 1861, Shelby declined a commission in the Union army and offered his services to the Confederacy. As a member of the State Guard, he fought with General Sterling PRICE at Wilson's Creek on August 10, 1861, and then participated in the siege of Lexington. His exemplary conduct as a cavalry leader marked him for additional service with the mounted arm. On March 7–8, 1862, he fought under General Ben McCULLOCH at the defeat of Pea Ridge, skillfully covering the Southern withdrawal. That June, he was commissioned a colonel in Confederate service and given a three-regiment force, which, by dint of hard fighting, gained renown as the "Iron Brigade." Under Shelby's untutored but excellent leadership, it quickly emerged as the finest Southern cavalry unit of the Trans-Mississippi theater.

As the tide of Confederate fortunes in Missouri and Arkansas ebbed and flowed, Shelby was usually on hand as a scout, a combat officer, or a commander of the rear guard. Audacious by nature, in December 1862 he briefly seized the outer defenses of Springfield, Missouri, and subsequently conducted numerous forays behind Union lines in support of General Thomas C. HINDMAN. He next fought under Price during the ill-fated attack on Helena, Arkansas, where he was wounded. That September, Shelby performed his greatest military deed by raiding across the length and breadth of Missouri with the Iron Brigade, capturing Federal garrisons at Boonville, Neosho, Warsaw, and Tipton. His hard-riding troopers covered 1,500 miles in only 36 days, inflicted nearly 600 casualties and destroying nearly $2 million of Union property. It is estimated that his activities tied down the services of 50,000 Union troops who had been sent to oppose him and precluded any reinforcements to Federal armies besieged at Chattanooga, Tennessee. Moreover, this proved not only the longest cavalry raid of the war but also one that gave Shelby a reputation to vie with that of General J. E. B. STUART in the East. In recognition of his accomplishments, he gained promotion to brigadier general on December 15, 1863.

In the spring of 1864, Shelby performed more useful service by successfully opposing 15,000 Union troops under General Frederick Steele at Princeton, Arkansas. That September, he accompanied Price's final invasion of Missouri and waged several successful actions against isolated Union detachments. On October 21–23, 1864, Shelby acquitted himself well during Price's defeat at Westport, Missouri, and his ferocious rearguard

actions undoubtedly saved his army from destruction. At that time, General Alfred PLEASONTON declared Shelby the best Confederate cavalry opponent he ever encountered. After falling back to Texas, he learned of General Robert E. LEE's surrender at Appomattox in April 1865 and vowed never to capitulate. He even threatened General Edmund KIRBY-SMITH with arrest if he attempted to surrender. Once reality prevailed, Shelby took 1,000 of his followers south into Mexico to found a colony for Emperor Maximilian. However, once the French began to withdraw in 1866, Shelby abandoned the effort and returned to Missouri. He farmed for many years in Bates County before serving as a U.S. federal marshal in 1893. He also gained a degree of notoriety by testifying as a defense witness in the trial of noted outlaw Frank James, which led to his acquittal. Shelby continued as sheriff and a popular frontier figure until his death in Adrian County, Missouri, on February 13, 1897. As a cavalry leader, many historians rate him as equal or better than such contemporaries as Nathan B. FORREST and Joseph WHEELER.

Further Reading

Beasley, Conger, Jr., ed. *Shelby's Expedition to Mexico: An Unwritten Leaf of the War.* Fayetteville: University of Arkansas Press, 2002.
Nichols, Bruce. *Guerrilla Warfare in Civil War Missouri, 1863.* Jefferson, N.C.: McFarland, 2006.
Scott, Mark E. *The Fifth Season: General "Jo" Shelby, the Great Raid of 1863.* Independence, Mo.: Two Trails Pubs., 2001.
Sellmeyer, Deryl P. J. *Shelby's Iron Brigade.* Gretna, La.: Pelican Publishing, 2007.
Shea, William L. "Prelude to Prairie Grove: Cane Hill, November 28, 1862." *Arkansas Historical Quarterly* 63, no. 4 (2004): 352–379.

Sheridan, Philip H. (1831–1888)
Union general

Philip Henry Sheridan was born near Albany, New York, on March 6, 1831, the son of Irish immigrants. He matured in Somerset, Ohio, and clerked several years in a dry goods store before winning an appointment to the U.S. Military Academy in

1849 after lying about his age. A mediocre student, Sheridan possessed a ferocious temper and at one point attacked a larger cadet captain with a fixed bayonet because of an alleged insult. He was suspended for a year in consequence and finally graduated in 1854 as a second lieutenant in the 1st U.S. Infantry. After fighting Native Americans along the Rio Grande in Texas, he transferred to the 4th U.S. Infantry and performed similar service against the Yakima tribes of the Oregon Territory. When the Civil War commenced in April 1861, Sheridan was an obscure captain, but he managed to wrangle a staff position under Generals Nathaniel LYON and Henry W. HALLECK. He performed well as a quartermaster but chafed as a bureaucrat and sought a combat command. After badgering Halleck for weeks (for Sheridan was anything if not dogged), he received command of the 2nd Michigan Cavalry in May 1862. With this force, he engaged and defeated 5,000 of General

Union general Philip H. Sheridan *(National Archives)*

William J. HARDEE's Confederate cavalry at Booneville, Mississippi, on July 1, 1862, becoming a brigadier general of volunteers in consequence. He subsequently commanded an infantry division under General Don C. BUELL at the bloody Battle of Perryville, Kentucky, on October 8, 1862, where his relentless attacks convinced General Braxton BRAGG to retreat. At the equally sanguine Battle of Murfreesboro (December 31, 1862–January 3, 1863), his valiant stand against General Leonidas POLK's superior numbers saved the army of General William S. ROSECRANS from certain destruction. His superior performance resulted in a promotion to major general of volunteers in March 1863 at the age of 32.

Sheridan commanded a division in the XX Corps throughout Rosecrans's brilliantly executed Tullahoma campaign in central Tennessee. But both leaders came to grief on September 20, 1863, when Bragg suddenly assailed Union forces at Chickamauga and Sheridan's men were routed by two divisions under General James LONGSTREET. Nevertheless, he rounded up the stragglers and assisted General George H. THOMAS in conducting a successful rear-guard action. Sheridan next fought well at the Battle of Missionary Ridge on November 25, 1863, herding his division up the slopes in an unauthorized advance that routed the Confederates and captured the crest. Sheridan's stomach for fighting brought him to the attention of General Ulysses S. GRANT, who ordered him east as head of his cavalry corps in the much abused Army of the Potomac.

Once in charge, Sheridan completely revamped, retrained, and reequipped the Union cavalry, converting it from a scouting force to a true combat arm. He also brusquely argued with General George G. MEADE about exactly what role troopers should play in the upcoming Overland campaign against Richmond, Virginia. Sheridan, at one point, openly declared that he would destroy Confederate troopers under legendary general J. E. B. STUART, if only allowed to. Grant, impressed by such aplomb, gave him this permission, and Sheridan set out. He defeated Stuart at Yellow Tavern on May 11, 1864, fatally wounding him. The following month, he waged a hard-fought but inconclusive battle with General Wade HAMPTON's troopers at Trevilian Station, Virginia, although he inflicted heavy damage on Confederate lines of communications and railroads in the process. In August Grant tasked him with driving Confederates under General Jubal A. EARLY out of the strategic Shenandoah Valley and laying waste to that fertile region. Sheridan's Army of the Shenandoah accordingly pounced on Early at Winchester on September 19, 1864, and at Fisher's Hill three days later, routing him. Pursuant to orders, he burned large swaths of valuable farmland to deny its use to the South, becoming a thoroughly hated figure in the process. Early subsequently turned and struck at the unsuspecting Federals at Cedar Creek on October 19, 1864, nearly routing them, but Sheridan galloped 15 miles from the rear, rallied his men, and shattered the Confederates in a sweeping counterattack. "Sheridan's Ride," as it came to be known, was celebrated in a famous poem by Thomas Buchanan Read, and victory also brought him the thanks of Congress and promotion to major general.

Sheridan finally dispensed with Early's survivors at Waynesboro, Virginia, on March 2, 1865. He then rejoined Grant outside of Petersburg. Massing his forces on the Confederate right flank, he was rebuffed by General George E. PICKETT at Dinwiddie Court House on March 31, 1865, but on the following day, April 1, he smashed through Confederate lines at the Battle of Five Forks. This masterstroke forced General Robert E. LEE's Army of Northern Virginia to abandon Richmond hastily and to flee westward with Sheridan in hot pursuit. On April 6, 1865, his cavalry caught and captured a third of the Confederate army at Sayler's Creek, and three days later, he cut off Lee's retreat at Appomattox Court House. Lee surrendered and Sheridan, thunderbolt of the Union army, helped close the Civil War in his typically decisive fashion.

After the war, Sheridan was dispatched to Texas where his threatening displays of military strength induced the government of Napoleon III to remove its armies from Mexico. He then oversaw Reconstruction activities in Texas and Louisiana although, as a Radical Republican, his conduct proved so heavy-handed that President Andrew Johnson removed him. In September 1867 Sheridan transferred to the Department of the Missouri as a lieutenant general, and for the next 16 years, he conducted a ruthless war of subjugation against hostile Native-American tribesmen with Generals Alfred H. TERRY, George CROOK, and George A. CUSTER. In 1870 he took a brief furlough to observe the Franco-Prussian War, and in 1878 he assumed command of the Military Division of the Southwest. Sheridan succeeded General William T. SHERMAN as commanding general of the army in November 1883, and in June 1888, he became only the third person, after Grant and Sherman, to pin four stars on his shoulders as a full general. Sheridan died in Noquitt, Massachusetts, on August 5, 1888, at the age of 57, an outstanding combat commander of the Civil War whose triumphs invariably centered around careful preparation, unswerving adherence to the offense, and unflinching concern for the soldiers serving under him.

Further Reading

Alexander, Robert. *Five Forks: Waterloo of the Confederacy: A Civil War Narrative.* East Lansing: Michigan State University Press, 2003.

Coffey, David. *Sheridan's Lieutenants: Philip Sheridan, His Generals, and the Final Year of the Civil War.* Wilmington, Del.: Rowman and Littlefield, 2005.

Hampson, Jeffery J. "Grant and His Disciples in Terror: A Study of the Civil War Campaigns of Grant, Sheridan, and Sherman." Unpublished master's thesis, James Madison University, 2003.

King, Curtis S. "Reconsider, Hell!" *MHQ* 13, no. 4 (2001): 88–95.

Longacre, Edward G. *The Cavalry at Appomattox: A Tactical Study of Mounted Operations during the Civil War's Climactic Campaign, March 2–April 9, 1865.* Mechanicsburg, Pa.: Stackpole Books, 2003.

Wittenberg, Eric J. *Little Phil: A Reassessment of the Civil War Leadership of General Philip H. Sheridan.* Washington, D.C.: Brassey's, 2002.

————. *Glory Enough for All: Sheridan's Second Raid and the Battle of Trevilian Station.* London: Brassey's, 2002.

Sherman, William T. (1820–1891)

Union general

Tecumseh Sherman was born in Lancaster, Ohio, on February 8, 1820, the son of a state judge. Orphaned at an early age, he became a ward of Senator Thomas Ewing, who subsequently christened him William. Sherman, with his stepfather's patronage, gained appointment to the U.S. Military Academy in 1836, and graduated near the top of his class four years later. He joined the 3rd U.S. Artillery as a second lieutenant and fought in Florida's Second Seminole War until 1841. Sherman then fulfilled a long string of garrison duties throughout the Deep South, where he thoroughly familiarized himself with the people and the geography. When the Mexican War broke out in 1846, Sherman sailed to California to join the staff of General Stephen W. Kearny, but he saw no combat. He next performed as a captain in the commissary department, but discouraged by low pay and slow promotions, Sherman resigned his commission in 1853. He then failed in banking and law, but in 1859 he accepted a position as superintendent of the Alexandria Military Academy, Louisiana. Sherman greatly admired the South and evinced genuine affection for the Southern people, but after the Civil War commenced in 1861, he departed Louisiana for St. Louis, Missouri, and he sought to regain his army commission. Before leaving, his many Southern friends implored him to accept a commission in the Confederate army, but he politely declined.

Through the influence of his younger brother John, a U.S. senator, Sherman was reinstated as a colonel of the 13th U.S. Infantry on May 14, 1861. He commanded a brigade under General Irvin McDowell at Bull Run on July 21, 1861, being one of few officers to distinguish himself in combat. Sherman rose to brigadier general the following August and transferred to the Department of the Ohio to assist General Robert Anderson. By October, he succeeded Anderson in command and entered into a bitter war of words with the local press, which openly regarded him as insane. When the volatile Sherman experienced a nervous breakdown, he was replaced by General Don C. Buell and sent to Missouri as a staff officer under General Henry W. Halleck. Sherman there received command of the District of Cairo, Illinois, where he gained acquaintance with General Ulysses S. Grant during the campaign against Forts Henry and Donelson in February 1862. The high-strung Sherman and the low-key Grant struck up a cordial relationship that lasted the remainder of their lives. He commanded a division in Grant's Army of the Tennessee and fought conspicuously at the bloody Battle of Shiloh (April 5–6, 1862). Sherman, who had commanded the pickets that day, had been surprised by Confederates under General Albert S. Johnston, but he effectively rallied his command and contributed to the final Union victory.

Sherman was promoted to major general the following May and performed useful service during the Union advance on Corinth, Mississippi. Grant then ordered him to secure Memphis, Tennessee, as a major base of operations against the Confederate citadel of Vicksburg. In this capacity, he ruthlessly suppressed guerrilla activity and punished civilian collaborators harshly—noting carefully the effect such moves had on discouraging the population from further resistance. That fall, Sherman performed initial moves against Vicksburg by attacking its northern tier of defenses along Chickasaw Bluffs, Mississippi, but he was badly repulsed on December 29, 1862. When the press widely accused him of incompetence, he publicly swore he would hang the next reporter who annoyed him. President Abraham Lincoln then supplanted Sherman with the politically oriented General John A. McClernand, who appointed him commander of the XV Corps in the newly constituted Army of the Mississippi. Sherman then accompanied combined operations resulting in the capture of Fort Hindman, Arkansas, on January 11, 1863, before Grant reassigned him to his own Army of the Tennessee. Sherman again distinguished himself by driving Confederates under General Joseph E. JOHNSTON from Jackson, Mississippi, on May 14, 1863, which left Grant free to concentrate on Vicksburg. After that city surrendered on July 4, 1863, Sherman advanced to brigadier general in the regular army and succeeded Grant as commander of the Army of the Tennessee. On November 24, 1863, Sherman figured conspicuously in the defeat of General Braxton BRAGG at Chattanooga, Tennessee, and his subsequent advance on Knoxville broke the siege of General James LONGSTREET. In March 1864, once Grant was called east to serve as commanding general, Sherman succeeded him in leading the Military Division of the Mississippi and as head of all Union forces in the western theater.

In the spring of 1864, Sherman conducted a large offensive toward Meridian, Mississippi, against General Leonidas POLK. His campaign occasioned little fighting; rather, it featured the marked destruction of railways, factories, and storage facilities of possible use to the Confederacy—in sum, a dry run for what happened on a much vaster scale that fall. Thus, Sherman's most vital contribution to the war effort unfolded in the spring and summer of 1864 while commanding the Armies of the Ohio, Cumberland, and Tennessee, under Generals John M. SCHOFIELD, George H. THOMAS, and James B. MCPHERSON. With these 100,000 veteran troops, he was to capture the strategic railroad junction at Atlanta, Georgia, before pressing on to Savannah and the sea. For the next few months, Union forces were engaged in an intricate campaign of maneuver against General Johnston's 60,000 men in the Army of Tennessee, who skillfully fell back on a succession of defensive positions. Only once, at Kennesaw Mountain, Georgia, on June 27, 1864, did Sherman grow impatient and attack—suffering heavy losses. However, Johnston's Fabian tactics did not sit well with the Confederate high command, and they replaced him with the aggressive General John B. HOOD in July. Hood then proceeded to squander his army in a series of headlong attack's

Union general William T. Sherman *(Library of Congress)*

against Sherman's men, and on September 2, 1864, Atlanta finally fell. Not only was this a significant Union victory, but it also virtually insured President Abraham Lincoln's reelection that fall. Sherman, having dispatched Schofield and Thomas to pursue Hood back to Nashville, marched next with General Oliver O. HOWARD's Army of the Tennessee and General Henry W. Slocum's Army of Georgia toward Savannah. Imitating Grant at Vicksburg, he also severed his own lines of supply and advanced while foraging off the land. But, most significant, Sherman initiated his policy of "total war," whereby property and food stuffs of potential use to the Confederacy were either confiscated or burned outright. "War is cruelty and you cannot refine it," he insisted. In truth, Sherman was determined to break, not simply Confederate armies, but the very will of Southerners to resist. Union forces then carved a 60-mile wide swath of destruction through Georgia, and on December 21, 1864, he forced General William J. HARDEE to abandon Savannah without a fight. Sherman proudly telegraphed his accomplishment to the president and offered to him the city as a Christmas present. For his efforts, so essential to the ultimate Union victory, Sherman again received the thanks of Congress.

In the spring of 1865, Sherman resumed advancing, this time northward into South Carolina. He drove General Wade HAMPTON's troops out of the state capital at Columbia on February 17, 1865, which was then burned to the ground. The Union columns then pressed into North Carolina where, on March 19–20, General Johnston launched his final, last-ditch blow at Bentonville, which was easily parried. On April 26, 1865, Johnston finally capitulated to Sherman at Durham Station, although under terms so generous that the new administration of President Andrew Johnston refused to acknowledge them. Continuing press criticism so angered the general that he also threatened to boycott the grand victory march through Washington, D.C., if retractions were not made. Sherman, never one to forgo a grudge, next snubbed Secretary of War Edwin M. Stanton on the reviewing stand and refused to shake his hand for criticizing the terms under which Johnston surrendered.

Sherman rose to lieutenant general in July 1866 while heading the Division of the Missouri. Three years later, newly elected President Grant appointed him commanding general of the army with four stars, becoming only the second individual in American history to be so honored. For the next decade, Sherman worked earnestly to improve conditions in the army and foster greater professionalism, including the wholesale adoption of German staff methods. In concert with General Philip H. SHERIDAN, he also waged a ruthless pacification program against hostile Native Americans and finally bought the western frontier under American domination. He proved as merciless toward Native Americans as he had toward Con-

federates, with identical results. Sherman retired from the military in November 1883 and resisted repeated calls to enter politics as a Republican. He died in New York City on February 14, 1891, a highly capable, successful—and ruthless—Civil War commander, second only to Grant in the Union's equation of victory. His systematic application of "total war" also anticipated the trend that warfare would follow throughout the 20th century, whereby civilian populations—and the industrial capability they represented—would become legitimate military targets.

Further Reading

Bailey, Anne J. *War and Ruin: William T. Sherman and the Savannah Campaign.* Wilmington, Del.: Scholarly Resources, 2003.

Flood, Charles B. *Grant and Sherman: The Friendship That Won the Civil War.* New York: Farrar, Straus, and Giroux, 2005.

Foster, Buckley T. *Sherman's Mississippi Campaign.* Tuscaloosa: University of Alabama Press, 2006.

Kennett, Lee B. *Sherman: A Soldier's Life.* New York: HarperCollins, 2001.

Marszalek, John F. *Sherman's March to the Sea.* Abilene, Tex.: McWhiney Foundation Press, 2005.

Scales, John R. *Sherman Invades Georgia: Planning the North Georgia Campaign, A Modern Perspective.* Annapolis, Md.: Naval Institute Press, 2006.

Sherman, William T. *Memoirs of General William T. Sherman, Written by Himself.* 2 vols. Bloomington: Indiana University Press, 1957.

Simms, William G. *A City Laid Waste: The Capture, Sack, and Destruction of the City of Columbia.* Columbia: University of South Carolina Press, 2005.

Woodworth, Steven E. *Nothing but Victory: The Army of the Tennessee, 1861–1865.* New York: Alfred A. Knopf, 2005.

Sibley, Henry H. (1816–1886)

Confederate general

Henry Hopkins Sibley was born in Natchitoches, Louisiana, on May 25, 1816, and educated at private schools in Ohio. He gained admission to the U.S. Military Academy in 1833, was held back a year for poor academics, and finally graduated in 1838 as a second lieutenant in the 2nd U.S. Dragoons. Sibley then fought in Florida's Second Seminole War before performing garrison duty throughout the Old Southwest. During the Mexican War, he marched with General Winfield SCOTT's army, winning brevet promotion to major for bravery at the Battle of Medellín on March 25, 1847. Afterward, Sibley resumed routine garrison duties in Texas where, at Fort Belknap, he perfected the so-called Sibley Tent. This was an Indian teepee modified for military use—as a device, it was widely employed by both sides in the Civil War. Sibley suffered from kidney stones, drank heavily to relieve the pain, and became alcoholic. In 1858 he accompanied General Albert S. JOHNSTON's Mormon expedition, where he engaged in a standing feud with his immediate superior, Major Philip St. George Cooke, and was court-martialed. Acquitted, he spent several months at

Confederate general Henry H. Sibley *(Library of Congress)*

Fort Craig, New Mexico, under Colonel Edward R. S. CANBY. Sibley resigned his commission shortly after the Civil War commenced in May 1861, apparently on the same day that his promotion to major arrived.

Now a Confederate colonel, Sibley ventured to Richmond, Virginia, to confer with President Jefferson DAVIS. He impressed on Davis the necessity of a Confederate campaign to sweep Union influence from the Arizona and New Mexico territories and possibly deliver California to the Confederacy. Davis, impressed by the scheme, promoted Sibley to brigadier general on June 17, 1861, and the following July, he was installed as head of the Department of New Mexico. He then hurriedly returned to San Antonio, Texas, to recruit soldiers. By January 1863 he had gathered 2,000 men, enough to outfit three regiments for his so-called Sibley Brigade. He then embarked on his quixotic quest by departing from El Paso and marching westward into New Mexico. Sibley had earlier promised Davis that his men could easily forage off the countryside, an unrealistic assertion considering the barrenness of the region—and the major cause for his ultimate defeat. His first objective was Fort Craig, where Canby awaited his approach with 3,800 soldiers and militia. The opposing forces clashed heavily at Valverde on February 21, 1862, after which Canby retreated within the confines of Fort Craig. Sibley, meanwhile, bypassed that strong point altogether and continued advancing up the Rio Grande. This move left a strong enemy force positioned astride Confederate lines of communications, a major strategic mistake.

Sibley continued advancing deeper into New Mexico, taking Albuquerque on March 10, 1862, despite the fact that Federal troops conducted a scorched earth policy in his path, destroying anything of potential use to the invaders. Facing logistical shortages, he next turned his attention to Fort Union, a major Union supply depot whose seizure would relieve his present difficulties. En route, the Confederates encountered the Colorado militia of Major John M. Chivington at

Glorieta Pass in the Sangre de Cristo Mountains on March 28, 1862. Sibley defeated part of this force, but a column led by Chivington marched through Apache Pass, behind the Confederates, and captured their supply train. Now lacking food and ammunition, Sibley had no recourse but to withdraw back to Texas before the 3,000 man "California Column" of Colonel James H. CARLETON made its appearance. The Texans then were harried by Canby's soldiers at every turn, losing additional men at Peralta on April 15, 1862. Sibley's exhausted column finally trudged into San Antonio that July, having lost 500 men—a quarter of its strength. The Confederacy never renewed its attempt to seize the Southwest, which remained firmly in Union hands until the end of the war.

Sibley was recalled back to Richmond to answer charges of intoxication, but he was cleared by a court of inquiry. He subsequently headed a brigade under General Richard TAYLOR in western Louisiana. Unfortunately, his mishandling of troops at the Battle of Bisland on April 12–14, 1864—attributed to drinking—led to his arrest and court-martial. Sibley was again acquitted, but his reputation was ruined, and he spent the remainder of the war in the Trans-Mississippi Department without a command.

In 1869 Sibley found employment with Ismail I, the khedive of Egypt, and he served as his chief of artillery. He was dismissed from the service in 1874 on account of drinking and settled down in poverty at Fredericksburg, Virginia. He spent the last few months of his life trying to recoup royalties owed him from government purchases of his Sibley tent, which a court ruled null and void after he entered Confederate service. He died at Fredericksburg on August 23, 1886, one of the Confederacy's most ineffectual figures.

Further Reading

Alberts, Don E. *The Battle of Glorieta: Union Victory in the West.* College Station: Texas A & M University Press, 2000.

Hall, Martin H. *Sibley's New Mexico Campaign.* Albuquerque: University of New Mexico Press, 2000.

Healey, Donald W. *The Road to Glorieta: A Confederate Army Marches through New Mexico.* Bowie, Md.: Heritage Books, 2003.

Hubbard, Joe A. "Intelligence and the Confederate Invasion of New Mexico." Unpublished master's thesis, New Mexico State University, 2001.

Thompson, Jerry D., ed. *Civil War in the South War: Recollections of the Sibley Brigade.* College Station: Texas A & M University Press, 2001.

Wilson, John P., and Jerry Thompson, eds. *The Civil War in West Texas and New Mexico: The Lost Letterbook of Brigadier General Henry Hopkins Sibley.* El Paso, Tex.: Texas Western Press, 2001.

Sickles, Daniel E. (1825–1914)

Union general

Daniel E. Sickles was born in New York City on October 20, 1825, the son of a successful lawyer and politician. After briefly studying at New York University, he passed the bar exam in 1846 and became intrigued by politics. As a state legislator, Sickles helped arrange the purchase of what became Central Park in 1853 and subsequently relocated to London, England, as private secretary to U.S. minister James Buchanan. Mercurially disposed, he lost that post by refusing to toast Queen Victoria during an official Fourth of July celebration. Sickles nonetheless advanced his political fortunes in 1856 by winning a seat in the U.S. House of Representatives as a Democrat, serving two terms. He also gained national notoriety for gunning down the son of Francis Scott Key over an alleged affair with his wife. During his trial, he was defended by Edwin M. Stanton, the future secretary of war, and was acquitted on the basis of temporary insanity, the first time such a defense had been employed. He then forgave his wife for infidelity, which ended his political career, and he returned to New York. When the Civil War broke out in 1861, Sickles sensed a return to the public forum and helped raised five regiments for the city's "Excelsior Brigade" with himself as colonel of the 17th New York Infantry. President Abraham LINCOLN, eager to solicit high-profile Democrats to the war effort, subsequently elevated him to brigadier general on September 3, 1861.

Union general Daniel E. Sickles *(Library of Congress)*

Sickles first saw action in the Peninsula campaign of 1862 as part of General Joseph HOOKER's division, III Corps. He performed well at the clashes of Fair Oaks and Malvern Hill (May–June) and also fought admirably at Antietam that September. Sickles then advanced to major general as of November 29, 1862, assuming command of Hooker's old division. In this capacity, he remained in reserve at Fredericksburg on December 13, 1862, and then succeeded Hooker to the command of III Corps once Hooker became army commander in January 1863. Sickles was present at the debacle of Chancellorsville (May 2–3, 1863), where the III Corps was detached from the Union line and was ordered to pursue Confederates under General Thomas J. JACKSON. This movement actually weakened Hooker's position just as Jackson delivered his famous flank attack, which rolled up the Union XI Corps. No blame was attached to Sickles for the debacle, and he continued heading the III Corps during General Robert E. LEE's invasion of Pennsylvania.

On July 1, 1863, Sickles commanded one of three corps constituting the left wing of the Army of the Potomac under General George G. MEADE. He saw little fighting that day, and on July 2 Meade ordered him to defend the hills of Round Top and Little Round Top on the extreme Union left flank. Then, in the most controversial action of his career, Sickles pushed his men beyond his assigned sector and occupied an exposed salient at the Peach Orchard. He felt that this was a better position, but no sooner had the III Corps taken its positions than Confederates under General James LONGSTREET drove them back in confusion. This precipitated a crisis as the center of the Union line nearly collapsed until General Winfield S. HANCOCK arrived in person with reinforcements and finally halted the hard-charging Southerners. Sickles consequently lost nearly half of his command and, after being struck by a cannonball, a leg as well. Historians have disagreed ever since about the impact of Sickles's indiscretion, with many feeling that he should have been court-martialed for disobeying orders. Nevertheless, in 1897 he received a Congressional Medal of Honor for his behavior and, in a macabre twist, also donated his severed limb to the National Museum of Medicine.

Sickles, his active military service ended, subsequently engaged in an acrimonious dispute with Meade about the events of July 2. He appeared before the Joint Committee on the Conduct of the War and roundly accused Meade of incompetence. His testimony, and the vitriol with which he delivered it, damaged the reputations of both men. In 1865 President Lincoln dispatched him to South America on a diplomatic mission—increasing his distance from Meade—and after the war, he also served as governor of the Carolinas during Reconstruction. Sickles, now a Radical Republican, worked so enthusiastically for the civil rights of African Americans that President Andrew Johnson removed him. Still, in July 1866 he advanced to colonel of the 42nd U.S. Infantry, and the following year, he received brevet promotion to brigadier general for services at Gettysburg. Sickles retired from the service in April 1869 with a rank of major general. That year, President Ulysses S. GRANT appointed him minister to Spain where he bungled his handling of American support for Cuban rebels and resigned. He then traveled through Europe for several years before being reelected to Congress as a Democrat in 1892. The combative and controversial Sickles died in New York on May 3, 1914, a talented political general but far from the best.

Further Reading

Gallagher, Gary H., ed. *The Second Day at Gettysburg: Essays on Confederate and Union Leadership*. Kent, Ohio: Kent State University Press, 1993.

Hyde, Bill. *The Union Generals Speak: The Meade Hearings on the Battle of Gettysburg*. Baton Rouge: Louisiana State University Press, 2003.

Jones, Wilmer L. *Generals in Blue and Gray*. 2 vols. Westport, Conn.: Praeger, 2004.

Keneally, Thomas. *American Scoundrel: The Life of the Notorious Civil War General Daniel Sickles*. New York: Doubleday, 2002.

Sauers, Richard A. *Gettysburg: The Meade-Sickles Controversy*. Washington, D.C.: Brassey's, 2003.

Sears, Stephen W. *Gettysburg*. Boston: Houghton Mifflin, 2004.

Sigel, Franz (1824–1902)
Union general

Franz Sigel was born in Sinsheim, Grand Duchy of Baden, Germany, on November 18, 1824, the son of a magistrate. He passed through the military college at Karlsruhe in 1843 and served in the ducal army as a lieutenant but was caught up in swell of radical liberalism. He dueled with a fellow officer over politics in 1847 and was forced to resign his commission. During the Revolution of 1848, Sigel served as a revolutionary commander and was defeated twice by Prussian troops before escaping to Switzerland. The following year, he returned to Baden after a liberal regime had been installed, and he served as the minister of war before the Prussians returned

and drove him out in 1849. Sigel fled again to Switzerland, was deported to England, and in May 1852, he arrived in New York City. He worked there as a schoolteacher while also serving in the local militia, rising to major. In 1857 he relocated to St. Louis, Missouri, home to a large German-speaking population, and he soon served as a prominent spokesperson for the community. When the Civil War erupted in April 1861, Sigel, like most German Americans, strongly favored the Union, and he offered his services to President Abraham LINCOLN. He then helped to raise the 3rd Regiment of Missouri Volunteers, in which he acted as colonel. In this capacity, Sigel assisted Captain Nathaniel LYON in the capture of Camp Jackson on May 10, 1861, and he pursued the rebels to the capital of Jefferson City. There, he received his first independent command, the 2nd Missouri Brigade, and attacked superior numbers under General Sterling PRICE at Carthage, Missouri, on July 5, 1861. Sigel was

Union general Franz Sigel *(Library of Congress)*

badly repulsed and then reunited with Lyon at Springfield in time for an even bigger confrontation with General Ben McCulloch at Wilson's Creek on August 10, 1861. He prevailed on his superior to perform an intricate flanking movement that ultimately failed and led to a Union defeat. Despite his checkered beginning, Sigel was hailed in the press as a hero and a rallying figure for German Americans to gather around.

In the spring of 1862, Sigel was entrusted with command of two infantry divisions in the army of General Samuel R. Curtis. On March 7–8, 1862, he fought competently at the Battle of Pea Ridge/Elkhorn Tavern, Arkansas, helping defeat Confederate forces under General Earl Van Dorn. President Lincoln, always eager to bolster his political support among German Americans, readily agreed to promoting him to major general on March 22, 1862. In June 1862 Sigel shipped east to the Shenandoah Valley, Virginia, to succeeded General John C. Frémont as commander of I Corps in General John Pope's Army of Virginia. He fought marginally well on the Union right wing during the disastrous Battle of Second Manassas, August 29–30, 1862, and the following fall, he transferred to the Army of the Potomac under General George B. McClellan. By December, he commanded a grand division under General Ambrose E. Burnside, although, during the defeat at Fredericksburg (December 13, 1862), he remained in reserve. When his grand division was broken up in the spring of 1863, Sigel assumed command of the largely German-speaking XI Corps. Poor health necessitated his removal shortly afterward, and he was succeeded by General Oliver O. Howard. By June, Sigel had recovered sufficiently to head the Pennsylvania Reserves during General Robert E. Lee's invasion of that state, but he still used his significant political connections to secure a combat command.

In February 1864 Sigel gained appointment as head of the Department and Army of West Virginia in the Shenandoah Valley. He then received orders to wrest that productive region from the Confederates and launched a invasion with 5,100 men. Sigel's advance was greatly delayed by the skillfull tactics of General John D. Imboden's cavalry, which allowed additional Southern troops under General John C. Breckinridge to gather at New Market, Virginia. On May 15, 1864, as Sigel dithered before New Market, Breckinridge attacked under the cover of a driving rainstorm, assisted by 247 Virginia Military Institute cadets, and he heavily defeated the Federals. Sigel consequently was stripped of his field command and was placed in charge of the garrison at Harper's Ferry, West Virginia. This post he yielded to General Jubal A. Early in July 1864 and hastily withdrew across the Potomac without a fight. Sigel consequently lacked a command for the remainder of the war and finally resigned his commission on May 4, 1865.

After the war, Sigel worked as an editor of German-language publications in Baltimore, Maryland, and New York. Political connections within the Democratic Party resulted in his appointment as collector of internal revenue in May 1871, and he also won election as city register. Sigel died in New York on August 21, 1902, little remembered as the highest-ranking Union immigrant soldier of the Civil War. Marginally competent at best, he performed more useful service as a symbol for German Americans to rally around.

Further Reading

Duncan, Richard R. "The Raid on Piedmont and the Crippling of Franz Sigel in the Shenandoah Valley." *West Virginia History* 55 (1996): 25–40.

Engle, Stephen D. *Yankee Dutchman: The Life of Franz Sigel.* Baton Rouge: Louisiana State University Press, 1997.

Hinze, David C., and Karen Farnham. *The Battle of Carthage.* Gretna, La.: Pelican Publishing, 2004.

Lepa, Jack H. *The Shenandoah Valley Campaign of 1864.* Jefferson, N.C.: McFarland, 2003.

Piston, William G. *Wilson's Creek: The Second Battle of the Civil War and the Men Who Fought It.* Chapel Hill: University of North Carolina Press, 2004.

Shea, William L., and Grady McWhiney. *Civil War in the West: Pea Ridge and Prairie Grove.* Abilene, Tex.: McWhiney Foundation Press, 2001.

Stuart, J. E. B. (1833–1864)

Confederate general

James Ewell Brown Stuart was born in Patrick County, Virginia, on February 6, 1833, the son of an attorney. After briefly attending Emory and Henry College, he was admitted to the U.S. Military Academy in 1850. Stuart proved himself an adept student and graduated near the top of his class four years later. In 1854 he served as a second lieutenant in the Mounted Rifle Regiment before transferring to the 1st U.S. Cavalry. In this capacity, he saw extensive service in Kansas and Texas against the Cheyenne, and he was badly wounded in a skirmish at Solomon's Fork. He was also actively employed in suppressing frontier violence during the period of frontier difficulties known as "Bleeding Kansas." In 1855 Stuart married the daughter of his commander and fellow Virginian, Colonel Philip St. George Cooke. Four years later, while on leave in Virginia, Stuart served as an aide to Colonel Robert E. LEE during the capture of abolitionist John Brown at Harper's Ferry. He returned to the frontier and rose to captain in April 1861 just as the Civil War was commencing. Stuart remained in the army until Virginia seceded; then he resigned his commission and joined the Confederacy.

Stuart rose quickly to become colonel of the 1st Virginia Cavalry assigned to the army of General Joseph E. JOHNSTON in the Shenandoah Valley. That summer, he expertly screened Johnston's moves to reinforce General Pierre G. T. BEAUREGARD at Bull Run and staged a spectacular cavalry charge that aided in the Confederate victory of July 21, 1861. Stuart then advanced to brigadier general on September 24, 1861, and began to mold his enthusiastic command into highly trained soldiers. Many of his troops fully inculcated his dash and tendency toward flamboyant displays on the battlefield. Stuart gained instant notoriety during the Peninsula campaign of 1862, when he skillfully executed a daring ride around the army of General George B. McCLELLAN (June 12–15). This act gave Lee accurate intelligence

necessary to commence his Seven Days' offensive when he drove Union forces from the gates of Richmond. Ironically, Stuart was pursued throughout by Colonel Cooke, his father-in-law, who remained loyal to the Union. Consequently, he became a major general on July 25, 1862, and received command of all 15,000 cavalry in the Army of Northern Virginia. Stuart next gained additional plaudits for his role in the Second Manassas Campaign against the army of General John POPE. Riding hard, he captured Pope's headquarters at Catlett Station on August 22 and his supply base at Manassas Junction on August 27. He effectively supported General Thomas J. JACKSON throughout the battle itself (August 29–30, 1862). His troopers rendered additional valuable service throughout Lee's invasion of Maryland that September, performing another circuitous ride around McClellan's army following severe combat at South Mountain and Antietam. In October he led a dashing raid as far north as Chambersburg, Pennsylvania, and seized more than 1,000 valuable horses. On December 13, 1862, Stuart's command formed the extreme right flank of Lee's army at Fredericksburg, again performing credibly.

The new year ushered in additional opportunities for Stuart to distinguish himself. In May 1863 he detected the advance of General Joseph HOOKER's army across the Rapidan River, granting Lee sufficient time to formulate a counterstrike at Chancellorsville. Soon after, a mounted brigade under General Fitzhugh LEE discovered that the flank General Oliver O. HOWARD's XI Corps was "in the air," setting the stage for a massive Confederate flank attack. During the battle of May 2, Stuart succeeded both Jackson and General Ambrose P. HILL to command the II Corps after they were wounded, and he conducted affairs competently. Lee then orchestrated his second invasion of the North and entrusted Stuart to screen his advance. On June 9, 1863, however, his command was surprised at Brandy Station by Union cavalry under General Alfred PLEASONTON

Confederate general J. E. B. Stuart *(National Archives)*

and nearly defeated in one of the largest cavalry actions of the war. Stuart's fine generalship allowed the Southerners finally to prevail, although he sustained heavy losses and was roundly criticized in the press—and military circles—for being caught unaware. Stung by these remarks, the haughty, sensitive Stuart, who relished official sanction, determined to redeem his reputation with some kind of grand gesture.

In late June 1863, Stuart received discretionary orders from Lee to screen the army's advance and provide intelligence as to the disposition of Union forces, but he remained at liberty to raid inland as circumstances allowed. Stuart, eager for action, chose the latter course and galloped off into Pennsylvania, losing contact with Lee's headquarters for several days. Consequently, the Confederates operated blindly when they encountered Union forces under General George G. MEADE at Gettysburg on

July 1, 1863. Stuart did not make his appearance on the battlefield until the following evening, and on July 3, 1863, he unsuccessfully jousted with General George A. CUSTER's troopers in the Union rear. He concluded the campaign by successfully covering the Southern withdrawal back to Virginia. Many historians have since concluded that Lee's ultimate defeat at Gettysburg revolved around his lack of reliable military intelligence. Only Stuart could have provided him with such information and, on this occasion, he clearly failed in his mission.

Stuart's experience at Gettysburg and the harsh criticism it engendered induced him to maintain closer contact with headquarters at all times. During the initial phases of General Ulysses S. GRANT's overland campaign to Richmond, he served brilliantly in that capacity, keeping Lee abreast of all Union movements. An exasperated Grant then unleashed General Philip H. SHERIDAN and 12,000 troopers on a raid against the Confederate capital to lure his elusive opponent out into the open and destroy him. On May 9, 1864, both sides clashed indecisively at Todd's Tavern, but two days later, a pitched battle erupted at Yellow Tavern, only six miles from Richmond. Stuart's embattled cavalrymen held their ground against double their numbers until he was mortally wounded and evacuated. "I would rather die than be whipped," he declared at the time. Stuart lingered a day in Richmond before dying on May 12, 1864, and he was replaced by General Wade HAMPTON. His passing was a significant blow to the Army of Northern Virginia. Brave, vainglorious Stuart personified the taste and temperament of "Southern Cavaliers."

Further Reading

Crouch, Richard E. *Brandy Station: A Battle Like None Other.* Westminster, Md.: Willow Bend Books, 2002.

McKinney, Joseph W. *Brandy Station Virginia, June 9, 1863: The Largest Cavalry Battle of the Civil War.* Jefferson, N.C.: McFarland, 2006.

Mitchell, Adele. *The Letters of Major General James E. B. Stuart.* Fairfax, Va.: Stuart-Mosby Historical Society, 1990.

Robinson, Warren C. *Jeb Stuart and the Confederate Defeat at Gettysburg.* Lincoln: University of Nebraska Press, 2007.

Smith, Derek. *The Gallant Dead: Union and Confederate Generals Killed in the Civil War.* Mechanicsburg, Pa.: Stackpole Books, 2005.

Walker, Paul D. *The Cavalry Battle That Saved the Union: Custer vs Stuart at Gettysburg.* Gretna, La.: Pelican Publishing, 2002.

Wittenberg, Eric J., and J. David Petruzzi. *Plenty of Blame to Go Around: Jeb Stuart's Controversial Ride to Gettysburg.* New York: Savas Beatie, 2006.

T

Taylor, Richard (1826–1879)
Confederate general

Richard Taylor was born near Louisville, Kentucky, on January 27, 1826, the son of general and future president Zachary Taylor. He was well educated at private schools and graduated from Yale University in 1843. Taylor, who exhibited a mania for military history, joined his father's staff during the onset of the Mexican War in 1846, and witnessed the battles of Palo Alto and Resaca de la Palma. However, he declined joining the military and returned to Jefferson County, Mississippi, to manage the family's plantation. During this period, another future president, Jefferson DAVIS, married his sister, while he became one of the state's wealthiest planters. Politically, Taylor opposed radical secessionists in the Democratic Party, and during the 1860 presidential convention in Baltimore, Maryland, he tried to arrange compromise between warring factions. Thereafter, he concluded that secession was inevitable, and during the Louisiana secession convention of January 1861, he voted to leave the Union and join the Confederacy. Shortly after, Taylor gained appointment as colonel of the 9th Louisiana Infantry and departed for the East.

Taylor arrived in Virginia too late to fight at Bull Run in July 1861, but the following October, President Davis made him a brigadier general. The appointment raised eyebrows in military circles as Taylor lacked professional military experience, and the move was denounced as favoritism. But drawing on years of studying military history, strategy, and tactics, Taylor settled quickly into his new role. He first saw combat under General Thomas J. JACKSON during the famous Shenandoah campaign of 1862, in which his Louisiana brigade served as an elite strike force. In the fighting at Front Royal, Winchester, and Port Republic (May–June 1862), Taylor's men invariably stormed strong Federal positions and tipped the contest in Jackson's favor. He next joined the Army of Northern Virginia under General Robert E. LEE, again performing credibly during the Seven Days' battles. Taylor then became the Confederacy's youngest major general on July 28, 1862, but prolonged exposure to cold weather triggered bouts of acute arthritis. Therefore, at Taylor's request, Davis appointed him head of the District of West Louisiana and sent him home. His native state had by then reached its lowest ebb, with New Orleans under firm Union control and Federal forces pushing ever farther up the Mississippi River. But Taylor's aggressive handling of troops defeated General Benjamin F. BUTLER in a number of small engagements that kept him confined him to the city, although he ended up dismissing General Henry H. SIBLEY for drunkenness. The impasse continued until the spring of 1864 when a large combined expedition under General Nathaniel C. BANKS and Admiral David D. PORTER began to ascend the Red River in a bid to invade East Texas.

Taylor, who only commanded 9,000 men, entered into a hostile exchange with General Edmund KIRBY-SMITH, commanding the Trans-Mississippi Department, over his scanty allocation of troops and resources. Taylor was then ordered to give ground and avoid combat, a strategy he performed only reluctantly. But on April 8, 1864, as Banks carelessly deployed his men near Mansfield, Louisiana, Taylor could not pass on an opportunity to attack, and he scattered his larger adversary after severe fighting. The next day, Banks fell back to stronger positions on Pleasant Hill, which Taylor promptly attacked on April 9, 1864, and was himself repulsed. Nonetheless, Union forces continued withdrawing to New Orleans as the gunboat armada of Admiral Porter nearly became stranded due to falling water levels. Taylor wanted to attack and capture the fleet intact, but at that exact moment, Kirby-Smith ordered the bulk of his forces to Arkansas to contain a Union offensive under General Frederick Steele. Taylor reluctantly complied and then unleashed a hostile and disrespectful diatribe at his commanding officer. He was asked to be relieved of command. The request was refused, and while events at Red River soured relations between the two men, Taylor's aggressive leadership preserved this productive part of the Confederacy for another year.

In July 1864 President Davis elevated Taylor to lieutenant general, becoming only one of three individuals who did not attend West Point to achieve such status. As such, he assumed command of the Department of Alabama, Mississippi, and East Louisiana. The ensuing year found Taylor coping with increasingly larger Union raids in his jurisdiction and steadily shrinking manpower resources. In January 1865 he assumed control of General John B. HOOD's Army of Tennessee, now decimated by recent fighting at Nashville. Within weeks, most of these troops were marched east to reinforce General Joseph E. JOHNSTON in the Carolinas. Taylor used the remnants to stave off Union raids, assisted by cavalry under General Nathan B. FORREST. Neither men could halt the depredations of Generals James H. WILSON's raiders, and in April, Confederate hopes for independence were finally dashed. On May 4, 1865, Taylor formally surrendered to General Edward R. S. CANBY at Citronelle, Alabama, being the last Confederate commander east of the Mississippi to do so.

After the war, Taylor resumed his activities in the Democratic Party and vocally opposed Reconstruction and the rights of African Americans. He moved to New York City in 1875 to campaign actively for presidential aspirant Samuel J. Tilden. Taylor died there on April 12, 1879, a capable Confederate leader.

Further Reading

Ayres, Thomas. *Dark and Bloody Ground: The Battle of Mansfield and the Forgotten Civil War in Louisiana.* Dallas: Taylor Trade, 2001.

Joiner, Gary D. *One Damn Blunder from Beginning to End: The Red River Campaign of 1864.* Wilmington, Del.: Scholarly Resources, 2003.

———. *Through the Howling Wilderness: The 1864 Red River Campaign and Union Failure in the West.* Knoxville: University of Tennessee Press, 2006.

Jones, Wilmer L. *Generals in Blue and Gray.* 2 vols. Westport, Conn.: Praeger, 2004.

Milbourn, Curtis W. "The Lafourche Offensive: Richard Taylor's Attempt to Relieve Port Hudson." *North & South* 7, no. 5 (2004): 70–83.

Persons, Benjamin S. *From This Valley They Say You Are Leaving: The Union Red River Campaign, March 1863–May 1865.* Bloomington, Ind.: 1st Books Library, 2003.

Prushankin, Jeffrey S. *A Crisis in Confederate Command: Edmund Kirby Smith, Richard Taylor, and the Army of the Trans-Mississippi.* Baton Rouge: Louisiana State University Press, 2005.

Terry, Alfred H. (1827–1890)
Union general

Alfred Howe Terry was born in Hartford, Connecticut, on November 10, 1827, the son of a bookseller. After passing through the local school system, he studied law at Yale University but did not graduate. Instead, he was admitted to the bar and clerked in the New Haven County Court (1853–60) while also serving in the local militia.

Terry was attracted by military service, and he served as colonel of the 2nd Connecticut Militia by the time the Civil War erupted in April 1861. His unit mustered into service as 90-day volunteers, and he fought at Bull Run on the following July 21, 1861. Once his unit disbanded, Terry gained appointment as colonel of the 7th Connecticut Infantry, a three-year outfit. In this capacity, he accompanied General Thomas W. Sherman on the expedition against Port Royal, South Carolina, on November 7, 1861, and he subsequently distinguished himself in the capture of Fort Pulaski, Georgia, on April 11, 1862. He consequently received promotion to brigadier general of volunteers and served as garrison commander. Terry's next assignment was at the siege of Charleston, South Carolina, where he was involved in actions against Morris Island, Fort Sumter, and Fort Wagner. In December 1863 Terry transferred to the Army of the James under General Benjamin F. BUTLER, commanding a division. He fought well in many actions around Petersburg and in the vicinity of the peninsula of Bermuda Hundred. On May 16, 1864, his men successfully covered the retreat of Union forces from Drewry's Bluff, which signaled the end of Butler's offensive operations.

Terry's exceptional performance led to his promotion to major general in August 1864, along with command of the X Corps, Army of the James. In this capacity, he accompanied Butler's ill-fated expedition against Fort Fisher, Wilmington, North Carolina, on December 25, 1864. General Ulysses S. GRANT then allowed him to sail with Admiral David D. PORTER on a renewed attempt against the fort in January 1865. Once ashore, he constructed defenses against possible Confederate reinforcements under General Robert F. HOKE and stood by him while Porter's entire fleet intensely bombarded Fort Fisher for three days. On January 15, 1865, assisted by a naval brigade, Terry successfully stormed and captured Fort Fisher after a hard-fought battle that resulted in 2,000 prisoners and 165 cannon captured. Success also resulted in the thanks of Congress and promotion to brigadier general in the regular army. The latter was quite

distinctive because Terry had never previously served in the military establishment.

After Fort Fisher fell, Terry's command was placed under the auspices of General John M. SCHOFIELD, and he continued with mop-up operations before finally linking up with General William T. SHERMAN's army at Goldsborough. Once the war ended, Terry rose to major general before mustering out of the volunteers and into the regular service. Throughout most of 1865, he performed Reconstruction work in the Department of Virginia, winning praise for his even-handed approach to delicate matters. However, he experienced a major career shift in 1866 when he was transferred to the Department of Dakota. Thereafter, he became indelibly associated with events along the western frontier for the next 22 years, save for 1869–72, when he served as head of the Department of the South in Georgia.

In the West, Terry became inextricably caught up in the tide of white encroachment on Native-

Union general Alfred H. Terry *(Massachusetts Commandery Military Order of the Loyal Legion and the U.S. Army Military History Institute)*

American lands and the inevitable strife that followed. When Chiefs Crazy Horse and Sitting Bull refused to return to their reservations, General Philip H. SHERIDAN ordered him to conduct a three-pronged offensive against the tribes of the Black Hills region. Assisted by Generals John GIBBON and George CROOK, Terry's column, which constituted the main strike force, reached the Big Horn, River and dispatched Colonel George A. CUSTER on a reconnaissance mission. On June 25, 1876, Custer's detachment was wiped out at Little Big Horn, and Terry's force arrived the next day to bury the dead. Through the ensuing political firestorm, he declined to become embroiled and remained silent as to Custer's culpability for the disaster. Subsequent campaigning throughout the winter gradually drove the exhausted tribes back onto reservations, and in 1877 Terry visited Canada and parleyed with Sitting Bull for his return. The following year, he remained east long enough to sit on the board that reversed General Fitz John PORTER's dismissal of 1863.

Terry remained with the Department of Dakota until March 1886, when he rose to major general and succeeded General Winfield S. HANCOCK as head of the Division of the Missouri, headquartered in Chicago. Declining health necessitated his resignation in April 1888 after a long and successful tenure on the frontier, distinguished by his fair treatment of Native Americans. Terry died in New Haven on December 16, 1890, one of few volunteer officers to achieve both distinction and high grade in the regular service.

Further Reading

Fonvielle, Chris E. *The Wilmington Campaign: Last Departing Rays of Hope.* Mechanicsburg, Pa.: Stackpole Books, 2001.

Majeske, Penelope A. "'Your Obedient Servant': The United States Army in Virginia during Reconstruction, 1865–1867." Unpublished Ph.D. diss., Wayne State University, 1980.

Marino, Carl W. "General Alfred Terry Howe: Soldier from Connecticut." Unpublished Ph.D. diss., New York University, 1968.

McCaslin, Richard B. *The Last Stronghold: The Campaign for Fort Fisher.* Abilene, Tex.: McWhiney Foundation Press, 2003.

Robertson, William G. *Back Door to Richmond: The Bermuda Hundred Campaign, April–June, 1864.* Newark: University of Delaware Press, 1987.

Schiller, Herbert M. *Sumter Is Avenged! The Siege and Reduction of Fort Pulaski.* Shippensburg, Pa.: White Mane Books, 1995.

Thomas, George H. (1816–1870)

Union general

George Henry Thomas was born in Southampton County, Virginia, on July 31, 1816, the son of farmers. He originally wished to study botany, but the death of his parents prevented him from attending college, and in 1836 he attended the U.S. Military Academy. Four years later, he became a second lieutenant with the 3rd U.S. Artillery and fought for two years in Florida's Second Seminole War before fulfilling routine garrison duty throughout the South. When the Mexican War broke out in 1846, he formed part of the Army of Occupation in Texas under General Zachary Taylor and served in the artillery company commanded by Captain Braxton BRAGG. Thomas fought well at Monterrey that year and at Buena Vista in 1847, winning two brevets to major. He then returned to West Point as a tactics instructor, rising there to captain by 1853. Two years later, he transferred as major to the newly raised 2nd U.S. Cavalry under Colonel Albert S. JOHNSTON. This distinguished unit possessed so many Southern officers that it was touted as "Jeff DAVIS's Own" and included such future Civil War luminaries as Robert E. LEE, William J. HARDEE, Edmund KIRBY-SMITH, Fitzhugh LEE, and John B. HOOD. Thomas performed quietly but capably, and in 1860 he was furloughed after receiving back injuries that left him with a trademark, lumbering stride. When the Civil War began in April 1861, he was disowned by his family for remaining with the Union. His courageous decision won little applause in Washington, D.C., however, where leaders viewed his Southern roots with suspicion. In contrast, soldiers who knew Thomas gave him the affectionate nickname "Old Pap" for his mild manners and the kindly treatment he afforded them.

Thomas assumed command of the 2nd U.S. Cavalry's remnants at Carlisle Barracks, Pennsylvania, and he advanced to brigadier general in August 1861 after useful service in the Shenandoah Valley. He then transferred to the Army of the Ohio under General Don C. BUELL, and he commanded a division. On January 19, 1862, Thomas won the first significant Union victory in the West by defeating General George B. CRITTENDEN at Mill Springs, Kentucky, although he failed to received a promotion. Thomas then accompanied Buell down the Tennessee River, arriving too late to fight at the bloody Battle of Shiloh (April 6–7, 1862). General Henry W. HALLECK next appointed him to command the left wing of his army during the advance on Corinth, Mississippi, as a major general of volunteers. Thomas returned to the Army of the Ohio that June and, six months later, fought conspicuously in Buell's victory over General Bragg at Perryville on October 8, 1862. Previously, he had refused an offer to command the Army of the Ohio in deference to Buell, whom he considered more experienced. However, once Buell was dismissed for failing to pursue Bragg energetically, Thomas was also passed over in favor of General William S. ROSECRANS. Thomas angrily protested the unwarranted snub and then continued serving as commander of the XIV Corps in the newly renamed Army of the Cumberland.

Thomas next fought well at the sanguine encounter at Murfreesboro (December 31, 1862–January 3, 1863), convincing Rosecrans not to retreat and greatly assisting in the victory. He continued on through the Tullahoma campaign during the summer of 1863, whereby Chattanooga was acquired by the North. But Thomas's greatest contribution occurred at the bloody Battle of Chickamauga (September 19–20, 1863), where Rosecrans inadvertently created a gap in his own line, and the veteran corps of General

Union general George H. Thomas *(Library of Congress)*

James LONGSTREET poured through, shattering his army. Thomas, commanding the right wing, methodically shored up his XIV Corps on Horseshoe Ridge and beat back every Confederate attempt to dislodge him. His magnificent, set-piece defense discouraged Bragg from pursuing, saved the Union army, and gained for him the popular sobriquet "Rock of Chickamauga." For his efforts, he received promotion to brigadier general in the regular army—but no command. It was not until the following October that General Ulysses S. GRANT appointed Thomas head of the Army of the Cumberland, then besieged in Chattanooga. On November 25, 1863, he helped rout Bragg's Confederates through a splendid— and unauthorized—charge up Missionary Ridge. But despite this latest bravura performance, Thomas still was denied a command position and ended up a subordinate under General William T. SHERMAN, an officer with less seniority. Thomas, as usual, took the snub in stride and carried on.

Through the spring and summer of 1864, Thomas accompanied Sherman on his march to Atlanta, Georgia, as his second in command and sparred constantly with Confederate defenders under General Joseph E. JOHNSTON. When Johnston was replaced by the more aggressive general Hood, Thomas effectively parried a serious Confederate counterattack at Peach Tree Creek on July 20, 1864. Sherman then dispatched him in pursuit of Hood once the latter marched into Tennessee. Thomas, tasked with cobbling together a new army as troops arrived in driblets, ordered General John M. SCHOFIELD to slow Hood's advance until his force was assembled and ready. The Confederates arrived outside Nashville in November and dared Thomas to attack them while officials in Washington also pressured him to advance. Thomas, however, remained methodical and imperturbably calm as ever despite repeated warnings from Grant that he would be replaced for failing to attack. Grant, in fact, issued orders to have General John A Logan succeed him when Thomas finally struck on December 15–16, 1864. The ensuing Battle of Nashville proved disastrous for the Confederacy, and Hood's army was nearly annihilated. He consequently received both the thanks of Congress and promotion to major general, along with command of the Departments of the Tennessee and the Cumberland. Lingering doubts as to Thomas's loyalty had finally been laid to rest.

Thomas remained in the peacetime establishment, and in 1868 he requested and received command of the Department of the Pacific, head-quartered at San Francisco, California. He then quietly and unobtrusively administered his charge until his death there on March 28, 1870. Low-key by nature, Thomas was less known nationally than many of his more flamboyant contemporaries, but he accrued a combat record second to none. Sherman, with great justification, eulogized him as "slow but true as steel."

Further Reading

Arnold, James R. *Jeff Davis's Own: Cavalry, Comanches, and the Battle for the Texas Frontier.* New York: Wiley, 2000.

Brennan, Patrick. "Hell on Horseshoe Ridge." *North & South* 7, no. 2 (2004): 22–44.

Daniel, Larry J. *Days of Glory: The Army of the Cumberland, 1861–1865.* Baton Rouge: Louisiana State University Press, 2004.

Einolf, Christopher J. *George Thomas, Virginian for the Union.* Norman: University of Oklahoma Press, 2007.

Hafendorfer, Kenneth A. *Mill Springs: Campaign and Battle of Mill Springs, Kentucky.* Louisville, Ky.: KH Press, 2001.

Lepa, Jack H. *Breaking the Confederacy: The Georgia and Tennessee Campaign of 1864.* Jefferson, N.C.: McFarland, 2005.

McDonough, James L. *Nashville: The Western Confederacy's Final Gamble.* Knoxville: University of Tennessee Press, 2004.

Mills, Brett. "'Time and History Will Do Me Justice': George H. Thomas and His Place in History." *Journal of America's Military Past* 29, no. 4 (2003): 6–24.

Prokopowicz, Gerald J. *All for the Regiment: The Army of the Ohio, 1861–1862.* Chapel Hill: University of North Carolina Press, 2001.

V

Van Dorn, Earl (1820–1863)

Confederate general

Earl Van Dorn was born in Port Gibson, Mississippi, on September 17, 1820, the son of a local magistrate. He gained appointment to the U.S. Military Academy in 1838 and graduated near the bottom of his class four years later. In 1842 Van Dorn became a second lieutenant in the 7th U.S. Infantry and fought briefly against the Seminoles in Florida before joining General Zachary Taylor's army in Texas. In 1847 he transferred to General Winfield SCOTT's army and won two brevet promotions for gallantry at the battles of Cerro Gordo and Churubusco. In 1855 Van Dorn advanced to captain in the 2nd U.S. Cavalry for service along the Texas frontier. He distinguished himself in many pitched battles with hostile Comanche, being seriously wounded. Van Dorn was promoted to major in 1860, but on January 3, 1861, he resigned his commission and returned to Mississippi. There, he succeeded his friend Jefferson DAVIS as major general of state forces, and the following March, he was installed as colonel in the Confederate service. In this capacity, he performed useful service in Texas by accepting the surrender of Union forces under General David E. Twiggs. President Davis next arranged Van Dorn's promotion to brigadier general on June 5, 1861, and major general the following September 19. He also received command of the Confederate Trans-Mississippi Department as of January 1862, a sprawl-ing jurisdiction encompassing Texas, Arkansas, and Missouri. For many months, Van Dorn's principal task was to sort out confusion in Confederate ranks, most notably bickering between Generals Sterling PRICE and Ben McCULLOCH.

Van Dorn was a brave and capable soldier, but he proved somewhat lacking in administrative ability. Once ordered to clear Union forces out of northern Arkansas, he assembled a scratch force of 16,000 men and attacked a smaller force of Federals under General Samuel R. CURTIS at Pea Ridge (March 6–7, 1862). His Confederate Army of the West, assisted by Confederate Cherokee under Colonel Stand WATIE, was poorly handled after an exhausting march and was badly defeated. Van Dorn then surrendered command of the Trans-Mississippi Department to General Theophilus H. Holmes while he was sent across the Mississippi to join General Braxton BRAGG in Tennessee. At length, Bragg felt it best to leave the mercurial Van Dorn behind in Mississippi to guard his communications. Van Dorn, however, took to the offensive by attacking General William S. ROSECRANS at Corinth on October 3–4, 1862. The Federals, strongly entrenched, handily beat off several determined Confederate attacks, inflicting heavy losses. Van Dorn then retreated in confusion, and his men were roughly handled in another encounter along the Hatchie River two days later. The losses incurred resulted in a court of inquiry that exonerated Van Dorn from charges of drunkenness, but he never again held a significant field command.

Despite his tactical ineptitude with large bodies of men, Van Dorn still enjoyed the confidence of President Davis, who then assigned him command of the strategic citadel at Vicksburg, Mississippi. He enjoyed some success when he repulsed an attempt by Admiral David G. FARRAGUT to bombard the city with gunboats, but in November he was succeeded by General John C. PEMBERTON and reassigned to a cavalry command. For the first time in the war, Van Dorn was back in his element, and he demonstrated flashes of brilliance. On December 20, 1863, he artfully orchestrated a surprise attack on the huge Union supply dump at Holly Springs, burning it to the ground. The loss proved so catastrophic to General Ulysses S. GRANT that he rescheduled his impending campaign against Vicksburg by several months. In March 1863, Van Dorn staged another successful action at Thompson's Station in concert with General Nathan B. FORREST, culminating in the capture of 1,000 Federals. This victory seemed to catapult Van Dorn to the front rank of Confederate cavalry commanders. However, his career reached its tragic end at Spring Hill, Tennessee, on May 7, 1863, when he was shot and killed by Dr. George B. Peters, allegedly for having an affair with his wife. This latest indiscretion deprived the Confederacy of a useful leader at a critical juncture of the Vicksburg campaign; at the time of his death, Van Dorn was also the ranking Confederate major general.

Further Reading

Arnold, James R. *Jeff Davis's Own: Cavalry, Comanches, and the Battle for the Texas Frontier.* New York: Wiley, 2000.

Carter, Arthur B. *The Tarnished Cavalier: Major General Earl Van Dorn, C.S.A.* Knoxville: University of Tennessee Press, 1999.

Cozzens, Peter. *The Darkest Days of the War: Iuka and Corinth.* Chapel Hill: University of North Carolina Press, 1997.

DeBlack, Thomas R. *With Fire and Sword: Arkansas, 1861–1874.* Fayetteville: University of Arkansas Press, 2003.

Lowe, Richard. "Van Dorn's Raid on Holly Springs, December, 1862." *Journal of Mississippi History* 61 (1999): 59–71.

Shea, William L., and Grady McWhiney. *War in the West: Pea Ridge and Prairie Grove.* Abilene, Tex.: McWhiney Foundation Press, 2001.

Winschel, Terrence J. "Earl Van Dorn: From West Point to Mexico." *Mississippi History* 62, no. 3 (2000): 179–197.

Wallace, Lew (1827–1905)

Union general

Lewis Wallace was born in Brookville, Indiana, on April 10, 1827, the son of an attorney. As a youth, he obtained rudimentary education, but he was essentially self-taught. Wallace prepared himself for a legal career but interrupted his studies in 1846 to raise a company of infantry for service in the Mexican War as its lieutenant. He saw no combat and was so angered by General Zachary Taylor's disparaging remarks about Indiana troops that he quit the Whig Party and became a Democrat. Wallace subsequently was admitted to the bar in 1849 while also maintaining close ties to the militia. He also set down political roots in 1856 by successfully standing for a seat in the state senate, and in April 1861 the governor appointed him adjutant general of state forces. Wallace then used his skill at raising troops and his political connections to become colonel of the 11th Indiana Infantry, a colorful Zouave unit. Unlike many political appointees, he proved himself a capable soldier who fought well and distinguished himself in minor actions at Romney and Harper's Ferry, Virginia. He rose to brigadier general in consequence on September 3, 1861, and he reported back to the Department of the Ohio to lead a division. In this capacity, Wallace handled his men capably during General Ulysses S. GRANT's campaign against Forts Henry and Donelson in February 1862. That month, he became the first Indiana native promoted to the rank of major general of volunteers, and he accompanied Grant down the Tennessee River to Pittsburg Landing, Tennessee. There, on April 6–7, Confederates under General Albert S. JOHNSTON surprised Grant's men in camp during the Battle of Shiloh while Wallace's division was encamped six miles downstream. Grant immediately ordered him to reinforce General William T. SHERMAN's division, but Wallace, saddled by inaccurate maps, took the wrong road and was forced to backtrack. He did not reach the Union camp until midnight, having failed to contribute to the day's fighting. On the following morning, his fresh troops spearheaded a counterattack that drove Confederates from the field, although Grant characterized his overall performance as lethargic.

Wallace had previously criticized General Henry W. HALLECK, who now replaced Grant as theater commander, and consequently Halleck removed him from command. He next reported for duty at Cincinnati, Ohio, and on September 2, 1862, he organized the city's defenses against a possible raid from Kentucky under General Edmund KIRBY-SMITH. Among the troops Wallace recruited was a brigade of African Americans, among the first such formations in the West. The following month, he chaired a military commission investigating the activities of General Don C. BUELL, which led to his ultimate dismissal. Wallace then assumed command of the Middle Department at Baltimore, Maryland, as head of the small VIII Corps. He discharged his duties capably and with little fanfare until midsummer 1864 when 11,000 Confederates under General Jubal A. EARLY marched up the Shenandoah Valley toward Washington, D.C. Though outnumbered two to one, Wallace assembled a scratch force of 6,000 men and confronted the invaders at Monocacy on July 9, 1864. The Federals were swept aside after a stiff fight, and Wallace withdrew back to Baltimore, but the delays incurred allowed General Horatio G. Wright to strengthen the capital's defenses, and a Confederate assault was thwarted. In May 1865, Wallace served on the court that tried conspirators charged with the assassination of President Abraham LINCOLN. The following August, he also sat on a tribunal that condemned Captain Henry Wirz, commander of notorious Andersonville Prison, to hang.

After mustering out, Wallace enjoyed a highly varied, wide-ranging career. He first ventured to Mexico to support Republican forces trying to oust the French-backed emperor Maximilian. Unsuccessful, Wallace then returned to Indiana to resume political activities, and in 1878 his influence helped deliver the state to President Rutherford B. Hayes. He was then appointed governor of the New Mexico Territory as a sinecure, and he expended considerable energy ending a hostile range war with the likes of Billy the Kid. In 1880 Wallace gained lasting renown by writing the novel *Ben Hur,* one of the most popular books ever published in American literature. President James A. Garfield then appointed him minister to Turkey, where he served from 1881 to 1885. Wallace then returned to Crawford, Indiana, to continue writing, and he died there on February 15, 1905. Despite his mixed military record, he was among the most colorful of political generals.

Further Reading

Arnold, James R. *Shiloh, 1862: The End of Innocence.* Westport, Conn.: Praeger, 2004.

Boomhower, Ray E. *The Sword and the Pen: A Life of Lew Wallace.* Indianapolis: Indiana Historical Society Press, 2005.

Leeke, Jim, ed. *Smoke, Sound & Fury: The Civil War Memoirs of Major-General Lew Wallace, U.S. Volunteers.* Philadelphia: Polyglot Press, 2004.

Stephens, Gail M. "Lew Wallace's Fall from Grace." *North & South* 7, no. 3 (2004): 32–46.

Stephens, Gail M., and Gloria B. Swift. "Honor Redeemed: Lew Wallace's Military Career and the Battle of Monocacy." *North & South* 4, no. 2 (2001): 34–46.

Woodworth, Steven L., ed. *Grant's Lieutenants: From Cairo to Vicksburg.* Lawrence: University Press of Kansas, 2001.

Watie, Stand (1806–1871)

Confederate general

Degataga (Stand Firm) was born to the Deer Clan of the Cherokee at Oothcaloga, Georgia, on December 12, 1806, a son of farmers. Educated at mission schools and converted to the Moravian Church, he gradually Anglicized his name to Stand Watie. He also claimed one-quarter Scottish ancestry through his mother, and he became closely associated with the light-skinned tribal elite. In time, both he and his brother Elias Boudinot, editor of the tribal newspaper *Cherokee Phoenix,* aligned themselves with factions who were willing to sell their land to the U.S. government and peacefully relocate to the Indian Territory (Oklahoma) reserved for them. This placed him at odds with Chief John Ross and the bulk of the Cherokee, who resisted deportation from Georgia. Watie was nonetheless one of a handful of chiefs who willingly signed the Treaty of New Echota in December 1835, mandating their removal. He arrived at his new home without incident, but many Cherokee, forced to endure the so-called Trail of Tears under General Winfield SCOTT, resented his cooperation with whites. Thereafter, the tribe was strongly split into two feuding factions under Ross and Watie, with the latter losing a brother, a cousin, and an uncle to assassination. Peace was not restored to the tribe until 1846.

After resettling, Watie established himself as a wealthy, slave-owning planter and was therefore naturally sympathetic to the newly established Confederate State of America. In August 1861 he prevailed on Chief Ross to embrace the Southern cause, and he received command of the 1st Cherokee Mounted Rifle Regiment as its colonel. When Ross subsequently reneged on his commitments and fled to Union-controlled territory, a civil war broke out among the Cherokee in which Watie ultimately prevailed. Thereafter, he mustered all available warriors and joined Confederates armies in the field. Watie fought with General Earl VAN DORN at Pea Ridge (March 7–8, 1862), and, there, he captured a Union battery and covered the Confederate withdrawal. He was also conspicuously engaged in the Southern defeat at Honey Springs on July 17, 1863, in which Confederate Native Americans were pitted against Union African Americans. That year, shifting tides of fortune finally convinced the majority of Cherokee to renounce their alliance with the Confederacy, but Watie remained loyal and advanced to brigadier general as of May 1864. He was also elected the principal tribal war chief and commanded an entire brigade of two mounted regiments and three battalions of Cherokee, Osage, and Seminole infantry. With them, he attacked and captured the Federal steamer *J. R. Williams* in June 1864, along with $41.2 million in supplies. The following September 19, 1864, Watie also seized 200 supply wagons and 1,200 mules at Cabin Crossing. Once hostilities concluded, Watie surrendered to Union officials on June 23, 1865, the last Confederate commander to do so.

After the war, Watie resumed his highly visible profile in tribal politics and worked at reconciling the various factions. He made his greatest contribution in helping to negotiate the Cherokee Reconstruction Treaty of 1866, whereby all slaves in tribal possession were manumitted. He thereafter became a fairly prosperous tobacco grower, minus his slaves. Watie died at Honey Creek, Indian Territory, on September 9, 1871, the only Native American to obtain general's rank during the Civil War. His activities tied down the services of thousands of Federal troops, marking him as one of the conflict's most skilled leaders of irregulars.

Further Reading

Confer, Clarissa W. *The Cherokee Nation in the Civil War.* Norman: University of Oklahoma Press, 2007.

Epple, Jess C. *Honey Springs Depot:, Elk Creek, Creek Nation, Indiana Territory.* Muskogee, Okla.: Thomason Print Co., 2002.

Hatch, Tom. *The Blue, the Gray, and the Red.* Mechanicsburg, Pa.: Stackpole Books, 2003.

Jackson, Rex T. *A Trail of Tears: The American Indian in the Civil War.* Bowie, Md.: Heritage Books, 2004.

Spencer, John D. *American Civil War in Indian Territory.* New York: Osprey, 2006.

Taylor, Ethel. *Dust in the Wind: The Civil War in Indian Territory.* Westminster, Md.: Heritage Books, 2005.

Wheeler, Joseph (1836–1906)
Confederate general

Joseph Wheeler was born in Augusta, Georgia, on September 10, 1836, the son of a banker. After attending private academies in Connecticut, he matriculated through the U.S. Military Academy in 1854 and graduated four years later near the bottom of his class. Wheeler then served as a second lieutenant in the Regiment of Mounted Riflemen in New Mexico, where his willingness to skirmish with hostile Apaches led to the nickname "Fighting Joe." However, once Georgia seceded from the Union in February 1861, he likewise resigned his commission and joined the Confederate army. Wheeler first served as an artillery lieutenant at Pensacola, Florida, under General Braxton BRAGG. He favorably impressed his superiors and consequently became colonel of the 19th Alabama Infantry in September 1861. In this capacity, Wheeler fought well at the Battle of Shiloh (April 6–7, 1862), garnering praise for his conduct of the Confederate rear guard. Bragg, now head of the Army of Mississippi, then appointed Wheeler to command all his cavalry. This proved a fortuitous appointment, for he became one of the hardest riding, most astute mounted leaders on either side. In August 1862 Wheeler's men spearheaded Bragg's drive into Kentucky, where, on October 8, 1862, he distinguished himself at the Battle of Perryville and then expertly covered the Confederate retreat. His

Confederate general Joseph Wheeler *(Library of Congress)*

good performance led to a promotion to brigadier general on October 30, 1862, and throughout the following December, he competently delayed the advance of Union forces under General William S. ROSECRANS. Wheeler then fought well at the bloody encounter of Murfreesboro (December 31, 1862–January 3, 1863), again covered Bragg's retreat, and served as cavalry commander in his newly organized Army of Tennessee. He also became the South's youngest major general as of January 20, 1863, at the age of 26.

Wheeler next accompanied Bragg throughout the Tullahoma campaign against Rosecrans before fighting again at Chickamauga on September 19–20, 1863. Once Union forces were besieged at Chattanooga, Tennessee, he conducted one of the war's most destructive cavalry raids by crossing the Tennessee River, brushing aside General George CROOK's command on the other bank, and then galloping through the Sequatchie Valley

of eastern Tennessee virtually unopposed. During the course of several days, his men inflicted nearly 2,000 casualties, burned 1,000 supply wagons, and destroyed $3 million of property at a cost of only 212 men. This master stroke nearly destroyed Rosecrans's ability to feed his army at Chattanooga and greatly increased its hardships. Wheeler then accompanied General James LONGSTREET on his aborted siege of Knoxville and, after the crushing Confederate defeat at Missionary Ridge on November 25, 1863, again covered Bragg's retreat into Georgia. Wheeler then acted in concert with General Patrick R. CLEBURNE at Ringgold Gap, Georgia, successfully defending it for several hours against superior numbers under General Joseph HOOKER.

In the spring of 1864, Wheeler found himself attached to the Army of Tennessee under General Joseph E. JOHNSTON. For several weeks, he campaigned hard against the advancing columns of General William T. SHERMAN as they marched toward Atlanta, Georgia. On July 30, 1864, he captured General George Stoneman's cavalry column, along with 700 prisoners, which incapacitated Sherman's mounted arm for several weeks. A new commander, General John B. HOOD, then dispatched Wheeler on another long and fruitless raid against Union communications in Tennessee. He then reunited with Johnston in the Carolinas, offering the only organized Confederate resistance to Union troopers under General Hugh J. KILPATRICK. Wheeler gained promotion to lieutenant general in February 1865, but concern over indiscipline in his command resulted in subordination under General Wade HAMPTON. Wheeler was again closely engaged at the Battle of Bentonville, North Carolina, on March 19–21, 1865, before fleeing back to Georgia. He finally was captured there on May 1865 while assisting the flight of President Jefferson DAVIS. In the course of his Civil War career, Wheeler fought in 200 engagements, lost 16 horses shot from beneath him, was wounded three times, and witnessed 36 staff officers shot down at his side.

Wheeler was imprisoned briefly in Delaware during the postwar period, but he relocated to New Orleans, Louisiana, where he flourished as a merchant and lawyer. In 1881 he gained election to the U.S. House of Representatives, returning there eight consecutive times and serving as chairman of the influential Ways and Means Committee. In this capacity, Wheeler became an important symbol of national reconciliation between North and South. For this reason, President William McKinley appointed him a major general of volunteers during the Spanish-American War of 1898. Wheeler again acquitted himself well as a cavalry commander, whose units included Colonel Theodore Roosevelt's "Rough Riders." After the war, he briefly led a convalescent camp at Montauk Point, New York, before leading a brigade in the Philippines. In 1900 Wheeler rose to brigadier general in the regular army as head of the Department of the Lakes. He retired the following year to live in Brooklyn, dying there on January 25, 1906. Wheeler, along with J. E. B. STUART, Joseph O. SHELBY, and Nathan B. FORREST, was among the most talented cavalry leaders of the Civil War. He is one of only a handful of Southern leaders to hold general's rank in both armies or to be interred at Arlington National Cemetery in Washington, D.C.

Further Reading

Black, Robert W. *Cavalry Raids of the Civil War.* Mechanicsburg, Pa.: Stackpole Books, 2004.

Blumberg, Arnold. "Wheeler's 1863 Sequatchie Valley Raid." *Military Heritage* 4, no. 4 (2003): 60–67, 90.

Brookshear, William R., and David K. Schneider. *Glory at a Gallop: Tales of the Confederate Cavalry.* Washington, D.C.: Brassey's, 1993.

Longacre, Edward G. *A Soldier to the Last. Maj. Gen. Joseph Wheeler.* Washington, D.C.: Potomac Books, 2006.

Poole, John R. *Cracker Cavaliers: The 2nd Georgia Cavalry under Wheeler and Forrest.* Macon, Ga.: Mercer University Press, 2000.

Wittenberg, Eric J. *The Battle of Monroe's Crossroads: And the Civil War's Final Campaign.* New York: Savas Bentie, 2006.

Wilkes, Charles (1798–1877)

Union naval officer

Charles Wilkes was born in New York City on April 3, 1798, the son of a banker. Early on, he developed a love of the sea, and after failing to receive a midshipman's commission in 1815, Wilkes joined the merchant marine to acquire nautical experience. Three years later, he was allowed to join the service as a midshipman and during the next 20 years fulfilled a series of routine assignments both afloat and ashore. Wilkes rose

Union naval officer Charles Wilkes *(Massachusetts Commandery Military Order of the Loyal Legion and the U.S. Army Military History Institute)*

to lieutenant by 1826, and in 1838 the government appointed him to command an ambitious exploring expedition that several senior naval leaders declined to accept. The fact that Wilkes had acquired the reputation as a querulous, disagreeable officer rankled contemporaries far less than the fact that he enjoyed less seniority than many officers now serving under him. Nevertheless, Wilkes departed Hampton Roads, Virginia, with a flotilla of six vessels and a bevy of scientists. During the next four years, he ably conducted the U.S. exploring expedition to the farthest reaches of the Pacific, which included the discovery of a new landmass, Antarctica (originally christened Wilkes Land), in December 1839. All told, it was a remarkable episode of discovery covering 80,000 miles, visiting 180 islands, and resulting in the creation of 180 nautical charts that were so accurate that many were still employed during World War II. Moreover, the plants and animals he brought back formed the core collection of what became the Smithsonian Institution. But no sooner had Wilkes docked at New York in June 1842 than he was brought up on charges of abuse leveled by many officers and crew members. A court-martial found him guilty of meting out unauthorized punishment, which only enhanced his reputation as a stiff-necked martinet. Worse, enemies in Congress obstructed the funding to publish his 20-volume record of the expedition. Wilkes simply accepted an assignment ashore and spent 17 years editing and publishing it on his own. During this period, he rose to commander in 1843 and captain in 1855.

When the Civil War commenced in April 1861, Wilkes was assigned to the USS *Merrimac* at Norfolk, but he arrived to find that it had already been scuttled by retreating Union forces. He then received command of the steamer *San Jacinto* with orders to patrol the west coast of Florida for Confederate commerce and possibly to intercept the raider CSS *Sumter* under Commander Raphael SEMMES. While in Havana, he learned that Confederate diplomats John M. Mason and John Slidell were aboard the British mail ship *Trent* off the Bahamas. Rough-hewn and hardly beholden to the nuances of diplomacy, Wilkes aggressively charted an intercept course, and on November 8, 1861, he fired a shot across the British vessel's bow. Mason and Slidell then were forcibly removed in an egregious violation of international neutrality, but Wilkes arrived at Boston to a hero's welcome. The British government, however, vehemently protested and threatened war if Mason and Slidell were not immediately released. President Abraham LINCOLN, wishing at all hazards to avoid British military intervention on the Confederacy's behalf, ordered both men released on January 1, 1862. The incident subsided much to the relief of both sides.

The contentious Wilkes received promotion to commodore in July 1862 and successively commanded the James River and Potomac River squadrons to assist the Peninsula campaign of General George B. McCLELLAN. That September, he was accorded a rank of acting rear admiral along with command of the West Indies Squadron. Wilkes then was tasked with intercepting Confederate privateers and blockade-runners, which he pursued with vigor. However, he also roughly accosted several British vessels in the process, and he was recalled in June 1863 amid a storm of diplomatic protests. Wilkes then vented his anger against Secretary of the Navy Gideon Welles, whom he publicly denounced as a buffoon, and he was court-martialed a second time in March 1864. He then was demoted to captain and placed on three years' suspension, although President Lincoln reduced the sentence to a single year. His active navy career ended, Wilkes retired in 1864 and resumed editing and publishing his expedition accounts. He advanced to rear admiral on the retired list in July 1866 and composed his lengthy memoirs in 1871 at the age of 73. Wilkes died in Washington, D.C., on February 8, 1877, a highly efficient naval officer, a thoroughly unlikable individual, and the man who almost embroiled the United States in a war with Britain.

Further Reading

Bradford, James C., ed. *Captains of the Old Steam Navy: Makers of the American Naval Tradition, 1840–1880.* Annapolis, Md.: Naval Institute Press, 1986.

Fuller, Howard. *Navies and Naval Operations of the Civil War, 1861–1865.* London: Conway Marine, 2005.

Joyce, Barry A. *The Shaping of American Ethnology: The Wilkes Exploring Expedition, 1838–1842.* Lincoln: University of Nebraska Press, 2001.

Morgan, William J., et al., eds. *Autobiography of Rear Admiral Charles Wilkes, U.S. Navy, 1798–1877.* Washington, D.C.: Naval History Division, 1978.

Philbrick, Nathaniel. *Sea of Glory: America's Voyage of Discovery: The U.S. Exploring Expedition, 1838–1842.* New York: Viking Press, 2003.

Warren, Gordon H. *Fountain of Discontent: The Trent Affair and Freedom of the Seas.* Boston: Northeastern University Press, 1981.

Wilson, James H. (1837–1925)

Union general

James Harrison Wilson was born in Shawneetown, Illinois, on September 2, 1837, the son of farmers. He briefly attended McKendree College before enrolling at the U.S. Military Academy in 1855. An excellent student, Wilson graduated sixth in his class in 1860 and was posted with the elite Corps of Engineers. He then spent a year at Fort Vancouver, Washington Territory, before the Civil War broke out in April 1861, when Wilson hastened back east to fight. He saw his first action as a topographical engineer on the staff of General Thomas W. Sherman at the capture of Port Royal, South Carolina, in November 1861 and subsequently distinguished himself under General David Hunter during the siege of Fort Pulaski, Georgia, in April 1862. Eager for advancement, Wilson next served as a volunteer aide-de-camp to General George B. McClellan throughout the Antietam campaign of September. Good conduct resulted in promotion to lieutenant colonel of volunteers and transfer to the staff of General Ulysses S. Grant the following November 1862. Wilson performed well throughout the ensuing Vicksburg campaign and served as inspector general of the Army of the Tennessee as of July 1863. He rose to brigadier

Union general James Wilson *(Library of Congress)*

general of volunteers that October and fought with distinction at the decisive Union victory of Chattanooga on November 25, 1863. Grant then recommended him as chief of the Cavalry Bureau within the War Department, which office he assumed in January 1864.

Wilson, possessing no prior experience with the mounted arm, nonetheless instituted reforms that completely overhauled the cavalry's equipment and mission. He believed that the days of sword-wielding charges had passed and that troopers were infinitely more valuable serving as mobile infantry, combining movement with firepower. To that end, he issued rapid-fire Spencer rifles to all ranks and trained them vigorously in the art of skirmishing. In April 1864 Grant reassigned Wilson to command the 3rd Cavalry Division as part of General Philip H. Sheridan's cavalry corps, Army of the Potomac. In his first mounted foray, Wilson conducted some minor raids near Richmond, losing his wagon train in one instance and then tangling heavily with General Wade HAMPTON's Confederate cavalry at Ream's Station on August 25, 1864. He subsequently accompanied Sheridan to the Shenandoah Valley and bore a prominent role in the crushing of Confederate forces under General Jubal A. EARLY. Wilson, as he acquired greater experience in handling mounted troops, exhibited signs of operational brilliance, and, in the fall of 1864, he was posted as cavalry chief in the Military Division of the Mississippi under General William T. SHERMAN.

Wilson provided useful services during the Union advance to Atlanta, Georgia, until General John B. HOOD's Confederates marched into Tennessee to attack Union supply lines. After detaching the division of General Hugh J. KILPATRICK to remain with Sherman, he then accompanied Generals George H. THOMAS and John M. SCHOFIELD westward. Wilson's cavalry expertly delayed the Confederate approach to Spring Hill and Franklin, where they suffered terrible losses on November 29, 1864, and he subsequently covered Schofield's retreat to Nashville. On December 16 his men were actively engaged in the decisive Battle of Nashville, which saw Hood's Army of Tennessee virtually destroyed by a vigorous pursuit. Wilson then gained promotion to brevet brigadier general of regulars in March 1865 along with command of his own cavalry corps, 15,000 strong. With it, he launched a series of devastating raids across northern Alabama and Georgia, heavily defeating General Nathan B. FORREST at Selma on April 2, 1865. This success was followed up by the captures of Montgomery on April 12 and Columbus, Georgia, on April 16, along with 7,000 prisoners and 300 cannon. Thus, to Wilson goes the distinction of fighting and winning the Civil War's last land engagement east of the Mississippi River. His men also gained a final measure of distinction on May 10, 1865, by capturing Confederate president Jefferson DAVIS at Irwinville, Georgia. He ended the war as a major general of volunteers at the age of 27.

Wilson was retained in the postwar service as a lieutenant colonel of the 35th U.S. Infantry, and he resigned from the service in December 1870 to pursue railroad engineering. He returned to the colors when the Spanish-American War commenced in 1898 as a major general of volunteers, seeing service in Cuba and Puerto Rico. In 1900 he ventured to China to fight in the Boxer Rebellion under General Adna R. Chaffee and commanded a punitive expedition against the city of Patachow. He then retired with a rank of brigadier general by a special act of Congress. Wilson died in Wilmington, Delaware, on February 23, 1925, a noted "boy general" of the Civil War and one of the longest surviving Union generals.

Further Reading

Black, Robert W. *Cavalry Raids of the Civil War.* Mechanicsburg, Pa.: Stackpole Books, 2004.

Bellware, Daniel A. "The Last Battle of the War. Period. Really." *Civil War Times Illustrated* 42, no. 1 (2003): 48–43, 56.

Coffey, David. *Sheridan's Lieutenants: Phil Sheridan, His Generals, and the Final Year of the Civil War.* Wilmington, Del.: Rowman and Littlefield, 2005.

Jones, James P. *Yankee Blitzkrieg: Wilson's Raid through Alabama and Georgia.* Lexington: University Press of Kentucky, 2000.

Kennan, Jerry. *Wilson's Cavalry Corps: Union Campaigns in the Western Theater, October 1864 through Spring 1865.* Jefferson, N.C.: McFarland, 1998.

Longacre, Edward G. *Lincoln's Cavalrymen: A History of the Mounted Forces of the Army of the Potomac, 1861–1865.* Mechanicsburg, Pa.: Stackpole Books, 2000.

Worden, John L. (1818–1897)

Union naval officer

John Lorimer Worden was born in Westchester County, New York, on March 12, 1818, and he joined the U.S. Navy as a midshipman in 1834. For the next 27 years, he fulfilled a series of routine assignments afloat and ashore, rising to lieutenant in 1846. He still held that rank when the Civil War commenced in April 1861 and immediately requested duty at sea. Worden was dispatched overland to Fort Pickens, Florida, with a secret communiqué for the Federal squadron offshore.

Confederate authorities apprehended him at Montgomery, Alabama, on his return trip, and he experienced close confinement for seven months. Once exchanged, Worden received command of inventor John Ericsson's new and experimental ironclad warship, USS *Monitor*. This unique vessel, frequently derided as a "cheese box on a raft," sat extremely low in the water with a single, revolving turret amidships. Its bizarre appearance greatly belied the dramatic military revolution it embodied.

On February 25, 1862, Worden sailed his charge from Long Island, New York, to Hampton Roads, Virginia, delayed by choppy seas and last-minute mechanical failures. He arrived on the evening of March 7, 1862, to behold the devastation wrought by the Confederate captain Franklin

Union naval officer John L. Worden *(U.S. Navy)*

BUCHANAN and the ironclad CSS *Virginia* (née *Merrimac*), which had sank or had severely damaged the Federal frigates *Cumberland* and *Congress* that afternoon. The following morning, the *Virginia*, now captained by Lieutenant Catesby ap Roger Jones, reappeared to finish off the Union vessels, and Worden placed his *Monitor* squarely in its path. For the next three hours, the armored giants flailed away at each other, inflicting little damage. The *Virginia* also tried to ram its smaller opponent, but it was thwarted by the latter's higher speed and shallower draft. Finally, a lucky Southern shot shattered Worden's pilothouse, wounding him in the eye. He relinquished command to Lieutenant Samuel D. Greene, and after a few more hours of combat, the *Virginia* withdrew back to Norfolk before low tides stranded it. This engagement, though technically a draw, proved a strategic victory for the North as it maintained the blockade of Norfolk and ensured its eventual capture. It also sounded the death knell of wooden warships. Worden's wound required several months of rehabilitation, but he received the thanks of Congress and promotion to commander in July 1862 for his fine performance. President Abraham LINCOLN was so impressed by the doughty sailor that he paid him a bedside visit.

After recovery, Worden assumed command of the new *Passaic*-class monitor *Montauk* in January 1863, and he sailed as part of Admiral Samuel F. Du PONT's South Atlantic Blockading Squadron. A massive naval attack on heavily defended Charleston, South Carolina, was then in the planning stages, and Worden was ordered to attack Fort McAllister, Savannah, Georgia, as an experiment, on January 27, 1863. He traded shots with the fort for several hours, inflicting little damage and sustaining 46 hits. Another attack on February 1, 1863, yielded similar results, but on February 28, he managed to destroy the Confederate raider CSS *Nashville* beneath the fort's guns. That month, he also rose to captain. But despite Du Pont's predictions of disaster, the Navy Department authorized the assault on Charleston, which transpired on the afternoon of April 7, 1863. Worden was actively engaged, receiving a further 14 direct hits, and the rest of the fleet was also heavily damaged. Shortly after, he was relieved of command and recalled to New York to supervise the construction of new monitor vessels. This vital service kept him out of combat for the remainder of the war.

In the postwar period, Worden commanded the *Pensacola* as part of the Pacific Squadron until May 1868, when he advanced to commodore and was appointed superintendent of the U.S. Naval Academy, Annapolis. His five year of tenure was characterized by his implementation of elevated academic standards and rules against hazing, and the founding of the U.S. Naval Institute, in which he served as first president. Worden rose to rear admiral in November 1872 and spent the next 14 years commanding various squadrons. He retired in December 1886 after a special act of Congress allowed him to retain full-pay status for life. Worden died in Washington, D.C., on October 18, 1897, an important leadership figure in the navy's transition from wood to iron.

Further Reading

Clancy, Paul R. *Ironclad: The Epic Battle Calamities, Loss, and Historic Recovery of the USS Monitor.* Camden, Maine: International Marine/McGraw-Hill, 2006.

Holzer, Harold, ed. *The Battle of Hampton Roads: New Perspectives on the USS Monitor and CSS Virginia.* New York: Fordham University Press, 2006.

Nelson, James L. *Reign of Iron: The Story of the First Battling Ironclads, The Monitor and the Merrimack.* New York: William Morrow, 2004.

Roberts, William H. *Civil War Ironclads: The U.S. Navy and Industrial Mobilization.* Baltimore: Johns Hopkins University Press, 2002.

Symonds, Craig L. *Decision at Sea: Five Naval Battles That Shaped American History.* New York: Oxford University Press, 2005.

West, W. Wilson. "Monitor Madness: Union Ironclad Construction at New York City, 1862–1864." Unpublished Ph.D. diss., University of Alabama, 2003.

APPENDIX

Casualties and Major Land Battles of the Civil War

TROOPS AVAILABLE FOR DUTY (JANUARY 1)

	Union	Confederacy
1862	527,204	209,852
1863	698,808	253,208
1864	611,250	233,586
1865	620,924	154,910
Total Forces	1,556,678	1,082,119

DEATHS DURING THE CIVIL WAR

	Union	Confederacy
Total forces	1,556,678	1,082,119
Deaths from Wounds	110,070	94,000
Deaths from Disease	249,458	164,000
Death Rate	23 percent	24 percent
Wounded	275,175	100,000

DEATHS IN AMERICAN WARS (U.S. MILITARY CASUALTIES)

Civil War	618,000
World War II	405,000
World War I	112,000
Vietnam War	58,000
Korean War	36,517
American Revolution	25,000
War of 1812	20,000
Mexican War	13,000
Spanish-American War	2,446
Gulf War	299

Major Land Battles

The Ten Costliest Land Battles, Measured by Casualties (Killed, Wounded, Captured, and Missing)

BATTLE (STATE)	DATES	CONFEDERATE COMMANDER	UNION COMMANDER	CONFEDERATE FORCES	UNION FORCES	VICTOR	CASUALTIES
Battle of Gettysburg (Pennsylvania)	July 1–3, 1863	Robert E. Lee	George G. Meade	75,000	82,289	Union	51,112 U: 23,049 C: 28,063
Battle of Chickamauga (Georgia)	September 19–20, 1863	Braxton Bragg	William Rosecrans	66,326	58,222	Conf.	34,624 U: 16,170 C: 18,454
Battle of Chancellorsville (Virginia)	May 1–4, 1863	Robert E. Lee	Joseph Hooker	60,892	133,868	Conf.	30,099 U: 17,278 C: 12,821
Battle of Spotsylvania Court House (Virginia)	May 8–19, 1864	Robert E. Lee	Ulysses S. Grant	50,000	83,000	Draw	27,399 U: 18,399 C: 9,000
Battle of Antietam (Maryland)	September 17, 1862	Robert E. Lee	George B. McClellan	51,844	75,316	Draw	23,134 U: 12,410 C: 10,724
Battle of the Wilderness (Virginia)	May 5–7, 1864	Robert E. Lee	Ulysses S. Grant	61,025	101,895	Draw	25,416 U: 17,666 C: 7,750
Second Battle of Manassas (Virginia)	August 29–30, 1862	Robert E. Lee	John Pope	48,527	75,696	Conf.	25,251 U: 16,054 C: 9,197
Battle of Stones River (Tennessee)	December 31, 1862	Braxton Bragg	William S. Rosecrans	37,739	41,400	Union	24,645 U: 12,906 C: 11,739
Battle of Shiloh (Tennessee)	April 6–7, 1862	Albert Sidney Johnston, P. G. T. Beauregard	Ulysses S. Grant	40,335	62,682	Union	23,741 U: 13,047 C: 10,694
Battle of Fort Donelson (Tennessee)	February 13–16, 1862	John B. Floyd, Simon B. Buckner	Ulysses S. Grant	21,000	27,000	Union	19,455 U: 2,832 C: 16,623

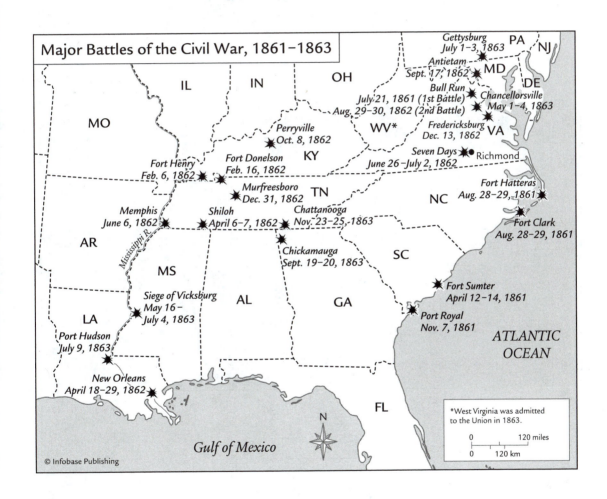

Major Battles of the Civil War, 1861–1863

Gettysburg
July 1–3, 1863
PA
NJ
Antietam
Sept. 17, 1862
MD
DE
Bull Run
July 21, 1861 (1st Battle)
Aug. 29–30, 1862 (2nd Battle)
Chancellorsville
May 1–4, 1863
IL
IN
OH
MO
WV*
Fredericksburg
Dec. 13, 1862
VA
Perryville
Oct. 8, 1862
KY
Seven Days
June 26–July 2, 1862
Richmond
Fort Henry
Feb. 6, 1862
Fort Donelson
Feb. 16, 1862
Fort Hatteras
Aug. 28–29, 1861
Murfreesboro
Dec. 31, 1862
TN
NC
Memphis
June 6, 1862
Shiloh
April 6–7, 1862
Chattanooga
Nov. 23–25, 1863
Fort Clark
Aug. 28–29, 1861
AR
Chickamauga
Sept. 19–20, 1863
SC
MS
Siege of Vicksburg
May 16–
July 4, 1863
AL
GA
Fort Sumter
April 12–14, 1861
LA
Port Royal
Nov. 7, 1861
Port Hudson
July 9, 1863
ATLANTIC
OCEAN
New Orleans
April 18–29, 1862
FL
N
*West Virginia was admitted
to the Union in 1863.
0   120 miles
0   120 km
Gulf of Mexico
© Infobase Publishing

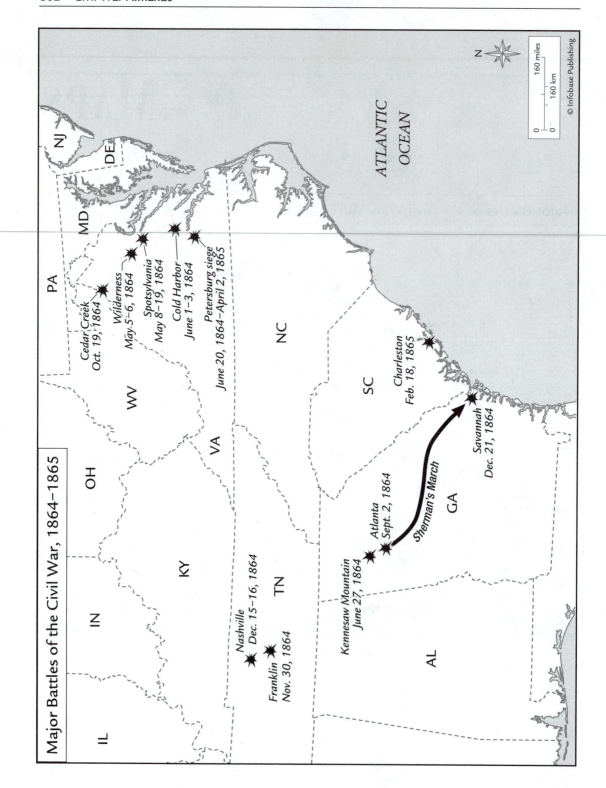

Major Battles of the Civil War, 1864–1865

N

160 miles

160 km

© Infobase Publishing

ATLANTIC OCEAN

NJ

DE

MD

PA

Cedar Creek
Oct. 19, 1864

Wilderness
May 5–6, 1864

Spotsylvania
May 8–19, 1864

Cold Harbor
June 1–3, 1864

Petersburg siege
June 20, 1864–April 2, 1865

WV

VA

NC

SC

Charleston
Feb. 18, 1865

Savannah
Dec. 21, 1864

Sherman's March

Atlanta
Sept. 2, 1864

GA

Kennesaw Mountain
June 27, 1864

OH

KY

TN

Nashville
Dec. 15–16, 1864

Franklin
Nov. 30, 1864

IN

IL

AL

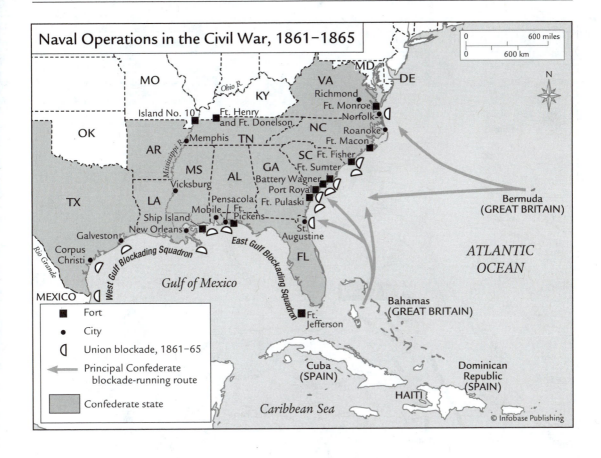

Naval Operations in the Civil War, 1861–1865

600 miles

600 km

MO

Ohio R.

KY

MD

VA

DE

Richmond

Ft. Monroe

OK

Island No. 10

Ft. Henry and Ft. Donelson

Norfolk

NC

AR

Memphis

TN

Roanoke

Ft. Macon

MS

Vicksburg

AL

GA

SC

Ft. Fisher

Ft. Sumter

Battery Wagner

Port Royal

Ft. Pulaski

Mississippi R.

TX

LA

Pensacola

Mobile

Ft. Pickens

Ship Island

Galveston

New Orleans

St. Augustine

East Gulf Blockading Squadron

FL

Corpus Christi

Rio Grande

West Gulf Blockading Squadron

Gulf of Mexico

MEXICO

ATLANTIC OCEAN

Bermuda (GREAT BRITAIN)

Bahamas (GREAT BRITAIN)

Ft. Jefferson

N

South Atlantic Blockading Squadron

Caribbean Sea

Cuba (SPAIN)

HAITI

Dominican Republic (SPAIN)

© Infobase Publishing

Legend:

- ■ Fort
- ● City
- ◖ Union blockade, 1861–65
- ← Principal Confederate blockade-running route
- Confederate state

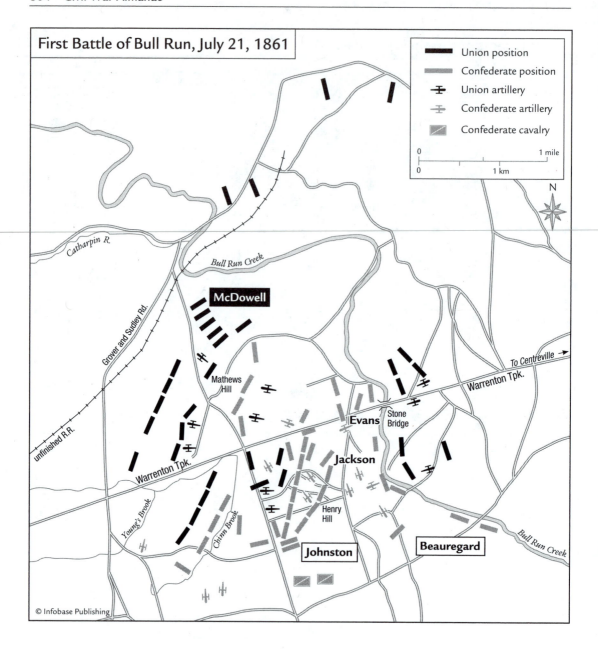

First Battle of Bull Run, July 21, 1861

Union position
Confederate position
Union artillery
Confederate artillery
Confederate cavalry

0   1 mile
0   1 km

N

Catharpin R.

Bull Run Creek

McDowell

Grover and Sudley Rd.

Mathews Hill

To Centreville →

Warrenton Tpk.

unfinished R.R.

Evans

Stone Bridge

Warrenton Tpk.

Jackson

Young's Brook

Henry Hill

Chinn Brook

Bull Run Creek

Johnston

Beauregard

© Infobase Publishing

Monitor and *Virginia (Merrimack)* at Hampton Roads, March 8–9, 1862

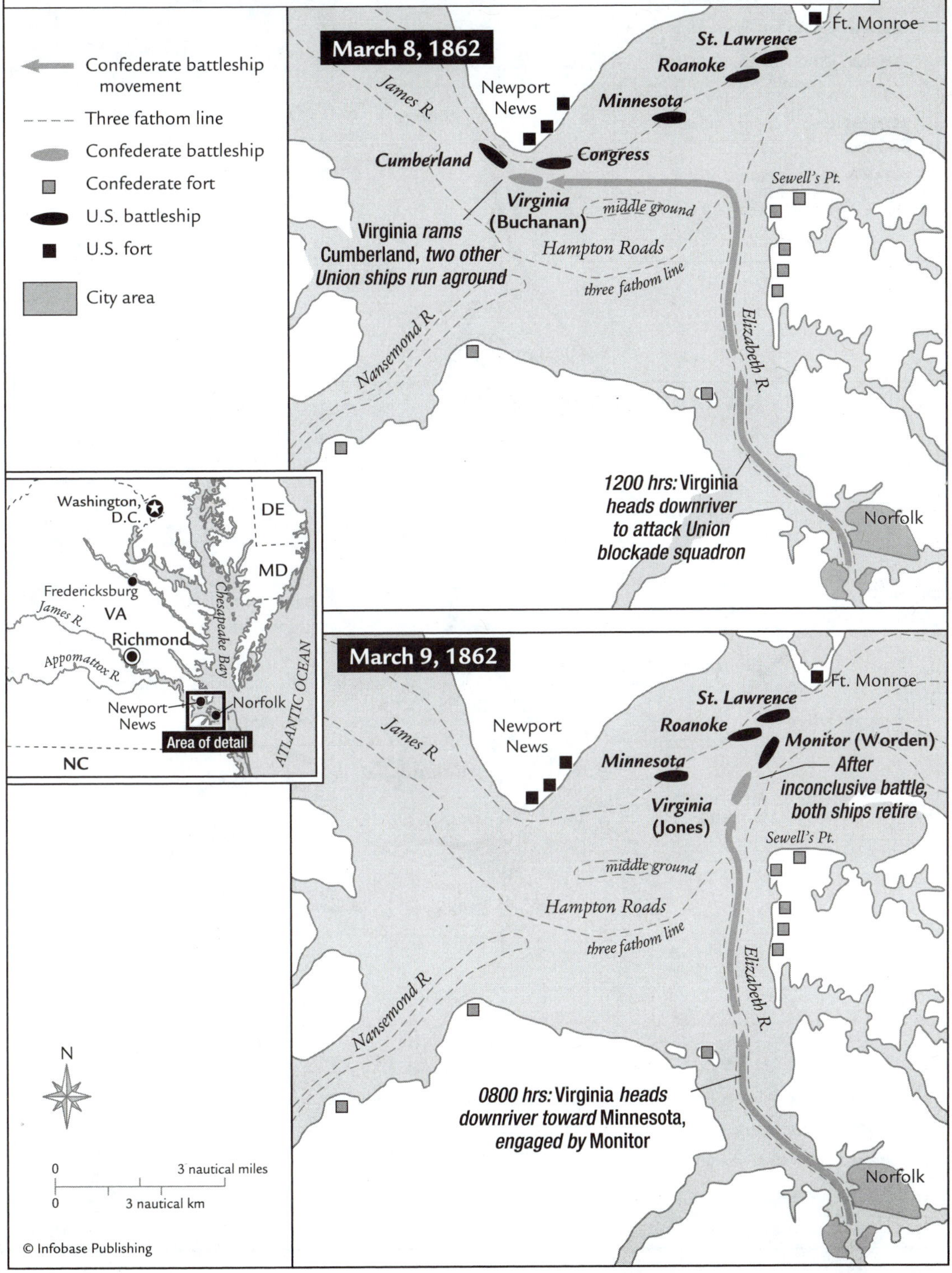
Confederate battleship movement
Three fathom line
Confederate battleship
Confederate fort
U.S. battleship
U.S. fort
City area
March 8, 1862
Ft. Monroe
St. Lawrence
Roanoke
Minnesota
Newport News
James R.
Cumberland
Congress
Virginia (Buchanan)
Virginia rams Cumberland, two other Union ships run aground
middle ground
Hampton Roads
three fathom line
Sewell's Pt.
Nansemond R.
Elizabeth R.
1200 hrs: Virginia heads downriver to attack Union blockade squadron
Norfolk
Washington, D.C.
DE
MD
Fredericksburg
James R.
VA
Richmond
Appomattox R.
Chesapeake Bay
ATLANTIC OCEAN
Newport News
Norfolk
Area of detail
NC
March 9, 1862
Ft. Monroe
St. Lawrence
Roanoke
Monitor (Worden)
Minnesota
After inconclusive battle, both ships retire
Virginia (Jones)
Newport News
James R.
Sewell's Pt.
middle ground
Hampton Roads
three fathom line
Elizabeth R.
Nansemond R.
0800 hrs: Virginia heads downriver toward Minnesota, engaged by Monitor
Norfolk
N
0
3 nautical miles
0
3 nautical km

© Infobase Publishing

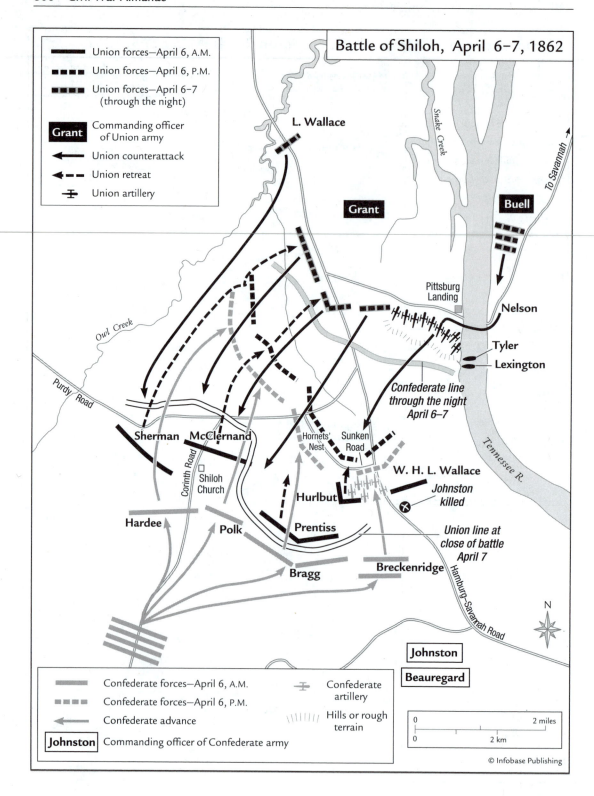

Battle of Shiloh, April 6–7, 1862

Union forces—April 6, A.M.
Union forces—April 6, P.M.
Union forces—April 6–7 (through the night)
Grant Commanding officer of Union army
Union counterattack
Union retreat
Union artillery

L. Wallace

Grant

Buell

To Savannah

Snake Creek

Pittsburg Landing

Nelson

Tyler
Lexington

Confederate line through the night April 6–7

Owl Creek

Purdy Road

Sherman   McClernand

Corinth Road

Shiloh Church

Hardee

Polk

Hornets' Nest   Sunken Road

W. H. L. Wallace

Johnston killed

Hurlbut

Prentiss

Union line at close of battle April 7

Bragg

Breckenridge

Tennessee R.

Hamburg-Savannah Road

N

Johnston

Beauregard

Confederate forces—April 6, A.M.
Confederate forces—April 6, P.M.
Confederate advance
Johnston Commanding officer of Confederate army
Confederate artillery
Hills or rough terrain

0   2 miles
0   2 km

© Infobase Publishing

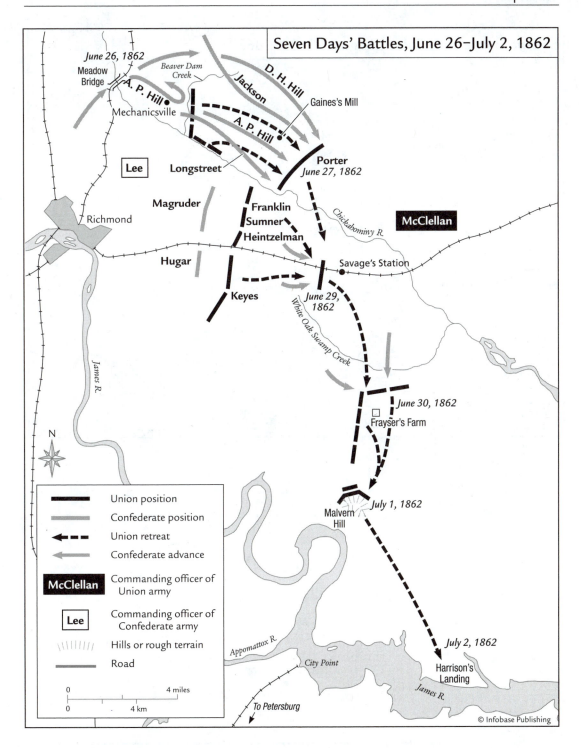

Seven Days' Battles, June 26–July 2, 1862

June 26, 1862
Meadow Bridge
Beaver Dam Creek
A. P. Hill
Mechanicsville
Jackson
D. H. Hill
Gaines's Mill
A. P. Hill
Lee
Longstreet
Porter
June 27, 1862
Magruder
Richmond
Franklin
Sumner
Heintzelman
Chickahominy R.
McClellan
Savage's Station
Hugar
Keyes
June 29, 1862
White Oak Swamp Creek
James R.
N
June 30, 1862
Frayser's Farm
July 1, 1862
Malvern Hill

Union position
Confederate position
Union retreat
Confederate advance
McClellan   Commanding officer of Union army
Lee   Commanding officer of Confederate army
Hills or rough terrain
Road

0   4 miles
0   4 km

Appomattox R.
City Point
July 2, 1862
Harrison's Landing
James R.
To Petersburg
© Infobase Publishing

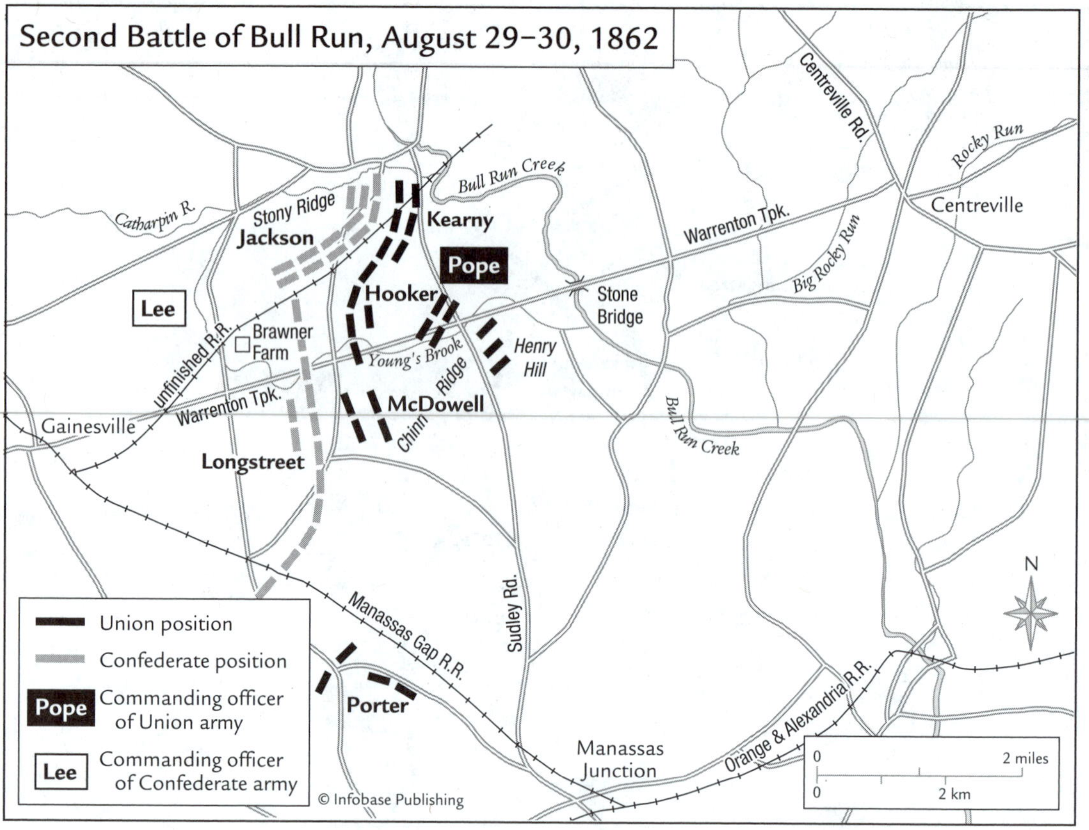
Second Battle of Bull Run, August 29–30, 1862
Centreville Rd.
Rocky Run
Bull Run Creek
Catharpin R.
Stony Ridge
Jackson
Kearny
Centreville
Warrenton Tpk.
Pope
Big Rocky Run
Hooker
Stone Bridge
Lee
Brawner Farm
Henry Hill
unfinished R.R.
Young's Brook
Chinn Ridge
Warrenton Tpk.
McDowell
Gainesville
Bull Run Creek
Longstreet
Sudley Rd.
Manassas Gap R.R.
N
Union position
Confederate position
Pope
Commanding officer of Union army
Lee
Commanding officer of Confederate army
Porter
Orange & Alexandria R.R.
Manassas Junction
0
2 miles
0
2 km
© Infobase Publishing

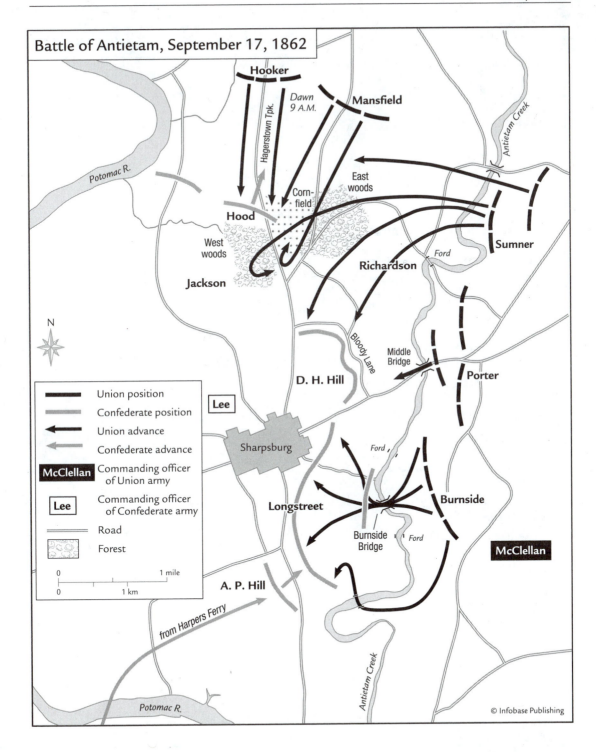

Battle of Antietam, September 17, 1862

Hooker

Dawn 9 A.M.

Mansfield

Antietam Creek

Potomac R.

Hagerstown Tpk.

East woods

Corn-field

Hood

West woods

Sumner

Jackson

Richardson

Ford

Bloody Lane

Middle Bridge

D. H. Hill

Porter

N

Lee

Union position

Confederate position

Union advance

Confederate advance

McClellan Commanding officer of Union army

Lee Commanding officer of Confederate army

Road

Forest

0   1 mile
0   1 km

Sharpsburg

Ford

Longstreet

Burnside

Burnside Bridge

Ford

McClellan

A. P. Hill

from Harpers Ferry

Antietam Creek

Potomac R.

© Infobase Publishing

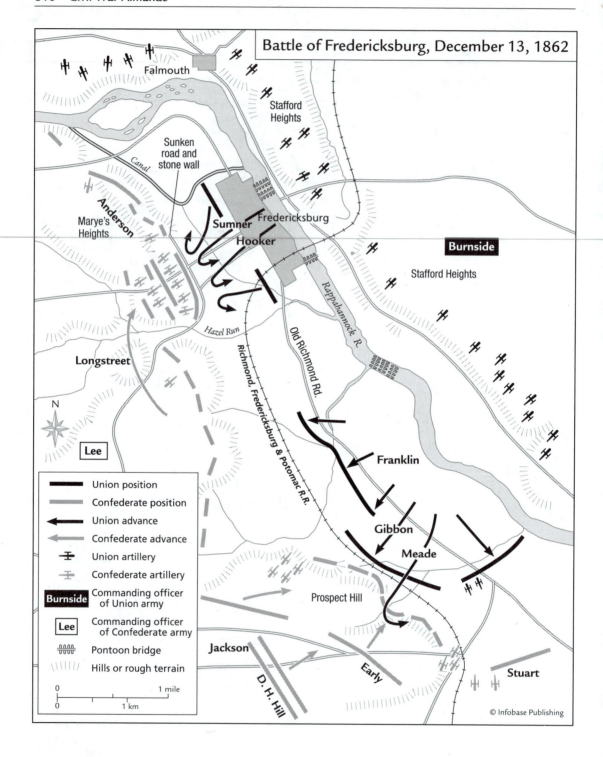

Battle of Fredericksburg, December 13, 1862

Falmouth

Stafford
Heights

Sunken
road and
stone wall

Canal

Marye's
Heights

Anderson

Sumner

Fredericksburg

Hooker

Burnside

Stafford Heights

Rappahannock R.

Hazel Run

Longstreet

Old Richmond Rd.

Richmond, Fredericksburg & Potomac R.R.

N

Lee

Franklin

Gibbon

Meade

	Union position
	Confederate position
	Union advance
	Confederate advance
	Union artillery
	Confederate artillery
Burnside	Commanding officer of Union army
Lee	Commanding officer of Confederate army
	Pontoon bridge
	Hills or rough terrain

Prospect Hill

Jackson

Early

Stuart

D. H. Hill

0   1 mile

0   1 km

© Infobase Publishing

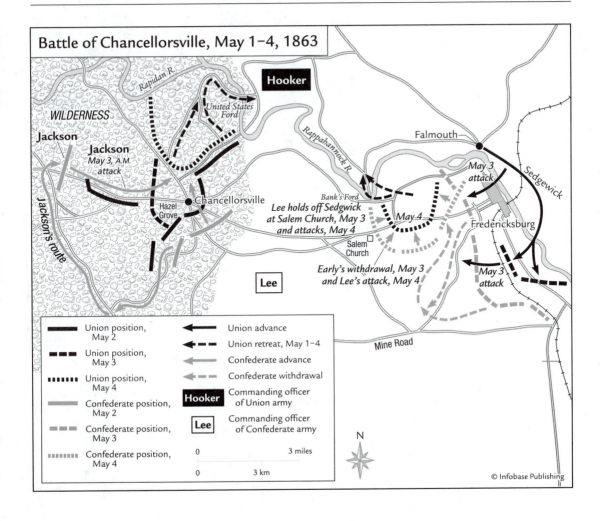

Battle of Chancellorsville, May 1–4, 1863

WILDERNESS

Rapidan R.

United States Ford

Hooker

Jackson

Jackson
May 3, A.M.
attack

Jackson's route

Hazel Grove

Chancellorsville

Rappahannock R.

Falmouth

May 3 attack

Sedgewick

Bank's Ford

Lee holds off Sedgwick
at Salem Church, May 3
and attacks, May 4

May 4

Fredericksburg

Lee

Salem Church

Early's withdrawal, May 3
and Lee's attack, May 4

May 3
attack

Mine Road

Union position,
May 2

Union position,
May 3

Union position,
May 4

Confederate position,
May 2

Confederate position,
May 3

Confederate position,
May 4

Union advance

Union retreat, May 1–4

Confederate advance

Confederate withdrawal

Hooker Commanding officer
of Union army

Lee Commanding officer
of Confederate army

| 0 | 3 miles |
| 0 | 3 km |

N

© Infobase Publishing

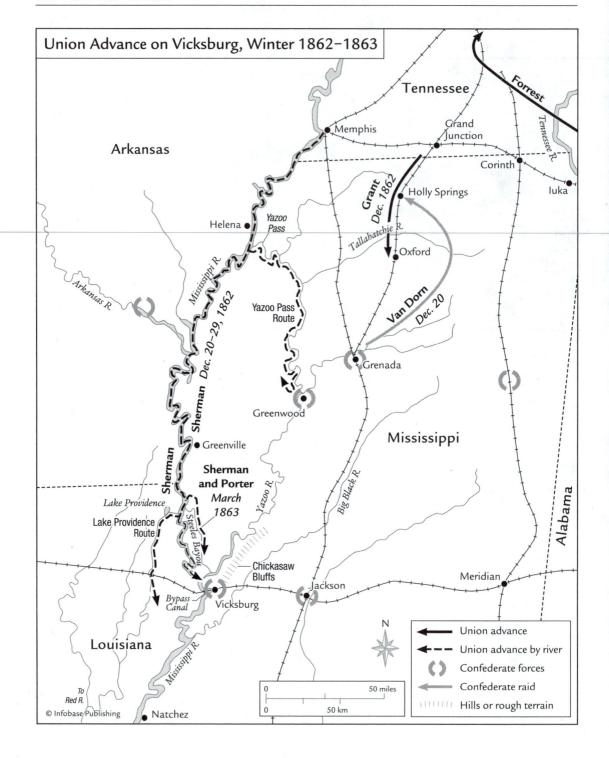

Union Advance on Vicksburg, Winter 1862–1863

Tennessee

Forrest

Arkansas

Memphis

Grand Junction

Corinth

Grant Dec. 1862

Holly Springs

Iuka

Tennessee R.

Helena

Yazoo Pass

Tallahatchie R.

Oxford

Mississippi R.

Van Dorn Dec. 20

Arkansas R.

Sherman Dec. 20–29, 1862

Yazoo Pass Route

Grenada

Greenwood

Greenville

Mississippi

Sherman

Sherman and Porter March 1863

Lake Providence

Steele's Bayou

Yazoo R.

Big Black R.

Lake Providence Route

Alabama

Chickasaw Bluffs

Bypass Canal

Vicksburg

Jackson

Meridian

Louisiana

Mississippi R.

To Red R.

© Infobase Publishing

Natchez

N

0   50 miles

0   50 km

→ Union advance
→ Union advance by river
◖◗ Confederate forces
→ Confederate raid
||||| Hills or rough terrain

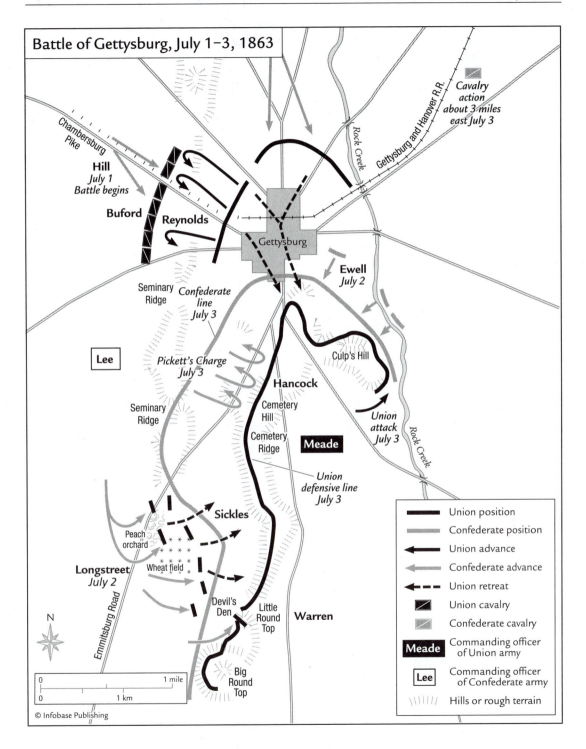

Battle of Gettysburg, July 1–3, 1863

Chambersburg Pike

Hill
July 1
Battle begins

Buford   **Reynolds**

Gettysburg

Rock Creek

Gettysburg and Hanover R.R.

Cavalry action about 3 miles east July 3

Ewell
July 2

Seminary Ridge   *Confederate line July 3*

Lee

Pickett's Charge July 3

Culp's Hill

Seminary Ridge

Hancock

Cemetery Hill

Cemetery Ridge

Meade

Union attack July 3

Rock Creek

Union defensive line July 3

Sickles

Peach orchard

Longstreet
July 2

Wheat field

Emmitsburg Road

Devil's Den

Little Round Top

Warren

Big Round Top

N

	1 mile
0	
0	1 km

© Infobase Publishing

▬▬▬	Union position
▬▬▬	Confederate position
◀▬▬	Union advance
◀▬▬	Confederate advance
◀- - -	Union retreat
▨	Union cavalry
▨	Confederate cavalry
Meade	Commanding officer of Union army
Lee	Commanding officer of Confederate army
||||	Hills or rough terrain

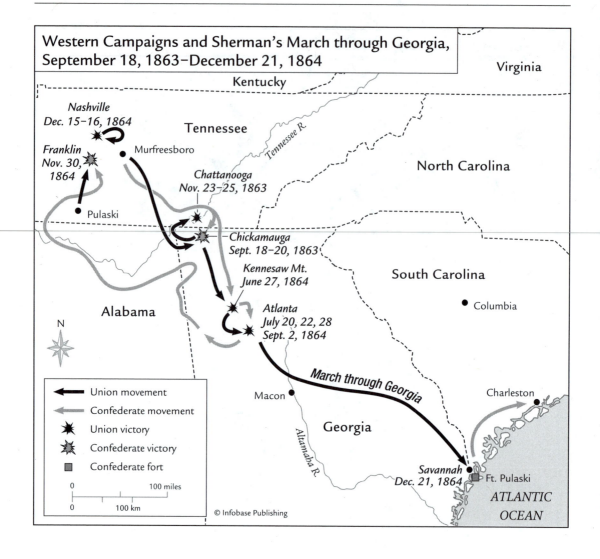

Western Campaigns and Sherman's March through Georgia,
September 18, 1863–December 21, 1864

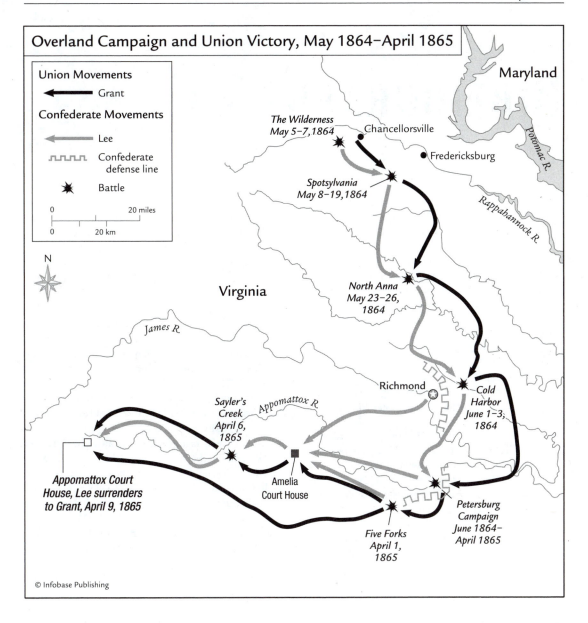

Overland Campaign and Union Victory, May 1864–April 1865

Union Movements

← Grant

Confederate Movements

← Lee

ⅢⅢⅢ Confederate defense line

✸ Battle

0   20 miles

0   20 km

N

Maryland

Potomac R.

The Wilderness
May 5–7, 1864

Chancellorsville

Fredericksburg

Rappahannock R.

Spotsylvania
May 8–19, 1864

Virginia

North Anna
May 23–26,
1864

James R.

Richmond

Cold
Harbor
June 1–3,
1864

Sayler's
Creek
April 6,
1865

Appomattox R.

Amelia
Court House

Appomattox Court
House, Lee surrenders
to Grant, April 9, 1865

Five Forks
April 1,
1865

Petersburg
Campaign
June 1864–
April 1865

© Infobase Publishing

BIBLIOGRAPHY

Adelman, Garry E. *The Myth of Little Round Top: Gettysburg.* Gettysburg, Pa.: Thomas Publications, 2003.

Alberts, Don E. *General Wesley Merritt: Brandy Station to Manila Bay.* Columbus, Ohio: General's Books, 2000.

Alduino, Frank W., and David J. Coles. "'Ye Come from Many a Far Off Clime; and Speak in Many Tongue': The Garabaldi Guard and Italian-American Service in the Civil War." *Italian Americana* 22, no. 1 (2004): 47–63.

Alexander, Ted. "Antietam: The Bloodiest Day." *North & South* 5, no. 7 (2002): 76–89.

Allmon, William B. "Hold Allatoona!" *Military Heritage* 4, no. 1 (2002): 52–59.

Archer, John M. *Culp's Hill at Gettysburg: "The Mountain Trembled.* Gettysburg, Pa.: Thomas Publications, 2002.

Ayers, Edward L., Gary W. Gallagher, and Andrew J. Torget, eds. *Crucible of the Civil War: Virginia from Secession to Commemoration.* Charlottesville: University of Virginia Press, 2006.

Baehr, Theodore. *Faith in God and Generals: An Anthology of Faith, Hope, and Love in the American Civil War.* Nashville, Tenn.: Broadman, Holman, 2003.

Bak, Richard. *The CSS Hunley: The Greatest Undersea Adventure of the Civil War.* New York: Cooper Square Press, 2003.

Baldwin, John. *Last Flag Down: The Epic Journey of the Last Confederate Warship.* New York: Crown Publishers, 2007.

Banasik, Michael E., ed. *Cavaliers of the Brush: Quantrill and His Men.* Iowa City, Iowa: Camp Pope Bookshop, 2003.

Barefoot, Daniel W. *Let Us Die Like Brave Men: Behind the Dying Words of Confederate Warriors.* Winston-Salem, N.C.: John F. Blair, 2005.

Barnes, Wyatt E. "Harboring the Czar's Fleet." *MHQ* 13, no. 4 (2001): 64–70.

Barnhart, Donald. "Junkyard Ironclad." *Civil War Times Illustrated* 40, no. 2 (2001): 30–37, 67–68.

Barry, Peter J. "The Charleston Riot and Its Aftermath: Civil, Military, and Presidential Responses." *Journal of Illinois History* 7, no. 2 (2004): 82–106.

Baumgartner, Richard A. *Buckeye Blood: Ohio at Gettysburg.* Huntington, W.Va.: Blue Acorn Press, 2003.

Bell, John. *Confederate Seadog: John Taylor Wood in War and Exile.* Jefferson, N.C.: McFarland, 2002.

Bennett, Brian A. *The Beau Ideal of a Soldier and a Gentleman: The Life of Coil. Patrick Henry O'Rourke from Ireland to Gettysburg.* Wheatland, N.Y.: Triphammer Pub., 2002.

Bennett, Michael J. *Union Jacks: Yankee Sailors in the Civil War.* Chapel Hill: University of North Carolina Press, 2004.

———. "Dissenters from the American Mood: Why Men Became Yankee Sailors during the Civil War." *North & South* 8, no. 2 (2005): 12–21.

Bishop, Ronald R. "August Sebelin's Civil War: A German Sailor in the Union Navy, 1861–1865." Unpublished master's thesis, Baylor University, 2002.

Blair, Dan. "'One Good Port': Beaufort Harbor, North Carolina." *North Carolina Historical Review* 79, no. 3 (2002): 301–326.

Blair, Jayne E. *Tragedy at Montpelier: The Untold Story of Ten Confederate Deserters from North Carolina.* Bowie, Md.: Heritage Books, 2003.

Bleser, Carol K. *Intimate Strategies of the Civil War: Military Commanders and Their Wives.* New York: Oxford University Press, 2001.

Bonds, Russell S. *Stealing the General: The Great Locomotive Clause of the First Medal of Honor.* Yardley, Pa.: Westholme, 2007.

Boswell, Evault. *Quantrill's Raiders in Texas.* Austin, Tex.: Eakin Press, 2003.

Bowden, Scott, and Bill Ward. *Last Chance for Victory: Robert E. Lee and the Gettysburg Campaign.* Campbell, Calif.: Savas, 2001.

Bragg, C. L. *Distinction in Every Service: Brigadier General Marcellus A. Stovall, C.S.A.* Shippensburg, Pa.: White Mane Books, 2002.

Brennan, Patrick. "The Army Commander Who Never Was." *North & South* 5, no. 5 (2002): 12–25.

———. "It Wasn't Stuart's Fault." *North & South* 6, no. 5 (2003): 22–37.

———. "'I Had Rather Die than Be Whipped': The Battle of Yellow Tavern." *North & South* 7, no. 4 (2004): 56–73.

Brewer, James D. *Tom Worthington's War: Shiloh, Sherman, and the Search for Vindication.* Jefferson, N.C.: McFarland, 2001.

Brooke, George M., ed. *Ironclads and Big Guns of the Confederacy: The Journals and Letters of John M. Brooke.* Columbia: University of South Carolina Press, 2002.

Brooks, Charles E. "The Social and Cultural Dynamics of Soldiering in Hood's Texas Brigade." *Journal of Southern History* 67, no. 3 (2001): 535–572.

Browning, Robert M. "Defunct Strategy and Divergent Goals: The Role of the United States Navy along the Eastern Seaboard during the Civil War." *Prologue* 33, no. 3 (2001): 168–179.

Brownstein, Elizabeth S. *Lincoln's Other White House.* Hoboken, N.J.: John Wiley and Sons, 2005.

Brubaker, Jack. "Defending the Susquehanna." *Civil War Times* 43, no. 3 (2003): 74–80.

Bruce, Susannah U. "The Harp and the Eagle: The Impact of Civil War Military Service in the Union Army on the Irish in America." Unpublished Ph.D. diss., Kansas State University, 2002.

Budiansky, Stephen. "America's Unknown Intelligence Czar." *American Heritage* 55, no. 5 (2004): 55–63.

Buker, George E. "The Inner Blockade of Florida and the Wildcat Blockade-Runners." *North & South* 4, no. 2 (2001): 70–85.

———. *Blockaders, Refugees, and Contrabands: Civil War on Florida's Gulf Coast.* Tuscaloosa: University of Alabama Press, 2004.

Bundy, Carol. *The Nature of Sacrifice: A Biography of Charles Russell Lowe, Jr., 1835–1864.* New York: Farrar, Straus, and Giroux, 2005.

Burkhardt, George S. *Confederate Rage, Yankee Wrath: No Quarter in the Civil War.* Carbondale: Southern Illinois University Press, 2007.

Butko, Brian, and Nicholas P. Ciotola, eds. *Industry and Infantry.* Pittsburgh: Historical Society of Western Pennsylvania, 2003.

Butts, Michele T. *Galvanized Yankees on the Upper Missouri: The Face of Loyalty.* Boulder: University of Colorado Press, 2003.

Calcutt, Rebecca B. *Richmond's Wartime Hospitals: In Depth Study of Medical Care during the War of 1812.* Gretna, La.: Pelican Publishing, 2005.

Callaghan, Daniel M. *Thomas Francis Meagher and the Irish Brigade in the Civil War.* Jefferson, N.C.: McFarland, 2006.

Callan, J. Sean. *Courage and Country: James Shields: More than Irish Luck.* Lake Forest, Ill.: 1st Books Library, 2004.

Calore, Paul. *Naval Campaigns of the Civil War.* Jefferson, N.C.: McFarland, 2002.

Campbell, Jacqueline G. "'The Most Diabolical Act of All the Barbarous War': Soldiers, Civilians, and the Burning of Columbia, February, 1865." *American Nineteenth Century History* 3, no. 3 (2002): 53–72.

Campbell, R. Thomas. *Sea Hawk of the Confederacy: Lt. Charles Read and the Confederate Navy.* Shippensburg, Pa.: Burd Street Press, 2000.

———. *Hunters of the Night: Confederate Torpedo Boats in the War between the States.* Shippensburg, Pa.: White Mane Books, 2000.

———. *Confederate Navy Quizzes and Facts.* Shippensburg, Pa.: Burd Street Press, 2001.

———. *The Hunley Story: Journey of a Confederate Submarine.* Shippensburg, Pa.: Burd Street Press, 2002.

Campbell, R. Thomas, ed. *Engineer in Gray: Memoirs of Chief Engineer James H. Tomb, CSN.* Jefferson, N.C.: McFarland, 2005.

Campbell, Thomas A. *Storm over Carolina: The Confederate Navy's Struggle for Eastern North Carolina.* Nashville, Tenn.: Cumberland House, 2006.

Canfield, Eugene B. "*Alabama*'s Defeat Was No Surprise." *Naval History* 18, no. 4 (2004): 43–46.

Carlisle, Rodney P. *The Civil War and Reconstruction.* New York: Facts On File, 2007.

Carmichael, Peter S. *The Last Generation: Young Virginians in Peace, War, and Reunion.* Chapel Hill: University of North Carolina Press, 2005.

Carson, Ray M. *The Civl War Soldier: A Photographic Journey.* New York: Gramercy Books, 2007.

Carter, Alice E. *The Civil War on the Web: A Guide to the Very Best Sites.* Wilmington, Del.: SR Books, 2003.

Casstevens, Frances H. *"Out of the Mouth of Hell": Civil War Prisons and Escapes.* Jefferson, N.C.: McFarland, 2005.

———. *Edward A. Wild and the African Brigade in the Civil War.* Jefferson, N.C.: McFarland, 2003.

———. *Clingman's Brigade in the Confederacy, 1862–1865.* Jefferson, N.C.: McFarland, 2002.

Castel, Albert. "Why the North Won and the South Lost." *Civil War Times Illustrated* 39, no. 2 (2000): 56–60.

———. *Articles of War: Winners, Losers, and Some Who Were Both in the Civil War.* Mechanicsburg, Pa.: Stackpole Books, 2001.

———. "So Glorious an Adventure: Major Tom Taylor's March to the Sea." *Timeline* 18, no. 5 (2001): 18–31.

———. "Vicksburg: Myths and Realities." *North & South* 6, no. 7 (2003): 62–69.

Chaffin, Tom. *Sea of Gray: The Around-the-World Odyssey of the Confederate Raider Shenandoah.* New York: Hill and Wang, 2006.

Christ, Mark K., ed. *"All Cut to Pieces and Gone to Hell": The Civil War, Race Relations, and the Battle of Poison Springs.* Little Rock, Ark.: August House, 2003.

Clancy, Paul R. *The Epic Battle, Calamitous Loss, and Historic Recovery of the USS Monitor.* Camden, Maine: International Marine, 2005.

Clark, John E. "Management in the War: The Legacy of the Civil War Railroads." *North & South* 5, no. 5 (2002): 50–59.

Clarke, Francis M. "Sentimental Bonds: Suffering, Sacrifice, and Benevolence in the Civil War North." Unpublished Ph.D. diss., John's Hopkins University, 2002.

Clarke, Hewitt. *He Saw the Elephant: Confederate Naval Saga of Lt. Charles "Savvy" Read, CSN.* Spring, Tex.: Lone Star Press, 2000.

Claxton, Melvin, and Mark Puls. *Uncommon Valor: The Exploit of the New Market Heights Medal of Honor Winners.* Hoboken, N.J.: John Wiley and Sons, 2006.

Clemmer, Gregg S. *Old Alleghany: The Life and Wars of General Ed Johnson.* Staunton, Va.: Hearthside Pub., 2004.

Coddington, Ronald S. *Faces of the Civil War: An Album of Union Soldiers and Their Stories.* Baltimore: Johns Hopkins University Press, 2004.

Coffin, Howard. *The Battered Stars: One State's Civil War Ordeal during Grant's Overland Campaign from the Home Front in Vermont to the Battlefields of Virginia.* Woodstock, Vt.: Countryman, 2002.

Cole, Philip M. *Command and Communication Frictions in the Gettysburg Campaign.* Orrtanna, Pa.: Colecraft Industries, 2006.

Coleman, Wim, and Pat Perrin. *The American Civil War.* Detroit: Greenhaven Press, 2005.

Collins, Robert. *General James G. Blunt: Corrupt Conqueror.* Gretna, La.: Pelican Pub., 2005.

Conrad, James L. *The Young Lions: Confederate Cadets at War.* Columbia: University of South Carolina Press, 2004.

———. *Rebel Reefers: The Organization and Midshipmen of the Confederate States Naval Academy.* Boulder, Colo.: Da Capo Press, 2003.

Cooper, Edward S. *William Babcock Hazen: The Best Hated Man.* Madison, N.J.: Fairleigh Dickinson University Press, 2005.

Coski, John M. *The Confederate Battle Flag: America's Most Embattled Emblem.* Cambridge, Mass.: Belknap Press of Harvard University Press, 2005.

Couper, William. *The Corps Forward: The Biographical Sketches of the VMI Cadets Who Fought in the Battle of New Market.* Buena Vista, Va.: Mariner Publishing, 2005.

Cozzens, Peter. "Jackson Alone." *Civil War Times Illustrated* 40, no. 6 (2001): 30–39, 74–76.

Creighton, Margaret S. *The Colors of Courage: Gettysburg's Forgotten History: Immigrants, Women, and African Americans in the Civil War's Defining Battle.* New York: Basic Books, 2005.

Cross, Coy F. *Lincoln's Man in Liverpool: Consul Dudley and the Legal Battle to Stop Confederate Warships.* Dekalb: Northern Illinois University Press, 2007.

Cunningham, Alvin R. *Conrad Elroy, Powder Monkey: The Role of the Navy in the Civil War.* Logan, Iowa: Perfection Learning, 2003.

Curry, Angus. *The Officers of the CSS Shenandoah.* Gainesville: University Press of Florida, 2006.

Cutler, Thomas J. "A Duel of Iron." *Naval History* 18, no. 4 (2004): 26–31.

Dahlstrom, Neil. "Rock Island Prison, 1863–1865: Andersonville of the North Dispelled." *Journal of Illinois History* 4, no. 4 (2001): 291–306.

Davis, Robert S. *Ghosts and Shadows of Andersonville: Essays on the Secret Social Histories of American's Deadliest Prison.* Macon, Ga.: Mercer University Press, 2006.

Davis, William C. *The Illustrated Encyclopedia of the Civil War: The Soldiers, Generals, Weapons, and Battles.* Guildford, Conn.: Lyons Press, 2001.

———. *The Commanders of the Civil War.* London: Salamander, 2001.

———. *Look Away! A History of the Confederate States of America.* New York: Free Press, 2002.

Davis, William C., Brian C. Pohanka, and Don Troiani, eds. *Civil War Journal: The Leaders.* New York: Gramercy Books, 2003.

Day, Carl F. *Tom Custer: Ride to Glory.* Spokane, Wash.: Arthur H. Clark, 2003.

Dedmondt, Glenn. *The Flags of Civil War North Carolina.* Gretna, La.: Pelican Publishing, 2003.

De Kay, James T. *The Rebel Raiders: The Astonishing History of the Confederacy's Secret Navy.* New York: Ballantine Books, 2002.

Desjardin, Thomas A. *These Honored Dead: How the Story of Gettysburg Shaped American Memory.* Cambridge, Mass.: Da Capo Press, 2003.

Dew, Charles B. "How Samuel E. Pittman Validated Lee's 'Lost Orders' Prior to Antietam: A Historical Note." *Journal of Southern History* 70, no. 4 (2004): 865–870.

Discofarno, Ken. *They Saved the Union at Little Round Top, Gettysburg, July 2, 1863.* Gettysburg, Pa.: Thomas Publications, 2002.

Dollar, Susan E. "The Red River Campaign, Natchitoches Parish, Louisiana: A Case of Equal Opportunity Destruction." *Louisiana History* 43, no. 4 (2002): 411–432.

Dougherty, James J. *Stone's Brigade and the Fight for the McPherson's Farm: Battle of Gettysburg, July 1, 1863.* Conshohocken, Pa.: Combined Publishing, 2001.

Doughtery, Kevin. *The Coastal War in North and South Carolina: An Analysis of the Evolution of Joint Navy-Army Operations, 1861–1865.* Danville, Va.: BGES, 2002.

Dreese, Michael A. *Civil War Leadership and Mexican War Experience.* Jackson: University Press of Mississippi, 2007.

———. *Never Desert the Old Flag: 50 Stories of Union Battle Flags and Color-Bearers at Gettysburg.* Gettysburg, Pa.: Thomas Publications, 2002.

Dreese, Michael E. *Torn Families: Death and Kinship at the Battle of Gettysburg.* Jefferson, N.C.: McFarland, 2007.

Duncan, Richard R. *Beleaguered Winchester: A Virginia Community at War, 1861–1865.* Baton Rouge: Louisiana State University Press, 2007.

Dunkelman, Mark H. "Death to All Foragers." *American History* 37, no. 3 (2002): 28–35.

Durkin, Joseph T. *Confederate Navy Chief: Stephen R. Mallory.* Tuscaloosa: University of Alabama Press, 2005.

Duvall, Sam. "Incident at Hatcher's Run." *Alabama Heritage,* no. 63 (2002): 18–28.

Ecelbarger, Gary L. *Black Jack Logan: An Extraordinary Life in Peace and War.* Guilford, Conn.: Lyon's Press, 2005.

———. "Stonewall Jackson's Fog of War: The Operational Triangle of May 24, 1862." *North & South* 5, no. 3 (2002): 46–55.

Echelberry, Earl. "Death in the Woods." *Military Heritage* 6, no. 5 (2005): 52–59, 82.

Edwards, Whit. *The Prairie Was on Fire: Eyewitness Accounts of the Civil War in the Indian Territory.* Oklahoma City: Oklahoma Historical Society, 2001.

Ehlers, Mark. "The Colors of Courage: White Soldiers' Response to Black Troops in the Civil War." Unpublished master's thesis, James Madison University, 2005.

Eicher, David J. *The Longest Night: A Military History of the Civil War.* New York: Simon and Schuster, 2001.

Ellem, Warren. "The Fall of Fort Fisher: Contested Memories of the Civil War." *North Carolina Historical Review* 79, no. 2 (2002): 198–233.

Elmore, Charles J. *General David Hunter's Proclamation: The Quest for African American Freedom before and during the Civil War.* Fort Washington, Pa.: Eastern National, 2002.

Elmore, Tom. "Head to Head." *Civil War Times Illustrated* 40, no. 7 (2002): 44–52, 54–55.

Escobedo, Santiago. "Iron Men and Wooden Carts: Tejano Freighters during the Civil War." *Journal of South Texas* 17, no. 2 (2004): 51–60.

Escott, Paul D. *The Plea of Military Necessity: Civil-Military Relations in the Confederacy.* Westport, Conn.: Praeger Security International, 2006.

Faust, Drew G. "'We Should Grow Too Fond of It': Why We Love the Civil War." *Civil War History* 50, no. 4 (2004): 368–383.

Feege, Edward H. "The Rehabilitation of James Waddell." *Naval History* 17, no. 3 (2003): 31–35.

Feis, William B. "Lee's Army Is Really Whipped': Grant and Intelligence Assessment from the Wilderness to Cold Harbor." *North & South* 7, no. 4 (2004): 28–37.

———. "Charles S. Bell: Union Scout." *North & South* 4, no. 5 (2001): 26–37.

————. "'There Is a Bad Enemy in This City': Colonel William Truesdail's Army Police and the Occupation of Nashville, 1862–1863." *North & South* 8, no. 2 (2005): 34–45.

Field, Ron. *Uniforms of the Civil War: An Illustrated Guide for Historians, Collectors, and Reenactors.* Guilford, Conn.: Lyon's Press, 2005.

————. *The Confederate Army, 1861–65.* Oxford, UK: Osprey, 2005.

Fitzpatrick, David J. "Emory Upton and the Citizen Soldier." *Journal of Military History* 65, no. 2 (2001): 355–389.

Fordyce, Samuel W., ed. *An American General: The Memoirs of David Sloan Stanley.* Santa Barbara, Calif.: Narrative Press, 2003.

Frazier, Donald S. "'The Battles of Texas Will Be Fought in Louisiana': The Assault of Fort Butler, June 28, 1863." *Southwestern Historical Quarterly* 104, no. 3 (2001): 332–362.

————. "'The Carnival of Death': The Cavalry Battle at Cheneyville, Louisiana, May 20, 1863." *Louisiana History* 42, no. 2 (2001): 193–207.

Freehling, William W. "Why Civil War Military History Must Be Less than 85 Percent Military." *North & South* 5, no. 2 (2001): 14–24.

Freemon, Frank R. *Gangrene and Glory: Medical Care during the American Civil War.* Urbana: University of Illinois Press, 2001.

Fuller, Howard J. "'The Whole Character of Maritime Life': British Reactions to the USS *Monitor* and the American Ironclad Experience." *Mariner's Mirror* 88, no. 3 (2002): 285–300.

————. "'This Country Now Occupies the Vantage Ground': Understanding John Ericsson's Monitors and the American Union's War against British Naval Supremacy." *American Neptune* 62, no. 1 (2002): 91–110.

Furgueron, James R. "The 'Best Hated Man' in the Union Army: The Remarkable Career of General William Babcock Hazen." *North & South* 4, nos. 3–4 (2001): 22–34; 66–79.

Furgurson, Ernest B. *Not War but Murder: Cold Harbor, 1864.* New York: Alfred A. Knopf, 2000.

Garavaglia, Louis A. "Sherman's March and the Georgia Arsenals." *North & South* 6, no. 1 (2002): 12–22.

Garcia, Pedro. "Highway to Victory." *Military Heritage* 4, no. 2 (2002): 74–79.

————. "Confederacy in the Balance." *Military Heritage* 6, no. 2 (2004): 60–67, 87.

Garrison, Nancy S. *With Courage and Delicacy: Civil War on the Peninsula: Women and the S. S. Sanitary Commission.* Cambridge, Mass.: Da Capo Press, 2003.

Giambrone, Jeff T. "Defense of the Mississippi Valley." *North & South* 7, no. 6 (2004): 50–65.

Gibson, Charles D. "Soldiers Take the Tidewater." *Naval History* 16, no. 6 (2002): 27–30.

Gottfried, Bradley M. *Brigades of Gettysburg: The Union and Confederate Brigades at the Battle of Gettysburg.* Cambridge, Mass.: Da Capo Press, 2002.

Goulka, Jeremiah H., ed. *The Grand Old Man of Maine: Selected Letters of Joshua Lawrence Chamberlain, 1865–1914.* Chapel Hill: University of North Carolina Press, 2004.

Grabeau, Warren. *Confusion Compounded: The Pivotal Battle of Raymond, 12 May, 1863: A Scholarly Monograph.* Saline, Mich.: McNaughton and Gunn, 2001.

Gragg, Rod. *A Commitment to Valor: A Character Portrait of Robert E. Lee.* Nashville, Tenn.: Rutledge Hill Press, 2001.

Garrison, Webb. *Mutiny in the Civil War.* Shippensburg, Pa.: White Mane, 2001.

Green, A. Wilson. *Breaking the Backbone of the Rebellion: The Final Battles of the Petersburg Campaign.* Mason City, Iowa: Savas Pub., 2000.

————. *Civil War Petersburg: Confederate City on the Crucible of War.* Charlottesville: University of Virginia Press, 2006.

Griffin, John C. *A Pictorial History of the Confederacy.* Jefferson, N.C.: McFarland, 2004.

Grimsley, Mark. "Second-Guessing Bobby Lee: A Counterfactual Assessment of Lee's Generalship during the Overland Campaign." *North & South* 7, no. 4 (2004): 38–45.

Grimsley, Mark, and Brooks D. Simpson. *The Collapse of the Confederacy.* Lincoln: University of Nebraska Press, 2001.

Grocki, Stan. *1863, Year of Lost Opportunities.* Baltimore: America House Book Publishers, 2002.

Hartwig, D. Scott. "'It Looked like a Task to Storm': The Pennsylvania Reserves Assault South Mountain, September 14, 1862." *North & South* 5, no. 7 (2002): 36–49.

Hattaway, Herman. "The Changing Face of Battle." *North & South* 4, no. 6 (2001): 34–43.

————. *Reflections of a Civil War Historian: Essays on Leadership, Society, and the Art of War.* Columbia: University of Missouri Press, 2003.

Hawkins, Rusty. "A Slight History of Coastal Battles in Texas during the Civil War." Unpublished master's thesis, West Texas A & M University, 2003.

Heiss, Walter R. *Veterinary Service during the American Civil War*. Baltimore: PublishAmerica, 2005.

Hennessy, John J. "Lincoln Wins Back His Army." *Civil War Times Illustrated* 39, no. 7 (2001): 34–42, 65.

Henris, John. "A Legacy of Rebellion: The Short, Tragic Career of William Edmondson (Grumble) Jones." Unpublished master's thesis, Slippery Rock, University of Pennsylvania, 2002.

Hess, Earl J. *Field Armies & Fortifications of the Civil War: The Eastern Campaigns, 1861–1864*. Chapel Hill: University of North Carolina Press, 2005.

Hicks, Brian. *Raising the Hunley: The Remarkable History and Recovery of the Lost Confederate Submarine*. New York: Ballantine Books, 2002.

Hogan, Neil. "Colonel Patrick O'Rorke: Fallen Hero of Gettysburg." *Irish Sword* 23, no. 91 (2002): 33–52.

Holberton, William B. *Homeward Bound: The Demobilization of the Union and Confederate Armies, 1865–66*. Mechanicsburg, Pa.: Stackpole Books, 2001.

Holzer, Harold. "Windows on the Civil War at Sea." *Naval History* 18, no. 4 (2004): 16–21.

Horres, C. Russell. "An Affair at Ft. Sumter." *South Carolina Historical Magazine* 102, no. 1 (2001): 6–26.

Howard, Nathan. "A Two Front Dilemma: The Texas Rangers in the Civil War." *Southern Historian* 23 (2002): 43–55.

Hoyt, Edwin P. *The Voyage of the Hunley*. Short Hills, N.J.: Buford Books, 2002.

Hubbs, Mark. "A Rebel Shot Causes 'Torture and Despair.'" *Naval History* 16, no. 2 (2002): 46–50.

Hughes, Nathaniel C., and Gordon D. Whitney. *Jefferson Davis in Blue: The Life of Sherman's Relentless Warrior*. Baton Rouge: Louisiana State University Press, 2002.

Jackson, Rex T. *The Sultana Saga: The Titanic of the Mississippi*. Bowie, Md.: Heritage Books, 2003.

Jamieson, Perry D. "Background to Bloodshed: The Tactics of the U.S.–Mexican War and the 1850s." *North & South* 4, no. 6 (2001): 24–31.

Johnson, Clint. *In the Footsteps of Robert E. Lee*. Winston-Salem, N.C.: John F. Blair, 2001.

Johnson, John M. *Lead, Salt, and the Railroad: Toland's Raid on Wytheville, July 18, 1863*. Wytheville, Va.: Wythe County Historical Society, 2003.

Jones, Robert A. *Confederate Corsair: The Life of Lt. Charles W. "Savez" Read*. Mechanicsburg, Pa.: Stackpole Books, 2000.

Jones, Terry L., ed. *Campbell Brown's Civil War: With Ewell in the Army of Northern Virginia*. Baton Rouge: Louisiana State University Press, 2001.

Jordan, David M. *"Happiness Is Not My Companion": The Life of G. K. Warren*. Bloomington: Indiana University Press, 2001.

Joyner, Elizabeth H. *The USS Cairo: History of Artifacts of a Civil War Gunboat*. Jefferson, N.C.: McFarland, 2006.

Kelly, Dorothy E. "General William P. Sanders: Son of the South, Defender of the Union." *North & South* 7, no. 2 (2004): 84–92.

Kinard, Jeff. *Lafayette of the South: Prince Camille de Polignac and the American Civil War*. College Station: Texas A & M University Press, 2001.

Konstam, Angus. *Confederate Ironclad, 1861–65*. Oxford, U.K.: Osprey, 2001.

———. *Union Monitor, 1861–65*. Oxford, U.K.: Osprey, 2002.

Konstam, Angus, and Tony Bryan. *USS Monitor & CSS Virginia at Hampton Roads, 1862*. Oxford, U.K.: Osprey, 2003.

———. *Confederate Submarines and Torpedo Vessels, 1861–65*. Oxford, U.K.: Osprey, 2004.

———. *Confederate Raider, 1861–65*. Oxford, U.K.: Osprey, 2003.

———. *Confederate Blockade Runner, 1861–65*. Oxford, U.K.: Osprey, 2004.

Krick, Robert K. *The Smoothbore Volley That Doomed the Confederacy: The Death of Stonewall Jackson and Other Chapters on the Army of Northern Virginia*. Baton Rouge: Louisiana State University Press, 2002.

Kroll, C. Douglas. *Friends in Peace and War: The Russian Navy's Landmark Visit to Civil War San Francisco*. Washington, D.C.: Potomac Books, 2007.

Krumwiede, John F. *Old Waddy's Coming! The Military Career of Brigadier General James S. Wadsworth*. Baltimore: Butternut and Blue, 2002.

Kunstler, Mort, and James I. Robertson. *Gods and Generals: The Paintings of Mort Kunstler*. Shelton, Conn.: Greenwich Workshop Press, 2002.

LaFantasie, Glenn W. "William C. Oates and the Death of General Elon Farnsworth." *North & South* 8, no. 1 (2005): 48–55.

———. "Night and Death on Little Round Top." *American History* 39, no. 6 (2004): 48–55, 71.

———. *Gettysburg Requiem: The Life and Lost Causes of Confederate Colonel William C. Oates*. New York: Oxford University Press, 2006.

Lamm, Alan K. "Wesley Merritt: The Union Army's Other 'Boy General.'" *Journal of America's Military Past* 28, no. 2 (2001): 19–44.

Lane, Mills. *Savannah and the Civil War Sea.* Savannah, Ga.: Ships of the Sea Maritime Museum, 2001.

Lang, J. Stephen. *The Complete's Idiot's Guide to the Confederacy.* Indianapolis, Ind.: Alpha Books, 2003.

Lanning, Michael L. *The Civil War 100: The Stories Behind the Most Influential Battles, People, and Events in the War Between the States.* Naperville, Ill.: Sourcebooks, 2007.

Larabee, Ann. *The Gentleman Bomber: The Chilling Tale of a Confederate Spy, Con Artist, and Mass Murderer.* New York: Palgrave Macmillan, 2005.

Lash, Jeffrey N. *A Politician Turned General: The Civil War Career of Stephen Augustus Hurlbut.* Kent, Ohio: Kent State University Press, 2003.

Lentz, Perry. *Private Fleming at Chancellorville: The Red Badge of Courage and the Civil War.* Columbia: University of Missouri Press, 2006.

Levine, Bruce C. *Confederate Emancipation: Southern Plans to Free and Arm Slaves during the Civil War.* New York: Oxford University Press, 2005.

Longacre, Edward G. *General William Dorsey Pender: A Military Biography.* Conshohocken, Pa.: Combined Publishing, 2001.

Longacre, Glenn, and John C. Haas. *To Battle for God and the Right: The Civil War Letterbooks of Emerson Opdycke.* Urbana: University of Illinois Press, 2003.

Lord, Francis A. *Civil War Collector's Encyclopedia: Arms, Uniforms, and Equipment of the Union and Confederacy.* Mineola, N.Y.: Dover Publications, 2004.

Lowe, Richard G. *Walker's Texas Division, C.S.A.: Greyhounds of the Trans-Mississippi.* Baton Rouge: Louisiana State University Press, 2006.

Lowry, Thomas P. "'I Hope to Get Wounded in the Arse': Military Justice during the Overland Campaign." *North & South* 7, no. 4 (2004): 50–54.

Lundahl, Jeffrey D. "Engineers in Blue: The Engineer Corps Contributions to the Union Victory." Unpublished master's thesis, California State University, Hayward, 2005.

Lundberg, John R. *The Finishing Stroke: Texans in the 1864 Tennessee Campaign.* Abilene, Tex.: McWhiney Foundation Press, 2002.

Lynn, John W. *Confederate Commando and Fleet Surgeon: Dr. Daniel Burr Conrad.* Shippensburg, Pa.: Burd Street Press, 2001.

Macomber, Robert. "Action on the Florida Coast." *Naval History* 17, no. 1 (2003): 38–41.

Maharay, George S. *Vermont Hero: Major General George J. Stannard.* Shippensburg, Pa.: White Mane Books, 2001.

Mahood, Wayne. *General Wadsworth: The Life and Times of Brevet Major General James S. Wadsworth.* Cambridge, Mass.: Da Capo Press, 2003.

———. *Alexander "Fighting Elleck" Hays: The Life of a Civil War General, from West Point to the Wilderness.* Jefferson, N.C.: McFarland, 2005.

Manning, Chandra. *What This Cruel War Was Over: Soldiers, Slavery, and the Civil War.* New York: Alfred A. Knopf, 2007.

Markle, Donald E. *Spies and Spymasters of the Civil War.* New York: Hippocrene Books, 2004.

Marten, James A. *Children for the Union: The War Spirit on the Northern Home Front.* Chicago: Ivan R. Dee, 2004.

Martin, Samuel J. *Matthew Calbraith Butler, Confederate General, Hampton Red Shirt, and U.S. Senator.* Mechanicsburg, Pa.: Stackpole Books, 2001.

Matthews, Gary R. *Basil Wilson Duke, C.S.A.: The Right Man in the Right Place.* Lexington: University Press of Kentucky, 2005.

Mayeux, Steven M. *Earthen Walls, Iron Men: Fort De Russey, Louisiana, and the Defense of the Red River.* Knoxville: University of Tennessee Press, 2007.

McCaslin, Richard B. "In the Shadow of Washington: Robert E. Lee and the Confederacy." *North & South* 4, no. 4 (2001): 14–23.

McKenzie, Kenneth F. "Among the Last to Run." *Naval History* 17, no. 5 (2003): 24–29.

McMurray, Philip. "'Where My Natural Roots Lead Me': Joshua L. Chamberlain—the Origins of a Civil War Officer." Unpublished master's thesis, Kent State University Press, 2001.

McNeil, Jim. *Masters of the Shoals: Tales of the Cape Fear Pilots Who Ran the Union Blockade.* Cambridge, Mass.: Da Capo Press, 2003.

McPherson, James M. *The Mighty Scourge: Perspectives on the Civil War.* New York, Oxford University Press, 2007.

———. *The Atlas of the Civil War.* Philadelphia: Courage Books, 2005.

McPherson, James M., ed. *The Most Fearful Ordeal: Original Coverage of the Civil War by the New York Times.* New York: St. Martin's Press, 2005.

Melton, Brian C. *Sherman's Forgotten General: Henry W. Slocum.* Columbia: University of Missouri Press, 2007.

Melton, Maurice. "Casualties of War: Two Georgia Coast Pilots and the Capture of the USS *Water Witch.*" *Journal of South Georgia History* 16 (2004): 1–14.

Milbourne, Curtis W. "'I Have Been Worse Treated than Any Officer': Confederate Colonel Thomas Green's Assessment of the New Mexico Campaign." *Southwestern Historical Quarterly* 105, no. 2 (2001): 322–337.

Miller, Edward S. "The *Monitor*'s Lucky Sister." *Naval History* 18, no. 4 (2004): 32–36.

Miller, Joel M. "Gustavus Vasa Fox and the Expedition to Relieve Fort Sumter." Unpublished master's thesis, Tulane University, 2004.

Miller, William J. *Great Maps of the Civil War: Pivotal Battles and Campaigns Featuring 32 Removable Maps.* Nashville, Tenn.: Rutledge Hill Press, 2004.

Milton, David H. *Lincoln's Spymaster: Thomas Haines Dudley and the Liverpool Network.* Mechanicsburg, Pa.: Stackpole Books, 2003.

Milton, Keith. "Duel at Hampton Roads." *Military Heritage* 3, no. 3 (2001): 38–44, 97.

Monroe, Dan. *Shapers of the Great Debate on the Civil War: A Biographical Dictionary.* Westport, Conn.: Greenwood Press, 2005.

Mulesky, Ray. *Thunder from a Clear Sky: Stovepipe Johnson's Confederate Raid on Newburgh, Indiana.* New York: iUniverse, 2005.

Murray, R. L. *"A Perfect Storm of Lead": George Sears Greene and His New York Brigade in Defense of Culp's Hill.* Wolcott, N.Y.: Benedum Books, 2000.

———. *"The Greatest Battle of the Age": New Yorkers at First Bull Run.* Wolcott, N.Y.: Benedum Books, 2002.

———. *Holding the Line: New Yorkers in Defense of Pickett's Charge.* Wolcott, N.Y.: Benedum Books, 2001.

———. *Antietam: A Strategic and Tactical Analysis of the Maryland Campaign of 1862.* Wolcott, N.Y.: Benedum Books, 2000.

———. *Letters from the Front: New Yorkers at First Bull Run.* Wolcott, N.Y.: Benedum Books, 2002.

———. *Letters from Berdan's Sharpshooters.* Wolcott, N.Y.: Benedum Books, 2005.

Mushkat, Jerome, ed. *A Citizen-Soldier's Civil War: The Letters of Brevet Major General Alvin C. Voris.* Dekalb: Northern Illinois University Press, 2002.

Neely, Mark E. "Was the Civil War a Total War?" *Civil War History* 50, no. 4 (2004): 434–458.

Nelson, Scott R., and Carol Sheriff. *A People at War: Civilians and Soldiers in America's Civil War.* New York: Oxford University Press, 2007.

Newton, Steven H. "Joseph Johnston and Snake Creek Gap." *North & South* 4, no. 3 (2001): 56–67.

———. "The Confederate Home Guard: Forgotten Soldiers of the Lost Cause?" *North & South* 6, no. 1 (2002): 40–50.

Newton, Steven H., et al. "The Ten Greatest Blunders of the Civil War." *North & South* 8, no. 1 (2005): 12–23.

Nosworthy, Brent. *The Bloody Crucible of Courage: Fighting Methods and Combat Experience of the Civil War.* New York: Carroll and Graf, 2003.

Noyalas, Jonathan A. *"'My Will is Absolute Law:' A Biography of Union General Robert H. Milroy."* Jefferson, N.C.: McFarland, 2006.

O'Donnell, Patrick D. "Dick Dowling and the Battle of Sabine Pass: The Thermopylae of Lieutenant Dick Dowling." *Irish Sword* 23, no. 91 (2002): 69–86.

Oeffinger, John C. *A Soldier's General: The Civil War Letters of Major General Lafayette McLaws.* Chapel Hill: University of North Carolina Press, 2002.

Owens, Richard H. "An Astonishing Career." *Military Heritage* 3, no. 2 (2001): 64–73.

Palmer, David W. *The Forgotten Hero of Gettysburg: A Biography of General George Sears Greene.* Trenton, N.J.: Xlibris Corp., 2004.

Palmer, Juliette M. "Beyond Black and White in Blue and Gray: The Absence of Ethnic Regiments in Civil War Films." Unpublished master's thesis, Regent University, 2001.

Paradis, James M. *African Americans and the Gettysburg Campaign.* Lanham, Md.: Scarecrow Press, 2005.

Parsons, Philip W. *The Union Sixth Army Corps in the Chancellorsville Campaign.* Jefferson, N.C.: McFarland, 2006.

Patterson, Gerard A. *From Blue to Gray: The Life of Confederate General Cadmus M. Wilcox.* Mechanicsburg, Pa.: Stackpole Books, 2001.

Peladeau, Marius B., and Edwin C. Bearss. *Burnished Rows of Steel: Vermont's Role in the Battle of Gettysburg, July 1–3, 1863.* Newport: Vermont Civil War Enterprises, 2002.

Petrie, Stewart J. *Bloody Path to the Shenandoah: Fighting with the Union VI Corps in the American Civil War.* Shippensburg, Pa.: Burd Street Press, 2004.

Platt, Carolyn V. "'Three Cheers for the Cracker Line': William Gates Le Duc and the Relief of Chattanooga." *Timeline* 22, no. 2 (2005): 36–39.

Polsky, Andrew J. "'Mr. Lincoln's Army': Revisited: Partisanship, Institutional Position, and Union Army Command, 1861–1865." *Studies in American Political Development* 16, no. 2 (2002): 176–207.

Prince, Cathryn J. *Burn the Town and Jack the Banks!: Confederates Attack Vermont!* New York: Carroll and Grant, 2006.

Pritchard, Russ A. *Raiders of the Civil War: Untold Stories of Actions behind the Lines.* Guilford, Conn.: Lyons Press, 2005.

Raab, James W. *J. Patton Anderson, Confederate General: A Biography.* Jefferson, N.C.: McFarland, 2004.

———. *Confederate General Lloyd Tilgham: A Biography.* Jefferson, N.C.: McFarland, 2006.

Rafuse, Ethan S. *The American Civil War.* Aldershot, U.K.: Ashgate, 2005.

Rafuse, Ethan S., ed. *The American Civil War.* Burlington, Vt.: Ashgate, 2005.

Ragan, Mark K. *Submarine Warfare in the Civil War.* Cambridge, Mass.: Da Capo Press, 2002.

Ramold, Steven J. *Slaves, Citizens: African Americans in the Union Navy.* Dekalb: Northern Illinois University Press, 2002.

Raus, Edmund J. *Banners South: A Northern Community at War.* Kent, Ohio: Kent State University Press, 2005.

Reidy, Joseph P. "Black Men in Navy Blue during the Civil War." *Prologue* 33, no. 3 (2001): 154–167.

Rhea, Gordon C. *Carrying the Flag: The Story of Private Charles Whilden, the Confederacy's Unlikely Hero.* New York: Basic Books, 2004.

———. "'Butcher' Grant and the Overland Campaign." *North & South* 4, no. 1 (2000): 44–55.

———. "'The Hottest Place I Ever Was In': The Battle of Haw's Shop, May 28, 1864." *North & South* 4, no. 4 (2001): 42–57.

———. "A Hot Time in Ashland: The Battles of Hanover Court House and Ashland, May 31–June 1, 1864." *North & South* 4, no. 7 (2001): 24–37.

———. *Cold Harbor: Lee and Grant, May 26–June 3, 1864.* Baton Rouge: Louisiana State University Press, 2002.

———. "The Truce at Cold Harbor." *North & South* 7, no. 1 (2004): 76–85.

———. "The Overland Campaign of 1864." *North & South* 7, no. 4 (2004): 12–26.

Richter, William L. *Historical Dictionary of the Civil War and Reconstruction.* Lanham, Md.: Scarecrow Press, 2004.

Ridgway, James M. *Little Mac: Demise of an American.* Princeton, N.J.: Xlibris Corp., 2000.

Ripple, Charles C. "Lion of War and Lamb of God: Thomas Jonathan Jackson, Christian Warrior." Unpublished master's thesis, Wake Forrest University, 2003.

Robinson, Armstead L. *Bitter Fruits of Bondage: The Demise of Slavery and the Collapse of the Confederacy, 1861–1865.* Charlottesville: University of Virginia Press, 2005.

Rodgers, Thomas E. "Billy Yank and G. I. Joe: Am Exploratory Essay on the Sociopolitical Dimensions of Soldier Motivation." *Journal of Military History* 69, no. 1 (2005): 93–121.

Rogers, J. H. "War Comes to Norfolk Harbor, 1861." *Virginia Cavalcade* 50, no. 2 (2001): 64–75.

Roland, Charles P. "Becoming a Soldier." *Register of the Kentucky Historical Society* 101, nos. 1–2 (2003): 75–92.

———. *An American Iliad: The Story of the Civil War.* Lexington: University Press of Kentucky, 2004.

Rosecrans, William S. "King of the Hill." *Civil War Times Illustrated* 49, no. 3 (2001): 24–26, 68–70.

Ross, D. Reid. "Kansas Abolitionists Fight Confederates in Missouri." *Journal of the West* 40, no. 3 (2001): 58–67.

Rubin, Anne S. *A Shattered Nation: The Rise and Fall of the Confederacy, 1861–1868.* Chapel Hill: University of North Carolina Press, 2005.

Rutkow, Ira M. *Bleeding Blue and Gray: The Untold Story of Civil War Medicine.* New York: Random House, 2005.

Samito, Christian G., ed. *Fear Was Not in Him: The Civil War Letters of Major General Francis C. Barlow, U.S.A.* New York: Fordham University Press, 2004.

Sanders, Charles W. *While in the Hands of the Enemy: Military Prisons of the Civil War.* Baton Rouge: Louisiana State University Press, 2005.

Schiller, Laurence D. "Two Tales of Tennessee: The Ups and Downs of Cavalry Command." *North & South* 4, no. 4 (2001): 78–86.

Schmidt, Leone. *For the Honor of the Flag: The Life of General Mason Brayman, 1813–1895.* Warrenville, Ill.: Warrenville Historical Society, 2004.

Schneller, Robert J. *Cushing: Civil War SEAL.* Washington, D.C.: Brassey's, 2004.

Schooler, Lynn. *The Last Shot: The Incredible Story of the C.S.S. Shenandoah and the True Conclusion of the American Civil War.* New York: Ecco, 2005.

Schultz, Duane P. *The Most Glorious Fourth: Vicksburg and Gettysburg, July 4, 1863.* New York: Norton, 2002.

Sears, Stephen W. "Glendale: Opportunity Squandered." *North & South* 5, no. 1 (2001): 12–24.

———. "'We Should Assume the Aggressive': Origins of the Gettysburg Campaign." *North & South* 5, no. 4 (2002): 58–66.

———. "The Lee of Gettysburg." *North & South* 6, no. 5 (2003): 12–19.

Shaw, David. *Sea Wolf of the Confederacy: The Daring Civil War Raids of Naval Lt. Charles W. Read.* New York: Free Press, 2004.

Sheldon, George. *Fire on the River: The Defense of the World's Longest Covered Bridge and How it Changed the Battle of Gettysburg.* Lancaster, Pa.: Quaker Hill Press, 2006.

Shover, Michele. "John Bidwell: Civil War Politics, and the Indian Crisis of 1862." *Dogtown Territorial Quarterly*, no. 46 (2001): 4–24, 34–37.

Sifakis, Stewart. *Compendium of the Confederate Armies.* Bowie, Md.: Willow Bend Books, 2003.

Silber, Nina. *Daughters of the Union: Northern Women Fight the Civil War.* Cambridge, Mass.: Harvard University Press, 2005.

Silverman, Jason H., and Susan R. Silverman. "Blacks in Gray, Myth or Reality." *North & South* 5, no. 3 (2002): 35–43.

Simson, Jay W. *Naval Strategies of the Civil War: Confederate Innovations and Federal Opportunism.* Nashville, Tenn.: Cumberland House, 2001.

Siry, David R. "Confederates in Pennsylvania: Lee's 1863 Invasion of the North, a Thesis in History." Unpublished master's thesis, Pennsylvania State University, 2003.

Sizer, Lyde C., and Jim Cullen. *The Civil War Era: An Anthology of Sources.* Malden, Mass.: Blackwell, 2004.

Sleevi, Nola M. "The Commanders of the Second Corps of the Army of Northern Virginia: Their Religious Beliefs, as Reflected in Their Leadership." Unpublished master's thesis, University of Missouri–Kansas City, 2002.

Small, Stephen C. "The *Wampanoag* Goes on Trial." *Naval History* 16, no. 4 (2002): 32–36.

Smith, Derek. "'This Brilliant Exploit': Attack on the USS *Underwriter*." *North & South* 8, no. 2 (2005): 76–82.

Smith, John D., ed. *Black Soldiers in Blue: African American Troops in the Civil War Era.* Chapel Hill: University of North Carolina Press, 2002.

Sneden, Robert K. "Pen and Sword at Savage's Station." *Civil War Times Illustrated* 39, no. 5 (2000): 42–51.

Snell, Mark A. *From First to Last: The Life of Major General William B. Franklin.* New York: Fordham University Press, 2002.

Speer, Lonnie R. *Portals to Hell: Military Prisons of the Civil War.* Lincoln: University of Nebraska Press, 2005.

Staats, Richard J. *The Life and Times of Ephraim Cooper: One of Lincoln's First Volunteers.* Bowie, Md.: Heritage Books, 2003.

Stephens, Larry, and Mike Skinner. *Hold the Fort—I Am Coming: The Battle of Altoona Pass, October 5, 1864.* Carrollton, Ga.: Battle Flag Press, 2001.

Suderow, Bryce A. "War Along the James." *North & South* 6, no. 3 (2003): 12–23.

Summers, Mark W. "The Spoils of War." *North & South* 6, no. 2 (2003): 82–89.

Sunderland, Jonathan. *Union Troops of the American Civil War.* Ramsbury, U.K.: Crowood, 2005.

Surdam, David G. "The Confederate Naval Buildup: Could More Have Been Accomplished?" *Naval War College Review* 54, no. 1 (2001): 107–127.

Sutherland, Daniel E. "Guerrilla Warfare, Democracy, and the Fate of the Confederacy." *Journal of Southern History* 68, no. 2 (2002): 259–292.

Swisher, James K. *Warrior in Gray: General Robert Rodes of Lee's Army.* Shippensburg, Pa.: White Mane Books, 2000.

Symonds, Craig L. *American Heritage History of the Battle of Gettysburg.* New York: HarperCollins, 2001.

———. "Generalship at Gettysburg." *North & South* 6, no. 5 (2003): 80–92.

Tagg, Larry. *The Generals of Gettysburg: The Leaders of America's Greatest Battle.* Cambridge, Mass.: Da Capo Press, 2003.

Tanner, Robert G. *Retreat to Victory? Confederate Strategy Reconsidered.* Wilmington, Del.: Scholarly Resources, 2001.

Tap, Bruce. "Amateurs at War: Abraham Lincoln and the Committee on the Conduct of the War." *Journal of the Abraham Lincoln Association* 23, no. 2 (2002): 1–18.

Taylor, John M. "British Observers in Wartime Dixie." *MHQ* 14, no. 2 (2002): 66–71.

Taylor, Lenette S. "Uncle Sam's Landlord: Quartering the Union Army in Nashville in the Summer of 1863."

Tennessee Historical Quarterly 61, no. 4 (2002): 242–265.

Teague, Chuck. "Leadership Impaired? The Health of Robert E. Lee during the Gettysburg Campaign." *North & South* 6, no. 5 (2003): 68–78.

Thompson, Jerry D. *Civil War to the Bloody End: The Life and Times of Major General Samuel P. Heintzelman.* College Station: Texas A&M University Press, 2006.

Thomsen, Brian M., ed. *Blue and Gray at Sea: Naval Memoirs of the Civil War.* New York: Forge, 2003.

Toomey, Daniel C. *The Johnson-Gilmore Raid, July 9–13, 1864.* Baltimore, Md.: Toomey Press, 2005.

Trask, Benjamin H., and Dina B. Hill. *USS Monitor Bibliography.* Newport News, Va.: The Mariners Museum, 2002.

Tucker, Leslie R. *Major General Isaac Ridgeway Trimble: Biography of a Baltimore Confederate.* Jefferson, N.C.: McFarland, 2005.

Tucker, Phillip T. *God Help the Irish!: The History of the Irish Brigade.* Abilene, Tex.: McWhiney Foundation, 2006.

Tucker, Phillip T. *Irish Confederates: The Civil War's Forgotten Soldiers.* Abilene, Tex.: McWhiney Foundation Press, 2006.

Tucker, Spencer C. *A Short History of the Civil War at Sea.* Wilmington, Del.: Scholarly Resources, 2002.

Tulloch, Hugh. *The Routledge Companion to the Civil War.* New York: Routledge, 2006.

Underwood, Rodman L. *Waters of Discord: The Union Blockade of Texas during the Civil War.* Jefferson, N.C.: McFarland, 2003.

———. *Stephen Russell Mallory: A Biography of the Confederate Navy Secretary and United States Senator.* Jefferson, N.C.: McFarland, 2005.

Van Tassel, David D., and John Vacha. *Behind Bayonets: The Civil War in Northern Ohio.* Kent, Ohio: Kent State University Press, 2005.

Varon, Elizabeth R. *Southern Lady, Yankee Spy: The True Story of Elizabeth Van Lew, A Union Agent in the Heart of the Confederacy.* New York: Oxford University Press, 2005.

Wagner, Richard. *For Honor, Flag, and Family: Civil War General Samuel W. Crawford.* Shippensburg, Pa.: White Mane Books, 2005.

Wakefield, John L. *Confederates against the Confederacy: Essays on Leadership and Loyalty.* Westport, Conn.: Praeger, 2002.

Waldrep, Christopher. *Vicksburg's Long Shadow: The Civil War Legacy of Race and Remembrance.* Lanham, Md.: Rowman and Littlefield, 2005.

Walsh, George. *Those Damn Horse Soldiers: True Tales of the Civil War Cavalry.* New York: Forge, 2006.

Walt, Eugene M. *Bull Run and Beyond.* Huntington, N.Y.: Nova History Publications, 2001.

Ward, Mary G. *Civil War Legends of Rich Mountain and Beverly, West Virginia.* Parson, W. Va.: McClain Printing Co., 2004.

Webber, Jennifer L. "'If Ever War Was Holy': Quaker Soldiers and the Union Army." *North & South* 5, no. 3 (2002): 62–72.

Weitz, Mark A. *More Damning than Slaughter: Desertion in the Confederate Army.* Lincoln: University of Nebraska Press, 2005.

———. "'A Justifiable Crime': Desertion in the Confederate Army." *North & South* 8, no. 1 (2005): 66–74.

Welch, Richard F. *The Boy General: The Life and Careers of Francis Channing Barlow.* Kent, Ohio: Kent State University Press, 2005.

Westrick, Robert F. "The U.S.S. *Peterhoff*: An Historical and Archaeological Investigation of a Civil War Shipwreck." Unpublished master's thesis, East Carolina University, 2001.

Whisker, James B. *U.S. and Confederate Arms and Armories during the American Civil War.* 4 vols. Lewiston, N.Y.: E. Mellen Press, 2002–2003.

Whittington, Terry. "In the Shadow of Defeat: Tracking the Vicksburg Parolees." *Journal of Mississippi History* 64, no. 4 (2002): 307–330.

Wideman, John C. *The Sinking of the USS Cairo.* Jackson: University Press of Mississippi, 2004.

Williams, Don. "Devil's Den." *Military Heritage* 3, no. 5 (2002): 68–75.

Williams, Frank J. "Abraham Lincoln: The President Who Changed the Role of Commander in Chief." *White House Studies* 2, no. 1 (2002): 3–15.

Wills, Brian S. *Gone with the Glory: The Civil War in Cinema.* Lanham, Md.: Rowman & Littlefield, 2007.

Wilson, Mark R. *The Business of the Civil War: Military Mobilization and the State, 1861–1865.* Baltimore: Johns Hopkins University Press, 2006.

Winik, Jay. *April, 1865: The Month That Saved America.* New York: HarperCollins, 2001.

Woodworth, Steven E. "The Scapegoat of Arkansas Post." *MHQ* 13, no. 3 (2001): 58–67.

———. *The Loyal, True, and Brave: American's Civil War Soldiers.* Wilmington, Del.: SR Books, 2002.

———. "The Army of the Tennessee and the Elements of Military Success." *North & South* 6, no. 4 (2003): 44–55.

Woodworth, Steven E., and Warren Wilkinson. "Calm Before the Storm." *MHQ* 14, no. 3 (2002): 34–41.

Wylie, Paul R. *The Irish General: Thomas Francis Meagher.* Norman: University of Oklahoma Press, 2007.

Yates, Bernice-Marie., ed. *The Perfect Gentleman: The Life and Letters of George Washington Custis Lee.* Fairfax, Va.: Xulon Press, 2003.

Youngblood, Norman E. "The Development of Landmine Warfare." Unpublished Ph.D. diss., Texas Tech University, 2002.

INDEX

Italic page numbers indicate illustrations. **Boldface** page numbers denote biographies.

A

Adobe Walls, Battle of 523*c*–524*c*
African-American regiments
    Battery Wagner, Charleston
      Harbor 327*c*, 332*c*–333*c*
    Baxter Springs, Kansas 357*c*
    Charleston, siege of 303*c*,
      304*c*
    Honey Springs, Battle of
      331*c*–332*c*
    Milliken's Bend, Battle of 306*c*
    Olustee, Battle of 400*c*
    Petersburg, siege of 461*c*
    Port Hudson, siege of 302*c*
Alabama-Kearsarge battle *458,*
  458*c*–459*c*
Aldie, Virginia 312*c*, 336*c*
Alexander, Edward P. 238*c*, 403*c*,
  603, **603–605,** 732, 741
Allatoona Pass, Georgia 447*c*,
  506*c*
Allegheny, Camp, Battle of 90*c*
Amelia Court House, Virginia
  576*c*, 578*c*
Anaconda Plan 24*c*, 28*c*
Anderson, Fort, North Carolina
  270*c*, 554*c*
Anderson, Richard H. *605,*
  605–606
    Berryville, Virginia 493*c*
    Chancellorsville, Battle of
      290*c*
    Cold Harbor, Battle of 447*c*,
      449*c*
    Darbytown Road, Virginia
      509*c*

    Fort Pickens 71*c*
    Front Royal, Virginia 486*c*
    Fitzhugh Lee and 708
    James Longstreet and 717
    Richmond, Virginia 497*c*,
      502*c*
    Sayler's Creek, Virginia 579*c*
    Shenandoah Valley campaign
      (1864) 485*c*, 489*c*, 493*c*
    Spotsylvania Court House,
      Battle of 432*c*
    Sumter, Fort, South Carolina
      584*c*
Anderson, Robert **606–608,** *607,*
  607
    Pierre G. T. Beauregard and
      613
    Abner Doubleday and 645
    John B. Floyd and 657
    Benjamin Huger and 693
    Abraham Lincoln and 713
    William T. Sherman and 770
    Sumter, Fort 4*c*, 6*c*, 8*c*–11*c*,
      16*c*, 17*c*, 19*c*–21*c*
Anderson, William 501*c*–502*c*,
  514*c*, **608–609,** 755
Antietam, Battle of 210*c*–212*c*,
  211, 624, 809*m*
Appomattox Court House,
  Virginia 572*c*, 580*c*, 581*c*, *582,*
  583*c*
Arkansas, CSS 182*c*, 189*c*
Ashby, Turner **609–610**
    Harrisonburg, Virginia 163*c*
    John D. Imboden and 695
    McDowell, Virginia 149*c*

    Shenandoah Valley campaign
      (1862) 125*c*, 129*c*, 144*c*,
      155*c*
    Woodstock, Virginia 162*c*
Athens, Tennessee 499*c*, 500*c*
Atlanta campaign 431*c*, 432*c*,
  438*c*, 439*c*, 445*c*, 452*c*, 453*c*,
  456*c*, 457*c*, 462*c*–477*c*, 479*c*,
  480*c*, 484*c*, 486*c*, 488*c*–495*c*, *496*

B

Bald Hill, Battle of 472*c*
Ball's Bluff, Battle of 74*c*–75*c*
Baltimore and Ohio Railroad
  283*c*, 509*c*
Banks, Nathaniel P. **611–613,** *612*
    Turner Ashby and 610
    Bisland, Fort 279*c*–281*c*
    Brazos Island, Texas 367*c*
    Brownsville, Texas 368*c*
    Benjamin F. Butler and 627
    Edward R. S. Canby and 629
    Cedar Mountain, Battle of
      190*c*–191*c*
    Corpus Christi, Texas 372*c*
    Richard S. Ewell and 653
    David G. Farragut and 656
    Franklin, Louisiana 281*c*
    Ulysses S. Grant and 669
    Benjamin H. Grierson and
      670
    Harper's Ferry 114*c*
    Thomas J. Jackson and 698
    Edmund Kirby-Smith and
      707
    Abraham Lincoln and 714

John B. Magruder and 730
Mansfield, Battle of 415*c*
Mustang Island, Texas 373*c*
Opelousas, Louisiana 283*c*
Pleasant Hill, Battle of 416*c*
David D. Porter and 750
Sterling Porter and 753
Port Hudson, siege of 269*c*,
    271*c*, 300*c*, 302*c*, 309*c*,
    310*c*, 326*c*
Red River campaign 393*c*,
    406*c*–417*c*, 442*c*
Shenandoah Valley campaign
    (1862) 130*c*, 140*c*, 143*c*,
    148*c*, 155*c*, 158*c*, 159*c*
Richard Taylor and 781
Washington, D.C. defense
    125*c*, 205*c*
Washington, Louisiana 283*c*
Winchester, First Battle of
    157*c*
Woodstock, Virginia 154*c*
Yellow Bayou, Louisiana
    441*c*
Bardstown, Kentucky 214*c*, 216*c*,
    217*c*, 219*c*, 479*c*
Baton Rouge, Battle of 188*c*–189*c*
Battery Wagner, Charleston
    Harbor 332*c*–333*c*, *333*
battles, major (1861–1863) 801*m*
battles, major (1864–1865) 802*m*
Baxter Springs, Battle of 357*c*–
    358*c*
Bean's Station, Battle of 383*c*
Beauregard, Pierre G. T. 20*c*, *613*,
    613–615
    Edward P. Alexander and 603
    Richard H. Anderson and
        605
    Robert Anderson and 607
    Bermuda Hundred, Virginia
        440*c*
    Bottom Church, Virginia
        442*c*
    Braxton Bragg and 615
    Don C. Buell and 621
    Bull Run, First Battle of
        45*c*–49*c*

Benjamin F. Butler and 627
Columbia, South Carolina
    554*c*
Corinth, Mississippi 145*c*,
    146*c*, 150*c*, 157*c*, 159*c*, 160*c*
Jefferson Davis and 643
Abner Doubleday and 645
Drewry's Bluff, Battle of
    438*c*, 440*c*
Samuel F. Du Pont and 647
Edisto River 553*c*
Nathan G. Evans and 651
Richard S. Ewell and 653
Josiah Gorgas and 666
Ulysses S. Grant and 668
Henry W. Halleck and 674
Henry, Fort, Battle of 107*c*
Daniel H. Hill and 684
Robert F. Hoke and 687
CSS *Hunley* 340*c*, 361*c*
John D. Imboden and 695
Thomas J. Jackson and 697
Albert S. Johnston and 700
Joseph E. Johnston and 701
Edmund Kirby-Smith and
    706
Abraham Lincoln and 713
James Longstreet and 716
Irvin McDowell and 727
Petersburg, siege of 456*c*
Petersburg, Virginia 487*c*
George E. Pickett and 742
Sterling Porter and 753
Rienzi, Mississippi 162*c*
Shiloh, Battle of 132*c*–134*c*
J. E. B. Stuart and 778
Sumter, Fort 16*c*, 21*c*
Beaver Dam Creek. *See*
    Mechanicsville, Battle of
Belmont, Missouri, Battle of 80*c*
Bermuda Hundred, Virginia 440*c*,
    442*c*
Big Bethel, Battle of 36*c*–37*c*
Big Blue River, Missouri 512*c*,
    513*c*
Bird Creek, Battle of 89*c*
Bisland, Fort 279*c*–281*c*
Blackburn's Ford, Battle of 46*c*

Black Hawk War 607
"Bleeding Kansas" 608
Blue Springs, Battle of 359*c*
Booneville, Mississippi, Battle of
    178*c*
Boonville, Missouri, Battle of 39*c*
Boyd, Belle 156*c*, 198*c*, 380*c*
Bragg, Braxton *615*, **615–617**
    Edward P. Alexander and
        604
    Richard H. Anderson and
        605
    Bardstown, Kentucky 214*c*,
        216*c*, 219*c*
    Baton Rouge barracks
        confiscation 9*c*
    Pierre G. T. Beauregard and
        614
    Bentonville, North Carolina
        567*c*, 568*c*
    John C. Breckinridge and
        618
    Don C. Buell and 621
    Burnsville, Tennessee 250*c*
    Caswell, Fort 544*c*
    Catlett's Gap, Georgia 350*c*
    Chattanooga, Battle of
        374*c*–377*c*
    Chattanooga, siege of 354*c*,
        359*c*, 363*c*, 367*c*
    Chattanooga, Tennessee
        344*c*, 347*c*, 349*c*, 370*c*,
        371*c*
    Chickamauga, Battle of
        351*c*–352*c*
    Patrick R. Cleburne and 631
    Cumberland Gap retreat
        222*c*–224*c*
    Jefferson Davis and 642, 643
    Fisher, Fort, North Carolina
        542*c*
    Nathan B. Forrest and 660,
        661
    Glasgow, Kentucky 213*c*
    Goldsborough, North
        Carolina 564*c*
    Ulysses S. Grant and 668
    William J. Hardee and 679

Daniel H. Hill and 684

Thomas C. Hindman and
686

Robert F. Hoke and 687

John B. Hood and 688

Albert S. Johnston and 700

Joseph E. Johnston and 467*c*,
469*c*, 701, 702

Jonesboro, Alabama 185*c*

Kentucky offensive 222*c*

Kinston, North Carolina
563*c*, 564*c*

Edmund Kirby-Smith and
706

James Longstreet and 717

Lookout Mountain, Battle of
375*c*–376*c*

Missionary Ridge, Battle of
376*c*–377*c*

John H. Morgan and 735

Munfordville, Kentucky
208*c*, 209*c*, 212*c*, 214*c*

Murfreesboro, Battle of
246*c*–251*c*

Murfreesboro, Tennessee
230*c*, 233*c*

Perryville 219*c*, 220*c*

Leonidas Polk and 746

William S. Rosecrans and
761

Shelbyville, Tennessee 316*c*

Philip Sheridan and 768

William T. Sherman and 771

Shiloh, Battle of 132*c*–133*c*

Snow Hill, Tennessee 304*c*

George H. Thomas and 784

Tullahoma Campaign 323*c*

Earl Van Dorn and 787

Wauhatchie, Battle of 365*c*

Joseph Wheeler and 791

Brandy Station, Battle of 243*c*,
623

Breckinridge, John C. 2*c*, 617,
617–619

Baton Rouge, Battle of 188*c*

Braxton Bragg and 616

Bull's Gap, Tennessee 519*c*

Benjamin F. Butler and 626

Clinton, Mississippi 328*c*

Jefferson Davis and 643

Jubal A. Early and 650

Winfield S. Hancock and 678

Thomas C. Hindman and
685

John D. Imboden and 696

Albert S. Johnston and 700

Kernstown, Second Battle
of 474*c*

Lynchburg, Virginia 457*c*

Missionary Ridge, Battle of
376*c*

Monocacy, Battle of 467*c*

Murfreesboro, Battle of
247*c*–250*c*

New Market, Battle of 439*c*

Gideon J. Pillow and 742

Franz Sigel and 777

Strawberry Plains, Tennessee
517*c*

Winchester, Third Battle of
498*c*

Wytheville, Virginia 534*c*

Brice's Cross Roads 451*c*, 453*c*

Bristoe Campaign 359*c*, 362*c*–
363*c*

Bristoe Station, Battle of 360*c*

Buchanan, Franklin 619, **619–620**

John A. B. Dahlgren and 639

David G. Farragut and 656

John L. Worden and 797

Buckland Mills, Battle of 362*c*

Buell, Don C. 5*c*, **620–622,** 621

Bardstown, Kentucky 217*c*,
219*c*

Bowling Green, Kentucky
208*c*

Braxton Bragg and 616

Ulysses S. Grant and 668

Henry W. Halleck and 673

William J. Hardee and 679

Albert S. Johnston and 700

Edmund Kirby-Smith and
706

Louisville, Kentucky 214*c*–
216*c*

John H. Morgan and 735

Murfreesboro 204*c*

Perryville 219*c*, 220*c*

John Pope and 747

William S. Rosecrans and
761

Philip Sheridan and 768

William T. Sherman and 770

Shiloh, Battle of 134*c*

George H. Thomas and 785

Lew Wallace and 789

Buffington Island, Battle of 333*c*

Buford, John 622, **622–623**

Brandy Station, Battle of
306*c*–307*c*

Brandy Station, Virginia
337*c*

death of 384*c*

Abner Doubleday and 645

Gettysburg, Battle of 318*c*–
319*c*

John Gibbon and 663

Goose Creek, Virginia 313*c*

Gordonsville, Virginia 351*c*

Henry Heth and 681

John D. Imboden and 696

George G. Meade and 732

Alfred Pleasonton and 744

Thoroughfare Gap, Battle
of 198*c*

Williamsport, Battle of 325*c*,
329*c*–330*c*

Bull Run, First Battle of 47*c*–49*c*,
48, 603, 614, 624, 804*m*

Bull Run, Second Battle of 198*c*–
201*c*, 199, 606, 808*m*

Burnside, Ambrose E. **623–625,**
624

Antietam 210*c*–211*c*

Blue Springs, Battle of 359*c*

Campbell's Station, Battle
of 372*c*

Chattanooga, siege of 354*c*

Cold Harbor, Battle of 449*c*

Copperhead suppression
280*c*

Cumberland Gap, Tennessee
348*c*

Falmouth, Virginia 231*c*

Fredericksburg, Battle of
   232*c*–234*c*, 237*c*–240*c*
Ulysses S. Grant and 669
Ambrose P. Hill and 683
Benjamin Huger and 693
Thomas J. Jackson and 698
Knoxville, siege of 373*c*–
   374*c*, 379*c*
Robert E. Lee and 711
Abraham Lincoln and 714
George B. McClellan and
   724
George G. Meade and 732
"mud March" 256*c*, 257*c*
New Bern, Battle of 123*c*
North Anna River 443*c*
North Carolina expedition
   98*c*, 107*c*, 121*c*, 122*c*, 125*c*,
   126*c*, 142*c*
Petersburg, siege of 461*c*
Petersburg, Virginia 477*c*
Shenandoah Valley campaign
   (1862) 477*c*
Franz Sigel and 777
South Mountain, Battle of
   207*c*
Spotsylvania Court House,
   Battle of 432*c*
Wilderness, Battle of the
   428*c*, 429*c*
Butler, Benjamin F. **625–627,** *626*
Baltimore martial law 30*c*
Nathaniel P. Banks and 611
Pierre G. T. Beauregard and
   614
Big Bethel, Battle of 36*c*–37*c*
Bottom Church, Virginia
   442*c*
Chausseurs d'Afrique 216*c*
Clifton, Fort 456*c*
Donaldsonville, Louisiana
   225*c*
Drewry's Bluff, Battle of
   437*c*–438*c*, 440*c*
Samuel F. Du Pont and 647
Dutch Gap, Virginia 538*c*
Fair Oaks, Virginia 514*c*
David G. Farragut and 656

Fisher, Fort, North Carolina
   535*c*–537*c*
General Order No. 28 issued
   152*c*
Ulysses S. Grant and 669
Hatteras Inlet 60*c*
Daniel H. Hill and 684
Robert F. Hoke and 687
Abraham Lincoln and 714
Mansfield Lovell and 720
John B. Magruder and 730
Monroe, Fortress, Virginia
   530*c*, 532*c*
New Orleans 88*c*, 125*c*, 127*c*,
   145*c*
Newport News 34*c*
Petersburg, Virginia 432*c*
George E. Pickett and 742
David D. Porter and 750
Richmond, Virginia 428*c*,
   503*c*
Richard Taylor and 781
Alfred H. Terry and 783

C

Camden, Arkansas 420*c*, 422*c*,
   424*c*, 425*c*
Campbell's Station, Battle of
   372*c*
Canby, Edward R. S. **628–629**
Nathaniel P. Banks and 612
Blakely, Fort, Alabama 581*c*
James H. Carleton and 630
Fort Craig, New Mexico 110*c*
Benjamin H. Grierson and
   671
Edmund Kirby-Smith and
   593*c*, 707
William L. Loring and 718
Mobile, Alabama 562*c*, 567*c*,
   569*c*, 584*c*
Mobile Bay, Battle of 479*c*
Henry H. Sibley and 773
Spanish Fort, Alabama 571*c*,
   581*c*
Richard Taylor and 589*c*,
   590*c*, 782
Valverde, Battle of 112*c*, 113*c*

Cane Hill, Arkansas 233*c*, 235*c*,
   236*c*, 518*c*
Carleton, James H. 73*c*, 144*c*, 628,
   629–630, 774
Carnifex Ferry, Battle of 63*c*
Carthage, Battle of 42*c*
Catlett's Station, Virginia 195*c*,
   360*c*, 367*c*
Cedar Creek, Virginia 484*c*, 486*c*,
   508*c*, 510*c*, 511*c*
Cedar Mountain, Battle of 190*c*–
   191*c*
Chambersburg, Pennsylvania
   221*c*, 476*c*–478*c*
Chancellorsville, Battle of 288*c*–
   292*c*, *291*, 604, 606, 811*m*
Chantilly, Battle of 202*c*
Charleston, South Carolina 260*c*,
   278*c*, 327*c*, 341*c*
   John A. B. Dahlgren and
      544*c*
   William J. Hardee and 554*c*,
      555*c*
   William T. Sherman and
      552*c*
Charlotte, North Carolina 558*c*,
   586*c*
Chattahoochie River, Georgia
   465*c*, 467*c*, 469*c*
Chattanooga, Battle of 374*c*–377*c*,
   616
Chattanooga, siege of 354*c*–359*c*,
   362*c*–364*c*, 366*c*, 367*c*
Chattanooga, Tennessee 164*c*,
   184*c*, 320*c*, 344*c*, 347*c*, 349*c*,
   353*c*, 370*c*, 371*c*
Cheat Mountain, Battle of 63*c*–65*c*
Cheraw, South Carolina 553*c*, 561*c*
Cherokee Indians
   Gunter's Prairie, Indian
      Territory 490*c*
   Honey Springs, Battle of
      331*c*
   Pea Ridge, Battle of 119*c*
   Pleasant Bluffs, Arkansas
      456*c*
   Smith, Fort, Arkansas 476*c*,
      478*c*, 479*c*

Cheyenne Indians 525c–526c, 539c, 549c

Chickamauga, Battle of 351c–352c, 616, 618

Chickasaw Bluffs, Mississippi 245c, 246c, 281c

Chickasaw Indians 44c, 83c, 89c

Choctaw Indians 44c, 83c, 89c, 331c

Cleburne, Patrick R. **630–632**, *631*

    Atlanta, Battle of 473c

    Bald Hill, Battle of 472c

    Bardstown, Kentucky 217c

    Chickamauga, Battle of 351c

    Franklin, Tennessee 526c–527c

    Thomas C. Hindman and 686

    John B. Hood and 689

    Joseph Hooker and 691

    Jonesboro, Battle of 492c

    Kennesaw Mountain, Battle of 462c

    Missionary Ridge, Battle of 376c

    Pickett's Mills, Battle of 445c

    Richmond, Kentucky, Battle of 201c

    Ringgold Gap, Battle of 378c–379c

    Joseph Wheeler and 792

Clifton, Tennessee 248c, 250c

Clinton, Mississippi 326c, 328c

Coggins Point, Virginia 494c, 497c

Cold Harbor, Battle of 446c–449c, *448*, 604, 618

Columbia, South Carolina 545c, 554c–556c

Copperheads 280c, 292c, 303c

Corinth, Mississippi

    Pierre G. T. Beauregard and 157c, 159c

    Henry W. Halleck and 149c–151c, 155c, 157c, 159c

    Earl Van Dorn's attack on 218c, 219c

Corricks Ford, Battle of 44c–45c

Crater, Battle of the 478c, 604, 625

Creek Indians 83c, 84c, 89c

Crittenden, George B. 99c, 100c, **632–633**, 700, 785

Crittenden Compromise 5c–6c, 9c, 10c

Crook, George **633–635**, *634*

    Cedar Creek, Virginia 510c

    George A. Custer and 638

    Jubal A. Early and 650

    Fisher's Hill, Battle of 500c

    John Gibbon and 663

    Henry Heth and 680–681

    Jetersville, Virginia 578c

    Lynchburg, Virginia 457c

    Meadow Bluff, West Virginia 442c

    John Pope and 748

    Shenandoah Valley campaign (1864) 472c–474c, 482c, 499c

    Philip Sheridan and 769

    Smith's Cross Roads, Tennessee 356c

    Alfred H. Terry and 784

    Virginia and Tennessee Railroad 425c

    Joseph Wheeler and 792

    Winchester, Third Battle of 498c

Cross Keys, Battle of 165c

Cross Lanes, Battle of 59c

Culpeper Court House, Virginia 227c, 246c

Cumberland Gap, Tennessee 125c, 190c, 348c

Curtis, Samuel R. **635–637**

    Arkansas shore raids 185c

    Baxter Springs, Battle of 358c

    Big Blue River, Missouri 512c

    Cache, Arkansas 179c

    Fayetteville, Arkansas 225c

    Henry W. Halleck and 673

    Ben McCulloch and 726

    Pea Ridge, Battle of 108c, 114c, 117c–119c

Alfred Pleasonton and 745

Sterling Porter and 753

William S. Rosecrans and 761

Franz Sigel and 777

Earl Van Dorn and 787

Westport, Missouri, Battle of 513c

Custer, George A. *637*, **637–638**

    Amelia Court House, Virginia 577c

    Buckland Mills, Battle of 362c

    Cedar Creek, Virginia 511c

    George Crook and 635

    Jubal A. Early and 650

    Five Forks, Virginia 573c

    Germanna Ford, Virginia 373c

    Gettysburg, Battle of 318c, 322c

    John Gibbon and 663

    Winfield S. Hancock and 678

    Hanovertown, Virginia 445c

    Haw's Shop, Battle of 446c

    Hugh J. Kilpatrick and 705

    Fitzhugh Lee and 708

    Lynchburg, Virginia 559c

    John S. Mosby and 737

    Mount Crawford, Virginia 560c

    Richmond raid 403c

    Sayler's Creek, Virginia 579c

    Shenandoah Valley campaign (1864) 486c

    Philip Sheridan and 769

    J. E. B. Stuart and 779

    Alfred H. Terry and 784

    Tom's Brook, Virginia 507c, 508c

    Trevilian Station, Battle of 453c, 454c

    Waynesboro, Virginia 560c

    Wilderness, Battle of 431c

    Williamsport, Battle of 329c–330c

    Yellow Tavern, Battle of 436c

Cynthiana, Kentucky 183c, 454c

D

Dahlgren, John A. B. 11*c*, **639–640**, *640*
  Alexandria, Virginia 33*c*
  Battery Wagner, Charleston Harbor 332*c*–333*c*
  Pierre G. T. Beauregard and 614
  Charleston, South Carolina 327*c*, 341*c*, 544*c*
  Samuel F. Du Pont and 647
  Georgetown, South Carolina 558*c*
  Hugh J. Kilpatrick and 705
  St. John's River, Florida 394*c*
  South Atlantic Blockading Squadron 547*c*
  Sumter, Fort 343*c*, 345*c*, 347*c*, 349*c*, 365*c*, 368*c*, 370*c*
Dallas, Georgia 443*c*, 445*c*, 446*c*
Dalton, First Battle of 401–403*c*
Danville, Virginia 576*c*, 577*c*
Davis, Charles H. **640–642**, *641*
  Arkansas shore raids 185*c*
  David G. Farragut and 656
  Andrew H. Foote and 659
  Memphis, First Battle of 163*c*–164*c*
  David D. Porter and 749
Davis, Jefferson **642–644**, *643*
  Abbeville, South Carolina 589*c*
  African-American prisoners 423*c*
  Pierre G. T. Beauregard and 613, 614
  Braxton Bragg and 615, 616
  Bread Riot 277*c*
  John C. Breckinridge and 618
  Bull Run, First Battle of 46*c*, 49*c*
  Benjamin F. Butler and 626
  Charlotte, North Carolina 586*c*
  Chattanooga, siege of 359*c*
  Chattanooga, Tennessee 370*c*

  Patrick R. Cleburne and 632
  Cokesbury, South Carolina 589*c*
  Danville, Virginia 576*c*, 577*c*
  declaration of war with the U.S. 28*c*
  diplomatic recognition for Confederacy 18*c*
  election as provisional President of Confederate States of America 13*c*
  Nathan G. Evans and 652
  John B. Floyd and 658
  Nathan B. Forrest and 661
  General-in-Chief Act 546*c*
  Josiah Gorgas and 666
  Greensborough, North Carolina 583*c*
  Wade Hampton and 676
  William J. Hardee and 679, 680
  Henry, Fort, Battle of 107*c*
  Henry Heth and 680
  Daniel H. Hill and 684
  Thomas C. Hindman and 685
  Robert F. Hoke and 687
  John B. Hood and 688
  inauguration as president of Confederate States of America 113*c*
  inauguration as provisional president of Confederate States of America 14*c*
  Joseph E. Johnston and 232*c*, 467*c*, 469*c*–471*c*, 701
  Hugh J. Kilpatrick and 705
  Edmund Kirby-Smith and 706
  Abraham Lincoln and 713
  Ben McCulloch and 725
  Mechanicsville, Battle of 172*c*
  Monroe, Fortress, Virginia 592*c*
  John H. Morgan and 735
  Negro Soldier Law 565*c*
  New Orleans expedition 95*c*

  peace negotiations 424*c*, 518*c*, 521*c*, 541*c*, 544*c*, 547*c*, 549*c*, 551*c*
  John C. Pemberton and 739
  Peninsula Campaign 138*c*
  Gideon J. Pillow and 743
  Leonidas Polk and 745
  David D. Porter and 749
  Sterling Porter and 753
  Port Royal, South Carolina 591*c*
  prisoners of war 187*c*
  Richmond raid 405*c*
  Sandersville, Georgia 590*c*
  Senate address on South Carolina crisis 9*c*
  Henry H. Sibley and 773
  slavery resolutions 1*c*, 2*c*
  Sumter, Fort 15*c*, 367*c*
  Richard Taylor and 781
  George H. Thomas and 784
  Earl Van Dorn and 786, 787
  Vicksburg, Battle of 236*c*
  Vicksburg, siege of 284*c*
  Joseph Wheeler and 792
Deep Bottom Run, Virginia 485*c*, 487*c*
District of Columbia 129*c*, 205*c*, 465*c*–469*c*
Donelson, Fort 261*c*, 262*c*
Donelson, Fort, Battle of 109*c*–111*c*
Doubleday, Abner **644–646**, *645*
  Robert Anderson and 608
  Gettysburg, Battle of 319*c*
  Winfield S. Hancock and 677
  Oliver O. Howard and 692
  George G. Meade and 732
  John F. Reynolds and 758
  Sumter, Fort 21*c*
Douglass, Frederick 192*c*, 338*c*
Dranesville, Virginia 92*c*, 276*c*, 400*c*
Drewry's Bluff, Battle of 437*c*–440*c*, 614, 627
Du Pont, Samuel F. *646*, **646–648**
  Pierre G. T. Beauregard and 614

Charleston, South Carolina
260c, 278c
John A. B. Dahlgren and 639
Charles H. Davis and 641
Andrew H. Foote and 659
Abraham Lincoln and 714
McAllister, Fort 258c
Port Royal expedition 73c,
77c, 78c, 80c
John Rodgers and 758, 759
John L. Worden and 797

E

Early, Jubal A. **649–651,** *650*
Bethesda Church 446c
John C. Breckinridge and
618
Bull Run, First Battle of 46c,
49c
Cedar Creek, Virginia 486c,
510c, 511c
Cedar Mountain, Battle of
190c
Chambersburg, Pennsylvania
476c
Chancellorsville, Battle of
291c
Chancellorsville campaign
287c
Cold Harbor, Battle of 449c
George Crook and 634
George A. Custer and 637
Abner Doubleday and 646
Richard S. Ewell and 654
Fisher's Hill, Battle of 500c
Fredericksburg, Battle of
238c
John B. Gordon and 664
Hagerstown, Maryland 465c,
467c
Henry W. Halleck and 674
Harper's Ferry, West Virginia
490c
Robert F. Hoke and 686
John D. Imboden and 696
Fitzhugh Lee and 708
Robert E. Lee and 712
James Longstreet and 717

Lynchburg, Virginia 457c–
458c
Montgomery C. Meigs and
734
Monocacy, Battle of 467c
Moorefield, Battle of 483c
Port Republic, Virginia 501c
Richmond, Virginia 455c,
497c
Salem Church, Battle of 292c
Shenandoah Valley campaign
(1864) 471c, 473c, 474c,
479c, 482c, 484c, 488c,
489c, 499c, 512c, 519c
Shepherdstown, Maryland
465c
Philip Sheridan and 769
Franz Sigel and 777
Spotsylvania Court House,
Battle of 432c
Staunton, Virginia 461c
Lew Wallace and 790
Washington, D.C. 468c, 469c
Waynesboro, Virginia 502c,
503c
Williamsburg, Virginia 147c
James H. Wilson and 796
Winchester, Second Battle
of 310c
Winchester, Third Battle of
498c
Winchester, Virginia 464c,
487c
Winchester, West Virginia
488c, 494c
York, Pennsylvania 317c
Elkhorn Tavern, Battle of 118c–
119c
emancipation
congressional resolution
136c
in Department of the South
150c
Department of the South
order 154c
Federal Bureau of
Emancipation plans 384c
First Confiscation Act 54c

Frémont's Missouri
declaration 60c, 63c, 64c
Lincoln's initial proclamation
181c
plantation owner policy 391c
in Fort Pulaski, Georgia
region 138c
slavery outlawed in
Washington, D.C. 139c
in West Virginia 275c
Emancipation Proclamation 184c,
214c
Antietam 212c
Jefferson Davis's opposition
to and 254c
effect on Great Britain
218c–219c
enactment as law 248c
Evans, Nathan G. 47c–48c, 74c–
75c, 168c–169c, **651–652**
Ewell, Richard S. **652–654,** *653*
Amelia Court House,
Virginia 576c, 578c
Bristoe Campaign 359c
John Buford and 623
Cedar Mountain, Battle of
190c
Cross Keys, Battle of 165c
Abner Doubleday and 645
Jubal A. Early and 649
Gaines's Mill, Battle of 173c
Gettysburg, Battle of 319c,
320c
John B. Gordon and 665
Groveton, Battle of 198c
Oliver O. Howard and 692
Thomas J. Jackson and 698
Manassas Junction, Virginia
197c
North Anna River 443c
Port Republic, Battle of 166c
Richmond, Virginia 455c,
575c
Sayler's Creek, Virginia 579c
Shenandoah Valley campaign
(1862) 155c
Spotsylvania Court House,
Battle of 432c, 440c, 441c

Wapping Heights, Battle of
334c
Wilderness, Battle of the
428c, 430c
Winchester, First Battle of
157c
Winchester, Second Battle of
310c–311c

F

Fairfax Court House, Virginia
83c, 257c, 269c, 317c, 338c
Fair Garden, Battle of 392c
Fair Oaks, Battle of 160c
Falmouth, Virginia 231c, 234c
Farragut, David G. 191c, **655–
657,** 656
    Franklin Buchanan and 620
    Benjamin F. Butler and 626
    John A. B. Dahlgren and 640
    Charles H. Davis and 641
    Donaldsonville, Louisiana
    191c
    Galveston, Texas 253c
    Grand Gulf, Battle of 272c
    Abraham Lincoln and 714
    Mansfield Lovell and 720
    Mobile Bay, Alabama 484c,
    489c, 491c
    Mobile Bay, Battle of 481c–
    483c
    New Orleans expedition
    82c–83c, 97c, 101c, 104c,
    112c, 113c, 121c, 129c,
    132c, 135c, 139c, 140c–143c
    New York City 532c, 535c,
    537c
    David D. Porter and 748
    Port Hudson, siege of 271c,
    302c, 316c
    Richmond, Virginia 578c
    Earl Van Dorn and 788
    Vicksburg, Mississippi 169c,
    170c, 174c, 175c
    Vicksburg, siege of 279c,
    292c, 303c
    Warrenton, Mississippi 276c
    Warrenton, Virginia 274c

Fayetteville, North Carolina 562c,
565c
Fisher, Fort, Battle of 542c–543c,
543, 616, 627
Fisher, Fort, North Carolina
535c–536c, 538c, 539c, 541c–
543c, 543
Fisher's Hill, Battle of 499c–500c
Florence, Alabama 506c, 522c
Floyd, John B. **657–658**
    Robert Anderson and 607
    Carnifex Ferry, Battle of 60c,
    63c
    death of 344c
    Donelson, Fort, Battle of
    107c, 109c–111c
    Ulysses S. Grant and 668
    Henry Heth and 680
    Albert S. Johnston and 700
    Joseph E. Johnston and 701
    Robert E. Lee and 710
    Montgomery C. Meigs and
    733
    Gideon J. Pillow and 743
    William S. Rosecrans and
    760
    Winfield Scott and 764
Foote, Andrew H. **658–660,** 659
    Charles H. Davis and 641
    death of 316c
    Donelson, Fort, Battle of
    108c–110c
    John B. Floyd and 658
    Ulysses S. Grant and 668
    Henry, Fort, Battle of 97c,
    102c, 104c–106c
    Island No. 10, Battle of 124c,
    125c
    Mississippi River operations
    114c, 138c
    Gideon J. Pillow and 743
    John Pope and 747
    John Rodgers and 758
Forrest, Nathan B. 660, **660–661**
    Athens, Tennessee 499c,
    500c
    Atlanta campaign 472c
    Bell's Mill, Tennessee 529c

Bradyville, Tennessee 267c
Braxton Bragg and 616
Brentwood, Tennessee 274c
Brice's Cross Roads 451c,
453c
Cedar Bluff, Alabama 292c
Chickamauga, Battle of
351c
Clifton, Tennessee 248c,
250c
Collierville, Tennessee 455c
Columbia, Tennessee 523c
Corinth, Mississippi 518c
Donelson, Fort 261c, 262c
Donelson, Fort, Battle of
110c
Ebenezer Church, Alabama
574c
Estenaula, Tennessee 385c
Florence, Alabama 506c
John B. Floyd and 658
Franklin, Tennessee 526c
Benjamin H. Grierson and
671
Wade Hampton and 676
Humbolt, Tennessee 242c
Huntsville, Alabama 504c
Johnsonville, Tennessee
517c, 518c
Kentucky raids 85c
Ku Klux Klan 601c
Lexington, Tennessee 241c
Memphis, Tennessee 489c
Montevallo, Alabama 573c
Murfreesboro, First Battle
of 181c
Murfreesboro, Second Battle
of 247c–248c, 250c
Murfreesboro, Tennessee
530c
Nashville, Battle of 533c
Nashville, Tennessee 114c,
228c, 528c
Nashville and Chattanooga
Railroad 447c
New Castle, Tennessee 386c
Okolona, Mississippi 401c,
468c, 469c

Paducah, Battle of 412*c*

Paris Landing, Tennessee 515*c*

Pillow, Fort, Battle of 418*c*
   Gideon J. Pillow and 743

Pulaski, Tennessee 501*c*

Ripley, Mississippi 454*c*

Round Mountain, Tennessee 197*c*

Scottsville, Alabama 572*c*

Selma, Alabama 575*c*–576*c*
   Joseph O. Shelby and 767

Shoal Creek, Tennessee 521*c*

Spring Hill, Tennessee 525*c*
   Richard Taylor and 782

Tennessee raids 232*c*, 246*c*, 497*c*

Thompson's Station, Tennessee 268*c*

Triune, Tennessee 308*c*

Tupelo, Battle of 469*c*, 470*c*

Union City, Tennessee 411*c*
   Earl Van Dorn and 788

West Point, Mississippi 400*c*
   Joseph Wheeler and 793

James H. Wilson and 796

Yazoo Pass 265*c*

Frankfort, Kentucky 203*c*, 207*c*, 218*c*

Franklin, Battle of 526*c*–527*c*

Franklin, Tennessee 268*c*, 279*c*

Frederick, Maryland 204*c*, 205*c*

Fredericksburg, Battle of 232*c*–234*c*, 237*c*–240*c*, 239, 810*m*
   Edward P. Alexander and 604
   Richard H. Anderson and 606
   Ambrose E. Burnside and 624

Fredericksburg, Virginia 229*c*–231*c*, 287*c*

Freeman's Ford, Battle of 195*c*–197*c*

Front Royal, Virginia 156*c*, 160*c*, 399*c*, 434*c*, 486*c*

Fugitive Slave Law 13*c*, 139*c*, 182*c*, 463*c*

G

Gaines's Mill, Battle of 173*c*–174*c*, 604

Galveston, Texas 249*c*, 253*c*

General Order No. 11 241*c*, 251*c*

Georgia, Sherman's march through. *See* Sherman's march through Georgia

Gettysburg, Battle of 318*c*–323*c*, *321*, 604, 606, 623, 813*m*

Gibbon, John **662–663**, *663*
   Fredericksburg, Battle of 238*c*
   Groveton, Battle of 198*c*
   Oliver O. Howard and 693
   Petersburg, siege of 460*c*, 489*c*
   Reams's Station, Virginia 490*c*
   Alfred H. Terry and 784

Glasgow, Kentucky 180*c*, 213*c*

Glendale, Battle of 176*c*

Goldsborough, North Carolina 564*c*, 569*c*

Gordon, John B. *664*, **664–665**
   Amelia Court House, Virginia 576*c*
   Appomattox Court House, Virginia 581*c*, 583*c*
   Cedar Creek, Virginia 510*c*
   Jubal A. Early and 650
   Hatcher's Run, Virginia 551*c*
   High Bridge, Virginia 580*c*
   Kernstown, Second Battle of 474*c*
   Monocacy, Battle of 467*c*
   Petersburg, Virginia 570*c*
   Sayler's Creek, Virginia 579*c*
   Spotsylvania Court House, Battle of 437*c*
   Wilderness, Battle of the 430*c*
   Winchester, Third Battle of 498*c*

Gordonsville, Virginia 182*c*, 351*c*

Gorgas, Josiah **665–666**

Grand Gulf, Battle of 272*c*, 287*c*

Grand Gulf, Mississippi 284*c*, 285*c*, 292*c*

Grand Junction, Tennessee 226*c*, 227*c*, 231*c*

Grant, Ulysses S. *582*, **666–670**, *667*
   Edward P. Alexander and 604
   Appomattox, Virginia 572*c*
   Baltimore, Maryland 466*c*
   Nathaniel P. Banks and 612
   Pierre G. T. Beauregard and 614
   Belmont, Battle of 79*c*, 80*c*
   Braxton Bragg and 616
   Don C. Buell and 621
   Ambrose Burnside and 625
   Benjamin F. Butler and 539*c*, 627
   Cedar Creek, Virginia 486*c*
   Chattanooga, Battle of 374*c*–377*c*
   Chattanooga, siege of 363*c*, 364*c*
   Chattanooga, Tennessee 353*c*
   City Point, Virginia 544*c*
   Cold Harbor, Battle of 444*c*, 446*c*–449*c*
   George B. Crittenden and 633
   George Crook and 635
   George A. Custer and 637
   John A. B. Dahlgren and 640
   Donelson, Fort, Battle of 109*c*–111*c*
   Jubal A. Early and 650
   Farmville, Virginia 580*c*
   David G. Farragut and 656
   Fisher, Fort, North Carolina 537*c*
   John B. Floyd and 658
   Andrew H. Foote and 659
   Nathan B. Forrest and 660
   General Order No. 11 241*c*, 251*c*, 256*c*
   John Gibbon and 663
   John B. Gordon and 664
   Grand Gulf, Mississippi 292*c*
   Grand Junction, Tennessee 226*c*, 227*c*, 231*c*

Benjamin H. Grierson and 670

Henry W. Halleck and 673

Winfield S. Hancock and 678

Hatcher's Run, Virginia 550c, 551c

Henry, Fort, Battle of 97c, 103c–106c

Ambrose P. Hill and 683

Holly Springs, Mississippi 230c, 241c, 242c

Joseph Hooker and 691

Oliver O. Howard and 692

Iuka, Mississippi 208c, 213c

Jackson, Mississippi 293c

James River, Virginia 571c

Jetersville, Virginia 578c

Albert S. Johnston and 700

Joseph E. Johnston and 701

Kentucky 67c

Hugh J. Kilpatrick and 705

La Grange, Tennessee 229c

Robert E. Lee and 581c, 711

Abraham Lincoln and 714

Robert Lincoln and 545c

James Longstreet and 717

William L. Loring and 719

Mattaponi River, Virginia 442c

George B. McClellan and 725

James B. McPherson and 728, 729

George G. Meade and 732

Montgomery C. Meigs and 734

Milford Station, Virginia 442c–443c

Missionary Ridge, Battle of 376c–377c

Missouri 71c

John S. Mosby and 737

Nashville, Tennessee 530c, 532c

North Anna River 443c

Overland Campaign 447c

Oxford, Mississippi 234c

Pemberton, Fort 271c

John C. Pemberton and 740

Petersburg, siege of 457c, 459c–461c

Petersburg, Virginia 475c–477c, 537c, 550c, 570c, 574c

Gideon J. Pillow and 743

Leonidas Polk and 746

John Pope and 747

David D. Porter and 749, 750

prisoner of war exchanges 420c, 547c

Red River campaign 407c

Richmond, Virginia 495c, 537c

Richmond, Virginia campaign 455c

William S. Rosecrans and 760

John M. Schofield and 763

Raphael Semmes and 766

Shenandoah Valley campaign (1862) 477c

Shenandoah Valley campaign (1864) 476c, 483c, 485c, 495c, 500c

Philip Sheridan and 768

William T. Sherman and 770, 772

Shiloh, Battle of 132c–135c

Daniel E. Sickles and 776

Spotsylvania Court House, Battle of 432c, 434c, 436c, 440c, 441c

J. E. B. Stuart and 779

Alfred H. Terry and 783

George H. Thomas and 785, 786

Earl Van Dorn and 788

Vicksburg, Battle of 226c, 228c–230c

Vicksburg, siege of 242c, 259c, 277c, 281c, 282c, 284c, 285c, 287c–290c, 294c–296c, 298c–300c, 311c, 323c–324c

Virginia Central Railroad raid 450c

Lew Wallace and 789

Wilderness, Battle of the 431c

Wilderness region, Virginia 428c

James H. Wilson and 795

Greeley, Horace 52c, 465c

Greenbrier River, Battle of 70c

Greensborough, North Carolina 583c–585c

Grierson, Benjamin H. **670–672,** 671

   Brice's Cross Roads 453c

   Comite River, Louisiana 290c

   Estenaula, Tennessee 385c

   Ulysses S. Grant and 668

   Holly Springs, Mississippi 204c

   La Grange, Tennessee 274c

   Mobile and Ohio Railroad raids 538c

   Nashville and Chattanooga Railroad 447c

   New Albany, Mississippi 283c

   New Castle, Tennessee 386c

   New Orleans and Jackson Railroad 294c

   Newton Station, Mississippi 285c

   Palo Alto, Mississippi 284c

   John C. Pemberton and 740

   John Pope and 748

   Vicksburg, siege of 245c, 282c, 287c

Groveton, Battle of 198c

H

Hagerstown, Maryland 205c, 465c, 467c

Halleck, Henry W. **673–675,** 674

   Nathaniel P. Banks and 612

   Pierre G. T. Beauregard and 614

   Booneville, Battle of 178c

   Don C. Buell and 621

   Corinth, Mississippi 146c, 149c–151c, 154c, 155c, 157c, 159c, 160c

Samuel R. Curtis and 636
Donelson, Fort, Battle of 108*c*
General Order No. 11 251*c*
Ulysses S. Grant and 667, 668
Henry, Fort, Battle of 102*c*, 103*c*
Joseph Hooker and 691
Abraham Lincoln and 714
George B. McClellan and 723
James B. McPherson and 728
John H. Morgan and 735
John Pope and 747
William C. Quantrill and 755
William S. Rosecrans and 760
St. Charles, Arkansas 169*c*
Philip Sheridan and 768
William T. Sherman and 770
George H. Thomas and 785
Lew Wallace and 789
Hampton, Wade *675*, **675–676**
Bentonville, North Carolina 567*c*
Brandy Station, Battle of 307*c*
Coggins Point, Virginia 497*c*
Columbia, South Carolina 554*c*, 555*c*
Nathan G. Evans and 651
Fayetteville, North Carolina 565*c*
Nathan B. Forrest and 661
Germanna Ford, Virginia 373*c*
Goose Creek, Virginia 313*c*
Winfield S. Hancock and 678
Hatcher's Run, Virginia 514*c*
Haw's Shop, Battle of 446*c*
John D. Imboden and 696
Fitzhugh Lee and 708
Monroe's Cross Roads, North Carolina 563*c*, 564*c*
Occoquan Creek 244*c*
Richmond raid 404*c*

Shenandoah Valley campaign (1864) 494*c*, 497*c*
Philip Sheridan and 769
William T. Sherman and 772
Stoney Creek Station, Virginia 463*c*
J. E. B. Stuart and 779
Trevilian Station, Battle of 453*c*, 454*c*
Virginia Central Railroad raid 452*c*
Joseph Wheeler and 792
Wilderness, Battle of the 431*c*
James H. Wilson and 796
Hampton Roads, Battle of 805*m*
Hancock, Winfield S. **676–678**, *677*
Cold Harbor, Battle of 447*c*–449*c*
George A. Custer and 638
Deep Bottom Run, Virginia 485*c*, 487*c*
Gettysburg, Battle of 319*c*, 320*c*
John Gibbon and 542*c*, 662
John B. Gordon and 664
Wade Hampton and 676
Hatcher's Run, Virginia 514*c*–515*c*
Haymarket, Maryland 315*c*
Henry Heth and 681
Ambrose P. Hill and 683
Oliver O. Howard and 692
James Longstreet and 717
George G. Meade and 732
North Anna River 443*c*
Petersburg, siege of 456*c*, 489*c*
Petersburg, Virginia 475*c*
George E. Pickett and 741
Reams's Station, Virginia 490*c*
Shenandoah Valley campaign (1864) 476*c*, 485*c*, 487*c*
Daniel E. Sickles and 775
Spotsylvania Court House, Battle of 432*c*, 434*c*, 436*c*, 437*c*, 440*c*

Alfred H. Terry and 784
Wilderness, Battle of the 428*c*–430*c*
Hanover Court House, Virginia 158*c*, 566*c*
Hardee, William J. **678–680**, *679*
Atlanta, Battle of 473*c*
Atlanta campaign 431*c*, 471*c*, 473*c*
Averasboro, North Carolina 566*c*
Bentonville, North Carolina 567*c*
John C. Breckinridge and 618
Charleston, South Carolina 554*c*, 555*c*
Patrick R. Cleburne and 631
George B. Crittenden and 633
Dallas, Georgia 446*c*
Georgia campaign 491*c*
Henry, Fort, Battle of 107*c*, 108*c*
Thomas C. Hindman and 685
John B. Hood and 688–689
Albert S. Johnston and 699
Jonesboro, Battle of 492*c*, 493*c*
Kennesaw Mountain, Battle of 462*c*
Macon, Georgia 522*c*
James B. McPherson and 729
Munfordville, Kentucky 209*c*
Murfreesboro, Battle of 247*c*
Peachtree Creek, Battle of 471*c*
Perryville 219*c*, 220*c*
Resaca, Battle of 438*c*
Savannah, Georgia 531*c*, 534*c*, 535*c*
Philip Sheridan and 768
William T. Sherman and 772
Sherman's Georgia campaign 465*c*

George H. Thomas and 784
Whippy Swamp, South
Carolina 549c
Harper's Ferry, Battle of 206c–
209c
Harper's Ferry, John Brown's raid
on 609
Harrisonburg, Virginia 148c,
163c, 501c
Harrodsburg, Kentucky 181c,
221c
Hatcher's Run, Virginia 514c,
550c, 551c
Haw's Shop, Battle of 446c
Henry, Fort, Battle of 105c–107c,
107
Heth, Henry **680–681**
Bristoe Station, Battle of
360c
John Buford and 623
Gettysburg, Battle of 318c–
319c
Hatcher's Run, Virginia 514c
Ambrose P. Hill and 683
Jackson's River Depot,
Virginia 152c
Lewisburg, Virginia 156c
Petersburg, siege of 488c
Petersburg, Virginia 476c,
487c
Poplar Springs Church,
Virginia 502c
Princeton, Virginia 153c
Reams's Station, Virginia
490c
Shelton Laurel massacre
255c
Sutherland Station, Virginia
575c
Williamsport, Battle of 329c
High Bridge, Virginia 579c, 580c
Hill, Ambrose P. *682*, **682–683**
Richard H. Anderson and
606
Antietam 209c, 211c
Boteler's Ford, Maryland
213c
Bristoe Campaign 359c

Bristoe Station, Battle of
360c
Bull Run, Second Battle of
199c
Cedar Mountain, Battle of
190c
Chancellorsville, Battle of
289c
Cold Harbor, Battle of 449c
Jubal A. Early and 649
Richard S. Ewell and 653
Franklin's Crossing, Virginia
304c–305c
Gaines's Mill, Battle of 173c
Gettysburg, Battle of 318c
Glendale, Battle of 176c
Winfield S. Hancock and
678
Harper's Ferry 208c
Hatcher's Run, Virginia 514c
Henry Heth and 681
Robert E. Lee and 711
James Longstreet and 717
Manassas Junction, Virginia
197c
Mechanicsville, Battle of
172c
North Anna River 443c
Petersburg, siege of 460c,
488c
Petersburg, Virginia 575c
Poplar Springs Church,
Virginia 502c, 504c
Reams's Station, Virginia
490c
J. E. B. Stuart and 778
Washington, North Carolina
276c
Wilderness, Battle of the
428c, 429c
Hill, Daniel H. **683–685**, *684*
Anderson, Fort 270c
Antietam 210c
Big Bethel, Battle of 37c
Blackwater, Virginia 308c
John C. Breckinridge and
618
Chickamauga, Battle of 352c

Fredericksburg, Battle of
238c
Gaines's Mill, Battle of 173c
John B. Gordon and 664
Robert F. Hoke and 686
Benjamin Huger and 694
Thomas J. Jackson and 697
Kinston, North Carolina
282c, 563c, 564c
Malvern Hill, Battle of 177c
Maryland campaign 206c
Mechanicsville, Battle of
172c
New Bern, North Carolina
269c
Peninsula Campaign 160c
Seven Pines, Battle of 160c,
161c
South Mountain, Battle of
207c
Washington, North Carolina
273c, 281c
Williamsburg, Virginia 147c
Yorktown, Battle of 137c
Hindman, Fort 251c, 253c
Hindman, Thomas C. 233c, 235c–
237c, 245c, **685–686**, 767
Hoke, Robert F. **686–687**
Drewry's Bluff, Battle of
437c, 438c, 440c
Fair Oaks, Virginia 514c
Fisher, Fort, North Carolina
536c, 541c, 542c
Harrison, Fort, Virginia 506c
Kinston, North Carolina
563c, 564c
New Bern, Battle of 123c
New Bern, North Carolina
393c–394c
Plymouth, North Carolina
420c, 422c
Rappahannock Station,
Second Battle of 369c
Richmond, Virginia 503c
Alfred H. Terry and 783
Hoke's Run, Battle of 41c
Holly Springs, Mississippi 204c,
230c, 241c, 242c

Honey Springs, Battle of 331*c*–332*c*

Hood, John B. **687–689,** *688*
- Allatoona Pass, Georgia 506*c*
- Antietam 210*c*
- Atlanta, Battle of 473*c*
- Atlanta campaign 431*c*, 470*c*–473*c*, 475*c*, 476*c*, 484*c*
- Atlanta evacuation 492*c*, 495*c*
- Bell's Mill, Tennessee 529*c*
- Braxton Bragg and 616
- John C. Breckinridge and 618
- Bull Run, Second Battle of 199*c*, 200*c*
- Chickasaw, Alabama 536*c*
- Patrick R. Cleburne and 632
- Columbia, Tennessee 525*c*
- Corinth, Mississippi 518*c*
- Decatur, Alabama 514*c*
- Eltham's Landing 148*c*
- Florence, Alabama 522*c*
- Nathan B. Forrest and 661
- Franklin, Tennessee 526*c*–527*c*
- Gaines's Mill, Battle of 173*c*
- Georgia campaign 491*c*
- Gettysburg, Battle of 320*c*
- Benjamin H. Grierson and 671
- William J. Hardee and 679, 680
- Joseph E. Johnston and 701
- Jonesboro, Battle of 492*c*, 493*c*
- Kennesaw Mountain, Battle of 459*c*, 460*c*
- James Longstreet and 717
- William L. Loring and 719
- James B. McPherson and 729
- Nashville, Battle of 533*c*–534*c*
- Nashville, Tennessee 527*c*, 528*c*, 530*c*–532*c*
- New Hope Church, Battle of 444*c*
- Peachtree Creek, Battle of 472*c*
- Pickett's Mills, Battle of 445*c*
- Resaca, Battle of 438*c*, 439*c*
- resignation of 542*c*
- Rome, Georgia 508*c*
- John M. Schofield and 762
- William T. Sherman and 771
- South Mountain, Battle of 207*c*
- Richard Taylor and 782
- George H. Thomas and 784
- Tupelo, Mississippi 540*c*
- Tuscumbia, Alabama 516*c*
- Joseph Wheeler and 792
- James H. Wilson and 796

Hooker, Joseph **689–691,** *690*
- Edward P. Alexander and 604
- Richard H. Anderson and 606
- Antietam 210*c*
- Brandy Station, Battle of 307*c*
- John Buford and 623
- Bull Run, Second Battle of 198*c*–200*c*
- Ambrose Burnside and 624
- Chancellorsville, Battle of 289*c*, 290*c*
- Chantilly, Battle of 202*c*
- Chattanooga, siege of 354*c*, 357*c*, 363*c*, 364*c*
- Patrick R. Cleburne and 631
- Franklin's Crossing, Virginia 305*c*
- Fredericksburg, Battle of 238*c*
- Fredericksburg, Virginia 287*c*
- John Gibbon and 662
- Glendale, Battle of 176*c*
- Henry W. Halleck and 674
- Winfield S. Hancock and 677
- Henry Heth and 681
- Ambrose P. Hill and 683
- Oliver O. Howard and 692
- Thomas J. Jackson and 698
- Philip Kearny and 703

- Kennesaw Mountain, Battle of 459*c*, 460*c*
- Kettle Run, Virginia 197*c*
- Robert E. Lee and 711
- Abraham Lincoln and 714
- James Longstreet and 716
- Lookout Mountain, Battle of 375*c*–376*c*
- George G. Meade and 731
- Missionary Ridge, Battle of 376*c*
- New Hope Church, Battle of 444*c*
- Oak Grove, Battle of 171*c*
- Alfred Pleasonton and 744
- Resaca, Battle of 439*c*
- John F. Reynolds and 757
- Ringgold Gap, Battle of 378*c*–379*c*
- Daniel E. Sickles and 775
- South Mountain, Battle of 207*c*
- J. E. B. Stuart and 778
- Wauhatchie, Battle of 366*c*
- Joseph Wheeler and 792
- Williamsburg, Virginia 147*c*

Howard, Oliver O. **691–693,** *692*
- Atlanta campaign 476*c*
- Beaufort, South Carolina 538*c*
- Bentonville, North Carolina 568*c*
- Bull Run, First Battle of 49*c*
- Chancellorsville, Battle of 289*c*
- Chattahoochie River, Georgia 466*c*
- Columbia, South Carolina 554*c*
- Richard S. Ewell and 653
- Georgia campaign 491*c*
- Gettysburg, Battle of 319*c*
- Ambrose P. Hill and 683
- Joseph Hooker and 691
- Thomas J. Jackson and 698
- Jonesboro, Battle of 492*c*
- Fitzhugh Lee and 708
- McAlister, Fort, Georgia 531*c*

George G. Meade and 732
Pickett's Mills, Battle of 445*c*
Alfred Pleasonton and 744
John Pope and 748
John F. Reynolds and 758
William T. Sherman and 771
Sherman's Georgia campaign
  464*c*–465*c*
Franz Sigel and 777
J. E. B. Stuart and 778
Huger, Benjamin 160*c*, 176*c*, 177*c*,
  606, **693–694**
Hunley, CSS 340*c*, 345*c*, 361*c*,
  362*c*, 399*c*

I

Imboden, John D. **695–696**, *696*
  Turner Ashby and 609
  Baltimore and Ohio Railroad
    raid 283*c*, 284*c*
  Burlington, West Virginia
    372*c*
  Charles Town, West Virginia
    362*c*
  Cheat River, West Virginia
    354*c*
  Coventry, Virginia 448*c*
  Lost River Gap, West Virginia
    435*c*
  Lynchburg, Virginia 457*c*
  Port Royal, Virginia 436*c*
  Franz Sigel and 777
  Williamsport, Battle of 325*c*
Independence, Missouri 125*c*,
  191*c*
Island No. 10, Battle of 122*c*–
  126*c*, 129*c*–131*c*, 134*c*–135*c*
Iuka, Mississippi 208*c*, 209*c*, 212*c*,
  213*c*
Ivy Mountain, Battle of 81*c*

J

Jackson, Mississippi 293*c*, 295*c*,
  325*c*, 327*c*, 330*c*, 331*c*
Jackson, Thomas J. **697–699**, *698*
  Edward P. Alexander and 604
  Richard H. Anderson and
    606

Antietam 210*c*
Turner Ashby and 610
Nathaniel P. Banks and 611
Big Bend, Virginia 162*c*
Boteler's Ford, Maryland
  212*c*–213*c*
Bull Run, First Battle of
  48*c*–49*c*
Bull Run, Second Battle of
  198*c*, 200*c*, 201*c*
Cedar Mountain, Battle of
  190*c*–191*c*
Chancellorsville, Battle of
  288*c*–290*c*
Chantilly, Battle of 202*c*
  death of 294*c*
Jubal A. Early and 649
Richard S. Ewell and 653
Frederick, Maryland 204*c*
Fredericksburg, Battle of
  232*c*, 234*c*, 238*c*, 240*c*
Front Royal, Virginia 156*c*
Gaines's Mill, Battle of 173*c*
John Gibbon and 662
Glendale, Battle of 176*c*
Groveton, Battle of 198*c*
Wade Hampton and 675
Harper's Ferry 205*c*–207*c*,
  209*c*
Henry Heth and 681
Ambrose P. Hill and 682
Daniel H. Hill and 683
Joseph Hooker and 690
Oliver O. Howard and 692
John D. Imboden and 695
Philip Kearny and 704
Robert E. Lee and 710, 711
James Longstreet and 716
William L. Loring and 718
Manassas Junction, Virginia
  197*c*
Irvin McDowell and 728
McDowell, Virginia 149*c*
George G. Meade and 732
Oak Grove, Battle of 172*c*
George E. Pickett and 740
Alfred Pleasonton and 744
John Pope and 748

Fitz John Porter and 751
Port Republic, Battle of
  165*c*–166*c*
Port Republic, Virginia 163*c*
Shenandoah Valley campaign
  (1862) 124*c*–126*c*, 129*c*,
  140*c*, 144*c*, 145*c*, 148*c*,
  152*c*, 155*c*, 158*c*, 159*c*,
  161*c*, 164*c*–166*c*
Daniel E. Sickles and 775
J. E. B. Stuart and 778
Richard Taylor and 781
Winchester, First Battle of
  157*c*
Winchester, Virginia 160*c*
Woodstock, Virginia 154*c*
Jenkin's Ferry, Arkansas, Battle
  of 426*c*
Jews. *See* General Order No. 11
Johnston, Albert S. **699–700**
  Edward P. Alexander and 603
  Richard H. Anderson and
    605
  Pierre G. T. Beauregard and
    614
  Braxton Bragg and 615
  John C. Breckinridge and
    618
  John Buford and 622
  Edward R. S. Canby and 628
  Patrick R. Cleburne and 631
  George B. Crittenden and
    633
  Donelson, Fort, Battle of
    110*c*, 111*c*
  John B. Floyd and 657
  Ulysses S. Grant and 668
  William J. Hardee and 679
  Henry, Fort, Battle of 107*c*,
    108*c*
  Henry Heth and 680
  John B. Hood and 687
  Joseph E. Johnston and 701
  Edmund Kirby-Smith and
    706
  Fitzhugh Lee and 708
  Robert E. Lee and 710
  Ben McCulloch and 725

John C. Pemberton and 739
Leonidas Polk and 745, 746
Fitz John Porter and 751
John F. Reynolds and 757
William T. Sherman and 770
Shiloh, Battle of 117c, 132c
Henry H. Sibley and 773
George H. Thomas and 784
Lew Wallace and 789
Johnston, Joseph E. *701*, **701–702**
   Edward P. Alexander and 604
   Turner Ashby and 610
   Atlanta campaign 431c, 432c,
      470c
   Pierre G. T. Beauregard and
      614
   Bentonville, North Carolina
      567c–569c
   Birdsong Ferry, Mississippi
      324c
   Braxton Bragg and 616
   John C. Breckinridge and
      618
   Bull Run, First Battle of 46c,
      47c, 49c
   Charlotte, North Carolina
      558c
   Chattahoochie River, Georgia
      466c, 467c
   Patrick R. Cleburne and 632
   Clinton, Mississippi 326c,
      328c
   Dalton, First Battle of 401–
      402c
   Jefferson Davis and 232c–
      233c, 469c, 470c
   Dranesville, Battle of 92c
   Jubal A. Early and 649
   Nathan G. Evans and 652
   Fair Oaks, Battle of 161c
   John B. Floyd and 657
   Goldsborough, North
      Carolina 564c
   Ulysses S. Grant and 668
   Henry W. Halleck and 674
   Wade Hampton and 676
   William J. Hardee and 679,
      680

   Harper's Ferry, Virginia 38c,
      45c
   Daniel H. Hill and 684
   Thomas C. Hindman and
      686
   Robert F. Hoke and 687
   John B. Hood and 688
   Benjamin Huger and 694
   Jackson, Mississippi 325c,
      327c, 330c, 331c
   Thomas J. Jackson and 697
   Kennesaw Mountain, Battle
      of 459c, 462c, 464c
   Edmund Kirby-Smith and
      706
   Fitzhugh Lee and 708
   Robert E. Lee and 710, 712
   James Longstreet and 716
   William L. Loring and 719
   Mansfield Lovell and 720
   John B. Magruder and 730
   George B. McClellan and 724
   Irvin McDowell and 727
   James B. McPherson and 729
   Montgomery C. Meigs and
      734
   New Hope, Georgia 450c
   John C. Pemberton and 740
   Peninsula Campaign 128c,
      132c, 136c, 138c, 144c
   Pickett's Mills, Battle of 445c
   Pine Mountain, Georgia
      458c
   Leonidas Polk and 745, 746
   Port Hudson, siege of 300c
   Raleigh, North Carolina 583c
   Resaca, Battle of 438c–440c
   Richmond, Virginia 152c,
      159c
   John M. Schofield and 762
   Raphael Semmes and 766
   Seven Pines, Battle of 160c
   William T. Sherman and 771,
      772
   Sherman's Georgia campaign
      465c
   Smyrna, Georgia 464c
   J. E. B. Stuart and 778

   Richard Taylor and 782
   George H. Thomas and 786
   Vicksburg, siege of 295c–
      299c, 311c, 320c
   Joseph Wheeler and 792
   Williamsburg, Virginia 147c
Jonesboro, Battle of 492c–493c

K

Kearny, Philip **703–704**
   Bull Run, Second Battle of
      199c
   Chantilly, Battle of 202c
   Richard S. Ewell and 652
   Fair Oaks, Battle of 161c
   Glendale, Battle of 176c
   Oak Grove, Battle of 171c
   Williamsburg, Virginia 147c
Kearsarge, USS *458*, 458c–459c
Kelly's Ford, Battle of 272c, 369c
Kennesaw Mountain, Battle of
   459c–462c, 464c
Kernstown, Battle of 126c, 610
Kernstown, Second Battle of 474c
Kilpatrick, Hugh J. *704*, **704–705**
   Aldie, Virginia 312c
   Augusutus, Georgia 527c
   Averasboro, North Carolina
      566c
   Buck Head Creek, Georgia
      525c
   Buckland Mills, Battle of
      362c
   Carlton's Store, Virginia 407c
   Carmel Church, Virginia
      184c
   George A. Custer and 637
   John A. B. Dahlgren and 640
   Fairburn, Georgia 488c
   Fayetteville, North Carolina
      562c
   Georgia campaign 489c, 491c
   Gettysburg, Battle of 318c
   Gordonsville, Virginia 351c
   Griswoldville, Georgia 522c
   Henry Heth and 681
   John D. Imboden and 696
   Jonesboro, Battle of 492c

Millen, Georgia 528c
Monroe's Cross Roads, North Carolina 563c, 564c
   Alfred Pleasonton and 744
   Richmond raid 403c–404c
   Upperville, Virginia 314c
   Waynesboro, Georgia 528c–529c
   Joseph Wheeler and 792
   Williamsport, Battle of 325c, 329c–330c
   James H. Wilson and 796
Kinston, North Carolina 282c, 563c, 564c
Kirby-Smith, Edmund 15c, 706, **706–707**
   Bardstown, Kentucky 214c
   Big Hill, Kentucky 196c
   Braxton Bragg and 616
   Don C. Buell and 621
   Bull Run, Second Battle of 199c
   Camden, Arkansas 422c
   Edward R. S. Canby and 629
   Chattanooga, Tennessee 164c
   Covington, Kentucky 209c
   Richard S. Ewell and 653
   Frankfort, Kentucky 203c, 207c
   William J. Hardee and 679
   Henry Heth and 681
   Jenkin's Ferry, Arkansas, Battle of 426c
   Joseph E. Johnston and 701
   Kentucky offensive 193c, 222c
   Milliken's Bend, Louisiana 305c
   Pleasant Hill, Battle of 416c
   Sterling Porter and 753
   Red River campaign 410c
   Richmond, Kentucky 200c, 201c
   Joseph O. Shelby and 767
   Richard Taylor and 782
   George H. Thomas and 784
   Lew Wallace and 789
Knoxville, siege of 372c–374c, 379c

L

La Grange, Tennessee 228c, 229c, 274c
Laurel Hill, Battle of 43c
Lawrence, Kansas massacre 342c, 609
Lee, Fitzhugh **708–709**, 709
   Appomattox Court House, Virginia 572c, 581c
   Cold Harbor, Battle of 447c
   Five Forks, Virginia 573c
   Gettysburg, Battle of 318c
   Hardy County, West Virginia 387c
   Hartwood Church, Virginia 266c
   John D. Imboden and 696
   Jetersville, Virginia 578c
   Kelly's Ford 272c
   Robert E. Lee and 710
   James Longstreet and 717
   George E. Pickett and 742
   Shenandoah Valley campaign (1864) 482c
   J. E. B. Stuart and 778
   George H. Thomas and 784
   Trevilian Station, Battle of 453c–454c
   Wilderness, Battle of the 431c
   Winchester, Third Battle of 498c
Lee, Robert E. 23c, 582, **709–712**, 710
   Edward P. Alexander and 603, 604
   Amelia Court House, Virginia 578c
   Richard H. Anderson and 606
   Antietam 210c–212c
   Appomattox Court House, Virginia 572c, 580c, 581c
   Pierre G. T. Beauregard and 614
   Bethesda Church 446c
   Boteler's Ford, Maryland 213c

   John C. Breckinridge and 618
   Bristoe Campaign 359c, 362c
   Bristoe Station, Battle of 360c
   John Buford and 623
   Bull Run, Second Battle of 200c, 201c
   Ambrose Burnside and 624
   Cedar Mountain, Battle of 191c
   Chancellorsville, Battle of 288c, 290c
   Cheat Mountain, Battle of 63c–64c
   Cold Harbor, Battle of 444c, 446c, 448c, 449c
   George Crook and 634
   Cunningham's Cross Roads, Pennsylvania 324c
   George A. Custer and 638
   Jefferson Davis and 643
   Deep Bottom Run, Virginia 487c
   Jubal A. Early and 649, 651
   Richard S. Ewell and 653, 654
   Five Forks, Virginia 573c, 574c
   John B. Floyd and 657
   Frederick, Maryland 204c
   Fredericksburg, Battle of 232c, 234c, 237c, 238c–240c
   Fredericksburg, Virginia 287c
   Gaines's Mill, Battle of 173c
   General-in-Chief Act 546c
   Gettysburg, Battle of 319c–322c
   John Gibbon and 663
   Glendale, Battle of 176c
   John B. Gordon and 664, 665
   Ulysses S. Grant and 669
   Henry W. Halleck and 674
   Wade Hampton and 676
   William J. Hardee and 679
   Harper's Ferry 208c

Harrison, Fort, Virginia
506c–507c
Henry Heth and 681
Ambrose P. Hill and 682
Daniel H. Hill and 684
Robert F. Hoke and 686
John B. Hood and 688
Joseph Hooker and 690
Benjamin Huger and 694
John D. Imboden and 695
Thomas J. Jackson and 698,
699
Albert S. Johnston and 699
Philip Kearny and 704
Kelly's Ford, Battle of 369c
Fitzhugh Lee and 708
Abraham Lincoln and 714
James Longstreet and 716,
717
William L. Loring and 718
Mansfield Lovell and 720
John B. Magruder and 730
Malvern Hill, Battle of 177c
Maryland campaign 205c–
206c
George B. McClellan and 724
Irvin McDowell and 728
Mechanicsville, Battle of
172c
Montgomery C. Meigs and
733, 734
Milford Station, Virginia
443c
Mine Run campaign 378c–
380c
John S. Mosby and 737
North Anna River 445c
Pamunkey River, Virginia
445c
John C. Pemberton and 739
Peninsula Campaign 138c
Petersburg, siege of 457c,
488c
Petersburg, Virginia 475c,
537c, 570c, 574c, 575c
George E. Pickett and 741,
742
Alfred Pleasonton and 744

John Pope and 748
Fitz John Porter and 751
Port Royal Expedition 81c
Rappahannock Station,
Second Battle of 369c
John F. Reynolds and 757
Richmond, Virginia 296c,
427c, 455c, 503c, 537c
Salem Church, Battle of 292c
Seven Pines, Battle of 161c–
162c
Joseph O. Shelby and 767
Shenandoah Valley campaign
(1864) 482c, 487c
Philip Sheridan and 769
Daniel E. Sickles and 775
Franz Sigel and 777
South Mountain, Battle of
207c
Spotsylvania Court House,
Battle of 432c, 434c, 436c,
437c, 440c, 441c
J. E. B. Stuart and 778
surrender 581c, 583c
Richard Taylor and 781
George H. Thomas and 784
Thoroughfare Gap, Battle
of 198c
Warrenton, Virginia 225c
Washington College, Virginia
598c
Wilderness, Battle of the
428c, 430c
Williamsport, Battle of 326c,
328c, 330c
Lexington, Missouri, Battle of
64c–67c
Lincoln, Abraham 1c–6c, 3, 13c–
16c, **712–715**, *713*
amnesty for deserters 269c,
564c
Robert Anderson and
607–608
Antietam 212c
Ball's Bluff, Battle of 75c
Nathaniel P. Banks and 611
John C. Breckinridge and
617

John Buford and 623
Bull Run, First Battle of 45c
Ambrose Burnside and 624,
625
Benjamin F. Butler and 626
cabinet crisis over William H.
Seward 240c–241c
Chattanooga, siege of 354c
Cold Harbor, Battle of 449c
Samuel R. Curtis and 636
John A. B. Dahlgren and 639
Jefferson Davis and 643
death of 585c
declares "state of
insurrection" 23c
election of 1864 401c, 447c,
452c, 462c, 471c, 480c,
489c, 492c–494c, 500c
Emancipation Proclamation
184c, 214c, 248c
emancipation proposal
presented to Congress
234c
Enrollment Act 267c
David G. Farragut and 539c,
655
Federal Bureau of
Emancipation proposed
384c
federal income tax 176c
Ford's Theater shooting 584c
Fredericksburg, Battle of
233c, 239c
John C. Frémont and 41c,
60c, 61c, 64c, 75c
Fugitive Slave Law repealed
463c
funeral 586c
funeral train 588c, 589c
General Order No. 1 102c
General Order No. 11 256c
General Order No. 100 284c
Gettysburg Address 373c–
374c
Ulysses S. Grant and 324c,
668
habeas corpus suspension
27c, 73c, 215c

Henry W. Halleck and 673
Winfield S. Hancock and 677
Joseph Hooker and 690
Hugh J. Kilpatrick and 705
loyalty oaths 178*c*
George B. McClellan and
51*c*, 69*c*, 95*c*, 96*c*, 104*c*,
121*c*, 135*c*, 156*c*–157*c*,
202*c*, 217*c*–219*c*, 222*c*,
225*c*, 226*c*, 723
Irvin McDowell and 727
Montgomery C. Meigs and
733
military pay legislation 255*c*
John H. Morgan and 735
peace negotiations 465*c*,
539*c*, 544*c*, 545*c*, 549*c*–
551*c*, 561*c*
Peninsula campaign 178*c*
pension legislation 181*c*
Petersburg, siege of 459*c*
John Pope and 747
David D. Porter and 749
prisoners of war 77*c*
Reconstruction 382*c*
reelection of 518*c*, 553*c*
John F. Reynolds and 758
William S. Rosecrans and
760
John M. Schofield and 762
Winfield Scott and 764
Second Confiscation Act
182*c*
Raphael Semmes and 765
Sewell's Point, Virginia
bombarded 149*c*
Shenandoah Valley campaign
(1864) 483*c*, 495*c*
William T. Sherman and 770
Daniel E. Sickles and 774,
775
Franz Sigel and 776
Sioux uprising pardons 235*c*
slave enlistment 402*c*
Special War Order No. 1
103*c*
Edwin M. Stanton and 540*c*
Sumter, Fort 17*c*–22*c*

Thanksgiving Day designated
by 356*c*
Wade-Davis Reconstruction
Act pocket veto 466*c*
Lew Wallace and 790
Washington, D.C. defense
129*c*, 130*c*, 467*c*–469*c*
Charles Wilkes and 794
John L. Worden and 797
Little Crow (Taoyateduta) 189*c*,
193*c*, 195*c*, 196*c*, 324*c*
Longstreet, James **715–717,** *716*
Edward P. Alexander and 604
Amelia Court House,
Virginia 576*c*
Richard H. Anderson and
605
Bean's Station, Battle of 383*c*
Braxton Bragg and 616
John Buford and 623
Bull Run, First Battle of 46*c*
Bull Run, Second Battle of
198*c*–201*c*
Ambrose Burnside and 625
Campbell's Station, Battle
of 372*c*
Cedar Mountain, Battle of
191*c*
Chickamauga, Battle of
351*c*–352*c*
Patrick R. Cleburne and 631
Culpeper, Virginia 227*c*, 231*c*
Dandridge, Tennessee 390*c*
Jubal A. Early and 651
Nathan G. Evans and 652
Fair Garden, Battle of 392*c*
Falmouth, Virginia 231*c*
Fredericksburg, Battle of
234*c*, 238*c*, 239*c*
Gaines's Mill, Battle of 173*c*
Gettysburg, Battle of 320*c*,
322*c*
Glendale, Battle of 176*c*
Ulysses S. Grant and 668
Hagerstown, Maryland 205*c*
Winfield S. Hancock and 677
High Bridge, Virginia 579*c*
Ambrose P. Hill and 682

John B. Hood and 688
Joseph Hooker and 690
Benjamin Huger and 694
Knoxville, siege of 373*c*, 379*c*
Robert E. Lee and 711
Malvern Hill, Battle of 177*c*
Manassas Junction, Virginia
197*c*
Irvin McDowell and 727
George G. Meade and 732
Mechanicsville, Battle of
172*c*
North Anna River 443*c*
Peninsula Campaign 160*c*
George E. Pickett and 741
John Pope and 748
Fitz John Porter and 751
Richmond, Virginia 264*c*,
514*c*
William S. Rosecrans and
761
Sanders, Fort, Battle of 379*c*
Sayler's Creek, Virginia 579*c*
Seven Pines, Battle of 160*c*–
161*c*
Philip Sheridan and 768
William T. Sherman and 771
Daniel E. Sickles and 775
South Mountain, Battle of
207*c*
Suffolk, Virginia 279*c*, 289*c*,
291*c*–292*c*
George H. Thomas and 785
Thoroughfare Gap, Battle
of 198*c*
Wauhatchie, Battle of 365*c*
Joseph Wheeler and 792
Wilderness, Battle of the
428*c*, 429*c*
Williamsburg, Virginia 147*c*
Yorktown, Battle of 137*c*
Lookout Mountain, Battle of
375*c*–376*c*
Loring, William W. 19*c*, *718*,
718–719
Charleston, Virginia 207*c*
Cheat Mountain, Battle of
63*c*–64*c*

Nathan G. Evans and 652
Thomas J. Jackson and 697
Kanawha Valley campaign
 204c
Kennesaw Mountain, Battle
 of 462c
Packs Ferry, Virginia 189c
Pemberton, Fort 270c
John C. Pemberton and 740
Vicksburg, siege of 297c,
 298c
western Virginia operations
 95c, 97c, 98c, 101c, 103c
Louisville, Kentucky 214c–216c
Lovell, Mansfield **719–721**
Coffeeville, Mississippi 235c
Corinth, Mississippi 217c,
 218c
Thomas C. Hindman and
 686
New Orleans expedition
 125c, 143c
Lynchburg, Virginia 457c–458c,
 559c
Lyon, Nathaniel 18c, **721–722**
Camp Bacon 39c
death of 59c
Dug Springs 54c
Camp Jackson 30c
Jefferson City, Missouri 38c
Ben McCulloch and 726
Sterling Porter and 752, 753
John M. Schofield and 762
Philip Sheridan and 768
Franz Sigel and 776
Wilson's Creek, Battle of 55c

M

Macon, Georgia 479c, 522c, 586c
Macon and Western Railroad
 490c–492c
Magruder, John B. **730–731**
Big Bethel, Battle of 37c
Benjamin F. Butler and 626
Galveston, Texas 233c–234c,
 249c
Glendale, Battle of 176c
Daniel H. Hill and 684

John B. Hood and 688
Malvern Hill, Battle of 177c
George B. McClellan and 724
Peninsula Campaign 126c,
 128c
Yorktown, Battle of 131c–
 132c, 137c, 138c
Malvern Hill, Battle of 177c–178c
Manassas, Second Battle of. See
 Bull Run, Second Battle of
Mansfield, Battle of 415c
McAllister, Fort, Georgia 258c,
 260c, 531c, 532c
McClellan, George B. **723–725,**
 724
Antietam 210c–212c
Nathaniel P. Banks and 611
Don C. Buell and 620
Ambrose Burnside and 624
Culpeper Court House,
 Virginia 227c
George A. Custer and 637
Dranesville, Battle of 92c
election of 1864 494c
Fair Oaks, Battle of 161c
Frederick, Maryland 204c,
 206c
Gaines's Mill, Battle of 174c
Glendale, Battle of 176c
Winfield S. Hancock and 677
Hanover Court House,
 Virginia 158c
Ambrose P. Hill and 682
Daniel H. Hill and 684
Joseph Hooker and 690
Oliver O. Howard and 692
Benjamin Huger and 694
Thomas J. Jackson and 697
Joseph E. Johnston and 701
Philip Kearny and 703
Hugh J. Kilpatrick and 704
Fitzhugh Lee and 708
Robert E. Lee and 710, 711
Abraham Lincoln and 69c,
 87c, 104c, 156c–157c,
 217c–219c, 222c, 225c,
 226c, 714
John B. Magruder and 730

Malvern Hill, Battle of 177c
Irvin McDowell and 727
George G. Meade and 731
Mechanicsville, Battle of
 172c, 173c
John S. Mosby and 736
Oak Grove, Battle of 172c
Peninsula campaign 130c,
 131c, 138c, 145c, 146c,
 148c, 157c, 178c
George E. Pickett and 740
Alfred Pleasonton and 744
Poolesville, Virginia 222c
John Pope and 747
Fitz John Porter and 751,
 752
removed as general in chief
 121c
John F. Reynolds and 757
Richmond, Virginia 152c,
 155c
Rich Mountain 43c, 44c
John Rodgers and 758
William S. Rosecrans and
 760
Winfield Scott and 765
Seven Pines, Battle of 160c
Franz Sigel and 777
South Mountain, Battle of
 207c
Special War Order No. 1
 103c
J. E. B. Stuart and 778
Warrenton, Virginia 225c
White House, Virginia 151c,
 153c
Charles Wilkes and 794
Williamsburg, Virginia 148c
James H. Wilson and 795
Yorktown, Battle of 132c,
 145c
McCulloch, Ben 14c, **725–726**
Nathaniel Lyon and 721
Pea Ridge, Battle of 116c,
 118c–119c
Sterling Porter and 753
Joseph O. Shelby and 766–
 767

Franz Sigel and 777
Earl Van Dorn and 787
Wilson's Creek, Battle of
    54*c*–56*c*
McDowell, Irvin **726–728,** *727*
    Pierre G. T. Beauregard and
        613, 614
    Bull Run, First Battle of
        45*c*–49*c*
    Jefferson Davis and 643
    Nathan G. Evans and 651
    John Gibbon and 662
    Oliver O. Howard and
        691–692
    Abraham Lincoln and 714
    James Longstreet and 716
    George B. McClellan and
        723, 724
    Peninsula Campaign 157*c*,
        168*c*
    Winfield Scott and 765
    Shenandoah Valley campaign
        (1862) 156*c*, 158*c*, 159*c*,
        161*c*
    William T. Sherman and 770
McPherson, James B. **728–730,**
729
    Atlanta, Battle of 473*c*
    Atlanta campaign 431*c*, 432*c*,
        470*c*–473*c*
    Bald Hill, Battle of 472*c*
    Camp Cotton, Mississippi
        380*c*
    Chattahoochie River, Georgia
        465*c*
    Dallas, Georgia 445*c*, 446*c*
    William J. Hardee and 680
    Joseph Hooker and 691
    Oliver O. Howard and 692
    Raymond, Mississippi 295*c*
    William T. Sherman and 771
    Vicksburg, siege of 281*c*,
        287*c*, 295*c*–297*c*, 299*c*, 300*c*
Meade, George G. *731,* **731–733**
    Edward P. Alexander and 604
    Bristoe Campaign 362*c*
    Bristoe Station, Battle of
        360*c*

John Buford and 623
Ambrose Burnside and 625
Abner Doubleday and 645
Richard S. Ewell and 653
Fredericksburg, Battle of
    238*c*
Gettysburg, Battle of 319*c*–
    322*c*
Ulysses S. Grant and 669
Henry W. Halleck and 674
Winfield S. Hancock and 677
Robert F. Hoke and 686
Joseph Hooker and 691
Oliver O. Howard and 692
Jetersville, Virginia 578*c*
Kelly's Ford, Battle of 369*c*
Hugh J. Kilpatrick and 705
Robert E. Lee and 711
Abraham Lincoln and 714
James Longstreet and 716–
    717
Mine Run campaign 378*c*–
    380*c*
Morton's Ford, Battle of 395*c*
Petersburg, siege of 456*c*
Petersburg, Virginia 477*c*
George E. Pickett and 741
Alfred Pleasonton and 745
Poplar Springs Church,
    Virginia 502*c*
John F. Reynolds and 757
Richmond, Virginia 427*c*
Richmond raid 405*c*
Shenandoah Valley campaign
    (1862) 477*c*
Philip Sheridan and 768
Daniel E. Sickles and 775
J. E. B. Stuart and 779
Wilderness, Battle of the
    428*c*
Williamsport, Battle of 328*c*
Mechanicsville, Battle of 172*c*–
    173*c*
Meigs, Montgomery C. 31*c*, *733,*
    733–734, 749
Memphis, First Battle of 163*c*–
    164*c*
Memphis, Tennessee 163*c*, 489*c*

Middle Creek, Battle of 97*c*
Milliken's Bend, Battle of 306*c*
Mills Springs, Battle of 100*c*
Missionary Ridge, Battle of
    376*c*–377*c*
Mobile, Alabama 562*c*, 567*c*, 584*c*
Mobile Bay, Alabama 484*c*, 489*c*,
    491*c*, 620
Mobile Bay, Battle of 479*c*, *481,*
    481*c*–483*c*, 620
Monitor, USS *120,* 248*c*
Monitor and *Merrimack. See*
    Hampton Roads, Battle of
Monocacy, Battle of 467*c*
Monocacy, Maryland 465*c*, 467*c*
Monroe, Fortress, Virginia 530*c*,
    532*c*, 592*c*
Monroe's Cross Roads, North
    Carolina 563*c*, 564*c*
Montgomery, Alabama 583*c*, 584*c*
Moorefield, Battle of 483*c*
Morgan, John H. **734–736,** *735*
    John C. Breckinridge and
        618
    Don C. Buell and 621
    Buffington Island, Battle of
        333*c*–334*c*
    Ambrose Burnside and 625
    Corydon, Indiana 326*c*
    death of 494*c*
    escape from prison 378*c*
    Kentucky raids 88*c*, 102*c*,
        150*c*, 180*c*, 181*c*, 183*c*,
        222*c*, 223*c*, 227*c*, 242*c*–
        247*c*, 250*c*, 273*c*, 320*c*,
        325*c*, 443*c*, 447*c*, 452*c*, 454*c*
    Louisiana and Nashville
        Railroad raid 194*c*
    Ohio cavalry raid 329*c*
    Pomeroy, Ohio 332*c*
    Salem, Indiana 327*c*
    Salineville, Battle of 335*c*
    Tennessee raids 124*c*, 191*c*,
        236*c*, 264*c*
    Vernon, Indiana 328*c*
    Wytheville, Virginia 435*c*
Mormon expedition 603, 622
Morton's Ford, Battle of 395*c*

Mosby, John S. **736–738**, *737*
 Aldie, Virginia 336*c*
 Annandale, Virginia 339*c*
 Baltimore and Ohio Railroad
  train burned 509*c*
 Bealton, Virginia 303*c*
 Bunker Hill, West Virginia
  426*c*
 Catlett's Station Virginia
  367*c*
 Charles Town, West Virginia
  580*c*
 Dranesville, Virginia 276*c*,
  400*c*
 Fairfax Court House, Virginia
  257*c*, 269*c*, 338*c*
 Front Royal, Virginia 399*c*,
  434*c*
 Germantown, Virginia 383*c*
 Goresville, Virginia 525*c*
 Herndon Station, Virginia
  272*c*
 Hunter's Mills, Virginia
  423*c*
 Leesburg, Virginia 385*c*
 Lewinsville, Virginia 382*c*
 Little River Turnpike,
  Virginia 274*c*
 Loudoun Heights, Virginia
  389*c*
 New Baltimore, Virginia
  364*c*
 Passpatansy Creek, Maryland
  562*c*
 Piedmont, Virginia 399*c*
 Rectortown, Virginia 387*c*
 Salem, Virginia 410*c*
 Seneca Mills, Maryland 308*c*
 Shenandoah Valley campaign
  (1864) 483*c*, 485*c*
 Upperville, Virginia 352*c*
 Warrenton, Virginia 291*c*,
  336*c*, 388*c*
 Waterford, Virginia 419*c*
 "mud March" 256*c*, 257*c*
 Munfordville, Kentucky 208*c*,
  209*c*, 212*c*, 214*c*
 Murfreesboro, First Battle of 181*c*

Murfreesboro, Second Battle of
 (Stone's River) 245*c*–250*c*, 616,
 618
Murfreesboro, Tennessee 204*c*,
 233*c*, 239*c*, 530*c*

N

Nashville, Tennessee 228*c*, 229*c*,
 527*c*–528*c*, 530*c*–532*c*
Nashville, Tennessee, Battle of
 533*c*–534*c*, 618
Navajo Indians 341*c*, 388*c*
naval operations 803*m*
New Baltimore, Virginia 346*c*,
 364*c*
New Bern, Battle of 123*c*
New Bern, North Carolina 269*c*,
 393*c*–394*c*
New Hope Church, Battle of 444*c*
New Market, Battle of 439*c*, 618
New Orleans, Louisiana
 Nathaniel P. Banks replaces
  Butler 229*c*, 240*c*
 Benjamin F. Butler and 145*c*,
  152*c*, 227*c*, 626
 first slave regiment mustered
  into Union 216*c*
 strategic importance to
  Union 82*c*–83*c*
New Orleans expedition
 David G. Farragut and 121*c*,
  129*c*
 Union approach to city 132*c*,
  135*c*, 139*c*–144*c*
Newtonia, Missouri 216*c*, 218*c*,
 515*c*
New York City 328*c*, 532*c*, 535*c*,
 537*c*
Norfolk, Virginia 144*c*, 150*c*
North Anna River 443*c*–445*c*

O

Oak Grove, Battle of 171*c*–172*c*
Okolona, Mississippi 401*c*, 468*c*,
 469*c*
Olustee, Battle of 400*c*
Orange and Alexandria Railroad
 195*c*, 196*c*

Overland campaign 428*c*–447*c*,
 449*c*, 815*m*

P

Paducah, Battle of 412*c*
Pamunkey River, Virginia 445*c*–
 446*c*
peace negotiations
 Jefferson Davis and 424*c*,
  518*c*, 521*c*, 541*c*, 544*c*,
  547*c*, 549*c*, 551*c*
 Horace Greeley and 52*c*, 465*c*
 Abraham Lincoln and 465*c*,
  539*c*, 544*c*, 545*c*, 549*c*–
  551*c*, 561*c*
Peachtree Creek, Battle of 471*c*–
 472*c*
Pea Ridge, Battle of 118*c*–119*c*
Pemberton, Fort 270*c*, 271*c*
Pemberton, John C. **739–740**
 Ulysses S. Grant and 668
 Benjamin H. Grierson and
  670
 Joseph E. Johnston and 701
 William L. Loring and 719
 Newton Station, Mississippi
  285*c*
 David D. Porter and 750
 Salisbury, North Carolina
  584*c*
 Earl Van Dorn and 788
 Vicksburg, siege of 284*c*,
  286*c*, 294*c*–299*c*, 311*c*,
  317*c*, 323*c*
Peninsula (Peninsular) campaign
 Edward P. Alexander and
  603–604
 Richard H. Anderson and
  605
 conclusion of 192*c*
 Drewry's Bluff 151*c*
 Joseph E. Johnston and 136*c*,
  138*c*, 144*c*
 George B. McClellan's
  approach to Richmond
  158*c*
 McClellan's Harrison
  Landing withdrawal 178*c*

Richmond 131*c*, 157*c*,
160*c*–161*c*
Daniel E. Sickles and 775
Yorktown, siege of 145*c*
Perryville, Battle of 219*c*, 220*c*,
616, 621
Petersburg, siege of 455*c*–457*c*,
459*c*–461*c*, 488*c*, 489*c*, 575*c*
Edward P. Alexander and 604
Richard H. Anderson and 606
Pierre G. T. Beauregard and
614
Ambrose E. Burnside and 625
Petersburg, Virginia 432*c*, 478*c*,
487*c*, 537*c*, 550*c*, 570*c*, 574*c*
Philippi, Battle of 35*c*–36*c*
Pickett, George E. **740–742,** *741*
Edward P. Alexander and 604
Richard H. Anderson and
606
Appomattox, Virginia 572*c*
Dinwiddie Court House,
Virginia 573*c*
Abner Doubleday and 645
Five Forks, Virginia 573*c*
Gaines's Mill, Battle of 173*c*
Gettysburg, Battle of 322*c*
John Gibbon and 663
Winfield S. Hancock and 677
Robert F. Hoke and 687
Fitzhugh Lee and 709
Robert E. Lee and 711
James Longstreet and 717
George G. Meade and 732
New Bern, North Carolina
393*c*–394*c*
Sayler's Creek, Virginia 579*c*
Philip Sheridan and 769
Suffolk, Virginia 285*c*
Pickett's Mills, Battle of 445*c*
Piedmont, Virginia 399*c*, 450*c*–
451*c*
Pillow, Fort, Battle of 417*c*–418*c*
Pillow, Fort, massacre 418*c*, 427*c*
Pillow, Gideon J. **742–744**
Belmont, Battle of 80*c*
John C. Breckinridge and
617

Donelson, Fort, Battle of
107*c*–111*c*
John B. Floyd and 658
Ulysses S. Grant and 667,
668
Joseph Hooker and 690
Albert S. Johnston and 700
John B. Magruder and 730
Leonidas Polk and 746
Pleasant Hill, Battle of 416*c*
Pleasant Hill, Missouri 180*c*, 297*c*
Pleasonton, Alfred *744*, **744–745**
Big Blue River, Missouri 513*c*
John Buford and 623
Samuel R. Curtis and 636
George A. Custer and 637
Jefferson City, Missouri 507*c*
Hugh J. Kilpatrick and 705
Little Blue River, Missouri
512*c*
Missouri antiguerilla
operations 485*c*
Sterling Porter and 754
William S. Rosecrans and
761
Joseph O. Shelby and 767
J. E. B. Stuart and 778–779
Plymouth, North Carolina 420*c*,
422*c*
Poison Springs, Arkansas, Battle
of 421*c*
Polk, Leonidas **745–747**
Atlanta campaign 431*c*
Belmont, Battle of 79*c*, 80*c*
Chickamauga, Battle of
351*c*–352*c*
Columbus, Kentucky 116*c*
Jefferson Davis and 643
death of 455*c*
Ulysses S. Grant and 667
Henry, Fort, Battle of 104*c*
Thomas C. Hindman and
686
William L. Loring and 719
Meridian campaign 397*c*
Munfordville, Kentucky 209*c*
Murfreesboro, Battle of 247*c*,
250*c*

Perryville 220*c*
Gideon J. Pillow and 743
Resaca, Battle of 438*c*
Philip Sheridan and 768
William T. Sherman and 771
Pope, John *747*, **747–748**
Nathaniel P. Banks and 611
John Buford and 622
Bull Run, Second Battle of
199*c*–201*c*
Ambrose Burnside and 624
Cedar Mountain, Battle of
191*c*
Richard S. Ewell and 653
Andrew H. Foote and 659
Gordonsville, Virginia 182*c*
John B. Hood and 688
Joseph Hooker and 690
Island No. 10, Battle of 124*c*,
131*c*
Philip Kearny and 704
Fitzhugh Lee and 708
Robert E. Lee and 711
Lexington, Missouri 92*c*
Abraham Lincoln and 714
James Longstreet and 716
Manassas Junction, Virginia
197*c*
George B. McClellan and 724
Irvin McDowell and 728
George G. Meade and 731
New Madrid, Missouri 117*c*,
123*c*
Orange Court House,
Virginia 187*c*
Fitz John Porter and 751
John F. Reynolds and 757
Rienzi, Mississippi 162*c*
William S. Rosecrans and
760
Shenandoah Valley 180*c*
Franz Sigel and 777
J. E. B. Stuart and 778
Poplar Springs Church, Virginia
502*c*, 504*c*
Porter, David D. **748–750,** *749*
CSS *Arkansas* 189*c*
Arkansas, Fort 252*c*

Nathaniel P. Banks and 612
Beaufort, North Carolina
    540c
Blair's Landing, Louisiana
    419c
Benjamin F. Butler and 627
Charles H. Davis and 641
David G. Farragut and 655,
    656
Fisher, Fort, North Carolina
    535c, 536c, 539c, 542c–545c
Grand Gulf, Battle of 287c
Grand Gulf, Mississippi
    284c, 285c, 292c
Ulysses S. Grant and 668
Hindman, Fort 251c, 253c
Edmund Kirby-Smith and
    707
Mansfield Lovell and 720
Malvern Hill, Battle of 177c
Montgomery C. Meigs and
    733
Mississippi River operations
    98c
Mobile, Alabama 34c
New Orleans expedition 83c,
    84c, 101c, 121c, 135c, 139c,
    144c
John C. Pemberton and 740
Fitz John Porter and 750
Port Hudson, siege of 324c
Red River, Louisiana 424c–
    426c
Red River campaign 393c,
    406c–408c, 413c, 414c,
    417c, 438c, 440c, 442c
Richmond, Virginia 577c
Steele's Bayou 271c, 273c
Strong, Fort, North Carolina
    557c
Richard Taylor and 781
Alfred H. Terry and 783
Vicksburg, siege of 244c,
    245c, 255c, 257c, 259c–
    260c, 277c, 282c, 288c,
    292c
Wilmington, North Carolina
    541c

Porter, Fitz John **750–752,** *751*
    Antietam 210c
    Boteler's Ford, Maryland
        212c
    Bull Run, Second Battle of
        199c, 200c
    court-martial of 252c, 256c
    Gaines's Mill, Battle of 173c,
        174c
    Hanover Court House,
        Virginia 158c
    John B. Hood and 688
    Robert E. Lee and 710–711
    Mechanicsville, Battle of 172c
    Montgomery C. Meigs and
        733
    John C. Pemberton and 740
    Peninsula campaign 157c,
        168c
    John Pope and 748
    David D. Porter and 748
    John M. Schofield and 763
    Richard Taylor and 781
    Alfred H. Terry and 783, 784
Port Hudson, siege of 271c, 300c,
    302c, 307c, 309c, 310c, 316c,
    324c, 326c, 612
Port Republic, Battle of 165c–
    166c
Port Republic, Virginia 163c, 501c
Port Royal, South Carolina 77c–
    80c, 591c
Powder River, Battle of 598c
Prairie Grove, Battle of 236c–237c
Price, Sterling **752–754,** *753*
    William Anderson and 609
    Big Blue River, Missouri 512c
    Bonham, Texas 523c
    Boonsboro, Missouri 508c
    Camden, Arkansas 420c,
        424c
    Cane Hill, Arkansas 518c
    Carrollton, Missouri 510c
    Corinth, Mississippi 216c,
        217c
    Samuel R. Curtis and 636
    Davidson, Fort, Missouri
        501c

Fredericktown, Missouri 501c
Helena, Arkansas 324c
Iuka, Mississippi 208c, 209c,
    212c, 213c
Jefferson City, Missouri 507c
Edmund Kirby-Smith and
    707
Lake Springs, Missouri 504c
Laynesport, Arkansas 528c
Leasburg, Missouri 503c
Lexington, Missouri 64c–67c,
    511c
Nathaniel Lyon and 721
Ben McCulloch and 726
Miller's Station, Missouri
    505c
Newtonia, Missouri 515c
Ozark, Missouri 252c
Paris, Missouri 510c
Pea Ridge, Battle of 108c,
    116c
Alfred Pleasonton and 745
John Pope and 747
Prairie D'Ane, Arkansas 417c
prisoner exchange 75c, 77c
William C. Quantrill and
    755
William S. Rosecrans and
    760–761
Joseph O. Shelby and 766
Franz Sigel and 776
Earl Van Dorn and 787
Washington, Missouri 505c
Westport, Missouri, Battle
    of 513c
Wilson's Creek, Battle of
    54c–56c
prisoners of war 336c, 420c, 487c,
    547c

Q

Quantrill, William C. **755–756**
    William Anderson and 609
    Baxter Springs, Battle of
        357c–358c
    death of 590c, 594c
    Independence, Missouri
        191c

Kansas 205*c*, 228*c*
Lawrence massacre 342*c*
manhunt for 102*c*
Missouri 227*c*, 233*c*, 485*c*
Pleasant Hill, Missouri 180*c*,
297*c*
John M. Schofield and 762

R

railroads 504*c*, 505*c*, 509*c*. *See also
specific railroads, e.g.:* Macon
and Western Railroad
Rappahannock Station, First
Battle of 195*c*–197*c*
Rappahannock Station, Second
Battle of 369*c*
Reams's Station, Virginia 489*c*,
490*c*
Red River, Louisiana 424*c*, 425*c*
Red River campaign 393*c*, 406*c*–
417*c*, 418, 438*c*, 440*c*, 442*c*, 612
Resaca, Battle of 438*c*
Reynolds, John F. **757–758**
John Buford and 623
Bull Run, First Battle of 49*c*
Bull Run, Second Battle of
199*c*
Abner Doubleday and 645
Gettysburg, Battle of 318*c*–
319*c*
John Gibbon and 662, 663
Winfield S. Hancock and
677
Ambrose P. Hill and 683
Oliver O. Howard and 692
George G. Meade and 732
Mechanicsville, Battle of
172*c*
Richmond, Kentucky, Battle of
200*c*, 201*c*
Richmond, Virginia
Richard A. Anderson's
reinforcement of defenses
497*c*
Bread Riot 277*c*
Benjamin F. Butler and 503*c*
evacuation of 575*c*
David G. Farragut and 578*c*

Ulysses S. Grant probes
defenses 502*c*
Robert F. Hoke and 503*c*
Robert E. Lee and 503*c*
James Longstreet and defense
of 264*c*
George B. McClellan advance
152*c*, 155*c*
Oak Grove, Battle of 171*c*–
172*c*
Peninsula campaign 131*c*,
157*c*, 159*c*–161*c*
David D. Porter and 577*c*
siege of 537*c*
Rich Mountain, Battle of 44*c*
Ringgold Gap, Battle of 378*c*–
379*c*
Roanoke Island, North Carolina,
Battle of 107*c*–108*c*
Rodgers, John **758–760**, *759*
CSS *Atlanta* 312*c*
Drewry's Bluff, Virginia 153*c*
Samuel F. Du Pont and 647
Andrew H. Foote and 659
Malvern Hill, Battle of 178*c*
Rome, Georgia 508*c*, 519*c*
Rosecrans, William S. *760*,
760–761
Braxton Bragg and 616
Don C. Buell and 621
Burnsville, Tennessee 250*c*
Carnifex Ferry, Battle of 60*c*,
62*c*, 63*c*
Catlett's Gap, Georgia 350*c*
Chattanooga, siege of 354*c*–
355*c*, 362*c*
Chattanooga, Tennessee
319*c*, 344*c*, 347*c*, 349*c*, 353*c*
Chickamauga, Battle of
351*c*–352*c*
Patrick R. Cleburne and 631
Corinth, Mississippi 217*c*,
218*c*
George Crook and 634
Nathan B. Forrest and 661
Ulysses S. Grant and 668
William J. Hardee and 679
John B. Hood and 688

Iuka, Mississippi 208*c*, 213*c*
Kentucky offensive 242*c*
James Longstreet and 717
Mansfield Lovell and 720
James B. McPherson and 728
Murfreesboro, Battle of
245*c*–251*c*
Alfred Pleasonton and 745
Sterling Porter and 753
Rich Mountain, Battle of
43*c*, 44*c*
Shelbyville, Tennessee 316*c*
Philip Sheridan and 768
Snow Hill, Tennessee 304*c*
George H. Thomas and 785
Tullahoma Campaign 323*c*
Earl Van Dorn and 787
Joseph Wheeler and 792

S

Salem Church, Battle of 292*c*
Salineville, Battle of 335*c*
Sanders, Fort, Battle of 379*c*–380*c*
Santee (Sioux) Indians 265*c*, 477*c*
Savannah, Georgia 515*c*, 531*c*,
534*c*, 535*c*, 544*c*, 547*c*
Saylor's Creek, Battle of 606
Schofield, John M. **762–763**, *763*
Anderson, Fort, North
Carolina 554*c*
Atlanta campaign 431*c*, 480*c*,
491*c*, 492*c*
Chattahoochie River, Georgia
465*c*, 466*c*
Patrick R. Cleburne and 632
Columbia, Tennessee 523*c*,
524*c*
Samuel R. Curtis and 636
East Point, Georgia 483*c*
Franklin, Tennessee 526*c*–
527*c*
Goldsborough, North
Carolina 569*c*
Greeneville, Tennessee 420*c*
John B. Hood and 689
Kennesaw Mountain, Battle
of 461*c*–462*c*
Nathaniel Lyon and 722

Nashville, Tennessee 527*c*, 528*c*
Neuse River Bridge, North Carolina 567*c*
New Hope Church, Battle of 445*c*
Newtonia, Missouri 218*c*
Fitz John Porter and 752
Resaca, Battle of 438*c*
William T. Sherman and 771
Spring Hill, Tennessee 525*c*
Alfred H. Terry and 783
George H. Thomas and 786
Utoy Creek, Georgia 482*c*
Wilmington, North Carolina 554*c*, 557*c*
James H. Wilson and 796
Scott, Winfield 7*c*, 8*c*, 16*c*, 17*c*, **763–765,** *764*
Anaconda Plan 24*c*, 28*c*
Richard H. Anderson and 605
Robert Anderson and 607
Pierre G. T. Beauregard and 613
John C. Breckinridge and 617
Bull Run, First Battle of 45*c*
Edward R. S. Canby and 628
Samuel R. Curtis and 636
Jefferson Davis and 642
Richard S. Ewell and 652
Josiah Gorgas and 665
Ulysses S. Grant and 667
Henry W. Halleck and 673
Winfield S. Hancock and 677
William J. Hardee and 679
Daniel H. Hill and 683
Joseph Hooker and 689
Benjamin Huger and 693
Thomas J. Jackson and 697
Albert S. Johnston and 699
Joseph E. Johnston and 701
Philip Kearny and 703
Edmund Kirby-Smith and 706
Robert E. Lee and 710

Abraham Lincoln and 713, 714
James Longstreet and 716
William L. Loring and 718
Mansfield Lovell and 719
Nathaniel Lyon and 721
George B. McClellan and 723
Irvin McDowell and 726
George G. Meade and 731
John C. Pemberton and 739
George E. Pickett and 740–741
Gideon J. Pillow and 742
Fitz John Porter and 750
Raphael Semmes and 765
Henry H. Sibley and 773
Earl Van Dorn and 787
Stand Watie and 790
Secessionville, Battle of 168*c*–168*c*
Selma, Alabama 569*c*, 575*c*–576*c*
Seminole War, Second 607, 615, 620
Semmes, Raphael **765–766**
Alabama-Kearsarge battle 458*c*, 459*c*
Azores 204*c*, 205*c*, 207*c*, 209*c*, 210*c*, 212*c*
Bermuda 227*c*, 229*c*
Brazil 271*c*, 274*c*, 278*c*, 281*c*, 286*c*, 292*c*, 425*c*
USS *Brilliant* seizure 218*c*
Cape Verde 424*c*
Caribbean 51*c*, 259*c*
Cherbourg, France 454*c*, 457*c*
Cuba 42*c*, 237*c*
Gibraltar 100*c*
Golden Eagle/Olive Jane seizures 265*c*
Haiti 236*c*, 258*c*
USS *Hatteras* 253*c*
Leeward Islands 85*c*, 86*c*
Martinique 231*c*, 232*c*
Nova Scotia 221*c*, 223*c*–226*c*
David D. Porter and 750
Puerto Rico 262*c*
South America 68*c*

CSS *Sumter* abandoned at Gibraltar 135*c*
Washington seizure and release 267*c*
West Indies 88*c*
Charles Wilkes and 794
Seven Days' Battles 172*c*–173*c*, 807*m*
Seven Pines, Battle of 160*c*–162*c*
Shelby, Joseph O. **766–767**
Arrow Rock, Missouri 360*c*
Big Blue River, Missouri 512*c*
Boonville, Missouri 359*c*
Cane Hill, Arkansas 233*c*
Humansville, Missouri 357*c*
Ironton, Missouri 501*c*
Edmund Kirby-Smith and 707
Mark's Mills, Arkansas 424*c*
Moffat's Station, Arkansas 355*c*
Neosho, Missouri 356*c*
New Haven, Kentucky 479*c*
Newtonia, Missouri 216*c*, 218*c*, 515*c*
Red River campaign 414*c*
Westport, Missouri, Battle of 513*c*
Joseph Wheeler and 793
Shenandoah Valley campaign (1862) 125*c*, 126*c*, 140*c*, 143*c*–145*c*, 158*c*–160*c*
Turner Ashby and 610
Harrisonburg 163*c*
Luray Valley 155*c*
George B. McClellan at Williamsburg 148*c*
McDowell, western Virginia 149*c*, 152*c*
New Market 154*c*
John Pope and 180*c*
Shenandoah Valley campaign (1864) 471*c*–474*c*, 476*c*, 479*c*, 483*c*–487*c*, 489*c*, 491*c*, 494*c*, 495*c*, 497*c*, 499*c*, 500*c*, 506*c*, 507*c*, 512*c*, 519*c*
Shepherdstown, Battle of 212*c*–213*c*

Sheridan, Philip H. **767–770,** *768*
  Amelia Court House,
    Virginia 577*c*
  Richard H. Anderson and
    606
  Appomattox, Virginia 572*c*,
    581*c*
  Beaver Dam Station, Virginia
    565*c*
  Berryville, Virginia 493*c*
  Booneville, Battle of 178*c*
  John C. Breckinridge and
    618
  Cedar Creek, Virginia 486*c*,
    508*c*, 510*c*511*c*
  Charlottesville, Virginia
    561*c*
  Cold Harbor, Battle of 447*c*
  George Crook and 634
  Cumberland Church,
    Virginia 580*c*
  George A. Custer and 637,
    638
  Dinwiddie Court House,
    Virginia 572*c*–573*c*
  Jubal A. Early and 650
  Richard S. Ewell and 654
  Fisher's Hill, Battle of 499*c*–
    500*c*
  Five Forks, Virginia 573*c*
  Goochland Court House,
    Virginia 564*c*
  John B. Gordon and 664
  Ulysses S. Grant and 669
  Benjamin H. Grierson and
    671
  Wade Hampton and 676
  Winfield S. Hancock and
    678
  Hanover Court House,
    Virginia 566*c*
  Harrisonburg, Virginia 501*c*
  John D. Imboden and 696
  James River, Virginia 571*c*
  Jetersville, Virginia 578*c*
  Fitzhugh Lee and 708, 709
  Robert E. Lee and 712
  Abraham Lincoln and 714

  Lynchburg, Virginia 559*c*
  George G. Meade and 732
  Montgomery C. Meigs and
    734
  Missionary Ridge, Battle of
    376*c*
  John S. Mosby and 737
  Murfreesboro, Battle of 247*c*
  North Anna River 443*c*
  Perryville 219*c*, 220*c*
  Petersburg, siege of 461*c*
  Petersburg, Virginia 475*c*
  George E. Pickett and 742
  Richmond, Virginia 432*c*
  John M. Schofield and 763
  Shenandoah Valley campaign
    (1864) 476*c*, 479*c*, 482*c*–
    486*c*, 488*c*, 489*c*, 491*c*,
    493*c*, 495*c*, 499*c*, 500*c*,
    506*c*, 507*c*
  William T. Sherman and 772
  J. E. B. Stuart and 779
  Alfred H. Terry and 784
  Trevilian Station, Battle of
    453*c*, 454*c*
  Virginia Central Railroad
    raid 450*c*–452*c*
  Waynesboro, Virginia 503*c*,
    560*c*
  Wilderness, Battle of the
    431*c*
  James H. Wilson and 795
  Winchester, Third Battle of
    498*c*
  Winchester, Virginia 487*c*,
    492*c*
  Winchester, West Virginia
    488*c*, 494*c*
  Yellow Tavern, Battle of 436*c*
Sherman, William T. **770–772,**
  771
  Robert Anderson and 608
  Angley's Post Office, South
    Carolina 550*c*
  Arkansas, Fort 252*c*
  Arkansas expedition 251*c*
  Atlanta, Battle of 490*c*
  Atlanta, siege of 484*c*

  Atlanta campaign 431*c*, 438*c*,
    439*c*, 445*c*, 452*c*, 453*c*,
    456*c*, 457*c*, 462*c*–465*c*,
    468*c*, 469*c*, 472*c*, 474*c*,
    476*c*, 479*c*, 480*c*, 484*c*,
    486*c*, 488*c*–495*c*
  Pierre G. T. Beauregard and
    614
  Bentonville, North Carolina
    568*c*
  Birdsong Ferry, Mississippi
    324*c*
  Branchville, South Carolina
    553*c*
  John C. Breckinridge and
    618
  Don C. Buell and 621
  Buford's Bridge, South
    Carolina 550*c*
  Charleston, South Carolina
    552*c*
  Chattahoochie River, Georgia
    465*c*
  Chattanooga, siege of 363*c*,
    364*c*
  Chattanooga, Tennessee
    353*c*, 371*c*
  Cheraw, South Carolina 561*c*
  Chesterfield, South Carolina
    560*c*
  Patrick R. Cleburne and 631
  Clinton, Mississippi 326*c*,
    328*c*
  Columbia, South Carolina
    554*c*–556*c*
  Combahee River, South
    Carolina 548*c*
  John A. B. Dahlgren and 640
  Dallas, Georgia 445*c*
  Edisto River Bridge, South
    Carolina 551*c*
  Fairburn, Georgia 488*c*
  Fayetteville, North Carolina
    562*c*, 565*c*
  Nathan B. Forrest and 497*c*,
    661
  Goldsborough, North
    Carolina 569*c*

Ulysses S. Grant and 668, 669

Greensborough, North Carolina 584*c*

Henry W. Halleck and 674

Wade Hampton and 676

Hanging Rock, South Carolina 559*c*

William J. Hardee and 679–680

Hill, Fort, Mississippi 302*c*

John B. Hood and 688, 689

Joseph Hooker and 691

Oliver O. Howard and 692

Jackson, Mississippi 325*c*, 327*c*, 330*c*, 331*c*

Joseph E. Johnston and 584*c*, 585*c*, 588*c*, 701

Jonesboro, Battle of 492*c*–493*c*

Kennesaw Mountain, Battle of 462*c*, 463*c*

Hugh J. Kilpatrick and 705

Knoxville, siege of 379*c*

Robert E. Lee and 712

Abraham Lincoln and 714

James Longstreet and 717

William L. Loring and 719

Stephen B. Luce and 542*c*

march from Savannah, Georgia 544*c*

march to Columbia, South Carolina 545*c*

March to the Sea *520*, 520*c*–535*c*, 814*m*

James B. McPherson and 729

Montgomery C. Meigs and 734

Memphis, Tennessee 489*c*

Meridian campaign 394*c*–397*c*

John C. Pemberton and 740

Leonidas Polk and 746

David D. Porter and 749

Raleigh, North Carolina 583*c*

Red River campaign 393*c*, 406*c*, 407*c*

Resaca, Battle of 438*c*, 439*c*

Richmond, Virginia 495*c*

Rocky Mount, South Carolina 558*c*

Rome, Georgia 508*c*, 519*c*

Savannah, Georgia 515*c*, 531*c*, 534*c*

John M. Schofield and 762, 763

Philip Sheridan and 769

Shiloh, Battle of 132*c*, 134*c*–135*c*

Smyrna, Georgia 464*c*

Special Field Order No. 15 544*c*

Edwin M. Stanton and 540*c*

Steele's Bayou 271*c*, 273*c*

Tallahatchie Bridge, Mississippi 168*c*

Alfred H. Terry and 783

George H. Thomas and 785, 786

Vicksburg, siege of 241*c*–246*c*, 277*c*, 281*c*, 287*c*, 295*c*–297*c*, 299*c*, 300*c*, 303*c*, 320*c*

Lew Wallace and 789

Joseph Wheeler and 792

Whippy Swamp, South Carolina 549*c*

James H. Wilson and 796

Sherman's march through Georgia (March to the Sea) *520*, 520*c*–535*c*, 814*m*

Shiloh, Battle of 132*c*–135*c*, *133*, 614, 615, 621, 806*m*

Sibley, Henry H. **772–774**, *773*

Bisland, Fort 280*c*

Edward R. S. Canby and 628

James H. Carleton and 630

Cubero, New Mexico Territory 117*c*

Sterling Porter and 754

Santa Fe, New Mexico 117*c*

Santee campaign 214*c*–215*c*

Richard Taylor and 781

Valverde, Battle of 112*c*, 113*c*

Sickles, Daniel E. **774–776,** *775*

Richard H. Anderson and 606

Chancellorsville, Battle of 289*c*

Gettysburg, Battle of 320*c*

Winfield S. Hancock and 677

John B. Hood and 688

James Longstreet and 717

George G. Meade and 732

Oak Grove, Battle of 171*c*

John F. Reynolds and 758

Seven Pines, Virginia 168*c*

Sigel, Franz *776*, **776–777**

John C. Breckinridge and 618

Bull Run, Second Battle of 199*c*, 200*c*

Bunker Hill, West Virginia 426*c*

Carthage, Battle of 42*c*

Samuel R. Curtis and 636

Oliver O. Howard and 692

John D. Imboden and 696

Abraham Lincoln and 714

Nathaniel Lyon and 722

Ben McCulloch and 726

New Market, Battle of 439*c*

Pea Ridge, Battle of 119*c*

Sterling Porter and 753

John M. Schofield and 762

Virginia Central Railroad 426*c*

Wilson's Creek, Battle of 55*c*

Sioux Indians 189*c*, 193*c*, 549*c*, 592*c*, 598*c*

Sioux uprising 193*c*–196*c*

slaves/slavery. *See also* Thirteenth Amendment

in 1st South Carolina Volunteer Infantry 254*c*

abolished in Washington, D.C. 130*c*

abolition in Louisiana 414*c*

abolition petitions and bills introduced in Congress 88*c*

abolition proposed in Tennessee 391*c*

assimilation of freed 541*c*
Confederate Constitution
    provision 17*c*
constitutional amendments
    to outlaw 540*c*
as "contraband of war" 33*c*
Crittenden Compromise 6*c*,
    10*c*
Crittenden Resolution 50*c*
Jefferson Davis's resolutions
    1*c*, 2*c*
enlistment 356*c*, 402*c*
excluded from military
    camps 84*c*
fugitives expelled from Fort
    Holt, Kentucky 93*c*
fugitive slaves as Union
    laborers 191*c*
Impressment Act 275*c*
Kansas constitution 12*c*
legal status of fugitives 80*c*
Lincoln's early stance 16*c*
Maryland abolishes 517*c*
Meridian campaign 397*c*
Missouri State Convention
    votes to end 319*c*
reaffirmation amendment
    15*c*
Second Confiscation Act
    182*c*
Union stance on fugitives
    35*c*, 39*c*
slave trade 13*c*, 25*c*, 38*c*, 113*c*,
    134*c*
Smith, Fort, Arkansas 476*c*, 478*c*,
    479*c*
South Mountain, Battle of 207*c*–
    208*c*
Spanish Fort, Alabama 571*c*, 581*c*
Spotsylvania Court House, Battle
    of 432*c*–441*c*, *435*, 604, 606,
    625
Stanton, Edwin M. 215*c*, 540*c*
Staunton, Virginia 148*c*, 461*c*
Steele's Bayou 271*c*, 273*c*
Stoneman's raid 623
Stone's River, Battle of. *See*
    Murfreesboro, Second Battle of

Strong, Fort, North Carolina
    557*c*, 558*c*
Stuart, J. E. B. **778–780,** *779*
    Brandy Station, Battle of
        243*c*, 306*c*–307*c*
    Buckland Mills, Battle of 362*c*
    John Buford and 622–623
    Carmel Church, Virginia
        184*c*
    Catlett's Station Virginia
        195*c*, 360*c*
    Chambersburg, Pennsylvania
        221*c*
    Chancellorsville, Battle of
        288*c*–290*c*
    Chantilly, Battle of 202*c*
    Culpeper Court House,
        Virginia 246*c*
    George A. Custer and 637
    Dranesville, Battle of 92*c*
    Dumfries, Virginia 244*c*
    Edward's Ferry, Maryland
        344*c*
    Fairfax Court House, Virginia
        317*c*
    Gettysburg, Battle of 319*c*,
        321*c*, 322*c*
    Hall's Woods, Maryland
        318*c*
    Wade Hampton and 675,
        676
    Joseph E. Johnston and 701
    Hugh J. Kilpatrick and 705
    Fitzhugh Lee and 708
    Robert E. Lee and 711
    George B. McClellan and 724
    John S. Mosby and 736
    Murfreesboro, Battle of 249*c*
    New Baltimore, Virginia
        346*c*
    Occoquan Creek 244*c*
    Alfred Pleasonton and 744
    Poolesville, Virginia 221*c*
    Richmond, Virginia 432*c*
    Robertson's River, Virginia
        355*c*
    Rockville, Maryland 315*c*
    Joseph O. Shelby and 767

    Philip Sheridan and 768
    Utz's Ford, Virginia 358*c*
    Warrenton Junction, Virginia
        231*c*
    Joseph Wheeler and 793
    Williamsport, Battle of 325*c*
    Yellow Tavern, Battle of 436*c*
Suffolk, Virginia 279*c*, 285*c*, 289*c*,
    291*c*–292*c*
Sumter, Fort, South Carolina 22
    Richard H. Anderson and
        584*c*
    Robert Anderson and
        607–608
    Pierre G. T. Beauregard and
        613
    first battle 21*c*–22*c*
    Abraham Lincoln and 713
    Union bombardment (1863)
        340*c*–343*c*, 345*c*, 347*c*, *348*,
        349c, 365*c*–368*c*, *370c*,
        371c, 373*c*, *375c*, 382*c*–383*c*

T

Taylor, Richard **781–782**
    Nathaniel P. Banks and 612
    Bisland, Fort 279*c*–281*c*
    Edward R. S. Canby and 629
    Cross Keys, Battle of 165*c*
    Nathan B. Forrest and 661
    Front Royal, Virginia 156*c*
    Wade Hampton and 676
    Henderson's Hill, Louisiana
        410*c*
    John B. Hood and 689
    Edmund Kirby-Smith and
        707
    John B. Magruder and 730
    Mansfield, Battle of 415*c*
    Milliken's Bend, Louisiana
        305*c*
    Pleasant Hill, Battle of 416*c*
    Port Republic, Battle of 166*c*
    Red River campaign 412*c*
    Henry H. Sibley and 774
Terry, Alfred H. **782–784,** *783*
    Beaufort, North Carolina
        540*c*

Bottom Church, Virginia 442*c*
Benjamin F. Butler and 627
Charles City, Virginia 514*c*
George A. Custer and 638
Darbytown Road, Virginia 509*c*
Fayetteville, North Carolina 565*c*
Fisher, Fort, North Carolina 538*c*, 542*c*, 543*c*
Harrison, Fort, Virginia 507*c*
Robert F. Hoke and 687
James Island, South Carolina 331*c*
David D. Porter and 750
Philip Sheridan and 769
Wilmington, North Carolina 541*c*
Thirteenth Amendment 389*c*, 415*c*, 455*c*, 548*c*
Thomas, George H. **784–786**, *785*
Atlanta campaign 431*c*, 470*c*, 471*c*, 491*c*
Don C. Buell and 621
Bull's Gap, Tennessee 519*c*
Centerville, Tennessee 366*c*
Charleston, Tennessee 386*c*
Chattahoochie River, Georgia 465*c*
Chattanooga, Battle of 374*c*
Chattanooga, siege of 362*c*, 363*c*, 367*c*
Chattanooga, Tennessee 353*c*
Chickamauga, Battle of 352*c*
George B. Crittenden and 633
Dalton, First Battle of 401–403*c*
Jefferson Davis and 642
Ulysses S. Grant and 668
William J. Hardee and 679
John B. Hood and 689
Oliver O. Howard and 692
Albert S. Johnston and 699
Hugh J. Kilpatrick and 705
Mills Springs, Battle of 99*c*, 100*c*

Missionary Ridge, Battle of 376*c*
Murfreesboro, Battle of 247*c*
Nashville, Battle of 527*c*, 528*c*, 530*c*–534*c*
Resaca, Battle of 439*c*
William S. Rosecrans and 761
John M. Schofield and 762
Philip Sheridan and 768
William T. Sherman and 771
James H. Wilson and 796
Thoroughfare Gap, Battle of 198*c*
Tom's Brook, Virginia 507*c*, 508*c*
Trevilian Station, Battle of 452*c*–454*c*
Tupelo, Battle of 469*c*–470*c*
Tuscumbia, Alabama 265*c*, 516*c*

U

Utoy Creek, Georgia 480*c*–481*c*, 483*c*

V

Van Dorn, Earl 19*c*, 21*c*, **787–788**
Baton Rouge, Battle of 188*c*
Samuel R. Curtis and 636
death of 293*c*
Nathan B. Forrest and 660
Franklin, Tennessee 268*c*, 279*c*
Benjamin H. Grierson and 670
William J. Hardee and 679
Holly Springs, Mississippi 242*c*
Mansfield Lovell and 720
Ben McCulloch and 726
James B. McPherson and 728
Pea Ridge, Battle of 116*c*–119*c*
John C. Pemberton and 739, 740
Sterling Porter and 753
William S. Rosecrans and 761
Franz Sigel and 777
Star of the West seizure 24*c*
Thompson's Station, Tennessee 268*c*

Tuscumbia, Alabama 265*c*
Vicksburg, Mississippi 175*c*
Vicksburg, siege of 245*c*
Stand Watie and 791
Vicksburg, Battle of 226*c*, 228*c*–230*c*
Vicksburg, siege of 242*c*–246*c*, 255*c*, 259*c*–260*c*, 276*c*–277*c*, 279*c*, 281*c*, 284*c*–286*c*, 303*c*, 311*c*, 316*c*, 317*c*, 320*c*, 323*c*–324*c*, 812*m*
Virginia, CSS 620
Virginia Central Railroad 426*c*, 445*c*, 450*c*, 451*c*

W

Wallace, Lew **789–790**
Turner Ashby and 610
Donelson, Fort, Battle of 110*c*
Jubal A. Early and 650
Ulysses S. Grant and 668
Henry W. Halleck and 673
Monocacy, Battle of 467*c*
Shiloh, Battle of 133*c*
Wapping Heights, Battle of 334*c*
Warrenton, Mississippi 275*c*, 276*c*
Warrenton, Virginia 225*c*, 231*c*, 274*c*, 291*c*, 336*c*, 388*c*
Washington, D.C. *See* District of Columbia
Washington, North Carolina 125*c*, 273*c*, 276*c*, 281*c*, 424*c*
Waterloo Bridge, Battle of 195*c*–197*c*
Watie, Stand 118*c*–119*c*, 476*c*, 478*c*, 479*c*, 725, 787, **790–791**
Wauhatchie, Battle of 365*c*–366*c*
Waynesboro, Virginia 502*c*, 503*c*, 560*c*
Weldon Railroad 488*c*, 489*c*
western campaigns 814*m*
Westport, Missouri, Battle of 513*c*
Wheeler, Joseph **791–793**, *792*
Antioch Station, Tennessee 278*c*
Ashland, Tennessee 254*c*

Atlanta campaign 431*c*, 477*c*, 484*c*
Buck Head Creek, Georgia 525*c*
Cape Fear River, North Carolina 570*c*
Charleston, Tennessee 386*c*
Chattanooga, siege of 355*c*
Patrick R. Cleburne and 631
Corinth, Mississippi 219*c*
George Crook and 634
Cumberland Iron Works, Tennessee 261*c*
Dalton, Georgia 485*c*
Jonesville, Virginia 380*c*
Hugh J. Kilpatrick and 705
Fitzhugh Lee and 709
Leet's Tan Yard, Georgia 406*c*
James Longstreet and 717
Lovejoy Station, Georgia 521*c*
Macon, Georgia 522*c*
Mill Creek, Tennessee 236*c*
John H. Morgan and 735
Murfreesboro 247*c*, 249*c*
Perryville 220*c*
Joseph O. Shelby and 767
Smith's Cross Roads, Tennessee 356*c*

Stone's River Railroad bridge 357*c*
Tennessee raids 252*c*, 495*c*
USS *Hastings* capture 254*c*
Waynesboro, Georgia 528*c*–529*c*
White House, Virginia 151*c*, 153*c*
Wilderness, Battle of the 428*c*–431*c*, 604, 606, 625
Wilkes, Charles 81*c*, *793*, **793–795**
Williamsburg, Virginia 147*c*–148*c*
Williamsport, Battle of 325*c*, 326*c*, 328*c*–330*c*
Wilmington, North Carolina 541*c*, 554*c*, 557*c*
Wilson, James H. *795*, **795–796**
  George A. Custer and 637
  Jefferson Davis and 644
  Nathan B. Forrest and 661
  Benjamin H. Grierson and 671
  Macon, Georgia 586*c*
  Montgomery, Alabama 583*c*, 584*c*
  Nashville, Tennessee 528*c*
  Nashville, Tennessee, Battle of 533*c*, 534*c*
  Petersburg, siege of 460*c*
  John M. Schofield and 762

Selma, Alabama 569*c*, 575*c*
Spring Hill, Tennessee 525*c*
Stoney Creek Station, Virginia 463*c*
  Richard Taylor and 782
  Yazoo Pass expedition 259*c*, 260*c*
Wilson's Creek, Battle of 55*c*–56*c*
Winchester, First Battle of 157*c*, 610, 611
Winchester, Second Battle of 310*c*–311*c*
Winchester, Third Battle of 498*c*
Winchester, Virginia 160*c*, 464*c*, 474*c*, 492*c*
Winchester, West Virginia 488*c*, 494*c*
Woodstock, Virginia 154*c*, 162*c*
Worden, John L. 20*c*, 114*c*, 119*c*–121*c*, 258*c*, 260*c*, 647, **796–798**, *797*
Wytheville, Virginia 435*c*, 534*c*

Y

Yazoo Pass 259*c*, 260*c*, 263*c*
Yellow Tavern, Battle of 436*c*
Yorktown, Battle of 131*c*–132*c*
Yorktown, Virginia 137*c*, 145*c*